Life

The Essentials of Human Development

SECOND EDITION

Gabriela **Martorell**

Mc
Graw
Hill

LIFE: THE ESSENTIALS OF HUMAN DEVELOPMENT, SECOND EDITION

Published by McGraw Hill LLC, 1325 Avenue of the Americas, New York, NY 10121. Copyright ©2022 by McGraw Hill LLC. All rights reserved. Printed in the United States of America. Previous edition ©2019. No part of this publication may be reproduced or distributed in any form or by any means, or stored in a database or retrieval system, without the prior written consent of McGraw Hill LLC, including, but not limited to, in any network or other electronic storage or transmission, or broadcast for distance learning.

Some ancillaries, including electronic and print components, may not be available to customers outside the United States.

This book is printed on acid-free paper.

1 2 3 4 5 6 7 8 9 LWI 24 23 22 21

ISBN 978-1-260-38830-5 (bound edition)
MHID 1-260-38830-1 (bound edition)
ISBN 978-1-264-00280-1 (loose-leaf edition)
MHID 1-264-00280-7 (loose-leaf edition)

Senior Portfolio Manager: *Ryan Treat*
Product Development Manager: *Dawn Groundwater*
Senior Product Developer: *Lauren A. Finn*
Marketing Manager: *Olivia Kaiser*
Content Project Managers: *Mary E. Powers (Core), Jodi Banowetz (Assessment)*
Buyer: *Susan K. Culbertson*
Designer: *Beth Blech*
Content Licensing Specialist: *Carrie Burger*
Cover Image: *Yulia-Images/Getty Images*
Compositor: *Aptara®, Inc.*

All credits appearing on page or at the end of the book are considered to be an extension of the copyright page.

Library of Congress Cataloging-in-Publication Data

Names: Martorell, Gabriela, author.
Title: Life : the essentials of human development / Gabriela Martorell.
Description: Second Edition. | New York : McGraw Hill Education, 2022. |
    First edition published 2018.
Identifiers: LCCN 2020036761 (print) | LCCN 2020036762 (ebook) | ISBN
    9781260388305 (Hardcover) | ISBN 9781264002801 (Spiral Bound) | ISBN
    9781264002795 (eBook) | ISBN 9781264002825 (eBook Other)
Subjects: LCSH: Developmental psychology. | Developmental psychobiology.
Classification: LCC BF713 .M3343 2022 (print) | LCC BF713 (ebook) | DDC
    155—dc23
LC record available at https://lccn.loc.gov/2020036761
LC ebook record available at https://lccn.loc.gov/2020036762

The Internet addresses listed in the text were accurate at the time of publication. The inclusion of a website does not indicate an endorsement by the authors or McGraw Hill LLC, and McGraw Hill LLC does not guarantee the accuracy of the information presented at these sites.

mheducation.com/highered

brief contents

Mc Graw Hill **connect** McGraw Hill Education Psychology APA Documentation Style Guide

iii

contents

③ Early Childhood

part

chapter 7
Physical and Cognitive Development in Early Childhood 159

chapter 8
Psychosocial Development in Early Childhood 190

Middle Adulthood

Mc Graw Hill **connect** McGraw Hill Education
Psychology
APA Documentation
Style Guide

Guide to Diversity

Feature coverage of diversity can be found in the following boxes:

Life: The Essentials of Human Development is designed to be a brief but thorough account of human development from conception to death, exposing students to culture and diversity, and immersing them in practical application. Written from a developmental framework and borrowing from multiple traditions and theoretical perspectives, *Life: The Essentials of Human Development* also addresses the major periods of development and focuses on the important biological, psychological, and social forces driving change, highlighting theoretical distinctions, research findings, and new directions in the field. *Life: The Essentials of Human Development* will engage your students intellectually and encourage the application of psychological concepts to everyday life.

Paired with McGraw Hill Education Connect, a digital assignment and assessment platform that strengthens the link between faculty, students, and coursework, instructors and students accomplish more in less time. Connect Psychology is particularly useful for remote and hybrid courses, and includes assignable and assessable videos, quizzes, exercises, and interactivities, all associated with learning objectives. Interactive assignments and videos allow students to experience and apply their understanding of psychology to the world with fun and stimulating activities.

Diversity

In response to requests from faculty, substantial space has been devoted to addressing issues of diversity. When relevant, each chapter includes current U.S. statistics drawn from census data and other federal databases, including not just major population trends but also demographic and statistical information on ethnic and racial minorities. Moreover, in many cases, global statistics, trends, and cultural differences in development have been explored as well.

Other forms of diversity have also been considered. For example, information is included on different family systems, including gay and lesbian parents, stepparents, divorced parents, and those families in which adults remain single by choice.

Additionally, each chapter includes a **Window on the World** feature. In this feature, a cross-cultural issue of interest is addressed from a global perspective. These features cover a wide variety of topics, including, for example, cultural differences in wedding traditions and funeral ceremonies along with research-based features on topics such as immigrant families, prenatal care, and bullying. Each feature ends with What's Your View—a series of questions that can be used as springboards for class discussion or writing prompts.

A complete Guide to Diversity can be found on page xii.

Current Research

Life: The Essentials of Human Development draws a current picture of the state of the field. In well-established areas of psychology, there is an emphasis on the inclusion of review articles and meta-analyses in order to capture the major trends found through decades of psychological research. In research areas with less information available, the emphasis is on the inclusion of the newest research. Moreover, scientifically important trends, such as the open science movement and modern critiques of historical models of development, are also discussed. Additionally, topics that have recently arisen in the public consciousness have been included. For example, there is new information on COVID-19 across the life span, on technology and young children, on the opioid epidemic, and on the development of transgender people.

Each chapter in *Life: The Essentials of Human Development* includes a **Research in Action** feature, in which a closer look is taken at an issue or area relevant to the chapter. The Research in Action features are designed to stimulate critical thinking about a wide variety of engaging topics, and they include such topics as Barbie dolls, childhood trauma, the impact of technology on development, and intimate partner violence. As with Window on the World features, each Research in Action feature ends with What's Your View question prompts.

Apply Concepts and Theory in an Experiential Learning Environment

An engaging and innovative learning game, **Quest: Journey Through the Lifespan** provides students with opportunities to apply content from their human development curriculum to real-life scenarios. Students play unique characters who range in age and make decisions that apply key concepts and theories for each age as they negotiate events in an array of authentic environments. Additionally, as students analyze real-world behaviors and contexts, they are exposed to different cultures and intersecting biological, cognitive, and socioemotional processes. Each quest has layered replayability, allowing students to make new choices each time they play—or offering different students in the same class different experiences. Fresh possibilities and outcomes shine light on the complexity of and variations in real human development. This new experiential learning game includes follow-up questions, assignable in Connect and auto-graded, to reach a higher level of critical thinking.

Real People, Real World, Real Life

At the higher end of Bloom's taxonomy, the **McGraw Hill Education Milestones video series** offers an observational tool that allows students to experience life as it unfolds, from infancy to late adulthood. This groundbreaking, longitudinal video series tracks the development of real children as they progress through the early stages of physical, social, and emotional development in their first few weeks, months, and years of life. Assignable and assessable within Connect Psychology, Milestones also includes interviews with adolescents and adults to reflect development throughout the entire life span.

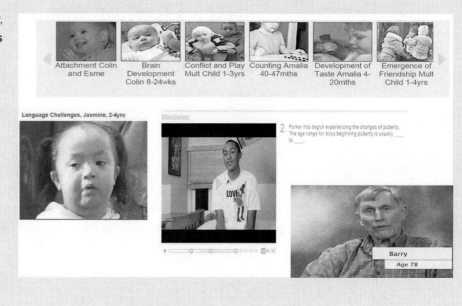

New to this edition, Milestones are available in a more engaging, WCAG-compliant format. Ask your McGraw Hill representative about this new upgrade!

Writing Assignment

McGraw Hill's new **Writing Assignment Plus** tool delivers a learning experience that improves students' written communication skills and conceptual understanding with every assignment. Assign, monitor, and provide feedback on writing more efficiently and grade assignments within McGraw Hill Connect®. Writing Assignment Plus gives you time-saving tools with a just-in-time basic writing and originality checker.

Preparing Students for Higher-Level Thinking

Also at the higher end of Bloom's, **Power of Process** for Psychology helps students improve critical-thinking skills and allows instructors to assess these skills efficiently and effectively in an online environment. Offered through Connect, instructors can upload their own material for use within the system or assign preloaded journal articles. Using a scaffolded framework such as understanding, synthesizing, and analyzing, Power of Process moves students toward higher-level thinking and analysis.

Provide a Smarter Text and Better Value

SMARTBOOK®

Available within Connect, **SmartBook** helps students distinguish the concepts they know from the concepts they don't, while pinpointing the concepts they are about to forget. SmartBook's real-time reports help both students and instructors identify concepts that require more attention, making study sessions and class time more efficient.

New to this edition, SmartBook is now optimized for mobile and tablet use and is accessible for students with disabilities. Content-wise, it has been enhanced with improved learning objectives that are measurable and observable to improve student outcomes. SmartBook personalizes learning to individual student needs. Study time is more productive and, as a result, students are better prepared for class and coursework.

Online Instructor Resources

The resources listed here accompany *Life: The Essentials of Human Development*. Please contact your McGraw Hill representative for details concerning the availability of these and other valuable materials that can help you design and enhance your course.

Instructor's Manual   Broken down by chapter, this resource provides chapter outlines, suggested lecture topics, classroom activities and demonstrations, suggested student research projects, essay questions, and critical-thinking questions.

Test Builder   New to this edition and available within Connect, **Test Builder** is a cloud-based tool that enables instructors to format tests that can be printed and administered within a Learning Management System. Test Builder offers a modern, streamlined interface for easy content configuration that matches course needs, without requiring a download. Test Builder enables instructors to:

- Access all test bank content from a particular title
- Easily pinpoint the most relevant content through robust filtering options
- Manipulate the order of questions or scramble questions and/or answers
- Pin questions to a specific location within a test
- Determine your preferred treatment of algorithmic questions
- Choose the layout and spacing
- Add instructions and configure default settings

PowerPoint Slides   The PowerPoint presentations, now WCAG compliant, highlight the key points of the chapter and include supporting visuals. All of the slides can be modified to meet individual needs.

Remote Proctoring New remote proctoring and browser-locking capabilities are seamlessly integrated within Connect to offer more control over the integrity of online assessments. Instructors can enable security options that restrict browser activity, monitor student behavior, and verify the identity of each student. Instant and detailed reporting gives instructors an at-a-glance view of potential concerns, thereby avoiding personal bias and supporting evidence-based claims.

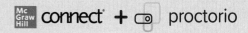

Major Chapter Changes

1 The Study of Human Development
- Expanded description of the interrelationship among different domains of development
- Example of COVID-19 influencing a historical generation
- Expanded information on adolescence in developing countries
- Research on recent changes in family household composition updated and expanded
- Research on global and U.S. poverty updated and expanded
- New key term and information on ethnic gloss

2 Theory and Research
- Cross-cultural research on Erikson's psychosocial theory of development added
- Information on tabula rasa view of learning theories added
- Information on the influence of culture in Vygotsky's approach added
- Information on the influence of culture in the evolutionary psychology approach added
- Section added on the open science movement,
- The reproducibility problem, publication bias, and p-hacking

3 Forming a New Life
- Research on multiple births added
- Cephalocaudal and proximodistal key terms added
- Research added on the ability of fetuses to feel pain, and to perceive, form preferences to, and remember sounds and tastes
- Expanded section on global prevalence and consequences of malnutrition
- Cross-cultural research on the use of alcohol during pregnancy added
- Research added on the use of e-cigarettes during pregnancy
- Research added on COVID-19 pandemic and risk of death for pregnant women and neonates; new key terms COVID-19, coronavirus, and pandemic
- Research added on racial and ethnic disparities in prenatal care

4 Birth and Physical Development during the First Three Years
- Cross-cultural research on childbirth and postpartum care added
- Research added on risks of childbirth in the United States and globally
- New section on effect of COVID-19 pandemic on childbirth
- Research added on international prevalence of cesarean deliveries
- Research added on doulas
- Cross-cultural research on infant sleep schedules added
- Updated and expanded information on the long-term consequences of low birth weight and postmaturity

- Information added on influence of COVID-19 on vaccination rates
- Research added on malnutrition in developing countries
- Cross-cultural research on cultural beliefs about teething in babies added
- Research added on prevalence of breastfeeding across racial and ethnic groups
- Information added on breastfeeding for mothers infected with COVID-19
- Research added on early preference for faces in infancy
- Section added on cultural influences on motor development in infancy

5 Cognitive Development during the First Three Years
- Cross-cultural research on the Bayley scales and the HOME inventory added
- Updated and expanded information on early intervention programs
- Updated and expanded information on imitation in infancy
- Research on the use of electronic media devices in infancy added
- Section added on tools of infant research
- Updated and expanded information on categorization and the understanding of causality and number in infancy
- Cross-cultural research on implicit and explicit memory system development added
- Cross-cultural research on the application of Vygotskian principles in early childhood education added
- Section on language development reorganized
- Section added on cultural differences in perceptual development
- Cross-cultural research on the use of gestures and learning new nouns and verbs added
- Research on bilingual language development added
- Research on brain development and its relationship to language development added
- Section on the role of social interaction in language development reorganized and expanded
- Cross-cultural research on the use of infant-directed speech added

6 Psychosocial Development during the First Three Years
- Cross-cultural research on emotional expression added
- Cross-cultural research on crying and infant physiology added
- Research on altruistic helping and empathy in infants updated and expanded
- Section added on collaborative activities and cultural transmission
- Section added on cultural influences on temperament
- Research on gender differences in infancy and toddlerhood and parental influences on gender differences updated and expanded
- Section on attachment reorganized
- Cross-cultural research on separation anxiety added
- Research on biological aspects of mutual regulation added
- Research on infants' responses to faces of different race and ethnicity added
- Cross-cultural research on the development of the self added
- Cross-cultural research on the development of self-regulation added
- Updated and expanded section on socialization influences
- Updated and expanded sections on contact with other children, including research on cross-cultural differences
- Cross-cultural research on early child care added
- Revised and updated section on factors impacting child care
- Research on cultural influences on abuse and neglect updated and expanded

7 Physical and Cognitive Development in Early Childhood
- Research on sleep disturbances updated and expanded
- Research on the development of gross motor skills updated and expanded
- Cross-cultural research on handedness added
- Research on malnutrition and the difference between wasting, stunting, and hidden hunger added
- Updated information on race, ethnicity, socioeconomic status, and access to health care
- Section on understanding of number updated and reorganized
- Section added on distinguishing between fantasy and reality
- Research on brain development and theory of mind added
- Section added on cultural influences on theory of mind
- Section added on media influences on cognition
- Cross-cultural research on influences on measured intelligence added
- Cross-cultural research on pragmatics and social speech added
- Section added on cultural variations in preschool

8 Psychosocial Development in Early Childhood
- Section added on racial and cultural influences on self-definition
- Section added on cultural influences on self-esteem
- Section added on cultural influences on self-regulation
- Section on understanding emotions reorganized and updated
- Section added on initiative versus guilt
- Research on transgender identity development updated and expanded
- Updated and expanded section on cultural influences on gender development
- Updated and expanded section on cultural influences on play
- Cross-cultural research added on the use of corporal punishment
- Research added on how cultural context affects the use of discipline
- Cross-cultural research on parenting styles updated and expanded
- Research on being an only child in China added

9 Physical and Cognitive Development in Middle Childhood
- Sections on physical development and health, fitness, and safety reorganized
- Section added on tooth decay and dental care
- Section added on physical activity and fitness in different countries
- Research on global overweight and obesity added
- Cross-cultural research on asthma and diabetes added
- Section added on childhood hypertension
- Information added on COVID-19 and children's health
- Section added on cultural influences on Piagetian tasks
- Section added on historical and global literacy trends
- Section added on the influence of technology and literacy
- Section added on educational reform
- Cross-cultural research on differences in class size added
- Section added on the impact of COVID-19 on education

10 Psychosocial Development in Middle Childhood

- Section added on cultural influences on emotional development
- Section added on family conflict
- Cross-cultural research on variations in family structure added
- Cross-cultural research on variations in divorce added
- Research on gay and lesbian families updated and expanded
- Research on historical trends in adoptive families added
- Section added on gender differences in peer groups
- Section on aggression reorganized and updated
- Section added on the influence of COVID-19 on children's mental health
- Revised and updated Research in Action

11 Physical and Cognitive Development in Adolescence

- Research on influences on and effects of pubertal timing updated and expanded
- Section added on the cultural context of puberty
- Section on the adolescent brain revised and updated
- Research on global trends in physical activity during adolescence added
- Section on nutrition, weight, and eating disorders revised and updated
- Section added on influences on substance abuse
- Section added on immature aspects of adolescent cognition
- Research added on the influence of COVID-19 and education
- Section added on gender and career choice

12 Psychosocial Development in Adolescence

- Section added on racial and ethnic influences on identity formation
- Section added on identity development in sexual minority youth
- Section added on risks for sexual minority youth
- Research on religiosity as a protective factor for sexual risk-taking added
- Section added on female genital mutilation
- Section on sexually transmitted infections updated and expanded to include global prevalence rates
- Research on global prevalence of teen pregnancy added
- Section on preventing teen pregnancy updated and expanded to include global data
- Critique of unidirectional model of parenting styles added
- Research on sibling relationships in non-Western cultures added
- Section added on social media and electronic interactions
- Research on global prevalence of sexual violence in adolescence added
- Section on biological influences on aggression updated and expanded

13 Physical and Cognitive Development in Emerging and Young Adulthood

- Cross-cultural research on emerging adulthood updated and expanded
- Updates on health care access in young adulthood added
- Research added on risk of complications from COVID-19 in young adults
- Section on food insecurity added
- Section on physical activity in young adulthood updated and expanded
- Research on global prevalence of smoking and alcohol abuse added
- New key term: Internet addiction

- Research on the influence of negative interactions in relationships and health added
- Cross-cultural research on gender differences in depression added
- Cross-cultural research on sexual behaviors and attitudes added
- Section on reflective thinking updated and expanded
- Cross-cultural research on the ethical systems of autonomy, community, and divinity added
- Research added on the impact of COVID-19 on college enrollment

14 Psychosocial Development in Emerging and Young Adulthood
- Section on paths to adulthood updated and expanded
- Section added on cultural issues and ethnic identity formation
- Section added on religious identity formation
- Section added on sexual and gender identity formation
- Cross-cultural research on emerging adults living with parents added
- Cross-cultural research on gay and lesbian marriage added
- Section on cohabitation reorganized and updated
- Section added on contextual and cultural differences in marriage
- Information on bride-price, dowry, and arranged marriage added
- Section added on cultural and contextual influences on parenthood

15 Physical and Cognitive Development in Middle Adulthood
- Research on global prevalence and correlates of sensory and perceptual problems in middle-age adults added
- Section on the brain at midlife updated and expanded
- Section on sexual activity at midlife revised and updated
- Cross-cultural data on hypertension, heart disease, and diabetes added
- All health-related statistics updated
- Research on stress resulting from prejudice and discrimination added
- Section on stress reorganized and updated with information on COVID-19
- Section on creativity updated and expanded

16 Psychosocial Development in Middle Adulthood
- Sections on theoretical approaches and issues and themes at midlife reorganized and updated
- Section added on cultural differences in generativity
- Cross-cultural research on the social clock added
- Cross-cultural research on the midlife crisis added
- Section on culture and personality added
- Section on identity process theory added
- Section on generativity and identity processes in women revised and updated
- Research on the relationship between religion and well-being added
- Research on arranged marriage and marital satisfaction added
- Cross-cultural research on cohabitation and divorce added
- Research on helicopter parenting added
- Multicultural and cross-cultural research on the empty nest added
- Section On ethnic and cultural differences in caregiving for aging parents added
- Section added on cultural differences in grandparenting

17 Physical and Cognitive Development in Late Adulthood
- Section on the aging brain revised and updated
- Research on racial and ethnic variations in cataract prevalence added
- Cross-cultural research on the prevalence of visual and hearing problems added
- New section added on COVID-19 risk and age
- Cross-cultural research on depression added
- Cross-cultural research on dementia added
- Research on the influence of personality on dementia added

18 Psychosocial Development in Late Adulthood
- Section on personality stability and change updated and expanded
- Research on the predictive value of personality change updated and expanded
- Section on well-being in late adulthood updated and expanded
- Section on well-being in sexual minorities added
- Section on the influence of religion on well-being updated and expanded
- New information on the influence of COVID-19 on jobs for older adults
- Cross-cultural research on retirement added
- Cross-cultural research on living arrangements in late adulthood added
- Research on the influence of pets on loneliness added
- Section on living with adult children updated and expanded
- Section on living in institutions updated and expanded
- Section on cultural differences in multigenerational families updated and expanded
- Research on living apart together relationships added
- Cross-cultural research on kinlessness in late adulthood added

19 Dealing with Death and Bereavement
- Section on the meaning of death and dying reorganized and updated
- Cross-cultural research on children's understanding of death added
- Section on the terminal drop added
- Section on near-death experiences added
- Section on losing a child revised and updated
- Cross-cultural research on aging added
- Section on international variations in end-of-life decisions added

Acknowledgments

Thank you to Rebecca Howell, Forsyth Technical Community College, and Dr. Khia Thomas, Broward College, for their important cultural and research contributions to Window on the World and Research in Action.

A special thanks to Jeffery S. Mio, California State Polytechnic University, Pomona, Danice L. Brown, Towson University, Galina Smith, Health Programs Manager for Boston Alliance of GLBTQ Youth, and Joy Wilson, The Human Rights Campaign's National Parents for Transgender Equality Council member for their careful review of diversity coverage and thoughtful suggestions about where I could do better.

Many thanks to those faculty instructors whose insight and feedback contributed to the second edition of *Life: The Essentials of Human Development*:

Mizuho Arai, Bunker Hill Community College

Renee Babcock, Central Michigan University

Phaer Bonner, Jefferson State Community College

Thea Boyer, Johnston Community College

Holly Brand, Missouri Baptist University

Virginia Cashion, Liberty University

Paul J. Chara, University of Northwestern—St. Paul

Tiffany Chenneville, University of South Florida, St. Petersburg

Nicki Favero, University of Lynchburg

Nadia Flanigan, Georgia Southern University

Lynn Haller, Morehead State University

Nicole Hamilton, St. Philips College

Aylene Harper, CCAC, South

Deborah Krause, Mid-State Technical College

Heekyeong Park, Tulsa Community College

Jodi Price, University of Alabama, Huntsville

Erin Richman, University of North Florida

James Rodgers, Hawkeye Community College

Kim Rybacki, Dutchess Community College

Peggy Skinner, South Plains College

Andrew Supple, University of North Carolina, Greensboro

Victoria Van Wie, Lone Star College, CyFair

Lora Vasiliauskas, Virginia Western Community College

From Gabi Martorell to my friends and family: I finished writing this book as the COVID-19 pandemic roared into our lives. While physically distanced, your support and love made the experience bearable. I have never been more grateful for our bonds. May you stay healthy and safe as we navigate the roiling waters ahead.

Gabriela Martorell

Life

The Essentials of Human Development

The Study of Human Development

Erik Isakson/Getty Images

learning objectives

Describe human development and how its study has evolved.

Describe the domains and periods of human development.

Give examples of the influences that make one person different from another.

Discuss the principles of the life-span perspective.

In this chapter we describe how the field of human development evolved. We identify aspects of development and show how they interrelate. We summarize major developments during each period of life. We look at influences on development and the contexts in which each occurs.

Human Development:
An Ever-Evolving Field

From the moment of conception, human beings begin a lifelong process of change until the last flicker of life ends. A single cell develops into a living, breathing, walking, talking person who moves through an ever-changing world, both being influenced by and influencing it. Although we all follow our own unique trajectory, we also share a species heritage, many common experiences, and broad patterns of development. These patterns of development are explored throughout this book.

human development
Scientific study of processes of change and stability throughout the human life span.

The field of **human development** focuses on the scientific study of the systematic processes of change and stability in people. Developmental scientists investigate the ways in which people change or stay the same from conception to death. The work of developmentalists can have a dramatic impact on people's lives. Research findings often have applications to child rearing, education, health, and social policy.

STUDYING THE LIFE SPAN

When the field of developmental psychology emerged as a scientific discipline, most researchers focused their energies on infant and child development. Growth and development are more obvious during these times given the rapid pace of change. As the field matured, however, it became clear that developmental science should include more than infancy and childhood. Now researchers consider **life-span development** to be from "womb to tomb," comprising the entire human life span from conception to death.

life-span development
Concept of human development as a lifelong process that can be studied scientifically.

Moreover, they acknowledge that development can be either positive (e.g., becoming toilet trained or enrolling in a college course after retirement) or negative (e.g., once again wetting the bed after a traumatic event or isolating yourself after retirement).

HUMAN DEVELOPMENT TODAY

As the field of human development itself developed, its goals came to include description, explanation, prediction, and intervention. For example, to *describe* when most children say their first word or how large their vocabulary is at a certain age, developmental scientists observe large groups of children and establish norms, or averages, for behavior at various ages. They then attempt to *explain* how children acquire language and why some children learn to speak later than usual. This knowledge may make it possible to *predict* future behavior, such as the likelihood that a child will have serious speech problems. Finally, an understanding of how language develops may be used to *intervene* in development, for example, by giving a child speech therapy.

Development is messy. It's complex and multifaceted and shaped by interacting arcs of influence. Thus development is best understood with input from a variety of theoretical and research orientations. Students of human development draw from a wide range of disciplines, including psychology, psychiatry, sociology, anthropology, biology, genetics, family science, education, history, and medicine. This book includes findings from research in all these fields.

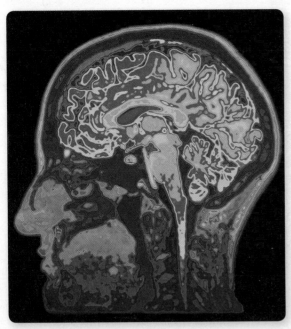

Technology has allowed scientists to investigate previously hidden processes. Brain imaging techniques are used to map where certain thought processes take place. SpeedKingz/Shutterstock

The Study of Human Development:
Basic Concepts

Developmentalists study processes of change and stability in all domains, or aspects, of development throughout all periods of the life span.

DOMAINS OF DEVELOPMENT

Developmental scientists study three major *domains*, or aspects, of development: physical, cognitive, and psychosocial. Growth of the body and brain, sensory capacities, motor skills, and health are parts of **physical development.** Learning, attention, memory, language, thinking, reasoning, and creativity make up **cognitive development.** Emotions, personality, and social relationships are aspects of **psychosocial development.**

Although in this book we talk separately about physical, cognitive, and psychosocial development, these domains are interrelated. Child development is a complex and tangled web of multiple influences, and understanding these influences requires thinking carefully about their interactions. Just as a fly caught on one thread of a web sends reverberations across the entire structure, development in one area sends ripples though all other areas.

For example, physical development affects cognitive and psychosocial development. A child with frequent ear infections may develop language more slowly than a child without this physical problem. In late adulthood, physical changes in the brains of some adults may lead to intellectual and personality deterioration.

Similarly, cognitive advances and declines are related to physical and psychosocial development. A child who is precocious in language development may bring about positive reactions in others and thus gain in self-worth. Memory development reflects gains or losses in physical connections in the brain. An adult who has trouble remembering people's names may feel shy in social situations.

And finally, psychosocial development can affect cognitive and physical functioning. Without meaningful social connections, physical and mental health suffers. Motivation and self-confidence are important contributors to school success, whereas negative emotions such as anxiety can impair performance. Researchers have even identified links between a conscientious personality and length of life.

physical development
Development of the body and brain, including patterns of change in sensory capacities, motor skills, and health.

cognitive development
Pattern of change in mental abilities, such as learning, attention, memory, language, thinking, reasoning, and creativity.

psychosocial development
Pattern of change in emotions, personality, and social relationships.

PERIODS OF THE LIFE SPAN

Division of the life span into periods is a **social construction**: a concept or practice that is an invention of a particular culture or society. There is no objectively definable moment when a child becomes an adult or a young person becomes old. Because the concept of childhood is a social construction, the form it takes varies across cultures. For example, in contrast to the relative freedom children have in the United States today, young children in Colonial times were expected to do adultlike tasks such as knitting socks and spinning wool (Ehrenreich & English, 2005). Inuit parents in the Canadian Arctic believe that young children are not yet capable of thought and reason and therefore are lenient when their children cry or become angry (Briggs, 1970). And Maniq parents in southern Thailand regularly allow their toddlers to play with knives, and by 4 years of age most children can easily gut small animals (Lancy, 2016).

A similar construction involves *adolescence*, which is a recent concept that emerged as society became more industrialized. In most nonindustrial tribal cultures, the transition from childhood to adulthood is most clearly marked by marriage (Schlegel & Barry, 1991). In the United States until the early twentieth century, young people were considered adults once they left school, married, or got a job. However, shifting social trends altered this pattern. By the 1920s, with the establishment of comprehensive high schools to meet the needs of a growing economy and with more families able to support extended formal education for their children, the teenage years became a distinct period of development (Keller, 1999). This trend has been mirrored globally in developed countries as the average age of marriage has edged upward and the education gap between men and women has narrowed (Curtis, 2015). Little research exists on the passage from adolescence to adulthood for young people in developing countries; however, there are suggestions that collectivistic concerns, such as

social construction
A concept or practice that may appear natural and obvious to those who accept it, but that in reality is an invention of a particular culture or society.

These children are engaging in all three domains of development: motor activity (physical development), playing games (cognitive development), and social relationship building (psychosocial development).
Jacob Maentz/The Image Bank Unreleased/Getty Images

caring for family members, figure more prominently as markers of the transition in these cultural contexts (Seiter & Nelson, 2011; Zhong & Arnett, 2014).

In this book, we follow a sequence of eight periods generally accepted in Western industrial societies. After describing the crucial changes that occur in the first period, before birth, we trace all three domains of development through infancy and toddlerhood, early childhood, middle childhood, adolescence, emerging and young adulthood, middle adulthood, and late adulthood (Table 1.1). For each period after infancy and toddlerhood, we have combined physical and cognitive development into a single chapter.

TABLE 1.1 Typical Major Developments in Eight Periods of Human Development

Age Period	Physical Developments	Cognitive Developments	Psychosocial Developments
Prenatal Period (conception to birth)	Conception occurs. Genes interact with environmental influences; vulnerability to environmental influences is great. Basic body structures and organs form; brain growth spurt begins; physical growth is the most rapid in the life span.	Abilities to learn and remember and to respond to sensory stimuli are developing.	Fetus responds to mother's voice and develops a preference for it.
Infancy and Toddlerhood (birth to age 3)	All senses and body systems operate at birth to varying degrees. The brain grows in complexity and is highly sensitive to environmental influence. Physical growth and development of motor skills are rapid.	Abilities to learn and remember are present, even in early weeks. Use of symbols and ability to solve problems develop by end of second year. Comprehension and use of language develop rapidly.	Attachments to parents and others form. Self-awareness develops. Shift from dependence toward autonomy occurs. Interest in other children increases.
Early Childhood (ages 3 to 6)	Growth is steady; appearance becomes more slender and proportions more adultlike. Appetite diminishes, and sleep problems are common. Handedness appears; fine and gross motor skills and strength improve.	Understanding of other people's perspectives grows. Cognitive immaturity results in some illogical ideas about the world. Memory and language improve, intelligence becomes more predictable. Preschool experience is common, and kindergarten experience is more so.	Self-concept and understanding of emotions become more complex; self-esteem is global. Independence, initiative, and self-control increase. Gender identity develops. Play becomes more imaginative, elaborate, and social; altruism, aggression, and fearfulness are common. Family is still the focus of social life, but other children become more important.
Middle Childhood (ages 6 to 11)	Growth slows; strength and athletic skills improve. Respiratory illnesses are common, but health is generally better than at any other time in the life span.	Egocentrism diminishes. Children begin to think logically but concretely; memory and language skills increase. Some children show special educational needs and strengths.	Self-concept becomes more complex, affecting self-esteem. Coregulation reflects gradual shift in control from parents to child. Peers assume central importance.

The age divisions shown in Table 1.1 are approximate and arbitrary. This is especially true of adulthood, when there are no clear-cut social or physical landmarks, such as starting school or entering puberty, to signal a shift from one period to another. Although individual differences exist in the way people deal with the characteristic events and issues of each period, developmentalists suggest that certain basic needs must be met and certain tasks mastered for normal development to occur.

TABLE 1.1 Typical Major Developments in Eight Periods of Human Development			
Age Period	Physical Developments	Cognitive Developments	Psychosocial Developments
Adolescence (ages 11 to about 20)	Physical growth and other changes are rapid and profound; reproductive maturity occurs. Major health risks arise from behavioral issues, such as eating disorders and drug abuse.	Ability to think abstractly and use scientific reasoning develops but immature thinking persists in some attitudes and behaviors. Education focuses on preparation for college or vocation.	Search for identity becomes central. Relationships with parents are generally good; peer group may exert a positive or negative influence.
Emerging and Young Adulthood (ages 20 to 40)	Physical condition peaks, then declines slightly. Lifestyle choices influence health.	Thought and moral judgments become more complex. Educational and occupational choices are made, sometimes after period of exploration.	Personality traits and styles become relatively stable. Intimate relationships and personal lifestyles are established but may not be lasting. Most people marry, and most become parents.
Middle Adulthood (ages 40 to 65)	Slow deterioration of sensory abilities, health, stamina, and strength may begin, but individual differences are wide. Women experience menopause.	Mental abilities peak; expertise and practical problem-solving skills are high. Creative output may decline but improve in quality. Varied career trajectories may occur, including career success and peak earning power, burnout or career change.	Sense of identity continues to develop; midlife transition may occur. Dual responsibilities of caring for children and parents may cause stress. Launching of children leaves empty nest.
Late Adulthood (age 65 and over)	Most people are healthy and active, although health and physical abilities generally decline. Slowing of reaction time affects some aspects of functioning.	Most people are mentally alert. Although intelligence and memory may deteriorate in some areas, most people find ways to compensate.	Retirement from workforce may occur. Relationships with family and close friends can provide important support. Search for meaning in life assumes central importance.

The Study of Human Development: Basic Concepts

Influences on Development

Although students of development are interested in the universal processes of development experienced by all typical human beings, they also study **individual differences** in characteristics, influences, and developmental outcomes. Every person has a unique developmental trajectory. Developmental psychology aims to identify the universal influences on development and then apply those to understanding individual differences in developmental trajectories.

individual differences
Differences in characteristics, influences, or developmental outcomes.

HEREDITY, ENVIRONMENT, AND MATURATION

Some influences on development originate primarily with **heredity**: inborn traits or characteristics inherited from the biological parents. Other influences come largely from the **environment**: the world outside the self, beginning in the womb, and the learning that comes from experience. Which of these two factors has more impact on development? The issue of the relative importance of *nature* (heredity) and *nurture* (environmental influences both before and after birth) historically generated intense debate.

heredity
Inborn traits or characteristics inherited from the biological parents.

environment
Totality of nonhereditary, or experiential, influences on development.

Today scientists have found ways to more precisely measure the roles of heredity and environment in the development of specific traits within a population. Research with regard to almost all characteristics points to a blend of inheritance and experience. For example, even though intelligence is strongly influenced by heredity, it is also affected by parental stimulation, education, peer influence, and other variables. Contemporary theorists and researchers are more interested in finding ways to explain how nature and nurture work together than in arguing about which factor is more important.

Many typical changes of infancy and early childhood, such as the abilities to walk and talk, are tied to **maturation** of the body and brain—the unfolding of a natural sequence of physical changes and behavior patterns. As children grow into adolescents and then into adults, individual differences in innate characteristics and life experience play a greater role. Throughout life, however, maturation continues to influence certain biological processes, such as brain development.

maturation
Unfolding of a natural sequence of physical and behavioral changes.

Even in processes that all people undergo, rates and timing of development vary. Throughout this book, we talk about average ages for the occurrence of certain events: the first word, the first menstruation or nocturnal emission, the development of logical thought, and menopause. But there is wide variation among people with respect to these norms. Only when deviation from the average is extreme should we consider development exceptionally advanced or delayed.

To understand development, then, we need to look at the *inherited* characteristics that give each person a start in life. We also need to consider the many *environmental* factors that affect development, especially such major contexts as family, neighborhood, socioeconomic status, race/ethnicity, and culture. We need to consider how heredity and environment interact. We need to understand which aspects of development are primarily maturational and which are not. We need to look at influences that affect many or most people at a certain age or a certain time in history and also at those that affect only certain individuals. Finally, we need to look at how timing can accentuate the impact of certain influences.

CONTEXTS OF DEVELOPMENT

Human beings are social animals. For an infant, the immediate context of development is typically the family, but the family in turn is subject to the wider and ever-changing influences of social and cultural influences.

Family The **nuclear family** is a household unit consisting of one or two parents and their children, whether biological, adopted, or stepchildren. Historically, the two-parent nuclear family has been the normative family unit in the United States and other Western societies. In 1960, 73 percent of children lived in families with two

nuclear family
Two-generational kinship, economic, and household unit consisting of one or two parents and their biological children, adopted children, or stepchildren.

married parents in their first marriage and 37 percent of households were composed of nuclear families. In 2014, only 69 percent of children and 16 percent of households could be described in the same fashion (Pew Research Center, 2015). Instead of a large, rural family in which parents and children work side by side on the family farm, we are now more likely to see smaller, urban families in which both parents work outside the home and children spend much of their time in school or child care. The increased incidence of divorce also has affected the nuclear family. Children of divorced parents may live with one or the other parent or may move back and forth between them. The household may include a stepparent and stepsiblings or a parent's live-in partner. There are increasing numbers of single and childless adults, unmarried parents, and gay and lesbian households (Dye, 2010; Brown et al., 2015; Umberson et al., 2015). Moreover, there are increased numbers of grandparents raising their grandchildren (Sadruddin et al., 2019).

In many societies in Asia, Africa, and Latin America and among some U.S. families that trace their lineage to those countries, the **extended family**—a multigenerational network of grandparents, aunts, uncles, cousins, and more distant relatives—is the traditional family form. Many people live in *extended-family households*, where they have daily contact with kin. Adults often share breadwinning and child-raising responsibilities, and older children are responsible for younger brothers and sisters. Today the extended-family household is becoming slightly less typical in many developing countries (Bradbury et al., 2014) in part due to industrialization and migration to urban centers (Kinsella & Phillips, 2005). However, this does not imply that all countries will converge toward a nuclear family structure in concert with their country's economic and technological development, as unique cultural and contextual influences still shape family dynamics (Pesando et al, 2019).

extended family
Multigenerational kinship network of parents, children, and other relatives, sometimes living together in an extended-family household.

Meanwhile, in the United States, economic pressures, housing shortages, immigration patterns, out-of-wedlock childbearing, and an increase in life expectancy have helped to fuel a trend toward three- and even four-generational family households. In 2016, a record 20 percent of the U.S. population, or 64 million people, lived in multigenerational households (Kohn & Passel, 2018). This number has been steadily increasing since the low of 12 percent reached in 1980 (Fry, 2019). At the same time, the rate of single parenthood has also been rising, and currently the United States has the world's highest rate of single parenthood (Kramer, 2019).

socioeconomic status (SES)
Combination of economic and social factors describing an individual or family, including income, education, and occupation.

Socioeconomic Status and Neighborhood A family's **socioeconomic status (SES)** is based on family income and the educational and occupational levels of the adults in the household. SES is related to developmental processes (such as mothers' verbal interactions with their children) and to developmental outcomes (such as health and cognitive performance). SES affects these processes and outcomes indirectly, through such related factors as the kinds of homes and neighborhoods people live in and the quality of nutrition, medical care, and schooling available to them.

An extended-family household might include grandparents, aunts, and cousins. Tim Macpherson/Cultura/Getty Images

FIGURE 1.1

Number of Extreme Poor, 1990–2015

Source: World Bank. (2019). *Poverty and Shared Prosperity 2018: Taking on Inequality.* Washington, DC: World Bank.

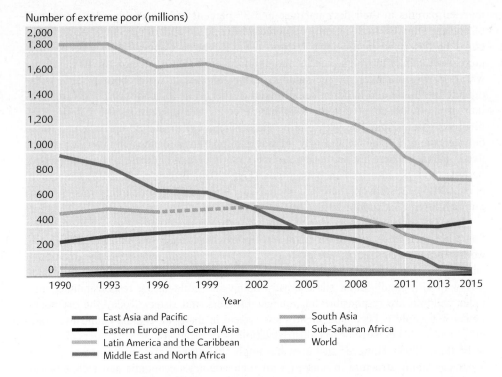

Number of extreme poor (millions)

Legend:
- East Asia and Pacific
- Eastern Europe and Central Asia
- Latin America and the Caribbean
- Middle East and North Africa
- South Asia
- Sub-Saharan Africa
- World

More than 736 million people worldwide lived on less than $1.90 a day in 2015. The majority of these people are young, live in rural areas, and are poorly educated. Although this represents a large number of people, it has fallen by almost 1.1 billion people since 1990 (Figure 1.1). The target of reducing the extreme poverty rate to below 3 percent has been reached in some previously troubled areas, including East Asia and Pacific, Europe, and Central Asia. However, sub-Saharan Africa remains challenged and showed an increase in extreme poverty in 2015. According to projections, by 2030, nearly 9 out of 10 people living in extreme poverty will be from sub-Saharan Africa (World Bank, 2019).

In the United States, 13 million children—18 percent of all children under age 18—live in poverty (Kids Count Data Center, 2019). Over 5 million of those children are in extreme poverty. Youngest children, who are the most vulnerable, are most likely to live in poverty (Children's Defense Fund, 2019). In the United States, race or ethnicity are often associated with SES. African American children (32 percent), American Indian (31 percent), and Hispanic children (26 percent) are far more likely to live in poverty than their white counterparts (11 percent) (Kids Count Data Center, 2019).

Poverty, especially if it is long-lasting, can be harmful to the physical, cognitive, and psychosocial well-being of children and families. Poor children are more likely than other children to go hungry, to have frequent illnesses, to lack access to health care, to experience violence and family conflict, to show emotional or behavioral problems (National Academies of Sciences, Engineering, and Medicine, 2019; Schickedanz et al., 2015; Eckenrode et al., 2014; Yoshikawa et al., 2012), and to have their cognitive potential and school performance suffer as well (Wolf et al., 2017; Luby, 2015). The harm done by poverty may be indirect, through its impact on parents' emotional state and parenting practices and on the home environment they create. Threats to well-being multiply if, as often happens, several **risk factors**—conditions that increase the likelihood of a negative outcome—are present. However, the negative effects of poverty are not inevitable. For example, factors such as supportive parenting (Hostinar & Miller, 2019; Morris et al., 2017; Barton et al., 2018) or particular temperament profiles (Moran et al., 2017; Rudasill et al., 2017) can buffer children against ill effects.

Children from middle- and lower-income families, even if above the poverty line, can also suffer the negative effects of employment insecurity and income inequality and may show decreased educational attainment, increased hostile and antisocial behaviors, and

risk factors
Conditions that increase the likelihood of a negative developmental outcome.

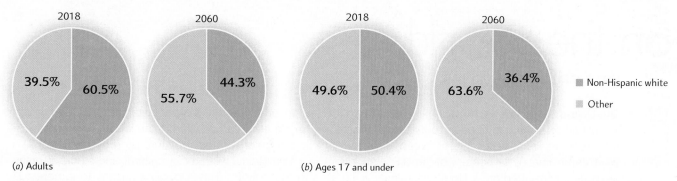

2018	2060	2018	2060	
39.5% 60.5%	55.7% 44.3%	49.6% 50.4%	63.6% 36.4%	■ Non-Hispanic white ■ Other

(a) Adults   *(b)* Ages 17 and under

FIGURE 1.2

Population Projections for Non-Hispanic White and Minority Groups, 2018–2060

(a) According to Census Bureau projections, racial/ethnic minorities will reach 55.7 percent of the U.S. population, exceeding the proportion of non-Hispanic white people by 2060. (b) Also by 2060, "minority" children under age 18 are expected to make up 63.6 percent of the child population.

Source: Colby, S. L., & Ortman, J. M. (2015, March). *Projections of the size and composition of the U.S. population: 2014–2060. Current Population Reports.* Washington, DC: U.S. Census Bureau. And Frey, W. (2018). The US will become "minority white" in 2045, Census projects. [Blog post].*The Avenue*. Retrieved from *www.brookings.edu/ blog/the-avenue/2018/03/14/the-us-will-become-minority-white-in-2045-census-projects/*

negative effects on their self-confidence (Foundation for Child Development, 2019). Even affluence does not necessarily protect children from risk. Some children in wealthy families face pressure to achieve and are often left on their own by busy parents. Such children may be at increased risk for substance abuse, anxiety, and depression (Luthar & Latendresse, 2005).

Culture and Race/Ethnicity **Culture** refers to a society's or group's total way of life, including its customs, traditions, laws, knowledge, beliefs, values, language, and physical products, from tools to artworks—all of the behavior and attitudes that are learned, shared, and transmitted among members of a social group. Culture is constantly changing, often through contact with other cultures. Today cultural contact has been enhanced by computers and telecommunications providing almost instantaneous communication across the globe.

An **ethnic group** consists of people united by a distinctive culture, ancestry, religion, language, or national origin, all of which contribute to a sense of shared identity and shared attitudes, beliefs, and values. By 2044 ethnic minorities in the United States are expected to become the majority. It is predicted that by 2060, 64 percent of the nation's children will be members of what are now minority groups, and the proportion of Hispanic or Latino/a children—33.5 percent—will be nearly equal to the 35.6 percent who will be non-Hispanic white (Colby & Ortman, 2015; Figure 1.2). An increasing number of the children being born today come from mixed racial or ethnic backgrounds (Alba, 2018). The theoretical and practical implications of these changing demographic trends are yet to be determined.

The United States has always been a nation of immigrants and ethnic groups, but the primary ethnic origins of the immigrant population have shifted from Europe and Canada to Asia and Latin America (Hernandez, 2004). In 2017, almost 14 percent of the population were immigrants (see Window on the World), roughly a quarter of whom are undocumented. Nearly every area in the world is represented among U.S. immigrant populations (Radford & Noe-Bustamante, 2019).

culture
A society's or group's total way of life, including customs, traditions, beliefs, values, language, and physical products—all learned behavior, passed on from parents to children.

ethnic group
A group united by ancestry, race, religion, language, or national origins, which contribute to a sense of shared identity.

The existence of Marcia and Millie Biggs, who as fraternal twins share approximately 50 percent of their genes, calls into question the concept of race as a biological construct. Ken McKay/ITV/Shutterstock

window on the world

IMMIGRANT FAMILIES

The United States is a nation of immigrants, known for its cultural diversity and appeals to those seeking refuge, freedom, financial security, or a second chance. In 2017, approximately 14 percent of the U.S. population were immigrants (Radford & Noe-Bustamante, 2019).

The ethnic origins of the immigrant population have shifted significantly over the past 100 years. In 1910, most U.S. immigrants came from Europe and Canada. By 2010, the largest numbers of immigrants were from Mexico, Asia, and the Caribbean. Since that time, the largest percentage increases have occurred in immigration from Southern Asia, the Middle East, and Northern Africa (Camarota & Ziegler, 2016). However, more immigrants come from Mexico (25.3 percent) than from any other country (Radford & Noe-Bustamante, 2019).

Roughly one-fourth (26 percent) of U.S. children lived in immigrant families in 2017, and 88 percent of these children were born in the United States, making them U.S. citizens (Migration Policy Institute, 2019). Children of immigrants are the fastest growing group of children in the United States.

Immigrant families must navigate a different culture, religion, and language, and often different ethics and values. Currently, 23 percent of U.S. immigrants are undocumented (Radford, 2019). Immigrants are more likely to work at low-paying jobs requiring manual labor. Not surprisingly, 15 percent of immigrant families live in poverty and almost 20 percent are uninsured (Radford & Noe-Bustamante, 2019). Though immigration can be difficult, the longer immigrants are in the United States, the more progress they make.

Immigrants bring racial, cultural, and ethnic diversity to the country. This allows Americans to experience different ways of life, languages, religions, and foods. Immigrants also bring innovative ideas and economic benefits. One-fourth of innovative U.S. companies founded between 1995 and 2005 had at least one immigrant in a senior position on product development or management teams (Anderson, 2011). More than half of all patent grants in 2014 were to foreign-born individuals (Grenier, 2014). Immigrants often work in farming, food service, maintenance, construction, and manufacturing industries. Many of these industries would collapse without immigrant labor (Jacobi, 2012). It is sometimes easy to forget the United States was founded by immigrants and what role our ancestors played in that process. Immigration will continue to bring a depth and richness to the nation and its culture.

what's your view

How do you see immigration influencing the United States? How do you imagine life may be different for immigrants 40 years from now?

It is important to remember that wide diversity exists within broad ethnic groups. Cuban Americans, South Americans, and Central Americans—all Hispanic Americans—have different histories and cultures and may be of African, European, Native American, or mixed descent. African Americans from the rural South differ from those of Caribbean ancestry. Asian Americans hail from a variety of countries with distinct cultures, from modern industrial Japan to communist China to the remote mountains of Nepal, where many people still practice their ancient way of life. Given this diversity within groups, a term such as *Black* or *Hispanic* can be an **ethnic gloss**—an overgeneralization that obscures or blurs such variations.

The term *race*, historically and popularly viewed as an identifiable biological category, is best defined as a social construct. There is no clear scientific consensus on its definition, and it is impossible to measure reliably (Yudell et al., 2016). Human genetic variation occurs along a broad continuum, and 90 percent of such variation occurs *within* rather than between socially defined races (Bonham et al., 2005; Ossorio & Duster, 2005). Nevertheless, race as a social category remains a factor in research because it makes a difference in "how individuals are treated, where they live, their employment opportunities, the quality of their health care, and whether [they] can fully participate" in their society (Smedley & Smedley, 2005, p. 23).

ethnic gloss
An overgeneralization that obscures or blurs variations between cultural or ethnic groups.

NORMATIVE AND NONNORMATIVE INFLUENCES

To understand similarities and differences in development, we need to look at two types of **normative** influences: biological or environmental events that affect many or most people in a society in similar ways and events that touch only certain individuals (Baltes & Smith, 2004).

Normative age-graded influences are highly similar for people in a particular age group. The timing of biological events is fairly predictable within a normal range. For example, people don't experience puberty at age 35 or menopause at 12.

Normative history-graded influences are significant events (such as World War II or the COVID-19 pandemic) that shape the behavior and attitudes of a **historical generation:** a group of people who experience the event at a formative time in their lives. For example, the generations that came of age during the Depression and World War II tend to show a strong sense of social interdependence and trust that has declined among more recent generations (Rogler, 2002). Depending on when and where they live, entire generations may feel the impact of famines, disease, nuclear explosions, or terrorist attacks.

A historical generation is not the same as an age **cohort:** a group of people born at about the same time. A historical generation may contain more than one cohort, but cohorts are part of a historical generation only if they experience major, shaping historical events at a formative point in their lives (Rogler, 2002).

Nonnormative influences are unusual events that have a major impact on *individual* lives because they disturb the expected sequence of the life cycle. They are either typical events that happen at an atypical time of life (such as the death of a parent when a child is young) or atypical events (such as surviving a plane crash). Some of these influences are largely beyond a person's control and may present rare opportunities or severe challenges that the person perceives as turning points. On the other hand, people sometimes help create their own nonnormative life events—say, by deciding to have a baby in their midfifties or taking up a risky hobby such as skydiving—and thus participate actively in their own development. Taken together, the three types of influences—normative age-graded, normative history-graded, and nonnormative—contribute to the complexity of human development.

CRITICAL OR SENSITIVE PERIODS

In a well-known study, Konrad Lorenz (1957), an Austrian ethologist, showed that newly hatched goslings will instinctively follow the first moving object they see. This phenomenon is called **imprinting.** Usually, this automatic and irreversible bond is with the mother. When the natural course of events is disturbed, however, other attachments, or none at all, can form. Imprinting, said Lorenz, is the result of a *predisposition toward learning*: the readiness of an organism's nervous system to acquire certain information during a brief *critical period* in early life.

A **critical period** is a specific time when a given event, or its absence, has a specific impact on development. If a necessary event does not occur during a critical period of maturation, normal development will not occur, and the resulting abnormal patterns may be irreversible (Kuhl et al., 2005).

Do human beings experience critical periods? If a pregnant woman receives X-rays, takes certain drugs, or contracts certain diseases, the fetus may show specific ill effects, depending on the nature of the insult, its timing, and characteristics of the fetus itself. However, because many aspects of development, even in

normative
Characteristic of an event that occurs in a similar way for most people in a group.

historical generation
A group of people strongly influenced by a major historical event during their formative period.

cohort
A group of people born at about the same time.

nonnormative
Characteristic of an unusual event that happens to a particular person or a typical event that happens at an unusual time of life.

imprinting
Instinctive form of learning in which, during a critical period in early development, a young animal forms an attachment to the first moving object it sees, usually the mother.

critical period
Specific time when a given event or its absence has a specific impact on development.

Newborn goslings followed and became attached to the first moving object they saw, which happened to be ethologist Konrad Lorenz. Lorenz called this behavior imprinting. Album/ Alamy Stock Photo

the physical domain, have been found to show **plasticity,** or modifiability of performance, it may be more useful to think about **sensitive periods,** when a developing person is particularly responsive to certain kinds of experiences (Bruer, 2001).

There is growing evidence that plasticity is not just a general characteristic of development that applies to all members of a species, but that there are individual differences in plasticity of responses to environmental events as well. For example, some children—especially those with difficult temperaments, those who are highly reactive, and those with particular gene variants—may be more profoundly affected by childhood experiences, whether positive or negative, than other children (Belsky & Pluess, 2009). This new research also suggests that characteristics generally assumed to be negative—such as a difficult or reactive temperament—can be adaptive (positive) when the environment is supportive of development. One study found that children who were highly reactive to environmental events showed, as expected, negative responses such as aggression and behavior problems when faced with stressors such as marital conflict in their families. Surprisingly, however, when the levels of family adversity were low, highly reactive children showed even more adaptive profiles than children low in reactivity. These highly reactive children were more prosocial, more engaged in school, and showed lower levels of externalizing symptoms (Obradovic et al., 2010). Research such as this clearly points to a need to reconceptualize the nature of plasticity in early development with an eye toward examining issues of resilience as well as risk. Research in Action discusses how the concepts of critical and sensitive periods apply to language development.

The Life-Span Developmental Approach

Paul B. Baltes (1936–2006) and his colleagues (1987; Baltes & Smith, 2004) have identified seven key principles of a life-span developmental approach that sum up many of the concepts discussed in this chapter.

1. *Development is lifelong.* Development is a lifelong process of change. Each period of the life span is affected by what happened before and will affect what is to come. No period is more or less important than any other.

2. *Development is multidimensional.* It occurs along multiple interacting dimensions—biological, psychological, and social—each of which may develop at varying rates.

3. *Development is multidirectional.* Although we generally think of development as proceeding in a positive direction, people can show gains or losses at any point in the life span.

4. *Relative influences of biology and culture shift over the life span.* The process of development is influenced by both biology and culture, but the balance between these influences changes. Biological abilities, such as sensory acuity and muscular strength and coordination, weaken with age, but cultural supports, such as education, relationships, and technologically age-friendly environments, may help compensate.

5. *Development involves changing resource allocations.* Individuals choose to invest their resources of time, energy, talent, money, and social support in varying ways. The allocation of resources to these three functions changes throughout life as the total available pool of resources decreases. In childhood and young adulthood the bulk of resources typically goes to growth; in old age, to regulation of loss.

6. *Development shows plasticity.* Many abilities, such as memory, strength, and endurance, can be improved significantly with training and practice, even late in life. One of the tasks of developmental research is to discover to what extent particular kinds of development can be modified at various ages.

7. *Development is influenced by the historical and cultural context.* Each person develops within multiple contexts—circumstances or conditions defined in part by maturation and in part by time and place. Human beings not only influence but also are influenced by their historical-cultural context.

BABY TALK: CULTURAL DIFFERENCES IN INFANT-DIRECTED SPEECH

Imagine you're cradling a baby in your arms. She gives you a toothless grin as you begin to speak. Do you notice a difference in your speech patterns? Are your words simpler? Do you make silly sounds to attract her attention?

When interacting with a baby, most adults naturally slip into "baby talk," a distinctive speech pattern typically used with preverbal infants. This infant-directed (ID) speech includes simplified grammar, slower tempo, pitch variations, exaggerated sound intonation, and repetition of key words and phrases (Estes & Hurley, 2013; Ma et al., 2011).

American English is the most studied language with respect to ID speech, but there is ample evidence of ID speech patterns cross-culturally. Similarities are also found in prosody (stressed syllables and intonation) across different languages (Broesch & Bryant, 2015; Soderstrom, 2007; Saint-Georges et al., 2013). Although there are some minor differences, both women and men use ID speech patterns (Gergely et al., 2016; Kokkinaki, 2019), a finding that has also been validated cross-culturally (Fernald et al., 1989; Broesch & Bryant, 2018).

Infants find ID speech highly engaging, and it draws their attention to spoken language. Adults speak in this fashion even to newborns (Johnson et al., 2014), and infants as young as 7 weeks display ID speech preferences. In fact, babies pay special attention to ID speech even in languages other than their own (Pegg et al., 1992). A study of mother-infant vocalization across 11 countries suggests that ID speech engages infants in the social function of language. Baby talk captures attention and elicits vocalization in a conversational, turn-taking manner (Bornstein et al., 2015).

ID speech may help convey cultural norms. Fernald and Morikawa (1993) found that American mothers use noun-labeling more frequently ("Look at the car.... Those are wheels."). Japanese mothers use ID speech to emphasize social interactions ("Car goes 'vrooom'.... I give to you.... You give back"). Japanese mothers also emphasized cultural norms of empathy and politeness within ID speech, promoting cultural values of interdependence, connectedness, and harmony (Fernald & Morikawa, 1993). Mastin and Vogt (2016) drew a similar conclusion from a study of Mozambican infants. Rural Mozambicans used more words related to kinship, emphasizing collectivist values even more so than those in urban areas. Another study comparing Canadian and Vietnamese families found language interactions in Canadian families involved more turn-taking, interpreted by the researchers as illustrating the Canadian parents' encouragement of individuality in their children (Ganek et al., 2018).

Despite being common, ID speech is not completely universal. The Gusii of Kenya do not believe it is useful or necessary to speak to infants (Richman et al., 2010). The Ifaluk of Micronesia see no point in talking to babies as it is believed infants lack understanding (Le, 2000), and remote Senegalese villagers express fears that evil spirits will possess babies who are spoken to (Weber et al., 2017; Zeitlin, 2011). As a result, little to no effort is made to speak to infants in these cultures, despite near constant contact with caregivers.

Still, the near ubiquity of ID speech suggests it has a function. ID speech supports the association of sounds of words with meanings (Estes & Hurley, 2013; Ma et al., 2011; Bergelson & Swingley, 2012), increases long-term word recognition (Singh et al., 2009), and causes increased neural activity (Zangl & Mills, 2007). Researchers and theorists believe the attention-grabbing features of ID speech exist to orient babies to spoken language, and the simplified and repetitive nature of ID speech is a supportive framework for language acquisition. We talk to babies this way and they love it as much as they do because those features make it easier to learn language.

Cross-cultural research helps us to tease out what aspects of our behavior are universal—common to humans everywhere—or culturally specific—the product of our upbringing. Without being able to compare the findings from different cultures, we would not know if the American findings on ID speech were a quirk of U.S. culture or a deeper human truth. To truly understand the complexity of human development, we cannot rely on the information from one culture alone.

what's your view

What other aspects of childcare and interaction do you think differ across cultures? What cultural norms are being transmitted by those differences?

summary and key terms

Human Development: An Ever-Evolving Field

- Human development is the scientific study of processes of change and stability and has important real-world applications.
- Life-span development has become a field of study.
- The study of human development seeks to describe, explain, predict, and, when appropriate, intervene in development.
- Students of human development draw on multiple disciplines.
- Methods of studying human development are still evolving, making use of advanced technologies.

human development, life-span development

The Study of Human Development: Basic Concepts

- Developmental scientists study change and stability in all domains of development throughout the life span.
- The three major domains of development are physical, cognitive, and psychosocial. Each affects the others.
- The concept of periods of development is a social construction.

physical development, cognitive development, psychosocial development, social construction

Influences on Development

- Influences on development come from both heredity and environment. Many typical changes during childhood are related to maturation. Individual differences tend to increase with age.

- In some societies, the nuclear family predominates; in others, the extended family.
- Socioeconomic status (SES) affects developmental processes and outcomes through the quality of home and neighborhood environments, nutrition, medical care, and schooling. Multiple risk factors increase the likelihood of poor outcomes.
- Important environmental influences stem from culture, race/ethnicity, and historical context. Race is a social construction. Ethic gloss is an overgeneralization that can blur differences between racial or ethnic groups.
- Influences may be normative (age-graded or history-graded) or nonnormative.
- There is evidence of critical or sensitive periods for certain kinds of early development.

individual differences, heredity, environment, maturation, nuclear family, extended family, socioeconomic status (SES), risk factors, culture, ethnic group, ethnic gloss normative, historical generation, cohort, nonnormative, imprinting, critical period, plasticity, sensitive periods

The Life-Span Developmental Approach

- The principles of the life-span developmental approach include the propositions that (1) development is lifelong, (2) development is multidimensional, (3) development is multidirectional, (4) the relative influences of biology and culture shift over the life span, (5) development involves changing resource allocations, (6) development shows plasticity, and (7) development is influenced by the historical and cultural context.

Theory and Research

Andrew Hetherington/Redux

learning objectives

Describe the purpose of theories in research and two theoretical issues on which developmental scientists differ.

Summarize the main theories of human development.

Describe the methods developmental researchers use to collect data and the advantages and disadvantages of each.

Explain ethical guidelines for researchers.

In this chapter we present an overview of the major theories of human development and of the research methods used to study it. We explore important issues and theoretical perspectives that underlie much research in human development, and we look at how researchers gather and assess information. Ethical issues that may arise in research are also addressed.

Basic Theoretical Issues

A scientific **theory** of development is a set of logically related concepts or statements that seek to describe and explain development and to predict the kinds of behavior that might occur under certain conditions. Theories organize and explain *data*, the information gathered by research. As painstaking research adds, bit by bit, to the body of knowledge, theoretical concepts help us make sense of, and see connections between, isolated pieces of data.

Theory and research are interwoven strands in the fabric of scientific study. Theories inspire further research and predict its results. They do this by generating **hypotheses,** explanations or predictions that can be tested by further research. Research can indicate whether a theory is accurate in its predictions but cannot conclusively show a theory to be true. Science is built upon falsifiability, and no theory is *ever* proven. However, theories can be *disproved*. Sometimes research supports a hypothesis and the theory on which it was based. At other times, scientists must modify their theories to account for unexpected data. This flexibility is one of the greatest strengths of science.

The way theorists explain development depends in part on their assumptions about two basic issues: (1) whether people are active or reactive in their own development and (2) whether development is continuous or occurs in stages.

ISSUE 1: IS DEVELOPMENT ACTIVE OR REACTIVE?

Psychology is an outgrowth of philosophy in many ways, and philosophers have frequently grappled with questions of psychology and development.

There have been a variety of perspectives. For example, the eighteenth-century English philosopher John Locke held that a young child is a *tabula rasa*—a "blank slate"—upon which society writes. How the child developed, in either positive or negative ways, depended entirely on experiences. In contrast, the French philosopher Jean Jacques Rousseau believed that children are born "noble savages" who develop according to their own positive natural tendencies if not corrupted by society. This debate remains important today, although in modern terms we speak of environmental influences and heredity.

Additional philosophical debates about development, and the same basic issues philosophers argued about, are reflected in the psychological theories of today. Psychologists today debate active and reactive development. Psychologists who believe in reactive development conceptualize the developing child as a hungry sponge that soaks up experiences and is shaped by this input over time. Psychologists who believe in active development argue that people create experiences for themselves and are motivated to learn about the world around them. Things aren't just happening to them; they are involved in making their world what it is.

Mechanistic Model Locke's view was the forerunner of the **mechanistic model.** In this model, people are like machines that react to environmental input (Pepper, 1961).

Machines do not operate of their own will; they react automatically to physical forces or inputs. Fill a car with gas, turn the ignition key, press the accelerator, and the car will move. In the mechanistic view, human behavior is much the same: It results from the operation of biological parts in response to external or internal stimuli. If we know enough about how the human "machine" is put together and about the forces acting on it, we can predict what the person will do.

Mechanistic researchers want to identify the factors that make people behave as they do. For example, to explain why some children are more competitive than others and why some are more cooperative, a mechanistic theorist might look for cultural influences such as where a culture falls on the individualism/collectivism scale.

Organismic Model Rousseau was the precursor of the **organismic model.** This model sees people as active, growing organisms that set their own development in motion (Pepper, 1961). The driving force for change is internal. Environmental influences do not

Continuity

Stage theory
(Discontinuity)

(a)

(b)

FIGURE 2.1
Quantitative and
Qualitative Change

*A major difference among
developmental theories is
(a) whether it proceeds
continuously, as learning
theorists and information-
processing theorists propose, or
(b) whether development occurs
in distinct stages, as Freud,
Erikson, and Piaget maintained.*

cause development, though they can speed or slow it. Development is believed to have an underlying, orderly structure, though it may not be obvious from moment to moment.

Because human behavior is viewed as an organic whole, it cannot be predicted by breaking it down into simple responses to environmental stimulation. An organismic theorist, in studying why some students drink too much, looks at what kinds of situations they choose to participate in, and with whom. Do they choose friends who prefer to party or to study?

ISSUE 2: IS DEVELOPMENT CONTINUOUS OR DISCONTINUOUS?

The mechanistic and organismic models also differ on the second issue: Is development *continuous*, that is, gradual and incremental, or *discontinuous*, that is, abrupt or uneven? Mechanist theorists see development as continuous: as occurring in small incremental stages (Figure 2.1a). Development is always governed by the same processes and involves the gradual refinement and extension of early skills into later abilities, allowing one to make predictions about future characteristics on the basis of past performance. This type of change is known as **quantitative change**—a change in number or amount, such as height, weight, or vocabulary size.

Organismic theorists see development as discontinuous; as marked by the emergence of new phenomena that could not be easily predicted on the basis of past functioning. Development at different points in the life span is, in this view, fundamentally different in nature. It is a change in kind, structure, or organization, not just in number. This type of change is known as **qualitative change.**

Organismic theorists are proponents of *stage theories* in which development is seen as occurring in a series of distinct stages, like stairsteps (Figure 2.1b). At each stage, what is going on is different from previous stages. Moreover, stages build upon each other. Stages cannot be skipped, and development only proceeds in a positive direction. It is believed that these processes are universal and account for the development of all humans everywhere, although the particular timing may vary a bit.

Theoretical Perspectives

Five major perspectives underlie much influential theory and research on human development. Following is a general overview of each of these perspectives. These are summarized in Table 2.1.

PERSPECTIVE 1: PSYCHOANALYTIC

Sigmund Freud (1856–1939) was a Viennese physician who was the originator of the **psychoanalytic perspective.** He believed in reactive development and qualitative change.

quantitative change
Changes in number or amount, such as in height, weight, size of vocabulary, or frequency of communication.

qualitative change
Discontinuous changes in kind, structure, or organization.

psychoanalytic perspective
View of human development as shaped by unconscious forces that motivate human behavior.

TABLE 2.1 Five Perspectives on Human Development

Perspective	Important Theories	Basic Propositions	Stage-Oriented	Causal Emphasis	Active/Reactive Individual
Psychoanalytic	Freud's psychosexual theory	Behavior is controlled by powerful unconscious urges.	Yes	Innate factors modified by experience	Reactive
	Erikson's psychosocial theory	Personality is influenced by society and develops through a series of crises.	Yes	Interaction of innate and experiential factors	Active
Learning	Behaviorism, or traditional learning theory (Pavlov, Skinner, Watson)	People are responders; the environment controls behavior.	No	Experience	Reactive
	Social learning, or social cognitive theory (Bandura)	Children learn by observation and imitation; they are active contributors to learning.	No	Experience modified by innate factors	Active and reactive
Cognitive	Piaget's cognitive stage theory	Qualitative changes in thought occur between infancy and adolescence. Children are active initiators of development.	Yes	Interaction of innate and experiential factors	Active
	Vygotsky's sociocultural theory	Social interaction is central to cognitive development.	No for general stages; yes for concept formation.	Experience	Active
	Information-processing theory	Human beings are processors and manipulators of symbols.	No	Interaction of innate and experiential factors	Active
Contextual	Bronfenbrenner's bioecological theory	Development occurs through interaction between a developing person and five interlocking contextual systems of influences.	No	Interaction of innate and experiential factors	Active
Evolutionary/ sociobiological	Evolutionary psychology; Bowlby's attachment theory	Human beings are the product of adaptive processes; there is an evolutionary basis for behavior and learning.	No	Interaction of innate and experiential factors	Active and reactive (theorists vary)

Freud proposed that humans were born with a series of innate, biologically based drives such as hunger, sex, and aggression. He thought that people were motivated to satisfy these drives, and that much of development involved learning how to do so in socially acceptable ways. In addition, Freud believed that early experiences shaped later functioning. Freud also promoted the idea that what we consciously know about and experience is only the small tip of the iceberg of who we are.

Psychosexual Development: Sigmund Freud Freud (1953, 1964a, 1964b) believed that people are born with biological drives that must be redirected to make it possible to live in society. He proposed three hypothetical parts of the personality: the *id*, the *ego*, and the *superego*. Newborns are governed by the *id*, which operates under the *pleasure principle*—the drive to seek immediate satisfaction of their needs and desires. When gratification is delayed, as it is when infants have to wait to be fed, they begin to see themselves as separate from the outside world. The *ego*, which represents reason, develops gradually during the first year or so of life and operates under the *reality principle*. The ego's aim is to find realistic ways to gratify the id that are acceptable to the *superego*, which develops at about age 5 or 6. The *superego* includes the conscience and incorporates socially approved "shoulds" and "should nots" into the child's value system. The superego is highly demanding; if its standards are not met, a child may feel guilty and anxious. The ego mediates between the impulses of the id and the demands of the superego.

Freud proposed that personality forms through unconscious childhood conflicts between the inborn urges of the id and the requirements of civilized life. These conflicts occur in a sequence of five stages of **psychosexual development** (Table 2.2), in which sensual pleasure shifts from one body zone to another—from the mouth to the anus and then to the genitals. At each stage, the behavior that is the chief source of gratification (or frustration) changes.

According to Freud, if children receive too little or too much gratification in the first three stages, they are at risk of *fixation*, an arrest in development that can show up in adult personality. Babies whose needs are not met during the *oral stage*, when feeding is the main source of pleasure, may grow up to become nail-biters or smokers. A person who, as a toddler, had too-strict toilet training may be fixated at the *anal stage*, and be obsessively clean, rigidly tied to schedules and routines, or defiantly messy.

A key event occurs in the *phallic stage* of early childhood. Boys develop sexual attachment to their mothers, and girls to their fathers, and they have aggressive urges toward the same-sex parent, whom they regard as a rival. Freud called these developments the *Oedipus* and *Electra complexes*.

Children eventually resolve their anxiety over these feelings by identifying with the same-sex parent and move into the *latency stage* of middle childhood, a period of relative emotional calm and intellectual and social exploration.

The *genital stage*, the final stage, lasts throughout adulthood. The sexual urges repressed during latency now resurface to flow in socially approved channels, which Freud defined as heterosexual relations with persons outside the family of origin.

Freud's theory made historic contributions; however, many of Freud's ideas now are widely considered obsolete or are impossible to investigate scientifically. Psychologists today reject his narrow emphasis on sexual and aggressive drives to the exclusion of other influences. Nevertheless, several of his central themes have stood the test of time. Freud made us aware of the importance of unconscious thoughts, feelings, and motivations; the role of childhood experiences in forming personality; the ambivalence of emotional responses, the role of mental representations of the self and others in the establishment of intimate relationships; and the path of typical development from an immature, dependent state to a mature, interdependent state. In all these ways, Freud left an indelible mark on psychoanalysis and developmental psychology (Gedo, 2001; Westen, 1998).

We need to remember that Freud based his theories about typical development on a clientele of Victorian upper-middle-class adults, mostly women, in therapy. His concentration on the influences of sexual urges and early experience did not take into account other, and later, influences on personality—including the influences of society and culture, which many heirs to the Freudian tradition, such as Erik Erikson, stress and which psychologists today acknowledge are of fundamental importance.

Psychosocial Development: Erik Erikson Erik Erikson (1902–1994) modified and extended Freudian theory and was a pioneer in taking a life-span perspective. Note that both theorists, as they proposed stage theories, believed in qualitative change.

TABLE 2.2 Developmental Stages According to Various Theories

Psychosexual Stages (Freud)	Psychosocial Stages (Erikson)	Cognitive Stages (Piaget)
Oral (birth to 12–18 months). Baby's source of pleasure involves the mouth (sucking and feeding).	*Basic trust versus mistrust (birth to 12–18 months).* Baby develops sense of whether world is a good and safe place. Virtue: hope.	*Sensorimotor (birth to 2 years).* Infant learns about the environment through sensory and motor activity.
Anal (12–18 months to 3 years). Child derives pleasure from withholding and expelling feces. Zone of gratification is anal region, thus toilet training is an important activity.	*Autonomy versus shame and doubt (12–18 months to 3 years).* Child develops a balance of independence and self-sufficiency over shame and doubt. Virtue: will.	*Preoperational (2 to 7 years).* Child develops a representational system and uses symbols to represent people, places, and events. Language and imaginative play are important manifestations of this stage. Thinking is still not logical.
Phallic (3 to 6 years). Child develops sexual feelings for other-sex parents leading to fear and identification with same-sex parent. Superego develops. Zone of gratification shifts to genitals.	*Initiative versus guilt (3 to 6 years).* Child develops initiative when trying out new activities and is not overwhelmed by guilt. Virtue: purpose.	
Latency (6 years to puberty). Time of relative calm between more turbulent stages.	*Industry versus inferiority (6 years to puberty).* Child must learn skills of the culture or face feelings of incompetence. Virtue: skill.	*Concrete operations (7 to 11 years).* Child can solve problems logically if they are focused on the here and now but cannot think abstractly.
Genital (puberty through adulthood). Reemergence of sexual impulses of phallic stage, channeled into mature adult sexuality.	*Identity versus identity confusion (puberty to young adulthood).* Adolescent must determine sense of self or experience role confusion. Virtue: fidelity. *Intimacy versus isolation (young adulthood).* Person makes commitments to others or may suffer from isolation and self-absorption. Virtue: love. *Generativity versus stagnation (middle adulthood).* Mature adult contributes to the next generation or risks personal impoverishment. Virtue: care. *Integrity versus despair (late adulthood).* Older adult achieves acceptance of death, or else despairs over inability to relive life. Virtue: wisdom.	*Formal operations (11 years through adulthood).* Person can think abstractly, deal with hypothetical situations, and think about possibilities.

Note: All ages are approximate.

psychosocial development
In Erikson's eight-stage theory, the socially and culturally influenced process of development of the ego, or self.

Erikson's (1950, 1982) theory of **psychosocial development** covers eight stages across the life span (refer to Table 2.2). Each stage involves what Erikson originally called a *crisis* in personality*—a major psychosocial challenge that is particularly important at that time. These issues must be satisfactorily resolved for healthy ego development.

Each stage requires balancing a positive and a negative tendency. The positive quality should dominate, but some degree of the negative quality is needed as well. The critical theme of infancy, for example, is *basic trust versus basic mistrust*. People need to trust the world and the people in it. However, they also need some mistrust to protect themselves from danger. The successful outcome of each stage is the development of a particular *virtue*, or strength—in this case, the virtue of *hope*.

*Erikson broadened the concept of "crisis" and later referred instead to conflicting or competing tendencies.

Successful resolution of each crisis puts the person in a particularly good position to address the next crisis, a process that occurs iteratively across the life span. So, for example, a child who successfully develops a sense of trust in infancy would be well prepared for the development of a sense of autonomy—the second psychosocial challenge—in toddlerhood. After all, if you feel that others have your back, you are more likely to try to develop your skills knowing that they will be there to comfort you if you fail.

While the crises that Erikson outlined were particular to his place and time—for example, not all cultures have a period of time that could be characterized as adolescence—Erikson argued for the influence of social and cultural factors on development. He highlighted the social clock, the conventional, culturally preferred timing of important life events. Moreover, Erikson's focus on lifelong development enriched the field of psychology and has been one of his enduring contributions.

PERSPECTIVE 2: LEARNING

The **learning perspective** maintains that development results from *learning*, a long-lasting change in behavior based on experience or adaptation to the environment. Learning theorists were not interested in the inner workings of the mind and preferred to focus on observable behaviors that could be counted and measured precisely, as well as tested in the laboratory in an objective manner.

learning perspective
View of human development that holds that changes in behavior result from experience or from adaptation to the environment.

Psychologists at this time viewed the mind as *tabula rasa,* a blank slate upon which experience could write. Thus, differences between individuals were ascribed to their different experiences. This implied that cultural and contextual influences were primary in importance. Learning theorists also saw development as continuous and incremental, and as capable of being influenced by changing environmental contingencies across the entire life span. Two important learning theories are *behaviorism* and *social learning theory*.

Behaviorism **Behaviorism** is a mechanistic theory that describes observed behavior as a predictable response to experience. Behaviorists consider development as reactive and continuous. Behavioral research focuses on *associative learning*, in which a mental link is formed between two events. Two kinds of associative learning are *classical conditioning* and *operant conditioning*.

behaviorism
Learning theory that emphasizes the predictable role of environment in causing observable behavior.

The Russian physiologist Ivan Pavlov (1849-1936) devised experiments in which dogs learned to salivate at the sound of a bell that rang at feeding time. These experiments were the foundation for **classical conditioning,** in which a response (in this case, salivation) to a stimulus (the bell) is evoked after repeated association with a stimulus that normally elicits the response (food).

The American behaviorist John B. Watson (1878-1958) applied such stimulus-response theories to children, claiming that he could mold any infant in any way he chose. In one of the earliest and most famous demonstrations of classical conditioning in human beings (Watson & Rayner, 1920), he taught an 11-month-old baby known as "Little Albert" to fear furry white objects. In this study, Albert was exposed to a loud noise that frightened him whenever he reached for a rat. After repeated pairings of the rat with the loud noise, Albert whimpered with fear when he saw the rat. Albert also started showing fear responses to white rabbits and cats, and the beards of elderly men. The study, although unethical, demonstrated that fear could be conditioned.

classical conditioning
Learning based on associating a stimulus that does not ordinarily elicit a response with another stimulus that does elicit the response.

Classical conditioning occurs throughout life. Fear responses to objects like a dog may be the result of a bad experience. Much advertising is based upon attempts to condition associations between products (like a car) and positive stimuli (like an attractive person).

Operant Conditioning Julio lies in his crib. When he starts to babble, his mother smiles and repeats the syllables. Julio learns that his behavior (babbling) can produce a desirable consequence (loving attention from a parent), and so he keeps babbling to attract his mother's attention. An originally accidental behavior (babbling) has become a conditioned response.

operant conditioning
Learning based on association of behavior with its consequences.

reinforcement
The process by which a behavior is strengthened, increasing the likelihood that the behavior will be repeated.

punishment
The process by which a behavior is weakened, decreasing the likelihood of repetition.

social learning theory
Theory that behaviors are learned by observing and imitating models. Also called *social cognitive theory*.

reciprocal determinism
Bandura's term for bidirectional forces that affect development.

observational learning
Learning through watching the behavior of others.

self-efficacy
Sense of one's capability to master challenges and achieve goals.

cognitive perspective
View that thought processes are central to development.

cognitive-stage theory
Piaget's theory that children's cognitive development advances in a series of four stages involving qualitatively distinct types of mental operations.

This type of learning is called **operant conditioning** because the individual learns from the consequences of "operating" on the environment. Unlike classical conditioning, operant conditioning involves voluntary behavior, such as Julio's babbling, and involves the consequences rather than the predictors of behavior.

The American psychologist B. F. Skinner (1904–1990) argued that an organism—animal or human—will tend to repeat a response that has been reinforced by desirable consequences and will suppress a response that has been punished. Thus **reinforcement** is the process by which a behavior is strengthened, *increasing* the likelihood that the behavior will be repeated. In Julio's case, his mother's attention reinforces his babbling. **Punishment** is the process by which a behavior is weakened, *decreasing* the likelihood of repetition. If Julio's mother frowned when he babbled, he would be less likely to babble again.

Reinforcement is most effective when it immediately follows a behavior. If a response is no longer reinforced, it will eventually be *extinguished*, that is, return to its original (baseline) level. If, after a while, no one repeats Julio's babbling, he may babble less often than if his babbles still brought reinforcement.

Although Skinnerian psychology has been useful in helping us understand how to eliminate undesirable behaviors or instill desirable behaviors, it is limited in application. As an overarching theory of development, it falls short. For example, it does not adequately address individual differences or biologically influenced behavioral patterns.

Social Learning (Social Cognitive) Theory The American psychologist Albert Bandura (b. 1925) developed many of the principles of **social learning theory.** Whereas behaviorists see the environment as the chief impetus for development, Bandura (1977, 1989) suggests that the impetus for development is bidirectional. Bandura called this concept **reciprocal determinism**—the person acts on the world as the world acts on the person.

Classic social learning theory maintains that people learn appropriate social behavior chiefly by observing and imitating models—that is, by watching other people. For example, by watching her older sister get disciplined for stealing a cookie cooling on the counter, Clara can learn to restrain herself from doing the same thing. This process is called **observational learning,** or *modeling*. Note that this is an active process, and that it can occur even if a person does not imitate the observed behavior.

Bandura's (1989) updated version of social learning theory is *social cognitive theory*. The change of name reflects a greater emphasis on cognitive processes as central to development. Cognitive processes are at work as people observe models, learn *chunks* of behavior, and mentally put the chunks together into complex new behavior patterns. Rita, for example, imitates the toes-out walk of her dance teacher but models her dance steps after those of Carmen, a slightly more advanced student. Even so, she develops her own style of dancing by putting her observations together into a new pattern.

Through feedback on their behavior, children gradually form standards for judging their actions and become more selective in choosing models who demonstrate those standards. They also begin to develop a sense of **self-efficacy,** or confidence in their ability to exert control.

PERSPECTIVE 3: COGNITIVE

The **cognitive perspective** focuses on thought processes and the behavior that reflects those processes. This perspective encompasses both organismic and mechanistically influenced theories. It includes the cognitive-stage theory of Piaget, Vygotsky's sociocultural theory of cognitive development, and the information-processing approach.

Cognitive-Stage Theory: Jean Piaget Our understanding of how children think owes a great deal to the work of the Swiss theoretician Jean Piaget (1896–1980). Through his careful observations and thoughtful questions, Piaget's **cognitive-stage theory** reintroduced the concept of scientific inquiry into mental states. Piaget viewed development organismically, as the product of children's efforts to understand and act on their world, and as discontinuous and occurring in stages.

Piaget suggested that cognitive development begins with an inborn ability to adapt to the environment. By rooting for a nipple, manipulating a toy, or exploring the boundaries of a room, young children learn about their environment and become more competent over time. This cognitive growth occurs through three interrelated processes: *organization, adaptation*, and *equilibration.*

Organization is the tendency to create categories, such as birds, by observing the characteristics that individual members of a category, such as sparrows and cardinals, have in common. According to Piaget, people create increasingly complex cognitive structures called **schemes,** ways of organizing information about the world. As children acquire more information, their schemes become more and more complex. Take sucking, for example. A newborn infant has a simple scheme for sucking but soon develops varied schemes for how to suck at the breast, a bottle, or a thumb. The infant may have to open her mouth wider, or turn her head to the side, or suck with varying strength. Schemes are originally concrete in nature (e.g., how to suck on objects) and become increasingly abstract over time (e.g., what a dog is).

Adaptation is Piaget's term for how children handle new information in light of what they already know. Adaptation occurs through two complementary processes: (1) **assimilation,** taking in new information and incorporating it into existing cognitive structures, and (2) **accommodation,** adjusting one's cognitive structures to fit the new information.

How does the shift from assimilation to accommodation occur? Piaget argued that children strive for **equilibration** between their cognitive structures and new experiences. Children want what they understand of the world to match what they observe around them. When children's understanding of the world does not match what they are experiencing, they find themselves in a state of disequilibrium, an uncomfortable motivational state that pushes children into accommodation. For example, Aiko knows what birds are and sees a plane for the first time. She labels the plane a "bird" (assimilation). Over time Aiko notes differences between planes and birds, which makes her somewhat uneasy (disequilibrium) and motivates her to change her understanding (accommodation) and provide a new label for the plane. She then is at equilibrium. Throughout life, the quest for equilibrium is the driving force behind cognitive growth.

Piaget described cognitive development as occurring in four universal, qualitatively different stages (listed in Table 2.2) driven by maturational processes. From infancy through adolescence, mental operations evolve from learning based on simple sensory and motor activity to logical, abstract thought.

Piaget's observations have yielded much information and some surprising insights. Piaget has shown us that children's minds are not miniature adult

Jean Piaget studied children's cognitive development by observing and talking with them in many settings, asking questions to find out how their minds worked.
Patrick Grehan/Corbis Historical/Getty Images

According to Lev Vygotsky, children learn through social interaction. Heritage Images/Hulton Archive/Getty Images

sociocultural theory
Vygotsky's theory of how contextual factors affect children's development.

zone of proximal development (ZPD)
Vygotsky's term for the difference between what a child can do alone and what the child can do with help.

scaffolding
Temporary support to help a child master a task.

information-processing approach
Approach to the study of cognitive development that analyzes processes involved in perceiving and handling information.

minds. Knowing how children think makes it easier for parents and teachers to understand and teach them. However, Piaget seems to have seriously underestimated the abilities of infants and children. Some contemporary psychologists also question his distinct stages, pointing instead to evidence that cognitive development is more gradual and continuous (Courage & Howe, 2002). Further, cross-cultural research indicates that performance on formal reasoning tasks is as much a function of culture as it is of development; people from industrialized societies who have participated in a formal educational system show better performance on those tasks (Buck-Morss, 1975). Last, research on adults suggests that Piaget's focus on formal logic as the climax of cognitive development is too narrow. It does not account for the emergence of such mature abilities as practical problem solving, wisdom, and the capacity to deal with ambiguous situations.

Sociocultural Theory: Lev Vygotsky The Russian psychologist Lev Semenovich Vygotsky (1896–1934) focused on the social and cultural processes that guide children's cognitive development. Vygotsky's (1978) **sociocultural theory,** like Piaget's theory, stresses children's active engagement with their environment. However, Vygotsky saw cognitive growth as a *collaborative* process. People, said Vygotsky, learn through social interaction, which occurs within their particular cultural context. They acquire cognitive skills as part of their induction into a way of life. These shared activities help children internalize their society's modes of thinking and behaving. Vygotsky placed special emphasis on *language*, not merely as an expression of knowledge and thought but as an essential tool for learning and thinking about the world.

According to Vygotsky, adults or more advanced peers must help direct and organize a child's learning before the child can master and internalize it. This guidance is most effective in helping children cross the **zone of proximal development (ZPD),** the gap between what they are already able to do by themselves and what they can accomplish with assistance. Sensitive and effective instruction, then, should be aimed at the ZPD and increase in complexity as the child's abilities improve. Responsibility for directing learning gradually shifts to the child, such as when an adult teaches a child to float: The adult first supports the child in the water and then lets go gradually as the child learns to relax into a horizontal position. **Scaffolding** is the support that parents, teachers, or others give a child in doing a task until the child can do it alone and it helps children work at the high end of their ZPD. The particular skills, tasks, or patterns of behavior that a child learns are shaped by cultural context. Thus, children from different cultures will follow different paths of development by virtue of their unique shared interactions with other cultural partners.

Vygotsky's theory has important implications for education and for cognitive testing. Tests that focus on a child's potential for learning provide a valuable alternative to standard intelligence tests, and many children may benefit from the sort of expert guidance Vygotsky prescribes. Moreover, Vygotsky's ideas have successfully been implemented in preschool children's curricula and show great promise for promoting the development of self-regulation, which affects later academic achievement (Barnett et al., 2008). Last, Vygotsky's theory highlights the importance of culture to development. He recognized that there are as many ways to successfully raise a child as there are different cultural experiences, values, and skills to be learned.

The Information-Processing Approach The **information-processing approach** seeks to explain cognitive development by analyzing the processes involved in making sense of incoming information and performing tasks effectively: such processes include attention, memory, planning strategies, decision making, and goal setting. The information-processing approach is not a single theory but a framework that supports a wide range of theories and research.

Some information-processing theorists compare the brain to a computer: There are certain inputs (such as sensory impressions) and certain outputs (such as behaviors). Information-processing theorists are interested in what happens in the middle. Why does the same input sometimes result in different outputs? In large part, information-processing researchers use observational data to *infer* what goes on between a stimulus and a response. For example, they may ask a person to recall a list of words and then observe any difference in performance if the person repeats the list over and over before being asked to recall the words or is kept from doing so. Through such studies, some information-processing researchers have developed *computational models* or flowcharts that analyze the specific steps people go through in gathering, storing, retrieving, and using information.

Like Piaget, information-processing theorists see people as active thinkers about their world. Unlike Piaget, they view development as continuous and incremental rather than as occurring in stages. They note age-related increases in the speed, complexity, and efficiency of mental processing and in the amount and variety of material that can be stored in memory.

PERSPECTIVE 4: CONTEXTUAL

According to the **contextual perspective,** development can be understood only in its social context. Contextualists see the individual not as a separate entity interacting with the environment, but as an inseparable part of it. (Vygotsky's sociocultural theory, which is discussed as part of the cognitive perspective, also can be classified as contextual.)

The American psychologist Urie Bronfenbrenner's (1917–2005) **bioecological theory** (1979, 1986, 1994) focused not just on immediate influences, as do most psychological approaches, but also on the wider circles of interacting influences of development. Bronfenbrenner identified five levels of environmental influence, ranging from very intimate to very broad (Figure 2.2). He argued that in order to understand the complexity of influences on development, we must see a person within the context of these multiple environments. For instance, we cannot look at the behavior of an individual child without considering the cultural context in which that child is embedded.

A *microsystem* is the everyday environment of home, school, work, or neighborhood, including face-to-face relationships with spouse, children, parents, friends, classmates, teachers, employers, or colleagues.

contextual perspective
View of human development that sees the individual as inseparable from the social context.

bioecological theory
Bronfenbrenner's approach to understanding processes and contexts of human development that identifies five levels of environmental influence.

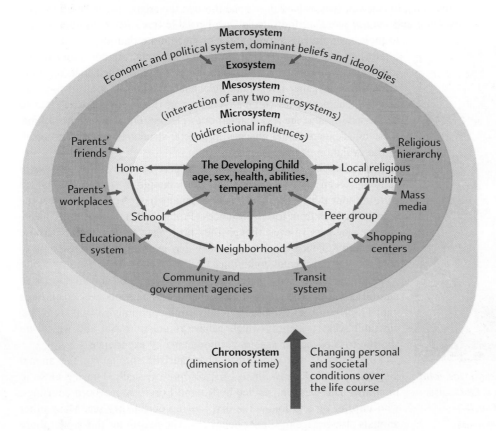

FIGURE 2.2
Bronfenbrenner's Bioecological Theory

Concentric circles show five levels of environmental influence on the individual, from the most intimate environment (the microsystem) to the broadest (the chronosystem)—all within the perpendicular dimension of time.

The *mesosystem* is the interlocking of various microsystems. For example, a parent's bad day at work might affect interactions with a child later that evening in a negative way. Despite never having actually gone to the workplace, the child is still affected by it.

The *exosystem* consists of interactions between a microsystem and an outside system or institution. For example, different countries have policies on what type, if any, of maternal or paternal leave accommodations are available for new parents. Thus governmental policies trickle down and can affect a child's day-to-day experiences.

The *macrosystem* consists of overarching cultural patterns, such as dominant beliefs, ideologies, and economic and political systems. How is an individual affected by living in a capitalist or socialist society?

Finally, the *chronosystem* adds the dimension of time: change or constancy in the person and the environment. Time marches on, and, as it does, changes occur. These can include changes in family composition, place of residence, or parents' employment, as well as larger events such as wars, ideology, political system, and economic cycles.

According to Bronfenbrenner, a person is not merely an outcome of development but is also a shaper of it. People affect their development through their biological and psychological characteristics, talents and skills, disabilities, and temperament.

By looking at systems that affect individuals in and beyond the family, this bioecological approach helps us to see the variety of influences on development. The contextual perspective also reminds us that findings about the development of people in one culture or in one group within a culture may not apply equally to people in other societies or cultural groups.

PERSPECTIVE 5: EVOLUTIONARY/SOCIOBIOLOGICAL

evolutionary/sociobiological perspective
View of human development that focuses on evolutionary and biological bases of behavior.

ethology
Study of distinctive adaptive behaviors of species of animals that have evolved to increase survival of the species.

The **evolutionary/sociobiological perspective** focuses on evolutionary and biological bases of behavior. Influenced by Darwin's theory of evolution, it draws on findings of anthropology, ecology, genetics, ethology, and evolutionary psychology to explain the adaptive, or survival, value of behavior for an individual or species.

According to Darwin, species have developed through the related processes of *survival of the fittest* and *natural selection*. Individuals with heritable traits *fitted* (better adapted) to their environments survive and reproduce more than those that are less fitted (less well adapted). Thus, through differential reproduction success, individuals with more adaptive characteristics pass on their traits to future generations at higher levels than individuals who are less fit. In this way, adaptive characteristics (ultimately coded in their genes) are selected to be passed on, and the less adapted ones die out. Over vast spans of time, these small, incremental changes in genetic structures add up and result in the evolution of new species.

Evolved mechanisms are behaviors that developed to solve problems in adapting to an earlier environment. For example, a sudden aversion to certain foods during pregnancy may originally have evolved to protect the vulnerable fetus from toxic substances (Profet, 1992). Such evolved mechanisms may survive even though they no longer serve a useful purpose (Bjorklund & Pellegrini, 2002), or they may evolve further in response to changing environmental conditions.

Ethology is the study of the adaptive behaviors of animal species in natural contexts. The assumption is that such behaviors evolved through natural selection. Ethologists generally compare animals of different species and seek to identify which behaviors are universal and which are specific to a particular species or modifiable by experience.

For example, one widespread characteristic throughout the animal kingdom is called *proximity-seeking*, or, more casually, "staying close to mommy." This was first studied by Konrad Lorenz in newborn ducklings, who imprint on and follow the first moving object they see. Many other animals also engage in similar behaviors. The reason for this is that those

Many animals, including humans and gorillas, form strong, loving bonds with their babies. Ethologists would highlight the survival value of such attachments. JRL Photographer/iStock/Getty Images

baby animals that did not stay close to their mothers tended not to survive, and therefore did not reproduce later in life.

But why discuss animal research in a human development text? The answer is that humans have also been subject to the forces of evolution and thus are likely to also have innate adaptive behaviors. In fact, one of the most important theories in developmental psychology was strongly influenced by the ethological approach. The British psychologist John Bowlby (1969) drew upon his knowledge of proximity-seeking behavior in animals of different species as he formed his ideas about attachment in humans.

A related extension of the ethological approach can be found in **evolutionary psychology.** Ethologists focus on cross-species comparisons, whereas evolutionary psychologists focus on humans and apply Darwinian principles to human behavior. Evolutionary psychologists believe that just as we have a heart specialized as a pump, lungs specialized for air exchange, and thumbs specialized for grasping, we also have aspects of our human psychology specialized for solving adaptive problems. According to this theory, people unconsciously strive to perpetuate their genetic legacy. They do so by seeking to maximize their chances of having offspring who will survive to reproduce and pass down their characteristics.

It is important to note that an evolutionary perspective does not reduce human behavior to the effects of genes seeking to reproduce themselves despite arguing that ultimately the transmission of genes is what drives many evolved behaviors. Evolutionary psychologists place great weight on the environment to which humans must adapt and the flexibility of the human mind. In this view, our evolved mechanisms are sensitive to the environmental and cultural contexts in which we develop. Moreover, our ability to engage in abstract thought and reasoning allows us to override evolutionary influences, such as might happen when we decide to forgo a tempting piece of chocolate cake despite having a gustatory system designed to appreciate sweets.

evolutionary psychology
Application of Darwinian principles of natural selection and survival of the fittest to individual behavior.

THEORIES AND THE RESEARCH PROCESS

Theories of human development grow out of, and are tested by, research. Research questions and methods reflect a researcher's particular theoretical orientation. For example, in trying to understand how a child develops a sense of right and wrong, a behaviorist might examine what kinds of behavior the parents punish or praise. A social learning theorist would focus on imitation of moral examples, possibly in stories or in movies. An information-processing researcher might try to identify the steps a child uses to determine the range of moral options available and then to decide which option to pursue. An evolutionary psychologist might be interested in the adaptive purpose of moral development and how it might affect social behavior.

With the vital connection between theory and research in mind, let's look at the methods developmental researchers use.

Research Methods

Researchers in human development work within two methodological traditions: quantitative and qualitative. Each of these traditions has different goals and different ways of seeing and interpreting reality and emphasizes different means of collecting and analyzing data.

QUANTITATIVE AND QUALITATIVE RESEARCH

Generally, when most people think of scientific research, they are thinking of what is called *quantitative research*. **Quantitative research** deals with objectively measurable, numerical data that can answer questions such as "how much?" or "how many?" and that is amenable to statistical analysis. For example, quantitative researchers might study the fear and anxiety children feel before surgery by asking them to answer questions, using a numerical scale, about how fearful or anxious they are. These data could then be compared to data for children not facing surgery to determine whether a statistically significant difference exists between the two groups.

quantitative research
Research that deals with objectively measurable data.

scientific method
System of established principles and processes of scientific inquiry, which includes identifying a problem to be studied, formulating a hypothesis to be tested by research, collecting data, analyzing the data, forming tentative conclusions, and disseminating findings.

Quantitative research on human development is based on the **scientific method,** which has traditionally characterized most scientific inquiry. Its usual steps are:

1. *Identification of a problem* to be studied, often on the basis of a theory or of previous research.

2. *Formulation of hypotheses* to be tested by research.

3. *Collection of data.*

4. *Statistical analysis of the data* to determine whether they support the hypothesis.

5. *Formation of tentative conclusions.*

6. *Dissemination of findings* so other observers can check, learn from, analyze, repeat, and build on the results.

qualitative research
Research that focuses on nonnumerical data, such as subjective experiences, feelings, or beliefs.

Qualitative research, in contrast, focuses on the how and why of behavior. It more commonly involves nonnumerical (verbal or pictorial) descriptions of participants' subjective understanding, feelings, or beliefs about their experiences. Qualitative researchers might study the same subject areas as quantitative researchers, but their perspective informs both how they collect data and how they interpret it. For example, if qualitative researchers were to study children's emotional state prior to surgery, they might do so with unstructured interviews or by asking children to draw their perceptions of the upcoming event. Whereas the goal in quantitative research is to generate hypotheses from previous research and empirically test them, the goal in qualitative research is to understand the "story" of the event. Qualitative data are more flexible and informal, and researchers may be more interested in exploring data to see what hypotheses emerge than in running statistical analyses on numerical data.

How does qualitative research compare with quantitative research? On the positive side, findings of qualitative research can be a rich source of insights into attitudes and behavior. The interactive relationship between investigators and participants can reveal information that would not emerge under the more impersonal conditions of quantitative research. On the other hand, qualitative research tends to be more subject to bias than quantitative research. Because samples are often small and usually not random, results are also less generalizable and replicable than the results of quantitative research.

The selection of quantitative or qualitative methods may depend on the purpose of the study, how much is already known about the topic, and the researcher's theoretical orientation. Quantitative research often is done in controlled laboratory settings; qualitative research typically is conducted in everyday settings, such as the home or school.

SAMPLING

sample
Group of participants chosen to represent the entire population under study.

Because studying an entire *population* (a group to whom the findings may apply) is usually too costly and time-consuming, investigators select a **sample,** a smaller group within the population. To be sure that the results of quantitative research are true generally, the sample should adequately represent the population under study—that is, it should show relevant characteristics in the same proportions as in the entire population. Otherwise the results cannot properly be *generalized*, or applied to the population as a whole.

random selection
Selection of a sample in such a way that each person in a population has an equal and independent chance of being chosen.

Often quantitative researchers seek to achieve representativeness through **random selection,** in which each person in a population has an equal and independent chance of being chosen. The result of random selection is a *random sample*. A random sample, especially a large one, is likely to represent the population well. Unfortunately, a random sample of a large population is often difficult to obtain. Instead, many studies use samples selected for convenience or accessibility (for example, children born in a particular hospital). The findings of such studies may not apply to the population as a whole.

In qualitative research, samples tend to be focused rather than random. Participants may be chosen for their ability to communicate the nature of a certain experience, such as how it feels to go through puberty or menopause. A carefully selected qualitative sample may have a fair degree of generalizability.

FORMS OF DATA COLLECTION

Common ways of gathering data (Table 2.3) include *self-reports* (verbal or visual reports by study participants), *observation* of participants in laboratory or natural settings, and *behavioral* or *performance measures*. Quantitative research typically uses standardized, structured methods involving numerical measurements of behavior or performance. Qualitative research tends to rely on self-reports, often in the form of in-depth, open-ended interviews or visual techniques and on observation in natural settings. Let's look more closely at several common methods of data collection.

Self-Reports The simplest form of self-report is a *diary* or log. Adolescents may be asked, for example, to record what they eat each day or the times when they feel depressed. In studying young children, *parental self-reports*—diaries, journals, interviews, or questionnaires—are commonly used, often together with other methods, such as videotaping or recording.

In a face-to-face or telephone *interview*, researchers ask questions about attitudes, opinions, or behavior. In a *structured* interview, each participant is asked the same set of questions. An *open-ended* interview is more flexible; the interviewer can vary the topics and order of questions and can ask follow-up questions based on the responses. To reach more people and to protect their privacy, researchers sometimes distribute a printed or online *questionnaire*, which participants fill out and return. Sometimes a participant may be asked to draw something, such as a child being asked to draw a self-portrait.

By questioning a large number of people, investigators can get a broad picture—at least of what the respondents *say* they believe or do or did. However, people willing to participate in interviews or fill out questionnaires may not accurately represent the population as a whole. Furthermore, heavy reliance on self-reports may be unwise because people may not have thought about what they feel and think or honestly may not know. They may forget when and how events took place or may consciously or unconsciously distort their replies to fit what is considered socially desirable.

TABLE 2.3 Major Methods of Data Collection

Type	Main Characteristics	Advantages	Disadvantages
Self-report: diary, visual reports, interview, or questionnaire	Participants are asked about themselves; questioning may be highly structured or flexible; self-report may be verbal or visual.	Provides firsthand information about a person. Visual techniques (e.g., drawing, mapping, graphing) avoid need for verbal skills.	Participant may not remember information accurately or distort responses in a socially desirable way; how question is asked or by whom may affect answer.
Naturalistic observation	People are observed in their normal setting, with no attempt to manipulate behavior.	Good description of behavior; does not subject people to unnatural settings that may distort behavior.	Lack of control; observer bias.
Laboratory observation	Participants are observed in the laboratory, with no attempt to manipulate behavior.	Good descriptions; greater control than naturalistic observation as all participants are observed under same conditions.	Observer bias; controlled situation can be artificial.
Behavioral and performance measures	Participants are tested on abilities, skills, knowledge, competencies, or physical responses.	Provides objectively measurable information; avoids subjective distortions.	Cannot measure attitudes or other nonbehavioral phenomena; results may be affected by extraneous factors.

naturalistic observation
Research method in which behavior is studied in natural settings without intervention or manipulation.

laboratory observation
Research method in which all participants are observed under the same controlled conditions.

Naturalistic and Laboratory Observation Observation takes two forms: *naturalistic observation* and *laboratory observation*. In **naturalistic observation,** researchers look at people in real-life settings. The researchers do not try to alter behavior or the environment; they simply record what they see. In **laboratory observation,** researchers observe and record behavior in a controlled environment, such as a laboratory.

Both kinds of observation are valuable, but they have limitations. For one, they do not explain *why* people behave as they do, though the observers may suggest interpretations. Moreover, when people know they are being watched, they may act differently. Finally, there is a risk of *observer bias*: the researcher's tendency to interpret data to fit expectations or to emphasize some aspects and minimize others.

Behavioral and Performance Measures For quantitative research, investigators typically use more objective measures of behavior or performance. Tests and other behavioral and neuropsychological measures may be used to assess abilities, skills, knowledge, competencies, or physiological responses, such as heart rate and brain activity.

Some written tests, such as intelligence tests, compare performance with that of other test-takers. Such tests can be meaningful and useful only if they are both *valid* (the tests measure the abilities they claim to measure) and *reliable* (the results are reasonably consistent from one time to another). To avoid bias, tests must be *standardized*, that is, given and scored by the same methods and criteria for all test-takers.

operational definition
Definition stated solely in terms of the operations or procedures used to produce or measure a phenomenon.

When measuring a characteristic such as intelligence, it is important to define exactly what is to be measured in a way that other researchers can repeat the experiment and compare their results. For this purpose, researchers use an **operational definition**—a definition stated solely in terms of the operations used to measure a phenomenon. Intelligence, for example, can be defined as the ability to achieve a certain score on a test covering logical relationships, memory, and vocabulary recognition. Some people may disagree with this definition, but no one can reasonably claim that it is not clear.

For most of the history of psychology, theorists and researchers studied cognitive processes apart from the physical structures of the brain in which these processes occur. Now, sophisticated imaging instruments, such as functional magnetic resonance imaging (fMRI) and positron emission tomography (PET), make it possible to see the brain in action, and the new field of **cognitive neuroscience** is linking our understanding of cognitive functioning with what happens in the brain.

cognitive neuroscience
Study of links between neural processes and cognitive abilities.

A baby under laboratory observation may or may not behave the same way as in a naturalistic setting, such as at home, but both kinds of observation can provide valuable information. Stephane Audras/REA/Redux

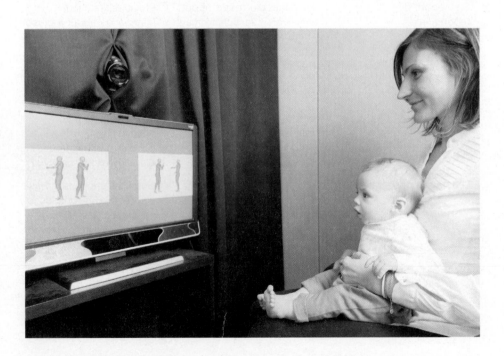

TABLE 2.4	Basic Research Designs		
Type	Main Characteristics	Advantages	Disadvantages
Case study	In-depth study of single individual.	Provides detailed picture of one person's behavior and development; can generate hypotheses.	May not generalize to others; conclusions not directly testable; cannot establish cause and effect.
Ethnographic study	In-depth study of a culture or subculture.	Can address cultural biases in theory and research and test universality of phenomena.	Subject to observer bias.
Correlational study	Attempt to find positive or negative relationship between variables.	Allows prediction of one variable from another; can suggest hypotheses about causal relationships.	Cannot establish cause and effect.
Experiment	Controlled procedure in the laboratory or the field in which an experimenter controls the independent variable to determine its effect on the dependent variable.	Establishes cause-and-effect relationships; highest degree of control, ideally can be replicated.	Findings, especially when derived from laboratory experiments, may not generalize to situations outside the laboratory.

BASIC RESEARCH DESIGNS

A research design is a plan for conducting a scientific investigation. Four basic designs used in developmental research are *case studies, ethnographic studies, correlational studies,* and *experiments.* The first two designs are qualitative; the last two are quantitative. Each design has advantages and drawbacks, and each is appropriate for certain kinds of research problems (Table 2.4).

Case Studies A **case study** is a study of an individual. Case studies also may use behavioral or physiological measures and biographical, autobiographical, or documentary materials. Case studies are particularly useful when studying something relatively rare, when it simply is not possible to find a large enough group of people with the characteristic in question to conduct a traditional laboratory study. They can explore sources of behavior and can test treatments, and they suggest directions for further research.

Case studies do have shortcomings, however. Using case studies, we can learn much about the development of a single person, but not how the information applies to people in general. Furthermore, case studies cannot explain behavior with certainty or make strong causal statements because there is no way to test their conclusions.

Ethnographic Studies An **ethnographic study** seeks to describe the pattern of relationships, customs, beliefs, technology, arts, and traditions that make up a society's way of life. In a way, it is like a case study of a culture. Ethnographic research can be qualitative, quantitative, or both. It uses a combination of methods, including informal, unstructured interviewing and **participant observation.** Participant observation is a form of naturalistic observation in which researchers live or participate in the societies or smaller groups they observe, as anthropologists often do for long periods of time.

Because of ethnographers' involvement in the events or societies they are observing, their findings are especially open to observer bias. On the positive side, ethnographic research can help overcome cultural biases in theory and research (Window on the World). Ethnographies demonstrate the error of assuming that principles developed from research in Western cultures are universally applicable.

case study
Study of a single subject, such as an individual or family.

ethnographic study
In-depth study of a culture, which uses a combination of methods including participant observation.

participant observation
Research method in which the observer lives with the people or participates in the activity being observed.

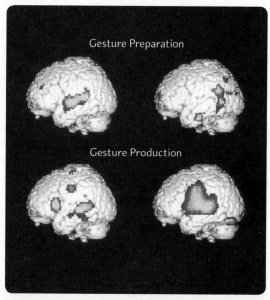

Researchers can analyze an fMRI (functional magnetic resonance imaging) brain scan taken during an activity or task to observe what happens in the brain. The regions shown in red are activated when thinking about making a gesture (preparation) and then in performing it (production).
WDCN/University College London/Science Source

When David, a European American child, was asked to identify the missing detail in a picture of a face with no mouth, he said, "The mouth." Ari, an Asian immigrant child in Israel, said the body was missing. As art in his culture did not typically present a head as a complete picture, he thought the absence of a body was more important (Anastasi, 1988, p. 360).

Cross-cultural research, where theorists investigate the differences among people from different countries, can help us learn how closely many components of development tie to society and culture. Multicultural research, another approach based on the examination of culture, investigates cultural differences within one society. Multicultural theorists, in addition to being interested in race and ethnicity, also examine issues relevant to gender, sexuality, age, religion, and other differences among people. Both methods can help us understand in what ways development is universal and in what ways it is culturally determined

For example, research has also shown us culture seems to exert an influence on early motor development. African babies, whose parents often prop them in a sitting position and bounce them on their feet, tend to sit and walk earlier than U.S. babies (Rogoff & Morelli, 1989). The society in which children grow up also influences the skills they learn. In the United States, children learn to read, write, and, increasingly,

operate computers. In rural Nepal, they learn how to drive water buffalo and find their way along mountain paths.

A majority of the research in child development has focused on Western industrialized societies. Typical development in these societies is often interpreted as the norm, or standard of behavior, for all societies. Measuring against this Westernized norm can lead to incorrect ideas about development in other cultures and beliefs that children are not developing appropriately if they deviate from these norms (Rogoff & Morelli, 1989).

Research has shown that there are cultural differences in gender roles, abstract thinking, moral reasoning, motor development, skill development as well as social and emotional development. As learners, we need to keep in mind that development is different across many cultures and take the time to understand and embrace these differences.

what's **your** view

Can you think of a situation in which you made an incorrect assumption about a person because you were unfamiliar with her or his cultural background? What types of characteristics do you think are most influenced by culture?

---

correlational study
Research design intended to discover whether a statistical relationship between variables exists.

Correlational Studies A **correlational study** seeks to determine whether a *correlation*, or statistical relationship, exists between *variables*, phenomena that change or vary among people or can be varied for purposes of research. Correlations are expressed in terms of direction (positive or negative) and magnitude (degree). Two variables that are correlated *positively* increase or decrease together. For example, studies show a positive correlation between televised violence and aggression. That is, children who watch more violent television tend to fight more than children who watch less violent television. Two variables have a *negative*, or inverse, correlation if, as one increases, the other decreases. Studies show a negative correlation between amount of schooling and the risk of developing dementia (mental deterioration) in old age. In other words, the less education, the more dementia (Katzman, 1993).

Correlations are reported as numbers ranging from −1.0 (a perfect negative relationship) to +1.0 (a perfect positive relationship). The closer a correlation comes to +1.0 or −1.0, the stronger the relationship, either positive or negative. A correlation of zero means that the variables have no relationship.

Correlations enable us to predict one variable in relation to another. On the basis of the positive correlation between watching televised violence and aggression, we can predict that children who watch violent shows are more likely to get into fights than children who do *not* watch such shows. The greater the magnitude of the correlation between the two variables, the greater the ability to predict one from the other.

Although strong correlations suggest possible cause-and-effect relationships, these are merely hypotheses. We cannot be sure from a positive correlation between televised violence and aggressiveness that watching televised violence *causes* aggression; we can conclude only that the two variables are related. It is possible that the causation goes the other way: Aggressive behavior may lead children to watch more violent programs. Or a third variable—perhaps an inborn predisposition toward aggressiveness—may cause a child *both* to watch violent programs and to act aggressively. The only way to show with certainty that one variable causes another is through experimentation.

Experiments An **experiment** is a controlled procedure in which the experimenter manipulates variables to learn how one affects another. Scientific experiments must be conducted and reported in such a way that another experimenter can *replicate* them, that is, repeat them in exactly the same way with different participants to verify the results and conclusions.

Groups and Variables A common way to conduct an experiment is to divide the participants into two kinds of groups. An **experimental group** consists of people who are to be exposed to the experimental manipulation or *treatment*—the phenomenon the researcher wants to study. Afterward, the effect of the treatment will be measured one or more times to find out what changes, if any, it caused. A **control group** consists of people who are similar to the experimental group but do not receive the experimental treatment or may receive a different treatment. An experiment may include one or more of each type of group. If the experimenter wants to compare the effects of different treatments (say, of two methods of teaching), the overall sample may be divided into *treatment groups*, each of which receives one of the treatments under study. To ensure objectivity, some experiments, particularly in medical research, use *double-blind* procedures, in which neither participants nor experimenters know who is receiving the treatment and who is instead receiving an inert *placebo*.

One team of researchers wanted to find out if 11-month-old infants could be trained to focus their attention (Wass et al., 2011). The researchers brought 42 infants to their laboratory and had them participate in a variety of tasks. Half of the infants were given about an hour of attentional training. This training required babies to use sustained gaze to make a fun event happen on a computer. For example, if babies fixated on an elephant, the elephant became animated. If the babies looked away, the elephant stopped moving. The other group of children were shown television clips and animations, but were not trained. At the end of 2 weeks, the babies were tested on a series of cognitive tasks. Babies who underwent the training performed better on the tasks than did the babies who were not trained. It is reasonable to conclude, then, that the attentional training improved the babies' performance on the tasks as it was the only thing varied between the two groups.

In this experiment, the type of activity (training versus watching television) was the *independent variable*, and the children's test performance the *dependent variable*. An **independent variable** is something over which the experimenter has direct control. A **dependent variable** is something that may or may not change as a result of changes in the independent variable; in other words, it *depends* on the independent variable. In an experiment, a researcher manipulates the independent variable to see how changes in it will affect the dependent variable. The hypothesis for a study states how a researcher thinks the independent variable affects the dependent variable.

Random Assignment If an experiment finds a significant difference in the performance of the experimental and control groups, how do we know that the cause was the independent variable? For example, in the attentional training experiment, how can we be sure that the training and not some other factor (such as intelligence) caused the difference in test performance of the two groups? The best way to control for effects of such

experiment
Rigorously controlled, replicable procedure in which the researcher manipulates variables to assess the effect of one on the other.

experimental group
In an experiment, the group receiving the treatment under study.

control group
In an experiment, a group of people, similar to those in the experimental group, who do not receive the treatment under study.

independent variable
In an experiment, the condition over which the experimenter has direct control.

dependent variable
In an experiment, the condition that may or may not change as a result of changes in the independent variable.

extraneous factors is **random assignment**: assigning the participants to groups in such a way that each person has an equal chance of being placed in any group.

If assignment is random and the sample is large enough, differences in such factors as age, gender, and ethnicity will be evenly distributed so that the groups initially are as alike as possible in every respect except for the variable to be tested. Otherwise, unintended differences between the groups might *confound*, or contaminate, the results, and any conclusions drawn from the experiment would have to be viewed with suspicion. To control for confounds, the experimenter must make sure that everything except the independent variable is held constant during the course of the experiment.

Of course, with respect to some variables we might want to study, such as age, gender, and race/ethnicity, random assignment is not possible. We cannot assign Kamau to be 5 years old and Ava to be 10, or one to be a boy and the other a girl. When studying such a variable researchers can strengthen the validity of their conclusions by randomly selecting participants and by trying to make sure that they are statistically equivalent in other ways that might make a difference in the study.

Laboratory, Field, and Natural Experiments A laboratory experiment is best for determining cause and effect. It generally consists of asking participants to visit a laboratory where they are subject to conditions manipulated by the experimenter. The tight control of a laboratory study allows researchers to be more certain that their independent variable caused change in their dependent variable; however, because of the artificiality of the laboratory experience, the results may be less generalizable to real life.

A field experiment is a controlled study conducted in an everyday setting, such as a home or school. Variables can still be manipulated, so causal claims can still be investigated. Because the experiments occur in the real world, there is more confidence that the behaviors that are seen are generalizable to natural behaviors. However, researchers have less control over events that may occur—the real world is often messy, and things do not always go as planned.

When, for practical or ethical reasons, it is impossible to conduct a true experiment, a natural experiment, also called a quasi-experiment, compares people who have been accidentally "assigned" to separate groups by circumstances of life—one group who were exposed, say, to famine or HIV or superior education, and another group who were not. A natural experiment, despite its name, is actually a correlational study because controlled manipulation of variables and random assignment to treatment groups are not possible.

Controlled experiments have two important advantages over other research designs: They can establish cause-and-effect relationships, and they permit replication. However, such experiments can be too artificial and too narrowly focused. In recent decades, many researchers have supplemented their research with a wider array of methods.

DEVELOPMENTAL RESEARCH DESIGNS

One of the primary goals of developmental research is to study change over time. The two most common research strategies used for this are *cross-sectional* and *longitudinal studies* (Figure 2.3). A **cross-sectional study** most clearly illustrates similarities or differences among people of different ages; a **longitudinal study** tracks people over time and focuses on individual change with age. A third type of study, a **sequential study,** combines the two approaches to minimize the drawbacks of the separate approaches.

Cross-Sectional, Longitudinal, and Sequential Studies In a cross-sectional study, children of different ages are assessed at one point in time. For example, in one cross-sectional study, researchers asked children from 7 months to 5 years to pick one of two objects, which were identical with the exception that one object was always pink, and the other was either green, blue, yellow, or orange. The researchers found that girls showed no preference for pink objects until age 2, when they began to reach for the pink object more frequently. Boys, however, showed a different pattern. Like girls, they initially showed no preference for pink over the other colors. Starting at about 2 years of age, however, they became less and less likely to choose the pink object. The researchers concluded that children's preferences for the color pink were learned over time, and they theorized that it was related to the acquisition of knowledge about gender (LoBue & DeLoache, 2011).

Can we draw this conclusion with certainty? The problem with cross-sectional studies is that we cannot know whether the 5-year-olds' preference for certain colors when they were under the age of 2 years was the same as that of the current babies in the study. We cannot be certain that this is a developmental change rather than merely a difference in formative experiences for the two age groups. For example, if a popular television program that targets children over the age of 2 and that strongly promotes gender stereotypes had been introduced in the year previous to the study, the older children might show color preferences as a result of watching the show and not because of an increased understanding of gender. Although it may appear to be a change related to age, it might instead be the result of television programming.

The only way to know whether change occurs with age is to conduct a longitudinal study of a particular person or group. In a longitudinal study, researchers study the same person or group of people over time, sometimes years apart.

One large longitudinal study examined the Internet habits of 754 people and how lonely they were. Researchers found that over the course of a year, more web browsing was associated with an increase in a global loneliness measure (Stepanikova et al., 2010). Just as with cross-sectional designs, there is a caveat. Because individual people are studied over time, researchers have access to each person's specific individual trajectory. However, the results from one cohort might not apply to a study of a different cohort. The study used data collected from 2004 to 2005, and the link between browsing history and loneliness might differ now. For example, new social media sites with more or fewer interactive features might affect the link between Internet use and loneliness.

Neither cross-sectional nor longitudinal design is superior in design to the other. Rather, both designs have strengths and weaknesses (Table 2.5). For example, cross-sectional design is fast—we don't have to wait 30 years for results. This also makes it a more economical choice. Moreover, because participants are assessed only once, we don't have to consider attrition (people dropping out of the study) or repeated testing (which can produce practice effects). But cross-sectional design uses group averages, so individual differences and trajectories may be obscured. More important, the results can be affected by the differing experiences of people born at different times, as previously explained.

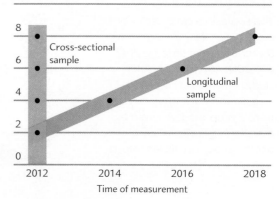

FIGURE 2.3

Developmental Research Designs

In the cross-sectional study, groups of 2-, 4-, 6-, and 8-year-olds were tested in 2012 to obtain data about age-related differences. In the longitudinal study, a sample of children were first measured in 2012, when they were 2 years old; follow-up testing is done when the children are 4, 6, and 8, to measure age-related changes. Note: Dots indicate times of measurement.

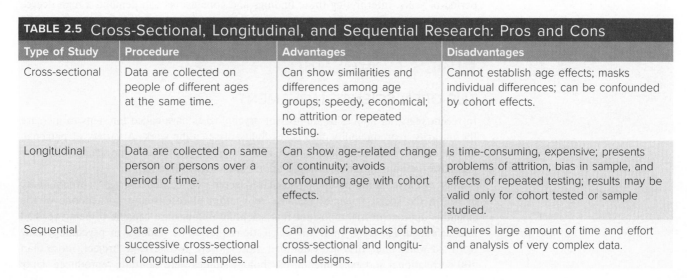

TABLE 2.5 Cross-Sectional, Longitudinal, and Sequential Research: Pros and Cons			
Type of Study	**Procedure**	**Advantages**	**Disadvantages**
Cross-sectional	Data are collected on people of different ages at the same time.	Can show similarities and differences among age groups; speedy, economical; no attrition or repeated testing.	Cannot establish age effects; masks individual differences; can be confounded by cohort effects.
Longitudinal	Data are collected on same person or persons over a period of time.	Can show age-related change or continuity; avoids confounding age with cohort effects.	Is time-consuming, expensive; presents problems of attrition, bias in sample, and effects of repeated testing; results may be valid only for cohort tested or sample studied.
Sequential	Data are collected on successive cross-sectional or longitudinal samples.	Can avoid drawbacks of both cross-sectional and longitudinal designs.	Requires large amount of time and effort and analysis of very complex data.

FIGURE 2.4
A Sequential Design

Two successive cross-sectional groups of 2-, 4-, 6-, and 8-year-olds were tested in 2012 and 2014. Also, a longitudinal study of a group of children first measured in 2012, when they were 2 years old, is followed by a similar longitudinal study of another group of children who were 2 years old in 2014.

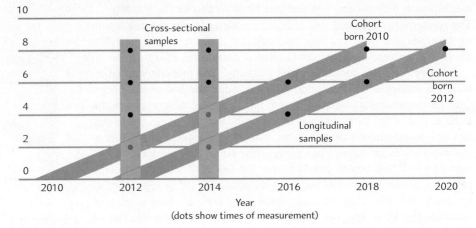

Longitudinal research shows a different and complementary set of strengths and weaknesses. Because the same people are studied over time, researchers can track individual patterns of continuity and change. This is more time-consuming and expensive than cross-sectional studies. In addition, repeated testing of participants can result in practice effects. For example, your performance on an intelligence test might get better over time from practice rather than from any increase in intelligence. Attrition can be problematic in longitudinal research as well because it tends to be nonrandom, which can introduce a positive bias to the study. Those who stay with the study tend to be above average in intelligence and socioeconomic status, and those who drop out tend to have more chaotic lives and worse overall outcomes. Moreover, practical issues, such as turnover in research personnel, loss of funding, or the development of new measures or methodologies, can introduce potential problems with data collection.

Some of the drawbacks of longitudinal and cross-sectional design can be overcome with sequential studies. Sequential designs track people of different ages (like cross-sectional designs) over time (like longitudinal designs). The combination of cross-sectional and longitudinal designs (as shown in Figure 2.4) allows researchers to separate age-related changes from cohort effects, and provides a more complete picture of development than would be possible with either design alone. The major drawbacks of sequential studies relate to time, effort, and complexity. Sequential designs require large numbers of participants and collection and analysis of huge amounts of data over a period of years. Interpreting these findings and conclusions can demand a high degree of sophistication.

Ethics of Research

THE OPEN SCIENCE MOVEMENT

In recent years, an increasing number of psychologists have called for steps to increase the integrity, reproducibility, and accessibility of scientific work. A variety of personal, institutional, and systemic factors have, at times, negatively affected the scientific process and have the potential to cast doubt upon psychological findings.

For example, some psychologists have become concerned over a "reproducibility crisis" in the social sciences. Because replication of results is a cornerstone of the scientific approach, it is important that scientific findings are capable of being verified and defended. However, there are suggestions that some findings in psychology may not hold water once they are examined more closely. In one large project, more than 100 correlational and experimental psychology studies were carefully reproduced. Only about half of the replications yielded the same statistical conclusion, even though results were generally in the same direction (Aarts et al., 2015). That the studies, even if statistically nonsignificant, pointed toward the same answers as the originals suggests the original researchers were on the correct track. However, how did so many statistically weak studies get published?

Part of the reason for this is the journals where psychological research is published are biased toward the publication of novel findings (Martin & Clarke, 2017), and replications of prior work are less likely to be published. This is especially true if they fail to reach significance (in other words, if they fail to find an expected effect).

Moreover, although it is considered unethical, because of the intense pressure to publish researchers sometimes engage in "p-hacking." P-hacking involves combing through data until a statistically significant result is found, and then developing a post hoc (after the fact) explanation for the finding. Because, by chance, a large enough data set will almost always provide a significant result of some sort, p-hacking can lead to the publication of misleading results with few applications to the real world.

Issues such as these have led a growing number of researchers to call for new guidelines to ensure the integrity of psychological findings. Among these guidelines are calls for a more open and transparent science, studies using larger numbers of participants, and a preference for stronger effects more likely to have an impact in the real world. Most importantly, registered pre-reports on statistical hypotheses to be tested before the collection of data would help ensure the integrity of data analysis (Lindsay, 2015; Button et al., 2013; van't Veer & Giner-Sorolla, 2016).

RESEARCH WITH HUMAN PARTICIPANTS

Should research that might harm its participants ever be undertaken? How do we balance the possible benefits against the risk or mental, emotional, or physical damage to individuals (see Research in Action).

Institutional review boards at colleges, universities, and other institutions review proposed research from an ethical standpoint. Guidelines of the American Psychological Association (APA, 2002) cover such issues as informed consent (consent freely given with full knowledge of what the research entails), avoidance of deception, protection of participants from harm and loss of dignity, guarantees of privacy and confidentiality, the right to decline or withdraw from an experiment at any time, and the responsibility of investigators to correct any undesirable effects, such as anxiety or shame.

In resolving ethical dilemmas, researchers should be guided by three principles. The first is *beneficence*, which is the obligation to maximize potential benefits to participants and to minimize potential harm. For example, suppose you are a researcher studying the effect of failure on self-esteem. If you are going to deceive some of your participants by telling them they failed on a laboratory task, what steps will you take to mitigate any potential harm you might cause them? The second principle is *respect* for participants' autonomy and protection of those who are unable to exercise their own judgment. For example, if you are conducting research with toddlers, and a 2-year-old refuses to participate, should you force the child to participate? What is the appropriate action in this case? The third principle is *justice*, which, in this case, is the inclusion of diverse groups together with sensitivity to any special impact the research may have on them. For example, it may be important that your study includes an appropriate and representative selection of diverse people. If this is the case, have you developed culturally appropriate materials and methods to use?

Developmental psychologists must be particularly careful as their research frequently involves vulnerable individuals, such as infants or children. In response, the Society for Research in Child Development (2007) has developed standards for age-appropriate treatment of children in research, covering such principles as avoidance of physical or psychological harm, obtaining the child's assent as well as a parent's or guardian's informed consent, and responsibility to follow up on any information that could jeopardize the child's well-being.

research in action

PREGNANCY AND ALCOHOL

What would you think if you saw a pregnant woman sitting down to dinner with a glass of wine? Is the woman being selfish and endangering her fetus? Should she be prevented from drinking alcohol?

On one side, proponents argue it is the woman's choice whether to drink alcohol, and furthermore, the risk of drinking small amounts of alcohol is minimal. On the other side, critics argue that any alcohol is an unacceptable risk and that fetuses need to be protected. Tennessee, Alabama, and South Carolina have even gone so far as to prosecute women who use drugs—alcohol included—while pregnant (Miranda et al., 2015), and in Minnesota, North Dakota, Oklahoma, South Dakota, and Wisconsin, pregnant women can be jailed during the course of their pregnancy for alcohol or drug consumption (Alcohol.org, 2019).

Despite the numbers of affected children born, scientists do not know what the precise level of safe exposure might be. Why can't scientists determine what, if any, is a safe level of alcohol for a developing fetus?

The answer to this question lies in experimental ethics. The gold standard in experimental research of this nature is a randomized, double-blind design, where, for example, half of pregnant women would be assigned to drink alcohol and half would be asked to abstain. By doing this across multiple studies with differing levels of alcohol exposure, we could theoretically determine what a "safe" amount might be. But this type of study would violate the principle of beneficence—that researchers do no harm to their participants. A study such as the one outlined above would expose the pregnancies to unacceptable risk.

Conducting research is a balancing act between what critical thinking and theoretical concerns would lead us to do in an ideal world to best answer a question and the ethical and pragmatic concerns of the real world. Given this, what options for research are left?

One option is the use of animal models. However, concerns about the use of alcohol in pregnancy are centered on the brain. Although other animals might tell us about basic processes, they cannot tell us how alcohol would ultimately affect a human brain.

Another option is correlational designs, where women are surveyed about their alcohol usage during pregnancy and their babies are assessed. Although this can answer many questions for us—for example, we know that heavy drinking is associated with fetal alcohol syndrome—the messiness of the real world does not allow us to tease out a detailed understanding. For instance, a woman may use multiple substances throughout pregnancy and thus the identification of negative effects often involves disentangling multiple drug interactions. Researchers also have difficulty distinguishing the effects of prenatal drug exposure from other risk factors, such as poor nutrition, lack of prenatal care, and chaotic social environment (Forray & Foster, 2015). Last, it is reasonable to suspect that women who continue to drink throughout their pregnancy might differ in other ways from women who abstain.

All these factors serve to muddle the conclusions that can be reached on the basis of correlational research. Thus, the best we can do now is to definitively state that high alcohol consumption is dangerous to a pregnancy, and that there is no "safe" limit known.

what's **your view**

What do you think about the impact of universal drug-screening policies or stiff criminal penalties on pregnant women with substance use disorders and their unborn babies? Do you think the same ethical questions exist for research into the use of illegal drugs, such as heroin or methamphetamine?

summary and key terms

Basic Theoretical Issues

- A theory is used to organize and explain data and generate testable hypotheses.
- Developmental theories differ on two basic issues: the active or reactive character of development and the existence of continuity or discontinuity in development.
- Two contrasting models of human development are the mechanistic model and the organismic model.

theory, hypotheses, mechanistic model, organismic model, quantitative change, qualitative change

Theoretical Perspectives

- The psychoanalytic perspective sees development as motivated by unconscious emotional drives or conflicts. Leading examples are Freud's and Erikson's theories.

psychoanalytic perspective, psychosexual development, psychosocial development

- The learning perspective views development as a result of learning based on experience. Leading examples are Watson's and Skinner's behaviorism and Bandura's social learning (social cognitive) theory.

learning perspective, behaviorism, classical conditioning, operant conditioning, reinforcement, punishment, social learning theory, reciprocal determinism, observational learning, self-efficacy

- The cognitive perspective is concerned with thought processes. Leading examples are Piaget's cognitive-stage theory, Vygotsky's sociocultural theory, and the information-processing approach.

cognitive perspective, cognitive-stage theory, organization, schemes, adaptation, assimilation, accommodation, equilibration, sociocultural theory, zone of proximal development (ZPD), scaffolding, information-processing approach

- The contextual perspective focuses on the individual in a social context. A leading example is Bronfenbrenner's bioecological theory.

contextual perspective, bioecological theory

- The evolutionary/sociobiological perspective, influenced by Darwin's theory of evolution, focuses on the adaptiveness of behavior. A leading example is Bowlby's attachment theory.

evolutionary/sociobiological perspective, ethology, evolutionary psychology

Research Methods

- Research can be either quantitative or qualitative or both.
- To arrive at sound conclusions, quantitative researchers use the scientific method.
- Random selection of a research sample can ensure generalizability.
- Three forms of data collection are self-reports, observation, and behavioral and performance measures.

quantitative research, scientific method, qualitative research, sample, random selection, naturalistic observation, laboratory observation, operational definition, cognitive neuroscience

- A design is a plan for conducting research. Two qualitative designs used in developmental research are the case study and the ethnographic study. Cross-cultural research can indicate whether certain aspects of development are universal or culturally influenced.
- Two quantitative designs are the correlational study and the experiment. Only experiments can firmly establish causal relationships.
- Experiments must be rigorously controlled to be valid and replicable. Random assignment of participants can help ensure validity.
- Laboratory experiments are easiest to control and replicate, but findings of field experiments may be more generalizable. Natural experiments may be useful in situations in which true experiments would be impractical or unethical.
- The two most common designs used to study age-related development are cross-sectional and longitudinal. Cross-sectional studies assess age differences; longitudinal studies describe continuity or change in the same participants. The sequential study is intended to overcome the weaknesses of the other two designs.

case study, ethnographic study, participant observation, correlational study, experiment, experimental group, control group, independent variable, dependent variable, random assignment, cross-sectional study, longitudinal study, sequential study

Ethics of Research

- The open science movement seeks to make research more transparent and rigorous.
- Researchers seek to resolve ethical issues on the basis of principles of beneficence, respect, and justice.
- Ethical issues in research include the rights of participants to informed consent, avoidance of deception, protection from harm and loss of dignity and self-esteem, and guarantees of privacy and confidentiality.
- There are special standards for protection of children used in research.

Design Credit: (globe) janrysavy/Getty Images

chapter 3

Forming a New Life

learning objectives

Explain how conception occurs and what causes multiple births.

Describe the mechanisms of heredity in normal and abnormal human development.

Explain how heredity and environment interact in human development.

Describe prenatal development, including environmental influences.

Discuss the importance of high-quality prenatal care.

master1305/iStock/Getty Images

We describe how conception normally occurs, how the mechanisms of heredity operate, and how biological inheritance interacts with environmental influences within and outside the womb. We trace the course of prenatal development, describe influences on it, and discuss ways to monitor it.

Conceiving New Life

Most people think of development as beginning on the day of birth, when the new child—squalling and thrashing—is introduced to the world. However, development starts at conception, as sperm and egg meet and an entirely new individual is created. Development continues as the fertilized egg grows and differentiates and edges closer to independent life outside the womb. And it persists in the dance between nature and nurture that shapes the unique individual that is the product of these processes. This chapter is about that story.

FERTILIZATION

Fertilization, or *conception,* is the process by which sperm and ovum—the male and female *gametes,* or sex cells—combine to create a single cell called a **zygote,** which then duplicates itself again and again by cell division to produce all the cells that make up a baby.

At birth, a girl is believed to have about 2 million immature ova in her two ovaries, each ovum in its own *follicle,* or small sac. In a sexually mature woman, *ovulation*—rupture of a mature follicle in either ovary and expulsion of its ovum—occurs about once every 28 days until menopause. The ovum is swept along through one of the fallopian tubes by the *cilia,* tiny hair cells, toward the uterus, or womb.

Sperm are produced in the testicles (testes), or reproductive glands, of a mature male at a rate of several hundred million a day and are ejaculated in the semen at sexual climax. Deposited in the vagina, they try to swim through the *cervix,* the opening of the uterus, and into the fallopian tubes, but only a tiny fraction make it that far. Fertilization normally occurs while the ovum is passing through the fallopian tube.

fertilization
Union of sperm and ovum to produce a zygote; also called *conception.*

zygote
One-celled organism resulting from fertilization.

MULTIPLE BIRTHS

Multiple births happen in two ways. Although twins are the most common variation, triplets, quadruplets, and other multiple births are possible.

Dizygotic twins, or fraternal twins, are the result of two separate eggs being fertilized by two different sperm to form two unique individuals. Genetically, they are like siblings who inhabit the same womb at the same time, and they can be the same or different sex. Dizygotic twins tend to run in families and are the result of multiple eggs being released at one time. This tendency may have a genetic basis and seems to be passed down from a woman's mother (Mbarek et al., 2016; Painter et al., 2010; National Center for Health Statistics, 1999). When dizygotic twins skip generations, it is normally because a mother of dizygotic twins has only sons to whom she cannot pass on the tendency (National Center for Health Statistics, 1999).

Monozygotic twins result from the cleaving of one fertilized egg and are generally genetically identical. They can still differ outwardly, however, because people are the result of the interaction between genes and environmental influences. For example, in one condition that affects only monozygotic twins (twin-to-twin transfusion syndrome), the blood vessels of the placenta form abnormally, and the placenta is shared unequally between the twins. One twin receives a smaller share of nutrients than does the other. Mortality is high, but if both twins survive, one twin will be significantly larger than the other at birth despite being genetically identical.

Moreover, environmental differences add up over time. The differences between identical twins generally magnify as twins grow older. So, for example, 3-year-old monozygotic twins appear more similar than 30-year-old monozygotic twins. These differences may result from chemical modifications in a person's genome shortly after conception or may be due to later experiences or environmental factors, such as exposure to smoke or other pollutants (Bell & Saffery, 2012; Talens et al., 2012). This process, known as *epigenesis,* is discussed later in this chapter.

dizygotic twins
Twins conceived by the union of two different ova with two different sperm cells; also called *fraternal twins*; they are no more alike genetically than any other siblings.

monozygotic twins
Twins resulting from the division of a single zygote after fertilization; also called *identical twins*; they are genetically similar.

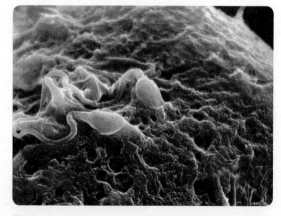

This color-enhanced scanning electron micrograph (SEM) shows two sperm (orange) attempting to breach the ovum's blue surface. The sperm's head releases enzymes that help it penetrate the ovum's surface for fertilization. Pascal Goetgheluck/Science Source

The rate of monozygotic twins (slightly under 4 per 1,000 live births) appears to be constant at all times and places, but the rate of dizygotic twins, the more common type, varies (Smits & Monden, 2011). The incidence of multiple births in the United States has grown rapidly since 1980. From 1980 to 2017 the twin birthrate rose by 76 percent, from 18.9 to 33.3 twins per 1,000 live births (Martin et al., 2018). Two related factors in the rise in multiple births are (1) the trend toward delayed childbearing and (2) the increased use of fertility drugs, which spur ovulation, and of assisted reproductive techniques such as in vitro fertilization (Pison et al., 2015).

Multiple births, especially triplets and higher multiples, are a concern because such births, which often result from assisted reproduction, are associated with increased risks: pregnancy complications, premature delivery, low-birth-weight infants, and disability or death of the infant. The multiple birthrate reached a peak in 1998, but declined 47 percent since then. Currently, it stands at slightly over 101 per 100,000 births (Martin et al., 2018). This decline can in part be attributed to changes in assisted reproduction procedures, specifically a reduced proportion of procedures involving three or more embryos (Martin et al., 2017).

Mechanisms of Heredity

The science of genetics is the study of *heredity:* the genetic transmission of heritable characteristics from parents to offspring. When ovum and sperm unite, they endow the baby-to-be with a genetic makeup that influences a wide range of characteristics from color of eyes and hair to health, intellect, and personality.

THE GENETIC CODE

The genetic code is transmitted via a molecule called **deoxyribonucleic acid (DNA).** The double-helix structure of a DNA molecule resembles a long, spiraling ladder whose steps are made of pairs of chemical units called *bases* (Figure 3.1). The bases— adenine (A), thymine (T), cytosine (C), and guanine (G)—are the "letters" of the **genetic code,** which cellular machinery "reads."

Chromosomes are coils of DNA that consist of smaller segments called **genes,** the functional units of heredity. Each gene is located in a definite position on its chromosome and contains thousands of bases. The sequence of bases in a gene tells the cell how to make the proteins that enable it to carry out specific functions. The complete sequence of genes in the human body constitutes the **human genome.** Of course, every human has a unique genome. The human genome is not meant to be a recipe for making a particular human. Rather, the human genome is a reference point, or representative genome, that shows the location of all human genes.

A useful analogy is to consider the DNA of an individual as a series of books in a library. Until those books are "read" by an enzyme called RNA polymerase and transcribed into a readable copy of messenger RNA (m-RNA), the knowledge contained within the books is not actualized. And what books will be pulled down from the shelf and read is in part determined by environmental factors that turn genes on and off at different points in development (Champagne & Mashoodh, 2009).

Every cell in the normal human body except the sex cells (sperm and ova) has 23 pairs of chromosomes—46 chromosomes in all. Through a type of cell division called *meiosis,* which the sex cells undergo when they are developing, each sex cell ends up with only 23 chromosomes—one from each pair. When sperm and ovum fuse at conception, they produce a zygote with 46 chromosomes, 23 from the father and 23 from the mother (Figure 3.2).

At conception, then, the single-celled zygote has all the biological information needed to guide its development into a unique individual. Through *mitosis,*

deoxyribonucleic acid (DNA)
Chemical that carries inherited instructions for the development of all cellular forms of life.

genetic code
Sequence of bases within the DNA molecule; governs the formation of proteins that determine the structure and functions of living cells.

chromosomes
Coils of DNA that consist of genes.

genes
Small segments of DNA located in definite positions on particular chromosomes; functional units of heredity.

human genome
Complete sequence of genes in the human body.

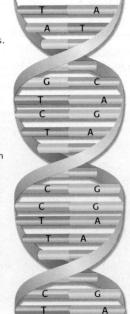

DNA is the genetic material in all living cells. It consists of four chemical units, called bases. These bases are the letters of the DNA alphabet. A (adenine) pairs with T (thymine) and C (cytosine) pairs with G (guanine). There are 3 billion base pairs in human DNA.

T = Thymine
A = Adenine
G = Guanine
C = Cytosine

FIGURE 3.1
DNA: The Genetic Code

Source: Adapted from Ritter, J. (1999, November 23). "Scientists close in on DNA code." *Chicago Sun-Times, 7.*

a process by which the non-sex cells divide in half over and over again, the DNA replicates itself. Each cell division creates a genetic duplicate of the original cell with the same hereditary information. As the cells divide, they differentiate, specializing in a variety of complex bodily functions that enable the child to grow and develop. Sometimes a mistake in copying is made, and a **mutation** may result. Mutations are permanent alterations in genetic material, most of which are harmful.

Genes spring into action when conditions call for the information they can provide. Sometimes this may be triggered by internal processes such as hormones. Other times they are affected by such environmental conditions as nutrition and stress. Thus, from the start, heredity and environment are interrelated.

WHAT DETERMINES SEX?

At the moment of conception, the 23 chromosomes from the sperm and the 23 from the ovum form 23 pairs. Twenty-two pairs are **autosomes,** chromosomes that are not related to sexual expression. The twenty-third pair are **sex chromosomes**—one from the father and one from the mother—that govern the baby's sex.

Sex chromosomes are either *X chromosomes* or *Y chromosomes.* Genetic females are XX, genetic males are XY. Thus, mothers pass on only X chromosomes, but a father's sperm may contain either an X or a Y chromosome. When an ovum (X) is fertilized by an X-carrying sperm, the zygote formed is XX, a genetic female. When an ovum (X) is fertilized by a Y-carrying sperm, the resulting zygote is XY, a genetic male (Figure 3.3). Thus, it is the father's sperm that genetically determines a child's sex.

Initially, the embryo's rudimentary reproductive system appears almost identical in males and in females. However, on the Y chromosome is a gene called the *SRY* gene. Research with mice has found that once hormones signal the *SRY* gene to turn on, cell differentiation and formation of the testes is triggered. At 6 to 8 weeks after conception, the testes start to produce the male hormone testosterone. Exposure of a genetically male embryo to steady, high levels of testosterone ordinarily results in the development of a male body with male sexual organs. Without this hormonal influence, a genetic male will develop genitals that appear female rather than male (Kashimada & Koopman, 2010; Arnold, 2017).

The development of the female reproductive system is equally complex and depends on a number of genetic variants. These variants promote ovarian development and inhibit testicular development (Ono & Harley, 2013). These include the HOX genes (Du & Taylor, 2016) and a signaling molecule called Wnt-4, a variant of which can masculinize a genetically female fetus (Kousta et al., 2010).

Further complexities arise from the fact that women have two X chromosomes, whereas men have only one. For many years researchers believed that the duplicate genes on one of a woman's two X chromosomes are inactive, or turned off. However, researchers discovered that only 75 percent of the genes on the extra X chromosome are inactive. About 15 percent remain active, and 10 percent are active in some women but not in

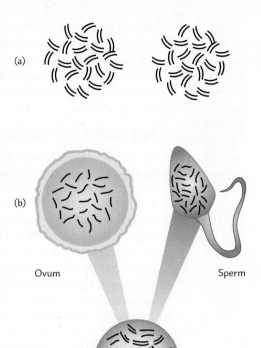

FIGURE 3.2
Hereditary Composition of the Zygote

(a) Body cells of women and men contain 23 pairs of chromosomes, which carry the genes, the basic units of inheritance. (b) Each sex cell (ovum and sperm) has only 23 single chromosomes because of a special kind of cell division (meiosis). (c) At fertilization, the 23 chromosomes from the sperm join the 23 from the ovum so that the zygote receives 46 chromosomes, or 23 pairs.

(a)

(b)

Ovum

Sperm

(c)

Zygote

Source: Adapted from Babu, A. & Hirschhorn, K. (1992). A guide to human chromosome defects. *Birth defects original article series, 28 (2).* 1.

mutation
Permanent alteration in genes or chromosomes that may produce harmful characteristics.

autosomes
In humans, the 22 pairs of chromosomes not related to sexual expression.

sex chromosomes
Pair of chromosomes that determines sex: XX in the normal human female, XY in the normal human male.

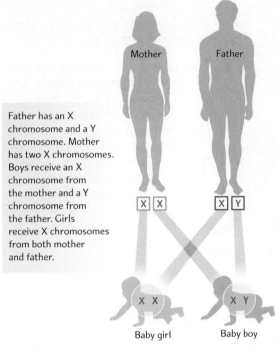

Father has an X chromosome and a Y chromosome. Mother has two X chromosomes. Boys receive an X chromosome from the mother and a Y chromosome from the father. Girls receive X chromosomes from both mother and father.

Mother   Father

X X   X Y

X X   X Y

Baby girl   Baby boy

FIGURE 3.3
Genetic Determination of Sex

Because all babies receive an X chromosome from the mother, sex is determined by whether an X or a Y chromosome is received from the father.

alleles
Two or more alternative forms of a gene that occupy the same position on paired chromosomes and affect the same trait.

homozygous
Possessing two identical alleles for a trait.

heterozygous
Possessing differing alleles for a trait.

dominant inheritance
Pattern of inheritance in which, when a child receives different alleles, only the dominant one is expressed.

recessive inheritance
Pattern of inheritance in which a child receives identical recessive alleles, resulting in expression of a nondominant trait.

polygenic inheritance
Pattern of inheritance in which multiple genes at different sites on chromosomes affect a complex trait.

phenotype
Observable characteristics of a person.

genotype
Genetic makeup of a person, containing both expressed and unexpressed characteristics.

others (Berletch et al., 2011). This variability in gene activity could help explain gender differences linked to the X chromosome and why women are generally healthier and longer lived than men: Harmful changes in a gene on one X chromosome may be offset by a backup copy on the other X chromosome (Migeon, 2006; Short et al., 2013)

PATTERNS OF GENETIC TRANSMISSION

During the 1860s, Gregor Mendel, an Austrian monk, crossbred pea plants that produced only yellow seeds with pea plants that produced only green seeds. The resulting hybrid plants produced only yellow seeds, meaning, he said, that yellow was *dominant* over green. Yet when he bred the yellow-seeded hybrids with each other 25 percent had green seeds. This showed, Mendel said, that a hereditary characteristic (in this case, the color green) can be *recessive;* that is, be carried by an organism that does not express, or show, it.

Mendel's groundbreaking work laid the foundations for our modern understanding of genetics. Although some human traits, such as the presence of facial dimples, are inherited via simple dominant transmission, most human traits fall along a continuous spectrum and result from the actions of many genes in concert.

Dominant and Recessive Inheritance Genes that can produce alternative expressions of a characteristic are called **alleles.** Alleles are alternate versions of the same gene. Every person receives one maternal and one paternal allele for any given trait. When both alleles are the same, the person is **homozygous** for the characteristic; when they are different, the person is **heterozygous.** In **dominant inheritance,** the dominant allele is always expressed, or shows up as a trait in that person. The person will look the same whether or not he or she is heterozygous or homozygous for the characteristic because the recessive allele doesn't show. For the trait to be expressed in **recessive inheritance,** the person must have two recessive alleles, one from each parent. If a recessive trait is expressed, that person cannot have a dominant allele.

Let's take red hair as an example. Because red hair is a recessive trait, you must receive two recessive copies (r) of the gene—one from each parent—in order to express red hair. Having hair that is not red (R; brown in this example) is a dominant trait, so you will have brown hair if you receive at least one copy (R) from either parent (Rr or RR) (Figure 3.4). If you receive one copy of the red hair allele (r) and one copy of an allele for brown hair (R), you are heterozygous (Rr); if you have two copies of the allele for brown hair, you are homozygous dominant (RR). In both of these cases, you will have brown hair. If you inherited one allele for red hair from each parent, you are homozygous recessive for this trait (rr) and will have red hair. Thus the only situation in which you would have red hair is if you received two recessive copies (r), one from each parent.

Relatively few traits are determined in this simple fashion. Most traits result from **polygenic inheritance,** the interaction of many genes. For example, there is not an "intelligence" gene that determines whether or not you are smart. Rather, a large number of genes work in concert to determine your intellectual potential. Although single genes often determine abnormal traits, there is no single gene that by itself significantly accounts for individual differences in any complex behavior.

Genotypes, Phenotypes, and Multifactorial Transmission If you have red hair, that is part of your **phenotype,** the observable characteristics through which your **genotype,** or underlying genetic makeup, is expressed. The phenotype is the product of the genotype and any relevant environmental influences. The difference between genotype and phenotype helps explain why a clone (a genetic copy of an individual) or even an identical twin can never be an exact duplicate of another person.

Mother

Rr

Father

Rr

RR   Rr   Rr   rr

FIGURE 3.4
Dominant and Recessive Inheritance

Because of dominant inheritance, the same observable phenotype (in this case, brown hair) can result from two different genotypes (RR and Rr). A phenotype expressing a recessive characteristic (such as red hair) must have a homozygous recessive genotype (rr).

As Figure 3.4 illustrates, people with different genotypes may exhibit the same phenotype. For example, a child who is homozygous dominant for brown hair (RR) will have brown hair, but so will a child who is heterozygous (Rr) for that same allele.

Furthermore, the recessive alleles can float around undetected for generations. For example, if you are heterozygous for red hair, and you find a mate who is also heterozygous for red hair, approximately one-fourth of your children should have red hair. Each child has a 25 percent chance to inherit both of the recessive alleles, and thus express the recessive trait (red hair). Because the dominant trait is always expressed, all that you would know, upon seeing a child with brown hair, is that the child had to have at least one brown hair allele.

Red hair has a strong genetic base, but experience modifies the expression of the genotype for most traits—a phenomenon called **multifactorial transmission.** Multifactorial transmission illustrates the action of nature and nurture and how they mutually and reciprocally affect outcomes. Imagine that Rio has inherited athletic talent and comes from a family of avid athletes. If his family nurtures his talent and he practices regularly, he may become a skilled athlete. However, if he is not encouraged and not motivated to engage in athletics, his genotype for athleticism may not be expressed (or may be expressed to a lesser extent) in his phenotype. Some physical characteristics (including height and weight) and most psychological characteristics (such as intelligence and musical ability) are products of multifactorial transmission. Many disorders arise when an inherited predisposition (an abnormal variant of a normal gene) interacts with an environmental factor, either before or after birth. Attention-deficit/hyperactivity disorder (ADHD) is one of several behavioral disorders thought to be transmitted multifactorially (Yang et al., 2013).

multifactorial transmission
Combination of genetic and environmental factors to produce certain complex traits.

Epigenetic Influences on Gene Expression Who you are is not just a function of your genes. It is also a function of which of your genes are expressed at any particular moment. Genes are turned off or on as they are needed by the developing body or when triggered by the environment. This phenomenon is called **epigenesis,** or *epigenetics.* Far from being fixed once and for all, epigenetic activity is affected by a continual bidirectional interplay with nongenetic influences (see Research in Action; Mazzio & Soliman, 2012).

epigenesis
Mechanism that turns genes on or off and determines functions of body cells.

research in action

EPIGENETICS AND IDENTICAL TWINS

Have you ever known a pair of identical twins? Were you able to tell them apart? Have you ever wondered why identical twins—who share 100 percent of their genetic code—look and act slightly different?

Epigenetic variation can help explain this. The field of epigenetics includes the study of biochemical modifications of genetic expression "above the genome"—without altering DNA sequence (van IJzendoorn et al., 2011). Epigenetics explains why a skin cell and a heart cell look different, even though both carry the entire genetic code. The differences arise as certain genes are turned on or off depending on need and environmental influences. These changes augment, dampen, or mute genetic expression entirely (Wong et al., 2010).

Epigenetic influences begin in utero, and even on the first day of birth, identical twins already differ. One likely factor is whether twins are monochorionic (share a placenta) and thus are subject to similar environmental influences or are dichorionic (have separate placentas) and are therefore exposed to somewhat different placental environments. In one study, monochorionic twins showed greater epigenetic similarity at birth; gene expression was more "alike" than dichorionic twins with separate womb environments (Gordon et al., 2011). These epigenetic differences continue after birth. For example, research has shown that at 14 years of age, monochorionic twins are still more similar to each other than dichorionic twins (Bui et al., 2015).

Environmental influences after birth also impact twins' similarity to each other. As twins age, even when identical and even when raised in the same family, they will have somewhat different experiences and be exposed to varied environmental influences. Over time, and particularly in adulthood where most twins will follow different life paths, these differences add up. The accumulated differences result in what has been termed epigenetic drift. The older the twins, the more different their epigenome becomes (Bell & Spector, 2011; Fraga et al., 2005; Martino et al., 2013; Wong et al., 2010).

Epigenetic studies create a strong case that identical twins are indeed *not* the same, even at birth and even given an identical genetic code. Epigenetic studies may confirm what many identical twins have asserted all along: They are truly individuals and have always been so.

what's your view

As epigenetic drift results in increasingly different identical twins, how might other people's responses to these increasing differences further shape the process? How might the concept of epigenetics explain differences in nonidentical siblings who share only roughly 50 percent of their genetic code?

Rainbow, on the left, nuzzles her clone, Cc, on the right. They are genetically identical, but have different appearances and personalities because of epigenetic changes on their genome. Pat Sullivan/AP Photo

Epigenesis (meaning "on, or above, the genome") refers to chemical molecules (or tags) attached to a gene that alter the way a cell "reads" the gene's DNA. If we think of the human genome as a piano keyboard, the epigenetic framework can be visualized as the particular tune being played at that time (Stelmach & Nerlich, 2015). Different situations call for different melodies. Thus, even though every cell in the body inherits the same DNA sequence, the chemical tags differentiate various types of body cells, such as brain cells, skin cells, and liver cells.

Epigenetic changes can occur throughout life in response to environmental factors such as nutrition, smoking, sleep habits, stress, and physical activity (Wong et al., 2014). Epigenetics may contribute to such common ailments as cancer, diabetes, and heart disease (Biswas & Rao, 2017; Rosen et al., 2018; Lippi & Cervellin, 2016). It may explain why one monozygotic twin is susceptible to a disease such as schizophrenia whereas the other twin is not, and why some twins get the same disease but at different ages (Demir & Demir, 2018; Wong et al., 2005). Environmental influences can also be social in nature. For example, childhood adversity can lead to a variety of health vulnerabilities including cardiovascular disease, decreased immune responses, and an increased risk of psychological disorders (Notterman & Mitchell, 2015; Vaiserman, 2015).

Cells are particularly susceptible to epigenetic modification during critical periods such as puberty and pregnancy (Padmanabhan et al., 2016; Morrison et al., 2014). Furthermore, epigenetic modifications, especially those that occur early in life, may be heritable. Studies of human sperm cells found age-related epigenetic variations capable of being passed on to future generations (Wei et al., 2015).

One example of epigenesis is *genome,* or *genetic, imprinting.* Imprinting is the differential expression of certain genetic traits, depending on whether the trait has been inherited from the mother or the father. In imprinted gene pairs, genetic information inherited from the parent of one sex is activated, but genetic information from the other parent is suppressed. Imprinted genes play an important role in regulating fetal growth and development. When a normal pattern of imprinting is disrupted, abnormal fetal growth or congenital growth disorders may result (Lee & Bartolemei, 2013).

An example of genomic imprinting can be found in Prader-Willi syndrome, a genetic disease that leads to feeding disturbances, behavioral problems, and intellectual disabilities. The most common form of the disorder occurs from the deletion of a gene segment on paternal chromosome 15, while the genes on the maternal chromosome 15 are turned off (Ishida & Moore, 2013).

Genomic imprinting may explain why a child with an asthmatic mother is more likely to develop asthma than a child with an asthmatic father.
Wavebreakmedia/iStock/Getty Images

GENETIC AND CHROMOSOMAL ABNORMALITIES

Most birth disorders are fairly rare (Table 3.1), affecting only about 3 percent of live births (Centers for Disease Control and Prevention, 2018). Nevertheless, they are the leading cause of infant death in the United States, accounting for almost 21 percent of all deaths in the first year in 2017 (Centers for Disease Control and Prevention, 2018). The most prevalent defects are Down syndrome, followed by cleft lip or cleft palate. Other serious malformations involve the eye, the face, the mouth, or the circulatory, gastronomical, or musculoskeletal systems (Parker et al., 2010).

It is in genetic defects and diseases that we see most clearly the operation of dominant and recessive transmission, and also of a variation, *sex-linked inheritance,* discussed in a subsequent section.

Dominant or Recessive Inheritance of Defects Most of the time, "good" genes are dominant over those carrying abnormal traits, but sometimes the gene for an abnormal trait is dominant. When one parent has one dominant abnormal gene and one recessive "good" gene and the other parent has two recessive "good" genes, each of their children has a 50-50 chance of inheriting the abnormal gene. Among the 1,800 disorders known to be transmitted by dominant inheritance are achondroplasia (a type of dwarfism) and Huntington's disease. Defects transmitted by dominant inheritance are less likely to be lethal at an early age than those transmitted by recessive inheritance because any affected children would be likely to die before reproducing. Therefore, that gene would not be passed on to the next generation and would soon disappear from the population.

Recessive defects are expressed only if the child is homozygous for that gene; in other words, a child must inherit a copy of the recessive gene from each parent. Defects transmitted by recessive genes tend to be lethal at an earlier age, in contrast to those transmitted by dominant genes, because recessive genes can be transmitted by heterozygous carriers who do not themselves have the disorder. Thus they are able to reproduce and pass the genes down to the next generation.

In **incomplete dominance,** a trait is not fully expressed. Normally the presence of a dominant/recessive gene pair results in the full expression of the dominant gene and the

incomplete dominance
Pattern of inheritance in which a child receives two different alleles, resulting in partial expression of a trait.

TABLE 3.1 Some Genetic Defects

Problem	Characteristics of Condition	Risk and Incidence	What Can Be Done
Alpha thalassemia	Severe anemia that reduces ability of the blood to carry oxygen; most affected infants are stillborn or die soon after birth.	More common in families from Mediterranean countries, as well as Asia, Africa, and the Middle East.	Frequent blood transfusions.
Beta thalassemia (Cooley's anemia)	Severe anemia resulting in weakness, fatigue, and frequent illness; usually fatal by young adulthood.	More common in families from Greece, Italy, Africa or Asia.	Frequent blood transfusions.
Cystic fibrosis	Overproduction of mucus, which collects in the lung and digestive tract; breathing and digestive difficulty, death usually occurs in the 30s.	1 in 2,500 to 3,500 white births.	Chest physical therapy, exercise, antibiotics, digestive enzymes, lung transplant.
Duchenne muscular dystrophy	Usually in males, muscle weakness; minor mental retardation; respiratory failure, death usually occurs in young adulthood.	1 in 3,500 to 5,000 male births	No treatment.
Hemophilia	Clotting disorder, usually males; in its most severe form can lead to crippling arthritis in adulthood.	1 in 4,000 to 5,000 male births.	Frequent transfusions of blood with clotting factors.
Anencephaly	Absence of brain tissues; infants are stillborn or die soon after birth.	1 in 10,000 live births.	No treatment.
Spina bifida	Incompletely closed spinal canal resulting in muscle weakness or paralysis and loss of bladder and bowel control; can co-occur with mental retardation.	1 in 2,500 births; more common in Hispanic families.	Surgery to close spinal canal; brain shunt to drain excess fluid.
Phenylketonuria (PKU)	Metabolic disorder resulting in mental retardation.	1 in 10,000 to 15,000 births; more common in European American families.	Special diet can prevent mental retardation.
Polycystic kidney disease	*Infantile form:* enlarged kidneys, respiratory problems, and congestive heart failure. *Adult form:* kidney pain, kidney stones, hypertension and chronic kidney failure.	Autosomal dominant affects 1 in 500 to 1,000 births; autosomal recessive affects 1 in 20,000 to 40,000 births.	Kidney transplants.
Sickle-cell anemia	Deformed red blood cells clog the blood vessels, symptoms include severe pain, stunted growth, frequent infections, leg ulcers, gallstones, susceptibility to pneumonia, and stroke.	1 in 500 African Americans	Painkillers, transfusions for anemia and to prevent stroke, antibiotics for infections.
Tay-Sachs disease	Degenerative disease of the brain and nerve cells, resulting in death before age 5.	Historically found mainly in Eastern European Jews	No treatment.

Source: Adapted from Centers for Disease Control and Prevention. (2020). Birth defects [Information sheet]. Retrieved from www.cdc.gov/ncbddd/birthdefects/index.html; National Institutes of Health. (2020). Genetic home reference [Information sheet]. Retrieved from https://ghr.nlm.nih.gov/

masking of the recessive gene. In incomplete dominance, the resulting phenotype is a combination of both genes. For example, people with one sickle-cell allele and one normal allele do not have sickle-cell anemia with its distinctive, abnormally shaped blood cells. However, their blood cells are not the typical round shape either. They are an intermediate shape, which shows that the sickle-cell gene for these people is incompletely dominant.

FIGURE 3.5
Sex-Linked Inheritance

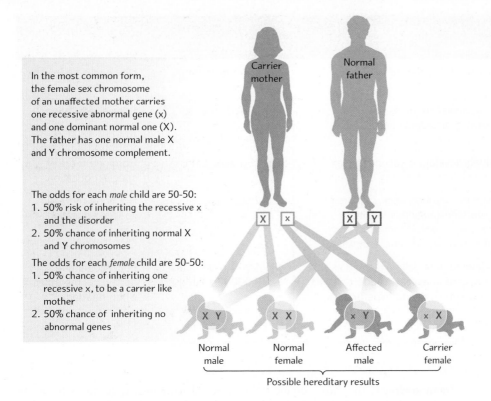

In the most common form, the female sex chromosome of an unaffected mother carries one recessive abnormal gene (x) and one dominant normal one (X). The father has one normal male X and Y chromosome complement.

The odds for each *male* child are 50-50:
1. 50% risk of inheriting the recessive x and the disorder
2. 50% chance of inheriting normal X and Y chromosomes

The odds for each *female* child are 50-50:
1. 50% chance of inheriting one recessive x, to be a carrier like mother
2. 50% chance of inheriting no abnormal genes

Carrier mother

Normal father

X x   X Y

X Y — Normal male
X X — Normal female
x Y — Affected male
x X — Carrier female

Possible hereditary results

Sex-Linked Inheritance of Defects In **sex-linked inheritance** (Figure 3.5), certain recessive disorders affect male and female children differently. This is due to the fact that in humans, males are XY and females are XX, and the Y chromosome is smaller and carries far fewer genes than the X chromosome. One outcome of this is that males receive only one copy of any gene that happens to be carried on the sex chromosomes, whereas females receive two copies. So, if a woman has a "bad" copy of a particular gene, she has a backup copy. However, if a male has a "bad" copy of a particular gene, that gene will be expressed.

Heterozygote women who carry one "bad" copy of a recessive gene and one "good" one are called carriers. If such a woman has children with an unaffected male (a man who has a "good" copy of the gene), she has a 50 percent chance of passing the disorder on to any sons they might have. If they have a son (who is XY by virtue of being male), the father contributed a Y chromosome, and the mother contributed the X chromosome. Because she has one "good" copy and one "bad" copy, either outcome is equally likely. Daughters (who are XX by virtue of being female) may be protected because the father will pass on his "good" copy to daughters, so the girls have a 50 percent chance either of being completely unaffected or of carrying a hidden recessive copy of the gene.

Sex-linked recessive disorders are more common in males than in females. For example, red-green color blindness, hemophilia (a disorder in which blood does not clot properly), and Duchenne muscular dystrophy (a disorder that results in muscle degeneration and eventually death) are all more common in males, and all result from genes located on the X chromosome. Occasionally, a female does inherit a sex-linked condition. For this to happen, the father must have a "bad" copy, *and* the mother must also be a carrier or herself have the condition.

Chromosomal Abnormalities Chromosomal abnormalities typically occur because of errors in cell division, resulting in an extra or missing chromosome. For example, Klinefelter syndrome is caused by an extra female sex chromosome (shown by the pattern XXY). Turner syndrome results from a missing sex chromosome (XO). The likelihood of errors increases in offspring of women age 35 or older. Characteristics of the most common sex chromosome disorders are shown in Table 3.2.

sex-linked inheritance
Pattern of inheritance in which certain characteristics carried on the X chromosome inherited from the mother are transmitted differently to her male and female offspring.

TABLE 3.2 Sex Chromosome Abnormalities

Pattern/Name	Typical Characteristics*	Incidence	Treatment
XYY	Male; tall stature; tendency toward low IQ, especially verbal.	1 in 1,000 male births	No special treatment.
XXX (triple X)	Female; normal appearance, menstrual irregularities, learning disorders, mental retardation.	1 in 1,000 female births	Special education.
XXY (Klinefelter)	Male; sterility, underdeveloped secondary sex characteristics, small testes, learning disorders.	1 in 650 male births	Hormone therapy, special education.
XO (Turner)	Female; short stature, webbed neck, impaired spatial abilities, no menstruation, infertility, underdeveloped sex organs, incomplete development of secondary sex characteristics.	1 in 2,500 female births	Hormone therapy, special education.
Fragile X	Minor-to-severe mental retardation; symptoms, which are more severe in males, include delayed speech, motor development, and hyperactivity.	1 in 4,000 male births; 1 in 8,000 female births	Educational and behavioral therapies when needed.

*Not every affected person has every characteristic.

Source: National Institutes of Health (2020). Genetic home reference [Information sheet]. Retrieved from https://ghr.nlm.nih.gov/

Down syndrome
Chromosomal disorder characterized by moderate-to-severe mental retardation and by such physical signs as a downward-sloping skin fold at the inner corners of the eyes. Also called *trisomy-21*.

genetic counseling
Clinical service that advises prospective parents of their probable risk of having children with hereditary defects.

Although Down syndrome is a major cause of mental retardation, people with this chromosomal abnormality can live happy and productive lives.
Stoked/George Doyle/Media Bakery

Down syndrome, the most common chromosomal abnormality, accounts for about 40 percent of all cases of moderate-to-severe mental retardation (Pennington et al., 2003). The condition is also called *trisomy-21* because it is characterized in more than 90 percent of cases by an extra 21st chromosome.

Approximately 1 in every 800 babies born alive has Down syndrome (de Graaf et al., 2015). Although the risk of having a child with Down syndrome rises with age, because of the higher birthrates of younger women, more young mothers have children with Down syndrome (Centers for Disease Control and Prevention, 2018). In 2011, noninvasive screening tests were developed, which allowed pregnant women to test for Down syndrome without risk of miscarriage. Approximately 30 percent of U.S. parents chose to terminate affected pregnancies (deGraaf et al., 2015).

The brains of children with Down syndrome appear nearly normal at birth but shrink in volume by young adulthood, particularly in the hippocampal area and prefrontal cortex, resulting in cognitive dysfunction, and in the cerebellum, leading to problems with motor coordination and balance (Davis, 2008; Pennington et al., 2003). Children with Down syndrome, like other children with disabilities, tend to benefit cognitively, socially, and emotionally when placed in regular classrooms rather than in special schools (Davis, 2008) and when provided with regular, intensive therapies designed to help them achieve important skills. As adults, many live in small group homes and support themselves; they tend to do well in structured job situations. Because of increases in the average life span, there now exists a much wider range of ages in the U.S. population of people with Down syndrome than used to be the case (de Graaf et al., 2015). Still, a recent international meta-analysis of 34 studies indicated that, across a variety of countries, people with Down syndrome live about 28 fewer years than the general population (O'Leary et al., 2018).

GENETIC COUNSELING AND TESTING

Genetic counseling can help prospective parents assess their risk of bearing children with genetic or chromosomal defects. People who have already had a child with a genetic defect, who have a family history of

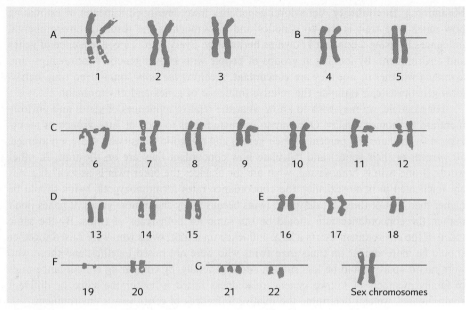

Source: Adapted from Babu, A., & Hirschhorn, K. (1992). A guide to human chromosome defects. *Birth Defects Original Article Series, 28(2)*, 1.

FIGURE 3.6
Karyotype of a Female with Down Syndrome

A karyotype is a photograph that shows the chromosomes. We know that this is a karyotype of a person with Down syndrome because there are three chromosomes instead of the usual two on pair 21. Because pair 23 consists of two Xs, we know that this is the karyotype of a female.

hereditary illness, who suffer from conditions known or suspected to be inherited, or who come from ethnic groups at higher-than-average risk of passing on genes for certain diseases can get information about their likelihood of producing affected children.

Geneticists have made great contributions to the avoidance of birth defects. For example, genetic testing has virtually eliminated Tay-Sachs disease in the Jewish population (Cao et al., 2002). Similarly, screening and counseling of women of childbearing age from Mediterranean countries, where beta thalassemia (refer to Table 3.1) is common, has brought a decline in births of affected babies and greater knowledge of the risks of being a carrier (Cao & Kan, 2013).

A genetic counselor takes a family history and gives the prospective parents and any biological children physical examinations. Chromosomes from body tissues may be photographed and analyzed according to size and structure on a chart called a *karyotype*. This chart can show chromosomal abnormalities and can indicate whether a person who appears unaffected might transmit genetic defects to a child (Figure 3.6). The counselor tries to help clients understand the mathematical risk of a particular condition, explains its implications, and presents information about alternative courses of action. Ideally, this process would occur prior to conception, allowing parents to make informed choices about their options. In reality however, research across a number of different countries shows that such testing most often occurs antenatally, when a child is identified as being affected by a genetic disorder (Hussein et al., 2018).

Nature and Nurture

Phenotypes for most traits are subject to a complex array of hereditary and environmental forces. Let's see how scientists study and explain the influences of heredity (nature) and environment (nurture).

STUDYING HEREDITY AND ENVIRONMENT

One approach to the study of heredity and environment seeks to measure *how much* heredity and environment influence particular traits and determine the relative influence of each. This is the traditional goal of the science of **behavioral genetics.**

behavioral genetics
Quantitative study of relative hereditary and environmental influences on behavior.

heritability
Statistical estimate of contribution of heredity to individual differences in a specific trait within a given population.

concordant
Term describing tendency of twins to share the same trait or disorder.

Measuring Heritability Behavioral geneticists have developed a means of estimating how much of a trait is due to genetics and how much is the result of environmental influences by using a concept known as **heritability.** Every trait is a consequence of genes and environment. By looking at groups of people with known genetic relationships, and assessing whether or not they are **concordant,** meaning *the same,* on a given trait, behavioral geneticists can estimate the relative influence of genes and environment.

For example, we may wish to know what the relative influences of genes and environment are for homosexuality. One way to estimate this is to look at large groups of monozygotic (who share 100 percent of their genes) and dizygotic twins (who share, on average, 50 percent of their genes) and calculate how concordant they are on the trait. In other words, if one twin is homosexual, what are the chances the other twin is as well? If genes are implicated in homosexuality, the concordance rates for monozygotic twins should be higher than that of those for dizygotic twins because they share more genes. If genes don't matter, the concordance rate should be the same for both types of twins. By the same token, if the environment exerts a large influence on a trait, twins who were raised together should be more similar on traits than twins who were not raised together, and those who were raised apart should be less similar. More generally, by comparing concordance rates of family members of known genetic relatedness raised in either the same or different environments, we can determine the relative influences of genes versus environment.

There are multiple variations of this basic approach. For example, immediate family members might be compared to more distant relatives, adopted children might be compared to their biological and adopted parents, or twins adopted by two different families might be compared to twins raised in the same family—but the essential logic is the same. If we know, on average, how many genes people share by virtue of knowing their genetic relationship, and whether or not they are raised together or apart, we can measure how similar they are on traits and work backward to determine the relative environmental influence.

Heritability is expressed as a percentage ranging from 0.0 to 1.0. A heritability estimate of 1.0 indicates that genes are 100 percent responsible for variances in the trait within the population. A heritability estimate of 0.0 percent would indicate the environment shaped a trait exclusively. Twin and adoption studies support a moderate to high hereditary basis for many normal and abnormal characteristics (Polderman et al., 2015; refer to Table 3.1). Note that heritability does not refer to the influences on any one particular person, rather, it indicates the statistical extent to which genes contribute to a trait at a certain time within a given population.

INTERACTIONS OF HEREDITY AND ENVIRONMENT

Today many developmental scientists see heredity and environment as fundamentally intertwined. Instead of looking at genes and experience as operating directly on an organism, they see both as part of a complex developmental system (Gottlieb, 1991, 1997; Lickliter & Honeycutt, 2003). Let's consider several ways in which inheritance and experience work together.

reaction range
Potential variability, depending on environmental conditions, in the expression of a hereditary trait.

Reaction Range Many characteristics vary, within limits, under varying hereditary or environmental conditions. The concept of *reaction range* can help us visualize how this happens.

Reaction range refers to a range of potential expressions of a hereditary trait. Body size, for example, depends largely on biological processes, which are genetically regulated. Tall people have tall children, and short people have short children. Even so, a range of sizes is possible. In societies in which nutrition has dramatically improved, an entire generation has grown up to tower over the generation before. The better-fed children share their parents' genes but have responded to a healthier world. And ultimately, height has genetic limits; we don't see people who are only 1 foot tall or who are 10 feet tall.

Heredity can influence whether a reaction range is wide or narrow. For example, a child born with a defect producing mild cognitive limitations is more able to respond to a favorable environment than a child born with more severe limitations. Likewise, a child with greater native intelligence is likely to benefit more from an enriched home and school environment than a child with normal intelligence (Figure 3.7).

Canalization Some traits have an extremely narrow range of reaction. The concept of **canalization** illustrates how heredity restricts the range of development for some traits. To use a metaphor, after a heavy storm, the rainwater has to go somewhere. If the street has potholes, the water will fill them. If deep canals have been dug along the edges of the street, the water will flow into the canals. Highly canalized traits, such as eye color, are analogous to the deep canals. They are strongly programmed by genes, and there is little opportunity for variance in their expression. Because of the deep, genetically dug channel, it would take an extreme change in environment to alter their course.

Many highly canalized traits tend to be those necessary for survival. In the case of very important traits such as these, natural selection has designed them to develop in a predictable and reliable way within a variety of environments and a multitude of influences. They are too important to be left to chance. Thus, typical babies follow a predictable sequence of motor development: rolling, walking, and running, in that order, at certain approximate ages, irrespective of variations in the environment.

Other traits are more subject to variations in experience. Consider reading. Environment plays a large part in reading skills development. Parents who play letter and word games and who read to their children are likely to have children who learn to read earlier than if these skills are not encouraged or reinforced. And children who are not taught to read do not learn to do so spontaneously.

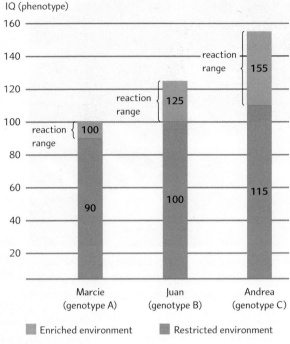

FIGURE 3.7

Intelligence and Reaction Range

Children with different genotypes for intelligence will show varying reaction ranges when exposed to a restricted (blue portion of bar) or enriched (entire bar) environment.

Genotype-Environment Interaction **Genotype-environment interaction** usually refers to the effects of similar environmental conditions on genetically different individuals, and a discussion of these interactions is a way to conceptualize and talk about the different ways nature and nurture interact. To take a familiar example, many children are exposed to pollen and dust, but those with a genetic predisposition are more likely to develop allergic reactions. Interactions can work the other way as well. Genetically similar children can develop differently depending on their home environments. Thus it is the interaction of hereditary and environmental factors, not just one or the other, that produces certain outcomes.

canalization
Limitation on variance of expression of certain inherited characteristics.

genotype-environment interaction
The portion of phenotypic variation that results from the reactions of genetically different individuals to similar environmental conditions.

Genotype-Environment Correlation Because genes influence a person's exposure to particular environments, the environment often reinforces genetic differences (Rutter, 2012). This is called **genotype-environment correlation** and it works in three ways to strengthen the phenotypic expression of a genotypic tendency (Bergeman & Plomin, 1989; Scarr, 1992; Scarr & McCartney, 1983). The first two ways are common among younger children, the third among older children, adolescents, and adults.

- *Passive correlations:* Biological parents provide both genes and environments to their children. For example, a musical parent is likely to create a home environment in which music is heard regularly, to give a child music lessons, and to take the child to musical events. If the child inherited the parent's musical genes, then the child will be uniquely well-suited to respond to those particular environmental influences. This type of correlation is called *passive* because the child does not control it. Passive correlations are most applicable to young children, whose parents have a great deal of control over their early experiences. Additionally, passive correlations function only when a child is living with a biologically related parent.

genotype-environment correlation
Tendency of certain genetic and environmental influences to reinforce each other; may be passive, reactive (evocative), or active. Also called *genotype-environment covariance.*

An adolescent with musical abilities may seek out musical friends and might even start a band. This is an example of niche-picking. Tim Pannell/Fuse/Getty Images

niche-picking
Tendency of a person, especially after early childhood, to seek out environments compatible with his or her genotype.

nonshared environmental effects
The unique environment in which each child grows up, consisting of distinctive influences or influences that affect one child differently than another.

- *Reactive, or evocative, correlations:* Children with differing genetic makeups evoke different reactions from others. For example, parents who are not musically inclined may make a special effort to provide musical experiences for a child who shows genuine interest and ability in music. This response, in turn, strengthens the child's genetic inclination toward music. This type of correlation is called *reactive* because the other people react to the child's genetic makeup.

- *Active correlations:* As children get older and have more freedom to choose their own activities and environments, they *actively* select or create experiences consistent with their genetic tendencies. An adolescent with a talent for music will probably seek out musical friends, take music classes, and go to concerts. This tendency to seek out environments compatible with one's genotype is called **niche-picking.**

Nonshared Environment Influences in the Family Although two children in the same family may bear a striking physical resemblance, siblings can differ greatly in intellect and especially in personality (Plomin & Daniels, 2011). One reason may be genetic differences, which lead children to need different kinds of stimulation or to respond differently to a similar home environment. For example, one child may be more affected by family discord than another (Horowitz et al., 2010). Children may live in the same family, but that does not imply that their experiences are identical.

These **nonshared environmental effects** result from the unique environment in which each child in a family grows up. Children in a family have a shared environment—the home they live in, the people in it, and the activities family members jointly engage in—but they also, even if they are twins, have experiences that are not shared by their brothers and sisters. Parents and siblings may treat each child differently. Certain events, such as illnesses and accidents, and experiences outside the home affect one child and not another. For example, if you are the oldest child in a family, one of your early influences was the ability to have your parents' undivided attention. Later siblings must share their parents' attention. Therefore, despite being in the same family, the influences are not identical. Indeed, some behavioral geneticists have concluded that although heredity accounts for most of the similarity between siblings, the nonshared environment accounts for much of the difference (Hetherington et al., 2013).

Children also mold their environments by the choices they make—what they do and with whom—and their genetic makeup influences these choices. These differences tend to be accentuated as children grow older and have more experiences outside the family (Plomin et al., 2016).

Prenatal Development

gestation
Period of development between conception and birth.

gestational age
Age of an unborn baby, usually dated from the first day of an expectant mother's last menstrual cycle.

During **gestation,** the period between conception and birth, an unborn child undergoes dramatic processes of development. The normal range of gestation is between 37 and 41 weeks (Martin et al., 2009). **Gestational age** is usually dated from the first day of an expectant mother's last menstrual cycle.

In this section we trace the course of prenatal development, and discuss environmental factors that can affect the developing person-to-be. In the next section, we assess techniques for determining whether development is proceeding normally and explain the importance of prenatal care.

STAGES OF PRENATAL DEVELOPMENT

Prenatal development takes place in three stages: *germinal, embryonic,* and *fetal.* (Table 3.3 gives a month-by-month description.) During these three stages of gestation, the original single-celled zygote grows into an *embryo* and then a *fetus.*

TABLE 3.3 Prenatal Development

Month	Description
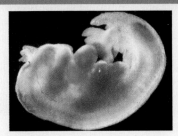 *1 month* Petit Format/Science Source	During the first month, growth is more rapid than at any other time during life; the embryo reaches a size 10,000 times greater than the zygote. By the end of the first month, it measures about ½ inch in length. It has a minuscule heart, beating 65 times a minute. It has the beginning of a brain, kidneys, liver, and digestive tract. The umbilical cord is working. Swellings on the head will eventually become eyes, ears, mouth, and nose. Its sex cannot yet be detected.
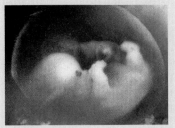 *7 weeks* Claude Edelmann/Science Source	By the end of the second month, the embryo becomes a fetus. It is less than 1 inch long and weighs only ⅓ ounce. Its head is half its total body length. Facial parts are developed, with tongue and teeth buds. The arms have hands, fingers, and thumbs, and the legs have knees, ankles, feet, and toes. Bone cells appear at about 8 weeks. Sex organs are developing. The stomach produces digestive juices; the liver, blood cells. The kidneys remove uric acid from the blood. The thin covering of skin is now sensitive enough to react to tactile stimulation.
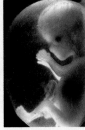 *3 months* Claude Edelmann/Science Source	By the end of the third month, the fetus weighs about 1 ounce and measures about 3 inches in length. It has fingernails, toenails, eyelids, vocal cords, lips, and a nose. Its head is about one-third its total length. Sex is detectable. The organ systems are functioning but not at full capacity. The fetus can now move its legs, feet, thumbs, and head; its mouth can open and close and it can swallow. If its palm is touched, it makes a partial fist; if its lip is touched, it will suck; and if the sole of the foot is stroked, the toes will fan out. These reflexes will be present at birth but will later disappear.
 *4 months* Steve Allen/Getty Images	The head is now only one-fourth the total body length, the same proportion it will be at birth. The fetus measures 8 to 10 inches and weighs about 6 ounces. The placenta is now fully developed. The mother may be able to feel the fetus kicking, a movement known as *quickening*.
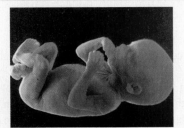 *5 months* James Stevenson/Science Source	The fetus, now weighing about 12 ounces to 1 pound and measuring about 1 foot, now has definite sleep-wake patterns, a favorite position in the uterus (called its *lie*), and becomes more active—kicking, stretching, and even hiccuping. The respiratory system is not yet adequate to sustain life outside the womb; a baby born at this time does not usually survive. Coarse hair has begun to grow for eyebrows and eyelashes, fine hair is on the head, and a woolly hair called *lanugo* covers the body.

(continued)

TABLE 3.3 Prenatal Development (*continued*)

Month	Description
 *6 months* Anatomical Travelogue/Science Source	By the end of the sixth month, the fetus is about 14 inches long and weighs 1 ¼ pounds. It has fat pads under the skin; the eyes can open, close, and look in all directions. It can hear, and it can make a fist with a strong grip. A fetus born early in the sixth month has only a slight chance of survival because the lungs have not matured.
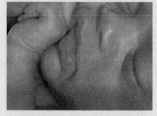 *7 months* Petit Format/Science Source	By the end of the seventh month, the fetus, about 16 inches long and weighing 3 to 5 pounds, has fully developed reflex patterns. It cries, breathes, and swallows, and it may suck its thumb. The lanugo may disappear, or it may remain until shortly after birth. Head hair may continue to grow. The chances that a fetus weighing at least 3½ pounds will survive are good with intensive medical attention.
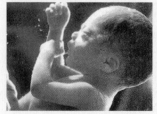 *8 months* Petit Format/Science Source	The 8-month-old fetus is 18 to 20 inches long and weighs between 5 and 7 pounds. Its living quarters are becoming cramped, and so its movements are curtailed. During the next two months a layer of fat develops, which will help the fetus to adjust to varying temperatures outside the womb.
 *9 months—newborn* Luke Schmidt/Shutterstock	About a week before birth, the fetus stops growing, having reached an average weight of about 7½ pounds and a length of about 20 inches, with boys tending to be slightly larger. Fat pads continue to form, the organ systems are operating more efficiently, the heart rate increases, and more wastes are expelled through the umbilical cord. At birth, the fetus will have been in the womb for about 266 days, though gestational age is estimated at 280 days as most doctors date the pregnancy from the mother's last menstrual period.

Note: Even in these early stages, individuals differ. The figures and descriptions given here represent averages.

cephalocaudal principle
Development proceeds "head to tail"; the upper parts of the body develop before the lower parts.

proximodistal principle
The parts of the body near the center develop before the extremities.

Both before and after birth, development proceeds according to two fundamental principles.

The **cephalocaudal principle,** from Latin, meaning "head to tail," dictates that development proceeds from the head to the lower part of the trunk. An embryo's head, brain, and eyes develop earliest and are disproportionately large until the other parts catch up. According to the **proximodistal principle,** from Latin, meaning "near to far," development proceeds from parts near the center of the body to outer ones. The embryo's head and trunk develop before the limbs, and the arms and legs before the fingers and toes.

Germinal Stage (Fertilization to 2 Weeks) During the **germinal stage,** from fertilization to about 2 weeks of gestational age, the zygote divides, becomes more complex, and is implanted in the wall of the uterus.

Within 36 hours after fertilization, the zygote enters a period of rapid cell division and duplication (mitosis). It continues this rapid pace of growth throughout the germinal stage. While the fertilized ovum is dividing, it is also making its way through the fallopian tube to the uterus, a journey of 3 or 4 days. Its form changes into a *blastocyst,* a fluid-filled sphere, which floats freely in the uterus until the sixth day after fertilization, when it begins to implant itself in the uterine wall. Only about 10 to 20 percent of fertilized ova complete the task of **implantation** and continue to develop. Where the egg implants will determine the placement of the placenta.

Before implantation, as cell differentiation begins, some cells around the edge of the blastocyst cluster on one side to form the *embryonic disk,* a thickened cell mass from which the embryo begins to develop. This mass will differentiate into three layers. The *ectoderm,* the upper layer, will become the outer layer of skin, the nails, hair, teeth, sensory organs, and the nervous system, including the brain and spinal cord. The *endoderm,* the inner layer, will become the digestive system, liver, pancreas, salivary glands, and respiratory system. The *mesoderm,* the middle layer, will develop and differentiate into the inner layer of skin, muscles, skeleton, and excretory and circulatory systems.

Other parts of the blastocyst begin to develop into organs that will nurture and protect development in the womb. The *amniotic sac* is a fluid-filled membrane that encases the developing embryo, protecting it and giving it room to move and grow. The *placenta* is a life support system that allows oxygen, nourishment, and wastes to pass between mother and embryo. It is connected to the embryo by the *umbilical cord.* Nutrients from the mother pass from her blood to the embryonic blood vessels, which carry them, via the umbilical cord, to the embryo. In turn, embryonic blood vessels in the umbilical cord carry embryonic wastes to the placenta, where they can be eliminated by maternal blood vessels. The placenta also produces the hormones that support pregnancy, prepare the mother's breasts for lactation, and eventually stimulate the uterine contractions that will expel the baby from the mother's body.

Embryonic Stage (2 to 8 Weeks) During the **embryonic stage,** from about 2 to 8 weeks, the organs and major body systems—respiratory, digestive, and nervous—develop rapidly. This process is known as *organogenesis.* This is a critical period, when the embryo is most vulnerable to destructive influences in the prenatal environment (Figure 3.8). Any organ system or structure that is still developing at the time of exposure is most likely to be affected. Because of this, defects that occur later in pregnancy are likely to be less serious as the major organ systems and physical structures of the body have already formed. Brain growth and development begins during the embryonic stage and continues after birth and beyond.

The most severely defective embryos usually do not survive beyond the first *trimester,* or 3-month period, of pregnancy. A **spontaneous abortion,** commonly called a *miscarriage,* is the expulsion from the uterus of an embryo or fetus that is unable to survive outside the womb. Most miscarriages occur during the first trimester (American College of Obstetricians and Gynecologists, 2018). A miscarriage that occurs after 20 weeks of gestation is generally characterized as a stillbirth.

As many as 1 in 4 recognized pregnancies end in miscarriage, and the actual figure may be as high as 1 in 2 because many spontaneous abortions take place before the woman realizes she is pregnant. Most miscarriages result from abnormal pregnancies; about 50 to 70 percent involve chromosomal abnormalities (Hogge, 2003). Smoking, drinking alcohol, and drug use increase the risks of miscarriage. Miscarriages are more common in African American, Native American, and Alaskan native women, in both young and older (greater than 35 years of age) mothers, and are more likely to occur in pregnancies involving twins or higher order multiples (MacDorman & Gregory, 2015).

germinal stage
First 2 weeks of prenatal development, characterized by rapid cell division, blastocyst formation, and implantation in the wall of the uterus.

implantation
The attachment of the blastocyst to the uterine wall, occurring at about day 6.

embryonic stage
Second stage of gestation (2 to 8 weeks), characterized by rapid growth and development of major body systems and organs.

spontaneous abortion
Natural expulsion from the uterus of an embryo that cannot survive outside the womb; also called *miscarriage.*

FIGURE 3.8
When Birth Defects Occur

Body parts and systems are most vulnerable during organogenesis, when they are developing most rapidly, generally within the first trimester of pregnancy.

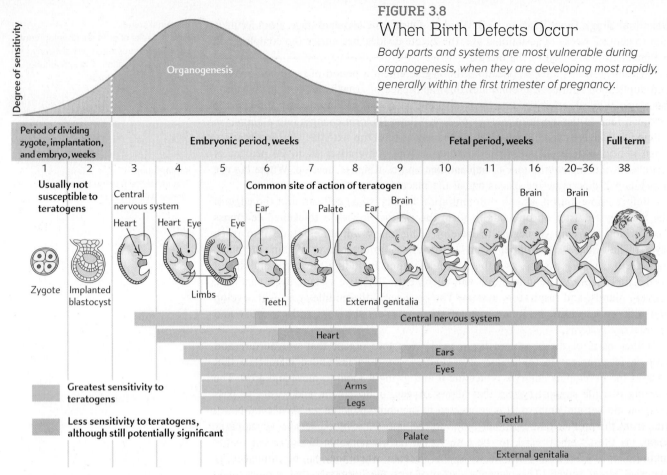

Note: Intervals of time are not all equal.

Source: Adapted from Bleyl, S. B., & Schoenwolf, G. C. (2010). What is the timeline of important events during pregnancy that may be disrupted by a teratogenic exposure. *Birth Defects Research, 7.*

fetal stage
Final stage of gestation (from 8 weeks to birth), characterized by increased differentiation of body parts and greatly enlarged body size.

ultrasound
Prenatal medical procedure using high-frequency sound waves to detect the outline of a fetus and its movements, so as to determine whether a pregnancy is progressing normally.

Fetal Stage (8 Weeks to Birth) The appearance of the first bone cells at about 8 weeks signals the beginning of the **fetal stage,** the final stage of gestation. During this period, the fetus grows rapidly to about 20 times its previous length, and organs and body systems become more complex.

Fetuses are not passive passengers in their mothers' wombs. They breathe, kick, turn, flex their bodies, do somersaults, squint, swallow, make fists, hiccup, and suck their thumbs. The flexible membranes of the uterine walls and amniotic sac, which surround the protective buffer of amniotic fluid, permit and stimulate limited movement.

Scientists can observe fetal movement through **ultrasound,** the use of high-frequency sound waves to detect the outline of the fetus. Other instruments monitor heart rate, changes in activity level, states of sleep and wakefulness, and cardiac reactivity. The movements and activity level of fetuses show marked individual differences, and their heart rates vary in regularity and speed (DiPietro et al., 2015).

Beginning at about the 12th week of gestation, the fetus swallows and inhales some of the amniotic fluid in which it floats. Because the amniotic fluid contains substances that cross the placenta from the mother's bloodstream, swallowing it may stimulate the budding senses of taste and smell. Exposure to strong flavors (e.g., garlic) repeatedly during pregnancy, as may happen if pregnant women's diets contain high levels of such foods, have been shown later to lead to higher acceptance of them in children's diets (De Cosmi et al., 2017; Nehring et al., 2015).

Fetuses can feel pain, but it is highly unlikely that they do so before the third trimester. This is because many of the relevant structures are immature at this point. For example, receptors in the skin lack nerve pathways to the spinal cord necessary for transferring pain stimuli to the brain until 16 to 25 weeks of gestation (Tadros et al., 2015), and the cortex (where consciousness is believed to reside) is immature at this point (Bellieni & Buonocore, 2012). Moreover, the thalamocortical pathways responsible for pain perception do not appear to be functional until 29 to 30 weeks of gestation (Kostović & Judaš, 2010). Furthermore, facial expressions of pain at 24 weeks of gestation are almost absent (5 percent of facial events) but appear more frequently (21.2 percent of facial events) at 36 weeks of gestation (Reissland et al., 2013).

Fetuses respond to the mother's voice and heartbeat and the vibrations of her body, suggesting that they can hear and feel. Responses to sound and vibration seem to begin at 26 weeks of gestation, increase, and then reach a plateau at about 32 weeks (Kisilevsky & Haines, 2010; Kisilevsky et al., 1992). Fetuses nearing full term recognize the voice of their mother (Voegtline et al., 2013) and prefer it to that of their father (Lee & Kisilevsky, 2014). At approximately 33 weeks of gestation fetuses orient toward and attend to music (Kisilevsky et al., 2004) and show increases in heart rate and motor activity when they hear familiar music (Brillo et al., 2019). Once born, neonates prefer female voices to male voices and their mother's native language to other languages (Pino, 2016) as illustrated by their willingness to suck longer on a modified pacifier rigged to play a tape as long they suck on it.

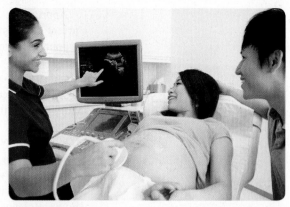
Ultrasound, the procedure this woman is undergoing, is a diagnostic tool that presents an image of the fetus in the womb. Ultrasound is widely used to monitor fetal development. Monkey Business Images/Shutterstock

Fetuses learn and remember as they near the end of the pregnancy. Heart rate data indicate that fetuses have some ability to remember auditory material for short periods of time (Pino, 2016). Current estimates suggest that fetal memory begins to function at approximately 30 weeks of gestational age, when fetuses are able to hold information in memory for 10 minutes. By 34 weeks, they are able to remember information for 1 month (Dirix et al., 2009). Moreover, fetuses not only remember and recognize voices, but they also have some limited ability to reproduce them. Newborn infants use distinctly different intonation patterns in their cries that mirror aspects of their mothers' native language (Mampe et al., 2009). For example, Cameroonian infants whose mothers spoke tonal languages produced more complex cries than Mandarin children, reflecting the more complex tonal structure of their language environment (Wermke et al., 2016).

MATERNAL INFLUENCES

Because the prenatal environment is the mother's body, virtually everything that influences her well-being, from her diet to her moods, may alter her unborn child's environment and affect its growth.

A **teratogen** is an environmental agent, such as a virus, a drug, or radiation, that can interfere with normal prenatal development. An event, substance, or process may be teratogenic for some fetuses but have little or no effect on others. Sometimes vulnerability may depend on a gene either in the fetus or in the mother. The timing of exposure, dose, duration, and interaction with other teratogenic factors also may make a difference.

teratogen
Environmental agent, such as a virus, a drug, or radiation, that can interfere with normal prenatal development and cause developmental abnormalities.

Maternal Weight Gain During Pregnancy Pregnant women typically need 300 to 500 additional calories a day, including extra protein. Women of normal weight and body build who gain 16 to 40 pounds are less likely to have birth complications or to bear babies whose weight at birth is dangerously low or overly high.

In the United States, 21 percent of women do not gain enough weight and 48 percent gain too much (Branum et al., 2016). If a woman does not gain enough, her baby may suffer growth retardation in the womb, be born prematurely, experience distress during labor and delivery, or die at or near birth. Women who gain too much weight risk having a large baby that needs to be delivered by induced labor or cesarean section, and increase their risk for preeclampsia, gestational diabetes, and postpartum hemorrhage. Additionally, both the mother and baby are at increased risk for later weight problems and the development of cardio-metabolic risk factors (Centers for Disease Control and Prevention, 2019; Catalano & Shanker, 2017; Gaillard et al., 2015; Marchi et al., 2015).

Appropriate weight gain depends on body mass index (BMI) before pregnancy. Current recommendations are that women who are underweight should gain 28 to 40 pounds, normal weight women should gain 25 to 35 pounds, overweight women should gain 15 to 25 pounds, and obese women should gain only 11 to 20 pounds (American College of Obstetrics and Gynecology, 2013). Women who are overweight or obese before becoming pregnant are more likely to gain too much weight once pregnant than women with a BMI in the normal range (Deputy et al., 2015).

Malnutrition Nutritional status during pregnancy can have long-term consequences. In rural Gambia, in western Africa, people born during the *hungry season,* when foods from the previous harvest are depleted, are 10 times more likely to die in early adulthood than people born during other parts of the year (Moore et al., 1997). Adults born to mothers who were pregnant during a famine in Ukraine from 1932 to 1933 were at elevated risk for diabetes, and their risk varied with the degree of famine severity they were exposed to (Lumey et al., 2015). Men exposed to malnutrition during the 1944–45 famine in the Netherlands showed higher mortality rates than men whose mothers were well nourished during pregnancy (Ekamper et al., 2015).

Malnutrition is a global problem driven by factors such as poverty, conflict, and climate change (World Health Organization, 2018). Worldwide, approximately 820 million people suffer from calorie deficiency (Food and Agricultural Organization of the United Nations, 2019). Malnutrition is not just a problem of the developing world. Some women in the United States have difficulty affording and accessing healthy food, particularly when living in food deserts. Food deserts are generally low-income areas, usually in ethnic minority neighborhoods, lacking accessible supermarkets or grocery stores (Walter et al., 2010). This issue is addressed in more detail in Chapter 7.

Studies indicate risks of insufficient calories during pregnancy differentially affect men and women. For example, women born during a famine in China from 1956–1963 were at higher risk for schizophrenia but men were not (Huang et al., 2014). Additionally, women, but not men, born to malnourished mothers are at increased risk for higher BMI, body weight, and waist circumference (Lumey et al., 2011).

Malnutrition can also involve the lack of essential nutrients. Estimates are that approximately 2 billion people suffer from chronic micronutrient deficiencies (World Health Organization, 2018). Micronutrients are vitamins or minerals that are needed in small quantities but have a profound negative effect if absent. For example, folic acid, or folate (a B vitamin), is critical in a pregnant woman's diet. A lack of folic acid can result in anencephaly and spina bifida. Addition of folic acid to enriched grain products has been mandatory in the United States since 1998 and has been instituted in more than 50 countries worldwide, sharply reducing the incidence of these defects (Chitayat et al., 2016). Vitamin A and zinc deficiencies result in a higher risk of death for both child and mother (Black et al., 2013), and babies born to mothers with a vitamin D deficiency may suffer from weak or soft bones (Anastasiou et al., 2017).

Malnutrition due to a calorie deficit or to micronutrient deficiencies are both urgent issues as this can not only hurt the expectant mother and her child, but also exert effects across generations (Martorell & Zongrone, 2012). For example, children who are malnourished in early childhood can be stunted, and this stunting, in women, is associated with a higher risk of birth complications (Black et al., 2008) and the birth of smaller babies (Victora et al., 2008). Thus, it is important to identify malnutrition early in pregnancy so it can be treated. Malnourished women who take dietary supplements while pregnant tend to have bigger, healthier infants and fewer stillbirths (Imdad & Bhutta, 2011; Haider & Bhutta, 2017).

Physical Activity and Strenuous Work Moderate exercise at any time during pregnancy does not seem to endanger the fetuses of healthy women (Committee on Obstetric Practice, 2002; Riemann & Kanstrup Hansen, 2000). Regular exercise prevents constipation and improves respiration, circulation, muscle tone, and skin elasticity, all of which contribute to a more comfortable pregnancy and an easier, safer delivery (American

College of Obstetricians and Gynecologists, 2019). Employment during pregnancy generally entails no special hazards. However, strenuous working conditions, occupational fatigue, and long working hours may be associated with a greater risk of premature birth (Bell et al., 2008).

Current recommendations advise women in low-risk pregnancies to get at least 150 minutes of moderate to intense aerobic exercise a week, taking care to avoid overheating and making sure to drink plenty of water. Contact sports or activities that might result in a fall should be avoided (American College of Obstetricians and Gynecologists, 2019).

Drug Intake Almost everything an expectant mother takes in makes its way to the uterus. Drugs may cross the placenta, just as oxygen, carbon dioxide, and water do. Vulnerability is greatest in the first few months of gestation, when development is most rapid.

Medical Drugs In the early 1960s a tranquilizer called *thalidomide* was banned after it was found to have caused stunted or missing limbs, severe facial deformities, and defective organs in some 12,000 babies. The thalidomide disaster sensitized medical professionals and the public to the potential dangers of taking drugs while pregnant.

Pregnant and breastfeeding women should generally avoid medication unless it is essential for her health or her child's (Koren et al., 1998). Among the medical drugs that may be harmful during pregnancy are the antibiotic tetracycline; certain barbiturates, opiates, and other central nervous system depressants; several hormones, including diethylstilbestrol (DES) and androgens; certain anticancer drugs, such as methotrexate; Accutane, a drug often prescribed for severe acne; drugs used to treat epilepsy; and several antipsychotic drugs (Briggs et al., 2012; Einarson & Boskovic, 2009; Koren et al., 1998). Angiotensin-converting enzyme (ACE) inhibitors and nonsteroidal anti-inflammatory drugs (NSAIDs), such as naproxen and ibuprofen, have been linked to birth defects when taken anytime from the first trimester on (Cooper et al., 2006; Ofori et al., 2006). In addition, certain antipsychotic drugs used to manage severe psychiatric disorders may have serious potential effects on the fetus, including withdrawal symptoms at birth (Hudak & Tan, 2012).

Opioids In recent years, the number of pregnant women abusing legal and illegal opioids has risen (Haight et al., 2018). Although opioid use has not been strongly implicated in birth defects, it is associated with small babies, fetal death, and preterm labor. Moreover, babies born to drug-addicted mothers are often addicted themselves and go through withdrawal once they are born and no longer receiving the drug. This results in neonatal abstinence syndrome, a condition in which newborns may show sleep disturbances, tremors, difficulty regulating their bodies, irritability and crying, diarrhea, fever, and feeding difficulties (Reddy et al., 2018). Long-term effects include deficiencies in growth as well as attentional, memory, and perceptual problems. However, studies on cognitive outcomes are conflicting, and results may be due to other variables (such as socioeconomic status or other drug use) that are correlated with opiate use (Maguire et al., 2016). To date, punitive measures such as jailing pregnant women who use these drugs have been shown to be ineffective. This has led to calls to address the opioid crisis in pregnant women as a public health problem rather than a law enforcement issue (O'Connor, 2019; Patrick & Schiff, 2017).

Alcohol Prenatal alcohol exposure is the most common cause of mental retardation and the leading preventable cause of birth defects in the United States. **Fetal alcohol syndrome (FAS)** is characterized by a combination of retarded growth, face and body malformations, and disorders of the central nervous system. FAS and other less severe alcohol-related conditions are estimated to occur in nearly 1 in every 20 births in the United States (Sacks et al., 2015). Worldwide, approximately 119,000 children are born with FAS every year (Tsang & Elliot, 2017). Alcohol exposure is also an issue in approximately 10 percent of pregnancies, and about 15 out of 10,000 live births will have FAS.

fetal alcohol syndrome (FAS)
Combination of mental, motor, and developmental abnormalities affecting the offspring of some women who drink heavily during pregnancy.

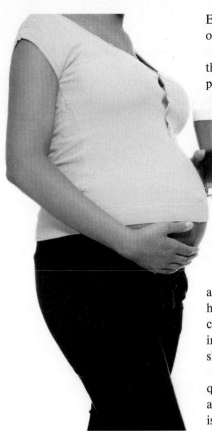

A mother who drinks during pregnancy risks having a child born with fetal alcohol syndrome. PhotoMediaGroup/Shutterstock

Exposure rates vary widely by region, from 25.2 percent in European countries to a low of 0.2 percent in the Eastern Mediterranean regions (Popova et al., 2017).

Even small amounts of social drinking may harm a fetus (Charness et al., 2016), and the more the mother drinks, the greater the effect. Moderate or heavy drinking during pregnancy seems to disturb an infant's neurological and behavioral functioning, and this may affect early social interaction with the mother, which is vital to emotional development (Hannigan & Armant, 2000). Heavy drinkers who continue to drink after becoming pregnant are likely to have babies with reduced skull and brain growth as compared with babies of nondrinking women or expectant mothers who stop drinking (Handmaker et al., 2006; Treit et al., 2016).

FAS-related problems can include reduced responsiveness to stimuli and slow reaction time in infancy and, throughout childhood, short attention span, distractibility, restlessness, hyperactivity, learning disabilities, memory deficits, mood disorders, aggressiveness, and problem behavior (Gupta et al., 2016). Prenatal alcohol exposure is a risk factor for development of alcohol and psychiatric disorders in adulthood (Rangmar et al., 2015).

Some FAS problems recede after birth, but others, such as retardation, behavioral and learning problems, and hyperactivity, tend to persist. However, interventions can help children develop to their fullest potential. Interventions may focus on the affected child or may provide parental support, training, and education. Research has shown that interventions can improve attention, self-regulation, adaptive functioning, and social skills in affected children (Reid et al., 2015; Petrenko, 2015; Murawski et al., 2015).

Although it is clear that alcohol use during pregnancy can have devastating consequences, more research is needed. For instance, research on interventions targeting affected adolescents and adults is scarce, which is problematic given the evidence that issues faced by children compound with age if left untreated (Reid et al., 2015). Additionally, at an international level, research on cultural barriers is sorely needed. For example, one key prevention tactic involves educating parents on the risks of drinking during pregnancy. However, in cultures where alcohol use during pregnancy is not stigmatized, education is less effective. Moreover, even if drinking during pregnancy is stigmatized, the effect varies with the cultural context. The social pressure exerted by stigma may result in lower levels of drinking during pregnancy. However, stigma may also make it difficult to obtain reliable information on prenatal alcohol exposure or a reluctance to officially label a child as affected (Petrenko & Alto, 2017).

Nicotine Maternal smoking during pregnancy has been identified as the single most important factor in low birth weight in developed countries (DiFranza et al., 2004). The global prevalence of smoking during pregnancy is estimated to be 1.7 percent, with the highest rates found in Europe and lowest rates in Africa (Lange et al., 2018). Recently, the use of e-cigarettes has sharply increased, in part because of marketing promoting it as a safer alternative. Research on the effects this has on pregnancy outcomes is scarce; however, the exposure to nicotine, even without exposure to additional substances, carries risks to immune system functioning, neural development, lung function, and the cardiovascular system (Whittington et al., 2018).

Women who smoke during pregnancy are more than 1½ times as likely as nonsmokers to bear low-birth-weight babies (weighing less than 5½ pounds at birth). Although even light smoking (fewer than five cigarettes a day) is associated with a greater risk of low birth weight (Martin et al., 2005; Shankaran et al., 2004), the effect is dose dependent. Thus those mothers who smoke more than 20 cigarettes a day have the smallest babies (Ko et al., 2014). This is problematic, as almost 73 percent of women who smoke at all during pregnancy are daily smokers (Lange et al., 2018).

Tobacco use during pregnancy also brings increased risks of miscarriage, growth retardation, stillbirth, small head circumference, sudden infant death, colic (uncontrollable, extended crying for no apparent reason) in early infancy, hyperkinetic disorder (excessive movement), and long-term respiratory, neurological, cognitive, attentional, and behavioral problems, and later obesity and cardiovascular issues (Froehlich et al., 2009;

Linnet et al., 2005; Shah et al., 2006; Smith et al., 2006; Banderali et al., 2015; Rayfield & Plugge, 2017). The effects of prenatal exposure to secondhand smoke on development tend to be worse when children also experience socioeconomic hardship during the first 2 years of life (Rauh et al., 2004), when they are exposed to additional teratogens such as lead (Froehlich et al., 2009), or deprived of necessary nutrients such as folic acid (Mook-Kanamori et al., 2010) at the same time.

Caffeine Can the caffeine a pregnant woman consumes in coffee, tea, cola, or chocolate cause trouble for her fetus? Several large-scale reviews have indicated that caffeine intake under 300 milligrams a day is not associated with an increased risk of miscarriage, stillbirth, or birth defects (Peck et al., 2010; Wikoff et al., 2017). However, other studies have found a slightly increased risk of miscarriage, stillbirth, and low birth weight in mothers who consume caffeine while pregnant (Greenwood et al., 2014; Li et al., 2015), and there are suggestions that risk may increase with dosage (Chen et al., 2017). Thus, although results are unclear, current recommendations on limiting caffeine to 200 milligrams or less (about one cup of coffee) are still in place.

Marijuana Marijuana is the most commonly used illegal drug during pregnancy, and rates of women who report using marijuana while pregnant have risen sharply in the last 10 years (Martin et al., 2015), perhaps as a result of more liberal laws in many states. Some women cite medical concerns, including nausea, anxiety, and pain management, as the impetus to smoke marijuana during pregnancy (Metz & Borgelt, 2018).

Research on marijuana is difficult. For example, many pregnant women who smoke marijuana also smoke cigarettes or consume alcohol, and socioeconomic factors also seem to be important (Metz & Stickrath, 2015). However, some research does suggest that marijuana exposure, especially at high levels, is associated with low birth weight, preterm delivery, difficult births and admission into neonatal intensive care (Metz & Borgelt, 2018; Gunn et al., 2016). Although marijuana exposure has not been associated with decreases in general intelligence (Behnke et al., 2013), it has been implicated in subtle neurological differences and deficits in problem-solving skills (Viteri et al., 2015; McLemore & Richardson, 2016), and it may alter patterns of cerebral blood flow (Smith et al., 2016). This may explain why marijuana exposure during the prenatal period is also associated with decreases in academic achievement (Goldschmidt et al., 2012).

Overall, the effects of prenatal marijuana exposure appear to be relatively weak and are difficult to interpret (Sharapova et al., 2018). However, there are clear theoretical reasons to suspect exposure will alter brain development (Naik et al., 2018). This, in conjunction with the somewhat controversial but still troubling research on the effects of prenatal marijuana exposure, suggests pregnant women should avoid its use.

Cocaine Cocaine use during pregnancy has been associated with spontaneous abortion, delayed growth, premature labor, low birth weight, small head size, birth defects, and impaired neurological development (Chiriboga et al., 1999; March of Dimes Birth Defects Foundation, 2004; Shankaran et al., 2004). In some studies, cocaine-exposed newborns show acute withdrawal symptoms and sleep disturbances (O'Brien & Jeffery, 2002). Cocaine does not appear to affect global cognitive development; however, it may preferentially affect areas of the brain involved in attention and executive functioning and has been associated with declines in academic performance in adolescence (Richardson & Day, 2018; Behnke et al., 2013; Buckingham-Howes et al., 2013). It has also been linked to other problems in adolescence and adulthood, including aggression, conduct disorders, greater likelihood of arrest, substance abuse, and risky sexual behaviors (Richardson et al., 2019; Min et al., 2014). Other studies, however, have found little specific connection between prenatal cocaine exposure and physical, motor, cognitive, emotional, or behavioral deficits that could not also be attributed to other risk factors, such as low birth weight; exposure to tobacco, alcohol, or marijuana; or a poor home environment (Konijnenberg, 2015; Ackerman et al., 2010; Messinger et al., 2004; Singer et al., 2004).

Methamphetamine Prenatal methamphetamine exposure is associated with fetal growth restriction (Smith et al., 2006). Additionally, exposure is also implicated in neonatal neurobehavioral abnormalities, such as quality of movement, lethargy, stress, and arousal. Fortunately, many of these abnormalities appear to resolve themselves by a month of age (Kiblawi et al., 2014). However, prenatal exposure to methamphetamines has been associated with fetal brain damage to areas of the brain involved in learning, memory, and control, which are likely to have longer-term consequences (Roussotte et al., 2011). For instance, methamphetamine-exposed children are more likely to have behavioral problems, high levels of aggression, and deficits in executive functioning, particularly if also exposed to early adversity (Eze et al., 2016; Abar et al., 2013).

Maternal Illnesses **Acquired immune deficiency syndrome (AIDS)** is a disease caused by the human immunodeficiency virus (HIV), which undermines functioning of the immune system. If an expectant mother has the virus in her blood, *perinatal transmission* may occur: The virus may cross over to the fetus's bloodstream through the placenta during pregnancy, labor, or delivery or, after birth, through breast milk.

The biggest risk factor for perinatal HIV transmission is a mother who is unaware she has HIV. In the United States, the perinatal transmission of HIV has declined by more than 95 percent due to routine testing and treatment of pregnant women and newborn babies. With proper precautions and treatment, the estimated rate of perinatal HIV infection can be one percent or less (Centers for Disease Control and Prevention, 2019).

An infection called *toxoplasmosis,* caused by a parasite harbored in the bodies of cats, cattle, sheep, and pigs typically produces either no symptoms or symptoms like those of the common cold in adults. In an expectant woman, however, it can cause fetal brain damage, severely impaired eyesight or blindness, seizures, miscarriage, stillbirth, or death of the baby. There may also be later problems, including eye infections, hearing loss, and learning disabilities. Treatment with antiparasitic drugs during the first year of life can reduce brain and eye damage for affected infants (McLeod et al., 2006). To avoid infection, expectant mothers should not eat raw or very rare meat, should wash hands and all work surfaces after touching raw meat, should peel or thoroughly wash raw fruits and vegetables, and should not dig in a garden where cat feces may be buried. Women who have a cat should have it checked for the disease, and, if possible, should have someone else empty the litter box (Centers for Disease Control and Prevention, 2019).

Offspring of mothers with diabetes are 3 to 4 times more likely than offspring of other women to develop a wide range of birth defects, although heart and neural tube defects are the most common (Ornoy et al., 2015). Women with diabetes need to be sure their blood glucose levels are under control *before* becoming pregnant (Li et al., 2005) and they should retain tight control of their blood glucose during the course of the pregnancy as well (American Diabetes Association, 2018).

In late 2019, a novel, highly infectious airborne respiratory coronavirus, **COVID-19**, became a **pandemic**. Many **coronaviruses**, such as those that cause the common cold, are relatively innocuous. However, some have been responsible for large disease outbreaks. In previous coronavirus outbreaks, such as severe acute respiratory syndrome (SARS) and Middle East respiratory syndrome (MERS), pregnant women and their fetuses were at higher risk of death than nonpregnant women (Schwartz & Graham 2020; Karimi-Zarchi et al., 2020). Despite the sparse data available to date, preliminary research suggests the COVID-19 pandemic does not seem to carry an elevated risk of death for either pregnant women or their fetuses (Zeng et al., 2020; Liu et al., 2020).

Maternal Stress and Depression Some tension and worry during pregnancy are normal and do not necessarily increase risks of birth complications (Littleton et al., 2006). Moderate maternal anxiety may even spur organization of the developing brain. In one study, newborns whose mothers experienced moderate levels of both positive and negative stress showed signs of accelerated neurological development (DiPietro et al., 2010). There are also suggestions that mild prenatal stress may be associated with enhanced later resilience in the face of stressful events (Monaghan & Haussman, 2015).

On the other hand, high levels of maternal **stress** and anxiety during pregnancy are negatively associated with cognitive development, and are positively linked to a more active and irritable temperament in newborns, negative emotionality, impulsivity, and behavioral disorders in early childhood (DiPietro et al., 2010; Van den Bergh et al., 2017). Additionally, chronic stress can result in preterm delivery, perhaps through the action of elevated levels of stress hormones or the resulting dampened immune functioning, which makes women more vulnerable to inflammatory diseases and infection that can also trigger labor (Schetter, 2009; Hoffman et al., 2016).

Depression may also have negative effects on development. Some studies report depressed pregnant women are more likely to give birth to a preterm child; however, other studies have not found this effect and it remains controversial (Gentile, 2017; Staneva et al., 2015). Other research has reported that children born to depressed mothers are at elevated risk for developmental delays as toddlers, increased incidence of both internalizing (e.g., depression) and externalizing (e.g., impulsive behavior and aggression) symptoms as children, and elevated levels of violent and antisocial behaviors in adolescence (Gentile, 2017; Deave et al., 2008; Hay et al., 2010).

Maternal Age Birthrates of U.S. women in their thirties and forties are at their highest levels since the 1960s, in part due to fertility treatments—an example of a history-graded influence (Figure 3.9) (Martin et al., 2010). From 2000 to 2014, there was a 23 percent increase in first births for women over the age of 35 years, for all ethnic and racial groups, and in all states (Mathews & Hamilton, 2016).

The chance of miscarriage or stillbirth rises with maternal age and reaches 90 percent for women age 45 or older. Women 30 to 35 are more likely to suffer complications due to diabetes, high blood pressure, or severe bleeding. There is also higher risk of premature delivery, retarded fetal growth, birth defects, and chromosomal abnormalities, such as Down syndrome (Lean et al., 2017; Heffner, 2004).

Adolescent mothers tend to have premature or underweight babies—perhaps because a young girl's still-growing body consumes vital nutrients the fetus needs (Martin et al., 2007) or because of inadequate or missing prenatal care (Malabarey et al., 2012). These newborns are at heightened risk of preterm delivery, low birth weight, disabilities, or health problems (Goossens et al., 2015). Although rates of teen pregnancy in the United States have been in a steady, long-term decline for young women of all ethnicities, they are still among the highest of industrialized nations (Martin et al., 2018; Hamilton & Ventura, 2012).

Outside Environmental Hazards Air pollution, chemicals, radiation, extremes of heat and humidity, and other environmental hazards can affect prenatal development. Pregnant women who regularly breathe air that contains high levels of fine combustion-related particles are more likely to bear infants who are premature or undersized (Jacobs et al., 2017; Malmqvist et al., 2017), have chromosomal abnormalities (Bocskay et al., 2005), and who in childhood show poor

stress
Physical or psychological demands on a person or organism.

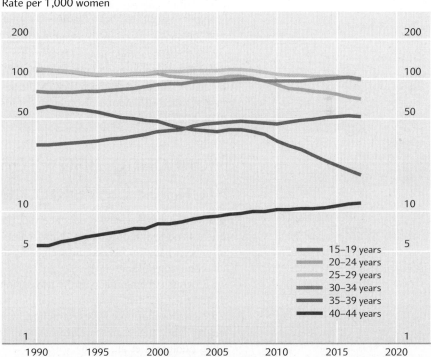

FIGURE 3.9

U.S. Birthrates, by Age of Mother, 1990–2017

Source: Martin, J. A., Hamilton, B. E., & Osterman, M. J. K, Driscoll, A. K., & Drake, P. (2018). Births: Final data 2017. *National Vital Statistics Reports, 67*(8). Hyattsville, MD: National Center for Health Statistics.

self-regulation and are low in social competence (Margolis et al., 2016). Similarly, exposure to high concentrations of disinfection by-products is associated with low birth weight and congenital abnormalities (Nieuwenhuijsen et al., 2013).

Fetal exposure to low levels of environmental toxins, such as lead, mercury, and dioxin, as well as nicotine and ethanol, may help explain the sharp rise in asthma, ear infections, and allergies (Parker-Lalomio et al., 2018; Wu et al., 2019). Childhood cancers, including leukemia, have been linked to pregnant mothers' drinking chemically contaminated groundwater (Boyles, 2002) and use of home pesticides (Menegaux et al., 2006). Infants exposed prenatally even to low levels of lead are born smaller and shorter than unexposed babies and tend to show IQ deficits during childhood (Xie et al., 2013; Schnaas et al., 2006).

Women who have routine dental X-rays during pregnancy triple their risk of having full-term, low-birth-weight babies (Hujoel et al., 2004). In utero exposure to radiation has been linked to miscarriage, mental retardation, small head size, increased cancer risk, and lowered IQ (Groen et al., 2012).

PATERNAL INFLUENCES

A man's exposure to lead, marijuana or tobacco smoke, large amounts of alcohol or radiation, DES, pesticides, or high ozone levels may result in abnormal or poor-quality sperm (Siddeek et al., 2018; Sokol et al., 2006). Offspring of men stationed on military vessels were at elevated risk of infant mortality and their mothers were at risk for dangerously high blood pressure during pregnancy (Baste et al., 2014). Babies whose fathers had diagnostic X-rays or had high lead exposure at work tended to have low birth weight and slowed fetal growth (Chen et al., 2018; Chen & Wang, 2006; Lin et al., 1998; Shea et al., 1997).

Men who smoke have an increased likelihood of transmitting genetic abnormalities and heart defects (Beal et al., 2017; Deng et al., 2013). A pregnant woman's exposure to the father's secondhand smoke has been linked with asthma (Simons et al., 2014), attentional problems (Langley et al., 2012), low birth weight (Rubin et al., 1986; Zhou et al., 2014), and cancer in childhood (Metayer et al., 2013).

Older fathers may be a significant source of birth defects due to damaged or deteriorated sperm. Birthrates for older fathers have risen in the United States for all races and across educational levels (Khandwala et al., 2017). Having an older father is a risk factor for schizophrenia (Janecka et al., 2017; Sharma et al., 2015) as is having, at least for male children, a young father (Miller et al., 2010). Advanced age of the father also may be a factor in bipolar disorder, and autism and related disorders (Andersen & Urhoj, 2017; Malaspina et al., 2015).

Monitoring and Promoting Prenatal Development

Historically, once a baby was conceived, parents were in the dark regarding the characteristics and health of the baby. Now scientists have developed an array of tools to assess an unborn baby's progress and well-being and even to intervene to correct some abnormal conditions (Table 3.4).

Progress is being made in the use of noninvasive procedures, such as ultrasound and blood tests, to detect chromosomal abnormalities. Contrary to previous findings, amniocentesis and chorionic villus sampling, which can be used earlier in pregnancy, carry only a slightly higher miscarriage risk than these noninvasive procedures (Caughey et al., 2006; Eddleman et al., 2006).

Screening for defects and diseases is only one important reason for early prenatal care. Early, high-quality prenatal care, which includes educational, social, and nutritional services, can help prevent maternal or infant death and other birth complications. The amount of prenatal care received by a woman is related linearly to positive outcomes (Partridge et al., 2012).

TABLE 3.4 Prenatal Assessment Techniques

Technique	Description	Uses and Advantages	Risks and Notes
Amniocentesis	Sample of amniotic fluid is withdrawn under guidance of ultrasound and analyzed. Most commonly used procedure to obtain fetal cells for testing.	Can detect chromosomal and sex-linked disorders and many genetic defects; more than 99 percent accuracy rate. Usually performed in women ages 35 and over; recommended if prospective parents are known carriers of genetic diseases.	Performed after 15 weeks' gestation. Results usually take 1 to 2 weeks. Small (0.5–1%) added risk of fetal loss or injury. Can be used for sex-screening of unborn babies.
Chorionic villus sampling (CVS)	Tissues from hairlike chorionic villi (projections of membrane surrounding fetus) are removed from placenta and analyzed.	Early diagnosis; can be performed between 10-12 weeks' gestation; yields highly accurate results within a week.	Some studies suggest 1–4% more risk of fetal loss than with amniocentesis.
Embryoscopy, fetoscopy	Tiny viewing scope is inserted in woman's abdomen to view embryo or fetus to aid in diagnosis of nonchromosomal disorders.	Can guide fetal blood transfusions and bone marrow transplants.	Riskier than other prenatal diagnostic procedures.
Maternal blood test	A sample of the prospective mother's blood is tested for hormone levels associated with fetal abnormalities.	May indicate defects in formation of brain or spinal cord; also can predict Down syndrome and other abnormalities. Permits monitoring of at-risk pregnancies.	No known risks, but false negatives are common. Ultrasound and/or amniocentesis needed to confirm suspected conditions.
Preimplantation genetic diagnosis	After in vitro fertilization, a sample cell is removed from the blastocyst and analyzed.	Can avoid transmission of genetic defects or predispositions; a defective blastocyst is *not* implanted in uterus.	No known risks.
Ultrasound (sonogram)	High-frequency sound waves produce a picture of fetus in uterus	Monitor fetal growth, movement, position, and form; assess amniotic fluid volume; detect major abnormalities or fetal death, judge gestational age; detect multiple pregnancies. Guide amniocentesis and chorionic villus sampling.	Done routinely in many places. Can be used for sex-screening of unborn babies.
Umbilical cord sampling (cordocentesis)	Needle guided by ultrasound is inserted into blood vessels of umbilical cord.	Allows direct access to fetal DNA for diagnostic measures, allows therapeutic measures such as blood transfusions.	Fetal loss or miscarriage is reported in 1–2% of cases; increases bleeding risk from umbilical cord and fetal distress.

Sources: Carlson, L. M., & Vora, N. L. (2017). Prenatal diagnosis: Screening and diagnostic tools. *Obstetrics and Gynecology Clinics*, *44*(2), 245–256; Wilson, R. D. (2017). Prenatal diagnosis and genetic counseling. In *Fundamentals of Pediatric Surgery* (pp. 17–24). Cham, Switzerland: Springer.

DISPARITIES IN PRENATAL CARE

In the United States prenatal care is widespread, but not universal as in many European countries, and it lacks uniform national standards and guaranteed financial coverage (see Window on the World). In 2017, 6.3 percent of expectant mothers received late or no prenatal care during their pregnancies, a slight increase from the previous year (Child Trends Databank, 2019; Martin et al., 2018).

Despite the availability of prenatal care, rates of low birth weight and premature birth continue to rise. Why? One answer is the high number of multiple births, which

window on the world

PRENATAL CARE AROUND THE WORLD

The United Nations (2018) estimates that approximately 130 million babies are born worldwide each year. About 830 women die each day from childbirth-related complications, with 99 percent of these deaths occurring in low-resource areas (World Health Organization, 2016). Hemorrhage, hypertensive disorders, and infection are responsible for more than half of all maternal deaths; most of these deaths could have been prevented with proper education and prenatal care (UNICEF Millennium Development Goals, 2015).

Proper prenatal care is vital to the survival of pregnant women and their babies. The World Health Organization (WHO) recommends a minimum of four, and preferably eight, prenatal visits to a skilled health care provider. At the minimum, prenatal services should include education about proper nutrition, activity levels, and substance use. Additionally, medical services should include a tetanus vaccination and vitamin supplements of at least folic acid and iron (March of Dimes, 2014).

Standards of prenatal care are not equal worldwide. In developed countries, pregnant women receive this standard of care routinely. In low-income/developing countries, only 40 percent of women receive the minimum WHO standard of four visits (World Health Organization, 2016). Poverty often limits both access and availability of services. Women living in remote areas have limited access to health care, sometimes the distance to facilities is too great, or there are not enough skilled workers to serve the population. Skilled care at birth leads to a 54 percent reduction of maternal mortality (World Health Organization, 2016).

The most common risks of not having proper prenatal care are low birth weight, birth defects, infections, premature birth, and placental concerns. These factors can lead to long-term health problems or death for the mother and/or newborn (March of Dimes, 2014).

The maternal/infant mortality rate has been declining over the past 20 years, but is still too high. An estimated 5 million babies died or were stillborn during 2015 (UNICEF, 2014). Childbirth is still the leading cause of death among adolescent girls in developing countries (Patton et al., 2009). All women need access to prenatal care, education, family planning, and support during pregnancy and the weeks following childbirth.

 **what's your view** What can you do to help promote healthy pregnancies around the world? The United States has one of the worst maternal mortality rates of the developed countries. What factors do you see contributing to this?

---

often are early births, with heightened risk of death within the first year. The twinning rate rose by 76 percent from 1980 to 2009, showed some slight variations in the intervening years, and reached an all-time high in 2014 (Martin et al., 2018). However, the birth of multiple births may have finally leveled off in the United States. From 2014 to 2018, there were steady declines in the rate of twin births, reaching the lowest level in in more than a decade at 32.6 births per 1,000 births (Martin & Osterman, 2019).

A second answer is that the benefits of prenatal care are not evenly distributed. Although usage of prenatal care has grown, the women most at risk of bearing low-birth-weight babies—teenage and unmarried women, those with little education, and some minority women—are still least likely to receive it. For example, women who receive no or little prenatal care are much more likely to be Native Hawaiian/Pacific Islander (19.6 percent), American Indian/Alaska native (12.6 percent), or African American (10.2 percent) than white (4.5 percent) or Asian (5.1 percent) (Martin et al., 2018). These disparities are likely to be responsible for the differences in maternal mortality rate by race (Moaddab et al., 2016). For example, African American women have a maternal mortality rate 3 to 4 times that of white women (Berg et al., 2010).

A related concern is an ethnic disparity in fetal and postbirth mortality. After adjusting for such risk factors as SES, overweight, smoking, hypertension, and diabetes, the chances of perinatal death (death between 20 weeks of gestation and 1 week after birth) remain 3.4 times higher for Blacks, 1.5 times higher for Hispanics, and 1.9 times higher for other minorities than for whites (Healy et al., 2006).

Ideally, women would receive not only prenatal care, but also care *before* conceiving. Such care should include physical examinations, vaccination for rubella and hepatitis B, risk screening for genetic disorders and infectious disease, and counseling to avoid smoking and alcohol, maintain a healthy body weight, and take folic acid supplements (Centers for Disease Control and Prevention, 2017). Preconception and prenatal care can give every child the best chance for entering the world in good condition to meet the challenges of life outside the womb.

summary and key terms

Conceiving New Life

- Fertilization, the union of an ovum and a sperm, results in the formation of a one-celled zygote, which then duplicates itself by cell division.
- Multiple births generally occur either by the fertilization of two ova or by the splitting of one fertilized ovum.
- Dizygotic (fraternal) twins have different genetic makeups and may be of different sexes. Although monozygotic (identical) twins typically have the same genetic makeup, they may have phenotypic differences.

fertilization, zygote, dizygotic twins, monozygotic twins

Mechanisms of Heredity

- The basic functional units of heredity are the genes, which are made of deoxyribonucleic acid (DNA). DNA carries the genetic code. Each gene is located by function in a definite position on a particular chromosome. The complete sequence of genes in the human body is called the *human genome.*

deoxyribonucleic acid (DNA), genetic code, chromosomes, genes, human genome, mutation

- At conception, each normal human being receives 23 chromosomes from the mother and 23 from the father. These form 23 pairs of chromosomes—22 pairs of autosomes and 1 pair of sex chromosomes. A child who receives an X chromosome from each parent is genetically female. A child who receives a Y chromosome from the father is genetically male.
- The simplest patterns of genetic transmission are dominant and recessive inheritance. When a pair of alleles are the same, a person is homozygous for the trait; when they are different, the person is heterozygous.

autosomes, sex chromosomes, alleles, homozygous, heterozygous, dominant inheritance, recessive inheritance

- Most normal human characteristics are the result of polygenic or multifactorial transmission. Dominant inheritance and multifactorial transmission explain why a person's phenotype does not always express the underlying genotype.
- The epigenome can turn genes on or off; it is affected by environmental factors.

polygenic inheritance, phenotype, genotype, multifactorial transmission, epigenesis

- Birth defects and diseases may result from simple dominant, recessive, or sex-linked inheritance, from mutations, or from genome imprinting.
- Through genetic counseling, prospective parents can receive information about the mathematical odds of bearing children with certain defects.
- Genetic testing involves risks as well as benefits.

incomplete dominance, sex-linked inheritance, Down syndrome, genetic counseling

Nature and Nurture

- Research in behavioral genetics is based on the assumption that the relative influences of heredity and environment within a population can be measured statistically. If heredity is an important influence on a trait, genetically closer persons will be more similar in that trait. Family studies, adoption studies, and studies of twins enable researchers to measure the heritability of specific traits.
- The concepts of reaction range, canalization, genotype-environment interaction, genotype-environment correlation, and niche-picking describe ways in which heredity and environment work together.
- Siblings tend to be more different than alike in intelligence and personality. According to some behavioral geneticists, heredity accounts for most of the similarity, and nonshared environmental effects account for most of the difference.

behavioral genetics, heritability, concordant, reaction range, canalization, genotype-environment interaction, genotype-environment correlation, niche-picking, nonshared environmental effects

Prenatal Development

- Prenatal development occurs in three stages of gestation: the germinal, embryonic, and fetal stages.
- As fetuses grow, they move less, but more vigorously. Swallowing amniotic fluid, which contains substances from the mother's body, stimulates taste and smell. Fetuses seem able to hear, exercise sensory discrimination, learn, and remember. It is unlikely fetuses feel pain before the third trimester.

gestation, gestational age, germinal stage, cephalocaudal principle, proximodistal principle, germinal stage, implantation, embryonic stage, spontaneous abortion, fetal stage, ultrasound

- The developing organism can be greatly affected by its prenatal environment. The likelihood of a birth defect may depend on the timing and intensity of an environmental event and its interaction with genetic factors.
- Important environmental influences involving the mother include nutrition, smoking, intake of alcohol or other drugs, transmission of maternal illnesses or infections, maternal stress, anxiety, depression, maternal age and physical activity, and external environmental hazards, such as chemicals and radiation. External influences also may affect the father's sperm.

teratogen, fetal alcohol syndrome (FAS), acquired immune deficiency syndrome (AIDS), COVID-19, coronavirus, pandemic, stress

Monitoring and Promoting Prenatal Development

- Ultrasound, amniocentesis, chorionic villus sampling, fetoscopy, preimplantation genetic diagnosis, umbilical cord sampling, and maternal blood tests can be used to determine whether an unborn baby is developing normally.
- Early, high-quality prenatal care is essential for healthy development. It can lead to detection of defects and disorders and may help reduce maternal and infant death, low birth weight, and other birth complications.
- Racial/ethnic disparities in prenatal care is a factor in disparities in low birth weight and perinatal death.
- Preconception care for every woman of childbearing age would increase the chances of good pregnancy outcomes.

Birth and Physical Development during the First Three Years

chapter 4

Insung Jeon/Getty Images

In this chapter we describe how babies come into the world, how newborn babies look, and how their body systems work. We discuss ways to safeguard their life and health and observe their rapid early physical development. We see how infants become busy, active toddlers and how caregivers can foster healthy growth and development.

learning objectives

Specify how childbirth has changed in developed countries.

Describe the birth process.

Describe the adjustment of a healthy newborn and the techniques for assessing its health.

Explain potential complications of childbirth and the prospects for infants with complicated births.

Identify factors affecting infants' chances for survival and health.

Discuss the patterns of physical growth and development in infancy.

Describe infants' motor development.

Childbirth, Culture and Change

Across all cultures, birth and the surrounding period as a whole are viewed not only as a time of joy, but also as a time of great vulnerability. Perhaps not surprisingly, birth practices tend to be ritualized and relatively standard across women within the bounds of each particular culture (Lozoff et al., 1988). Attempts to exert control over the process, via either rituals or medicalization, are common (Behruzi et al., 2013). Laboring women are almost always assisted by others. In traditional societies, these others are most often family members or other well-known associates. In modern societies, this assistance is most often medicalized (Liamputtong, 2007). Additionally, customs or beliefs meant to ensure positive outcomes for mother and baby are common across both traditional and industrialized cultures, and often take on a moral tone (Lozoff et al., 1988).

Despite these commonalities, wide variations exist. Customs surrounding childbirth reflect a culture's beliefs, values, and resources. A Mayan woman in Yucatan gives birth in the hammock she sleeps in every night, and both the father-to-be and a midwife are expected to be present (Jordan & Davis-Floyd, 1993). In northern Thailand, the husband assists his pregnant partner and her attendant, boils water, and cleans up after the birth (Liamputtong, 2009). By contrast, among the Ngoni in East Africa, although women are assisted by attendants, men are excluded from the birth experience. Should the birth prove difficult men are pressured to divulge any adulterous relationships, which are believed to be a contributing factor in difficult deliveries (Barnes, 1949). In the Kung San of the Kalahari Desert, laboring women seek out a favorite location in the bush—alone—and are expected to be brave, as fear is believed to lead to a difficult and painful delivery (Konner & Shostak, 1987). The postpartum experience also varies. Before the twentieth century, peasant mothers in Europe and the United States were expected to be back at work in the fields within a few hours or days of giving birth (Fontanel & d'Harcourt, 1997). By contrast, in southeast Thailand, traditional beliefs for the postpartum period involve rest for the new mother, and "regaining heat" for the body by consuming hot drinks, taking hot baths, and lying by the fire (Kaewesarn et al., 2003).

Childbirth also varies across historical time periods. At the start of the twentieth century, childbirth began to be professionalized in the United States, at least in urban settings. The growing use of maternity hospitals led to safer, more antiseptic conditions for childbirth, which reduced mortality for women. In 1900, only 5 percent of U.S. deliveries occurred in hospitals; by 1920, in some cities 65 percent did (Scholten, 1985). A similar trend took place in Europe. Most recently, in the United States 98.6 percent of babies were born in hospitals, and 91 percent of births were attended by physicians (Martin et al., 2019).

The dramatic reductions in risks surrounding pregnancy and childbirth in industrialized countries are largely due to the availability of antibiotics, blood transfusions, safe anesthesia, improved hygiene, and drugs for inducing labor. In addition, improvements in prenatal assessment and care make it far more likely that a baby will be born healthy. U.S. mortality rates for both mothers and children have decreased dramatically as noted in Figure 4.1.

Still, childbirth is not risk-free. Among the nearly 4 million U.S. women who give birth yearly more than 50,000 will experience a life-threatening complication (Lu, 2018). This number has risen steadily since the mid-1990s. The increase—almost 200 percent from 1993 to 2014—is likely due to a variety of factors, including increases in maternal age, prepregnancy obesity, preexisting medical conditions, and cesarean delivery. Black women, obese women, those with difficult medical histories, those who had previous cesarean deliveries, and those who had several children are at elevated risk of cardiovascular events, infection, sepsis, hemorrhage, and other dangerous complications (Centers for Disease Control and Prevention, 2018). Unlike trends in all other developed countries, maternal mortality in the United States is increasing (MacDorman & Declercq, 2018). Approximately 700 women will die every year as a result of pregnancy, in large part due to chronic diseases associated with obesity and poor access to health care (Lu, 2018; Nelson et al., 2018). Race and ethnicity are significant risk factors; the mortality ratio (the number of pregnancy-related deaths per 100,000 women) is much higher in African American (42.4) and American Indian/Alaskan native women (30.4) than in white (13) and Hispanic (11.3) women (Centers for Disease Control and Prevention, 2019).

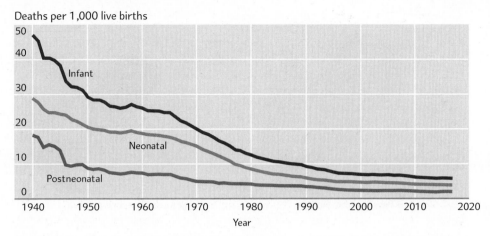

Deaths per 1,000 live births

Source: Kochanek, K. D., Murphy, S. L., Xu, J. Q. & Arias, E. (2019). Deaths: Final data for 2017. *National Vital Statistics Reports, 68*(9). Hyattsville, MD: National Center for Health Statistics.

FIGURE 4.1
U.S. Infant Mortality Rates, 1940–2017

The U.S. infant mortality rate has decreased from 47.0 infant deaths per 1,000 live births in 1940 to 5.79 in 2017. During the same period, the neonatal rate decreased from 28.8 to 3.84 deaths per 1,000 live births, and the postneonatal rate decreased from 18.3 to 1.95 deaths per 1,000 live births.

Childbirth remains a dangerous endeavor in many developing countries, especially sub-Saharan Africa and South Asia (World Health Organization, 2019). There, 60 million women deliver at home each year without the benefit of skilled care, and until recently more than 500,000 women and 4 million newborns died in or shortly after childbirth (Sines et al., 2007). However, there are promising trends. Estimates suggest almost 295,000 women died during and following pregnancy and childbirth in 2017, a number that, albeit high, nonetheless represents a decline of 38 percent since 2000 (World Health Organization, 2019).

Although childbirth is undoubtedly safer with the advances of modern medicine, the medicalization of childbirth has nonetheless had social and emotional costs that some women are rejecting. Today, a small but growing percentage of women in developed countries are going back to the intimate, personal experience of home birth (MacDorman et al., 2010). Home births usually are attended by a trained nurse-midwife, with the resources of medical science close at hand. Arrangements may be made with a physician and a nearby hospital in case an emergency arises. Some studies suggest that planned home births with speedy transfer to a hospital in case of need can be as safe as hospital births for low-risk deliveries attended by skilled, certified midwives or nurse-midwives (American College of Nurse-Midwives, 2016). However, the American College of Obstetricians and Gynecologists (ACOG, 2018) and the American Medical Association (AMA House of Delegates, 2008) point out that complications can arise suddenly, even in low-risk pregnancies, and hospitals or accredited birthing centers are best equipped to respond to such emergencies. In the immediate wake of the COVID-19 pandemic indications are that home births, believed by many women in low-risk pregnancies to be safer than risking potential viral exposure in the hospital, may make a resurgence.

The Birth Process

Labor is brought on by a series of uterine, cervical, and other changes called **parturition.** Parturition is the act or process of giving birth.

parturition
The act or process of giving birth.

The uterine contractions that expel the fetus begin—typically about 266 days after conception—as a tightening of the uterus. A woman may have felt false contractions (known as *Braxton-Hicks contractions*) at times during the final months of pregnancy, or even as early as the second trimester, when the muscles of the uterus tighten for up to 2 minutes. In comparison with the relatively mild and irregular Braxton-Hicks contractions, real labor contractions are more frequent, rhythmic, and painful, and they increase in frequency and intensity.

STAGES OF CHILDBIRTH

Labor takes place in three overlapping stages (Figure 4.2).

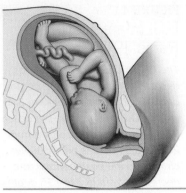

Stage one: Baby positions itself

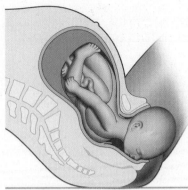

Stage two: Baby begins to emerge

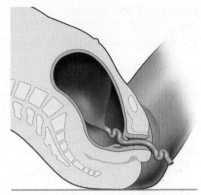

Stage three: Placenta is expelled

FIGURE 4.2

The Three Stages of Childbirth

During the first stage of labor, a series of increasingly stronger contractions dilates the cervix, the opening to the mother's womb. During the second stage, the baby's head moves down the birth canal and emerges from the vagina. During the brief third stage, the placenta and umbilical cord are expelled from the womb. Then the cord is cut.

Stage 1: Dilation of the Cervix The first stage, dilation of the cervix, is the longest, typically lasting 12 to 14 hours for a woman having her first child. In subsequent births, the first stage tends to be shorter. During this stage, regular and increasingly frequent uterine contractions—15 to 20 minutes apart at first—cause the cervix to shorten and dilate, or widen, in preparation for delivery. Toward the end of the first stage, contractions occur every 2 to 5 minutes. This stage lasts until the cervix is fully open (10 centimeters, or about 4 inches) so the baby can descend into the birth canal.

Stage 2: Descent and Emergence of the Baby The second stage typically lasts up to an hour or two. It begins when the baby's head begins to move through the cervix into the vaginal canal, and it ends when the baby emerges completely from the mother's body. If this stage lasts longer than 2 hours, signaling that the baby may need help, a doctor may use vacuum extraction with a suction cup to pull the baby out of the mother's body. The use of forceps—an instrument shaped like a large pair of salad tongs—is increasingly rare, occurring at less than 1 percent of births (Martin et al., 2017). At the end of this stage, the baby is born but is still attached to the placenta in the mother's body by the umbilical cord, which must be cut and clamped.

Stage 3: Expulsion of the Placenta The third stage, expulsion of the placenta, lasts between 10 minutes and 1 hour. During this stage, the placenta and the remainder of the umbilical cord are expelled from the mother.

ELECTRONIC FETAL MONITORING

Most births have a happy outcome, but labor and delivery are nonetheless risky. To lessen these risks, technologies have been developed to monitor the fetus prior to delivery. **Electronic fetal monitoring** (EFM) can be used effectively in high-risk deliveries to track the fetus's heartbeat and to indicate how the fetal heart is responding to the stress of uterine contractions. Monitoring is most commonly done with the use of sensors attached to the woman's midsection and held in place with an electric belt. The procedure was used in 89 percent of live births in the United States in 2004 (Chen et al., 2013).

However, the use of continuous EFM in a healthy, low-risk pregnancy is associated with an *increase* in risk for mother and baby. EFM has a high false-positive rate, suggesting that fetuses are in trouble when they are not. Such warnings may prompt doctors to deliver by the riskier cesarean method rather than vaginally. Why, then, do doctors continue to

electronic fetal monitoring Mechanical monitoring of fetal heartbeat during labor and delivery.

use it in almost all pregnancies? Generally, concerns regarding possible malpractice lawsuits, particularly if a child is born with cerebral palsy, are believed to be the driving force behind the overuse of EFM (Spector-Bagdady et al., 2017; Nelson et al., 2016).

VAGINAL VERSUS CESAREAN DELIVERY

The usual method of childbirth, previously described, is *vaginal delivery*. Alternatively, **cesarean delivery** can be used to surgically remove the baby from the uterus through an incision in the mother's abdomen. In the United States, the cesarean birth rate peaked in 2009 at 32.9 percent. Although still high, the rate in 2018 declined to 31.9 percent for all groups except first-time African American mothers (Martin et al., 2019; Thompson et al., 2019). Internationally, the rate of cesarean deliveries is rising, and at 21.2 percent is almost double what it was in 2000. The rate varies sharply by country. For example, cesareans in Latin American and Caribbean countries are markedly higher at an average of 44.3 percent than in African nations at an average of 4.1 percent of births (Boerma et al., 2018).

cesarean delivery
Delivery of a baby by surgical removal from the uterus.

The operation is commonly performed when labor progresses too slowly, when the fetus seems to be in trouble, or when the mother is bleeding vaginally. Often a cesarean is needed when the fetus is in the breech position (feet or buttocks first) or in the transverse position (lying crosswise in the uterus) or when the head is too big to pass through the mother's pelvis.

The increase in cesarean rates is attributed largely to rising proportions of older first-time mothers, who tend to have multiple births, and of very premature infants (Martin et al., 2010) for whom cesarean delivery significantly reduces the risk of dying during the 1st month of life (Malloy, 2008). Physicians' fear of malpractice suits also may play a part in the choice of cesarean deliveries, as may the increased revenue hospitals generate when a woman has a cesarean rather than a vaginal birth (Betran et al., 2018).

Although cesarean deliveries reduce the risk of urinary incontinence and pelvic organ prolapse (where weakened muscles allow one or more of the pelvic organs to drop into or press out of the vagina) in comparison to vaginal delivery, they carry significant risks of serious complications for the mother. Cesarean delivery can lead to bleeding, uterine rupture, and heightened risks of problems in future pregnancies. Moreover, there are indications that cesarean delivery alters newborn physiology and puts children at risk for future obesity and asthma (Keag et al., 2018; Sandall et al., 2018).

Many physicians warn that a vaginal birth after cesarean (VBAC) should be attempted only with caution. VBACs have been associated with greater (though still low) risks of uterine rupture and maternal death (Habak & Kole, 2018; Sabol et al., 2015). However, other research shows that there are also risks associated with repeat cesarean deliveries, including postpartum endometriosis (a painful condition in which uterine cells are found outside of the uterus), complications related to the use of anesthesia, bladder or bowel injury, or hysterectomy (Fong et al., 2016; Zwergel & von Kaisenberg, 2019). Overall, women who attempt a trial of labor following one or two cesarean deliveries are successful 60 to 80 percent of the time (ACOG, 2017) and represented 13.3 percent of total births in 2018 (Martin et al., 2019). VBAC is not recommended for home births or women who have conditions that make it less likely to be successful, such as advanced age, high body mass index, a very large baby, or a previous cesarean that was the result of a failure of the cervix to dilate (ACOG, 2017).

MEDICATED VERSUS NONMEDICATED DELIVERY

For centuries, pain was considered an unavoidable part of giving birth. Then, in the mid-nineteenth century, sedation with ether or chloroform became common practice as more births took place in hospitals (Fontanel & d'Harcourt, 1997).

During the twentieth century, several alternative methods of **natural childbirth** or **prepared childbirth** were developed. These methods minimize or eliminate the use of drugs that may pose risks for babies and enable both parents to participate fully in a natural, empowering experience.

natural childbirth
Method of childbirth that seeks to prevent pain by eliminating the mother's fear through education about the physiology of reproduction and training in breathing and relaxation during delivery.

prepared childbirth
Method of childbirth that uses instruction, breathing exercises, and social support to induce controlled physical responses to uterine contractions and reduce fear and pain.

The Lamaze method, introduced by the French obstetrician Fernand Lamaze in the late 1950s, acknowledges that labor is painful and teaches an expectant mother to relax her muscles through controlled breathing. Using the LeBoyer method a woman gives birth in a quiet room under low lights to reduce stress, and the newborn is gently massaged to ease crying. Other methods use submersion of the laboring mother in a soothing pool of water, mental imagery, massage, gentle pushing, and deep breathing. Perhaps most extreme is the Bradley method, which rejects all obstetrical procedures and other medical interventions.

Today, improvements in medicated delivery have led many mothers to choose pain relief, sometimes along with natural methods. A woman may be given local (vaginal) anesthesia, also called a *pudendal block*, usually during the second stage of labor. Or she can receive an *analgesic* (painkiller), which reduces the perception of pain by depressing the activity of the central nervous system. However, analgesics may slow labor, cause maternal complications, and make the baby less alert after birth.

Among women who give birth vaginally to a singleton, 61 percent have regional (*epidural or spinal*) injections (Osterman & Martin, 2011). Regional anesthesia, which is injected into a space in the spinal cord between the vertebrae in the lumbar (lower) region, blocks the nerve pathways that would carry the sensation of pain to the brain. With any of these forms of anesthesia, a woman can see and participate in the birth process and can hold her newborn immediately afterward. Although previous researchers believed epidurals given early in labor could block pain and even shorten labor with no added risk of cesarean (Wong et al., 2005), newer data suggest that the use of epidurals significantly slows the second stage of labor and can lead to unnecessary interventions (Cheng et al., 2014).

In many traditional cultures, childbearing women are attended by a **doula,** an experienced mentor, coach, and helper who can furnish emotional support and information and can stay at a woman's bedside throughout labor. Studies have found that the use of a doula is associated with a decreased likelihood of a low-birth-weight baby, birth complications, and cesarean delivery, and a greater chance of breastfeeding success (Gruber et al., 2013; National Partnership for Women, 2018). Doulas also provide an economic benefit. Infants born before 37 weeks of gestation—currently 1 in 9 in the United States—incur medical costs that average approximately 10 times what the costs are for a full-term infant. Additionally, cesarean deliveries are double the cost of vaginal births. Doulas, if

doula
An experienced mentor who furnishes emotional support and information for a woman during labor.

A doula, or experienced helper, stays at a woman's bedside throughout labor and provides emotional support. Research has found that women attended by doulas tend to have shorter labor and easier deliveries. Andersen Ross/ Stockbyte/Getty Images

funded by insurance, would result in significant overall savings (Kozhimannil et al., 2016). Unfortunately, doulas are not usually covered by insurance, and cost is the largest barrier most women face in securing the support of a doula (Strauss et al., 2015).

CHILDBIRTH AND THE COVID-19 PANDEMIC

In many countries, the COVID-19 pandemic has changed the way in which pregnant women are cared for within medical settings. Early research suggests that the COVID-19 pandemic does not directly increase the risk of death for either pregnant women or their neonates, and that infected newborns generally show mild symptoms (Zeng et al., 2020; Liu et al., 2020). However, despite the preliminary nature of the data, indications are that infected women are more likely to experience birth complications and preterm birth than uninfected women (Di Mascio et al., 2020), perhaps in part due to elevated stress and anxiety.

Most hospitals changed their policies surrounding labor and delivery in an attempt to keep uninfected pregnant women and their newborns safe. For example, health recommendations changed to move preliminary health checks and prenatal visits online when possible to avoid unnecessary social contact in the weeks leading to delivery. Additionally, during delivery, most hospitals limited the number of people permitted to be present during labor, a decision with repercussions for those women who hoped to use a doula during their birth. These women had to choose between the expertise of a doula and the comfort of a family member. Most hospitals kept new mothers and their babies physically separated from other patients, and if the mother was suspected or confirmed to have COVID-19, it was recommended the child should not room with her (American College of Obstetrics and Gynecology, 2020). Although rigorous data on trends do not yet exist, early indications are that more women are opting to give birth at home out of a fear of hospital infections (Gammon, 2020).

The Newborn Baby

The **neonatal period,** the first 4 weeks of life, is a time of transition from the uterus, where a fetus is supported entirely by the mother, to an independent existence. What are the physical characteristics of newborn babies, and how are they equipped for this crucial transition?

neonatal period
First 4 weeks of life, a time of transition from intrauterine dependency to independent existence.

SIZE AND APPEARANCE

An average **neonate,** or newborn, in the United States is about 20 inches long and weighs about 7½ pounds. Boys tend to be slightly longer and heavier than girls. In their first few days, neonates lose as much as 10 percent of their body weight. They begin to gain weight again at about the 5th day and are generally back to birth weight by the 10th to the 14th day.

neonate
Newborn baby, up to 4 weeks old.

New babies have a large head (one-fourth the body length) and a receding chin (which makes it easier to nurse). Newborn infants also have soft spots on their heads known as *fontanels* where the bones of the skull do not meet. Fontanels are covered by a tough membrane that allows for flexibility in shape, which eases the passage of the neonate through the vaginal canal. In the first 18 months of life, the plates of the skull gradually fuse together.

Newborns have skin so thin that it barely covers the capillaries through which blood flows. Often they are hairy because the *lanugo,* a fuzzy prenatal hair, has not yet fallen off. Most new babies are covered with *vernix caseosa* ("cheesy varnish"), an oily protection against infection that dries within the first few days.

"Witch's milk," a secretion that sometimes leaks from the swollen breasts of newborn boys and girls around the 3rd day of life, was believed during the Middle Ages to have special healing powers. Like the whitish or blood-tinged vaginal discharge of some newborn girls, this fluid emission results from high levels of the hormone estrogen, which is secreted by the placenta just before birth and goes away within a few days or weeks. A newborn, especially if premature, also may have swollen genitals.

BODY SYSTEMS

Before birth, blood circulation, respiration, nourishment, elimination of waste, and temperature regulation are accomplished through the mother's body. All these systems, with the exception of the lungs, are functioning to some degree by the time a full-term birth occurs, but the fetus is not yet an independent entity. After birth, all of the baby's systems and functions must operate on their own.

During pregnancy, the fetus gets oxygen through the umbilical cord, which carries used blood to the placenta and returns a fresh supply. Once born, a neonate must take over this function fully. Most babies start to breathe as soon as they are exposed to air. If a neonate does not begin breathing within about 5 minutes, the baby may suffer permanent brain injury caused by **anoxia,** lack of oxygen, or *hypoxia,* a reduced oxygen supply. This form of *birth trauma* can leave permanent brain damage, causing intellectual disability, behavior problems, or even death.

In the uterus, the fetus relies on the umbilical cord to bring food from the mother and to carry fetal body wastes away. At birth, babies instinctively suck to take in milk, and their own gastrointestinal secretions digest it. During the first few days infants secrete *meconium,* a stringy, greenish-black waste matter formed in the fetal intestinal tract.

The layers of fat that develop during the last 2 months of fetal life help healthy full-term infants to keep their body temperature constant after birth despite changes in air temperature. Newborn babies also maintain body temperature by increasing their activity when air temperature drops.

Three or four days after birth, about half of all babies (and a larger proportion of babies born prematurely) develop **neonatal jaundice:** Their skin and eyeballs look yellow. This kind of jaundice is caused by the immaturity of the liver. Usually it is not serious, does not need treatment, and has no long-term effects. However, severe jaundice that is not monitored and treated promptly may result in brain damage.

MEDICAL AND BEHAVIORAL ASSESSMENT

The first few minutes, days, and weeks after birth are crucial for development. It is important to know as soon as possible whether a baby has any problem that needs special care.

The Apgar Scale One minute after delivery, and then again 5 minutes after birth, most babies are assessed using the **Apgar scale** (Table 4.1). Its name, after its developer, Dr. Virginia Apgar (1953), helps us remember its five subtests: *a*ppearance (color), *p*ulse (heart rate), *g*rimace (reflex irritability), *a*ctivity (muscle tone), and *r*espiration (breathing). The newborn is rated 0, 1, or 2 on each measure, for a maximum score of 10. A 5-minute score of 7 to 10 indicates that the baby is in good to excellent condition. A score below 5 to 7 means the baby needs help to establish breathing; a score below 4 means the baby needs immediate lifesaving treatment.

anoxia
Lack of oxygen, which may cause brain damage.

neonatal jaundice
Condition, in many newborn babies, caused by immaturity of liver and evidenced by yellowish appearance; can cause brain damage if not treated promptly.

Apgar scale
Standard measurement of a newborn's condition; it assesses appearance, pulse, grimace, activity, and respiration.

TABLE 4.1 Apgar Scale

Sign*	0	1	2
Appearance (color)	Blue, pale	Body pink, extremities blue	Entirely pink
Pulse (heart rate)	Absent	Slow (below 100)	Rapid (over 100)
Grimace (reflex irritability)	No response	Grimace	Coughing, sneezing, crying
Activity (muscle tone)	Limp	Weak, inactive	Strong, active
Respiration (breathing)	Absent	Irregular, slow	Good, crying

*Each sign is rated in terms of absence or presence from 0 to 2; highest overall score is 10.

Source: Apgar, V. (1953). A proposal for a new method of evaluation of the newborn infant. *Current Researches in Anesthesia and Analgesia, 32*(4), 260–267.

Neonatal Screening for Medical Conditions Children who inherit the enzyme disorder phenylketonuria, or PKU, will develop intellectual disability unless they are fed a special diet beginning in the first 3 to 6 weeks of life (National Institute of Child Health and Human Development, 2017). Screening tests administered soon after birth often can discover this and other correctable defects.

Routine screening of all newborn babies for such rare conditions as PKU (1 case in 15,000 births), congenital hypothyroidism (1 in 3,600 to 5,000), galactosemia (1 in 60,000 to 80,000), and other even rarer disorders is expensive. Yet the cost of testing thousands of newborns to detect one case of a rare disease may be less than the cost of caring for one intellectually disabled person for a lifetime. The Recommended Uniform Screening Panel, developed by the U.S. government in conjunction with professionals in the field, includes 35 core conditions and 26 secondary conditions for which it recommends screening all newborns. However, states vary with respect to which conditions they include (U.S. Department of Health and Human Services, 2018).

STATES OF AROUSAL

Babies have an internal clock that regulates their daily cycles of eating, sleeping, and elimination. These periodic cycles of wakefulness, sleep, and activity, which govern an infant's **state of arousal,** or degree of alertness, seem to be inborn and highly individual. Changes in state are coordinated by multiple areas of the brain (Tokariev et al., 2016) and are accompanied by changes in the functioning of virtually all body systems (Scher et al., 2004).

Youngest babies sleep the most and wake up the most frequently. Parents report that from 0 to 2 months of age, infants sleep about 14.5 hours a day and wake 1.7 times per night. However, by a year of age, that number has dropped to 12.6 hours of sleep per night and 0.7 times night wakings each evening. Likewise, their longest sleep period rises from 5.7 hours at 2 months of age to 8.3 hours at 6 to 24 months of age. With respect to daytime napping, a similar developmental trend emerges. At 0 to 5 months, the typical child will nap about 3 hours every day. By 1 to 2 years of age, most children are napping only about an hour (Galland et al., 2012).

Newborns' sleep alternates between quiet (regular) and active (irregular) sleep. Active sleep is the equivalent of rapid eye movement (REM) sleep, which in adults is associated with dreaming. Active sleep appears rhythmically in cycles of about 1 hour and accounts for up to 50 percent of a newborn's total sleep time. The amount of REM sleep declines to less than 30 percent of daily sleep time by age 3 and continues to decrease steadily throughout life (Hoban, 2004).

Babies' sleep rhythms and schedules vary across cultures. Among the Micronesian Truk and the Canadian Hare peoples, babies and children have no regular sleep schedules; they fall asleep whenever they feel tired. Mothers in rural Kenya allow their babies to nurse as they please, and their 4-month-olds continue to sleep only 4 hours at a stretch (Broude, 1995). Similarly, Kung mothers in the Kalahari co-sleep with their infants, who wake frequently to nurse throughout the night (Konner, 2017). In many predominantly Asian countries, bedtimes are later and total sleep time is shorter than in predominantly Caucasian countries, but children continue to nap later into childhood (Mindell et al., 2013). Even within the United States, there are variations across different groups. Racial and ethnic minorities, as well as people from lower socioeconomic levels, report more sleep problems and shorter sleep times in their infants (Grandner et al., 2016).

state of arousal
An infant's physiological and behavioral status at a given moment in the periodic daily cycle of wakefulness, sleep, and activity.

Complications of Childbirth

Although the great majority of births result in healthy babies, some, sadly, do not. Let's look at these potential complications of birth and how they can be avoided or treated to maximize the chances of favorable outcomes.

LOW BIRTH WEIGHT

low-birth-weight babies
Weight of less than 5½ pounds (2,500 grams) at birth because of prematurity or being small for date.

preterm (premature) infants
Infants born before completing the 37th week of gestation.

small-for-date (small-for-gestational-age) infants
Infants whose birth weight is less than that of 90 percent of babies of the same gestational age, as a result of slow fetal growth.

Low-birth-weight babies (LBW) are those neonates born weighing less than 2,500 grams (5½ pounds) at birth. There are two types of LBW babies: those born early and those born small. Typical gestation is 40 weeks, and babies born before the 37th week of gestation are known as **preterm (premature) infants.** Some babies, known as **small-for-date (small-for-gestational-age) infants,** are born at or around their due dates, but are smaller than would be expected. These babies weigh less than 90 percent of babies of the same gestational age. They are small, not because they were born early and did not have a chance to finish putting on weight, but for other reasons, most commonly inadequate prenatal nutrition, which slows fetal growth.

An estimated 14.6 percent of all infants worldwide are born with low birth weight, and the percentages are far greater in less economically developed countries (Figure 4.3). The true extent of low birth weight may be much higher because about half of the newborns in the developing world are not weighed at birth (UNICEF, 2019; Blencowe et al., 2019). In the United States, 8.28 percent of infants born in 2018 were low-birth-weight babies. After declining from 2007 to 2014, the preterm birthrate rose for the fourth straight year to 10.02 percent (Martin et al., 2019).

Low birth weight in developing regions stems primarily from the mother's poor nutrition. In the industrialized world, low birth weight is more often a result of advanced maternal age, maternal smoking, the birth of multiples, or the use of cesarean sections (UNICEF & WHO, 2019). The risk of both preterm delivery and low birth weight increases rapidly with the number of babies being carried, approaching 100 percent for quadruplets (Martin et al., 2019).

Birth weight and length of gestation are the two most important predictors of an infant's survival and health (Mathews & MacDorman, 2008). Together they constitute the second leading cause of death in infancy in the United States after birth defects (Ely & Driscoll, 2019). Preterm birth is involved in nearly half of neurological birth defects, such as cerebral palsy, and more than one-third of infant deaths; altogether, low-birth-weight infants account for more than two-thirds of infant deaths. Internationally, low birth weight is an underlying factor in 60 to 80 percent of neonatal deaths worldwide (UNICEF, 2008).

Preventing preterm births would greatly increase the number of babies who survive the first year of life. Globally, progress in reducing the incidence of low birth weight has stalled since 2000 (UNICEF & WHO, 2019). Training and the provision of equipment

FIGURE 4.3

Low Birth Weight Prevalence, by Country and United Nations Region, 2015

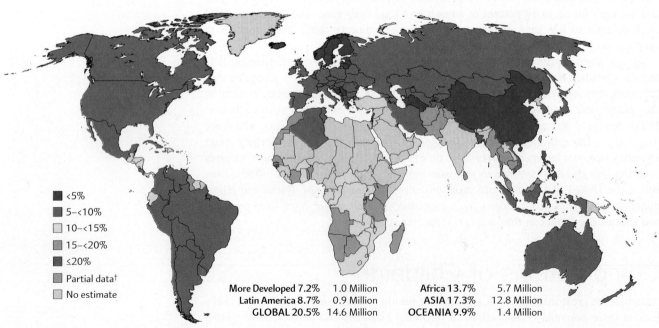

Legend:
- <5%
- 5–<10%
- 10–<15%
- 15–<20%
- ≤20%
- Partial data†
- No estimate

More Developed 7.2%	1.0 Million	Africa 13.7%	5.7 Million
Latin America 8.7%	0.9 Million	ASIA 17.3%	12.8 Million
GLOBAL 20.5%	14.6 Million	OCEANIA 9.9%	1.4 Million

Source: UNICEF & WHO (2019). Low birthweight estimates: Levels and trends, 2000-2015 [Fact sheet].

and supplies could do much to improve progress in this area. For example, even low-tech changes such as ensuring appropriate warmth, support for breastfeeding, and training in basic care for infections and breathing problems can reduce mortality rates.

Risk Factors for Low Birth Weight Factors increasing the likelihood that a woman will have an underweight baby include (1) *demographic and socioeconomic factors,* such as being African American, under age 15 or over 35, and being poor, unmarried, or undereducated (Martin et al., 2019; Centers for Disease Control and Prevention, 2016); (2) *individual factors predating the pregnancy,* such as having no children or more than four, being short or thin, having had previous low-birth-weight infants or multiple miscarriages, having had low birth weight oneself and having particular genetic variants associated with higher risk (National Institutes of Health, 2010; Shah, 2010; Han et al., 2012); (3) *prenatal behavioral and environmental factors,* such as poor nutrition, inadequate prenatal care, smoking, use of alcohol or other drugs, or exposure to stress, high altitude, or toxic substances (Centers for Disease Control and Prevention, 2016; Mumbare et al., 2012); and (4) *medical conditions associated with the pregnancy,* such as infections, high or low blood pressure, anemia, depression, anxiety, and too little weight gain (Arias et al., 2003; Schetter & Tanner, 2012; Mumbare et al., 2012; Bramham et al., 2014).

The high proportion of low-birth-weight newborns—14.07 percent (Martin et al., 2019)—is a major factor in the high mortality rates of Black babies. Reasons for the greater prevalence of low birth weight, preterm births, and infant mortality among African American babies include (1) health behaviors and socioeconomic status; (2) higher levels of stress in African American women; (3) greater susceptibility to stress; (4) the impact of racism, which may contribute to or exacerbate stress; and (5) ethnic differences in stress-related body processes, such as blood pressure and immune reactions (Giscombé & Lobel, 2005).

Immediate Treatment and Outcomes The most pressing fear regarding very small babies is that they will die in infancy. A low-birth-weight or at-risk preterm baby may be placed in an *isolette* (an antiseptic, temperature-controlled crib) and fed through tubes. These infants' nervous systems may be too immature for them to perform functions basic to survival, such as sucking, so they may need to be fed intravenously (through the veins). Because they do not have enough fat to insulate them and to generate heat, it is hard for them to stay warm. Preterm babies are especially at risk for slowed growth and developmental delays (Scharf et al., 2016). Gentle massage seems to foster growth and weight gain, and is also associated with improvements in developmental scores, reduced stress, improved immune system functioning, decreased pain responses, and earlier release from the hospital (Niemi, 2017). Girls tend to be hardier than boys (Glass et al., 2015).

Kangaroo care, a method of skin-to-skin contact in which a newborn is laid face down between the mother's breasts for an hour or so at a time after birth, can help preemies—and full-term infants—make the adjustment from fetal life to the outside world. This soothing maternal contact seems to reduce stress on the central nervous system and help with self-regulation of sleep and activity (Boundy et al., 2016).

Respiratory distress syndrome is common in preterm babies who lack an adequate amount of an essential lung-coating substance called *surfactant,* which keeps air sacs from collapsing. These babies may breathe irregularly or stop breathing altogether. Administering surfactant to high-risk preterm newborns has dramatically increased survival rates since the late 1990s (Glass et al., 2015) as well as neurological and developmental status at 18 to 22 months (Vohr et al., 2005). Moreover, new, less invasive techniques have been developed that appear as effective as prior methods but do not require intubation of the infant (Lau et al., 2017; Marquez et al., 2019).

kangaroo care
Method of skin-to-skin contact in which a newborn is laid face down between the mother's breasts for an hour or so at a time after birth.

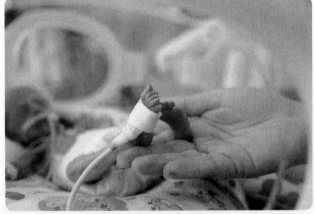

The antiseptic, temperature-controlled crib, or isolette, in which this premature baby lies has holes through which the infant can be examined, touched, and massaged. Frequent human contact helps low-birth-weight infants thrive.
Kristina Bessolova/Shutterstock

Thanks to their own resilience, many children born in less than ideal circumstances, such as this child in war-torn Afghanistan, can develop into self-confident, successful adults. U.S. Air Force photo by Staff Sgt. Marcus McDonald

postmature
A fetus not yet born as of 2 weeks after the due date or 42 weeks after the mother's last menstrual period.

stillbirth
Death of a fetus at or after the 20th week of gestation.

Long-Term Outcomes Even if low-birth-weight babies survive the dangerous early days, their trials may not be over. Although the majority of preterm infants are healthy, they are nonetheless at higher risk in adulthood of high blood pressure, metabolic syndrome, adult-onset diabetes, and cardiovascular disease (Raju et al., 2017; Parkinson et al., 2013; Markopoulou et al., 2019; Levy et al., 2017). In addition, preterm birth is associated with a heightened risk of death from infancy to adulthood, diminished reproductive rates in adulthood, and, for women, increased risk of bearing preterm infants themselves (Crump et al., 2019; Drukker et al., 2018; Swamy et al., 2008). Generally, the shorter the period of gestation, the greater the likelihood of cerebral palsy, mental retardation, and low educational and job-related income levels (Johnson & Marlow, 2017).

In longitudinal studies of extremely low-birth-weight infants (about 1 to 2 pounds at birth) and infants born before 26 weeks of gestation, the survivors tend to be smaller than full-term children and more likely to have neurological, sensory, cognitive, educational, and behavioral problems (Hutchinson et al., 2013; Johnson & Marlow, 2017). Cognitive deficits, especially in memory and information-processing speed, have been noted among very low-birth-weight babies (those weighing less than 1,500 grams or 3.5 pounds at birth) by age 5 or 6 months, persisting into adulthood (Rose et al., 2002; Litt et al., 2012; Johnson & Marlow, 2017). Very-low-birth-weight children and adolescents also tend to have more behavioral and mental health problems than those born at normal weight (Johnson & Marlow, 2014), and impaired motor development in young adulthood (Husby et al., 2016).

However, birth weight alone does not necessarily determine the outcome. Factors such as maternal education, family structure, SES, and parenting also help determine outcomes (Voss et al., 2012; Saigal et al., 2006; Poehlmann-Tynan et al., 2015; Faure et al., 2017), and given supportive postnatal environments, a significant proportion of low-birth-weight babies can become well-functioning adults.

POSTMATURITY

When people think about birth complications, they generally think about issues related to being born too early or too small. However, babies can also be negatively affected by staying too long in the womb. In fact, 5.9 percent of women have not gone into labor by 41 weeks of gestation (Martin et al., 2019). Because data show that inducing pregnancy at this point does not increase the risk of cesarean section and is associated with better outcomes (Galal et al., 2012; Bleicher et al., 2017), most doctors will opt to induce labor at this point. If they do not, as is true for approximately 0.3 percent of babies (Martin et al., 2019), the baby will be considered **postmature.** Postmature babies tend to be long and thin because they have kept growing in the womb but have had an insufficient blood supply toward the end of gestation. Possibly because the placenta has aged and become less efficient, it may provide less oxygen. The baby's greater size also complicates labor; the mother has to deliver a baby the size of a normal 1-month-old. This puts the mother at higher risk of a cesarean delivery, perineal tears, and postpartum hemorrhage, and the neonate at greater risk of shoulder dystocia (a condition in which the baby's shoulders become stuck behind the mother's pelvic bone during delivery), meconium aspiration, low Apgar scores, brain damage, and death (American College of Obstetricians and Gynecologists, 2014).

STILLBIRTH

Stillbirth, the sudden death of a fetus at or after the 20th week of gestation, is a tragic union of opposites—birth and death. Sometimes fetal death is diagnosed prenatally; in other cases, the baby's death is discovered during labor or delivery.

Worldwide, about 2.6 million fetuses were stillborn in 2018 (UNICEF, 2019). The risk of stillbirth is about 10 times higher in low- and middle-income countries than in wealthier counterparts (Saleem et al., 2018). In 2013, there were almost 24,000 stillbirths in the United States, a number representing 5.96 fetal deaths for every 1,000 live births. Boys are more likely to be stillborn than girls, non-Hispanic Black fetuses are more likely to be stillborn than fetuses of other racial/ethnic groups, and twins and higher multiples are more likely to be stillborn than singletons (MacDorman & Gregory, 2015).

Although the cause of stillbirth is often not clear, many stillborn fetuses are small for gestational age, indicating malnourishment in the womb (MacDorman & Gregory, 2015). Fetuses believed to have problems can have prenatal surgery in the womb to correct congenital problems or be delivered prematurely (Goldenberg et al., 2004). Interventions such as these could prevent a large proportion of stillbirths.

Survival and Health

Infancy and toddlerhood are risky times of life. How can we ensure that infants and toddlers live, grow, and develop as they should?

REDUCING INFANT MORTALITY

In 2018, there were 5.3 million worldwide deaths of children 5 years of age and younger. Of those deaths, 2.5 million were infants 28 days or younger in age. The vast majority of these early deaths are in developing countries, especially in sub-Saharan Africa (UNICEF, 2019; Figure 4.4).

The chief causes of neonatal death worldwide are preterm birth complications (35 percent), childbirth complications (24 percent), and sepsis (15 percent). Many of these deaths are preventable, resulting from a combination of poverty, poor maternal health and nutrition, infection, and inadequate medical care (UNICEF, 2019). Although maternal mortality declined by 38 percent from 2000 to 2017, the number of women and girls who die in childbirth is still about 290,000 a year (UNICEF, 2019). Most of these deaths (27 percent) are due to hemorrhage, with preexisting medical conditions, eclampsia, embolisms, and complications of unsafe abortions also playing a role (UNICEF, 2015). About two-thirds of maternal deaths occur during the immediate postnatal period, and infants whose mothers have died are more likely to die than infants whose mothers remain alive (Sines et al., 2007).

In the United States, the **infant mortality rate**—the proportion of babies who die within the 1st year—has fallen almost continuously since the beginning of the twentieth century, when 100 infants died for every 1,000 born alive. In 2017, the rate fell to a record low of 5.79 infant deaths per 1,000 live birth. Birth defects and genetic abnormalities are the leading cause of infant deaths in the United States, followed by disorders related to prematurity or low birth weight, maternal complications of pregnancy, sudden

infant mortality rate
Proportion of babies born alive who die within the 1st year.

FIGURE 4.4
Under-5 Mortality Rate, 2018

Most neonatal deaths occur in sub-Saharan Africa and central and southern Asia.

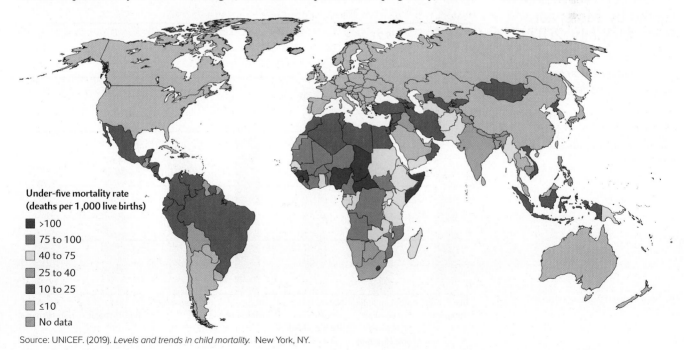

Under-five mortality rate
(deaths per 1,000 live births)
- >100
- 75 to 100
- 40 to 75
- 25 to 40
- 10 to 25
- ≤10
- No data

Source: UNICEF. (2019). *Levels and trends in child mortality.* New York, NY.

infant death syndrome (SIDS), and accidents (Ely & Driscoll, 2019). More than half of U.S. infant deaths take place in the first week of life, and about two-thirds occur during the neonatal period (Heron et al., 2009).

The improvement in U.S. infant mortality rates since 1990 is attributable largely to prevention of SIDS (discussed in the next section) as well as to effective treatment for respiratory distress and medical advances in keeping very small babies alive (Arias et al., 2003). Still, U.S. babies have less chance of reaching their 1st birthday than do babies in many other developed countries (MacDorman & Mathews, 2009). The U.S. infant mortality rate in 2008 was higher than that in 44 countries worldwide (Kaiser Family Foundation, 2017).

Racial/Ethnic Disparities in Infant Mortality Although infant mortality has declined for all races and ethnic groups in the United States, large disparities remain. Black babies (10.97 deaths per 1,000 live births) are nearly 2½ times as likely to die in their 1st year as white (4.67) and Hispanic (5.10) babies (Figure 4.5). This disparity largely reflects the greater prevalence of preterm delivery and low birth weight among African Americans. The rate for Asian babies, at 3.78 deaths per 1000 live births, is the lowest of any group.

Because causes and risk factors for infant mortality vary among ethnic groups, efforts to further reduce infant deaths need to focus on factors specific to each ethnic group (Hesso & Fuentes, 2005). For example, preexisting conditions such as obesity, cardiovascular disease, and high blood pressure can increase the risk associated with pregnancy, and the prevalence of these conditions varies across different racial and ethnic groups (Hales et al., 2017; Lackland, 2014). Thus some of the disparities in infant mortality rates may be attributable to factors such as these (Creanga et al., 2017). Additionally, racial or ethnic disparities in access to and quality of health care for minority children (National Center for Health Statistics, 2016) may help account for differences in infant mortality, and behavioral factors such as obesity, smoking, and alcohol consumption also play a part. However, even when these factors are controlled for, disparities remain. Researchers are increasingly identifying the chronic stress that structural racism exerts on minority women as an influence on the health of a pregnancy, and hence, the newborn baby (Kamal et al., 2019).

FIGURE 4.5

U.S. Infant Mortality Rates per 1,000 Live Births by Maternal Race/Ethnicity, 2017

Ethnicity influences mortality, and African American babies have the highest death rates.

Source: Kamal, R., Hudman, J., & McDermott, E. (2019). What do we know about infant mortality in the U.S. and comparable countries? [Report]. *Peterson-KFF Health System Tracker.*

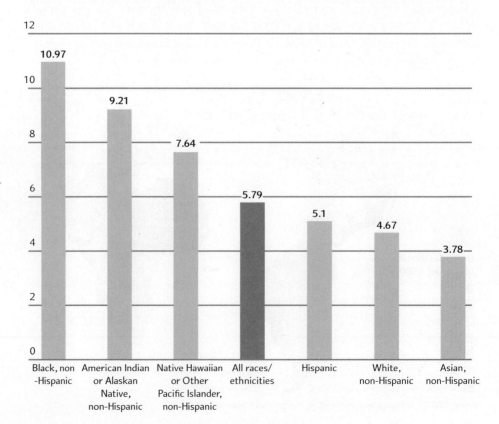

Sudden Infant Death Syndrome (SIDS) Sudden infant death syndrome (SIDS) is the sudden death of an infant under age 1 in which the cause of death remains unexplained after a thorough investigation that includes an autopsy. SIDS accounts for 6 percent of infant mortality rates (Ely & Driscoll, 2019). It peaks between 2 and 4 months and is most common among African Americans, low-birth-weight babies, preterm babies, twins or triplets, and babies whose mothers are young, have previously had three or more children, have high blood pressure during pregnancy, or receive late or no prenatal care (Hakeem et al., 2015).

sudden infant death syndrome (SIDS) Sudden and unexplained death of an apparently healthy infant.

An underlying biological defect may make some infants vulnerable during a critical period to certain contributing or triggering experiences. In approximately 14 percent of SIDS cases, there appear to be genetic mutations affecting the heart that under some conditions can lead to death (Baruteau et al., 2017). More commonly, some infants appear to be born with delays or defects in the brain stem, which regulates breathing, heartbeat, body temperature, and arousal (Machaalani & Waters, 2014). These defects may prevent SIDS babies who are sleeping face down or on their sides from waking or turning their heads when they breathe stale air containing carbon dioxide trapped under their blankets (Panigrahy et al., 2000). Similarly, babies who have low levels of serotonin may not awaken under conditions of oxygen deprivation and carbon dioxide buildup and are thus at greater risk as well (Duncan et al., 2010). Exposure to smoke, either during pregnancy or after birth, is a key risk factor (Zhang & Wang, 2013). Babies who die from SIDS frequently have multiple risk factors (Ostfeld et al., 2010).

Another environmental trigger for these vulnerable babies is sleeping on their stomachs. SIDS rates declined in the United States by more than 50 percent in the 10 years following the Back to Sleep campaign advocating that healthy babies be laid down to sleep on their backs (Trachtenberg et al., 2012). Illustrating the importance of considering race and ethnicity in intervention practices, targeting messages used in the campaign resulted in greater changes in the parenting practices of African American parents than for Native American/Pacific Island parents, the two groups at the highest risk (Parks et al., 2017).

The American Academy of Pediatrics (Moon & Task Force on Sudden Infant Death Syndrome, 2016) also recommends that infants not sleep on soft surfaces, such as pillows, quilts, or sheepskin, or under loose covers, which, especially when the infant is face down, may increase the risk of overheating or rebreathing (breathing the infant's own exhaled carbon dioxide). Current recommendations for risk reduction also include sleeping in the parent's room, but on a separate surface; skin-to-skin care, avoiding tobacco smoke, and the use of a pacifier as strategies to reduce the risk of SIDS. Breastfeeding and immunizations appear to offer some protection as well (Moon & Hauck, 2016).

Deaths from Injuries Unintentional injuries are the fifth leading cause of death in infancy in the United States (Ely & Driscoll, 2019). About 90 percent of all injury deaths in infancy are due to one of five causes: suffocation, motor vehicle traffic, drowning, residential burns or fires, and falls. Among children aged 1 to 4, traffic accidents are the leading cause of unintentional injury deaths, followed by drowning and suffocation (Kochanak et al., 2019). Falls are by far the major cause of nonfatal injuries in both infancy (52 percent) and toddlerhood (43 percent). Boys of all ages are more likely to be injured and to die from their injuries than girls (Borse et al., 2008). African American, American Indian, and Alaskan Native infants are 2 to 3 times more likely than white infants and 4 to 6 times more likely than Asian, Pacific Islander, and Hispanic infants to die of accidental injuries (Hauck et al., 2011).

IMMUNIZATION FOR BETTER HEALTH

Such once-familiar and sometimes fatal childhood illnesses as measles, pertussis (whooping cough), and polio are now largely preventable, thanks to vaccines that mobilize the body's natural defenses. Unfortunately, many children still are not adequately protected.

Worldwide, 86 percent of children—116 million—received routine vaccinations during their 1st year in 2018. Estimates are that this averts 2 million to 3 million deaths every year. Unfortunately, 13.5 million children under the age of 1 year did not receive any

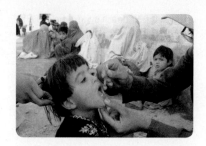

The rates of infectious diseases have dropped in many developing countries as a result of immunization programs. Here, a child receives an oral polio vaccine. Asianet-Pakistan/Shutterstock

immunizations, in many cases because they lived in conflict-ridden countries where health services are disrupted (UNICEF, 2019).

In the United States, thanks to a nationwide immunization initiative, over 90 percent of 19- to 35-month-olds had completed a recommended series of childhood vaccinations, including measles, mumps, rubella, hepatitis B, and chicken pox. Still, many children, especially poor or African American children, lack one or more of the required shots and there are regional differences in coverage (Centers for Disease Control and Prevention, 2018). More recently, indications are that the COVID-19 pandemic is likely to sharply reduce immunization rates as parents avoid clinics and hospitals out of a fear of infection. A comparison of vaccination rates from February to April 2020, as the COVID-19 virus spread rapidly in the United States, showed a 50 percent drop in measles, mumps, and rubella shots, and a drop of 42 percent for diphtheria and whooping cough (Hoffman, 2020).

Some parents hesitate to immunize their children because of speculation that certain vaccines—particularly the diphtheria-pertussis-tetanus (DPT) and measles-mumps-rubella (MMR) vaccines—may cause autism or other neurodevelopmental disorders. However, a recent meta-analysis representing data from over 1.26 million children showed no link between autism, autism-spectrum disorders, mental retardation, and vaccines (Taylor et al., 2014). Another parental worry is that infants receive too many vaccines for their immune system to handle safely. Actually, the opposite is true. Multiple vaccines fortify the immune system against a variety of bacteria and viruses and reduce related infections (Offit et al., 2002).

Despite these findings, however, many parents elect not to vaccinate their children, or vaccinate them incompletely or on a delayed schedule. Although most children do eventually get fully vaccinated, more than a third of children from the ages of 19 to 35 months do not follow the recommended schedule, leaving themselves and their communities unprotected until the full series is taken (Hargreaves et al., 2020). This, as well as imported disease from international travel, has resulted in a resurgence of some diseases (Ventola, 2016). For example, in 2019, almost 1,300 cases of measles were reported across 31 states, primarily in unvaccinated individuals. By contrast, only 375 cases were logged in all of 2018 (Centers for Disease Control and Prevention, 2020). Currently, vaccine exemptions for religious or philosophical reasons are allowed in many states, and in some areas, the exemption rate is as high as 20 percent (Ventola, 2016).

Early Physical Development

Fortunately, most infants survive, develop normally, and grow up healthy. What principles govern their development? What are the typical growth patterns? How do babies' needs and abilities change?

PRINCIPLES OF DEVELOPMENT

As before birth, physical growth and development follow the *cephalocaudal principle* and the *proximodistal principle*.

cephalocaudal principle
Principle that development proceeds in a head-to-tail direction, that is, that upper parts of the body develop before lower parts of the trunk.

According to the **cephalocaudal principle,** growth occurs from the top down. Because the brain grows rapidly before birth, a newborn baby's head is disproportionately large. The head becomes proportionately smaller as the child grows in height and the lower parts of the body develop (Figure 4.6). Sensory and motor development proceed according to the same principle: Infants learn to use the upper parts of the body before the lower parts. So, for example, a baby learns to use her arms for grasping before learning to use her legs for walking, and holds her head up before she can sit unaided.

proximodistal principle
Principle that development proceeds from within to without, that is, that parts of the body near the center develop before the extremities.

According to the **proximodistal principle** (inner to outer), growth and motor development proceed from the center of the body outward. In the womb, the head and trunk develop before the arms and legs, then the hands and feet, and then the fingers and toes. During infancy and early childhood, the limbs continue to grow faster than the hands and feet. Babies learn to use the parts of their bodies closest to the center of their body before they learn to use the outermost parts. For example, babies first learn to control

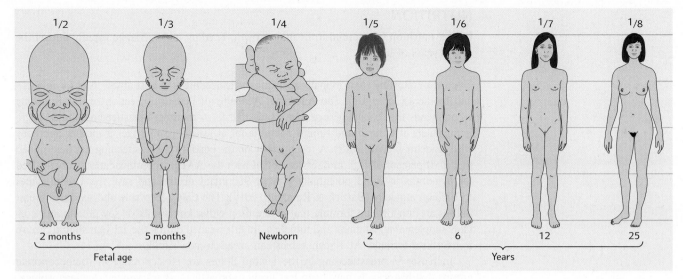

FIGURE 4.6

Changes in Proportions of the Human Body during Growth

The most striking change is that the head becomes smaller relative to the rest of the body. The fractions indicate head size as a proportion of total body length at several ages. The increasing leg proportion is almost exactly the reverse of the decreasing head proportion.

their arms when reaching, then use their hands in a scooping motion, then finally learn to use their thumb and pointer finger in a pincer grip.

GROWTH PATTERNS

Children grow faster during the first 3 years, especially during the first few months, than they ever will again (Figure 4.7). This rapid growth rate tapers off during the 2nd and 3rd years. As a baby grows into a toddler, body shape and proportions change too; a 3-year-old typically is slender compared with a chubby, potbellied 1-year-old.

The genes an infant inherits have a strong influence on whether the child will be tall or short, thin or stocky, or somewhere in between. This genetic influence interacts with nutrition and living conditions. Today children in many developed countries are growing taller and maturing at an earlier age than children did a century ago, primarily because of better nutrition, improved sanitation and medical care, and the decrease in child labor. In developing countries, however, children are more likely to suffer from malnutrition, wasting, or stunting. Height and weight differences between groups seem to be primarily driven by the environment. Although infants of different races or ethnicities may grow at slightly different rates, any innate differences between groups are overwhelmed by environmental variations (World Health Organization and UNICEF, 2009).

Teething usually begins around 3 or 4 months, when infants begin grabbing almost everything in sight to put into their mouths, but the first tooth may not actually arrive until sometime between 5 and 9 months or even later. By their first birthday, babies generally have 6 to 8 teeth; by age 2½, they have a mouthful of 20. In medieval Europe, teething was believed to lead to illness or death (Fontanel & d'Hartcount, 1997); these beliefs are shared by some indigenous cultures and immigrant groups today. Thus concerned parents, when faced with a sick baby, will sometimes opt to remove teeth or tooth buds, usually the canines, in their child (Garve et al., 2016; Elgamri et al., 2018).

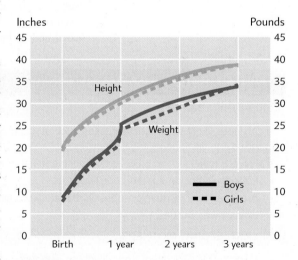

FIGURE 4.7

Growth in Height and Weight during Infancy and Toddlerhood

Babies grow most rapidly in both height and weight during the first few months of life and then taper off somewhat by age 3. Baby boys are slightly larger, on average, than baby girls.

Note: Curves shown are for the 50th percentiles for each sex.

NUTRITION

Proper nutrition is essential to healthy growth. Feeding needs change rapidly during the first 3 years of life.

Breast or Bottle? Nutritionally speaking, breastfeeding is almost always best for infants—and mothers (Table 4.2). The American Academy of Pediatrics Section on Breastfeeding recommends that babies be *exclusively* breastfed for 6 months. Breastfeeding should begin immediately after birth and should continue for at least 1 year, longer if mother and baby wish (Eidelman et al., 2012). A recent study on the benefits of breastfeeding has determined that if 90 percent of U.S. mothers complied with the AAP's recommendation to breastfeed for 6 months, it could potentially prevent 911 infant deaths and save the United States $13 billion annually (Bartick & Reinhold, 2010). The only acceptable alternative to breast milk is an iron-fortified formula that is based on either cow's milk or soy protein and contains supplemental vitamins and minerals. Infants weaned during the 1st year should receive iron-fortified formula. At 1 year, babies can switch to cow's milk.

Increases in breastfeeding in the United States are most notable in socioeconomic groups that historically have been less likely to breastfeed: Black women, teenage women, poor women, working women, and those with no more than high school education. Despite this, however, many women do not breastfeed or do not breastfeed exclusively for the recommended 6 months. Moreover, there are differences among ethnic groups; Black women are the least likely to breastfeed, whereas Hispanic women, particularly if they speak Spanish, breastfeed at high levels (McKinney et al., 2016).

Postpartum maternity leave, flexible scheduling, the ability to take relatively frequent and extended breaks at work to pump milk, privacy for nursing mothers at work and at school, as well as education about the benefits of breastfeeding might increase its prevalence (Guendelman et al., 2009; Ryan et al. 2002; Taveras et al., 2003). However, race and ethnicity are important variables that also must be considered. For example, welfare reform laws that require new mothers to return to work rapidly interfere with the establishment of a milk supply (Bentley, Dee & Jensen, 2003), and although there is a relationship between going back to work and the cessation of breastfeeding in all groups, Black mothers are more likely to report going back to work as the primary reason for discontinuing breastfeeding (Dagher et al., 2016; Hurley et al., 2008). Culturally variable perceptions of the breast as sexual and of breastfeeding as painful or difficult, along with a lack of role models and

---

TABLE 4.2 Benefits of Breastfeeding over Formula-Feeding

BREASTFED BABIES . . .

- Are less likely to contract illnesses such as diarrhea, respiratory infections, otitis media (ear infections), sepsis, bacterial diseases, and urinary tract infections.
- Have a lower risk of SIDS and of postneonatal death.
- Perform better on IQ and cognitive tests.
- Are less likely to develop obesity, diabetes, or childhood cancer.
- Have fewer cavities.

BREASTFEEDING MOTHERS . . .

- Enjoy quicker recovery from childbirth with less risk of postpartum bleeding.
- Are more likely to return to their prepregnancy weight and less likely to develop long-term obesity.
- Have reduced risk of anemia and lower risk of repeat pregnancy while breastfeeding.
- Are less likely to develop osteoporosis or ovarian and premenopausal breast cancer.

Sources: American Academy of Pediatrics (2019). Benefits of breastfeeding [Information sheet]. Retrieved from https://www.aap.org/en-us/advocacy-and-policy/aap-health-initiatives/Breastfeeding/Pages/Benefits-of-Breastfeeding.aspx; Horta, B. L., Loret de Mola, C., & Victora, C. G. (2015). Breastfeeding and intelligence: A systematic review and meta-analysis. *Acta Paediatrica, 104*, 14–19; Khan, J., Vesel, L., Bahl, R., & Martines, J. C. (2015). Timing of breastfeeding initiation and exclusivity of breastfeeding during the first month of life: Effects on neonatal mortality and morbidity—a systematic review and meta-analysis. *Maternal and Child Health Journal, 19*(3), 468–479; Schwarz, E. B., & Nothnagle, M. (2015). The maternal health benefits of breastfeeding. *American Family Physician, 91*(9), 603–604; and Avila, W. M., Pordeus, I. A., Paiva, S. M., & Martins, C. C. (2015). Breast and bottle feeding as risk factors for dental caries: A systematic review and meta-analysis. *PloS One, 10*(11), e0142922.

aggressive marketing of formula, interact with structural barriers to make breastfeeding difficult for some women to maintain (Bentley et al., 2003).

Contraindications for breastfeeding are rare. Breastfeeding is inadvisable if a baby has been diagnosed with galactosemia (a genetic metabolic disorder), if the mother is infected with the AIDS virus or any other infectious illness, if she has been exposed to radiation, or if she is taking any drug that would not be safe for the baby (Centers for Disease Control and Prevention, 2018). The risk of transmitting HIV infection to an infant continues as long as an infected mother breastfeeds, and in the United States, where clean water and formula are available, the risk of transmission is not worth the benefits associated with breastfeeding (Centers for Disease Control and Prevention, 2018). However, in many developing countries, the risk of disease or death without breastfeeding outweighs that of contracting HIV, and mothers are encouraged to breastfeed, ideally while complying with an anti-retroviral medication protocol. When the protocol is followed, as it is by almost 80 percent of pregnant or breastfeeding mothers, the risk of contagion is low (Global Breastfeeding Collective et al., 2018).

Preliminary evidence indicates that the COVID-19 virus is not found in breast milk, and thus new mothers are advised to breastfeed when possible. Ideally new mothers can avoid infection, however, if infected mothers choose to directly breastfeed, it is recommended they wash their hands before coming in contact with their children and between each feeding, and wear a face mask. If mothers chose to use expressed milk, care should be taken to keep the breast pump sanitized, and ideally a noninfected person would feed the child (Centers for Disease Control and Prevention, 2020).

Pediatric experts recommend that iron-enriched solid foods—usually beginning with cereals—be introduced gradually during the second half of the 1st year. Water may be introduced at this time (American Academy of Pediatrics, 2019). Unfortunately, despite improvements in what young children eat in the past decade, many parents do not follow recommendations. Recent data show 17 percent of infants are given solid food before 4 months, 5.5 percent drink juice before 6 months, and 17 percent drink cow's milk before 12 months. Moreover, most young children do not eat enough fruits or vegetables, or a sufficient variety of vegetables, and, as they age into toddlerhood, many consume increasing amounts of sugar-sweetened beverages (Roess et al., 2018).

Obesity, defined in infants as having a weight for height in the 95th percentile, has increased in infancy as it has in all age groups in the United States. In 2011–2012, the prevalence of obesity in children from birth to age 2 was 8.1 percent (Ogden et al., 2014), with the highest rates found in American Indians or Alaska Natives (20.7 percent) and Latinos (17.9 percent) (Polhamus et al., 2011). Children born to mothers who had a higher prepregnancy body mass index (BMI) or who gained a great deal of weight during the pregnancy were at higher risk, as were infants who were exposed prenatally to tobacco, who weighed a great deal at birth, or who gained weight quickly as infants (Baidal et al., 2016).

Infants and toddlers in the United States may eat too much, however, in many low-income communities around the world, they may not eat enough. The accompanying Window on the World addresses the effects of malnutrition and the efforts to study its effects.

Breast milk offers many benefits to babies—physical, cognitive, and emotional. Westend61/Getty Images

THE BRAIN AND REFLEX BEHAVIOR

The **central nervous system** includes the brain and *spinal cord* (a bundle of nerves running through the backbone) and the peripheral network of nerves extending to every part of the body. Through this network, sensory messages travel to the brain, and motor commands travel back.

central nervous system
Brain and spinal cord.

Building the Brain The growth of the brain is a lifelong process fundamental to physical, cognitive, and emotional development. The brain at birth is only about one-fourth to one-third of its eventual adult volume (Toga et al., 2006). By age 6, it is almost adult size, but specific parts of the brain continue to grow and develop functionally into adulthood. The brain's growth occurs in fits and starts called *brain growth spurts*. Different parts of the brain grow more rapidly at different times.

on the w🌐rld

MALNUTRITION: THE FIRST YEARS

Chronic malnutrition is caused by factors such as poverty, low-quality foods, poor dietary patterns, contaminated water, unsanitary conditions, insufficient hygiene, inadequate health care, and diarrheal diseases and other infections. Approximately 3.1 million children around the world die each year from chronic malnutrition, accounting for 45 percent of all deaths of children under 5 (UNICEF, 2017). Worldwide, 25 percent of children under 5 are malnourished; most of these children live in West/Central Africa, Southeast Asia, Latin America, and the Caribbean (Lake, 2015). Malnutrition is not confined to developing countries. In the United States, 13.9 million children live in food insecure households and 3.5 percent are stunted as a result of too little food (U.S. Department of Agriculture, 2019).

Conducting research on malnutrition is a challenging proposition, given both ethical and practical considerations. However, the Institute of Nutrition of Central America and Panama (INCAP) successfully conducted a long-term longitudinal quasi-experiment to address this issue. In this study, two large (900 people) and two small (500 people) Guatemalan villages were identified. The villages were matched on variables known to be important to development, such as overall health and socioeconomic status. Children under the age of 7 in all the villages were given a vitamin and mineral supplement twice a day and closely monitored. In one of each village size, the supplement also contained additional protein.

This research showed that early protein supplementation resulted in substantial improvements in cognitive skills, physical development, and economic productivity. A number of follow-up studies conducted over the course of three decades demonstrated that children who were under the age of 3 when they participated in the study and who received the protein supplementation were taller, had better performance on a wide variety of cognitive tasks, and had greater fat-free mass. As adults, they were at lower risk of living in poverty and (in men) showed greater work capacity. Currently, additional follow-up work on susceptibility to chronic diseases of adulthood is being conducted on these children, who are now 39 to 53 years of age. Early results indicate that the supplementation had a positive result here as well (Martorell, 2016).

This research along with numerous other lines of inquiry has led the United Nations International Children's Emergency Fund (UNICEF) to implement initiatives designed to assess the nutritional and health needs of affected people, educate and support breastfeeding women, provide essential vitamins and nutrients, and provide food and clean water for malnourished children (UNICEF, 2015). Despite a 42 percent decrease in the prevalence of malnourished people in developing nations between 1990 and 2014, 13.5 percent of the overall population in developing nations remains chronically undernourished (Hunger Notes, 2016). Currently, most countries are off target for reaching global nutrition goals, and a concerted effort is needed to allow hungry children to reach their full potential (Fanzo et al., 2018).

what's your view
What do you think some of the ethical considerations are when conducting research with malnourished children? What responsibility do wealthy nations have toward developing nations?

Beginning about 3 weeks after conception, the brain gradually develops from a long hollow tube into a spherical mass of cells (Figure 4.8). By birth, the growth spurt of the spinal cord and *brain stem* (the part of the brain responsible for such basic bodily functions as breathing, heart rate, body temperature, and the sleep-wake cycle) has nearly run its course. The *cerebellum* (the part of the brain that maintains balance and motor coordination) grows fastest during the 1st year of life (Knickmeyer et al., 2008).

The *cerebrum,* the largest part of the brain, is divided into right and left halves, or hemispheres, each with specialized functions. This specialization of the hemispheres is called **lateralization.** The left hemisphere is mainly concerned with language and logical thinking, the right hemisphere with visual and spatial functions such as map reading and drawing. Joining the two hemispheres is a tough band of tissue called the *corpus callosum,*

lateralization
Tendency of each of the brain's hemispheres to have specialized functions.

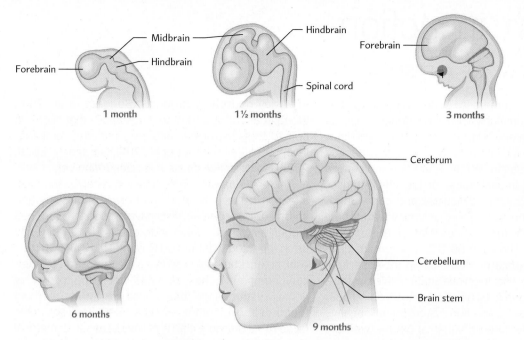

FIGURE 4.8
Brain Development during Gestation

Fetal nervous system development begins at about 3 weeks. At 1 month, major regions of the brain appear: the forebrain, midbrain, and hindbrain. As the brain grows, the front part expands to form the cerebrum, the seat of conscious brain activity. The cerebellum grows most rapidly during the 1st year of life.

Source: Cowan, W. M. (1979). "The development of the brain." *Scientific American, 241*(3), 113–133.

which allows them to continuously share information and coordinate commands. The corpus callosum grows dramatically during childhood, reaching adult size by about age 10. Each cerebral hemisphere has four lobes or sections, which control different functions. They include the *occipital, parietal, temporal,* and *frontal lobes* (Figure 4.9). The occipital lobe is the smallest of the four lobes and is primarily concerned with visual processing. The parietal lobe is involved with integrating sensory information from the body. It helps us move our bodies through space and manipulate objects in our world. The temporal lobe helps us interpret smells and sounds and is involved in memory. The frontal lobe, the newest region of the brain, is involved with a variety of higher-order processes, such as goal setting, inhibition, reasoning, planning, and problem solving. The regions of the *cerebral cortex* (the outer surface of the cerebrum) that govern vision, hearing, and other sensory information grow rapidly in the first few months after birth and are mature by age 6 months, but the areas of the frontal cortex responsible for abstract thought, mental associations, remembering, and deliberate motor responses grow very little during this period and remain immature for several years (Gilmore et al., 2007).

The brain growth spurt that begins at about the third trimester of gestation and continues until at least the 4th year of life is important to the development of neurological functioning. Smiling, babbling, crawling, walking, and talking—all the major sensory, motor, and cognitive milestones of infancy and toddlerhood—reflect the rapid development of the brain, particularly the cerebral cortex. (Research in Action discusses autism, a disorder related to abnormal brain growth.)

Brain Cells The brain is composed of *neurons* and *glial cells*. **Neurons,** or nerve cells, send and receive information. *Glia,* or glial cells, nourish and protect the neurons. They are the support system for neurons.

neurons
Nerve cells.

FIGURE 4.9
The Human Brain

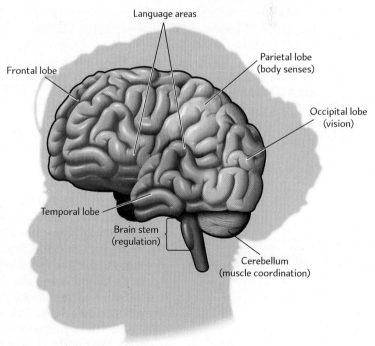

research in action

THE ETIOLOGY OF AUTISM

Autism spectrum disorders (ASD) are characterized by deficits in social communication and language; difficulties with social interaction; and restrictive, repetitive patterns of behavior, interests, or activities (American Psychiatric Association, 2013). There are indications that culture may impact some of the characteristic traits; for instance, social difficulties and communication problems seem to be more universal than repetitive behaviors and strict routines (Matson et al., 2011).

Recent figures show 1 in 59 U.S. children are diagnosed with ASD (Baio et al., 2018), an increase from previous years. To what might we attribute this increase, and what can research tell us about what is going on?

Changes in the classification system for autism have led to an increase in the number of people who are now officially classified as falling on the autism spectrum. Changes in ASD rates can also be explained by increased public awareness, referrals by doctors and schools, and more sensitive diagnostic tools (Zylstra et al., 2014). However, the rise in rates cannot be fully explained by these factors (Hansen et al., 2015).

Research has indicated that ASD has a strong genetic basis (Ozonoff et al., 2011; Sandin et al., 2014). However, genes are not fully deterministic, and proposed key genetic variations are also found in individuals without ASD (Nardone & Elliott, 2016). Moreover, the rise in prevalence rates is unlikely to be attributable solely to genetics, as it has occurred too rapidly to reflect significant genomic change.

What other factors have been investigated? Ng and others (2017) conducted a meta-analysis of 315 international studies, noting a "vast literature riddled with inconsistent findings." Nevertheless, several key factors emerged. These include physiological factors such as advanced parental age, preterm birth, low birth weight, and clustering of pregnancy complications. Other culprits include pesticides, lead, heavy metals, traffic-related air pollutants, chemicals found in everyday household products (Boggess et al., 2016; Wong et al, 2015), and other substances that might be able to cross the placental barrier and affect brain development (Kalkbrenner et al., 2014; Nardone & Elliott, 2016). No definitive cause has been found yet.

The environmental factor that has received the most attention is the purported link between vaccines and autism. Anti-vaccine activists have argued that vaccines trigger autism in certain individuals. This theory has been repeatedly debunked (Taylor et al., 2014). Thimerosal, an antibacterial preservative composed of a mercury compound, has at times been the center of controversy, despite being less toxic than mercury found in fish or other sources. Meta-analyses have failed to substantiate claims of links between thimerosal and ASD (Ng et al., 2017; Roy et al., 2016). Nonetheless, it has been largely removed from vaccines in response to the public debate. Vaccines are safe for almost all children and far less risky than failing to immunize against potentially life-threatening diseases (Roy et al., 2016). However, anti-vaccination attitudes proliferate and are spread via websites, forums, and social media (Basch et al., 2017; Venkatraman et al., 2015).

More research is needed to lay claim to definitive causes of ASD. The relevant research questions to explore are daunting, in consideration of critical windows of exposure, ASD subtypes, gender variations, and individual genetic susceptibility (Kalkbrenner et al., 2014). Science can give us answers, but not all of them, and not right away.

what's your view Given what you know today, how would you respond to claims that vaccinations are linked to autism? Why do you think some people are resistant to scientific evidence about the lack of association?

Beginning in the 2nd month of gestation, an estimated 250,000 immature neurons are produced every minute through cell division (mitosis). At birth, most of the more than 100 billion neurons in a mature brain are already formed but are not yet fully developed. The number of neurons increases most rapidly between the 25th week of gestation and the first few months after birth. This cell proliferation is accompanied by a dramatic growth in cell size.

Originally the neurons are simply cell bodies with a nucleus, or center, composed of deoxyribonucleic acid (DNA), which contains the cell's genetic programming. As the brain grows, these rudimentary cells migrate to various parts of the brain (Bystron et al., 2006). Most of the neurons in the cortex are in place by 20 weeks of gestation, and its structure becomes fairly well defined during the next 12 weeks.

Once in place, the neurons sprout *axons* and *dendrites*—narrow, branching, fiberlike extensions. Axons send signals to other neurons, and dendrites receive incoming messages from them, through *synapses,* tiny gaps, which are bridged with the help of chemicals called *neurotransmitters* that are released by the neurons. Eventually, a particular neuron may have anywhere from 5,000 to 100,000 synaptic connections.

The multiplication of dendrites and synaptic connections, especially during the last 2½ months of gestation and the first 6 months to 2 years of life, accounts for much of the brain's growth and permits the emergence of new perceptual, cognitive, and motor abilities. As the neurons multiply, migrate to their assigned locations, and develop connections, they undergo the complementary processes of *integration* and *differentiation*. Through **integration,** the neurons that control various groups of muscles coordinate their activities. Through **differentiation,** each neuron takes on a specific, specialized structure and function. Over time and through experience, these neurons form functional networks to process and synthesize information. For example, one network might specialize on language, and another on sensorimotor information (Gao et al., 2015).

At first the brain produces many more neurons and synapses than it needs. The large number of excess neurons provided by this early proliferation gives the brain flexibility—with more connections available than will ever be needed, many potential paths are open for the growing brain. As early experience shapes the brain, the paths are selected, and unused paths are pruned away. This process involves **cell death,** which may sound negative but is a way to calibrate the developing brain to the local environment. This process begins during the prenatal period and continues after birth. Only about half the neurons originally produced survive and function in adulthood (Society for Neuroscience, 2008). Even as unneeded neurons die, others may continue to form during adult life (Deng et al., 2010; Gould et al., 1999). This flexibility is a double-edged sword. The brain's amazing plasticity implies people are vulnerable to negative environmental experiences; however, it also suggests great recovery is possible in those who have experienced difficulties and accounts for our ability to adapt to a wide variety of cultural experiences.

Myelination Much of the credit for efficiency of neural communication goes to the glia that coat the neural pathways with a fatty substance called *myelin*. This process of **myelination** enables signals to travel faster and more smoothly.

Myelination begins about halfway through gestation (Dubois et al., 2014). In the fetus, myelin development progresses from the center out. Sensory pathways, including the somatosensory, visual, and auditory pathways, are generally myelinized before motor pathways, and the occipital pole (the posterior end of the occipital lobe) is myelinized before the temporal and frontal poles. Last, projection fibers (nerve tracts that connect the cortex with lower parts of the brain and spinal cord) are myelinized before association fibers (nerve tracts that connect cortical areas within the cerebral hemisphere) (Qui et al., 2015). It has been argued that this sequence exists because before higher cortical areas can use information, they must be able to access stable inputs. Therefore, the primary cortical areas are myelinated first (Guillery, 2005).

Myelination continues to occur rapidly throughout infancy, accelerating at 12 to 16 months, and then slowing again from 2 to 5 years of age (Deoni et al., 2012). At 5 years of age, the myelinated white matter volume in the brain is approximately 80 percent of that found in adults (Deoni et al., 2011). Myelination continues through adolescence and persists through the third decade of life (Bartzokis et al., 2010).

Early Reflexes When your pupils contract as you turn toward a bright light, they are acting involuntarily. Such an automatic, innate response to stimulation is called a **reflex behavior.** Reflex behaviors are controlled by the lower brain centers that govern other involuntary processes, such as breathing and heart rate.

Human infants have an estimated 27 major reflexes, many of which are present at birth or soon after (Noble & Boyd, 2012; Table 4.3). *Primitive reflexes,* such as sucking and rooting for the nipple, are related to instinctive needs for survival and protection or may support the early connection to the caregiver. Some primitive reflexes are likely part of humanity's evolutionary legacy. One example is the grasping reflex, which enables infant

integration
Process by which neurons coordinate the activities of muscle groups.

differentiation
Process by which cells acquire specialized structures and functions.

cell death
In brain development, normal elimination of excess brain cells to achieve more efficient functioning.

myelination
Process of coating neural pathways with a fatty substance called myelin, which enables faster communication between cells.

reflex behaviors
Automatic, involuntary, innate responses to stimulation.

TABLE 4.3 Early Human Reflexes

Reflex	Stimulation	Baby's Behavior	Typical Age of Appearance	Typical Age of Disappearance
Moro	Baby is dropped or hears loud noise.	Extends legs, arms, and fingers, arches back, draws back head.	7th month of gestation	3 months
Darwinian (grasping)	Palm of baby's hand is stroked.	Makes strong fist; can be raised to standing position if both fists are used.	7th month of gestation	4 months
Tonic neck	Baby is laid down on back.	Turns head to one side, assumes fencer position, flexes opposite limbs.	7th month of gestation	5 months
Babinski	Sole of baby's foot is stroked.	Toes fan out; foot twists in.	Birth	4 months
Rooting	Baby's cheek or lower lip is stroked with finger or nipple.	Head turns; mouth opens to prepare for sucking.	Birth	9 months
Walking	Baby is held under arms, with bare feet touching flat surface.	Makes well-coordinated steplike motions.	1 month	4 months
Swimming	Baby is put into water face down.	Makes well-coordinated swimming movements.	1 month	4 months

Moro reflex
Denise Hager/Catchlight Visual Services/Alamy Stock Photo

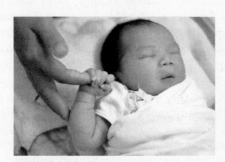

Darwinian (grasping) reflex.
Supachok Pichetkul/EyeEm/Getty Images

Tonic neck reflex.
Custom Medical Stock Photo/Alamy Stock Photo

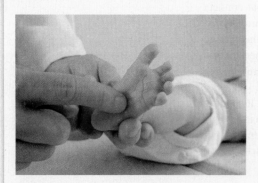

Babinski reflex.
Custom Medical Stock Photo/Alamy Stock Photo

Rooting (and sucking) reflex.
Science Photo Library/Shutterstock

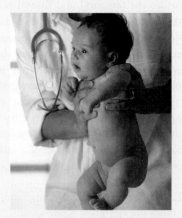

Walking reflex.
Picture Partners/Alamy Stock Photo

monkeys to hold on to their mothers' fur. Human infants show a similar reflex wherein they tightly grasp any object placed in their palm, a holdover from our ancestral past.

Most of the early reflexes disappear during the first 6 to 12 months. Reflexes that continue to serve protective functions—such as blinking, yawning, coughing, gagging, sneezing, shivering, and dilation of the pupils in the dark—remain. Disappearance of unneeded reflexes on schedule is a sign that motor pathways in the cortex have been partially myelinated, enabling a shift to voluntary behavior. Thus we can evaluate a baby's neurological development by seeing whether certain reflexes are present or absent.

Brain Plasticity Our brains are not static; rather, they are living, changeable organs that respond to environmental influences and are a reflection of our experiences. The technical term for this malleability of the brain is **plasticity.** Plasticity may be an evolutionary mechanism to enable adaptation to environmental change (Gomez-Robles et al., 2013).

plasticity
Modifiability, or "molding," of the brain through experience.

Plasticity enables learning. Individual differences in intelligence may reflect differences in the brain's ability to develop neural connections in response to experience (Garlick, 2003). Early experience can have lasting effects on the capacity of the central nervous system to learn and store information. But there are two sides to every coin. Just as plasticity allows learning in response to appropriate environmental input, it can also lead to damage in the case of harmful input. During the formative period of early life when the brain is most plastic, the brain is especially vulnerable. Exposure to hazardous drugs, environmental toxins, or maternal stress before or after birth can threaten the developing brain, and malnutrition can interfere with normal cognitive growth. Early abuse or sensory impoverishment can leave an imprint on the brain as it adapts to the environment in which the developing child must live, delaying neural development or affecting brain structure (Kolb et al., 2017).

Ethical constraints prevent controlled experiments on the effects of environmental deprivation on human infants. However, the discovery of thousands of infants and young children raised in overcrowded Romanian orphanages offered a natural experiment (Becket et al., 2006). These abandoned children had spent much of their time lying quietly in their cribs or beds with nothing to look at. They were rarely taken out of their cribs or talked to and had almost no personalized caregiving. Most of the 2- and 3-year-olds did not walk or talk, and the older children played aimlessly. PET scans of their brains showed extreme inactivity in the temporal lobes, which regulate emotion and receive sensory input.

Some of these children were placed in adoptive homes in Canada or the United Kingdom. In one longitudinal study, Romanian children who had been removed from institutions *before* age 6 months and adopted by English families showed no cognitive impairment by age 11 as compared with a control group of English children adopted within the United Kingdom. By contrast, the average IQs of Romanian children adopted into English families *after* age 6 months were 15 points lower (Beckett et al., 2006). Other research has shown that Romanian adoptees have significantly lower white and gray matter volume in their brains (Mehta et al., 2009), a physical analogue to the cognitive deficits. Additionally, they also show difficulty attaching properly to their adoptive parents and a range of disturbances, including attentional issues, aggression, poor executive control, and autistic-like social abnormalities (Nelson et al., 2019). There is recovery in some areas however. Although adults who were institutionalized for more than 6 months as children had lower educational attainment and higher unemployment, the cognitive impairments disappeared by early adulthood. These findings suggest that high-quality care may partly overcome the adverse effects of early institutionalization (Sonuga-Barke et al., 2017).

EARLY SENSORY CAPACITIES

The rearward regions of the developing brain, which control sensory information, grow rapidly during the first few months of life, enabling newborn infants to make fairly good sense of what they touch, see, smell, taste, and hear (Gilmore et al., 2007).

Touch and Pain Touch is the first sense to develop, and for the first several months it is the most mature sensory system. By 32 weeks of gestation, all body parts are sensitive to touch, and this sensitivity increases during the first 5 days of life (Haith, 1986; Field, 2010).

In the past, physicians performing surgery (such as circumcision) on newborn babies often used no anesthesia because of a mistaken belief that neonates cannot feel pain or feel it only briefly. However, there is evidence that the capacity for pain perception emerges late in pregnancy (Bellieni & Buonocore, 2012; Lee et al., 2005). Newborns can and do feel pain, and they become more sensitive to it during the first few days. Anesthesia is dangerous for young infants, however, so when possible, alternative methods of pain management are used for minor procedures such as circumcision, a heel stick, or vaccines. For example, infants show a decreased pain response when they are held or cuddled, especially with skin-to-skin contact, and either breastfed or given a sweet solution to suck on (Riddell et al., 2015; Campbell-Yeo et al., 2011).

Smell and Taste The senses of smell and taste also begin to develop in the womb. A preference for certain tastes and smells can be learned in utero and during the first few days after birth, and the odors transmitted through the mother's breast milk may further contribute to this learning (Ventura & Worobey, 2013). Exposure to the flavors of healthy foods through breastfeeding may improve acceptance of healthy foods after weaning and later in life (Dunn & Lessen, 2017). The taste preferences developed in infancy may last into early childhood; children repeatedly offered a wide variety of foods with different flavors and textures are less restricted in their food preferences (Mura Paroche et al., 2017). This process allows for the cultural programming of food preferences.

Other taste preferences seem to be largely innate and appear to reflect an adaptive preference for signals for high-calorie, high-protein foods and an aversion toward a food that may be poisonous or toxic (Mennella & Bobowski, 2015; Ventura & Worobey, 2013). Newborns much prefer sweet tastes, such as breast milk, to sour, bitter, or salty tastes (Mennella, 2014). Newborns also strongly dislike bitter flavors, likely a survival mechanism given the toxic nature of many bitter substances (Beauchamp & Mennella, 2011).

Hearing Hearing, too, is functional before birth; fetuses respond to sounds and seem to learn to recognize them. From an evolutionary perspective, early recognition of voices and language heard in the womb may lay the foundation for the relationship with the mother, which is critical to early survival (Rakison, 2005).

Auditory discrimination develops rapidly after birth. Even in the womb, fetuses can tell new speech sounds from those they have heard before (Partanen et al., 2013). In addition, infants as young as 2 days old were able to recognize a word they heard up to a day earlier (Swain et al., 1993). At 1 month, babies can distinguish sounds as close as *ba* and *pa* (Eimas et al., 1971). There are even indications that infants can recognize music that is typical of their culture (Virtala et al., 2013) and by 4 months of age prefer music typical of their cultural experiences (Soley & Hannon, 2010).

Because hearing is a key to language development, hearing impairments should be identified as early as possible. Hearing loss occurs in 1 to 2 of 1,000 live births in developed countries and is slightly higher in developing countries (Kanugo & Patel, 2017).

Sight Vision is the least developed sense at birth, perhaps because there is so little to see in the womb. Visual perception and the ability to use visual information—identifying caregivers, finding food, and avoiding dangers—become more important as infants become more alert and active (Rakison, 2005).

The eyes of newborns are smaller than those of adults, the retinal structures are incomplete, and the optic nerve is underdeveloped. A neonate's eyes focus best from about 1 foot away—just about the typical distance from the face of a person holding a newborn. Newborns blink at bright lights. Their field of peripheral vision is very narrow; it more than doubles between 2 and 10 weeks and is well developed by 3 months (Maurer & Lewis, 1979; Tronick, 1972). The ability to follow a moving target also develops rapidly in the first months, as does color perception (Haith, 1986). The development of these abilities is tied closely to cortical maturation (Braddick & Atkinson, 2011).

Visual acuity at birth is approximately 20/400 but improves rapidly, reaching the 20/20 level by about 8 months (Kellman & Arterberry, 1998). *Binocular vision*—the use of both eyes to focus, enabling perception of depth and distance—usually does not develop until 4 or 5 months (Bushnell & Boudreau, 1993).

Generally, infants seem to show privileged attention to faces, a tendency which is likely the result of a dedicated neural system for the processing of facial stimuli. From the very beginning, infants prefer to look at and are able to discriminate between human faces more than almost any other stimuli (Pascalis & Kelly, 2009; Sugden & Marquis, 2017). Infants use faces to learn important information. Within a few months after birth, infants begin to pay close attention to human eyes over other features (Dupierrix et al., 2014). Between about 4 to 8 months of age, when learning the foundations of language, infants pay particular attention to the mouth. Then, at approximately a year of age, as they begin to master some of the basics, their attention shifts back to the eyes (Lewkowicz & Hansen-Tift, 2012). Infants also show some ability to categorize racial groups on the basis of facial data. At 3 months, infants look longer at own-race faces. By 9 months, they look longer at other race faces and seem to process own-race faces more efficiently (Liu et al., 2015). Moreover, using visual fixation as an index, they also seem to like own-race faces more, associating own-race faces with happy music, but other-race faces with sad music (Xiao et al., 2018).

Early screening is essential to detect problems that interfere with vision. Infants should be examined between 6 and 12 months for visual fixation preference, ocular alignment, and signs of eye disease. Formal vision screening should begin by age 3 (American Optometric Association, 2019). Doctors' offices have modified eye charts for toddlers specifically for this purpose; in place of letters are shapes easily recognized by most toddlers such as stars, hearts, and circles.

Motor Development

Babies do not have to be taught such basic motor skills as grasping, crawling, and walking. They just need room to move and freedom to see what they can do.

MILESTONES OF MOTOR DEVELOPMENT

Motor development is marked by a series of milestones: achievements that develop systematically, each newly mastered ability preparing a baby to tackle the next. Babies first learn simple skills and then combine them into increasingly complex **systems of action,** which permit a wider or more precise range of movement and more effective control of the environment. In developing the precision grip, for example, an infant first tries to rake things up with the whole hand, fingers closing against the palm. Later the baby masters the *pincer grasp,* in which thumb and index finger meet at the tips to form a circle, making it possible to pick up tiny objects.

The **Denver Developmental Screening Test** (Frankenburg et al., 1975) is used to chart progress between ages 1 month and 6 years and to identify children who are not developing normally. The test measures **gross motor skills** (those using large muscles), such as rolling over and catching a ball, and **fine motor skills** (using small muscles), such as grasping a rattle and copying a circle. It also assesses language development (for example, knowing the definitions of words) and personality and social development (such as smiling spontaneously and dressing without help). The newest edition, the Denver II Scale (Frankenburg et al., 1992), includes revised (Table 4.4).

When we talk about what the "average" baby can do, we refer to the 50 percent Denver norms, but normality covers a wide range: About half of babies master these skills before the ages given, and about half afterward.

Head Control At birth, most infants can turn their heads from side to side while lying on their backs. When lying chest down, many can lift their heads enough to turn them. Within the first 2 to 3 months, they lift their heads higher and higher—sometimes to the

systems of action
Increasingly complex combinations of motor skills, which permit a wider or more precise range of movement and more control of the environment.

Denver Developmental Screening Test
Screening test given to children 1 month to 6 years old to determine whether they are developing normally.

gross motor skills
Physical skills that involve the large muscles.

fine motor skills
Physical skills that involve the small muscles and eye-hand coordination.

TABLE 4.4 Milestones of Motor Development

Skill	50 Percent	90 Percent
Rolling over	3.2 months	5.4 months
Grasping rattle	3.3 months	3.9 months
Sitting without support	5.9 months	6.8 months
Standing while holding on	7.2 months	8.5 months
Grasping with thumb and finger	8.2 months	10.2 months
Standing alone well	11.5 months	13.7 months
Walking well	12.3 months	14.9 months
Building tower of two cubes	14.8 months	20.6 months
Walking up steps	16.6 months	21.6 months

Note: This table shows the approximate ages when 50 percent and 90 percent of children can perform each skill.

Source: Frankenburg, W. K., Dodds, J., Archer, P., Bresnick, B., Maschka, P., Edelman, N., & Shapiro, H. (1992). *Denver II training manual.* Denver, CO: Denver Developmental Materials.

point where they lose their balance and roll over on their backs. By 4 months, almost all infants can keep their heads erect while being held or supported in a sitting position.

Hand Control Babies are born with a grasping reflex. If the palm of an infant's hand is stroked, the hand closes tightly. At about 3½ months, most infants can grasp an object of moderate size, such as a rattle, but have trouble holding a small object. Next, they begin to grasp objects with one hand and transfer them to the other. Sometime between 7 and 11 months, their hands become coordinated enough to pick up a tiny object, such as a pea, using the pincer grasp. By 15 months, the average baby can build a tower of two cubes. A few months after the 3rd birthday, the average toddler can copy a circle fairly well.

Locomotion After 3 months, the average infant begins to roll over deliberately—first from front to back and then from back to front. The average baby can sit without support by 6 months and can assume a sitting position without help by about 8½ months.

Between 6 and 10 months, most babies begin to get around under their own power by means of creeping or crawling. This new achievement of *self-locomotion* has striking cognitive and psychosocial ramifications (Bertenthal et al., 1994; Karasik et al., 2011). Crawling infants become more sensitive to where objects are, how big they are, whether they can be moved, and how they look. Crawling helps babies learn to judge distances and perceive depth. They learn to look to caregivers for clues as to whether a situation is secure or frightening—a skill known as *social referencing* (Campos et al., 2013).

Yu Zhang/Shutterstock

Ale Ventura/PhotoAlto/Alamy Stock Photo

Bonfanti Diego/Cultura/Getty Images

Lifting and holding up the head from a prone position, crawling along the floor to reach something enticing, such as a colorful toy, and walking well enough to push a wagon are important early achievements of motor development.

By holding onto a helping hand or a piece of furniture, the average baby can stand at a little past age 7 months. The average baby can let go and stand alone well at about 11½ months.

All these developments lead up to the major motor achievement of infancy: walking. For some months before they can stand without support, babies practice cruising while holding onto furniture. Soon after they can stand alone well most infants take their first unaided steps. Within a few weeks, shortly after the first birthday, the average child is walking fairly well and thus achieves the status of toddler.

During the 2nd year, children begin to climb stairs one at a time, putting one foot after another on the same step; later they will alternate feet. Walking down stairs comes later. Also in their 2nd year, toddlers run and jump. By age 3½, most children can balance briefly on one foot and begin to hop.

ETHNIC AND CULTURAL INFLUENCES

Examining the influence of culture on motor development provides an excellent opportunity to consider the intersection of nature and nurture. Although motor development generally follows a universal sequence, its pace does respond to certain cultural factors. What variables might impact differences in the pace of motor development?

According to some research, babies of African descent, and to a lesser extent those from India, tend to be more advanced motorically than U.S. and European infants in sitting, walking, and running (Kelly et al., 2006). Such differences have been found in babies from Jamaica, Uganda, Kenya, Mali, Nigeria, and the Caribbean (Mendonca et al., 2016). In Uganda, for example, babies typically walk at 10 months, as compared with 12 months in the United States and 15 months in France. By contrast, some research suggests that Asian infants are delayed in the development of voluntary motor activity relative to American and European infants (Toy et al., 2000; Williams & Williams, 1987). The origin of these differences is unclear. They may be due to differences in typical activity level, and thus related to practice in performing motor skills. For instance, Brazilian children, who are encouraged to play physically active and expressive games, outperform British children in running and walking (Victora et al., 1990). Alternatively, such differences may be related in part to ethnic differences in temperament (Kaplan & Dove, 1987) or may reflect a culture's child-rearing practices (Venetsanou & Kambas, 2010).

Some cultures actively encourage early development of motor skills. In many African and West Indian cultures in which infants show advanced motor development, adults use special *handling routines,* such as bouncing and stepping exercises, to strengthen babies' muscles. (Hopkins & Westra, 1988, 1990). In Western countries, motor intervention programs that encourage locomotor skills in young children have been shown to accelerate some forms of motor development, such as head control, reaching, walking, horizontal jumping, or skipping (Lobo & Galloway, 2012; Deli et al., 2006).

On the other hand, some cultures discourage early motor development, either through parenting practices or via direct instruction. For instance, some infants raised in northern China were traditionally placed in "sand bags" to toilet them, a practice that, although keeping them clean, constrained and delayed their locomotor development (Mei, 1984). Children of the Ache in eastern Paraguay, whose mothers pull them back to their laps if they crawl away and who carry them much of the time, do not begin to walk until age 18 to 20 months (Kaplan & Dove, 1987). These types of effects are not limited to traditional cultures. Children who wear diapers and restrictive clothing, an influence more typical of developed countries, show less mature gait patterns, fall more often, and show decreased quality and quantity of stepping (Cole et al., 2012; Groenen et al., 2010). Historical change can also be a factor. The Back to Sleep campaign was effective in reducing the incidence of SIDS but had the unintended consequence of delaying a variety of motor milestones. Because infants were no longer on their stomachs, they were slower to develop the arm and core strength necessary for some milestones (Davis et al., 1998).

Some researchers argue because of these early differences, motor development milestones developed within one culture may not be valid when applied to a different cultural

Brazilian children are encouraged to play physically active games, which may be an influence in why they tend to outperform British children in running and walking in the toddler years.
Palie Massa/Shutterstock

context (Mendonca et al., 2016). Other researchers argue that the majority of motor milestones are similar across different countries and cultural groups, and thus the use of normative milestones is warranted (WHO Multicentre Growth Reference Study Group & de Onis, 2006), particularly for younger infants who have had less time to hone specialized skills (Ertem et al., 2018). For now, this remains a debate in the field. What is clear, however, is that typical development need not follow the same timetable for all children.

MOTOR DEVELOPMENT AND PERCEPTION

Sensory perception enables infants to learn about themselves and their environment so they can make better judgments about how to navigate in it. Motor experience sharpens and modifies their perceptual understanding of what is likely to happen if they move in a certain way.

Sensory and motor activity seem fairly well coordinated from birth (von Hofsten, 2004). Infants begin reaching for and grasping objects at about 4 to 5 months; by 5½ months they can adapt their reach to moving or spinning objects although they still are not very good at it (Wentworth et al., 2000).

visual guidance
Use of the eyes to guide movements of the hands or other parts of the body.

For many years, researchers believed that reaching depended on **visual guidance:** the use of the eyes to guide the movement of the hands (or other parts of the body). More recently, researchers have realized that in younger infants, clumsy corrective movements are more likely to be illustrating immature cerebellar development. The immature cerebellum is only able to provide a rough guideline of movements used in reaching, which must be then corrected to be successful (Berthier, 2011). Younger infants are more likely to correct their reaching movements using proprioceptive feedback from their muscles and joints and haptic (relating to touch) information rather than vision (Berthier & Carrico, 2010; Corbetta et al., 2014). Rather than use their eyes to correct their movements, infants reach first, and then the eyes follow.

depth perception
Ability to perceive objects and surfaces three-dimensionally.

Depth perception, the ability to perceive objects and surfaces in three dimensions, depends on several kinds of cues that affect the image of an object on the retina of the eye. These cues involve not only binocular coordination but also motor control (Bushnell & Boudreau, 1993). *Kinetic cues* are produced by movement of the object or the observer, or both. To find out whether an object is moving, a baby might hold his or her head still for a moment, an ability that is well established by about 3 months.

haptic perception
Ability to acquire information about properties of objects, such as size, weight, and texture, by handling them.

Sometime between 5 and 7 months, after babies can reach for and grasp objects, they develop **haptic perception,** the ability to acquire information through touch, for example, by handling objects rather than by simply looking at them. Haptic perception enables babies to respond to such cues as relative size and differences in texture and shading (Bushnell & Boudreau, 1993).

THE ECOLOGICAL THEORY OF PERCEPTION

In a classic experiment by Richard Walk and Eleanor Gibson (1961), 6-month-old babies were seated on a plexiglass tabletop laid over two ledges. From the far side of the table, the infants' mothers beckoned their children. To the babies, it appeared that their mothers were asking them to crawl over a **visual cliff**—a steep drop down to the floor. Walk and Gibson wanted to know if babies would willingly crawl over the deep end of the visual cliff when urged to do so by their mothers.

visual cliff
Apparatus designed to give an illusion of depth and used to assess depth perception in infants.

ecological theory of perception
Theory developed by Eleanor and James Gibson, which describes developing motor and perceptual abilities as interdependent parts of a functional system that guides behavior in varying contexts.

Experiments such as these were pivotal in the development of Eleanor Gibson and James J. Gibson's **ecological theory of perception** (E. J. Gibson, 1969; J. J. Gibson, 1979; Gibson & Pick, 2000). In this approach, locomotor development depends on infants' increasing sensitivity to the interaction between their changing physical characteristics and various features of their environment. Babies' bodies continually change with age—their weight, center of gravity, muscular strength, and abilities. And each new environment provides a new challenge for babies to master. For example, sometimes a baby might have to make her way down a slight incline and other times might have to navigate stairs. Instead of relying on solutions that previously worked, babies must learn to continually gauge their abilities and adjust their movements to their current environment.

This process of "learning to learn" (Adolph, 2008) involves visual and manual exploration, testing alternatives, and flexible problem solving. What worked at one time may not work now, and what worked in one environment may not work well in another. For example, when faced with steep downward slopes, infants who have just begun to crawl or walk seem unaware of the limits of their abilities and are more likely to plunge recklessly down steep slopes. Infants who have been crawling for some time are better at judging slopes and know how far they can push their limits (Adolph, 2008; Adolph et al., 2003). For example, they may gauge the steepness with their hands first or turn around to go down backward as if they are going down stairs.

According to Gibson, "Each problem space has its own set of information-generating behaviors and its own learning curve" (Gibson, 1969). So, for example, babies who learn how far they can reach for a toy across a gap while in a sitting position without tumbling over must acquire this knowledge anew for situations involving crawling. Likewise, when crawling babies who have mastered slopes begin to walk, they have to learn to cope with slopes all over again (Adolph & Eppler, 2002).

No matter how enticing a mother's arms are, this baby is staying away from them. As young as she is, she can perceive depth and wants to avoid falling off what looks like a cliff. Denver Post/Getty Images

dynamic systems theory (DST)
Esther Thelen's theory, which holds that motor development is a dynamic process of active coordination of multiple systems within the infant in relation to the environment.

DYNAMIC SYSTEMS THEORY

Esther Thelen, in her influential **dynamic systems theory (DST),** argued that "behavior emerges in the moment from the self-organization of multiple components" (Spencer et al., 2006, p. 1523). Infant and environment form an interconnected, dynamic system. Opportunities and constraints presented by the infant's physical characteristics, motivation, energy level, motor strength, and position in the environment at a particular moment in time affect whether and how an infant achieves a goal. Ultimately, a solution emerges as the baby explores various combinations of movements and assembles those that most efficiently contribute to that end. Furthermore, the solution must be flexible and subject to modification in changing circumstances. Rather than being solely in charge of it, the maturing brain is but one component of a dynamic process. Indeed, no one factor determines the pace of development, and no predetermined timetable specifies when a particular skill will emerge. Rather, typical babies tend to develop the same skills in the same order because they are built approximately the same way and have similar challenges and needs. However, because these factors can vary from baby to baby, this approach also allows for variability in the timeline of individual development.

Thelen used the walking reflex to illustrate her approach. When neonates are held upright with their feet touching a surface, they spontaneously make coordinated stepping movements. This behavior usually disappears by the 4th month. Not until the latter part of the 1st year, when a baby is getting ready to walk, do the movements appear again. The traditional explanation focused on cortical control, and the belief was that an older baby's deliberate walking was a new skill masterminded by the developing brain. However, this explanation did not make sense to Thelen. She wondered why the stepping reflex—which used the same series of movements that would become walking—should stop, particularly as other early behaviors, such as kicking, persisted. The answer, she suggested, might be found by considering other relevant variables that could affect movement. For example, babies' legs become thicker and heavier during the early months of life, but the large leg muscles used to control movements are not yet strong enough to handle the increased weight (Thelen & Fisher, 1982, 1983). In support of this hypothesis, when infants who had stopped stepping were held in warm water, stepping reappeared. Presumably, the water helped support their legs and lessened the pull of gravity on their muscles, allowing them to once again demonstrate the skill. Their ability to produce the movement had not changed—only the physical and environmental conditions that inhibited or promoted it. These same systems of dynamic influences affect all motor movements, from reaching for a rattle to sitting independently to learning to walk. In this view, motor development, rather than being genetically determined and largely automatic, is seen as a continuous process of interaction between the baby and environment.

summary and key terms

Childbirth, Culture, and Change

- Childbirth is often ritualized within a culture; however, wide variations exist across cultures. Customs surrounding childbirth reflect a culture's beliefs, values, and resources.
- The science of obstetrics professionalized childbirth. Births took place in hospitals and were attended by physicians. Medical advances dramatically improved safety.
- Today, delivery at home or in birth centers attended by midwives can be a relatively safe alternative to physician-attended hospital delivery for normal, low-risk pregnancies.

The Birth Process

- Birth normally occurs after a preparatory period of parturition.
- The birth process consists of three stages: (1) dilation of the cervix, (2) descent and emergence of the baby, and (3) expulsion of the umbilical cord and the placenta.
- Electronic fetal monitoring can detect signs of fetal distress but may indicate problems where none exist.
- About 32 percent of U.S. births are by cesarean delivery.
- Alternative methods of childbirth can minimize the need for painkilling drugs and maximize parents' active involvement.
- Modern epidurals can give effective pain relief with smaller doses of medication than in the past.
- The presence of a doula can provide physical and emotional support, and is an economically sound intervention.

parturition, electronic fetal monitoring, cesarean delivery, natural childbirth, prepared childbirth, doula

The Newborn Baby

- The neonatal period is a time of transition from intrauterine to extrauterine life.
- At birth, the circulatory, respiratory, digestive, elimination, and temperature regulation systems become independent of the mother's. If a newborn cannot start breathing within about 5 minutes, brain injury may occur.
- Newborns have a strong sucking reflex and secrete meconium from the intestinal tract. They are commonly subject to neonatal jaundice due to immaturity of the liver.
- At 1 minute and 5 minutes after birth, a neonate's Apgar score can indicate how well he or she is adjusting to extrauterine life.
- Neonatal screening is done for certain rare conditions, such as PKU and congenital hypothyroidism.
- A newborn's state of arousal is governed by periodic cycles of wakefulness, sleep, and activity. Sleep takes up the major, but a diminishing, amount of a neonate's time.
- Cultural customs affect sleep patterns.

neonatal period, neonate, anoxia, neonatal jaundice, Apgar scale, state of arousal

Complications of Childbirth

- Complications of childbirth include low birth weight, postmature birth, and stillbirth.
- Low-birth-weight babies may be either preterm (premature) or small for gestational age. Low birth weight is a major factor in infant mortality and can cause long-term physical and cognitive problems.
- A supportive postnatal environment and other protective factors often can improve the outcome for babies suffering from birth complications.

low-birth-weight babies, preterm (premature) infants, small-for-date (small-for-gestational-age) infants, kangaroo care, postmature, stillbirth

Survival and Health

- The vast majority of infant deaths occur in developing countries. Postnatal care can reduce infant mortality.
- Although infant mortality has diminished in the United States, it is still disturbingly high, especially among African American babies. Birth defects are the leading cause of death in infancy.
- Sudden infant death syndrome (SIDS) is a leading cause of postneonatal death in the United States. SIDS rates have declined markedly following recommendations to lay babies on their backs to sleep.
- Vaccine-preventable diseases have declined as immunization rates have improved, but many children are not fully protected.

infant mortality rate, sudden infant death syndrome (SIDS)

Early Physical Development

- Physical growth and sensory and motor development proceed according to the cephalocaudal and proximodistal principles.
- A child's body grows most dramatically during the 1st year of life; growth proceeds at a rapid but diminishing rate throughout the first 3 years.
- Breast-feeding offers many health advantages and sensory and cognitive benefits.
- Babies are at risk of becoming obese adults if they have obese parents or grow very quickly in the first year.
- The central nervous system controls sensorimotor activity. Lateralization enables each hemisphere of the brain to specialize in different functions.

- The brain grows most rapidly during the months before and immediately after birth as neurons migrate to their assigned locations, form synaptic connections, and undergo integration and differentiation. Cell death and myelination improve the efficiency of the nervous system.
- Reflex behaviors—primitive, locomotor, and postural—are indications of neurological status. Most early reflexes drop out during the 1st year as voluntary, cortical control develops.
- Especially during the early period of rapid growth, environmental experiences can influence brain development positively or negatively.
- Sensory capacities, present from birth and even in the womb, develop rapidly in the first months of life. Very young infants are good at discriminating between stimuli.
- Touch is the first sense to develop and mature. Smell, taste, and hearing begin to develop in the womb. Newborns are sensitive to pain.
- Vision is the least well-developed sense at birth.

cephalocaudal principle, proximodistal principle, central nervous system, lateralization, neurons, integration, differentiation, cell death, myelination, reflex behavior, plasticity

Motor Development

- Motor skills develop in a certain sequence, which may depend on maturation, context, experience, and motivation. Simple skills combine into increasingly complex systems.
- Self-locomotion brings about changes in all domains of development.
- Perception is intimately related to motor development. Depth perception and haptic perception develop in the first half of the 1st year.
- According to the Gibsons' ecological theory, sensory perception and motor activity are coordinated from birth, helping infants figure out how to navigate in their environment.
- Thelen's dynamic systems theory holds that infants develop motor skills, not by maturation alone but by coordination of multiple systems of action in a changing environment.
- Cultural practices may influence the pace of early motor development.

systems of action, Denver Developmental Screening Test, gross motor skills, fine motor skills, visual guidance, depth perception, haptic perception, visual cliff, ecological theory of perception, dynamic systems theory (DST)

chapter 5

Cognitive Development during the First Three Years

learning objectives

Identify six approaches to the study of cognitive development.

Describe how infants learn and remember.

Discuss infant assessment measures and how intelligence is predicted.

Summarize and evaluate Piaget's theory of cognitive development.

Explain how infants process information and begin to understand the characteristics of the physical world.

Describe language development in infancy.

Oksana Kuzmina/Shutterstock

In this chapter we look at infants' and toddlers' cognitive abilities from a variety of perspectives: behaviorist, psychometric, Piagetian, information processing, cognitive neuroscientific, and social-contextual. We trace the early development of language.

Cognitive Development: Six Approaches

Developmental psychologists take one of six approaches to their study:

- The **behaviorist approach** studies the basic *mechanics* of learning. Behaviorists are concerned with how behavior changes in response to experience.

- The **psychometric approach** measures *quantitative differences* in abilities that make up intelligence by using tests that indicate or predict these abilities.

- The **Piagetian approach** looks at changes, or stages, in the *quality* of cognitive functioning. It is concerned with how the mind structures its activities and adapts to the environment.

- The **information-processing approach** focuses on the nuts and bolts of cognition—perception, learning, memory, and problem solving. It aims to discover how children process information.

- The **cognitive neuroscience approach** seeks to identify what brain structures are involved in specific aspects of cognition.

- The **social-contextual approach** examines the effects of environmental aspects of the learning process, particularly the role of parents and other caregivers.

Behaviorist Approach

Babies are born with the ability to see, hear, smell, taste, and touch, and they have some ability to remember what they learn. Learning theorists are interested in mechanisms of learning.

CLASSICAL AND OPERANT CONDITIONING

Eager to capture Ella's growth, her father took many pictures. Whenever the flash went off, Ella blinked. One evening Ella saw her father hold the camera up to his eye—and she blinked *before* the flash. She had learned to associate the camera with the bright light, so the sight of the camera alone activated her blinking reflex.

This is an example of **classical conditioning,** in which a person learns to make a response (in this case, blinking) to a stimulus (the camera) that originally did not bring about the response. Classical conditioning enables infants to anticipate an event before it happens. Classically conditioned learning will become *extinct,* or fade, if it is not reinforced by repeated association. Thus, if Ella frequently saw the camera without the flash, she would eventually stop blinking at the sight of the camera alone.

Operant conditioning focuses on how the consequences of a behavior affect the likelihood of that behavior occurring again. Specifically, behaviors may be reinforced and become more likely to occur, or they may be punished and become less likely to occur. For example, a baby may learn that when she babbles her parents respond with smiles and attention, and she may increase this behavior to receive even more smiles and attention. In other words, she has been reinforced for her babbling. By contrast, a baby may see that when she throws her food her parents tend to frown and speak sharply to her. To avoid this punishment, she might learn not to throw her food.

INFANT MEMORY

Can you remember anything that happened to you before you were about 2 years old? Chances are you can't. Part of the reason is that early procedural knowledge (e.g., how to hold a pencil) and perceptual knowledge (e.g., what an apple tastes like) are not the same as the later language-based memories used by adults (e.g., what you did last Sunday).

Luckily, we can use operant conditioning techniques to "ask" infants questions about what they remember. For example, Carolyn Rovee-Collier (1999) brought 2- to 6-month-old infants to the laboratory and attached a string between one of their ankles and a

behaviorist approach
Approach to the study of cognitive development that is concerned with basic mechanics of learning.

psychometric approach
Approach to the study of cognitive development that seeks to measure intelligence quantitatively.

Piagetian approach
Approach to the study of cognitive development that describes qualitative stages in cognitive functioning.

information-processing approach
Approach to the study of cognitive development that analyzes processes involved in perceiving and handling information.

cognitive neuroscience approach
Approach to the study of cognitive development that links brain processes with cognitive ones.

social-contextual approach
Approach to the study of cognitive development that focuses on environmental influences, particularly parents and other caregivers.

classical conditioning
Learning based on associating a stimulus that does not ordinarily elicit a response with another stimulus that does elicit the response.

operant conditioning
(1) Learning based on association of behavior with its consequences. (2) Learning based on reinforcement or punishment.

Researchers have creatively used everyday objects such as infant mobiles that move when a baby kicks to "ask" babies what they know and remember about their world. Lifebrary/Shutterstock

mobile. The babies soon learned that when they kicked their leg, the mobile moved. As this was reinforcing to them, the number of kicks increased. When they were later brought back, they kicked more than other infants who had not been conditioned in this fashion, even if their ankles were no longer attached. This demonstrated that the recognition of the mobiles triggered a memory of their initial experience with them. Similar research has shown the length of time a conditioned response lasts increases with age. At 2 months of age, the typical infant can remember a conditioned response for 2 days; 18-month-olds can remember it for 13 weeks (Hartshorn et al., 1998; Rovee-Collier, 1999; Rovee-Collier, 1996).

Research using operant conditioning techniques has illustrated that infants' memory processes do not differ fundamentally from those of older children and adults except their retention time is shorter and memory is more dependent on encoding cues. With increasing age, these abilities become more sophisticated. Additionally, studies have found that just as with adults, memory can be aided by reminders. Brief, nonverbal exposure to the original stimulus can sustain a memory from early infancy through age 1½ to 2 years (Rovee-Collier, 1999).

Psychometric Approach

Intelligence enables people to acquire, remember, and use knowledge; to understand concepts and relationships; and to solve everyday problems. Moreover, **intelligent behavior** is presumed to be goal oriented and adaptive.

intelligent behavior
Behavior that is goal oriented and adaptive to circumstances and conditions of life.

The goals of psychometric testing are to quantitatively measure the factors that are thought to make up intelligence (such as comprehension and reasoning) and, from the results of that measurement, to predict future performance (such as school achievement). **IQ (intelligence quotient) tests** consist of questions or tasks that show how much of the measured abilities a person has by comparing that person's performance with norms established by a large group of test-takers.

IQ (intelligence quotient) tests
Psychometric tests that seek to measure intelligence by comparing a test-taker's performance with standardized norms.

TESTING INFANTS AND TODDLERS

Although it is extremely difficult to measure infants' intelligence, we can still test their functioning by assessing their behavior on tasks and comparing their performance with established norms. So, for example, if a child is unable to perform a task that the "average baby" can do by a particular age, that child may be delayed in that area.

The **Bayley Scales of Infant and Toddler Development** (Bayley, 2005) is a developmental test designed to assess children from 1 month to 3½ years. Scores on the Bayley-III indicate a child's competencies in each of five developmental areas: *cognitive, language, motor, social-emotional,* and *adaptive behavior.* An optional *behavior rating scale* can be completed by the examiner, in part on the basis of information from the child's caregiver. Separate scores, called *developmental quotients* (DQs), are calculated for each scale. DQs are most commonly used for early detection of emotional disturbances and sensory, neurological, and environmental deficits and can help parents and professionals plan for a child's needs.

Bayley Scales of Infant and Toddler Development
Standardized test of infants' and toddlers' mental and motor development.

The Bayley-III may not be appropriate for all cultural groups. For example, Balinese children are discouraged from crawling because it is considered to be animal-like. An American child who failed to crawl at the appropriate age would be labeled as delayed; however, a Balinese child is likely to skip crawling altogether (Fernald et al., 2017).

ASSESSING THE EARLY HOME ENVIRONMENT

Using the **Home Observation for Measurement of the Environment (HOME)** (R. H. Bradley, 1989; Caldwell & Bradley, 1984), trained observers interview the primary caregiver and rate on a yes-or-no checklist the intellectual stimulation and support observed in a child's home. HOME scores are significantly correlated with measures of cognitive development (Totsika & Sylva, 2004).

Research has identified a number of variables important to cognitive development. These include the number of books in the home, the presence of playthings that encourage the development of concepts, parents' involvement in children's play, and overall parental responsiveness, including kissing and caressing the child during the interview (Bradley et al., 2001).

The HOME has been used in research across more than 50 countries. Such research has unearthed some common features across different cultures. For instance, socioeconomic status and HOME scores tend to be correlated. Additionally, HOME scores are correlated with cognitive function, language ability, and academic achievement. Last, stimulation and parental responsiveness are important predictive variables (Fernald et al., 2017). However, other HOME items may be less culturally relevant in non-Western families than in Western families (Bradley et al., 2001), and the scale has been modified at times so as to more appropriately capture positive developmental influences across cultures. For example, although encouraging exploration of the environment is generally a positive variable, an intervention program targeting severely malnourished Bangladeshi children modified the HOME to include items focused on parental limit setting, a necessary feature for this population given the poverty and physical danger the children were exposed to (Nahar et al., 2012). As another example, parents from a number of cultures, including Nigeria, Uganda, and Macedonia, believe that physical punishment is an important socialization tool necessary for teaching children to be respectful of adults (Drotar et al., 1999; Aina et al., 1993; Bradley, 2009). Thus, items focused on physical punishment must be modified to reflect cultural values, and do not carry the same negative weight as they do in countries such as the United States.

Some items of the HOME inventory must be modified to capture cultural differences. For example, parental limit setting, generally characterized as a negative influence, is a necessary safeguard in some Bangladeshi families. Ricky Simms/Majority World CIC/Alamy Stock Photo

Home Observation for Measurement of the Environment (HOME) Instrument to measure the influence of the home environment on children's cognitive growth.

EARLY INTERVENTION

Early intervention is a systematic process of planning and providing therapeutic and educational services for families that need help in meeting young children's developmental needs. Examples include Project CARE (Wasik et al., 1990), the Abcedarian (ABC) Project (Ramey, 2018), and Head Start (Lee et al., 2014).

Generally, these programs involve full-day, year-round early childhood education from infancy through the preschool years as well as family-oriented social services, early childhood education, medical care and services, and family education on child development. Control groups vary, but may, for example, consist of children who receive pediatric or social work services but do not participate in day care (Ramey & Ramey, 2003), or children who are cared for at home by parents or attend center-based day care (Lee et al., 2014; Zhai et al., 2014).

The typical pattern of findings for early intervention programs involves an advantage for children who participated in them over children in control groups. Generally, participants show positive outcomes on cognitive developmental outcomes, including reading and math scores, IQ, and school progress (Lee et al., 2014; Ramey, 2018;

early intervention Systematic process of providing services to help families meet young children's developmental needs.

Camilli et al., 2010). The gains are strongest initially and fade over time (Lee et al., 1990). It appears that without sufficient ongoing environmental support, initial gains diminish.

Despite the initial decline in gains, there are lasting effects of early intervention programs. Children who participate in early intervention programs are less likely to require special education services in grade school and high school, more likely to graduate from high school, more likely to be employed, less likely to be incarcerated, and report higher lifetime earnings (Melhuish et al., 2015). Thus, from an economic standpoint, despite their high cost, early intervention programs are worth the benefits (Ramey, 2018).

Piagetian Approach

The first of Piaget's four stages of cognitive development is the **sensorimotor stage.** During this stage (birth to approximately age 2), infants learn about themselves and their world through their developing sensory and motor activity. Babies change from creatures who respond primarily through reflexes and random behavior into goal-oriented toddlers.

SUBSTAGES OF THE SENSORIMOTOR STAGE

The sensorimotor stage consists of six substages that flow from one to another as a baby's **schemes,** organized patterns of thought and behavior, become more elaborate. During the first five substages, babies learn to coordinate input from their senses and organize their activities in relation to their environment. During the sixth substage, they progress to using symbols and concepts to solve simple problems.

Much of this early cognitive growth comes about through **circular reactions,** in which an infant learns to reproduce events originally discovered by chance. Initially, an activity such as sucking produces an enjoyable sensation that the baby wants to repeat. The repetition produces pleasure, which motivates the baby to do it yet again (Figure 5.1). The originally chance behavior has been consolidated into a new scheme. These are called circular reactions because they stimulate their own repetition.

In the *first substage* (birth to about 1 month), neonates practice their reflexes. For example, newborns suck reflexively when their lips are touched. But they soon learn to find the nipple even when they are not touched, and they suck at times when they are not hungry. Infants thus modify and extend the scheme for sucking.

In the *second substage* (about 1 to 4 months), babies learn to purposely repeat pleasant actions first achieved by chance (as shown in Figure 5.1a). Also, they begin to turn toward sounds, showing the ability to coordinate different kinds of sensory information (vision and hearing).

In the *third substage* (about 4 to 8 months) babies intentionally repeat an action not merely for its own sake, as in the second substage, but to get results *beyond the infant's own body* (as shown in Figure 5.1b). For example, a baby this age might repeatedly shake a rattle to hear the noise.

By the time infants reach the *fourth substage* (about 8 to 12 months), they have learned to generalize from past experience to solve new problems. They modify and coordinate previous schemes, such as the schemes for crawling, pushing, and grabbing, to find one that works. This substage marks the development of complex, goal-directed behavior.

sensorimotor stage
Piaget's first stage in cognitive development, in which infants learn through senses and motor activity.

schemes
Piaget's term for organized patterns of thought and behavior used in particular situations.

circular reactions
Piaget's term for processes by which an infant learns to reproduce desired occurrences originally discovered by chance.

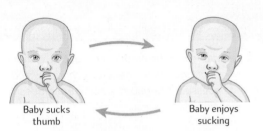

(a) **Primary circular reaction:** Action and response both involve infant's own body (1 to 4 months).

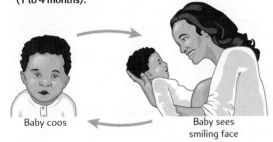

(b) **Secondary circular reaction:** Action gets a response from another person or object, leading to baby's repeating original action (4 to 8 months).

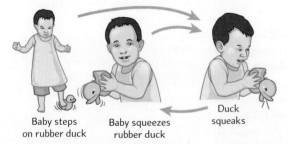

(c) **Tertiary circular reaction:** Action gets one pleasing result, leading baby to perform similar actions to get similar results (12 to 18 months).

FIGURE 5.1
Primary, Secondary, and Tertiary Circular Reactions

TABLE 5.1 Key Developments of the Sensorimotor Stage

Concept or Skill	Piaget's View	More Recent Findings
Imitation	Invisible imitation develops around 9 months; deferred imitation begins with mental representations at 18 to 24 months.	Controversial studies have found invisible imitation of facial expressions in newborns and deferred imitation as early as 6 weeks. Deferred imitation of complex activities seems to exist as early as 6 months.
Object permanence	Develops gradually between the third and sixth substage.	Infants as young as 3½ months seem to show object knowledge through their looking behavior.
Symbolic development	Develops at 18 to 24 months with representational thinking.	Understanding that pictures stand for something else occurs at about 19 months. Children under 3 have difficulty interpreting scale models.
Categorization	Develops at 18 to 24 months with representational thinking.	Infants as young as 3 months recognize perceptual categories; by the end of the first year they categorize by function.
Causality	Develops between 4 to 6 months and 1 year, based on an infant's discovery, first of effects of own actions and then of effects of outside forces.	Some evidence suggests early awareness of specific causal events in the physical world, but general understanding of causality may be slower to develop.
Number	Develops at 18 to 24 months with the use of symbols.	Infants as young as 5 months recognize and mentally manipulate small numbers; interpretation of findings is controversial.

In the *fifth substage* (about 12 to 18 months), babies begin to experiment to see what will happen. They now vary a behavior to see what might happen. For example, a toddler may squeeze a rubber duck that squeaked when stepped on, to see whether it will squeak again (as shown in Figure 5.1c). By trial and error, they try behaviors until they find the best way to attain a goal.

The *sixth substage* (about 18 months to 2 years) is a transition to the preoperational stage of early childhood. **Representational ability**—the ability to mentally represent objects and actions in memory, largely through symbols such as words, numbers, and mental pictures—frees toddlers from immediate experience. They can pretend, and their representational ability affects the sophistication of their pretending (Bornstein et al., 1996). They can think about actions before taking them and try solutions in their mind.

During these six substages, infants develop the ability to think and remember, and develop knowledge about the physical world. Researchers have found that some of these developments conform fairly closely to Piaget's observations, but others may occur earlier than Piaget claimed. (Table 5.1 compares Piaget's views on these and other topics with more current findings.)

representational ability
Piaget's term for capacity to store mental images or symbols of objects and events.

IMITATION

One-year-old Clara watches as her older sister brushes her hair. When her sister puts the brush down, Clara picks it up and tries to brush her hair too.

Imitation becomes increasingly valuable late in the first year of life as babies try new skills (Nelson, 2005). Piaget noted this behavior in his own observations and maintained that **visible imitation**—imitation that uses body parts such as hands or feet that babies can see—develops first and is then followed by **invisible imitation**—imitation that involves parts of the body that babies cannot see—at 9 months.

Piaget believed that children under 18 months could not engage in **deferred imitation.** Deferred imitation is the reproduction of an observed behavior after the passage of time. As the behavior is no longer happening, deferred imitation requires that a stored representation of the action be recalled. Piaget argued that young children could not engage in deferred imitation because they lacked the ability to retain mental representations.

visible imitation
Imitation with parts of one's body that one can see.

invisible imitation
Imitation with parts of one's body that one cannot see.

deferred imitation
Piaget's term for reproduction of an observed behavior after the passage of time by calling up a stored symbol of it.

However, deferred imitation of novel or complex events seems to begin by about 6 to 9 months (Bauer, 2002). For example, in one study 6-month-old German and Cameroonian infants were able to imitate how an adult interacted with a doll after a 10-minute delay (Goertz et al., 2011).

The ability to hold material in memory over a longer time span increases with age. By 9 months, more than 40 percent of infants can reproduce two steps, such as dropping a toy car down a vertical chute and then pushing a car with a rod to make it roll to the end of a ramp and turn on a light. Moreover, they can do this after a delay of 1 month (Bauer 2002; Bauer et al., 2003). By 14 months, toddlers show preferences about whom they imitate. For example, they are more likely to imitate people who speak the same language they do (Buttelmann et al., 2013). At 15 months, they show a bias toward imitating a peer; however, at 24 months they prefer to imitate an adult (Seehagen & Herbert, 2011). At 4 years of age, they are more likely to imitate those who are the same gender they are (Grace et al., 2008). Theorists argue children's imitation varies depending on their goals. When children are trying to communicate similarity or forge social bonds, they are more likely to imitate others who are like them, such as other children. When children are trying to learn new things, they are likely to imitate those whom they think they can learn the most from, such as adults (Zmyj & Seehagen, 2013).

OBJECT CONCEPT

The *object concept*—the idea that objects have independent existence, characteristics, and locations in space—is fundamental to an orderly view of physical reality.

The Development of Object Permanence One aspect of the object concept is **object permanence,** the realization that an object or a person continues to exist when out of sight. Piaget believed object permanence develops gradually during the sensorimotor stage. At first, infants appear to have no such concept. At about 4 months, they will look for something they have dropped, but if they cannot see it, they act as if it no longer exists.

Some research suggests that babies may fail to physically search for hidden objects because they cannot yet carry out a two-step sequence of actions, such as lifting the cover of a box and then grasping the object. Methods based only on infants' looking behavior eliminate the need for coordination with motor activity and thus can be used at very early ages.

Over the next few months, this ability continues to develop. For example, infants will continue to look for an object in the place where they first found it after seeing it hidden, even if they were later shown the object being moved to a new location (the A-not-B error). Somewhere between 5 and 8 months they start *looking* at the correct location where the object was moved, but do not reach for it. At about 9 to 10 months, infants will start looking and reaching for the object in the correct location (Cuevas & Bell, 2010). At 12 to 18 months, most infants will reliably search for an object in the last place they saw it hidden. However, they will not search for it in a place where they did *not* see it hidden. At 18 to 24 months, object permanence is fully achieved; toddlers will look for an object even if they did not see it hidden.

Infants' growing understanding that objects can be hidden and reappear may be why games like peekaboo are common across many cultural groups. Three-month-old infants enjoy their mothers' looming faces. At 5 to 7 months they show anticipatory looking and smiling in the direction where they expect their play partner to appear and are particularly delighted by unexpected reemergences that surprise them. By about a year of age, infants take an increasingly active role in the game, initiating play by covering their eyes or putting a cloth over their face (Fernald & O'Neill, 1993; Millar, 1988). Peekaboo type games have been documented in a wide variety of cultures, including Germany, Brazil, Greece, India, South Africa, Japan, Korea, Italy,

object permanence
Piaget's term for the understanding that a person or an object still exists when out of sight.

This little girl seems to be showing some concept of object permanence by searching for an object that is partially hidden.
Doug Goodman/Science Source

the Netherlands, Iran, Indonesia, and immigrant groups in the United States (Fernald & O'Neill, 1993).

Symbolic Development, Pictorial Competence, and Understanding of Scale Much of the knowledge people acquire about their world is gained through *symbols,* intentional representations of reality. One aspect of symbolic development is the growth of *pictorial competence,* the ability to understand the nature of pictures (DeLoache et al., 2003). For example, consider how suns are represented in children's books. Generally they are drawn as a yellow circle with radiating spires. A child who understands that this graphic stands in for the ball of light in the sky has attained some degree of pictorial competence.

There are indications that even very young children can understand some aspects of pictorial representations. Infants as young as 4 months of age stare longer at and show expressions of interest to "impossible objects" like a picture of a cube that would defy the rules of geometry, suggesting that even at this age they have some ability to mentally represent three-dimensional objects (Krause et al., 2019). Still, this understanding is incomplete. Until about 15 months, infants use their hands to explore pictures as if they were objects—rubbing, patting, or attempting to lift a depicted object off the page. By about 19 months children are able to point at a picture of an object while saying its name, clearly demonstrating their understanding that a picture is a symbol of something else (DeLoache et al., 2003). By age 2, children understand that a picture is both an object and a symbol (Preissler & Bloom, 2007).

Picture books support children's acquisition of information about the world. However, research suggests the ability to learn from books is influenced by cultural experiences. Twenty-month-old Tanzanian children who had previously not had experience with books were able to recognize familiar objects in books presented to them by a researcher but were not able to learn a label for a novel object (a gold S-shaped hook) first presented to them in a book and then in real life. By approximately 27 months they were able to learn the word for the novel object from a picture book and apply it to the real object correctly, and by 34 months they were able to apply what they learned to a different exemplar of that novel object (a silver S-shaped hook) (Walker et al., 2013).

Tablet computers and cell phones offer an interesting contrast in that objects on the screen are two-dimensional, like photographs, but can be manipulated like real objects. For example, by using two fingers in a pinch and spread move, objects on the screen can be shrunk and magnified (Ziemer & Snyder, 2016). Young children rapidly become adept at interacting with content on electronic devices. In one study of more than 450 toddlers, 68 percent could flick their finger to turn a page on an electronic book, 41 percent could press and drag objects around the screen, and 71 percent were adept at using a tap (Cristia & Seidl, 2015). However, despite their facility with electronics, young children still treat content on a screen more like a photograph than a real object (Ziemer & Snyder, 2016) and are limited in what they can learn. For example, when 2- to 3-year-old children are shown how to solve a puzzle on a touchscreen, they have difficulty transferring this information to a real puzzle board with actual puzzle pieces (Moser et al., 2015). In another study, children under the age of 2 years did not learn the word for a novel object presented via an e-book, although they easily learned the word presented in a traditional print book (Strouse & Ganea, 2017).

What about television? Although toddlers may spend a good deal of time watching television, at first they seem unaware that what they are seeing is a representation of reality (Troseth et al., 2006). This makes it difficult for them to use the information presented on television effectively. For example, 12- to 18-month-old children were better able to imitate an adult's actions (helping a puppet ring a bell) when they saw an adult performing the action in front of them than when they saw a video of the same thing (Barr et al., 2007). In one series of experiments, 2 1⁄2-year-olds were able to locate an object hidden in an adjoining room after watching a video of an adult hiding it, but 2-year-olds could not. Yet the younger children were able to find the object if they watched through a window as it was hidden (Troseth & DeLoache, 1998). Apparently,

research in action

RESEARCH-BASED RECOMMENDATIONS FOR BABIES AND MEDIA USE

About 90 percent of parents report their children under 2 using electronic media (AAP, 2011). Media technology geared toward young children is expansive, including TV, DVDs, tablets, apps, and streaming video (AAP, 2013). TV outranks other media in consumption (Vittrup et al., 2016), with near constant access possible through the proliferation of mobile media devices (AAP, 2013; Northwestern University Center on Human Development, 2014).

"Baby media" geared toward infants and toddlers directly or indirectly implies early education benefits, and parents perceive its educational value as a jump start to learning. While young children *can* learn from media starting at around 15 months of age, this process primarily occurs when parents watch *and* review content with them. Moreover, heavy media usage in infancy has been shown to be associated with an increased risk of negative outcomes, including obesity, sleep problems, and cognitive, language, and social-emotional delays (AAP, 2016).

The American Academy of Pediatrics (AAP) recommends limited use of media—with the exception of live video chatting—in children younger than 24 months (AAP, 2016). The academy echoes expert advice that children learn best through hands-on play and recommends that young children engage in interpersonal activities, such as talking, reading, or playing with toys. Nevertheless, few parents enforce TV viewing limitations with infants (Barr et al., 2010). As children display interest and become more competent, parents tend to encourage media use (Lauricella et al., 2015). Positive attitudes toward "baby media" use are maintained despite cautionary messages. Experts question whether parents are unfamiliar with or outright disagree with AAP recommendations (Vittrup et al., 2016).

Parents represent the most influential social partner in their children's lives, modeling media use from birth (Vittrup et al., 2016). Increasingly, it is understood that change in infant and toddler media use requires a family effort, as parents' media use is mirrored in children's use across media types (Lauricella et al., 2015; Northwestern University Center on Human Development, 2014).

what's your view

What restrictions, if any, would you place on infant or toddler TV, video, or mobile media use? Do you believe that there are negative consequences if young children engage in *limited* media use?

---

what the 2-year-olds lacked was representational understanding of screen images. See Research in Action for recommendations about media use in young children.

Have you ever seen toddlers try to put on a hat that is too small for their head, or sit in a chair much too tiny to hold them? This is known as a *scale error*—a momentary misperception of the relative sizes of objects (DeLoache et al., 2013). In one study, 18- to 36-month-olds were first allowed to interact with play objects that fit their body size, such as a toy car to ride in or a plastic slide. Then the life-size objects were replaced with miniature replicas. The children tried to slide down the tiny slides and squeeze their bodies into the miniature cars.

The researchers suggested that these actions might in part be based on a lack of impulse control—the children wanted to play with the objects so badly that they ignored perceptual information about size. However, toddlers might also be exhibiting faulty communication between immature brain systems. One brain system enables the child to recognize and categorize an object ("That's a chair") and to plan what to do with it ("I'm going to sit in it"). A separate system may be involved in perceiving the size of the object and using visual information to control actions pertaining to it ("It's big enough to sit in"). When communication between these areas breaks down, children momentarily, and amusingly, treat the objects as if they were full size (DeLoache et al., 2004).

The **dual representation hypothesis** offers yet another proposed explanation for scale errors. An object such as a toy chair has two potential representations. The chair is both an object in its own right, as well as a symbol for a class of things ("chairs"). According to this hypothesis, it is difficult for toddlers to simultaneously mentally represent both the actual object and the symbolic nature of what it stands for. In other words, they can focus on either the particular chair they are faced with ("This is a miniature chair") or the symbol and what it represents ("Chairs are for sitting in"), and so they may confuse the two (DeLoache, 2011).

EVALUATING PIAGET'S SENSORIMOTOR STAGE

According to Piaget, the journey from reflex behavior to the beginnings of thought is a long, slow one. However, research using simplified tasks and modern tools suggests that limitations Piaget saw in infants' early cognitive abilities may instead have reflected immature linguistic and motor skills. The answers that Piaget received were as much a function of the ways in which he asked the questions as they were a reflection of the actual abilities of young children.

In terms of describing what children do under certain circumstances, and the basic progression of skills, Piaget was correct. As Piaget observed, immature forms of cognition precede more mature forms. However, Piaget may have been mistaken in his emphasis on motor experience as the primary engine of cognitive growth. Infants' perceptions are far ahead of their motor abilities, and today's methods enable researchers to make observations and inferences about those perceptions, as we discuss it in the next section.

Information-Processing Approach

Information-processing researchers analyze the parts of a complex task to figure out what abilities are necessary for each part of the task and at what age these abilities develop.

HABITUATION

At about 6 weeks, Amalia lies peacefully in her crib near a window, sucking a pacifier. It is a cloudy day, but suddenly the sun breaks through, and an angular shaft of light appears on the end of the crib. Amalia stops sucking for a few moments, staring at the pattern of light and shade. Then she looks away and starts sucking again.

We cannot directly observe what was going on in Amalia's mind when she saw the shaft of light, but we can tell by her sucking and looking behavior at what point she began paying attention and when she stopped. Much information-processing research with infants is based on **habituation,** a type of learning in which repeated or continuous exposure to a stimulus (such as a shaft of light) reduces attention to that stimulus (such as looking away). It can be compared to boredom, and the rate of habituation (how quickly infants look away) can be used to "ask" infants how interesting they think various objects are.

Researchers study habituation in newborns by presenting a stimulus such as a sound or visual pattern, and then monitoring responses such as sucking or eye movements. A baby who has been sucking typically stops or sucks less vigorously when a stimulus is first presented in order to pay attention to the stimulus. After the stimulus loses its novelty, the infant generally resumes sucking vigorously. This indicates that habituation has occurred. If a new sight or sound is presented, the baby's attention is generally captured once again, and the baby will reorient toward the interesting stimulus and once again sucking slows. This response to a new stimulus is called **dishabituation.**

Researchers gauge the efficiency of infants' information processing by measuring how quickly babies habituate to familiar stimuli, how fast their attention recovers when they are exposed to new stimuli, and how much time they spend looking at new or old stimuli. Liking to look at new things and habituating to them quickly correlates with later signs of cognitive development, such as a preference for complexity, rapid exploration of the environment, sophisticated play, quick problem solving, and the ability to match pictures. In fact, as we will see, speed of habituation and other information-processing abilities show promise as predictors of intelligence (Rose et al., 2012).

TOOLS OF INFANT RESEARCH

visual preference
Tendency of infants to spend more time looking at one sight than another.

The tendency to spend more time looking at one sight rather than another is known as **visual preference.** Researchers can use this natural tendency to ask babies which of two objects they prefer. For example, if babies given a choice between looking at a curved or straight line spend more time focused on the curved line, the implication is that babies like curved lines more than straight lines. With this technique, researchers have determined that babies less than 2 days old prefer curved lines to straight lines, complex patterns to simple patterns, three-dimensional objects to two-dimensional objects, pictures of faces or facelike configurations to pictures of other things, and new sights to familiar sights (Rakison, 2005; Turati et al., 2002). The tendency to prefer new sights to familiar ones is called *novelty preference.*

The realization that babies like to look at new things afforded researchers with yet another tool with which to ask them questions. Babies can be shown a stimulus and be allowed to habituate to it. Then they can be concurrently presented with the familiar stimulus, as well as an additional novel stimulus. If the baby spends longer looking at the novel stimulus, that suggests the baby recognizes the familiar stimulus. In other words, because the novel stimulus is new and babies like new things, it is more interesting and thus warrants a better look than the previously seen, more boring, stimulus. This behavior demonstrates **visual recognition memory,** an ability that depends on the capacity to form and refer to mental representations (Zelazo et al., 1995).

visual recognition memory
Ability to distinguish a familiar visual stimulus from an unfamiliar one when shown both at the same time.

PERCEPTUAL PROCESSES

Contrary to Piaget's view, such studies suggest that a rudimentary representational ability exists at birth or very soon after and quickly becomes more efficient. Speed of processing increases rapidly during infants' 1st year (Bornstein & Colombo, 2012). It continues to increase during the 2nd and 3rd years, as toddlers become better able to distinguish new information from information they have already processed (Rose et al., 2002; Zelazo et al., 1995). Moreover, there are individual differences in the speed with which infants form and refer to mental images. When shown two sights at the same time, infants who quickly shift attention from one to another tend to have better recognition memory and stronger novelty preference than infants who take longer looks at a single sight (Jankowski et al., 2001).

Auditory discrimination studies are also usually based on attentional preference. This ability may emerge prenatally. In one study, fetuses were played recordings of various adults reading a story in either their parents' native language or a novel language. Heart rate data indicated the fetuses paid increased attention to both their mother's voice and stories read in a novel language (Kisilevsky et al., 2009). Newborn infants also have the ability to remember some sounds. Infants who heard a certain speech sound one day after birth remembered that sound 24 hours later, as shown by a reduced tendency to turn their heads toward the sound (Swain et al., 1993). Brain imaging research mirrors that finding, as right frontal regions of the brain active in adults during word recognition tasks are similarly activated in infants, particularly for vowel sounds (Benavides-Varela et al., 2012). However, these memory traces, at least initially, are brief and subject to interference and forgetting (Benavides-Varela et al., 2011).

Piaget held that the senses are unconnected at birth and are only gradually integrated through experience. However, this integration begins almost immediately. The fact that neonates will look at a source of sound shows that at the very least they associate hearing and sight. A more sophisticated ability is **cross-modal transfer,** the ability to use information gained from one sense to guide another—as when a person negotiates a dark room by feeling for the location of familiar objects.

cross-modal transfer
Ability to use information gained by one sense to guide another.

Cross-modal transfer of some, but not all, modalities appears to be available almost from birth. For example, in one study newborns were able to visually recognize a cylinder or a prism they had previously held but could not use tactile (touch) information to recognize a shape they had previously seen. However, they were able to use textured objects bidirectionally. In other words, if the objects used as stimulus were either smooth or nubby, they could transfer vision to touch and touch to vision equally well (Sann & Streri, 2007). Similarly, 1-month-olds can transfer information gained from sucking (touch) to vision (Gibson & Walker, 1984), and 2- to 8-month-old infants expect bouncing objects and their sounds to be synchronous (Lewkowicz, 1996).

Researchers also study how attention itself develops. From birth to about 2 months, the amount of time infants typically gaze at a new sight increases (Colombo, 2002). Between about 4 and 8 months looking time shortens, with the fastest decline seen at 4 to 6 months (Colombo et al., 2010). Presumably, this is because infants learn to scan objects more efficiently and thus shift attention more rapidly. Indeed, those infants who look for *less* time at novel stimuli show better memory for it later (Reynolds et al., 2011). Near the end of the 1st year and into the 2nd, when sustaining attention becomes more voluntary and task-oriented, looking time plateaus or increases (Colombo et al., 2004).

The capacity for *joint attention*—which is of fundamental importance to social interaction, language acquisition, and the understanding of others' intentions and mental states—develops between 10 and 12 months, when babies follow an adult's gaze by looking or pointing in the same direction (Behne et al., 2012). Young children who follow an adult's gaze at 10 or 11 months have a larger vocabulary at 18 months, 2 years and 2½ years than those who do not, especially if they spontaneously point at the object as well (Brooks & Meltzoff, 2005, 2008, 2015).

INFORMATION PROCESSING AS A PREDICTOR OF INTELLIGENCE

Because of a weak correlation between infants' scores on developmental tests such as the Bayley Scales and their later IQ (Bjorkland & Causey, 2017), many psychologists assumed that the cognitive functioning of infants had little in common with that of older children and adults. However, when cognitive functioning is examined more closely, some aspects of mental development do seem to be fairly continuous from birth (Courage & Howe, 2002).

Four core cognitive domains appear to be associated with later IQ: attention, processing speed, memory, and representational competence (as indexed by cross-modal transfer and the ability to anticipate future events). In one study, performance on these tasks in infancy (7 and 12 months) was related to performance on the same tasks in toddlerhood (24 and 36 months) as well as to performance on IQ tests at 11 years of age (Rose et al., 2012). Similar relationships to school performance have been found for the ability to shift attention rapidly (Hitzert et al., 2014) and the ability to inhibit attention toward irrelevant stimuli (Markant & Amso, 2014; Amso & Scerif, 2015). This provides evidence for the continuity of cognitive processes. Essentially, children who, from the start, are efficient at attending to, taking in, and interpreting sensory information score well on later intelligence tests.

INFORMATION PROCESSING AND PIAGETIAN ABILITIES

Here we consider categorization, causality, object permanence, and number, all of which depend on formation of mental representations (refer to Table 5.1).

Categorization Adults can understand that plants and animals are both living things but a television is not. Furthermore, they can understand that some animals are pets, that among those pets are cats and dogs, and that a chihuahua is a type of dog. These nested relationships are known as *categories*. Dividing the world into meaningful categories is the foundation of language, reasoning, problem solving, and memory.

According to Piaget, the ability to group things into categories does not appear until around 18 months. However, visual preference paradigms using behaviorally based looking measures have been able to assess infants at earlier ages. This research has shown that newborns distinguish between closed (e.g., triangles and squares) and open (e.g., crosses) shapes, but are unable to categorize different types of closed shapes (e.g., equilateral and isosceles triangles) until about 3 to 4 months of age. By 3 to 4 months, they can also distinguish between, for example, a dog and a cat, or between a chair and a bed by looking longer at items in a new category (Rakison & Yermolayeva, 2010). Infants at first seem to categorize on the basis of *perceptual* features, such as shape, color, and pattern, then by 12 to 14 months their categories become *conceptual,* based on real-world knowledge, particularly of function (Mandler, 1998, 2007).

Categorization is not limited to visual stimuli. Infants can categorize musical chords into dissonant versus consonant and major versus minor dimensions (Virtala et al., 2013). Vocalizations, however, are special, and there is evidence they help even 3-month-old babies categorize objects better than musical tones (Ferry et al., 2010), Additionally, once children start to understand words, they use those words to help form new categories (Bergelson & Swingley, 2012). Furthermore, in the 2nd year, language becomes a factor in their ability to categorize. In one study, 14-month-olds who understood more words were more flexible in their categorizing than those with smaller understood vocabularies (Ellis & Oakes, 2006).

Causality Eight-month-old Aviva accidentally squeezes her toy duck and it quacks. Startled, she drops it, and then, staring at it intently, she squeezes it again. Aviva is beginning to understand causality—the principle that one event (squeezing) causes another (quacking). Piaget maintained that this understanding develops slowly during infants' 1st year.

However, information-processing studies suggest that an understanding of causality emerges earlier. In one study, infants as young as 4½ months were able to understand simple causality (a ball knocking another ball out of position). However, only those infants who had practiced playing with a Velcro-covered ball and Velcro mittens—allowing them to easily manipulate the ball and therefore practice performing causal actions—were able to do so (Rakison & Krogh, 2012). By 6 months of age, this ability is more robust and does not require training (Leslie, 1995). By 8 months, infants make causal attributions for simple events even when they cannot see the actual moment of contact between the two objects (Muentener & Carey, 2010). And by 10 to 12 months old, the types of inferences made by infants become even more sophisticated. For example, 10- to 12-month-old infants looked longer when a hand emerged from the opposite side of a stage onto which a beanbag had been thrown than when the hand emerged from the same side as the beanbag, suggesting the infants understood that the hand had probably thrown the beanbag. The infants did *not* have the same reaction when a toy train rather than a hand appeared or when the thrown object was a self-propelled puppet (Saxe et al., 2005).

It may be that, with age, infants accumulate more information about how objects behave, thus they are better able to see causality as a general principle operating in a variety of situations (Cohen & Amsel, 1998; Cohen et al., 2002). Increasing experience with the environment may also be a factor. For example, 7-month-olds who had begun to crawl recognized self-propulsion of objects, but noncrawling 7-month-olds did not. This finding suggests that infants' ability to identify self-propelled motion is linked to the development of self-locomotion, which gives them new ways of understanding objects in their world (Cicchino & Rakison, 2008). Self-locomotion has also been linked to infants' ability to predict the goal of other people's intentional failed actions (like trying, but failing, to reach an object), perhaps because of having had the experience of being thwarted in an attempt to complete an action too (Brandone, 2015).

Object Permanence When Piaget investigated object permanence, he used infants' motor responses to gauge whether or not infants understood that a hidden object still existed. Their failure to reach for the hidden object was interpreted to mean they did not. However, it was possible that infants understood object permanence but could not demonstrate this knowledge with motor activity. At that time, infant development

Seven-month-old babies appear to understand that an object incapable of self-motion, such as a tennis ball, must be set in motion by a causal agent, such as a hand.
Pixelbliss/Shutterstock

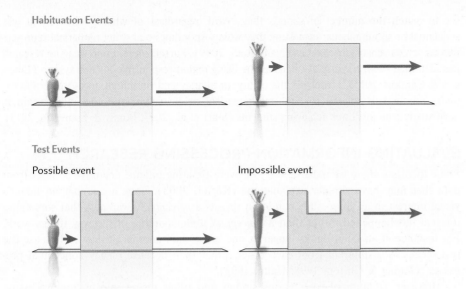

Habituation Events

Test Events

Possible event   Impossible event

Source: Adapted from Baillargeon, R., & DeVos, J. (1991). Object permanence in young infants: Further evidence. *Child Development, 62,* 1227–1246.

FIGURE 5.2

How Early Do Infants Show Object Permanence?

In this experiment, 3½-month-olds watched a short carrot and then a tall carrot slide along a track, disappear behind a screen, and then reappear. After they became accustomed to seeing these habituation events, the opaque screen was replaced by a screen with a large notch at the top for the test events. The short carrot did not appear in the notch when passing behind the screen; the tall carrot, which should have appeared in the notch, also did not. The babies looked longer at the tall than at the short carrot event, suggesting they were surprised that the tall carrot did not appear in the notch.

violation of expectations
Research method in which dishabituation to a stimulus that conflicts with experience is taken as evidence that an infant recognizes the new stimulus as surprising.

research methodologies were more limited. Researchers needed to ask babies the question in a different way, using the violation-of-expectations paradigm.

Violation of expectations begins with a familiarization phase in which infants see an event happen normally. After the infant becomes bored and has habituated to this procedure (most commonly as indexed by looking away), the event is changed in a way that conflicts with—or violates—normal expectations. If the baby looks longer at this changed event, researchers assume the additional interest implies that the baby is surprised.

For example, in one experiment, infants as young as 3½ months were first shown an animation of a carrot moving back and forth behind a screen (Hespos & Baillargeon, 2008). The center of the screen was notched, and a tall carrot should have shown momentarily as it moved in front of the notch, as shown in Figure 5.2. In the "possible" event, the short carrot, as expected, could not be seen as it passed in front of the notch. In the "impossible" event, the tall carrot would appear at one side, never show in the middle, and then emerge out the other side. Infants showed surprise by looking longer at the "impossible" event, indicating that the "impossible" event violated their expectations.

This procedure was important to the study of object permanence because for babies to be surprised by the carrot's failure to show, they needed to be able to remember that the carrot continued to exist. Thus, it provides evidence for the development of this ability at much younger ages than Piaget thought possible.

Number The violation-of-expectations paradigm can also be used to ask babies questions about their understanding of numbers. In one classic study, infants watched as Mickey Mouse dolls were placed behind a screen, and a doll was either added or taken away. The screen then was lifted to reveal either "right" or "wrong" number of dolls. Babies looked longer at surprising "wrong" answers than at expected "right" ones, suggesting they had mentally computed the right answers (Wynn, 1992). Subsequent to this study, multiple programs of research supported infants' ability to discriminate between small sets of numbers (Baillargeon & Carey, 2012). Wynn interpreted this research as suggesting that numerical concepts are inborn. However, critics argued the infants might simply have been responding *perceptually* to the puzzling presence or the absence of the doll behind the screen (Cohen & Marks, 2002; Haith, 1998). In other words, they may merely notice differences in the overall contours, area, or collective mass of sets of objects rather than compare the number of objects in the sets (Mix et al., 2002).

However, increasing evidence suggests that human *do* have an innate intuitive sense of number. For instance, newborns in one study expected the number of objects they could see to match the number of sounds they heard, regardless of whether the stimuli was sequential or simultaneous, suggesting they were responding to abstract numerical representations across sensory modalities (Izard et al., 2009). Furthermore, brain imaging research has identified the intraparietal sulcus as the likely region responsible for this system (Emerson & Cantlon, 2015). Moreover, the ability, in infancy and preschool, to estimate approximate numbers is related to later mathematical achievement, and this relationship is particularly true for lower achieving students (Starr et al., 2013; Bonny & Lourenco, 2013).

EVALUATING INFORMATION-PROCESSING RESEARCH

Some theorists argue we must be wary of overestimating infants' cognitive abilities from data that may have simpler explanations (Kagan, 2008). They argue that an infant's visual interest in an impossible condition reveals a *perceptual* awareness that something unusual has happened rather than a *conceptual* understanding of the way things work. For instance, if an infant looks longer at one scene than another, it may be because the two scenes look different from each other rather than because of any conceptual processes (Goubet & Clifton, 1998; Haith, 1998).

However, violation-of-expectations studies and other recent information-processing research with infants raise the possibility that at least rudimentary forms of categorization, causal reasoning, object permanence, and number sense may be present in the early months of life. One proposal is that infants are born with reasoning abilities—*innate learning mechanisms* that help them make sense of the information they encounter—or that they acquire these abilities very early (Baillargeon et al., 2011). Some investigators go further, suggesting that infants at birth may already have intuitive *core knowledge* of basic physical principles in the form of specialized brain modules that help infants organize their perceptions and experience (Spelke, 2017).

Cognitive Neuroscience Approach

Current brain research bears out Piaget's assumption that neurological maturation is a major factor in cognitive development. Brain growth spurts (periods of rapid growth and development) do indeed coincide with changes in cognitive behavior (Fischer, 2008).

Some researchers have used brain scans to determine which brain structures are tied to cognitive functions and to chart developmental changes. These brain scans provide physical evidence of the location of two separate long-term memory systems—*implicit* and *explicit*—that acquire and store different kinds of information and mature at different rates (Bauer et al., 2007). **Implicit memory** refers to remembering that occurs without effort or even conscious awareness, such as knowing how to tie your shoe or throw a ball. It most commonly pertains to habits and skills. Implicit memory seems to develop early and is demonstrated by such actions as an infant's kicking on seeing a familiar mobile (Nelson, 2005). **Explicit memory,** also called *declarative memory,* is conscious or intentional recollection, usually of facts, names, events, or other things that can be stated or declared. Delayed imitation of complex behaviors is evidence that declarative memory has developed. This is because delayed imitation requires a representation of a behavior to be stored in memory. Although infants cannot yet speak, and thus the memory cannot technically be "declared," this is nonetheless a demonstration of symbolic representation (Bauer et al., 2007). By 6 months, infants show evidence of deferred imitation by imitating actions an adult performs after a 24-hour delay, such as shaking a puppet, but have difficulty if the object or context is changed in any way, such as if the puppet is swapped out for a different one or they are tested in a different location (Hayne et al., 2000).

Explicit memory is a more conscious and deliberative process, and as such, it would be expected to be more affected by cultural influences. By contrast, the more automatic and early-appearing implicit memory processes, because they appear primarily outside of awareness, would be predicted to be less affected by cultural influences (Kolling et al., 2016). For example, one study comparing 6- and 9-month-old middle-class German and Cameroonian Nso infants found that although all infants imitated actions and all infants imitated with greater frequency as they aged, the German infants showed more spontaneous actions

implicit memory
Unconscious recall, generally of habits and skills; sometimes called *procedural memory.*

explicit memory
Intentional and conscious memory, generally of facts, names, and events.

directed at toys at 9 months old but not 6 months of age. The researchers attributed this to the German infants' greater experience with toys (Graf et al., 2014). Experience does not affect implicit memory in the same way. German infants, at 3 months of age, kick more frequently than Nso infants, presumably because they spend more time laying down alone. Nso infants spend the majority of their time being carried, which strengthens their core but restricts their legs. However, these early experiences do not seem to have an effect on infants' ability to establish and remember implicit responses. When their legs were attached to a mobile so that kicks made it move, the key factor in learning and memory was how much an infant kicked, not cultural experiences. Infants who kicked too frequently were less able to notice the mobile's contingent responses to their movements. Culture affected memory, but only insofar as it affected the frequency of kicking (Graf et al., 2012).

In early infancy, when the structures responsible for memory storage are not fully formed, memories are relatively fleeting. The maturing of the *hippocampus,* a structure deep in the temporal lobes, along with the development of cortical structures coordinated by the hippocampal formation make longer-lasting memories possible (Lavenex & Lavenex, 2013; Bauer et al., 2003).

The *prefrontal cortex* (the large portion of the frontal lobe directly behind the forehead) is believed to control many aspects of cognition. This part of the brain develops more slowly than any other (Diamond, 2002), making it more sensitive to environmental disruption (Kolb et al., 2012). During the second half of the 1st year, the prefrontal cortex and associated circuitry develop the capacity for **working memory** (Pelphrey et al., 2004). Working memory is short-term storage of information the brain is actively processing, or working on. For example, when you try to estimate how much an item on sale will cost, you are using working memory to make the calculations. Working memory can be overwhelmed, as when someone speaks to you while you try to calculate the sale price.

working memory
Short-term storage of information being actively processed.

Working memory appears relatively late in development and may be responsible for the slow development of object permanence, which seems to be seated in a rearward area of the prefrontal cortex (Bell, 2012; Nelson, 1995). By 12 months, this region may be developed enough to permit an infant to avoid the A-not-B error by controlling the impulse to search in a place where the object previously was found (Bell & Fox, 1992; Diamond, 1991).

Social-Contextual Approach

Researchers influenced by Vygotsky's sociocultural theory have studied how cultural context affects early social interactions. From the very beginning, choices made about child care are socialization tools that transmit cultural information. For example, in the United States, slightly over 20 percent of mothers report sharing a bed with their babies (Smith et al., 2016). In line with individualistic goals, parents often report sleeping separately is necessary for the child to build independence. However, in many nonindustrialized and traditional societies, bed sharing is the norm, and indeed forcing a baby to sleep separately from her mother is seen as abusive or neglectful. In this case, the collectivistic ideals call for integrating the baby into the social group (Ball, 2006).

How children are expected to learn about their world also varies with culture. In many cultures, children learn in regimented ways within a formal educational system. By contrast, some cultures use **guided participation.** Guided participation refers to mutual interactions with adults that help structure children's activities and bridge the gap between a child's understanding and an adult's. This concept was inspired by Vygotsky's view of learning as a collaborative process. Guided participation often occurs in shared play and in ordinary, everyday activities in which children informally learn the skills, knowledge, and values important in their culture.

guided participation
Adult's participation in a child's activity that helps to structure it and bring the child's understanding of it closer to the adult's.

For example, in a series of cross-cultural studies (Göncü et al., 2000; Rogoff et al., 1993), researchers visited the homes of 1- to 2-year-old children in four culturally different places: a Mayan town in Guatemala, a tribal village in India, and middle-class urban neighborhoods in Salt Lake City and Turkey. The investigators interviewed caregivers about their child-rearing practices and watched them help the toddlers learn to dress themselves and to play with unfamiliar toys.

Cultural differences affected the types of guided participation the researchers observed. In the Guatemalan town and the Indian village, the children customarily played while the mother worked nearby. When children needed to be shown how to do something, such as tie their shoes, the mothers tended to provide an initial demonstration and instruction, and then allow the children to take over while they remained available to help if needed. The instruction was primarily nonverbal. The U.S. toddlers, who had full-time caregivers, tended to interact and learn most from caregivers while playing with them. Caregivers managed and motivated children's learning with praise and excitement. Their instruction was highly verbal in nature, often consisting of "lessons." Turkish families, who were in transition from a rural to an urban way of life, showed a pattern somewhere in between.

The cultural context influences the way caregivers contribute to cognitive development. Direct adult involvement in children's play and learning may be better adapted to a middle-class urban community, in which parents or caregivers have more time, greater verbal skills, and possibly more interest in children's play and learning, than to a rural community in a developing country, in which children frequently observe and participate in adults' work activities (Rogoff et al., 1993).

The social constructionist approach has been influential in early childhood education. Research has shown that preschool programs that are highly focused on academic skills are not necessarily ideal (Bodrova, 2008; Hirsch-Pasek, 1991) and may even result in lower academic achievement later in school (Marcon, 2002). However, programs based on Vygotsky's philosophies can transmit academic concepts within the context of classroom routines and play. Guided play programs take advantage of children's natural motivation to play—supporting their autonomy, and cultivating their love of learning while also scaffolding specific learning outcomes (Weisberg et al., 2016). For example, a geometry lesson in which 4- to 5-year-old children donned detective hats and were guided through solving a "mystery of the shapes" sorting task where they were asked to discover the secret distinguishing "real" shapes from "fake" ones was more effective in teaching shape knowledge than either didactic teaching or free play (Fisher et al., 2013)

Language Development

language
Communication system based on words and grammar.

Language is a communication system based on words and grammar. Once children know words, they can use them to represent objects and actions. They can reflect on people, places, and things, plus they can communicate their needs, feelings, and ideas.

CLASSIC THEORIES OF LANGUAGE ACQUISITION

Is linguistic ability learned or inborn? In the 1950s, a debate raged between two schools of thought: one led by B. F. Skinner, the foremost proponent of learning theory, the other by the linguist Noam Chomsky.

Skinner (1957) maintained that language learning, like other learning, is based on experience and learned associations. According to classic learning theory, children learn language through the processes of operant conditioning. At first, babies utter sounds at random. Caregivers reinforce the sounds that happen to resemble adult speech. Infants then repeat these reinforced sounds, and language is gradually shaped. Social learning theorists extended this early model to account for imitation. According to social learning theory, babies imitate the sounds they hear adults make and, again, are reinforced for doing so.

For example, Lila, while babbling, inadvertently says "da." Her parents hear and provide her with smiles and praise. Lila is thus reinforced and continues to say "da." Eventually, her parents no longer provide as much reinforcement. But then Lila happens to say "dada," perhaps imitating her parents. Now her parents once again reward her lavishly. Again, their praise eventually tapers off, and now the word is only reinforced when her father is present. Over time, her parents' selective reinforcement of closer and closer approximations to speech results in the shaping of language.

Observation, imitation, and reinforcement do contribute to language development, but, as Chomsky (1957) persuasively argued, they cannot fully explain it. For one thing, word combinations and nuances are so numerous and so complex that they cannot all be acquired by specific imitation and reinforcement. In addition, caregivers often reinforce utterances that are not strictly grammatical, as long as they make sense ("Grandma go bye-bye"). Adult speech itself is an unreliable model to imitate, as it is often ungrammatical and contains false starts, unfinished sentences, and slips of the tongue. Also, learning theory does not account for children's imaginative ways of saying things they have never heard, such as when 2-year-old Clara insisted "I *am* hayve" after being told she needed to behave.

Chomsky's view is called **nativism.** Unlike Skinner's learning theory, nativism emphasizes the active role of the learner. Chomsky (1957, 1972, 1995) proposed that the human brain has an innate capacity for acquiring language. He suggested that an inborn **language acquisition device (LAD)** programs children's brains to analyze the language they hear and to figure out its rules.

Support for the nativist position comes from newborns' ability to differentiate phonemes easily, suggesting that they are born with perceptual "tuning rods" that pick up characteristics of speech. Nativists point out that almost all children master their native language in the same age-related sequence without formal teaching. Furthermore, our brains have structures that have been shown to be directly implicated in language use (Friederici, 2011), which is what would be predicted on the basis of the nativist position. Still, the nativist approach does not tell us why some children acquire language more rapidly and efficiently than others, why children differ in linguistic skill and fluency, or why speech development appears to depend on having someone to talk with, not merely on hearing spoken language.

Most developmental scientists today maintain that language acquisition, like most other aspects of development, depends on an intertwining of nature and nurture. Children have an inborn capacity to acquire language, which may be activated or constrained by experience.

EARLY LANGUAGE DEVELOPMENT

Before babies can use words, they still make their needs and feelings known with other vocalizations. These sounds are known as **prelinguistic speech.** Over time, infants become better able to recognize, understand and imitate speech sounds and to use meaningful gestures (Table 5.2).

Early Vocalization *Crying* is a newborn's first means of communication. Different pitches, patterns, and intensities signal hunger, sleepiness, or anger (Lester & Boukydis, 1985). Adults find crying aversive for a reason—it motivates them to find the source of the problem and fix it (Leerkes et al., 2012). Thus crying has great adaptive value. Although all newborns cry instinctively, even at this early age they are influenced by culture. The intonation patterns and fundamental frequency of their cries vary with the language they have been exposed to (Mampe et al., 2009; Wermke et al., 2016).

Between 6 weeks and 3 months, babies start *cooing* when they are happy—squealing, gurgling, and making vowel sounds like "ahhh." *Babbling*—repeating consonant-vowel strings, such as "da-da-da-da"—occurs between ages 6 and 10 months and is often mistaken for a baby's first word. Until about 9 months, babbling is language-general, meaning babies across different cultures babble in roughly the same way. However, after this time, babbling gradually becomes calibrated to sound patterns the baby has repeatedly heard (Cychosz et al., 2019).

Imitation is key to early language development. First, infants accidentally imitate language sounds. Generally, they are reinforced by their parents' positive responses and thus encouraged to produce such sounds more over time. Then, at about 9 to 10 months, infants deliberately imitate sounds without understanding them. Once they have a repertoire of sounds, they string them together in prelinguistic speech patterns that sound like language but appear to have no meaning. Finally, after infants become familiar with the sounds of words and phrases, they begin to attach meanings to them (Fernald et al., 2006; Jusczyk & Hohne, 1997).

nativism
Theory that human beings have an inborn capacity for language acquisition.

language acquisition device (LAD)
In Chomsky's terminology, an inborn mechanism that enables children to infer linguistic rules from the language they hear.

prelinguistic speech
Forerunner of linguistic speech; utterance of sounds that are not words. Includes crying, cooing, babbling, and accidental and deliberate imitation of sounds without understanding their meaning.

TABLE 5.2 Language Milestones from Birth to 3 Years

Age in Months	Development
Birth	Can perceive speech, cry, make some response to sound.
1½ to 3	Coos and laughs.
5 to 7	Recognizes frequently heard sound patterns and phonemes of native language.
6 to 10	Babbles in strings of consonants and vowels.
9 to 10	Intentionally imitates sounds.
9 to 12	Uses a few social gestures.
10 to 12	No longer can discriminate sounds not in own language.
10 to 14	Says first word (usually a label for something).
12 to 13	Understands symbolic function of naming; passive vocabulary grows.
13 to 14	Uses more elaborate and symbolic gestures.
16 to 24	Learns many new words, expanding expressive vocabulary rapidly from about 50 words to as many as 400; uses verbs and adjectives.
18 to 24	Says first sentence (two words).
20	Uses fewer gestures; names more things.
20 to 22	Has comprehension spurt.
24	Uses many two-word phrases; no longer babbles; wants to talk.
30	Learns new words almost every day; speaks in combinations of three or more words; makes grammatical mistakes.
36	Says up to 1,000 words, 80 percent intelligible; makes some mistakes in syntax.

Sources: Bates, E., O'Connell, B., & Shore, C. (1987). Language and communication in infancy. In J.D. Osofsky (Ed.), *Handbook of infant development* (2nd ed., pp. 149–203). New York, NY: Wiley; Capute, A. J., Palmer, F. B., Shapiro, B. K., & Piermattie, L. A. (1987). Using language to track development. Patient Care, *21*(19), 60–70; Kuhl, P. K. (2004). Early language acquisition: Cracking the speech code. *Nature Reviews Neuroscience, 5*(11), 831–843; Lalonde, C. E., & Werker, J. F. (1995). Cognitive influences on cross-language speech perception in infancy. *Infant Behavior and Development, 18*(4), 459–475; Newman, J. (2005). Three-place predicates: A cognitive-linguistic perspective. *Language Sciences, 27*(2), 145–163.

Perceiving Language Sounds and Structure Imitation of language sounds requires the ability to perceive subtle differences between sounds. Infants' brains are wired for language. They seem to be preset to discriminate basic linguistic units, perceive linguistic patterns, and categorize them as similar or different (Kuhl, 2010).

Phonemes are the smallest units of sound in speech. For example, the word *dog* has three phonemes: the *d*, the *o*, and the *g* sound. Every language has its own unique phonology, or system of sounds, that are used in the production of speech. At first, infants can discriminate the sounds of any language. In time, however, exposure to a native language commits the brain's neural networks to further learning of the patterns of the infant's native language and constrains future learning of nonnative language patterns (Kuhl, 2011). This exposure can occur either prenatally or postnatally. If a mother speaks two languages regularly during pregnancy, her newborn baby will recognize both languages and be more interested in listening to speakers in the languages he or she was previously exposed to. Even more important, the baby will show differential responses to both languages, suggesting that even newborns have some understanding that two language systems are involved, and that they are sensitive not just to the overall sounds but to the patterns and rhythms that distinguish the two languages (Byers-Heinlein et al., 2010).

By 6 to 7 months, hearing babies have learned to recognize the phonemes used in their native language (Kuhl et al., 1992), and by 8 months they begin to lose sensitivity to phonemes that are not used in their native language (Gervain & Mehler, 2010). By the end of the 1st year, babies lose their sensitivity to sounds that are not part of the language or languages they usually hear spoken. This process begins earlier for vowels and later for consonants (Kuhl & Rivera-Gaxiola, 2008). The ability to discriminate native-language sounds at this age predicts individual differences in language abilities during the 2nd year (Tsao et al., 2004), whereas nonnative sound discrimination does not (Kuhl et al., 2005). The increased sensitivity to native sounds helps the child more efficiently acquire language. Interestingly, analogous processes occur in deaf children with gestures (Kuhl & Rivera-Gaxiola, 2008).

How does this change occur? One hypothesis is that infants mentally compute the relative frequency of particular phonetic sequences in their language and learn to ignore sequences they infrequently hear (Werker et al., 2012; Kuhl, 2004). Another hypothesis is that early language experience modifies neural structures, facilitating detection of word patterns in the native language while suppressing attention to nonnative patterns that would slow native language learning. In support of this, toddlers who at 7½ months had shown better neural discrimination of native phonemes were more advanced in word production and sentence complexity at 24 months and at 30 months than toddlers who, at 7½ months, had been better able to discriminate phonetic contrasts in nonnative languages (Kuhl & Rivera-Gaxiola, 2008).

In addition to learning what the phonemes in their language are, babies also learn the rules for how they fit together. For example, in English, the sound combination in "kib" is acceptable, although "kib" is not a word. However, the nonsense word "bnik" breaks the phonological rules in English as a "b" and an "n" are not typically found next to each other within the same word. Between 6 and 12 months, babies begin to become aware of the phonological rules of their language. Research with infants supports this and suggests that they may have a mechanism for discerning abstract rules of sentence structure. Moreover, as they learn the intonation patterns and syntactical rules of language, they use their emerging knowledge to help them learn new words. For example, knowledge of the syntactical structure of "I'm VERBing it" might help them learn new verbs (Erickson & Thiessen, 2015).

Cultural Differences in Perceptual Development A less well-studied aspect of language development involves the developmental progression of infants learning tonal languages. This is surprising given the majority of world languages are tonal in nature (Singh & Fu, 2016). In tonal languages, a word can assume different meanings based on the pitch used when speaking it. For example, Thai has five different lexical tones (low, mid, high, rising, and falling), and the tone used when speaking a word changes its meaning (Kitamura et al., 2014). Many aspects of learning this type of language mirror learning in nontonal languages, but culture still exerts an effect.

Although calibrated perception for phonemes used in a baby's native language emerges at about 6 to 12 months of age, a similar language-specific perception for tone appears to emerge even earlier. In one experiment, 4-month-old babies raised in English-speaking homes were able to recognize tonal contrasts, but at 9 months were unable to do so. Cantonese and Thai babies, who were learning a tonal language, retained their ability to discriminate tonal contrasts over this time period (Yeung et al., 2013). However, nontonal learning infants' tonal sensitivity rebounds at about 17 to 18 months. It appears as if their increasing sensitivity to prosodic features of speech may be responsible. As nontonal language children learn more about the

At about a year of age, most babies will spontaneously start pointing at objects to direct the attention of others. Photodisc/Getty Images

How babies are raised influences their use of gestures. Mayan babies, who are often carried on their mothers' backs and hence have less direct social interaction, tend to gesture less than babies from other cultures. meunierd/Shutterstock

social context of speech and the nonverbal information that is relayed by vocal tone, they may once again direct their attention to pitch and thus regain some sensitivity (Liu & Kager, 2014).

As with other aspects of language, these early experiences appear to shape the brain architecture along culturally prescribed paths. Brain scans showed that neurons in the auditory portion of the brain stems of adult speakers of Mandarin and Thai were more sensitive to changes in pitch than were those of English speakers (Krishnan et al., 2010)

Gestures Before babies can speak, they point (Liszkowski et al., 2008). Pointing is important to language acquisition, and indeed pointing and later language development are correlated (Colonnesi et al., 2010). By using gestures, babies show an understanding that symbols refer to specific objects, events, desires, and conditions.

By 12 months, most babies have learned some *conventional social gestures;* for example, waving bye-bye, nodding the head for "yes," and shaking the head for "no." By about 13 months, they use more elaborate *representational gestures;* for example, holding an empty cup to the mouth to indicate thirst. *Symbolic gestures,* such as blowing to mean "hot" or sniffing to mean "flower," often emerge around the same time that babies say their first words. Toddlers often combine gestures with words. Gesture-word combinations serve as a signal that a child is about to begin using multiword sentences (Goldin-Meadow, 2007). Girls show a developmental advantage and use gestures at a slightly earlier age than do boys (Ozcaliskan & Goldin-Meadow, 2010).

Generally, research has found infants across all cultures use gestures and the use of gestures increases with age. Gestures usually appear before children have a vocabulary of 25 words and drop out when children learn the word for the idea they were gesturing (Lock et al., 1990).

However, culture influences the particular form those gestures take. For example, children in the United States and Germany are more likely to use gestures such as reaching, pointing, showing, holding their arms out to be picked up, or "stop." By contrast, babies in Taiwan are more likely to sign "quiet." These differences reflect cultural values, and they increase with age (Kwon et al., 2018). Italian babies, whose parents gesture more than American babies, use more spontaneous signs than do babies from the United States (Iverson et al., 2008). A comparison of three cultural groups found that the degree of direct social interaction was the key predictor for the development of gestures. Mayan infants, who had the least direct social interaction, gestured the least, followed by Dutch children. Chinese infants had the greatest degree of social interaction and also the most and earliest gestures (Salomo & Liszkowski, 2013). Just as spoken language does, gestures also impart important cultural information.

First Words Long before infants can connect sounds to meanings, they learn to recognize sound patterns they hear frequently, such as their name. Infants 5 months old listen longer to their name than to other names (Newman, 2005). Babies also understand many words before they can use them. Six-month-olds are more likely to look at a video of a bear when they hear the word "bear" than when they hear the word "dog" (Bergelson & Swingley, 2015). Infants at 8 months or younger start discerning perceptual cues such as syllables that usually occur together (such as *ba* and *by*) and store these possible word forms in memory. They also notice pronunciation, stress placed on syllables, and changes in pitch. This early auditory learning lays the foundation for vocabulary growth (Swingley, 2008).

The average baby says a first word sometime between 10 and 14 months, initiating **linguistic speech**—verbal expression that conveys meaning. At about 10 months, infants tend to assume a new word refers to whatever object they find most interesting, whether or not the name is correct. At 12 months, they begin to pay attention to cues from adults, such as looking or pointing at an object while saying its name.

linguistic speech
Verbal expression designed to convey meaning.

Around this time, most children understand that a word stands for a specific thing or event, and they can quickly learn the meaning of a new word (Woodward et al., 1994; Gurteen et al., 2011). Additionally, they may use a single syllable, known as a **holophrase**, to mean more than one thing depending on the context or vocal intonation. For example, "Da!" may mean "I want Daddy now!" and "Da?" may mean "Where is Daddy?" (Bruner, 1974).

By 18 to 24 months, children follow social cues in learning words, regardless of the intrinsic interest of the objects (Golinkoff & Hirsh-Pasek, 2006; Pruden et al., 2006). At 24 months, children quickly recognize names of familiar objects in the absence of visual cues (Swingley & Fernald, 2002). Additionally, if presented with a familiar object and novel object, 24-month-old children will assume a novel term refers to the novel object and quickly learn and remember that term (Spiegel & Halberda, 2011).

Receptive vocabulary—what infants understand—continues to grow as verbal comprehension gradually becomes faster and more accurate and efficient (Fernald et al., 2006). Generally, infants have a far greater receptive vocabulary than an expressive—or spoken—vocabulary. By 18 months, 3 out of 4 children can understand 150 words and can say 50 of them (Kuhl, 2004). Children with larger vocabularies and quicker reaction times can recognize spoken words from just the first part of the word. For example, when they hear "daw" or "ki," they will point to a picture of a dog or kitten (Fernald et al., 2001). This early language learning is closely related to later cognitive development. Late talkers who are quick to recognize words at 18 months are more likely to show accelerated vocabulary growth in the next year than those who are slower at word recognition (Fernald & Marchman, 2012), and children's speed of recognition of spoken words and vocabulary size at 25 months predict linguistic and cognitive skills at 8 years (Marchman & Fernald, 2008).

Addition of new words to the *expressive* (spoken) *vocabulary* is slow at first. Then, sometime between 16 and 24 months, a "naming explosion" may occur (Ganger & Brent, 2004). Within a few months, many toddlers go from saying about 50 words to saying several hundred (Samuelson & McMurray, 2017). Rapid gains in spoken vocabulary reflect increases in speed and accuracy of word recognition during the 2nd year (Fernald et al., 2006). Children also use their growing knowledge of syntax to puzzle out word meaning (Fisher et al., 2010) as well as an understanding that things belong in categories (Samuelson & McMurray, 2017).

Nouns seem to be the easiest type of word to learn, perhaps because it is easier to form a mental image of nouns (McDonough et al., 2011). In a cross-cultural study, Spanish, Dutch, French, Hebrew, Italian, Korean, and U.S. parents all reported that their 20-month-old children knew more nouns than any other class of words (Bornstein et al., 2004). A similar advantage has emerged for nouns in laboratory studies where children have been taught novel nouns and verbs (Imai et al., 2008). Generally, research has shown that across different languages, children are consistently adept at quickly and easily learning nouns. However, when learning novel verbs, children have a more difficult time. Children tend to learn verbs most easily in languages in which surrounding noun phrases are explicitly mentioned ("The girl is petting the dog"), and they have a more difficult time mapping meaning to verbs when the surrounding verb phrases are dropped ("She's petting it") (Waxman et al., 2013).

First Sentences The next important linguistic breakthrough comes when a toddler puts two words together to express one idea ("Want juice"). Generally, children do this between 18 and 24 months. However, this age range varies greatly.

A child's first sentences typically deal with everyday events, things, people, or activities. Children typically use **telegraphic speech,** consisting of only a few essential words. When Lamaya says, "go outside," she means, "Let's go outside."

Sometime between 20 and 30 months, children become more comfortable with articles (*a, the*), prepositions (*in, on*), conjunctions (*and, but*), plurals, verb forms, and forms of the verb *to be* (*am, are, is*). They also become increasingly aware of the communicative purpose of speech and of whether their words are being understood (Dunham et al., 2000)—a sign of growing sensitivity to the mental lives of others. By age 3,

holophrase
Single word that conveys a complete thought.

telegraphic speech
Early form of sentence use consisting of only a few essential words.

speech is fluent, longer, and more complex. In the third year of life, the average child's sentence will be approximately three or four words long (Rice et al., 2010).

CHARACTERISTICS OF EARLY SPEECH

Early speech has a character all its own, no matter what language a child is speaking (Slobin, 1990). As we have seen, young children *simplify*. They use telegraphic speech to say just enough to get their meaning across ("No drink milk!").

Young children *understand grammatical relationships they cannot yet express.* The rules of language are known as **syntax** and children illustrate their knowledge of them with their word use. For example, Nina understands that a dog is chasing a cat but does not yet produce multiple-word sentences easily, so her sentence comes out as "Puppy chase" rather than "The puppy is chasing the kitty." She does not say "kitty chase." The order of the words shows she understands the underlying syntactic rules.

Children also make mistakes with respect to what category a word describes by either underextending or overextending word meaning. When they *underextend word meanings,* they use words in too narrow of a category. For example, Amalia knows their family pet is a "doggy." However, she shakes her head no when her mother points out other dogs outside their home. To her, her dog, and *only* her dog, is a "doggy." Amalia is underextending the word *doggy* by restricting it to only her pet.

Alternatively, children also *overextend word meanings* by using words in too broad of a category. At 14 months, Amir jumped in excitement at the sight of a gray-haired man on the television screen and shouted, "Gampa!" Amir was overgeneralizing, or overextending, a word. He thought that because his grandfather had gray hair, all gray-haired men could be called "Grandpa."

Young children also *overregularize rules.* Overregularization is a language error, but it nonetheless illustrates children's growing knowledge of syntax. It occurs when children inappropriately apply a syntactical rule. For instance, when children say sentences such as "Daddy goed to the store" or "I drawed that," they are applying the English language rule "add *-ed* to a verb to make it past tense." It takes a while for children to learn the rule as well as the exceptions to it. For example, children commonly use the exceptions to the rule first. They generally learn these by rote for phrases they commonly hear ("Daddy went to the store"). Then they learn the rule and use that to fill in the blanks when they can't recall the exception ("Daddy goed to the store"). By early school age, as they become more proficient in language, they memorize the exceptions and begin to apply them, once again saying the phrase correctly ("Daddy went to the store").

VARIATIONS IN LANGUAGE DEVELOPMENT

Deaf babies seem to learn sign language in much the same fashion and in the same sequence as hearing infants learn speech, providing they are raised in a language-rich environment (Lederberg et al., 2013). Just as hearing babies of hearing parents imitate vocal utterances, deaf babies of deaf parents seem to imitate the sign language they see their parents using, first stringing together meaningless motions and then repeating them over and over in what has been called hand-babbling. As parents reinforce these gestures, the babies attach meaning to them (Petitto & Marentette, 1991; Petitto et al., 2001).

Deaf babies begin hand-babbling between age 7 and 10 months, about the age when hearing infants begin voice-babbling (Petitto et al., 2001). Deaf babies also begin to use sentences in sign language about the same time that hearing babies begin to speak in sentences (Meier, 1991). These observations suggest that an inborn language capacity may underlie the acquisition of both spoken and signed language and that advances in both kinds of language are tied to brain maturation (Kuhl, 2010).

In households where more than one language is spoken, babies achieve similar milestones in each language on the same schedule as children who hear only one language (Petitto & Kovelman, 2003). However, children learning two languages tend to have smaller vocabularies in each language than children learning only one language

syntax
Rules for forming sentences in a particular language.

(Hoff, 2006). Although they may have smaller vocabularies, they show advantages in other areas. Bilingual children tend to have more advanced nonverbal executive control skills, theory of mind, and an earlier understanding of syntactical and morphological rules of language (Barac et al., 2014).

Bilingual children often use elements of both languages, sometimes in the same utterance—a phenomenon called **code mixing** (Petitto & Kovelman, 2003). In Montreal, children as young as 2 in dual-language households differentiate between the two languages, using French with a French-speaking parent and English with an English-speaking parent (Genesee et al., 1995). This ability to shift from one language to another is called **code switching.**

code mixing
Use of elements of two languages, sometimes in the same utterance, by young children in households where both languages are spoken.

code switching
Changing one's speech to match the situation, as in people who are bilingual.

INFLUENCES ON EARLY LANGUAGE DEVELOPMENT

What determines how quickly and how well children learn to understand and use language? Research has focused on both neurological and environmental influences.

Brain Development Our brains have structures that have been shown to be directly implicated in language use (Friederici, 2011). A newborn's cries are controlled by the *brain stem* and *pons,* the most primitive parts of the brain and the earliest to develop. Repetitive babbling may emerge with the maturation of parts of the *motor cortex*, which controls movements of the face and larynx (Imada et al., 2006).

How effectively various brain systems develop has implications for later language development. For example, newborn babies who showed more activity in the parietal regions of the brain had better declarative memory and auditory comprehension at 15 months (Brito et al., 2016). Similarly, babies who were better at processing auditory information at 6 weeks of age, as indexed by brain activity, were more advanced in their language development at 9 months of age (Chonchaiya et al., 2013). A link also exists between the brain's phonetic perception and motor systems as early as 6 months—a connection that becomes even stronger at 6 to 12 months (Imada et al., 2006).

Brain scans also confirm the sequence of vocabulary development outlined earlier in this chapter. In toddlers with large vocabularies, brain activation focuses on the left temporal and parietal lobes, whereas in toddlers with smaller vocabularies, brain activation is more scattered (Kuhl & Rivera-Gaxiola, 2008). Cortical regions associated with language continue to develop until at least the late preschool years or beyond—some even until adulthood.

In many ways, the brains of young children, even before they begin to speak, process language similarly to adult brains. For example, both infants and adults process speech sounds in parallel and hierarchical streams. In other words, they process multiple features of speech (e.g., who the speaker is, emotion, intensity, sound, timbre, familiarity) across multiple brain regions. Additionally, frontal brain regions are involved in the processing of speech in infants as they are in adults, although in infants this process is slower. Last, the processing of linguistic information is localized in the left hemisphere in infants as it is in almost all adults (Dehaene-Lambertz, 2017; Dehaene-Lambertz & Spelke, 2015).

Social Interaction Language is a social act. Language takes not only the necessary biological machinery and cognitive capacity but also interaction with a live communicative partner. Children who grow up without normal social contact do not develop language normally. Neither do children who are exposed to language only through television. For example, in one experiment, 9-month-old English-speaking infants learned and retained Mandarin when they played and interacted with adults speaking

Is linguistic ability learned or inborn? Though inborn language capacity may underlie this baby's ability to speak, when this mother repeats the sounds her baby makes, she is reinforcing the likelihood the baby will repeat those sounds—highlighting the influences of both nature and nurture. Jani Bryson/E+/Getty Images

window on the world

CHILDREN'S BOOKS AS SOCIALIZATION TOOLS

Most babies love to be read to. The frequency with which caregivers read to them can influence how well children speak and eventually how well and how soon they develop **literacy**—the ability to read and write. Reading to children improves their language skills and cognitive abilities, encourages creativity, and promotes social, emotional, and moral development (Crippen, 2017).

Books are also important cultural socialization tools. Through the themes and characters and plot lines, children are taught important cultural scripts and ideals. For example, one analysis of 145 Chinese children's stories showed that traditional Chinese cultural values such as harmony with nature, conformity, harmonious personal relationships, stoicism, and respect for the elderly were prominent (Zhang & Morrison, 2010).

Because different cultures have different values, books that hail from different places vary in their themes. For example, one study comparing American, Indonesian, and Japanese children's books found that, in line with cultural ideals of collectivism and individualism, Japanese books contained more challenge events for characters than Indonesian books, but fewer of those challenges were internal when compared to the American books. In the Japanese books, more of the challenges were solved individually, whereas in the American books, assistance was often sought from others (Suprawati et al., 2014). Sometimes the messages are not transmitted in the words themselves but are in the accompanying images. For instance, a comparison of best-selling storybooks in the United States and Taiwan showed that although characters in all books smiled an equivalent amount of time, the American books had pictures of characters with wider smiles and engaged in more exciting activities (Tsai et al., 2007).

Because children love to be read to, the transmission of cultural ideals becomes not a lecture on morality, but a nurturing, shared activity engaged in by choice. Thus, it is an ideal place for socialization processes.

what's your view

What was your favorite children's book? What lessons did you learn from reading this book? Do you still follow those lessons today?

---

literacy
(1) Ability to read and write. (2) In an adult, ability to use printed and written information to function in society, achieve goals, and develop knowledge and potential.

Mandarin, but not when they merely watched television in Mandarin (Kuhl & Rivera-Gaxiola, 2008). A series of experiments on baby vocabulary videos showed that infants and toddlers did not learn new words from videos (DeLoache et al., 2010; Richert et al., 2010), even when researchers made sure the infants were paying attention to the content of the video (Krcmar, 2011). It was not the video that is at fault; rather, it was the lack of contingent social interaction that impeded learning. When infants engage in socially contingent video chats, they are able to learn new words (Roseberry et al., 2014).

As Bronfenbrenner's bioecological model would predict, the age of caregivers, the way they interact with an infant, child care experience, and, later, schooling, peers, and television exposure all affect the course of language acquisition. At the babbling stage, adults help an infant advance toward true speech by repeating the sounds the baby makes and rewarding her efforts. The baby finds this imitation engaging and soon joins in the game, repeating the sounds back. Parents' imitation of babies' sounds affects the amount of infant vocalization (Goldstein et al., 2003) and the pace of language learning (Schmitt et al., 2011). It also helps babies experience the social aspect of speech (Kuhl, 2004).

Later, a strong relationship exists between the frequency of specific words in mothers' speech and the order in which children learn these words (Brent & Siskind, 2001) as well as between mothers' talkativeness and the size of toddlers' vocabularies (Schmitt et al., 2011). The milestones of language development described in this chapter are typical of Western, middle-class children who are spoken to directly. They are not necessarily typical in all cultures, nor at all socioeconomic levels (Hoff, 2006). Mothers with higher socioeconomic status tend to use richer vocabularies and longer utterances, and their 2-year-olds have larger spoken vocabularies (Hoff, 2003; Ramey & Ramey, 2003; Rowe, 2012). By age 3, vocabularies of low-income children vary greatly, depending in part on the diversity of word types they have heard their mothers use (Pan et al., 2005) as well as their joint activities, shared routines, and connectedness (Hirsh-Pasek et al., 2015).

Child-Directed Speech If, when you talk to an infant or toddler, you speak slowly in a singsong, high-pitched voice with exaggerated ups and downs, simplify your speech, exaggerate vowel sounds, and use short words and sentences and repetition, you are engaging in **child-directed speech (CDS),** sometimes called *parentese, motherese,* or *baby talk.* Most adults and even children do it naturally, and other babyish stimuli, such as puppies or kittens, also can elicit it. Such baby talk has been documented in many languages and cultures including the United States, Russia, Sweden, Australia, Thailand, Spain, Syria, England, Italy, France, Germany, and others (Kuhl et al., 1997; Kitamura et al., 2001; Cooper & Asling, 1990; Ferguson,1964).

> **child-directed speech (CDS)**
> Form of speech often used in talking to babies or toddlers; includes slow, simplified speech, a high-pitched tone, exaggerated vowel sounds, short words and sentences, and much repetition; also called parentese or motherese.

Infants, even before a month of age, clearly prefer to hear CDS (Dunst et al., 2012; Cooper & Aslin, 1990; Kuhl et al., 1997). This may be a key feature of its function: Infants are "captured" attentionally by the sound and find it highly engaging, resulting in more rapid learning (Golinkoff et al., 2015). For example, infants who experienced more CDS had larger expressive vocabularies at 2 years of age and seemed to be more adept at processing language (Weisleder & Fernald, 2013). Laboratory data also highlight the support that CDS provides. For example, 21-month-old children were able to learn new words only when CDS speech was used. However, 27-month-old children, who were more sophisticated in their language abilities, were able to use adult-directed speech to learn new words (Ma et al., 2011).

What about cultural differences? As with adults in nontonal languages, CDS is used by adults who speak tonal languages where word meaning is transmitted in part via tone. However, a more constrained pitch range is used (Kitamura et al., 2014). In some cultures, young children are simply not spoken to very much. For instance, among the Tsimané forager-horticulturalists of Bolivia, children under the age of 4 receive less than one minute of one-on-one verbal interaction per hour (Cristia et al., 2019). Similarly, Gusii mothers of Kenya, although they are highly responsive physically to their infants and hold and cuddle them when they are upset, tend not to speak to or make eye contact with them to the same degree as American parents (Richman et al., 2010). Regardless of their exposure, however, all babies learn to talk. Moreover, even if babies are not spoken to directly, they are nonetheless immersed in a rich linguistic environment that feeds their hungry minds and shapes their developing intellect.

summary and key terms

Cognitive Development: Six Approaches

- Six approaches to the study of cognitive development are behaviorist, psychometric, Piagetian, information-processing, cognitive neuroscience, and social-contextual.

  behaviorist approach, psychometric approach, Piagetian approach, information-processing approach, cognitive neuroscience approach, social-contextual approach

Behaviorist Approach

- Two simple types of learning that behaviorists study are classical conditioning and operant conditioning.
- Rovee-Collier's research suggests that infants' memory processes are much like those of adults.

  classical conditioning, operant conditioning

Psychometric Approach

- Psychometric tests measure factors presumed to make up intelligence.
- Developmental tests, such as the Bayley Scales of Infant and Toddler Development, can indicate current functioning but are generally poor predictors of later intelligence.
- The home environment may affect measured intelligence.

intelligent behavior, IQ (intelligence quotient) tests, Bayley Scales of Infant and Toddler Development, Home Observation for Measurement of the Environment (HOME), early intervention

Piagetian Approach

- During Piaget's sensorimotor stage, infants' schemes become more elaborate. They progress from primary to secondary to tertiary circular reactions and finally to the development of representational ability, which makes possible deferred imitation, pretending, and problem solving.
- Object permanence develops gradually, according to Piaget, and is not fully operational until 18 to 24 months.
- Research suggests that a number of abilities, including imitation and object permanence, develop earlier than Piaget described.

sensorimotor stage, schemes, circular reactions, representational ability, visible imitation, invisible imitation, deferred imitation, object permanence, dual representation hypothesis

Information-Processing Approach

- Information-processing researchers measure mental processes through habituation and other signs of visual and perceptual abilities.
- Indicators of the efficiency of infants' information processing, such as speed of habituation, tend to predict later intelligence.
- Information-processing research techniques such as habituation, novelty preference, and the violation-of-expectations method have yielded evidence that infants as young as 3 to 6 months may have a rudimentary grasp of such Piagetian abilities as categorization, causality, object permanence, a sense of number, and an ability to reason about characteristics of the physical world.
- Some researchers suggest that infants may have innate learning mechanisms for acquiring such knowledge.

habituation, dishabituation, visual preference, visual recognition memory, cross-modal transfer, violation of expectations

Cognitive Neuroscience Approach

- Explicit memory and implicit memory are located in different brain structures.
- Working memory emerges between 6 and 12 months of age.
- Neurological developments help explain the emergence of Piagetian skills and memory abilities.

implicit memory, explicit memory, working memory

Social-Contextual Approach

- Social interactions with adults contribute to cognitive competence through shared activities that help children learn skills, knowledge, and values important in their culture.

guided participation

Language Development

- The acquisition of language is an important aspect of cognitive development.
- Two classic theoretical views about how children acquire language are learning theory and nativism. Today, most developmental scientists hold that an inborn capacity to learn language may be activated or constrained by experience.
- Prelinguistic speech includes crying, cooing, babbling, and imitating language sounds. By 6 months, babies have learned the basic sounds of their language and have begun to link sound with meaning. Perception of categories of sounds in the native language may commit the neural circuitry to further learning in that language only.
- Before they say their first word, babies use gestures.
- The first word typically comes sometime between 10 and 14 months. For many toddlers, a naming explosion occurs sometime between 16 and 24 months.
- The first brief sentences generally come between 18 and 24 months. By age 3, syntax and communicative abilities are fairly well developed.
- Early speech is characterized by oversimplification, underextending and overextending word meanings, and overregularizing rules.
- Influences on language development include neural maturation and social interaction.
- Family characteristics, such as socioeconomic status, adult language use, and maternal responsiveness, affect a child's vocabulary development.
- Child-directed speech (CDS) seems to have cognitive, emotional, and social benefits, and infants prefer it.

language, nativism, language acquisition device (LAD), prelinguistic speech, linguistic speech, holophrase, telegraphic speech, syntax, code mixing, code switching, literacy child-directed speech (CDS),

Psychosocial Development during the First Three Years

chapter 6

TerryJ/iStock/Getty Images

learning objectives

Discuss the development of emotions and personality in infancy.

Describe infants' social relationships with caregivers, including attachment.

Discuss the emerging sense of self, autonomy, and moral development in toddlerhood.

Explain how social contexts influence early development.

Explain child maltreatment and its effects.

In this chapter, we examine foundations of psychosocial development and consider Erikson's views about the development of trust and autonomy. We look at relationships with caregivers, the emerging sense of self, and the foundations of conscience. We explore relationships with siblings and other children and consider the impact of parental employment and early child care. Finally, we discuss child maltreatment and what can be done to protect children from harm.

Foundations of Psychosocial Development

Although babies share common patterns of development, from the start each shows a distinct set of behavioral tendencies, known as temperament. One baby may usually be cheerful; another easily upset. One toddler plays happily with other children; another prefers to play alone. Eventually, temperament becomes what we think of as **personality:** the relatively consistent blend of emotions, thought, and behavior that makes each person unique. From infancy on, personality development is intertwined with social relationships; this combination is called *psychosocial development.* See Table 6.1 for highlights of psychosocial development during the first 3 years.

personality
The relatively consistent blend of emotions, temperament, thought, and behavior that makes a person unique.

EMOTIONS

Emotions, such as fear, anger, or joy, are subjective reactions to experience that are associated with physiological and behavioral changes. For example, the subjective feeling of fear is associated with changes in heart rate, breathing, and startle response. A person's characteristic pattern of emotional reactions begins to develop during infancy and is a basic element of personality. People differ in how often and how strongly they feel a particular emotion, in the kinds of events that may produce it, in the physical manifestations they show, and in how they act as a result. Culture, too, influences the way people feel about a situation and the way they show their emotions. Some cultures that stress social harmony, including those in Asia, Germany, and Israel, discourage open expressions of anger. When expressions of anger do occur, they seem to draw notice. The opposite is often true in cultures such as the United States and Greece, which stress self-expression, self-assertion, and self-esteem, and where emotions such as sadness garner more attention (Hareli et al., 2015; Cole et al., 2002).

emotions
Subjective reactions to experience that are associated with physiological and behavioral changes.

Crying Crying is the earliest and most powerful way infants can communicate their needs. There are four patterns of crying (Wolff, 1969): the basic *hunger cry* (a rhythmic cry), the *angry cry* (a variation of the rhythmic cry, in which excess air is forced through the vocal cords), the *pain cry* (a sudden onset of loud crying, sometimes followed by holding the breath), and the *frustration cry* (two or three drawn-out cries, with no prolonged breath-holding) (Wood & Gustafson, 2001).

TABLE 6.1 Highlights of Psychosocial Development, Birth to 36 Months	
Approximate Age, Months	**Characteristics**
0–3	Infants show interest and curiosity, and they smile readily at people.
3–6	Infants can anticipate events and may become angry when disappointed. They smile, coo, and laugh. Reciprocal exchanges between the baby and the caregiver begin.
6–9	Infants play social games and elicit responses from people. They talk to and touch other babies. They show joy, fear, anger, and surprise.
9–12	Infants become attached to their primary caregiver and may become afraid of strangers and new situations.
12–18	Toddlers explore their environment, using attachment figures as a secure base. As they master the environment, they become more confident.
18–36	Toddlers sometimes become anxious at longer separations from caregivers. They engage in fantasy within their increasingly sophisticated play and may identify with adults.

Source: Sroufe, L. A. (1979). Socioemotional development. In J. Osofsky (Ed.), *Handbook of infant development* (pp. 462–516). New York, NY: Wiley.

Features of infants' cries are related to their physiological state. A higher pitch and a more monotonic vocalization is associated with autonomic system activity during stressful procedures in infants (Stewart et al., 2013) and is more characteristic of the cries of preterm infants, who generally have higher needs, than full- term infants of the equivalent age (Shinya et al., 2016). Additionally, developmental changes in cry frequency appear to be universal. A meta-analysis conducted across a number of countries, including the United States, Japan, Germany, Denmark, Canada, the Netherlands, and the United Kingdom, showed high fuss and cry durations over the first 6 weeks of life, with crying significantly diminishing between 6 and 12 weeks of age (Wolke et al., 2017). This does not appear to be a function of living in developed countries, as a similar pattern has been found in the nomadic Kung of the Kalahari (Barr et al., 1991).

As children age, they begin to realize that crying serves a communicative function. By 5 months of age, babies have learned to monitor their caregivers' expressions, and if ignored they will first cry harder in an attempt to get attention and then stop crying if their attempt is unsuccessful (Goldstein et al., 2009). Boys and girls, as infants, show similar patterns of sadness and anger; however, by the toddler years, boys express more anger than girls (Chaplin & Aldao, 2013).

Some parents worry that picking up a crying baby will spoil the infant. However, this is not the case, especially when levels of distress are high. For example, if parents wait it may become more difficult to soothe the baby, and such a pattern, if experienced repeatedly, may interfere with an infant's developing ability to regulate his or her own emotional state (Thompson, 2011). Indeed, mothers' rapid and sensitive response to crying is associated with later social competence and positive adjustment, regardless of whether or not babies cry frequently or rarely (Leerkes et al., 2009).

Smiling and Laughing The earliest faint smiles occur spontaneously soon after birth, often during REM sleep, apparently as a result of subcortical nervous system activity.

Social smiling, when newborn infants gaze at their parents and smile at them, develops during the 2nd month of life. Babies generally start using a social smile at the same time and in the same way regardless of culture. However, by 12 weeks of age, infants smile at others more or less frequently depending on the responses of adults around them (Wörmann et al., 2012). Laughter becomes more common between 4 and 12 months (Salkind, 2005).

Parents often try to elicit smiles and laughs from their young children by clowning. Clowning includes silly, nonverbal behaviors such as odd facial expressions or sounds, actions like revealing a usually hidden body part (such as a belly button), and imitating another's odd actions. Babies try to join in the humor starting at 3 months of age, by shrieking or making faces (Mireault et al., 2012). Babies' humor gradually becomes more complex with age. A 6-month-old may giggle in response to the mother making unusual sounds or appearing with a towel over her face; a 10-month-old may laughingly try to put the towel back on her face when it falls off. This reflects cognitive development: By laughing at the unexpected, babies show that they know what to expect; by turning the tables, they show awareness that they can make things happen (Sroufe, 1997).

Anticipatory smiling—in which infants smile at an object and then gaze at an adult while continuing to smile—rises sharply between 8 and 10 months and seems to be among the first types of communication in which the infant refers to an object or experience. By 12 to 15 months, infants are intentionally communicating to the partner about objects.

The Differentiation of Emotions Emotional development is an orderly process; complex emotions unfold from simpler ones. According to one model (Lewis, 1997; Figure 6.1), babies show signs of contentment, interest, and distress soon after birth. These are diffuse, reflexive, mostly physiological responses to sensory stimulation or internal processes. During the next 6 months or so, these early emotional states differentiate into true emotions: joy, surprise, sadness, disgust, and then anger and fear.

Crying is the most powerful way that babies can communicate their needs. Parents learn to recognize whether their baby is crying because of hunger, anger, frustration, or pain.
Tatiana Dyuvbanova/EyeEm/Getty Images

social smiling
Beginning in the 2nd month, newborn infants gaze at their parents and smile at them, signaling positive participation in the relationship.

anticipatory smiling
Infant smiles at an object and then gazes at an adult while still smiling.

FIGURE 6.1
Differentiation of Emotions during the First 3 Years

The primary, or basic, emotions emerge during the first 6 months or so; the self-conscious emotions develop beginning in the 2nd year, as a result of the emergence of self-awareness together with accumulation of knowledge about societal standards. Note: There are two kinds of embarrassment. The earlier kind is more often a response to being singled out as the object of attention. The later kind involves the evaluation of behavior by others.

Source: Lewis, M. (1997). "The self in self-conscious emotions." In S. G. Snodgrass & R. L. Thompson (Eds.), *The self across psychology: Self-recognition, self-awareness, and the self-concept: Vol. 818.* New York, NY: New York Academy of Sciences.

(top): Frare/Davis Photography/Brand X Pictures/Corbis; (middle): Amos Morgan/Photodisc/Getty Images; (bottom): file404/Shutterstock

Contentment	Interest	Distress	
↓	↓	↓	**First 6 months**
Joy	Surprise	Sadness, disgust	
		↓	
		Anger, fear	

Embarrassment
Envy
Empathy

From 15 to 24 months

Embarrassment
Pride
Shame
Guilt

From 2½ to 3 years

Children who do not live up to behavioral standards may feel guilty and try to make amends. Guilt is thought to develop between ages 2½ and 3.
enterphoto/Shutterstock

Self-conscious emotions, such as embarrassment, empathy, and envy, arise only after children have developed **self-awareness:** the cognitive understanding that they have an identity that is separate and different from others. This consciousness of self emerges between 15 and 24 months.

By about age 3, having acquired self-awareness plus knowledge about their society's accepted standards, rules, and goals, children become better able to evaluate their own thoughts, plans, desires, and behavior against what is considered socially appropriate. Only then can they demonstrate the **self-evaluative emotions** of pride, guilt, and shame (Lewis, 1995, 1997, 1998, 2007).

Altruistic Helping and Empathy A guest of 18-month-old Alex's father dropped his pen on the floor, and it rolled under a cabinet. Alex crawled under the cabinet, retrieved the pen, and gave it to the guest. By acting out of concern for a stranger with no expectation of reward, Alex showed **altruistic behavior** (Warneken & Tomasello, 2006).

The roots of altruism can be seen in early empathic reactions in infancy. For example, infants at 1, 3, 6, and 9 months of age respond to the cries of other infants with cries of their own and facial expressions of distress (Geangu et al., 2010). At 6 and 12 months of age they respond to other infants' expressions of anger and distress with pupillary dilation, a sign consistent with emotional arousal (Geangu et al., 2011). Infants also form "opinions" about others on the basis of their social behaviors. In one series of experiments (Hamlin & Wynn, 2011), infants watched as a puppet tried to open a box. In one condition, a second "opener" puppet helped the first puppet open the box, and in another condition a "closer" puppet interfered by jumping on the box to slam it shut. When later given the choice, 3-month-old infants preferred to look at and 5-month-old infants preferred to reach for the "opener" puppet.

Altruistic behavior seems to come naturally to toddlers. At 12 months, infants spontaneously help an adult reach or find a toy that has fallen out of reach. By 15 months of age, infants also have expectations about fairness, as illustrated by their tendency to stare longer at an unfair distribution of goods than to an equal distribution. Moreover, those infants who looked the longest at the unequal sharing were also more likely to themselves share toys later (Sommerville et al., 2013). Other research has also documented that well before the 2nd birthday, children are likely to help others, share belongings and food, and offer comfort at the distress of others (Dunfield et al., 2011; Warneken & Tomasello, 2008). Researchers (Cole et al., 1992) have concluded that such behavior may collectively reflect **empathy,** the ability to imagine how another person might feel in a particular situation.

Research in neurobiology has identified special brain cells called *mirror neurons,* which may underlie empathy and altruism. **Mirror neurons** fire not only when a person does something but also when he or she observes someone else doing the same thing. By "mirroring" the activities and motivations of others, they may help a person to see the world from someone else's point of view (Iacoboni, 2008; Iacoboni & Mazziotta, 2007; Oberman & Ramachandran, 2007). Infants also show similar sympathetic nervous system arousal when they help someone directly *and* when they see a third party doing the helping but not if the person is not helped (Hepach et al., 2012).

Some theorist doubt the conclusions that have been reached about mirror neurons. They point out, for example, that people sometimes feel empathy for others even without the action of mirror neurons. Moreover, they argue, despite its intrigue, the theory lacks direct empirical support (Lamm & Majdandzic, 2015).

Collaborative Activities and Cultural Transmission The motivation to help and share plus the ability to understand others' intentions contribute to an important development between 9 and 12 months of age—collaboration with caregivers in joint activities, such as a child passing a pair of socks to her mother to help while getting dressed in the morning. Collaborative activities increase during the 2nd year of life as toddlers become more adept at communication (Tomasello, 2007).

These types of interactions are quintessentially human. Although many of our closest relatives, such as chimpanzees, are able to communicate and learn from each other in impressive and sophisticated ways, they do not share with us our ability and motivation to engage in socially coordinated actions with shared goals. For example, young children engage in what is known as over-imitation, closely copying all actions they see an adult do, even if some of the actions are clearly irrelevant or impractical. Chimps, by contrast, will skip steps that don't accomplish anything (Nielsen & Tomaselli, 2010). Some researchers have argued that our universal propensity to engage in collaborative activities accounts for our impressive creation of cultural artifacts and institutions. In this view, our biologically shaped transmission of collaborative learning has led to our unique success as a species in this area (Tomasello & Moll, 2010).

TEMPERAMENT

From the very first day of life, all babies are unique. Some babies are fussy; others are happy and placid. Some are active; others lay calmly. Some babies like meeting new people; some shrink from contact.

Psychologists call these early individual differences **temperament.** Temperament can be defined as an early-appearing, biologically based tendency to respond to the environment in predictable ways. Temperament is closely linked to emotional responses to the environment, and many responses, such as smiles or cries, are emotional in nature. However, unlike emotions such as fear, excitement, and boredom, which come and go, temperament is relatively consistent and enduring. Individual differences in temperament, which are thought to derive from a person's basic biological makeup, form the core of the developing personality.

self-conscious emotions
Emotions, such as embarrassment, empathy, and envy, that depend on self-awareness.

self-awareness
Realization that one's existence and functioning are separate from those of other people and things.

self-evaluative emotions
Emotions, such as pride, shame, and guilt, that depend on both self-awareness and knowledge of socially accepted standards of behavior.

altruistic behavior
Activity intended to help another person with no expectation of reward.

empathy
Ability to put oneself in another person's place and feel what the other person feels.

mirror neurons
Neurons that fire when a person does something or observes someone else doing the same thing.

temperament
Characteristic disposition, or style of approaching and reacting to situations.

Studying Temperamental Patterns Longitudinal research on infant behavior and its later correlates has shown babies can be placed into one of three temperamental categories (Thomas, et al., 1968).

- Forty percent are **"easy" children**: generally happy, rhythmic in biological functioning, and accepting of new experiences.

- Ten percent are **"difficult" children**: more irritable and harder to please, irregular in biological functions and more intense in expressing emotions.

- Fifteen percent are **"slow-to-warm-up" children**: mild, but slow to adapt to new people and situations (Thomas & Chess, 1977, 1984).

Some children do not fit neatly into any of these three categories. A baby may eat and sleep regularly but be afraid of strangers. Another child may warm up slowly to new foods but adapt quickly to new babysitters (Thomas & Chess, 1984). A child may laugh intensely but not show intense frustration, and a child with rhythmic toilet habits may show irregular sleeping patterns (Rothbart et al., 2000). All these variations are normal.

Stability of Temperament From the beginning, babies show different patterns of sleeping, fussing, and activity, and these differences tend to persist to some degree (Bornstein et al., 2015). Studies have found strong links between infant temperament and childhood personality at age 7 (Rothbart et al., 2001). Similarly, researchers investigating positive emotionality, negative emotionality, and constraint (a dimension reflecting the tendency to behave in a controlled fashion) have found stability in these traits from toddlerhood to early childhood, and then from early childhood to middle childhood (Neppl et al., 2010).

Temperament is generally conceptualized as being inborn and influenced by genetics. That does not mean, however, that temperament is fully formed at birth or that the environment does not matter. Temperament develops as various emotions and self-regulatory capacities appear (Rothbart et al., 2000) and can change in response to parental treatment and other life experiences (Belsky et al., 1991; Kagan & Snidman, 2004). Current conceptions of temperament view it as being strongly influenced by genetics early in life, with greater influence wielded by the environment over time (Shiner et al., 2012).

Charlotte's habit of smiling at strangers and playing happily in a shopping cart are signs of her easy temperament. Ipatov/Shutterstock

Goodness of Fit According to the many researchers, the key to healthy adjustment is **goodness of fit**—the match between a child's temperament and the environmental demands and constraints the child must deal with. If a very active child is expected to sit still for long periods, if a slow-to-warm-up child is constantly pushed into new situations, or if a persistent child is constantly taken away from absorbing projects, tensions may occur.

Children also differ in their susceptibility to environmental influences. For example, infants with difficult or inflexible temperaments may be more sensitive to parenting than easier infants (Stright et al., 2008). They are at higher risk for both internalizing and externalizing disorders, as well as social and cognitive issues, but *only* when exposed to negative parenting (Slagt et al., 2016). Some research even suggests that children at risk as a result of temperamental characteristics may even show enhanced outcomes when compared with their lower risk peers, but in this case only in the presence of optimal parenting (Kochanska et al., 2015; Belsky & Pluess, 2009).

Behavioral Inhibition Temperament has a biological basis. One biologically based individual difference that has been identified is *behavioral inhibition.* Behavioral inhibition has to do with how boldly or cautiously a child approaches unfamiliar objects and situations (Kagan et al., 1984).

When babies high in behavioral inhibition are presented with a novel stimulus, they became physiologically aroused, pumping their arms and legs vigorously and often arching their backs. This feeling of overarousal is unpleasant for them, and most start to fuss and cry. Approximately 20 percent of babies respond in this way. The 40 percent of babies low in behavioral inhibition, however, show little distress or motor activity to novel stimuli and often calmly stare at it, sometimes with a smile (Kagan & Snidman, 2004).

These differences between babies are theorized to be the result of an underlying difference in physiology. The amygdala detects and reacts to unfamiliar events and, in the case of behaviorally inhibited children, responds vigorously and easily to most novel events (Kagan, 2012). Meta-analyses on brain differences between highly inhibited and uninhibited children has supported this finding and has additionally found greater activation in parts of the brain associated with the processing of novelty, threat, rewards, and inhibitory control. Specifically, this includes regions in the basal ganglia (the globus pallidus, putamen, and caudate) and the prefrontal cortex (the middle frontal gyrus) (Clauss et al., 2015). Moreover, children who are highly behaviorally inhibited tend to show greater right frontal EEG (electroencephalographic) asymmetry (Fox et al., 2001; Smith & Bell, 2010), a pattern that has been associated more broadly with a tendency toward retreat and withdrawal (Coan & Allen, 2004).

Infants who are identified as inhibited or uninhibited seemed to maintain these patterns over time (Kagan, 1997; Kagan & Snidman, 2004). Many highly inhibited infants remain so through the first two years of age (Fox et al., 2001). Inhibited toddlers are then likely to turn into shy 7-year-olds (Kagan et al., 1988), and behaviorally inhibited 8- to 12-year-old children are less likely as young adults to have a positive, active social life and more likely to live close to their family of origin in adulthood (Gest, 1997). Behavioral inhibition has also been associated with a heightened risk of developing a social anxiety disorder later in life (Clauss & Blackford, 2012). Not surprisingly, their amygdalae continue to respond in a vigorous and sustained fashion into adulthood (Blackford et al., 2010).

However, experience can moderate or accentuate early tendencies. Behaviorally inhibited children are more likely to outgrow their inhibition if parents do not completely shield them from new situations and instead provide gentle support and encouragement during anxiety-provoking situations (Kiel et al., 2016; Park et al., 1997), and they are no more likely to suffer from anxiety disorders if their mothers encourage independence but are not overly controlling (Lewis-Morrarty et al., 2012). Other environmental influences, such as culture, addressed in the following section, also can reinforce or soften a child's original temperament bias.

Cultural Influences on Temperament Culturally influenced child-rearing practices may influence temperament. For example, in the United States, individuality and assertiveness are valued. Research has shown that infants from the United States are rated by their parents as higher in activity level, vocalization, frustration, and pleasure than babies from both Italy and Norway, who are rated as more cuddly and easy to soothe (Montirosso et al., 2011; Cozzi et al., 2013; Sung et al., 2015). Similarly, American babies are rated as higher in positive affectivity and vocal reactivity than are babies from Japan and Russia, who tend to show more fear (Gartstein et al., 2010); they show higher extraversion and lower negative affectivity than Polish babies (Dragan et al., 2011); and they smile and laugh more than babies from Ethiopia, who show more negative emotionality and fear (Gartstein et al., 2016). The free expression of positive emotions and needs and the suppression of fearfulness are in line with the American cultural valuation of individuality and assertiveness.

Although the concept of goodness-of-fit is most commonly applied to the family environment, it can also be applied to the match between a child's temperament and cultural milieu. For example, in the seminomadic Maasai people of Kenya and Tanzania, infants with "difficult" temperaments are viewed positively. In the perilous subsistence conditions traditionally encountered by these infants, an active and fussy temperament is associated with enhanced survival, as infants such as these demand increased care. Rather than being a risk, "difficult temperament" is protective, especially during periods of drought or deprivation (deVries, 1994).

EARLY SOCIAL EXPERIENCE: THE FAMILY

Infant care practices and patterns of interaction within the family vary greatly around the world. In Bali, infants are believed to be ancestors or gods brought to life in human form and thus must be treated with utmost dignity and respect. The Beng of West Africa think young babies can understand all languages, whereas people in the Micronesian atoll of Ifaluk believe babies cannot understand language at all, and therefore adults do not speak to them (DeLoache & Gottlieb, 2000).

Among the Efe people of central Africa, infants typically receive care from multiple caregivers and are routinely breastfed by other women and the mother (Tronick et al., 1992). In Maori families in New Zealand, babies are the collective responsibility of the family and are cared for not just by their parents but also by siblings, aunts, and grandparents (Jones et al., 2017). In cultures where infant mortality is high, such as the Gusii in western Kenya (LeVine, 1994), and who are nomadic, such as the Aka hunter-gatherers in central Africa (Hewlett et al., 1998), parents keep their infants close to them, respond quickly when they cry, and feed them on demand. However, Ngandu farmers, who tend to live far apart and to stay in one place for long periods of time, are more likely to leave their infants alone and to let them fuss or cry, smile, vocalize, or play (Hewlett, et al., 1998).

This Maasai toddler's fussiness may be interpreted differently by adults in his culture, where difficult temperament is associated with a greater chance of survival. Keith Levit/Perspectives/Design Pics Inc/Alamy Stock Photo

Many of the patterns of adult-infant interaction are culture-based. There is wide diversity in family systems, even within the United States, where the number of nontraditional families, such as those headed by single parents, gay and lesbian couples, and grandparents, has increased in recent years (Spicer, 2010; Saddrudin et al., 2019). In families where both parents work and with single parents, separated or divorced parents, African American parents, and incomes exceeding $100,000 a year, children are more likely to be regularly cared for by someone other than their parents (Spicer, 2010).

Human infants have socioemotional needs that must be satisfied if they are to grow up typically. One of these needs is for a mother who responds warmly and promptly to the infant. Later in this chapter we discuss the mutual attachment between infants and mothers.

The fathering role is in many ways a social construction (Doherty et al., 1998), with different meanings in different cultures. The role may be taken or shared by someone other than the biological father: the mother's brother, as in Botswana, or a grandfather, as in Vietnam (Engle & Breaux, 1998; Richardson, 1995; Townsend, 1997). In some societies fathers are more involved in their young children's lives than in others.

Among the Huhot of Inner Mongolia, fathers traditionally are responsible for economic support and discipline and mothers for nurturing (Jankowiak, 1992). Men almost never hold infants. Fathers interact more with toddlers but perform child care duties only if the mother is absent. However, urbanization and maternal employment are changing these attitudes. Fathers—especially college-educated fathers—now seek more intimate relationships with children, especially sons (Engle & Breaux, 1998). Among the Aka of central Africa, in contrast with the Huhot, "fathers provide more direct infant care than fathers in any other known society" (Hewlett, 1992, p. 169).

In the United States, fathers' involvement in caregiving has greatly increased as more mothers have begun to work outside the home and as concepts of fathering have changed (Cabrera et al., 2000). A father's frequent and positive involvement with his child, from infancy on, is directly related to the child's well-being and physical, cognitive, and social development (Kelley et al., 1998; Shannon et al., 2002).

GENDER

Identifying as male or female affects how people look, how they move their bodies, and how they work, dress, and play. All these characteristics—and more—are included in the word **gender**: what it means to be male or female. Although sex is coded by the chromosomes and is a biological attribute, gender is a socially constructed psychological characteristic.

gender
Significance of being male or female.

Gender Differences in Infants and Toddlers Infant boys are a bit longer and heavier and may be slightly stronger. However, boys are more physically vulnerable from conception on, whereas girls are less reactive to stress and more likely to survive infancy (Akinbami et al., 2017; Bale & Epperson, 2015; Stevenson et. al., 2000). Boys' brains at birth are about 10 percent larger than girls' brains, a difference that continues into adulthood (Gilmore et al., 2007; Ruigrok et al., 2014). Despite these differences, they achieve the motor milestones of infancy about the same times.

There is some evidence for differences in social behavior between boys and girls. For instance, girls are rated as more cuddly (Benenson et al., 1999), are more interested in faces and better at discriminating facial expressions (Connellan et al., 2000; McClure, 2000), show fewer externalizing emotions (Chaplin & Aldao, 2013), and are better than boys at regulating their distress during and quicker to recover from still-face procedures than boys (Weinberg et al., 1999). Still, such differences are relatively small and have not always been found consistently (Alexander & Wilcox, 2012).

However, there are some consistently identified and robust early behavioral difference between boys and girls, including a preference for toys, play activities, and playmates of the same sex. A preference for sex-typed toys, such as trucks for boys and dolls for girls, appears as young as 3 months of age (Alexander et al., 2009), and a preference for sex-typed colors emerges by about 2½ years (LoBue & DeLoache, 2011). By 3 years of age, girls, but not boys, show more interest in novel toys labeled as being for their sex and decorated with masculine or feminine colors (Weisgram et al., 2014).

Toddlers, and to a lesser extent babies, prefer to play with others of the same sex (Campbell et al., 2000). This may be because boys as young as 17 months tend to play more actively and aggressively than girls (Baillargeon et al., 2007). Some theorists have argued that the segregation seen in boys' and girls' play is a result of these differences in play styles. Girls play with girls and boys play with boys, not because they necessarily want to play with someone who is the same sex but because most children enjoy playing with someone who plays like they do (Maccoby, 1990).

Play style is likely to be influenced by prenatal androgen exposure. One clue can be found by looking at girls with congenital adrenal hyperplasia (CAH), a genetic condition involving the overproduction of androgens (such as testosterone) in utero. These girls generally have play styles that are more typical of boys. Additionally, despite identifying as girls, they have a greater preference for male playmates than unaffected girls (Paterski et al., 2011).

Parental Influences on Gender Generally, parents use broadly similar parenting styles with their boys and girls. They seem, overall, to be equally warm, sensitive, and responsive to both and to use relatively similar levels of control (Jennings et al., 2008; Hallers-Haalboom et al., 2014; Endendijk et al., 2016). However, parents in the United States do nonetheless tend to stereotype baby boys and girls. For example, despite no actual differences in pitch, high-pitched infant cries are more frequently attributed to girls and lower-pitched infant cries are more frequently attributed to boys (Reby et al., 2016), and despite identical performance, mothers of 11-month-old infants expect sons to crawl more effectively than daughters (Mondschein et al., 2000).

Rather than explicitly telling their children how they should behave with respect to their gender, especially in cultures in which gender equality is valued, parents often unconsciously impart this knowledge through their parenting practices. For example, a mother might respond less negatively to her son's rough play than she would to that of her daughter. A father might draw extra praise and attention to the brave boy in a book and be more likely to label a sad-looking rabbit in the story as a girl. Children also watch their parents' behaviors carefully—who does the housework, what they say, and their interests and hobbies. All of these actions provide implicit messages about gender that children internalize over time (Mesman & Groeneveld, 2018).

Additionally, despite broad commonalities, parents do nonetheless show some gendered differences in their treatment. For example, girls are generally allowed a bit more latitude in the expression of negative emotions (Brown et al., 2015; Grady, 2018). Fathers, especially, promote **gender-typing,** the process by which children learn behavior their culture considers appropriate for each sex (Chaplin et al., 2005; Lytton & Romney, 1991). Fathers treat boys and girls more differently than mothers do, even during the 1st year (Snow et al., 1983). During the 2nd year, fathers talk more and spend more time with sons than with daughters (Lamb, 1981). Fathers, overall, play with their children more and more actively than mothers do (Lamb & Lewis, 2010) and play more roughly with sons and show more sensitivity to daughters (Kelley et al., 1998; Lindsey et al., 2010). Mothers talk more, and more supportively, to daughters than to sons (Leaper et al., 1998), and girls at this age tend to be more talkative than boys (Leaper & Smith, 2004).

Culture influences these interactions. In the United States, a highly physical style of play is characteristic of many fathers, but Swedish and German fathers usually do not play with their babies this way (Lamb et al., 1982). African Aka fathers (Hewlett, 1987) and those in New Delhi, India, also tend to play gently with small children (Roopnarine et al., 1993). Both the Efe and Lese foraging fathers of Zaire spend a great deal of time in proximity to their children engaged in direct care and nurturance, and relatively little time is spent in active play (Tronick, et al., 1992; Roopnarine & Davidson, 2015). Such cross-cultural variations suggest that although nurturing behaviors on the part of mothers and rough play on the part of fathers may be biologically based gender differences, they are strongly culturally influenced.

Developmental Issues in Infancy

How does a dependent newborn become a child with complex feelings and the ability to understand and control them? Much of this development revolves around relationships with caregivers.

DEVELOPING TRUST

Erikson (1950) argued that at each stage in the life span, we are faced with a challenge and a complementary risk. Our first challenge involves forming a **basic sense of trust versus mistrust.** The critical element in developing trust is sensitive, responsive, consistent caregiving, and it is formed primarily within the feeding situation. Can the baby count on being fed when hungry, and can the baby therefore trust the mother as a representative of the world?

The stage begins in infancy and continues until about 18 months. Ideally, babies develop a balance between trust (which lets them form intimate relationships) and mistrust (which enables them to protect themselves). If trust predominates, as it should, children develop hope and the belief that they can fulfill their needs and obtain their desires (Erikson, 1982). If mistrust predominates, children view the world as unfriendly and unpredictable and have trouble forming quality relationships.

DEVELOPING ATTACHMENTS

When Ahmed's mother is near, he looks at her, smiles at her, babbles to her, and crawls after her. When she leaves, he cries; when she comes back, he squeals with joy. When he is frightened or unhappy, he clings to her. Ahmed has formed his first attachment to another person.

Attachment is a reciprocal, enduring emotional tie between an infant and a caregiver, each of whom contributes to the quality of the relationship. From an evolutionary point

gender-typing
Socialization process by which children, at an early age, learn appropriate gender roles.

basic sense of trust versus mistrust
Erikson's first stage in psychosocial development, in which infants develop a sense of the reliability of people and objects.

attachment
Reciprocal, enduring tie between two people—especially between infant and caregiver—each of whom contributes to the quality of the relationship.

of view, attachments have adaptive value for babies, ensuring that their psychosocial as well as physical needs will be met (Ainsworth et al., 2015). To ensure this occurs, infants and parents are biologically predisposed to become attached to each other.

The Attachment System In a series of experiments by Harry Harlow and his colleagues, rhesus monkeys were separated from their mothers 6 to 12 hours after birth. The infant monkeys were put into cages with two kinds of surrogate "mothers": a plain cylindrical wire-mesh form that offered food, and a form covered with terry cloth that offered nothing but a cuddly figure to cling to. The baby monkeys spent the majority of their time clinging to the terry-cloth mother.

None of the monkeys in either group grew up normally (Harlow & Harlow, 1962), and none were effectively able to nurture their own offspring (Suomi & Harlow, 1972). It is hardly surprising that a dummy mother would not provide the same kinds of stimulation and opportunities for positive development as a live mother. However, what is striking and important about these experiments was that they brought about a conceptual shift in the understanding of mothers. They showed that the previous model of mothering—that attachment resulted from an association with food—was fundamentally incorrect. Feeding is not the only, or even the most important, thing babies get from their mothers. Mothering includes the comfort of close bodily contact and, at least in monkeys, the satisfaction of an innate need to cling.

When infant monkeys could choose whether to go to a wire "mother" or a warm, soft, terry-cloth "mother," they spent more time clinging to the cloth mother, even if their food came from the wire mother. Harlow Primate Laboratory, University of Wisconsin-Madison

The pioneering ethologist John Bowlby (1951) knew of Harlow's seminal work with rhesus monkeys demonstrating the importance of contact comfort rather than food. He also worked with children who had been separated from their parents by war and observed firsthand the devastating consequences such separation had on their development. Over time, he became convinced of the importance of the mother-baby bond, its deep evolutionary roots, its importance to multiple domains of healthy development, and the transmission of patterns across generations.

By the time babies are 1 year old, they have established a characteristic style of attachment. According to Bowlby, attachment styles are the result of repeated interactions with a caregiver. For example, if every time a baby cries the mother responds quickly and sensitively to that bid for comfort, over time the baby comes to expect it. By contrast, if a mother responds inconsistently to crying, babies form a very different set of expectations.

Bowlby called these sets of expectations working models. As long as the mother continues to act the same way, the model holds up. If her behavior changes—not just once or twice but repeatedly—the baby may revise the model, and security of attachment may change. Because the working model emerges as a result of interactions between both partners in the relationship, babies can have different working models (and attachment styles) with different people. Later, the working model of this early relationship becomes the blueprint for other important relationships, most notably, any children that baby might someday have.

When the baby is near the attachment figure and feels safe, the baby feels free to explore the environment. When the baby feels threatened or scared, the attachment figure is approached and the baby seeks *contact comfort*—or being held or cuddled. This helps the baby regulate his or her emotional state. Because a healthy attachment means a baby will feel secure more often and hence explore the environment more often, a secure working model of attachment should thus be associated with cognitive development.

Stranger Anxiety and Separation Anxiety
Maria used to be a friendly baby, smiling at strangers and going to them, continuing to coo happily as long as someone—anyone—was around. Now, at 8 months, she turns away when a new person approaches and howls when her parents try to leave her with a babysitter.

Maria's reluctance to allow her mother's friend to hold her is a sign of stranger anxiety. Christina Kennedy/Alamy Stock Photo

stranger anxiety
Wariness of strange people and places, shown by some infants during the second half of the 1st year.

separation anxiety
Distress shown by someone, typically an infant, when a familiar caregiver leaves.

Strange Situation
Laboratory technique used to study infant attachment.

secure attachment
Pattern in which an infant may cry or protest when the primary caregiver leaves and actively seeks out the caregiver on his or her return.

avoidant attachment
Pattern in which an infant rarely cries when separated from the primary caregiver and avoids contact on his or her return.

ambivalent (resistant) attachment
Pattern in which an infant becomes anxious before the primary caregiver leaves, is extremely upset during his or her absence, and both seeks and resists contact on his or her return.

Maria is experiencing both **stranger anxiety,** wariness of a person she does not know, and **separation anxiety,** distress when a familiar caregiver leaves her. Babies rarely react negatively to strangers before age 6 months but commonly do so by 8 or 9 months (Sroufe, 1997). Bowlby believed this was an adaptive process. Once babies can crawl, they can get away from their attachment figures, and perhaps into danger. Evolution thus built in wariness to keep them close to attachment figures, and hence safety.

Separation protest—crying and attempting to maintain contact with the attachment figure during a separation—appears to be universal. Research with American, Ladino and Mayan Guatemalans, Israeli, Kalahari Kung, and Navaho infants has shown a similar emergence and pattern of separation anxiety and protest peaking at about a year of age (Kagan, 1976; Chisholm, 2017; Lester et al., 1974). However, the timeline can vary slightly with cultural and individual factors. One key cultural influence appears to be how accustomed to being separated from the attachment figure a child is. The greatest degree of separation protest is exhibited by children who either are very frequently or almost never separated from their attachment figure (Jacobson & Wille, 1984). For example, Guatemalan infants showed an earlier onset of separation protest than American infants, perhaps because they tended to live in small, one-bedroom homes and thus were infrequently separated from their mothers (Lester et al., 1974).

Studying Attachment Patterns Although Bowlby theorized that sensitive mothering should lead to secure attachment, he did not specify how attachment might be measured. Mary Ainsworth, a student of Bowlby's, did so with the development of the **Strange Situation,** a now-classic, laboratory-based technique designed to assess attachment patterns between a 10- to 24-month-old infant and an adult.

The Strange Situation consists of a sequence of episodes and takes less than half an hour. The episodes are designed to trigger the emergence of attachment-related behaviors. During that time, the mother twice leaves the baby in an unfamiliar room, the first time with a stranger. The second time she leaves the baby alone, and the stranger comes back before the mother does. The mother then encourages the baby to explore and play again and gives comfort if the baby needs it (Ainsworth et al., 1978). Of particular concern is the baby's response each time the mother returns.

When Ainsworth and her colleagues observed 1-year-olds in the Strange Situation and at home, they found three main patterns of attachment. These are *secure attachment* (the most common category, into which about 60 to 75 percent of low-risk North American babies fall) and two forms of anxious, or insecure, attachment: *avoidant* (15 to 25 percent) and *ambivalent,* or *resistant* (10 to 15 percent) (Vondra & Barnett, 1999).

Babies with **secure attachment** are resilient in the face of stress. They sometimes cry when a caregiver leaves, but they quickly obtain the comfort they need once the caregiver returns. Some babies with secure attachment are comfortable being left with a stranger for a short period of time; however, they clearly indicate they prefer the caregiver to the stranger, often smiling at, greeting, or approaching the caregiver during the reunion episode. Babies with **avoidant attachment,** by contrast, are outwardly unaffected by a caregiver leaving or returning. They generally continue to play in the room and frequently interact with the stranger. However, upon the caregiver's return, they ignore or reject the caregiver, sometimes deliberately turning away. Avoidantly attached babies tend to show little emotion, either positive or negative. Babies who exhibit **ambivalent (resistant) attachment** are often anxious even before the caregiver leaves. They are extremely reactive to the caregiver's departure from the room and generally become very upset. Upon the caregiver's return, these babies tend to remain upset for long periods of time, kicking, screaming, refusing to be distracted with toys, and sometimes arching back and away from contact. They show a mix of proximity-seeking and angry behaviors and are very difficult to settle.

Note that in all of these cases what the baby does during the caregiver's *absence* is not diagnostic of attachment categorization. What is diagnostic is what the babies do when the caregiver *returns*. The important component of the attachment relationship is how the babies use a caregiver to obtain comfort while *in* his or her presence.

These three attachment patterns are universal in all cultures in which they have been studied, though the percentage of infants in each category varies. Generally, however, secure attachment is the largest category (van IJzendoorn & Kroonenberg, 1988; van IJzendoorn & Sagi, 1999).

Other research (Main & Solomon, 1986) later identified a fourth pattern, **disorganized-disoriented attachment.** Babies with the disorganized pattern seem to lack a cohesive strategy to deal with stress and are unable to effectively use their attachment figure for comfort. Instead, they show contradictory, repetitive, or misdirected behaviors (such as seeking closeness to the stranger instead of the mother or showing a fear response upon the caregiver's entry). They often seem confused and afraid (Carlson, 1998; van IJzendoorn et al., 1999).

Disorganized attachment is thought to occur in at least 10 percent of infants (Vondra & Barnett, 1999). It is most prevalent in babies with mothers who are insensitive, intrusive, or abusive; who are fearful or frightening and thus leave the infant with no one to alleviate the fear the mother arouses; or who have suffered unresolved loss or have unresolved feelings about their childhood attachment to their own parents. Disorganized attachment is a reliable predictor of later behavioral and adjustment problems (Solomon & George, 2011; Carlson, 1998; van IJzendoorn & Sagi, 1999).

disorganized-disoriented attachment Pattern in which an infant, after separation from the primary caregiver, shows contradictory, repetitious, or misdirected behaviors on his or her return.

Alternative Methods of Attachment Study The Waters and Deane (1985) Attachment Q-set (AQS) asks mothers or other home observers to sort a set of descriptive words or phrases ("cries a lot"; "tends to cling") into categories ranging from most to least characteristic of the child and then compare these descriptions with expert descriptions of the prototypical secure child.

In a study using the AQS, mothers in China, Colombia, Germany, Israel, Japan, Norway, and the United States described their children as behaving much like the prototypical "most secure child." Furthermore, the mothers' descriptions of "secure-base" behavior were about as similar across cultures as within cultures. These findings suggest that the tendency to use the mother as a secure base is universal (Posada et al., 1995).

Neurobiological studies may offer another way to study attachment. Functional MRIs given to mothers showed that certain areas of a mother's brain were activated at the sight of her own infant smiling or crying but not at the sight of other infants showing similar behaviors (Strathearn, 2011). Research has also shown that mothers with a secure adult attachment style (a related measure discussed below) showed a different pattern of brain activation to photographs of their babies' faces than those with an insecure attachment (Strathearn et al., 2009). Additional research has found that adults with insecure attachment representations also show greater amygdala activation and respond with greater irritation than do securely attached adults to infant cries (Riem et al., 2012). These neurological differences may have implications for child neglect (Strathearn, 2011).

Long-Term Effects of Attachment As attachment theory proposes, security of attachment seems to affect emotional, social, and cognitive competence, presumably through the action of internal working models (Sroufe et al., 2010). The more secure a child's attachment to a nurturing adult, the more likely that the child will develop good relationships with others. A recent meta-analysis including over 80 studies and 4,000 children concluded that attachment security in infancy is associated with peer competence across childhood and early adolescence, whereas insecurity, regardless of subtype, is associated with lower peer competence (Groh et al., 2014).

Securely attached toddlers tend to have larger, more varied vocabularies than those who are insecurely attached (Meins, 1998) and show less stress in adapting to child care (Ahnert et al., 2004). They have more positive interactions with peers, and their friendly overtures are more likely to be accepted (Fagot, 1997).

Between ages 3 and 5, securely attached children are likely to be more curious, competent, empathic, resilient, and self-confident; to get along better with other children; and to form closer friendships than children who were insecurely attached as infants (Elicker et al., 1992; Jacobson & Wille, 1986; Youngblade & Belsky, 1992). They interact more positively with parents, preschool teachers, and peers; are better able to resolve conflicts; and tend to have a more positive self-image (Elicker et al., 1992; Verschueren et al., 1996; Sroufe et al., 2005). In middle childhood and adolescence, securely attached children tend to have the closest, most stable friendships (Schneider et al., 2001; Sroufe et al., 1993), to be socially well adjusted (Jaffari-Bimmel et al., 2006), and to be good at self-regulation (Zeinali et al., 2011). Secure attachment in infancy also influences the quality of attachment to a romantic partner in young adulthood (Simpson et al., 2007).

Insecurely attached children, in contrast, often are more likely to have inhibitions and negative emotions in toddlerhood, hostility toward other children at age 5, and dependency during the school years (Calkins & Fox, 1992; Fearon et al., 2010; Kochanska, 2001; Lyons-Ruth et al., 1993; Sroufe et al., 1993). They also are more likely to show evidence of externalizing behaviors such as aggression and conduct problems and be poor self-regulators. This appears to be more true for boys, for clinically referred children, and when the attachment assessments are based on observational data (Fearon et al., 2010; Zeinali et al., 2011). Those with disorganized attachment are more likely to have behavior problems at all levels of schooling and psychiatric disorders at age 17 (Carlson, 1998). As adults, individuals who were insecurely attached as infants are also more likely to have cognitive vulnerabilities tied to depression (Morley & Moran, 2011).

Intergenerational Transmission of Attachment Patterns The *Adult Attachment Interview* (AAI) (George et al., 1985; Main, 1995; Main et al., 1985) asks adults to recall and interpret feelings and experiences related to their childhood attachments. Studies using the AAI have found that the way adults recall early experiences with parents or caregivers is related to their emotional well-being and may influence the way they respond to their own children (Dykas & Cassidy, 2011; Adam et al., 2004). Longitudinal data have shown infant attachment as measured by the Strange Situation is not necessarily predictive of adult attachment status (Booth-LaForce & Roisman, 2014); however, a mother who can reflect upon a secure attachment or who has resolved her memories of an insecure attachment to her own mother can more accurately recognize the baby's attachment behaviors, respond encouragingly, and help the baby form a secure attachment to her (Bretherton, 1990).

By contrast, mothers who are preoccupied with their past attachment relationships tend to show anger and intrusiveness in interactions with their children. Depressed mothers who dismiss memories of their past attachments tend to be cold and unresponsive to their children (Adam et al., 2004; see Research in Action). Parents' attachment history also influences their perceptions of their baby's temperament, and those perceptions may affect the parent-child relationship as well (Pesonen et al., 2004). Fortunately, caregiving interventions can help break the cycle of insecure attachment (Cassibba et al., 2015).

EMOTIONAL COMMUNICATION WITH CAREGIVERS

The ability of both infant and caregiver to respond appropriately and sensitively to each other's mental and emotional states is known as **mutual regulation.** Ideally, caregivers and infants have high **interactional synchrony**—where both unconsciously coordinate their behavior and affect in a rhythmic back-and-forth manner, responding appropriately and effectively to each other's signals in an interactive dance. Infants take an active part in this by sending behavioral signals, like smiling, that influence the way caregivers behave toward them. There are some suggestions that during the first month of life, this process is universal. In the second and third months of life, cultural differences, such as the degree of eye contact made with a baby and how much face-to-face contact is typical, affect the developmental course of interactional synchrony (Kartner et al., 2010).

mutual regulation
Process by which infant and caregiver communicate emotional states to each other and respond appropriately.

interactional synchrony
The synchronized coordination of behavior and affect between a caregiver and infant.

research in action

POSTPARTUM DEPRESSION

Much media attention has focused on the issue of postpartum depression (PPD). Celebrity moms, including Chrissy Teigen, Hayden Panettierre, and Alyssa Milano have spoken publicly about their struggles in an effort to raise awareness, decrease stigma, and advocate for new moms to seek treatment.

PPD includes symptoms of major depressive disorder experienced within 4 weeks of giving birth that interfere with maternal functioning (Vliegen et al., 2014). Between 13 and 19 percent of mothers experience this condition (O'Hara & McCabe, 2013). The significant emotional and lifestyle changes after the birth of a baby may trigger depressive symptoms. First-time mothers may be especially at risk; they are generally less likely to have experience in taking care of a newborn and thus may struggle with parenting (Leahy-Warren et al., 2012). Other risk factors include prior history of depression, poor partner relationship, parental stress, financial worries, and recent negative life events (Parsons et al., 2012; Vliegen et al., 2014).

PPD has profoundly negative effects on mother-infant interactions and is linked to long-term disruptions in cognitive and emotional outcomes. Depression itself is associated with poor concentration, lethargy, sleep disturbance, and low mood. These symptoms interfere with the ability to carry out child care tasks (Parsons et al., 2012). Inadequate or inconsistent caregiving practices impact feeding, sleep routines, health care checkups, and safety practices (Field, 2010). Depressed mothers are also more irritable and less engaged in parenting, and their social interactions with infants are generally less positive (Field, 2010).

PPD can also interfere in the bonding process. Some mothers report little to no emotional connection with the baby, and attachment issues may persist up to a full year (O'Higgins et al., 2013). In the short term, infants growing up with depressed parents show impaired social interaction and developmental delays (Earls, 2010). Long-term studies highlight emotional and behavioral problems in elementary school (Fihrer et al., 2009; Closa-Monasterolo et al., 2017).

Untreated PPD poses a threat to optimal development, with long-lasting effects that may persist throughout childhood. Early intervention is essential to improve children's cognitive, social, and behavioral outcomes (Earls, 2010). Experts advocate for multi-pronged interventions, including mental health screening for pregnant and postpartum women, parenting practice education, and increased social support and partner involvement for mothers (Field, 2010; O'Hara & McCabe, 2013)

what's your view Can you suggest ways to help depressed mothers and babies, other than those mentioned here? Do you think PPD is the same as or different from major depressive disorder?

Some of this interactional synchrony may be expressed at a biological level. For example, when mothers and infants are interacting face-to-face in a synchronous fashion, their heart rates become synchronized with lags of less than one second. This process does not occur during asynchronous periods of interaction (Feldman et al., 2011). Additionally, the release of oxytocin, a hormone related in bonding processes in mammals, has been found to be related to parenting behaviors in humans. In fathers, oxytocin levels are related to playful behaviors. In mothers, oxytocin levels are related to positive affect, affectionate touch, and "baby talk"—all markers of sensitive parenting (Gordon et al., 2010).

Typically, interaction shifts between well-regulated states and poorly regulated states. When an interaction is highly synchronous, the baby tends to be joyful, or at least interested (Tronick, 1989; Lowe et al., 2012). However, when a mother or caregiver is not synchronous in her interaction with the baby—for example, if an invitation to play is ignored or an adult is overly intrusive—the baby can become stressed or physiologically aroused (Conradt & Ablow, 2010). From this process, babies learn over time how to send signals and what to do when their signals are not effective.

Young children whose mothers were high in interactional synchrony are more likely later to be better at regulating their behavior, to comply with parental requests, to have higher IQ and perform better on a variety of cognitive tasks; to have fewer behavioral problems, better school adjustment, and higher quality play; and to show more empathy in adolescence (Feldman, 2007; Leclere et al., 2014). It may be that mutual regulation processes help them learn to read others' behavior and to respond appropriately.

SOCIAL REFERENCING

social referencing
Understanding an ambiguous situation by seeking another person's perception of it.

Ann toddles warily toward the new playground and stops at the entrance, staring at the laughing, screaming children scaling the bright structure. Unsure of herself, she turns toward her mother and makes eye contact. Her mother smiles at her, and Ann, emboldened by her mother's response, walks in and starts to climb the structure. When babies check in with their caregivers upon encountering an ambiguous event, they are engaging in **social referencing,** seeking emotional information to guide behavior. In social referencing, one person forms an understanding of how to act in an ambiguous, confusing, or unfamiliar situation by seeking and interpreting another person's perception of it.

Infants show evidence of social referencing by 5½ months of age, but only if they are provided with both auditory and visual information (Vailliant-Molina & Bahrick, 2012). At 12 months, toddlers can use either a facial expression or vocal tone as a cue to the safety of an action, but respond more quickly to voice (Vaish & Striano, 2004). By 14 months, they avoid touching a plastic creature dropped within their reach if an adult expressed negative emotions toward it an hour earlier (Hertenstein & Campos, 2004).

Although cross-cultural research specifically focused on social referencing has not been undertaken, research on closely related developmental achievements, such as pointing and gaze following, suggests that social referencing is likely to be a cultural universal (Fawcett & Liszkowski, 2015). Social referencing, and the ability to retain information gained from it, may play a role in such key developments of toddlerhood as the rise of self-conscious emotions (embarrassment and pride), the development of a sense of self, and the processes of *socialization* and *internalization,* to which we turn in the next section of this chapter.

Developmental Issues in Toddlerhood

At about 18 months, babies become toddlers. Let's look at the emerging *sense of self;* the growth of *autonomy,* or self-determination; and *socialization,* or *internalization of behavioral standards.*

THE EMERGING SENSE OF SELF

self-concept
Sense of self; descriptive and evaluative mental picture of one's abilities and traits.

The **self-concept** is our image of ourselves. It describes what we know and feel about ourselves and guides our actions (Harter, 1996).

From a jumble of seemingly isolated experiences (say, from one breastfeeding session to another), infants begin to extract consistent patterns that form rudimentary concepts of self and other. Depending on what kind of care the infant receives and how she or he responds, pleasant or unpleasant emotions become connected with experiences that play an important part in the growing concept of the self (Harter, 1998).

By at least 3 months of age, infants pay attention to their mirror image (Courage & Howe, 2002). Between 4 and 10 months, when infants learn to reach, grasp, and make things happen, they experience a sense of personal *agency,* the realization that they can control external events. At about this time infants develop *self-coherence,* the sense of being a physical whole with boundaries separate from the rest of the world. These developments occur in interaction with caregivers in games such as peekaboo, in which the infant becomes increasingly aware of the difference between self and other.

Four- to 9-month-olds show more interest in images of others than in images of themselves, suggesting they have attained some degree of self-awareness. Zdravinjo/Shutterstock

Visual preference research shows by 3 months, babies generally prefer faces of their own ethnicity. However, at this age there is no evidence they understand race. Rather, if infants habitually see one race, then those are the faces they prefer. So, for example, white babies exposed to predominantly white faces prefer white faces (Kelly et al., 2005) and Chinese babies exposed to predominantly Chinese faces prefer Chinese faces (Kelly et al., 2007). At 6 months, infants start showing a positive bias toward own-race faces; they look longer when own-race faces are shown with happy music and other-race faces are shown with sad music (Xiao et al., 2017). At about 9 months babies can categorize faces on the basis of race and become better at recognizing people of their own race (Quinn et al., 2016). Thus it appears that recognition of own- versus other-race faces is not just a perceptual process, but is linked with emotional content and gradually refined over time.

The emergence of *self-awareness*—conscious knowledge of the self as a distinct, identifiable being—is tested by studying whether an infant recognizes his or her own image. In classic research, investigators dabbed rouge on the noses of 6- to 24-month-olds in front of a mirror. Three-fourths of 18-month-olds and all 24-month-olds touched their red noses more often than before, whereas babies younger than 15 months never did. This behavior suggests that these toddlers had self-awareness. They knew they did not normally have red noses and recognized the image in the mirror as their own (Lewis, 1997; Lewis & Brooks, 1974).

By 20 to 24 months, toddlers begin to use first-person pronouns, another sign of self-awareness (Lewis, 1997). Between 19 and 30 months children begin to apply descriptive terms ("big" or "little") and evaluative terms ("good," "naughty," or "strong") to themselves. The rapid development of language enables children to think and talk about the self and to incorporate parents' verbal descriptions ("What a hard worker!") into their emerging self-image (Stipek et al., 1990). This process is interactive; children who attain self-recognition earlier also comprehend and label more body parts (Waugh & Brownell, 2015). Toddlers of this age also demonstrate self-understanding through acknowledging objects that belong to them ("Mine!") and those that belong to others (Fasig, 2000).

A positive correlation between the use of pronouns and mirror self-recognition has been found cross-culturally. However, there are variations in the timeline of development. Children from individualistic autonomy-supporting cultures, such as German and Indian urban samples, recognize themselves in a mirror earlier than do children from collectivistic cultures stressing relatedness and interactional goals, such as Indian and Nso rural samples (Kärtner et al., 2012). Moreover, research with young children from a variety of cultures, including the United States, Canada, Germany, Cameroon, Costa Rica, Greece, Kenya, Fiji, Santa Lucia, Grenada, and Peru, showed wide variability in performance on the mirror self-recognition task, although it was not always clear what their behaviors illustrated (Broesch et al., 2011; Keller et al., 2005; Keller et al., 2004). For example, children from Kenya, who rarely passed the mirror self-recognition test, were more likely to freeze at the sight of their image rather than reach for their noses. Cameroonian children, who were generally highly compliant, might have resisted touching their nose as a result of assuming it had been placed there on purpose by an adult.

DEVELOPMENT OF AUTONOMY

Erikson (1950) identified the period from about 18 months to 3 years as the second stage in personality development, **autonomy versus shame and doubt,** marked by a shift from external control to self-control. Having come through infancy with a sense of basic trust in the world and an awakening self-awareness, toddlers begin to substitute their own judgment for their caregivers'. The virtue that emerges during this stage is *will.* Because unlimited freedom is neither safe nor healthy, said Erikson, shame and doubt have a necessary place. Toddlers need adults to set appropriate limits, and shame and doubt help them recognize the need for those limits.

autonomy versus shame and doubt
Erikson's second stage in psychosocial development, in which children achieve a balance between self-determination and control by others.

window on the world

THE TERRIBLE TWOS?

In the United States, toddlers often enjoy testing the notions that they are individuals, that they have some control over their world, and that they have new, exciting powers. This often shows itself in the form of *negativism,* the tendency to shout, "No!" just for the sake of resisting authority. Almost all U.S. children show negativism to some degree, commonly described by many caregivers as the "terrible twos." However, the negativism generally begins before age 2, peaks at about 3½ to 4, and declines by age 6.

Are the "terrible twos" a normal phase in child development? Many Western parents and psychologists think so, but research shows this phase doesn't appear to be universal.

A cross-cultural study compared 16 Mayan families in San Pedro, Guatemala, with 16 American families in Salt Lake City, Utah (Mosier & Rogoff, 2003). Each family had toddlers 14 to 20 months old and older children 3 to 5 years old. Researchers interviewed each mother about her child-raising practices. With the parents and both siblings present, the researchers handed the mother a series of toys (such as a puppet on strings). In the presence of the older sibling, the researchers asked the mother to help the toddler operate the toys. Researchers found striking differences across cultures.

The older American siblings often tried to take and play with the toys themselves. By contrast, the older Guatemalan children would often offer to help their younger siblings, or the two children would play with the toys together. When there was a conflict over possession of the toys, the Guatemalan mothers favored the toddlers 94 percent of the time. However, in more than one-third of the American families, the mothers treated both children equally, negotiating with them or suggesting they take turns or share.

What explains these cultural contrasts? Two differences emerged: the age parents felt children can be held responsible for their actions, and the amount of direct parental supervision children received. Most of the American mothers maintained that by age 1, their toddlers understood the consequences of their actions. Most Guatemalan mothers placed the age of understanding consequences of actions between 2 and 3 years of age. All of the American children were under direct caregiver supervision. Alternatively, 11 of the 16 Guatemalan children were without supervision much of the time and had more mature household responsibilities.

The researchers suggest that the terrible twos may be a phase specific to societies that place individual freedom before the needs of the group. In societies that place higher value on group needs, interdependence, responsibility, and expectations of cooperation are more important. American parents seem to believe that responsible behavior develops gradually from engaging in fair competition and negotiations. Guatemalan parents seem to believe that responsible behavior develops rapidly when children are old enough to understand the need to respect others' desires as well as their own.

what's **your** view

From your experience or observation of toddlers, which of the two ways of handling sibling conflict would you expect to be more effective? Can you think of other ways in which independence and interdependence might be expressed in childhood socialization processes?

In the United States, this growing sense of autonomy is sometimes called the terrible twos. Many parents might be surprised to hear the terrible twos do not seem to be universal (Window on the World).

SOCIALIZATION PROCESSES

socialization
Development of habits, skills, values, and motives shared by responsible, productive members of a society.

internalization
During socialization, process by which children accept societal standards of conduct as their own.

Socialization is the process by which children develop habits, skills, values, and motives that make them responsible, productive members of society. Socialization rests on **internalization** of societal standards. Children who are successfully socialized no longer obey rules or commands merely to get rewards or avoid punishment; rather, they have internalized standards and made them their own. They comply with rules not because they are afraid of getting in trouble but because they believe them to be right and true.

Developing Self-Regulation Laticia, age 2, is about to poke her finger into an electric outlet. When Laticia hears her father shout, "No!" the toddler pulls her arm back. The next time she goes near an outlet, she starts to poke her finger, hesitates, and then says, "No." She is beginning to show **self-regulation:** control of her behavior even when her caregiver is not present.

Self-regulation is the foundation of socialization. To stop herself from poking her finger into an outlet requires that Laticia consciously remember and understand what her father told her. But memory is not enough; restraining herself also requires emotional control. By reading their parents' emotional responses to their behavior, children continually absorb information about what conduct their parents approve of. Maternal sensitivity, parents' use of mental terms when talking to the child, and support of the child's autonomous behavior are all important influences on self-regulation (Bernier et al., 2010).

Before they can control their own behavior, children may need to be able to regulate, or control, their *attentional processes* and to modulate negative emotions (Eisenberg, 2000; Rueda et al., 2005). Attentional regulation enables children to develop willpower and cope with frustration (Duckworth et al., 2014; Sethi et al., 2000). For example, control of attentional processes might allow a child to distract herself enough that she manages not to steal the cookies temptingly cooling on the counter.

The growth of self-regulation parallels the development of the self-conscious emotions, such as empathy, shame, and guilt (Lewis, 1995, 1997, 1998). It requires the ability to wait for gratification. It is correlated with measures of conscience development, such as resisting temptation and making amends for wrongdoing (Eisenberg, 2000). In most children, the full development of self-regulation takes at least 3 years (Rothbart et al., 2011).

Most of the research conducted on the development of self-regulatory capacities in children has focused on European-American families. However, cultural values affect the development of key processes that impact the ability to engage in self-regulation (LeCuyer & Zhang, 2015). For example, one study comparing Israeli (an individualistic culture) and Palestinian (a collectivistic culture) parent-child pairs found that although self-regulation abilities emerged at roughly the same age in all toddlers, the predictors varied by culture. In the Israeli families, the children who received the most face-to-face contact were the best self-regulators; in the Palestinian families, the children who had more close physical contact with their parents were the best self-regulators. In other words, optimal parenting differed by culture (Feldman et al., 2006).

The Origins of Conscience A **conscience** involves the ability to refrain from certain acts as well as the feeling of emotional discomfort in the event of failure.

Kochanska and her colleagues looked for the origins of conscience by studying children ages 26 to 41 months with their mothers playing together with toys (Kochanska & Aksan, 1995). After a free-play period, a mother would give her child 15 minutes to put away the toys. The laboratory had a special shelf with other, unusually attractive toys, such as a bubble gum machine, a walkie-talkie, and a music box. The child was told not to touch anything on that shelf. After about an hour, the experimenter asked the mother to go into an adjoining room, leaving the child alone. A few minutes later, a woman entered, played with several of the forbidden toys, and then left the child alone again for 8 minutes.

Some children could put the toys away as long as their parents were there to remind them. These children showed what is called **situational compliance.** They needed the extra assistance provided by their parents' presence and prompts to complete the task. However, other children seemed to have internalized their parents' requests more fully. These children showed **committed compliance**—that is, they could follow requests without their parents' direct intervention (Kochanska et al., 2001).

The roots of committed compliance go back to infancy. Committed compliers, most typically girls, tend to be those who, at 8 to 10 months, could refrain from touching when told, "No!" (Kochanska et al., 1998). Mothers of committed compliers, as

self-regulation
A child's independent control of behavior to conform to understood social expectations.

conscience
Internal standards of behavior, which usually control one's conduct and produce emotional discomfort when violated.

situational compliance
Kochanska's term for obedience of a parent's orders only in the presence of signs of ongoing parental control.

committed compliance
Kochanska's term for wholehearted obedience of a parent's orders without reminders or lapses.

contrasted with mothers of situational compliers, were more sensitive and responsive with their children as infants (Kochanska et al., 2010) and, once the children were toddlers, tended to rely on gentle guidance rather than force, threats, or negative control (Eisenberg, 2000; Kochanska et al., 2004). Committed compliance increases with age, whereas situational compliance decreases.

Receptive cooperation goes beyond committed compliance. It is a child's eager willingness to cooperate with a parent, not only in disciplinary situations, but also in daily interactions, including routines, chores, hygiene, and play. Early attachment security seems to be a key feature. Children who have a secure attachment relationship with their parent as an infant trust in and have a positive orientation toward that parent. That, in turn, leads to a cascade of positive effects—a cooperative, willing child elicits supportive, responsive parenting, and these influences reciprocally interact over time (Goffin et al., 2018).

Other Socialization Influences How parents socialize a child and the quality of the parent-child relationship may help predict how hard or easy socialization will be. However, not all children respond in the same way. For example, temperamentally fearful toddlers respond better to gentle reminders than to strong admonitions, whereas bold toddlers require more assertive parenting (Kochanska et al., 2007).

How parents talk to children is also an influence. Constructive conflict over a child's misbehavior—conflict that involves negotiation, reasoning, and resolution—can help children develop moral understanding by enabling them to see another point of view (Laible & Thompson, 2002). In one observational study, 2-year-olds whose mothers explained why they were doing tasks, used noncontrolling language, and provided simple descriptions were more likely to comply with requests at 3½ years than children whose mothers had threats, punishments, criticism, sarcasm, or bribes (Laurin & Joussemet, 2017).

Emotional socialization seems to be important too. Discussion of emotions in conflict situations ("How would you feel if . . .") is associated with conscience development, most likely by fostering the development of moral emotions (Laible & Thompson, 2002). Additionally, parents who talk to their 18- to 30-month-old children about emotions tend to have toddlers who are quicker to help others (Brownell et al., 2013).

There are also cultural differences. For example, Japanese mothers in one study patiently elicited cooperation from their toddlers with hints and questions, and avoided the use of reprimands. This was in line with a cultural belief that the positive nature of the relationship needed to be maintained for learning to occur. By contrast, Taiwanese mothers deliberately sought confrontations with their toddlers, believing these interactions to be an ideal opportunity to deliver moral lessons and provide explicit instructions on behavior (LeVine & LeVine, 2016).

Peer Influences

Although parents exert a major influence on children's lives, relationships with other children—both in the home and out of it—also are important from infancy on.

SIBLING INTERACTIONS

Although exasperated adults may not always see it that way, sibling disputes and their settlement are socialization opportunities, in which children learn to stand up for principles and negotiate disagreements (Howe et al., 2002). Lessons and skills learned from interactions with siblings carry over to relationships outside the home (Brody, 1998; Ji-Yeon et al., 2007).

Babies usually become attached to their older siblings. Although rivalry may be present, so is affection. Nevertheless, as babies begin to move around and become more assertive, they inevitably come into conflict with siblings—at least in U.S. culture. Sibling conflict increases dramatically after the younger child reaches 18 months (Volling et al., 2010). During the next few months, younger siblings begin to participate more fully in family interactions and become more involved in family disputes. As they do, they become more aware of others' intentions and feelings. They begin to recognize what kind of behavior will upset or annoy an older brother or sister and what behavior is considered "naughty" or "good" (Dunn & Munn, 1985; Recchia & Howe, 2009).

Despite the frequency of conflict, sibling rivalry is not the main pattern between young siblings. Prosocial and play-oriented behaviors are more common than rivalry, hostility, and competition. Older siblings initiate more behavior, both friendly and unfriendly; whereas younger siblings tend to imitate the older ones. As the children age, they tend to become less physical and more verbal in showing both aggression and affection (Abramovitch et al., 1986). Because older siblings tend to dominate younger ones, the quality of the relationship is more affected by the emotional and social adjustment of the older child than the younger one (Pike et al., 2005). Generally, same-sex siblings, particularly girls, are closer and play together more peaceably than boy-girl pairs (Kier & Lewis, 1998).

In many non-Western cultures such as Morocco, it is common to see older siblings caring for younger siblings.
Wigbert Roth/imageBROKER/Shutterstock

Lessons and skills learned from interactions with siblings carry over to relationships outside the home. A child who is aggressive with siblings is likely to be aggressive with friends as well (Abramovitch et al., 1986). For example, children who victimize their siblings are more likely to be bullied or to bully others, and children who are victimized by their siblings are more likely to be bullied (Tippett & Wolke, 2015). By the same token, siblings who frequently play amicably together and who have high-quality relationships tend to develop prosocial behaviors, which then tend to positively affect their peer relationships (Pike et al., 2005; Smorti & Ponti, 2018). One longitudinal study of over 10,000 children found that kindergarteners and 5th graders with siblings had significantly better social skills than did children without siblings (Downey et al., 2015). Constructive conflict with siblings helps children recognize each other's needs, wishes, and point of view, and it helps them learn how to fight, disagree, and compromise within the context of a safe, stable relationship (Kramer, 2010; Vandell & Bailey, 1992).

Likewise, friendships can influence sibling relationships. Older siblings who have experienced a good relationship with a friend before the birth of a sibling are likely to treat their younger siblings better and are less likely to develop antisocial behavior in adolescence (Kramer & Kowal, 2005). For a young child at risk for behavioral problems, a positive relationship with either a sibling or a friend can buffer the effects of a negative relationship with the other (McElwain & Volling, 2005).

In many cultures, including agrarian communities in Africa, Southeast Asia, the Pacific, and indigenous North America, young children are given the task of caring for their infant siblings (LeVine &LeVine, 2016). Research in the United States has shown that infants become attached to their siblings and can use them as a secure base, and that their older siblings generally offer them comfort when they are distressed (Samuels, 1980; Stewart, 1983). However, siblings are generally a secondary attachment, and babies prefer the attention of a primary caretaker, most commonly the mother, when truly distressed. Although there is sparse research available on sibling attachments in other cultures, what little exists suggests the same is true in traditional cultures as well (LeVine, 1994).

INTERACTIONS WITH NONSIBLINGS

Infants and—even more so—toddlers show interest in people outside the home, particularly people their own size. During the first few months, they look, smile, and coo at other babies (Field, 1978). From about 6 to 12 months, they increasingly smile at, touch, and babble to them (Hay et al., 1982). At about 1 year, babies offer objects to other babies, try to take objects away from them, make eye contact and smile, and touch or hit other babies (Williams et al., 2010). From about 1½ years to almost 3, children show growing interest in what other children do and an increasing understanding of how to deal with them (Eckerman et al., 1989).

Toddlers learn by imitating one another. Games such as follow-the-leader help toddlers connect with other children and pave the way for more complex games during the preschool years (Eckerman et al., 1989). Imitation of each other's actions leads to more frequent verbal communication (such as "You go in playhouse"), which helps peers coordinate joint activity (Eckerman & Didow, 1996). Cooperative activity develops during the 2nd and 3rd years as social understanding grows (Brownell et al., 2006). As with siblings, conflict also can have a purpose: helping children learn how to negotiate and resolve disputes (Kramer, 2010).

Preschoolers usually like to play with children of the same gender (Martin et al., 2013) and prefer prosocial playmates who can provide them with positive experiences (Paulus, 2017) and who are advanced in theory of mind (Slaughter et al., 2015). Preschoolers reject disruptive, demanding, intrusive, or aggressive children (Coelho et al., 2017; Bierman, 2004; Roopnarine & Honig, 1985). As children become older, their preferences become more sophisticated and start focusing less on physical traits and more on characteristics such as doing things together, liking and caring for each other, and sharing and helping one another (Furman & Bierman, 1983). Beginning at about 4 years, children will start to conform to peer pressure and sometimes go along with the group even when they disagree with an action (Haun & Tomasello, 2011).

Cultural differences in peer relationships abound. In Western countries, with their individualistic orientations, peer relationships are viewed as a way for children to develop autonomy from the family. In collectivistic societies, peer relationships are viewed more as a way for children to learn social standards and desired behaviors (Chen et al., 2014). Moreover, although children in developed countries like the United States spend much of their time in organized play, and often have little time for free, unstructured play, children in hunter-gatherer communities spend much of the day playing and most often play in mixed-age groups out of necessity (Gray, 2011).

There are also cross-cultural commonalities. As in developed countries, young children in hunter-gatherer cultures segregate by gender. Research with Hadza children of Tanzania and the Bayaka of the Republic of Congo showed that children preferred to play with same gender children, when they were available, and tended to play in ways that conformed to gender norms in their societies, often pretending to do gendered adult work (Lew-Levy et al., 2019). Additionally, the existence of cooperative games and conflictual interactions appear to be universal, and have been documented in cultures as varied as the United States, Britain, Canada, Israel, Italy, and Papua New Guinea (Hay et al., 2018).

Maternal Employment and Child Care

Because of women's traditional role in the home, most of the research on parental employment has focused on the influence of working mothers. How do their work and child care arrangements affect infants and toddlers?

EFFECTS OF MATERNAL EMPLOYMENT

Labor force participation by mothers of children of all ages has increased dramatically in the past three decades. In 1975, fewer than half of all mothers were working or looking for work. In 2019, 62.2 percent of married mothers and 66.6 percent of mothers with other marital statuses who had children under age 3 and 66.4 percent of women with children under age 6 were in the labor force (U.S. Bureau of Labor Statistics, 2020).

How does early maternal employment affect children? Longitudinal data from two large studies have shown negative cognitive and behavioral effects as a result of maternal employment during the first year of life. However, maternal sensitivity, a high-quality home environment, and high-quality child care attenuated the negative effects in 3-year-old children. Additionally, 8-year-old children in disadvantaged families showed fewer negative cognitive effects than children in more advantaged families (Brooks-Gunn et al., 2002).

Much of the research on maternal employment has been inconsistent. A meta-analysis conducted on 69 studies investigating the impact of maternal employment on child achievement outcomes found a small achievement advantage for children whose mothers worked part-time versus full-time, but no consistent significant associations between the maternal work status and child achievement (Goldberg et al., 2008). Some studies have found negative behavioral and cognitive effects for children of working mothers (Brooks-Gunn et al., 2002). Other studies have found advantages for children of working mothers. In one study, maternal employment during infancy and early childhood was associated with higher levels of academic achievement and lower levels of internalizing behaviors, and these findings were most striking for single mothers and for mothers on public assistance. Although some studies have shown differential effects for children of different races or ethnicities, when viewed as a whole, the literature does not support this relationship (Lucas-Thompson et al., 2010).

It is important to note that employment is a necessity in many families, and given the importance of socioeconomic variables to many child outcomes, there are negative effects associated with a drop in income when a mother does not work. Notably, meta-analyses results separated by socioeconomic status showed partial support for a positive effect of maternal employment in working-class samples, who presumably benefitted most from an increase in income, and a small, negative trend for decreased achievement in the middle- and upper-class samples (Goldberg et al., 2008).

EARLY CHILD CARE

Among the Gusii women of Kenya, siblings often care for babies while mothers work in the field. However, they do not trust other co-wives in their household, with whom they are often in competition for land inheritance, to watch their babies. Hausa mothers in Nigeria and Beng mothers in the Ivory Coast assume older women in their community will help with child care. In Haryana State in north India, mothers care for their babies only 40 percent of the time. Grandmothers, aunts, and the father fill in and assist when needed (LeVine & LeVine, 2016). However, in countries such as the United States, working mothers often must seek assistance in the form of child care provided by non-kin. The impact of this care depends on a variety of factors, including the child's temperament and gender, the quality of care, and the characteristics of the caregiver.

Factors Impacting Child Care About 60 percent of children under the age of 6 not yet enrolled in kindergarten are in some sort of regular child care arrangement (National Center for Education Statistics, 2019). Of those children, 42 percent are cared for by relatives, primarily grandparents and fathers. About a third are regularly cared for by nonrelatives, and approximately 12 percent are cared for by a mix of relatives and nonrelatives. Approximately a quarter are cared for in some form of organized care facility (Laughlin, 2013). About 32 percent of parents with young children report having difficulty affording child care, and the proportion of parents who report this increases as income goes down (National Center for Education Statistics, 2018).

Temperament and gender of the child make a difference (Crockenberg, 2003). Shy children in child care experience greater stress, as shown by cortisol levels, than sociable children (Watamura et al., 2003). There are some indications that children who are highly reactive or difficult respond worse to poor-quality child care, but *also* respond with enhanced positive outcomes to high-quality child care (Phillips et al., 2012; Davis et al., 2012). In other words, they are more strongly affected by their caregiving environment than other children. Similarly, boys are more vulnerable to stress, in child care and elsewhere, than are girls (Crockenberg, 2003) and tend to show more negative effects as a result of low-quality child care (Broekhuizen et al., 2015).

A critical factor in determining the effects of child care is the quality of care a child receives. Quality of care can be measured by *structural characteristics,* such as staff training and the ratio of children to caregivers, and by *process characteristics,* such as the warmth, sensitivity, and responsiveness of caregivers and the developmental appropriateness of activities.

TABLE 6.2 Checklist for Choosing a Good Child Care Facility

- Is the program licensed?

- Are parents welcome to visit, unannounced, at any time?

- Is the child-to-adult ratio adequate for the age of your child? Are children supervised at all times, even when sleeping?

- Have all employees working in the program been given state and national background checks, including fingerprints?

- Are program directors or teachers credentialed or trained in child development? Are all adults working in the program provided the opportunity for continuing education in the field?

- Is there a varied schedule that includes active and quiet play time, group and individual activities, structured learning and free play, rest time, and meal times?

- Is the environment, safe, clean, well-maintained? Are the program staff trained in infant and child first aid and CPR? Does the program have a written plan for actions to be followed if a child is sick, injured or lost, or for how to handle emergencies or disasters?

- Is there a written policy on how discipline is maintained, and are the techniques used intended to teach and guide children rather than punish them? Are there specific directives against the use of physical punishment?

- Do the adults and program seem warm and welcoming to children? Are staff actively involved in interactions with children? Does the program provide age-appropriate toys and activities?

Source: Childcare.gov. (2020). Selecting a child care program: Visiting and asking questions [Information sheet]. Retrieved from https://childcare.gov/consumer-education/selecting-a-child-care-program-visiting-and-asking-questions

Stimulating interactions with responsive adults are crucial to early cognitive, linguistic, and psychosocial development. In one study, warm and caring interaction with staff at home-based day care centers was associated with a lower incidence of problem behavior in children but *not* with decreases in stress hormone activation (as measured by cortisol, the primary stress hormone). By contrast, intrusive and overcontrolling care did lead to increases in cortisol production. The authors suggested that overly structured day cares with multiple transitions overwhelm the children's abilities and lead to heightened stress. However, this is not necessarily maladaptive. We all need to learn how to manage stress during the course of our lives, so this early practice may not be harmful (Gunnar et al., 2010).

Low staff turnover is another important factor in quality of care. Infants need consistent caregiving in order to develop trust and secure attachments (Burchinal et al., 1996; Shonkoff & Phillips, 2000). Stability of care facilitates coordination between parents and child care providers, which may help protect against any negative effects of long hours of care (Ahnert & Lamb, 2003). Table 6.2 provides guidelines for selecting a high-quality child care facility.

Maltreatment: Abuse and Neglect

Although most parents are loving and nurturing, some cannot or will not take proper care of their children, and some deliberately harm them. *Maltreatment,* whether perpetrated by parents or others, is deliberate or avoidable endangerment of a child.

Maltreatment can take several specific forms, and the same child can be a victim of more than one type (USDHHS, 2019).

- **Physical abuse,** injury to the body through punching, beating, kicking, or burning.

- **Neglect,** failure to meet a child's basic needs, such as food, clothing, medical care, protection, and supervision.

- **Sexual abuse,** any sexual activity involving a child and an older person.

- **Emotional maltreatment,** including rejection, terrorization, isolation, exploitation, degradation, ridicule, or failure to provide emotional support, love, and affection.

physical abuse
Action taken deliberately to endanger another person, involving potential bodily injury.

neglect
Failure to meet a dependent's basic needs.

sexual abuse
Physically or psychologically harmful sexual activity or any sexual activity involving a child and an older person.

emotional maltreatment
Rejection, terrorization, isolation, exploitation, degradation, ridicule, or failure to provide emotional support, love, and affection; or other action or inaction that may cause behavioral, cognitive, emotional, or mental disorders.

State and local child protective service agencies received an estimated 3.5 million referrals for alleged maltreatment of 6.2 million children in the United States in 2017, a 10 percent increase from 2013. About 75 percent of children were neglected, 18.3 percent were physically abused, and 8.6 percent were sexually abused. Emotional maltreatment was not included in this analysis, however, as it often co-occurs with the other forms of abuse. An estimated 1,720 children died of maltreatment, and the actual number may well have been considerably higher (USDHHS, 2019).

MALTREATMENT IN INFANCY AND TODDLERHOOD

Children are abused and neglected at all ages, but the highest rates of victimization and of death from maltreatment are for age 3 and younger (Child Welfare Information Gateway, 2019; Figure 6.2).

Babies who do not receive nurturance and affection or who are neglected sometimes suffer from **nonorganic failure to thrive,** slowed or arrested physical growth with no known medical cause, accompanied by poor developmental and emotional functioning. Symptoms may include lack of appropriate weight gain, irritability, excessive sleepiness and fatigue, avoidance of eye contact, lack of smiling or vocalizing, and delayed motor development. In short, they neither grow nor develop normally despite a lack of underlying physical or medical causes. Failure to thrive can result from a combination of inadequate nutrition, difficulties in breastfeeding, improper formula preparation or feeding techniques, and disturbed interactions with parents. Poverty is the greatest single risk factor for failure to thrive worldwide. Infants whose mother or primary caregiver is depressed, abuses alcohol or other substances, is under severe stress, or does not show warmth or affection toward the baby are also at heightened risk (Block et al., 2005; Lucile Packard Children's Hospital at Stanford, 2009).

Shaken baby syndrome is a form of maltreatment found mainly in children under 2 years old, most often in infants. Because the baby has weak neck muscles and a large, heavy head, shaking makes the brain bounce back and forth inside the skull. This causes bruising, bleeding, and swelling and can lead to permanent and severe brain damage, paralysis, and even death (National Institute of Neurological Disorders and Stroke, 2006). The damage is typically worse if the baby is thrown into bed or against a wall. Head trauma is the leading cause of death in child abuse cases in the United States (Dowshen et al., 2004). About 20 percent of babies with head trauma die within a few days. Survivors may be left with a wide range of disabilities from learning and behavioral disorders to neurological injuries, paralysis or blindness, or a permanent vegetative state (King et al., 2003; National Institute of Neurological Disorders and Stroke, 2006).

ECOLOGICAL PERSPECTIVE ON ABUSE

As Bronfenbrenner's bioecological theory would suggest, abuse and neglect are not caused by one thing, but by many intersecting factors.

Characteristics of Abusive and Neglectful Parents There is no identifying behavior or characteristic that determines who will or will not abuse a child. In 2018, almost 78 percent of perpetrators were the child's parents, with slightly over half (53.8 percent) women. About 6.4 percent were a relative other than the parent, and another 3.7 percent had an "other" relationship to the child. This category includes foster siblings, babysitters, neighbors, family friends, and other nonrelatives. Perpetrators were predominantly white (49.6 percent), African American (20.6 percent), and Hispanic (19.2 percent) (USDHHS, 2020).

Maltreatment by parents is a symptom of extreme disturbance in child rearing, usually aggravated by other family problems, such as poverty, lack of education, alcoholism, depression, or antisocial behavior. A disproportionate number of abused and neglected

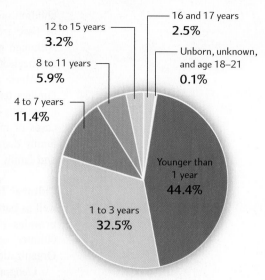

FIGURE 6.2
Deaths from Maltreatment by Age, 2016

More than three-quarters of fatalities are children younger than age 3.

Source: Child Welfare Information Gateway. (2017). Child abuse and neglect fatalities, 2017: Statistics and interventions [Fact sheet].

nonorganic failure to thrive
Slowed or arrested physical growth with no known medical cause, accompanied by poor developmental and emotional functioning.

shaken baby syndrome
Form of maltreatment in which shaking an infant or toddler can cause brain damage, paralysis, or death.

children are in large, poor, or single-parent families, which tend to be under stress and to have trouble meeting children's needs (USDHHS, 2020; Dubowitz et al., 2011). Although many neglect cases occur in very poor families, most low-income parents do not neglect their children.

Abuse and neglect sometimes occur in the same families (USDHHS, 2020). Such families tend to have no one to turn to in times of stress and no one to see what is happening (Dubowitz, 1999). Substance abuse is a factor in approximately a quarter of cases of maltreatment (USDHHS, 2020). Sexual abuse often occurs along with other family disturbances such as physical abuse, emotional maltreatment, substance abuse, and family violence (Kellogg & the Committee on Child Abuse and Neglect, 2005).

Cultural Influences Culture can impact the likelihood of child abuse and neglect, as well as parents' understanding of what maltreatment is. The World Health Organization provides a broad definition of abuse, however the interpretation of behaviors varies by cultures, and thus so do perceptions and reports of abuse and neglect (World Health Organization, 2016).

Geographical and economic factors influence rates of abuse. A recent meta-analysis of 288 cross-cultural studies showed countries in Europe and Asia had lower rates of abuse, whereas countries in South America had higher rates. Additionally high-income countries had lower rates of neglect than did low- or middle-income countries. Last, estimates of physical abuse and neglect were lower than estimates of emotional abuse and sexual abuse. However, differing rates of physical abuse and neglect could be an artifact of cultural differences. In many countries, the use of physical force is a normative practice and is not seen as abuse (Viola et al., 2016). Similarly, in some countries, leaving infants and children in the care of young siblings is routine; in countries such as the United States, this would likely be considered neglectful (Korbin & Spilsbury, 1999).

Other important cultural values include the glorification of violence, rigid gender roles, and beliefs that diminish the status of the child within the parenting relationship, all of which increase the risk of maltreatment (World Health Organization, 2019). Another particularly important factor is attitudes on corporal punishment. Both within individual families in a culture and across different cultures, a belief that corporal punishment is necessary and normative is associated with a greater likelihood of its use and a consequently greater risk of abuse and neglect (Lansford et al., 2015). In the United States, homicide, domestic violence, and rape are common, and many states still permit corporal punishment in schools. Although corporal punishment, overall, has been trending down in recent decades, nearly 8 out of 10 parents of preschoolers and nearly half of parents of school-age children still report using physical punishment at home (Zolotor et al., 2011). By contrast, in countries where violent crime is infrequent and children are rarely spanked, such as Japan, China, and Tahiti, child abuse is rare (Celis, 1990).

HELPING FAMILIES IN TROUBLE

State and local child protective service agencies investigate reports of maltreatment. After making a determination of maltreatment, they determine what steps, if any, need to be taken. Agency staff may try to help the family resolve their problems or arrange for alternative care for children who cannot safely remain at home (USDHHS, 2020). Services for children who have been abused and their parents include shelters, education in parenting skills, and therapy. However, availability of services is often limited (Burns et al., 2004).

When authorities remove children from their homes, the usual alternative is foster care. Foster care removes a child from immediate danger, but it is often unstable, further alienates the child from the family, and may turn out to be another abusive situation. Often a child's basic health and educational needs are not met (David and Lucile Packard Foundation, 2004; National Research Council, 1993).

In part because of a scarcity of traditional foster homes and an increasing caseload, a growing proportion of placements are in kinship foster care, under the care of grandparents or other family members (Berrick, 1998; Geen, 2004). Although most foster children who leave the system are reunited with their families, about 28 percent reenter foster care within the next 10 years (Wulczyn, 2004). Children who have been in foster care are more likely than other children to become homeless, to commit crimes, and to become teenage mothers (David and Lucile Packard Foundation, 2004), as well as to suffer mental or physical health problems in adulthood (Zlotnick et al., 2012).

LONG-TERM EFFECTS OF MALTREATMENT

Long-term consequences of maltreatment may include poor physical, mental, and emotional health; impaired brain development (Romano et al., 2015; Glaser, 2000); cognitive, language, and academic difficulties; problems in attachment and social relationships (Child Welfare Information Gateway, 2013; Romano et al., 2015); and, in adolescence, heightened risks of poor academic achievement, delinquency, teenage pregnancy, alcohol and drug use, and suicide (Romano et al., 2015; Garwood et al., 2015; Halpern et al., 2018; Gomez et al., 2017). Abuse and neglect in childhood results in an elevated risk that the victims will, when grown, engage in criminal activity or themselves become abusers (Widom, 2017; Child Welfare Information Gateway, 2013). Moreover, adult survivors of child maltreatment report a lower quality of life (Weber et al., 2016) and poorer health as adults, including a higher incidence of heart disease, cancer, chronic lung disease, and liver disease (Chartier et al., 2010; Levine et al., 2017).

What are the long-term consequences of sexual abuse? Sexually abused children often become sexually active at an earlier age and tend to have higher numbers of sexual partners than children who were not sexually abused. As adults they tend to be more anxious, depressed, or suicidal and are more likely to be diagnosed with post-traumatic stress disorder and abuse drugs and alcohol (Fergusson et al., 2013). Moreover, sexual abuse may also compromise physical health: Sexual abuse survivors are more likely to be obese or suffer from stress-related or autoimmune disorders (Wilson, 2010).

Many maltreated children show remarkable resilience. Optimism, self-esteem, intelligence, creativity, humor, and independence are protective factors. Another key factor may be the social support of a caring adult (Levine et al., 2017; Child Welfare Information Gateway, 2019). Just as a dysfunctional, abusive relationship may pull a young child's developmental trajectory in a negative direction, a supportive loving relationship from a different adult may buffer that child from the storms of a difficult childhood.

summary and key terms

Foundations of Psychosocial Development

- Emotional development is orderly; complex emotions seem to develop from earlier, simpler ones.
- Crying, smiling, and laughing are early signs of emotion. Other indices are facial expressions, motor activity, body language, and physiological changes.
- Self-conscious and self-evaluative emotions arise after the development of self-awareness.

  personality, emotions, social smiling, anticipatory smiling, self-conscious emotions, self-awareness, self-evaluative emotions, altruistic behavior, empathy, mirror neurons

- Many children seem to fall into one of three categories of temperament: "easy," "difficult," and "slow-to-warm-up."
- Temperamental patterns appear to have a biological basis. They are generally stable but can be modified by experience.
- Goodness of fit between a child's temperament and environmental demands aids adjustment.
- Cross-cultural differences in temperament may reflect child-raising practices.

  temperament, "easy" children, "difficult" children, "slow-to-warm-up" children, goodness of fit

- Child-raising practices and caregiving roles vary around the world.

- Infants have strong needs for maternal closeness, warmth, and responsiveness as well as physical care.
- Fathering roles differ in various cultures.
- Although significant gender differences typically do not appear until after infancy, U.S. fathers, especially, promote early gender-typing.

gender, gender-typing

Developmental Issues in Infancy

- According to Erikson, infants in the first 18 months are in the first stage of personality development, basic sense of trust versus mistrust.
- By 12 months of age, infants form an internal working model of attachment based on a history of interactions with their attachment figure. The attachment figure acts as a secure base from which they explore their environment when they feel safe and retreat to when they feel frightened or upset.
- Research based on the Strange Situation has found four patterns of attachment: secure, avoidant, ambivalent (resistant), and disorganized-disoriented.
- Stranger anxiety and separation anxiety may arise during the second half of the 1st year.
- Newer instruments measure attachment in natural settings, in cross-cultural research, and with brain imaging.
- A parent's memories of childhood attachment can influence his or her own child's attachment.
- Infant attachment may have long-term implications for development.
- Mutual regulation enables babies to play an active part in regulating their emotional states.
- Social referencing has been observed as early as 5 months.

basic sense of trust versus mistrust, attachment, stranger anxiety, separation anxiety, Strange Situation, secure attachment, avoidant attachment, ambivalent (resistant) attachment, disorganized-disoriented attachment, mutual regulation, interactional synchrony, social referencing

Developmental Issues in Toddlerhood

- Erikson's second stage concerns autonomy versus shame and doubt.
- The sense of self arises between 4 and 10 months, as infants begin to perceive a difference between self and others.
- The self-concept builds on the perceptual sense of self and develops between 15 and 24 months with the emergence of self-awareness and self-recognition.
- Socialization, which rests on internalization of societally approved standards, begins with the development of self-regulation.

- A precursor of conscience is committed compliance to a caregiver's demands. Children who show receptive cooperation can be active partners in their socialization.
- Parenting practices, a child's temperament, the quality of the parent-child relationship, and cultural and socioeconomic factors may affect the ease and success of socialization.

self-concept, autonomy versus shame and doubt, socialization, internalization, self-regulation, conscience, situational compliance, committed compliance, receptive cooperation

Peer Influences

- Sibling relationships play a distinct role in socialization and influence relationships outside the home.
- Between ages 1½ and 3 years, children tend to show more interest in and understanding of other children.

Maternal Employment and Child Care

- Different cultures use a variety of caregivers, usually kin, for infants. Developed countries tend to use non-kin child care arrangements.
- There have not been consistent findings demonstrating a negative effect of maternal employment on child outcomes.
- Substitute child care varies in quality. The most important elements include warm, responsive caregivers and low staff turnover.

Maltreatment: Abuse and Neglect

- Forms of maltreatment are physical abuse, neglect, sexual abuse, and emotional maltreatment.
- Most victims of maltreatment are infants and toddlers. Some die due to failure to thrive. Others are victims of shaken baby syndrome.
- Characteristics of the abuser or neglecter, the family, the community, and the larger culture all contribute to child abuse and neglect.
- Maltreatment can interfere with physical, cognitive, emotional, and social development, and its effects can continue into adulthood. Still, many maltreated children show remarkable resilience.
- Preventing or stopping maltreatment may require multifaceted, coordinated community efforts.

physical abuse, neglect, sexual abuse, emotional maltreatment, nonorganic failure to thrive, shaken baby syndrome

Physical and Cognitive Development in Early Childhood

learning objectives

Identify physical changes in early childhood.

Describe three views of the cognitive changes that occur in early childhood.

Summarize how language develops in early childhood.

Evaluate different approaches to early childhood education.

bonzodog/Shutterstock

In this chapter we look at physical and cognitive development from ages 3 to 6. Children grow more slowly than before, but make enormous progress in muscle development and coordination. We trace their advances in the abilities to think, speak, and remember and consider several health concerns. We end with a discussion of early childhood education.

Physical Development

In early childhood, children slim down and shoot up. They need less sleep than before and are more likely to develop sleep problems. They get better at running, hopping, skipping, jumping, and throwing balls. They become more proficient at tying shoelaces, drawing with crayons, and pouring cereal, and they show a preference for using either the right or left hand.

BODILY GROWTH AND CHANGE

Children grow rapidly between ages 3 and 6, but less quickly than before. At about 3, children normally begin to lose their babyish roundness and take on the slender, athletic appearance of childhood. As abdominal muscles develop, the toddler potbelly tightens. The trunk, arms, and legs grow longer. The head is still relatively large, but the other parts of the body continue to catch up and body proportions become more adultlike.

The average 3-year-old child now weighs about 35 pounds. Both boys and girls typically grow about 2 to 3 inches a year during early childhood and gain approximately 4 to 6 pounds annually (Table 7.1). Boys have a slight edge in height and weight, which continues until the growth spurt of puberty.

Muscular and skeletal growth progresses, making children stronger. Cartilage turns to bone at a faster rate than before, and bones become harder. These changes, coordinated by the still-maturing brain and nervous system, promote the development of a wide range of motor skills.

SLEEP PATTERNS AND PROBLEMS

Sleep patterns change throughout the growing-up years (Figure 7.1). Most U.S. children average about 11 hours of sleep at night by age 5 and give up daytime naps (Hoban, 2004). In other cultures the timing of sleep may vary. Among the Gusii of Kenya, the Javanese in Indonesia, and the Zuni in New Mexico, young children have no regular bedtime and are allowed to stay up until they are sleepy. Among the Canadian Hare, 3-year-olds don't take naps but are put to sleep right after dinner and sleep as long as they wish in the morning (Broude, 1995). Children from predominantly Asian countries sleep, on average, less than children from predominantly non-Asian countries (Galland et al., 2012).

About a third of parents or caregivers report sleep problems in their young child (Mindell et al., 2015). Sleep disturbances may be caused by incomplete arousal from a deep sleep (Hoban, 2004) or by disordered breathing or restless leg movements (Guilleminault et al., 2003). These disturbances tend to run in families (Lane et al., 2017) and are associated with anxiety (Willis & Gregory, 2015), nasal abnormalities, and overweight (Bixler et al., 2009). Problems are particularly prevalent in children with

TABLE 7.1 Physical Growth, Ages 3 to 6 (50th percentile*)

Age	HEIGHT (INCHES)		WEIGHT (POUNDS)	
	Boys	Girls	Boys	Girls
3	39.0	36.6	35.3	34.5
4	42.0	41.7	40.8	40.3
5	44.8	44.2	46.6	45.0
6	47.2	46.7	52.8	52.4

*Fifty percent of children in each category are above this height or weight level, and 50 percent are below it.

Source: Fryar, C. D., Gu, Q., Ogden, C. L., & Flegal, K. M. (2016). Anthropometric reference data for children and adults: United States, 2011–2014. *Vital Health Statistics, 3*(39).

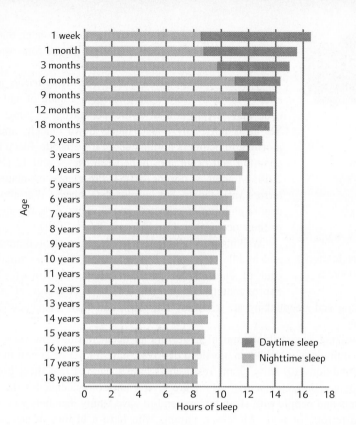

FIGURE 7.1

Typical Sleep Requirements in Childhood

The number of hours of sleep steadily decreases throughout childhood.

Source: Thiedke, C. C. Sleep disorders and sleep problems in childhood. American Academy of Family Physicians, 63(2), 2001, 277-287.

physical or learning disabilities, including both attention-deficit/hyperactivity disorder and autism (Neto et al., 2016; Mazurek & Sohl, 2016). Culture also matters. Parents from predominantly Asian countries report more sleep disturbances in their children than do white parents, and the sleep problems reported by Asian parents are more strongly associated with individual demographic variables than with actual sleep measures in children. This suggests parental perceptions and cultural expectations about sleep are driving the cultural differences (Sahdeh et al., 2011).

Fortunately, in most cases sleep disturbances are occasional and are usually outgrown (Mason & Pack, 2007). The majority of sleep problems are behavioral in nature and most commonly include refusing to go to bed, taking a long time to go to sleep, or frequent night waking (Owens et al., 2019). Many sleep issues are the result of ineffective parenting practices that exacerbate rather than ease the problem (Mindell et al., 2010; Table 7.2). For instance, allowing young children to nap in the daytime to catch up on

TABLE 7.2 Encouraging Good Sleep Habits
HELPING CHILDREN GO TO SLEEP
• Encourage children to exercise during the day and avoid food or beverages with caffeine.
• Avoid electronic media before bedtime, and do not keep a television in the child's bedroom.
• Establish a regular, unrushed bedtime routine of quiet activities, such as taking a warm bath or reading a story.
• Do not stay in the room with your child until he or she falls asleep—encourage the ability to fall asleep independently.
• Keep the bedroom darkened and at a comfortable temperature.
• Offer rewards for good bedtime behavior, such as stickers or praise.
• Maintain consistent sleep and waking schedules.

Sources: Mindell, J. A., Meltzer, L. J., Carskadon, M. A., & Chervin, R. D. (2009). Developmental aspects of sleep hygiene: findings from the 2004 National Sleep Foundation Sleep in America Poll. *Sleep Medicine, 10*(7), 771–779; Galland, B. C., & Mitchell, E. A. (2010). Helping children sleep. *Archives of Disease in Childhood, 95* (10), 850–853.

Nightmares are common in children and have been related to difficult temperament, anxiety, dependency, and stress.
Yuliya Evstratenko/Shutterstock

sleep can result in difficulty getting to sleep later that evening. Possible sleep disturbances include night terrors, walking and talking while asleep, and nightmares.

A child who experiences *sleep* (or *night*) *terrors* appears to awaken abruptly from a deep sleep in a state of agitation. The child may scream and sit up in bed, staring or thrashing about. Yet he is not really awake, quiets down quickly, and the next morning remembers nothing about the episode. Sleep terrors are common and occur mostly between ages 4 and 12 (Petit et al., 2010; Mindell & Owens, 2015). Prevalence estimates of night terrors vary widely, but current data suggest that about 30 percent of children are affected, and boys and girls are equally prone to their occurrence (VanHorn & Street, 2019).

Walking and talking during sleep are also common in early and middle childhood. It is estimated that approximately 5 percent of children sleepwalk (Stallman & Kohler, 2016) and approximately 37 percent sleeptalk (Laberge et al., 2000). Sleepwalking and sleeptalking are generally harmless, and their frequency declines as children age.

Sleepwalking, sleeptalking, and night terrors all occur during slow wave sleep and are more common when children are sleep deprived, have a fever or are on medications, or when conditions are noisy. Some researchers have suggested that these events represent the same underlying disorder. There are several lines of evidence for this assertion. Sleepwalkers and people with sleep terrors tend to have family members who sleepwalk, have sleep terrors, or both. Moreover, parents who have a history of sleepwalking or sleeptalking tend to have children who have night terrors. Young children who have night terrors also tend to later sleepwalk (Petit et al., 2015).

Nightmares are also common (Petit et al., 2007). The occurrence of nightmares has been related to difficult child temperament, high overall childhood anxiety, and bedtime parenting practices that promote dependency (Moore, 2012). Some studies suggest that overexcitement, perhaps seeing a frightening television show or a video game, is related to nightmares, but results on this are inconsistent (Schredl et al., 2008). Frequent or persistent nightmares may signal excessive stress (Hoban, 2004) and are correlated with emotional, attentional, and conduct problems (Schredl et al., 2009).

enuresis
Repeated urination in clothing or in bed.

Most children stay dry, day and night, by ages 3 to 5, but **enuresis**—repeated, involuntary urination at night by children old enough to be expected to have bladder control—is not unusual. About 10 to 15 percent of 5-year-olds, more commonly boys, wet the bed regularly. More than half outgrow the condition by age 8 without help (Community Paediatrics Committee, 2005). The discovery of genes linked to enuresis points to heredity as a major factor (von Gontard et al., 2011).

Children (and their parents) need to be reassured that enuresis is common and not serious. The child is not to blame and should not be punished. Enuresis that is particularly persistent is most commonly treated with an antidiuretic hormone or nighttime alarm (Wright, 2016).

BRAIN DEVELOPMENT

During the first few years of life, brain development is rapid and profound. At about 5 years of age, the brain is approximately 90 percent of adult size. From ages 3 to 6, the most rapid brain growth occurs in the frontal areas that regulate planning and goal setting, with the density of synapses in the prefrontal cortex peaking at age 4 (Lenroot & Giedd, 2006). This "exuberant connectivity" is gradually pruned over time as a result of experience, a process that underlies the great plasticity of the human brain (Innocenti & Price, 2005; Stiles et al., 2015). In addition, myelin (a fatty substance that coats the axons of nerve fibers and accelerates neural conduction) continues to form (Giedd & Rapoport, 2010). By age 6, the brain has attained about 90 percent of its peak volume

(Stiles et al., 2015). From ages 6 to 11, rapid brain growth occurs in areas that support associative thinking, language, and spatial relations (Thompson et al., 2000). Much of this development occurs in the prefrontal cortex, a change that appears to support children's increasing cognitive flexibility (Buttleman & Karbach, 2017).

The *corpus callosum* is a thick band of nerve fibers that connects both hemispheres of the brain and allows them to communicate more rapidly and effectively with each other. The corpus callosum continues to be myelinized throughout childhood and adolescence, with peak volume occurring later in boys than in girls (Luders et al., 2010).

MOTOR SKILLS

Preschool children make great advances in **gross motor skills** involving the large muscles (Table 7.3). Because their bones and muscles are stronger and their lung capacity is greater, they can run, jump, and climb farther and faster. And because of the development of the sensory and motor areas of the cerebral cortex, they are better able to coordinate their motor actions. Children vary in adeptness, depending on their genetic endowment and opportunities to learn and practice motor skills. Physical development flourishes best in active, unstructured free play.

gross motor skills
Physical skills that involve the large muscles.

The gross motor skills developed during early childhood are the basis for sports, dancing, and other activities that often begin in middle childhood. Thus it is perhaps not surprising that motor coordination predicts participation in sports (Vandorpe et al., 2012; Henrique et al., 2016). Motor coordination has also been associated with both childhood and adolescent levels of physical activity, although it does not necessarily predict adult physical activity (Lopes et al., 2011; Hofhelder & Schott, 2014). Moreover, poor motor coordination has been associated with an increased risk of obesity or overweight in children in what is likely to be a reciprocal relationship (Cattuzzo et al., 2016).

Children from non-Western countries are exposed to different motor activities, and thus we might expect their development to likewise differ. Unfortunately, such data are limited. What information does exist, however, illustrates the influence of culture on motor development. For example, 4- to 6-year-old American children performed better at throwing and catching tasks, presumably due to encouragement in sports activities (Chow et al., 2001), and 4 year-old Brazilian children were more advanced motorically than British children, perhaps because of more frequent opportunities for free play activities (Victora et al., 1990).

Fine motor skills, such as buttoning shirts and drawing pictures, involve eye-hand and small-muscle coordination. Gains in these skills allow young children to take more responsibility for their personal care. Similarly to gross motor skills, culture can influence development. For example, 4- to 6-year-old children from Hong Kong performed better on fine motor tasks than did American children, presumably because of their practice with chopsticks and entry into preschool (Chow et al., 2001). Alternatively, a lack of

fine motor skills
Physical skills that involve the small muscles and eye-hand coordination.

TABLE 7.3 Gross Motor Skills in Early Childhood		
3-Year-Olds	**4-Year-Olds**	**5-Year-Olds**
Cannot turn or stop suddenly	Have more effective control of stopping, starting, and turning	Can start, turn, and stop effectively
Can jump a distance of 15 to 24 inches	Can jump a distance of 24 to 33 inches	Can make a running jump of 28 to 36 inches
Can ascend a stairway unaided, alternating feet	Can descend a long stairway alternating feet, if supported	Can descend a long stairway unaided, alternating feet
Can hop, using an irregular series of jumps	Can hop four to six steps on one foot	Can easily hop a distance of 16 feet

Source: Corbin, C. (1973). *A textbook of motor development.* New York, NY: W. C. Brown Co.

As children develop physically, they are better able to make their bodies do what they want. Large-muscle development lets them run to kick a soccer ball; increasing eye-hand coordination helps them use a pencil or weave cloth. (top left): Robert Christopher/Cultura/Image Source; (bottom left): Liderina/Shutterstock; (top right): Lew Robertson/Stone/Getty Images

systems of action
Increasingly complex combinations of motor skills, which permit a wider or more precise range of movement and more control of the environment.

handedness
Preference for using a particular hand.

practice can lead to slower motor development. Children of Arab descent, who family members often dressed and who thus had little practice, performed poorly on tasks such as putting on or taking off clothes on a standardized test of motor abilities when compared to Western samples (Al-Naquib et al., 1999).

As they develop motor skills, preschoolers continually merge abilities they already have with those they are acquiring to produce more complex capabilities. Such combinations of skills are known as **systems of action.**

Handedness **Handedness,** the preference for using one hand over the other, is usually evident by about age 3. Because the left hemisphere of the brain, which controls the right side of the body, is usually dominant, 90 percent of people favor their right side (Coren, 2012). Boys are more likely to be left-handed than are girls (Papadatou-Pastou et al., 2008).

Is handedness genetic or learned? Some researchers argue for genetic explanations, citing, for example, high heritability estimates between twins or family members (Medland et al., 2009; Lien et al., 2015). However, rather than being a single gene, some evidence suggests handedness may be the result of many genes working together (McManus, et al., 2013; Armour, et al., 2014). Others argue that environmental influences are likely to be key given that such factors as low birth weight, difficult deliveries, and multiples (i.e., twins and triplets) are associated with left-handedness (Alibeik & Angaji, 2010; De Kovel et al., 2019).

Cultural influences, too, play a role. In one study of traditional cultures, including the G/wi San of Botswana, the Himba of Namibia, and the Yanomamo of Venezuela, most people were generally ambidextrous, with the notable exception of right-hand dominance for precision tool work (Marchant et al., 1995). In another similar culture, the Tucano of Colombia, where the use of the right hand was encouraged and reinforced in childhood, all participants were right-hand dominant (Bryden et al., 1993). Similarly, children who attend schools are more likely to be right-handed than children who do not receive a formal education (Geuze et al., 2012). Some cultures, such as Japan and India, are biased against left-handedness, and people from those cultures are also less likely to be left-hand dominant than those from Western countries (Ida & Mandal, 2003).

Health and Safety

Because of widespread immunization, many of what once were the major diseases of childhood are now much less common in many, but not all, countries. In some countries, obesity and overweight are challenges; in others, malnutrition remains a key childhood risk. Allergies, exposure to pollution, and accidental death are also risks.

OBESITY AND OVERWEIGHT

Worldwide, an estimated 41 million children under age 5 were obese or overweight in 2016 (World Health Organization, 2018). If current trends continue, 70 million children under age 5 will be overweight or obese by 2025 (World Health Organization, 2017). Prevalence rates have leveled off in the United States (Ogden et al., 2015); however, rates continue to rise in developing countries with less income (World Health Organization, 2017). Overall, poorer countries have more quickly rising prevalence rates for obesity than richer countries, and this socioeconomic disparity has been increasing in the last 2 decades (Chung et al., 2016).

Obesity is a serious problem among U.S. preschoolers. In 2015–2016, almost 14 percent of 2- to 5-year-olds had a body mass index (BMI) at or above the 95th percentile for their age; this number was slightly higher in boys than in girls. This number was highest in Hispanic children (25.8 percent), followed by African American (22 percent) and white children (14.1 percent), with the lowest obesity rates found in Asian American children (11 percent) (Hales et al., 2017).

Overweight was also an issue; approximately 26 percent of children aged 2 to 5 years have a body mass index at or above the 85th percentile for their age, with findings for gender and ethnicity mirroring those for obesity (Skinner et al., 2018). Children who come from families lower on the socioeconomic ladder are more likely to be obese (Ogden et al., 2010). Although researchers thought for a time prevalence rates had leveled off in the United States, more recent data suggest they are still rising (Hales et al., 2017; Skinner et al., 2018).

A tendency toward obesity can be hereditary, but the main factors driving the obesity epidemic are environmental (AAP, 2004). Excessive weight gain hinges on increases in caloric intake, changes in diet composition, declining levels of physical activity, and changes in the gut microbiome (Sahoo et al., 2015; Ng et al., 2014). Increasingly, the pattern of weight change with age is emerging as a key risk factor. At approximately 5 to 6 years of age, children tend to be at their leanest. After this, children tend to gain more weight relative to body size, a process known as adiposity rebound. Children who reach adiposity rebound at earlier ages are more likely to become obese in adulthood (Delamater et al., 2013). Another important factor is the availability of highly processed, energy-dense, nutrient-poor foods (Crino et al., 2015). Research in Action addresses the influence of available food sources on obesity in children.

Prevention of obesity in the early years is critical (Quattrin et al., 2005). Overweight children tend to become obese adults (Kumar & Kelly, 2017) and excess body mass is a threat to health (Biro & Wein, 2010). Thus early childhood is a good time to treat overweight, when a child's diet is still subject to parental influence or control (Quattrin et al., 2005). Trends toward childhood obesity can be identified as early as 6 months of age, and the earlier interventions start for at-risk children, the more likely they are to be effective (De Onis et al., 2010).

Data suggest that three factors are important in the prevention of obesity: (1) regularly eating an evening meal as a family, (2) getting adequate sleep, and (3) watching less than 2 hours of television a day (Anderson & Whitaker, 2010).

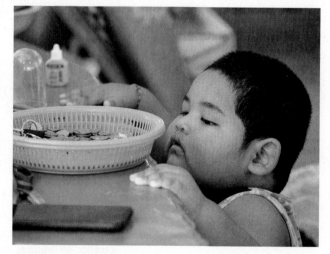

Obesity among young children has increased. Sergey Colonel/ Shutterstock

UNDERNUTRITION

In developed countries such as the United States, overweight and obesity are common patterns. However, in many developing countries a different pattern emerges. Some children appear to be of normal weight but are shorter than they should be for their age and may have cognitive and physical deficiencies. We call these children stunted. This form of malnutrition is often the result of chronic, persistent hunger. Other children are an appropriate height for their age but are thinner than they should be. We call these

research in action

FOOD DESERTS, FOOD SWAMPS, AND OBESITY

As with any complex human trait, obesity is not caused by any one thing. Although genetics or activity level matter, researchers should not ignore structural and systemic features in the development of obesity. One such feature is the local food environment and food system. It is easy to blame individuals for poor food choices; however, it is hardly fair to do so when they do not have the access or means to secure healthy, high-quality food.

Food deserts are physical locations where access to fresh fruits and vegetables and healthy, whole foods is limited. Food deserts are found more frequently in low-income areas, rural or inner-city areas lacking accessible supermarkets or grocery stores, as well as ethnic minority neighborhoods, even when socioeconomic status is controlled for (Walter et al., 2010). Moreover, in many areas healthy food choices are supplanted with retailers such as fast-food restaurants and convenience stores selling low-quality, high-calorie, highly processed food. Locations such as these are known as food swamps and the presence of fast food and junk food is as important as the absence of healthy alternatives (Cooksey-Stowers et al., 2017).

Research shows that children in food deserts have a higher body mass index (Thomsen et al., 2016) and face greater likelihood of being overweight (Schafft et al., 2009). Similarly, children in food swamps are more likely to be obese (Newman et al., 2014), and food swamps are even more predictive of obesity risk than food deserts (Cooksey-Stowers et al., 2017).

In the developing world, people with the most money, and hence the greatest ability to buy food, are the most likely to be obese. However, the converse is true in developed countries. Research on food deserts and food swamps reconciles the apparently contradictory finding that in developed countries, people with the least money are the most likely to be obese (Dinsa et al., 2012; Wang & Lim, 2012). For families on the financial brink, traveling outside of their neighborhood or town to obtain fresh, healthy foods constitutes a time and economic burden (Walker et al., 2010). As a result, families subsist on foods available within their local area. Moreover, when budgets stretch thin, healthy whole grains, lean meats, and fresh vegetables and fruits may be nixed in favor of empty-calorie foods such as highly processed foods and baked goods. Empty calorie foods tend to cost less, but are high in calories and low in nutrients (Drewnowski, 2009).

Many associate malnutrition with starvation; however, poor nutritional status can also arise through a consistent high-calorie, nutrient-poor diet of "empty foods" associated with the promotion of rapid weight gain during early childhood (Lobstein et al., 2015). This is not the consequence of poor parenting or a failure to understand or care about children's food choices. As with starvation in developing countries, obesity can involve issues of socioeconomic status and equity.

what's your view What do you think matters more—limited access to healthy food, or easy availability of unhealthy food? What policies or programs might be useful in alleviating issues related to food deserts or food swamps?

children wasted. This form of malnutrition is generally the result of a recent, rapid weight loss. In 2018, approximately 149 million children under the age of 5 were stunted and another 49 million were wasted from lack of adequate nutrients and calories (World Health Organization, 2019).

Another form of undernutrition is known as hidden hunger. In hidden hunger, children do not receive sufficient amounts of essential vitamins or minerals even if they receive sufficient calories in their diets. Hidden hunger is found in both high- and low-income countries. Although statistics are difficult to determine, the estimated number of children suffering from vitamin A and iron deficiency, as an example, is 340 million (UNICEF, 2019).

Nutrition-related factors are the underlying cause in about 45 percent of worldwide deaths for children under 5 (World Health Organization, 2019). South Asia has the highest level of stunting (34.4 percent) and wasting (15.2 percent). In North America, by comparison, 2.6 percent of children are stunted and 0.4 percent are wasted. Hidden hunger is most prevalent in Africa, where approximately 76 percent of children under the age of 5 lack at least one essential micronutrient in their diet (UNICEF, 2019).

Because undernourished children usually live in deprived circumstances, the specific effects of poor nutrition are hard to determine. However, taken together, these deprivations may negatively affect not only growth and physical well-being but cognitive and psychosocial development as well (Martorell et al., 2010), and the effects may be long lasting (Liu et al., 2003).

ALLERGIES

A food allergy is an abnormal immune system response to a specific food. Reactions can range from tingling in the mouth and hives to more serious, life-threatening reactions such as shortness of breath and even death. Ninety percent of food allergies can be attributed to eight foods: milk, eggs, peanuts, tree nuts, fish, soy, wheat, and shellfish (Boyce et al., 2010). Food allergies are more prevalent in children than in adults, and most children will outgrow their allergies (Branum & Lukacs, 2008). In 2018 about 5.8 percent of children under the age of 5 suffered from some type of food allergy (Centers for Disease Control and Prevention, 2019).

Research on children under age 18 has demonstrated an increase in the prevalence of skin and food allergies over the past 10 years. There is no clear pattern to this increase, and it exists equally for boys and girls and across different races and ethnicities (Branum & Lukacs, 2008; Jackson et al., 2013). However, children across a variety of different cultures with a variety of allergies, including indoor and outdoor allergies, skin allergies, and food allergies, are more likely to come from families of higher socioeconomic status (Uphoff et al., 2015).

Changes in diet, how foods are processed, and decreased vitamin D based upon less exposure to the sun have all been suggested as contributors to the increase in allergy rates. A theory that society is too clean and that children's immune systems are less mature because they are not exposed to enough dirt and germs has also been explored. The link between eczema and food allergies has also led some researchers to theorize that sensitization to allergens develops through skin exposure. Additionally, better awareness by doctors and parents might factor into the reported increases. Although possible explanations abound, not enough evidence exists to pinpoint a cause (Sicherer & Sampson, 2018; Lack, 2008).

DEATHS AND ACCIDENTAL INJURIES

In 2018, estimates are that approximately 5.5 million children under the age of 5 died worldwide. Although large, this number nonetheless represents a 59 percent drop from 1990. Most child deaths are the result of infectious diseases or neonatal complications (World Health Organization, 2019). Window on the World discusses children's chances of surviving the first 5 years of life the world over.

In the United States, deaths in childhood are relatively few compared with deaths in adulthood, and accidents are the leading cause of death from the ages of 5 to 12 years (Kochanek et al., 2019). Most deaths from injuries among preschoolers in the United States and across Europe occur in the home—often from fires, drowning in bathtubs, suffocation, poisoning, falls, or homicide (Nagaraja et al., 2005; Sengoelge et al., 2010). Everyday medications, such as aspirin, acetaminophen, and cough medicine, and even vitamins can be dangerous to inquisitive young children. U.S. laws requiring the use of car seats, childproof caps on medicine bottles and other dangerous household products, regulation of product safety, mandatory helmets for bicycle riders, and safe storage of medicines have improved child safety.

Other common causes of death in early childhood include cancer, congenital abnormalities and chromosomal disorders, assault and homicide, heart disease, respiratory diseases (including both chronic respiratory disease as well as influenza and pneumonia), and septicemia (a bacterial infection that poisons the blood leading to organ failure) (Heron, 2018).

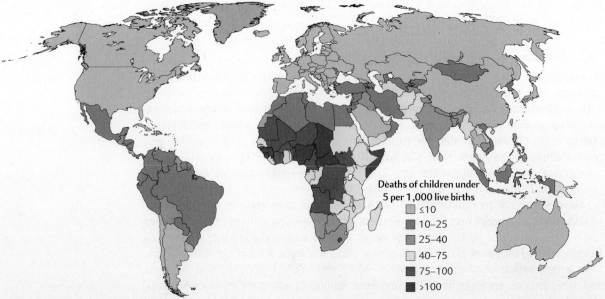

Under 5 Mortality Rates by Country, 2018
Source: UNICEF Data. (2019, September). Retrieved from https://data.unicef.org/topic/child-survival/under-five-mortality/

International efforts to improve child health focus on the first 5 years of life because nearly 90 percent of deaths in children under age 15 occur during those years. Worldwide, in 2018 about three-quarters of deaths in children under the age of 5 were attributed to seven issues: preterm birth complications (18 percent), pneumonia (15 percent), intrapartum complications (13 percent), congenital abnormalities (9 percent), diarrhea (8 percent), neonatal sepsis (7 percent), and malaria (5 percent) (UNICEF, 2019).

There are great disparities in children's survival prospects depending on the region in which they live. About 82 percent of all under-5 deaths in the world occur in sub-Saharan Africa (54 percent) and South Asian (28 percent). The risk of a child dying in sub-Saharan Africa is 15 times higher than it is for children in higher-income countries (UNICEF, 2019).

The risk of a child dying under the age of 5 years is strongly affected by poverty. Almost all child deaths occur in the poorest regions of developing countries, where nutrition is inadequate, water is unsafe, and sanitary facilities are lacking. Poor air quality appears to be strongly associated with increased mortality risk. Maternal variables are also important, particularly with respect to newborn deaths. Children born to mothers who are young, uneducated, or who have had children closely spaced are at higher risk (Hug et al., 2018). Over half of these deaths are preventable. Often, simple interventions such as immunization campaigns, better nutrition, safe and sanitary food and water supplies, and appropriate access to health care providers would be effective (World Health Organization, 2019).

The under-5 child mortality rate has decreased by 59 percent since 1990, and more than 80 countries have been able to reduce their under-5 mortality rates by at least two-thirds. Of these countries, 31 are low- or lower-middle-income countries, demonstrating that although poverty remains an obstacle, it is not insurmountable. However, despite these gains, approximately 15,000 children under the age of 5 will die every day (UNICEF, 2019).

Thus a global effort is being made to reduce child mortality rates. The goals, which vary by country, broadly include ending preventable child deaths while also addressing emerging child health priorities. These emerging priorities include addressing congenital abnormalities and noncommunicable diseases such as diabetes, heart disease, and cancer. Additionally, reducing childhood obesity has emerged as an important priority (World Health Organization, 2019).

what's your view

What else do you think could help to combat child mortality around the world? What are the responsibilities of individual countries to help decrease child mortality worldwide?

ENVIRONMENTAL INFLUENCES ON HEALTH

Although some children are genetically predisposed toward certain medical conditions, environmental factors also play a major role.

Socioeconomic Status and Race/Ethnicity The lower a family's SES, the greater a child's risks of illness, injury, and death (Braveman et al., 2010; Olson et al., 2010). Poor children are more likely than other children to have chronic conditions and activity limitations, to lack health insurance, and to have unmet medical and dental needs. Social factors linked to poverty, such as increased stress, also impact health outcomes (Murray et al., 2013). In particular, children from racial and ethnic minorities may experience stress-related health issues at higher rates due to cumulative effects of discrimination, stigma, and prejudice (Cheng & Goodman, 2015).

A key factor in health is, not surprisingly, access to necessary medical services. Health insurance is thus an important predictor of child health. Medicaid has been a safety net for many poor children since 1965. However, despite this, many children remained uninsured. With the passage of the Affordable Care Act of 2010, the number of uninsured children dropped to a historic low of 4.5 percent in 2015 (Federal Interagency Forum on Child and Family Statistics, 2019). Unfortunately this promising trend reversed in 2017 with the repeal of the individual mandate, the requirement that all Americans carry a minimum level of health insurance or pay a fee. By 2018, the rate of uninsured children rose to 5.5 percent, or 4.3 million children (Berchick et al., 2019). The loss of coverage was most striking in families of low and moderate income and in states that did not expand Medicaid (Alker & Roygardner, 2019).

Race and ethnicity are associated with access to health insurance. American Indians/ Native American children (13.2 percent) have the highest uninsured rate, followed by Hispanic (8.2 percent) children. The sharpest rise in the uninsured rate from 2017 to 2018 was in Hispanic children (Alker & Roygardner, 2019). Although language and cultural barriers and the need for more Latino care providers may help explain some of these disparities (Betancourt et al., 2016), researchers believe a "chilling effect" has occurred for families in which the child is a citizen but the parent is not. Despite children being eligible for Medicaid, such families may avoid enrollment out of fears of deportation. African American families were the only group to show an improvement in health insurance status with a significant increase in coverage from 2017 to 2018 (Alker & Roygardner, 2019).

Homelessness Homelessness results from circumstances that force people to choose between food, shelter, and other basic needs. Factors that contribute to homelessness include lack of employment opportunities, declines in public assistance funds, lack of affordable health care, domestic violence, mental illness, and addiction (National Coalition for the Homeless, 2017). Current estimates are that there are approximately 2.5 million homeless children each year in the United States (Bassuk et al., 2014).

Families now make up 33 percent of the homeless population on any given night. African American families, at 51 percent, are the most likely racial group to be homeless despite accounting for only 13 percent of the U.S. population. Latino families, at 29 percent, are also at high risk of homelessness (Henry et al., 2018). Young families, especially those headed by single mothers, are more likely to be homeless (United States Interagency Council on Homelessness, 2018).

Many homeless children spend their early years in unstable, insecure, and often unsanitary environments. They may be cut off from ready access to medical care and schooling. These children suffer more physical health problems than poor children who have homes, and they are more likely to

Families with children are the fastest-growing part of the homeless population. Jim West/Alamy Stock Photo

have a low birth weight or need neonatal care in infancy. Homeless children are more likely to experience separations from their parents and witness violence. They also tend to suffer from depression and anxiety and to have academic and behavior problems (Dwomoh & Dinoflo, 2018; Richards et al., 2011). More research is needed on evidence-based interventions to tackle the multitude of risk factors that homeless children are exposed to (Zlotnick et al., 2012).

Exposure to Environmental Pollutants Parental smoking is a preventable cause of childhood illness and death. The potential damage caused by exposure to tobacco is greatest during the early years of life (Constant et al., 2011). Children exposed to parental smoke are at increased risk of respiratory infections such as bronchitis and pneumonia, ear problems, worsened asthma, and slowed lung growth. In 1988 to 1994, approximately 85 percent of children between the ages of 4 and 11 years showed evidence of exposure to secondhand smoke. In 2013 to 2014, this number dropped to 37 percent, with African American children and children living in poverty at the highest risk (Federal Interagency Forum on Child and Family Statistics, 2019).

Air pollution is associated with increased risks of death and of chronic respiratory disease. Environmental contaminants also may play a role in certain childhood cancers, neurological disorders, attention-deficit/hyperactivity disorder, and mental retardation (Woodruff et al., 2004). In 2017, 62 percent of U.S. children lived in counties that failed to meet one or more national air quality standards at least once during the year (Federal Interagency Forum on Child and Family Statistics, 2019).

Children are more vulnerable than adults to chronic pesticide damage (Federal Interagency Forum on Child and Family Statistics, 2019). There is some evidence that pesticide exposure may negatively affect the developing brain (Jurewicz & Hanke, 2008). Pesticide exposure is greater among children in agricultural and inner-city families (Dilworth-Bart & Moore, 2006).

Children can get elevated concentrations of lead from contaminated food or water, from airborne industrial wastes, or from inhaling dust or playing with paint chips in places where there is peeling lead-based paint. Lead poisoning can interfere with cognitive development and can lead to irreversible neurological and behavioral problems (Federal Interagency Forum on Child and Family Statistics, 2019). Very high levels of blood lead concentration may cause headaches, abdominal pain, loss of appetite, agitation, or lethargy and eventually vomiting, stupor, and convulsions (AAP Committee on Environmental Health, 2005).

Children's median blood lead levels have dropped by 89 percent in the United States compared to 1976–1980 levels due to laws mandating removal of lead from gasoline and paints and reducing smokestack emissions. The number of children with elevated levels of lead in their blood has declined from about 25 percent of children aged 1 to 5 in 1994 to 0.9 percent 2016. Still, many children are at risk due to lead in dust, paint chips, and other sources, and rates of elevated lead levels are highest among non-Hispanic Blacks and children living in poverty (Federal Interagency Forum on Child and Family Statistics, 2019).

Cognitive Development: Piagetian Approach

preoperational stage
In Piaget's theory, the second major stage of cognitive development, in which symbolic thought expands but children cannot yet use logic.

In this chapter we turn our attention to Piaget's second stage, the **preoperational stage.** Lasting from approximately ages 2 to 7, it is characterized by an expansion in symbolic thought. However, children are not fully ready to engage in logical mental operations. Let's look at some advances and some immature aspects of preoperational thought (Tables 7.4 and 7.5) and at recent research, some of which challenges Piaget's conclusions.

ADVANCES OF PREOPERATIONAL THOUGHT

Advances in symbolic thought are accompanied by a growing understanding of space, causality, identities, categorization, and number.

TABLE 7.4 Cognitive Advances during Early Childhood

Advance	Significance	Example
Use of symbols	Children do not need sensorimotor contact with something in order to think about it. Children can imagine that things are something different than they are.	Simon asks his mother about the elephants they saw on their trip to the circus several months earlier. Rolf pretends that a slice of apple is a vacuum cleaner "vrooming" across the kitchen table.
Understanding of identities	Children are aware that superficial alterations do not change the nature of things.	Antonio knows that his teacher is dressed up as a pirate but is still his teacher underneath the costume.
Understanding of cause and effect	Children realize that events have causes.	Seeing a ball roll from behind a wall, Aneko looks behind the wall for the person who kicked the ball.
Ability to classify	Children organize objects, people, and events into meaningful categories.	Rosa sorts the pinecones she collected on a nature walk into two piles: "big" and "little."
Understanding of number	Children can count and deal with quantities.	Lindsay shares some candy with her friends, counting to make sure that each girl gets the same amount.
Empathy	Children become more able to imagine how others might feel.	Emilio tries to comfort his friend when he sees that his friend is upset.
Theory of mind	Children become more aware of the mental activity of others.	Blanca wants to save some cookies for herself, so she hides them from her brother in a pasta box. She knows her brother will not look in a place where he doesn't expect to find cookies.

TABLE 7.5 Immature Aspects of Preoperational Thought (According to Piaget)

Limitation	Description	Example
Centration: inability to decenter	Children focus on one aspect of a situation and neglect others.	Jacob thinks he has more juice than his sister because his juice box has been poured into a tall, skinny glass, but hers has been poured into a short, wide glass.
Irreversibility	Children fail to understand that actions can be reversed.	Jacob does not realize that the juice in each glass can be poured back into the original juice box, and that as they held the same amount then, they must still have the same amount now even if they look different.
Focus on states rather than transformations	Children fail to understand the significance of the transformation between states.	Jacob does not understand that transforming the shape of a liquid (pouring it from one container into another) does not change the amount.
Transductive reasoning	Children see causes where none exist.	Luis was mean to his sister. Then she got sick. Luis concludes that he made his sister sick.
Egocentrism	Children assume everyone else thinks, perceives, and feels as they do.	Kara holds a book so only she can see the picture she is asking her father to explain to her.
Animism	Children attribute life to objects not alive.	Amanda says the car is hungry and wants some gas to eat.
Inability to distinguish appearance from reality	Children confuse what is real with outward appearance.	Courtney believes that if she wears blue-tinted glasses, everything she sees really did turn blue.

Cognitive Development: Piagetian Approach   LIFE: THE ESSENTIALS OF HUMAN DEVELOPMENT   **171**

symbolic function
Piaget's term for ability to use mental representations (words, numbers, or images) to which a child has attached meaning.

pretend play
Play involving imaginary people and situations; also called fantasy *play, dramatic play,* or *imaginative play.*

transduction
Piaget's term for a preoperational child's tendency to mentally link particular phenomena, whether or not there is logically a causal relationship.

The Symbolic Function "I want ice cream!" announces Gemma, age 4, trudging indoors from the hot, dusty backyard. She has not seen or smelled or tasted anything that triggered this desire. Rather, she has called up the concept from her memories.

Being able to think about something in the absence of sensory or motor cues characterizes the **symbolic function.** Children who have attained symbolic function can use symbols, or mental representations, such as words, numbers, or images to which a person has attached meaning. This is a vital achievement because without symbols people could not communicate verbally, make change, read maps, or treasure photos of distant loved ones.

Deferred imitation, in which children imitate an action at some point after having observed it, is related to symbolic function because it requires the child to have kept a mental representation of that action. Another marker of symbolic function is **pretend play.** In pretend play, also called *fantasy play, dramatic play,* or *imaginary play,* children use an object to represent something else. For example, a child may hold up a remote control to her ear while pretending to talk on a cell phone. By far the most extensive use of the symbolic function is language. Language, at its heart, is a system of symbols. For example, the word "key" is a symbol for the class of objects used to open doors. When we see the emergence of language in young children, we have a wide and clear window into their increasing use of the symbolic function.

Understanding of Objects in Space In addition to their growing ability to use the symbolic function, children also slowly begin to be able to understand the symbols that describe physical spaces. It is not until at least age 3 that most children reliably grasp the relationships between pictures, maps, or scale models and the objects or spaces they represent. So, for example, older preschoolers can view a scale model of a room, be shown on that model where a toy is hidden, and then find the toy in the actual room. They can transfer the spatial understanding gained from working with models to the real world and vice versa (DeLoache, 2011).

Understanding of Causality Piaget maintained that preoperational children cannot yet reason logically about cause and effect. Instead, he said, they reason by **transduction.** They mentally link two events, especially events close in time, whether or not there is logically a causal relationship. For example, Jamal may think that his "bad" behavior caused his parents' divorce.

Piaget was incorrect in believing that young children could not understand causality. When tested in situations that are appropriate to their overall level of cognitive development, young children do grasp cause and effect. For example, in one study, children were shown two small and one large light. Pressing on one of the small lights, which was attached to the large light by a wire, caused the large light to illuminate. Four-year-old children were able to understand that a relevant change (switching the wire connection to the other small light) would alter the causal sequence, but an irrelevant change (moving a block near the light) would not (Buchanan & Sobel, 2011).

Understanding of Identities and Categorization Preschool children also develop a better understanding of *identities:* the concept that people and many things are fundamentally the same even if they change in outward form, size, or appearance. For example, putting on a wig does not make a person a different person; rather, it is just a surface change in appearance. This understanding underlies the emerging self-concept, and many of the processes involved in understanding the identity of others are mirrored in the understanding of one's own identity.

Categorization, or classification, requires a child to identify similarities and differences. By age 4, many children can classify by two criteria, such as color and shape. Children use this ability to order many aspects of their lives, categorizing people as "good," "bad," "nice," "mean," and so forth.

One type of categorization is the ability to distinguish living from nonliving things. When Piaget asked young children whether the wind and the clouds were alive, their answers led him to think they were confused. The tendency to attribute life to objects

As this girl pretends to listen to the bear's heart, she is showing deferred imitation, the ability to act out a behavior she observed some time before while visiting her doctor. Duplass/Shutterstock

that are not alive is called **animism.** However, when later researchers questioned 3- and 4-year-olds about something more familiar to them—differences between a rock, a person, and a doll—the children showed they understood that people are alive and rocks and dolls are not (Gelman et al., 1983; Jipson & Gelman, 2007). In general, it appears that children attribute animism to items that share characteristics with living things, including movement, sounds, and lifelike features such as eyes (Opfer & Gelman, 2011). They are also more likely to attribute life to objects they are attached to, such as a favorite stuffed animal or security blanket (Gjersoe et al., 2015).

Understanding of Number Multiple lines of research have shown that by the age of 4½ months, infants have a rudimentary concept of number. They seem to know that if one doll is added to another doll, there should be two dolls, not just one (Wynn, 1992). By 6 months of age, they can "count" higher and know that 8 dots are different from 16 dots (Libertus & Brannon, 2010). Other research has found that *ordinality*—the concept of comparing quantities (*more* or *less, bigger* or *smaller*)—seems to begin around 9 to 11 months (Suanda et al., 2008).

The *cardinality* principle, where children understand that the number of items in a set is the same regardless of how they are arranged, and that the last number counted is the total number of items in the set, starts to develop at about 2½ years of age. However, this ability is based in practical situations, such as checking to see which one of two plates has more cookies in it (Gelman, 2006). Not until age 3½ or older do most children consistently apply the cardinality principle in counting (Sarnecka & Carey, 2007; Wynn, 1990). That is, when asked to count six items, children at about 3½ are able to recite the number names (for example, one through six) and are then able to say how many items there are altogether (six).

By age 4, most children have added words for comparing quantities. They can say that one tree is *bigger* than another or one cup holds *more* juice than another. They also can solve simple numerical ordinality problems ("Megan picked six apples, and Joshua picked four apples; which child picked more?") (Byrnes & Fox, 1998). By age 5, most children can count to 20 or more and know the relative sizes of the numbers 1 through 10 (Siegler, 1998).

Children intuitively devise strategies for adding by counting on their fingers or by using other objects (Naito & Miura, 2001). By the time they enter elementary school, most children have developed basic *number sense* (Jordan et al., 2006). This basic level of number skills includes *counting, number knowledge* (ordinality), *number transformations* (simple addition and subtraction), *estimation* ("Is this group of dots more or less than 5?"), and recognition of *number patterns* (2 plus 2 equals 4, and so does 3 plus 1).

Socioeconomic status (SES) and preschool experience affect how rapidly children advance in math. By age 4, children from middle-income families have markedly better number skills than low-SES children, and their initial advantage tends to continue. Children whose preschool teachers do a lot of "math talk" (such as asking children to help count days on a calendar) tend to make greater gains (Klibanoff et al., 2006). Likewise, the amount of "math talk" mothers use in their naturalistic interactions with their children is positively associated with their later preschool math abilities (Susperreguy & Davis-Kean, 2016). Also, playing number board games with children enhances their numerical knowledge and can help low-income children catch up to their middle-income peers (Siegler, 2009). Numerical competence is important; how well children understand numbers in kindergarten predicts their academic performance in math through 3rd grade (Jordan et al., 2010) and deficient number sense has been associated with mathematical learning disabilities (Mazzocco et al., 2011).

IMMATURE ASPECTS OF PREOPERATIONAL THOUGHT

One of the main characteristics of preoperational thought is **centration:** the tendency to focus on one aspect of a situation and neglect others. According to Piaget, preschoolers come to illogical conclusions because they cannot **decenter**—think about several aspects of a situation at one time.

egocentrism
Piaget's term for inability to consider another person's point of view; a characteristic of young children's thought.

FIGURE 7.2
Piaget's Three-Mountain Task

A preoperational child is unable to describe the mountains from the doll's point of view—an indication of egocentrism, according to Piaget.

conservation
Piaget's term for awareness that two objects that are equal according to a certain measure remain equal in the face of perceptual alteration so long as nothing has been added to or taken away from either object.

irreversibility
Piaget's term for a preoperational child's failure to understand that an operation can go in two or more directions.

Egocentrism **Egocentrism** is a form of centration. According to Piaget, young children center so much on their own point of view that they cannot take in another's. When 3-year-old Luis believes that his "bad thoughts" have made his sister sick, he is thinking egocentrically.

To study egocentrism, Piaget designed the *three-mountain task* (Figure 7.2). A child sits facing a table that holds three large mounds. A doll is placed on a chair at the opposite side of the table. The investigator asks the child how the "mountains" would look to the doll. Piaget found that young children only described the mountains from their own perspective. Piaget saw this as evidence that preoperational children cannot imagine a different point of view (Piaget & Inhelder, 1967).

However, posing the problem in a different way can yield different results. In one study, a child was given instructions to select one object from a set by an experimenter who could only see some of the objects. The researchers found that children as young as 3 were able to take the experimenter's perspective. For example, two of the objects were rubber ducks. In one condition, the experimenter could see only one of the rubber ducks. When the child heard the instructions to retrieve the rubber duck, the child more often selected the rubber duck that the experimenter could see even though the child could see both (Nilsen & Graham, 2009). When the question was posed in a familiar, less abstract way, children were able to take others' perspectives.

Conservation Another classic example of centration is the failure to understand **conservation,** the fact that two things that are equal remain so if their appearance is altered, as long as nothing is added or taken away. Piaget found that children do not fully grasp this principle until the stage of concrete operations and that they develop different kinds of conservation at different ages. Table 7.6 shows how some of the dimensions of conservation have been tested.

In one type of conservation task, conservation of liquid, 5-year-old Justin is shown two identical clear glasses, each short and wide and each holding the same amount of water. Justin is asked, "Is the amount of water in the two glasses equal?" When he agrees, the researcher pours the water in one glass into a third glass, a tall, thin one. Justin is now asked, "Do both glasses contain the same amount of water? Or does one contain more? Why?" In early childhood—even after watching the water being poured or even after pouring it himself—Justin will say that either the taller glass or the wider one contains more water.

Why do children make this error? Their responses are influenced by two immature aspects of thought: centration and **irreversibility.** Centration involves focusing on one

TABLE 7.6 Tests of Various Kinds of Conservation				
Conservation Task	**What Child Is Shown***	**Transformation**	**Question for Child**	**Preoperational Child's Usual Answers**
Number	Two equal, parallel rows of candies	Space the candies in one row farther apart.	"Are there the same number of candies in each row or does one row have more?"	"The longer one has more."
Length	Two parallel sticks of the same length	Move one stick to the right.	"Are both sticks the same size or is one longer?"	"The one on the right (or left) is longer."
Liquid	Two identical glasses holding equal amounts of liquid	Pour liquid from one glass into a taller, narrower glass.	"Do both glasses have the same amount of liquid or does one have more?"	"The taller one has more."
Matter (mass)	Two balls of clay of the same size	Roll one ball into a sausage shape.	"Do both pieces have the same amount of clay or does one have more?"	"The sausage has more."

*Child then acknowledges that both items are equal.

dimension while ignoring the other. Preoperational children cannot consider height and width at the same time as they cannot *decenter,* or consider multiple attributes of an object or situation. In addition, children are limited by irreversibility: failure to mentally reverse an action. Because their thinking is concrete, preoperational children cannot realize that the original state of the water can be restored by pouring it back into the other glass, and thus it must be the same. Preoperational children commonly think as if they were watching a slide show with a series of static frames: They *focus on successive states,* said Piaget, and do not recognize the transformation from one state to another.

THEORY OF MIND

Clara, age 4, hates brussels sprouts, but when her mother asks for them to be passed at the dinner table, she places the bowl in her mother's hands. She now understands her mother might like brussels sprouts, even though she herself finds them highly suspect. In understanding this, Clara is illustrating her growing understanding of others' minds.

Theory of mind is the awareness of the broad range of human mental states—beliefs, intents, desires, dreams, and so forth—and the understanding that others have their own distinctive beliefs, desires, and intentions. Having a theory of mind allows us to understand and predict the behavior of others and makes the social world understandable.

Piaget (1929) asked children such questions as "Where do dreams come from?" and "What do you think with?" On the basis of the answers, he concluded that children younger than 6 cannot distinguish between thoughts or dreams and real physical entities and have no theory of mind. However, more recent research suggests an earlier timeline. Let's take a closer look.

theory of mind
Awareness and understanding of mental processes of others.

Knowledge about Thinking and Mental States At age 2, children readily engage in pretend play, and at 3, they can use deception in simple games and predict others' actions on the basis of their desires (Frye, 2014). Between ages 3 and 5, children come to understand that thinking goes on inside the mind; that it can deal with either real or imaginary things, and that thinking is different from seeing, talking, touching, and knowing (Flavell, 2000). They understand that thinking about the past or the future might make someone feel sad or happy (Lagattuta, 2014) and that another child would be sad if her toy was taken from her (Pesowski & Friedman, 2015). They start to expect people to act in accordance with their beliefs, and when asked to explain people's behavior they use words like "want" or "think." They also know that people's expressions might not necessarily match their internal state (Wellman, 2014) and realize that you can manipulate others' mental states to deceive or tease them (Miller, 2009). They infer knowledge on the basis of mistakes; for instance, by realizing that a puppet that plays a game incorrectly probably does not understand the rules (Ronfard & Corriveau, 2016). By 5 years of age, they understand that if they are sad about something, they can try to think about something else (Davis et al., 2010). However, it is not until a few years later that they understand that they can be wrong about what someone else thinks (Miller, 2009) and are introspective enough about mental processes to understand that the mind is continuously active (Flavell, 2016).

The recognition that others have mental states accompanies the decline of egocentrism, the development of empathy, and the tendency to behave in prosocial ways (Povinelli & Giambrone, 2001; Imuta et al., 2016).

False Beliefs and Deception The understanding that people can hold false beliefs flows from the realization that people can hold incorrect mental representations of reality. For example, if you see your mother searching for an umbrella, but you know it's not raining outside, you can understand that she *thinks* it's raining, even if it is not. This ability is generally tested with what is called a false belief task. Although infants as young as 13 months can illustrate some understanding of the mental states of others (Scott & Baillargeon, 2009), it is not until about 4 years of age that children consistently pass false belief tasks (Baillargeon et al., 2010). And it is not until 5 to 6 years of age that

Is Mickey Mouse real? The ability to distinguish fantasy from reality develops by age 3, but 4- to 6-year-olds may enjoy pretending a character is real nonetheless.
Broadimage/Shutterstock

children understand second-order false beliefs—that they may have an incorrect belief about what someone else believes (Miller, 2009).

Deception is an effort to plant a false belief in someone else's mind. Not surprisingly, performance on the false belief task has been repeatedly shown to predict the ability to lie (Leduc et al., 2017; Bigelow & Dugas, 2009). Thus, although most people do not view the ability to lie as a positive trait, it is nonetheless a developmental milestone illustrative of advances.

Generally children become capable of telling simple lies, such as denying looking at a hidden toy they were instructed to avoid, at about 3 years of age. However, when asked follow-up questions to their lie that if answered would reveal their deception, such as what kind of toy it was, young children fail to hide their knowledge (Evans & Lee, 2013). It is not until almost 8 years of age that children become better able to think about what they should and should not know, and thus conceal their transgressions more effectively (Talwar & Lee, 2002). Furthermore, as children age and become more aware of social conventions as well as others' feelings, they become more likely to lie out of politeness or a desire to avoid hurting others' feelings. For example, they are more likely to tell an experimenter that they liked an unattractive gift when in reality they did not (Xu et al., 2010).

Distinguishing between Appearance and Reality According to Piaget, not until about age 5 or 6 do children begin to understand the distinction between what *seems* to be and what *is*. However, more recent studies have found this ability emerging between 3 and 4 years of age.

In one classic series of experiments (Flavell et al., 1986), 3-year-olds seemed to confuse appearance and reality in a variety of tests. For example, when the children put on special sunglasses that made milk look green, they said the milk *was* green. Similarly, 3-year-olds thought that a sponge that looked like a rock was a rock, even after being shown the sponge in use (Flavell et al., 1983).

Later research showed that 3-year-old children could answer questions about reality and appearance correctly under certain circumstances. For example, when children were presented with two objects, such as an eraser that looked like a chocolate bar and a real chocolate bar, and asked to hand an experimenter "the real one" they were able to select the correct item (Moll & Tomasello, 2012). Similarly, 3-year-old children were able to understand that an adult looking through a yellow screen at a blue object saw it as green, as evidenced by correctly selecting the blue toy after being asked "can you put the green one in the bag for me?" (Moll & Meltzoff, 2011). It may be that children do understand the difference between appearance and reality, but have difficulty displaying their knowledge in traditional tasks that require verbal responses. When you ask them to display their knowledge via their actions, they are better able to do so.

Distinguishing between Fantasy and Reality Sometime between 18 months and 3 years, children learn to distinguish between real and imagined events. Three-year-olds know the difference between a real dog and a dog in a dream and between something invisible (such as air) and something imaginary. They can pretend and can tell when someone else is pretending (Flavell, 2000).

Although more inclined to believe in storybook characters than older children, 3-year-olds are still skeptical about whether or not characters in books are real or pretend, especially if those books contain fantastical elements (Woolley & Cox, 2007). By the age of 4, most children, if given the choice, complete stories with real-world causal laws rather than magical or fantastical elements (Weisberg et al., 2013). Religion can influence this process. Children raised in religious households are more likely to believe the protagonists in stories with fantastical elements are real if they think the stories are religious in nature than are children raised in secular households (Corriveau et al., 2015). For example, if told a particular story is a Bible story, 5-year-olds are more likely to assert magical events in the story are possible in real life (Woolley & Cox, 2007).

Individual Differences in Theory-of-Mind Development Some children develop theory-of-mind abilities earlier than others. What explains these individual differences?

Several lines of research show that infants who are better at paying attention to others show more facility with theory-of-mind tasks at 4 years of age (Wellman et al., 2008; Aschersleben et al., 2008). Social competence also matters (Cassidy et al., 2003). Children whose teachers and peers rate them high on social skills are better able to recognize false beliefs, to distinguish between real and pretend emotion, and to take another person's point of view (Cassidy et al., 2003; Watson et al., 1999). Having siblings is also associated positively with theory of mind development, perhaps as a result of practicing social interactions with a partner who is either less or more advanced (McAlister & Peterson, 2013). Findings such as these suggest continuity in social cognition and that skills build on each other over time.

Language is also important. There are links between the ability to pass false belief tasks and language development (Grazzani et al., 2018). Additionally, a mother's reference to others' thoughts and knowledge is a consistent predictor of a child's later mental state language (Dunn, 1991, 2006). For example, talking with children about how the characters in a story feel helps them develop social understanding (Lillard & Curenton, 1999). Theory of mind has been positively related to reading storybooks, perhaps because parents and children often discuss characters and their desires, beliefs, or emotions (Mar et al., 2010).

Being bilingual can also help. Bilingual children do somewhat better on certain theory-of-mind tasks, particularly when they are more advanced in language development relative to other children (Kovacs, 2012; Nguyen & Astington, 2014). Bilingual children know that an object or idea can be represented linguistically in more than one way, and this may help them see that different people may have different perspectives. Bilingual children also recognize the need to match their language to that of their partner, making them more aware of others' mental states (Bialystok & Senman, 2004; Goetz, 2003).

Brain development is also necessary for theory of mind. Some researchers have pointed to either general processing mechanisms whereas others have focused on the development of attentional and inhibitory processes (Berthiaume et al., 2013; Leslie et al., 2004). As somewhat different areas of the brain are active during different types of false belief tasks (Schurz et al., 2013), it is likely a variety of different processes underlie children's developing abilities in this area. In particular, neural activity in the prefrontal cortex has been identified as important. Children who are able to correctly reason about the mental states of others (such as where a puppet might look for a toy airplane that was moved without their knowledge) or distinguish between appearance and reality (such as with a sponge that looks like a rock) show brain wave activation in their dorsal medial prefrontal cortex and the right temporal parietal juncture. However, those children who are not able to correctly pass the task do not (Liu et al., 2009). Moreover, age-related changes in the organization and connectivity of white matter in the brain is associated with improvements in the performance of false belief tasks, even when linguistic ability and executive functioning are controlled for (Weismann et al., 2017). Although children who are better at theory-of-mind tasks show brain wave patterns more similar to those of adults, children's brain wave activity nonetheless differs from that of adults' and continues to change over childhood (Weismann et al., 2017; Meinhardt et al., 2011).

An incomplete or ineffective theory of mind may be a sign of a cognitive or developmental impairment. Individuals with this type of impairment have difficulty determining the intentions of others, lack an understanding of how their behavior affects others, and have a difficult time with social reciprocity. Research suggests that a core feature of autism is a deficiency in theory of mind (Baron-Cohen, 2000).

Cultural Influences on Theory of Mind Studies investigating the influence of culture on the development of the theory of mind have been contradictory. Some studies have suggested a universal timeline of development (Devine & Hughes, 2014). For example, children from fishing/gathering cultures in Micronesia and the hunter/gatherer Baka of

Cameroonian rain forests, as well as children from Canada, India, Peru, Samoa, and Thailand appear to have highly similar theory-of-mind development (Oberle, 2009; Avis & Harris, 1991; Callaghan et al., 2005).

However, other studies have shown differences. For example, a meta-analysis showed children from China and Hong Kong developed theory-of-mind abilities as much as 2 years later than Western samples (Liu et al., 2008). Similar data have been discovered for Samoan children (Mayer & Trauble, 2013). Moreover, differences have emerged with respect to the pathway to proficiency. Children in Iran and China develop the abilities underlying theory-of-mind development in a different order than children in Australia and the United States (Shahaeian et al., 2011; Wellman et al., 2006).

In research on these cultural differences, no clear correlates have emerged (Devine & Hughes, 2014). Some studies have suggested differences might be driven by exposure to formal education. For instance, unschooled Mofu children from Cameroon and Tolai children from Papua New Guinea show delayed theory-of-mind development contrasted to their schooled peers, and British children, who enter school a year earlier than Italian and Japanese children, are able to pass false beliefs at an earlier age (Vinden, 1999; Hughes et al., 2014; Lecce & Hughes, 2010).

Other studies have investigated language variations across different cultural groups. For example, in Chinese there are three different forms of the word "belief," two of which signify the belief is false. When the neutral form of the word is used, Chinese children have a more difficult time correctly answering theory-of-mind questions. However, when the false forms of the word are used, the performance of Chinese children is more similar to that of children from Western cultures (Lee et al., 1999). These performance differences may be reflected in emerging neural architecture. Brain imaging studies have found that although some areas of the brain (such as the ventromedial prefrontal cortex) show similar activation during theory-of-mind tasks across American and Japanese children, other areas (such as the inferior frontal gyrus and the tempero-parietal junction) differ across cultures (Kobayashi et al., 2007).

Another candidate influence is cultural values, such as the emphasis on group harmony found in collectivistic cultures and the individual orientation found in individual-istic cultures (Nisbett, 2003; Fu et al., 2008).

MEDIA AND COGNITION

Preschool-age children comprehend the symbolic nature of television and can readily imitate behaviors they see. Exposure to television during the first few years of life has been negatively associated with academic outcomes (Pagani et al., 2010) and cognitive development, especially when the television is left on for long periods of time or when young children are exposed to high levels of adult programming (Barr et al., 2010). Some researchers have also found that the fast-paced programming common now in many children's shows negatively impacts executive functioning and the ability to sustain attention in preschool children (Lillard & Peterson, 2011).

Although certain kinds of programming do appear to be harmful to young children's cognitive development, the type of television watched is also important, and high-quality children's programming can result in cognitive enhancements (Kirkorian et al., 2008). For example, Sesame Street, developed specifically to improve school readiness in inner city children, has been repeatedly shown to improve outcomes. Viewing Sesame Street is associated with a host of positive outcomes, including cognitive proficiency, literacy, and numeracy (Mares & Pan, 2013). Similar findings have emerged for other educational programming such as Blue's Clues and Dora the Explorer (Kirkorian et al., 2008). It is clear that program content is an important mediator. Additionally, parents who limit screen time, select well-designed, age-appropriate programs, and view the programs with their children can maximize the benefits of media.

While for many years television was the most frequently used media source, the use of home computers, tablets, cellular phones, and other such devices has grown rapidly in recent years. The American Academy of Pediatrics (2016) recommends that children from 2 to 5 years of age should spend no more than an hour a day on any screen media, and that parents should watch programming with their children and discuss it. For children 6 and older, there should be consistent limits and designated media-free times.

Memory Development: Information-Processing Approach

During early childhood, thinking improves in attention, speed, efficiency, and long-term memory. However, some aspects are still immature.

BASIC PROCESSES AND CAPACITIES

Information-processing theorists focus on the processes that affect cognition. According to this view, memory can be described as a filing system that has three steps or processes: *encoding, storage,* and *retrieval.* **Encoding** is like putting information in a folder to be filed in memory; it attaches a "code" to the information so it will be easier to find when needed. For example, if you were asked to list "things that are red," you might list apples, stop signs, and hearts. Presumably, all these items were tagged in memory with the concept "red" when they were originally encoded. **Storage** is putting the folder away in the filing cabinet. It is where the information is kept. When the information is needed, you access storage, and through the process of **retrieval,** you search for the file and take it out.

Information-processing models depict the brain as containing three types of storage: *sensory memory, working memory,* and *long-term memory.* **Sensory memory** is a temporary storehouse for incoming sensory information. For example, the light trail that is visible when a sparkler is moved quickly on a dark night illustrates visual sensory memory. Sensory memory shows little change from infancy on (Siegler, 1998). Without processing (encoding), sensory memories fade quickly.

Information being encoded or retrieved is kept in **working memory,** a short-term storehouse for information a person is actively working on, trying to understand, remember, or think about. Working memory has a limited capacity. Researchers can assess the capacity of working memory by asking children to recall a series of scrambled digits (for example, 2-8-3-7-5-1 if they heard 1-5-7-3-8-2). The capacity of working memory—the number of digits a child can recall—increases rapidly. At age 4, children typically remember only two digits; at 12 they typically remember six (Zelazo et al., 2003). The growth of working memory may permit the development of **executive function,** the conscious control of thoughts, emotions, and actions to accomplish goals or to solve problems (McCabe et al., 2010). Executive function enables children to plan and carry out goal-directed mental activity (Zelazo & Carlson, 2012). It probably emerges around the end of an infant's 1st year and develops in spurts with age.

Long-term memory is a storehouse of virtually unlimited capacity that holds information for long periods of time. This information is transferred from working memory if it is deemed important enough. But who decides its importance? According to a widely used model, a **central executive** controls processing operations in working memory (Baddeley, 1998, 2001). The central executive orders information encoded for transfer to long-term memory, retrieves information from long-term memory for further processing, and can temporarily expand the capacity of working memory by moving information into two separate subsidiary systems while the central executive is occupied with other tasks. One of these subsidiary systems holds verbal information (as in the digit task), and the other holds visual-spatial images.

RECOGNITION AND RECALL

Recognition and *recall* are types of retrieval. **Recall** is the ability to reproduce knowledge from memory (for example, describing a lost mitten at the lost-and-found desk). **Recognition** is the ability to identify something encountered before (for example, to pick out the

encoding
Process by which information is prepared for long-term storage and later retrieval.

storage
Retention of information in memory for future use.

retrieval
Process by which information is accessed or recalled from memory storage.

sensory memory
Initial, brief, temporary storage of sensory information.

working memory
Short-term storage of information being actively processed.

executive function
Conscious control of thoughts, emotions, and actions to accomplish goals or solve problems.

long-term memory
Storage of virtually unlimited capacity that holds information for long periods.

central executive
In Baddeley's model, element of working memory that controls the processing of information.

recall
Ability to reproduce material from memory.

recognition
Ability to identify a previously encountered stimulus.

missing mitten from a lost-and-found box). Preschool children, like all age groups, do better on recognition than on recall, and both abilities improve with age.

Young children often fail to use strategies for remembering unless reminded, and they sometimes choose inefficient memory strategies (Whitebread at al., 2009). This tendency not to generate efficient strategies may reflect lack of awareness of how a strategy would be useful (Sophian et al., 1995). Older children, particularly once they begin formal schooling, tend to become more efficient in the spontaneous use of memory strategies (Schneider, 2008).

FORMING AND RETAINING CHILDHOOD MEMORIES

Most of the early conscious childhood memories seem to be short-lived. One investigator has distinguished three types of childhood memory that serve different functions: *generic, episodic,* and *autobiographical* (Nelson, 1993).

generic memory
Memory that produces scripts of familiar routines to guide behavior.

script
General remembered outline of a familiar, repeated event, used to guide behavior.

episodic memory
Long-term memory of specific experiences or events, linked to time and place.

autobiographical memory
Memory of specific events in one's life.

Generic memory, which begins at about age 2, produces a **script,** or general outline of a familiar, repeated event, such as riding the bus to preschool. It helps a child know what to expect and how to act.

Episodic memory refers to awareness of having experienced a particular event at a specific time and place. Given a young child's limited memory capacity, episodic memories are usually temporary. Unless they recur several times, they last for a few weeks or months and then fade (Nelson, 2005). For example, getting vaccinated at the pediatrician's office might originally be an episodic memory. Over time and repeated visits, a child might form a generic memory of the doctor's office being a place where shots are administered.

Autobiographical memory, a type of episodic memory, refers to memories of distinctive experiences that form a person's life history. Autobiographical memories have a special, personal meaning to the child (Fivush, 2011) and generally emerge between ages 3 and 4 (Nelson, 2005). Theorists believe that autobiographical memory emerges slowly because it depends on the development of the self and the emergence of language (Fivush, 2011). Language is important because it enables children to share memories and organize them into personal narratives (Fivush & Nelson, 2004; Nelson & Fivush, 2004).

social interaction model
Model, based on Vygotsky's sociocultural theory, that proposes children construct autobiographical memories through conversation with adults about shared events.

The **social interaction model,** based on Vygotsky's sociocultural approach, provides a rationale. Theorists argue that children collaboratively construct autobiographical memories with parents or other adults as they talk about events (Fivush & Haden, 2006), such as might occur when a mother and child leaf through a photo album and talk about past events. For example, parents who spend more time reminiscing about and discussing past events have children who form more coherent autobiographical memories (Fivush et al., 2011).

Why do some memories last longer than others? One important factor is uniqueness. When events are rare or unusual, children seem to remember them better (Peterson, 2011). Children, as they get older, are also more likely to remember unique details of an event they have a generic script for (Brubacher et al., 2011). Moreover, events with emotional impact seem to be remembered better (Buchanan, 2007), although some evidence suggests attention is focused on central aspects of the situation rather than on peripheral details (Levine & Edelstein, 2009). So, for example, if you were frightened by a scary film, you might show enhanced memory for events in the film but forget if you bought candy or who you went with. Still another factor is children's active participation. Preschoolers tend to remember things they *did* better than things they merely saw (Murachver et al., 1996).

"Remember when you danced at Holi last year?" Young children are most likely to remember an event when parents discuss it with them or the event was unique. Rudra Narayan Mitra/Shutterstock

Intelligence: Psychometric and Vygotskian Approaches

Although the definition of intelligence is controversial, most psychologists agree that intelligence involves the ability to learn from situations, adapt to new experiences, and manipulate abstract concepts.

TRADITIONAL PSYCHOMETRIC MEASURES

Three- to 5-year-old children are more proficient with language than younger children, so intelligence tests for this age group can include more verbal items. These tests, beginning at age 5, tend to be fairly reliable in predicting measured intelligence and school success later in childhood. Two commonly used individual tests are the Stanford-Binet Intelligence Scales and the Wechsler Preschool and Primary Scale of Intelligence.

The **Stanford-Binet Intelligence Scales** are used for ages 2 and up and take 45 to 60 minutes. The child is asked to define words, string beads, build with blocks, identify the missing parts of a picture, trace mazes, and show an understanding of numbers. The child's score is intended to measure fluid reasoning (the ability to solve abstract or novel problems), knowledge, quantitative reasoning, visual-spatial processing, and working memory. The fifth edition, revised in 2003, includes nonverbal methods of testing all five of these dimensions of cognition and permits comparisons of verbal and nonverbal performance. In addition to providing a full-scale IQ, the Stanford-Binet yields separate measures of verbal and nonverbal IQ plus composite scores spanning the five cognitive dimensions.

The **Wechsler Preschool and Primary Scale of Intelligence, Revised (WPPSI-IV)** is an individual test taking 30 to 60 minutes. It has separate levels for ages 2½ to 4 and 4 to 7 and yields verbal, performance, and combined scores. It includes subtests designed to measure both verbal and nonverbal fluid reasoning, receptive versus expressive vocabulary, and processing speed. The WPPSI-IV has been validated for special populations, such as children with intellectual disabilities, developmental delays, language disorders, and autistic disorders.

Stanford-Binet Intelligence Scales Individual intelligence tests for ages 2 and up used to measure fluid reasoning, knowledge, quantitative reasoning, visual-spatial processing, and working memory.

Wechsler Preschool and Primary Scale of Intelligence, Revised (WPPSI-IV) Individual intelligence test for children ages 2½ to 7 that yields verbal and performance scores as well as a combined score.

INFLUENCES ON MEASURED INTELLIGENCE

A common misconception is that IQ scores represent inborn intelligence. In reality, an IQ score is simply a measure of how well a child can do certain tasks in comparison with other children of the same age. Indeed, test scores of children in many industrialized countries have risen steadily since testing began, forcing test developers to raise standardized norms (Flynn, 1984, 1987). This trend reflects better nutrition, preschools, better-educated parents, smaller families in which each child received more attention, and changes in the tests themselves. Although the trend slowed in 1970s and 1980s (Sundet et al., 2004; Teasdale & Owen, 2008), recent meta-analyses suggest average IQ continues to rise at a rate of 2.3 points per decade (Trahan et al., 2014).

The degree to which family environment influences a child's intelligence is in question. Some of parents' influence on intelligence comes from their genetic contribution and some results from the fact that they provide a child's earliest environment for learning. Twin and adoption studies suggest that family life has its strongest influence in early childhood, and this influence diminishes greatly by adolescence (Bouchard & McGue, 2003; Haworth et al., 2010).

The correlation between socioeconomic status and IQ is well documented (Strenze, 2007). Family income is associated with cognitive development and achievement in the preschool years and beyond. Family economic circumstances can exert a powerful influence, not so much in themselves as in the way they affect other factors such as health, stress, parenting practices, and the atmosphere in the home (Jenkins et al., 2014; NICHD Early Child Care Research Network, 2005).

The relationship between IQ and socioeconomic status interacts with other variables. For example, children in deprived families tend to have lower IQs. However, poor children with an outgoing temperament, warm mothering, and stimulating activities in the home (which may be influenced by parental IQ) tend to do better than other economically deprived children (Kim-Cohen et al., 2004). Environmental differences also seem to matter more for some children than others. Research has shown that children with low IQ show greater negative effects as a result of low socioeconomic status than do those with high IQ (Hanscombe et al., 2012).

However, this is not universally true. In the United States, where low socioeconomic status is associated with greater deprivation, poverty and IQ are closely associated. Poor children in the United States do not show strong genetic influences on intelligence, although children from more affluent homes do. However, in countries with more robust social services, such as the Netherlands, the links between genes and intelligence remain strong for children who live in poverty (Tucker-Drob & Bates, 2016). Presumably this is because despite living in poverty, they nonetheless have access to enriching experiences, and thus are able to express their innate abilities.

TESTING AND TEACHING BASED ON VYGOTSKY'S THEORY

According to Vygotsky, children learn through interactions with others. This interactive learning is most effective in helping children cross the **zone of proximal development (ZPD),** the imaginary psychological space between what children can do or know by themselves and what they could do or know with help. The ZPD can be assessed by *dynamic tests* that provide a better measure of children's intellectual potential than do traditional psychometric tests that measure what children have already mastered. Dynamic tests emphasize potential. Examiners help the child when necessary by asking questions, giving examples or demonstrations, and offering feedback, making the test itself a learning situation.

The ZPD, in combination with the related concept of **scaffolding,** can help parents and teachers more efficiently guide children's cognitive progress. Scaffolding is the supportive assistance that a more sophisticated interaction partner provides, and ideally it should be aimed at the ZPD. The less able a child is to do a task, the more scaffolding, or support, an adult must give. As the child can do more and more, the adult helps less and less. When the child can do the job alone, the adult takes away the scaffold that is no longer needed.

Scaffolding helps children learn. For example, first-grade students struggling with reading showed greater gains in their abilities when their teachers prompted them to use sources of information they were ignoring to decode difficult words when they got stuck (Rodgers et al., 2016). Teachers who scaffolded the group discussions of their fourth-grade classrooms had students who later modeled their behavior on that of the teachers', for example, by remembering to use evidence to support their statements (Jadalla et al., 2011).

Language Development

Young children's growing facility with language helps them express their unique view of the world. Between ages 3 and 6, children make rapid advances in vocabulary, grammar, and syntax.

VOCABULARY

At age 3 the average child knows and can use 900 to 1,000 words. By age 6, a child typically has an expressive (speaking) vocabulary of 2,600 words and understands more than 20,000. With the help of formal schooling, a child's passive, or receptive, vocabulary (words she can understand) will quadruple to 80,000 words by the time she enters high school (Owens, 1996).

zone of proximal development (ZPD)
Vygotsky's term for the difference between what a child can do alone and what the child can do with help.

scaffolding
Temporary support to help a child master a task.

By giving suggestions for playing a game his son can do it on his own, this father supports his child's cognitive progress. Africa Studio/ Shutterstock

This rapid expansion of vocabulary may occur through **fast mapping,** which allows a child to pick up the approximate meaning of a new word after hearing it only once or twice in conversation (Spiegel & Halberda, 2011). Using the context, children seem to form a quick hypothesis about the meaning of the word. For example, suppose a child is at the zoo and encounters an emu for the first time. The mother might point to the emu and say, "Look at the emu over there." The child might use what she knows about the rules for forming words, about the context, and about the subject to form a hypothesis about the meaning of the word *emu.* Names of objects (nouns) seem to be easier to fast map than names of actions (verbs), even across different languages (Imai et al., 2008).

fast mapping
Process by which a child absorbs the meaning of a new word after hearing it once or twice in conversation.

GRAMMAR AND SYNTAX

The ways children combine syllables into words and words into sentences grow increasingly sophisticated during early childhood as their understanding of grammar and syntax becomes more complex. In this context, grammar does not refer to the lessons learned in seventh-grade language arts class; rather, it refers to the deep underlying structure of a language that enables us to both produce and understand utterances. Syntax is a related concept and involves the rules for putting together sentences in a particular language.

At age 3, children typically begin to use plurals, possessives, and past tense and know the difference between *I, you,* and *we.* They can ask and answer what and where questions. However, their sentences are generally short, simple, and declarative ("I want juice").

Between ages 4 and 5, sentences average four to five words and may be declarative, negative ("I'm not hungry"), interrogative ("Why can't I go outside?"), or imperative ("Catch the ball!"). Four-year-olds use complex, multiclause sentences ("I'm eating because I'm hungry") more frequently if their parents often use such sentences (Huttenlocher et al., 2002). Children are also affected by their peers. When children interact with peers who have strong language skills, this results in a small but significant positive effect on their own language (Mashburn et al., 2009). Children this age tend to string sentences together in long run-on narratives (". . . And then . . . And then . . ."). In some respects, comprehension may be immature. For example, 4-year-old Noah can carry out a command that includes more than one step ("Pick up your toys and put them in the cupboard"). However, if his mother tells him, "You may watch TV after you pick up your toys," he may process the words in the order in which he hears them and think he can first watch television and then pick up his toys.

By ages 5 to 7, children's speech has become adultlike. They speak in longer and more complicated sentences. They use more conjunctions, prepositions, and articles. Still, although children this age speak fluently, comprehensibly, and fairly grammatically, they have yet to master many fine points of language. They rarely use the passive voice ("I was dressed by Grandpa"), conditional sentences ("If I were big, I could drive the bus"), or the auxiliary verb *have* ("I have seen that lady before") (Chomsky, 1969).

Young children sometimes make errors because they have not yet learned exceptions to rules. Saying "holded" instead of "held" or "eated" instead of "ate" is a typical sign of linguistic progress. When young children discover a rule, such as adding *-ed* to a verb for past tense, they tend to overgeneralize—to use it even with words that do not conform to the rule. Eventually, they notice that *-ed* is not always used to form the past tense of a verb (Vasilyeva et al., 2006) and memorize the exceptions.

PRAGMATICS AND SOCIAL SPEECH

Language is a social process. As children learn vocabulary, grammar, and syntax, they also become more competent in **pragmatics.** Pragmatics involves the practical knowledge of how to use language to communicate. For example, a child is more likely to be successful with a request such as "May I please have a cookie?" than with "Give me a cookie now."

Pragmatics is related to theory of mind because to understand how to use language socially, you must put yourself in other people's shoes. This includes knowing how to ask for things, how to tell a story or joke, how to begin and continue a conversation,

pragmatics
The practical knowledge needed to use language for communicative purposes.

social speech
Speech intended to be understood by a listener.

and how to adjust comments to the listener's perspective (Rice, 1982). These are all aspects of **social speech,** speech intended to be understood by a listener.

Most 3-year-olds try to explain themselves more clearly if people cannot understand them. Four-year-olds, especially girls, simplify their language and use a higher register when speaking to 2-year-olds. Most 5-year-olds can adapt what they say to what the listener knows or who the listener is. They can use words to resolve disputes, and they use more polite language and fewer direct commands in talking to adults than to other children, although they are more likely to ask for something politely from an experimenter than with their parents. They become sensitive to the power dynamics in relationships, and are more likely to use an aggravated tone of voice with those lower in hierarchy, such as a younger sibling, and a deferential tone with someone higher in social dominance, such as a popular peer. Almost half of 5-year-olds can stick to a conversational topic for about a dozen turns (Owens, 1996; Shatz & Gelman, 1973; Zuffery, 2016).

Because pragmatics reflects cultural knowledge, there are cultural differences in pragmatic development. For example, in collectivistic cultures. people are more likely to use indirect appeals and body language when making a request of someone. This is because maintaining harmony with others and considering others' feelings are important cultural values. By contrast, in individualistic cultures, people are more likely to make a direct, assertive request (Ogawa & Gudykunst, 2000).

Politeness can also be transmitted with honorifics, which are readily learned by children. For example, in the southern United States, children are encouraged to use "ma'am" and "sir" to a greater degree than much of the rest of the country. In some families, they must address their parents with the terms; in others, it is meant to convey respect for other adults outside of the family. However, this is much less common in northern states (Hudley & Mallinson, 2015). There are varied ways to indicate respect. Japanese children also use honorifics (such as suffixes like "-san" attached to the ends of names) but they also incorporate physical body position (such as bowing) to indicate deference or respect for others (Burdelski, 2012). By contrast, the Hobongan of Indonesia lack honorifics to indicate politeness and instead show respect by avoiding the use of names in talking to or about someone as a means by which to prevent evil spirits from identifying them (Perkins, 2016).

Similarly, rudeness can also be expressed in language. The Hobongan language has three language modifiers used to curse, and their use is interpreted as impolite (Perkins, 2016). Children readily learn what words are taboo from their parents. In most Western cultures, adults actively dissuade their children from the use of curse words, often with punishment (Jay et al., 2006). By contrast, in some native Australian cultures, swearing in front of your mother is not considered rude (White, 2010).

PRIVATE SPEECH

Clara, age 4, was alone in her room, building a house from a set she had received for her birthday. Puzzling over the blocks, she was overheard saying aloud, "Now the blue blocks have to go on the sides. There are four of them on each side."

private speech
Talking aloud to oneself with no intent to communicate with others.

Private speech—talking aloud to oneself with no intent to communicate with others—is normative and common in childhood. Piaget (1962) saw private speech as a sign of cognitive immaturity, and he believed that children were simply vocalizing whatever was on their minds. Vygotsky (1962) viewed private speech as a special form of communication: conversation with the self. He believed private speech was part of the learning process.

Research generally supports Vygotsky. There is evidence for the role of private speech in self-regulation (Day & Smith, 2013; Lidstone et al., 2011). Private speech tends to increase when children are trying to solve problems or perform difficult tasks, especially without adult supervision (Berk, 1992). The use of private speech in young children also predicts their autobiographical memory (Al-Namlah et al., 2012), creativity (Daugherty & White, 2008), spelling proficiency (Aram et al., 2014), and writing level (Aram et al., 2017).

DELAYED LANGUAGE DEVELOPMENT

About 11 percent of of 3- to 6-year-old children have a communication disorder, most frequently a problem with speech or language (Black et al., 2015). Children who speak late do not necessarily lack linguistic input at home. Hearing problems and head and facial abnormalities may be associated with speech and language delays, as are premature birth, family history, socioeconomic factors, and other developmental delays (Dale et al., 1998; U.S. Preventive Services Task Force, 2006). Heredity seems to play a role (Kovas et al., 2005; Spinath et al., 2004). Boys are more likely than girls to be late talkers (U.S. Preventive Services Task Force, 2006).

Many children who speak late—especially those whose comprehension is normal—eventually catch up. About 80 percent of children with language delays at age 2 catch up with their peers by age 7 (Rice et al., 2008). However, some children with early language delays, if left untreated, may experience far-reaching cognitive, social, and emotional consequences (U.S. Preventive Services Task Force, 2006).

PREPARATION FOR LITERACY

To understand what is on the printed page, children first need to master certain prereading skills. The development of fundamental skills that eventually lead to being able to read is known as **emergent literacy.**

Prereading skills can be divided into two types: (1) oral language skills, such as vocabulary, syntax, narrative structure, and the understanding that language is used to communicate; and (2) specific phonological skills (linking letters with sounds) that help in decoding the printed word.

Social interaction is an important factor in literacy development. Children are more likely to become good readers and writers if, during the preschool years, parents provide appropriate conversational challenges—if they use a rich vocabulary and read and talk about books, and center dinner-table talk on the day's activities, on mutually remembered past events, or on questions about why people do things and how things work (Reese, 1995; Reese et al., 2010).

Reading to children is one of the most effective paths to literacy. Eighty-one percent of U.S. children age 3 to 5 and not in kindergarten are read to three or more times a week by a family member (Federal Interagency Forum on Child and Family Statistics, 2019).

Children who are read to from an early age learn that reading and writing in English move from left to right and from top to bottom and that words are separated by spaces. They also are motivated to learn to read (Whitehurst & Lonigan, 2001; Baker, 2013). There are suggestions that these processes may be altered (Korat & Or, 2010) or interrupted (Parish-Morris et al., 2013), when reading is conducted on electronic devices.

emergent literacy
Preschoolers' development of skills, knowledge, and attitudes that underlie reading and writing.

Early Childhood Education

PRESCHOOL

Going to preschool is an important step, widening a child's physical, cognitive, and social environment. A high-quality preschool prepares a child for the next transition—into kindergarten. Let's look at these influences.

Cultural Variations in Preschool As we will discuss later in the chapter, early childhood education is essential for the development of school readiness skills and sets the stage for academic performance in later school settings. Yet there are wide global variations in the proportion of children who attend preschool, as well as in the cultural ideals and skills taught to young children.

In Western countries such as the United States, 83 percent of young children are enrolled in some form of preschool program. In low-income countries, only 22 percent of children are able to access this experience, and socioeconomic disparities within low-income countries mean poor children are 8 times less likely to be enrolled in preschool than are children from wealthy families. Only 12 percent of children in low-income countries who do not attend preschool will be on track for literacy and numeracy skills, as compared with 44 percent of their preschool-attending peers. Globally, half of preschool-age children— roughly 175 million—are not enrolled in preschool (UNICEF, 2019). The limited early childhood educational opportunities for many of these children perpetuate a cycle of poverty and inequality.

Preschools in different countries also vary with respect to their developmental goals and socialization practices. In some countries, such as the United States, play is viewed as essential for development, whereas hunter-gatherer cultures and Asian countries are more likely to view play as separate from developmental processes (Roopnarine, 2011). Not surprisingly, American preschools stress exploring the environment, having fun, and self-expression. By contrast, preschools in China, Japan, and France focus more closely on disciplined learning and following rules (Tobin et al., 1989; Tobin, 2005; Hess & Azuma, 1991).

Types of Preschool One of the most popular preschool programs is the Montessori method. The Montessori method is based on the belief that children's natural intelligence involves rational, spiritual, and empirical aspects (Edwards, 2003). Montessori stresses the importance of children learning independently at their own pace, as they work with developmentally appropriate materials and self-chosen tasks. Teachers serve as guides, and older children help younger ones. Teachers provide an environment of calm productivity, and the classrooms are organized to be orderly, pleasing environments.

Montessori's approach has been shown to be effective. An evaluation of Montessori education in Milwaukee found that 5-year-old Montessori students were well prepared for elementary school in reading and math, and they outperformed children who attended other types of preschools (Lillard & Else-Quest, 2006).

Reggio Emilia is a less formal model than Montessori. Teachers follow children's interests and support them in exploring and investigating ideas and feelings through words, movement, dramatic play, and music. Learning is purposeful but less defined than with the Montessori curriculum. Teachers ask questions that draw out children's ideas and then create flexible plans to explore these ideas with the children. Classrooms are carefully constructed to offer complexity, beauty, organization, and a sense of well-being (Ceppi & Zini, 1998; Edwards, 2002).

Compensatory Preschool Programs Compensatory preschool programs are designed to aid children who would otherwise enter school poorly prepared to learn. Teachers and researchers in early childhood education generally work within a model of the whole child, seeking not just to enhance cognitive skills but also to improve physical health and to foster self-confidence and social skills.

The best known of the early intervention programs in the United States is Project Head Start, a federally funded program launched in 1965. Head Start provides medical, dental, and mental health care; social services; and at least one hot meal a day. About 72.1 percent of Head Start children are from English-speaking homes and 13 percent of enrolled children were diagnosed with disabilities (Administration for Children and Families, 2019).

Has Head Start lived up to its name? Research on Head Start and other similar programs has demonstrated that children show academic and social gains in multiple, but not all, target areas immediately following their participation. Head Start children make gains in vocabulary, letter recognition, early writing, early mathematics, and social skills (Figure 7.3). The gap between their vocabulary and early reading scores and national norms narrows significantly. Furthermore, their skills continue to progress in kindergarten. Gains are closely related to parental involvement and are stronger for children who are low in cognitive potential, have parents with a low educational level, or attend programs for more hours per week (Camilli et al., 2010; Lee et al., 2014; Bitler et al., 2014).

Some reports suggest that these gains are not maintained over time. However, an analysis of long-term effects of Head Start suggests the benefits outweigh the costs (Puma et al., 2012). Children from Head Start and other compensatory programs were less

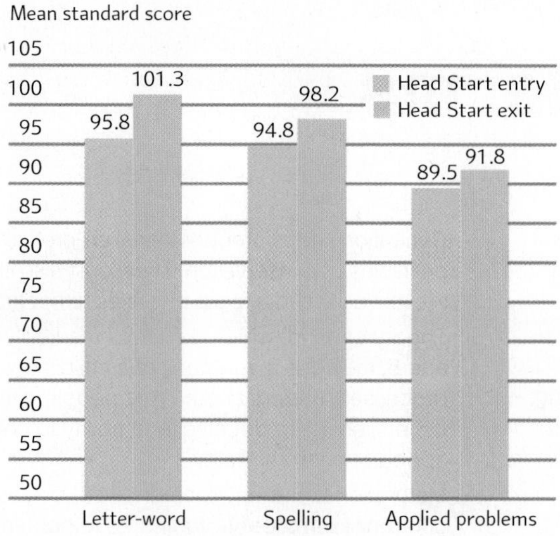

Mean standard score

FIGURE 7.3

Mean literacy and math standard scores for children in Head Start

These outcomes represent all children who entered Head Start for the first time in the fall of 2009, completed 1 or 2 years of the program, and entered kindergarten in the fall of either 2010 or 2011. Immediate gains are most striking; however, better outcomes do persist over time.

Source: Aikens, N., Kopack Klein, A., Tarullo, L., & West, J. (2013). Getting ready for kindergarten: Children's progress during Head Start. *FACES 2009 Report. OPRE Report 2013-21a.* Washington, DC: Office of Planning, Research and Evaluation, Administration for Children and Families, U.S. Department of Health and Human Services.

likely to be placed in special education or to repeat a grade and were more likely to finish high school and attend or graduate from college than low-income children who did not attend such programs (McCoy et al., 2017; Bauer & Shanzenbach, 2016). "Graduates" of similar programs were much less likely to become juvenile delinquents or to become pregnant in their teens (Schweinhart, 2007), perhaps in part due to changes in overall socio-emotional functioning. These changes include better self-control and self-esteem, as well as a decreased likelihood of being rejected by peers and developing oppositional or attentional problems (Bauer & Shanzenbach, 2016; Nix et al., 2016). Outcomes are best with earlier and longer-lasting intervention through high-quality, center-based programs (Brooks-Gunn, 2003; Zigler & Styfco, 2001).

Head Start and other similar programs carry a high cost upfront. Intervention programs are expensive, ranging from approximately $5,200 to $10,500 per child per year (Karoly, 2016). In terms of child outcomes, it can be argued that one cannot put a price on a higher quality of life and better opportunities for the most vulnerable children among us. However, politicians, voters, and funding agencies do want to know the economic consequences of investing money in such programs. Although the initial improvement in outcomes is not maintained at the same high level, overall, research shows the programs are still effective in the long term and thus yield long-term economic payoffs. Economic analyses show that for every dollar invested in early intervention programs, there is a return of $3 to $17 (Karoly, 2016).

KINDERGARTEN

Although some states do not require kindergarten programs or kindergarten attendance, most 5-year-olds attend kindergarten. Since the late 1970s, an increasing number of kindergarteners spend a full day in school, rather than the traditional half day (Kena et al., 2014). A practical impetus for this trend is the growing number of single-parent and dual-earner households. Full-day kindergarten has been associated with small to moderate increases in reading and math skills when compared to a half-day schedule (Votruba-Drzal et al., 2008); however, by the end of third grade these differences disappear (Rathbun et al., 2004).

Findings highlight the importance of the preparation a child receives *before* kindergarten. The resources with which children come to kindergarten—preliteracy skills and the richness of a home literacy environment—predict reading achievement in first grade (Rathbun et al., 2004). Emotional and social adjustment also affect readiness for kindergarten and strongly predict school success. It is important that children have the ability to sit still, follow directions, wait one's turn, and regulate one's own learning (Raver, 2002). Broadly, kindergarten readiness is associated with positive academic and social outcomes for children (Goldstein et al., 2017; Jones et al., 2015).

summary and key terms

Physical Development

- Physical growth continues during the years from 3 to 6, but more slowly than before. Boys are slightly taller, heavier, and more muscular than girls. Internal body systems are maturing.
- Sleep patterns change during early childhood and are affected by cultural expectations. Occasional sleepwalking, sleep terrors, and nightmares are common, but persistent sleep problems may indicate emotional disturbances.
- Bed-wetting is usually outgrown without special help.
- Brain development continues steadily throughout childhood.
- Children progress rapidly in gross and fine motor skills.
- Handedness is usually evident by age 3.

  enuresis, gross motor skills, fine motor skills, systems of action, handedness

Health and Safety

- Although major contagious illnesses are rare today in industrialized countries, preventable disease continues to be a major problem in the developing world.
- The prevalence of obesity among preschoolers has increased.
- Undernutrition can affect all aspects of development.
- Food allergies are becoming increasingly common.
- Accidents are the leading cause of death in childhood in the United States.
- Environmental factors such as exposure to poverty, homelessness, smoking, air pollution, and pesticides increase the risks of illness or injury. Lead poisoning can have serious physical, cognitive, and behavioral effects.

Cognitive Development: Piagetian Approach

- Children in the preoperational stage show several important advances, as well as some immature aspects of thought.
- The symbolic function enables children to reflect on people, objects, and events that are not physically present. It is shown in deferred imitation, pretend play, and language.
- Symbolic development helps preoperational children make more accurate judgments of spatial relationships. They can link cause and effect with regard to familiar situations, understand the concept of identity, categorize, compare quantities, and understand principles of counting.
- Preoperational children appear to be less egocentric than Piaget thought.

- Centration keeps preoperational children from understanding principles of conservation. Their logic also is limited by irreversibility and a focus on states rather than transformations.
- Theory of mind, which develops markedly between ages 3 and 5, includes awareness of a child's own thought processes, understanding that people can hold false beliefs, ability to deceive, and ability to distinguish appearance from reality.
- Maturational and environmental influences affect individual differences in theory-of-mind development.

  preoperational stage, symbolic function, pretend play, transduction, animism, centration, decenter, egocentrism, conservation, irreversibility, theory of mind

Memory Development: Information-Processing Approach

- Information-processing models describe three steps in memory: encoding, storage, and retrieval.
- Although sensory memory shows little change with age, the capacity of working memory increases. The central executive controls the flow of information to and from long-term memory.
- At all ages, recognition is better than recall, but both increase during early childhood.
- Early episodic memory is only temporary; it fades or is transferred to generic memory.
- Autobiographical memory typically begins at about age 3 or 4; it may be related to self-recognition and language development.
- According to the social interaction model, children and adults co-construct autobiographical memories by talking about shared experiences.
- Children are more likely to remember unusual activities that they actively participate in. The way adults talk with children about events influences memory formation and retention.

  encoding, storage, retrieval, sensory memory, working memory, executive function, long-term memory, central executive, recall, recognition, generic memory, script, episodic memory, autobiographical memory, social interaction model

Intelligence: Psychometric and Vygotskian Approaches

- The two most commonly used psychometric intelligence tests for young children are the Stanford-Binet Intelligence Scales and the Wechsler Preschool and Primary Scale of Intelligence, Revised (WPPSI-IV).

- Intelligence test scores have risen in industrialized countries.
- Intelligence test scores may be influenced by a number of factors, including the home environment and SES.
- Newer tests based on Vygotsky's concept of the zone of proximal development (ZPD) focus on potential rather than achievement.

Stanford-Binet Intelligence Scales, Wechsler Preschool and Primary Scale of Intelligence, Revised (WPPSI-IV), zone of proximal development (ZPD), scaffolding

Language Development

- During early childhood, vocabulary increases greatly, and grammar, syntax, and pragmatics become more sophisticated.
- Private speech is normal and common, and may aid in self-regulation.

- Causes of delayed language development are multiple. If untreated, language delays may have serious cognitive, social, and emotional consequences.
- Interaction with adults can promote emergent literacy.
- Well-designed, age-appropriate programming is associated with enhanced cognitive development.

fast mapping, pragmatics, social speech, private speech, emergent literacy

Early Childhood Education

- Goals of and access to preschool education vary across cultures.
- Compensatory preschool programs have had positive outcomes, although some gains fade over time.
- Many children today attend full-day kindergarten. Success in kindergarten depends largely on emotional and social adjustment and kindergarten readiness.

chapter 8
Psychosocial Development in Early Childhood

learning objectives

Discuss emotional and personality development in early childhood.

Discuss gender development in early childhood.

Describe play in early childhood.

Explain how parenting practices influence development.

Evaluate young children's relationships with siblings and peers.

Paul Springett 08/Alamy Stock Photo

In this chapter we discuss preschool children's understanding of themselves and their feelings. We see how their sense of male or female identity arises and how it affects behavior. We describe play, the activity in which children in industrialized countries typically spend most of their time. We consider the influence, for good or ill, of what parents do. Finally, we discuss relationships with siblings and other children.

The Developing Self

THE SELF-CONCEPT

The **self-concept** is our total picture of our abilities and traits. It is "a *cognitive construction* ... a system of descriptive and evaluative representations about the self" that determines how we feel about ourselves and guides our actions (Harter, 1996, p. 207). The sense of self also has a social aspect: Children incorporate into their self-image their growing understanding of how others see them.

Developmental Changes in Self-Definition Children's **self-definition**—the way they describe themselves—typically changes between about ages 5 and 7, reflecting self-concept development and advances in cognitive ability. At age 4, Jason says,

> My name is Jason and I live in a big house with my mother and father and sister, Lisa. I have a kitty that's orange and a television set in my own room. . . . I like pizza and I have a nice teacher. I can count up to 100, want to hear me? I love my dog, Skipper. I can climb to the top of the jungle gym, I'm not scared! Just happy. You can't be happy *and* scared, no way! I have brown hair, and I go to preschool. I'm really strong. I can lift this chair, watch me! (Harter, 1996, p. 208)

The way Jason describes himself is typical of U.S. children his age. They are very concrete in their thinking. Jason focuses on what he does, what he looks like, things he owns, and the people and animals in his life. He speaks in specifics, mentioning a particular skill (climbing) rather than general abilities (being athletic) and he is unrealistically positive about his abilities. Moreover, he has difficulty understanding how conflicting emotions can exist simultaneously. In a few years at about age 7, Jason will begin to describe himself in terms of generalized traits such as popular, smart, or dumb; recognize that he can have conflicting emotions; and be self-critical despite holding a positive overall self-concept.

At 4, Jason's statements about himself are one-dimensional. He cannot consider different aspects of himself at the same time. His thinking about himself is all-or-nothing. He cannot acknowledge that his **real self,** the person he actually is, is not the same as his **ideal self,** the person he would like to be.

At about age 5 or 6, Jason begins to make logical connections between one aspect of himself and another: "I can run fast, and I can climb high. I'm also strong. I can throw a ball real far, I'm going to be on a team some day!" (Harter, 1996, p. 215). However, his image of himself is still expressed in completely positive, all-or-nothing terms. He cannot see how he might be good at some things and not at others.

In middle childhood, children begin to integrate specific features of the self into a general, multidimensional concept. As all-or-nothing thinking declines, Jason's self-descriptions will become more balanced and realistic: "I'm good at hockey but bad at arithmetic."

Racial and Cultural Influences on Self-Definition Part of what shapes children's growing understanding of race involves conversations with parents. Parents of children from ethnic and racial minorities often engage in direct socialization of their children with such discussions. When children are younger, parents focus on affirming content such as promoting cultural traditions, discussing important historical figures, eating ethnic foods, and promoting racial pride and heritage. As children become more cognitively sophisticated, the conversations include information about discrimination and preparation for racial bias. These conversations, as a whole, help children understand where they

Jason describes himself in terms of his appearance (brown hair) and his possessions (his dog, Skipper).
Rob Hainer/Shutterstock

self-concept
Sense of self; descriptive and evaluative mental picture of one's abilities and traits.

self-definition
Cluster of characteristics used to describe oneself.

real self
The self one actually is.

ideal self
The self one would like to be.

come from, and are associated with more positive attitudes about their race (Hughes et al., 2006).

Culture helps shape the understanding of the self. In highly individualistic cultures like the United States, individuals are seen as separate from one another, and independence and self-reliance are highly valued. So, for example, European American parents tend to encourage individuality, self-expression, and self-esteem. In collectivistic cultures, such as India and China, individuals are seen as fundamentally interrelated, and group harmony and cohesiveness take precedence over individual concerns. Thus Chinese parents tend to encourage compliance with authority, appropriate conduct, humility, and a sense of belonging to the community (Oyserman, et al., 2002).

Children absorb such differing cultural styles of self-definition as early as age 3 or 4, and these differences increase with age. When asked to describe themselves, American children are likely to focus on their individual characteristics, abstract traits, and inner qualities. Moreover, they are likely to describe themselves in positive terms. Chinese children, by contrast, describe themselves in terms of their relationships to others and the way they behave in different contexts, and their tone is likely to be neutral or negative (Wang, 2004). Differences in self-definitions across cultures can even be seen in children's drawings. Children from cultures where autonomy, individualism, and self-expression are valued tend to draw themselves larger, whereas children from cultures where relatedness and social connections are viewed as more important draw themselves smaller (Gernhardt et al., 2014). For example, in one study, Cameroonian Nso farmer children drew their heads and bodies smaller than did urban German children (Rübeling et al., 2011).

self-esteem
The judgment a person makes about his or her self-worth.

This mother's approval of her 5-year-old daughter's schoolwork is an important contributor to her self-esteem.
David Malan/Getty Images

SELF-ESTEEM

Self-esteem is the self-evaluative part of the self-concept, the judgment children make about their overall worth. Self-esteem, in part, is based on children's growing cognitive ability to describe and define themselves.

Developmental Changes in Self-Esteem Children show relative stability in their perceptions of themselves. In a longitudinal study (Verschueren et al., 2001), 5-year-olds' self-perceptions of variables such as their physical appearance, scholastic and athletic competence, social acceptance, and behavioral conduct predicted their self-perceptions and socio-emotional functioning at age 8.

Young children's self-esteem is not firmly based on reality, and most young children wildly overestimate their abilities. One reason for this is that self-esteem is, in part, the result of feedback received from others, and adults tend to give positive feedback (Harter, 1998, 2006). For example, a kindergartener's crude lettering is not generally critiqued as being messy; rather, parents are more likely to praise the child's efforts.

Children's self-esteem also tends to be unidimensional. In other words, children believe they are either all good or all bad. In middle childhood, self-esteem will become more realistic (Harter, 1998).

Self-Esteem and Mindset Consider the praise parents give children for succeeding. If a child is generally praised for working hard, and she fails at a task, the logical implication is that she did not try hard enough. That child might then be motivated to work harder next time. If the same child is praised for being smart, and she fails at a task, the implication is the child is no longer smart. The motivation for working hard has been stripped away.

If self-esteem is contingent on success, children may view failure or criticism as an indictment of their worth and may feel helpless to do better. Some children have a *fixed mindset*—a belief that their abilities are finite, and that putting effort into a task shows they are bad at that task. For example, when given a difficult puzzle, these children are likely to give up. They are frightened of failure because failure implies they aren't smart or capable (Dweck, 2008).

Children with noncontingent self-esteem, in contrast, tend to attribute failure or disappointment to factors outside themselves or to the need to try harder. If initially unsuccessful or rejected, they persevere, trying new strategies until they find one that works (Harter, 1998; Pomerantz & Saxon, 2001). These children have a *growth mindset* and believe they can get better at a task. Thus working hard at a task, rather than indicating a lack of ability, is instead seen as an opportunity to learn (Dweck, 2008). Children with a growth mindset tend to have parents who praise their efforts, not their inherent abilities, and who focus on specific, focused feedback rather than generic praise (Gunderson et al., 2013).

Cultural Influences on Self-Esteem Parents from different cultures may place more or less importance on their children's self-esteem. For example, European American parents report nurturing high self-esteem in their children as an important parenting goal (Harwood et al., 2001). This orientation stems from individualistic cultural values that focus on individual autonomy and achievement (Rychlak, 2003). By contrast, Puerto Rican, Taiwanese, Japanese, and Chinese parents do not view high self-esteem as essential for good child outcomes (Harwood et al., 2001; Miller et al., 2002; Stevensen et al., 1990). Indeed, self-esteem is viewed as harmful in traditional Japanese culture. Promoting individual successes is not in concert with cultural norms focused on solidifying bonds between individuals and promoting group harmony (Heine et al., 1999). Similarly, in line with Confucian ideals, modesty is viewed as a positive trait by Chinese parents and that, rather than high self-esteem, is seen as an important goal of parenting (Luo et al., 2013).

Parents' beliefs shape how they respond to child behaviors. So, for example, European American parents are more likely to praise their children's successes and to minimize their failures, whereas Chinese parents show the opposite pattern (Ng et al., 2007). The interpretation of why children do or do not do well may also differ. Japanese and Chinese parents are more likely to focus on process, effort, and working hard, an orientation that has implications for children's mindset (Shimahara, 1986; Stigler & Stevenson, 1992). These early influences may be the reason people from Western countries like the United States, Canada, and Western Europe report higher self-esteem in adulthood than do people from East Asian countries such as Japan and China (Schmitt & Allik, 2005).

REGULATING EMOTIONS

At 5-year-old Kayla's birthday party, Kayla opens a present from her grandmother and finds not the doll she was hoping to receive, but a board game. Her face drops as her mother whispers in her ear, "Smile and tell grandma thank you. You don't want to hurt her feelings." Kayla tries, but her smile is unconvincing.

The ability to regulate, or control, one's feelings is one of the key advances of early childhood (Dennis, 2006). Children who can understand their emotions are better able to control the way they show them and to be sensitive to how others feel (Garner & Estep, 2001). Emotional self-regulation helps children guide their behavior (Eisenberg et al., 2006) and contributes to their ability to get along with others (Denham et al., 2003). Children's ability to exert control over themselves is related to adjustment (Baker, 2018). For example, children who, at 3 to 4 years of age, had difficulty in delay-of-gratification tasks were more likely to have behavior problems at 5 to 8 years. Similarly, young children who were poor at deliberately slowing down, inhibiting their movements in a game, or paying close attention were more likely to have academic difficulties when older (Kim et al., 2013). Children develop the ability to regulate their emotions slowly, via a shift from early reliance on orienting processes supported by the parietal and frontal areas of the brain to control of affect using frontal brain networks in the anterior cingulate cortex (Rothbart et al., 2011; Woltering & Shi, 2016).

Cultural Influences on Emotion Regulation Culture influences the way in which parents socialize their children's emotion regulation. Individualistic cultures like the United States tend to value the free expression of emotions. By contrast, cultures with collectivistic and interdependent values tend to value group harmony and harmonious relationships. Parents from these cultures are more likely to encourage minimizing strong emotional expressions, especially if those emotions are negative (Fung et al., 2018). For example, parents from the United States and Germany encourage their children to express their emotions when upset and see this as a healthy expression of autonomy, whereas parents from India and Nepal tend to become distressed when their children express negative emotions (Heikamp et al., 2013).

These socialization patterns also impact how children express their emotions. For example, in one study Chinese children expressed less disgust, smiled less, and were overall less emotionally expressive than were European American children (Camras et al., 2006). Another study found that children in the United States expressed the most pride, Japanese children the most shame, and Korean children the most guilt (Furukawa et al., 2012).

UNDERSTANDING EMOTIONS

Emotional understanding appears to proceed in an ordered and hierarchical manner. Emotions directed toward the self, such as guilt, shame, and pride, typically develop by the end of the 3rd year, after children gain self-awareness and accept the standards of behavior their parents have set.

By about 4 to 5 years, most children can recognize the facial expressions of joy, sadness, fear, anger, surprise, and disgust (Widen & Russell, 2008), although girls tend to outperform boys slightly (Denham et al., 2015). Preschoolers can talk about their feelings and often those of others, they understand that emotions are connected with experiences and desires, and they know reminding someone of something that happened can elicit that emotion again (Saarni et al., 2006; Pons et al., 2004). They are also now able to recognize emotions as reflected in vocal cues (Sauter et al., 2013) and body posture, such as found in a sad person's slumped shoulders or an angry person's aggressive stance (Parker et al., 2013).

By about 7 years of age, children start to understand that mental states can drive emotions. For example, they understand that someone can feel one way and look another. They also understand that what someone believes, even if it is not true, can affect emotional state, and what someone wants, even if they themselves do not want it, can also affect emotional state (Pons et al., 2004).

Last, by about 9 years of age, children start to understand more complex aspects of emotion. For example, they understand that situations can be viewed from multiple perspectives, that people might have conflicting emotions like feeling angry at someone despite loving them, and that they can use cognitive strategies to regulate their emotional state (Pons et al., 2004).

ERIKSON: INITIATIVE VERSUS GUILT

The need to deal with conflicting feelings about the self is at the heart of the third stage of psychosocial development identified by Erik Erikson (1950): **initiative versus guilt**. Preschool children can do—and want to do—more and more. At the same time, they are learning that some of the things they want to do meet social approval, whereas others do not.

This conflict marks a split between two parts of the personality: the part that remains a child, full of exuberance and a desire to test new powers, and the part that is becoming an adult, constantly examining the propriety of motives and actions. Children who learn

initiative versus guilt
Erikson's third stage in psychosocial development, in which children balance the urge to pursue goals with reservations about doing so.

how to regulate these opposing drives develop the virtue of purpose, the courage to envision and pursue goals without being unduly inhibited by guilt or fear of punishment (Erikson, 1982).

Gender

Gender identity, awareness of one's femaleness or maleness and all it implies in one's society of origin, is an important aspect of the developing self-concept.

GENDER DIFFERENCES

Gender differences are psychological or behavioral differences between males and females. This is a controversial area of psychology. Measurable differences between baby boys and girls are few. Although some gender differences become more pronounced after age 3, boys and girls on average remain more alike than different (Hyde, 2005).

Physically, among the larger differences are boys' higher activity level, superior motor performance, especially after puberty, and their greater propensity for physical aggression (Hyde, 2005; Archer, 2004; Baillargeon et al., 2007; Pellegrini & Archer, 2005). These physical differences impact the nature of play. Boys engage in more rough-and-tumble, physically active play than girls do (LaFreniere, 2011). There are also sex-typed toy preferences; girls prefer to play with dolls and doll accessories, and boys prefer to play with construction and transportation toys (Paterski et al., 2011). Sex-typed play preferences increase between toddlerhood and middle childhood, and the degree of sex-typed behavior exhibited early in life is a strong indicator of later gender-based behavior (Golombok et al., 2008).

Cognitive gender differences are small and are affected by task characteristics (Miller & Halpern, 2014; Ardila et al., 2011). There are no gender differences in overall intelligence (Nisbett et al., 2012).

Boys and girls do equally well on tasks involving basic mathematical skills and are equally capable of learning math, but show variations in specific abilities starting in

One clear behavioral difference between young boys and young girls is boys' greater propensity to engage in rough-and-tumble play. Knot. P. Saengma/Shutterstock

elementary school (Spelke, 2005). Girls tend to perform better on tests of verbal fluency, mathematical computation, memory for locations of objects, and problems requiring algebraic solutions or short-answer responses. Boys generally show an advantage in mental rotations, especially when the task involves three-dimensional objects and when it is timed (Miller & Halpern, 2014), mathematical word problems, and memory for spatial configurations (Spelke, 2005). Boys' mathematical abilities vary more than girls', with more boys at both the highest and lowest ends of the ability range (Halpern et al., 2007). However, in most studies, mathematics test performance tends to be about the same (Miller & Halpern, 2014).

Across different languages, girls tend to start using language earlier, say more, and combine words earlier (Eriksson et al., 2012). Boys are more likely to stutter or to have a reading disability than girls (Wallentin, 2009; Rutter et al., 2004). Girls tend to use more praise, agreement, acknowledgment, and elaboration on what someone else has said (Leaper & Smith, 2004). Girls also tend to show an advantage in school and tend to earn higher grades, especially in language classes (Voyer & Voyer, 2014).

PERSPECTIVES ON GENDER DEVELOPMENT

gender roles
Behaviors, interests, attitudes, skills, and traits that a culture considers appropriate for each sex; differ for males and females.

gender-typing
Socialization process by which children, at an early age, learn appropriate gender roles.

gender stereotypes
Preconceived generalizations about male or female role behavior.

Gender roles are the behaviors, interests, attitudes, skills, and personality traits that a culture considers appropriate for males or females. Historically, in most cultures, women have been expected to devote most of their time to caring for the household and children, whereas men were providers and protectors. Women were expected to be compliant and nurturing; men, to be active, aggressive, and competitive. Today, gender roles, especially in Western cultures, have become more diverse and flexible.

Gender-typing, the acquisition of a gender role, takes place early in childhood (Iervolino et al., 2005). **Gender stereotypes** are preconceived generalizations about male or female behavior: "All females are passive and dependent; all males are aggressive and independent." Gender stereotypes appear to some degree in children as young as 2 or 3, increase during the preschool years, and reach a peak at age 5 (Campbell et al., 2004; Ruble & Martin, 1998).

Let's look at five theoretical perspectives on gender development (summarized in Table 8.1): *biological*, *evolutionary*, *psychoanalytic, cognitive,* and *social learning*.

TABLE 8.1 Five Perspectives on Gender Development

Theories	Major Theorists	Key Processes	Basic Beliefs
Biological approach		Genetic, neurological, and hormonal activity	Many behavioral differences between the sexes can be traced to biology.
Evolutionary approach	Charles Darwin	Natural and sexual selection	Gender differences stem from evolutionary differences in reproductive and parenting behaviors for each sex.
Psychoanalytic approach	Sigmund Freud	Resolution of unconscious emotional conflict	Gender identity occurs when the child identifies with the same-sex parent.
Cognitive approach/ cognitive-developmental theory	Lawrence Kohlberg	Self-categorization	Once a child learns she is a girl or he is a boy, the child interprets and uses information about behavior by gender.
Social learning approach/ social cognitive theory	Albert Bandura	Observation of models, reinforcement	Child observes and imitates gendered behavior and is reinforced for appropriate behavior and punished for inappropriate behavior.

Biological Approach The existence of similar gender roles across different cultures suggests that some gender differences are biologically based. If gender differences were purely cultural inventions, we would expect to see more variability.

The biological approach explains some gender differences using neurological, hormonal, and evolutionary explanations. One obvious place to look for the source of gender differences is the brain. Across the life span, and starting early in development, men, on average, have larger brain volume than women (Ruigrok et al., 2014). By age 5, when the brain reaches approximate adult size, boys' brains are about 10 percent larger than girls' brains (Reiss et al., 1996). However, girls' brains have a higher proportion of gray matter (neurons) and show greater cerebral blood flow, whereas boys' brains contain more white matter (axons for communication between neurons) (Cosgrove et al., 2007).

One important influence may be what occurs in the womb, where hormones affect the developing brain. An analysis of fetal testosterone levels and the development of gender-typical play has shown a link between higher testosterone levels and male-typical play in boys (Auyeng et al., 2009). Additionally, fetal testosterone exposure has been linked to dominance, status striving behavior, and, more weakly, aggression and violence in adults (Eisenegger et al., 2011; Turanovic et al., 2017). Some research focuses on girls with a disorder called *congenital adrenal hyperplasia (CAH)*. These girls have high prenatal levels of *androgens* (male sex hormones). They tend to show preferences for boys' toys, rough play, and male playmates, as well as strong spatial skills. *Estrogens* (female sex hormones), on the other hand, seem to have less influence on boys' gender-typed behavior (Pasterski et al., 2011; Berenbaum et al., 2012).

Biological Influences on Variations in Gender Identity Development Any good theory of gender development should be capable of addressing not just the typical path to gender identity, but also provide an explanatory framework for atypical development. Thus the study of intersex and transgender individuals can provide us with valuable information about how biology affects our understanding of who we are.

Perhaps the most compelling examples of biologically based research have to do with intersex infants born with ambiguous sexual organs that cannot be immediately interpreted or assigned as male or female. John Money and his colleagues (Money et al., 1955) recommended that these children be assigned as early as possible to the gender that holds the potential for the most nearly normal functioning. They based this recommendation on the appearance of the genitals.

However, newer studies demonstrate the profound difficulty of predicting the outcome of sex assignment at birth, particularly on the basis of external genitalia. In one study, 14 genetically male children born without normal penises but with testes were legally and surgically assigned female sex during the 1st month of life and were raised as girls. Ultimately, eight declared themselves male, five declared unwavering female identity but expressed difficulty fitting in with other girls, and one refused to discuss the subject with anyone. Meanwhile, the two boys whose parents had refused the initial sexual assignment remained male (Reiner & Gearhart, 2004). This and other similar cases strongly suggest that gender identity is rooted in biological factors and is not easily changed (Meyer-Bahlburg, 2005; Reiner, 2005). Merely telling children what they are is not enough to alter gender identity. Because of findings such as these, genetically male infants born with a disorder of sex development, even if they have an absent or very small penis, are increasingly gender-assigned male (Kolesinska, 2014).

But what about those people without a biological disorder of sexual development, who nonetheless do not show the typical pattern of gender identity development? Transgender people are individuals whose gender identity is different from their biological sex. Although many young children play with their identity—for example, dressing up in different clothes or pretending to be something they are not—children, especially girls, who will later identify as transgender are far more likely to show strong and persistent gender dysphoria early in childhood (Steensma et al., 2013). It is estimated that approximately 0.3 to 0.5 percent of the global population identifies as transgender (Reisner et al., 2016). In the United States, estimates are that 1 million to 1.4 million adults identify as transgender, with a greater proportion of younger adults identifying as such (Flores et al., 2016; Meerwik & Sevelius, 2017).

The reported number of transgender individuals has risen in the United States in recent decades, most likely as a result of increased referral rates to clinics (Zucker 2017). However, the existence of alternate gender identities is not a new phenomenon. Greek and Roman mythology contains accounts of men turned into women, and writers of the time also spoke of men who dressed and acted as women. In the Renaissance period, there are indications that a number of notable public figures, including King Henry III of France and the ambassador for Louis XIV to Siam, were transgender (Denny, 2013). Anthropologists have, for decades, written about variations in gender identity and the difficulties of using a binary system to describe gender categories in other cultures, although gender identity (a person's identification as male and female) and sexual orientation (who a person is sexually attracted to) were often conflated in the literature (Martin & Vorhees, 1975; Devereux, 1988). In the United States and Canada, anthropological accounts of indigenous peoples discussed gender variant "two spirit" people across a variety of different native groups (Towle & Morgan, 2002). And in India, such variations have even been codified into law with hijras. Hijras have a history that spans centuries and are biologically male but adopt a feminine gender expression (Goel, 2016).

There are indications that the disparity between gender and sex in transgender people is biologically influenced. For example, biological women who later identify as male have markers that suggest high androgen exposure in the womb (Leinung & Wu, 2017; Wu & Leinung, 2015). Additionally, research on twins suggests there may be genetic influences at play as well (Diamond, 2013). In one study, if one member of a pair of identical twins (who shared all their genes) was transgender, the other twin was also transgender 40 percent of the time. By contrast, none of the transgender fraternal twins (who shared roughly half of their genes) also had a transgender twin (Heylens et al., 2012).

There also appear to be brain differences in transgender people. For example, the volume of the stria terminalis (an area of the brain involved in sexual behavior) in biological men who later identify as women is more similar to that of other women than to that of other men (Zhou et al., 1995). Other research has shown that transgender female-to-male individuals show masculinized organization of subcortical grey matter, and male-to-female individuals show feminized cortical thickness (Zubiarre-Elorza et al., 2012). Differences may be more pronounced in areas that have to do with body perception. For example, transgender female-to-male adults have more white matter in a number of areas in the somatosensory cortex. In addition, they show less activation of the supramarginal gyrus and secondary somatosensory cortex and more activation of the temporal pole when compared to cisgender (non-transgender) women when their breasts are stimulated, a response consistent with anxiety and alarm. These findings suggest altered sensory processing of gender incongruous body parts (Case et al., 2017). In short, there is emerging evidence that gender identity—a psychological construct housed in the brain—is strongly influenced by biology and is not merely the result of biological sex or child-rearing practices.

Evolutionary Approach The evolutionary approach sees gendered behavior as adaptive and reflecting the evolved mating and child-rearing strategies of adult males and females.

theory of sexual selection
Darwin's theory that gender roles developed in response to men's and women's differing reproductive needs.

According to Darwin's (1871) **theory of sexual selection,** the selection of sexual partners is a response to the differing reproductive pressures that early men and women confronted in the struggle for survival of the species (Wood & Eagly, 2012). Although women *must* invest a great deal in children, including pregnancy and breastfeeding, men may invest minimally via fertilization only. This puts into play different reproductive dynamics for each sex. The more widely a man can engage in sexual activity, the greater his chances to pass on his genetic inheritance. Thus, men tend to prefer more sexual partners than women do. They value physical prowess because it enables them to compete for mates and for control of resources and social status, which women value.

Because a woman invests more time and energy in pregnancy and can bear only a limited number of children, each child's survival is of utmost importance to her, so she looks for a mate who will remain with her and support their offspring. For women, having more sexual partners does not result in more children (Bjorklund & Pellegrini, 2000; Wood & Eagly, 2002). According to evolutionary theory, male competitiveness and aggressiveness and female nurturance develop during childhood as preparation for these adult roles (Pellegrini & Archer, 2005). Boys play at fighting; girls play at parenting.

Some people misinterpret evolutionary approaches as being deterministic in nature. If evolution plays a role in the development of gender roles, they conclude that means gender roles should be inflexible and highly resistant to change. But this is not the case. Clearly, men can care for children and women can be aggressive. Evolution does not specify how things must be. Rather, evolution builds in a slight "push" for men and women in one direction or another that can be minimized or maximized by cultural and environmental influences. It is only when large numbers of individuals are examined that gender differences emerge.

Critics of evolutionary theory argue that society and culture are more important than biology in determining gender roles. But evolutionary theorists have never argued that culture is insignificant. Rather, they have argued that men and women have cognitive adaptations designed to be sensitive to environmental input. Research suggests that men's primary ancestral role was to provide for subsistence whereas women's was to tend to the children, but this does not mean that we are bound to these roles.

Psychoanalytic Approach "Daddy, where will you live when I grow up and marry Mommy?" asks Mario, age 4. From the psychoanalytic perspective, Mario's question is part of his acquisition of gender identity. That process, according to Freud, is one of **identification,** the adoption of characteristics, beliefs, attitudes, values, and behaviors of the parent of the same sex. Freud considered identification an important personality development of early childhood.

According to Freud, identification will occur for Mario when he represses or gives up the wish to possess the parent of the other sex (his mother) and identifies with the parent of the same sex (his father). Although this explanation for gender development has been influential, it has been difficult to test and has little research support (Maccoby, 2000). Most developmental psychologists today favor other explanations.

Cognitive Approach Sarah realizes she is a girl because people call her a girl and treat her like a girl. As she observes and thinks about her world, she constructs her own gender-typing.

Kohlberg's Cognitive-Developmental Theory In Lawrence Kohlberg's (1966) theory, gender knowledge ("I am a boy") precedes gendered behavior ("so I like to do boy things"). As children realize which gender they belong to, they adopt behaviors they perceive as consistent with being male or female. Thus 3-year-old Sarah should prefer dolls to trucks because she sees other girls playing with dolls (Martin & Ruble, 2004).

The acquisition of gender roles, said Kohlberg, hinges on **gender constancy**—a child's realization that his or her gender will always be the same. According to this theory, once this occurs, children are motivated to adopt behaviors appropriate to their gender. Gender constancy seems to develop in three stages (Martin et al., 2002):

- *Gender identity:* awareness of one's own gender and that of others typically occurs between ages 2 and 3.

- *Gender stability:* awareness that gender does not change. However, children at this stage base judgments about gender on superficial appearances (clothing or hairstyle) and stereotyped behaviors.

- *Gender consistency:* the realization that a girl remains a girl even if she plays with trucks, and a boy remains a boy even if he has long hair. This typically occurs between ages 3 and 7 once children realize that changes in outward appearance do not affect gender.

identification
In Freudian theory, the process by which a young child adopts characteristics, beliefs, attitudes, values, and behaviors of the parent of the same sex.

gender constancy
Awareness that one will always be male or female.

Much research challenges Kohlberg's view that gender-typing depends on gender constancy. Long before children attain the final stage of gender constancy, they show gender-typed preferences (Martin & Ruble, 2004). For example, gender preferences in toys and playmates appear as early as 12 months (Jadva et al., 2010).

Today, cognitive-developmental theorists no longer claim that gender constancy must precede gender-typing (Martin et al., 2002). Rather, gender-typing is heightened by the more sophisticated understanding that gender constancy brings (Martin & Ruble, 2004). The achievement of gender identity may motivate children to learn more about gender; whereas gender stability and gender consistency may motivate them to be sure they are acting "like a boy" or "like a girl" (Martin et al., 2002).

Gender-Schema Theory Another cognitive approach is **gender-schema theory.** Like cognitive-developmental theory, it views children as actively extracting knowledge about gender from their environment *before* engaging in gender-typed behavior. However, gender-schema theory places more emphasis on the influence of culture. Once children know what sex they are, they develop a concept of what it means to be male or female *in their culture.* Children then match their behavior to their culture's view of what boys and girls are "supposed" to be and do (Bem, 1993; Martin et al., 2002). According to this theory, gender schemas promote gender stereotypes by influencing judgments about behavior. When meeting a new boy his age, 4-year-old Brandon offers him a toy truck, assuming that the new boy will like the same toys he likes.

Bem argued children who show stereotypical behavior may do so as a result of pressure for gender conformity. However, there is little evidence that gender schemas are at the root of stereotyped behavior or that children who are highly gender-typed necessarily feel pressure to conform (Yunger et al., 2004). Indeed, as many parents will attest, it can be difficult to encourage a young child to behave in ways that are not stereotypically masculine or feminine.

Another problem with both gender-schema theory and Kohlberg's theory is that gender-stereotyping does not always become stronger with increased gender knowledge (Bandura & Bussey, 2004; Banse et al., 2010). In fact, gender-stereotyping rises and then falls in a developmental pattern. Around ages 4 to 6, young children notice and remember only information consistent with gender schemas. Indeed, they tend to *mis*remember information that challenges gender stereotypes, such as photos of a girl sawing wood or a boy cooking. They are also quick to accept gender labels; when told that an unfamiliar toy is for the other sex, they will quickly discard it (Martin & Ruble, 2004). By ages 5 and 6, children develop rigid stereotypes about gender that they apply to themselves and others. A boy will pay more attention to what he considers boys' toys and a girl to girls' toys. Then, around age 7 or 8, schemas become more complex as children take in and integrate contradictory information, such as the fact that many girls have short hair. At this point, children develop more complex beliefs about gender and become more flexible in their views about gender roles (Martin & Ruble, 2004; Trautner et al., 2005).

Cognitive approaches to gender development have been an important contribution. However, these approaches may not fully explain the link between knowledge and conduct. There is disagreement about precisely what mechanism prompts children to act out gender roles and why some children become more strongly gender-typed than others (Bussey & Bandura, 1992, 1999; Martin & Ruble, 2004). Some investigators point to socialization.

Social Learning Approach According to Walter Mischel (1966), a traditional social learning theorist, children acquire gender roles by imitating models and being rewarded for gender-appropriate behavior. Children may pattern their behavior after a parent, other adults, or peers. Behavioral feedback, together with direct teaching by parents and other adults, reinforces gender-typing. A boy who models his behavior after his father is commended for acting "like a boy." A girl gets compliments on a pretty dress or hairstyle.

Since the 1970s, however, studies have cast doubt on the power of same-sex modeling alone to account for gender differences. As cognitive explanations have come to the fore, traditional social learning theory has lost favor (Martin et al., 2002). Albert Bandura's (1986; Bussey & Bandura, 1999) newer **social cognitive theory,** an expansion of social learning theory, incorporates some cognitive elements.

According to social cognitive theory, observation enables children to actively learn much about gender-typed behaviors before performing them. Instead of viewing the environment as a constant, social cognitive theory recognizes that children select or even create their environments through their choice of playmates and activities. However, critics say that social cognitive theory does not explain how children differentiate between boys and girls before they have a concept of gender, or what initially motivates children to acquire gender knowledge (Martin et al., 2002).

For social cognitive theorists, the way a child interprets and internalizes experiences with parents, teachers, peers, and cultural institutions plays a central part in gender development. In the following sections we address three primary sources of social influences.

Family Influences Usually experiences in the family seem to reinforce gender-typical preferences and attitudes. We say *seems* because it is difficult to separate parents' genetic influence from the influence of the environment they create. Also, parents may be responding to rather than encouraging children's gender-typed behavior (Iervolino et al., 2005).

Boys tend to be more strongly gender-socialized concerning play preferences than girls. Parents, especially fathers, generally show more discomfort if a boy plays with a doll than if a girl plays with a truck (Ruble et al., 2006; Sandnabba & Ahlberg, 1999). Girls have more freedom than boys in their clothes, games, and choice of playmates (Fagot et al., 2000; Miedzian, 1991).

The division of labor in a household matters too. Parents who adhere to traditional gender schemas are more likely to have strongly gender-typed children (Tenenbaum & Leaper, 2002). There are indications that the father's role in gender socialization is especially important, and that viewing fathers engaged in household and child care work is associated with decreased gender-typing (Deutsch et al., 2001; Turner & Gervai, 1995). In general, parents' behaviors are better predictors of children's gender role attitudes than are parents' beliefs (Halpern & Perry-Jenkins, 2016).

Peer Influences Even in early childhood, the peer group is a major influence on gender-typing. Preschoolers generally play in sex-segregated groups that reinforce gender-typed behavior (Martin et al., 2013), and the influence of the peer group increases with age (Martin et al., 2002). Children who play in same-sex groups (Maccoby, 2002; Martin & Fabes, 2001) or by themselves (Goble et al., 2012) tend to be more gender-typed than children who do not. Additionally, the more children chose to play with particular friends, the more they mutually influence each other (Martin et al., 2013).

Peers can exert either positive or negative pressure on each other to behave in normative ways. Being gender atypical is most commonly associated with peer victimization, although the relationship is not always simple. At times friends can serve as a protective buffer against victimization (Zosuls et al., 2016)

Cultural Influences When a young girl in Nepal touched the plow that her brother was using, she was scolded. In this way she learned that as a girl she must refrain from acts her brother was expected to perform (D. Skinner, 1989). Social learning theory predicts that the cultural influences around us will influence the degree to which we become gender-typed.

Children's books have long been a source of gender stereotypes. Analyses of children's books have uncovered nearly twice as many male as female main characters, greater representation of males in book titles, and strong gender-stereotyping (McCabe et al., 2011). Female main characters nurtured more, were portrayed in indoor settings, and appeared to have no paid occupations (Hamilton et al., 2006). Fathers were largely

social cognitive theory
Albert Bandura's expansion of social learning theory; holds that children learn gender roles through socialization.

absent, and when they appeared, they were shown as withdrawn and ineffectual (Anderson & Hamilton, 2005). Similar results have been found in coloring books, where females are more typically portrayed as children and males as superheroes, animals, or adults (Fitzpatrick & McPherson, 2010). Some of the gender stereotypicality may be due to child preferences. Cross-cultural research conducted in China, the United States, and Germany showed that across the different cultures, boys strongly preferred aggressive stories whereas girls strongly preferred nurturing stories (Knobloch et al., 2005).

In the United States, television is also a major format for the transmission of cultural attitudes toward gender (Collins, 2011). This includes the influences within the content of programming as well as in commercials (Eisend, 2010) and music videos (Wallis, 2011). In both children's and in prime-time programming, boys and men receive greater screen time. Moreover, in children's programming, boys display a wider range of emotions than girls do, and in adult programming, men are portrayed as dominant, and women are likely to be portrayed as sexually provocative (Martin, 2017; Sink & Mastro, 2017). Not surprisingly, children who watch more television become more strongly gender-typed (Kimball, 1986).

Movies also have an impact. Research has shown that males in G-rated movies are more likely to be main characters, and females are more likely to be portrayed as young and as possessing traits such as intelligence and beauty (Smith et al., 2010). Disney movies have been frequent targets of criticism because of their stereotypical portrayal of male and female roles. Although Disney has made attempts at introducing more egalitarian ideals in its line of princess movies (England et al., 2011), more work remains. One recent study showed that preschool girls who were highly engaged with Disney princess movies showed higher gender-stereotypical behavior a year later than did children less engaged with princess movies (Coyne et al.,2016).

Major strengths of the socialization approach include the breadth and multiplicity of processes it examines and the scope for individual differences it reveals. But this very complexity makes it difficult to establish clear causal connections. Just what aspects of the home environment and the peer culture promote gender-typing? Does differential treatment produce or reflect gender differences? Further research may help us see how socializing agents mesh with children's biological tendencies and cognitive understandings with regard to gender-related attitudes and behavior.

Play

Through play, children stimulate the senses, exercise their muscles, coordinate sight with movement, gain mastery over their bodies, make decisions, and acquire new skills. Play is not what children do to burn off energy so they can get to the real business of learning; rather, it is the context in which much of the most important learning occurs (see Research in Action).

Researchers categorize children's play in varying ways. One common classification system is by *cognitive complexity*. Another classification is based on the *social dimension* of play.

COGNITIVE LEVELS OF PLAY

Courtney, at 3, talked for a doll, using a deeper voice than her own. Miguel, at 4, wore a kitchen towel as a cape and flew around as Batman. These children were engaged in play involving make-believe people or situations—one of four levels of play Smilansky (1968) identified as showing increasing amounts of cognitive complexity. Although certain types of play are more common at particular ages, the types of play can occur anytime.

functional play
Play involving repetitive large muscular movements.

The simplest level, which begins during infancy, is **functional play** (sometimes called *locomotor play*), consisting of repeated practice of large muscular movements, such as rolling a ball (Bjorklund & Pellegrini, 2002).

research in action

THE ADAPTIVE VALUE OF PLAY

Play is ubiquitous, not just in young humans—who take almost any opportunity they can to play—but also in the young of many species, especially intelligent ones (Bjorklund & Pellegrini, 2000; Graham & Burghardt, 2010). Why is this pattern of behavior so common across different species?

From an evolutionary standpoint, play serves a purpose. During play, physical attributes plus cognitive and social skills necessary for adult life are practiced. Kittens pounce and stalk, puppies wrestle, horses run and kick. Play is a means of experimenting in a relatively risk-free fashion with new behavioral routines that will be needed in adulthood (Pellegrini et al., 2007).

In humans, early locomotor play supports gross motor skill and neuromuscular development (Burdette & Whitaker, 2005). Exercise play increases from early childhood to the early primary school years, and vigorous activity helps develop muscle strength, endurance, efficiency of movement, and athletic coordination (Graham & Burghardt, 2010; Smith & Pellegrini, 2013).

Object play may serve an evolutionary purpose for skills related to tool use by enabling children to learn the properties of objects and what can be done with them (Bjorklund & Pellegrini, 2000). In non-Western societies, where children as young as 2 or 3 years old spend time observing adults at work, they begin to emulate their activities through object manipulation and socio-dramatic play (Morelli et al., 2003).

The most complex and difficult thing we will ever have to learn how to navigate is our social world, and social play helps us practice how to do this. Social play is abundant in childhood. Children develop and sustain friendships, practice cooperation, negotiate conflict, and build complex social skills in coordination with peers (Jarvis et al., 2014). Across cultures, social play provides an opportunity to learn and practice societal norms of cooperation, competition, power, and social strategies (Kamp, 2001).

Evolutionary psychologists posit for play to be an adaptation, its benefits must outweigh its costs. Potential costs include excess energy expenditure, injury, aggression, and decreased vigilance from predators or other dangers (Graham & Burghardt, 2010). Comparatively, numerous adaptive developmental functions are learned, practiced, and refined through play (Hewes, 2014). There is still much more to learn, but one thing seems clear: Play is not frivolous activity but time well spent.

what's your view From your observations of children's play, have you noticed differences in the way boys and girls play together? What might be an evolutionary rationale for that?

The second level, **constructive play** (also called *object play*), is the use of objects or materials to make something, such as a house of blocks or a crayon drawing (Bjorklund & Pellegrini, 2002).

The third level, **dramatic play** (also called *pretend play, fantasy play,* or *imaginative play*), involves imaginary objects, actions, or roles. It involves a combination of cognition, emotion, language, and sensorimotor behavior. More advanced cognitive development affords more sophisticated play, but play also helps strengthen the development of dense connections in the brain and promotes later capacity for abstract thought. Play is not just the response to a developing intellect; it is the driver of it as well. For example, studies have found the quality of dramatic play to be associated with social and linguistic competence (Bergen, 2002; Christie, 1998). Pretend play also may further the development of theory-of-mind skills (Smith, 2005). Pretending that a remote control is a telephone, for example, and understanding that you and I both agree on that pretense, can help children begin to understand others' thoughts.

Dramatic play peaks during the preschool years (Bjorklund & Pellegrini, 2002; Smith, 2005) and then declines as school-age children become more involved in **formal games with rules**—organized games with known procedures and penalties, such as tag and four square. However, many children continue to engage in pretending well beyond the elementary school years.

constructive play
Play involving use of objects or materials to make something.

dramatic play
Play involving imaginary people or situations; also *called pretend play, fantasy play, or imaginative play*.

formal games with rules
Organized games with known procedures and penalties.

TABLE 8.2 Parten's Categories of Social and Nonsocial Play

Category	Description
Unoccupied behavior	The child does not seem to be playing but watches anything of interest.
Onlooker behavior	The child spends most of the time watching other children play.
Solitary independent play	The child plays alone with toys that are different from those used by nearby children and makes no effort to get close to them.
Parallel play	The child plays alongside other children, but not with other children. The parallel player does not try to influence the other children's play.
Associative play	The child plays with other children. All the children play similarly but there is no organization around a goal. Each child is interested more in being with the other children than in the activity itself.
Cooperative or organized supplementary play	The child plays in a group organized for some goal—to make something, play a formal game, or dramatize a situation. By a division of labor, children take on different roles.

Source: Parten, M. B. (1932). Social play among preschool children. *Journal of Abnormal and Social Psychology, 27,* 243–269.

THE SOCIAL DIMENSION OF PLAY

In a classic study done in the 1920s, Mildred B. Parten (1932) identified six types of play ranging from the least to the most social (Table 8.2). She found that as children get older their play tends to become more interactive and cooperative. Although this general progression is common, children of all ages also engage in all of Parten's categories of play (Rubin et al., 1998).

Parten incorrectly regarded nonsocial play as less mature than social play. She suggested that young children who continue to play alone may develop social, psychological, or educational problems. It is true that solitary play can be a sign of shyness, anxiety, fearfulness, or social rejection (Coplan et al., 2014; Degnan et al., 2014; Coplan et al., 2004). However, researchers now consider not only *whether* a child plays alone but *why*. Some children may just prefer to play alone (Coplan et al., 2015). A preference for solitude is not necessarily associated with negative outcomes in adulthood, so it is reasonable to think the same might be true for children (Ooi et al., 2018). In fact, most

These superheroes are participating in dramatic play. Alistair Berg/DigitalVision/Getty Images

children who like to play alone are rated as socially and cognitively competent by others (Harrist et al., 1997). Similarly, *reticent play,* a combination of Parten's unoccupied and onlooker categories, is often a manifestation of shyness (Coplan et al., 2004) but does not seem to affect whether or not children are well-liked or have problem behaviors (Spinrad et al., 2004).

One kind of play that becomes more social during the preschool years is dramatic play (Rubin et al., 1998). Children typically engage in more dramatic play when playing with someone else than when playing alone (Bjorklund & Pellegrini, 2002). In pretending together, children develop joint problem-solving, planning, and goal-seeking skills; gain an understanding of other people's perspectives; and construct an image of the social world (Bergen, 2002; Bjorklund & Pellegrini, 2002; Smith, 2005).

GENDER DIFFERENCES IN PLAY

As we have mentioned, sex segregation is common among preschoolers and becomes more prevalent in middle childhood. By 3 years of age girls are much more likely to play with dolls and tea sets whereas boys prefer toy guns and trucks (Dunn & Hughes, 2001). Children will sometimes reprimand each other for playing with the "wrong" toys for their gender (Mayeza, 2017). Girls and boys also prefer to dress in stereotypically gender-typed ways—girls in twirly dresses, boys in fireman hats—and this tendency occurs regardless of the parents' own desires about how their children dress (Halim et al., 2014).

Girls tend to select other girls as playmates, and boys prefer other boys (Maccoby & Jacklin, 1987; Martin & Fabes, 2001), a phenomenon known as **gender segregation.** Boys' tendency to be more active and physically aggressive in their play as compared to girls' more nurturing play styles are major contributors (Martin et al., 2011). Boys engage in higher levels of rough-and-tumble play; girls tend to choose more structured, adult-supervised activities (Fabes et al., 2003; Smith, 2005).

gender segregation
Tendency to select playmates of one's own gender.

Girls' pretend stories generally focus on social relationships and nurturing, and they highlight domestic roles as in playing house (Pellegrini & Archer, 2005; P.K. Smith, 2005). Boys' pretend play often involves danger or discord and competitive, dominant roles, as in mock battles. Additionally, boys' play is more strongly gender-stereotyped than girls' (Bjorklund & Pellegrini, 2002). Thus, in mixed-sex groups, play tends to revolve around traditionally masculine activities (Fabes et al., 2003).

CULTURAL INFLUENCES ON PLAY

Cultural values influence beliefs about the importance of play. In Western cultures such as the United States, some argue that adequate amounts of child-directed free play are necessary for optimal development. In other cultures, play may be viewed differently. For example, in one study, parents from China, Korea, Pakistan, Nepal, and India were asked about their beliefs and reported they saw little developmental value in play, preferring to encourage academics. The European parents in the same study, by contrast, believed that play was important for development (Parmar et al., 2004). Similarly, teachers in Sweden and the United States in another study saw play as "children's work," although Japanese educators did not (Izumi-Taylor et al., 2010). Cultural values also affect the play environments adults set up for children, and these environments in turn affect the frequency of specific forms of play across cultures (Bodrova & Leong, 2005).

Culture also influences development via peer interactions. Children who behave in ways that are contrary to cultural values may be met with rejection from peers, whereas those who embody those values are likely to be accepted (Chen, 2012). One observational study compared middle-class Korean American and middle-class Anglo American children in

When preschool girls and boys play together, they usually play with "masculine" toys such as cars or trains. Pixtal/AGE Fotostock

separate preschools (Farver et al., 1995). The Korean American children played more cooperatively, often offering toys to other children—a reflection of their culture's emphasis on group harmony. Anglo American children were more aggressive and often responded negatively to other children's suggestions, reflecting the competitiveness of American culture. Similarly, in another study, Andalusian children (from a collectivistic culture) who unexpectedly engaged in more aggressive encounters than Dutch children (from an individualistic culture) during a naturalistic play interaction were nonetheless also able to more frequently negotiate a resolution. This reflected their culture's emphasis on social goals and accommodation (Martinez-Lozano et al., 2011).

Gender differences in play do not not seem to be driven by cultural influences. Regardless of where they come from, boys tend to engage in more exploratory play, and girls enjoy more symbolic and pretend play (Cote & Bornstein, 2009; P. K. Smith, 2005). However, the more salient gender is made (for example, with the use of different clothing for men and women, or when children are separated into groups by gender), the more children believe in gender stereotypes and the less they play with other-sex peers (Hillard & Liben, 2010).

Parenting

Parenting can be a complex challenge. Parents must deal with small people who have independent minds and wills, but who still have a lot to learn about what kinds of behavior work well in society.

FORMS OF DISCIPLINE

discipline
Methods of molding children's character and of teaching them to exercise self-control and engage in acceptable behavior.

In the field of human development, **discipline** refers to methods of molding character and of teaching self-control and acceptable behavior. In casual speech we tend to think of discipline as involving only punishment, but the psychological definition of the word also includes techniques such as rewarding desired behaviors and drawing attention to how actions affect others.

Reinforcement and Punishment "You're such a wonderful helper! Thank you for putting away your toys." Nick's mother smiles warmly at her son as he plops his dump truck into the toy box.

Parents sometimes punish children to stop undesirable behavior, but children usually learn more from being reinforced for good behavior. *External* reinforcements may be tangible (treats, a toy) or intangible (a smile or a word of praise). Whatever the reinforcement, the child must see it as rewarding and must receive it consistently after showing the desired behavior. Eventually, the behavior should provide an *internal* reinforcement: a sense of pleasure or accomplishment.

Sometimes punishment, such as isolation or denial of privileges, can also be effective. Children cannot be permitted to run into traffic or hit another child. In situations such as these, immediate cessation of the behavior is generally the goal. In such situations, punishment, if consistent, immediate, and clearly tied to the offense, may stop the behavior. It is most effective when accompanied by a short, simple explanation (AAP Committee on Psychosocial Aspects of Child and Family Health, 1998; Baumrind, 1996). It is important to remember that, in addition to punishment for undesired behaviors children need to know what should be substituted for misbehavior.

Punishment that is too harsh can be harmful. Children who are punished harshly and frequently show more externalizing behaviors such as physical aggression and impulsivity (Erath et al., 2009). The link between harsh parenting and aggression is cross-cultural and has been found in China, India, Italy, Kenya, the Philippines, and Thailand (Gershoff et al., 2010). Harsh parenting has also been linked to relational aggression, in which attempts are made to damage another's social status or reputation (Kawabata et al., 2011).

The influence of harsh parenting is bidirectional; difficult children elicit more coercive parenting (Pettit & Arsiwalla, 2008). Moreover, different children respond differently to harsh parenting. For example, children are particularly likely to respond to coercive parenting with behavior problems if they also suffer from attentional issues (Scott et al., 2012). Shyer children may become frightened if parents lose control and may eventually try to avoid a punitive parent, undermining the parent's ability to influence behavior (Grusec & Goodnow, 1994). The influence of parenting tactics varies with child temperament (Kochanska, 1993).

Corporal punishment can include spanking, hitting, slapping, pinching, shaking, and other physical acts. Corporal punishment is common across many cultures and found at all income levels (Runyan et al., 2010). It is popularly believed to be more effective than other methods to instill respect for parental authority and to be harmless if done in moderation by loving parents (Kazdin & Benjet, 2003; McLoyd & Smith, 2002).

corporal punishment
Use of physical force with the intention of causing pain but not injury so as to correct or control behavior.

The rates of corporal punishment for American preschoolers have trended sharply down in recent decades. From 1975 to 2014, rates of spanking declined by approximately 28 percent in American families (Finklehor et al., 2019). In 2015, 4 percent of parents reported spanking their children "often" and almost 17 percent of parents reported spanking their children at least some of the time (Parker et al., 2015). In the United States, spanking is more common in the South, among conservative Christians, and in African American families (Finklehor et al., 2019).

A large body of evidence suggests that corporal punishment is often counterproductive and should be avoided (Straus, 1999; Gershoff, 2010). Apart from the risk of injury, children who experience corporal punishment may fail to internalize moral messages, develop poor parent-child relationships, and show increased physical aggressiveness or antisocial behavior. As adults they are more likely to suffer from mental health issues, engage in criminal behavior, and abuse their own children (Gershoff, 2013). A link between spanking and externalizing behaviors has been found in children from different cultural and ethnic groups, both internationally, as well as within white, African American, Latino, and Asian American families in the United States (Gershoff et al., 2010; Gershoff et al. 2012; Berlin et al., 2009). In addition, spanking has been negatively associated with cognitive development (MacKenzie et al., 2013) and there is no clear line between mild and harsh spanking—mild spanking often leads to the other (Kazdin & Benjet, 2003).

The United Nations Convention on the Rights of Children opposes all forms of physical violence against children; the United States and Somalia remain the only nations yet to ratify the convention (Zolotor et al., 2011). In the United States, 15 states specifically allow the use of corporal punishment in schools, 7 states do not prohibit it, and 28 states specifically prohibit it (U.S. Department of Education, 2017). Some educators believe it is an effective deterrent to harmful misbehaviors, such as fighting, but others assert that corporal punishment degrades the educational environment. Moreover, critics point to the fact that ethnic minority children and children with disabilities are subject to corporal punishment more frequently (U.S. Department of Education, 2017).

Inductive Reasoning, Power Assertion, and Love Withdrawal When Sara took candy from a store, her father explained how the owner of the store would be harmed and how sad he would feel that the candy was gone. He asked Sara how she would feel in the same situation. When he took her back to the store to return the candy, Sara, even though she had not been asked to do so, told the store owner she was sorry she had made him sad.

Inductive techniques, such as those Sara's father used, are designed to encourage desirable behavior or discourage undesirable behavior by setting limits, demonstrating logical consequences of an action, explaining, discussing, negotiating, and getting ideas from the child about what is fair. They also tend to include appeals to consider how one's actions affect how others feel.

inductive techniques
Disciplinary techniques designed to induce desirable behavior by appealing to a child's sense of reason and fairness.

Inductive techniques are usually the most effective method of getting children to accept parental standards (Hoffman, 1970; Kerr et al., 2004). Inductive reasoning tends to arouse empathy for the victim of wrongdoing as well as guilt on the part of the wrongdoer (Kochanska et al., 2002). Parents who use inductive techniques are more likely to have children who see the moral wrongness of behavior that hurts other people (Grusec, 2006; Volling et al., 2009).

Two other broad categories of discipline are *power assertion* and *temporary withdrawal of love*. **Power assertion** is intended to stop or discourage undesirable behavior through physical or verbal enforcement of parental control; it includes demands, threats, withdrawal of privileges, spanking, and other types of punishment. **Withdrawal of love** may include ignoring, isolating, or showing dislike for a child. Neither of these is as effective as inductive reasoning in most circumstances, and both may be harmful (Baumrind et al., 2010; McCord, 1996).

However, it is important to consider disciplinary strategies within their cultural context. Research with Western samples shows that psychological control tactics, such as love withdrawal or shaming, are generally associated with negative outcomes in European American children (Scharf & Goldner, 2019). However, these techniques can be effective in other contexts. For example, Chinese and Russian parents are more likely than American parents to use psychological control tactics. However, although American preschool children whose parents use psychological control tactics show an increase in internalizing and externalizing behaviors, Chinese children show no such pattern, and in Russian children, psychological control is linked only to externalizing problems (Olsen et al., 2002).

PARENTING STYLES

Parents differ in their approach to parenting. Children interpret and respond to parenting within the context of an ongoing relationship with their parents. Thus the different styles of parenting may affect children's competence in dealing with their world.

Baumrind's Model of Parenting Styles In her research, Diana Baumrind (1971, 1996; Baumrind & Black, 1967) studied 103 preschool children from 95 families. Through interviews, testing, and home studies, she measured how the children were functioning, identified three parenting styles, and described typical behavior patterns of children raised according to each (Baumrind, 1989; see Table 8.3).

Authoritarian parenting emphasizes control and obedience. Authoritarian parents insist children conform to a set standard of conduct and punish them for violating it. They are less warm than other parents. Their children tend to be more discontented, withdrawn, and distrustful.

Permissive parenting emphasizes self-expression and self-regulation. Permissive parents make few demands and rarely punish. They are warm, noncontrolling, and undemanding. Their preschool children tend to be immature—the least self-controlled.

Authoritative parenting Authoritative parents are loving yet demand good behavior and have firm standards. They impose limited, judicious punishment when necessary, within the context of a warm, supportive relationship. Preschoolers with authoritative parents tend to be the most self-reliant, self-controlled, self-assertive, exploratory, and content.

Eleanor Maccoby and John Martin (1983) added a fourth parenting style—*neglectful, or uninvolved*—to describe parents who, sometimes, perhaps because of stress or depression, focus on their needs rather than on those of the child. Neglectful parenting has been linked with a variety of behavioral disorders in childhood and adolescence (Steinberg et al., 2006).

Why does authoritative parenting seem to enhance children's social competence? It may be because authoritative parents set sensible and realistic standards. By using clear, consistent rules, they let children know what is expected of them. In authoritarian homes, children are so strictly controlled that often they cannot make independent choices about their own behavior. In permissive homes, children receive so little guidance

TABLE 8.3 Parenting Styles

		WARMTH	
		High	Low
CONTROL	High	Authoritative	Authoritarian
	Low	Permissive	Neglectful

that they may become uncertain and anxious about whether they are doing the right thing. In authoritative homes, children know when they are meeting expectations and can decide whether it is worth risking parental displeasure to pursue a goal. They also know the satisfaction of accepting responsibilities and achieving success.

Criticisms of Baumrind's Model In research based on Baumrind's work, the benefits of authoritative parenting have generally been supported. However, because Baumrind's findings are correlational, they only establish associations between each parenting style and a particular set of child behaviors. They do not show that different styles of child rearing *cause* children to be more or less competent. As with all correlations, the direction of effects is not certain.

Moreover, Baumrind did not consider innate factors, such as temperament, that might have influenced the parents. An easy child, for example, might elicit authoritative parenting, and a difficult child, more power assertive techniques as parents search for a way to manage her defiance.

Cultural Differences in Parenting Styles Another concern is that Baumrind's categories reflect a biased view of child development. Some researchers have argued that although authoritative parenting may be a beneficial parenting strategy for children within dominant U.S. culture, it may not function in the same way across different ethnic or cultural groups.

Parenting strategies reflect cultural values, and thus they are interpreted by children within that context. In countries such as the United States, the traits of independence and initiative are highly valued, and constraints on behavior are seen as negative by children. Among Asian Americans, obedience and strictness are not necessarily associated with harshness and domination but instead with caring, concern, and involvement. Traditional Chinese culture, with its emphasis on respect for elders, stresses the responsibility to maintain the social order. This obligation is modeled through firm and just control and governance of the child and even by physical punishment if necessary (Zhao, 2002). Although Asian American parenting is frequently described as authoritarian, the warmth and supportiveness that characterize Asian family relationships may more closely resemble Baumrind's authoritative parenting but without the emphasis on the European American values of individuality, choice, and freedom (Chao, 1994) and with stricter parental control (Chao, 2001).

Traditional Asian culture stresses adults' responsibility to maintain the social order by teaching children socially proper behavior.
kumikomini/iStock/Getty Images

As another example, Mexican American families use more authoritarian parenting than European American families, perhaps in line with the respect for authority characteristic of Mexican culture, to no ill effect (Varela et al., 2004). In African American families, which tend to use more physical punishment, authoritarian parenting is not related to negative behavioral outcomes, although this relationship does exist for white families (Baumrind, 1972; McLeod et al., 1994). Other evidence suggests that despite the association between parenting style and later academic achievement in European American teens, it is not necessarily associated with such outcomes in Latino, Asian, or African American adolescents (Dornbusch et al., 1987; Steinberg et al., 1994).

OTHER BEHAVIORAL CONCERNS

Three issues of special concern are how to promote altruism, curb aggression, and deal with fears that often arise at this age.

Prosocial Behavior Alex, at 3½, responded to two preschool classmates' complaints that they did not have enough modeling clay, his favorite plaything, by giving them half of his. Alex was showing **altruism:** motivation to help another person with no expectation of reward. Altruism often entails cost, self-sacrifice, or risk. Altruism is at the heart of **prosocial behavior,** voluntary, positive actions to help others.

Even before the 2nd birthday, children often help others, share belongings and food, and offer comfort. Children who are more advanced in their emotional understanding at the age of 3 years generally engage in more prosocial behaviors at the age of 4 (Ensor et al., 2011). Also, those children with better theory of mind, who are more effectively able to model other people's points of view, are more effective at helping, cooperating, and comforting others (Imuta et al., 2016).

Heritability research suggests some of these behaviors are coded in the genes (Knafo-Noam et al., 2018). However, although genes matter, so does the environment. Traditional cultures in which people live in extended family groups and share work seem to instill prosocial values more than cultures that stress individual achievement (Eisenberg et al., 2015). Moreover, parents who show affection and use positive (inductive) disciplinary strategies encourage their children's natural tendency to prosocial behavior (Knafo & Plomin, 2006). Additionally, parents of prosocial children tend to point out models of prosocial behavior and steer children toward stories, films, and television programs that depict cooperation, sharing, and empathy and encourage sympathy, generosity, and helpfulness (Singer & Singer, 1998), which have been shown to increase children's altruism, cooperation, and even tolerance for others (Wilson, 2008). Relationships with siblings, peers, and teachers also can model and reinforce prosocial behavior (Eisenberg, 1992).

The goal of instrumental aggression is not to hurt or dominate another child, but rather to acquire a goal, such as a desired toy. Randy Faris/Cardinal/Corbis

Aggression Noah walks over to Jake, who is playing quietly with a toy car. Noah hits Jake and snatches the car away. He has used aggression as a tool to gain access to a wanted object. This is **instrumental aggression,** or aggression used to reach a goal—the most common type of aggression in early childhood. Between ages 2½ and 5, children frequently struggle over toys and control of space. Aggression surfaces mostly during social play; children who fight the most also tend to be the most sociable and competent. In fact, the ability to show some instrumental aggression may be a necessary step in social development. As children develop more self-control and become better able to express themselves verbally, they typically shift from showing aggression with blows to doing it with words (Coie & Dodge, 1998; Tremblay et al., 2004).

Gender Differences in Aggression Aggression is an exception to the generalization that boys and girls are more similar than different (Hyde, 2005). In all cultures studied, as among most mammals, boys are more aggressive than girls. This gender difference is apparent by age 2 (Baillargeon et al., 2007; Pellegrini & Archer, 2005).

However, when aggression is looked at more closely, it becomes apparent that boys and girls also tend to use different kinds of aggression. Boys engage in more **overt (direct) aggression,** tending to openly direct aggressive acts at a target. Girls, by contrast, tend to engage in a form of indirect social aggression known as **relational (social or indirect) aggression** (Putallaz & Bierman, 2004). This more subtle kind of aggression consists of damaging or interfering with relationships, reputation, or psychological well-being, often through teasing, manipulation, ostracism, spreading rumors, name-calling, and put-downs. It can be either overt or covert (indirect)—for example, making mean faces or ignoring someone. Among preschoolers, it tends to be direct and face-to-face ("You can't come to my party if you don't give me that toy") (Archer, 2004; Brendgen et al., 2005).

Cross-cultural research has supported the clear propensity for boys to engage in higher levels of physical aggression. However, the data on relational aggression are less clear. Some studies have found girls engage in higher levels of relational aggression; other studies have not found a difference between the genders (Lansford et al., 2012; Hyde, 2014; Archer, 2004). It is safe to say that if a difference does exist, it is quite small.

Influences on Aggression Why are some children more aggressive than others? Temperament may play a part. Children who are intensely emotional and low in self-control, or who have a difficult temperament, tend to express anger aggressively (Eisenberg et al., 1994; Rubin et al., 2003; Yaman et al., 2010). This is true not only for physical aggression, but also for relational aggression, which has been associated with negative emotionality and poor self-regulation (Tackett et al., 2014; Han et al., 2014).

Both physical and social aggression have genetic and environmental sources, but their relative influence differs. Research has shown the heritability of physical aggression is about 50 to 60 percent, whereas genes explain only 20 percent of social aggression (Brendgen et al., 2005). Aggressiveness is also the product of stressful and unstimulating home atmosphere, harsh discipline, lack of maternal warmth and social support, family dysfunction, exposure to aggressive adults and neighborhood violence, poverty, and transient peer groups, which prevent stable friendships (Dodge et al., 1994; Grusec & Goodnow, 1994; Romano et al., 2005).

Culture can also influence how much aggressive behavior a child shows. For example, in countries such as Japan and China, there is a cultural emphasis on harmony, self-control, and group cohesiveness. Anger and aggression contradict these cultural values. Thus Chinese and Japanese mothers are more likely than U.S. mothers to use inductive discipline, pointing out how aggressive behavior hurts others. They also show strong disappointment when children fail to meet behavioral standards. Moreover, teachers and peers are more likely to reject or exclude such children, and they are more likely than less aggressive children to have low social status (Zahn-Waxler et al., 1996; Chen, 2010).

Fearfulness Passing fears are common in early childhood. Many 2- to 4-year-olds are afraid of animals, especially dogs. By age 6, children are more likely to be afraid of the dark. Other common fears are of thunderstorms, doctors, and imaginary creatures (DuPont, 1983; Stevenson-Hinde & Shouldice, 1996).

Young children's fears stem largely from their intense fantasy life and their tendency to confuse appearance with reality. They are more likely to be frightened by something that looks scary, such as a cartoon monster, than by something capable of doing great harm, such as a nuclear explosion (Cantor, 1994). For the most part, older children's fears are more realistic (being kidnapped) and self-evaluative (failing a test) (Stevenson-Hinde & Shouldice, 1996).

Fears may come from hearing about other people's experiences (Muris et al., 1997) or from negative events experienced directly by children, such as vaccinations (LoBue et al., 2010). Children who have lived through an earthquake, kidnapping, war, or some other frightening event may fear that it will happen again (Kolbert, 1994).

Parents can help prevent children's fears by instilling a sense of trust and normal caution without being too protective. They can help a fearful child with reassurance and the open expression of feelings. Ridicule, coercion, and logical persuasion are not helpful (Cantor, 1994).

Relationships with Other Children

Relationships with siblings and peers become more important in early childhood (see Window on the World). Let's look first at some of these relationships and then at children without siblings.

A young girl is brave enough to pick up a crab despite the risk of being pinched.
Johner Images/Getty Images

window on the world

CULTURAL VARIATIONS IN AGE SEGREGATION

Historically, children of different ages mixed together. If they went to school, children were often assigned to classes based on how much they knew rather than when they were born (Neyfakh, 2014), and particularly in rural areas, many schools consisted of one or a few rooms where children of different ages were taught together.

In most developed countries today, as soon as children enter day care or school, many of their activities are stratified by age. This is a recent change over the past 100 years and is related to the increased industrialization in society and the advent of compulsory education (Rogoff, 2003; Reese, 1998). Same-age play allows for easier competition and collaboration as both children tend to be at similar levels of developmental complexity.

However, in the developing world and in many traditional cultures, children of different ages routinely play with each other. For example, in the Efe and Aka children of the Congo and in Mayan children in Guatemala, children generally play in mixed-age groupings. It is also common for children in cultures such as these to be related to their playmates. Children from developed countries like the United States are more likely to play with unrelated children of the same age as themselves (Rogoff et al., 2010; Boyette, 2010).

Parents sometimes believe that younger and older children do not have much to learn from each other.

However, both younger and older children benefit from age mixing. Younger children learn by watching and modeling the older children's behavior and by participating in activities alongside them. They can learn physical and cognitive skills, hone their social skills, and receive care and emotional support from older children. Older children can develop their leadership abilities and serve as mentors. They expand their comprehension through teaching. This interaction helps to enhance their creativity and allows them to develop their ability to nurture and care for others (Gray, 2011).

"We have a lot to learn from people who are in different phases of life than us," said Barbara Rogoff (Neyfakh, 2014). Although children can learn a great deal from those who are similar to them in age, there is also value in interactions with others of different ages. Cultures tend to gravitate toward one or the other dimension, but it may be that the ideal situation is a mix of the two approaches.

what's your view If you were a parent, would you prefer your child play with same-age or mixed-age peers? Would your preferences change in a free play versus an academic setting? Why or why not?

SIBLING RELATIONSHIPS

The earliest, most frequent, and most intense disputes among siblings are over property rights or access to the mother. Although exasperated adults may not always see it that way, sibling disputes are socialization opportunities, in which children learn to stand up for principles and negotiate disagreements (Howe et al., 2002).

Despite the frequency of conflict, sibling rivalry is *not* the main pattern between brothers and sisters early in life. Prosocial and play-oriented behaviors are more common than rivalry, hostility, and competition. As the children age, they tend to become less physical and more verbal in showing both aggression and care and affection (Abramovitch et al., 1986). Because older siblings tend to dominate younger ones, the quality of the relationship is more affected by the emotional and social adjustment of the older child than the younger one (Pike & Oliver, 2017). Generally, same-sex siblings, particularly girls, are closer and play together more peaceably than boy-girl pairs (Kier & Lewis, 1998). Sibling conflict is more common in large families and in families with more boys (Tippett & Wolke, 2015).

The quality of sibling relationships tends to carry over to relationships with other children. A child who is aggressive with siblings is likely to be aggressive with peers as well (Vlachou et al., 2011; Tippett & Wolke, 2015) whereas siblings who frequently play amicably together tend to develop prosocial behaviors (Pike et al., 2005). Likewise, friendships can influence sibling relationships. Older siblings who have experienced a good relationship with a friend before the birth of a sibling are likely to treat their younger siblings better (Kramer & Kowal, 2005). For a young child at risk for behavioral problems, a positive relationship with *either* a sibling or a friend can buffer the effects of a negative relationship with the other (McElwain & Volling, 2005). Similarly, the parenting relationship also influences sibling relationships. Harsh parenting increases sibling conflict and aggression, but positive parenting is associated with more harmonious sibling relationships (Tippett & Wolke, 2015).

THE ONLY CHILD

In the United States, approximately 18 percent of families have only one child (Gao, 2015). Generally, the stereotype of only children as selfish, lonely, or spoiled appears to be false. A meta-analysis of 115 studies found that most "onlies" do well. With respect to academic outcomes and success in work, they perform slightly better than children with siblings, and they are more motivated to achieve, have slightly higher self-esteem, and do not differ in emotional adjustment, sociability, or popularity (Mancillas, 2006).

Some theorists suggest only children do better because parents focus more attention on only children, talk to them more, and expect more of them than do parents with more than one child (Falbo, 2006). Because most children today spend considerable time in play groups, child care, and preschool, only children do not lack opportunities for social interaction with peers.

Research in China also has produced largely encouraging findings about only children. In 1979, to control an exploding population, the People's Republic of China established an official policy of limiting families to one child each. Although the policy has since been relaxed, most urban families now have only one child, and most rural families no more than two (Feng et al., 2016). This situation offered researchers the opportunity to study the adjustment of large numbers of only children.

Only children seem to be at an advantage, at least in China. Those with siblings reported higher levels of fear, anxiety, and depression than only children, regardless of sex or age (Yang et al., 1995). Among 4,000 third and sixth graders, only children's academic achievement and physical growth were about the same as, or better than, children with siblings although the differences were small (Falbo, 2012). As adults, only children, overall, were less likely to show signs of anxiety or depression than those children born in families with siblings (Falbo & Hooper, 2015). These findings may reflect the greater attention, stimulation, hopes, and expectations that parents shower on a baby they know will be their first and last.

PLAYMATES AND FRIENDS

Friendships develop as people develop. Toddlers play alongside or near each other, but not until about age 3 do children begin to have friends. Through friendships with casual playmates, young children learn how to get along with others. They learn moral values and gender-role norms, and they practice adult roles.

Preschoolers usually like to play with children of the same age and sex, although this varies by culture (see Window on the World). They also prefer prosocial playmates who can provide them with positive experiences (Hartup & Stevens, 1999; Hart et al. 1992), and highly prosocial children tend to seek out prosocial peers as their best friends (Eivers et al., 2012). Well-liked preschoolers and kindergarteners and those who are rated by parents and teachers as socially competent generally cope well with anger. They avoid insults and threats. Instead, they respond directly, in ways that minimize further conflict and keep relationships going (Fabes & Eisenberg, 1992).

Both temperament and emotional and behavioral self-control impact peer relationships (Ladd & Sechler, 2013). Preschoolers reject disruptive, impulsive, intrusive, or

Young children learn the importance of being a friend to have a friend.
Courtesy Gabriela Martorell

aggressive children (Sterry et al., 2010; Ramsey & Lasquade, 1996; Roopnarine & Honig, 1985). Less well-liked children also tend to hit back or tattle when a conflict develops (Fabes & Eisenberg, 1992).

As children become older, their preferences become more sophisticated. In one study, 4- to 7-year-olds rated the most important features of friendships as doing things together, liking and caring for each other, sharing and helping one another, and to a lesser degree, living nearby or going to the same school. Younger children rated physical traits, such as appearance and size, higher than older children did and rated affection and support lower (Furman & Bierman, 1983).

summary and key terms

The Developing Self

- The self-concept undergoes a major change in early childhood. Self-definition shifts from single representations to representational mappings. Young children do not see the difference between the real self and the ideal self.
- Children from individualistic cultures tend to view the self in terms of innate traits and personal characteristics, whereas those from collectivistic cultures tend to view themselves in terms of contextual influences and relationships.
- Self-esteem in early childhood tends to be global and unrealistic, reflecting adult approval.
- In individualistic cultures, parents are more concerned with self-esteem and children tend to describe themselves positively. In collectivistic cultures, modesty is often seen as a virtue, and children more often describe themselves in neutral or negative terms.
- Understanding of emotions directed toward the self and of simultaneous emotions develops gradually.
- According to Erikson, the developmental conflict of early childhood is initiative versus guilt. Successful resolution of this conflict results in the virtue of *purpose*.

self-concept, self-definition, real self, ideal self, self-esteem, initiative versus guilt

Gender

- Gender identity is an aspect of the developing self-concept.
- The main gender difference in early childhood is boys' greater aggressiveness. Girls tend to be more empathic and

prosocial and less prone to problem behavior. Cognitive differences are small.
- Children learn gender roles at an early age through gender-typing. Gender stereotypes peak during the preschool years.
- Five major perspectives on gender development are biological, evolutionary, psychoanalytic, cognitive, and social learning.
- Evidence suggests that some gender differences may be biologically based.
- There is increasing evidence that intersex and transgender gender identity development is influenced by brain-based biological processes.
- Evolutionary theory sees children's gender roles as preparation for adult mating and parenting behavior.
- In Freudian theory, a child identifies with the same-sex parent after giving up the wish to possess the other parent.
- Cognitive-developmental theory maintains that gender identity develops from thinking about one's gender. According to Kohlberg, gender constancy leads to acquisition of gender roles. Gender-schema theory holds that children categorize gender-related information by observing what males and females do in their culture.
- According to social cognitive theory, children learn gender roles through socialization. Parents, peers, and culture influence gender-typing.

gender identity, gender roles, gender-typing, gender stereotypes, theory of sexual selection, identification, gender constancy, gender-schema theory, social cognitive theory

Play

- Play has physical, cognitive, and psychosocial benefits. Changes in the types of play children engage in reflect cognitive and social development.
- According to Smilansky, children progress cognitively from functional play to constructive play, dramatic play, and then formal games with rules. Dramatic play and rough-and-tumble play begin during early childhood.
- According to Parten, play becomes more social during early childhood. However, later research has found that nonsocial play is not necessarily immature.
- Children prefer to play with others of their sex.
- Cognitive and social aspects of play are influenced by the culturally approved environments adults create for children.

functional play, constructive play, dramatic play, formal games with rules, gender segregation

Parenting

- Discipline can be a powerful tool for socialization.
- Both positive reinforcement and prudently administered punishment can be appropriate tools of discipline within the context of a positive parent-child relationship.
- Power assertion, inductive techniques, and withdrawal of love are three categories of discipline. Reasoning is generally the most effective and power assertion the least effective. Spanking and other forms of corporal punishment can have negative consequences.
- Baumrind identified three parenting styles: authoritarian, permissive, and authoritative. A fourth style, neglectful or uninvolved, was identified later. Authoritative parents tend to raise more competent children. However, Baumrind's findings may be misleading when applied to some cultures.

- The roots of altruism and prosocial behavior appear early. This may be an inborn disposition, which can be cultivated by parental modeling and encouragement.
- Instrumental aggression—first physical, then verbal—is most common in early childhood.
- Boys tend to practice overt aggression, whereas girls often engage in relational aggression.
- Preschool children show temporary fears of real and imaginary objects and events; older children's fears tend to be more realistic.

discipline, corporal punishment, inductive techniques, power assertion, withdrawal of love, authoritarian parenting, permissive parenting, authoritative parenting, altruism, prosocial behavior, instrumental aggression, overt (direct) aggression, relational (social or indirect) aggression

Relationships with Other Children

- Most sibling interactions are positive. Older siblings tend to initiate activities, and younger siblings to imitate. Same-sex siblings, especially girls, get along best.
- Sibling dispute resolution promotes moral development.
- The kind of relationship children have with siblings often carries over into other peer relationships.
- Only children seem to develop at least as well as children with siblings.
- Preschoolers choose playmates and friends who are like them and with whom they have positive experiences.
- Aggressive children are less popular than prosocial children.
- Cultures vary with respect to childhood age-segregation. Both younger and older children can benefit from mixed-age groupings.

Physical and Cognitive Development in Middle Childhood

learning objectives

Describe physical changes and health in school-age children.

Describe cognitive development in school-age children.

Explain how language abilities continue developing in school-age children.

Summarize children's adjustment to school and influences on school achievement.

Describe how schools educate children with special needs.

Rachel Frank/Corbis/Glow Images

In this chapter we look at strength, endurance, motor proficiency, and other physical developments. Cognitively, we examine concrete operations, memory, problem solving, intelligence testing, and literacy. We discuss school achievement, methods of teaching reading, and second-language education. Finally, we look at special needs education.

Physical Development

HEIGHT AND WEIGHT

Children grow about 2 to 3 inches each year between ages 6 and 11 and approximately double their weight during that period (Table 9.1). Girls retain somewhat more fatty tissue than boys, a characteristic that will persist through adulthood. The average 10-year-old weighs about 18 pounds more than 40 years ago (Fryar et al., 2016).

BRAIN DEVELOPMENT

Changes in the brain's structure and function affect a number of cognitive advances seen in middle childhood. In general, these changes can be characterized as resulting in faster, more efficient information processing and an increased ability to ignore distracting information (Amso & Casey, 2006; Wendelken et al., 2011). For example, it becomes easier for children to concentrate on the teacher—even if it's a boring lesson—while filtering out the antics of the class clown.

Magnetic resonance imaging (MRI) technology shows us that the brain consists of both gray matter and white matter. Gray matter is composed of closely packed neurons in the cerebral cortex. White matter is made of glial cells, which provide support for neurons, and of myelinated axons, which transmit information across neurons.

The amount of gray matter in the frontal cortex, which is strongly influenced by genetics, is likely linked with differences in IQ (Toga & Thompson, 2005; Deary et al., 2010). Gray matter volume shows a U-shaped trajectory. The overall volume increases prepuberty and then declines by postpuberty (Gogtay & Thompson, 2010). The decline in overall volume is driven primarily by a loss in the density of gray matter (Figure 9.1). Although "less" gray matter may sound negative, the result is actually the opposite. We are born with more connections than we need. The "loss" reflects pruning of unused dendrites. In other words, those connections that are used remain active; the unused connections eventually disappear. The result is that the brain becomes "tuned" to the experiences of the child. In this way, we can calibrate our growing brains to local conditions.

Beneath the cortex, gray matter volume in the caudate—a part of the basal ganglia involved in control of movement and muscle tone and in mediating higher cognitive functions, attention, and emotional states—peaks at age 7 in girls and age 10 in boys (Lenroot & Giedd, 2006). Gray matter volume in the parietal lobes, which deal with spatial understanding, and in the frontal lobes, which handle higher-order functions, peaks at age 11. Gray matter in the temporal lobes, which deal with language, peaks at age 14, while the cerebellum, which regulates motor movements takes longer. Generally, gray matter volume peaks 1 to 2 years earlier in girls than in boys (Gogtay & Thompson, 2010).

TABLE 9.1 Physical Growth, Ages 6 to 11 (50th percentile*)				
	HEIGHT (INCHES)		WEIGHT (POUNDS)	
Age	Girls	Boys	Girls	Boys
6	46.7	47.2	52.4	52.8
7	49.0	49.8	58.7	61.9
8	51.8	51.9	69.9	69.4
9	54.2	53.7	82.7	74.4
10	56.8	56.3	90.9	88.7
11	59.3	59.2	104.5	107.0

*Fifty percent of children in each category are above this height or weight level and 50 percent are below it.

Source: Fryar, C. D., Gu, Q., Ogden, C. L., & Flegal, K. M. (2016). Anthropometric reference data for children and adults: United States, 2011–2014. *Vital and Health Statistics, 3*(39).

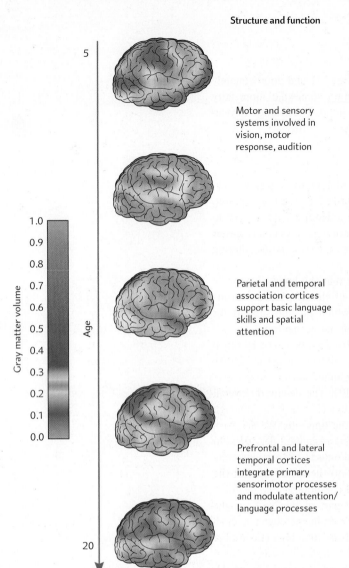

Structure and function

Motor and sensory systems involved in vision, motor response, audition

Parietal and temporal association cortices support basic language skills and spatial attention

Prefrontal and lateral temporal cortices integrate primary sensorimotor processes and modulate attention/ language processes

FIGURE 9.1

Gray-Matter Maturation in the Cerebral Cortex, Ages 5 to 20

Losses in gray matter density reflect maturation of various regions of the cortex, permitting more efficient functioning. Blue areas correspond to specific parts of the cortex undergoing loss of gray matter at a given age.

Sources: Amso, D., & Casey, B. J. (2006). Beyond what develops when: Neuroimaging may inform how cognition changes with development. *Current Directions in Psychological Science, 15*(1), 24-29; adapted from Gogtay, N., Giedd, J. N., Lusk, L., Hayashi, K. M., Greenstein, D., Vaituzis, A. C., . . . Rapoport, J. L. (2004). Dynamic mapping of human cortical development during childhood through early adulthood. *Proceedings of the National Academy of Sciences, 101*(21), 8174–8179.

The loss in density of gray matter with age is balanced by another change—a steady increase in white matter. The connections between neurons thicken and myelinate, beginning with the frontal lobes and moving toward the rear of the brain. Between ages 6 and 13, striking growth occurs in connections between the temporal and parietal lobes. In fact, white matter growth may not begin to drop off until well into adulthood (Giedd & Rapoport, 2010; Kuhn, 2006; Lenroot & Giedd, 2006).

Children's brains also show changes in the thickness of the cortex. Overall, the volume of the cortex peaks in late childhood to early adolescence (Raznahan et al., 2011). However, this is not a linear process, and different areas show different rates of change.

Health, Fitness, and Safety

SLEEP

Six- to 13-year-olds require 9 to 11 hours of sleep a day (National Sleep Foundation, 2020). However, many do not get the required amount. Sleep problems, such as resistance to going to bed, insomnia, and daytime sleepiness, are common in the United States during these years (Hoban, 2004).

Sleep is necessary for optimal outcomes. Failure to get adequate sleep is associated with an increased risk of obesity and overweight, poor neurological functioning, and a variety of adjustment problems, and this effect is particularly marked when children are African American or come from homes of low socioeconomic status (Liu et al., 2012; Maski & Kothare, 2013). At the same time, children from racial and ethnic minority groups and who live in poverty tend to get less and worse quality sleep, a disparity that increases with age (Guglielmo et al., 2018).

TOOTH DECAY AND DENTAL CARE

Tooth decay remains one of the most common chronic untreated conditions. Globally, about 560 million children have untreated tooth decay in their permanent teeth (World Health Organization, 2017). In the United States, approximately 15.5 percent of 6- to 9-year-old children have untreated dental decay. There are disparities by racial and ethnic group: 12.1 percent of non-Hispanic white children have untreated decay, 22.6 percent of African American children, and 18.4 percent of Hispanic children have untreated cavities (U.S. Department of Health and Human Services, 2020). Socioeconomic status matters as well; 25 percent of children aged 5 to 19 years from low-income families have untreated cavities as compared with 11 percent of children from higher-income families (Dye et al., 2012).

Untreated dental caries can result in pain, difficulties chewing food, missed school, problems with concentration, and discomfort with appearance. Parents can help prevent dental caries with regular dental care, fluoridated water supplies or fluoride supplements, and the use of adhesive sealants on rough chewing surfaces (National Center for Chronic Disease Prevention and Health Promotion, 2019).

NUTRITION

The recommended calories per day for schoolchildren 9 to 13 years of age range from 1,400 to 2,600, depending on gender and activity level. Nutritionists recommend a varied diet, including plenty of grains, fruits, and vegetables plus high levels of complex carbohydrates such as whole grains. Children should consume about 25 to 30 percent of their calories from fat and less than 10 percent of their calories from added sugars (DeSalvo et al., 2016), as sugar consumption has been linked to weight gain (Malik et al., 2013).

Approximately 20 percent of children skip breakfast, a habit associated with a greater risk of obesity (Deshmukh-Taskar et al., 2010). Most children get almost a third of their daily calories through snacks (Shriver et al., 2018). Eating out, especially fast food, is another culprit (Braithwaite et al., 2014). Children who eat outside the home consume an estimated 200 more calories a day than when the same foods are eaten at home (French et al., 2001). Unfortunately, one-third of children eat at fast-food restaurants on any given day (Vikraman et al., 2015). The media strongly influence children's food choices, and not for the better. Exposure to fast-food and soft drink advertising is associated with increased consumption of both types of products, especially in overweight or obese children (Cairns et al., 2013; Andreyeva et al., 2011).

PHYSICAL ACTIVITY AND FITNESS

While motor skills continue to improve in middle childhood school-age children in the United States spend less time on sports and other outdoor activities than in the early 1980s, and more hours on schooling, homework, television, and computer activities (Juster et al., 2004; Basterfield et al., 2011). In 2016, only 21.6 percent of U.S. children age 6 to 19 reached the recommendations for physical activity on 5 out of 7 days in a week (Centers for Disease Control and Prevention, 2017). Activity levels decrease significantly as children get older, from an average level of approximately 180 minutes of activity per day for 9-year-olds to 40 minutes per day for 15-year-olds (Nader et al., 2008).

In a meta-analysis surveying over 25 million 6- to 19-year-olds in 27 countries across Africa, the Middle East, Asia, Australasia, Europe, and North America, aerobic fitness declined in all countries from 1958 to 2003 at the rate of about 0.46 percent a year (Tomkinson & Olds, 2007). Recent research shows that in much of the world, few children attain the recommended physical activity guidelines. In the United States, Australia, Canada, England, South Korea, Spain, Thailand, and Wales, only about a third of children are sufficiently active. In Belgium, Chile, China, Estonia, Qatar, Scotland, and the United Arab Emirates, fewer than 20 percent are (Tremblay et al., 2016).

In poorer countries with less infrastructure, children are more likely to get sufficient exercise. Researchers have suggested that many features of modern life, including the availability of electronics, parent work schedules, the growth of organized sports, and safety concerns may be influential (Tremblay et al., 2016). Although data are sparse, indications are that the adoption of a modern lifestyle results in decreased physical activity for children. In one study, Australian aboriginal and Torres Straight Islander children were more active than their nonindigenous counterparts (Gwynn et al., 2010). Similarly, Inuit children in Canada, when living their traditional lifestyle in the high Arctic, were more physically fit than urban Canadian children. However, as they acculturated, they became increasingly sedentary and their fitness levels approached that of the urban Canadian children (Shepherd, 2007).

Recess Most primary schools in the United States include a daily 30-minute recess period and two physical education classes a week. However, on average, primary school students spend only 15 minutes per school day engaged in vigorous- or moderate-intensity physical activity, a number that falls to 5 minutes per school day by high school (Kohl & Cook, 2013).

The games children play at recess tend to be informal and spontaneously organized. Most recess activity involves socializing with peers, although younger children spend more time running and chasing each other (Holmes, 2012). About 10 percent of

Games at recess, such as jump rope, tend to be informal. They promote both agility and social competence. Blue Jean Images/Collage/Corbis

rough-and-tumble play
Vigorous play involving wrestling, hitting, and chasing, often accompanied by laughing and screaming.

schoolchildren's free play in the early grades consists of **rough-and-tumble play**—wrestling, kicking, tumbling, grappling, and chasing, often accompanied by laughing and screaming. Rough-and-tumble play peaks in middle childhood (Bjorklund & Pellegrini, 2002). It seems to be universal, and boys engage in higher levels of it than girls (Pellegrini et al., 2002; Smith, 2005). Girls favor games that include verbal expression or counting aloud, such as hopscotch and jump rope.

When given the choice, most children opt to play in natural or green areas rather than concrete (Lucas & Dyment, 2010). However, when provided with more playground equipment, especially unfixed equipment such as balls, children are more physically active during recess (Ridgers et al., 2012). More space to play in also leads to higher levels of activity, and children tend to decrease their activity levels as the temperature rises (Ridgers et al., 2010).

Recess is associated with improvements in academic performance (Murray & Ramstetter, 2013). A meta-analysis showed that after recess, children were better able to focus on class material; they were less fidgety, less listless, more focused and on task, and this was true whether or not recess involved physical interaction or social activity (Rasberry et al., 2011).

Organized Sports Estimates are that approximately 37 percent of 6- to 12-year-old children played team sports on a regular basis in 2017, a slow but steady decline from 44.5 percent in 2008. Household income is a major factor. In 2017, slightly under 70 percent of children from families that made less than $25,000 participated in organized sports on at least one day that year; in families making more than $100,000, almost 90 percent of children did (The Aspen Institute, 2018a, 2018b).

Developmental changes determine what types of organized sports are most effective. Six- to 9-year-olds need more flexible rules, shorter instruction time, and more free time for practice than older children. At this age girls and boys are about equal in weight, height, endurance, and motor skill development. Older children are better able to process instruction and learn team strategies.

OBESITY AND OVERWEIGHT

Overweight, a body mass index between the 85th and 95th percentile, and obesity, a body mass index over the 95th percentile, has become a health issue for children worldwide. The global prevalence rate has risen sharply—in 1975, just over 4 percent of children and teens ages 5 to 19 were overweight or obese. In 2016, 18 percent—or more than 340 million children and adolescents—were overweight or obese. While overweight and obesity were once considered to be problems of high-income and urban countries, low- and middle-income countries are now affected as well. Many of these countries now carry a double burden and must manage the twin issues of obesity and overweight and undernutrition at the same time (World Health Organization, 2020).

In the United States, about 18.5 percent of children between the ages of 2 and 19 are obese and another 16.6 percent are overweight. Boys are slightly more likely to be obese than girls. Although obesity has increased in all ethnic groups, it is most prevalent among Mexican American boys (29.2 percent) and Hispanic boys (28 percent) and non-Hispanic Black girls (25.1 percent) and Mexican American girls (24.3 percent). Although Asian boys (11.7 percent) and girls (10.1 percent) show the lowest obesity rates, there are indications health risks may begin at a lower weight compared to other ethnic groups (Fryar et al, 2018; Fryar et al., 2016).

Causes of Obesity Obesity often results from an inherited tendency for weight gain aggravated by too little exercise and too much or the wrong kinds of food (Sahoo et al., 2015). Children are more likely to be overweight if they have overweight parents or other relatives. Poor nutrition and inactivity also contribute (Braithwaite et al., 2014; Bradley et al., 2011). Where children live also matters. Children who live in rural areas have a 26 percent higher risk of obesity than children who live in urban areas

(Johnson & Johnson, 2015). Television viewing appears to be an important variable and has been associated with an increased risk of obesity in both developing and developed nations (Katzmarzyk et al., 2015).

A number of individual and social variables influence the likelihood of physical activity. Preadolescent girls, children with disabilities, children who live in public housing, and children in unsafe neighborhoods with no facilities for outdoor exercise are most likely to be sedentary (American Academy of Pediatrics, 2006). Additionally, physical inactivity and sedentary behaviors differ among children in various ethnic groups. For example, immigrant children are significantly more likely to be physically inactive and less likely to participate in sports than native children (Singh et al., 2013).

Promoting an active lifestyle through both informal and organized sports is an important way to combat the problem of childhood obesity. mikkeell/Shutterstock

Overweight and Obesity Outcomes Overweight children tend to become obese adults, at risk for **hypertension** (high blood pressure), heart disease, orthopedic problems, diabetes, and other problems (Sahoo et al., 2015). Indeed, childhood obesity may be a stronger predictor of some diseases than adult obesity (AAP, 2004; Baker et al., 2007) and may put children at risk of premature death (Franks et al., 2010).

Obese children commonly have medical problems, most notably diabetes, sleep apnea, and cardiovascular disease, or they may develop these diseases at a younger age (Sahoo et al., 2015). Some data show that obese boys have higher levels of cardio-metabolic risk factors than obese girls (Skinner et al., 2015).

There are also socio-emotional consequences to obesity. Overweight and obese children are often bullied, and they must contend with negative stereotypes and social marginalization. They often report fewer friends than do children in a healthy weight range. Not surprisingly, they are at elevated risk for depression and anxiety disorders, low self-esteem, and body dissatisfaction. Additionally, there are often academic consequences. Some of the academic consequences can be attributed to a higher likelihood of school problems. However, obese children are also more likely to miss school due to health issues that co-occur with obesity, such as diabetes and asthma. Overweight children may compensate by indulging themselves with treats or by withdrawing to their homes, making their problems even worse (Sahoo et al., 2015).

Concern with **body image**—how one believes one looks—becomes important early in middle childhood, especially for girls, and may develop into eating disorders in adolescence. Playing with physically unrealistic dolls, such as Barbie, may be an influence (see Research in Action).

hypertension
Chronically high blood pressure.

body image
Descriptive and evaluative beliefs about one's appearance.

Prevention and Treatment Childhood obesity rates are a significant public health issue. Childhood obesity rates continue to rise at alarming rates, particularly in African American and Hispanic children, and children from urban areas (Skinner et al., 2018; Ogden et al., 2018).

Fifty-five percent of obese children will become obese adults. However, a typical weight in childhood does not guarantee a healthy weight in adulthood. Seventy percent of obese adults were not obese in childhood (Simmonds et al., 2016). Thus, prevention and intervention should target health in *all* children, not just overweight children.

Research supports efforts focused on overall lifestyle changes rather than narrowly defined diets or exercise programs. Recommendations include less time in front of television and computers, changes in food labeling and advertising, healthier school meals, education to help children make better food choices, and more time spent in physical education and informal exercise with family and friends, such as walking and unorganized sports (AAP, 2004; Evans et al., 2012; De Bourdeauhuij et al., 2011). The most effective interventions are those in which parents are helped to change their own behaviors as well as those of their children (Kitzmann et al., 2010).

research in action

BARBIES AND BODY IMAGE

Barbie has remained the best-selling fashion doll for generations of girls. Barbie's body proportions present an unrealistic and unattainable female ideal. If she were a real woman, Barbie would have a 39-inch bust, impossibly small 18-inch waist, and 33-inch hips (Dittmar, et al., 2006; Lind & Brzuzy, 2008). Girls who do not measure up—which given Barbie's proportions includes all girls—may experience body dissatisfaction.

Rice and colleagues (2016) examined the impact of Barbie on thin ideals and body dissatisfaction among 5- to 8-year-old girls. . Barbie's mere presence, whether via photo, physical observation, or play engagement, was associated with higher thin-ideal internalization. This effect extends to judgments made about others as well. Worobey and Worobey (2014) showed preschool-age girls a variety of Barbie-like dolls of different body types and asked them to assign positive and negative traits to the dolls. The results were striking. Positive traits were frequently ascribed to thin and average-sized dolls (i.e., smart, pretty, happy, has a best friend), whereas fat dolls were almost exclusively linked with negative traits (i.e., sad, no friends, gets teased).

In 2016, Barbies of three body types premiered—petite, tall, and curvy—with a wider range of skin tones, hair textures, and eye colors to represent a diverse and more inclusive range of beauty. Curvy Barbie has a rounder stomach and wider hips and thighs, but her figure remains slim, though not as unrealistically so (Jarman, 2016).

Unfortunately, Curvy Barbie may not be enough to counteract harmful weight attitudes. When 3- to 10-year-old girls were asked how they felt about a series of different Barbie dolls (original, tall, petite, and curvy), they held the strongest negative attitudes for the curvy Barbie and wanted to play with it the least, and they were more positive about the thinner dolls. The girls with the most negative body image felt the most positive about the original doll (Harriger et al., 2019).

Other dolls marketed to girls are also often noticeably thin (Boyd & Murnen, 2017), and a myriad of other social and cultural influences exist. Moreover, there are also self-socialization influences—young girls often request the very objects and experiences that negatively influence their own developing body image. In short, there is no easy answer as to how to improve body image and promote healthy weight attitudes in young children.

what's your view If you had (or have) a young daughter and she requested a Barbie, would you try to discourage her? What proactive measures do you think parents could take to instill healthy body image?

OTHER MEDICAL CONDITIONS

Most U.S. children are healthy—more than 86 percent enjoy very good or excellent health (Centers for Disease Control and Prevention, 2018). When illness does occur in middle childhood, it tends to be brief. **Acute medical conditions**—occasional, short-term conditions, such as infections and warts—are common. Six or seven bouts a year with colds, flu, or viruses are typical as germs pass among children at school or at play (Behrman, 1992).

Fortunately, most children without underlying medical conditions appear to be at low risk of complications or death as a result of contracting the novel coronavirus COVID-19 (Centers for Disease Control and Prevention, 2020). However, children with preexisting conditions, especially when those conditions are medically complex, are at significantly elevated risk of complications (Shekerdemian et al., 2020). Additionally, there are early suggestions a small percentage of healthy children may develop a multi-system inflammatory disorder after exposure (Verdoni et al., 2020; Riphagen et al., 2020).

An estimated 12.8 percent of U.S. children have or are at risk for **chronic medical conditions** that persist for 3 months or more (Kogan et al., 2005). These rates have been rising, as have the rates of hospital admissions for children with more than one medically complex condition (Burns et al., 2010). Children who are males, Black, Hispanic, or have overweight mothers are at higher risk (Van Cleave et al., 2010).

acute medical conditions
Illnesses that last a short time.

chronic medical conditions
Illnesses or impairments that persist for at least 3 months.

Asthma **Asthma** is a chronic, allergy-based respiratory disease characterized by sudden attacks of coughing, wheezing, and difficulty breathing. Its prevalence in the United States more than doubled between 1980 and 1995 and has remained high (Akinbami, 2006). More than 9.5 percent of U.S. children and adolescents up to age 17 have been diagnosed with asthma at some time (Akinbami et al., 2012). It is 20 percent more likely to be diagnosed in Black children than in white children (McDaniel et al., 2006). Its prevalence has leveled off in developed countries but is still increasing in developing countries (Asher, 2010).

The causes of the asthma increases are uncertain, but a genetic predisposition is likely. For example, researchers have identified a gene variant that increases the risk of developing asthma, an effect that is exacerbated in homes where children are exposed to smoke (Caliskan et al., 2013). Environmental factors, too, are involved. Smoke exposure is a major environmental risk factor, as is pollution from car emissions (Burke et al., 2012; Gasana et al., 2012). Approximately 62 percent of U.S. children live in counties where the pollutant concentrations are above air quality standards at least once a year (Federal Interagency Forum on Child and Family Statistics, 2019). Increasing evidence points to an association between obesity and asthma (Weinmayr et al., 2014). There is also an association between low levels of vitamin D and increased incidence of asthma in children (Bener et al., 2014).

Diabetes **Diabetes** is one of the most common diseases in school-age children. In 2015, more than 132,000 children in the United States had diabetes (Centers for Disease Control and Prevention, 2017). Diabetes is characterized by high levels of glucose in the blood as a result of defective insulin production, ineffective insulin action, or both.

Type 1 diabetes is the result of an insulin deficiency that occurs when insulin-producing cells in the pancreas are destroyed. Symptoms include increased thirst and urination, hunger, weight loss, blurred vision, and fatigue. Treatment includes insulin administration, nutrition management, and physical activity (American Diabetes Association, 2020).

The available information on prevalence and incidence rates of type 1 diabetes varies by country. However, estimates are that there are approximately 500,000 children under age 15 with type 1 diabetes globally. The majority of documented cases can be found in Europe and North America (Patterson et al., 2014).

Type 2 diabetes is characterized by insulin resistance and used to be found primarily in overweight and older adults. As type 2 diabetes is associated with lifestyle factors, especially obesity, there is great variability in risk across countries. This factor, in conjunction with differential access to medical care and varied screening and research methodologies, makes accurate estimates challenging. However, some trends have emerged. Across different countries, ethnic minority children have higher rates of type 2 diabetes than white children, girls are at higher risk than boys, and the incidence risk rises over the course of childhood with age (Farsani et al., 2013).

Each year about 3,700 American children are diagnosed with type 2 diabetes, with higher incidence among white, Hispanic, and African American children (Dabelea et al., 2014). If current trends continue, estimates are that by 2050, over 84,000 American children will be diagnosed with type 2 diabetes (Imperatore et al., 2012). Symptoms are similar to those of type 1 diabetes. Nutrition management and increased physical activity can be effective treatments, although glucose-lowering medication or insulin may be needed.

Childhood Hypertension Hypertension, or high blood pressure, was once rare in childhood, but current estimates are that 19.2 percent of boys and 12.6 percent of girls have blood pressure at or above the 90th percentile. Risk factors include obesity or overweight, salt intake, sedentary lifestyle, poor sleep quality, and race (Rosner et al., 2013).

Although high blood pressure in childhood is not generally associated with mortality as it is in adulthood, it does put children at risk for later disease and damages organs. For example, it can lead to left ventricular hypertrophy (thickening and hardening of the left wall of the heart), damage to the retina of the eyes, or damage to arteries (Woroniecki et al., 2017; Falkner, 2010). Additionally, indications are that high blood

asthma
A chronic respiratory disease characterized by sudden attacks of coughing, wheezing, and difficulty in breathing.

diabetes
One of the most common diseases of childhood. It is characterized by high levels of glucose in the blood as a result of defective insulin production, ineffective insulin action, or both.

pressure may negatively affect the brain. Children with hypertension are more likely to have learning disabilities and show decreased performance on attention, memory, and executive functioning tasks (Lande et al., 2018; Lande et al., 2017).

Weight reduction through dietary modification and regular physical activity is the primary treatment for overweight-related hypertension. If blood pressure does not come down, drug treatment can be considered (Flynn et al., 2017). However, care must be taken in prescribing such drugs, as their long-term effects on children are uncertain.

ACCIDENTAL INJURIES

As in early childhood, accidental injuries are the leading cause of death among school-age U.S. children (Heron, 2019). In 2017, 1,578 U.S. children between the ages of 5 and 14 years died in accidents, the majority—855—in car accidents (Kochanek et al., 2019). International data are similar. Car accidents are the second leading cause of death overall in children age 5 to 14 years and the most common cause of accidental death. Drowning and fire-related burns are also significant contributors to international child deaths (Branche et al., 2008).

An estimated 70 percent of children in the United States ride bicycles (Mattei et al., 2012). Unfortunately, despite the existence of laws requiring their use in 21 states and the District of Columbia, bicycle helmet use is still low (Kaushik et al., 2015). An estimated 23,000 children each year suffer serious brain injuries from bicycle accidents, and as many as 88 percent of these injuries could be prevented by using helmets (AAP Council on Injury and Poison Prevention, 2001). Protective headgear also is vital for baseball and softball, football, roller skating, in-line skating, skateboarding, scooter riding, horseback riding, hockey, speed sledding, snowmobiling, skiing, snowboarding, and tobogganing. For soccer, "heading" the ball should be minimized because of the danger of brain injury (AAP Council on Sports Medicine and Fitness, 2001). Also, because of the need for stringent safety precautions and constant supervision for trampoline use, the AAP Council on Injury, Violence and Poison Prevention and the Council on Sports Medicine and Fitness (Briskin et al., 2012) recommend that parents not buy trampolines and that children only be allowed to use trampolines as part of structured training programs.

Cognitive Development: Piagetian Approach

At about age 7, according to Piaget, children enter the stage of **concrete operations** when they can use mental operations, such as reasoning, to solve concrete (actual) problems but are still limited in their thinking to the real world.

COGNITIVE ADVANCES

In the stage of concrete operations, children have a better understanding than preoperational children of spatial concepts, causality, categorization, inductive and deductive reasoning, conservation, and number (Table 9.2).

Spatial Relationships Eight-year-old Ella stares intently at the map. "The star means we are here," she points, "so that must mean the store is there!" Ella turns to her mother with a smile and they both begin walking.

Ella is now in the stage of concrete operations. She is better able to understand spatial relationships. This allows her to interpret a map, find her way to and from school, estimate the time to get from one place to another, and remember routes and landmarks. At this age, children are more easily able to navigate a physical environment with which they have experience, and training can help improve spatial skills as well (Uttal et al., 2013).

Causality Another key development during middle childhood involves the ability to make judgments about cause and effect. For example, when 5- to 12-year-old children were asked

concrete operations
Third stage of Piagetian cognitive development (approximately ages 7 to 12), during which children develop logical but not abstract thinking.

TABLE 9.2 Advances in Selected Cognitive Abilities during Middle Childhood

Ability	Example
Spatial thinking	Danielle can use a map or model to help her search for a hidden object. She can find her way to and from school, estimate distances, and judge how long it will take her to get somewhere.
Cause and effect	Douglas knows which physical attributes of objects on a balance scale matter (i.e., number of objects matters but color does not). He does not yet know which spatial factors (e.g., position, placement of the objects) matter.
Categorization	Elena can sort objects into categories, such as shape, color, or both. She knows that a subclass (roses) has fewer members than the class of which it is a part (flowers).
Seriation and transitive inference	Catherine can arrange a group of sticks in order, from the shortest to the longest. She knows that if one stick is longer than a second stick, and the second stick is longer than a third, then the first stick is longer than the third.
Inductive and deductive reasoning	Dominic can solve both inductive and deductive problems and knows that inductive conclusions (based on particular premises) are less certain than deductive conclusions (based on general premises).
Conservation	Felipe, at age 7, knows that a clay ball rolled into a sausage still contains the same amount of clay (conservation of substance). At age 9, he knows that the ball and the sausage weigh the same. In early adolescence he will understand that they displace the same amount of liquid if dropped in water.
Number and mathematics	Kevin can count in his head, can add by counting up from the smaller number, and can solve simple story problems.

to predict how balance scales worked, younger children understood that the number of objects on each side of a scale mattered, but it was not until later that they understood that the distance of objects from the center of a scale was also important (Amsel et al., 1996).

As children learn more about the world, their growing knowledge informs the quality of their reasoning. For example, in one study, children ages 3 to 11 years were given information about oral health that was either consistent (e.g., going to the dentist is good for teeth) or inconsistent (e.g., drinking cola is good for teeth) with reality, and scenarios in which the outcome was either good or bad oral health. Children were then asked how the causal association provided in the scenarios might be tested. When the information was consistent with reality and had a good outcome, or inconsistent and had a bad outcome, children were more likely to use appropriate hypothesis testing (i.e., manipulate only one variable at a time). In other conditions, they used scientifically invalid procedures (e.g., changing all variables at a time) (Croker & Buchanan, 2011).

Categorization John sits at the table, working on his class project. He is making a timeline of his life. His mother has given him six photographs of himself from infancy on, and John carefully lays them in order from earliest to latest.

John is now able to complete such a task because he is better able to categorize objects using a series of relatively sophisticated abilities. One such ability is **seriation,** arranging objects in a series according to one or more dimensions. Children become increasingly better at seriation for time (earliest to latest), length (shortest to longest), or color (lightest to darkest) (Piaget, 1952). Children's later mathematical achievement is dependent on early numeracy, including seriation (Aunio & Niemivirta, 2010), and difficulties in seriation predict later learning disabilities in mathematics (Desoete, 2015).

seriation
Ability to order items along a dimension.

Another emerging ability is that of **transitive inferences** (if a < b and b < c, then a < c). For example, Mateo is shown three sticks: a short yellow stick, a medium-length green stick, and a long blue stick. He is shown that the yellow stick is shorter than the green stick and is then shown that the green stick is shorter than the blue stick. However, he is not shown all three sticks together. If Mateo is able to understand transitive inferences, he should be able to easily infer that the yellow stick is shorter than the blue stick without

transitive inference
Understanding the relationship between two objects by knowing the relationship of each to a third object.

physically comparing them (Piaget & Inhelder, 1967). While Piaget believed that children did not develop this ability until middle childhood, more recent research on visual preferences has shown that children as young as 15 months have some limited ability to reason in this fashion, at least for social stimuli (Gazes et al., 2017; Mou et al., 2014).

class inclusion
Understanding of the relationship between a whole and its parts.

Class inclusion also becomes easier. **Class inclusion** is the ability to see the relationship between a whole and its parts, and to understand the categories within a whole. For example, Piaget (1964) showed preoperational children 10 flowers—seven roses and three carnations—and asked them whether there were more roses or more flowers. Children in the preoperational stage of development tended to say there were more roses because they were comparing the roses with the carnations rather than all flowers. However, at about age 7 or 8, when children have reached the concrete operations stage, they are able to understand that roses are a subcategory and that there are therefore more flowers than there are roses (Flavell et al., 2002). More recent research indicates that children are able to understand the logic of class inclusion, but usually fail to inhibit the incorrect response in favor of the misleading perceptual comparison (Borst et al., 2013).

inductive reasoning
Type of logical reasoning that moves from particular observations about members of a class to a general conclusion about that class.

deductive reasoning
Type of logical reasoning that moves from a general premise about a class to a conclusion about a particular member or members of the class.

Inductive and Deductive Reasoning **Inductive reasoning** involves making observations about particular members of a class of people, animals, objects, or events, and then drawing conclusions about the class as a whole. For example, if one neighbor's dog barks and another neighbor's dog barks, then the conclusion might be that all dogs bark. Inductive reasoning must be tentative, however, because it is always possible to come across new information, such as a dog that does not bark.

Deductive reasoning, by contrast, starts with a general statement—a premise—about a class and applies it to particular members of the class. If a premise is true of the whole class, and the reasoning is sound, then the conclusion must be true. So, for example, if the belief is that all dogs bark, and a new dog comes along, it would be reasonable to conclude that the new dog will also bark.

Piaget believed that children in the concrete operations stage of cognitive development used only inductive reasoning, and deductive reasoning did not develop until adolescence. However, research suggests Piaget underestimated the abilities of children. In one study, researchers gave reasoning problems to kindergarteners, second graders, fourth graders, and sixth graders. Because they did not want the children to use real-world knowledge, they used imaginary terms and words. For example, one of the inductive problems was "Tombor is a popgop. Tombor wears blue boots. Do all popgops wear blue boots?" The corresponding deductive reasoning problem was "All popgops wear blue boots. Tombor is a popgop. Does Tombor wear blue boots?" Contrary to Piagetian theory, second graders (but not kindergartners) were able to answer both kinds of problems correctly (Galotti et al., 1997; Pillow, 2002). Given age-appropriate testing methods, evidence of inductive and deductive reasoning is present considerably earlier than Piaget predicted. Moreover, children can be encouraged to reason at higher levels via training or intervention programs (Molnar, 2011; Barkl et al., 2012).

Conservation In the preoperational stage of development, children are focused on appearances and have difficulty with abstract concepts. For example, Camilla, who is at the preoperational stage of development, is likely to think that if one of two identical clay balls is rolled into a long thin snake, it will now contain more clay because it is longer. She is deceived by appearances and thus fails this conservation task. However, Michael, who is in the stage of concrete operations, will say that the ball and the snake still contain the same amount of clay. What accounts for this emerging ability?

Three primary achievements allow children to solve conservation problems. First, they understand the principle of *identity.* For instance, Michael understands that the clay is still the same clay even though it has a different shape because nothing was added or taken away from it. Second, they understand the principle of *reversibility.* Michael can picture what would happen if he went backward in time and rolled the snake back into a ball, thus the snake must still be the same amount of clay. Third, children at this stage can *decenter*. When Camilla looked at the snake, she centered on one dimension (length) while excluding the other (thickness). Michael, however, is able to decenter and look at more than one aspect of the two objects at once. Thus, although the ball is shorter than the snake, it is also thicker.

Typically, children can solve problems involving conservation of matter, such as the clay task, at about age 7 or 8. By age 8 or 9 children correctly solve conservation of weight tasks in which they are asked, for instance, whether the ball and the snake weigh the same. For conservation of volume—in which children must judge whether the snake and ball displace the same amount of liquid—children rarely answer correctly before age 12. Children's thinking at this stage is so concrete, so closely tied to a particular situation, that they cannot readily transfer what they have learned about one type of conservation to another type, even though the underlying principles are the same.

A child who has achieved conservation of liquid knows that pouring water from a wide, short glass to a tall, thin glass does not change the volume of water, even though the shape is different.
Marmaduke St. John/Alamy Stock Photo

Number and Mathematics When 4- to 5-year-old children deal a deck of cards or distribute portions of pizza, they demonstrate that they have some intuitive understanding of fractions (Bialystok & Codd, 2000; McCrink et al., 2010). However, children have more difficulty when dealing with numbers, which are abstract. They tend not to think about the quantity a fraction represents; instead, they focus on the numerals that make it up. Thus, they may say that ½ plus ⅓ equals ⅖. It is also difficult for children to grasp that ½ is bigger than ¼ —that the smaller fraction (¼) has the larger denominator (Geary, 2006).

By about kindergarten, many children can count in their heads. They also learn to *count on:* to add 5 and 3, they start counting at 5 and then go on to 6, 7, and 8. By age 9 most children can count up and down (Geary, 2006). Children also become more adept at solving simple story problems, such as "Pedro went to the store with $5 and spent $2 on candy. How much did he have left?" When the original amount is unknown— "Pedro went to the store, spent $2 and had $3 left. How much did he start out with?"— the problem is harder because the operation needed to solve it (addition) is not as clearly indicated. Few children can solve this kind of problem before age 8 or 9 (Resnick, 1989).

The ability to estimate progresses with age. When asked to place 24 numbers along a line from 0 to 100, kindergartners exaggerate the distances between low numbers and minimize the distances between high numbers. Most second graders produce number lines that are more evenly spaced (Siegler & Booth, 2004). Second, fourth, and sixth graders show a similar progression in producing number lines from 0 to 1,000 (Siegler & Opfer, 2003), most likely reflecting the experience older children gain in dealing with larger numbers (Berteletti et al., 2010). Practice matters; children who play board games that include linear sequences show an advantage in their number line estimation, number estimation, and counting-on skills (Whyte & Bull, 2008; Laski & Siegler, 2014). In addition to improving in number line estimation with age, school-age children also improve in computational estimation, such as estimating the sum in an addition problem; numerosity estimation, such as estimating the number of candies in a jar; and measurement estimation, such as estimating the length of a line (Booth & Siegler, 2006).

CULTURAL INFLUENCES ON PIAGETIAN TASK PERFORMANCE

While early researchers assumed Piaget's theory of cognitive development applied universally to all children, later research showed significant cultural influences on the development of various abilities. In many cultures, children reach proficiency at tasks at a later age, and in some cultures, never at all (Dasen, 1972). However, this is affected by the nature of the task. Children can think more logically about things they know something about. For example, a series of studies compared children in Geneva who attended school in formal educational settings with Australian hunter/gatherer indigenous children. With respect to conservation tasks, the progression of abilities in indigenous children was similar to that of the children from Geneva, but occurred several years later. However, on tasks assessing the understanding of spatial relationships, the indigenous children showed an advantage.

The ability to add develops through concrete experience in a cultural context. Thus, a child learning practical math via market transactions may be able to provide a correct answer to a problem when asked verbally, but unable to produce the same answer when asked to calculate it on paper and pencil.
commerceandculturestock/Moment/Getty Images

The progression of these skills in each domain mapped onto important cultural values and tasks. For example, the apportionment of resources in the indigenous culture did not depend on accurately segmenting items into equal amounts, but depended on kinship relationships. Items were rarely counted, and there were no number words past "five." Accurately judging amounts was not an important task in that culture. By contrast, remembering where resources, such as water, were located was an important cultural task, and thus indigenous children were advanced in that area (Dasen, 1994).

Similarly West African children, who produced, stored, and exchanged food in markets, attained proficiency at conservation of liquid tasks at an earlier age than Inuit children, who traditionally lived a hunter-gatherer lifestyle (Dasen, 1984). Even within Western countries, cultural change over time can affect the timing of abilities. When 10,000 British 11- and 12-year-olds were tested on conservation of volume and weight, their performance was 2 to 3 years behind that of their counterparts 30 years earlier, presumably because teachers were focusing on the three Rs rather than hands-on experience with the way materials behaved (Shayer et al., 2007).

There are also cultural influences on mathematical abilities. Research with minimally schooled people in developing countries suggests that the ability to add develops through concrete experience in a cultural context (Guberman, 1996; Resnick, 1989). In a study of Brazilian street vendors ages 9 to 15, a researcher said, "I'll take two coconuts." Each coconut cost 40 cruzeiros; she paid with a 500-cruzeiros bill and asked, "What do I get back?" The child counted up from 80: "Eighty, 90, 100 . . ." and gave the customer 420 cruzeiros. However, when this same child was given a similar problem in the classroom ("What is 500 minus 80?"), he arrived at the wrong answer (Carraher et al., 1988).

Findings such as these illustrate different routes for cultural learning. Understanding emerges from culturally defined experiences, and children are more likely to learn about skills that are valued and required in their culture.

Information-Processing Approach

As children move through the school years, they make steady progress in **executive function,** the conscious control of thoughts, emotions, and actions to accomplish goals or solve problems. They also improve in their ability to regulate and sustain attention, and in memory processes.

EXECUTIVE FUNCTIONING

Executive functioning develops gradually from infancy to adolescence and is accompanied by brain development, most notably in the prefrontal cortex (Lamm et al., 2006). As unneeded synapses are pruned away and pathways become myelinated, processing speed improves dramatically (Camarata & Woodcock, 2006). This increases the amount of information children can keep in working memory (McAuley & White, 2011). As children develop the ability to mentally juggle concepts at the same time, they are also able to develop more complex thinking and goal-directed planning.

Another aspect of executive function involves the development of self-regulatory capacity, including the ability to regulate attention, inhibit responses, and monitor errors. Advances in these areas, as well as in working memory, occur in concert with increases in activity of frontoparietal and frontostraital circuits (Hughes, 2011; Tau & Peterson, 2010). Language, too, matters. Children with robust language skills do well with executive function; those with language delays have difficulty (Gooch et al., 2016).

Environmental influences also matter. For example, the quality of the family environment—including available resources, cognitive stimulation, parental scaffolding, maternal sensitivity, and attachment—predicts executive control (Fay-Stammbach et al., 2014; Bernier et al., 2012; Hammond et al., 2012). Moreover, just as high-quality family environments can promote the

executive function
Conscious control of thoughts, emotions, and actions to accomplish goals or solve problems.

development of executive functioning, less ideal circumstances can undermine its development. Children from chaotic families tend to show less advanced executive functioning abilities (Vernon-Feagans et al., 2016), as do those from families who exert high control over their children (Bindman et al., 2013). Environmental circumstances may interact with individual characteristics as well. In one series of studies, poverty did not impact the executive functioning abilities of children who were low in temperamental reactivity, but negatively affected temperamentally reactive children (Raver et al., 2013).

Children can benefit from training. A wide variety of techniques have been successfully used, including computerized training, physical activity such as martial arts or yoga, and mindfulness (meditation) training (Diamond & Lee, 2011).

SELECTIVE ATTENTION

School-age children can concentrate longer than younger children and can focus on the information they need and screen out irrelevant information. For example, in school, it may be necessary for a child to focus on a teacher's lesson while simultaneously ignoring the antics of the class clown. This growth in *selective attention*—the ability to deliberately direct one's attention and shut out distractions—may hinge on the executive skill of *inhibitory control,* the voluntary suppression of unwanted responses (Luna et al., 2004).

The increasing capacity for selective attention is believed to be due to neurological maturation and is one of the reasons memory improves during middle childhood (Sanders et al., 2006). Older children make fewer mistakes in recall than younger children because they are better able to expect and predict what might be important to remember, to then select and attend to the appropriate stimulus when presented with it, and, when asked, to recall the relevant information from memory while ignoring irrelevant information (Gazzaley & Nobre, 2012).

WORKING MEMORY

Working memory involves the short-term storage of information that is being actively processed. For example, if you are asked to compute what 42×60 is, you would use your working memory to solve the answer.

The efficiency of working memory increases greatly in middle childhood, laying the foundation for a wide range of cognitive skills. Between the ages of 6 and 10 there are improvements in processing speed (how quickly information is processed) and storage capacity (how many things can be simultaneously held in working memory) (Bayliss et al., 2005).

Because working memory is necessary for storing information while other material is being mentally manipulated, the capacity of a child's working memory can directly affect academic success (Alloway & Alloway, 2010). Children with low working memory struggle with structured learning activities, especially when there are lengthy instructions (Gathercole & Alloway, 2008). Individual differences in working memory capacity are also linked to a child's ability to acquire knowledge and new skills (Alloway, 2006).

Research has indicated that as many as 10 percent of school-age children suffer from poor working memory (Alloway et al., 2009). Training programs can improve working memory capacity and have been shown to be associated with changes in brain activity in frontal and parietal cortex, basal ganglia, and dopamine receptor density (Klingberg, 2010). This is especially true for visuospatial working memory, such as that needed to play concentration games in which pairs of cards must be matched. However, such training effects tend to be short-lived and are not transferable to areas other than the specific form of working memory addressed (Melby-Lervag & Hulme, 2013; Rapport et al., 2013). However, more research is needed in this area.

METAMEMORY AND MNEMONIC STRATEGIES

Were you ever taught the saying "please excuse my dear Aunt Sally" as a technique to help you remember the order of operations in solving an equation? This is an example of a **mnemonic device,** a strategy to aid memory.

mnemonic device
Strategy to aid memory.

Contestants in a spelling bee make good use of mnemonic strategies— devices to aid memory—such as rehearsal (repetition), organization, and elaboration. Jim Lo Scalzo/EPA/ Shutterstock

external memory aids
Mnemonic strategies using something outside the person.

rehearsal
Mnemonic strategy to keep an item in working memory through conscious repetition.

organization
Mnemonic strategy of categorizing material to be remembered.

elaboration
Mnemonic strategy of making mental associations involving items to be remembered.

metamemory
Understanding of processes of memory.

metacognition
Thinking about thinking, or awareness of one's own mental processes.

Wechsler Intelligence Scale for Children (WISC-IV)
Individual intelligence test for school-age children, which yields verbal and performance scores as well as a combined score.

Stanford-Binet Intelligence Scales
Individual intelligence test for children which yields scores for fluid reasoning, knowledge, quantitative reasoning, visual-spatial processing and working memory.

Common memory strategies are rehearsal, organization, and elaboration. Writing down a telephone number, making a list, setting a timer, and putting a library book by the front door are examples of **external memory aids:** prompts by something outside the person. Saying a telephone number over and over after looking it up, so as not to forget it before dialing, is a form of **rehearsal,** or conscious repetition. **Organization** is mentally placing information into categories (such as animals, furniture, vehicles, and clothing) to make it easier to recall. In **elaboration,** children associate items with something else, such as an imagined scene or story or even another memory. To remember the names of a type of cloud in science class, for example, a child might tie the memory of that term to a time she went camping with her family and the sunset sky was full of the same type of clouds.

Metamemory is one component of **metacognition** and can be described as the knowledge of and reflection about memory processes. From kindergarten through the elementary school years, children advance steadily in understanding memory (Schneider, 2008). Kindergarteners and first graders know that people remember better if they study longer, that people forget things with time, and that relearning something is easier than learning it for the first time (Flavell et al., 2002). However, younger children tend not to use organizational memory strategies such as grouping things by categories and they tend to overestimate their memory capacity (Karably & Zabrucky, 2017). Moreover, even when taught to use memory strategies, they tend to use those memory strategies only in the context in which they were taught, and do not generalize them to other tasks. By third grade, children know that some people remember better than others and that some things are easier to remember than others (Flavell et al., 2002), and they become more proficient in their use of memory strategies (Karably & Zabrucky, 2017). For example, they often use more than one strategy for a task, choose different kinds of strategies for different problems, and are better at assessing if they are reaching their memory goals (Bjorklund et al., 1997; Schneider, 2008).

Metamemory may allow learners to calibrate whether or not the subjective assessment of the accuracy of responses (does it "feel right") aligns with reality by monitoring failures. This ability is supported by cortical thinning in the anterior insula and an increase in the thickness of the ventromedial prefrontal cortex from childhood through adolescence (Fandakova et al., 2017). Children's metamemory abilities continue to progress through adolescence and quite possibly longer (van der Stel & Veenman, 2014).

Although it is difficult to teach young children to use mnemonic strategies, teaching older children about them if they are developmentally ready to learn such skills can result in memory gains. This technique works best if it is integrated into the curricula rather than being taught separately (Schneider, 2008).

Psychometric Approach

Psychometrics is a branch of psychology involved in the quantitative measurement of psychological variables. The most widely used psychometric test is the **Wechsler Intelligence Scale for Children (WISC-IV).** This test for ages 6 through 16 measures verbal and performance abilities, yielding separate scores for each as well as a total composite score. The separate subtest scores pinpoint a child's strengths and help diagnose specific problems. For example, if a child does well on verbal tests (such as general information and basic arithmetic operations) but poorly on performance tests (such as doing a puzzle or drawing the missing part of a picture), the child may be slow in perceptual or motor development.

Another commonly used individual test is the **Stanford-Binet Intelligence Scales.** The Stanford-Binet measures both verbal and nonverbal abilities and consists of five subtests: fluid reasoning, knowledge, quantitative reasoning, visual-spatial processing, and working memory (Becker, 2003).

A popular group test, the **Otis-Lennon School Ability Test (OLSAT8),** has levels for kindergarten through 12th grade. Children are asked to classify items, show an understanding of verbal and numerical concepts, display general information, and follow directions. Separate scores for verbal comprehension, verbal reasoning, pictorial reasoning, figural reasoning, and quantitative reasoning can identify specific strengths and weaknesses (Otis, 1993).

Otis-Lennon School Ability Test (OLSAT 8)
Group intelligence test for kindergarten through 12th grade.

THE IQ CONTROVERSY

The use of psychometric intelligence tests such as those just described is controversial. On the positive side, because IQ tests have been standardized and widely used, there is extensive information about their norms, validity, and reliability. Cross-culturally, scores on IQ tests are good predictors of school achievement (Lynn et al., 2007). Childhood IQ is also predictive of a host of health outcomes, including general health, the risk of late-onset dementia, and chronic health conditions such as diabetes and cardiovascular disease (Deary et al., 2010; Wraw et al., 2015; Dobson et al., 2017).

On the other hand, critics claim that the tests underestimate the intelligence of children who are in ill health or who do not perform well on tests (Sternberg, 2004). Because the tests are timed, they equate intelligence with speed and penalize a child who works slowly and deliberately. Their appropriateness for diagnosing learning disabilities also has been questioned (Benson, 2003). Moreover, such variables as working memory (Alloway & Alloway, 2010) and self-control (Duckworth et al., 2012) have also been found to be important in predicting academic achievement.

A more fundamental criticism is that IQ tests do not directly measure native ability; instead, they measure what children already know. Further, the tests are validated against measures of achievement, such as school performance, affected by such factors as schooling and culture. There is also controversy over whether intelligence is a single, general ability or whether there are types of intelligence not captured by IQ tests.

INFLUENCES ON IQ

Brain Development Intelligence is highly heritable, and one mechanism of genetic action may be via brain development and structure. Brain imaging research shows a moderate correlation between brain size or amount of gray matter and general intelligence (Rushton & Ankney, 2009), especially reasoning, problem-solving abilities, and nonverbal performance measures (Gray & Thompson, 2004; Lange et al., 2010). One study found that the amount of gray matter in the frontal cortex is largely inherited, varies widely among individuals, and is linked with differences in IQ (Thompson et al., 2001).

The developmental changes found in cortical thickness are also strongly influenced by genes (Fjell et al., 2015). Recent research has found that intelligence is highest in those children whose cortex thins most quickly (Schnack et al., 2014) or whose white matter develops most rapidly (Tamnes et al., 2010). Moreover, while IQ is generally a stable trait, there are sometimes fluctuations. Research has shown that children and adolescents who show declines in IQ over time also show reductions in cortical thickness, suggesting a neural substrate for their declines in intellectual performance (Burgaleta et al., 2014).

Although reasoning, problem solving, and executive function are linked to the prefrontal cortex, other brain regions under strong genetic influence also contribute to intelligent behavior (Davis et al., 2009) as do the speed and reliability of transmission of messages in the brain. The efficiency and integration of brain processes, both at the global and specific levels, are associated with intellectual functioning (Kim et al., 2016).

Influence of Schooling on IQ Schooling increases tested intelligence (Adey et al., 2007). IQ scores drop during summer vacation and rise again during the academic year (Ceci & Williams, 1997; Huttenlocher et al., 1998). Additionally, scores attained on various educational assessment tests—which test knowledge, like math and science, unlikely to be learned outside of an educational environment—are strongly correlated

IQ scores in children are influenced by a variety of factors, including school. Children's scores drop during summer vacation and then rise again during the academic year. Monkey Business Images/Shutterstock

with IQ, and this relationship exists in all countries for which data are available (Lynn & Meisenberg, 2010; Lynn & Vanhanen, 2012).

However, the cognitive gains associated with schooling do not appear to be general in nature and instead consist of direct gains in specific cognitive skills that are then tapped by IQ tests (Ritchie et al., 2015). Not surprisingly, the type of schooling also matters. Children who are enrolled in schools with an academic focus tend to show greater gains in intellectual performance than children in schools with a vocational focus (Becker et al., 2012).

Racial, Ethnic, and Socioeconomic Influences on IQ Average test scores vary among racial/ethnic groups. Historically, Black children scored about 15 points lower than white children and showed a comparable lag on school achievement tests (Neisser et al., 1996). However, these gaps have narrowed in recent years (Dickens & Flynn, 2006). Average IQ scores of Hispanic American children fall between those of Black and white children (Ang et al., 2010).

What accounts for racial/ethnic differences in IQ? Some researchers have argued for a substantial genetic factor (Herrnstein & Murray, 1994; Jensen, 1969; Rushton & Jensen, 2005). Although there is strong evidence of a genetic influence on *individual* differences in intelligence, there is no direct evidence that IQ differences among ethnic, cultural, or racial *groups* are hereditary (Gray & Thompson, 2004; Neisser et al., 1996; Sternberg, 2005). Instead, many studies attribute ethnic differences in IQ to inequalities in environment (Nisbett et al., 2012; Colman, 2016)—in income, nutrition, living conditions, health, parenting practices, early child care, intellectual stimulation, schooling, culture, or other circumstances such as the effects of oppression and discrimination that can affect self-esteem, motivation, and academic performance.

The strength of genetic and environmental influences appears to vary with socioeconomic status (Nisbett et al., 2012). Some research suggests that genetic influences are more important for wealthy children, who have a more standardly high-quality environment, but the environment may matter more for children of lower SES—at least in countries like the United States (Hanscombe et al., 2012). However, in countries where social services are offered more consistently to people at the lower ends of the socioeconomic scale, and poverty is thus not associated with the same level of deprivation, genetic influences on intelligence function similarly for children of high and low socioeconomic status (Tucker-Drob & Bates, 2016).

What about Asian Americans, whose scholastic achievements consistently top those of other ethnic groups? Asian American children's strong scholastic achievement seems to be best explained by their culture's emphasis on obedience and respect for elders, the importance Asian American parents place on education as a route to upward mobility, and the devotion of Asian American students to homework and study (Nisbett et al., 2012). Window on the World discusses other issues related to cultural influences on IQ.

SPECIFIC INTELLIGENCE FACTORS

One critique of IQ tests is their sole focus on abilities useful in school. Yet, there are other aspects of intelligent behavior.

theory of multiple intelligences
Gardner's theory that each person has several distinct forms of intelligence.

Gardner's Theory of Multiple Intelligences Is a child who is good at analyzing paragraphs and making analogies more intelligent than one who can play a challenging violin solo or pitch a curve ball at the right time? The answer is no, according to Gardner's (1993, 1998) **theory of multiple intelligences.**

According to Gardner, there are eight different types of intelligences, and conventional intelligence tests tap only three of them: *linguistic, logical-mathematical,* and, to some extent, *spatial.* The other five, which are not reflected in IQ scores, are *musical,*

window on the world

CULTURE AND IQ

Intelligence and culture are inextricably linked, and behavior seen as intelligent in one culture may be viewed as foolish in another (Sternberg, 2004). For example, when given a sorting task, North Americans would be likely to place a robin in the category of birds, whereas the Kpelle people in North Africa would consider it more intelligent to place the robin in the functional category of flying things (Cole, 1998). Thus a test of intelligence developed in one culture may not be equally valid in another. Furthermore, the competencies taught and tested in school are not necessarily the same as the practical skills needed to succeed in everyday life (Sternberg, 2004, 2005). Intelligence might thus be better defined as the skills and knowledge needed for success within a particular social and cultural context. The mental processes that underlie intelligence may be the same across cultures, but their products may be different and so should be the means of assessing performance (Sternberg, 2004).

These arguments have led to assertions that ethnic differences in IQ are not reflecting intelligence, but rather are an artifact of cultural bias. It may be that some questions use vocabulary or call for information or skills more familiar to some cultural groups than to others (Sternberg, 1985, 1987). Because these intelligence tests are built around the dominant thinking style and language of white people of European ancestry, minority children are at a disadvantage (Heath, 1989; Helms, 1992; Matsumoto & Juang, 2008).

Test developers have tried to design **culture-free tests**—tests with no culture-linked items—by posing tasks that do not require language, such as tracing mazes, putting the right shapes in the right spaces, and completing pictures, but they have been unable to eliminate all cultural influences. It is virtually impossible to produce **culture-fair tests** consisting only of experiences common to all people. Psychologists continue to work on constructing suitable tests and on interpreting the findings on intelligence.

 what's your view Do you think intelligence will be defined the same way 100 years in the future? Is there anything about intelligence that is always the same across time and place?

---

bodily-kinesthetic, interpersonal, intrapersonal, and *naturalist* (Table 9.3 gives definitions of each intelligence and examples of fields in which it is most useful).

Gardner argued that high intelligence in one area does not necessarily accompany high intelligence in another. A person may be extremely gifted in art (a spatial ability), precision of movement (bodily-kinesthetic), or social relations (interpersonal), but not have a traditionally high IQ. Thus an artist, an athlete, or a therapist could be equally intelligent, each in a different area.

Critics of Gardner argue that his multiple intelligences are actually more accurately labeled as talents or abilities and assert that *intelligence* is more closely associated with skills that lead to academic achievement. They further question his criteria for defining separate intelligences that largely overlap such as mathematical and spatial intelligence (Willingham, 2004).

Sternberg's Triarchic Theory of Intelligence Sternberg's (1985, 2004) **triarchic theory of intelligence** consists of three elements: *componential, experiential,* and *contextual* intelligence.

- The **componential element** is the analytic aspect of intelligence; it determines how efficiently people process information. It helps people solve problems, monitor solutions, and evaluate the results.

- The **experiential element** is insightful or creative; it determines how people approach novel or familiar tasks. It enables people to come up with new ways of putting facts together—in other words, to think originally.

- The **contextual element** is practical; it helps people deal with their environment. It is the ability to size up a situation and decide what to do in a real-world context.

culture-free tests
Intelligence tests that, if they were possible to design, would have no culturally linked content.

culture-fair tests
Intelligence tests that deal with experiences common to various cultures, in an attempt to avoid cultural bias.

triarchic theory of intelligence
Sternberg's theory describing three elements of intelligence: componential, experiential, and contextual.

componential element
Sternberg's term for the analytic aspect of intelligence.

experiential element
Sternberg's term for the insightful or creative aspect of intelligence.

contextual element
Sternberg's term for the practical aspect of intelligence.

TABLE 9.3 Eight Intelligences, According to Gardner

Intelligence	Definition	Fields or Occupations Where Used
Linguistic	Ability to use and understand words and nuances of meaning	Writing, editing, translating
Logical-mathematical	Ability to manipulate numbers and solve logical problems	Science, business, medicine
Spatial	Ability to find one's way around in an environment and judge relationships between objects in space	Architecture, carpentry, city planning
Musical	Ability to perceive and create patterns of pitch and rhythm	Musical composition, conducting
Bodily-kinesthetic	Ability to move with precision	Dancing, athletics, surgery
Interpersonal	Ability to understand and communicate with others	Teaching, acting, politics
Intrapersonal	Ability to understand the self	Counseling, psychiatry, spiritual leadership
Naturalist	Ability to distinguish species and their characteristics	Hunting, fishing, farming, gardening, cooking

Source: Gardner, H. (1993). *Frames of mind: The theory of multiple intelligences.* New York, NY: Basic Books. (Original work published 1983); and Gardner, H. (1998). Are there additional intelligences? In J. Kane (Ed.), *Education, information, and transformation: Essays on learning and thinking.* Englewood Cliffs, NJ: Prentice Hall.

Sternberg Triarchic Abilities Test (STAT)
An intelligence test designed to measure three elements of intelligence; componential, experiential and contextual intelligence.

tacit knowledge
Sternberg's term for information that is not formally taught but is necessary to get ahead.

Kaufman Assessment Battery for Children (K-ABC-II)
Nontraditional individual intelligence test designed to provide fair assessments of minority children and children with disabilities.

dynamic tests
Tests based on Vygotsky's theory that emphasize potential rather than past learning.

According to Sternberg, everyone has these three abilities to a greater or lesser extent. The **Sternberg Triarchic Abilities Test (STAT)** (Sternberg, 1993) seeks to measure each ability through multiple-choice and essay questions. For example, an item to test practical quantitative intelligence might be to solve an everyday math problem having to do with buying tickets to a ball game. A creative verbal item might ask children to solve deductive reasoning problems that start with factually false premises (such as "Money falls off trees"). An analytical figural item might ask children to identify the missing piece of a figure. Validation studies have found positive correlations between the STAT and critical thinking, creativity, practical problem solving, and academic achievement (Sternberg et al., 2001; Ekinci, 2014).

Sternberg argued that conventional IQ tests, by focusing only on book knowledge, have less utility predicting outcomes in the real world. For example, children in many cultures have to learn practical skills, known as **tacit knowledge,** to succeed. In studies in Usenge, Kenya, and among Yup'ik Eskimo children in southwestern Alaska, children's tacit knowledge of medicinal herbs, hunting, fishing, and preserving plants showed no correlation with conventional measures of intelligence but were necessary for survival (Grigorenko et al., 2004; Sternberg, 2004).

The Kaufman Assessment Battery for Children (K-ABC-II) is designed to evaluate cognitive abilities in children with diverse needs, such as hearing impairments and language disorders. Jovanmandic/iStock/Getty Images

OTHER INTELLIGENCE TESTS

The second edition of the **Kaufman Assessment Battery for Children (K-ABC-II)** (Kaufman & Kaufman, 1983, 2003), an individual test for ages 3 to 18, is designed to evaluate cognitive abilities in children with diverse needs (such as autism, hearing impairments, and language disorders) and from varying cultural and linguistic backgrounds.

Dynamic tests based on Vygotsky's theories emphasize potential rather than present achievement. The focus in these tests is the child's zone of proximal development (ZPD): the difference between the items a child can answer alone and the items the child can answer with help. Examiners help the child when necessary by asking leading questions, giving examples or demonstrations, and offering feedback; thus, the test itself is a learning situation (Resing, 2013).

Language and Literacy

VOCABULARY, GRAMMAR, AND SYNTAX

As vocabulary grows during the school years, children use increasingly precise verbs. They learn that a word like *run* can have more than one meaning, and they can tell from the context which meaning is intended (Owens, 1996). *Similes* and *metaphors,* figures of speech in which a word or phrase that usually designates one thing is compared or applied to another, become increasingly common and more complex (Katis & Selimis, 2005). Although grammar is quite complex by age 6, children during the early school years rarely use the passive voice (as in "The sidewalk is being shoveled").

Children's understanding of rules of *syntax* (the deep underlying structure of language that organizes words into understandable phrases and sentences) becomes more sophisticated with age (Chomsky, 1969). For example, most children under age 5 or 6 think the sentences "John promised Bill to go shopping" and "John told Bill to go shopping" both mean that Bill is the one to go to the store. By age 8 most children can interpret the first sentence correctly and by age 9 virtually all children can. They now look at the meaning of a sentence as a whole instead of focusing on word order alone.

Sentence structure continues to become more elaborate. Older children use more subordinate clauses ("The boy *who delivers the newspapers* rang the doorbell"). Still, some constructions, such as clauses beginning with *however* and *although,* do not become common until early adolescence (Owens, 1996).

PRAGMATICS

The major area of linguistic growth during the school years is in **pragmatics:** the social context of language. Pragmatics includes both conversational and narrative skills.

pragmatics
The social context of language.

There are wide individual differences in conversational skills. Some 7-year-olds are better conversationalists than some adults (Anderson et al., 1994). There are also gender differences. Boys tend to use more controlling statements, negative interruptions, and competitive statements, whereas girls phrase their remarks in a more tentative, conciliatory way and are more polite and cooperative (Leman et al., 2005; Cook-Gumperz & Syzmanski, 2001). However, not all children show this gender difference. Both Dutch girls and boys tend to be equally assertive and controlling in their play (Ladegaard, 2004).

Children also improve at telling stories. Most 6-year-olds can retell the plot of a short book, movie, or television show. They are beginning to describe motives and causal links. By second grade, children's stories become longer and more complex. Fictional tales often have conventional beginnings and endings ("Once upon a time . . ." and "They lived happily ever after"). Word use is more varied than before, but characters do not show change, and plots are not fully developed.

Older children usually set the stage with introductory information about the setting and characters, and they clearly indicate changes of time and place during the story. They construct more complex episodes than younger children do, but with less unnecessary detail. They focus more on the characters' motives and thoughts, and they think through how to resolve problems in the plot.

SECOND-LANGUAGE LEARNING

In 2017, 23 percent of U.S. children ages 5 to 17 spoke a language other than English at home, most commonly Spanish (Federal Interagency Forum on Child and Family Statistics, 2019). About 9.4 percent of the public school population is defined as *English-language learners* (ELLs) (NCES, 2017).

Some schools use an **English-immersion approach** (sometimes called ESL, or English as a second language), in which language-minority children are immersed in English from the beginning, in special classes. Other schools have adopted programs of **bilingual education,** in which children are taught in two languages, first learning in their native language and then switching to regular classes in English when they become more

English-immersion approach
Approach to teaching English as a second language in which instruction is presented only in English.

bilingual education
System of teaching non-English-speaking children in their native language while they learn English, and later switching to all-English instruction.

proficient. These programs can encourage children to become **bilingual** (fluent in two languages) and to feel pride in their cultural identity.

Advocates of early *English immersion* claim that the sooner children are exposed to English, the better they learn it. Proponents of *bilingual* programs claim that children progress faster academically in their native language and later make a smoother transition to all-English classrooms. Research shows children in bilingual programs typically outperform those in all-English programs on tests of English proficiency (Crawford, 2007; Krashen & McField, 2005).

BECOMING LITERATE

Historical and Global Trends in Literacy Although there are written texts going back as far as 3000 to 3500 BCE, literacy was, during that time, a skill held by only the powerful. In the Middle Ages, roughly from 500 to 1500 AD, literacy levels began to slowly increase, but it was not until the Age of Enlightenment in the 17th to 19th century that the goal of a literate population emerged. Estimates are that in 1870, only 1 in 5 people could read. Literacy rates grew slowly until the beginning of the 20th century and then accelerated as global efforts to promote literacy began (Roser & Ortiz-Espina, 2018).

Today, the global literacy rate is approximately 86 percent. While this is a vast improvement, 750 million people worldwide are still illiterate. Two-thirds of the illiterate population are women. Geography matters as well. Almost half (49 percent) of the illiterate population is in southern Asia, followed by sub-Saharan Africa (27 percent). Age makes a difference too. Children and adolescents are less likely to be illiterate than adults (UNESCO Institute for Statistics, 2017).

Reading and Writing Think of what must happen in order for a child to learn to read. First, a child must remember the distinctive features of letters—for example, that, a "c" consists of a curved half-circle and an "o" is a closed circle. Then a child must be able to recognize the different phonemes by breaking down words into their constituent parts. For example, a child must be able to understand that the word *dog* is composed of three different sounds, the "d," the "o," and the "g." Finally, the child must be able to match the visual features of letters and the phonemes and remember which ones go together. This process is known as **decoding.**

In the traditional approach to literacy, called the **phonetic (code-emphasis) approach,** the child learns to sound out the word, translating it from print to speech before retrieving it from long-term memory. To do this, the child must master the phonetic code that matches the printed alphabet to spoken sounds (as described above). Instruction generally involves rigorous, teacher-directed tasks focused on memorizing sound-letter correspondences.

The **whole-language approach** emphasizes visual retrieval and the use of contextual cues. This approach is based on the belief that children can learn to read and write naturally, much as they learn to understand and use speech. By using **visually based retrieval,** the child simply looks at the word and without analyzing the constituent pieces, pulls it out of memory. Whole-language proponents assert that children learn to read with better comprehension and more enjoyment if they experience written language from the outset as a way to gain information and express ideas and feelings, not as a system of isolated sounds and syllables to be learned by memorization and drill.

Research has found little support for the whole-language approach. Although humans have brains wired for spoken language, there is no theoretical reason to assume that written language, a relatively new invention in human history, has similar evolutionary roots and thus should be learned as naturally as spoken language. A long line of research supports the view that phonemic awareness and early phonetics training are keys to reading proficiency for most children (Brady, 2011).

Many experts recommend a blend of the best features of both approaches (National Reading Panel, 2000). For example, children might be not only drilled in sound-letter correspondences, but also asked to memorize certain common words like *the* and *one* that are more difficult to decode. Children who can summon both visually based and phonetic strategies become better, more versatile readers (Siegler, 1998, 2000).

Learning how to write well is difficult for young children. Unlike conversation, which offers constant feedback, writing requires the child to judge independently whether the communicative goal has been met. The child also must keep in mind a variety of other constraints: spelling, punctuation, grammar, and capitalization, as well as the basic physical task of forming letters (Siegler, 1998). Older preschoolers begin using letters, numbers, and letterlike shapes as symbols to represent words or parts of words (syllables or phonemes). Often their spelling is quite inventive—so much so that they may not be able to read it themselves (Ouellette & Sénéchal, 2008; Whitehurst & Lonigan, 1998). Metacognitive skills, such as reading more slowly, rereading difficult passages, trying to visualize information, or thinking of additional examples when trying to learn information in a challenging written passage, can help children read more effectively (National Reading Panel, 2000).

The Influence of Technology Today's children are growing up in a world saturated with technology, and many of their literary experiences will take place on digital screens rather than on printed books. While some researchers have argued that e-books undermine children's understanding of the thematic content of a story and encourage a passive approach to reading (Labbo & Kuhn, 2000), other researchers have suggested that e-books can be used effectively to help children, especially reluctant readers, develop literacy skills (Maynard, 2010).

Research has supported this assertion; a number of school-based interventions have found that e-books supported literacy development to a greater degree than printed books, especially for children at risk for learning disabilities (Ihmeideh, 2014; Shamir et al., 2012; Shamir & Shlafer, 2011). However, for technology to be useful, it must consist of carefully designed applications that encourage collaborative activity and be carefully scaffolded by parents or teachers (Moody, 2010; Flewitt et al., 2015).

The Child in School

INFLUENCES ON SCHOOL ACHIEVEMENT

Self-Efficacy Beliefs Think of how you felt the last time you studied for a big exam. Did you feel you could do well as long as you studied, and were you confident in your ability to master the material? Or did you feel that nothing you could do would matter, and that the material was just too hard? Your attitude can be described as involving a construct called *self-efficacy*. Those students high in self-efficacy believe they can master schoolwork and regulate their own learning (Korramaju & Nadler, 2013). They are more likely to succeed than students who do not believe in their abilities (Caprara et al., 2008), in part because high self-efficacy has a positive effect on motivation (Skaalvik et al., 2015). Self-regulated learners try hard, persist despite difficulties, and seek help when necessary. Doing well in school results in increases in self-efficacy, which once again results in attitudes and behaviors likely to lead to academic success (Schöber et al., 2018). Unfortunately, the converse is also true. Students who do not believe in their ability to succeed tend to become frustrated and depressed—feelings that make success increasingly elusive over time.

Gender Girls tend to do better in school than boys; they receive higher marks, on average, in every subject (Voyer & Voyer, 2014; Halpern et al., 2007), are less likely to repeat grades, have fewer school problems (Freeman, 2004), and outperform boys in national reading and writing assessments (Scheiber, et al., 2015). In addition, girls and women tend to do better than boys and men on timed tests (Camarata & Woodcock, 2006). Some research has suggested that boys outperform girls on science and math (Reilly et al., 2015), but other research has not found a gender gap (Lindberg et al., 2010) or has found it varies by culture (Else-Quest et al., 2010). In second grade, boys' and girls' performance on mental rotation tasks does not differ. However, by fourth grade, boys begin to outperform girls on this task (Neuberger et al., 2011).

Interest, attention, and active participation all contribute to a child's academic success in school.
Andersen Ross/Blend Images/Getty Images

Gender differences tend to become more prominent in high school. A combination of several factors—early experience, biological differences (including differences in brain size and structure), and cultural expectations—helps explain these differences (Nisbett et al., 2012; Halpern et al., 2007).

Parenting Practices Parents of high-achieving children create an environment for learning. They provide a place to study and to keep books and supplies; they set times for meals, sleep, and homework; they monitor their children's activities; and they talk with their children about school and are involved in school activities (Hill & Taylor, 2004; Hill & Tyson, 2009).

Generally, regardless of how it is defined, parental involvement has a positive effect on academic achievement (Wilder, 2014; LaRocque et al., 2011). However, some forms of involvement appear to be more effective than others. For example, homework assistance has not been consistently related to academic achievement (Hill & Tyson, 2009; McNeal, 2012). School involvement, including parental participation in school events and activities and good communication with teachers, is more strongly associated with strong academic performance (Overstreet et al., 2005; Topor et al., 2010). The strongest effects for parent involvement, however, center on parental expectations. Those parents who expect that their children will do well in school have children who live up to those beliefs (Wilder, 2014; Davis-Keane, 2005) perhaps because children also adopt the same attitude about their abilities (Topor et al., 2010).

Socioeconomic Status Socioeconomic status (SES) can be a powerful factor in educational achievement—not in and of itself, but through its influence on family atmosphere, choice of neighborhood, and parenting practices (Evans, 2004; Rouse et al., 2005). Generally, achievement gaps between advantaged and disadvantaged students widen from kindergarten to third grade (Rathbun et al., 2004). Summer vacation contributes to these gaps because of differences in the typical home environment and in the summer learning experiences the children have, particularly with respect to reading (Johnston et al., 2015). This can help account for later differences in high school achievement and completion and college attendance (Alexander et al., 2007). As the income gap between wealthy and poor families has gotten larger, the achievement gap between wealthy and poor children has also grown (Reardon, 2011).

In addition to these factors, socioeconomic status may influence brain development itself. For example, children who live in poverty are more likely to be exposed to environmental toxins such as lead, which can negatively impact brain development. Poor children are also less likely to have access to healthy foods and more likely to suffer from nutrient deficiencies. Moreover, poverty is associated with higher stress, and high levels of chronic stress can have a direct negative effect on development as well as indirect effects on development via its impact on relational processes (Hackman et al., 2010; Blair & Raver, 2016). Research has demonstrated that children living in poverty have 3 to 4 percent less gray matter volume in their frontal lobe, temporal lobe, and hippocampus, a finding that has implications for academic functioning (Hair et al., 2015).

Peer Acceptance Both boys and girls who are disliked by their peers tend to do poorly in school (Nakamoto & Schwartz, 2010; van Lier et al., 2012). Among 248 fourth graders, those whose teachers reported that they were not liked by peers had poorer academic self-concepts, more symptoms of anxiety or depression in fifth grade, and lower reading and math grades in sixth grade (Flook et al., 2005). It may be that the characteristics of some children, including aggression and oppositional behavior, lead to doing poorly in school *and* not being liked by peers. Then their academic underachievement and peer victimization lead to anxiety, depression, and further declines in academic performance (van Lier et al., 2012).

Teachers can serve as buffers against some of the effects of negative peer interactions, either by establishing a warm relationship with a rejected child or by promoting a classroom climate in which victimization of disliked children is discouraged and positive social identities are encouraged (Elledge et al., 2016; Serdiouk et al., 2015).

Educational Reform The No Child Left Behind (NCLB) Act of 2001 was a sweeping educational reform emphasizing accountability, expanded parental options, local control, and flexibility. The intent was to funnel federal funding to research-based programs and practices. Third- through eighth-grade students were tested annually to determine if they were meeting statewide progress objectives.

What was the influence of these regulatory systems? The pattern of improvements in achievement scores was highly variable across states, grades, and subjects (Lee & Reeves, 2012). However, test scores did show improvement. In 2007, for example, math scores for fourth and eighth graders on the National Assessment of Educational Progress (NAEP) rose to their highest levels since the test began in 1990. Black, white, and Hispanic students all improved (NCES, 2007), but ethnic group gaps remained (Hernandez & Macartney, 2008). Efforts to improve the teaching of reading seemed to be paying off more slowly (Dee & Jacob, 2011).

NCLB was replaced in 2015 by the Every Student Succeeds Act (ESSA) with bipartisan support. ESSA retained the standardized testing requirements of NCLB but shifted the responsibility and accountability of oversight to the state governments.

Many educators say the only real solution to a high failure rate is to identify at-risk students early and intervene before they fail. One way is to provide alternative schools or programs for at-risk students, offering smaller classes, remedial instruction, counseling, and crisis intervention (NCES, 2003).

Class Size The average class size varies widely across different countries. Average class sizes are larger in Chile (30.5 students), Japan (27.2 students), and the United Kingdom (26.7 students), and smaller in Costa Rica (15.4 students), Luxembourg (15.9 students), and Latvia (16.3). The average class size in the United States is 20.8 students (Organisation for Economic Co-Development and Learning, 2020).

The evidence on the importance of class size for educational achievement is mixed (Schneider, 2002). Some researchers have not found evidence that reducing class size benefits academic performance (Chingos, 2012; Hoxby, 2000). Other research has shown that reducing class size has a beneficial effect on academic performance and results in improved test scores in reading mathematics and word recognition (Shin & Raudenbush, 2011). However, it has been argued that the effects are small and not likely to lead to sizable increases in student learning (Cho et al., 2012). Moreover, the effect of class size varies depending on cultural context. In some Asian countries, including China and Japan, classes are larger, yet students perform at a high level (Organisation for Economic Co-Operation and Learning, 2013).

Many educators nonetheless argue that smaller classes benefit students. There is evidence that in smaller classes, students spend more time interacting with the teacher, are more likely to be the focus of a teacher's attention, and spend more time on-task and less time off-task (Blatchford et al., 2011; Folmer-Annevelink et al., 2010). Some data suggest the students most at risk, including students of lower socioeconomic status or from marginalized or disenfranchised groups, benefit the most from small classrooms. Additionally, small class size seems to be most useful for younger children (Nandrup, 2016; Zyngier, 2014; Blatchford et al., 2011; Watson et al., 2013).

Media Use Access to the Internet in public schools has skyrocketed. In 1994 only 4 percent of classrooms had Internet access, compared with 97 percent in 2008 (National Center for Education Statistics, 2016). However, fewer black, Hispanic, and American Indian children than white and Asian children, and fewer poor children than non-poor children use these technologies. Girls and boys spend about the same amount of time on computer and Internet use (Day et al., 2005; DeBell & Chapman, 2006).

In recent decades, the amount of time children spend watching television has drastically decreased, although most children 6 to 11 years of age still watch at least 2 hours of television a day (Loprinzi & Davis, 2016). Television has been displaced with the use of other media platforms including DVDs, computers, video games, and mobile devices, which make up an increasingly large percentage of children's media time (Common Sense Media, 2013).

This exposure to media has varying influences depending on what type of media is examined as well as the gender of the child. For example, television is associated with the displacement of other more beneficial experiences such as playing or sleeping for all children. Computer usage is associated with increases in achievement and problem-solving abilities for girls. However, for boys, who are more likely to play violent video games, computer usage is associated with increased aggressive behavior problems (Hofferth, 2010; Chassiakos et al., 2016).

Charter Schools and Homeschooling More than 3.2 million U.S. children attend charter schools (National Alliance for Public Charter Schools, 2020). Charter schools tend to be smaller than regular public schools and tend to have a unique philosophy, curriculum, structure, or organizational style. Some studies have found achievement gains, especially in mathematics, for elementary and middle school students enrolled in charter schools (Betts & Tang, 2019), some studies have found mixed results (Berends, 2015), and some studies have found negative results (Clark et al., 2015). Currently, not enough data are available for general recommendations to be made.

Homeschooling is legal in all 50 states. In 2016, 1.8 million U.S. students representing 3 percent of the school-age population were homeschooled (McQuiggan et al., 2017). The main reasons parents give for choosing to homeschool their children is a poor or unsafe learning environment in the schools and the desire to provide religious or moral instruction (NCES, 2008). While advocates of homeschooling argue that homeschooling is associated with good academic outcomes (Christian Home Educators Association of California, 2013; Ray, 2010) the studies that have been conducted have serious methodological flaws and tend to come from a limited pool of researchers and organizations with potential biases (Kunzman & Gaither, 2013; Lubienski et al., 2013). Thus the efficacy of homeschooling remains in question.

The Influence of COVID-19 on Education In 2020, many countries instituted physical distancing protocols, including school closures, to slow the spread of COVID-19, caused by a novel coronavirus. By May 2020, 160 countries closed all educational institutions nationwide, and multiple other countries enacted localized closures in viral hot spots (UNESCO, 2020). As of July 2020, several large U.S. school districts announced they would be implementing online school in the fall, and many districts announced hybrid models or delayed in-person schooling (Grayer, 2020).

School closures and distance learning are likely to exacerbate existing social and economic inequalities. For instance, children from food-insecure households often rely upon food provided during the school day to meet their nutritional needs. When school is not in session, these children are more likely to go hungry. Additionally, the learning gap between lower- and higher-income children is likely to become larger. Children from lower-income homes are less likely to have access to rapid and reliable Internet service and to have a quiet place in which to complete schoolwork, and they are more likely to experience housing instability or homelessness. Moreover, the economic impact of the health crisis most strongly affected those households least able to manage a decrease in income (Van Lancker & Parolin, 2020). The pandemic was also likely to exacerbate the obesity epidemic in children, especially in children of lower socioeconomic status, and those from urban areas with little available outdoor space (Rundle et al., 2020).

Children's mental health is also likely to be negatively affected. Based on previous research on the effect of quarantines, children are likely to experience boredom, fear of infection, frustration, lack of personal space, loneliness, and family financial problems. These, in turn, can lead to increases in anxiety, depression, and post-traumatic stress responses. The longer a quarantine lasts, the more likely it is such problems will emerge (Brooks et al., 2020). Unfortunately, disruptions are expected to continue across another academic year, and it is estimated children will spend roughly double the time out of school than would otherwise occur (Rundle et al., 2020). The long-term effects of these educational interruptions remains to be seen.

Educating Children with Special Needs

CHILDREN WITH LEARNING PROBLEMS

Intellectual Disability **Intellectual disability** is significantly subnormal cognitive functioning. It is indicated by an IQ of about 70 or less, coupled with a deficiency in age-appropriate adaptive behavior (such as communication, social skills, and self-care), appearing before age 18 (American Psychiatric Association, 2013). Intellectual disability is sometimes referred to as cognitive disability or mental retardation. Less than 1 percent of U.S. children are intellectually disabled (NCHS, 2004). Worldwide, about 1 of every 10 people are intellectually disabled (Maulik et al., 2011).

In 30 to 50 percent of cases, the cause of intellectual disability is unknown. Known causes include genetic disorders, traumatic accidents, prenatal exposure to infection or alcohol, and environmental exposure to lead or high levels of mercury (Woodruff et al., 2004). Many cases may be preventable.

Intervention programs have helped many of those mildly or moderately disabled and those considered borderline (with IQs from 70 up to about 85) to hold jobs, live in the community, and function in society. The profoundly disabled need constant care and supervision, usually in institutions.

Learning Disabilities **Learning disabilities (LDs)** are disorders that interfere with specific aspects of school achievement, such as listening, speaking, reading, writing, or mathematics, resulting in performance substantially lower than would be expected given a child's age, intelligence, and amount of schooling. Approximately 2.4 million children in the United States in the public school system, two-thirds of them boys, were identified as having a learning disability in 2011. This represents a decline of 18 percent since 2002, which can be attributed to early screening and diagnostic services, and early childhood education. In recent years, rather than waiting for children to fail and then providing services, it is more typical to provide early—and more effective—assistance to these children (National Center for Learning Disabilities, 2014).

Children with LDs often have near-average to higher-than-average intelligence and normal vision and hearing, but they have trouble processing sensory information. Causal influences include both genetic and environmental factors. For example, the genes most responsible for the high heritability of the most common LDs are also responsible for typical variations in learning abilities (Plomin & Kovas, 2005). Environmental factors include complications of pregnancy or birth, injuries after birth, nutritional deprivation, and exposure to lead (National Center for Learning Disabilities, 2014).

About 4 out of 5 children with LDs have been identified as dyslexic. **Dyslexia** is a developmental language disorder in which reading achievement is substantially below the level predicted by IQ or age. It is a chronic condition and tends to run in families (Shaywitz, 2003). It hinders the development of oral as well as written language skills and may cause problems with writing, spelling, grammar, and understanding speech as well as with reading (National Center for Learning Disabilities, 2014). Reading disability is more frequent in boys than in girls (Rutter et al., 2004). Although reading and intelligence are related to each other in children without dyslexia, they are not coupled in this fashion for children with dyslexia. In other words, dyslexia is not an issue of intelligence (Ferrer et al., 2010).

Brain imaging studies have found that dyslexia is due to a neurological defect that disrupts recognition of speech sounds (Shaywitz et al., 2006). Several identified genes contribute to this disruption (Eicher & Gruen, 2013; Carrion-Castillo et al., 2013). Many children—and even adults—with dyslexia can be taught to read through systematic phonological training, but the process does not become automatic, as it does with most readers (Eden et al., 2004).

Attention-Deficit/Hyperactivity Disorder **Attention-deficit/hyperactivity disorder (ADHD)** is a chronic condition usually marked by persistent inattention, distractibility, impulsivity, and low tolerance for frustration. ADHD affects an estimated 2 to 7 percent of school-age children worldwide (Sayal et al., 2018). In 2016 about 5.4 million children

intellectual disability
Significantly subnormal cognitive functioning. Also referred to as cognitive disability or mental retardation.

learning disabilities (LDs)
Disorders that interfere with specific aspects of learning and school achievement.

dyslexia
Developmental disorder in which reading achievement is substantially lower than predicted by IQ or age.

attention-deficit/hyperactivity disorder (ADHD)
Syndrome characterized by persistent inattention and distractibility, impulsivity, low tolerance for frustration, and inappropriate overactivity.

in the United States had a current diagnosis of ADHD, a rate of about 8.4 percent (Danielson et al., 2018). The rate of ADHD has increased about 3 percent per year over the past 10 years (Pastor & Reuben, 2008).

Similar to LD, ADHD diagnosis rates vary greatly by gender, ethnicity, geographic area, and other contextual factors. Boys (12.9 percent) are more likely than girls (5.6 percent) to have ADHD (Centers for Disease Control and Prevention, 2019). Prevalence rates are higher in non-Hispanic white children (12.5 percent) than Black (9.6 percent) and Hispanic (6.4 percent) children (Pastor et al., 2015).

Imaging studies reveal that certain regions in the brains of children with ADHD—most notably areas in the frontal cortex—show delays in development. The motor cortex is the only area that matures faster than normal, and this mismatch may account for the restlessness and fidgeting characteristic of the disorder (Shaw et al., 2007). During tasks that require the deployment of attentional processes, children with ADHD show reduced activation in frontoparietal and ventral attention networks areas (Cortese et al., 2012). These frontal regions enable a person to set goals, focus attention, monitor progress, and inhibit negative impulses—all functions disturbed in children with ADHD.

ADHD seems to have a substantial genetic basis with heritability at about 72 percent for both inattention and hyperactivity (Nikolas & Burt, 2010). Birth complications also may play a part in ADHD. Prematurity, a prospective mother's alcohol or tobacco use, and oxygen deprivation (Barkley, 1998; Thapar et al., 2003; USDHHS, 1999; Woodruff et al., 2004) have all been linked to ADHD.

ADHD is often managed with drugs, sometimes combined with behavioral therapy, counseling, training in social skills, and special classroom placement. Interventions with children with ADHD are most useful if they include behavioral interventions, modification of teaching instructions and student tasks, good communication with parents, and collaboration across school professionals such as teachers and psychologists (DuPaul & Stoner, 2014).

Educating Children with Disabilities In 2017, about 14 percent of public school students in the United States were receiving special educational services under the Individuals with Disabilities Education Act, which ensures a free, appropriate public education for all children with disabilities (National Center for Education Statistics, 2019). Most of these children had learning disabilities or speech or language impairments. An individualized program must be designed for each child, with parental involvement. Children must be educated in the "least restrictive environment" appropriate to their needs—which means, whenever possible, the regular classroom.

Programs in which children with special needs are included in the regular classroom are known as inclusion programs. Here, children with disabilities are integrated with nondisabled children for all or part of the day, sometimes with assistance. In 2017, 63 percent of students with disabilities spent at least 80 percent of their time in regular classrooms (National Center for Education Statistics, 2019).

GIFTED CHILDREN

The traditional criterion of giftedness is an IQ score of 130 or higher. This definition tends to exclude highly creative children (whose unusual answers often lower their test scores), children from minority groups (whose abilities may not be well developed, though the potential is there), and children with specific aptitudes (who may be only average or even show learning problems in other areas). All 50 states have moved beyond a single-score definition of giftedness (McClain & Pfeiffer, 2012).

It benefits children with disabilities or special needs when accommodations can be made for their inclusion in classrooms with nondisabled or neurotypical children. FatCamera/E+/Getty Images

Generally, multiple criteria are used for admission to programs for the gifted, including achievement test scores, grades, classroom performance, creative production, parent and teacher nominations, and student interviews. An estimated 6.4 percent of the public school student population is considered gifted. In the 2013–2014 academic year, approximately 3.33 million children were enrolled in gifted and talented programs in the United States (National Center for Education Statistics, 2017).

High levels of performance require strong intrinsic motivation and years of rigorous training (Gardner, 1993; Clinkenbeard, 2012; Al-Dhamit & Kreishan, 2016). However, motivation and training will not produce giftedness unless a child is endowed with unusual ability (Winner, 2000). Conversely, children with innate gifts are unlikely to show exceptional achievement without motivation and hard work (Achter & Lubinski, 2003).

Gifted children tend to grow up in enriched family environments with intellectual or artistic stimulation. Their parents recognize and often devote themselves to nurturing the children's gifts but also give their children an unusual degree of independence. Parents of gifted children typically have high expectations and are hard workers and high achievers themselves (Winner, 2000; Al-Dhamit & Kreishan, 2016; Garn et al., 2010).

Defining and Measuring Creativity One definition of **creativity** is the ability to see things in a new light—to produce something never seen before or to discern problems others fail to recognize and find new and unusual solutions to those problems. High creativity and high IQ do not necessarily go hand in hand (Anastasi & Schaefer, 1971; Getzels & Jackson, 1963). However, it does appear that a threshold level of intelligence, which varies with the complexity of the creative activity, is necessary. Once the intelligence threshold is met, personality factors become more important (Jauk et al., 2013).

The reason creativity is not highly correlated with traditional IQ tests is that traditional tests are measuring a different kind of thinking than is characteristic of creativity. Guilford (1956, 1986) distinguished two kinds of thinking: convergent and divergent. **Convergent thinking**—the kind IQ tests measure—seeks a single correct answer. For example, when solving an arithmetic problem, there is one correct answer upon which everyone is expected to converge. **Divergent thinking** involves coming up with a wide array of fresh possibilities, such as when children are asked to list how many different uses there might be for a paper clip. There is no one right answer. Tests of creativity call for divergent thinking. This ability can be assessed via the *Torrance Tests of Creative Thinking* (TTCT) (Torrance, 1974; Torrance & Ball, 1984), one of the most widely known tests of creativity.

Educating Gifted Children Programs for gifted children generally stress either enrichment or acceleration. **Enrichment programs** may deepen students' knowledge and skills through extra classroom activities, research projects, field trips, or expert coaching. **Acceleration programs** speed up their education through early school entrance, grade skipping, placement in fast-paced classes, or advanced courses. Other options include ability grouping, which has been found to help children academically and not harm them socially (Vogl & Preckel, 2014); dual enrollment (for example, an eighth grader taking algebra at a nearby high school); magnet schools; and specialized schools for the gifted.

creativity
Ability to see situations in a new way, to produce innovations, or to discern previously unidentified problems and find novel solutions.

convergent thinking
Thinking aimed at finding the one right answer to a problem.

divergent thinking
Thinking that produces a variety of fresh, diverse possibilities.

enrichment programs
Programs for educating the gifted that broaden and deepen knowledge and skills through extra activities, projects, field trips, or mentoring.

acceleration programs
Programs for educating the gifted that move them through the curriculum at an unusually rapid pace.

summary and key terms

Physical Development

- Physical development is less rapid in middle childhood than in earlier years. Wide differences in height and weight exist.
- Proper nutrition and sleep are essential.
- Changes in brain structure and functioning support cognitive advances.
- Because of improved motor development, boys and girls in middle childhood can engage in a wide range of motor activities.
- Informal recess-time activities help develop physical and social skills. Boys' games tend to be more physical and girls' games more verbal.

- About 10 percent of schoolchildren's play, especially among boys, is rough-and-tumble play.
- Many children engage in organized, competitive sports, although socioeconomic factors can affect children's ability to participate in organized sports.

Health, Fitness, and Safety

- Middle childhood is a relatively healthy period; most children are immunized and the death rate is low.
- Overweight entails multiple risks. It is influenced by genetic and environmental factors and is more easily prevented than treated. Many children do not get enough physical activity.

- Hypertension is becoming more common along with the rise in overweight.
- Respiratory infections and other acute medical conditions are common at this age. Most children with COVID-19 recover easily, although a small minority are at higher risk.
- Chronic conditions such as asthma are most prevalent among poor and minority children. Diabetes is one of the most common childhood chronic conditions.
- Accidents are the leading cause of death in middle childhood. Use of helmets and other protective devices and avoidance of trampolines, snowmobiling, and other dangerous sports can greatly reduce injuries.

rough-and-tumble play, body image, hypertension, acute medical conditions, chronic medical conditions, asthma, diabetes

Cognitive Development: Piagetian Approach

- A child from about age 7 to age 12 is in the stage of concrete operations. Children are less egocentric than before and are more proficient at tasks requiring logical reasoning, such as spatial thinking, understanding of causality, categorization, inductive and deductive reasoning, and conservation. However, their reasoning is largely limited to the here and now.
- Culture and schooling seem to contribute to the rate of development of Piagetian skills.

concrete operations, seriation, transitive inference, class inclusion, inductive reasoning, deductive reasoning

Information-Processing Approach

- Executive skills, reaction time, processing speed, selective attention, metamemory, and use of mnemonic devices improve during the school years.

executive function, mnemonic device, external memory aids, rehearsal, organization, elaboration, metamemory, metacognition

Psychometric Approach

- IQ tests are fairly good predictors of school success but may be unfair to some children.
- Differences in IQ among ethnic groups appear to result to a considerable degree from socioeconomic and other environmental differences.
- Schooling increases measured intelligence.
- Attempts to devise culture-free or culture-fair tests have been unsuccessful.
- IQ tests tap only three of the eight intelligences in Howard Gardner's theory of multiple intelligences.
- According to Robert Sternberg's triarchic theory, IQ tests measure mainly the componential element of intelligence, not the experiential and contextual elements.
- Other directions in intelligence testing include the Sternberg Triarchic Abilities Tests (STAT), Kaufman Assessment Battery for Children (K-ABC-II), and dynamic tests based on Vygotsky's theory.

Design Credit: (globe) janrysavy/Getty Images

Wechsler Intelligence Scale for Children (WISC-IV), Stanford-Binet Intelligence Test, Otis-Lennon School Ability Test (OLSAT 8), culture-free tests, culture-fair tests, theory of multiple intelligences, triarchic theory of intelligence, componential element, experiential element, contextual element, Sternberg Triarchic Abilities Test, tacit knowledge, Kaufman Assessment Battery for Children (K-ABC-II), dynamic tests

Language and Literacy

- Use of vocabulary, grammar, and syntax become increasingly sophisticated, but the major area of linguistic growth is in pragmatics.
- Methods of second-language education are controversial.
- Despite the popularity of whole-language programs, early phonetics training is a key to reading proficiency. Mixed approaches may be most effective.

pragmatics, English-immersion approach, bilingual education, bilingual, decoding, phonetic (code-emphasis) approach, whole-language approach, visually based retrieval, metacognition

The Child in School

- Entry into first grade is an important milestone.
- Children's self-efficacy beliefs affect school achievement.
- Girls tend to do better in school than boys.
- Parents influence children's learning by becoming involved in their schooling and transmitting attitudes about academics.
- Socioeconomic status can influence achievement.
- Peer acceptance and class size affect learning.
- Current educational issues and innovations include social promotion, charter schools, homeschooling, and computer literacy.
- School closures as a result of measures to contain COVID-19 are expected to exacerbate existing inequalities between children from different socioeconomic levels.

Educating Children with Special Needs

- Three frequent sources of learning problems are intellectual disability, learning disabilities (LDs), and attention-deficit/hyperactivity disorder (ADHD). Dyslexia is the most common learning disability.
- In the United States, all children with disabilities are entitled to a free, appropriate education in the least restrictive environment possible, often in the regular classroom.
- An IQ of 130 or higher is a common standard for identifying gifted children.
- Creativity and IQ are not closely linked. Tests of creativity measure divergent thinking.
- Special educational programs for gifted children stress enrichment or acceleration.

intellectual disability, learning disabilities (LDs), dyslexia, attention-deficit/hyperactivity disorder (ADHD), creativity, convergent thinking, divergent thinking, enrichment programs, acceleration programs

Psychosocial Development in Middle Childhood

chapter 10

Scott B. Rosen/Alamy Stock Photo

learning objectives

Discuss emotional and personality development in school-age children.

Describe changes in family relationships in the school-age years.

Identify changes in peer relationships among school-age children.

Describe the development and treatment of emotional disorders that can develop in school-age children.

In this chapter we see how children develop a more realistic self-concept. Through interacting with peers, they make discoveries about their own attitudes, values, and skills. The kind of household a child lives in and the relationships in it can profoundly affect psychosocial development. We look at several mental health problems and at resilient children, who can emerge from stress healthy and strong.

The Developing Self

The cognitive growth that takes place during middle childhood enables children to develop more complex concepts of themselves and to gain in emotional understanding and control.

SELF-CONCEPT DEVELOPMENT

"At school I'm feeling pretty smart in certain subjects, Language Arts and Social Studies," says 8-year-old Lisa. "I got As in these subjects on my last report card and was really proud of myself. But I'm feeling really dumb in Arithmetic and Science, particularly when I see how well the other kids are doing. . . . I still like myself as a person, because Arithmetic and Science just aren't that important to me. How I look and how popular I am are more important" (Harter, 1996, p. 208).

Young children have difficulty with abstract concepts and with integrating various dimensions of the self. Their self-concepts focus on physical attributes, possessions, and global descriptions. However, around age 7 or 8, children's judgments about the self become more conscious, realistic, balanced, and comprehensive as children form **representational systems:** broad, inclusive self-concepts that integrate various aspects of the self (Harter, 1993, 1996, 1998). We can see these changes in Lisa's self-description.

representational systems
In neo-Piagetian terminology, the third stage in development of self-definition, characterized by breadth, balance, and the integration and assessment of various aspects of the self.

INDUSTRY VERSUS INFERIORITY

According to Erikson (1998), a major determinant of self-esteem is children's view of their capacity for productive work, which develops in his fourth stage of psychosocial development: **industry versus inferiority.** As with all of Erikson's stages, there is an opportunity for growth represented by a sense of industry and a complementary risk represented by inferiority.

If children are unable to obtain the praise of others, or lack motivation and self-esteem, they may develop a feeling of low self-worth, and thus develop a sense of inferiority. This is problematic because during middle childhood children must learn skills valued in their society.

Developing a sense of industry, by contrast, involves learning how to work hard to achieve goals. The details may vary across societies: Arapesh boys in New Guinea learn to make bows and arrows and to lay traps for rats; Inuit children of Alaska learn to hunt and fish; and children in industrialized countries learn to read, write, do math, and use computers. If the stage is successfully resolved, children develop a view of themselves as being able to master skills and complete tasks. This can go too far—if children become too industrious, they may neglect social relationships and turn into workaholics.

industry versus inferiority
Erikson's fourth stage of psychosocial development, in which children must learn the productive skills their culture requires or else face feelings of inferiority.

EMOTIONAL DEVELOPMENT

As children grow older, they are more aware of their own and other people's feelings. They can better regulate or control their emotions and can respond to others' emotional distress (Saarni et al., 2006). Children learn what makes them angry, fearful, or sad and how other people react to displays of these emotions. They also start to understand that they and others can have conflicting emotions (Zajdel et al., 2013).

When parents are skilled at the recognition of emotions in others, label emotions, and allow children the latitude to express emotions, their children understand and recognize emotions better (Castro et al., 2015). However, if parents respond with excessive disapproval or punishment to the expression of emotions, emotions such as anger and fear may become more intense and may impair children's social adjustment (Fabes et al., 2001), or children may become secretive and anxious about negative feelings (Almas et al., 2011). Parents who acknowledge children's feelings of distress and help them focus on solving the root problem foster empathy, prosocial development, and social skills (Bryant, 1987; Eisenberg et al., 1996).

This young boy may develop a sense of competence and build his self-esteem by helping care for his family's cattle. Hong Hanh Mac Thi/Alamy Stock Photo

Have you ever received a gift you didn't like or had to hold in your anger to avoid getting in trouble? The ability to fake liking a gift or to smile when you are mad involves emotional self-regulation. Emotional self-regulation is effortful (voluntary) control of emotions, attention, and behavior (Eisenberg et al., 2004). Some children, especially girls, are better than others at emotional self-regulation, but most children get better with age (Colle & Del Giudice, 2011).

Children's ability to exert control over themselves is related to adjustment (Eisenberg et al., 2004). For example, children who, at 3 to 4 years of age, had difficulty in delay-of-gratification tasks were more likely to have behavior problems at 5 to 8 years. Similarly, children who were poor at deliberately slowing down, inhibiting their movements in a game, or paying close attention when young were more likely to have academic difficulties when older (Kim et al., 2013). In contrast, children who are good at self-regulation tend to be socially competent and do well in school (Eisenberg et al., 2016).

Children tend to become more empathic and more inclined to prosocial behavior in middle childhood. Empathy—the capacity to understand and feel the emotions of another person—is likely one of the key motivators for prosocial behavior (Eisenberg et al., 2010). Prosocial children tend to act appropriately in social situations, to be relatively free from negative emotion, and to cope with problems constructively (Eisenberg et al., 1996).

Cultural Influences on Emotional Development Different cultures hold different behavioral standards for children, and successful adjustment and socialization require that children learn to control their responses in culturally meaningful ways. So, for example, if a child who becomes angry out of frustration behaves aggressively or rudely, this can lead to social rejection in cultures in which the free display of negative emotions is not viewed favorably (Trommsdorf & Cole, 2011).

For example, by age 7 or 8, children typically are aware of feeling shame and pride, and they have a clearer idea of the difference between guilt and shame (Olthof et al., 2000). However, cultural values affect the expression of these emotions. For example, one study found that children in the United States expressed the most pride, Japanese children the most shame, and Korean children the most guilt (Furukawa et al., 2012). In another study, when Braham children from India were asked how they would feel in a difficult interpersonal situation, they reported they would feel anger, whereas Tamang children from Tibet reported shame as their most likely emotion (Cole et al., 2002). Brahman adults generally ignore shame and respond to angry children with reasoning and yield to their demands. Tamang adults expect children to be socially compliant and are intolerant of anger but will reason with and yield to children who are ashamed. Thus children learn to shape their emotional responses to what is expected and tolerated of them (Cole et al., 2006).

Cultural values also influence the development of emotional self-regulation. In individualistic cultures, the free expression of emotions is encouraged in children and viewed as healthy and normative. In collectivistic cultures, self-restraint is valued, as the strong expression of emotions, particularly if negative, might damage relationships (Trommsdorff & Cole, 2011).

Empathy and prosocial behavior are also shaped by cultural context. In collectivistic cultures, where interdependence is stressed, children would be expected to feel more empathy in response to the distress of others, and also to more readily engage in prosocial behavior. In individualistic cultures, where the self is viewed as primary and independent, the reverse should be true. A survey of 63 countries provided support for these predictions. A country's level of collectivism was associated with empathy and the tendency to engage in prosocial behaviors (Chopik et al., 2017).

Family Influences

School-age children spend more time away from home visiting and socializing with peers than when they were younger. Still, home and the people who live there remain an important part of most children's lives.

FAMILY ATMOSPHERE

Family atmosphere is a key influence on development. One key factor is whether or not conflict is present in the home. Other important influences include parents' work status and the family socioeconomic level.

Coregulation and Parental Control Strategies Babies don't have a lot of say in what happens to them; they experience what their parents decide they should experience. However, there is a shift in power as children grow and become more autonomous. Over the course of childhood, control gradually shifts from parents to child. Children begin to request certain types of experiences, demand particular foods, negotiate for desired objects, and communicate their shifting needs to parents.

In middle childhood, social power becomes more equal between parent and child. Parent and child engage in **coregulation,** a stage that can include strategies in which parents exercise oversight but children enjoy moment-to-moment self-regulation (Maccoby, 1984, 1992). For example, with regard to problems among peers, parents might now rely less on direct intervention and more on discussion with their child (Parke & Buriel, 1998). These broad patterns in coregulation appear to be similar across different cultures (Parke, 2004).

Coregulation is affected by the overall relationship between parent and child. Children are more apt to follow their parents' wishes when they believe their parents are fair and concerned about their welfare and that they may "know better" because of experience. This is particularly true when parents take pains to acknowledge children's maturing judgment and take strong stands only on important issues (Maccoby, 1984, 1992). The shift to coregulation affects the way parents handle discipline (Kochanska et al., 2008). Parents of school-age children are more likely to use inductive techniques. For example, they might explain how their actions affect others, highlight moral values, or let their children experience the natural consequences of their behaviors.

Parents also modify their use of physical discipline (such as spanking) as children age. Parents who use physical punishment tend to decrease its use as children grow older. Generally, the use of physical punishment is associated with negative outcomes for children. Those parents who continue to spank their children past the age of 10 years tend to have worse relationships with their children in adolescence and to have teens with worse behavioral problems (Lansford et al., 2009).

Cultural differences are also important, and tend to exert complex effects on the use of parental control strategies. Generally, researchers find that in cultures that stress family interdependence (such as in Turkey, India, and Latin America) authoritarian parenting, with its high degree of control, is not associated with negative maternal feelings or low self-esteem in children as it is in more individualistic cultures (Rudy & Grusec, 2006). Latino parents, for example, have well adjusted children as often as other groups although they tend to exert more control over their school-age children than European American parents do (Halgunseth et al., 2006), and expectations for girls are even more strict (Domenech et al., 2009). However, children in China, also a collectivistic culture, tend to be negatively affected by high control just as are children from the individualistic United States (Pomerantz & Wang, 2009). With respect to low control, children of Iranian (Kazemi et al., 2010), Spanish (Garcia & Garcia, 2009), and some European parents (Calafat et al., 2014) with a permissive parenting style have good outcomes, contrary to what has been found in American samples (Pinquart, 2017). Thus the influence of parental control strategies is shaped by the cultural context in which it occurs.

Family Conflict Exposure to violence and conflict is harmful to children, in terms of both direct exposure via parental discord (Harold & Sellers, 2018) and via indirect influences on variables like low family cohesion and anger regulation strategies (Houltberg et al., 2012).

coregulation
Transitional stage in the control of behavior in which parents exercise general supervision and children exercise moment-to-moment self-regulation.

Although school-age children spend less time at home, family influences continue to be important in their lives.
Denis Kuvaev/Shutterstock

Children exposed to family conflict show a variety of responses that can include externalizing or internalizing behaviors. **Internalizing behaviors** include anxiety, fearfulness, and depression—anger turned inward. **Externalizing behaviors** include aggression, fighting, disobedience, and hostility—anger turned outward. Both internalizing and externalizing behaviors are more likely in children who come from families with high levels of discord (Harold & Sellers, 2018; Fear et al., 2009; Houltberg et al., 2012).

How family conflict is resolved is also important. If family conflict is constructive, it can help children learn how to solve interpersonal problems, communicate effectively, and understand how to resolve conflict without damaging social relationships (McCoy et al., 2013). For example, when family conflict in one longitudinal study was solved in constructive ways, children reported being more emotionally secure one year later and, one year after that, reported more prosocial behavior (McCoy et al., 2009).

Maternal Employment Because there has not been much variability in paternal employment but women have increasingly joined the work force, most studies of the impact of parents' work on children's well-being have focused on employed mothers. In 1975, the labor force participation rate of mothers with children was 47 percent (U.S. Bureau of Labor Statistics, 2008). By 2018, 71.5 percent of U.S. mothers worked either full- or part-time (U.S. Bureau of Labor Statistics, 2019). Mothers are far more likely to take on part-time work than fathers (Weeden et al., 2016)

In general, the more satisfied a mother is with her employment status, the more effective she is likely to be as a parent. However, the impact of a mother's work depends on many other factors, including the child's age, sex, temperament, and personality; whether the mother works full-time or part-time; why she is working; whether she has a supportive or unsupportive partner, or none; the family's socioeconomic status; and the type of care the child receives before and/or after school (Parke, 2004; Gottfried & Gottfried, 2013). Often a single mother must work to stave off economic disaster. How her working affects her children may hinge on how much time and energy she has left to spend with them. How well parents keep track of their children and monitor their activities may be more important than whether the mother works for pay (Fosco et al., 2012).

When both parents work outside the home, child care arrangements are common. Half of grade school children are in some form of child care outside of school, often with relatives (Laughlin, 2013), while others attend organized programs. These programs vary widely in quality. Two important markers of quality are structural features (such as physical facilities and staff characteristics) and process features (such as the activities available for children and the overall culture of the program). When children are enrolled in high-quality programs, they show positive changes in social conscience, decision making, critical thinking, academic outcomes, attachment to their school, peer relationships, and self-confidence, and they show declines in problem behaviors and drug use (Smischney et al., 2018; Durlak et al., 2010).

Approximately 11 percent of school-age children and early adolescents are reported to be in *self-care,* regularly caring for themselves at home without adult supervision (Laughlin, 2013). This arrangement is advisable only for older children who are mature, responsible, and resourceful and know how to get help in an emergency—and, even then, only if a parent can stay in touch by telephone.

Poverty and Parenting About 17.5 percent of U.S. children up to age 17 lived in poverty in 2017. The poverty rate for white children was 10.9 percent. Rates were much higher for Black (28.7 percent) and Hispanic (25 percent) children. Children living with single mothers were almost 5 times more likely to be poor than children living with married couples—40.7 percent as compared with 8.4 percent (Federal Interagency Forum on Child and Family Statistics, 2019).

Poverty can harm children's development through a multitude of pathways. Parents who live in poverty are more likely to become anxious, depressed, and irritable and thus may become less affectionate with and responsive to their children. There may be increased levels of parent-child conflict and harsh discipline. Poverty also affects where

internalizing behaviors
Behaviors by which emotional problems are turned inward; for example, anxiety or depression.

externalizing behaviors
Behaviors by which a child acts out emotional difficulties; for example, aggression or hostility.

children go to school and the neighborhood they live in, features that can exacerbate child stressors. These features in turn also affect parents and their perceived stress. In short, there are cascades of negative interactions that can have a deleterious effect on child outcomes. These outcomes include physical health, behaviors, mental health, and cognitive and intellectual development (Chaudry & Wimer, 2016; Morris et al., 2017; Yoshikawa et al., 2012).

Fortunately, this pattern is not inevitable. Effective parenting can buffer children from the effects of poverty. Effective family interventions promote positive parent-child interactions (for example, by encouraging parents to praise their children while also helping them develop reasonable rules and limits) and provide social support for parents (Morris et al., 2017). Parents who can turn to relatives or to community resources for emotional support, help with child care, and child-rearing information often can parent their children more effectively (Brody et al., 2004). Community organizations, schools, and pediatricians can also be utilized to provide services and advocacy for children affected by poverty (Ellis & Dietz, 2017; Dreyer et al., 2016; Durlak et al., 2011).

FAMILY STRUCTURE

In most developed countries, family structure has changed dramatically, particularly with respect to marriage rates. Some countries, such as China, Italy, and Portugal, have marriage rates nearly half of those held by countries such as Lithuania and Turkey, but almost all countries show declines over the past few decades (Organisation for Economic Co-operation and Development, 2019).

Family structure in the United States has also changed dramatically. In earlier generations, the vast majority of children grew up in families with two married parents. In 1960, almost 88 percent of children lived with two married biological, adoptive, or step-parents. However, this has become less common, and in 2019, 70 percent of children lived with two married parents (see Figure 10.1; U.S. Census Bureau, 2019). About 8 percent of two-parent families are stepfamilies resulting from divorce and remarriage, and 5 percent are cohabiting families (Federal Interagency Forum on Child and Family Statistics, 2019). Other increasingly common family types are gay and lesbian families and grandparent-headed families.

Other things being equal, children tend to do better in families with two continuously married parents than in cohabiting, divorced, single-parent, or stepfamilies (Brown, 2010). The distinction is even stronger for children growing up with two *happily* married parents. This suggests that the parents' relationship, the quality of their parenting, and their ability to create a favorable family atmosphere may affect children's adjustment more than their marital status does (Amato, 2005).

In two-parent family structures, there are relatively few differences in child well-being regardless of whether children live with biological cohabiting families, married/cohabiting stepfamilies, or blended families (Artis, 2007). Family instability, however, may be harmful. Children who experience more family transitions, such as a divorce or a remarriage, were more likely to have behavior problems, be low in social competence, high in aggression, and to engage in delinquent behavior than children in stable families

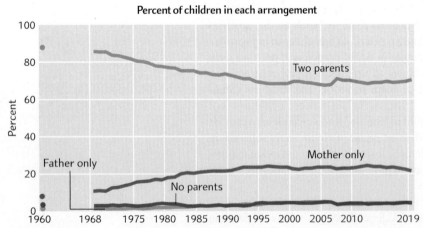

Percent of children in each arrangement

Note: Direct identification of both parents began in 2007, resulting in the ability to identify children living with two unmarried parents.

FIGURE 10.1

Living Arrangements of Children Under 18, 1960 to 2019

Most children under 18 in the United States live with two parents.

Source: U.S. Census Bureau. (2019). Living arrangements of children: 1960 to present [Graph]. Retrieved from www.census.gov/data/tables/time-series/demo/families/children.html

(Briggs et al., 2019; Fomby & Cherlin, 2007; Magnuson & Berger, 2009). The negative effect of family transitions appears to be stronger if they occur earlier in development and for boys (Cavanagh & Huston, 2008).

A father's frequent and positive involvement with his child is directly related to the child's well-being and physical, cognitive, and social development (McLanahan et al., 2013; Adamsons & Johnson, 2013). Unfortunately, in 2019, approximately 21.4 percent of children lived in homes without a biological father present (U.S. Census Bureau, 2019).

Divorce Divorce rates differ sharply across countries—from a low of 0.1 divorce per 1,000 people in Chile to a high of almost 5 divorces per 1,000 people in Russia (Organisation for Economic Co-operation and Development, 2019). In most European countries, the divorce rate has been increasing since the 1960s (Amato, 2014). In Asia and Southeast Asia, divorce rates have likewise climbed and are similar to those found in Europe and range from 2 to 3 divorces per 1,000 people. In South Asia, by contrast, divorce rates are low and stable, primarily because many women do not have the option of returning to their family of origin if they divorce and are generally not able to earn an income to support themselves independently (Jones, 2015). In sub-Saharan Africa, although divorce is common, divorce rates as a whole are stable or decreasing, a trend that appears to be associated with an increase in age at first marriage and higher levels of education for women (Clarke & Brauner-Otto, 2015).

Divorce is also found in traditional societies. For example, only about 20 percent of Hazda indigenous couples in Tanzania stay married to the same person for life, and divorce is a frequent consequence of infidelity (Marlowe, 2010). In the Igbo farming communities of rural Nigeria, divorce is also frequent, with infidelity, infertility, impotence, and laziness cited as common antecedents (Enwereji, 2008).

In the United States, the divorce rate rose from 1960 (2.2 per 1,000 people) to its peak level in 1980 (3.5 per 1,000 people) (Amato, 2014; Cherlin, 2010). Since then the divorce rate has slowly dropped, and it currently stands at 2.9 per 1,000 people (Centers for Disease Control and Prevention, 2019).

Adjusting to Divorce Divorce is stressful for children. First there is the stress of marital conflict and then of parental separation with the departure of one parent, usually the father, and the potential loss of friends if a move is necessary. Children may not fully understand what is happening. Divorce is, of course, stressful for the parents as well and may negatively affect their parenting. The family's standard of living is likely to drop, and, if a parent moves away, a child's relationship with the noncustodial parent may suffer (Kelly & Emery, 2003; Amato, 2014). A parent's remarriage or second divorce after remarriage can increase the stress on children, renewing feelings of loss (Ahrons & Tanner, 2003; Amato, 2003).

Family conflict is a consistently identified risk factor for children (Stallman & Ohan, 2016). Children's emotional or behavioral problems after a divorce may reflect the level of parental conflict *before* the divorce. Children whose parents later divorce show more anxiety, depression, or antisocial behavior before the divorce than those whose parents stay married (Strohschein, 2012). In fact, if predivorce parental discord is chronic, overt, or destructive, children may be as well or better off after a divorce (Amato, 2003, 2005). Indeed, it matters less if parents are married or separated than if they engage in frequent or extended conflict (Harold & Sellers, 2018). Additionally, the quality of parenting prior to divorce matters as well, with maternal sensitivity and support acting as a protective factor for some children whose families divorced (Weaver & Schofield, 2015).

Findings on children's adjustment to divorce tend to be quite similar across Europe and the United States, with most studies finding that when compared to children raised by two continuously married parents, children of divorced parents show poorer outcomes, including more conduct problems and emotional problems, lower academic achievement, and more difficulty with interpersonal relationships. As adults, they obtain less education and have a lower income than children of married parents, and they are more likely to suffer from physical health problems and have a higher chance of their own marriages ending in divorce. However, children's adjustment to divorce is highly

Children of divorce tend to be better adjusted if they have reliable, frequent contact with the noncustodial parent. Paul Bradbury/Glow Images

variable (Amato, 2014). This is because adjustment depends on a large number of individual difference variables, including the child's age, maturity, gender, temperament, and psychosocial adjustment before the divorce. Although children whose parents divorce are at slightly higher risk for negative outcomes, most do eventually show good adjustment (Amato & Anthony, 2014).

Custody and Co-parenting In most divorce cases, the mother gets custody, though paternal custody is a growing trend. Joint custody, shared by both parents, is another arrangement. When parents have joint legal custody, they share the right and responsibility to make decisions regarding the child's welfare. When they have joint physical custody (which is less common), the child lives part-time with each parent.

Research suggests children do better with joint custody (Warshak, 2014; Baude et al., 2016), perhaps because fathers are more likely to remain involved. Many children of divorce say that losing contact with a father is one of the most painful results of divorce (Fabricius, 2003). When one parent has custody, children do better after divorce if the custodial parent is warm, supportive, and authoritative; monitors the child's activities; and holds age-appropriate expectations. In addition, conflict between the divorced parents should be minimal, and the nonresident parent should remain closely involved (Stallman & Ohan, 2016; Ahrons & Tanner, 2003). Conflict, as before divorce, is damaging and can result in lower life satisfaction, negative affect, externalizing symptoms, and adolescent delinquency (Lamela et al., 2016; Teubert & Pinquart, 2010). High conflict between parents, especially if a child is drawn into the conflict and forced to choose sides, can be extremely damaging (Fosco & Grych, 2010).

Co-parenting is a parenting relationship in which two people who may or may not be romantically involved work together in a cooperative fashion to raise a child. Co-parenting has been consistently linked to positive child outcomes (Teubert & Pinquart, 2010), in part because it is strongly associated with more frequent contact between father and child (Sobolewski & King, 2005). For instance, children whose parents are able to parent cooperatively following a divorce tend to have closer ties to their fathers– and fewer behavioral problems–than children whose parents have more conflict following divorce (Amato et al., 2011). Unfortunately, cooperative parenting is not the norm (Amato, 2005). Parent education programs that teach separated or divorced couples how to prevent or deal with conflict, keep lines of communication open, and help children adjust to divorce have been introduced in many states with measurable success (Ferraro et al., 2016).

Long-Term Effects Most children of divorce adjust well (Amato & Anthony, 2014). However, parental divorce may affect later relationships as children enter adulthood. For example, children whose parents divorced have higher separation and divorce rates themselves (Mustonen et al., 2011). Although these differences are small, as adults, the children of divorce tend to have lower SES, poorer psychological well-being, particularly with respect to their risk of depression, and a greater chance of having a birth outside marriage. Their marriages tend to be less satisfying and are more likely to end in divorce (Amato, 2005; Uphold-Carrier & Utz, 2012). Additionally, adults whose parents divorced when they were children and who endured multiple or prolonged separation from a parent later show compromised parenting themselves, including lower sensitivity and warmth, and more parent-child conflict and physical punishment (Friesen et al., 2017). However, much depends on how young people resolve and interpret the experience of parental divorce. Some who saw a high degree of conflict between their parents are able to learn from that negative example and form highly intimate relationships themselves (Shulman et al., 2001).

One-Parent Families One-parent families result from divorce or separation, unwed parenthood, or death. With rising rates of divorce and of parenthood outside of marriage, the number of single-parent families in the United States has increased by over 3 times since 1960. Currently, almost 26 percent of children live in a single-parent household. More than half of all Black children live with a single parent, as compared with 21 percent of non-Hispanic white children and 28 percent of Hispanic children (U.S. Census Bureau, 2019). Although children are far more likely to live with a single mother than with a single father, the number of father-only families has more than quadrupled since 1960 (U.S. Census Bureau, 2019). Single parenthood is more common in low-income families (Mather, 2010).

Children in single-parent families do fairly well overall but tend to lag socially and educationally behind peers in two-parent families (Waldfogel et al., 2010; Brown, 2010). They also have a higher risk of obesity (Duriancik & Goff, 2019) and tend to make less money as adults than do children from two-parent families (Lerman et al., 2017).

However, negative outcomes for children in one-parent families are not inevitable. The child's age and level of development, the family's financial circumstances and educational level, whether there are frequent moves, and a nonresident father's involvement make a difference (Amato, 2005; Seltzer, 2000; Ricciuti, 2004). One important variable appears to be family stability. Children from stable single-parent families fare comparably to those from unstable two-parent families (Heiland & Liu, 2006). Income also matters; many of the negative effects of single-parenthood appear to be driven by lower socioeconomic status (Brown, 2010). In countries with a more robust welfare support system for single mothers, such as Norway, Sweden, and Denmark, children in such families report higher levels of well-being than children in countries who do not provide as much aid to single mothers (Bjarnason et al., 2012).

Cohabiting Families Approximately 32 percent of children in the United States live with cohabitating parents—in other words, unmarried partners living together (Livingston, 2018). Cohabiting families are similar in many ways to married families, but the parents tend to be more disadvantaged. They traditionally have less income and education, report poorer relationships, and have more mental health problems (Mather, 2010). Cohabiting families are more likely to be white (55 percent) than Hispanic (25 percent), Black (13 percent), or Asian (3 percent) (Livingston, 2018).

Research shows worse emotional, behavioral, and academic outcomes for children living with cohabiting biological parents than for those living with married biological parents (Waldfogel et al., 2010; Brown, 2004). However, this difference in outcomes is primarily the result of differences in economic resources and family instability (Manning, 2017). Parenting differences explain only a small amount of the variation in child outcomes for cohabiting versus married couples (Thomson & McLanahan, 2012).

Roughly two decades ago, research showed cohabiting families were more likely to break up than married families (Amato, 2005). Although it remains controversial (Wilcox & DeRose, 2017), newer research suggests this may no longer be the case (Smock & Schwartz, 2020). When issues such as the timing of children (Musick & Michaelmore, 2015) and the age of the cohabiting couple (Kuperberg, 2014) are taken into consideration, cohabiting families look much more like married couples. These new patterns may be because cohabitation has become more normative, and thus it no longer indicates the degree of commitment—or lack thereof—a couple holds for the relationship. Indeed, in a study of 16 European countries, cohabitation was associated with relationship dissolution in those countries in which it was rare. When cohabitation was normative, it did not confer a risk to the relationship. When cohabitation became exceedingly common, it once again was associated with relationship dissolution, presumably because of the increasing selectivity of the subpopulation of married couples relative to the rest of the coupled population (Liefbroer & Dourleijn, 2006).

Stepfamilies Most divorced parents eventually remarry, and many unwed mothers marry men who were not the father of their children, forming step-, or blended, families. Fifteen percent of U.S. children live in blended families (Pew Research Center, 2015).

Adjusting to a new stepparent may be stressful. Both children and parents have to navigate shifting relationships, adapt to a new power structure in the family, and adjust to household changes. Studies have found small to moderate, but consistent, negative effects for children living in stepparent families when compared to married families (Sweeney, 2010; Hofferth, 2006). Adjustment to the stepparents and the potential negative influence of that on development appear to be influenced by family relationships before the formation of the stepfamily. When there is a good relationship with the biological parent (usually the mother) prior to the introduction of a stepparent, children show more positive relationships with their stepparent and better adjustment (King et al., 2015).

Gay or Lesbian Parents Globally, same-sex marriage has become increasingly accepted. Currently, 30 countries, primarily in Europe and the Americas, legally recognize gay marriage (Pew Research Center, 2019). In the United States, an estimated 6 million children and adolescents have at least one gay or lesbian parent (Gates, 2013). About 23 percent of lesbian couples and 6 percent of gay couples have children living with them (U.S. Census Bureau, 2018). Although there is still much discrimination leveled toward same-sex relationships, the legalization of same-sex marriage and a decrease in social stigma have resulted in many LGBT people coming out an earlier age. In the past, such adults were more likely to have first entered into heterosexual relationships that produced children. Now same-sex couples are less likely to be raising children that were the product of such unions and more likely to jointly be raising children that are the product of reproductive technologies such as artificial insemination or adoption (Gates, 2015).

Research has shown that children living with homosexual parents are no more likely than other children to have social or psychological problems or to be homosexual themselves.
Jules Ingall/Moment/Getty Images

A considerable body of research has examined the development of children of gays and lesbians and has found no special concerns (APA, 2004). There is no consistent difference between homosexual and heterosexual parents in emotional health or parenting skills and attitudes, and where there are differences, they tend to favor gay and lesbian parents (Golombok et al., 2013; Meezan & Rauch, 2005; Pawelski et al., 2006; Biblarz & Stacey, 2010). Gay or lesbian parents usually have positive relationships with their children, and the children are no more likely than children raised by heterosexual parents to have emotional, social, academic, or psychological problems (Perrin et al., 2013; Fedewa et al., 2015; Manning et al., 2014; Meezan & Rauch, 2005). Furthermore, children of gays and lesbians are no more likely to be homosexual or to have difficulty establishing their gender identity than are children of heterosexuals (Fedewa et al., 2015; Meezan & Rauch, 2005; Wainright et al., 2004).

Such findings have social policy implications for legal decisions on custody and visitation disputes, foster care, and adoptions (Fettro & Manning, 2018). In the face of controversy over gay and lesbian marriages or civil unions, several states have considered or adopted legislation sanctioning second-parent adoption by same-sex partners. The American Academy of Pediatrics supports legislative and legal efforts to permit a partner in a same-sex couple to adopt the other partner's child (Perrin et al., 2013).

Adoptive Families Adoption is found in all cultures throughout history. It is not only for infertile people; single people, older people, gay and lesbian couples, and people who already have biological children have become adoptive parents. In 2007, 1.8 million U.S. children under 18 (about 2 percent) lived with at least one adoptive parent (Child Trends DataBank, 2012). Although it is difficult to compile accurate statistics as there is no one single source of data, estimates are that in 2012, approximately 119,500 children were adopted, which represents a 15 percent decrease since 2001 (Child Welfare Information Gateway, 2016).

Adoptions usually take place through public or private agencies. Traditionally, agency adoptions were intended to be confidential, with no contact between the birth mother and the adoptive parents. However, independent adoptions, made by direct agreement between birth parents and adoptive parents, have become more common. Often these are *open adoptions,* in which both parties share information or have direct contact with the child (Grotevant, 2012). Generally, open adoptions are beneficial for all parties. For example, birth mothers who participate in open adoptions have less unresolved grief than those that participate in closed adoptions (Grotevant et al., 2013). Contact can also help the child develop a sense of identity and provide information about family history. However, if contact goes poorly, it also runs the risk of undermining children's stability, particularly if negative interactions occur between birth and adoptive parents (Boyle, 2017).

Adopted children do tend to have more psychological and academic difficulties than non-adopted children, but these differences are small, and most adopted children fall within the normal range of development (Palacios & Brodzinsky, 2010; Haugaard, 1998). Younger children, especially those adopted in infancy, are least likely to have adjustment problems (Julian, 2013; Sharma et al., 1996). Any problems that do occur may surface during middle childhood, when children become more aware of differences in the way families are formed (Freeark et al., 2005), or in adolescence (Goodman et al., 1998; Sharma et al., 1996), particularly among boys (Freeark et al., 2005) and international adoptees (Juffer et al., 2011).

Before the 1960s, most adopted children in the United States were healthy, white infants, adopted as newborns and surrendered by unmarried teen mothers. Adoption rates for children born to women of color were extremely low. In the 1960s a variety of social and economic changes, including the growing acceptance of single motherhood and the rise of social support programs, led to an increase in the number of women who kept their babies. Additionally, the growing availability of birth control and the legalization of abortion led to a decrease in unintentional pregnancies. These changes resulted in fewer white babies available for adoption (Brodzinsky & Pinderhughes, 2002). About 48 percent of adopted children are non-Hispanic white. The majority of other adopted children are Black (19.1 percent) or Hispanic (21.7 percent) (Children's Bureau, 2018). Transracial adoptions, where at least one parent is of a different race than the child, are common and comprise about 40 percent of adoptions (Vandivere et al., 2009).

Changes in adoption protocols making it more difficult for Americans to adopt children from different countries have resulted in a steady decline in international adoptions. In 2016, 5,370 children were adopted from foreign countries, a drop of 77 percent from the peak in 2004 (Budiman & Lopez, 2017).

Does foreign adoption entail special problems? Aside from the possibility of malnourishment or medical conditions in children from developing countries (Bosch et al., 2003), a number of studies find no significant problems with the children's psychological adjustment, school adjustment, and performance (Palacios & Brodzinsky, 2010). When foreign adoptees reach adolescence, they may experience feelings of loss of their native culture and growing awareness of racism and discrimination in their adopted culture. Parents who expose their adopted children to experiences that help them identify with their native culture and speak with their children about racism and discrimination may help buffer adopted children from negative effects (Lee et al., 2006).

SIBLING RELATIONSHIPS

In remote rural areas of Asia, Africa, Oceania, and Central and South America, it is common to see older girls caring for three or four younger siblings (Cicirelli, 1994). This pattern is also seen in recent immigrants to industrialized societies such as the United States (Hafford, 2010). However, in most industrialized societies, parents generally try not to "burden" older children with the regular care of siblings (Weisner, 1993).

Sibling relations have both positive and negative aspects to them. Having a warm and supportive sibling relationship is associated with better adjustment, social competence, prosocial behavior, and empathy. In part, this is the result of conflict in the relationship. Although generally perceived as negative, conflict can nonetheless be a laboratory for conflict resolution. Through these conflicts, siblings learn about others' points of view, negotiation, and problem solving (McHale et al., 2012).

However, sibling conflict is not always beneficial. High sibling conflict has been associated with internalizing (e.g., depression and anxiety) and externalizing (e.g., delinquency and aggression) problems as well as risky behaviors (Buist et al., 2013; Solmeyer et al., 2012). Siblings can also exert a negative effect via modeling antisocial actions, introducing

In many nonindustrialized cultures, children routinely care for their younger siblings. imageBROKER/Alamy Stock Photo

undesirable behaviors to younger siblings, or encouraging antisocial acts or collusion against parents (McHale et al., 2012). For example, when older siblings use drugs or alcohol, or engage in early sexual activity, their younger siblings are more likely to do so as well (Low et al., 2012; McHale et al., 2009). Interestingly, there is also another side to the positive effects of sibling warmth. In the presence of antisocial behaviors, sibling warmth can actually be a risk factor (McHale et al., 2009). For example, an older teen who is abusing substances might be more likely to introduce those substances to a sibling he is close to than to one he is not.

Sibling conflict and warmth are direct influences. Siblings also influence each other indirectly, through their impact on each other's relationship with their parents. Parents' experience with an older sibling influences their expectations and treatment of a younger one (Brody, 2004). And behavior patterns a child establishes with parents tend to spill over into the child's behavior with siblings. When a parent-child relationship is warm and affectionate, siblings tend to have positive relationships as well. When the parent-child relationship is conflictual, sibling conflict is more likely (Pike et al., 2005).

Peer Influences

How does the peer group influence children? What determines acceptance by peers and the ability to make friends?

POSITIVE AND NEGATIVE PEER INFLUENCES

As children begin to move away from parental influence, the peer group opens new perspectives. The peer group helps children learn how to adjust their needs and desires to those of others, when to yield, and when to stand firm. Within the context of peer groups, children develop skills needed for sociability and intimacy, and they gain a sense of belonging and identity.

The peer group can sometimes foster antisocial tendencies. Although some degree of conformity to group standards is healthy, it is unhealthy when it becomes destructive or prompts young people to act against their better judgment. It is usually in the company of peers that some children shoplift and begin to use drugs (Dishion & Tipsord, 2011; Hartup, 1992).

Unfortunately, peer groups may reinforce **prejudice:** unfavorable attitudes toward outsiders, especially members of certain racial or ethnic groups. Children tend to be biased toward children like themselves. These biases peak at about 5 to 7 years of age and then decrease through late childhood. As children move into adolescence, social context and what children learn from others seem to matter more (Raabe & Beelmann, 2011).

Children can be negatively affected by discrimination. The perception of being discriminated against has been linked to reductions in well-being, self-esteem, and life satisfaction, and increases in anxiety, depression, and negative mood (Schmitt et al., 2014). However, prejudice is not inevitable. In one study, the degree of bias toward immigrants was related to whether the adolescents in the study had immigrant friends. Those who did were more tolerant of differences and showed less bias toward immigrants (van Zalk & Kerr, 2014). Group norms also matter. Children whose social groups or schools have a norm of inclusion are less likely to show prejudiced behavior (Nesdale, 2011; Tropp et al., 2014). Intervention programs, including extended contact and the promotion of empathy and perspective-taking, have been moderately successful at reducing prejudice (Beelmann & Heinemann, 2014).

GENDER AND PEER GROUPS

Boys' and girls' peer groups engage in different types of activities. Boys play in large groups with well-defined leadership hierarchies, engage in more competitive and rough-and-tumble play, and more consistently pursue gender-typed activities. Girls have more intimate conversations characterized by prosocial interactions, cooperation, and shared confidences (Rose & Smith, 2018).

prejudice
Unfavorable attitude toward members of certain groups outside one's own, especially racial or ethnic groups.

Boys and girls also prefer different characteristics in friends. Boys report liking friends high in positive affect and low in anxiety and are not overly concerned with how empathic their friends are. Girls, by contrast, prefer friends high in empathy and optimism, but lower in positive affect (Oberle et al., 2010).

Why do children segregate themselves by sex and engage in such different activities? One of the most clearly identified reasons is because of boys' higher activity levels and more vigorous play (Pellegrini & Archer, 2005). However, another reason may be that same-sex peer groups help children learn gender-appropriate behaviors and incorporate gender roles into their self-concept. A sense of being typical of one's gender and being content with that gender increases self-esteem and well-being, whereas feeling pressure—from parents, oneself, or, in this case, peers—to conform to gender stereotypes lessens well-being (Yunger et al., 2004)

POPULARITY

Much of research in child development depends on asking children the right questions in the right way. If a researcher asked schoolchildren to tell her the social ranking of all the children in a classroom, she would most likely be met with a blank stare. However, children can easily say who they like to play with, who they like the most, or who they think other kids like the most. This is known as a *positive nomination.*

Children can also easily describe which children they don't like to play with, like the least, or think other kids don't like—this is a *negative nomination.* By asking these types of questions of every child in a classroom, a researcher can use the aggregated responses to get an overall score, or tally, for each child. The tally may be composed of positive nominations, negative nominations, or no nominations. This measure is known as *sociometric popularity.*

Sociometrically *popular* children receive many positive nominations and few negative nominations. They generally have good cognitive abilities, are high achievers, are good at solving social problems, are kind and help other children, are assertive without being disruptive or aggressive, and have good theory-of-mind skills. Their superior social skills make others enjoy being with them (Cillessen & Mayeux, 2004; LaFontana & Cillessen, 2002; Slaughter et al., 2015)

Children can be unpopular in one of two ways. Some children are *rejected,* and they receive a large number of negative nominations. Other children are *neglected* and receive few nominations of any kind. Some unpopular children are aggressive; others are hyperactive, inattentive, or withdrawn (Dodge et al., 1990; LaFontana & Cillessen, 2002; McDonald & Gibson, 2017). Still others act silly and immature or anxious and uncertain. Unpopular children are often insensitive to other children's feelings and do not adapt well to new situations (Bierman et al., 1993).

Other children can be *average* in their ratings and do not receive an unusual number of either positive or negative nominations. Finally, some children are *controversial* and receive many positive and negative nominations, indicating that some children like them a great deal and some dislike them a great deal. Less is known about outcomes related to average and controversial sociometric categories.

Popularity is important in middle childhood. Schoolchildren whose peers like them are likely to be well adjusted as adolescents. Those who have trouble getting along with peers are more likely to develop psychological problems, drop out of school, or become delinquent (Dishion & Tipsord, 2011; Mrug et al., 2012; Hartup, 1992). Peer rejection has also been linked to lower levels of classroom participation and low academic achievement (Ladd et al., 2008; Wentzel & Muenks, 2016).

FRIENDSHIP

Children look for friends who are like them in age, sex, activity level, and interests (McDonald et al., 2013; Macdonald-Wallis et al., 2011). The strongest friendships involve equal commitment and mutual give-and-take. Though children tend to choose friends with similar ethnic backgrounds, cross-racial/ethnic friendships are associated with positive developmental outcomes (Kawabata & Crick, 2008).

With their friends, children learn to communicate and cooperate. They help each other weather stressful situations, such as starting at a new school or adjusting to parents' divorce. The inevitable quarrels help children learn to resolve conflicts. In short, friendships are a means by which children practice and hone social interaction skills (Glick & Rose, 2011; Newcomb & Bagwell, 1995).

Children's concepts of friendship and the ways they act with their friends change with age, reflecting cognitive and emotional growth. Preschool friends play together and have preferred playmates, but they are not friends in the same sense that older children are. Children cannot be or have true friends until they achieve the cognitive maturity to consider other people's views and needs as well as their own (Dodge et al., 2006; Hartup & Stevens, 1999). On the basis of interviews with people between the ages of 3 and 45, Robert Selman (1980; Selman & Selman, 1979) traced changing conceptions of friendship across development (Table 10.1).

AGGRESSION

Aggression declines and changes in form during the early school years. After age 6 or 7, most children become less aggressive as they grow less egocentric, more empathic, more cooperative, and better able to communicate. They can now put themselves in someone else's place, can understand another person's motives, and can find positive ways of asserting themselves. *Instrumental aggression*, aggression aimed at achieving an objective, becomes much less common. However, as aggression declines overall, *hostile aggression*, aggression intended to hurt another person, increases (Dodge et al., 2006), often taking verbal rather than physical form (Pellegrini & Archer, 2005). Boys continue to engage in more *direct aggression*, and girls are increasingly more likely to engage in *social* or *relational aggression*, although some researchers argue the differences have been overstated (Card et al., 2008).

Aggression may also be characterized as either being *instrumental*, or *proactive*, or as being *hostile*, or *reactive*. Proactive aggressors view force and coercion as effective ways to get what they want. For example, such a child might learn that he can force another child to trade lunch items with him by threatening to hit the other child. If that strategy works, the child has been reinforced for his aggressive acts. Children who are reactive aggressors,

TABLE 10.1 Selman's Stages of Friendship		
Stage	**Description**	**Example**
Stage 0: Momentary playmateship (ages 3 to 7)	In the *undifferentiated* level, children define their friends by physical closeness and value them for material or physical attributes.	"She lives on my street and has a big yard to run in" or "He has the Power Rangers."
Stage 1: One-way assistance (ages 4 to 9)	In the *unilateral* level, a "good friend" does what the child wants the friend to do.	"She's not my friend anymore, because she wouldn't do what I said" or "He's my friend because he always let me borrow his toys."
Stage 2: Two-way fair-weather cooperation (ages 6 to 12)	The *reciprocal* level involves give-and-take but still serves many separate self-interests, rather than the common interests of the two friends.	"We are friends; we do things for each other" or "A friend is someone who plays with you when you don't have anybody else to play with."
Stage 3: Intimate, mutually shared relationships (ages 9 to 15)	In the *mutual* level, children view a friendship as a committed relationship. Friends become possessive and demand exclusivity.	"It takes a long time to make a close friend, so you feel bad if you find out that your friend is trying to make other friends too."
Stage 4: Autonomous interdependence (beginning at age 12)	In this *interdependent stage,* children respect friends' needs for both dependency and autonomy.	"A good friendship is a risk you have to take; you have to support and trust and give, but you have to be able to let go too."

Sources: Selman, R. L. (1980). *The growth of interpersonal understanding: Developmental and clinical analyses.* New York, NY: Academic Press, 1980. Selman, R. L., & Selman, A. P. (1979, April). Children's ideas about friendship: A new theory. *Psychology Today,* 71–80.

by contrast, respond to provocation in a hostile manner. Such a child might, after being accidentally pushed by someone in the lunch line, assume that the bump was on purpose and push back angrily. Children who habitually assume the worst of others in situations such as these are said to have a **hostile attribution bias.** They quickly conclude, in ambiguous situations, that others were acting with ill intent and are likely to strike out in retaliation or self-defense. Generally, other children then respond to this hostility with aggression, thereby confirming the original hostile attributional bias and strengthening it (Crick & Dodge, 1996; de Castro et al., 2002). Because people often *do* become hostile toward someone who acts aggressively toward them, a hostile bias may become a self-fulfilling prophecy, setting in motion a cycle of aggression (de Castro et al., 2002).

Generally, aggressive children are not liked and aggression is associated with worse outcomes. For example, overt aggression in boys and relational aggression in girls are both related to social problems with peers (Preddy & Fite, 2012). School-age boys who are physically aggressive may become juvenile delinquents in adolescence (Hay et al., 2017). Children who are high in both physical aggression and indirect relational aggression are at higher risk for depression, delinquency, and narcissism in early adulthood (Cleverley et al., 2012; Ehrenreich et al., 2016).

However, it has been argued that aggression is not always a predictor for negative outcomes, and at times may be adaptive (Little et al., 2007). For instance, although children high in physical aggression are generally disliked, physically aggressive children sometimes can attain higher social status as they get older (Garandeau et al., 2011; Cillessen & Mayeux, 2004). Similarly, relationally aggressive girls are generally not well liked by other girls; however, as they approach adolescence, relational aggression becomes associated with increases in popularity, especially with boys (Smith et al., 2010; Cillessen & Rose, 2005).

Aggressive boys tend to gain in social status by the end of fifth grade, suggesting that bullying behavior may be seen as cool or glamorous by preadolescents. Design Pics Inc/Alamy Stock Photo

hostile attribution bias
Tendency to perceive others as trying to hurt one and to strike out in retaliation or self-defense.

The Influence of Media Violence on Aggression Children spend more time on entertainment media than on any other activities except school and sleeping. On average, children spend more than 7 hours a day in front of a television or computer screen (Anderson et al., 2015).

Violence is prevalent in U.S. media. In one study, even in shows rated for children 7 years of age and younger, violence was featured in over 70 percent of episodes (Gabrielli et al., 2016). Approximately 15 percent of music videos feature physical aggression (Smith & Boyson, 2002) and disproportionately feature violence against women and Blacks. The motion picture, music, and video game industries aggressively market violent, adult-rated products to children (AAP Committee on Public Education, 2009).

Evidence from research conducted over the past 60 years on exposure to violence on TV, movies, and video games supports a causal relationship between media violence and violent behavior on the viewer's part. Exposure to violent media has been demonstrated to increase aggressive thoughts, feelings and behaviors, physiological arousal, hostile attributions, and to desensitize children to violence. Violent media also decrease empathy and prosocial behavior (Anderson et al., 2017). Highly aggressive children are more strongly affected by media violence than are less aggressive children (Anderson et al., 2003).

Approximately 92 percent of American children play video games (Gentile, 2011). Some psychologists have argued that long-term increases in violent behavior could be even greater for video games than for TV and movies. Players of violent games are active participants who receive positive reinforcement for violent actions (Huesmann, 2007). Cross-cultural research has shown violent video game players show less prosocial behavior and empathy, more aggressive behaviors, feelings and thoughts, physiological arousal and stress response, hostile appraisals, desensitization to violence, and they are more likely to respond violently

Researchers disagree on how much of an influence violent video games have on real-world behavior. Andrey Popov/Shutterstock

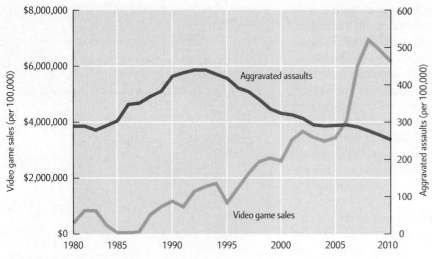

FIGURE 10.2

Annual Changes in Video Game Sales and Aggravated Assaults, 1978 to 2011.

Some researchers question the link between video games and violence, pointing out, for example, that video game sales have risen as assault and other violent crimes have fallen.

Source: Data from Markey, P. M., Markey, C. N., & French, J. E. (2015). Violent video games and real-world violence: Rhetoric versus data. *Psychology of Popular Media Culture, 4*(4), 277.

to provocation (Anderson et al., 2017; Ferguson, 2015; Gentile et al., 2017).

Although the majority of researchers endorse the link between viewing violence and aggression (Bushman et al., 2015), some believe the link between media violence and aggression may have been overstated (Ferguson, 2013). For example, some researchers argue that methodological flaws such as a failure to consider confounding variables, difficulty generalizing from laboratory studies of aggression to real-world aggressive acts, and inappropriate statistical modeling call into question some of the claims (Ferguson & Savage, 2012). In support of this assertion are data indicating that youth violence has declined even though exposure to violent media has remained stable (Ferguson, 2013) and video game consumption is inversely related to youth violence (Figure 10.2; Ferguson, 2015).

Recent experimental evidence casts even greater doubt on the existence of a direct causal relationship between the electronically mediated aggression in video games and aggression in the real world. In this study, 275 male undergraduates played one of two video games. One version was a violent first-person shooter game, the second a closely matched nonviolent version in which booger monsters needed to be sent back to their home dimension. Following the game, participants were provoked in real life by a confederate and given the chance to respond aggressively. The researchers did not find an effect for video game violence. In other words, violence within the context of the video game did not translate, at least in the short term, into real-world behavior (Hilgard et al., 2019).

However, this does not mean that children should be allowed to watch violent content without limits or that modeling of aggression across all media has no effects. Media-induced aggressiveness can be minimized by cutting down on television use and by parental monitoring and guidance of the shows children watch (Anderson et al., 2003). Additionally, just as viewing violent media promotes aggression, viewing media that promotes messages of empathy and helping promotes prosocial behavior in children (Anderson et al., 2015).

bullying
Aggression deliberately and persistently directed against a particular target, or victim, typically one who is weak, vulnerable, and defenseless.

Bullies and Victims Aggression becomes **bullying** when it is deliberately, persistently directed against a particular target: a victim (Window on the World). Bullying can be physical (hitting, punching, kicking, or damaging or taking of personal belongings), verbal (name-calling or threatening), or relational or emotional (isolating and gossiping, often behind the victim's back). Bullying can be *proactive*—done to show dominance, bolster power, or win admiration—or *reactive,* responding to a real or imagined attack. Bullying can also take the form of *cyberbullying*—such as posting negative comments or derogatory photos of the victim on a website.

Bullying may reflect a genetic tendency toward aggressiveness combined with environmental influences, such as coercive parents and antisocial friends (Berger, 2007). Bullies also tend to be low in empathy, especially with respect to the ability to experience the emotions that other people are feeling, or the affective component of empathy (Fink et al., 2015). Both bullies and victims tend to be deficient in social problem-solving skills, and those who also have academic problems are more likely to be bullies than victims (Cook

window on the world

BULLYING: A WORLDWIDE PROBLEM

In the United States, 28 percent of U.S. students in grades 6 to 12 report having been bullied in their schools (U.S. Department of Health and Human Services, 2014). How does this compare to other countries? In a global status report UNESCO (2019) collected data on bullying prevalence rates across a number of countries. Globally, 32 percent of children report being bullied in the previous month, although numbers vary by region. For example, high levels of bullying are reported by children in sub-Saharan Africa (48.2 percent), North Africa (42.7 percent), and the Middle East (41.1 percent). By contrast, bullying occurs less frequently in Centra America (22.8 percent), Europe (25 percent), and the Caribbean (25 percent). Cyberbullying is reported by about 8 percent of children globally.

Risk factors for victimization seem to be similar across cultures (Schwartz et al., 2001). Victims do not fit in. They tend to be anxious, depressed, cautious, quiet, and submissive and to cry easily, or to be argumentative and provocative (Hodges et al., 1999; Veenstra et al., 2005). Some victims are small, passive, weak, and submissive and may blame themselves for being bullied. Other victims are provocative; they goad their attackers, and they may even attack other children themselves (Berger, 2007; Veenstra

et al., 2005). Physical appearance is a common target for bullies, and children who are overweight are more likely to become victims. Disabilities, too, confer a higher risk. Girls and boys are equally likely to be bullied, and children who are sexually nonconforming are at higher risk. Bullying based on race, nationality, and color is also common (UNESCO, 2019).

Bullying and unsafe environments create a climate of fear and insecurity that can lead to negative developmental outcomes. Cross-cultural research conducted with adults in 30 European countries indicated that those adults who had been bullied as children showed lower life satisfaction (29 percent) than those who had not been bullied (40 percent) (UNESCO, 2017). Health promotion and prevention strategies need to address bullying problems to make the world safer for all.

what's **your view**

There are wide disparities in bullying rates across countries. What do you think some relevant country-level variables might be? Do you think culture might also impact which characteristics put children at risk of being bullying?

et al., 2010). Most bullies are boys who tend to victimize other boys; female bullies tend to target other girls (Berger, 2007; Pellegrini & Long, 2002; Veenstra et al., 2005).

Patterns of bullying and victimization may become established as early as kindergarten; as tentative peer groups form, aggressors soon get to know which children make the easiest targets. The frequency of bullying increases from elementary school to middle school before declining again in high school (Hong & Espelage, 2012). Although overall, boys cyberbully at higher levels than do girls, girls engage in more cyberbullying in early to midadolescence, while boys' cyberbullying peaks somewhat later (Barlett & Coyne, 2014).

Bullying, especially emotional bullying, is harmful to both bullies and victims (Berger, 2007). Both bullies and victims tend to have conduct problems and lower academic achievement. Bullies are at increased risk of delinquency, crime, or alcohol abuse (Golmaryami et al., 2016; Shetgiri et al., 2015). They are also more likely be diagnosed with anxiety or depression (Turcotte et al., 2015). Victims of chronic bullying tend to develop behavior problems. They may become more aggressive themselves or may become depressed (Schwartz et al., 1998; Veenstra et al., 2005). Furthermore, frequent bullying affects the school atmosphere, leading to widespread underachievement, alienation from school, stomachaches and headaches, reluctance to go to school, and frequent absences (Berger, 2007).

As more and more children gained access to electronic devices and participated in social media at younger and younger ages (Kowalski et al., 2014), there was a concurrent rise in cyberbullying. The yearly prevalence of cyberbullying is initially relatively low in primary public school students (5 percent), although it increases with age and peaks in middle school students at 33 percent before declining slightly in high school (Centers for Disease Control and Prevention, 2019). Research suggests that cyberbullying is often an extension of face-to-face bullying, as cyberbullies also tend to engage in aggressive acts in person as well as online (Modecki et al., 2014; Kowalski et al., 2014). Being a victim of cyberbullying is associated with a wealth of mental health and academic issues, and, for some children, an elevated risk of suicidal ideation and suicide (Van Geel et al., 2014).

The U.S. Department of Health and Human Services has promoted Steps to Respect, a program for grades 3 to 6 that aims to (1) increase staff awareness and responsiveness to bullying, (2) teach students social and emotional skills, and (3) foster socially responsible beliefs. Some research has found less physical bullying, better student climate, and a reduction in school bullying problems in schools that implemented the program (Brown et al., 2011). However, other data have indicated the impact on actual bullying behavior is minimal although the programs may enhance students' social competence and self-esteem (Merrell et al., 2008).

Mental Health

Let's look at several common emotional disturbances and then at types of treatment.

COMMON EMOTIONAL PROBLEMS

Estimates for the prevalence rate of mental health disorders in the United States range from 13 to 20 percent, and there are suggestions that this rate may be increasing (Perou et al., 2013). Unfortunately, only 53.5 percent of children with a conduct or behavioral disorder, 59.3 percent of children with an anxiety disorder, and about 80 percent of children with depression receive the help they need (Ghandour et al., 2019).

Disruptive Conduct Disorders Temper tantrums and defiant, argumentative, hostile, or deliberately annoying behavior—common among 4- and 5-year-olds—typically are outgrown by middle childhood as children get better at controlling these behaviors (Miner & Clarke-Stewart, 2009). When such a pattern of behavior persists until age 8, children (usually boys) may be diagnosed with **oppositional defiant disorder (ODD),** a pattern of defiance, disobedience, and hostility toward adult authority figures lasting at least 6 months and going beyond the bounds of normal childhood behavior. Children with ODD constantly fight, argue, lose their temper, snatch things, blame others, and are angry and resentful. They are spiteful and deliberately annoy others. They have few friends, are in constant trouble in school, and test the limits of adults' patience (Matthys & John, 2017).

Some children with ODD may later be diagnosed with **conduct disorder (CD),** a persistent, repetitive pattern, beginning at an early age, of aggressive, antisocial acts, such as truancy, setting fires, habitual lying, fighting, bullying, theft, vandalism, assaults, and drug and alcohol use (Matthys & John, 2017). About 7.4 percent of American children age 3 to 17 years currently have a conduct disorder, with boys (10.1 percent) at higher risk than girls (4.5 percent) (Ghandour et al., 2019). Conduct disorder in childhood is strongly predictive of antisocial and criminal behavior in adulthood (Mordre et al., 2011).

There are indications that children with conduct disorders have neurological deficits that affect their ability to feel empathy for others, leading to a characteristic callous unemotionality (Lockwood et al., 2013; Michalska et al., 2016). Such deficits may be genetically influenced or may be brought on by adverse environments such as hostile parenting or family conflict, or both (van Goozen et al., 2007; Miner & Clarke-Stewart, 2009). Also influential are stressful life events and association with deviant peers (Roosa et al., 2005; Murray & Farrington, 2010).

Anxiety Disorders About 7.1 percent of children aged 3 to 17 have an anxiety disorder, with slightly more girls (7.3 percent) than boys (6.9 percent) diagnosed. One in 3 of children with an anxiety disorder also suffers from depression (Ghandour et al., 2019).

oppositional defiant disorder (ODD)
Pattern of behavior, persisting into middle childhood, marked by negativity, hostility, and defiance.

conduct disorder (CD)
Repetitive, persistent pattern of aggressive, antisocial behavior violating societal norms or the rights of others.

Some children have **school phobia,** an unrealistic fear of going to school. True school phobia may be a type of **separation anxiety disorder,** a condition involving excessive anxiety for at least 4 weeks concerning separation from home or from people to whom the child is attached. Although separation anxiety is normal in infancy, it is cause for concern when it persists in older children. Separation anxiety disorder affects some 4 percent of children and young adolescents. These children often come from close-knit, caring families. They may develop the disorder spontaneously or after a stressful event, such as the death of a pet, an illness, or a move to a new school (American Psychiatric Association, 2000; Harvard Medical School, 2004).

Sometimes school phobia may be a form of **social phobia,** or *social anxiety:* extreme fear and/or avoidance of social situations such as speaking in class or meeting an acquaintance on the street. Social phobia affects about 5 percent of children. It runs in families, suggesting a genetic component (Beidel & Turner, 1998). Social anxiety tends to increase with age, whereas separation anxiety decreases (Costello et al., 2003).

Some children have a **generalized anxiety disorder,** not focused on any specific part of their lives. These children worry about almost everything: school grades, storms, earthquakes, and hurting themselves on the playground. They tend to be self-conscious, self-doubting, and excessively concerned with meeting the expectations of others. They seek approval and need constant reassurance, but their worry seems independent of performance or of how they are regarded by others (Harvard Medical School, 2004).

Far less common is **obsessive-compulsive disorder (OCD).** Children with this disorder may be obsessed by repetitive, intrusive thoughts, images, or impulses (often involving irrational fears), or they may show compulsive behaviors, such as constant hand-washing, or both (American Psychiatric Association, 2000; Harvard Medical School, 2004).

Childhood Depression **Childhood depression** is a disorder of mood that goes beyond normal, temporary sadness. Depression is estimated to occur in approximately 3.2 percent of children. As with anxiety disorders, girls (3.3 percent) are slightly more likely to be affected than boys (3 percent) (Ghandour et al., 2019).

Symptoms include inability to have fun or concentrate, fatigue, extreme activity or apathy, crying, sleep problems, weight change, physical complaints, feelings of worthlessness, a prolonged sense of friendlessness, or frequent thoughts about death or suicide. Childhood depression may signal the beginning of a recurrent problem that is likely to persist into adulthood (Kovacs et al., 2016).

The exact causes of childhood depression are determined by multiple factors, but depressed children tend to come from families with high levels of parental depression, anxiety, substance abuse, or antisocial behavior. The children themselves are also frequently anxious, have poor impulse control, and poor peer relationships (Bufferd et al., 2014). Researchers have also found specific genes related to depression (Aguilera et al., 2009).

Children as young as 5 or 6 can accurately report depressed moods and feelings that forecast later trouble, from academic problems to major depression and ideas of suicide (Ialongo et al., 2001). Depression often emerges during the transition to middle school and may be related to stiffer academic pressures (Cicchetti & Toth, 1998), weak self-efficacy beliefs, and lack of personal investment in academic success (Rudolph et al., 2001). Depression becomes more prevalent during adolescence.

The Influence of COVID-19 on Child Mental Health Worldwide, the prevalence rate of mental disorders in children and adolescents had previously been estimated to be approximately 13.4 percent (Polancyzk et al., 2015). The advent of the novel coronavirus COVID-19 might be expected to influence this number for a variety of reasons. In many countries, the pandemic led to widespread lockdowns. Families were asked to isolate in their homes and businesses shuttered. Some children experienced the hospitalization or death of loved ones, or were themselves hospitalized. The coronavirus also led to the closing of schools, with approximately 80 percent of school-aged children across the globe affected (Van Lancker & Parolin, 2020).

school phobia
Unrealistic fear of going to school; may be a form of *separation anxiety disorder* or *social phobia.*

separation anxiety disorder
Condition involving excessive, prolonged anxiety concerning separation from home or from people to whom a person is attached.

social phobia
Extreme fear and/or avoidance of social situations.

generalized anxiety disorder
Anxiety not focused on any single target.

obsessive-compulsive disorder (OCD)
Anxiety aroused by repetitive, intrusive thoughts, images, or impulses, often leading to compulsive ritual behaviors.

childhood depression
Mood disorder characterized by such symptoms as a prolonged sense of friendlessness, inability to have fun or concentrate, fatigue, extreme activity or apathy, feelings of worthlessness, weight change, physical complaints, and thoughts of death or suicide.

research in action

CHILDREN'S RESPONSES TO TRAUMA

Globally, up to 1 billion children experience physical, sexual, or emotional violence and neglect each year (World Health Organization, 2019). Some children will experience maltreatment within the family home. Others will experience terrorism or war acts, or may be worried about or experience school shootings. Some will live through natural disasters. Still others will be separated from loved family members. All of these experiences run the risk of traumatizing children and putting them at risk for the development of anxiety or depressive disorders and post-traumatic stress disorder (PTSD), or negatively affecting their developing competencies.

Children are more susceptible than adults to psychological harm from a traumatic event such as war or terrorism, and their reactions vary with age (Garbarino et al., 2015; Wexler et al., 2006). The impact of a traumatic event is influenced by the type of event, how much exposure children have to it, and how much they and their families and friends are personally affected. Human-caused disasters, such as terrorism and war, are harder on children psychologically than natural disasters, such as earthquakes and floods. Compared to natural disasters, terrorist events have been associated with higher levels of distress (Hagan et al., 2005), and the intermittent and unpredictable nature of these attacks may contribute to heightened stress and anxiety levels that continue long after the event (Fremont, 2004).

Children's responses to trauma across different cultures are similar (Navarro et al., 2016). Children exposed to trauma have been reported to show elevated post-traumatic stress symptoms for months afterward (Comer et al., 2016). Symptoms are often commensurate with direct threat to life, loss of loved ones, and local community devastation (Drury & Williams, 2012). Sleep disturbances, attention problems, headache and stomachache complaints, school avoidance, or irrational fears are also common responses (Saraiya et al., 2013).

Parents' responses to a violent event or disaster and the way they talk with a child about it strongly influence the child's ability to recover. Recommendations include being open to conversations with children to talk about and process the trauma. If children are young, drawing or playing with toys may be another option. Additionally, parents should honestly answer questions in age-appropriate language the child understands. Last, as much as possible, maintaining a regular routine provides consistency and familiarity for children and can help them feel safer (American Academy of Child and Adolescent Psychiatry (2017).

what's **your** **view**

What would you say to a child to soothe upset emotions and fears regarding trauma? How might you respond differently to a 6-year-old versus an 11-year-old who have questions about what happened?

Early research emerging from countries most strongly affected by COVID-19 illustrates the influence of the pandemic on children. For example, children in China, Italy and Spain subjected to quarantine were more likely to have difficulty concentrating and be fearful, anxious, clingy, agitated, restless, and lonely. Moreover, there were also behavioral changes. Children were less likely to be active. They also increased their screen time and slept more hours, although their sleep was more likely to be of poor quality (Orgilés et al., 2020; Jiao et al., 2020). In many cases, children were separated from ill parents or quarantined away from their families if they were found to be positive for COVID-19. Forced separation from parents is profoundly damaging to children. In the short term, it can result in the development of PTSD (Rojas-Flores et al., 2017; see Research in Action for responses to trauma). In the long term, forced separation can result in lifelong negative effects on physical and mental health (Putnam et al., 2013).

Parents can help their children manage their stress and anxiety by talking to them about COVID-19 in simple, concrete terms they can understand. A regular routine with a variety of indoor activities is also helpful. Allowing children the opportunity to maintain ties with peers electronically is also important, although monitoring their consumption of electronic media is advised so they do not gain access to false or frightening information. Counseling or therapy may also be needed for some children (Bahn, 2020).

TREATMENT FOR EMOTIONAL DISTURBANCES

Psychological treatment for emotional disturbances can take several forms. In **individual psychotherapy,** a therapist sees a child one-on-one to help the child gain insights into his or her personality and relationships and to interpret feelings and behavior. Such treatment may be helpful at a time of stress, such as the death of a parent or parental divorce.

In **family therapy,** the therapist sees the family together, observes how members interact, and points out healthy and destructive patterns of family functioning. Therapy can help parents confront their conflicts and begin to resolve them. This is often the first step toward resolving the child's problems as well.

Behavior therapy, or *behavior modification,* uses principles of learning theory to eliminate undesirable behaviors or to develop desirable ones. Behavior therapy is more effective than nonbehavioral methods, and results are best when treatment is targeted to specific problems and desired outcomes (Weisz et al., 1995). *Cognitive-behavioral therapy,* which seeks to change negative thoughts through gradual exposure, modeling, rewards, or talking to oneself, has proven the most effective treatment for anxiety disorders (Hofmann et al., 2012).

When children have limited verbal and conceptual skills or have suffered emotional trauma, **art therapy** can help them describe what is troubling them without the need to put their feelings into words. The child may express deep emotions through his or her choice of colors and subjects to depict (Kozlowska & Hanney, 1999). Art therapy has been demonstrated to be beneficial and is often used in conjunction with other forms of therapy (Slayton et al., 2010).

Play therapy, in which a child plays freely while a therapist occasionally comments, asks questions, or makes suggestions, has been shown to be effective with a variety of emotional, cognitive, and social problems, especially when consultation with parents or other close family members is part of the process (Lin & Bratton, 2015; Ray et al., 2015).

The use of **drug therapy**—antidepressants, stimulants, tranquilizers, or antipsychotic medications—to treat childhood emotional disorders is controversial. During the past two decades the rate at which antipsychotic medications are prescribed for children and adolescents has risen sharply and at a faster rate than for adults (Olfson et al., 2014). For example, from 1999 to 2001 approximately 1 in 650 children were receiving antipsychotic medications; this number rose to 1 in 329 for 2007 (Olfson et al., 2010). Sufficient research on the effectiveness and safety of many of these drugs, especially for children, is lacking.

RESILIENCE

Much of the early history of psychology was marked by investigations into the various risks that can pull a child into a negative developmental trajectory. However, psychologists have increasingly come to realize that there is also value in examining resilience. **Resilient children** are those who weather circumstances that might blight others, who maintain their composure and competence under challenge or threat, or who bounce back from traumatic events. The two most important **protective factors** that help children and adolescents overcome stress and contribute to resilience are *good family relationships* and *cognitive functioning* (Masten & Coatsworth, 1998).

Resilient children also tend to have high IQs and to be good problem solvers, and their cognitive ability may help them cope with adversity, protect themselves, regulate their behavior, and learn from experience. They may attract the interest of teachers, who can act as guides, confidants, or mentors (Masten & Coatsworth, 1998). They may even have protective genes, which may buffer the effects of an unfavorable environment (Caspi et al., 2002; Kim-Cohen et al., 2004).

In play therapy, the therapist observes as a child acts out troubled feelings, often using developmentally appropriate materials such as toy animals.
Photographee.eu/Shutterstock

individual psychotherapy
Psychological treatment in which a therapist sees a troubled person one-on-one.

family therapy
Psychological treatment in which a therapist sees the whole family together to analyze patterns of family functioning.

behavior therapy
Therapeutic approach using principles of learning theory to encourage desired behaviors or eliminate undesired ones; also called *behavior modification.*

art therapy
Therapeutic approach that allows a person to express troubled feelings without words, using a variety of art materials and media.

play therapy
Therapeutic approach that uses play to help a child cope with emotional distress.

drug therapy
Administration of drugs to treat emotional disorders.

resilient children
Children who weather adverse circumstances, function well despite challenges or threats, or bounce back from traumatic events.

protective factors
(1) Influences that reduce the impact of potentially negative influences and tend to predict positive outcomes. (2) Influences that reduce the impact of early stress and tend to predict positive outcomes.

Other frequently cited protective factors include the following (Ackerman et al., 1999; Eisenberg et al., 2004; Masten & Coatsworth, 1998; Werner, 1993):

- *The child's temperament or personality:* Resilient children are adaptable, friendly, well liked, independent, and sensitive to others. They are competent and have high self-esteem. When under stress, they can regulate their emotions well.

- *Compensating experiences:* A supportive school environment or successful experiences in studies, sports, or music or with other children or adults can help make up for a destructive home life.

- *Reduced risk:* Children who have been exposed to only one of a number of factors for psychiatric disorder (such as parental discord, a disturbed mother, a criminal father, and experience in foster care) are often better able to overcome stress than children who have been exposed to more than one risk factor.

This does not mean that bad things that happen in a child's life do not matter. In general, children with unfavorable backgrounds have more adjustment problems than children with more favorable backgrounds, and even some outwardly resilient children may suffer internal distress that may have long-term consequences (Masten & Coatsworth, 1998). Still, what is heartening about these findings is that negative childhood experiences do not necessarily determine the outcome of a person's life and that many children have the strength to rise above the most difficult circumstances.

summary and key terms

The Developing Self

- The self-concept becomes more realistic during middle childhood when children form representational systems.
- According to Erikson, the source of self-esteem is children's competence. This virtue develops through resolution of the fourth psychosocial conflict, industry versus inferiority.
- School-age children have internalized shame and pride and can better understand and regulate emotions.
- Empathy and prosocial behavior increase.
- Emotional growth is affected by parents' reactions to displays of negative emotions and involves effortful control
- Different cultures socialize emotions in ways that reflect important cultural ideals

representational systems, industry versus inferiority

Family Influences

- School-age children spend less time with parents and are less close to them than before, but relationships with parents continue to be important. Culture influences family relationships and roles.
- The family environment has two major components: family structure and family atmosphere.
- The emotional tone of the home, the way parents handle disciplinary issues and conflict, the effects of parents' work, and the adequacy of financial resources all contribute to family atmosphere.

- Development of coregulation may affect the way a family handles conflicts and discipline.
- The impact of mothers' employment depends on many factors.
- Poverty can harm children's development indirectly through its effects on parents' well-being and parenting practices.
- Many children today grow up in nontraditional family structures. Other things being equal, children tend to do better in continuously married two-parent families than in cohabiting, divorced, single-parent, or stepfamilies.
- Children's adjustment to divorce depends on factors concerning the child, the parents' handling of the situation, custody and visitation arrangements, financial circumstances, contact with the noncustodial parent (usually the father), and a parent's remarriage.
- The amount of conflict in a marriage and after divorce may influence whether children are better off if the parents stay together.
- In most divorces the mother gets custody, though paternal custody is a growing trend.
- Joint custody can be beneficial to children when the parents can cooperate. Joint legal custody is more common than joint physical custody.
- Although parental divorce increases the risk of long-term problems for children, most adjust reasonably well.

- Children living with only one parent are at heightened risk of behavioral and academic problems, largely related to socioeconomic status.
- Studies have found positive developmental outcomes in children living with gay or lesbian parents.
- Adopted children are generally well adjusted, though they face special challenges.
- The roles and responsibilities of siblings in nonindustrialized societies are more structured than in industrialized societies.
- Siblings learn about conflict resolution from their relationships with each other. Relationships with parents affect sibling relationships.

coregulation, internalizing behaviors, externalizing behaviors

The Child in the Peer Group

- The peer group becomes more important in middle childhood. Peer groups generally consist of children who are similar in age, sex, ethnicity, and socioeconomic status and who live near one another or go to school together.
- The peer group helps children develop social skills, allows them to test and adopt values independent of parents, gives them a sense of belonging, and helps develop their self-concept and gender identity. It also may encourage conformity and prejudice.
- Popularity in middle childhood tends to influence future adjustment. Popular children tend to have good cognitive abilities and social skills. Behaviors that affect popularity may be influenced by family relationships and cultural values.
- Intimacy and stability of friendships increase during middle childhood. Boys tend to have more friends, whereas girls tend to have closer friends.
- During middle childhood, aggression typically declines. Instrumental aggression generally gives way to hostile

aggression, often with a hostile bias. Highly physically aggressive children tend to be unpopular.
- Many researchers argue aggressiveness may be promoted by exposure to media violence although there is some controversy.
- Middle childhood is a prime time for bullying. Victims tend to be weak and submissive or argumentative and provocative and to have low self-esteem.

prejudice, hostile attribution bias, bullying

Mental Health

- Common emotional and behavioral disorders among school-age children include disruptive behavioral disorders, anxiety disorders, and childhood depression.
- COVID-19 has resulted in increased prevalence of mental health issues in children from highly affected countries. Parents can help by talking to children, providing structured indoor activities, and allowing children to maintain electronic contact with friends. Some children may need counseling or therapy.
- Treatment techniques include individual psychotherapy, family therapy, behavior therapy, art therapy, play therapy, and drug therapy. Often therapies are used in combination.
- Children may be traumatized by exposure to terrorism, war, or natural disasters.
- Resilient children are better able than others to withstand stress. Protective factors involve family relationships, cognitive ability, personality, degree of risk, and compensating experiences.

oppositional defiant disorder (ODD), conduct disorder (CD), school phobia, separation anxiety disorder, social phobia, generalized anxiety disorder, obsessive-compulsive disorder (OCD), childhood depression, individual psychotherapy, family therapy, behavior therapy, art therapy, play therapy, drug therapy, resilient children, protective factors

chapter **11**

Physical and Cognitive Development in Adolescence

learning objectives

Discuss the nature of adolescence.

Describe the changes involved in puberty, as well as the changes in the adolescent brain.

Identify adolescent problems related to health.

Explain cognitive changes in adolescence.

Summarize key aspects of how schools influence adolescent development.

FatCamera/E+/Getty Images

In this chapter, we describe the physical transformations of adolescence and how they affect young people's feelings. We look at the not-yet-mature adolescent brain and discuss health issues associated with this time of life. We examine the Piagetian stage of formal operations, information-processing skills, and linguistic and moral development. Finally, we explore educational and vocational issues.

Adolescence as a Social Construction

This chapter focuses on processes that occur in **adolescence**—a developmental transition that involves physical, cognitive, emotional, and social changes and takes varying forms in different social, cultural, and economic settings. In this book, we define adolescence roughly as encompassing the years between 11 and 20.

However, adolescence is not a clearly defined physical or biological category—it is a social construction. In traditional and preindustrial cultures, children generally entered the adult world when they matured physically or when they began a vocational apprenticeship. In the Western world, adolescence was first recognized as a unique period in the life span in the twentieth century. Today adolescence is recognized globally, but it may take different forms in different cultures.

In most parts of the world, adolescence lasts longer and is less clear-cut than in the past. There are myriad reasons for this social change. First, puberty generally begins earlier, which means the period of adolescence begins at a younger age than in the past. In addition, as the world becomes more driven by technology and information, the amount of training required to be eligible for higher-paying occupations has increased. Because of this, the period of adolescence has been extended upward as young adults tend to go to school for more years, delay marriage and childbirth, and settle into permanent careers later and less firmly than in the past.

adolescence
Developmental transition between childhood and adulthood entailing major physical, cognitive, and psychosocial changes.

Physical Development in Puberty

An important physical change in adolescence is the onset of **puberty,** the process that leads to sexual maturity, or fertility—the ability to reproduce. Puberty is part of a long, complex process of maturation that begins even before birth and has psychological ramifications that may continue into adulthood.

puberty
Process by which a person attains sexual maturity and the ability to reproduce.

HORMONAL CHANGES IN PUBERTY

The advent of puberty results from a cascade of hormonal responses (Figure 11.1). First, the hypothalamus releases elevated levels of gonadotropin-releasing hormone (GnRH). The increased GnRH then triggers a rise in lutenizing hormone (LH) and follicle-stimulating hormone (FSH). These hormones exert their actions differentially on boys and girls. In girls, increased levels of FSH lead to the onset of menstruation. In boys, LH initiates the release of two additional hormones: testosterone and androstenedione (Buck Louis et al., 2008).

Puberty can be broken down into two basic stages: adrenarche and gonadarche. Adrenarche occurs between ages 6 and 8. During this stage, the adrenal glands secrete increasing levels of androgens, most notably dehydroepiandrosterone (DHEA) (Susman & Rogol, 2004). Levels increase gradually but consistently, and by the time a child is 10 years of age, the levels of DHEA are 10 times what they were between ages 1 and 4. DHEA influences the growth of pubic, axillary (underarm), and facial hair. It also contributes to faster body growth, oilier skin, and the development of body odor.

The second stage, gonadarche, is marked by the maturing of the sex organs, which triggers a second burst of DHEA production (McClintock & Herdt, 1996). During this time, a girl's ovaries increase their input of estrogen, which in turn stimulates the growth of female genitals, breasts, and the development of pubic and underarm hair. In boys, the testes increase the production of androgens, especially testosterone. This increase leads to the growth of male genitals, muscle mass, and body hair.

TIMING AND SEQUENCE OF PUBERTY

A wide variation in age at puberty is normative, but puberty generally lasts 3 to 4 years and begins about age 8 in girls and age 9 in boys (Susman & Rogol, 2004).

Primary and Secondary Sex Characteristics The **primary sex characteristics** are the organs necessary for reproduction. In the female, the sex organs include the ovaries, fallopian

primary sex characteristics
Organs directly related to reproduction, which enlarge and mature during adolescence.

FIGURE 11.1
Regulation of Human Puberty Onset and Progression

HPG (hypothalamus-pituitary-gonadal) activation requires a signal from the central nervous system (CNS) to the hypothalamus, which stimulates the production of LH and FSH from the pituitary.

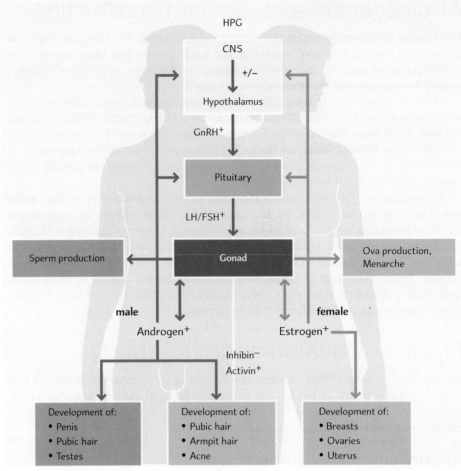

Source: Buck Louis, G., Gray, L., Marcus, M., Ojeda, S., Pescovitz, O., Witchel, S., . . . Euling, S. Y. Environmental factors and puberty timing: Expert panel research needs. *Pediatrics*, 121, 2008, S192–S207.

secondary sex characteristics
Physiological signs of sexual maturation (such as breast development and growth of body hair) that do not involve the sex organs.

tubes, uterus, clitoris, and vagina. In the male, they include the testes, penis, scrotum, seminal vesicles, and prostate gland. During puberty, these organs enlarge and mature.

The **secondary sex characteristics** are physiological signs of sexual maturation that do not directly involve the sex organs, for example, the breasts of females and the broad shoulders of males. Other secondary sex characteristics are changes in the voice and skin texture, muscular development, and the growth of pubic, facial, axillary, and body hair.

These changes unfold in a sequence that is much more consistent than their timing. One girl may develop breasts and body hair at about the same rate; in another girl, body hair may reach adultlike growth a year or so before breasts develop. Boys have similar variations in pubertal status.

Signs of Puberty The first external signs of puberty typically are breast tissue and pubic hair in girls and enlargement of the testes in boys (Susman & Rogol, 2004). A girl's nipples enlarge and protrude, the *areolae* (the pigmented areas surrounding the nipples) enlarge, and the breasts assume first a conical and then a rounded shape. Some adolescent boys experience breast enlargement; this development is normal and generally does not last longer than 18 months.

Pubic hair, at first straight and silky, eventually becomes coarse, dark, and curly. It appears in different patterns in males and females. Adolescent boys are usually happy to see hair on the face and chest, but girls are generally dismayed at the appearance of even a slight amount of hair on the face or around the nipples, though this, too, is normal.

The voice deepens, especially in boys, partly in response to the growth of the larynx and partly in response to the production of male hormones. The skin becomes coarser and oilier, giving rise to pimples and blackheads. Acne is more common in boys and seems related to increased amounts of testosterone.

The Adolescent Growth Spurt The **adolescent growth spurt**—a rapid increase in height, weight, and muscle and bone growth that occurs during puberty—generally begins in girls between ages 9½ and 14½ (usually at about 10) and in boys, between 10½ and 16 (usually at 12 or 13). It typically lasts about 2 years; soon after it ends, the young person reaches sexual maturity. Both growth hormone and the sex hormones (androgens and estrogens) contribute to this normal pubertal growth pattern (Susman & Rogol, 2004).

Because girls' growth spurt usually occurs 2 years earlier than that of boys, girls between ages 11 and 13 tend to be taller, heavier, and stronger than boys the same age. After their growth spurt, boys are again larger. Girls typically reach full height at age 15 and boys at age 17 (Gans, 1990).

Boys and girls also grow differently in form and shape. A boy becomes larger: his shoulders wider, his legs longer relative to his trunk, and his forearms longer relative to his upper arms and his height. A girl's pelvis widens to make childbearing easier, and layers of fat accumulate under her skin, giving her a more rounded appearance. Fat accumulates twice as rapidly in girls as in boys (Susman & Rogol, 2004).

Most girls experience a growth spurt 2 years earlier than most boys, so between ages 11 and 13 girls tend to be taller, heavier, and stronger than boys the same age. Justin Pumfrey/ The Image Bank/Getty Images

adolescent growth spurt
Sharp increase in height and weight that precedes sexual maturity.

Sexual Maturity The maturation of the reproductive organs brings the beginning of menstruation in girls and the production of sperm in boys. The principal sign of sexual maturity in boys is the production of sperm. The first ejaculation, or **spermarche,** occurs at an average age of 13. A boy may wake up to find a wet spot or a hardened, dried spot on the sheets—the result of a *nocturnal emission,* an involuntary ejaculation of semen (commonly referred to as a *wet dream*).

The principal sign of sexual maturity in girls is *menstruation,* a monthly shedding of tissue from the lining of the womb. The first menstruation, called **menarche,** occurs fairly late in the sequence of female development; its normal timing can vary from age 10 to 16½. Although menarche is a significant event, the reproductive system may not yet be functionally mature, as menstrual cycles may occur without ova, especially in very young girls (Eveleth, 2017).

spermarche
Boy's first ejaculation.

menarche
Girl's first menstruation.

Influences on Pubertal Timing Many studies have indicated that the start of puberty has shifted downward in the twentieth century (Papadimitriou, 2016). Developmental scientists call a pattern such as this a **secular trend**—a trend that spans several generations. The trend, which also involves increases in adult height and weight, began about 100 years ago. It has occurred in such places as the United States, Western Europe, and Japan (Anderson et al., 2003) with better evidence existing for girls than for boys (Papadimitriou, 2016; Euling et al., 2008). The age of puberty has declined as a whole for China and India as well; however, children from different regions or of different ethnicities vary widely in the age at which they hit puberty (Song et al., 2015; Pathak et al., 2014). This may not be the only change in pubertal processes; recent research indicates that there may be a compensatory delay in pubertal maturation that is associated with earlier puberty. In other words, children may be starting puberty earlier, but spending more time to reach full sexual maturity (Papadimitriou, 2016; Mendle, 2014).

One set of proposed explanations focuses on environmental factors that influence the pace of pubertal development, such as standard of living. Undernutrition, whether because of insufficient food supply or disease, has been associated with delayed onset of puberty and a reduced puberty growth spurt (Soliman et al., 2014). Alternatively, children who are healthier, better nourished, and better cared for might be expected to mature "on time" and grow bigger (Slyper, 2006). How much physical exertion children

secular trend
Trend that can be seen only by observing several generations, such as the trend toward earlier attainment of adult height and sexual maturity, which began a century ago in some countries.

engage in is also an influence, and puberty is delayed in environments in which children engage in high levels of physical activity (Soliman et al., 2014). Cross-cultural research has shown children from developed countries tend to be more physically active and less sedentary (Tremblay et al., 2014). Thus, because of both undernutrition and high physical activity level, the average age of sexual maturity tends to be later in developing countries than in developed countries.

In girls, reaching a critical amount of body fat is necessary for successful reproduction. Girls who have a higher percentage of body fat in early childhood tend to show earlier pubertal development. A contributing factor for the shift in pubertal timing in the United States during the last part of the twentieth century may have been the increase in obesity among young girls (Anderson et al., 2003; Lee et al., 2007). Increases in leptin, a hormone associated with obesity, appear to play a role in this process, as does kisspeptin, an antecedent hormone to GnRH. The degree of adipose (fat) tissue itself may also matter (Reinehr & Roth, 2019). Weight appears to influence pubertal timing differently in boys. In boys, having a high body mass index in childhood or being obese appears to delay puberty rather than accelerate it (Lee et al., 2010; Wang, 2002). Interestingly, recent research has found that being overweight, rather than either thin or obese, results in an earlier start to puberty in boys (Lee et al., 2016). More research is needed in this area.

Another environmental explanation focuses on exposure to endocrine-disrupting chemicals, such as those found in some plastics, flame retardants, and pesticides. Exposure to such substances can be related to earlier pubertal timing (Lee & Styne, 2013; Ozen & Darcan, 2011). Exposure may occur in utero or during childhood and adolescence, most commonly through foods and liquids or the inhalation of dust or sprays (Frye et al., 2012). Other toxins may also play a role. For example, studies have also shown that earlier menarche is associated with maternal smoking during pregnancy (Maisonet et al., 2010).

A variety of social factors also influence when puberty begins. For example, studies on maternal influences have shown that earlier menarche is associated with being the firstborn child (Maisonet et al., 2010) as well as being born to a single mother (Belsky et al., 2007; Ellis et al., 1999) and harsh maternal parenting practices (Belsky et al., 2010). Fathers also play a role. Girls with absent, distant, or conflictual relationships with their fathers tend to reach menarche earlier than girls with close supportive paternal relationships (Belsky et al., 2007; Mendle et al., 2006; Ellis et al., 1999; Tither & Ellis, 2008). The unifying theme in these influences is stress, which has been proposed to mediate the above associations. In other words, it is not being firstborn, or being born to a single mother, or having a conflictual relationship per se that influences puberty; rather, it is the presence or absence of high levels of stress. Those children who are exposed to high stress when young tend to reach pubertal milestones earlier than those who are not (Belsky et al., 2015; Ellis & Del Giudice, 2014; Bleil et al., 2013).

Another factor that influences timing of pubertal development is race and ethnicity. African American and Mexican American girls generally enter puberty earlier than white girls or Asian girls (Biro et al., 2013). By 7 years of age, 10.4 percent of white girls, 15 percent of Hispanic girls, and 23.4 percent of African American girls are showing signs of entering puberty (Biro & Wein, 2010). On average, Black girls experience menarche 6 months earlier than white girls (Cabrera et al., 2014). Recent data in boys suggest a similar pattern, with African American boys developing at a more rapid pace than white or Hispanic boys (Papadimitriou, 2016; Herman-Giddens et al., 2012).

Genetic factors are also important. Both maternal and paternal pubertal timing are associated with an individual's pubertal timing (Wohlfahrt-Veje et al., 2016). Additionally, twin studies have documented the heritability of age of menarche (Mendle et al., 2006), and further support for genetic influences is illustrated by the finding that the age of a girl's first menstruation tends to be similar to that of her mother's (Maisonet et al., 2010).

Consequences of Pubertal Timing The onset of puberty can vary by as many as 5 years among typical boys and girls. For both girls and boys, early maturation increases the likelihood of accelerated skeletal maturation and psychosocial difficulties, and it has been linked to adult health issues, including reproductive tract cancers, type 2 diabetes, and cardiovascular disease (Golub et al., 2008). Early puberty is also predictive of adult obesity (Prentice & Viner, 2013). Other effects of early and late maturation vary in boys and girls.

Research on early maturing boys has had mixed results. The most consistent trends to emerge from the literature are that early maturing boys are at significant risk for a wide variety of negative outcomes (Mendle & Ferrero, 2012), including substance use, delinquent behavior, and conduct and behavioral disorders (Hummel et al., 2013; Westling et al., 2008; Golub et al., 2008). The data for late maturing boys are less consistent and more characteristic of internalizing symptoms (Mendle & Ferrero, 2012). Late maturing boys have been found to feel more inadequate, self-conscious, rejected, and dominated; to be more dependent, aggressive, insecure, or depressed; to have more conflict with parents and more trouble in school; and to have poorer social and coping skills and be at higher risk for aggression problems (Graber et al., 1997; Sontag et al., 2011).

Early maturing girls are at increased risk of anxiety and depression, disruptive behavior, eating disorders, early smoking, drinking, substance abuse, antisocial behavior, precocious sexual activity, early pregnancy, and attempted suicide (Copeland et al., 2010; Galvao et al., 2014; Blumenthal et al., 2011; Belsky et al., 2010; Susman & Rogol, 2004; Golub et al., 2008). Early maturers tend to be particularly vulnerable to risky behavior and the influence of deviant peers (Mrug et al., 2014; Susman & Rogol, 2004). As adults, women who had early puberty are also somewhat more likely to have polycystic ovarian syndrome, a hormonal disorder causing acne, irregular periods, excess hair growth, and the growth of cysts on the ovaries (Fuqua, 2013; Franceschi et al., 2010). Less data exists on late maturing girls. Generally, they are not at risk for poor psychological outcomes when compared to "on-time" girls (Ge et al., 2001). However, the cause of late maturation matters. For example, eating disorders and a very low body weight can delay puberty, as can chronic illness (Kaplowitz, 2010). There is also evidence that delayed puberty can, in adulthood, result in lower bone mass density and a higher risk of bone fractures and cardiovascular disease, although it is also associated with a decreased risk of later breast cancer (Zu & Chan, 2017).

Effects of early or late maturation are most likely to be negative when adolescents are much more or less developed than their peers; when they do not see the changes as advantageous; and when several stressful events, such as the advent of puberty and the transition to junior high school, occur about the same time (Petersen, 1993; Simmons et al., 1983). Contextual factors such as ethnicity, school, and neighborhood can make a difference. For example, early-maturing girls are more likely to engage in sexual risk-taking (Belsky et al., 2010), and they show more problem behavior in mixed-gender schools than in all-girl schools and in disadvantaged urban communities than in rural or middle-class urban communities (Caspi et al., 1993; Dick et al., 2000; Ge et al., 2002).

Cultural Context of Puberty In many traditional and indigenous cultures, the end of puberty and the attainment of adult status is marked by an initiation ritual. For example, in the San bushmen of Southern Africa, when a girl enters menarche she is covered with a blanket so that others cannot see her and sequestered in a hut. She must not touch the ground. Her menstrual blood is considered to be powerful, with the ability to negatively affect the prowess of hunters in the tribe. The community gathers together to dance, and at the conclusion of the dance, the girl—now considered a woman—is formally introduced to each member of the community as if she were meeting them for the first time. Boys, too, must bleed in their ceremony. When a boy is considered mature enough for adult responsibilities such as hunting, small cuts are made on his forehead. While he bleeds, he too cannot be looked at. If a boy and girl are to be married, they may receive tattoos, or their blood may be mixed together (Keeney & Keeney, 2013).

Menarche is the most common marker for entry into adulthood for girls. Responses to it vary. In Zambia, a newly menstruating woman is expected to stay at home and kept from doing any work for the duration of her period. In some places in India, girls are celebrated and given gifts of jewelry; in others, they are subjected to dietary restrictions to strengthen their reproductive system. In rural Turkey, young girls are slapped when they enter menarche to remind them they should exercise care with this new stage of life (Marvan & Alcala-Herrera, 2019).

In boys, there is no clear sign of sexual maturity such as menarche. However, when they are deemed ready to enter adulthood, many cultures use initiation ceremonies to mark the occasion. Ceremonies for boys often involve painful events to be endured or tests they must pass. In the Gisu herders of northern Uganda, boys must demonstrate their willpower and courage by undergoing a ritual circumcision. In this circumcision, the foreskin is removed and some of the flesh is removed from the penis itself. No anesthetic is used, and the boy must stand perfectly still. If a boy flinches or refuses to go forward with the ceremony, he risks dishonoring his entire family line. In the agricultural Mende people of Sierra Leone, boys are stripped naked, thrown belly-down on the ground, and older men scarify their backs with a hook or blunt razor. If any boys try to escape, their heads are pushed into pre-dug holes in the ground and they are forcibly restrained. After the ceremonies, in both the Gisu and Mende peoples, boys are sent into the bush alone where they must demonstrate they can survive without assistance. After this, they are considered men (Gilmore, 1990).

Although the rituals used in traditional cultures may seem cruel or extreme when viewed from a modern perspective, they are meant to prepare young adults for adult life and generally are replete with symbolism and viewed with reverence. However, as the influence of the modern world has spread across the globe, such rituals are becoming less common (Schlegel, 2011). In modern society today, there are relatively few rituals to mark entry into adulthood. Debutante balls, quinceaneras, bar mitzvahs, and bat mitzvahs still exist, but the majority of teens in modern society lack a formal initiation into adulthood.

The Adolescent Brain

Dramatic changes in brain structures involved in emotions, judgment, organization of behavior, and self-control take place between puberty and young adulthood (Figure 11.2). On the positive side, a steady increase in white matter, nerve fibers that connect distant portions of the brain, permits faster transmission of information and better communication across hemispheres (Casey et al., 2011). In adolescence, this process continues in the frontal lobes (Bava et al., 2010), occurring earlier in women than men (Asato et al., 2010). In addition, there is a major spurt in production of gray matter in the frontal lobes (Blakemore & Choudhury, 2006; Kuhn, 2006). After the growth spurt, the density of gray matter

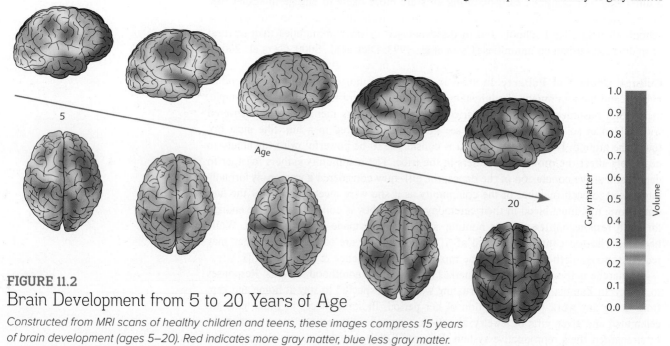

FIGURE 11.2

Brain Development from 5 to 20 Years of Age

Constructed from MRI scans of healthy children and teens, these images compress 15 years of brain development (ages 5–20). Red indicates more gray matter, blue less gray matter.

Source: Gogtay, N., Giedd, J. N., Lusk, L., Hayashi, K. M., Greenstein, D., Vaituzis, A. C., Thompson, P. M. Dynamic mapping of human cortical development during childhood through early adulthood. *Proceedings of the National Academy of Sciences, USA,* 101, 2004, 8174–8179.

declines greatly, particularly in the prefrontal cortex, as unused synapses (connections between neurons) are pruned and those that remain are strengthened. This process begins in the rear portions of the brain and moves forward (Konrad et al., 2013; Casey et al., 2011). Thus, by mid- to late adolescence young people have fewer but stronger, smoother, and more effective neuronal connections, making cognitive processing more efficient.

The teen years are often marked by impulsivity and risk-taking (Casey et al., 2011). One possible explanation for this rapid shift to risk-taking lies with patterns of brain development. Because development starts in the back of the brain and moves forward, subcortical brain areas, including the limbic and reward systems, mature earlier (Konrad et al., 2013; Albert et al., 2013). The underdevelopment of frontal cortical systems by comparison may help explain why adolescents tend to seek thrills and novelty and why many of them find it hard to focus on long-term goals. Although teens are *capable* of thinking in a sophisticated fashion, the more advanced development in reward areas biases them toward thinking with their subcortical "gas pedal" rather than with the "brakes" that might be provided by their prefrontal cortex (Casey et al., 2011). The tendency to engage in risky behaviors has been found cross-culturally in China, Colombia, Cyprus, India, Italy, Jordan, Kenya, the Philippines, Sweden, Thailand, and the United States (Duelle et al., 2018).

Adolescence is a time of social change. Adolescents grapple with changes in identity and feelings of self-consciousness, and they become more sensitive to acceptance and rejection from their peers (Blakemore, 2012). Peers tend to exert a stronger influence in adolescence in part because of a heightened neurobehavioral susceptibility to social reward cues and concurrent immaturity in the cognitive control system (Albert et al., 2013). The changes in the processing of social information are mirrored in brain structure; most clearly in the temporoparietal junction and the posterior superior temporal sulcus. Generally, these areas decrease in volume (suggesting dendritic pruning) from adolescence into the early twenties (Mills et al., 2012). Moreover, there is also a decline in medial prefrontal cortex activity and gray matter volume at the same time (Blakemore, 2012)

Our slowly developing brains give us the time and flexibility to learn about the wide variety of environments in which we find ourselves. However, because the brain develops so slowly during the teen years, this makes it particularly susceptible to both beneficial and harmful environmental influences (Dow-Edwards et al., 2019; Konrad et al., 2013). Thus cognitive stimulation in adolescence makes a critical difference in the brain's development. Likewise, adolescent drug use can have particularly devastating effects on the growing brain.

Physical and Mental Health

About 1.2 billion people in the world—1 in 6—are adolescents (WHO, 2019). Across many countries, adolescents from less affluent families generally report poorer health, and adolescents from more affluent families tend to have healthier diets and to be more physically active (Elgar et al., 2015).

Many health problems are preventable and stem from lifestyle choices (WHO, 2018). Because adolescents are generally healthy, they may not feel the effects of their choices for decades. Lifestyle patterns tend to solidify in adolescence, which may result in poor lifelong health habits and early death in adults

Let's look at several specific health concerns: physical fitness, sleep needs, eating disorders, drug abuse, depression, and causes of death in adolescence.

PHYSICAL ACTIVITY

The benefits of regular exercise include improved strength and endurance, healthier bones and muscles, weight control, and reduced anxiety and stress, as well as increased self-esteem, better academic performance, and enhanced well-being. A sedentary lifestyle may result in increased risk of obesity, type 2 diabetes, and an increased likelihood of heart disease and cancer in adulthood (USDHHS, 2018).

Adolescents who engage in physical activity tend to feel better than those who do not. gbh007/ iStock/Getty Images

Recent data collected from 146 countries, territories, and areas show a distressing pattern: 77.6 percent of boys and 84.7 percent of girls age 11 to 17 do not get enough exercise. Although boys' levels of physical activity rose slightly in recent years, girls' levels have not changed significantly since 2001. There are no consistent differences associated with country income (Guthold et al., 2020).

The U.S. Department of Health and Human Services (2018) recommends that adolescents do one hour or more of moderate to vigorous physical activity per day. U.S. adolescents exercise less than adolescents in most other industrialized countries (Guthold et al., 2020). Recent research shows only 26.1 percent of U.S. high school students engage in the recommended physical activity (Office of Disease Prevention and Health Promotion, 2020), and the proportion of young people who are inactive increases throughout the high school years (Kann et al., 2018). Additionally, girls, adolescents from less affluent families, and ethnic minorities tend to be less physically active (Office of Disease Prevention and Health Promotion, 2020; Foltz et al., 2011).

SLEEP

The American Academy of Sleep Medicine (Paruthi et al., 2016) recommends that adolescents age 13 to 18 years should regularly sleep a minimum of 8 to 10 hours a day. Only about 42 percent of middle school students and 25.4 percent of high school students get sufficient sleep every night (Kann et al., 2018; Wheaton et al., 2018).

Children generally go to sleep later and sleep less on school days the older they get. Only 16 percent of U.S. sixth graders report sleeping less than 8 hours a night, but by 12th grade, 75 percent do not sleep a full 8 hours, a pattern that is true internationally. Although many teens attempt to catch up with the sleep deficit on weekends, sleeping in on weekends does not make up for the loss of sleep on school nights (Owens & Adolescent Sleep Working Group, 2014).

Sleeping less than the recommended amount can result in declines in academic performance and has been linked to attentional issues and learning problems. Sleep deprivation is also associated with a higher risk of accidents and injuries, especially while driving. It is also related to physical health risks, including obesity, hypertension, and diabetes as well as mental health risks such as depression, self-harm, and suicidal thoughts. Too much sleep may also be harmful (Owens & Adolescent Sleep Working Group, 2014; Paruthi et al., 2016).

Why do adolescents stay up late? Often they do homework, listen to music, play video games, or talk to or text friends and surf the web (Bartel et al., 2015). However, sleep experts now recognize that biological changes are also behind adolescents' sleep problems. The timing of secretion of the hormone *melatonin* is a gauge of when the brain is ready for sleep. After puberty, this secretion takes place later at night, making it difficult for teens to get to sleep early (Owens & Adolescent Sleep Working Group, 2014). But adolescents still need adequate sleep, so when they go to bed later, they need to get up later as well. Yet most secondary schools start *earlier* than elementary schools. School schedules are out of sync with students' biological rhythms (Carskadon, 2011). Starting school later would positively influence student attendance, fatigue, and academic achievement (Adolescent Sleep Working Group, 2014).

NUTRITION, WEIGHT, AND EATING DISORDERS

Good nutrition is important. Unfortunately, many U.S. adolescents eat fewer fruits and vegetables and consume more foods high in cholesterol, fat, and calories and lower in nutrients than they should. The average American teen scores 52 out of a possible 100 points as measured on the Healthy Eating Index (Federal Interagency Forum on Child and Family Statistics, 2019).

Globally, a lack of sufficient nutrients and calories is sometimes an issue for many adolescents in developing countries. However, in low-, middle-, and higher-income countries, teens are increasingly becoming overweight and obese (see Window on the World).

window on the w🌐rld

ADOLESCENT OVERWEIGHT AND OBESITY

Worldwide, the prevalence of overweight and obesity has tripled since 1975. Recent global estimates are that slightly over 18 percent of children and adolescents age 5 to 19 are overweight or obese. This includes 216 million overweight and 124 million obese youth (WHO 2018). Some of the highest rates of child and adolescent obesity can be found in North America, Eastern Europe, Pacific island nations, and the Middle East. Within higher-income countries, such as the United States, Canada, Greece, and Italy, obesity rates are high, but have leveled off (UNICEF, 2019). In middle- and especially lower-income countries, undernutrition often co-occurs with overweight. However, in some countries, including many in East Asia, Latin America, and the Caribbean, a rapid shift from undernutrition to overnutrition is occurring (Murtagh & NCD Risk Factor Collaboration, 2017).

As countries become more technologically advanced, rates of overweight and obesity tend to increase. This trend is driven by the increased consumption of animal fat and protein, refined grains, and added sugar, and the concurrent decreases in physical activity. These diet and lifestyle changes are brought about by global trade liberalization, economic growth, and urbanization (Malik et al., 2013).

Health promotion campaigns to encourage parents to provide healthier food options to their children have been implemented in numerous countries,

including Australia, Canada, Chile, Denmark, France, Mexico, New Zealand, Spain, and the United States. Improved food labeling campaigns have been launched across Europe and Australia. Bans on advertising of foods and beverages on TV and radio during hours when children are the main audience have been put in place in Chile, Iceland, Ireland, and Mexico. Ireland has launched an obesity action plan including calorie labeling on products and the regulation of food advertising and marketing. Turkey has implemented several health promotion campaigns, including one called Move for Health, which distributed 275,000 bicycles to schools to get students moving (Kaiser Family Foundation, 2017).

In every region of the world except parts of sub-Saharan Africa and Asia, there are now more overweight and obese people than underweight people—a change from previous decades (WHO, 2018). It remains to be seen if interventions result in significant reductions in these emerging health risks.

what's your view What is more responsible for obesity—individual lifestyle choices or systemic cultural and environmental influences? Do you think the programs that have been implemented in the past few years will have an impact?

Overweight and Obesity In the United States, approximately 15.6 percent of high school students are between the 85th and 95th percentile for body mass index (**BMI**) and thus classified as overweight. Another 14.8 percent have a BMI greater than the 95th percentile and are medically obese. Although evidence is more clear with obesity than overweight, overweight teenagers tend to be in poorer health than their peers and be at heightened risk of hypertension, diabetes, asthma, and cardiac disease (Sahoo et al., 2015; Flynn, 2013; Pulgaron, 2013; Sharma et al., 2019). Obese teens may have difficulty attending school or engaging in strenuous activity or personal care (Swallen et al., 2005). One in 5 have abnormal lipid levels, including either too much bad cholesterol, too little good cholesterol, or high blood triglycerides (Centers for Disease Control and Prevention, 2010). Overweight teens tend to become overweight adults, and the negative effects of carrying too much weight increase with age (Singh et al., 2008). As adults, these youth are at increased risk for a variety of adverse health consequences, including diabetes, hypertension, heart disease, stroke, asthma, and (for women) polycystic ovarian syndrome (Reilly & Kelly, 2011).

There are also psychological consequences. Weight gain and obesity in adolescence are associated with depression, anxiety disorders, behavioral disorders, low self-esteem, lower reported quality of life and well-being, and higher stress. Overweight children are also more likely to be teased, bullied, and rejected by not just peers, but sometimes parents, teachers, and health care providers as well. As we will discuss shortly, some youth, especially girls, are at risk for developing disordered eating (Rankin et al., 2016).

There is no consensus view on the primary cause of obesity, but a vast literature indicates that two key factors are a high-calorie diet in conjunction with low physical activity levels (Ross et al., 2016). However, such factors as overweight or obesity history, genetic influences, behaviors, and a variety of sociocultural factors also impact risk. For example, a history of childhood obesity is predictive of later obesity (Kumar & Kelly, 2017). Genetics may be important here as being born to overweight or obese parents is a risk factor for childhood and adolescent obesity, and overweight and BMI appear to be strongly influenced genetically (Wardle et al., 2008; Silventoinen et al., 2010). Family environmental influences matter as well. Children with parents who eat poorly themselves or who exert too much control over their food choices are at risk for later obesity (Delamater et al., 2013). Socioeconomic level exerts an influence; however, it is more closely tied to education than income. Children whose parents are more well educated are less likely to be obese (Ogden et al., 2018). However, sociocultural factors such as safe outdoor recreational areas and access to grocery stores do affect weight (Delamater et al., 2013). Race, ethnicity, and gender also matter. Overall, high school boys (17.5 percent) are more likely to be obese than girls (12.1 percent), and Black (18.2 percent) and Hispanic (18.2 percent) teens are more likely to be obese than white (12.5 percent) teens (Centers for Disease Control and Prevention, 2018).

Dieting for adolescents is often counterproductive as it often leads to weight gain (Field et al., 2003). Programs that use behavioral modification techniques to help adolescents make lifestyle changes have better success. For example, interventions that have encouraged increases in physical activity, reductions in television viewing, and encouragement of healthier eating habits, either home- or school-based, have been shown to reduce body mass index and other weight-related outcome measures (Wang et al., 2013; Doak et al., 2006).

Body Satisfaction and Disordered Eating Overall, boys tend to be more satisfied with their bodies than girls (Makinen et al., 2012; Lawler & Nixon, 2011). Because of the normal increase in girls' body fat during puberty, many become unhappy with their appearance, reflecting the cultural emphasis on women's physical attributes (Susman & Rogol, 2004). Girls tend to express the highest levels of body satisfaction when underweight, some dissatisfaction when average weight, and the most dissatisfaction when overweight. Boys express the most dissatisfaction when overweight and underweight, but are more satisfied with an average weight body (Makinen et al., 2012; Lawler & Nixon, 2011).

Body satisfaction is important because it has been related to self-esteem (Wichstrøm & von Soest, 2016), dieting, and disordered eating (Bucchianeri et al., 2016). Body satisfaction may be protective for overweight girls. In one study, overweight girls with low body satisfaction gained significantly more weight over a decade—an almost 3 unit increase in body mass index—than overweight girls with high body satisfaction. Thus, being dissatisfied with one's body, at least in girls, does not motivate weight loss as is commonly believed (Loth et al., 2015).

By age 15, more than half the girls sampled in 16 countries were dieting or thought they should be (Vereecken & Maes, 2000). Asian American boys and girls have the highest levels of body dissatisfaction, followed by Hispanics, whites, and African Americans (Buccianeri et al., 2016). African American girls are generally more satisfied with their bodies and less concerned about weight and dieting than are white girls (Gillen & Lefkowitz, 2012).

There are clearly other influences at play as well. For example, friends' dieting, teasing about weight, and pressure to conform to weight ideals predict weight-control behaviors and negative body image (Balantekin et al., 2018; Kenny et al., 2017; Eisenberg & Neumark-Sztainer, 2010). Media also exert a powerful influence. When adolescents, especially young women, are exposed to images of a thin ideal in mass media content, they show more dissatisfaction with their bodies, more concern with their appearance, and greater endorsement of disordered eating behaviors (Grabe et al., 2008). Similarly,

TABLE 11.1 Eating Disorders: Risk Factors and Symptoms

SYMPTOMS

Anorexia	Bulimia
• Abuse of laxatives, diuretics, or enemas in an effort to lose weight	• Abuse of laxatives, diuretics, or enemas to prevent weight gain
• Binge eating	• Binge eating
• Going to the bathroom right after meals, dental cavities due to self-induced vomiting	• Going to the bathroom right after meals, dental cavities due to self-induced vomiting
• Frequent weighing, exercising compulsively	• Frequent weighing
• Restricting the amount of food eaten, cutting food into small pieces	• Self-induced vomiting
• Perfectionist behavior	• Overachieving behavior
• Low blood pressure, extreme sensitivity to cold	
• Weight loss, wasting of muscles and fat, blotchy or yellow skin, fine hair, no menstruation	
• Depression, confused or slow thinking	

the use of social media such as Facebook and Instagram is associated with body image concerns in adolescents (Fardouly & Vartanian, 2016).

Excessive concern with weight control and body image may be signs of *anorexia nervosa* or *bulimia nervosa*, both of which involve abnormal patterns of food intake. These chronic disorders occur worldwide, mostly in adolescent girls and young women. Table 11.1 outlines some of the symptoms for anorexia and bulimia.

Anorexia Nervosa **Anorexia nervosa,** or *self-starvation,* is potentially life threatening. An estimated 0.3 to 0.5 percent of adolescent girls and young women in Western countries will be diagnosed with anorexia at some point in their adolescent years (Swanson et al., 2011). Most research has found higher prevalence rates in women and girls. People with anorexia have a distorted **body image** and, though typically severely underweight, think they are too fat. They are often good students but may be withdrawn or depressed and may engage in repetitive, perfectionist behavior. They are extremely afraid of losing control and becoming overweight (National Institute of Mental Health, 2018). Early warning signs include determined, secret dieting; dissatisfaction after losing weight; setting new, lower weight goals after reaching an initial desired weight; excessive exercising; and interruption of regular menstruation.

Bulimia Nervosa and Binge Eating Disorder (BED) **Bulimia nervosa** affects about 1 percent of people from middle- to high-income countries (Kessler et al., 2013). A person with bulimia regularly goes on huge, short-lived eating binges (2 hours or less) and then may try to purge the high-caloric intake through self-induced vomiting, strict dieting or fasting, excessively vigorous exercise, or laxatives, enemas, or diuretics. These episodes occur at least once a week for at least 3 months. People with bulimia are not necessarily overweight, but they are obsessed with their weight and shape. They tend to have low self-esteem and may become overwhelmed with shame, self-contempt, and depression (Wilson et al., 2007).

anorexia nervosa
Eating disorder characterized by self-starvation.

body image
Descriptive and evaluative beliefs about one's appearance.

bulimia nervosa
Eating disorder in which a person regularly eats huge quantities of food and then purges the body by laxatives, induced vomiting, fasting, or excessive exercise.

People with anorexia, such as this girl, see themselves as fat even when they are emaciated. Ted Foxx/Alamy Stock Photo

binge eating disorder
Eating disorder in which a person loses control over eating and binges huge quantities of food.

The related **binge eating disorder** (BED) involves frequent binging but without subsequent fasting, exercise, or vomiting (APA, 2013). People who binge frequently tend to be overweight and to experience emotional distress and other medical and psychological disorders. BED is the most common eating disorder in the United States, affecting approximately 1.6 percent of adolescents and becoming more common in adulthood. Approximately 2 percent of adult men and 3.5 percent of adult women meet the criteria for diagnosis (Swanson et al., 2011). Estimates are that in middle- to high-income countries, approximately 2 percent of adults have BED (Kessler et al., 2013).

Treatment and Outcomes of Eating Disorders The immediate goal of treatment for anorexia is to get patients to eat and gain weight. Adolescents who show signs of severe malnutrition, are resistant to treatment, or do not make progress on an outpatient basis may be admitted to a hospital, where they can be given 24-hour nursing. Once their weight is stabilized, patients may enter less intensive daytime care (McCallum & Bruton, 2003).

One widely used treatment is a form of behaviorally focused, intensive, outpatient family therapy where parents take control of their teen's eating patterns, and autonomy over eating is relinquished back to the teen gradually. Alternatively, teens may participate in individual therapy, either inpatient or outpatient. Initially, both family and individual therapy show similar outcomes. However, at 6 to 12 months posttreatment, teens who participated in family therapy show more lasting gains than those who participated in individual therapy (Couturier et al., 2013).

Both cognitive-behavioral therapy and medications are helpful in the treatment of bulimia and BED (Shapiro et al., 2007; Vocks et al., 2010). In cognitive-behavioral therapy, patients keep daily diaries of their eating patterns and are taught ways to avoid the temptation to binge (Wilson et al., 2007). Medications such as fluoxetine and antidepressants are also used to control core symptoms such as binge eating and purging, ideally in conjunction with therapy. Although they have some success with reducing these behaviors, generally, the use of medications does not help people with BED, who are usually obese or overweight, lose weight (Mitchell et al., 2013).

substance abuse
Repeated, harmful use of a substance, usually alcohol or other drugs.

substance dependence
Addiction (physical, or psychological, or both) to a harmful substance.

Because patients with eating disorders are at risk for depression and have a suicide risk 10 times that of the general population (Chesney et al., 2014), antidepressant drugs are often combined with psychotherapy but evidence of their long-term effectiveness on either anorexia or bulimia is lacking (Wilson et al., 2007).

Mortality rates among those affected with anorexia nervosa have been estimated at about 10 percent of cases. Among the surviving anorexia patients, less than one-half make a full recovery and only one-third improve; 20 percent remain chronically ill (Steinhausen, 2002). Recovery rates from bulimia are a bit better and average 30 to 50 percent after cognitive-behavioral therapy (Wilson et al., 2007).

SUBSTANCE ABUSE

Substance abuse is harmful use of alcohol or other drugs. Abuse can lead to **substance dependence,** or *addiction,* which may be physiological, psychological, or both.

Trends in Illicit Drug Use In the mid-1990s, illicit drug use in high school students peaked. After declining through 2008, use once again began to rise and has changed little since 2011. Currently, nearly half (48.3 percent) of U.S. adolescents report trying illicit drugs by the time they leave high school (Johnston et al., 2017; Figure 11.3).

In the past two decades, there has also been a general increase in opioid abuse in the United States. This involves both prescription and street drugs (Dart et al., 2015; SAMHSA, 2013). However, the sharp rise in heroin usage has primarily been limited to older teens and emerging adults (Schulenberg et al., 2017). In adolescents, use of legal narcotics peaked in 2002 and has been slowly declining since then to the current 7.8 percent prevalence rate. Lifetime prevalence of heroin use in adolescents peaked in 2000 and has shown a downward path since that time. Currently it stands at 0.7 percent (Johnston et al., 2017).

Alcohol, Marijuana, and Tobacco Alcohol, tobacco and marijuana use among U.S. teenagers has followed a trend roughly parallel to that of harder drug use, with a dramatic

Marijuana is the most widely used illicit drug in the United States.
Doug Menuez/Forrester Images/Photodisc/ Getty Images

rise during most of the 1990s followed by a smaller, gradual decline (Johnston et al., 2017).

Alcohol use is a serious problem in many countries. Approximately 27 percent of 15- to 19-year-olds across the globe report drinking alcohol. Rates vary by region. Rates are highest in Europe (44 percent), the Americas (38 percent), and the Western Pacific (38 percent) (WHO, 2018).

By the end of high school, 61.2 percent of American teens will have tried alcohol, and 46.3 percent will have gotten drunk. **Binge drinking**—consuming five or more drinks on one occasion—is reported by 16 percent of 12th graders (Johnston et al., 2017).

Adolescent brains are still developing, thus exposure to alcohol can have a disproportionate effect. Brain imaging studies have documented changes in dose-dependent smaller gray matter volume and lower white matter integrity in teens who use alcohol. There are also changes in key prefrontal areas involved in executive control and structural differences in areas of the brain involved in reward mechanisms (Ewing et al., 2014). Additionally, alcohol interacts with inhibitory (e.g., GABA) and excitatory (e.g., N-methyl-D-aspartate) receptor systems that are developing in adolescence (Spear, 2014). Studies such as this provide an explanation for why adolescents who consume alcohol show deficits in verbal learning, attention, visuospatial, and memory tasks, and seem to be highly sensitive to the rewarding effects of alcohol and less sensitive to its negative features (Spear, 2014, 2018).

Marijuana is far the most widely used illicit drug in the United States. By the end of high school, students report a lifetime prevalence use of 44.5 percent (Johnston et al., 2017). Heavy use has been associated with damage to the brain, heart, and lungs, declines in school performance, memory problems, and increased risk for anxiety and depression (Volkow et al., 2014).

It is difficult to ascertain the impact of marijuana use in teens. Because marijuana potency quadrupled from 1980 to 2014 (ElSohly et al., 2016), older studies may not fully capture potential for harm at current levels. Additionally, it is difficult to disentangle the direct effects of marijuana with indirect effects, such as the common and concurrent use of other drugs. The debate about marijuana use is also complicated by the fact that marijuana does have legitimate medical applications (Volkow et al., 2014). The impact of recent movements to legalize marijuana has not at this point resulted in increasing use in adolescence (Sarvet et al., 2018).

Adolescent tobacco use is particularly concerning because the vast majority of smokers begin smoking before adulthood and become addicted in adolescence. Cigarettes will kill approximately half of all lifetime users and increase the risk of multiple cancers, especially lung cancer, as well as heart disease, stroke, emphysema, and multiple other diseases (Eriksen et al., 2013).

The use of cigarettes in the United States has been declining, and currently 28.3 percent of 12th graders report having tried cigarettes. Although this number is high, there is some good news. In the late 1990s, about 28 percent of high school students reported being current smokers (Johnston et al., 2017). Adolescent tobacco use is a less widespread problem in the United States than in most other industrialized countries (Gabhainn & François, 2000). However, the use of electronic vaporizers increased from almost 0 in 2011 to 33.8 percent in 2016 (Johnston et al., 2017). This is troubling, as there is reason to suspect that e-cigarette users may eventually graduate to cigarettes.

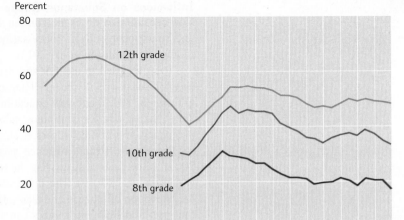

FIGURE 11.3

Trends in High School Students' Use of Illicit Drugs over Lifetime

Source: Johnston, L. D., O'Malley, P. M., Miech, R. A., Bachman, J. G., & Schulenberg, J. E. (2017). Monitoring the Future National Survey Results on Drug Use, 1975–2016: Overview, key findings on adolescent drug use. *Institute for Social research.*

binge drinking
Consuming five or more drinks on one occasion.

Influences on Substance Abuse Continued progress in eliminating drug abuse is slow because new drugs are continually introduced or rediscovered by a new generation, and young people do not necessarily generalize the adverse consequences of one drug to another (Johnston et al., 2017).

Teens exposed to alcohol and drugs before the age of 15 demonstrate an increased risk for substance disorders (Hingson et al., 2006), risky sexual behavior (Stueve & O'Donnell, 2005), and low educational attainment (King et al., 2006). Moreover, they are at higher risk for continuing substance abuse, sexually transmitted infections, early pregnancy, and crime (Odgers et al., 2008).

Peers are a strong influence as well (Monahan et al., 2014; Cleveland & Wiebe, 2003), with evidence suggesting the transmission of pro-drug attitudes may be important (Zapolski et al., 2019). The influence of older siblings and their friends also increases the likelihood of tobacco and alcohol use (Rende et al., 2005). Recent research indicates that peer and sibling influences can also now act via media such as online social media postings and messaging content (Huang et al., 2014).

Rational discussions with parents can counteract harmful influences and discourage or limit drinking (Austin et al., 2000). Similarly, adolescents who believe that their parents disapprove of smoking are less likely to smoke or use illicit drugs (Sargent & Dalton, 2001; Zapolski et al., 2019). However, parents also can be a negative influence. Having an alcoholic parent significantly increases the risk of early alcohol use and later alcohol problems (Wong et al., 2006).

The government can also influence substance abuse. National campaigns, including graphic warnings of risk associated with smoking, bans on tobacco advertising, eliminating illicit tobacco trade, and, most importantly, increasing taxes on cigarettes, have been shown to reduce tobacco use (WHO, 2019). Alternatively, movies and media that depict smoking increase early initiation of smoking as well as the overall risk of smoking (Leonardi-Bee et al., 2016).

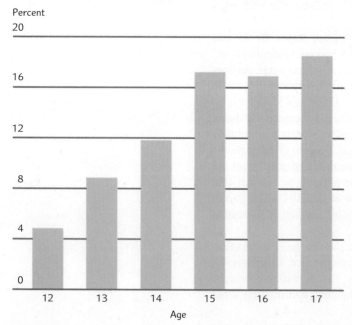

Percent

FIGURE 11.4

Past Year Prevalence of Major Depressive Episode for U.S. Adolescents

Source: Substance Abuse and Mental Health Services Administration. (2018). *Key substance use and mental health indicators in the United States: Results from the 2017 National Survey on Drug Use and Health* (HHS Publication No. SMA 18-5068, NSDUH Series H-53). Rockville, MD: Center for Behavioral Health Statistics and Quality, Substance Abuse and Mental Health Services Administration. Retrieved from www.samhsa.gov/data/

DEPRESSION

The prevalence of depression increases during adolescence. In 2017, 13.3 percent of young people ages 12 to 17 experienced at least one episode of major depression, and only about 40 percent of them had been treated (SAMHSA, 2018; Figure 11.4). Depression in young people may appear as sadness, irritability, boredom, or inability to experience pleasure. One reason depression needs to be taken seriously is the danger of suicide (Brent & Birmaher, 2002).

Being female is a risk factor. Adolescent girls, especially early maturing girls, are more likely to be depressed than adolescent boys (Galvao et al., 2014). This gender difference may be related to biological changes associated with puberty, socialization influences, or girls' greater vulnerability to stress in social relationships (Birmaher et al., 1996; Hankin et al., 2007). Other risk factors include a family history of depression; stress, especially if chronic or severe; anxiety; substance abuse; diet and sleep patterns; and poor physical health (Thaper et al., 2012; Cairns et al., 2014; Naicker et al., 2013). Youth who experience bouts of depression in childhood or adolescence are at risk for the development of bipolar disorder, in which depressive episodes ("low" periods) alternate with manic episodes ("high" periods) characterized by increased energy, euphoria, grandiosity, and risk-taking (Faedda et al., 2015).

One treatment option for depression is psychotherapy. Medications, specifically selective serotonin reuptake inhibitors

(SSRIs), are also used. Although there are concerns about their safety, research suggests the benefits outweigh the risks (Maughan et al., 2013). The most effective treatment for depressed adolescents, at least in the short term, seems to be a combination of medications and cognitive-behavioral therapy (Dubicka et al., 2010). Depressed adolescents who do not respond to outpatient treatment or who have substance dependence or psychosis or seem suicidal may need to be hospitalized.

DEATH IN ADOLESCENCE

Worldwide in 2016, some 1.1 million teens died, primarily from preventable causes. The top five causes of death were automobile accidents, suicide, interpersonal violence, HIV/AIDS, and diarrheal diseases (WHO, 2018). In the United States, the leading causes of deaths among adolescents are accidents, homicide, and suicide (Figure 11.5). After declining for years, the death rate for 10- to 19-year-olds rose by 12 percent from 2013 to 2016, an increase driven entirely by the top three causes of death (Curtin et al., 2018). The mortality rate of 15- to 19-year-old American males is almost 2½ times that of female adolescents (Heron, 2019).

Vehicle Accidents The frequency of violent and accidental deaths in this age group reflects adolescents' inexperience and immaturity, which can lead to risk-taking and carelessness. Motor vehicle collisions are the leading cause of death in 15- to 20-year-olds (Banz et al., 2019). Collisions are more likely to be fatal when teenage passengers are in the vehicle, and the more passengers, the greater the risk (Oimet et al., 2015). The risk is also higher for males and for new drivers. In the United States, about 1 in 5 teens involved in fatal traffic crashes had been drinking, suggesting that alcohol is a major factor in accident-related fatalities (National Highway Traffic Safety Administration, 2017). Another important risk factor is distracted driving, which includes actions such as texting, talking on a cell phone, or eating. Although all drivers risk a crash if distracted, novice drivers are at the highest risk. For example, they are 8 times more likely to crash or have a near miss when placing a phone call in comparison to experienced drivers who are 2 times more likely to do so (Klauer et al., 2014). Despite efforts aimed at increasing seat belt use among teens, only 58.8 percent of teens and young adults reported always wearing a seatbelt in 2017—the lowest of any age group (Centers for Disease Control and Prevention, 2018). In 2015, 58 percent of young people 16 to 20 years old involved in fatal motor vehicle crashes were unbuckled (National Highway Traffic Safety Administration, 2017).

Firearms Firearm-related deaths are far more common in the United States than in other industrialized countries (Grinshteyn & Hemenway, 2016). Boys are 3 times more likely to commit suicide and 6 times more likely to be fatally shot than girls. Race and ethnicity matter as well; the homicide rate for African American male teens is more than 20 times higher than that of white male teens (Child Trends DataBank, 2015). Gun fatalities make up about one-third of all injury deaths and more than 85 percent of homicides in that age group. The chief reason for these grim statistics seems to be the ease of obtaining a gun in the United States (AAP Committee on Injury and Poison Prevention, 2000). Indeed, having a firearm in the home is strongly associated with an increased risk of completed suicide and being the victim of a homicide (Anglemyer et al., 2014).

Suicide Suicide is the third leading cause of death among U.S. 15- to 19-year-olds (Curtin et al., 2018). The teenage suicide rate fell by 34 percent between 1990 and 2006, in part due to restrictions on children's access to firearms (Centers for Disease Control and Prevention, 2008). Firearms are the most common method used, followed by suffocation and poisoning. After this period of decline, the suicide rate increased by 50 percent from 2007 to 2016. Men are more likely to successfully complete a suicide than women (Curtin et al., 2018).

Although suicide occurs in all ethnic groups, Native American boys have the highest rates and African American girls the lowest (Curtin et al., 2018). Sexual minority youth,

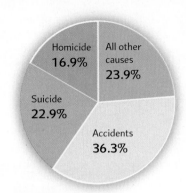

FIGURE 11.5

Leading Causes of Death, Ages 15 to 19 years

In the United States, accidents are responsible for the most deaths among adolescents.

Source: Heron, M. (2019). Deaths: Leading causes for 2017. *National Vital Statistics Reports, 68*(6), 1–77. Hyattsville, MD: National Center for Health Statistics.

including gay, lesbian, and bisexual teens, are at increased risk for suicide and are more likely to consider, plan, or attempt suicide (Caputi et al., 2017). Transgender adolescents, especially female to male youth, are at particularly high risk (Toomey et al., 2018).

Young people who consider or attempt suicide tend to have histories of emotional illness. They are likely to be either perpetrators or victims of violence and to have school problems, academic or behavioral. Many have suffered from maltreatment in childhood and have severe problems with relationships. They tend to think poorly of themselves, to feel hopeless, and to have poor impulse control and a low tolerance for frustration and stress. These young people are often alienated from their parents and have no one outside the family to turn to. They also tend to have attempted suicide before, to have friends or family members who did so, or to report suicidal ideation (Borowsky et al., 2001; Brent & Mann, 2006; Nock et al., 2013). Substance abuse, especially heroin, is also a risk factor, and that risk increases with the number of illicit substances being used (Wong et al., 2013). Protective factors that reduce the risk of suicide include a sense of connectedness to family and school, emotional well-being, and academic achievement (Taliaferro & Muehlenkamp, 2014; Borowsky et al., 2001).

Aspects of Cognitive Maturation

Adolescents' speed of information processing continues to increase. Although their thinking may remain immature in some ways, many are capable of abstract reasoning and sophisticated moral judgments and can plan more realistically for the future.

FORMAL OPERATIONS

formal operations
Piaget's final stage of cognitive development, characterized by the ability to think abstractly.

Adolescents enter what Piaget called the highest level of cognitive development—**formal operations**—when they move away from their reliance on concrete, real-world stimuli and develop the capacity for abstract thought. This development, usually around age 11, gives them a new, more flexible way to manipulate information. They can use symbols to represent other symbols (for example, letting the letter X stand for an unknown numeral) and thus can learn algebra and calculus. They can better appreciate the hidden messages in metaphor and allegory and thus can find richer meanings in literature. They can think in terms of what *might be*, not just what *is*. They can imagine possibilities and can form and test hypotheses.

hypothetical-deductive reasoning
Type of logical reasoning that moves from a general premise about a class to a conclusion about a particular member or members of the class.

Hypothetical-Deductive Reasoning **Hypothetical-deductive reasoning** involves a methodical, scientific approach to problem solving, and it characterizes formal operations thinking. It involves the ability to develop, consider, and systematically test hypotheses. To appreciate the difference formal reasoning makes, let's follow the progress of a typical child in dealing with a classic Piagetian problem, the pendulum problem (Ginsburg & Opper, 1988).

The child, Adam, is shown the pendulum—an object hanging from a string. He is then shown how he can change the length of the string, the weight of the object, the height from which the object is released, and the amount of force used. He is asked to figure out which factor determines how fast the pendulum swings.

When 6-year-old Adam first sees the pendulum, he is is in the preoperational stage. He tries one thing after another in a hit-or-miss manner. First, he puts a light weight on a long string and pushes it; then he tries swinging a heavy weight on a short string; then he removes the weight entirely. He is unable to solve the problem.

At 10, Adam is in the stage of concrete operations. This time he discovers that varying the length of the string and the weight of the object affects the speed of the swing. However, because he varies both factors at the same time, he cannot tell which factor is critical.

At 15, Adam goes at the pendulum problem systematically. He varies one factor at a time, each time holding the other three factors constant. In this way, he is able to solve the problem and determine that only the length of the string impacts how fast the pendulum swings. He is now capable of hypothetical-deductive reasoning.

What brings about the shift to formal reasoning? Brain development is required; however, formal education is also necessary. When adolescents in New Guinea and Rwanda were tested on the pendulum problem, none were able to solve it. On the other hand, Chinese children in Hong Kong, who had been to British schools, did at least as well as U.S. or European children. Schoolchildren in Central Java and New South Wales also showed some formal operational abilities (Gardiner & Kosmitzki, 2005). Formal reasoning is a learned ability that is not equally necessary or equally valued in all cultures.

Immature Aspects of Adolescent Cognition As children's thinking becomes more complex, they develop from egocentric beings to persons capable of solving abstract problems and imagining ideal societies. Yet in some ways, adolescents' thinking is strangely immature (Elkind, 1967).

For example, their developing abilities allow adolescents to envision an ideal world, and they can now realize how far the real world falls short. Moreover, adolescents can keep many alternatives in mind at the same time yet may lack effective strategies for choosing among them. Young adolescents also often do not recognize the difference between expressing an ideal, such as conserving energy, and making the sacrifices necessary to live up to it, such as driving less often. Thus they tend to be idealistic and critical of others.

Another characteristic of adolescent thought is self-consciousness. Adolescents can think about thinking—their own and other people's. However, in their preoccupation with their own mental state, adolescents often assume everyone else is thinking about the same thing they are thinking about: themselves. This is known as the *imaginary audience*, a conceptualized "observer" who is as concerned with a young person's thoughts and behavior as he or she is. The certainty, for example, that the entire high school is staring at a new, small pimple all day long is one example of this.

Last, the *personal fable* is the belief by adolescents that they are special, their experience is unique, and they are not subject to the rules that govern the rest of the world. This belief might encourage adolescents to believe they can drive fast and recklessly and not get into an accident. This form of egocentrism has been theorized to underlie risky, self-destructive behavior.

Evaluating Piaget's Theory Psychologists have critiqued Piaget's work on a variety of fronts. For example, although adolescents *do* tend to think more abstractly than younger children, there is debate about the precise age at which this advance occurs (Eccles et al., 2003). Piaget's own writings provide examples of children displaying aspects of scientific thinking well before adolescence. At the same time, many late adolescents and adults seem incapable of abstract thought as Piaget defined it (Gardiner & Kozmitzki, 2005). Thus the timing of formal operations thought processes does not always correspond to when Piaget argued it occurred.

In most of his early writings, Piaget paid little attention to social and cultural influences. However, neo-Piagetian research suggests that children's cognitive processes are closely tied to the context of a problem and the kinds of information and thought a culture considers important (Kuhn, 2006). The ability to pass a formal reasoning test is strongly tied to how much formal education a person has had, thus, in cultures in which there is no formal educational system few adults attain what Piaget would characterize as formal reasoning abilities (Rogoff & Morelli, 1989).

Finally, Piaget's theory does not adequately consider such cognitive advances as gains in information-processing capacity, accumulation of knowledge and expertise in specific fields, and the role of *metacognition,* the awareness and monitoring of one's own mental processes and strategies (Flavell et al., 2002). This ability to "think about thinking," and thus to manage one's mental processes, may be the chief advance of adolescent thought (Kuhn, 2006).

LANGUAGE DEVELOPMENT

In adolescence, vocabulary continues to grow. By ages 16 to 18 the average young person knows approximately 80,000 words (Owens, 1996). This is important for academic success; vocabulary knowledge is crucial for reading comprehension (Lesaux et al., 2010).

With the advent of abstract thought, adolescents can define and discuss such abstractions as *love, justice,* and *freedom.* They more frequently use such terms as *however, otherwise, therefore,* and *probably* to express logical relationships. They become more conscious of words as symbols that can have multiple meanings, and they take pleasure in using irony, puns, and metaphors (Owens, 1996).

Adolescents also become more skilled in social perspective-taking, the ability to tailor their speech to another person's point of view. So, for example, a teen might use simpler words when talking to a child, swear among friends, and show deference when speaking to an adult.

Language is not static; it is fluid and the words and phrases used by people change over time. These changes are striking in the speech of adolescents, who often develop their own specialized terms. Vocabulary may differ by gender, ethnicity, age, geographical region, neighborhood, and type of school (Eckert, 2003) and vary from one clique to another. Teenage slang is part of the process of developing an independent identity separate from parents and the adult world. This specialized vocabulary even extends to electronic communication, with its own rules for spelling, abbreviations, and the use of emoticons and emojis to convey emotional content (Haas et al., 2011).

MORAL REASONING

As children attain higher cognitive levels, they become capable of more complex reasoning about moral issues. Adolescents are better able than younger children to take another person's perspective, to solve social problems, to deal with interpersonal relationships, and to see themselves as social beings. All of these tendencies foster, although do not necessarily lead to, moral development.

Let's look at Lawrence Kohlberg's theory of moral reasoning, at Carol Gilligan's work on moral development in women and girls, and at research on prosocial behavior in adolescence.

Moral Reasoning A woman is near death from cancer. A druggist has discovered a drug that doctors believe might save her. The druggist is charging $2,000 for a small dose—10 times what the drug costs him to make. The sick woman's husband, Heinz, borrows from everyone he knows but can scrape together only $1,000. He begs the druggist to sell him the drug for $1,000 or let him pay the rest later. The druggist refuses. Heinz, desperate, breaks into the man's store and steals the drug. Should Heinz have done that? Why or why not? (Kohlberg, 1969).

Starting in the 1950s, Kohlberg and his colleagues posed hypothetical dilemmas like this one to 75 boys ages 10, 13, and 16 and continued to question them periodically for more than 30 years. Kohlberg came to believe that moral development was a consequence of moral reasoning, which depended heavily on cognitive development. Moreover, he believed that at the heart of every dilemma was the concept of justice—a universal principle.

On the basis of thought processes shown by responses to his dilemmas, Kohlberg (1969) described three levels of moral reasoning, each divided into two stages (Table 11.2):

In Kohlberg's theory, it is the reasoning underlying a person's response to a moral dilemma, not the response itself, that indicates the stage of moral development. As shown in Table 11.2, two people who give opposite answers may be at the same stage if their reasoning is based on similar factors. Later, Kohlberg proposed a seventh, "cosmic," stage, in which people consider the effect of their actions not only on other people but on the universe as a whole (Kohlberg, 1981; Kohlberg & Ryncarz, 1990).

Evaluating Kohlberg's Theory Kohlberg, building on Piaget, inaugurated a profound shift in the way we look at moral development. Instead of viewing morality solely as the attainment of control over self-gratifying impulses, investigators became interested in how children and adults based moral judgments on their growing understanding of the social world.

For example, neither Piaget nor Kohlberg considered parents important to children's moral development, but more recent research shows that adolescents with supportive, authoritative parents who stimulate them to question and expand on their moral reasoning

TABLE 11.2 Kohlberg's Six Stages of Moral Reasoning

Levels	Stages of Reasoning	Typical Answers to Heinz's Dilemma
Level I: **Preconventional morality** *(ages 4 to 10)*	*Stage 1: Orientation toward punishment and obedience.* Children obey rules to avoid punishment. They ignore the motives of an act and focus on its consequences.	*Pro:* "He should steal the drug. If he doesn't, his wife might die and he would be lonely." *Con:* "He shouldn't steal the drug. He might end up in jail."
	Stage 2: Instrumental purpose and exchange. Children conform to rules out of self-interest. They look at an act in terms of the needs it meets and differentiate this value from the act's physical form and consequences.	*Pro:* "It's all right to steal the drug, because his wife needs it and he wants her to live. *Con:* "He shouldn't steal it. The druggist isn't wrong or bad; he just wants to make a profit.
Level II: **Conventional morality** *(ages 10 to 13 or beyond)*	*Stage 3: Maintaining mutual relations, approval of others, the Golden Rule.* Children want to please others, can judge their intentions, and develop their own ideas of what a good person is. They evaluate an act according to motive or the person performing it, and take circumstances into account.	*Pro:* "He should steal the drug because he is doing it out of love. *Con:* "He shouldn't steal. If his wife dies, he can't be blamed. It isn't because he's heartless. The druggist is the heartless one."
	Stage 4: Social concern and conscience. People are concerned with doing their duty, showing respect for authority, and maintaining social order. They consider an act always wrong, regardless of motive or circumstances, if it violates a rule.	*Pro:* "He should steal it. It's your responsibility if she dies. *Con:* "It is a natural thing for Heinz to want to save his wife, but it's still always wrong to steal."
Level III: **Postconventional morality** *(early adolescence, or not until young adulthood, or never)*	*Stage 5: Morality of contract, of individual rights, and of democratically accepted law.* People think in rational terms, valuing the welfare of society. They see these values as best supported by law. Although they recognize that there are times when human need and the law conflict, they believe it is better for society if they obey the law.	*Pro:* "Taking the drug in this situation isn't really right, but it's justified." *Con:* "You can't have people stealing whenever they are desperate. The ends don't justify the means."
	Stage 6: Morality of universal ethical principles. People do what they as individuals think is right, regardless of legal restrictions or the opinions of others. They act in accordance with internalized standards, knowing that they would condemn themselves if they did not.	*Pro:* "Because this situation forces him to choose between stealing and letting his wife die, it is morally right to steal. He should preserve and respect life." *Con:* "Heinz should think about all the other people who need the drug just as badly as his wife and consider the value of all the lives involved."

Sources: Adapted from Kohlberg, L., & Lickona, T. (1976). Moral stages and moralization: The cognitive developmental approach in Moral development and behavior. *Moral development and behavior, Holt, Rinehart & Winston, New York.*

tend to reason at higher levels. Peers also affect moral reasoning by talking with each other about moral conflicts. Having more close friends, spending quality time with them, and being perceived as a leader are associated with higher moral reasoning (Eisenberg & Morris, 2004).

Initial research supported Kohlberg's theory. The American boys that Kohlberg and his colleagues followed through adulthood progressed through Kohlberg's stages and their moral judgments correlated positively with age, education, IQ, and socioeconomic status (Colby et al., 1983). Generally speaking, adolescents who are more advanced in moral reasoning do tend to be more moral in their behavior, and antisocial adolescents tend to use less mature moral reasoning (Eisenberg & Morris, 2004). Recent research, however, has cast doubt on the delineation of some of Kohlberg's stages (Eisenberg & Morris, 2004). For example, some children can reason flexibly about such issues as early as age 6 (Helwig & Jasiobedzka, 2001).

preconventional morality
First level of Kohlberg's theory of moral reasoning in which control is external and rules are obeyed in order to gain rewards or avoid punishment or out of self-interest.

conventional morality (or morality of conventional role conformity)
Second level in Kohlberg's theory of moral reasoning in which standards of authority figures are internalized.

postconventional morality (or morality of autonomous moral principles)
Third level of Kohlberg's theory of moral reasoning, in which people follow internally held moral principles and can decide among conflicting moral standards.

One reason the ages attached to Kohlberg's levels are so variable is that people who have achieved a high level of cognitive development do not always reach a comparably high level of moral development. A certain level of cognitive development is *necessary* but not *sufficient*. In other words, just because a person is capable of moral reasoning does not mean the person actually does so. People may sometimes come up with highly sophisticated and cognitively complex justifications for immoral actions. Some investigators suggest that moral activity is also influenced by empathy, guilt, distress, and the internalization of prosocial norms (Eisenberg & Morris, 2004; Gibbs, 1991, 1995; Gibbs & Schnell, 1985).

Last, Kohlberg's system does not seem to well represent moral reasoning in non-Western cultures (Eisenberg & Morris, 2004). Older people in countries other than the United States do tend to score at higher stages than younger people. However, people in non-Western cultures rarely score above stage 4 (Shweder et al., 2006), suggesting that some aspects of Kohlberg's model may not fit these societies' collectivistic cultural values.

An Ethic of Care Kohlberg viewed the apex of morality in terms of justice and fairness. Did this view reflect cognitive complexity or Kohlberg's own biases and beliefs about what was most important? This question was addressed by Carol Gilligan (1982/1993), who asserted that Kohlberg's theory was sexist and oriented toward values more important to men than to women. Women, Gilligan argued, held a different set of values that placed caring and avoiding harm as higher goals than justice. Kohlberg's typology unfairly categorized women as less morally and cognitive complex because of the exclusive focus on justice (Eisenberg & Morris, 2004).

Research has found little support for Gilligan's claim of a male bias in Kohlberg's stages (Brabeck & Shore, 2003; Jaffee & Hyde, 2000), and she has since modified her position. Generally, gender differences in moral reasoning are small (Jaffee & Hyde, 2000).

PROSOCIAL REASONING AND BEHAVIOR

Prosocial moral reasoning is reasoning about moral dilemmas in which one person's needs conflict with those of others in situations in which social rules or norms are unclear or nonexistent. For example, a child faced with the dilemma of deciding whether or not to intervene when a friend is being teased might run the risk of becoming a target of the bullies too. Such a child might engage in prosocial moral reasoning when deciding on a course of action.

Research has shown that, from childhood to early adulthood, prosocial reasoning based on personal reflection about consequences and on internalized values and norms increases with age, whereas reasoning based on stereotypes such as "it's nice to help" decreases with age (Eisenberg & Morris, 2004). Girls tend to show more prosocial behavior and empathic concern than boys (Landazabal, 2009; Van der Graaff et al., 2014), and this difference becomes more pronounced in adolescence (Eisenberg et al., 2006). Cross-culturally, parents of girls emphasize social responsibility more than parents of boys do. This has been validated in Australia, Bulgaria, the Czech Republic, Hungary, Russia, Sweden, and the United States (Flannagan et al, 1998). Parents who are warm and sympathetic and who use prosocial reasoning themselves are also more likely to have teens who behave in prosocial ways (Carlo et al., 2011). Peers also matter. Peer feedback about the value of prosocial behavior can, depending on whether the peer group is perceived as supporting or disliking such behavior, increase or decrease the occurrence of prosocial behavior (Hoorn et al., 2016).

Prosocial behavior does not just help the recipient—it is beneficial for the actor as well. Cross-cultural data from 136 countries indicated that prosocial behavior is associated with well-being and increases in happiness (Aknin et al., 2013). Prosocial behavior also helps mitigate the negative effects of stress by influencing emotional responses, allowing people to retain positive affect and dampening negative emotional responses (Raposa et al., 2016). Volunteering, a common form of prosocial behavior, is also associated with benefits. Students who do volunteer work tend to be more engaged in their communities, to have a higher degree of self-understanding and commitment to others (Eccles, 2004), and better academic and civic outcomes (Schmidt et al., 2007). The effects of community service also apply to inner city, racial minority youth (Chan et al., 2014), suggesting that intervention programs promoting community service might be an important means by which to promote characteristics associated with positive development.

Educational and Vocational Issues

Education is one of the most powerful ways in which to reduce poverty and promote health, gender equality, and well-being. Across the world, each year of additional education results in a 9 percent rise in income (Psacharopoulos & Patrinos, 2018). Unfortunately, access to educational opportunities varies widely.

There is good news. In 1950 the average adult in a low-income country received 2 years of schooling; this number has now risen to 7.2 years. More children are going to school, and gender disparities in educational access are much smaller than they used to be. High school is attended by over 50 percent of children in all regions of the world except for some areas of sub-Saharan Africa. Still, work remains to be done. In 2014, 202 million adolescents were not in high school. In low-income countries, only 35 percent of youth complete high school. By contrast, the completion rate is 96 percent in high-income countries. Wars and conflict have an influence as well. More than a third of children and teens who are not in school are in conflict-ridden areas of the world (World Bank, 2018). Likewise, the COVID-19 epidemic also disrupted schooling, and in early 2020, estimates were schools were closed for approximately 80 percent of schoolchildren and adolescents across the world (Van Lancker & Parolin, 2020).

In the 2016–2017 academic year, the 4-year graduation rate for U.S. public high school students hit a high of 85 percent. In the United States, minority status is generally correlated with poverty, which in turn is strongly associated with school achievement. Thus we might expect ethnicity to be an important factor. This is indeed the case. High school graduation rates in 2014–2015 were highest for Asian Americans (91 percent), followed by whites (89 percent), Hispanics (80 percent), Blacks (78 percent), and Native Americans (72 percent) (National Center for Education Statistics, 2019). However, despite our wealth and technological sophistication, U.S. adolescents remain solidly in the middle with respect to academics. Compared to other countries, U.S. students score average in scientific literacy and reading, and below average in math (OECD, 2016).

Students who take responsibility for their own learning are likely to do well in school.
Purestock/Getty Images

INFLUENCES ON SCHOOL ACHIEVEMENT

In adolescence, such factors as parenting and the quality of the home environment influence the course of school achievement. Other factors include gender, ethnicity, peer influence, quality of schooling, and students' belief in themselves.

Self-Efficacy and Motivation Western educational practices are based on the assumption that students are, or can be, motivated to learn. Educators emphasize the value of intrinsic motivation—the student's desire to learn for the sake of learning—because research has shown this orientation is associated with academic achievement (Cerasoli et al., 2014). Unfortunately, many U.S. students are *not* self-motivated, and motivation often declines as they enter high school (Eccles, 2004; Larson & Wilson, 2004).

Students high in *self-efficacy*—who believe that they can successfully achieve academic goals—are likely to do well in school (Komarraju & Nadler, 2013). So, for example, after failing a test, a student with high self-efficacy might conclude that he didn't study enough and that to do well in future tests he should study more. A student with low self-efficacy might conclude the material was too hard or the test was unfair, a belief system that undermines work ethic and motivation. Similarly, students' beliefs about their ability to self-regulate their learning (Zuffiano et al., 2013) as well as their actual levels of self-discipline (Duckworth & Seligman, 2005) impact academic achievement.

In the United States, where opportunities exist for many children, personal motivation can have a strong effect on how much children learn. But in many cultures, education is based on such factors as duty (India), submission to authority (Islamic countries), and participation in the family and community (sub-Saharan Africa). In the countries of east Asia, students are expected to learn to meet family and societal expectations. Learning is expected to require intense effort, and students who fail or fall behind feel obligated to try again. This expectation may help explain why, in international comparisons in science and math, east Asian students substantially surpass U.S. students (Larson & Wilson, 2004).

In developing countries, issues of motivation pale in the light of social and economic barriers to education: inadequate or absent schools, the need for child labor to support the family, barriers to schooling for girls, and early marriage (Larson & Wilson, 2004). Thus, as we discuss factors in educational success, which are drawn largely from studies in the United States and other Western countries, we need to remember that they do not apply to all cultures.

Gender and Academic Achievement Reading tests conducted on 15-year-olds in 72 countries show an advantage for girls, although the difference in scores for girls and boys narrowed between 2009 and 2015. Although gender differences in science are small, boys are more likely to be top performers in all countries with the exception of Finland (OECD, 2016). However, despite having a greater proportion of high performers, boys are simultaneously more likely to fail to achieve a baseline of proficiency in reading, mathematics, and science (OECD, 2015). Overall, beginning in adolescence, girls do better on verbal tasks that involve writing and language usage; boys do better in activities that involve visual and spatial functions helpful in math and science. However, an evaluation of SAT results and math scores from 7 million students found few gender differences in math performance (Hyde et al., 2008).

Why might we expect gender differences? As with all aspects of development, research points to interacting biological and environmental contributions. Male and female brains show some differences in structure and organization. Girls have more gray matter and the growth of gray matter peaks earlier. Their neurons also have more connections (Halpern et al., 2007). The brain structure of girls appears to better integrate verbal and analytic tasks (which occur in the left brain) with spatial and holistic tasks (which occur in the right brain) (Ingalhalikar et al., 2014).

On average, boys have bigger brains (Ruigrok et al., 2014), more connective white matter (Ingalhalikar et al., 2014), and more cerebrospinal fluid, which cushions the longer paths of nerve impulses. Boys' brains are more modular and show an advantage for visual and spatial performance (Halpern et al., 2007; Ingalhalikar et al., 2014). Earlier reports about sex differences in the size of the corpus callosum (a band of nerve fibers connecting both hemispheres of the brain) appear to be an artifact of overall brain size (Luders et al., 2014).

Social and cultural forces that influence gender differences include (Halpern et al., 2007):

- *Home influences:* Across cultures, parents' gender attitudes, expectations, educational level, and involvement correlate with their children's math achievement.

- *School influences:* Subtle differences in the way teachers treat boys and girls, especially in math and science classes, have been documented.

- *Neighborhood influences:* Boys benefit more from enriched neighborhoods and are hurt more by deprived neighborhoods.

- *Women's and men's roles* in society help shape girls' and boys' choices of courses and occupations.

- *Cultural influences:* The size of gender differences in math performance varies among nations and becomes greater with age. These differences correlate with the degree of gender equality in the society.

Parent and Peer Influences Previous research on parental influences on academic achievement focused on parenting style. However, these influences were small and had little predictive value (Pinquart, 2016). Parental involvement in academic activities is a far better predictor of which teens will do well academically (Castro et al., 2015), and this is particularly true for teens from lower socioeconomic classes (Benner et al., 2014). Teens who do well academically have parents who read in the home, hold high academic expectations for their child, communicate to their children about school, and are supportive of their child's learning (Boonk et al., 2018). Parents' educational level and family income also affect educational attainment, and the performance difference between wealthy and poor families has grown larger in the last few decades (Reardon, 2013).

Peers matter too. Generally, academically engaged students associate with peers who are also academically engaged (Veronneau & Dishion, 2011), and, especially for girls, this predicts later performance (Crosnoe et al., 2003; Riegle-Crumb et al., 2006). The quality of peer relationships also seems to be important. Socially competent students who are liked by their peers tend to be more motivated and do better in school. Those students who do poorly are more likely to be rejected or bullied (Wentzel, 2017; Veronneau et al., 2010; Nakamoto & Schwartz, 2010).

School Influences The quality of schooling influences student achievement. A good school has an orderly and safe environment, adequate resources, a stable teaching staff, and a positive sense of community. The school culture places a strong emphasis on academics and offers opportunities for extracurricular activities. Teachers trust, respect, and care about students and have high expectations for students and confidence in their ability to teach (Eccles, 2004).

The peer culture of a school—including both how students relate to each other and what they perceive the academic culture of the school to be—is also important (Lynch et al., 2013). If adolescents feel support from teachers and other students, and if the curriculum and instruction are meaningful and appropriately challenging and fit their interests and needs, they are more satisfied with school (Samdal & Dür, 2000) and get better grades (Jia et al., 2009).

The Influence of Technology In 2013, approximately 78 percent of teens had a cell phone, 23 percent had a tablet computer, and 93 percent had access to a computer at home (Madden et al., 2013). The expansion of technology and the major role it plays in children's lives has affected learning. Teachers often ask students to conduct research online, as well as to access (79 percent) and submit (76 percent) homework and assignments online (Purcell et al., 2013). Although data do not yet exist on the degree to which the COVID-19 pandemic increased reliance on electronic media, the rapid shift to online learning following widespread school closures suggests a sharp increase in their use. The impact of these changes, and how long they will persist, remains to be seen.

Research indicates that whereas critical-thinking and analysis skills have declined as a result of the increased use of computers and video games, visual skills have improved. Students are spending more time multitasking with visual media and less time reading for pleasure. Reading develops vocabulary, imagination, and induction, skills that are critical to solving more complex problems. Multitasking can prevent a deeper understanding of information, and students given access to the Internet during class do not process what was presented as well and perform more poorly than students without access (Greenfield, 2009). See Research in Action for more on multitasking.

DROPPING OUT OF HIGH SCHOOL

As noted, more U.S. youths are completing high school than ever before. The status dropout rate includes all people in the 16- to 24-year-old age group who are not enrolled in school and who have not completed a high school program. In 2017, the status dropout rate was 5.4 percent, and it was higher for boys (6.4 percent) than for girls (4.4 percent). Average dropout rates are lower for white students (4.3 percent) than for both Blacks (6.5 percent) and Hispanics (8.2 percent). Asian students at 2.1 percent are the least likely to drop out (McFarland et al., 2019).

Why are poor and minority adolescents more likely to drop out? Reasons include low teacher expectations, differential treatment of these students, less teacher support than at the elementary level, and the perceived irrelevance of the curriculum to culturally underrepresented groups. The transition to high school for African American and Latino students seems to be most risky for those students transitioning from smaller, more

research in action

TEENS AND MEDIA MULTITASKING

Multitasking, doing two things at one time, is not a new phenomenon. What has changed dramatically, however, is the impact that electronic media have had on multitasking. Adolescents, who have grown up with portable electronic media at their fingertips, are particularly prone to multitasking (Voorveld & van der Goot, 2013). Studies show that more than 25 percent of adolescents' media consumption occurs using at least two media types simultaneously (Rideout et al., 2010).

Two kinds of media multitasking patterns have been identified: consumption of at least two media types simultaneously (e.g., watching TV while surfing on the Internet) and use of a media during a non-media activity (e.g., instant messaging while completing homework) (Baumgartner et al., 2014). Teens are most likely to media multitask, frequently combining music with online activities (Voorveld & van der Goot, 2013). Over time, this changes how teens process information. Adolescents who frequently media multitask report more problems staying focused, inhibiting inappropriate behaviors, and switching effectively between tasks (Baumgartner et al., 2014). Additionally, media multitasking is associated with poor academic performance in math and English and to decreased working memory capacity (Cain et al., 2016).

Equally disturbing are statistics that link media multitasking to distracted driving. Over 90 percent of adolescents engage in distracted driving and have higher rates of distracted driving crashes than older drivers (Carter et al., 2014). Driving inexperience coupled with the visual, manual, and cognitive distraction of cell phone use is considered an especially dangerous combination for adolescent drivers (Garner et al., 2011). In a study comparing cell phone use while driving and drunk driving, impairments while using a cell phone were determined to be as profound as those associated with driving while drunk (Strayer et al., 2006).

what's your view

What about multitasking might lead to its negative effects on cognitive functioning? What actions can be taken to reduce the number of adolescent deaths associated with distracted driving and cell phone use?

---

supportive junior high schools with significant numbers of minority peers to larger, more impersonal high schools with fewer minority peers (Benner & Graham, 2009).

Society suffers when young people do not finish school. Dropouts are more likely to be unemployed or to have low incomes, to end up on welfare, to become involved with drugs, crime, and delinquency. They also tend to be in poorer health (Laird et al., 2006; McFarland et al., 2019).

There are also personal consequences. As young adults, those who successfully complete high school are most likely to obtain postsecondary education, to have jobs, to earn more money, and to be employed. (Finn, 2006; U.S. Department of Labor, 2013).

OTHER VOCATIONAL ISSUES

How do men and women differ in their career paths? How do young people decide whether to go to college and, if not, how to enter the world of work?

Gender and Career Choice Despite the greater flexibility in career goals today, there are still gender differences in career choices. Women receive more than half of all undergraduate degrees in biology, chemistry, and math. However, they are underrepresented—earning only 20 percent of degrees—in computer science, engineering, and physics (Cheryan et al., 2017).

Although the reasons for this are varied, one factor is gender-stereotyping, which still influences vocational choice. Girls and boys in the United States are now equally likely to plan careers in math and science. However, girls are still more likely to go into fields such as nursing, social welfare professions, and teaching (Eccles et al., 2003). Much the same is true in other industrialized countries (OECD, 2004). Another factor may be that those individuals who are high in both mathematical and verbal abilities—of whom more are female—have a wider variety of career options available to them. These individuals are less likely to pursue careers in science, technology, engineering, or mathematical areas (Wang et al., 2013).

Guiding Students Not Bound for College Adolescents decide to forgo college for a variety of reasons. Some young adults, who tend to come from low-income families and have low academic achievement, have financial constraints that prevent them from attending college despite their desire to do so. A second smaller group is composed of young people who have the financial means to go to college as well as the academic ability, but prefer to begin working and earning money. The remainder of non-college-bound young adults give a wide variety of reasons for their decision not to attend college (Bozick & DeLuca, 2011). Most recently, early indications are that many more graduating seniors, particularly those from lower-income homes, will delay or drop their plans to attend college as a result of the economic devastation of the COVID-19 pandemic (Whitmire, 2020).

Most industrialized countries offer guidance to non-college-bound students. Germany, for example, has an apprenticeship system in which high school students go to school part-time and spend the rest of the week in paid on-the-job training supervised by an employer-mentor. However, the United States lacks coordinated policies to help non-college-bound youth make a successful transition from high school to the labor market. Vocational counseling is generally oriented toward college-bound youth. Whatever vocational training programs do exist for high school graduates who do not immediately go on to college tend to be less comprehensive than the German model and less closely tied to the needs of businesses and industries. Most of these young people must get training on the job or in community college courses. Many, ignorant about the job market, do not obtain the skills they need. Others take jobs beneath their abilities. Some do not find work at all (National Research Council, 1993).

Adolescents in the Workplace In the United States, 20 percent of high school students are employed during a given school year (Child Trends DataBank, 2019), and the vast majority of adolescents are employed at some time during high school, mostly in service and retail jobs. Researchers disagree over whether part-time work is beneficial to high school students (by helping them develop real-world skills and a work ethic) or detrimental (by distracting them from long-term educational and occupational goals). How much time students work matters—those that work more than 20 hours a week generally suffer academically and are more likely to drop out of school (Warren & Lee, 2003). However, research suggests that this association is not causal and is a consequence of the fact that those students who are poor achievers may prefer to work more hours (Staff et al., 2010). Some data, however, suggest that although working may not affect academic performance in high school, it may nonetheless lower the probability of going to college (Lee & Orazem, 2010).

For high school students who must or choose to work outside of school, the effects are more likely to be positive if they try to limit working hours and remain engaged in school activities. Cooperative educational programs that enable students to work part-time as part of their school program may be especially beneficial (Staff et al., 2004).

Students whose strength is in creative activities frequently don't get a chance to show what they can do. Jacob Lund/Shutterstock

summary and key terms

Adolescence as a Social Construction

- Adolescence, in modern industrial societies, is the transition from childhood to adulthood. It lasts from about age 11 to about 20.
- Early adolescence involves physical, cognitive, and psychosocial growth, but risks. Risky behavior patterns, such as

drinking alcohol, drug abuse, sexual and gang activity, and use of firearms, tend to increase throughout the teenage years, but most young people experience no major problems.

adolescence

Physical Development in Puberty

- Puberty is triggered by hormonal changes. Puberty takes about 4 years, typically begins earlier in girls than in boys, and ends when a person can reproduce.
- Puberty is marked by two stages: (1) the activation of the adrenal glands and (2) the maturing of the sex organs a few years later.
- During puberty, both boys and girls undergo an adolescent growth spurt. The reproductive organs enlarge and mature, and secondary sex characteristics appear.
- A secular trend toward earlier attainment of adult height and sexual maturity began about 100 years ago, probably because of improvements in living standards.
- The principal signs of sexual maturity are production of sperm (for males) and menstruation (for females).

puberty, primary sex characteristics, secondary sex characteristics, adolescent growth spurt, spermarche, menarche, secular trend

The Adolescent Brain

- The adolescent brain is not yet fully mature. It undergoes a second wave of overproduction of gray matter, especially in the frontal lobes, followed by pruning of excess nerve cells. Continuing myelination of the frontal lobes facilitates the maturation of cognitive processing.
- The amygdala, which is involved in strong emotions, develops before the frontal lobes. Thus adolescents tend to make less reasoned judgments.
- Underdevelopment of frontal cortical systems connected with motivation, impulsivity, and addiction may help explain adolescents' tendency toward risk-taking.

Physical and Mental Health

- For the most part, the adolescent years are relatively healthy.
- Many adolescents do not engage in regular vigorous physical activity.
- Many adolescents do not get enough sleep because of electronics use and because the high school schedule is out of sync with their natural body rhythms.
- Concern with body image, especially among girls, may lead to eating disorders.
- Common eating disorders in adolescence are obesity, anorexia nervosa, bulimia nervosa, and binge-eating disorder. All can have serious long-term effects. Anorexia and bulimia affect mostly girls and young women. Outcomes for bulimia tend to be better than for anorexia.
- Adolescent substance use has lessened in recent years; still, drug use often begins as children move into middle school.
- Marijuana, alcohol, and tobacco are the most popular drugs with adolescents. All involve serious risks.
- The prevalence of depression increases in adolescence, especially among girls.
- Leading causes of death among adolescents include motor vehicle accidents, firearm use, and suicide.

Design Credit: (globe) janrysavy/Getty Images

anorexia nervosa, body image, bulimia nervosa, binge eating disorder, substance abuse, substance dependence, binge drinking

Aspects of Cognitive Maturation

- Adolescents who reach Piaget's stage of formal operations can engage in hypothetical-deductive reasoning. They can think in terms of possibilities, deal flexibly with problems, and test hypotheses.
- Because environmental stimulation plays an important part in attaining this stage, not all people become capable of formal operations.
- Adolescents have some immature cognitive tendencies, including egocentrism, the imaginary audience, and the personal fable.
- Piaget paid little attention to individual differences, between-task variations, and cultural factors.
- Vocabulary and other aspects of language development, such as social perspective-taking, improve in adolescence. Adolescents enjoy wordplay and create their own dialect.
- According to Kohlberg, moral reasoning progresses from external control to internalized societal standards to personal, principled moral codes.
- Kohlberg's theory has been criticized for failing to credit the roles of emotion, socialization, and parental guidance, and for being biased toward men and Western cultures.
- Prosocial behavior, especially in girls, increases throughout adolescence. It is associated with positive outcomes.

formal operations, hypothetical-deductive reasoning, preconventional morality, conventional morality (or morality of conventional role conformity), postconventional morality (or morality of autonomous moral principles)

Educational and Vocational Issues

- Although more people are being educated globally than in previous decades, there are still deficiencies. Teens in developing countries are less likely to graduate from secondary school.
- Self-efficacy beliefs, parental practices, cultural and peer influences, gender, and quality of schooling affect adolescents' educational achievement.
- Although most Americans graduate from high school, the dropout rate is higher among poor, Hispanic, and African American students. COVID-19 also appears to have negatively affected college plans for low-income students.
- Educational and vocational aspirations are influenced by several factors, including self-efficacy, parental values, and gender stereotypes.
- High school graduates who do not immediately go on to college can benefit from vocational training.
- Part-time work can have both positive and negative effects on educational, social, and occupational development. The long-term effects tend to be best when working hours are limited.

Psychosocial Development in Adolescence

chapter 12

Peathegee Inc/Blend Images LLC

learning objectives

Discuss identity formation in adolescence.

Describe adolescent sexuality.

Characterize changes in adolescents' relationships with family and peers.

Describe adjustment problems of adolescents and strategies for intervention and risk reduction.

In this chapter, we turn to psychosocial aspects of the quest for identity. We discuss how adolescents come to terms with their sexuality. We consider how teenagers' burgeoning individuality expresses itself in relationships with parents, siblings, peers, and friends. We examine sources of antisocial behavior and ways of reducing the risks to adolescents to make it a time of positive growth and expanding possibilities.

The Search for Identity

The search for **identity** comes into focus during the teenage years. Adolescence is a time to figure out exactly who you are.

PSYCHOSOCIAL THEORY

The chief task of adolescence, said Erikson (1968), is to confront the crisis of **identity versus identity confusion** so as to become a unique adult with a coherent sense of self and a valued role in society. At least in Western countries such as the United States, adolescence is a relatively long period of time during which young people begin to take on adult responsibilities but are not fully independent. Erikson believed this time-out period, which he called *psychosocial moratorium,* allowed young people the opportunity to search for commitments to which they could be faithful.

Adolescents who resolve the identity crisis satisfactorily develop the virtue of **fidelity:** sustained loyalty, faith, or a sense of belonging to a loved one, friends, or companions (Erikson, 1982). Individuals who do not develop a firm sense of their own identity may lack fidelity, be insecure, and fail to plan for the future. Erikson saw this identity or role confusion as the prime danger of this stage.

IDENTITY STATUS

What does the process of forming an identity look like? Erikson's perspective was extended by the work conducted by Marcia (1966). Through 30-minute, semistructured *identity-status interviews,* Marcia distinguished four types of **identity status**. The four categories differ according to the presence or absence of **crisis** and **commitment**.

Crisis, as defined by Marcia, does not refer to a stressful event such as losing your job or not being able to pay your bills. Rather, it refers to the process of actively grappling with what to believe and who to be. *Commitment* involves a personal investment in an occupation or ideology. Commitments can be held after they have been deeply considered, after crisis, or they can be adopted without much thought put into them. Here are some examples.

- **Identity achievement** (*crisis leading to commitment*). After a crisis period Olivia made thoughtful choices and expressed strong commitment to them. Her parents have encouraged her to make her own decisions. Research suggests she will be more mature and socially competent than people in the other three categories (Kroger, 2003; Marcia, 1993).

- **Foreclosure** (*commitment without crisis*). Isabella has made commitments by uncritically accepting her family's plans for her life. She is self-assured, but she becomes dogmatic when her opinions are questioned. She has close family ties and is obedient.

- **Moratorium** (*crisis with no commitment yet*). Josh is actively grappling with his identity and trying to decide for himself who he wants to be and the path he wants his life to take. He is not only lively, talkative, self-confident, but also anxious and fearful. He will probably come out of his crisis with the ability to make commitments and achieve identity.

- **Identity diffusion** (*no commitment, no crisis*). Jayden has not seriously considered options and has avoided commitments. He is unsure of himself and tends to be uncooperative. His parents do not discuss his future with him; they say it's up to him. People in this category tend to be unhappy and often lonely.

These categories are not stages; they represent the status of identity development at a particular time, and they may change in any direction as young people continue to develop (Marcia, 1979). Also, because our identity is multidimensional, our identity development is as well. For example, a young person may have decided upon a career path but not yet considered political or religious affiliation.

identity
According to Erikson, a coherent conception of the self, made up of goals, values, and beliefs to which a person is solidly committed.

identity versus identity confusion
Erikson's fifth stage of psychosocial development, in which an adolescent seeks to develop a coherent sense of self, including the role she or he is to play in society. Also called *identity versus role confusion.*

fidelity
Sustained loyalty, faith, or sense of belonging that results from the successful resolution of Erikson's *identity versus identity confusion* psychosocial stage of development.

identity status
Marcia's term for states of identity development that depend on the presence or absence of crisis and commitment.

crisis
Marcia's term for period of conscious decision making related to identity formation.

commitment
Marcia's term for personal investment in an occupation or system of beliefs.

identity achievement
Identity status, described by Marcia, that is characterized by commitment to choices made following a crisis, a period spent in exploring alternatives.

foreclosure
Identity status, described by Marcia, in which a person who has not spent time considering alternatives (that is, has not been in crisis) is committed to other people's plans for his or her life.

moratorium
Identity status, described by Marcia, in which a person is currently considering alternatives (in crisis) and seems headed for commitment.

identity diffusion
Identity status, described by Marcia, that is characterized by absence of commitment and lack of serious consideration of alternatives.

window on the world

CULTURAL VALUES AND IDENTITY FORMATION

Our understanding of who we are is not just a product of individual processes. It is also affected by cultural values. One important factor is captured by the cultural value dimension of individualism-collectivism (IC). Individualistic cultures value autonomy, individual rights, self-fulfillment, independence, and personal achievement. By contrast, collectivistic cultures place more importance on relationships, interdependence, and group harmony. Rather than achievement, people from collectivistic cultures are more likely to be focused on the collective good of the group.

In individualistic cultures, because of the strong emphasis on the self, people's self-concept is individual in nature and their personality is generally stable across situations. The self is seen as an individual construction. However, in collectivistic cultures, because identity is entwined with group processes, people view themselves within the context of their relationships with others. Thus, people's personality characteristics are more fluid because who they consider themselves to be depends in part on who they are with at the time. Their sense of self is interdependent (Marcus & Kitayama, 1991).

Although no culture is a monolith and individual differences abound, cross-cultural research in identity formation generally supports the influence of the IC dimension on the construal of the self. In individualistic countries, self-esteem is defined through individual accomplishments rather than through social roles (Oyserman et al., 2002). For example, in one study of 14 countries, college students from individualistic countries rated personal success as a vital component of self-esteem, whereas those from collectivistic cultures cited family life as more important (Watkins et al., 1998). Self-esteem as a whole is more important in collectivistic countries, where self-criticism and pride in the accomplishments of others are more normative (Heine et al., 1999; Neumann et al., 2009).

The IC dimension also affects another aspect of self-construal—how people describe themselves. In one study comparing American and Indian college students, the American students were more likely to use personal trait descriptors (e.g., "nice") to describe themselves, and students from India were more likely to describe themselves in terms of their relationships (e.g., "daughter") (Dhawan et al., 1995). Similar tendencies have been found in Asian American, Mexican American, Korean, and Chinese students (Rhee et al., 1995; Trafimow et al., 1991; Dabul et al., 1995). The influence of IC on self-construal extends in surprisingly far-reaching ways, from indigenous groups in a pretechnological society to the online persona presented by modern college students in social media sites. For instance, one study showed the collectivistic Masai and Samburu traditional African people were more likely to describe themselves in terms of social relationships, whereas urban Kenyan and American college students were more likely to use nonsocial descriptors (Ma & Schoeneman, 1997). In an online study, when students were low on extraversion (and hence less likely to self-disclose in general) and were also high on collectivism, they were the least honest on social media and the most likely to disclose audience-relevant information (Chen & Marcus, 2012).

No person is an island, and we are who we are within the context of our social group. Thus the predominant beliefs and values of a culture affect the construal of the self and our identity formation processes.

what's your view
Even within the bounds of one country, individuals can vary with respect to their IC orientation. Which do you think exerts a stronger effect—cultural values or individual orientation? Which orientation appeals more strongly to you?

In a broad sense, there is some evidence for this approach, at least within Western samples from developed countries. From late adolescence on, as Marcia proposed, more and more people are in moratorium or achievement. About half of late adolescents remain in foreclosure or diffusion, but when development does occur, it is typically in the direction Marcia described (Kroger, 2003). Additionally, when middle-age people look back on their lives, they most commonly trace a path from foreclosure to moratorium to identity achievement (Kroger & Haslett, 1991). However, the process of identity formation varies depending on cultural context (see Window on the World).

RACIAL AND ETHNIC INFLUENCES ON IDENTITY FORMATION

For young people in minority groups, race and ethnicity tend to be central in identity formation processes. Steve Skjold/Alamy Stock Photo

cultural socialization
Parental practices that teach children about their racial/ethnic heritage and promote cultural practices and cultural pride.

sexual orientation
Focus of consistent sexual, romantic, and affectionate interest, either hetero-sexual, homosexual, or bisexual.

transgender
Referring to individuals whose biological sex at birth and gender identity differ.

For a European American young person growing up in a predominantly white culture, the process of ethnic identity formation is not particularly troublesome. However, for many young people in minority groups, race or ethnicity is central to identity formation. Following Marcia's model, ethnic identity formation can also be conceptualized as being diffused, foreclosed, in moratorium, or having achieved identity (Phinney, 1998).

Studies of minority youth have found evidence of all four identity statuses across age groups, although teens are more likely to be in moratorium status than are adults. Regardless of age, teens who are in achieved status are most likely to view race as central to their identity (Yip et al., 2006).

Perceived discrimination during the transition to adolescence can interfere with positive identity formation and lead to conduct problems or depression. As an example, perceptions of discrimination are associated with depressive symptoms, alienation, and a drop in academic performance in Chinese American adolescents (Benner & Kim, 2009) and decreases in self-esteem and increases in depression in Asian American, Black, and Latino teens (Greene et al., 2006). Although the effect is stronger for males than for females, increases in racial identity over 1 year have been related to a decreased risk of depressive symptoms (Mandara et al., 2009). Other protective factors are nurturant, involved parenting; secure attachment with parents; prosocial friends; and strong academic performance (Myrick & Martorell, 2011; Brody et al., 2006).

Parents play an important role, often via **cultural socialization.** Cultural socialization includes practices that teach children about their racial or ethnic heritage, promote cultural customs and traditions, and foster racial/ethnic and cultural pride. When parents teach their children about their culture of origin and encourage them to explore it and feel pride in their heritage, teens are more likely to have a robust ethnic identity, especially if they are able to speak their ethnic language (Phinney et al., 2001). Adolescents who have experienced cultural socialization tend to have stronger and more positive ethnic identities than those who have not (Hughes et al., 2006)

IDENTITY DEVELOPMENT IN SEXUAL MINORITY YOUTH

It is in adolescence that a person's **sexual orientation** generally becomes more clear: whether that person will consistently be sexually attracted to persons of the other gender (*heterosexual*), of the same gender (*homosexual*), or of their gender as well as other genders (*bisexual*). As with other important areas of development, teens may hold varying identity statuses as they form their sexual identity.

Most gay, lesbian, and bisexual youth begin to identify as such between the ages of 12 and 17 years (Calzo et al., 2017). Gay, lesbian, and bisexual youth who are unable to establish peer groups that share their sexual orientation may struggle with the recognition of same-sex attractions (Bouchey & Furman, 2003), although the Internet has increasingly provided an anonymous and accessible means for young adults to explore their sexuality (Harper et al., 2016). Sexual minority youth who do not successfully integrate their sexual identity in their self-concept are at risk for issues with anxiety, depression, or conduct problems (Rosario et al., 2011).

Transgender is a term that refers to individuals whose biological sex assigned at birth and gender identity are not the same. Although some transgender people identify as male or female, others may feel neither fully male or female. Transgender and other gender non-conforming people may or may not seek medical assistance, including gender affirming hormone therapy or surgery, to move closer towards their desired presentation. Because being transgender is relatively rare—somewhere between 0.39 and 0.6 percent of the U.S. population (Flores et al., 2017; Meerwijk & Sevelius, 2017)—it is likely that many transgender children and youth do not have access to transgender adult models to base their understanding on in the same way homosexual children do. Moreover, because the very concept has been controversial, it is often not discussed in school-based sexual education programs (Boskey, 2014). Still, most transgender children from a young age know something is different. Although researchers report some children making statements about their gender being different from their biological sex as early as 2 years of age (Diamond et al., 2011), most transgender children begin to articulate their feelings about gender at about 3 to 4 years of age (Boskey, 2014). However, it may take a while to develop a full understanding. In a retrospective study of transgender adolescents, all reported feeling different from other people at an average age of 7 1/2 years but not coming to a full realization of being transgender until 13 to 15 years of age (Grossman et al., 2005).

Sexuality

Seeing oneself as a sexual being, recognizing one's sexual orientation, and forming romantic or sexual attachments all are parts of achieving *sexual identity.* Although this process is biologically driven, its expression is in part culturally defined.

SEXUAL ORIENTATION AND GENDER IDENTITY

In adolescence a person's sexual orientation generally becomes more clear. Heterosexuals will consistently be sexually attracted to persons of the other gender; homosexuals, to persons of the same gender; and bisexuals, to persons of their gender as well as other genders. Depending on whether it is measured by sexual or romantic *attraction or arousal* or by sexual *behavior* or sexual *identity,* the rate of homosexuality in the U.S. population ranges from 1 to 21 percent (Savin-Williams, 2006).

Many young people have one or more homosexual experiences, but isolated experiences or even occasional attractions or fantasies do not determine sexual orientation. In a national survey, 3 percent of 18- to 19-year-old males and 8 percent of females in that age group reported being gay, lesbian, or bisexual, but 4 percent of the men and 12 percent of the women reported same-sex sexual behaviors (Guttmacher Institute, 2016). Social stigma may bias such self-reports, underestimating the prevalence of homosexuality and bisexuality.

Risks Associated with Gender Identity and Sexual Orientation Although it once was considered a mental illness, several decades of research have found no association between homosexual orientation and emotional or social problems—apart from those caused by societal treatment of homosexuals (Meyer, 2003; C. J. Patterson, 1992, 1995a, 1995b). These findings led the psychiatric profession in 1973 to stop classifying homosexuality as a mental disorder.

However, despite the increased acceptance of homosexuality in the United States, many adolescents who openly identify as gay, lesbian, or bisexual often feel isolated or subject to discrimination and violence. Others may be reluctant to disclose their sexual orientation, even to their parents, for fear of strong disapproval or a rupture in the family (Hillier, 2002). They may find it difficult to meet and identify potential same-sex partners (Diamond & Savin-Williams, 2003). African American, Hispanic, and older adults are more likely to hold negative views of homosexuality (Glick et al., 2015; Brown, 2017).

Gay and lesbian youth who experience rejection and low support for their sexual orientation from their parents after coming out are more likely to adopt a negative view of their sexuality (Bregman et al., 2013). Family rejection is associated with low self-esteem, depression, substance abuse, and suicidal ideation (Ryan et al., 2010), perhaps because parents' negative views about homosexuality are incorporated into their self-image (Baiocco et al., 2016).

Transgender youth are at significantly elevated risk for a host of negative outcomes. And like homosexual youth, these outcomes appear to be driven by stigma, rejection, and a lack of social support. For instance, transgender youth are more likely to be bullied, and this bullying is in turn associated with an elevated risk of suicide attempts (Goldblum et al., 2012). Transgender youth are also at elevated risk of sexual victimization, violence,

Laverne Cox was bullied in her childhood and attempted suicide at age 11 years. Despite these early difficulties, she has become a successful, award-winning actor and prominent LGBTQ advocate. She was the first openly transgender person to be nominated for and win an Emmy award. Jeff Kravitz/FilmMagic/Getty Images

depression, anxiety, and substance abuse (Johns et al., 2019; Borgogna et al., 2019; Grossman et al., 2011). Parental rejection, which is common, appears to be a particularly important risk factor (Grossman & D'Augelli, 2007; Grossman et al., 2005). Finding a sense of community is a protective factor and has been related to less fearfulness, a decreased risk of suicidality, a sense of comfort, and increases in resilience (Testa et al., 2014; Bariola et al., 2015).

Origins of Sexual Orientation Sexual orientation seems to be at least partly genetic (Diamond & Savin-Williams, 2003). For example, research has found stretches of DNA on chromosomes 7, 8, 10, and 28 that appear to be involved (Mustanski et al., 2005; Sanders et al., 2015). Twin studies have led to similar conclusions about genetic influences. Researchers have found that the concordance rate of monozygotic (identical) twins is always higher than that of dizygotic (fraternal) twins. However, despite having the same copy of genes, identical twins are not perfectly concordant for sexual orientation (Ngun & Vilain, 2014). This implies that nongenetic factors must also play a part. What are the environmental experiences that might impact sexual orientation?

One environmental influence on development involves biological correlates of family structure. The more older biological brothers a man has, the more likely he is to be gay (Blanchard, 2017). Each older biological brother increases the chances of homosexuality in a younger brother by 33 percent (Bogaert, 2006). Furthermore, there are indications that male babies who will later identify as gay are more likely to weigh less at birth and are more likely to have mothers who experience miscarriages (VanderLaan et al., 2015; Skorska et al., 2017). These phenomena may be a cumulative immune-like response to the presence of successive male fetuses in the womb.

Another variable that has been implicated in sexual orientation is the 2D:4D ratio. This ratio—that of the pointer finger to the ring finger—is, through a quirk of development, affected by hormone exposure in utero. A lower 2D:4D ratio indicates high prenatal androgen exposure and is more typical of men than women. Interestingly, one meta-analysis showed that lesbian women had a significantly more masculinized 2D:4D ratio when compared to heterosexual women, suggesting androgen exposure in utero affected their sexual orientation. Gay men, by contrast, did not appear to have a different 2D:4D ratio than heterosexual men (Grimbos, et al., 2010). Other research with girls who have a condition called congenital adrenal hyperplasia (CAH) also speaks to the influence of prenatal hormone exposure. Girls with CAH, who are exposed to higher than average levels of androgens in utero, are more likely to later identify as lesbian or bisexual (Bao & Swaab, 2010).

Correlational imaging studies have found similarities of brain structure and function between homosexuals and heterosexuals of the other sex. Brains of gay men and straight women are more symmetrical, whereas in lesbians and straight men the right hemisphere is slightly larger. Also, in gays and lesbians, connections in the amygdala, which is involved in emotion, are more typical of the other sex (Savic & Lindström, 2008). Differences have also been found in the size of the hypothalamus, a brain structure that governs sexual activity, in heterosexual and gay men (LeVay, 1991).

SEXUAL BEHAVIOR

In 2007, 47.8 percent of teens reported being sexually active. By contrast, in 2017, 39.5 percent of high school students reported having had sexual intercourse. Although more male students (41.4 percent) than female students (37.7 percent) reported having had sex, 28.6 percent of *both* teen boys and girls reported being currently sexually active (Figure 12.1) (Kann, 2018). Masturbation is common, although teen boys (74 percent) report masturbating more than do teen girls (48 percent) (Robbins et al., 2011).

African Americans tend to begin sexual activity earlier than white youth (Kaiser Family Foundation et al., 2003) and are more likely to report being sexually active (Kann, 2018). Although Latino boys are also likely to have sex at an earlier age, Latino girls tend to have sex slightly later than their non-Latino white counterparts (Finer & Philbin, 2014).

The percentage of U.S. adolescents who are sexually active has declined over the past few decades (Kann et al., 2014); however, noncoital forms of genital sexual activity, such as oral and anal sex and mutual masturbation, are common. Many heterosexual teens do not regard these activities as "sex" but as substitutes for, or precursors of, sex, or even as abstinence (Remez, 2000). In one national survey, just under half of teenage boys and girls reported having given or received oral sex (Copen et al., 2012).

Correlates of Adolescent Sexual Activity Two major concerns about adolescent sexual activity are the risks of contracting sexually transmitted infections (STIs) and, for heterosexual activity, of pregnancy. Most at risk are young people who start sexual activity early, have multiple partners, do not use contraceptives regularly, and have inadequate information—or misinformation—about sex. Other risk factors are living in a socioeconomically disadvantaged community or rural community; being Black, Hispanic, or Native American; substance use; antisocial behavior; and association with deviant peers (Centers for Disease Control and Prevention, 2017; Burrus, 2018; Baumer & South, 2001; Meade & Ickovics, 2005).

Generally, an involved and engaged relationship between teens and parents is associated with a decreased risk of early sexual activity. For instance, participating in regular family activities predicts declines in teenage sexual activity (Coley et al., 2009), and more parent-child communication is associated with delayed sexual intercourse (Parkes et al., 2011). Teens who have supportive relationships with their parents are more likely to delay intercourse and to use safe sex practices when they finally do so (Deptula et al., 2010). Teenagers, particularly girls, who have close, warm relationships with their mothers are also likely to delay sexual activity, especially if they perceive that their mothers would disapprove (Jaccard & Dittus, 2000; Sieving et al., 2000; Kincaid et al., 2012). For those teens in two-parent families, having fathers who know more about their friends and activities is associated with delays in sexual activity (Coley et al., 2009), whereas the absence of a father, especially early in life, is a predictor of early sexual activity (Ellis et al., 2003).

Another proposed protective factor is a sense of meaning in life, which is theorized to provide protection against health risk behaviors. Religiosity is a source of meaning for many people and has been associated with decreased risk for early sexual activity (Haglund & Fehring, 2010). In support of this, common reasons teenagers give for not yet having had sex include that it is against their religion or morals (Abma et al., 2010). Meaning in life has also been associated with a decreased risk of unsafe sexual activity, but only in adolescent women (Brassai et al., 2011).

Peer group norms exert a powerful influence on adolescent behavior, and religious teens are less likely to be friends with peers who have positive views of sexual activity (Landor et al., 2011). On the other hand, if adolescents believe their peers are having and approve of sex, or are pressuring them to have sex, then they, especially boys, may feel pressure to engage in activities they do not feel ready for (Van de Bongardt et al., 2015; Widman et al., 2016). As a teen's number of close friends who initiate sex grows, the likelihood the teen will initiate sex also rises (Ali & Dwyer, 2011).

Female Genital Mutilation Female genital mutilation includes any and all procedures that involve removal of external female genitalia for non-health-related reasons. Often it involves the removal of the clitoris, the inner and/or outer folds of the vulva, or narrowing the vaginal opening with stitches. More than 200 million women and girls have been cut, primarily in Africa, the Middle East, and Asia. Although the stated reasons for its use vary, they often center upon maintaining chastity (by removing the temptation of sexual pleasure) and improving marriageability (World Health Organization, 2018).

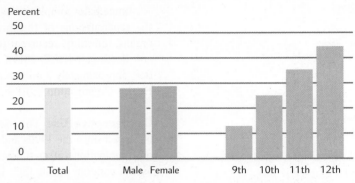

Percent

*Had sexual intercourse with at least one person, during the 3 months before the survey
Note: This graph contains weighted results.

FIGURE 12.1

Percentage of High School Students Who Were Sexually Active by Sex and Grade, 2017

Source: Kann, L., T. McManus, W. A. Harris, S. L. Shanklin, K. H. Flint, B. Queen, . . . C. Lim. Youth risk behavior surveillance—United States, 2017. MMWR Surveillance Summaries 67(8), 2018, 1.

Immediate complications include bleeding, infections, and slow healing. However, the repercussions of this practice can be lifelong. They include damage to adjacent organs, infertility, recurrent urinary tract infections, birth complications, dermoid cysts, and death (UNICEF, 2014). Although strides have been made in combatting this practice, approximately 3 million girls a year remain at risk of receiving the procedure (World Health Organization, 2018).

Contraceptive Use The use of contraceptives among sexually active teenage girls has increased since the 1990s and includes the pill and new hormonal and injectable methods or combinations of methods (Abma & Martinez, 2017). In 2017, 53.8 percent of teens used a condom during their last sexual encounter and 29.4 used hormonal birth control (Centers for Disease Control and Prevention, 2018). Approximately 5.8 percent of adolescent females use a long-term reversible method such as an intrauterine implant (Abma & Martinez, 2017). Adolescent girls who do not use contraception during their first sexual encounter are twice as likely to become teenage mothers (Martinez & Abma, 2015). As with sexual activity, peer influences are important. Teens who believe their peers approve of contraception are more likely to adopt their use as well (Ali et al., 2011).

The best safeguard for sexually active teens is regular use of condoms, which give some protection against sexually transmitted infections (STIs) as well as against pregnancy. Almost 80 percent of teens who are having sex for the first time use a condom (Martinez et al., 2011) although 21 percent of adolescent females and 16 percent of adolescent males report not using a condom during their last sexual encounter (Martinez & Abma, 2015). Adolescents who start using prescription contraceptives often stop using condoms, in some cases not realizing that they leave themselves unprotected against STIs (Klein & AAP Committee on Adolescence, 2005).

Barriers to contraceptive use include lack of access, concerns about confidentiality, financial concerns, a belief they will not get pregnant, or reluctance to discuss use with a sexual partner (Hasstedt, 2018; Kusunoki & Upchurch, 2011). Less commonly, some teens may be deliberately seeking to become pregnant (Barber et al., 2015).

SEXUALLY TRANSMITTED INFECTIONS (STIS)

sexually transmitted infections (STIs) Infections and diseases spread by sexual contact.

Sexually transmitted infections (STIs) are diseases spread by sexual contact. Globally, more than 1 million STIs are acquired each day with an estimated 376 million new infections a year (World Health Organization, 2020). Rates in the United States are higher than in other developed nations, although the majority of cases are found in developing countries (Advocates for Youth, 2010).

In the United States, an estimated 19.7 million new STIs are diagnosed each year, over half in young men and women (Centers for Disease Control and Prevention, 2019). Approximately 65 million Americans have an incurable STI (Wildsmith et al., 2010). An estimated 3.2 million adolescent girls in the United States—about 1 in 4 of those ages 14 to 19—has at least one STI (Forhan et al., 2008). The chief reasons for the prevalence of STIs among teenagers include early sexual activity, multiple partners, and failure to use condoms or to use them regularly and correctly. Additionally, there are often barriers to sexual health services such as lack of transportation to clinics, inability to pay, conflict between school and clinic hours, and concerns about confidentiality (Centers for Disease Control and Prevention, 2019). Despite the fact that teens are at higher risk for contracting STIs, they perceive their own personal risk as low (Wildsmith et al., 2010).

The most common STI, accounting for about half of all STI infections diagnosed in 15- to 24-year-olds each year, is human papilloma virus (HPV), or genital warts, the leading cause of cervical cancer in women (Weinstock et al., 2004). In low- or middle-income countries, where women lack adequate reproductive health care, cervical cancer is the most common—and most deadly—cancer in women (Chibwesha & Stringer, 2019).

Almost every adult who is sexually active will eventually get HPV in the absence of vaccination (Centers for Disease Control and Prevention, 2019). The Centers for Disease Control and Prevention (2019) recommends routine vaccination for all adolescents starting at age 11 or 12. Despite low vaccination rates, HPV incidence since the introduction of the vaccine in 2006 has dropped from 11.5 percent to 5.1 percent (Markowitz et al., 2013). A recent meta-analysis including more than 60 million individuals from 14 high-income countries showed that even when vaccination campaigns include only women, the incidence of HPV infection drops rapidly in all risk groups (Drolet et al., 2019). In 2018, slightly over half of American teens received the entire series and 68.1 percent received the first shot (Walker et al., 2019). Research has shown that vaccination for HPV does not lead to more or riskier sexual behavior in adolescents (Mechcatie & Rosenberg, 2018; Mayhew et al., 2014). Additionally, large-scale studies have shown little to no evidence of adverse side effects or safety risks (Markowitz et al., 2018; Gee et al., 2016; Lu et al., 2011).

The most common bacterial STIs are chlamydia (1.8 million cases in the United States) and gonorrhea (583,405 cases). Syphilis, another bacterial infection, is less common (35,063 cases) (Centers for Disease Control and Prevention, 2019). Globally, approximately 131 million people are infected with chlamydia, 78 million are inflected with gonorrhea, and 5.6 million are infected with syphilis every year (World Health Organization, 2016).

These diseases, if undetected and untreated, can lead to severe health problems, including, in women, pelvic inflammatory disease (PID), a serious abdominal infection. Currently treatable with antibiotics, gonorrhea and to a lesser extent chlamydia and syphilis are showing growing signs of antibiotic resistance. Currently, only one effective treatment exists for gonorrhea, and if new drugs are not developed, gonorrhea may no longer be a treatable disease (World Health Organization, 2016; Centers for Disease Control and Prevention, 2019).

Genital herpes simplex is a chronic, recurring, often painful, and highly contagious disease. It can be fatal to a person with a deficiency of the immune system or to newborn infants. There are two variants: herpes simplex virus type 1 (HSV-1), which causes cold sores, and herpes simplex virus type 2 (HSV-2), which causes genital sores. Teens today are less likely to have been infected with HSV-1 because of public health education efforts. However, their lack of exposure means they have not had the opportunity to form HSV-1 antibodies, which may result in a higher risk of HSV-2 if they are exposed when they become sexually active (Bradley et al., 2014).

Hepatitis B is a virus that affects the liver, causing cirrhosis, liver cancer, and death. Currently, it affects an estimated 257 million people globally and is most common in the Western Pacific and Africa (World Health Organization, 2019). There are approximately 2.2 million infected people in the United States. Although rates dropped sharply when the hepatitis vaccine was added to routine newborn immunization schedules in the 1990s, they have recently shown a slight uptick, possibly as a result of increased injectable drug abuse (Harris et al., 2016).

The human immunodeficiency virus (HIV), which causes acquired immune deficiency syndrome (AIDS), is transmitted through bodily fluids, usually by sharing intravenous drug needles or by sexual contact with an infected partner. The virus attacks the body's immune system, leaving a person vulnerable to a variety of fatal diseases. Symptoms of AIDS include extreme fatigue, fever, swollen lymph nodes, weight loss, diarrhea, and night sweats. There were 1.7 million new HIV infections worldwide in 2018, representing a 37 percent decline from 2000. Still, approximately 37.9 million people were living with HIV/AIDS worldwide in 2018, two-thirds of whom live on the African continent. As of now, AIDS is incurable, but increasingly the related infections that kill people are being stopped with antiviral therapy (World Health Organization, 2019).

In the United States approximately 1.1 million people were living with HIV. The incidence rate has dropped by 11 percent from 2010 to 2017, but risk varies across different groups, with gay and bisexual men at the highest risk. People who inject drugs, African Americans and Hispanics, and people living in the southern United States are also at higher risk. About 1 in 7 people infected with the virus are unaware of their status, and in infected people age 13 to 24 years, 54.6 percent are unaware of their status. About half of infected people who are receiving treatment have a suppressed viral load, a sign of successful management of the disease. Still, many remain untreated, and in 2017, slightly over 16,000 people died as a result of their HIV status (HIV.gov, 2020).

Comprehensive sex and STI/HIV education is critical to promoting responsible decision making and controlling the spread of STIs. Evidence for the positive impact of such programs is strong (Denford et al., 2017).

TEENAGE PREGNANCY AND CHILDBEARING

Teen pregnancy is a global problem. Approximately 12 million females aged 15 to 19 years give birth a year in developing countries, and 10 million of these pregnancies are unintentional. Young women often do not have access to contraceptives or reproductive health care. In some cultures, particularly in developing countries, girls marry at a young age and are encouraged to bear children early. Also, sexual violence is widespread, and up to a third of girls in some countries report being raped as their first sexual encounter. The consequences of these pregnancies can be immense. Approximately 5.6 million of these young girls obtain abortions every year, 3.9 million of which are unsafe. Childbirth also can be unsafe in developing areas of the world. Pregnancy and childbirth complications are the leading cause of death for 15- to 19-year-old women (World Health Organization, 2020).

More than 7 in 100 girls in the United States have been pregnant at least once before age 20 (Kost et al., 2013). Approximately 61 percent of young women choose to keep their pregnancies. Of the remainder of these pregnancies, 24 percent end in abortion, and 15 percent end in miscarriage or stillbirth (Figure 12.2). Teen pregnancy rates are highest among African American and Hispanic teens (Livingston & Thomas, 2019). Approximately 77 percent of these pregnancies are unplanned, and nearly 90 percent occur outside of marriage (U.S. Department of Health and Human Services, 2020).

A substantial decline in teenage pregnancy has accompanied steady decreases in early intercourse and in sex with multiple partners and an increase in contraceptive use. In 2018, birthrates for teens dropped to their lowest level yet, 17.4 per 1,000 females age 15 to 19 years (Martin et al., 2019). Abortion rates have also declined. There is no clear pattern linking reduced access to abortion services to the abortion rate. Rather, the decline appears to be a consequence of overall declines in pregnancies themselves (Nash & Dreweke, 2019).

Pregnancy prevention programs that focus on teen outreach have had some success. Such programs generally combine comprehensive sex education and access to family planning services. With the use of such a program, California—the only state that refused abstinence-only federal dollars—went from having the highest teen pregnancy rate to showing the steepest decline, effectively halving rates (Boonstra, 2010).

Research suggests that contributing factors for teen pregnancy are similar for both young men and women. They include low education and socioeconomic status, being in foster care, having a teen parent, having been physically or sexually abused and/or exposed to parental divorce or separation, domestic violence, substance abuse, or a household member who was mentally ill or engaged in criminal behavior (Centers for Disease Control and Prevention, 2019; Madigan et al., 2014; Fasula et al., 2019).

Outcomes of Teenage Pregnancy Teenage pregnancies often have poor outcomes. Many of the mothers are impoverished and poorly educated, and some are drug users. Teenage mothers are likely to drop out of school and to have repeated pregnancies, less likely to go to college, and more likely to live in poverty. During pregnancy, many do not eat properly, do not gain enough weight, and get inadequate prenatal care or none at all. Their babies are likely to be premature or dangerously small and are at heightened risk of other birth complications. They are also at heightened risk for health and academic problems, abuse and neglect, and developmental disabilities, substance abuse, gang activity,

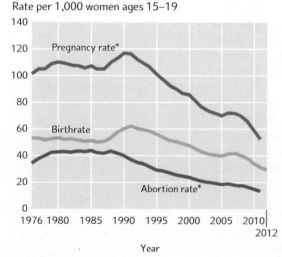

Rate per 1,000 women ages 15–19

*Data not available for 2010–2012.

FIGURE 12.2

Pregnancy, Birth, and Abortion Rates for U.S. Females Ages 15 to 19

Source: Centers for Disease Control and Prevention. (2013). *Pregnancy rates for U.S. women continue to drop,* Figure 3.

and of becoming adolescent parents themselves (Basch, 2011; Klein & AAP Committee on Adolescence, 2005; Menacker et al., 2004; Jeha et al., 2015; Wen et al., 2007). The effects, however, vary among different groups. Adolescent pregnancy is most likely to disrupt outcomes in teens of higher socioeconomic status (Diaz & Fiel, 2016).

Poor outcomes of teenage parenting are far from inevitable, however. Several long-term studies find that, two decades after giving birth, most former adolescent mothers are not on welfare; many have finished high school and secured steady jobs; and they do not have large families. Comprehensive adolescent pregnancy and home visitation programs seem to contribute to good outcomes (Basch, 2011; Klein & AAP Committee on Adolescence, 2005), as does contact with the father (Howard et al., 2006), and involvement in a religious community (Carothers et al., 2005).

SEXUAL EDUCATION

Approximately 22 percent of teen girls and 30 percent of teen boys report that their parents do not talk to them about any sexual or reproductive health topics (Lindberg et al., 2016). Increasingly, teens are using online sources to access confidential information, and such sources show potential for use as sexual education tools (Guilamo-Ramos et al., 2015).

Many teenagers get much of their sex education from the media, which present a distorted view of sexual activity, associating it with fun, excitement, competition, or violence and rarely showing the risks of unprotected sex. Surprisingly, teens report more exposure to sexual media from television, movies, and music than they do from the Internet (Ybarra et al., 2014). Teens who watch highly sexual television content are twice as likely to experience a pregnancy compared with lower level or no exposure (Chandra et al., 2008). Additionally, teens exposed to sexual explicit content—including pornography and erotica—are more likely to have oral sex and sexual intercourse at earlier ages (Brown & L'Engle, 2009). Moreover, those teens exposed to sexual explicit content or sexual violence in media are more likely to be perpetrators or victims of sexual violence themselves (Rodenhizer & Edwards, 2019).

From 2011 to 2013, approximately 80 percent of teens received formal sexual education—generally at a school, church, or community center—on preventing STIs or how to say no to sex. However, only 55 percent of males and 60 percent of females received information on the use of birth control methods (Lindberg et al., 2016). This is in part driven by policies promoting abstinence research over more comprehensive programs. Some critics claim that community- and school-based sex education leads to more or earlier sexual activity, even though evidence shows otherwise (Boonstra, 2010; Kirby & Laris, 2009). Programs that encourage abstinence but also discuss STI prevention and safer sexual practices—known as comprehensive sexual education—have been found to delay sexual initiation, promote positive behavioral change, and increase contraceptive use (Fox et al., 2019; Denford et al., 2017). However, only 14.1 percent of middle schools and 38.3 percent of high schools teach all 19 topics recommended by the Centers for Disease Control and Prevention (Brener et al., 2017).

Some school programs promote abstinence as the *only* option, even though abstinence-only courses do not delay sexual activity, reduce pregnancy rates, or decrease the rate of sexually transmitted infections (Fox et al., 2019; Denford et al., 2017). This may be because abstinence-only programs do not impact whether or not teens use safe sex practices such as condoms (Chin et al., 2012). Thus, if teens do have sex, they are less likely to be protected. Likewise, pledges to maintain virginity have shown little impact on sexual behavior other than a *decrease* in the likelihood to take precautions during sex (Rosenbaum, 2009).

In 2010, Congress withdrew financial support for abstinence-only programs and shifted toward evidence-based models. Thus comprehensive sexual education programs were funded and teen pregnancy rates hit historic lows (Guttmacher Institute, 2018). However, under the Trump administration, federal funding for abstinence education programming is again on the rise, and comprehensive sexual education programs are being

MTV's Teen Mom franchise, originally criticized for glamorizing teen pregnancy, may instead be partially responsible for declines in teenage motherhood. Internet searches for birth control and abortion spiked after episodes of the reality drama aired (Kearney & Levine, 2015). DFree/Shutterstock

defunded (Guttmacher Institute, 2017). The effect on adolescent pregnancy rates remains to be seen, but previous research suggests this approach will result in the erosion of the recent gains made in combating teen pregnancy.

In Europe, teen pregnancy and birthrates are many times lower than the United States despite similar levels of sexual activity (Guttmacher Institute, 2013). This has been attributed to the provision of universal, comprehensive sex education for young adults and access to reproductive services. Contraceptives are provided free to adolescents in many countries. For example, Sweden showed a fivefold reduction in the teenage birthrate following introduction of birth control education, free access to contraceptives, and free abortion on demand (Bracher & Santow, 1999). Comprehensive sexual education programs have also been shown to be effective in preventing pregnancy and disease across sub-Saharan Africa, Asia, Latin America, and the Caribbean (Fonner et al., 2014). Unfortunately, policies promoting abstinence programs have not only undermined the quality of the information taught in the United States, but also in foreign aid programs. These policies have harmed both family planning and HIV prevention programs in other countries (Santelli et al., 2017).

The problem of teenage pregnancy requires a multifaceted solution. It must include programs and policies to encourage postponing or refraining from sexual activity, but it also must recognize that many young people do become sexually active and need education and information to prevent pregnancy and STIs. It requires attention to underlying factors that put teenagers and families at risk—reducing poverty, school failure, behavioral and family problems, and expanding employment, skills training, and family life education.

Relationships

Adolescents spend more time with peers and less with family. However, even as adolescents increasingly turn toward peers to fulfill many of their social needs, they still look to parents for a secure base from which they can try their wings.

ADOLESCENTS AND PARENTS

Just as adolescents feel tension between dependency on their parents and the need to break away, parents want their children to be independent yet find it hard to let go.

The Myth of Adolescent Rebellion The teenage years have been called a time of **adolescent rebellion.** Yet full-fledged rebellion is relatively uncommon even in Western societies. Although family conflict and emotional distance do increase somewhat during adolescence, particularly in mother-daughter dyads (Holmbeck, 2018), most young people feel close to and positive about their parents, share similar opinions on major issues, and value their parents' approval (Blum & Reinhart, 2000; Offer & Church, 1991). Most family arguments concern control over everyday personal matters—chores, schoolwork, dress, money, curfews, dating, and friends—rather than issues of health and safety or right and wrong (Adams & Laursen, 2001; Steinberg, 2005).

Teenage rebellion, rather than being normative, is more likely to be associated with variables such as abusive, indifferent, or neglectful parenting (McDermott & Barik, 2014). The relatively few deeply troubled adolescents tend to come from disrupted families and, as adults, continue to have unstable family lives and reject cultural norms (Offer et al., 2002; Holmbeck, 2018).

Individuation and Connectedness If you were like most teens, you probably listened to different music from your parents, dressed in a different style of clothing, and felt it was reasonable to keep certain things private from them. This process, called **individuation,**

adolescent rebellion
Pattern of emotional turmoil, characteristic of a minority of adolescents, that may involve conflict with family, alienation from adult society, reckless behavior, and rejection of adult values.

individuation
Adolescents' struggle for autonomy and personal identity.

involves the struggle for autonomy and differentiation, or personal identity. An important aspect of individuation is carving out boundaries of control between self and parents (Nucci et al., 2005).

Parents of young adolescents must strike a delicate balance between too much freedom and too much intrusiveness. For instance, seventh- and eighth-grade students have been found to be at elevated risk because of decreased parental monitoring and involvement, which allows the behavior of antisocial peers to exert increased influence (Van Ryzin et al., 2012). By 11th grade, those young people who see themselves as having a great deal of autonomy tend to spend more time in unsupervised socializing with peers and are at risk for problem behavior. But too little autonomy can also have negative effects. Those students who perceive their parents as highly intrusive in their personal lives are also more likely to be influenced by negative peer interactions (Goldstein et al., 2005). Somewhat paradoxically, a warm, interconnected relationship with parents can help teens individuate successfully (Ponappa et al., 2014).

There are also cultural differences. One primary distinction is that drawn between collectivistic and individualistic societies. Research in this area shows that connectedness between teens and parents is higher in collectivistic countries such as India, Saudi Arabia, and Algeria than in individualistic Western countries such as France, Poland, and Argentina. In collectivistic cultures, emphasis is placed more on family than on individual desires (Dwairy & Achoui, 2010).

The COVID-19 pandemic is particularly challenging for teens. Because many adolescents have been asked to stay at home and remain socially distant from friends, individuation processes may have been curtailed as teens retreated back to their families.

Parenting Styles Authoritative parenting continues to foster healthy psychosocial development (Baumrind, 2005; Hoskins, 2014). Authoritative parents exercise appropriate control over a child's conduct (*behavioral control*) but not over the child's feelings, beliefs, and sense of self (*psychological control*) (Steinberg & Darling, 1994). So, for example, they might ground their teenage son for breaking a rule, but they would not insist that the teen agree with them about the wisdom of the broken rule.

Problems arise when parents overstep what adolescents perceive as appropriate bounds of legitimate parental authority. The existence of a mutually agreed personal domain in which authority belongs to the adolescent has been found in various cultures and social classes from Japan to Brazil. This domain expands as parents and adolescents continually renegotiate its boundaries (Nucci et al., 2005).

The original model of parenting styles has been critiqued on the grounds that it is primarily unidirectional. In other words, it considered the effect of parenting on adolescents but minimized the effect that teens' behaviors had on parenting. For example, a rebellious and confrontational adolescent is likely to elicit a far different set of parenting behaviors than will a compliant and cooperative teen. There is indeed evidence that many of the effects of parenting on teen behavior are bidirectional (Pinquart, 2017). Additionally, some research suggests that adolescents may actually exert a stronger effect on their parents' behavior than parenting exerts on their behavior (Kerr et al., 2012), perhaps via their own genetically influenced personality traits (Klahr & Burt, 2014).

Parental Monitoring and Adolescents' Self-disclosure A large body of research shows that parental monitoring is one of the most consistently identified protective factors for teens (Barnes et al., 2006; Racz & McMahon, 2011). Parental monitoring broadly involves keeping track of the young person's activities, for example, by signing the teen up for after-school activities, checking in with parents of their teen's friends, and keeping track of a teen's whereabouts (Barnes et al., 2006).

Part of monitoring involves knowing what a teen is up to. Both adolescents and parents see *prudential* issues, behavior related to health and safety (such as smoking, drinking, and drug use), as most subject to disclosure; followed by *moral* issues (such as lying); *conventional* issues (such

Adolescents raised in homes with a positive family atmosphere tend to come through adolescence without serious problems. gawrav/E+/Getty Images

TABLE 12.2 Items Used to Assess Perceived Areas of Parental versus Adolescent Authority

Moral Items	Conventional Items	Prudential Items	Multifaceted Items	Multifaceted Friendship	Personal Items
Stealing money from parents	Not doing chores	Smoking cigarettes	Not cleaning bedroom	When to start dating	Sleeping late on weekends
Hitting siblings	Talking back to parents	Drinking alcohol	Getting multiple ear piercings	Staying over at a friend's house	Choosing how to spend allowance money
Lying to parents	Using bad manners	Doing drugs	Staying out late	Seeing friends parents don't like	Choosing own clothes or hairstyles
Breaking a promise to parents	Cursing	Having sex	Watching cable TV	Seeing friends rather than family	Choice of music

Source: Smetana, J., Crean, H., Campione-Barr, N. (2005). Adolescents' and parents' changing conceptions of parental authority. In J. Smetana (Ed.), *Changing boundaries of parental authority during adolescence* (New Directions for Child and Adolescent Development, No. 108, pp. 31–46). San Francisco, CA: Jossey-Bass.

as bad manners or swearing); and *multifaceted,* or borderline, issues (such as seeing an R-rated movie), which lie at the boundary between personal matters and one of the other categories. Both adolescents and parents see *personal* issues (such as how teens spend their time and money) as least subject to disclosure (Smetana et al., 2005; Table 12.1). However, for each type of behavior parents tend to want more disclosure than adolescents are willing to provide, although this discrepancy diminishes with age (Smetana et al., 2006). Adolescent disclosure to parents is predictive of delinquency; those teens who disclose more are less likely to engage in problem behaviors (Keijsers et al., 2010).

Teens are more likely to disclose information when parents maintain a warm, responsive family climate and provide clear expectations without being overly controlling (Soenens et al., 2006)—in other words, when parenting is authoritative. This link between warmth and disclosure has been found in various ethnic groups in the United States, including Chinese American, Mexican American, and European American youth (Yau et al., 2009). Adolescents, especially girls, tend to have closer, more supportive relationships with their mothers than with their fathers (Smetana et al., 2006), and girls confide more in their mothers (Yau et al., 2009). Moreover, relationship quality seems to matter more in girls' willingness to confide in their parents. In other words, boys' secret keeping depends less on relationship warmth than does that of girls' (Keijsers et al., 2010).

Family Structure and Atmosphere Adolescents living with their continuously married parents tend to have significantly fewer behavioral problems than those in other family structures (single-parent, cohabiting, or stepfamilies). However, research suggests the structure of the family is less important than the family climate. The processes that promote or undermine positive development are the same across varied types of families (Murry & Lippold, 2018). For instance, when negative affect or conflict are high, teen outcomes are less positive regardless of the type of family structure (Phillips, 2012; Lansford & Ceballo, 2001). Transitioning into a new family structure, as occurs when parents divorce or remarry, can also have a negative influence on outcomes. This is particularly true when there is an associated change in economic status or if the transition negatively affects parenting practices (Murry & Lippold, 2018).

Divorce negatively impacts outcomes in part via its influence on the paternal relationship. Teens whose parents were still married reported a close relationship with their father 48 percent of the time, whereas those whose parents were divorced reported being close to their father only 25 percent of the time (Scott et al., 2007). Although involvement with nonresident fathers is generally beneficial, high levels of conflict are associated with externalizing problems and low academic achievement in teens (Modecki et al., 2015).

Adolescents, especially boys, from single-parent families are at higher risk for problem behaviors such as substance abuse or aggression. However, this risk can be mitigated by other family structures. For example, parental monitoring (Griffin et al., 2000) and mother's educational level, family income, and quality of the home environment (Ricciuti, 2004) have been associated with a reduction in risk.

Adolescents in cohabiting families, like younger children, tend to have greater behavioral and emotional problems than adolescents in married families. However, some of the data on cohabitation are driven by family instability—a documented negative influence on development—rather than cohabitation per se. Adolescents in stepparent families have also experienced family instability and thus may be considered a more appropriate comparison group. When compared to teens in married stepparent families, a recent review suggested that adolescents in cohabiting families are similar in outcomes. They have similar rates of delinquency, substance abuse, risky sexual activity, academic outcomes, physical health, and emotional well-being (Manning, 2017).

Adolescents from families headed by gay or lesbian parents do not appear to show differences in a wide variety of outcomes, including cognitive development, gender identity, and adjustment problems (Fedewa et al., 2015). Rather, as with traditional two-parent families, the quality of the relationship—not the sexual orientation of the parents—is the key variable influencing outcomes (Wainright & Patterson, 2006).

Maternal Employment and Economic Stress The impact of a mother's work outside the home may depend on how many parents are present in the household. Single mothers may find that work affects how much time and energy is left to spend with children or monitor their activities (Han et al., 2010). Additionally, maternal employment has repeatedly been associated with a less healthy nutritional environment in the home (Bauer et al., 2012) and an increased risk of overweight (Miller, 2011; Morrissey, 2013).

The type of after-school care and supervision is particularly important. Those teens who are on their own, away from home, tend to become involved in alcohol and drug use and in misconduct in school, especially if they have an early history of problem behavior (Coley et al., 2004). Participation in organized after-school activities can serve as a protective factor (Mahatmya & Lohman, 2011; Sharp et al., 2015).

As discussed earlier, a major problem in many single-parent families is lack of money. For example, teens are more likely to drop out of school and show declines in self-esteem and mastery if their mothers have unstable employment or are out of work for 2 years (Kalil & Ziol-Guest, 2005). Job displacement—where employees lose their jobs due to organizational changes such as restructuring, downsizing, or relocating—has also been associated with declines in educational attainment and well-being in adolescents from single-parent families (Brand & Simon Thomas, 2014). Thus any potential negative effects of maternal employment need to be weighed against the economic benefits of employment outside the home. For instance, higher maternal income during childhood is associated with fewer problems in adolescence and higher cognitive achievement (Shepherd-Banigan et al., 2019; Cook & Rabon, 2018).

SIBLING RELATIONSHIPS IN ADOLESCENCE

In many traditional cultures, older siblings have the responsibility of caring for younger siblings (Weisner et al., 1977). This care may involve merely keeping a younger sibling occupied while a nearby parent is busy to full responsibility for feeding, bathing, and caring for a younger sibling (Maynard, 2004). In Western, industrialized countries such as the United States, siblings are generally not given these types of responsibilities.

As adolescents spend more time with peers, they spend less time with siblings. Generally, and perhaps as a result of this, adolescents tend to be less close to siblings than to friends and are less influenced by them. This distance grows across adolescence (Laursen, 1996). Moreover, as children move through adolescence, their relationships with their siblings become progressively more equal (Campione-Barr, 2017).

Sibling conflict declines across middle adolescence. Research has shown that sisters report more intimacy than brothers or mixed pairs. Mixed-sex siblings become less intimate between middle childhood and early adolescence, but more so in middle adolescence, a time when most young people become more interested in the other sex (Kim et al., 2006).

Sibling relationships become more equal as younger siblings approach or reach adolescence and the relative age difference diminishes. Even so, younger siblings still look up to their older siblings and may try to emulate them. Peathegee Inc/Blend Images LLC

Teens who have opposite-sex siblings report increases in their perceived romantic competence from early adolescence into adulthood (Doughty et al., 2015).

Siblings can exert positive or negative effects on each other. Older siblings may influence a younger one to smoke, drink, or use drugs (Pomery et al., 2005; Rende et al., 2005). Younger siblings hanging out with an antisocial older brother are at serious risk for adolescent antisocial behavior, drug use, sexual behavior, and violence (Snyder et al., 2005; Solmeyer et al., 2014). Although generally a warm relationship is protective and contributes to good outcomes, at times an emotionally close sibling relationship can lead to an increased risk of a child modeling the antisocial behavior of a delinquent sibling (Dirks et al., 2015).

However, siblings can also be protective. A recent meta-analysis supports the strong connection between warm relationships with little conflict and healthier psychological adjustment in siblings (Buist et al., 2013). For example, when siblings show increases in warmth and decreases in conflict over time, this predicts a decrease in depressive symptoms (Harper et al., 2016). Additionally, adolescents who have positive relationships with their siblings are liked better by their peers (Yucel et al., 2018), suggesting that social skills learned in the context of sibling relationships can be transferred to the peer group.

PEER INFLUENCES IN ADOLESCENCE

In childhood, most peer interactions are *dyadic,* or one-to-one, though larger groupings begin to form in middle childhood. As children move into adolescence, the peer social system becomes more diverse. *Cliques*—structured groups of friends who do things together—become more important. A larger type of grouping, the *crowd,* which does not normally exist before adolescence, is based not on personal interactions but on reputation, image, or identity. Crowd membership is a social construction: for example, the jocks, the nerds, or the stoners (Brown & Klute, 2003).

Friendships The intensity of friendships and the amount of time spent with friends may be greater in adolescence than at any other time. Friendships become more reciprocal, equal, and stable. Higher-quality friendships are more stable (Hiatt et al., 2015). Those that are less satisfying become less important or are abandoned. Often, differences in such areas as peer acceptance, physical aggression, school competence, and especially sex predict friendship dissolution (Hartl et al., 2015).

Greater intimacy, loyalty, and sharing with friends mark a transition toward adultlike friendships. Girls' friendships tend to be more intimate than boys', with frequent sharing of confidences (Brown & Klute, 2003). Adolescents who are more intimate with their friends feel closer to and have less conflict with them (Chow et al., 2013). Additionally, they have a high opinion of themselves, do well in school, are sociable, and are unlikely to be hostile, anxious, or depressed (Berndt & Perry, 1990; Buhrmester, 1990; Hartup & Stevens, 1999). When adolescents have high-quality friendships, those friendships tend to be deeply embedded within their other supportive social relationships, including other friends, romantic partners, and family members (Flynn et al., 2017). For example, adolescents with high-quality friendships also tend to have established strong bonds with parents (Brown & Klute, 2003).

Not all the influence of friendships is positive, however. Risk-taking, especially in early adolescence, is higher in the company of peers than when alone (Gardner & Steinberg, 2005), even when potential negative consequences are made clear (Smith et al., 2014).

Social Media and Electronic Interactions We live in a brave new world of electronically mediated communication. Approximately 95 percent of teens own or have access to a smartphone and 88 percent have access to a computer in their home (Anderson & Jiang, 2018).

In general, screen-based media usage is related to poorer physical health, quality of life, and quality of family relationships (Iannotti et al., 2009). The type of media consumed appears to be important. For example, studies indicate that instant messaging (van den Eijnden et al., 2008) and video game usage (Mathers et al., 2009) are associated with depression, whereas television is associated with obesity, socio-emotional problems, and lower self-esteem (Russ et al., 2009). Additionally, some people can develop problematic Internet usage,

The increased intimacy of adolescent friendship reflects cognitive as well as emotional development. Closer intimacy means a greater ability and desire to share emotions and feelings. Mauritius/Pixtal/age fotostock

a condition akin to addiction, in which continued Internet and electronic use can impact everyday functioning, relationships, and overall well-being (Akin, 2012). Men, perhaps because of their generally greater interest in video games and online gaming, are at higher risk of developing addiction-related behaviors (Anderson et al., 2017). The transmission of sexual content over electronic media is a growing concern as well (see Research in Action).

However, not all access to the Internet is harmful. At times online communication can stimulate rather than reduce social connectedness (James et al., 2017). For example, studies have found instant messaging can have a positive effect on relationship quality in adolescence (Valkenburg & Peter, 2009), and social competence in lonely adolescents can be strengthened using the Internet to communicate with others and experiment with their identities (Valkenburg & Peter, 2008). This has been particularly true for sexual minority youth, possibly because they often have difficulty finding partners or safe supportive places in which to be themselves in real life (Korchmaros et al., 2015). It also served as a lifeline to many teens during the COVID-19 pandemic, allowing them to remain socially connected to others despite restrictions on movement and socialization (Hamilton et al., 2020).

Individuals often become unusually intimate in an online environment and feel free to express themselves. This, in conjunction with limited contextual cues, increases the risk of cyberbullying. Adolescents who are active users of social media sites, especially if they are not guarded about their personal privacy, are more vulnerable to online harassment and cyberbullying (Ang, 2015). Estimates for prevalence rates across middle school and high school vary widely, with cyberbullying perpetration reported from 1 to 41 percent, victimization from 3 to 72 percent, and cyberbully/victim rates from 2.3 percent to 16.7 percent (Selkie et al., 2016). Most studies on cyberbullying have been conducted in North America, but cross-cultural work also shows variable estimates across different countries, with Canada (23.8 percent) and China (23 percent) showing higher median prevalence rates and Australia (5 percent), Sweden (5.2 percent), and Germany (6.3 percent) lower levels (Brochado et al., 2017).

Romantic Relationships Romantic relationships are a central part of most adolescents' social worlds. This is not limited to Western countries. A survey of the anthropological literature spanning 166 cultures documented the evidence of romantic love in 147 of the cultures (Jankowiak & Fischer, 1992).

With the onset of puberty, most heterosexual boys and girls begin to think about and interact more with members of the other sex. Typically, they move from mixed groups or group dates to one-on-one romantic relationships that, unlike other-sex friendships, they describe as involving passion and a sense of commitment (Lantagne & Furman, 2017). Although they practice interacting with the opposite sex within the context of friendships, opposite-sex friends are unlikely to become romantic partners. Rather, romantic partners tend to come from different friendship networks (Kreager et al., 2016).

Romantic relationships tend to become more intense and intimate across adolescence. By age 16, adolescents interact with and think about romantic partners more than they do parents, friends, or siblings (Bouchey & Furman, 2003). Not until late adolescence or early adulthood, though, do romantic relationships begin to serve the full gamut of emotional needs that such relationships can serve and then only in relatively long-term relationships (Furman & Wehner, 1997). Relationships with parents, including divorce or conflict in the home, may affect the quality of romantic relationships (Johnson & Galambos, 2014; Cui & Fincham, 2010; Cui et al., 2011).

Dating Violence Dating violence is a significant global problem. The three common forms of dating violence are:

Physical—when a partner is hit, pinched, shoved, or kicked.

Emotional—when a partner is threatened or verbally abused.

Sexual—when a partner is forced to engage in a nonconsensual sex act.

Intimate partner violence is the most common form of gender-based violence perpetrated against young girls. Approximately 120 million girls and women worldwide have

research in action

TEEN DATING AND TECHNOLOGY

Adolescent dating is a normative development in many Western cultures. As with other social relationships, technology plays an increasingly large role in adolescent romantic relationships (Vaterlaus et al., 2017).

Although most teens meet romantic partners in school, some teenagers develop online relationships. Teenagers with online romantic partners fall into two camps: those who are popular offline, and those with difficulty forming offline relationships. LGBTQ adolescents have been identified as especially likely to initiate online relationships, possibly because of a lack of partners or safe, supportive spaces in which to be themselves in real life (Korchmaros et al., 2015).

Social media profiles are often used as a means of "checking out" new romantic interests early in relationships. After a first encounter, exchange of social media information may help gauge continued interest (Subrahmanyam & Greenfield, 2008). Photos and status updates are used to learn more about potential romantic partners. Adolescents also report "signaling" romantic interest by liking older photos and using embedded private messaging tools as a less intimidating means of initiating further communication (Van Ouystel et al., 2016). Once a relationship is established, social media may also be used to communicate daily, to convey affection, to referee arguments, and to initiate "breakups and makeups" (Vaterlaus et al., 2017). Adolescents report uploading joint photos of themselves as a couple to indirectly broadcast a relationship, rather than making an official status change (Van Ouystel et al., 2016).

More problematically, electronic communication can also be used for the exchange of sexually charged conversation or explicit photographs, often referred to as **sexting**. A large cross-national meta-analysis of 34 studies including more than 110,000 respondents from the United States, Europe, Canada, Australia, South Africa, and South Korea suggested that about 14.8 percent of teens starting at an average age of 15 years engaged in sexting (Madigan et al., 2018). Sexting has been linked with other risky behaviors, such as higher substance use, being sexually active, having concurrent sexual partners, and more current sexual partners (Ybarra & Mitchell, 2014; Kletke et al., 2014).

 How do you think social media, text messaging, and other technologies have affected the nature of adolescent dating? Do you think sexting is a form of adolescent risk-taking?

sexting
The sharing or sending of sexually explicit or suggestive photos or videos to others.

experienced rape or sexual assault, and almost 1 in 3 adolescent girls have been the victims of physical, sexual, or emotional violence at the hands of their husband or romantic partner (UNICEF, 2014).

Statistics indicate that about 1 in 11 adolescent females and slightly 1 in 15 adolescent males in the United States have experienced physical violence in their dating relationship (Centers for Disease Control and Prevention, 2020). The rates for emotional abuse are even higher: As many as 3 in 10 adolescents report being verbally or psychologically abused (Halpern et al., 2003). Teen females (1 in 9) are more at risk of sexual violence than males (1 in 36) (Centers for Disease Control and Prevention, 2020). White students generally report lower levels of teen dating violence than African American or Hispanic students (Vagi et al., 2015).

In addition to the physical harm caused by this type of abuse, teens who are victims of dating violence are more likely to do poorly in school and to engage in risky behaviors such as drug and alcohol use. These students are also subject to eating disorders, depression, anxiety, and suicide (Mulford & Giordano, 2008; Centers for Disease Control and Prevention, 2020).

Risk factors that may predict violence include substance abuse, conflict and/or abuse in the home, antisocial peers, and living in neighborhoods with high rates of crime and drug use (Child Trends DataBank, 2010a, 2010b). Additionally, attitudes about the acceptability of violence within relationships, poor family relationship quality, mental health problems, and the use of aggressive media also predict violence (Vagi et al., 2013). Peers are a particularly important influence. Peer dating violence, peers' aggressive and/or antisocial behavior, and being victimized by peers are all significantly related to both dating violence perpetration and victimization (Garthe et al., 2017).

Unhealthy relationships can last a lifetime as victims carry patterns of violence into future relationships. Adolescent dating violence is a predictor of adult partner violence (Exner-Cortens et al., 2017).

Antisocial Behavior and Juvenile Delinquency

What influences young people to enage in—or refrain from—violence or other antisocial acts?

BIOLOGICAL INFLUENCES

Analyses of many studies have concluded that genes influence 40 to 56 percent of the variation in antisocial behavior within a population, and 60 to 65 percent of the variation in aggressive antisociality (Ferguson, 2010; Rhee & Waldman, 2002; Tackett et al., 2005). Genes alone, however, are not predictive of antisocial behavior. Recent research findings suggest that although genetics influences delinquency, environmental influences including family, friends, and school affect gene expression (Guo et al., 2008; Silberg et al., 2012).

Neurobiological deficits, particularly in the portions of the brain that regulate reactions to stress, may help explain why some children become antisocial. As a result of these neurological deficits, children may not receive or heed normal warning signals to restrain impulsive or reckless behavior (Van Goozen & Fairchild, 2008). For example, they tend to have abnormal or blunted responses to events that generally evoke fear in others (Marsh et al., 2011).

Part of this abnormal physiological profile may involve arousal processes. Specifically, individuals who have low arousal levels may be prone to antisocial behaviors as a form of sensation seeking to achieve arousal levels that a typical person experiences. In support of this, high frontal EEG power (which is associated with low brain arousal) is associated with adolescent aggressive antisocial behavior in male twins (Niv et al., 2015). Low heart rate has also been found to be repeatedly associated with antisocial behavior in both men and women (Portnoy & Farrington, 2015; Hammerton et al., 2018).

Attentional processes may also be involved. Children with attention-deficit/hyperactivity disorder (ADHD) are at higher risk for the development of comorbid conduct disorder (CD) and depression that contribute to antisocial behavior (Drabick et al., 2006). There is some dispute about whether or not ADHD by itself is a direct risk factor for the development of antisocial behavior, although more recent research does seem to indicate this is the case (Storebø & Simonsen, 2016).

Also, findings of an MRI investigation of empathetic response have indicated youth with aggressive conduct disorders have atypical responses to seeing others in pain (Decety, et al., 2009). Moreover, those individuals who have traits associated with psychopathy seem to have reduced gray matter volume in the anterior rostral prefrontal cortex and temporal poles, areas involved in the processing of empathy, moral reasoning, and emotions such as shame and guilt (Gregory et al., 2012).

Researchers have identified two types of antisocial behavior: an early-onset type, beginning by age 11, which tends to lead to chronic juvenile delinquency in adolescence, and a milder, late-onset type, beginning after puberty, which tends to arise temporarily in adolescence (Moffitt, 1993). Evidence suggests that early-onset offenders are more strongly influenced by biological factors. For example, such adolescents show poor impulse control, are aggressive, and tend not to think about their future (Barker et al., 2010; Monahan et al., 2009).

ENVIRONMENTAL INFLUENCES

Parents of children who become chronically antisocial may have failed to reinforce good behavior in early childhood and may have been harsh or inconsistent in their discipline (Coie & Dodge, 1998; Snyder et al., 2005; Neppl et al., 2016). The children may get payoffs for antisocial behavior: When they act up, they may gain attention or get their own way. When constant criticism, angry coercion, or rude, uncooperative behavior characterizes parent-child interactions, the child tends to show aggressive behavior problems, which worsen the parent-child relationship (Buehler, 2006). However, when parents show high warmth and low hostility, even delinquent teens tend to reduce their problematic behavior and behave more positively (Williams & Steinberg, 2011).

Antisocial adolescents tend to have antisocial friends, and their antisocial behavior increases when they associate with each other (Monahan et al., 2009). The way antisocial teenagers talk, laugh, or smirk about rule-breaking and nod knowingly among themselves seems to constitute a sort of "deviancy training" (Dishion & Tipsord, 2011). Not all children respond in the same way, however. Teens who are genetically predisposed to antisocial behavior respond more strongly to maladaptive peer group norms than other children (Brendgen et al., 2015). Notably, peer influences can also be positive. For example, exposure to altruistic peers can buffer adolescents against the negative effects of violent or dangerous neighborhoods (Criss et al., 2017; Rious & Cunningham, 2018).

Poor children are more likely than other children to commit antisocial acts, and those whose families are continuously poor tend to become more antisocial with time (Macmillan et al., 2004). Even within individual children, those whose families rose in and out of poverty showed more delinquent behavior when their families had less money than when they were financially well off (Rekker et al., 2015).

Weak neighborhood social organization in a disadvantaged community can influence delinquency through its effects on parenting behavior and peer deviance (Chung & Steinberg, 2006) as well as on norms about the use of antisocial or violent acts (Stewart & Simons, 2010). For example, exposure to community violence and living in a dangerous community are strong predictors of future antisocial behavior (Slatterly & Meyers, 2014; Criss et al., 2017). By contrast, collective efficacy—the strength of social connections within a neighborhood and the extent to which residents monitor or supervise each other's children—can positively influence outcomes (Odgers et al., 2009).

PREVENTING AND TREATING DELINQUENCY

Adolescents who have taken part in well-designed early childhood intervention programs are less likely to get in trouble than their equally underprivileged peers (Piquero et al., 2016; Reynolds et al., 2011) Effective programs target high-risk urban children and last at least 2 years during the child's first 5 years. They influence children directly, through high-quality day care or education, and at the same time indirectly, by offering families assistance and support geared to their needs (Schweinhart et al., 1993; Yoshikawa, 1994; Zigler et al., 1992).

Once children reach adolescence, especially in poor, crime-ridden neighborhoods, interventions need to focus on spotting troubled adolescents and preventing gang recruitment (Tolan et al., 2003). Successful programs boost parenting skills through better monitoring, behavioral management, and neighborhood social support (Vieno et al., 2009).

Programs such as teen hangouts and summer camps for behaviorally disturbed youth and Scared Straight (in which at-risk teens visit prisons and speak with inmates) can be counterproductive because they bring together groups of deviant youth who tend to reinforce each other's deviancy. Moving juveniles through the juvenile court system rather than diversion programs (such as counseling referrals) also tends to increase future offending (Petrosino et al., 2013). More effective programs—scouts, sports, and church activities—integrate deviant youth into the nondeviant mainstream. Structured, adult-monitored, or school-based activities after school, on weekend evenings, and in summer, when adolescents are most likely to be idle and to get in trouble, can reduce their exposure to settings that encourage antisocial behavior (Dodge et al., 2006).

Fortunately, the great majority of adolescents do not get into serious trouble. Those who show disturbed behavior can—and should—be helped. With love, guidance, and support, adolescents can avoid risks, build on their strengths, and explore their possibilities as they approach adult life.

What are the chances this young man will become a hardened criminal? Teenagers who don't have positive alternatives are more likely to adopt antisocial lifestyles. ncognet0/E+/Getty Images

summary and key terms

The Search for Identity

- A central concern during adolescence is the search for identity. Erik Erikson described this psychosocial conflict as *identity versus identity confusion*. The virtue that should arise from this conflict is *fidelity*.
- James Marcia described four identity statuses: identity achievement, foreclosure, moratorium, and identity diffusion.
- Researchers differ on whether girls and boys take different paths to identity formation.
- Ethnicity is an important part of identity. Minority adolescents seem to go through stages of ethnic identity development much like Marcia's identity statuses.
- Identity development may be challenging for sexual minority youth.

identity, identity versus identity confusion, fidelity, identity status, crisis, commitment, identity achievement, foreclosure, moratorium, identity diffusion, cultural socialization, sexual orientation, transgender

Sexuality

- Sexual orientation appears to be influenced by an interaction of biological and environmental factors.
- Teenage sexual activity involves risks of pregnancy and sexually transmitted infections. Adolescents at greatest risk are those who begin sexual activity early, have multiple partners, do not use contraceptives, and are ill-informed about sex.
- Regular condom use is the best safeguard for sexually active teens.
- Comprehensive sex education programs delay sexual initiation and encourage contraceptive use. Abstinence-only programs are not as effective.
- Female genital mutilation involves procedures to remove external female genitalia for non-health-related reasons. It is associated with both immediate and long-term health risks.
- Teenage pregnancy and birthrates in the United States have declined.
- Teenage childbearing often has negative outcomes, including ill health and financial hardship, and risk of ineffective parenting.

sexually transmitted infections (STIs)

Relationships

- Full-scale adolescent rebellion is unusual. For the majority of teens, adolescence is a fairly smooth transition. For the few deeply troubled teens, it can predict a difficult adulthood.
- Adolescents spend an increasing amount of time with peers, but relationships with parents continue to be influential.
- Conflict with parents tends to be greatest during early adolescence. Parental monitoring and warmth are associated with positive outcomes.
- Effects of family structure and maternal employment on adolescents' development may depend on such factors as economic resources and the quality of the home environment.
- Relationships with siblings tend to become more distant during adolescence, and the balance of power between older and younger siblings becomes more equal.
- The influence of the peer group is strongest in early adolescence. The structure of the peer group becomes more elaborate, involving cliques and crowds as well as friendships.
- Friendships, especially among girls, become more intimate, stable, and supportive in adolescence.
- Romantic relationships meet a variety of needs and develop with age and experience.

adolescent rebellion, individuation, sexting

Antisocial Behavior and Juvenile Delinquency

- Chronic delinquency generally stems from early-onset antisociality. It is associated with multiple, interacting risk factors, including ineffective parenting, school failure, peer and neighborhood influence, and low socioeconomic status. Programs that attack risk factors from an early age have had success.

Design Credit: (globe) janrysavy/Getty Images

Physical and Cognitive Development in Emerging and Young Adulthood

learning objectives

Describe the transition from adolescence to adulthood.

Summarize physical development in young adults.

Discuss sexuality in young adults.

Characterize cognitive changes in early adulthood.

Identify examples of the roles of experience, culture, and gender in adult moral development.

Explain how emerging adults make the transitions to higher education and work.

Cecilie_Arcurs/E+/Getty Images

In this chapter, we look at emerging and young adults' physical functioning and factors that can affect health, fitness, sexuality, and reproduction. We discuss features of their cognition and how education can stimulate its growth. We examine moral development. Finally, we discuss entering the world of work.

Emerging Adulthood

In industrialized countries, the achievement of adult status takes longer and follows far more varied routes than in the past. Before the mid-twentieth century, a young man just out of high school typically would seek a stable job, marry, and start a family. For a young woman, the usual route to adulthood was marriage, which occurred as soon as she found a suitable mate.

Since the 1950s, the technological revolution made specialized training increasingly essential. The ages at first marriage and childbirth shifted sharply upward as both women and men pursued higher education or vocational opportunities and as cohabitation became more acceptable (Furstenberg et al., 2005; Lundberg & Pollack, 2014). Today the road to adulthood may be marked by multiple milestones—entering college, working, moving away from home, getting married, and having children—and the order and timing of these transitions vary (Schulenberg et al., 2005).

Thus some developmental scientists suggest that, for the many young people in industrialized societies, the late teens through the mid to late twenties has become a distinct period of the life span now known as **emerging adulthood.** It is a time during which young people are no longer adolescents but have not yet settled into adult roles. This period of the life span is marked by identity exploration and a focus on the self. Young adults commonly feel between life stages, and although life is often unstable, most acknowledge the possibilities the future may hold for them (Arnett, 2014).

This exploratory process is not shared by all young adults in the world. It is largely tied to development in Western countries, especially among relatively affluent young people. For example, in the United States, young adults from lower social classes generally report they attain adult status a few years earlier than those from higher social classes. This may be because poorer young adults experienced a difficult childhood or the shouldering of adult responsibilities at a young age, pushing them into maturity. Others, often due to financial constraints, do not attend college and so settle into a stable working life at an earlier age than do their wealthier counterparts (Arnett, 2016).

In Europe high unemployment rates make one common marker of adult status, economic self-sufficiency, difficult to attain. This may delay perceived entry into adulthood (Arnett, 2014). In Japan, which before the COVID-19 pandemic had a more robust employment rate than Europe, young people reported reaching adulthood earlier (Crocetti et al., 2015). Cultural values may also affect this process. Some of the concepts linked with emerging adulthood in Western countries, such as independence from parents and the establishment of a separate home, are viewed as less desirable in collectivistic cultures (Zhong & Arnett, 2014). Moreover, the negative impact of the COVID-19 pandemic on the global economy may alter this marker of adulthood.

Despite these differences, research across European countries, North America, and Asia suggests many commonalities in the paths young people take as they move toward adulthood (Arnett, 2014; Buhl & Lanz, 2007). Still, as we discuss aspects of emerging adulthood in this chapter, we must remember that, as with adolescence, emerging adulthood is a stage of the life span whose definition relies upon cultural context.

emerging adulthood
Proposed transitional period between adolescence and adulthood commonly found in industrialized countries.

Physical Health and Fitness

Young adults in the United States generally enjoy the benefits of good health, but they increasingly suffer from a range of health-related risks tied to modern lifestyles.

HEALTH STATUS AND INSURANCE COVERAGE

Behavioral factors—what young adults eat, whether they get enough sleep, how physically active they are, and whether they smoke, drink, or use drugs—contribute greatly to health and well-being. Moreover, these environmental factors can result in epigenetic changes in the expression of particular genes that can have lifelong consequences (Motta et al., 2017). The habits that young adults develop during this time tend to become ingrained

Many young adults, like this young man, are in prime physical condition. Digital Vision/Getty Images

and are highly predictive of the likelihood they will experience good health at older ages (Liu et al., 2012).

Approximately 96 percent of adults 19 to 24 years of age in the United States report that they are in good to excellent health. (National Center for Health Statistics, 2017). Lower socioeconomic status is consistently, although not invariably, associated with poor health (Braveman et al., 2010), and additional disparities are conferred by living in rural versus urban areas of the United States (Caldwell et al., 2016). Accidents, most commonly car accidents, are the leading cause of death for Americans age 15 to 24. Closely following this are suicides and homicides, both of which overwhelmingly occur via the use of firearms (Kochanek et al., 2019).

Although the risk of death or severe complications such as respiratory distress and stroke as a result of COVID-19 infection is lower in younger adults than in older adults, it is not nonexistent (CDC COVID-19 Response Team, 2020; Oxley et al., 2020). A small percentage of young adults will become seriously ill after infection, and this risk may increase when high blood pressure, cardiac disease, diabetes, or obesity is present (Fang et al., 2020; Lighter et al., 2020).

Whites and Asians are the young adults most likely to be in good health, although Asians report higher levels of depression than do white adults. African Americans and Latinos report higher levels of obesity and are more likely to report poor health and depression than whites and Asians. These effects are mirrored if, rather than self-reported race, skin color is used as a metric. Darker individuals, especially women, report higher obesity, poorer health, and higher levels of depression. This suggests that perceived discrimination and the consequent stress it can cause negatively affect darker skinned individuals. When respondents carry the intersectional characteristics of minority racial status as well as female gender, these effects are magnified (Perreira et al., 2019).

In the past, young people generally aged out of many social service programs at the same time they moved away from home and began living independently. Thus emerging and young adults had the highest poverty rate and the lowest levels of health insurance of any age group (Callahan & Cooper, 2005; Park et al., 2006). The implementation of the Affordable Care Act in 2010 resulted in sharp rises in health care access, utilization, and reported health indicators in young adults (Barbaresco et al., 2015; Sommers et al., 2015). From 2013 to 2016, the percentage of young adults without health insurance decreased by 8.6 percent (Griffith, 2020). However, in December 2017, the Trump administration effectively repealed the individual mandate requiring all adults to purchase health insurance or face a fine. As a result, the percentage of young adults without health insurance began to rise (Griffith, 2020; Klein, 2020). In response to fears about declining coverage, six states independently passed individual mandates, and additional states were actively considering similar legislation (National Conference of State Legislators, 2020). How these actions might have affected health insurance coverage has been eclipsed by the COVID-19 pandemic. Because of the resultant historic job losses and high unemployment, many previously insured people lost health insurance. Given continuing effects of the pandemic, and because most health insurance coverage is tied to employment, it is likely the percentage of uninsured people will continue to be high, particularly in those states that opted not to expand Medicaid (Bureau of Labor Statistics, 2020; Garfield et al., 2020).

GENETIC INFLUENCES ON HEALTH

The expression of any disorder—obesity, certain cancers, asthma—is the product of an interaction between genes and environment (Ritz et al., 2017). For example, a number of genetic variants increase the likelihood of major depressive disorder in adulthood in response to early life stress. When raised in a supportive environment, a child with these variants is at no additional risk when compared to a child without the variants. However, in the absence of a supportive early environment, depression risk is elevated (Heim & Binder, 2012). The mechanism of action for increased depression risk is likely via genetic influences on neurobiological factors. In other words, genes that affect the action of hormone receptors, stress response systems, and synaptic plasticity may influence a person's ability to respond adaptively to stressful events. This sensitivity may then make that person more reactive to the influence of environmental stress, especially when it occurs early in development (Hornung & Heim, 2014). It is not the gene in isolation nor is it the environment in isolation that leads to depression. Rather, it is the interaction of the two that is key.

BEHAVIORAL INFLUENCES ON HEALTH

Many health risks are affected by modifiable behavioral factors. Unfortunately *knowing* about good (and bad) health habits is not enough and people do not always do what they should.

Diet and Nutrition The World Health Organization recommends a diet rich in fruits, vegetables, whole grains, and unsaturated fats. Unfortunately, a healthy diet is not the norm across the globe. In 2017, 11 million deaths across the world could be attributed to dietary risk factors, including high salt intake, low consumption of whole grains, and a failure to include fruits in the diet (Afshin et al., 2019).

Worldwide, poor diets and a lack of physical activity are among the leading causes of preventable diseases, overweight, and obesity (World Health Organization, 2020). In the United States, estimates are that half of premature deaths could be prevented via modifiable lifestyle factors, including improvements in diet and exercise, and quitting smoking (Yoon et al., 2014)

Obesity and Overweight Research on overweight and obesity in emerging adulthood is an important area of research as people are most likely to become obese at this time (GBD 2015 Obesity Collaborators, 2017). This is particularly true in the early twenties, and especially so for those young adults who are already overweight (Lanoye et al., 2017). Factors such as moving out of the family home, decreases in income, and establishing independence make this stage of the life span a critical juncture for health.

Across the world, obesity has almost tripled since 1975. In 2016, there were 1.9 billion overweight adults, 650 million of whom were obese. Much of this increase can be attributed to unintended consequences of globalization, including increases in the availability of nutrient-poor, high-calorie processed foods and urbanization of the environment (World Health Organization, 2018; Figure 13.1).

In the United States, the average man or woman is more than 24 pounds heavier than in the early 1960s but is only about 1 inch taller (Flegal et al., 2010). In 2016 the prevalence of obesity was 39.6 percent among United States adults. Young adults age 20 to 39 had slightly lower rates (35.7 percent) than the general adult population, with a higher rate in women (36.5 percent) than men (34.8 percent). Overall adult obesity rates were highest in Hispanics (47 percent), African Americans (46.8 percent), and non-Hispanic whites (37.9), and lowest in Asian Americans (12.7 percent) (Hales et al., 2017). If overweight and obesity are considered together (BMI greater than 25), some 71.6 percent of the United States population meets the criteria (Fryar et al., 2018).

What explains the obesity epidemic? Experts point to an increase in snacking, availability of inexpensive fast foods, supersized portions, high-fat diets, labor-saving technologies including highly processed foods, sedentary recreational pursuits such as television and computers, and community and environmental factors such as a lack of sidewalks and safe bike trails (Zizza et al., 2001; Pereira et al., 2005; Centers for Disease Control and Prevention, 2020). An inherited tendency toward obesity may interact with environmental and behavioral factors (Choquet & Meyre, 2011; Albuquerque et al., 2015).

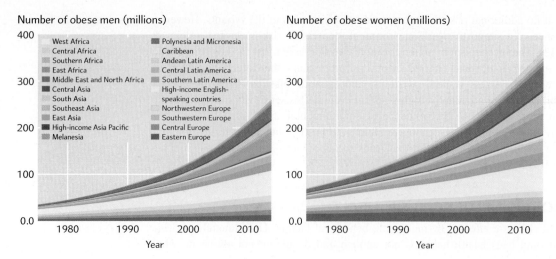

FIGURE 13.1

Global Trends in Body Mass Index, 1975–2015

Worldwide, obesity is growing. Rates of obesity have nearly tripled since 1975.

Source: NCD Risk Factor Collaboration. (2016). "Trends in adult body-mass index in 200 countries from 1975 to 2014: A pooled analysis of 1698 population-based measurement studies with 19.2 million participants." *The Lancet, 387*(10026), 1377–1396.

Obesity carries risks of high blood pressure, heart disease, stroke, diabetes, gallstones, arthritis and other muscular and skeletal disorders, and some cancers, and it diminishes quality and length of life. It is also associated with mental illness, most notably anxiety and depression (Centers for Disease Control and Prevention, 2020). Estimates are that obesity costs the United States approximately $342 billion a year in total health care spending on noninstitutionalized adults, or some 28.2 percent of total health care expenditures (Beiner et al., 2017).

Lifestyle changes (dietary change plus exercise) or drug treatments can result in weight loss (LeBlanc et al., 2018; Khera et al., 2016), but such losses are difficult for many people to sustain for long periods of time. People who lose weight must fight both their physiology, which includes altered satiety and metabolic influences, as well as their propensity to return to earlier behaviors that contributed to their weight in the first place (MacLean et al., 2015). Weight-loss maintenance is possible, but requires *permanent* lifestyle changes (Thomas et al., 2014; Dombrowski et al., 2014; Montesi, et al., 2016). Only about 1 in 6 people are able to successfully lose and keep off 10 percent of their body weight (Kraschnewski et al., 2010).

Another option available for weight loss for obese adults is bariatric surgery. Bariatric surgery is any surgery that is carried out to induce weight loss, and it generally involves rerouting or removing parts of the stomach or small intestine. Bariatric surgery results in more consistent and sustained weight loss and a reduction in risk profile for obesity-related disease in most adults than diet or lifestyle changes. However, 10 to 17 percent of adults experience complications as a result of the surgery (Chang et al., 2014). Generally, bariatric surgery is an effective route only for the most obese adults (Williams et al., 2015).

Food Insecurity Although most of the world lives in countries in which overweight and obesity kill more people than being underweight (World Health Organization, 2018), it is nonetheless the case many people do not have enough to eat. This is particularly true in Africa and Southern Asia. Moreover, food insecurity and hunger is rising in some countries, most notably in middle-income countries and countries that rely heavily on the international trade of raw materials (World Health Organization, 2019). Researchers predict that climate change and COVID-19 will increase global levels of food insecurity (Richardson et al., 2018; The World Bank, 2020).

Food security exists in developed countries as well. In the United States, one recent nationally representative study found 11 percent of adults 24 to 32 years old were food insecure. Food insecurity was associated with poor health, high blood pressure, and obstructive airway disease (Nagata et al., 2019).

Physical Activity In addition to helping maintain healthy body weight, physical activity builds muscles; strengthens heart and lungs; lowers blood pressure; protects against heart disease, stroke, diabetes, several cancers, and osteoporosis (a thinning of the bones that is most prevalent in middle-age and older women); relieves anxiety and depression; and lengthens life (Reiner et al., 2013; Centers for Disease Control and Prevention, 2019). Moreover, research suggests that exercise is also related to cognitive functioning (Guiney et al., 2015), and that a healthy body is one of the variables related to the establishment and maintenance of a healthy mind (Kramer et al., 2006). Incorporating more physical activity into daily life—for example, by walking instead of driving short distances—can be as effective as structured exercise. Health benefits accrue from exercise no matter how much a person weighs. However, weight loss generally requires calorie restriction (Swift et al., 2018) and maintaining a healthy weight requires permanent physical activity and diet changes.

Unfortunately, although people are aware of the need to establish healthy habits, this is easier said than done. Generally, adults age 18 to 64 should engage in 75 to 150 minutes of aerobic exercise (depending on intensity levels) and muscle-strengthening activities, preferably spread across a week, for substantial health benefits. Additional health benefits are gained by engaging in more than 300 minutes of physical activity a week, including muscle-strengthening activities on 2 or more days a week (Centers for Disease Control and Prevention, 2020). Despite the fact that the minimum guidelines represent less than half an hour a day of exercise, only about half of Americans meet these guidelines, slightly over 77 percent do not meet aerobic and strength training guidelines, and 15.2 percent report no physical activity at all (Centers for Disease Control and Prevention, 2014; Blackwell & Clark, 2018).

Estimates are that if adults exercised in line with recommendations, 1 in 10 cases of chronic disease could be prevented. There are also economic benefits—approximately $117 billion in annual U.S. health care costs could be prevented with exercise. Moreover, a lack of exercise is associated with military readiness. Approximately 1 in 4 young Americans cannot join the military because they weigh too much, and the number of ineligible young adults is projected to increase in the coming years (Centers for Disease Control and Prevention, 2019).

Stress A growing body of research suggests that our psychological health affects our physical health, and that high levels of chronic stress are related to a host of physical and immunological impairments (Ho et al., 2010).

Some young adults are more reactive to negative events than others (Howland et al., 2017). In some cases, stress may lead young adults to engage in risky behaviors such as drinking or smoking (Pedersen, 2017; Suzuki et al., 2016). Additionally, stressed-out college students are more likely to eat junk food, are less likely to exercise (Hudd et al., 2000), and tend to have poor quality or insufficient sleep (Lund et al., 2010), and their grades and health tend to suffer (Leppink et al., 2016).

Young adults who have high self-esteem, are high in extraversion and low in neuroticism, or are religious may be better able to handle negative aspects of stressful events (Balgiou, 2017; Koenig et al., 2012; Yadav et al., 2017). There are also gender differences in how young adults typically cope with stress. *Emotion-focused coping* consists of attempts to manage the emotions associated with experiencing a particular event by such tactics as refusing to think about an issue or reframing the event in a positive

Incorporating more activity into daily life, say, by biking to work instead of driving, can be as effective as structured exercise. LarsZ/Shutterstock

light. *Problem-focused coping* involves addressing an issue head-on and developing action-oriented ways of managing and changing a bad situation (Lazarus & Folkman, 1984). College-age women are more likely to use emotion-focused strategies than are college-age men (Crăciun, 2013; Nolen-Hoeksema & Aldao, 2011). At the same time, college-age women experience overall higher levels of stress (Brougham et al., 2009).

Sleep Many emerging and young adults often go without adequate sleep. Among college students, family life stress, together with academic stress, is associated with high levels of insomnia (Lund et al., 2010). In a study of more than 1,300 undergraduate college students, 47 percent reported mild insomnia and 22.5 percent reported moderate to severe insomnia (Gress-Smith et al., 2015).

Sleep deprivation affects not only physical health but cognitive, emotional, and social functioning as well. A lack of sleep affects executive control (Lowe et al., 2017) and attentional processes, including the ability to inhibit (Anderson & Platten, 2011) or sustain (Lowe et al., 2017) attention, as well as the ability to rapidly shift attention from one task to another (Whitney et al., 2017). Sleep deprivation also affects working (Frenda & Fenn, 2016), long-term (Lowe et al., 2017), and prospective (memory for future events) memory (Grundgeiger et al., 2014). Not surprisingly, sleep deprivation is associated with poor academic performance (van der Heijden et al., 2018). Perhaps of even more concern, adults are 3 times more likely to get into a car crash if sleep impaired, and driving after not sleeping for 20 hours is equivalent to a 0.08 blood alcohol level—the legal limit (National Safety Council, 2020). Adults 18 to 24 years, who are already in the highest accident risk group, are also the most likely to show declines in driving performance after not sleeping (Soleimanloo et al., 2017).

Sleep deprivation also feels bad. Sleep deprivation is associated with enhanced emotional reactivity to negative events and a dampened response to positive events (Kahn et al., 2013; O'Leary et al., 2017). Sleep deprived people also report feeling sleepy, stressed, cold, confused, hungry, and irritable, and this effect is larger in younger than in older adults (Schwarz et al., 2019). These effects are interactive. It is also the case that negative emotions, especially stress, can negatively impact sleep quantity and quality (Yap et al., 2018; Konjarski et al., 2018).

Sleep deprivation is also associated with mental illness and psychological disorders, including excessive use of electronics (see Window on the World). For instance, sleep deprivation has been linked to depression (Murphy & Peterson, 2015; Soehner & Harvey, 2012). Although sleep deprivation results in heightened negative responses to specific negative events in healthy people, in people with mood disorders sleep deprivation results in a generalized negative emotional response to almost all events (O'Leary et al., 2017). Sleep deprivation has also been linked to anxiety disorders (Soehner & Harvey, 2012) and an increase in psychotic symptoms in healthy, sleep-deprived adults (Reeve et al., 2018).

Adequate sleep improves learning of complex motor skills and consolidates previous learning (Tucker et al., 2017). Compared to adults who did not sleep well the previous night, adults who had a good night's sleep were more engaged with their work the next day (Kuhnel et al., 2017). Even a short nap can prevent burnout—oversaturation of the brain's perceptual processing systems (Mednick et al., 2002).

Smoking Smoking causes cancer, stroke, lung disease, diabetes, and chronic obstructive pulmonary disease, as does second-hand smoke (Centers for Disease Control and Prevention, 2018). Smoking is the leading preventable cause of death worldwide, and it kills half of users (World Health Organization, 2020). Globally, approximately 1.1 billion people smoke, 80 percent of whom live in low- and middle-income countries. Direct tobacco use kills approximately 7 million people a year, and another 1.2 million people die as a consequence of exposure to second-hand smoke (World Health Organization, 2020).

Health care expenditures that result from smoking account for 5.7 percent of total global health care costs, and when both health care and productivity are considered together, they account for 1.8 percent of the global annual gross domestic product (Goodchild et al., 2018). Smoking also exerts an economic burden on individuals,

Because nicotine is so addictive, it is hard to quit smoking despite awareness of health risks. Ryan McVay/Photodisc/Getty Images

window on the world

INTERNET ADDICTION

About half of the global population—3.8 billion people—use the Internet. In 2008, global statistics for the average Internet use for adults was 2.7 hours per day. By 2017, that number had more than doubled to 5.9 hours per day (Meeker, 2018). Although access to the Internet and to the information available there has undoubted benefits, it also carries risks. **Internet addiction** (IA) is one such risk. IA is characterized by a compulsive need to engage in nonwork online activities, to the point where such activities are interfering with family, social life, or work (Cash et al., 2012).

The prevalence of IA is estimated to be approximately 6 percent worldwide. However, differences are substantial across regions. Countries with lower life satisfaction, more pollution and traffic, and a lower median income are likely to have higher rates of IA. The highest rates of IA are found in the Middle East (10.9 percent) and the lowest in Northern and Western Europe (2.6 percent) (Cheng & Li, 2014). Overall, Asian countries appear to have higher rates of IA than do Western countries (Kuss et al., 2014). Moreover, IA is somewhat more common in men than in women, especially in Asia (Su et al., 2019). However, this gender difference can vary by country. In Spain, for example, women are more likely to have issues with IA than are men (Aparicio-Martinez et al., 2020). Data are not currently available for the African continent as a whole; however, Internet access is rapidly increasing there and thus IA is likely to become problematic in the near future (Cheng & Li, 2014).

Examples abound of the relationship between excessive Internet use and poor outcomes. For example, American college students who show signs of IA are more likely to have low life satisfaction, and American, Italian, Brazilian, Portuguese, and Turkish students who show signs of IA have lower self-esteem (Blachnio et al., 2019; Seabra et al., 2017; Bozoglan et al., 2013). In Hong Kong, IA is associated with poor academic performance, depression, and suicidal ideation (Chung et al., 2019). A study of nine European countries showed an association between obsessive-compulsive behaviors and paranoid ideation with problematic Internet usage and, in men, phobic anxiety (Laconi et al., 2018).

As the use of technology spreads more broadly beyond the borders of the developed world, we can expect to see the influence of this new risk spread. The world's most vulnerable developing countries were on track to achieve universal Internet and mobile phone access by 2020 (United Nations, 2018). Although this is vital to modernization efforts, the introduction of these technologies is a double-edged sword.

what's **your** **view**

What do your Internet habits look like? Are there things you need to change to live a healthier life?

---

particularly those from poor countries, who divert their income to tobacco products rather than essential needs such as food (World Health Organization, 2020).

Approximately 15.6 percent of men and 12 percent of women over age 18 in the United States are current smokers. Smoking rates are higher among Native Americans/ Alaska native (22.6 percent), whites (15 percent), and African Americans (14.6 percent) and lower in Hispanic adults (9.8 percent) and Asian Americans (7.1 percent) (Centers for Disease Control and Prevention, 2019). In recent years, e-cigarettes have become more popular, and currently 2.8 percent of adults smoke e-cigarettes (Centers for Disease Control and Prevention, 2020).

The primary reason people continue to smoke even when they would prefer to stop is the addictive nature of nicotine, a substance found in tobacco. Nicotine is as addictive as heroin and cocaine (National Institute on Drug Abuse, 2012; Centers for Disease Control and Prevention, 2010). A tendency to addiction may be genetic (Ware & Munafo, 2015), and the link between genetic susceptibility and likelihood of addiction is strongest for those who begin to smoke at a young age (Weiss et al., 2008). Smoking is strongly associated with socioeconomic level as well. Adults who are poor, lack health insurance,

internet addiction
A compulsive need to engage in nonwork online activities, to the point where such activities are interfering with family, social life, or work.

or have low levels of education are more likely to smoke (Centers for Disease Control and Prevention, 2019).

Nicotine chewing gum, nicotine patches, drugs such as buproprion (Zyban) or vareni-cline (Chantix), and nicotine nasal sprays and inhalers, especially when combined with counseling, can help addicted persons quit smoking (Centers for Disease Control and Prevention, 2019). Although early research on the effectiveness of replacing cigarettes with e-cigarettes as part of a smoking cessation program was somewhat promising (Siegel et al., 2011; Cahn & Siegel, 2011), more recent research seems to suggest that people who switch to e-cigarettes are *less* likely to quit smoking (Kalkhoran & Glantz, 2016).

Quitting smoking is difficult, and many smoking cessation programs have low success rates. Medication can increase the 6-month success rate to approximately 25 to 33 percent (American Cancer Society, 2011), and overall, almost 60 percent of U.S. adults who had ever smoked have quit (Babb, 2017). However, fewer than one-third of smokers who try to quit use proven smoking cessation therapies, and only 1 in 10 manage to quit over the course of a year (Babb, 2017).

A variety of methods have been shown to be effective means of reducing tobacco use. Media campaigns, especially graphic pictorials, have been shown to reduce smoking in countries in which they have been instituted, as have bans on promoting and advertising tobacco products. Increasing the price of cigarettes, generally via taxation, is another method that has been shown to reduce smoking. For every 10 percent increase in tobacco product prices, there is a 4 to 5 percent drop in smoking rates (World Health Organization, 2020).

Alcohol Use Alcohol use peaks in emerging adulthood. Among adults ages 18 to 25, approximately 55.1 percent reported drinking alcohol in the past month, and 34.9 reported a binge drinking episode (SAMHSA, 2019).

College is a prime time and place for drinking, and college students tend to drink more frequently and more heavily than their noncollegiate peers. In 2018, nearly 55 percent of full-time college students ages 18 to 22 had used alcohol in the past month as compared to 44.6 percent of their noncollegiate peers. Moreover, 9.6 percent of college students drank heavily, and almost 37 percent had engaged in binge drinking (NIAAA, 2020; Figure 13.2). Heavy drinking over the years may lead to high blood pressure, stroke, cirrhosis of the liver, other gastrointestinal disorders (including ulcers), pancreatic disease, certain cancers, heart failure, stroke, damage to the nervous system, psychoses, and other medical problems (Centers for Disease Control and Prevention, 2019).

Alcohol use is associated with other risks characteristic of emerging adulthood, such as traffic accidents, crime, HIV infection, illicit drug and tobacco use, and the likelihood of committing sexual assault (Centers for Disease Control and Prevention, 2019; Brecklin & Ullman, 2010). Academic consequences are common for college students (NIAAA, 2020). An estimated 11.1 percent of U.S. drivers age 16 or older said that in the past year they drove under the influence of alcohol. Driving under the influence of alcohol is highest in the early adult years, and peaks during ages 21 (19.4 percent) to 29 (17.6 percent) (Lipari et al., 2016).

Risky drinking is defined as consuming more than 14 drinks a week or four drinks on any single day for men and more than seven drinks a week or three drinks on any single day for women. Approximately 1 out of 4 people are risky drinkers, at risk for alcoholism and liver disease, as well as physical, mental, and social problems as a result of their drinking (NIAAA, 2016).

The group reporting the highest consumption of alcohol is Native Americans, followed by whites, and the lowest levels of use are reported by African Americans, Hispanics, and Asian Americans. Gender affects consumption patterns as well, with females generally consuming less alcohol overall as well as having lower levels of binge drinking (SAMHSA, 2019; NIAAA, 2016).

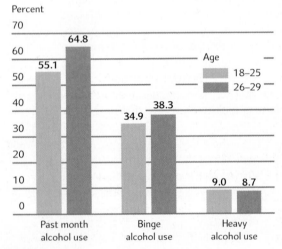

FIGURE 13.2

Current (Past Month) Alcohol Use, Binge Drinking, and Heavy Alcohol Use

Source: Substance Abuse and Mental Health Services Administration (SAMHSA). (2019). Results from the 2018 national survey on drug use and health: Detailed tables. Retrieved from www.samhsa.gov/data/sites/default/files/cbhsq-reports/NSDUHDetailedTabs2018R2/NSDUHDetTabsSect2pe2018.htm

risky drinking
Consuming more than 14 drinks a week or 4 drinks on any single day for men, and more than 7 drinks a week or 3 drinks on any single day for women.

INDIRECT INFLUENCES ON HEALTH

Indirect influences on health include income, education, and race/ethnicity. Relationships also seem to make a difference, as do the paths young people take into adulthood.

Living in poverty, as do this mother and her infant daughter in a shelter, can affect health through poor nutrition, substandard housing, and inadequate health care. Gabriella Angotti-Jones/The New York Times/Redux

Socioeconomic Status and Race/Ethnicity The connection between socioeconomic status (SES) and health has been widely documented (Williams et al., 2016). Higher-income people rate their health as better and live longer than lower-income people (National Center for Health Statistics, 2019). This finding exists across a wide variety of countries and is most marked in countries with high income inequality (Lago et al., 2018). Education is important too. The less schooling people have had, the greater the chance that they will develop and die from communicable diseases, injuries, or chronic ailments, or that they will become victims of homicide or suicide (National Center for Health Statistics, 2019; Pamuk et al., 1998). As with SES, the association between education and health also exists across countries (Rosengren et al., 2018; Vom dem Knesebeck et al., 2006).

This does not mean that income and education *cause* good health; instead, they are related to environmental and lifestyle factors that do. Better-educated and more affluent people tend to have healthier diets and better preventive health care and medical treatment. They exercise more, are less likely to be overweight, smoke less, are less likely to use illicit drugs, and are more likely to use alcohol in moderation (National Center for Health Statistics, 2019; SAMHSA, 2019). The less affluent are more likely to live close to a polluting facility (Mohai et al., 2009) and show elevated levels of lead and other toxins in their blood (Bellinger, 2008).

Race and ethnicity matter as well. However, because many minorities in the United States also tend to have a lower SES, many health issues stem from that rather than from minority status per se. Factors associated with SES do not tell the whole story, however. For example, although African Americans smoke less than white Americans, they metabolize more nicotine in the blood, face higher risks of lung cancer, and have more trouble breaking the habit. Similarly, given equal alcohol consumption, African Americans have more liver damage and higher alcohol-related mortality (Williams, 2012; Caraballo et al., 1998). Additionally, even when controlling for SES, African Americans are more likely to suffer from and die of heart disease (Williams et al., 2016). A review of more than 100 studies found that racial/ethnic minorities tend to receive lower-quality health care than white people do, even when insurance status, income, age, and severity of conditions are similar (Smedley et al., 2002).

Relationships and Health Social relationships are vital to health and well-being. Research has identified at least two interrelated aspects of the social environment that can promote health: *social integration* and *social support*. However, the social environment can also affect health adversely if *negative interactions* are common (Cohen, 2004).

Social integration is active engagement in a broad range of social relationships, activities, and roles. Social integration has repeatedly been associated with lower mortality rates (Holt-Lundstad et al., 2010; Holt-Lundstad et al., 2015). A recent multicountry meta-analysis of 51 studies found wide friendship networks were protective against depression (Santini et al., 2015). Having a wide social network and multiple social roles is also associated with a reduced risk of high blood pressure (Cuffee et al., 2014) and even a decreased susceptibility to colds (Cohen et al., 2015). In contrast, loneliness, social isolation, and low-quality relationships are associated with increased risk of heart disease, stroke, depression, and anxiety (Valtorta et al., 2016; Teo et al., 2013; Teo et al., 2013). It appears that online social networking sites, such as Facebook, can provide some of these benefits via online interaction and support (Hobbs et al., 2016; Ellison et al., 2007).

Although there is a clear association between relationships and health, it's not clear which is the cause and which the effect. Sam Edwards/Caia Image/Glow Images

Social support refers to material, informational, and psychological resources derived from the social network on which a person can rely for help in coping with stress. In highly stressful situations, people who are in touch with others may be more likely to eat and sleep sensibly, get enough exercise, and avoid substance abuse, and are less likely to be distressed, anxious, depressed, or even to die (Cohen, 2004; Thoits, 2011). Social support has been associated with lower risk for depression across multiple countries (Santini et al., 2015), and support from varied sources, including family, friends, and children, is associated with increases in well-being over time (Chopik, 2017).

It is important to note that relationships can also be a source of stress. *Negative interactions*, as a whole, are damaging. For instance, strain in relationships has been found to be predictive of chronic illness and lower well-being (Chopik, 2017; Walen & Lachman, 2000) and negative social exchanges are predictive of declines in physical health (Edwards et al., 2001). Relationship stress may also lead to unhealthy behavior patterns—such as smoking or drinking—in attempts to manage the unpleasant arousal that can result (Cacioppo & Cacioppo, 2014).

Because marriage offers a readily available system for both social integration and social support, it is not surprising that marriage tends to benefit health (Robles et al., 2014). Married people, particularly in young adulthood, tend to be healthier physically and psychologically than those who are never-married, cohabiting, widowed, separated, or divorced (Schoenborn, 2004). Dissolving a marriage, or a cohabitation, tends to have negative effects on physical or mental health or both—but so, apparently, does remaining in a bad relationship (Wu & Hart, 2002). People in an unhappy marriage have poorer health than single adults, and even a supportive network of friends and family does not buffer this effect (Holt-Lundstad et al., 2008). High conflict, in particular, is associated with a host of negative outcomes, including poor immune system functioning, higher blood pressure, poor cardiovascular health, and even death (Segrin & Flora, 2017).

The effects of marriage and health can be both direct and indirect. Most notably, two-income families are more likely to have access to health insurance, which is in turn related to general health. This can help explain the higher risk for negative health consequences in past years for some people in same-sex relationships, as they were less likely to have health insurance (Buchmueller & Carpenter, 2010). The passage of same-sex marriage laws seems to have resulted in broad health benefits to gay couples, perhaps also in part due to decreasing discrimination and prejudice, and thereby stress (Hatzenbuehler et al., 2012).

MENTAL HEALTH PROBLEMS

In emerging adulthood, the freedom to make life decisions and choose diverse paths is often liberating, but the responsibility to rely on oneself and to become financially self-supporting can be overwhelming.

Alcoholism Alcohol abuse and dependence are global issues. Approximately 2.3 billion people in the world drink alcohol, although rates vary by region. The average drinker consumes 32.8 grams of alcohol a day, but this number is 20 percent higher in Africa and 20 percent lower in Southeast Asia (World Health Organization, 2019). College, too, is a prime time and place for drinking, and college students tend to drink more heavily than their noncollegiate peers (SAMHSA, 2019; Figure 13.3). Alcohol consumption is responsible for 5.3 percent of deaths worldwide, numbering some 3 million people every year. This number is even more striking with adults age 20 to 39; 13.5 percent of deaths for this stage in the life span are attributable to alcohol. Moreover, alcohol is a causal factor in more than 200 diseases and injuries (World Health Organization, 2018).

In the United States, 5.8 percent of the adult population suffers from alcohol use disorder (NIAAA, 2020). Alcohol dependence, or **alcoholism,** is a long-term physical condition characterized by compulsive drinking that a person is unable to control. The heritability of a tendency to alcoholism is about 50 percent (Verhulst et al., 2015).

From 6 to 48 hours after the last drink, alcoholics can experience physical withdrawal symptoms (anxiety, agitation, tremors, elevated blood pressure, and sometimes seizures). Alcoholics, like drug addicts, develop a tolerance for the substance and need more and more to get the desired high (NIAAA, 1996).

Treatment for alcoholism may include detoxification (removing all alcohol from the body), hospitalization, medication, individual and group psychotherapy, and referral to a support organization, such as Alcoholics Anonymous. Although not a cure, treatment can give alcoholics new tools to cope with their addiction and lead productive lives.

Drug Use and Abuse Use of illicit drugs peaks at ages 18 to 25; almost 24 percent of this age group report using illicit drugs during the past month. As young adults settle down, get married, and take responsibility for their future, they tend to cut down on drug use. Usage rates drop sharply during the late twenties, and then continue to decline, albeit more slowly as people enter later adulthood and old age.

As in adolescence, marijuana is by far the most popular illicit drug among young adults. In 2018, 22.1 percent of 18- to 25-year-olds had used marijuana within the previous month (SAMHSA, 2019). In general, although a substantial proportion of young adults will experiment with alcohol, cigarettes, or marijuana, a much smaller proportion will try other drugs such as ecstasy, methamphetamines, or heroin. An even smaller number will become chronic and heavy users of illegal drugs (Johnston et al., 2013). However, despite the relatively moderate prevalence numbers for heavy abuse, drug abuse still results in significant costs to the user personally and to society at large. Estimates are that illicit drugs cost society some $193 billion a year (U.S. Department of Justice Drug Intelligence Center, 2011).

People with substance use disorders are likely to also have mood or anxiety disorders (Hunt et al., 2020; Hunt et al., 2016; Lai et al., 2015). The causal relationship here is unclear. It may be that the use of illegal drugs puts young people at risk for the development of psychopathology. Alternatively, it could be the case that those people who suffer from psychological distress self-medicate and thus are more prone to addiction and other risky behaviors.

Depression Adolescence and emerging adulthood appear to be sensitive periods for the onset of depressive disorders. Starting about age 13, rates of depression begin to rise, first in girls and then in boys. Rates continue to increase through adolescence and early adulthood, with the early gender difference peaking in adolescence and then declining somewhat in adulthood (Salk et al., 2017; Salk et al., 2016).

Depression is not just being sad. A major depressive disorder is a clinical diagnosis with a specific set of symptoms, is considered to be very serious, and generally requires medical intervention. People who are diagnosed with major depressive disorder often have depressed or irritable moods for most of the day, every day, show reduced interest in and enjoyment of previously pleasurable activities, often either gain or lose significant amounts of weight, have difficulties sleeping too little or too much, and frequently show a variety of cognitive biases and maladaptive recurrent thoughts.

A recent meta-analysis including data from 90 nations indicated young women are more likely to suffer from a major depressive episode. This difference in prevalence begins about age 12, peaks in adolescence, and then declines slightly. Somewhat

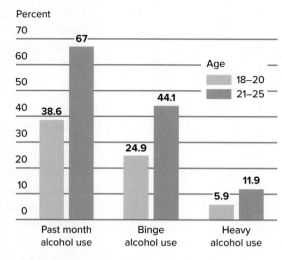

FIGURE 13.3

Current (Past Month) Alcohol Use, Binge Drinking, and Heavy Alcohol Use among Persons aged 18-25 Years

Source: Substance Abuse and Mental Health Services Administration (SAMHSA). (2019). Results from the 2018 national survey on drug use and health: Detailed tables. Retrieved from www.samhsa.gov/data/sites/default/files/cbhsq-reports/NSDUHDetailedTabs2018R2/NSDUHDetTabsSect2pe2018.htm

alcoholism
Chronic disease involving dependence on use of alcohol, causing interference with normal functioning and fulfillment of obligations.

paradoxically, gender differences in depression rates are largest in countries with more gender equity (Salk et al., 2017). Women are also more likely than men to show atypical symptoms, to have an additional psychopathology along with their depressive disorders, and to attempt (but not succeed in) suicide (Gorman, 2006). In addition, women and men may respond to antidepressants differently, with women showing a greater likelihood of adverse drug reactions (Franconi et al., 2007).

The Effect of COVID-19 on Mental Health The COVID-19 pandemic has changed life. In the United States, early data indicate the shelter-at-home orders instituted in most states, the economic devastation and unemployment, and the suspension of the ordinary rhythms of life resulted in a mental health crisis. Overall, Americans reported increased levels of depression (24 percent) and anxiety (30 percent) as a result of the pandemic, a significant rise from earlier years. Moreover, the effects were being felt most intensely by young adults. A poll conducted in May 2020 showed high levels of depression (36 percent) and anxiety (42 percent) in adults age 18 to 29 years (Centers for Disease Control and Prevention, 2020). This mental health crisis came at the same time many people lost their jobs and health insurance, and thus their access to mental health care services.

Sexual and Reproductive Issues

Sexual and reproductive activities are often a prime preoccupation of emerging and young adulthood. Three such concerns are disorders related to menstruation, sexually transmitted infections (STIs), and infertility.

SEXUAL BEHAVIOR AND ATTITUDES

Sexual behaviors and attitudes across different nations vary widely. Generally, extramarital affairs, homosexuality, and abortion are viewed the most negatively (Pew Research Center, 2014), although younger and more educated adults are more likely to accept homosexuality and same-sex marriage. Still, adults in most countries, especially with a majority Orthodox population, do not hold positive views about same-sex marriage (Pew Research Center, 2017).

Premarital sex is more likely to be considered acceptable in developed than developing countries. In some countries, including Iran, Morocco, Pakistan, Saudi Arabia, Somalia, and Sudan, premarital sex is illegal. Nonetheless, the number of adults who have premarital sex appears to be rising, with China serving as a particularly striking example. Even in countries with negative views about premarital sexual activity, such as India, Indonesia, and Iran, prevalence is rising (Chamie, 2018). Some of this change is likely due to the increase in availability of and knowledge about contraceptives. Across different countries, most adults view contraception as morally acceptable, and only about 14 percent of adults say the use of contraceptives is immoral (Pew Research Center, 2014).

In the United States today almost all never-married, non-cohabitating adults—81.5 percent—have had vaginal intercourse before marriage (Copen et al., 2016). Increasingly, American adults agree with statements about the acceptability of premarital sex for adults over the age of 18 (Daugherty & Copen, 2016). According to a nationally representative in-person survey of men and women ages 18 to 44 years, 86.2 percent of women and 87.4 percent of men have had oral sex, 35.9 percent of women and 42.3 percent of men have had anal sex, and 94.2 percent of women and 92 percent of men have had vaginal intercourse (Copen et al., 2016). Casual sex (hooking up) is fairly common, especially on college campuses. Sexual assaults on women are a problem in this age group.

Emerging adults tend to have more sexual partners than in older age groups, but they have sex less frequently. People who become sexually active during emerging adulthood tend to engage in fewer risky behaviors than those who began in adolescence (Lefkowitz & Gillen, 2006). The most common contraceptives are the birth control pill, female sterilization, and condoms. There has been a recent rise in the use of the IUD and a decline in the use of male sterilization (Kavanaugh & Jerman, 2018).

Acceptability of homosexual unions is growing, especially in younger cohorts and in women (Daugherty & Copen, 2016), although religious adults, especially evangelical Protestants, are less likely to be supportive of same-sex relationships (Pew Research Center, 2019). With respect to sexual orientation, 1.3 percent of women and 1.9 percent of men reported they were homosexual, and 5.5 percent of women and 2 percent of men reported they were bisexual (Copen et al., 2016). Although estimates of the transgender population are more difficult to determine, roughly 0.10 to 0.39 percent of the U.S. population is transgender (Flores et al., 2017; Meerwijk & Sevelius, 2017).

By emerging adulthood, most lesbian, gay, bisexual, and transgender persons are clear about their sexual identity. Indeed, the median age at which gay, lesbian, and bisexual adults report suspecting they might not be heterosexual is about 12 years, and the median age they report knowing for sure is 17 years (Pew Research Center, 2013). In general, more recent generations in the United States are coming out at an earlier age, and men are more likely to come out at an earlier age (by approximately 2 years) than women. Ethnic minority youth are equally likely to be open about their sexual orientation to their friends, but they are more likely to keep this information secret from their parents (Grov et al., 2006).

SEXUALLY TRANSMITTED INFECTIONS

Sexually transmitted infections (STIs), also known as sexually transmitted diseases (STDs), are illnesses that are transmitted by having sex. Because people can carry infections for years without displaying signs of active disease, STIs is becoming the preferred term.

Every day, 1 million people are infected with an STI. There are roughly 30 bacteria and viruses that can cause STIs. Four of the most common STIs—syphilis, gonorrhea, chlamydia, and trichomoniasis—are currently curable with antibiotics. The other four common STIs—hepatitis B, herpes, human immunodeficiency (HIV), and human papillomavirus (HPV)—are viral, and although some of their symptoms can be controlled, they cannot be cured. Although attempts to promote positive behavioral changes in sexually active people and to increase the availability of health screening tools and medications to treat infection have been taken, STIs remain an international problem (World Health Organization, 2019).

By far the highest rates of STIs in the United States are among emerging adults (Centers for Disease Control and Prevention, 2019). People age 15 to 24 years account for 20 percent of the total prevalence rate and about half of all new infections (Satterwhite et al., 2013). The risk has been rising—for five years in a row, chlamydia, gonorrhea, and syphilis all showed increases in prevalence and are currently at an all-time high. Moreover, the risk is higher among certain ethnic groups. For example, there are elevated rates of STIs in African American men and women, and the lowest rates are found in Asian Americans (Centers for Disease Control and Prevention, 2019).

Worldwide, approximately 37.9 million adults are living with HIV, 62 percent of whom have access to some form of medical treatment. Over two-thirds of people infected with HIV live in Africa (World Health Organization, 2019). Since the peak in 1997, the number of new HIV infections has fallen by 40 percent. Still, in 2018 approximately 1.7 million people were infected (UNAIDS, 2019). Key populations at risk include men who have sex with men, people who inject drugs, prison inmates, sex workers, and transgender people (World Health Organization, 2019). With highly active antiviral therapy, death rates of persons diagnosed with HIV have dropped dramatically, and their average median survival after diagnosis has increased to more than 35 years (Bhaskaran et al., 2008; Lohse et al., 2007).

MENSTRUAL DISORDERS

Premenstrual syndrome (PMS) is a disorder that produces physical discomfort and emotional tension for up to 2 weeks before a menstrual period. Symptoms may include fatigue, headaches, swelling and tenderness of the breasts, swollen hands or feet, abdominal bloating, nausea, cramps, constipation, food cravings, weight gain, anxiety,

premenstrual syndrome (PMS)
Disorder producing symptoms of physical discomfort and emotional tension for up to 2 weeks before a menstrual period.

depression, irritability, mood swings, tearfulness, and difficulty concentrating or remembering (ACOG, 2020). Cross-culturally, women report PMS at a rate of about 50 percent, with a range of 10 to 98 percent (Direkvand-Moghadam et al., 2014).

The cause of PMS is not fully understood, but it appears to be a response to normal monthly surges of the female hormones estrogen and progesterone as well as to levels of the male hormone testosterone and of serotonin, a brain chemical (Biggs & Demuth, 2011). Smoking and alcohol consumption may put women at increased risk for the development of PMS (Bertone-Johnson et al., 2008; del Mar Fernández et al., 2018). Caffeine, which women are sometimes counseled to avoid, does not appear to be associated with PMS (Purdue-Smith et al., 2016).

The symptoms of PMS can sometimes be alleviated through aerobic exercise, eating frequent small meals, a diet high in complex carbohydrates and low in salt and caffeine, and regular sleep routines. Calcium, magnesium, and vitamin E supplements may help. Medications may relieve specific symptoms—for example, a diuretic for bloating and weight gain (ACOG, 2020).

PMS may include the presence of cramps, but it is not the same thing. PMS can be confused with *dysmenorrhea* (painful menstruation, or "cramps"). Cramps tend to affect younger women, whereas PMS is more typical in women in their thirties or older. Dysmenorrhea is caused by contractions of the uterus, which are set in motion by prostaglandin, a hormone-like substance; it can be treated with prostaglandin inhibitors, such as ibuprofen (Wang et al., 2004). Dysmenorrhea is found cross-culturally and estimated to affect up to 91 percent of women. Depending on country, 2 to 28 percent of women report experiencing severe symptoms that interfere with activities (Ju et al., 2014).

INFERTILITY

infertility
Inability to conceive a child after 12 months of sexual intercourse without the use of birth control.

An estimated 6 percent of U.S. women 15 to 44 years old experience **infertility**: the inability to conceive a baby after 12 months of intercourse in the absence of birth control methods. Moreover, approximately 12 percent of women have difficulty carrying a pregnancy to term (Centers for Disease Control and Prevention, 2019). Worldwide, about 1 in 4 couples have difficulty getting pregnant or maintaining a pregnancy to term (Mascarenhas et al., 2012).

Women's fertility begins to decline in their late twenties, with substantial decreases during their thirties. By their forties, many women are not able to become pregnant without the use of assisted reproductive technology (ART). Men's fertility is less affected by age but begins to decline in the late thirties (Dunson et al., 2002). Approximately 30 percent of couples are unable to become parents, and they show worse mental health outcomes than those couples who do succeed (Gameiro & Finnigan, 2017).

The most common cause of infertility in men is production of too few sperm. In some instances an ejaculatory duct may be blocked, preventing the exit of sperm, or sperm may be unable to swim well enough to reach the cervix (O'Flynn et al., 2010).

A major cause of declining fertility in women after age 30 is deterioration in the quality of ova. Infertility can also result from blockage of the fallopian tubes, preventing ova from reaching the uterus. This blockage may occur as the result of scar tissue formation from sexually transmitted infections. In addition, some women suffer from physical disorders affecting fertility, such as polycystic ovarian syndrome or primary ovarian insufficiency (Centers for Disease Control and Prevention, 2019).

Delayed childbearing, use of fertility drugs, and assisted reproductive techniques such as in vitro fertilization increase the likelihood of multiple, usually premature, births. Nancy R. Cohen/Photodisc/Getty Images

IN VITRO FERTILIZATION

Assisted reproductive technologies (ARTs) offer hope for those who experience infertility. In vitro fertilization (IVF) is the most common type of assisted reproductive technology, accounting for 99 percent of ARTs (Centers for Disease Control and Prevention, 2017). With IVF, women receive fertility drugs to stimulate ova (egg) production. Ova are surgically removed, fertilized with sperm in a laboratory dish, put in a special culture, and monitored for growth. Approximately 3 to 5 days later, the largest and healthiest fertilized eggs—known as blastocysts—are then implanted in the uterus. If successful, the woman's body responds hormonally to the blastocyst, which continues to grow and divide, and pregnancy occurs.

Generally, more fertilized eggs are produced than are used during one cycle. Unused eggs may be frozen and stored for later implantation. Fresh embryo transfers have greater IVF success rates, but frozen-thawed embryo transfers have begun to approach these rates in recent years (Wong et al., 2014). More recently, women have also been employing cryopreservation, or egg freezing, to extend their years of fertility. Eggs are harvested with the intention of conceiving a child at a later date with the help of IVF (Brezina & Zhao, 2012).

IVF success rates are not very high. In 2015, approximately 30 percent of IVF procedures using fresh, nondonor eggs resulted in pregnancy (Centers for Disease Control and Prevention, 2017). Transfer of multiple embryos not only increases the odds of IVF success, but also carries risks to mother and baby, including multiple births, preterm delivery, and pregnancy complications (Reddy et al., 2007). Thus many advocates support single embryo transfers coupled with subsequent frozen-thawed embryo transfers for infertile couples wanting multiple children, and many countries pose restrictions on the number of embryos transferred per IVF cycle (Brezina & Zhao, 2012).

Assisted reproduction can result in a tangled web of legal and ethical dilemmas. Who retains ownership of frozen embryos in the event that a couple breaks up? What should be done with "leftover" embryos? Additionally, many people object to the creation and/or destruction of embryos in a laboratory on religious grounds. In many ways, our legal system has to play catch up with these new ethical dilemmas created by modern reproductive technologies.

what's your view

If you or your partner were infertile, would you seriously consider or undertake in vitro fertilization? Why or why not?

In both men and women, modifiable individual factors are related to infertility. For example, overweight men (Campbell et al., 2015) and women (Pantasri & Norman, 2014) are more likely to have issues with fertility. Smoking also appears to have a strong negative effect on fertility. Other factors, such as psychological stress, high levels of caffeine and alcohol consumption, and exposure to environmental pollutants have been implicated, but the evidence for their negative effects is less strong (Hoffman et al., 2007).

Sometimes hormone treatment, drug therapy, or surgery may correct the problem. For couples struggling with infertility, science today offers several alternative ways to parenthood; in vitro fertilization is discussed in Research in Action.

Perspectives on Adult Cognition

Developmentalists have studied cognition from a variety of perspectives. Here, we address different perspectives on cognition in young adulthood.

POSTFORMAL THOUGHT

Research and theoretical work since the 1970s suggest that mature thinking is more complex than the formal operations reasoning Piaget described. This higher stage of

postformal thought
Mature type of thinking that relies on subjective experience and intuition as well as logic and allows room for ambiguity, uncertainty, inconsistency, contradiction, imperfection, and compromise.

adult cognition, which tends to emerge in early adulthood and is associated with higher education, is sometimes called **postformal thought** (Labouvie-Vief, 2006).

Postformal thought is characterized by the ability to deal with inconsistency, contradiction, and compromise. Life is messy and complex, and some people are better able to deal with its inherent uncertainty. Thus postformal thinking is in some way as much a personality style as it is a mode of thinking.

Another characteristic of postformal thought is its flexibility. At times, formal logical thought is the best tool to solve a problem. But other times, especially in ambiguous circumstances, it is not enough. Postformal thought draws on intuition and emotion as well as logic to help people cope with situations such as social dilemmas, which are often less clearly structured and fraught with emotion (Berg & Klaczynski, 1996; Sinnot, 2003).

Postformal thought is also relativistic. Immature thinking tends to be Black and white—there is one right answer and one wrong one. Relativistic thought, by contrast, acknowledges that there may be more than one valid way of viewing an issue. Relativistic thinking often develops in response to events or interactions that open up unaccustomed ways of looking at things and challenge a simple, polarized view of the world. Research has found a progression toward postformal thought throughout young and middle adulthood (Blanchard-Fields & Norris, 1994).

REFLECTIVE THINKING

reflective thinking
Type of logical thinking that becomes more prominent in adulthood, involving continuous, active evaluation of information and beliefs in the light of evidence and implications.

Reflective thinking is a type of logical thinking that becomes more prominent in adulthood (Dewey, 1933). Reflective thinkers engage in continuous, active evaluation of actions and beliefs in the context of evidence and implications. Moreover, they are comfortable with reconciling apparently conflicting ideas and ascribe value to many different perspectives.

Reflective thinking comes online slowly and in predictable stages. First, young adults engage in *dualism*, and see the world in Black and white with little subtlety. Authorities are viewed as having the answers, and ambiguity is not well tolerated. This is followed by *multiplicity*, in which different viewpoints are seen as potentially all having value. Now, the world is full of gray areas. Next is the development of *contextual relativism*, where the merits of different solutions to problems are considered with an understanding that some answers may be better than others. Last is *commitment within contextual relativism*, in which young adults become skilled at using evidence to evaluate solutions or answers, but also understand that the best answer may depend on context and value systems.

What drives this change? Overall, exposure to diversity, especially with respect to race (often the most salient dimension), leads to increases in cognitive complexity. This influence is strongest when it takes the form of interpersonal interactions rather than, for example, coursework or workshops (Bowman, 2010; 2013). For example, discussions that include mixed-race participants produce greater novelty and complexity of ideas than all-white discussions (Antonio et al., 2004).

These findings have implications for affirmative action and enrollment decisions. Some have argued that a diverse group of students and high academic quality are competing priorities (Bowman, 2010). Research suggests, by contrast, a different story. Those campuses with more diverse student bodies tend to show greater amounts of interracial friendships rather than continued or increased segregation (Fischer, 2008). This integration then contributes to academic achievement and intellectual gains (Gurin et al., 2003).

Although American college students do seem to pass through these stages of logical thinking, later research has shown they are not a human universal. For instance, research with Chinese students shows an opposite pattern of cognitive development than American students, with relativistic thinking highest in freshmen and lowest in seniors (Zhang, 2004). Additionally, several programs of research have shown the tendency to engage in reflective thought is more a characteristic of educational experiences than age and is also contingent upon the domain in which the question is asked, and the knowledge a young person has of important components of the domain (King & Kitchener, 2004).

TRIARCHIC THEORY OF INTELLIGENCE

The triarchic theory of intelligence is comprised of three elements: *componential, experiential,* and *contextual knowledge* (Sternberg, 1985, 1987). Componential knowledge includes analytical abilities or "book smarts," which can help students sail through examinations and receive high grades when in school. However, componential knowledge is not always sufficient to do well in life. Also important are experiential elements (how insightful or creative a person is) and contextual knowledge (the practical aspect of intelligence). When original thinking is expected, experiential intelligence—including fresh insights and original ideas—may be more important. Practical, contextual intelligence, or "street smarts," is also important outside of academic settings. Practical knowledge allows people to do well across a variety of contexts and adapt to new conditions.

An important aspect of practical intelligence is **tacit knowledge:** "inside information" or know-how that is not formally taught or openly expressed. Tacit knowledge is commonsense knowledge of how to get ahead, such as how to win a promotion or cut through red tape. Sternberg's method of testing tacit knowledge in adults was to compare a test-taker's chosen course of action in hypothetical, work-related situations (such as how best to angle for a promotion) with the choices of experts in the field and with accepted rules of thumb. Tacit knowledge, when measured in this way, is not well correlated with measures of general cognitive ability but does predict managerial success and job performance (Sternberg et al., 2001; Herbig et al., 2001; Sternberg et al., 1995).

tacit knowledge
Sternberg's term for information that is not formally taught but is necessary to get ahead.

EMOTIONAL INTELLIGENCE

Peter Salovey and John Mayer (1990) coined the term **emotional intelligence (EI).** It refers to four related skills: the abilities to *perceive, use, understand,* and *manage,* or regulate, emotions—our own and those of others—so as to achieve goals. Emotional intelligence enables a person to harness emotions to deal more effectively with the social environment. It requires awareness of the type of behavior that is appropriate in a given social situation. Although mean scores for these four categories differ by country, the test remains valid cross-culturally (Karim & Weisz, 2010).

emotional intelligence (EI)
Salovey and Mayer's term for the ability to understand and regulate emotions; an important component of effective, intelligent behavior.

Emotional intelligence affects the quality of personal relationships. Studies have found that college students with high emotional intelligence are more likely to report positive relationships with parents and friends (Lopes et al., 2003), are more likely to provide emotional support to their close friends in time of need (Lopes et al., 2004), and score higher on well-being measures (Lanciano & Curci, 2015). Emotional intelligence is also protective against risky behaviors such as smoking, drinking, and drug use (Rivers et al., 2013). College-age couples in which both partners have high emotional intelligence report the happiest relationships, whereas couples who are low in emotional intelligence are the most unhappy (Brackett et al., 2005). Generally, women score higher on emotional intelligence measures than do men (Lanciano & Curci, 2015).

Emotional intelligence also affects occupational success, and is associated with constructive conflict management, especially among subordinates (Schlaearth et al., 2013); higher salaries and more promotions (Lopes et al., 2006); lower job stress, especially for married men (Naseem, 2018); psychological attachment to the workplace (Olatomide & Akomolafe, 2013); and going over and above job duties by choice (Miao et al., 2017). Low levels of emotional intelligence have been associated with engaging in nonwork activities while at work, boredom, procrastination, and undermining the goals or interests of an organization (Wan et al., 2014; Miao et al., 2017).

Moral Reasoning

Recall that Kohlberg broke moral development into three stages. In the final stage, postconventional morality, Kohlberg believed that people became capable of fully principled moral reasoning based on universal principles of justice. Kohlberg argued that most people did not reach this level until their twenties, if at all (Kohlberg, 1973). He believed that the acquisition of this was a function of experience. In particular, when young people encounter values that conflict with their own (as might happen in college or foreign travel) and when they are responsible for the welfare of others (as in parenthood), their development of moral reasoning abilities increases.

Shortly before his death, Kohlberg proposed an additional seventh state of moral reasoning. He believed it was possible for people to achieve "a sense of unity with the cosmos, nature, or God," which enabled them to see moral issues from "the standpoint of the universe as a whole" (Kohlberg & Ryncarz, 1990, pp. 191, 207).

CRITIQUES OF KOHLBERG'S APPROACH

Carol Gilligan was bothered by what she perceived as a male bias in Kohlberg's approach. She believed that women's central dilemma was the conflict between their needs and the needs of others, and that women saw morality in terms of an obligation to exercise care and avoid hurting others rather than independently derived abstract ideals. Women's moral reasoning was not less complex than men's, she argued, it merely had a different focus. However, a number of studies have not found consistent differences in moral reasoning in men and women. Thus the weight of evidence as a whole does not seem to back up Gilligan's assertions (Brabeck & Shore, 2003).

Another critique leveled at Kohlberg's approach involves his belief that people from certain cultures were more likely to attain the highest levels of moral reasoning (Jenson, 1997). This underlying belief in the superiority of a particular worldview has been criticized as being biased toward Western cultural norms of individuality and a nonreligious mindset. For example, many cultures provide moral dictates focused on divine authority and tradition, and there is no reason for these beliefs to be viewed as morally inferior or as reflecting a less sophisticated form of reasoning (Shweder et al., 2006).

CULTURE, RELIGION, AND MORAL REASONING

Cultures affect moral reasoning because important cultural values and goals, including those associated with religion, are reflected in the dominant ethical system of a culture. Because world views differ across cultures, so do the ethical systems. The *ethic of autonomy* is characteristic of individualistic cultures, and it focuses on the rights of the individual and abstract concepts of justice. The *ethic of community*, more characteristic of collectivistic cultures, focuses on social connections, duty to others, group harmony, and respect for the structures that maintain social harmony. Last, the *ethic of divinity* views the person as a temporary vessel for a divine soul or sacred being. Moral dictates, in this view, center upon attaining holiness and endorse concepts related to sanctity or purity (Shweder et al., 1997).

All three ethics exist in individuals from different cultures and have been documented, for example, in Brazil, Israel, Japan, New Zealand, and the United Kingdom (Guerra & Giner-Sorolla, 2015). However, their centrality varies by country, worldview, and age. For example, Americans are more likely to use the ethic of autonomy than Brazilians or people from India (Haidt et al., 1993; Jensen, 1998). Additionally, both within and across countries, religiously liberal people are more likely to endorse the ethic of autonomy than are more conservative religious groups. Religious people as a whole are more likely to use the ethic of divinity than liberals, although both groups frequently use the ethic of community (Jensen, 2011).

There are separate developmental trajectories for each ethic. The ethic of autonomy is present early in childhood, and a person's tendency to use it generally remains stable over time in all but the most collectivistic cultures. However, the type of autonomy reasoning may change with age. The ethic of community generally shows a slow and steady rise from childhood through adolescence and adulthood, perhaps as a consequence of an individual's primary interactions moving outside of the family to include friends, the formation of his or her own family, and the wider social world. The ethic of divinity, because it often consists of abstract religious principles, shows a different pattern. Here, at least in countries in which this ethic is common in adults, there are generally low levels in childhood and a sharper rise in adolescence and emerging adulthood that is concurrent with increased cognitive capabilities (Jensen, 2011).

Education and Work

COLLEGE

Access to higher education has not been and is not always available to everyone. It was not until 1823 that the first African American man in the United States graduated from college (Harper et al., 2009). Historically, women have generally also had less access. In Colonial America, literacy was valued for women, but only insofar as it allowed them to read religious texts. At Oberlin College in 1837, when women were for the first time admitted, their presence was as much for the purposes of doing the male students' laundry as it was for their own benefit (Conway, 1974). It was not until 1862 that the first African American woman attended college (Harper et al., 2009). In the United States of today, socioeconomic status remains a key factor in whether or not young people attend and graduate college (Walpole, 2003).

College is an increasingly important path to adulthood, though it is only one such path and, until recently, not the most common one (Montgomery & Côté, 2003). Between 1960 and 2017, the proportion of U.S. high school graduates who went straight into a 2- or 4-year college grew from less than half (45.1 percent) to more than two-thirds (67 percent) (McFarland et al., 2019).

College courses and even complete degree or certificate programs are now widely available by *distance learning,* in which courses are delivered via mail, e-mail, the Internet, or other technological means. About 6.35 million students took at least one online course in 2016, representing a third of all students (Seaman et al., 2018). Colleges also are increasingly experimenting with hybrid courses, which utilize a mixture of both online and in-person techniques. In general, research seems to suggest that learning outcomes are similar for online, hybrid, and traditional students, although a wide variety of variables can affect outcomes (Tallent-Runnels et al., 2006). The COVID-19 pandemic may accelerate movement toward online instruction.

Some colleges, including Stanford University and MIT, have offered massive, open, online courses (MOOCs) that allow any person with an Internet connection to take the course for free. Although such courses show some promise, especially with respect to opening avenues of affordable knowledge in far-flung locales, they also suffer from high rates of attrition and are subject to cheating (Daniel, 2012). Estimates are that only 6.5 percent of students enrolled in MOOCs finish the course, and the longer the course, the higher the attrition rate (Jordan, 2014).

Unlike young people in past generations, who typically moved directly from school to work and financial independence, many emerging adults today do not have a clear career path. Some alternate between education and work; others pursue both. Most of those who do not enroll in or finish postsecondary education enter the job market. Some take a year off from formal education or the workplace— a *gap year*—to gain new skills, do volunteer work, travel, or study abroad. And some combine college with marriage and child rearing.

Prior to the COVID-19 epidemic, college enrollments in the United States were at an all-time high. More than 2 out of 3 high school graduates went directly to college. The influence of the pandemic on college attendance rates is not yet known. Fuse/Getty Images

Gender, Socioeconomic Status, and Race/Ethnicity U.S. college enrollment rates have overall increased from 2000 to 2017. In a reversal of the traditional gender gap, a larger percentage of 18- to 24-year-old women (44 percent)

enroll in college than men (37 percent) (McFarland et al., 2019). Similarly, women have higher postsecondary enrollment rates than men in most European countries, as well as in Australia, Canada, New Zealand, Japan, and the Russian Federation (Buchmann & DiPrete, 2006; Sen et al., 2005). Since the mid-1980s, more U.S. women have earned associate's, bachelor's, and master's degrees than men, and since 2005–2006 this has also become true for doctoral degrees (McFarland et al., 2019).

Still, gender differences are evident within some fields at the highest educational levels and, following graduation, within jobs in science, technology, engineering, and math (STEM) (Funk & Parker, 2018). In the United States, women remain more likely than men to major in the health professions, psychology, and biology, whereas men are more likely to major in business and engineering (McFarland et al., 2019). Even so, women have made gains in almost every field, with math-intensive fields the only remaining where women have not attained equal or greater graduation rates compared with men (Wang & Degol, 2017).

In explaining the persistent disparities between men and women, a variety of factors appears to be important. Some researchers have pointed to cognitive differences in men and women at the upper end of the mathematical, visual, and spatial ability range, or to the more varied choices available to those women who are both mathematically and verbally skilled (Halpern et al., 2007; Wang et al., 2013). Other explanations center on women's interests and preferences, including those centering around work and family balance (Wang & Degol, 2017). The influence of gender stereotypes has also been proposed as important (Miller et al., 2015). Last, attention has also been drawn to women's persistent reports of gender discrimination in those fields where the largest disparities between men and women can be found (Funk & Parker, 2018).

In the 2017–2018 academic year, the average total net price of attendance at a four-year college or university for a full-time undergraduate at a public institution was $24,300. Private, nonprofit institutions were roughly double the cost at $50,300, and private, for-profit institutions cost an average of $32,200 (McFarland et al., 2019). From 2004 to 2015, prices for tuition, room, and board rose 33 percent at public institutions and 26 percent at private, not-for-profit institutions (Snyder et al., 2016), making the attainment of higher education increasingly difficult for low- and middle-income families. Thus many students from more modest circumstances are likely to work while attending college, which often slows their progress (Dey & Hurtado, 1999). In addition, students from wealthier families are less likely to drop out of college before graduating (Hamilton & Hamilton, 2006).

Enrollment figures for the fall of 2020 were expected to be substantially different from earlier data, given the influence of the COVID-19 pandemic. Before the spread of the novel coronavirus in the United States, more than half of parents of high school students reported their children planned to enroll in college in the fall of 2020, but as of May 10, 2020, this number had dropped. Latino (61 percent) and Black (59 percent) parents were more likely to report their children would not be enrolling in college than were white parents (43 percent) (Civis Analytics, 2020).

Completing College Although college entrance has become more common in the United States, *finishing* college has not. Currently, the six-year graduation rate at 4-year institutions is about 60 percent; however, the rate differs by ethnicity. The highest graduation rate is that of Asian students (73.3 percent) followed by white (64.3 percent), mixed race (57.1 percent), Hispanic (55 percent), and African American (39.8 percent) (McFarland et al., 2019).

Today, more women than men enter college and earn degrees. A college education is often the key to a successful career and a healthy, satisfying life. michaeljung/Shutterstock

Whether a person completes college may depend not only on motivation, academic aptitude and preparation, and ability to work independently, but also on social integration and social support: employment opportunities, financial support, suitability of living arrangements, quality of social and academic interactions, and the fit between what the college offers and what the student wants and needs. Intervention programs for at-risk students have improved college attendance rates by creating meaningful bonds between students and teachers, finding opportunities for students to work while in college, providing academic assistance, and helping students see how college can move them toward a better future (Montgomery & Côté, 2003).

WORK

By their midtwenties, most emerging adults are either working or pursuing advanced education or both (McFarland et al., 2019). Those who enter the workforce face a rapidly shifting landscape. Where previous generations of employees often could expect to remain at a company from their start date until retirement, that pattern of employment is becoming increasingly rare. More and more adults are self-employed, working at home, telecommuting, on flexible work schedules, or acting as independent contractors. Moreover, the COVID-19 pandemic resulted in high unemployment rates, with workers under the age of 25 most likely to show reductions in income or lose their jobs (Bureau of Labor Statistics, 2020; Sternberg, 2020).

In the United States in 2017, adults age 25 to 34 who had a master's or higher degree and who were working full-time had a median income of $65,000, a full 26 percent higher than those with a bachelor's degree ($51,800) and 62 percent higher than those who had completed high school but had not attended college ($32,000) (Figure 13.4). Moreover, for adults without sufficient education, unemployment rates are high. Young adults with a bachelor's degree or higher had an employment rate of 86 percent in 2017, whereas those who had not completed high school had an employment rate of 56 percent (McFarland et al., 2019)

Although income differentials between male and female workers exist at all levels of educational attainment, these gaps have narrowed considerably. In 1979, women earned 62 percent of what men did. In 2017, women earned 82 percent of men's income, and this gender gap in wages is greater for older women than for younger women (U.S. Bureau of Labor Statistics, 2017). One-fourth of the pay gap is unexplained by such factors as hours, occupations, and parenthood, suggesting that it stems from gender discrimination.

Combining Work and Schooling In 2014, about 43 percent of full-time college students and 81 percent of part-time college students worked while attending college (McFarland et al., 2019). Generally, there is a trade-off such that the more time students spend working, the less time they spend on academic pursuits (Greene & Maggs, 2015).

Working during college may affect the likelihood of attending graduate programs. Although grants and loans are available to some students, many students must work to help support their educational aspirations. Such work cuts into the time they have available to engage in other activities, such as participation in research groups, unpaid internships, and volunteer work. These activities are optional but allow students a more

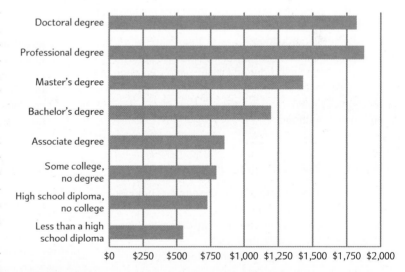

FIGURE 13.4

Median Weekly Earnings by Highest Educational Attainment, 2018.

Even considering the cost of an education, higher educational levels mean more earnings.

Torpey, E. Education pays. Career Outlook, U.S. Bureau of Labor Statistics, 2019.

competitive application into graduate school. Therefore, although work itself may not be detrimental to an undergraduate education, it may be related to difficulties meeting criteria for graduate programs.

Cognitive Growth at Work People seem to grow in challenging jobs, the kind that are becoming increasingly prevalent today. This research has revealed a reciprocal relationship between the **substantive complexity** of work—the degree of thought and independent judgment it requires—and a person's flexibility in coping with cognitive demands (Kohn, 1980).

A great deal of development in the frontal lobes occurs in young adulthood (Luciana, 2010). Magnetic resonance imaging shows that the most frontward part of the frontal lobes plays a major role in problem solving and planning. This portion of the brain springs into action when a person needs to put an unfinished task on hold and shift attention to another task. It permits a worker to keep the first task in working memory while attending to the second—for example, to resume reading a report after being interrupted by the telephone (Koechlin et al., 1999).

Cognitive growth need not stop at the end of the workday. According to the **spillover hypothesis,** cognitive gains from work carry over to nonworking hours. Studies support this hypothesis: Substantive complexity of work strongly influences the intellectual level of leisure activities (Kohn, 1980; K. Miller & Kohn, 1983).

substantive complexity
Degree to which a person's work requires thought and independent judgment.

spillover hypothesis
Hypothesis that there is a carryover of cognitive gains from work to leisure that explains the positive relationship between activities in the quality of intellectual functioning.

summary and key terms

Emerging Adulthood

- For many young people in advanced technological societies, entrance into adulthood is not clearly marked. Some developmental scientists suggest that the late teens through the midtwenties has become a transitional period called emerging adulthood.
- Emerging adulthood consists of multiple milestones or transitions, and their order and timing varies. Passage of these milestones may determine when a young person becomes an adult.

emerging adulthood

Physical Health and Fitness

- Health insurance coverage is an important component of health.
- Physical and sensory abilities are typically at their peak in emerging and young adulthood.
- Accidents are the leading cause of death in this age group.
- The mapping of the human genome is enabling the discovery of genetic bases for certain disorders.
- Lifestyle factors such as diet, obesity, exercise, sleep, smoking, and substance use or abuse can affect health, survival, and may have epigenetic consequences for the regulation of when genes turn on and off. Food insecurity is an issue in some countries.

- Good health is related to higher income and education. Some minorities tend to be less healthy. Although much of this is due to SES, there also are indications that people of different ethnicities sometimes respond differently to environmental influences on health.
- Social relationships, especially marriage, tend to be associated with physical and mental health.
- Mental health is generally good in early adulthood, but certain conditions, such as depression, become more prevalent. Alcohol abuse and alcoholism are the most common substance disorders.

internet addiction, risky drinking, alcoholism

Sexual and Reproductive Issues

- Sexual behaviors and attitudes vary widely across different countries. Almost all U.S. young adults have sexual relations before marriage.
- Sexually transmitted infections, menstrual disorders, and infertility can be concerns during young adulthood.
- The highest rates of STIs in the United States are among emerging adults.
- The most common cause of infertility in men is a low sperm count; the most common cause in women is blockage of the fallopian tubes.
- Infertile couples now have many options for assisted reproduction.

premenstrual syndrome (PMS), infertility

Perspectives on Adult Cognition

- Some investigators propose distinctively adult forms of cognition beyond formal operations. Reflective thinking emphasizes complex logic; postformal thought involves intuition and emotion as well.
- According to Sternberg's triarchic theory of intelligence, the experiential and contextual elements become particularly important during adulthood. Tests that measure tacit knowledge can be useful complements to traditional tests.
- Emotional intelligence plays an important part in life success.

postformal thought, reflective thinking, tacit knowledge, emotional intelligence (EI)

Moral Reasoning

- According to Kohlberg, moral development in adulthood depends primarily on experience.
- Kohlberg has been critiqued for biases against women and other cultures.

- Ethical world views across culture that affect moral reasoning include ethics of autonomy, community, and divinity. While found in all cultures, these ethical systems are more or less common in particular cultures and show distinct developmental trajectories.

Education and Work

- A majority of emerging adults now go to college. More women than men now go to college, and an increasing percentage pursue advanced degrees even in traditionally male-dominated fields. Minority participation is growing. Many students enter college, but fewer graduate with a degree.
- Research has found a relationship between substantive complexity of work and cognitive growth.
- Changes in the workplace call for higher education or training. Higher education greatly expands workplace opportunities and earnings.

substantive complexity, spillover hypothesis

chapter **14**

Psychosocial Development in Emerging and Young Adulthood

learning objectives

Describe identity development and the relationship with parents in emerging adulthood.

Summarize theoretical perspectives on adult personality development.

Identify key aspects of intimate relationships and love.

Characterize marital and nonmarital lifestyles.

Discuss parenthood and the pressures on dual-income families.

Identify trends in divorce and remarriage.

Chee Gin Tan/E+/Getty Images

Personal choices made in emerging and young adulthood establish a framework for the rest of life. In this chapter, we examine the choices that frame personal and social life: adopting a sexual lifestyle; marrying, cohabiting, or remaining single; having children or not; and establishing and maintaining friendships.

Developmental Tasks of Emerging Adulthood

PATHS TO ADULTHOOD

Traditionally, adulthood was defined by markers such as moving out of the family home, marriage, children, full-time employment, or the establishment of a career. Today, a wide variety of paths may be followed on the way to adulthood. Individual paths to adulthood are influenced by gender, academic ability, early attitudes toward education, race and ethnicity, expectations in late adolescence, and social class.

Three primary pathways increasingly characterize the trajectory of young adulthood in the United States (Scales et al., 2016). The first pathway includes those young adults who begin families early and generally do not go to college. Early marriage and family formation are associated with poverty and substance use (Oesterle et al., 2010; Oesterle et al., 2011). Early parenthood, in particular, limits future prospects (Boden et al., 2008; Dariotis et al., 2011), especially for women who do not marry (Assini-Meytin & Green, 2015; Driscoll, 2014). However, not all consequences of teen pregnancy are negative. Some young mothers who carry an unintended pregnancy to term report fewer sexual partners and less substance use when compared to women who terminated an unintended pregnancy or had never been pregnant (Gomez-Scott & Cooney, 2014).

The second pathway includes those young adults who delay children until young adulthood, but who, rather than investing in college, move into full-time work. When compared to college graduates, these young adults bear more children by their thirties, work more hours, reach an income plateau, and depend more on government aid (Mitchell & Syed, 2015).

The third pathway involves emerging adults of both sexes who delay parenthood and other traditional markers of adulthood in pursuit of educational or career goals (Oesterle et al., 2010; Eliason et al., 2015). This group tends to start in the most privileged place and have the most positive outcomes. In a longitudinal study that followed a nationally representative sample of high school seniors each year since 1975, emerging adults with the highest well-being were those who were not yet married, had no children, attended college, and lived away from their childhood home (Schulenberg et al., 2005).

IDENTITY DEVELOPMENT

The Contemporary Moratorium Identity status research has found that only about a third of Western youth seem to go through what Marcia named the *moratorium* status, a self-conscious crisis that ideally leads to a resolution and identity achievement status. Approximately 15 percent seem to regress during emerging adulthood, and about half show no significant changes (Kroger et al., 2009). Rather than actively and thoughtfully exploring their identity, many young adults seem to do little active, conscious deliberation, instead taking a passive (diffused) approach or taking the lead from their parents (foreclosure). Nevertheless, about 3 out of 4 eventually settle on some sort of occupational identity by the end of their twenties. Identity confusion persists for 10 to 20 percent, who lack what Erikson called *fidelity:* faith in something larger than themselves (Côté, 2006). Religious and community involvement (for example with volunteer activities or political campaigns) is associated with general increases in identity formation in emerging adults (Hardy et al., 2011), perhaps by giving young adults something to believe in.

Cultural Issues and Ethnic Identity Formation The approach to the study of identity development was conceptualized within the United States, with its emphasis upon individualism and personal autonomy. In a culture such as this, identity achievement status is adaptive and beneficial. However, in countries where the emphasis is on collectivism and focused more strongly on group membership, this model may not apply in the same fashion. For example, in a study conducted with China, Taiwan, Japan, and the United States, identity was accepted without much distress, exploration, or questioning in the less Westernized samples, yet still held a great deal of interpersonal meaning (Berman et al., 2011). Although we might find foreclosure less adaptive in the United States, it may confer benefits in a different cultural context (Cheng & Berman, 2012). Gender also interacts with identity formation processes across cultures. Although in Western countries, men's and women's identity formation processes are relatively similar, this is not the case cross-culturally. In some indigenous cultures and developing countries, women are more often expected to marry shortly after puberty, whereas men are accorded more time before beginning a family (Schlegel, 2013).

Ethnic identity can be defined as one's identity as a member of a particular ethnic group (Phinney, 2003). Identity exploration is different for racial/ethnic minorities than for the majority white population. Many minority youth, often out of economic concerns, must take on adult responsibilities earlier than their peers. At the same time, they tend to value close and interdependent family relations and may feel obligated to assist their families financially. They may be under pressure to marry and have children at an early age or to enter the workforce immediately rather than spending years in higher education. Thus, for them, some of the processes of emerging adulthood may be curtailed (Phinney, 2006).

The formation of an achieved and positive ethnic identity has beneficial effects on variables such as depression, perceived stress, coping, social competence, self-esteem, well-being, internalizing and externalizing symptomatology, academic achievement, and health risks. These effects are generally small to moderate in size but have been found across a multitude of studies, especially for African American adults (Rivas-Drake et al., 2014; Rivas-Drake et al., 2014; Smith & Silva, 2011). Because a secure ethnic identity involves positive feelings about both one's own personal identity (Yip, 2014) and the wider culture (Phinney, 1989), it is not surprising to find that secure ethnic identity is also related to greater acceptance of other groups (Phinney et al., 1997). Ideally, such feelings can result in more positive interactions between different groups and reductions in discrimination (Phinney et al., 2007).

Religious Identity Formation Although almost all adults endorse a religious identity for themselves, a recent study of 106 countries showed young adults are less likely to report affiliation with a religious identity or belief system than older adults, especially in North America, Europe, and predominantly Christian countries (Pew Research Center, 2018). In the United States, religiosity, particularly if measured by church attendance, declines from adolescence to young adulthood (Koenig et al., 2008).

However, despite declines in religiosity, it remains an important feature of life for many people. A survey of young adults across eight countries found that although many did not attend religious services or participate in structured religious activities, most emerging adults reported actively seeking a sense of meaning in religion and making attempts to live in accordance with religious principles (Benson et al., 2012). The inner lives of young adults—for example, frequent prayer and strong relational ties to faith—have a stronger influence on religious identity development than do external factors such as attending church regularly or going on missions (Smith et al., 2010). Moreover, emerging adults report a belief in god as being more important than necessarily following all of a formal religion's dictates (Smith & Snell, 2009).

As with racial and ethnic minorities, religious minorities are often subject to bias, discrimination, and stereotyping. Thus these adults sometimes feel separate or different from others. For example, young Jewish adults in Britain reported a sense of being different as an integral part of their social identity (Sinclair & Milner, 2005). This felt separateness may conflict with integration into society, particularly when paired with discrimination. For instance, Muslims in Germany, Norway, and Spain reported linkages between their nationalist identity and religious identity, but specific effects varied by country. In Norway, adults felt no conflict between their religious identity and Norwegian identity. However, those who reported more perceived discrimination were less likely to identify as Norwegian. In Germany and Spain, by contrast, strong religious identification was seen as incompatible with nationalistic identification, and thus was associated with weaker nationalistic identification (Chryssochoou & Lyons, 2011).

Sexual and Gender Identity Formation Sexual identity can be defined as the cognitive and emotional underpinnings of people's understanding of and meaning ascribed to their sexuality (Savin-Williams, 2011). Generally, sexual minority children first realize there is something different about them in childhood. In early adolescence, they often recognize they are attracted to, for example, others of the same sex, and by late adolescence, many have given themselves a label such as "gay" or "lesbian." In emerging adulthood, sexual identity becomes further solidified (Morgan, 2013). This process is tied to cultural beliefs and attitudes about different sexualities. For example, the greater acceptance of diverse sexualities in recent decades has led to a downward shift in the age at which sexual identity is consolidated (Floyd & Bakeman, 2006; Halpern & Kaestle, 2014). For heterosexual adults, sexual identity often halts at a foreclosed identity status— meaning many young adults assume their sexuality is the norm and do not question or think deeply about it (Eliason, 1995).

Transgender identity development is complicated. It is often assumed that the primary identity crisis for transgender people involves a mismatch between psychological gender and biological sex, and that identity achievement thus consists of changing the physical body such that gender and biology match and the person feels either fully male or fully female. However, many transgender people show shifts in their understanding of themselves over time and actively resist a binary gender classification (Diamond et al., 2011; Katz-Wise et al., 2017). Moreover, many transgender people must also weigh the social consequences of changing gender and consider the risks to their existing relationships with others, jobs, and safety (Levitt & Ippolito, 2014).

Transgender people have higher rates of depression, suicidality, self-harm, and eating disorders (Connolly et al., 2016), not as a direct consequence of being transgender, but in response to societal pressures, rejection, stigma, and discrimination. Pride in a transgender identity, gender-affirming medical therapy, and support from family and friends are protective factors (Bockting, 2014; Connolly et al., 2016). Key features appear to be whether others use correct identity labels (many transgender people change their names once they transition) and the correct use of pronouns, in part because this is indicative of respect and support from others (Katz-Wise et al., 2017). The successful identification and resolution of transgender identity is associated with positive feelings about congruency, resilience and personal growth, enhanced empathy for others, and, when their identity is accepted by friends and family, improved and more authentic relationships (Riggle et al., 2011).

Models of Personality Development

Four approaches to adult psychosocial development are represented by *normative-stage models,* the *timing-of-events model, trait models,* and *typological models* (Table 14.1).

NORMATIVE-STAGE MODELS

Normative-stage models are theoretical approaches that hold that adults follow a basic sequence of age-related psychosocial changes. The changes are normative in that they are common for most members of a population in a particular culture at a particular time. The most influential of these models has been Erik Erikson's (1950) model of psychosocial development. Erikson argued that at each stage in the life span people address particular crises. The normative crisis of young adulthood is **intimacy versus isolation**.

Erikson believed that young people who develop a strong sense of self during adolescence are in a better position, in early adulthood, to fuse their identity with that of

normative-stage models
Theoretical models that describe psychosocial development in terms of a definite sequence of age-related changes.

intimacy versus isolation
Erikson's sixth stage of psychosocial development, in which young adults either form strong, long-lasting bonds with friends and romantic partners or face a possible sense of isolation and self-absorption.

TABLE 14.1 Four Views of Personality Development

Models	Questions Asked	Methods Used	Change or Stability
Normative-stage models	Does personality change in typical ways at certain periods throughout the life course?	In-depth interviews, biographical materials	Normative personality changes involving personal goals, work, and relationships occur in stages.
Timing-of-events model	What if important life events occur earlier or later than usual?	Statistical studies, interviews, questionnaires	Nonnormative timing can cause stress and affect personality development.
Trait models	Do personality traits fall into groups, or clusters? Do these clusters change with age?	Personality inventories, questionnaires, factor analysis	Overall average personality changes are small, especially after age 30, although there are normative developmental changes for all five traits.
Typological models	Can basic personality types be identified, and how well do they predict the life course?	Interviews, clinical judgments, Q-sorts, behavior ratings, self-reports	Personality types tend to show continuity from childhood through adulthood, but certain events can change the life course.

Source: Sternberg, R. J. (1986). A triangular theory of love. *Psychological Review, 93,* 119–135.

another. In other words, knowing who you are and what you want makes it more likely you will end up with a compatible partner who fulfills your needs. This is important because if adults cannot make deep personal commitments to others, they risk becoming isolated and self-absorbed. Resolution of this stage results in the virtue of love: mutual devotion between partners who have chosen to share their lives and have children. Erikson believed that a failure to fulfill what he believed to be a natural procreative urge has negative consequences for development. Quite rightly, his theory has been criticized for excluding single, celibate, homosexual, and childless people.

Moreover, research has indicated that men and women may follow different developmental trajectories. For example, identity status achievement for men appears to be related to the initiation of relationships, whereas for women it is more strongly related to the stability of relationships (Kahn et al., 2014). Additionally, at least early in marriages, women tend to report higher intimacy than do men, which has implications for the health of the marriage later (Boden et al., 2010).

Last, the early work on normative life stages was based on small groups of men and women born in the 1920s, 1930s, and 1940s. Today, young adults follow much more diverse developmental paths and, as a result, may develop differently than did the people in these studies. In addition, the findings of normative-stage research may not apply to other cultures, some of which have very different patterns of life-course development.

Despite these critiques, normative-stage research has nonetheless had an impact on the field. Psychologists, have identified developmental tasks that need to be accomplished for successful adaptation in young adulthood (Roisman et al., 2004). Among these tasks are leaving the childhood home for advanced schooling, work, or military service; developing new and more intimate friendships and romantic relationships; and developing self-reliance and independence (Arnett, 2004; Scharf et al., 2004).

Young adults who have a strong sense of self are likely to be ready for the demands of an intimate relationship, according to Erikson. Florin Prunoiu/Image Source/Getty Images

TIMING-OF-EVENTS MODEL

Instead of looking at adult personality development purely as a function of age, the **timing-of-events model** (Neugarten et al., 1965; Neugarten & Neugarten, 1987) holds that the course of development depends on when certain events occur in people's lives. **Normative life events** (also called *normative age-graded events*) are those that typically happen at certain times of life—such events as marriage, parenthood, grandparenthood, and retirement. According to this model, people usually are keenly aware of both their timing and the **social clock**—their society's norms or expectations for the appropriate timing of life events.

Stress or depression may come from an unexpected event (such as losing a job), an event that happens off time (being widowed at age 35), or the failure of an expected and wanted event to occur (being unable to have a child) (Rubin et al., 2009). Personality differences influence how people respond to life events and may even influence their timing. For example, a resilient person is likely to experience an easier transition to adulthood and the tasks and events that lie ahead than an overly anxious person.

The timing of the social clock in U.S. culture has shifted somewhat in recent years (Arnett, 2010). The rise in the average age when adults first marry in the United States (U.S. Census Bureau, 2019) and the trend toward delayed first childbirth (Martin et al., 2019) are two examples of events for which timing has shifted. The social clock in many Western societies has also become more widely age-graded. Today people are more accepting of 40-year-old first-time parents and 40-year-old grandparents, or 50-year-old retirees and 75-year-old workers.

The timing-of-events model has made an important contribution to our understanding of adult personality by emphasizing the individual life course and challenging the idea of universal, age-related change. However, its usefulness may well be limited to cultures and historical periods in which norms of behavior are stable and widespread.

TRAIT MODELS

Traits can be thought of as mental, emotional, temperamental, or behavioral attributes that vary between people. **Trait models** are psychological models that focus on the measurement and examination of these different traits. One of the best known of these models is Paul T. Costa and Robert R. McCrae's **five-factor model** consisting of factors, or dimensions, that seem to underlie five groups of associated traits, known as the "Big Five" (see Figure 14.1).

Continuity and Change in the Big Five Overall, average personality changes are small (Cobb-Clark & Schurer, 2012). Analyses of longitudinal and cross-section data in U.S. adults have found considerable continuity within people (Costa & McCrae, 2006; McCrae, 2002; McCrae et al., 1986).

timing-of-events model
Theoretical model of personality development that describes adult psychosocial development as a response to the expected or unexpected occurrence and timing of important life events.

normative life events
In the timing-of-events model, commonly expected life experiences that occur at customary times.

social clock
Set of cultural norms or expectations for the times of life when certain important events, such as marriage, parenthood, entry into work, and retirement, should occur.

trait models
Theoretical models of personality development that focus on mental, emotional, temperamental, and behavioral traits, or attributes.

five-factor model
Theoretical model of personality, developed and tested by Costa and McCrae, based on the "Big Five" factors underlying clusters of related personality traits: neuroticism, extraversion, openness to experience, conscientiousness, and agreeableness.

Openness	**C**onscientiousness	**E**xtraversion	**A**greeableness	**N**euroticism (emotional stability)
• Imaginative or practical	• Organized or disorganized	• Sociable or retiring	• Softhearted or ruthless	• Calm or anxious
• Interested in variety or routine	• Careful or careless	• Fun-loving or somber	• Trusting or suspicious	• Secure or insecure
• Independent or conforming	• Disciplined or impulsive	• Affectionate or reserved	• Helpful or uncooperative	• Self-satisfied or self-pitying

FIGURE 14.1
Costa and McCrae's Five Factors of Personality

Each factor, or dimension, of personality represents a cluster of related traits. Use the acronym OCEAN to remember the main five: openness, conscientiousness, extraversion, agreeableness, and neuroticism.

Source: Costa, Jr., P. T., & McCrae, R. R. (1980). Still stable after all of these years: Personality as a key to some issues in adulthood and old age. In P. Baltes and O. Brim, Jr. (Eds.), *Life-span development and behavior* (Vol. 3, p. 71, Figure 1). New York. NY: Academic Press, .

Agreeableness and conscientiousness generally increase in young adults, whereas neuroticism, extraversion, and openness to experience decline (McCrae et al., 2000; Specht et al., 2011). These patterns of age-related change appeared to be universal across cultures and thus, according to these authors, maturational (McCrae, 2002).

The observation that people's personalities, on average, remain similar does not mean change does not occur (Roberts & Mroczek, 2008). There is normative developmental change in all five dimensions between adolescence and age 30, with much slower change thereafter. Change includes increases in social dominance, conscientiousness, emotional stability, and agreeableness and decreases in neuroticism, extraversion, and openness to experience (Soto et al., 2011; Specht et al., 2011; Borghuis et al., 2017; McCrae et al., 2000).

The Big Five are linked to various aspects of health and well-being including marital satisfaction (Gattis et al., 2004), parent-infant relationships (Kochanska et al., 2004), work-family conflict (Wayne et al., 2004), and personality disorders. With respect to specific factors, openness to experience has been related to verbal intelligence and creative achievement (DeYoung et al., 2014; Kaufman et al., 2016) as well as better health (Strickhouser et al., 2017). Conscientiousness has been linked most strongly with health-related behaviors that contribute to long life (Bogg & Roberts, 2013; Strickhouser et al., 2017). People low in extraversion are prone to agoraphobia (fear of open spaces) and social phobias (Bienvenu et al., 2001), whereas those high in extraversion tend to be high in well-being (Soto, 2015), but are likely to engage in more substance use (Atherton et al., 2014). Agreeableness has been associated with less negative responses to stress; however, it also appears associated to greater declines in positive affect following a stressor (Leger et al., 2016). Last, people high in neuroticism tend to be subject to anxiety and depression (Bienvenu et al., 2001) and are more likely to be dependent on drugs and low in well-being (Valero et al., 2014; Soto et al., 2011).

Costa and McCrae's body of work originally made a powerful case for continuity of personality. More recent research has questioned that conclusion, and Costa and McCrae have now acknowledged that change occurs throughout the life span.

TYPOLOGICAL MODELS

Jack Block (1971; Block & Block, 2006) was a pioneer in the **typological approach.** Typological research seeks to complement and expand trait research by looking at personality as a functioning whole.

Researchers have identified three personality types. These three types differ in **ego resiliency,** or adaptability under stress, and **ego control,** or self-control. *Ego-resilient* people are well-adjusted, self-confident, independent, articulate, attentive, helpful, cooperative, and task-focused. *Overcontrolled* people are shy, quiet, anxious, and dependable; they tend to keep their thoughts to themselves and to withdraw from conflict, and they are the most subject to depression. *Undercontrolled* people are active, energetic, impulsive, stubborn, and easily distracted.

Ego resiliency interacts with ego control to determine whether or not behavior is adaptive or maladaptive. For example, undercontrol can lead to creativity and resourcefulness or, if it is excessive, to externalizing and antisocial behaviors. By the same token, overcontrol can help make a person highly focused and planful, or it can lead to an inflexible and inhibited style of behavior. More extreme forms of either overcontrol or undercontrol are generally associated with low levels of ego resilience (Kremen & Block, 1998). These or similar personality types seem to exist in both sexes, across cultures and ethnic groups, and in children, adolescents, and adults (Caspi, 1998; Hart et al., 1997; Pulkkinen, 1996; Robins et al., 1996; van Lieshout et al., 1995).

Relationships in Emerging Adulthood

RELATIONSHIPS WITH PARENTS

Even though they are no longer children, emerging adults still need parental acceptance, empathy, and support, and attachment to the parents remains a key ingredient of well-being

typological approach
Theoretical approach that identifies broad personality types, or styles.

ego resiliency
(1) Dynamic capacity to modify one's level of ego control in response to environmental and contextual influences. (2) The ability to adapt flexibly and resourcefully to potential sources of stress.

ego control
Self-control and the self-regulation of impulses.

(Lindell & Campione-Barr, 2017). When emerging adults have parents who are closely involved, warm, and loving, they have higher levels of self-worth (Nelson, et al., 2015). Generally, parents and young adult children get along best when the young adult is following a normative life course but has deferred the responsibility of parenthood until other adult roles are well established (Belsky et al., 2003). Financial support from parents, especially for education, enhances emerging adults' chances of success in adult roles (Aquilino, 2006). Parents of disruptive or conflictual young adults may experience increased distress as a result of their child's actions (McClelland & McKinley, 2016), particularly given the shifting balance of power as young adults become more independent and are less subject to parental control.

Economic and social changes in the United States—including automation, globalization, and technological change—have made it more difficult for young adults to establish an economically viable independent household (Hill & Holzer, 2007). More than half of 18- to 24-year-olds and 16 percent of 25- to 34-year-olds live with their parents (U.S. Census Bureau, 2019). Although staying in the family home can afford the opportunity to continue to work on occupational advancement, it also can result in threats to autonomy and independence for young adults (Burn & Szoeke, 2016). For example, African Americans, Hispanics, and those with household incomes less than $50,000 a year, who are less likely to receive parental assistance, believe financial independence should begin at ages 16 to 18 years (Country Financial Security Index, 2018).

In contrast to developed cultures, developing cultures tend not to view the establishment of a separate household, either before or after marriage, as an essential step on the path to adulthood (Arnett, 2015). Despite this, the trend for increasing numbers of emerging adults to live in the parents' home for economic reasons also exists in other countries. Young adults from the ages of 18 to 24 years are the most likely to suffer the effects of an economic recession (Aasve et al., 2013). Across much of Europe, as well as in Hong Kong, the global financial crisis, weak employment and wages, and high housing costs led to an increase in the proportion of emerging adults remaining in the parental home (Lennartz et al., 2016; Victor, 2015; Figure 14.2). Economic projections suggest this trend will continue (Seiffge-Krenke, 2016), and the projected continuing negative influence of the COVID-19 pandemic on the global economy (Jackson et al., 2020) suggests it may accelerate.

FRIENDSHIP

Young adults generally have the largest friendship networks; however, friendships during this time are often less stable than in either adolescence or later adulthood, primarily because people in emerging adulthood relocate more frequently (Wrzus et al., 2017; Collins & Van Dulmen, 2006).

Over the course of young adulthood, the number of friends and the amount of time spent with them gradually decreases, presumably as leisure time decreases and responsibility to others increases. For example, having a child is associated with a sharp decrease in the size of the friendship network (Wrzus et al., 2013). Still, friends remain important. People with friends tend to have

Although emerging adults may no longer rely on parents for basic sustenance, they still benefit from parental companionship and social support. Ronnie Kaufman/Blend Images LLC

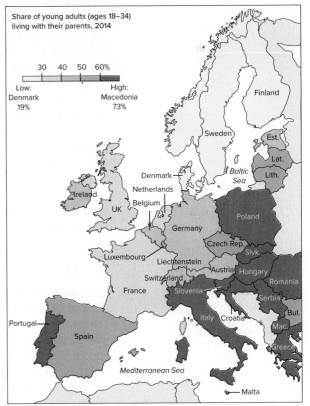

Note: In Iceland and Cyprus, not shown, 36% and 53% of young adults lived with their parents in 2014, respectively.

FIGURE 14.2

Share of European Young Adults (18 to 34 Years) Living with Their Parents (2014).

For the first time in the modern era, living with parents edges out other living arrangements for 18- to 34-year-olds.

Source: DeSilver, D. In the U.S. and Abroad, More Young Adults are Living with Their Parents. Washington, DC: Pew Research Center, 2016.

Intimate relationships involve self-awareness, empathy, and the ability to communicate. Eugenio Marongiu

fictive kin
Friends who are considered and behave like family members.

triangular theory of love
Sternberg's theory that patterns of love hinge on the balance among three elements: intimacy, passion, and commitment.

a sense of well-being—although it is unclear if friendship causes well-being or if people who feel good about themselves have an easier time making friends (Myers, 2000).

Women typically have more intimate friendships than men do (Hall, 2011). Women are more likely to share confidences with friends (Rosenbluth & Steil, 1995), to talk with their friends about marital problems, and to receive advice and support (Helms et al., 2003). Men, by contrast, are more likely to share information and activities (Rosenbluth & Steil, 1995). However, when men do share intimate details, as with women, this results in increased closeness (Bowman, 2009).

Close supportive friendships are sometimes incorporated into family networks. These types of friends are known as **fictive kin**—they are treated as family members despite a lack of blood relationship. For example, fictive kinship relationships often develop for gay and lesbian people who have straight friends of the opposite sex, particularly if those friends are unmarried or have an unconventional lifestyle (Muraco, 2006). Single adults without children are also more likely to develop stronger fictive kin relationships than are married adults with families (Casper et al., 2016).

In recent years, young adults' use of social networking sites has increased dramatically (Facebook, 2011). Currently, 90 percent of adults age 18 to 29 years use social media (Perrin, 2015). Studies have found the use of social media is associated with negative effects on well-being, depression, and negative body image (Kross et al., 2013; Primack et al., 2017; Holland & Tiggemann, 2016). However, social networking sites can also have advantages. For example, recent research indicates that social networking sites are often used to maintain and strengthen ties to others (Hampton et al., 2011; Subrahmanyam et al., 2008; Manago et al., 2012), and they are related to increased participation in political discussion and activities (Boulianne, 2015; Skoric et al., 2016). They have also been associated with increases in perceived social support, decreases in stress and loneliness, and better health outcomes (Nabi et al., 2013; Deters & Mehl, 2013; Korda & Itani, 2013).

Why people use social networking sites may help determine their effects. Some people use electronic communication as a means by which to augment and extend their interactions with others. However, other people use electronic communication as a means by which to avoid social interactions, in which case social media may be displacing face-to-face interactions and have negative effects on well-being (Ahn & Shin, 2013).

LOVE

According to Robert J. Sternberg's **triangular theory of love** (1986, 1998, 2006), the crucial elements of love are intimacy, passion, and commitment. *Intimacy*, the emotional element, involves self-disclosure, which leads to connection, warmth, and trust. *Passion*, the motivational element, is based on inner drives that translate physiological arousal into sexual desire. *Commitment*, the cognitive element, is the decision to love and to stay with the beloved. As adolescents move into adulthood, they tend to feel an increasing amount of intimacy, passion, and commitment in their romantic relationships (Sumter et al., 2013). Romantic love, dominated by passion, does not appear to be a Western invention. An anthropological survey of 166 cultures found evidence of romantic love in 88.5 percent of the accounts, suggesting that romantic love is a near-universal (Jankowiak & Fischer, 1992).

Although they are more alike than different, men and women show modest differences in intimacy, passion, and commitment within their romantic relationships. Generally, women report greater intimacy in their relationships, whereas men report greater passion. Levels of commitment, however, appear to be similar in both genders (Sumter et al., 2013). The length of the relationship affects the dynamics of the relationship. Generally, passion is higher at the beginning of the relationship and declines over time as commitment increases (Ahmetoglu et al., 2010).

Marital and Nonmarital Lifestyles

SINGLE LIFE

Across Europe and North America, many single adults are postponing marriage and children (Geist, 2017). In the United States, the proportion of young adults age 18 to 34 who have not yet married has similarly increased over the past decades, from 41 percent in 1978 to 71 percent in 2018 (U.S. Census Bureau, 2018). Some young adults stay single because they have not found the right mate; others are single by choice. At the same time, many single adults are postponing marriage and children due to economic instability (Cohn, 2018), a desire to coordinate career goals with long-term relationship goals (Shulman & Connolly, 2013), or out of a desire for self-fulfillment.

Since the 1960s, Americans are likely to have more sexual partners and casual sex, and be more accepting of premarital sex (Twenge et al., 2015). One pattern that has become increasingly common is that of "friends with benefits" (FWB), relationships in which there is a blend of friendship and physical intimacy, but little commitment. Men are more likely to seek FWB out of a desire for sexual activity, whereas women are more likely to express a desire for an emotional connection and for the relationship to eventually progress to a committed romantic relationship (Lehmiller et al., 2011; Gusarova et al., 2012). Given these different motivations, it is perhaps not surprising that women report greater levels of deception in FWB relationships (Quirk et al., 2014). Despite this, both men and women generally report positive emotions about their FWB relationships, although men are more likely to do so (Owen & Fincham, 2011). As a whole, young adults in such relationships do not appear to be at greater risk of psychological distress than their counterparts in committed romantic relationships (Eisenberg et al., 2009).

GAY AND LESBIAN RELATIONSHIPS

Forty-five years ago, same-sex couples were not legally recognized in any country (Saez, 2011). However, shifting attitudes have led to great changes. Currently, 30 countries and territories have legalized same-sex marriage (Pew Research Center, 2019; Figure 14.3). Most countries are in Western Europe (Italy and Switzerland are exceptions) and the Americas, where acceptance of homosexuality is high (Masci & DeSilver, 2019; Masci et al., 2017).

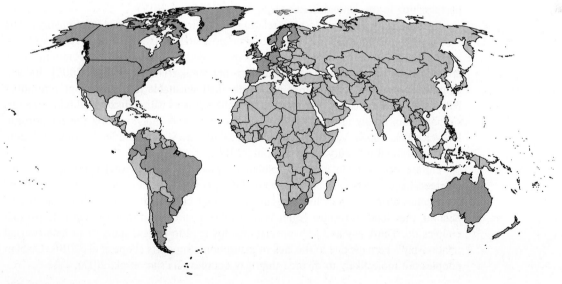

FIGURE 14.3

Where Gay Marriage Is Legal, 2019

Source: Masci, D., & D. DeSilver. A global snapshot of same-sex marriage. Pew Research Center, 2019. Retrieved from https://www.pewresearch.org/fact-tank/2019/10/29/global-snapshot-same-sex-marriage/

On June 26, 2015, the U.S. Supreme Court legalized *same-sex marriage.* Hinterhaus Productions/DigitalVision/Getty Images

Countries in Asia and Africa tend to be less tolerant of homosexuality (McGee, 2016). In Russia, it is a crime to distribute "propaganda of nontraditional sexual relationships among minors." Same-sex relations between men are banned in some areas of Indonesia, Malaysia, Myanmar, and much of the African continent, and in Brunei, Mauritania, Sudan, and parts of Nigeria, are punishable by death (Council on Foreign Relations, 2019).

In the United States, greater social acceptance of homosexuality has led to more gay and lesbian adults living openly. Approximately 87 percent of Americans know someone who is gay or lesbian and about half report a close family member or friend is gay or lesbian (Drake, 2013). It may be that the increasing openness with which gay and lesbian people are living their lives is affecting public opinion. Those who are close to a gay or lesbian person are more likely to be supportive of gay marriage and anti-discrimination laws (Neidorf & Morin, 2011), and currently 67 percent of Americans now support gay marriage (McCarthy, 2018).

In 2019, approximately 75 percent of Democrats supported same-sex marriage. By contrast, only 44 percent of Republicans supported it. Religion also plays a role. Of those people who characterize themselves as unaffiliated with any religion, 79 percent support gay marriage. Although religiously affiliated people are less likely to endorse gay marriage, the number that are in favor of it has also increased. For example, in 2004 approximately 11 percent of white evangelical Christians were in favor of gay marriage. In 2017, that number rose to 29 percent. In addition, age has been implicated in the debate, with younger generations becoming increasingly accepting of same-sex marriage (Pew Research Center, 2019).

In the United States, gays and lesbians struggled for decades to obtain legal recognition of their unions. They argued that same-sex marriage offered benefits that civil unions did not (Herek, 2006; King & Bartlett, 2006). Research supported their assertion: Gay and lesbian people in those states that had legalized gay marriage and who were thus able to marry showed lower levels of depression, stress, and internalized homophobia and felt they had more meaning in their lives (Riggle et al., 2010). Before the Supreme Court decision legalizing same-sex marriage, approximately 8 percent of gay, lesbian, bisexual, or transgender people were married to a same-sex partner (Gallup News, 2017). Currently, this number has risen to 53.6 percent of the slightly over 1 million same-sex partnerships in the United States (U.S. Census Bureau, 2019).

In most ways, gay and lesbian relationships mirror heterosexual relationships. The factors that predict the quality of both homosexual and heterosexual relationships—personality traits, perceptions of the relationship by the partners, ways of communicating and resolving conflicts, and social support—are similar (Kurdek, 2005, 2006). Indeed, committed same-sex relationships are hardly distinguishable in quality from committed heterosexual relationships (Roisman et al., 2008). Just as with heterosexual relationships, support from family and friends is related to how well and how long the relationship lasts (Kurdek, 2008). Variables related to breakups are similar and include poor relationship quality and infidelity (Balsam et al., 2017).

Differences between gay and lesbian couples and heterosexual couples also have emerged from research (Kurdek, 2006). First, gay and lesbian couples are more likely than heterosexual couples to negotiate household chores on a more egalitarian basis. Second, they tend to resolve conflicts in a more positive atmosphere than heterosexual couples do. Third, gay and lesbian relationships tend to be less stable than heterosexual relationships, perhaps due to the lack of institutional supports (Pope et al., 2010). Lesbian couples are more likely to divorce than gay couples (Balsam et al., 2017).

COHABITATION

Cohabitation is an increasingly common lifestyle in which an unmarried couple involved in a sexual relationship live together. The prevalence of cohabitation varies widely across countries. For example, within the Americas, rates are relatively low in Mexico and the United States, and higher in Central America, the Caribbean, and Amazonian areas (Lopez-Gay et al., 2014). Surveys in 14 European countries, Canada, New Zealand, and the United States also found wide variations in cohabitation rates, ranging from more than 14 percent in France to less than 2 percent in Italy. In Japan cohabitation rates are relatively high at 15 percent (Raymo et al., 2009). In sub-Saharan Africa, cohabitation rates are rising quickly, with the highest rates found in urban centers and Western Africa. Countries with a large Muslim population, such as Niger and Senegal, have the lowest rates (Popoola & Ayandele, 2019).

There is evidence that attitudes are changing, with younger adults showing greater acceptance for cohabitation and other marital alternatives (Treas et al., 2014). Not surprisingly, the patterns of cohabitation are changing as well. In many countries, including Canada, China, Spain, and parts of Africa, more recent cohorts are cohabiting at higher rates than older adults (Yu & Xie, 2015; Dominguez-Folgueras & Castro-Martin, 2013; Le Bourdais & Lapierre-Adamcyk, 2004; Odimegwu et al., 2018).

In 2019 an estimated 8.5 million unmarried couples were living together in the United States (Gurrentz, 2019). Cohabitation is now more common in adults age 18 to 24 years than marriage (U.S. Census Bureau, 2016). About half of cohabiting adults are younger than 35 years (Stepler, 2017). Cohabitation in the United States has become more common among all racial/ethnic groups and at all educational levels, but people with less education are more likely to cohabit than those with higher education (Fields, 2004; Manning, 2013). Cohabitants also are likely to be less religious, less traditional, have less confidence in their relationships, be more accepting of divorce, be more negative and aggressive in their interactions with their romantic partners, and communicate less effectively (Jose et al., 2010).

Beliefs about cohabitation, cohabitation patterns, and the stability of cohabitation vary among racial/ethnic groups. Couples who cohabitate, on average, are younger, more likely to be Black, and less religious (Horowitz et al., 2019). Perhaps for economic reasons, Black and Hispanic couples are less likely than non-Hispanic white couples to regard cohabitation as a trial marriage and more likely to regard it as a substitute for marriage (Phillips & Sweeney, 2005; Manning et al., 2019).

Cohabiting couples report lower levels of relationship satisfaction and less trust in their partners, and are less likely to stay together than married couples (Graf, 2019; Lau, 2012). Generally, the lowest relationship quality is reported by cohabitants without plans to marry or in relationships in which one partner wishes to marry and the other does not (Brown et al., 2017; Willoughby & Belt, 2016). However, both married couples and cohabiting couples who plan to marry report higher relationship satisfaction in comparison to cohabiting couples who do not plan to marry (Tai et al., 2014). This suggests there may be fundamental differences in types of cohabiting couples, with those couples who eventually marry having more stable and happier relationships than those who do not (Jose et al., 2010). These young adults are not using cohabitation to replace marriage, but view it as one step along the way to marriage (Graf, 2019).

U.S. family law currently gives cohabitants few of the legal rights and benefits of marriage (Stepien-Sporek & Ryznar, 2016). However, efforts are being undertaken to provide relationship partners as well as any resulting children legal protection in the event of relationship dissolution, and 65 percent of Americans support granting unmarried couples the same legal rights as married couples (Waggoner, 2016; Graf, 2019). Other countries, including Australia, Canada, New Zealand, and the United Kingdom, have enacted legislation giving committed cohabiting couples rights similar to married couples (Waggoner, 2015).

MARRIAGE

Cultural and Contextual Influences Marriage customs vary widely across cultures (see Window on the World). Marriage is sometimes linked to economic transactions. In some cultures, primarily concentrated in Africa and Asia, marriage is associated with either a bride price or a dowry. A *bride price* is a payment made by a groom or his

POPULAR WEDDING TRADITIONS ACROSS CULTURES

Most cultures have long-standing wedding traditions. Often these traditions were designed to ward off evil spirits and bring luck and good fortune to the new couple. Special clothing, symbolic elements, and traditional rites are usually part of the ceremony.

Brides wear white in much of Europe and America. Wearing white is symbolic of purity and virginity of the bride. This tradition began when Queen Victoria wore a white gown to her wedding in 1840. Before this, white was worn as a symbol of mourning; red was the most popular color to be married in (Smithsonian, 2014). In China, brides still wear red, which is considered to be a symbol of good luck and good fortune (Traditional Chinese Weddings, 2014).

In traditional West African weddings, couples would jump a broom together as a symbol of the joining of two families and the couple starting their new life together. This ritual has become a popular part of many African American couples' weddings today as a means of showing respect for their ancestors (African Wedding Traditions, 2013).

One of the most common traditions is to throw rice, oats, wheat, beans, peas, or other seeds at the new couple as they exit the ceremony. It symbolizes new life, fertility, and prosperity for the couple. Other things are used today such as birdseed, confetti, or bubbles. This tradition has been seen in Czechoslovakia, France, Germany, Greece, Italy, Spain, the United States, and numerous other countries (Monger, 2013) but its origin is still unclear.

The wedding veil is also a common tradition used today. Its ancient purpose is to ward off evil spirits by hiding the bride. This was combined with dressing the bridesmaids similarly to the bride to confuse and deter evil spirits. The tradition was also used in arranged marriages in Middle Eastern cultures to hide the bride from her new husband until after the ceremony so he could not change his mind if he did not like what he saw (Monger, 2013). Variations of this tradition include traditional Chinese brides wearing a full red veil to hide their face while being escorted to the ceremony under a red umbrella to ward off evil spirits and encourage fertility and prosperity for the new couple (Traditional Chinese Weddings, 2014).

A wedding reception or party is also common across most cultures. Depending on religion, status, and custom, these can include speeches, a toast, dancing, and traditional wedding foods. This is a time for friends and family to celebrate with the new couple. Length and formality of the reception can vary. For example, in India, the celebration will go on for several days, whereas in Russia the reception lasts 2 hours (Monger, 2013).

what's your view — Have you thought about getting married and the traditions that you might follow one day? Where do you think these traditions come from and what is their meaning?

family to the bride's family. A *dowry* is a payment by a bride's family to the newly married couple or to the groom's family (Conteh, 2016). More rarely, a *bride service* is a service provided to the family of a bride in exchange for the marriage (Dean, 2018).

If a girl marries and a bride price is paid to her family, the family has one fewer member to support and simultaneously receives a financial boon. This may be why marriage in cultures in which a bride price is paid tends to happen, for girls, at earlier ages (Corno & Voena, 2016). By contrast, if a young woman's parents must pay a dowry to find her a husband, she becomes an economic burden. Thus, in cultures such as these, many parents show a strong preference for sons and a reluctance to bear daughters. This reluctance, in its extreme manifestations, can result in selective female infanticide as a means by which to avoid the economic burden of daughters (Diamond-Smith et al., 2008).

For much of human history and in many cultures today, arranged marriages, where parents or professional matchmakers select their children's marital partners, was and is normative. Such marriages often occur at a younger age than is typical in Western industrialized countries. Generally marriage is focused on the union of two families, rather than on love between two individuals. Given this orientation, it is perhaps not surprising to find that couples in arranged marriages have very different expectations of their spouses. There are decreased expectations of intimacy and love, and responsibility and commitment are emphasized. However, despite these variations, couples in arranged marriages appear to be equally happy in their relationships (Regan et al., 2012; Myers et al., 2005).

People in collectivistic cultures are more likely to endorse arranged marriages and view them more positively than are those from individualistic cultures (Buuunk et al., 2010; Benjanyan et al., 2015). They are also less likely to view love as an essential precondition for marriage (Levine et al., 1995). However, in many cultures, the Western ideal of a relationship based on love and personal attraction seems to have changed the nature of arranged marriage, with "semi-arranged" marriages becoming more common (Naito & Geilen, 2005). In these situations, parents are heavily involved in the process of finding a marriage partner, but the young adult holds veto power over potential spouses.

The age at first marriage has been rising across Europe and North America. Across 25 countries in Europe and North America, the average age at first marriage was slightly over 25 years, although marriage ranged from 21 to 30 years (Geist, 2017). In the United States in 1960, the age at first marriage was 20 years for women and 23 years for men. By 2019, this number rose to 28 years for women and 29.8 years for men (U.S. Census Bureau, 2020). The increase in age at first marriage has occurred across all cohorts but is most prominent in young adults (Cohn et al., 2011), especially African Americans (Wang & Parker, 2014).

More recent cohorts of young women are likely to have attained a higher educational level than previous generations of women and are generally more economically successful. In 1970 in the United States, only 4 percent of women 35 to 44 years of age made more money than their husbands, but by 2017 this number had increased to 28 percent (Murray-Close & Heggeness, 2018; Parker & Stepler, 2017). Gender equity in a country is linked to delays in marriage, as are male unemployment rates (Geist, 2017). Almost a third of single adults cite getting on their feet financially and establishing themselves in stable jobs or careers as formidable obstacles to marriage (Kefalas et al., 2005; Wang & Parker, 2014). However, marriage as a whole is associated with increases in economic security for both men and women (Cohn & Fry, 2010). Religious beliefs also affect the marriage rate. Religious people are more likely both to endorse earlier marriage (Fuller et al., 2015), to marry at earlier ages (Uecker & Stokes, 2008), and to view marriage as central to their lives (Willoughby et al., 2015).

In the United States, merging adults today view marriage differently than did previous generations. Younger adults are less likely to view marriage and having children as essential for living a fulfilling life than are older adults (Barroso, 2020). They are also more likely to endorse premarital sex and cohabitation as alternatives to marriage (Daugherty & Copen, 2016). Many young adults expect greater space for individual interests and pursuits in their marriage and put more emphasis on friendship and compatibility (Kefalas et al., 2005). Women, more so than men, look for a partner who can support a family financially, whereas men care more about finding someone who shares their views on raising children (Parker & Stepler, 2017; Wang & Parker, 2014).

Extramarital Sexual Activity Estimates are that approximately 20 to 25 percent of marriages experience infidelity, with a 2 to 4 percent annual prevalence rate peaking in the summer (Fincham & May, 2017).

Extramarital activity is more prevalent among younger adults and husbands than among wives (Smith, 2003; Labrecque & Whisman, 2017) and is more likely in individuals high in neuroticism and low in agreeableness and conscientiousness (Fincham & May, 2017; Zare, 2011). Extramarital relations are

This mass wedding in India, organized by social workers for members of impoverished families, is an example of the variety of marriage customs around the world. Vishal Owe/EPA/Shutterstock

most likely to occur with a close personal friend, neighbor, coworker, or long-term acquaintance, although men are somewhat more likely to have an affair with a casual acquaintance (Labrecque & Whisman, 2017). Generally, extramarital activity occurs early in the relationship; marriages that last for long periods of time show decreasing risk (DeMaris, 2009). More than half of those engaging in extramarital sex will divorce or separate from their partner (Allen & Atkins, 2012).

Young adults of both sexes have become less permissive in their attitudes toward extramarital sex (Twenge et al., 2015). Across 40 nations adults agreed that it was morally unacceptable for an adult to have an extramarital affair, with the vast majority listing infidelity as a greater wrong than gambling, homosexuality, premarital sex, and abortion. The only country in which adults did not agree with this assessment was France, where only 47 percent of adults found infidelity immoral (Poushter, 2014).

The changing landscape of technology has led to increased use of the Internet to initiate extramarital affairs (Hertlein & Piercy, 2006). Electronic acts of infidelity generally include behaviors such as viewing or participating in pornography, sending or receiving sexually explicit photographs or videos, engaging in sexual activity while online or on the telephone, or messaging inappropriately intimate or sexual content to a person other than the spouse. Although online acts of infidelity at times do not consist of actual physical contact, they can nonetheless be perceived as betrayals and result in similar negative consequences for the marital relationship (Whitty, 2003), including a loss of trust, psychological distress, and trauma (Schneider et al., 2012).

Marital Satisfaction Marriages seem to be just about as happy as they were a quarter-century ago, but husbands and wives spend less time doing things together. Married people tend to be happier than unmarried people, though those in unhappy marriages are less happy than those who are unmarried or divorced (Ben-Zur, 2012; Myers, 2000). Generally, husbands and wives report similar levels of marital satisfaction (Jackson et al., 2014). Marital happiness is positively affected by increased economic resources, equal decision making, nontraditional gender attitudes, and support for the norm of lifelong marriage. Marital happiness is negatively affected by premarital cohabitation, extramarital affairs, wives' job demands, and wives' longer working hours. Increases in husbands' share of housework appear to lower marital satisfaction among husbands but improve it among wives (Amato et al., 2003). Sharing household chores is viewed as very important to marital success by approximately 56 percent of American respondents, although women spend more time on chores (Geiger, 2016).

Sixty-one percent of married Americans report having a satisfying sexual relationship as very important for the marriage (Geiger, 2016). The frequency of sex, sexual satisfaction, and marital satisfaction are closely related to and predict each other (McNulty et al., 2016). What may be more important than the actual amount of sex a married couple has is whether or not they both desire roughly similar levels of sexual activity. High discrepancy with respect to sexual activity is associated with lower relationship satisfaction, lower relationship stability, and greater conflict (Willoughby et al., 2014).

Another factor underlying marital satisfaction may be a difference in what the man and woman expect from marriage. Women tend to place more importance on emotional expressiveness—their own and their husbands'—than men do (Lavee & Ben-Ari, 2004). Empathy, validation, and caring are related to feelings of intimacy and better relationship quality (Sullivan et al., 2010). Men's efforts to express positive emotion to their wives, to pay attention to the dynamics of the relationship, and to set aside time for activities focused on building the relationship are important to women's perceptions of marital quality (Wilcox & Nock, 2006).

People who marry and stay married, especially women, tend to become better off financially than those who do not marry or who divorce (Hirschl et al., 2003; De Vaus et al., 2017). However, a large difference in wage earning potential between spouses is associated with decreases in happiness (Stutzer & Frey, 2006).

Parenthood

CULTURAL AND CONTEXTUAL INFLUENCES

Across the globe, parenthood has changed. Before 1965, women had an average of 4.5 to 7 children each. Currently, the global average is approximately 2 children per woman. Among the reasons for this sharp decline are women's education and empowerment. However, lower child mortality rates also seem to be at play. Where child mortality is high, parents are likely to have more children to ensure the survival of some (Roser 2017).

People in developed countries also typically have fewer children today than in earlier generations, and they start having them later in life. In 2018 the average age of first births in the United States rose to 26.9 years (Figure 14.4) (Martin et al., 2019). The rise has been most dramatic for women in their forties, whose birthrate rose 19 percent from 2007 to 2016 (National Center for Health Statistics, 2017).

A woman's age at first birth varies with ethnic and cultural background. In 2018, Asian American and Pacific Islander women had their first babies at an average age of 30.5 whereas American Indian and Alaska Native women gave birth for the first time, on average, at just 23.5 years. Black women and Hispanic women had their first child at roughly 25 years of age, and white women had their first child at 27.7 years (Martin et al., 2019). In 2018, 40.1 percent of U.S. births were to unmarried women, 23 percent lower than the peak of 51.8 percent in the 2007/2008 estimates (Martin et al., 2019).

Estimates are that there are somewhere from 2 million to 3.7 million children being raised by lesbian, gay, bisexual, or transgender (LGBT) parents (Gates, 2015). Approximately 191,000 of these children live with same-sex parents (U.S. Census Bureau, 2019). There has been a decline in the number of LGBT parents in the past 2 decades. This may be due to the declines in social stigma and increasing acceptance of alternative sexualities. LGBT people are coming out at an earlier age, and are thus less likely to have children as the result of a previous heterosexual match (Gates, 2015).

An increasing proportion of U.S. couples remain childless. The percentage of households with children fell from 45 percent in 1970 (Fields, 2004) to approximately 28.7 percent in 2016 (Schondelmyer, 2017). The aging of the population as well as delays in marriage and childbearing may help explain these data, but some couples undoubtedly remain childless by choice.

RELATIONSHIP DYNAMICS

Men's and Women's Involvement in Parenthood Most mothers now work outside the home. The labor force participation rate for mothers with children under the age of 6 years is 65.1 percent, (Bureau of Labor Statistics, 2019). Despite working outside the home, women spend more time on child care than their counterparts did in the 1960s, when 60 percent of children lived with a breadwinner father and a stay-at-home mother. Today, only about 30 percent of children live in such families. Yet married mothers spent 14 hours a week on child care in 2016 compared with 10 hours in 1965, and single mothers in 2000 spent 11.8 hours a week on child care as compared with 7.5 hours in 1965 (Livingston & Parker, 2019; Bianchi et al., 2006).

The amount of time fathers spend with their children has gone up. For example, in 1965, married fathers reported spending 2.5 hours a week on child care and 4 hours a week on housework. In 2016, married fathers spent more than three times as much time with child care (8 hours) and more than double the time doing housework (10 hours) (Livingston &

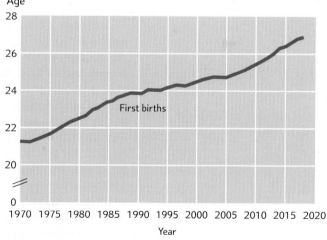

FIGURE 14.4

Mean Age of Mother at First Birth: United States

Many women today start families at a later age than in their parents' generation, raising the average age at first birth.

Source: National Center for Health Statistics, Division of Vital Statistics, *National Vital Statistics Report,* 2016; Martin, J. A., Hamilton, B. E., Osterman, M. J. K., & Driscoll, A. K. (2019). Births: Final data for 2018. *National Vital Statistics Reports, 68* (3), 1–47. Hyattsville, MD: National Center for Health Statistics.

Spending time with children is one of the many joys of parenthood. Sue Cunningham Photographic/Alamy Stock Photo

Parker, 2019). The gendered division of labor in child care by men and women has been found in the United States, as well as a variety of countries in Europe and Asia (Craig & Mullan, 2011; Garcia-Mainar et al., 2011; Oshio et al., 2013).

Work affects the time parents spend with children. Fathers with long working hours report wanting more time to spend with their children (Livingston & Parker, 2019). However, when women work more hours and bring home a larger income, fathers tend to step in and increase the time they spend caring for children (Raley et al., 2012). Although they are vastly outnumbered by mothers, there has been an uptick in the number of stay-at-home fathers, who now account for 7 percent of stay-at-home parents (Livingston, 2018).

Marital Satisfaction How does parenthood affect marriage Studies show that marital satisfaction typically declines during the child-raising years—and the more children, the greater the decline. Mothers of young infants tend to feel the effects most strongly. For example, only 38 percent of new mothers report high marital satisfaction compared with 62 percent of childless wives (Twenge et al., 2003).

Declines occur because new parents are likely to experience stressors such as sleep deprivation, uncertainty, and isolation. Nighttime crying, for example, is associated with a decrease in marital satisfaction in the 1st year of the child's life (Meijer & van den Wittenboer, 2007). If the woman was working outside the home and is now staying home, the burden of housework and child care may fall mostly on her (Schulz et al., 2006). Many couples find their relationship becoming more "traditional" following the birth of a child, with the woman often engaging in the bulk of caregiving and housekeeping (Cox & Paley, 2003). The perceptions of unfairness and inequity that result from this process can damage the marital relationship (Dew & Wilcox, 2011).

Although it has been documented across a wide variety of cultures, the decline in marital satisfaction in response to childbirth does not seem to be universal. For example, the Igbo people of Nigeria show increases in marital satisfaction with the birth of a child. In their case, marital satisfaction is more closely related to the birth of a child than to income or education, and the more children in a family, the higher the reported rates of marital satisfaction (Onyishi et al., 2012). This suggests many of the findings linking children and marital satisfaction have more to do with the context in which they occur than they do with any intrinsic effect of childbearing. For example, some research has shown the influence of children on a marriage depends on whether or not the couple was happy prior to the pregnancy, the couple's attachment representations, whether or not the pregnancy was planned, the age of parents at the birth of a child, and a good work-life balance (Lawrence et al., 2008; Nelson et al., 2013; Kohn et al., 2012; van Steenbergen et al., 2011). Other data indicate that parents have greater happiness, positive emotions, and meaning in life than nonparents (Nelson et al., 2013).

DUAL-INCOME FAMILIES

In married family life of the past, men were traditionally viewed as the main providers, and women, if they worked, as secondary providers. In the United States today, 63 percent of families with children have two working parents (Bureau of Labor Statistics, 2019), and women are providing an increasingly large percentage of family income. For example, in 1970 women's income accounted for only about 27 percent of family income, whereas in 2015 women brought in 35 percent of family income. Moreover, 29 percent of working wives earned *more* than their husbands (Bureau of Labor Statistics, 2017).

Generally, combining work and family roles is good for both men's and women's mental and physical health and has positive effects on the strength of their relationship (Barnett & Hyde, 2001). However, juggling multiple roles—partner, parent, and employee—is often difficult. The family role is most demanding, especially for women, when children are young (Borelli et al., 2017), and the career role is most demanding when a worker is getting established or being promoted. Although both men and women say balancing work and family is difficult, women report more difficulty with this challenge and say they take care of more responsibilities related to children (Livingston, 2018).

For those parents who are not able to establish a satisfactory work-family balance, negative effects may snowball. The more hours worked, the greater the negative effect on work-family balance (McNamara et al., 2013). To cope with this, new parents may cut back on working hours, refuse overtime, or turn down jobs that require excessive travel to increase family time and reduce stress. Or a couple may make a trade-off, trading a career for a job, or trading off whose work takes precedence depending on shifts in career opportunities and family responsibilities. Women are more likely to do the scaling back, which usually occurs during the early years of child rearing (Young & Schieman, 2018; Gauthier & Furstenberg, 2005).

Cross-cultural studies have suggested that the general relationship between work-family balance and well-being holds across different countries. However, the effects are stronger in individualistic cultures than collectivistic cultures and in cultures that are more egalitarian with respect to gender roles (Haar et al., 2014). Government policies can also have an effect. When parents live in countries with supportive policies such as paid time off and child care subsidies, they show less of a decline in well-being after the birth of a child relative to parents in countries without such policies (Glass et al., 2016).

Fathers in 65 countries—but not in the United States—get paid paternity leave. In the United States, approximately 48 percent of workers in the private sector do not have paid leave to care for themselves, and even more lack paid leave to care for other family members such as children. Moreover, even of those who are legally entitled to take family leave, 78 percent do not because they cannot afford to do so (Quamie, 2010). The United States is the only industrialized nation without paid maternity leave, although a few states and industries have adopted paid family plans. For example, in December 2019, 12 weeks of paid parental leave for federal employees was signed into law (U.S. Office of Personnel Management, 2019). Still, many parents, especially those with lower paying jobs, are not able to take any leave after the birth of a baby.

When Marriage Ends

DIVORCE

The U.S. divorce rate has decreased sharply since 1970 and was approximately 2.9 divorces per 1,000 people in 2018 (Centers for Disease Control and Prevention, 2018). The sharpest drop in divorce has occurred among younger cohorts—those born since the mid-1950s (U.S. Census Bureau, 2007). However, the divorce rate for adults over the age of 35 years has doubled in the past 20 years (Kennedy & Ruggles, 2014). Education matters too. College-educated women, who previously had the most permissive views about divorce, have become less so, whereas women with lower educational levels have become more permissive and thus more likely to divorce (Aughinbaugh et al., 2013; Martin & Parashar, 2006). Age at marriage is another predictor of whether a union will last. The decline in divorce may reflect higher educational levels as well as the later age of first marriages, both of which are associated with marital stability (Popenoe & Whitehead, 2004). It also may reflect the rise in cohabitation, which, if it ends, does not end in divorce (Kennedy & Ruggles, 2013). The rates of marital disruption for Black women remain higher than those for white or Latina women (Bulanda & Brown, 2007; Amato, 2010). In addition, interracial couples, particularly those involving white women with Asian or Black men, are more likely to divorce than same-race couples (Bratter & King, 2008).

research in action

INTIMATE PARTNER VIOLENCE

Intimate partner violence (IPV) is the infliction of physical, sexual, or psychological harm by a current or former partner or spouse. Approximately 27 percent of women and 11 percent of men in the United States have experienced some form of physical violence, sexual violence, or stalking by an intimate partner (Centers for Disease Control and Prevention, 2017). The true extent of IPV is difficult to ascertain because victims are often too afraid or ashamed to disclose to others or make an official report to legal authorities.

Women disproportionately experience multiple forms and more severe levels of IPV in individual relationships and across the life span (Centers for Disease Control and Prevention, 2017). Male to female partner violence is more repetitive and is more likely to result in injury or death (Caetano et al., 2001). Conservative estimates suggest that women are roughly 6 times more likely than men to die at the hands of an intimate partner, with homicide typically occurring as a culmination of a long history of abuse (Stock et al., 2013).

Comparatively, there are far fewer studies examining male IPV victimization. In research studies, men disclose both physical and psychological abuse. Psychological violence includes threats of blackmail, financial harm, or taking children away. With physical abuse, partners are especially likely to use objects to inflict injury. Embarrassment and fear of ridicule are among the chief reasons men do not disclose IPV. Serious physical assault incidents are much more likely to be reported to the police, who may not believe the claims or take them seriously (Drijber et al., 2013).

Same-sex relationships are also affected by IPV. Same-sex IPV rates are similar to those in heterosexual relationships (Edwards et al., 2015). National studies indicate lifetime prevalence of physical violence, rape, or stalking by an intimate partner as comparable among heterosexual and gay men. Bisexual women have a significantly higher prevalence of physical violence, rape, or stalking by an intimate partner than either heterosexual or lesbian women (Black et al., 2011). Although these rates indicate IPV occurrence, much less is known about specific risk factors and patterns of IPV perpetration among sexual minority couples (Edwards et al., 2015).

what's **your view** Which individual or psychological factors do you think relate to perpetration and victimization of intimate partner violence? What can be done on an individual and societal level to help protect victims of intimate partner violence?

Predictors of Divorce The most frequently cited reasons for divorce are incompatibility and lack of emotional support. Spousal abuse is third, suggesting that intimate partner violence may be more frequent than is generally realized (Dolan & Hoffman, 1998; Research in Action). Other common risk factors for divorce include premarital cohabitation (Tach & Halpern-Meekin, 2009) and infidelity (Balsam et al., 2017; Hall & Fincham, 2006).

Economic resources and work are also related to divorce risk. However, effects vary with respect to gender. Husbands' unemployment is associated with a greater risk of divorce (Killewald, 2016). Risks associated with wives' employment are most notably those linked to tension over the division of labor, a relationship that increases with the number of hours worked by wives. Additionally, greater economic independence means that when they do wish to leave a marriage, women are more able to do so. However, wives' work also has positive effects on marriage stability via the increased income and subsequent reductions in economic concerns generated when women work (Amato, 2010).

Generally, couples are more likely to stay married if they have children (Bernardi & Martinez-Pastor, 2011). However, instead of staying together "for the sake of the children," some embattled spouses conclude that exposing children to continued parental conflict does greater damage (Eisenberg, 1998).

Adjusting to Divorce Ending even an unhappy marriage can be painful for both partners, especially when there are young children in the home. Issues concerning custody and visitation often force divorced parents to maintain contact with each other, and these contacts may be stressful (Williams & Dunne-Bryant, 2006). However, by the same token, a positive co-parenting relationship following a divorce can be protective for both children and parents (Lamela et al., 2016).

Divorce tends to reduce long-term well-being, especially for the partner who did not initiate the divorce or does not remarry (Amato, 2010). Especially for men, divorce can have negative effects on physical or mental health or both (Sbarra, 2015). Women are more likely than men to experience a sharp reduction in economic resources and living standards after separation or divorce (De Vaus et al.,). People who were—or thought they were—happily married tend to react more negatively and adapt more slowly to divorce (Lucas et al., 2003). On the other hand, when a marriage was highly conflictual, its ending may improve well-being in the long run (Amato, 2000).

An important factor in adjustment is emotional detachment from the former spouse. People who argue with their ex-mates or who have not found a new partner or spouse experience more distress. An active social life, both at the time of divorce and afterward, helps (Amato, 2000). Finding a new partner, in particular, is associated with well-being following a divorce (Symoens et al., 2013).

REMARRIAGE AND STEPPARENTHOOD

Approximately 20 percent of U.S. marriages are remarriages for both bride and groom, and about 8 percent of newly married adults have been married 3 times or more. However, remarriage rates vary depending on the age group being examined. Although rates for older adults are relatively high, rates for younger adults have dropped in recent decades. For example, in 1960, 72 percent of young adults who had divorced or widowed were remarried again by the age of 35. In 2013, only 42 percent of adults age 35 and younger remarried under the same circumstances (Livingston, 2014).

Men and women living with children from a previous relationship are most likely to form a new union with someone who also has resident children, thus forming a his-and-hers stepfamily (Goldscheider & Sassler, 2006). And families in which both parents bring children into the marriage are marked by higher levels of conflict (Heatherington, 2006). Remarriages are more likely than first marriages to end in divorce (Lewis & Krieder, 2015).

The more recent the current marriage and the older the stepchildren, the harder stepparenting seems to be. Women, especially, seem to have more difficulties in raising stepchildren than in raising biological children, perhaps because women generally spend more time with the children than men do (MacDonald & DeMaris, 1996). The conflict experienced by stepparents can be mitigated with healthy and open communication between the two partners (Pace et al., 2015). The stepfamily, as any family, has the potential to provide a warm, nurturing atmosphere for children.

summary and key terms

Developmental Tasks of Emerging Adulthood

- Emerging adulthood is often a time of experimentation before assuming adult roles and responsibilities.
- Paths to adulthood are influenced by gender, academic ability, early attitudes toward education, expectations in late adolescence, and social class.
- Emerging adulthood offers a moratorium, a period in which young people are free from pressure to make lasting commitments.

- In collectivistic cultures, successful identity formation may not include identity achievement.
- Identity formation processes occur in multiple domains, including race/ethnicity, religion, sexuality, and gender.

Models of Personality Development

- Four theoretical perspectives on adult personality development are normative-stage models, the timing-of-events model, trait models, and typological models.

- Normative-stage models hold that age-related social and emotional change emerges in successive periods sometimes marked by crises. In Erikson's theory, the major issue of young adulthood is intimacy versus isolation.
- The timing-of-events model, proposes that adult psychosocial development is influenced by the occurrence and timing of normative life events.
- The five-factor model is organized around five groupings of related traits: open to new experiences, conscientiousness, extraversion, agreeableness, and neuroticism.
- Typological research, has identified personality types that differ in ego resiliency and ego control.

  normative-stage models, intimacy versus isolation, timing-of-events model, normative life events, social clock, trait models, five-factor model, typological approach, ego resiliency, ego control

Relationships in Emerging Adulthood

- Young adults ideally maintain close but autonomous relationships with their parents. Remaining in the parental home is increasingly common among emerging and young adults, which can complicate the negotiation of an adult relationship with parents.
- Young adults seek intimacy in relationships with peers and romantic partners. Women and unmarried adults are more likely to have more intimate friendships.
- The use of social media sites has both positive and negative effects on friendship.
- According to Sternberg's triangular theory of love, love has three aspects: intimacy, passion, and commitment.

  fictive kin, triangular theory of love

Marital and Nonmarital Lifestyles

- Today, more adults postpone marriage or never marry. The trend is particularly pronounced among African American women and people from lower socioeconomic classes.
- Reasons for staying single include career opportunities, a desire for self-fulfillment, financial constraints, fear of divorce, and difficulty in finding a suitable mate.
- The ingredients of long-term satisfaction are similar in homosexual and heterosexual relationships.

- Gays and lesbians in the United States are now able to marry.
- Cohabitation has increased and has become the norm in some countries.
- Cohabitation can be a trial marriage, an alternative to marriage, or, in some places, almost indistinguishable from marriage. Cohabiting relationships in the United States tend to be less stable than marriages.
- Marriage (in a variety of forms) is universal and meets basic economic, emotional, sexual, social, and child-raising needs.
- Mate selection and marrying age vary across cultures. People in industrialized nations now marry later than in past generations.
- Success in marriage may depend on partners' sensitivity to each other, their validation of each other's feelings, and their communication and conflict management skills. Men's and women's differing expectations may be important factors in marital satisfaction.

Parenthood

- Today women in industrialized societies are having fewer children and having them later in life, and an increasing number choose to remain childless.
- Fathers are usually less involved in child raising than mothers, but more so than in previous generations.
- Marital satisfaction typically declines during the childbearing years.
- In most cases, the burdens of a dual-earner lifestyle fall most heavily on the woman.
- Family-friendly workplace policies may help alleviate marital stress.

When Marriage Ends

- Divorce rates in the United States vary depending on the age of the cohort measured.
- Adjusting to divorce can be painful.
- Many divorced people remarry within a few years, but remarriages tend to be less stable than first marriages.

Physical and Cognitive Development in Middle Adulthood

learning objectives

Explain how midlife is changing and define middle adulthood.

Discuss physical changes in middle adulthood.

Characterize health and well-being in middle age.

Identify cognitive changes in middle adulthood.

Describe creative achievement and the relationship between creativity and age.

Discuss trends in work, retirement, and education in middle adulthood.

Maskot/Getty Images

In this chapter, we examine physical changes during midlife as well as physical, sexual, and mental health issues. We look at factors that affect intelligence, thought processes, and creativity. Finally, we look at work, retirement, and educational pursuits.

Middle Age: A Social Construct

Like adolescence, midlife is a social construct (Cohen, 2012). Today, in industrial societies, middle adulthood is considered to be a distinct stage of life with its own societal norms, roles, opportunities, and challenges. However, some traditional societies, such as upper-caste Hindus in rural India (Menon, 2001) and the Gusii in Kenya (Levine, 1980), do not recognize a middle stage of adulthood at all.

We define *middle adulthood* in chronological terms as the years between ages 40 and 65. In 2018, almost 84 million people in the United States, or 25.6 percent of the population, were between the ages of 45 and 64 years. This represents an overall increase of 9.7 percent since 2010, although proportionately, the percentage of middle-age adults in the population has dropped slightly since 2010 (U.S. Census Bureau, 2019).

The experience of middle age varies with health, gender, race/ethnicity, socioeconomic status, cohort, and culture, as well as with personality, marital and parental status, and employment. Moreover, middle age is marked by growing individual differences and a multiplicity of life paths. Some adults can run marathons, and others struggle to climb a flight of stairs. Middle-age adults may have launched their children, or they may be busy caring for aging parents. They may manage households, departments or businesses, or feel overwhelmed and lost. Middle age can be a time of decline and loss, or it can be a time of mastery, competence, and growth.

Physical Changes

Although some physiological processes are direct results of biological aging and genetic makeup, behavioral and lifestyle factors dating from youth strongly affect the likelihood, timing, and extent of physical change.

SENSORY FUNCTIONING

With increasing age, it is common for adults to experience a variety of perceptual declines, including hearing and visual difficulties (Pleis & Lucas, 2009). Age-related visual problems occur mainly in five areas: near vision, dynamic vision (reading moving signs), sensitivity to light, visual search (locating a car in a parking lot), and speed of processing visual information (Kline & Scialfa, 1996).

You may have seen older people using reading glasses, or holding a book or phone as far out as possible with one arm while trying to focus. This is a condition known as **presbyopia,** which occurs when the lens of the eye loses elasticity, and can no longer focus on near objects. Presbyopia generally begins in the forties and eventually affects all adults (Rosenthal & Fischer, 2014). In 2015, 1.8 billion people worldwide had vision impairment as a result of presbyopia, and only about 45 percent of them—most of whom lived in urban areas in more developed countries—had access to adequate vision correction (Fricke et al., 2018). The incidence of **myopia** (nearsightedness) also increases throughout middle age. Overall, approximately 12 percent of adults age 45 to 64 experience declines in their vision (Pleis & Lucas, 2009). By the age of 65, 36.6 percent of adults will have some form of visual disability (Rosenthal & Fischer, 2014).

Middle-age people often need brighter lighting to see well. Because of changes in the eye, they need about one-third more brightness to compensate for the loss of light reaching the retina. Reading glasses, bifocals, and trifocals are also used to aid the eye in focusing on objects.

Age-related, gradual hearing loss is known as **presbycusis.** It is rarely noticed earlier in life, but it generally speeds up and becomes noticeable in the fifties (Merrill & Verbrugge, 1999). Presbycusis usually begins with higher-pitched sounds less important for understanding speech and gradually extends into lower pitches. Although significant hearing loss is not common in middle-age adults, it is a significant factor affecting well-being in older adults. The loss of the ability to hear speech effectively can isolate adults and is associated with anxiety, depression, and cognitive declines (Fischer et al., 2016).

presbyopia
Age-related, progressive loss of the eyes' ability to focus on nearby objects due to loss of elasticity in the lens.

myopia
Nearsightedness.

presbycusis
Age-related, gradual loss of hearing, which accelerates after age 55, especially with regard to sounds at higher frequencies.

Hearing loss proceeds more quickly in men than in women (Ozmeral et al., 2016). Prevalence is also higher among Hispanics and non-Hispanic white adults than among African Americans (Goman & Lin, 2016). However, the most important factor in hearing loss is environmental noise. Estimates are that 7 to 21 percent of hearing loss in adults can be attributed to noise experienced at a work site. Noise-induced hearing loss is higher in developing countries and in military, manufacturing, and construction jobs (Lie et al., 2016; Neitzel & Fligor, 2019). Although hearing protectors such as earplugs have decreased the impact of occupational noise, "social noise" (including concerts and headphones) has increased (Sliwinska-Kowalska & Davis, 2012; Krug, 2015).

Sensitivity to taste and smell generally begins to decline in midlife. Approximately 13.5 percent of adults over the age of 40 years have problems with their sense of smell, 17.3 percent with their sense of taste, and 2.2 percent have issues with both smell and taste (Liu et al., 2016). By the age of 80, over 75 percent of adults show declines (Doty, 2018). These declines are more common in men, African Americans, people who consume large amounts of alcohol, adults with cardiovascular disease, and smokers (Liu et al., 2016; Ajmani et al., 2017). Additionally, the use of medicines to treat many diseases of aging can also have a negative effect on the gustatory senses (Imoscopi et al., 2012). These declines have implications for quality of life and are associated with Alzheimer's and Parkinson's diseases and mortality risk (Doty, 2018). In contrast to gradual declines, a sudden loss or decrease in the ability to smell has been associated with COVID-19 infection (Moein et al., 2020).

PHYSICAL FITNESS

Staying physically active has wide-ranging positive effects on almost every body system, including physical health markers such as reduced cardiovascular risk, psychological markers such as decreased risk of depression, and cognitive markers such as decreased risk of dementia (Bauman et al., 2016). The more people do, the more they *can* do, and the longer they can do it for.

Some loss of muscle strength is usually noticeable by age 45; 10 to 15 percent of maximum strength may be gone by 60. The reason is a loss of muscle fiber, which is replaced by fat (Guralnik et al., 2006; Schaap et al., 2012). Additionally, changes in the skeletal muscle fiber itself lead to decrements in the ability to shorten quickly and forcefully (Brocca et al., 2017) and the fibers lose some of their ATP-producing capacity with age, thus producing less molecular energy (Porter et al., 2015). Still, impairment is not inevitable; strength training and a high-protein diet can protect against these declines (Bradlee et al., 2018; Francis et al., 2017).

basal metabolism
Use of energy to maintain vital functions.

Basal metabolism is the minimum amount of energy, typically measured in calories, that your body needs to maintain vital functions while resting. As people age, the amount of energy needed to maintain the body goes down, particularly after age 40. So, for example, older people often put on weight later in life despite no change in eating or exercise habits (Merrill & Verbrugge, 1999). Weight gain in early adulthood is predictive of major chronic diseases later (Zheng et al., 2017) and in middle age is associated with an increased risk of complications in the event of COVID-19 infection (Satter et al., 2020; Lighter et al., 2020). Staying active can help adults maintain current weight, retain physical skills, and slow declines.

THE BRAIN AT MIDLIFE

In general, the aging brain can be described as working more slowly and having difficulty juggling multiple tasks (Zanto & Gazzaley, 2014). This affects tasks across many different

Though strength and coordination may decline, many middle-age people who remain active show benefits in both psychological and physical health. Ronnie Kaufman/Blend Images LLC

areas—such as understanding complex language, driving a car skillfully, and learning new skills. What these disparate tasks have in common is the necessity to quickly process complex information and pay attention to relevant stimuli while simultaneously ignoring irrelevant stimuli (Madden & Langley, 2003; Stevens et al., 2008).

Starting at about age 35, there is a steady decline in whole brain volume of approximately 0.2 percent per year that accelerates to 0.5 percent as adults near 60 years of age (Hedman et al., 2012). This loss is in part due to a decrease in the volume of gray matter, primarily in the prefrontal cortex (Terribilli et al., 2011). Additionally, myelin, the fatty sheath that lines nerve axons and helps impulses move more quickly through the brain, also begins to break down with age (Lu et al., 2013; Chopra et al., 2018; Salami et al., 2012). The specific location and extent of these changes in the gray and white matter are associated with the severity of processing slowdown and the area of cognition in which it occurs (Eckert, 2011; Hong et al, 2015).

In the past, it was believed that education helped slow the declines associated with age. However, education does not appear to delay declines in processing speed or cognitive functioning. Rather, adults with a high level of education start off ahead and hence may function at a higher level for a longer period of time (Zahodne et al., 2011; Lenehan et al., 2015; Ritchie et al., 2013).

Although effects sizes are small, meta-analyses have found that physical activity and fitness are associated with higher white and gray matter volume (Sexton et al., 2016; Erickson et al., 2014). Moreover, physical activity in midlife is positively associated with cognitive function during midlife itself, as well as with protection against future cognitive declines (Cox et al., 2016; Sofi et al., 2011). Last, reviews of both aerobic exercise and resistance training interventions have shown they are effective in improving attention, processing speed, executive function, and memory, although effects are generally modest in size (Smith et al., 2010; Chang et al., 2012). It may be that some of the benefits associated with exercise are due to general processes such as changes in blood volume or vessels, or changes in gray matter density (Thomas et al., 2012).

Adults who read and write on a regular basis or who work in a cognitively stimulating environment are also more likely to retain their cognitive functions (Cotrena et al., 2016; Smart et al., 2014). There is also some evidence that meditation affords cognitive benefits to middle-age adults and may help offset declines (Gard et al., 2014). Cognitive interventions and mental stimulation have also been shown to be effective in improving functioning (Lampit et al., 2014).

The aging brain compensates for functional declines in part by recruiting a larger number of brain areas to work together to distribute processing demands more widely for difficult tasks (Davis et al., 2011). However, when declines occur nonetheless, knowledge based on experience can help compensate for the physical changes. For example, middle-age adults are better drivers than younger ones (McFarland et al., 1964). More experienced drivers tend to anticipate potential hazards before they become dangerous, shifting their gaze around the environment, whereas novice drivers tend to stare straight ahead and respond only to clear and imminent hazards (Borowsky et al., 2010). Similarly, 60-year-old typists are as efficient as 20-year-olds (Spirduso & MacRae, 1990), and skilled industrial workers in their forties and fifties are often more productive than younger workers, and in fact tend to be more conscientious and careful (Salthouse & Maurer, 1996).

STRUCTURAL AND SYSTEMIC CHANGES

Changes in appearance may become noticeable during the middle years. By the fifth or sixth decade, the skin may become less taut and smooth as the layer of fat below the surface becomes thinner, collagen molecules more rigid, and elastin fibers more brittle. Hair may become thinner due to a slowed replacement rate and grayer as production of melanin, the pigmenting agent, declines. Middle-age people tend to gain weight as a result of accumulation of body fat and lose height due to shrinkage of the intervertebral disks (Merrill & Verbrugge, 1999; Whitbourne, 2001).

Bone density normally peaks in the twenties or thirties. From then on, people typically experience some bone loss as more calcium is absorbed than replaced, causing bones to become thinner and more brittle. Bone loss accelerates in the fifties and sixties; it occurs twice as rapidly in women as in men, sometimes leading to osteoporosis (Merrill & Verbrugge, 1999; Whitbourne, 2001). Smoking, alcohol use, and a poor diet earlier in adulthood tend to speed bone loss; it can be slowed by aerobic exercise, resistance training with weights, increased calcium intake, and vitamin C (Whitbourne, 2001; Yoon et al., 2012). Lower childhood socioeconomic level and adult educational attainment have been linked to lower bone mass density in late adulthood. This association may exist because stress, which is higher in people of low socioeconomic status, is damaging to bone health (Crandall et al., 2012).

Heart disease begins to emerge in the late forties or early fifties. Arterial walls may become thicker and more rigid. The heart may begin to pump more slowly and irregularly in the midfifties, and by 65, it can lose up to 40 percent of its aerobic power. **Vital capacity**—the maximum volume of air the lungs can draw in and expel—may begin to diminish at about age 40 and may drop by as much as 40 percent by age 70 (Merrill & Verbrugge, 1999; Whitbourne, 2001). The body temperature of older people is lower, and they are less able to maintain an appropriate body temperature in extremely hot or cold environments (Blatteis, 2012). Sleep is also affected by age; middle-age adults are less likely to fall asleep in the daytime, need less sleep to maintain alertness, and show reductions in slow wave sleep at night when compared to adolescents and emerging adults (Dijk et al., 2010).

vital capacity
Amount of air that can be drawn in with a deep breath and expelled.

SEXUALITY AND REPRODUCTIVE FUNCTIONING

Although both sexes experience losses in reproductive capacity during middle adulthood, sexual enjoyment continues throughout adult life. (Changes are summarized in Table 15.1.)

Menopause **Menopause** takes place when a woman permanently stops ovulating and menstruating and can no longer conceive a child. Most women experience it between 45 and 55 (Avis & Crawford, 2006).

Menopause is not a single event; it is a process called the *menopausal transition*. It begins with **perimenopause,** also known as the *climacteric.* During this time, a woman's production of mature ova begins to decline, and the ovaries produce less estrogen. Menstruation becomes less regular, with less flow than before, and there is a longer time between menstrual periods. Eventually, menstruation ceases. The menopausal transition generally begins in the midthirties to midforties, and can take approximately 3 to 5 years.

Symptoms The most commonly reported symptoms are hot flashes, sudden sensations of heat that flash through the body due to erratic changes in hormone secretion that affect the temperature control centers in the brain. Hot flashes are associated with anxiety, depression, and an increased risk of heart disease (Fu et al., 2018; Thurston et al., 2017). They are experienced by up to 80 percent of menopausal women and are the most common reason for which women seek medical attention related to menopause. The average duration of hot flash symptoms is over 5 years, although African American

menopause
Cessation of menstruation and of ability to bear children.

perimenopause
Period of several years during which a woman experiences physiological changes of menopause; includes first year after end of menstruation; also called *climacteric.*

TABLE 15.1 Changes in Human Reproductive Systems during Middle Age

	Female	Male
Hormonal change	Drop in estrogen and progesterone	Drop in testosterone
Symptoms	Hot flashes, vaginal dryness, urinary dysfunction	Undetermined
Sexual changes	Less intense arousal, frequent and quicker orgasms	Loss of psychological arousal, fewer erections, slower orgasms, longer recovery between ejaculations, erectile dysfunction
Reproductive capacity	Ends	Continues; some decrease in fertility occurs

window on the world

CULTURAL DIFFERENCES IN MENOPAUSE

Many women accept hot flashes, night sweats, and mood disturbances as normal accompaniments of menopause. However, these symptoms vary widely across cultures. For instance, women from the United States, the United Kingdom, and Canada report more numerous and severe menopause symptoms than women from other European countries, whereas women from Sweden and Italy report the fewest (Minkin et al., 2015). Previous research indicated that American and Canadian samples also reported more symptoms than Japanese samples (Lock, 1993), although recent data cast doubt upon whether or not this is still the case (Mueck & Ruan, 2017; Islam et al., 2017). In some cultures, such as that of Mayan women in Mexico or the indigenous women in Australia, menopausal symptoms are rare, with many noting only the cessation of menses (Beyene & Martin, 2001; Jones et al., 2012).

This difference may exist in part because of cultural differences. For example, in many Asian cultures, such as China, Japan, Singapore, and Taiwan, menopause is not regarded as a medical condition. There are no specific terms for "hot flash," although people recognize that there are changes and distinctions among body states. Muscle and joint pains are often reported by women in these countries but are not often interpreted as being related to menopause (Scheid, 2007). Menopause, for many women, marks the entry into a new stage of life, where fertility is over and children have left the nest. It is considered to be primarily socially rather than biologically driven (Zeserson, 2001).

Even within the United States itself, different racial and ethnic groups experience menopause differently. For instance, although 75 percent of women experience some hot flashes, the prevalence varies widely. The prevalence of hot flashes is 18 percent in Japanese Americans, 21 percent in Chinese Americans, 35 percent in Hispanic Americans, 46 percent in African Americans, and 53 percent in Caucasian women (Tepper et al., 2016).

Research shows that this seemingly universal biological event has major variations. In addition to a woman's beliefs, her diet, overall health, and activity levels all play a factor in her experiences with menopausal symptoms.

what's your view

What do you think might explain cultural differences in women's experience of menopause? What is a greater influence—changing biology or beliefs about aging, and why?

women, highly stressed women, and women of low educational status may experience them for longer (Col et al., 2009; Avis et al., 2015).

Up to 57 percent of postmenopausal women experience vaginal dryness and about half experience thinning of the vaginal walls, both of which have the potential to make intercourse painful. Water-soluble lubricants may help relieve this problem (Edwards & Panay, 2016). In addition, some women of menopausal age may experience mood disturbances, such as irritability, nervousness, tension, and depression (Gracia & Freeman, 2018). Some of the symptoms of menopause may reflect societal views of women and aging (see Window on the World).

Treatment of Menopause Menopause hormone therapy (MHT) appears to be the most effective intervention for night sweats, hot flashes, and deterioration of the urinary tract and vagina. MHT may also help address other symptoms such as joint and muscle pains, mood swings, problems with sleep, and sexual dysfunction. However, the use of MHT should be the lowest dose possible and considered within the context of other

Women of menopausal age report many different symptoms. Physical exercise may alleviate some of them. Adam Kaz/iStock/ Getty Images

life and health variables, including diet, exercise, family and personal history, and the use of cigarettes and alcohol. Women using MHT should also undergo a yearly health assessment, since the use of hormones is not without risks (Baber et al., 2016). Most notably, hormone therapy increases the risk of cardiac disease, dangerous blood clots, stroke, and bone loss, especially for women over the age of 60 or women who use them for extended periods of time (Pinkerton et al., 2017).

Changes in Male Sexual Functioning Men also have a biological clock and they also experience age-associated changes. Starting at about age 30, testosterone levels begin to decline at a rate of about 1 percent a year, although there are wide individual variations (Asthana et al., 2004; Lewis et al., 2006). Although men can still father children, sperm count declines with age. Moreover, the genetic quality of their sperm declines as well, and advanced paternal age has been implicated as a source of birth defects (Almeida et al., 2018; Yatsenko & Turek, 2018).

Men's changing hormone levels affect more than just their sexual organs. The decline in testosterone has been associated with reductions in bone density and muscle mass (Asthana et al., 2004) as well as decreased energy, lower sex drive, overweight, emotional irritability, and depressed mood. Low testosterone has also been linked to diabetes and cardiovascular disease and has been theorized to increase mortality (Lewis et al., 2006; Kelly & Jones, 2014; Johnson et al., 2013; Fui et al., 2014).

Some middle-age and older men experience erectile dysfunction (ED; commonly called *impotence*). **Erectile dysfunction** is defined as a persistent inability to achieve or maintain an erect enough penis for satisfactory sexual performance. A recent review of international studies on ED found widely divergent estimates across countries; however, all countries showed increases in ED with age. Overall, in men younger than 40 years, the prevalence rates were from 1 to 10 percent. From 40 to 49 years, prevalence rates across countries were 2 to 15 percent, and rose to 20 to 40 percent in the decade from 60 to 69 years. By their seventies and eighties, men in nearly all countries showed prevalence rates from 50 to 100 percent (McCabe et al., 2016). In the United States, approximately 61 percent of 40- to 69-year-olds and more than 77 percent of men over the age of 70 have ED (Wagle et al., 2012).

There are multiple potential causes for ED. Diabetes, hypertension, high cholesterol, kidney failure, depression, neurological disorders, and many chronic diseases have been implicated. In addition, alcohol and drug use, as well as smoking, may contribute. Poor sexual techniques, lack of knowledge, unsatisfying relationships, anxiety, and stress may be contributing factors as well (Rosen & Kupelian, 2016; Sartorius et al., 2012). Treatment guidelines state that clinicians should first counsel men to institute lifestyle modifications to improve health, which then may also improve ED. If this is ineffective, then sildenafil (Viagra) and other similar testosterone therapies can be prescribed (Burnett et al., 2018). There is some evidence that men with testosterone levels clearly below average may benefit from testosterone therapy; however, the data are less certain for those men whose testosterone shows the typical age-related drop (Corona et al., 2014; Lewis et al., 2006; Whitbourne, 2001; see Research in Action).

erectile dysfunction
Inability of a man to achieve or maintain an erect penis sufficient for satisfactory sexual performance.

Sexual Activity The single most important factor determining sexual activity is the presence of a partner. Married and cohabitating women have a roughly 8 times higher chance of being sexually active (Thomas et al., 2015). A couple's relationship quality is important too. When a couple communicates well, kisses and cuddles frequently, and is physically tender, this is associated with greater sexual satisfaction. Importantly, couples who can communicate about sexual activity and preferences, who care about each other's pleasure, and who desire approximately the same amount of sexual activity also tend to be more satisfied (Thomas et al., 2018; Fisher et al., 2015; Freak-Poli et al., 2017; Gillespie, 2017).

Individual differences matter as well. Women who feel confident about their bodies and are high in self-acceptance tend to have higher levels of sexual satisfaction, whereas those who are self-conscious about their appearance are more likely to report declines (Thomas et al., 2018).

research in action

ANDROPAUSE AND TESTOSTERONE REPLACEMENT

Testosterone replacement therapies (TPT) have been used for decades to address midlife declines in testosterone, sometimes called *andropause*. Many men seek these treatments, in part because of aggressive marketing by manufacturers. Testosterone supplement sales have increased, with 40- to 60-year-old men accounting for roughly 70 percent of prescriptions (Baillargeon et al., 2013). It has also become common to encounter advertisements for herbal supplements and over-the-counter "medications" marketed to help men regain youthful vitality, athletic performance, and sexual virility, and online searches for such supplements have also risen sharply in recent years (Teck & McCann, 2018).

The U.S. Food and Drug Administration issues stark warnings to consumers interested in boosting aging males' testosterone levels. Testosterone supplements were originally developed for men who produce no endogenous testosterone, and the FDA neither approves nor recommends these products for use to ward off the effects of male aging (U.S. Food and Drug Administration, 2016).

A major fear is that testosterone supplementation may increase men's risk for cardiovascular events, stroke, or death (Garnick, 2015). Some research does indicate a relationship between supplementation and stroke, although the data are somewhat inconclusive (Anderson et al., 2015; Wallis et al., 2016; Loo et al., 2017). However, studies have also shown benefits of TRT's use among middle-age men in terms of improved sexual function (Corona et al., 2017), decreased frequency of nighttime urination, better sleep quality (Shigehara et al. 2015), and reduced body fat (Fui et al., 2016). However, many studies use small, nonrandomized samples that do not assess long-term treatment risks (U.S. Food and Drug Administration, 2016).

Currently, men with untreated prostate or breast cancer are advised to avoid TRT (Osterberg et al., 2014). In the absence of those risk factors, the jury is still out on TRT. Every drug is a balance of costs and benefits, and TRT is no different. The question is whether the short-term benefits outweigh the potential for health risks potentially leading to an early death.

what's your view

Do you think andropause is analogous to the changes that women undergo in menopause? What advice would you give to a middle-age man interested in taking testosterone replacement supplements?

Health is also important, and good health has been repeatedly associated with sexual activity and satisfaction (Thomas et al., 2015; Fisher et al., 2015). Menopause may affect desire as well. Sixty-one percent of married or cohabiting premenopausal women but only 41 percent of postmenopausal women reported having sex once a week or more (Rossi, 2004), and hot flashes are associated with declines in sexual activity (Thomas et al., 2015). Other factors such as surgery, medications, and too much food or alcohol can also impact sexual activity (Rossi, 2004).

Physical and Mental Health

Most middle-age Americans, like middle-age people in other industrialized countries, are generally healthy. All but 15.3 percent of 45- to 54-year-olds and 19.1 percent of 55- to 64-year-olds consider themselves in good to excellent health (National Center for Health Statistics, 2020). In this section, we address issues related to health at midlife.

PHYSICAL HEALTH AT MIDLIFE

Many people in midlife, especially those with low SES, experience increasing health problems (Lachman, 2004). The prevalence of physical limitations increases with age. In 2018, 16.5 percent of 45- to 54-year-olds and 25.3 percent of 55- to 64-year-olds were limited in activities because of chronic conditions (National Center for Health Statistics, 2020).

Hypertension (chronically high blood pressure) is currently the world's leading preventable cause of early death. Approximately 1.13 billion people worldwide have hypertension, although the prevalence rates vary by region. The highest rates are found in Africa (27 percent) and the lowest rates in the Americas (18 percent), with men more likely to be affected than women (World Health Organization, 2019). In high-income countries, rates decreased by 2.6 percent from 2000 to 2010, presumably as a result of better diagnosis and treatment. By contrast, low- and middle-income countries showed an increase of 7.7 percent (Mills et al., 2016). These high rates are troubling given hypertension's status as a risk factor for cardiovascular disease and stroke (Forouzanfar et al., 2015). These two diseases are the leading causes of global death, and estimates are that 1 in 4 deaths can be attributed to them (Abubakar et al., 2015).

hypertension
Chronically high blood pressure.

In the United States in 2016, 37.2 percent of men and 29.4 percent of women ages 40 to 59 had high blood pressure, with the highest rates found in African American men and women (Fryar et al., 2017). Some adults can lower their blood pressure with lifestyle modifications, such as weight loss, increases in physical activity, eating a low-salt diet with plentiful fruits and vegetables, increasing potassium intake, and consuming light amounts of alcohol. If lifestyle modifications are not effective, medication is generally used as well (Frisoli et al.,2011).

Heart disease is associated with hypertension. Globally, heart disease is the leading cause of death, accounting for 31 percent of deaths. Most of these deaths occur in low-to middle-income countries where access to health care services is limited (World Health Organization, 2017). In the United States, heart disease is the leading cause of death between ages 45 and 64 (Centers for Disease Control and Prevention, 2019, 2019). Overall, heart disease and its associated death rates have been on a long-term decline, although progress seemed to stall in 2011 (Sidney et al., 2016). The slowed progress in reducing heart disease may be due to rising rates of obesity and diabetes (Sidney et al., 2017). As with hypertension, African Americans are at higher risk (National Center for Health Statistics, 2019). Although women are less likely to have or die from heart disease when younger, as they age their risk rises to meet that of men. Moreover, because they often present with atypical symptoms and are treated less aggressively, all else being equal, their outcomes are generally worse than men's (Khamis et al., 2016). For example, chest pain is the most common symptom of a heart attack in both men and women, but women may experience other symptoms, such as back and jaw pain, nausea and vomiting, indigestion, difficult breathing, or palpitations (Patel et al., 2004).

In 1980, global prevalence of **diabetes** was 108 million. By 2014, this number had more than quadrupled to 422 million, with rates rising more quickly in low- to middle-income countries (World Health Organization, 2018). In the United States, approximately 17.5 percent of adults—almost 15 million people—age 45 to 64 years have diabetes, although roughly 3 million are undiagnosed. The rates are highest for Native American/Alaska Natives, Hispanics, and African Americans. Prevalence rates, which have been rising, are higher for people from lower socioeconomic levels (Centers for Disease Control and Prevention, 2020). The most common type, mature-onset (type 2) diabetes, typically develops after age 30 and becomes more prevalent with age. People with mature-onset diabetes often do not realize they have it until they develop such serious complications as heart disease, stroke, blindness, kidney disease, or loss of limbs (American Diabetes Association, 1992).

diabetes
Disease in which the body does not produce or properly use insulin, a hormone that converts sugar, starches, and other foods into energy needed for daily life.

Many of the chronic diseases and conditions common at midlife confer an added risk to those adults who become infected with the novel coronavirus, COVID-19. For example, obesity, cardiovascular disease, diabetes, chronic respiratory disease, cancer, and hypertension are associated with an increased risk of death from COVID-19 for infected adults (Jordan et al., 2020).

BEHAVIORAL INFLUENCES ON HEALTH

On average, Americans who smoke, are overweight, and have high blood pressure and high blood sugar have a life expectancy 4 years less than those who do not (Danaei et al., 2010). By the same token, people who do not smoke, who exercise regularly, drink alcohol in moderation, and eat plenty of fruits and vegetables have 4 times less risk of dying in midlife and old age (Khaw et al., 2008). Perhaps more important from a quality-of-life perspective, people who guard their health not only live longer but also have shorter periods of disability at the end of life (Vita et al., 1998).

Excess weight in middle age increases the risk of impaired health and death (Jee et al., 2006). Being overweight, which is medically defined as having a body mass index (BMI) of between 25 and 29.9, is not a risk factor. However, obesity, defined as a BMI of 30 or more, does increase a wide variety of health risks and is associated with mortality (Flegal et al., 2013). Weight also interacts with ethnicity, making some ethnic groups more likely to become overweight or obese. African American adults are the most likely to be obese (49.6 percent), followed by Hispanic adults (44.8 percent) and white adults (42.2 percent). Asian Americans are the least likely to be obese (17.4 percent). The prevalence of severe obesity, with a BMI of 40 or higher, is higher in adults age 40 to 59 than in any other age group (Hales et al., 2020).

With age, there are declines in muscle strength and physical performance. However, physical activity in midlife can help aging adults retain their muscle tone and strength (Akune et al., 2014), increase the chances of remaining mobile in old age (Patel et al., 2006), avoid weight gain (Jakicic et al., 2019), and stay healthier longer (Rhodes et al., 2017). Adults who engage in regular, moderate, or vigorous exercise are about 35 percent less likely to die in the next 8 years than those with a sedentary lifestyle. And those with cardiovascular risk factors, including smoking, diabetes, high blood pressure, and a history of coronary heart disease, benefit the most from being physically active (Richardson et al., 2004). Last, physical activity is associated with better cognitive functioning at midlife (Hoang et al., 2016) and a decreased risk of dementia in late adulthood (Blondell et al., 2014; Tolppanen et al., 2015).

Unfortunately, few adults comply with health guidelines. Approximately 52 percent of adults age 35 to 49 years eat a poor diet, as defined by less than 40 percent adherence to dietary guidelines, and this number is higher in Hispanics and African Americans. Education matters as well; greater adherence with dietary guidelines is found in more educated groups (Rehm et al., 2016). Only 22.9 percent of adults meet physical activity guidelines (Blackwell & Clarke, 2018). Although rates have decreased, slightly over 16 percent of adults age 45 to 64 smoked (Creamer et al., 2019). Adhering to a healthy lifestyle throughout life is ideal, but changes later in life can reverse some of the damage (Tolppanen et al., 2015).

SOCIOECONOMIC STATUS AND HEALTH

People with low socioeconomic status tend to have poorer health, shorter life expectancy, and more activity limitations due to chronic disease than people with higher SES. In part this is due to the cost of health care. In 2018, 41.3 percent of poor and near-poor people either delayed or did not receive medical care because of its expense (National Center for Health Statistics, 2018).

People with low SES also tend to live in more stressful environments and thus report higher levels of perceived stress. These higher levels of stress, in turn, are associated with a greater likelihood of engaging in unhealthy behaviors, such as consuming a poor diet, smoking, and not exercising (Algren et al., 2018). People with higher SES, by contrast, experience less stress and have a greater sense of control over what happens to them, attenuating their stress response (Mooney et al., 2018). They also tend to choose healthier lifestyles, to seek medical attention and social support when they need it (Lachman & Firth, 2004; Marmot & Fuhrer, 2004), and to show higher compliance with lifestyle modifications recommended to improve health indices (Wright et al., 2009).

RACE/ETHNICITY AND HEALTH

Even though racial and ethnic disparities have decreased in the United States since 1990, substantial differences persist (National Center for Health Statistics, 2018). In trying to determine the cause of these disparities, researchers have looked to the human genome.

Research in this area has found distinctive variations in the DNA code among people of European, African, and Chinese ancestry (Hinds et al., 2005). These variations are linked to predispositions to various diseases, from cancer to obesity, and such data may ultimately open the way to targeted treatments of preventive measures (Antonarakis & Cooper, 2019).

Although genetics may offer some clues to differences in health as a function of race or ethnicity, by far the most research has focused on correlates of ethnicity. Poverty is most likely the largest single underlying factor in this link. People who live in poverty generally have poorer access to health care, more stressful lives, and greater exposure to potential toxins in their everyday environment. For African Americans, for example, poverty has been related to poor nutrition, substandard housing, and poor access to health care (Smedley & Smedley, 2005). Moreover, people of different races may have differential responses to poverty. Some data suggest, for example, that the health of African Americans is more affected by poverty than that of white adults (Mode et al., 2016; Rodriguez et al., 2019).

From young adulthood throughout middle age, African Americans have higher overall death rates and higher incidence of hypertension, obesity, and diabetes. Hispanic Americans, like African Americans, have a disproportionate incidence of stroke, liver disease, diabetes, HIV infection, homicide, and cancers of the cervix and stomach (National Center for Health Statistics, 2016). They are also much less likely, particularly if they are limited English proficient, to have health insurance and a regular source of health care (Martorell & Martorell, 2006). Not surprisingly, they are also less likely to be screened for cholesterol and for breast, cervical, and colorectal cancers, or to receive influenza and pneumonia vaccines (Balluz et al., 2004).

GENDER AND HEALTH

Women have a higher life expectancy than men and lower death rates throughout life (World Health Organization, 2019; Kochanek et al., 2019). This has not always been the case. It is likely that for much of human history, men and women had similar life spans. However, improvements in maternal mortality rates and reductions in infectious diseases more greatly impacted women's mortality than men's (Warraich & Califf, 2019; Goldin & Lleras-Muney, 2019). Women's greater longevity has also been attributed to genetic protection given by the second X chromosome (which men do not have) and, before menopause, to the beneficial effects of the female hormone estrogen on both cardiovascular and cognitive health (World Health Organization, 2019; Hara et al., 2015). However, psychosocial and cultural factors, such as men's greater propensity for risk-taking, also played a part (Mahalik et al., 2013; Courtenay, 2011).

Although women live longer, they are slightly more likely to report being in fair or poor health than men (National Center for Health Statistics, 2018). Middle-age women tend to report more specific symptoms and chronic conditions than men, and they devote more effort to maintaining their health (Cleary et al., 2004). Men may feel that admitting illness is not masculine and seeking help means a loss of control (Addis & Mahalik, 2003), and they are less likely to seek professional help for health problems or stay overnight in a hospital (National Center for Health Statistics, 2018). They are also more likely to suffer from chronic health problems such as cancer or high blood pressure (Seigel et al., 2015; Maranon & Reckelhoff, 2013) and to report drug or alcohol problems (Cleary et al., 2004). Men are also more likely to report limitations in daily living as the result of a chronic condition (13.4 percent) than are women (12.4 percent) (National Center for Health Statistics, 2018).

Women's greater longevity has been attributed to genetic protection given by the second X chromosome (which men do not have) and, before menopause, to beneficial effects of the female hormone estrogen, particularly on cardiovascular health. Dave and Les Jacobs/Blend Images LLC

Women are at increased risk for osteoporosis, breast cancer, and heart disease after menopause. With longer life spans, women in many developed countries now can expect to live half their adult lives after menopause. As a result, increasing attention is being paid to women's health issues at this time of life (Barrett-Connor et al., 2002). There has also been more awareness of men's health issues as well. For example, as they age, men face an increasing risk of erectile dysfunction, particularly if their health is already poor (Gupta et al., 2011).

For many years, older men were subject to aggressive screening procedures for prostate cancer. Sometimes small cancers would be discovered, and many men were treated for those cancers. However, given the slow growth of prostate cancer, it is likely that many of these growths would never have become dangerous. New recommendations were recently developed to reduce the emphasis on aggressive screening procedures with the goal of reducing unnecessary medical treatment. Now, unless men meet one of a number of particular risk factors, prostate screening is not always recommended (Moyer, 2012; Heidenreich et al., 2011).

Bone Loss and Osteoporosis In women, bone loss rapidly accelerates in the first 5 to 10 years after menopause as levels of estrogen, which helps in calcium absorption, fall. Extreme bone loss may lead to **osteoporosis** (porous bones), a condition in which the bones become thin and brittle as a result of calcium depletion. Common signs of osteoporosis are marked loss in height and a hunchbacked posture that results from compression and collapse of a weakened spinal column. Approximately 200 million women across the world have osteoporosis, and the disease is responsible for 8.9 million fractures a year (Johnell & Kanis, 2006; Kanis, 2007).

Osteoporosis is more common in white women, most often in those with a small frame, low weight and BMI, and a family history of the condition. Other risk factors, besides age, include smoking, lack of exercise, and alcohol use (Centers for Disease Control and Prevention, 2019; Looker et al., 2017; Johansson et al., 2014). A predisposition to osteoporosis seems to have a genetic basis, particularly as there are indications that genetic markers may have implications for which drugs will be most effective in an individual (Richards et al., 2012).

The treatment approaches for osteoporosis have come under scrutiny in recent years (Guallar & Laine, 2014). Previous treatment philosophies assumed increasing available calcium via supplements should increase bone strength. However, research indicated that calcium supplements did not affect the risk of a bone fracture. Moreover, calcium supplements increased the risk of other health issues, including kidney stones, cardiovascular problems, and gastrointestinal issues (Reid, 2014). Additionally, there was also confusion about the role of hormone replacement therapy (HRT) in women. Although HRT can ameliorate some of the symptoms of menopause as well as slow bone loss, its use also carries significant risks (De Villiers et al., 2013).

In 2017 the American College of Physicians (ACP) released new, evidence-based guidelines for the treatment and management of osteoporosis in both men and women (Qaseem et al., 2017). Strong recommendations included the use of biphosphonates (drugs that slow or prevent bone loss) such as alendronate, risendronate, zoledronic acid, or denosumab in women who have been diagnosed with osteoporosis. These medications reduce the risk of hip or vertebral fractures in women, but the evidence for their effectiveness in men is weaker. In contrast to earlier recommendations, the ACP strongly recommends HRT not be used for treating osteoporosis in women, as new evidence does not show it to be effective. The ACP also recommends biphosphonate therapy for 5 years; however, bone density monitoring does not appear to confer any additional benefits to patients and is not necessary. Last, the ACP recommends that treatment decisions be holistic and take into account patient preferences and profile, and the financial and medical costs and benefits of medications.

Good lifestyle habits can reduce risk, especially if started early in life. Longitudinal studies suggest that exercise can help slow bone density loss (Kemmler et al., 2015) as well as maintain strength, agility, and balance, and thus be protective against falls that often lead to broken bones. Older adults also benefit from proper nutrition and the avoidance of smoking or heavy drinking (Cosman et al., 2014).

Breast Cancer and Mammography Breast cancer is the most common cancer in women, and was responsible for 627,000 deaths in 2018 (World Health Organization, 2020). Almost 13 percent of American women will develop breast cancer at some point in their lives (Howlader et al., 2019). In 2017, 42,510 people in the United States died of breast cancer (Kochanek et al., 2019).

osteoporosis
Condition in which the bones become thin and brittle as a result of rapid calcium depletion.

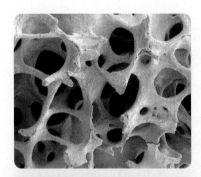
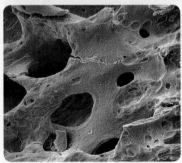

Images of normal (top) and osteoporotic (bottom) bones.
(both): Steve Gschmeissner/Science Photo Library/Brand X Pictures/Getty Images

About 5 to 10 percent of breast cancer cases are thought to be hereditary, resulting from inherited mutations. The most common of these are mutations of the BRCA1 and BRCA2 genes. Women without these mutations have roughly a 10 percent chance of developing breast cancer. However, those who have a BRCA1 or BRCA2 mutation have as much as a 70 percent chance of developing breast cancer. Another gene, PALB2, can also predispose women to a higher risk of breast cancer (American Cancer Society, 2017).

However, the vast majority of breast cancer cases are environmentally influenced. Once found mostly in affluent countries, breast cancer is becoming a worldwide problem as Western lifestyles move into the developing world (Porter, 2008). Overweight women, those who drink alcohol, those who experience early menarche and late menopause, those with a family history of breast cancer, and those who have no children, did not breastfeed, or who bore children later in life have a greater risk of breast cancer, whereas those who are moderately physically active and eat low-fat, high-fiber diets are at less risk (American Cancer Society, 2017; McTiernan et al., 2003). Weight gain, especially after menopause, increases a woman's risk of breast cancer, and weight loss decreases the risk (Eliassen et al., 2006).

Advances in treatment and early diagnosis have dramatically improved prospects for breast cancer patients. Fully 89 percent of U.S. women with breast cancer now survive at least 5 years past diagnosis. If the cancer is still localized and has not yet spread, the 5-year survival rate is 99 percent (Miller et al., 2016). Cancer can be treated with removal of part or all of the breast, along with radiation or chemotherapy.

The benefits of **mammography,** diagnostic X-ray examination of the breasts, appear to be greatest for women over 50. In 2009, the U.S. Preventive Services Task Force issued a new set of guidelines recommending that women begin routine screening for breast cancer at 50, rather than at 40 years of age as had been previously suggested. However, adherence to this diagnostic schedule varies, and medical professionals and organizations often disagree with recommended diagnostic guidelines (Corbelli et al., 2014).

Hormone Therapy The most troublesome physical effects of menopause are linked to reduced levels of estrogen, and **hormone therapy (HT)** has been used to address these effects. HT is treatment with artificial estrogen, sometimes in combination with progesterone, to help relieve symptoms of menopause. HT has a complicated pattern of risks and benefits.

On the positive side, HT is the most effective means of addressing symptoms such as night sweats and hot flashes, especially for women below the age of 60 or who went through menopause less than 10 years ago (De Villiers et al., 2013). However, it is not as effective at managing osteoporosis. HT, when started at menopause and continued for at least 5 years, can slow bone loss after menopause (Barrett-Connor et al., 2002; Lindsay et al., 2002). However, bone loss resumes within 3 years if and when HT stops (Heiss et al., 2008). Moreover, HT fails to reduce the risk of fracture (Reid, 2014).

Although earlier research was equivocal, the most recent research suggests that HT does not impact the risk of either cardiovascular disease or mortality (Manson et al., 2017; Benkhadra et al., 2015). Because of the complicated risk profile of these drugs, HT should not be used for disease prevention but is appropriate for menopausal symptom management in affected women (Manson et al., 2013). Lifestyle changes such as losing weight and stopping smoking, together with any necessary drugs to lower cholesterol and blood pressure, appear to be wiser courses for heart disease prevention in most women (Manson & Martin, 2001). HT, especially when taken orally, has also been associated with a greater, although still overall small, risk of stroke or blood clot (De Villiers et al., 2013).

As with the cardiac data, the links between HR and breast cancer risk are complex. Heightened risk of breast cancer seems to occur mainly among current or recent estrogen users, if estrogen and progestin are used together, and the risk increases with length of use (Chen et al., 2002; De Villiers et al., 2013). However, the overall risk is still quite low, with an incidence of less than 1 woman per 1,000 over a year. This risk is comparable

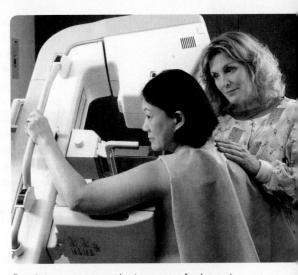

Routine mammography to screen for breast cancer is generally recommended for older women. If cancer is detected before it spreads, women have about a 98 percent chance of surviving at least 5 years after diagnosis.
Source: Rhoda Baer/National Cancer Institute (NCI)

mammography
Diagnostic X-ray examination of the breasts.

hormone therapy (HT)
Treatment with artificial estrogen, sometimes in combination with the hormone progesterone, to relieve or prevent symptoms caused by decline in estrogen levels after menopause.

to increased risk due to lifestyle factors such as being sedentary or consuming alcohol (De Villiers et al., 2013).

Results on the effects of HT on cognitive function and dementia risk are also difficult to interpret. Some studies have found that HT reduces the risk of cognitive impairment (Zandi et al., 2002), others have found it increases the risk (Espeland et al., 2004; Shumaker et al., 2004). Timing may matter here. HT that begins in early menopause does not seem to have a negative effect on cognition; however, later initiation of HT is associated with increased risk of dementia (De Villiers et al., 2013). Additional research in this area indicates that when women use HT in midlife *only*, they show a lower risk of dementia than women who use HT in early menopause and then continue to do so into late adulthood, and in women who begin using HT in late adulthood. It may be there is a critical window of time where HT is protective, but taken outside of that window, it is damaging (Whitmer et al., 2011; Shao et al., 2012).

MENTAL HEALTH AT MIDLIFE

In 2017, approximately 22.3 million U.S. adults age 26 to 49 had some form of mental, behavioral, or emotional disorder that met *DSM-IV* criteria in the past year (excluding developmental disorders and substance use disorders). Of those, 7.6 million had a major depressive episode, and slightly over 67 percent of them received treatment for it (Substance Abuse and Mental Health Services Administration, 2018). Depression negatively affects health, making prevention and treatment an important issue. Adults with depression are more likely than their peers to be diagnosed with heart disease, arthritis, or stroke, and to report needing help with activities of daily living such as bathing and dressing (Hare et al., 2014; Matcham et al., 2016; Dong et al., 2012; Pratt et al., 2007).

Even those adults not diagnosed with a mental disorder may experience negative effects at a subclinical level. For example, when asked about the presence of mental-health-related symptoms in the past month, 42 percent of adults reported feeling nervous or anxious, 37 percent reported feeling depressed or sad, 33 percent reported constant worrying, and 37 percent reported irritability or anger (American Psychological Association, 2016).

Emotions and Mental Health Although negative emotions are unpleasant to experience, under the right circumstances they are a healthy response to events and serve important adaptive functions. For example, when negative emotions are elicited in negative contexts, they can have beneficial consequences, such as when fear motivates an individual to schedule a screening for a disease (Coifman et al., 2016). However, when negative moods are excessive, long-lasting, or occur too frequently, they can have damaging effects on the body, suppress immune functioning, and increase susceptibility to disease.

Negative emotions such as anxiety and despair are often associated with poor physical and mental health (Ray, 2004; Salovey et al., 2000; Spiro, 2001). People high in neuroticism and hostility, who are prone to such feelings on a regular basis, are more likely to suffer from serious illness and reduced longevity. Hostility has also been associated with an increased risk of coronary heart disease and mortality for postmenopausal women (Lahey, 2009; Smith, 2006) and in an increased risk of death from heart attack in men (Assari, 2017).

The opposite pattern has been found for positive emotions. Positive emotions and well-being are associated with both short-term and long-term positive health outcomes and reduced mortality (Diener & Chan, 2011; Howell et al., 2007; Chida & Steptoe, 2008; Sin, 2016). Hope and curiosity have been found to predict a decreased likelihood of hypertension, diabetes, and respiratory tract infections (Richman et al., 2005). Personality traits also affect health—optimism and conscientiousness are consistently associated with better health and longer life (Kern & Friedman, 2008; Lahey, 2009; Smith, 2006). A positive emotional outlook can even affect the propensity to get sick from a common cold.

A positive outlook may guard against disease and buffer the impact of stress. Rolf Bruderer/Blend Images LLC

For example, when adult volunteers were exposed to a virus that can cause colds, those with a positive emotional outlook were less likely to get sick (Cohen et al., 2003).

There are also indirect effects of positive emotions on health (DeSteno et al., 2013). A positive emotional outlook motivates people to engage in more healthful practices, such as regular sleep and exercise, and to pay more attention to health-related information. Positive emotions may also affect health indirectly by softening the impact of stressful life events and helping people feel more connected to others (Armenta et al., 2016; Cohen & Pressman, 2006; Richman et al., 2005).

STRESS AT MIDLIFE

One of the ways in which people become more vulnerable to poor physical and mental health is via stress. **Stress** is the damage that occurs when perceived environmental demands, or **stressors,** exceed a person's capacity to cope with them. The body's capacity to adapt to stress involves the brain, which perceives danger (either real or imagined); the adrenal glands, which mobilize the body to fight it; and the immune system, which provides the defenses.

People early in middle age tend to experience higher levels of stress and more frequent stress than other age groups. For example, in a nationally representative study (American Psychological Association, 2020), 39 percent of U.S. 35- to 55-year-olds reported extreme stress approximately 25 percent of the time. Younger adults (ages 18 to 34) and late middle-age and older adults (age 55 and up) reported lower stress levels, with 29 percent and 25 percent, respectively, reporting high stress.

Prior to 2020, common sources of reported stress included health, work and money, personal debt, housing instability, and hunger. The largest source of stress, reported by 71 percent of adults, was mass shootings (American Psychological Association, 2020). However, the advent of the COVID-19 pandemic shifted the sources of stress for most Americans. In April 2020, unemployment rose to almost 15 percent, reflecting job losses for over 23 million people (Bureau of Labor Statistics, 2020). Not surprisingly, the stress reported due to work and the economy increased sharply from the previous year, from 46 to 70 percent of adults. Additionally, 70 percent of people reported the way in which the government was handling the crisis was a source of stress as well. The effects of the pandemic were also felt more strongly by adults with children. Forty-six percent of adults with children reported their average stress level as high, whereas only 26 percent of adults without children reported the same (American Psychological Association, 2020).

For minority group members, discrimination and racism can also lead to increased chronic stress and are associated with an increased risk for disease (Thoits, 2010). Racial minority (63 percent) and sexual minority (64 percent) adults report discrimination has kept them from having a full and productive life (American Psychological Association, 2020). Moreover, the disparity in experienced stress has continued during the COVID-19 pandemic, with minority group members reporting higher levels of stress than white adults (American Psychological Association, 2020).

Stress and the Immune System The stress response system and the immune system are closely linked and work together to keep the body healthy. Acute, or short-term, stress, such as the challenge of taking a test or running a competitive race, generally strengthens the immune system. We are adapted to dealing with such events, and our bodies quickly and efficiently respond to and then recover from the event. However, intense or prolonged stress, such as might result from poverty or disability, can weaken or break down the body, increasing the susceptibility to disease (Segerstrom & Miller, 2004; Sapolsky, 1992).

Chronic stress can lead to persistent inflammation and, over time, to disease (Cohen et al., 2012). Stress has been increasingly recognized as a factor in age-related diseases including hypertension, heart disease, stroke,

stress
Physical or psychological demands on a person or organism.

stressors
Perceived environmental demands that may produce stress.

Positive emotions and well-being are associated with both short- and long-term positive health outcomes and reduced mortality. moodboard/Cultura/ Getty Images

osteoporosis, peptic ulcers, and cancer (Liu et al., 2017; Wirtz & von Kanel, 2017; Kotlega et al., 2016; Kelly et al., 2019; Deding et al., 2016; Moreno-Smith et al., 2010). Moreover, a propensity to respond in a negative fashion to stress may interact with genetic predispositions. So, even if similar stressors are experienced, some people respond more negatively than others. Daily stressors such as irritations, frustrations, and overloads may be less severe in their impact than life changes, but their buildup can also affect health and emotional adjustment, particularly for emotionally reactive adults (Piazza et al., 2013).

Cognitive Performance

The status of cognitive abilities in middle age has been a subject of much debate. Here, we look at two important lines of research, Schaie's Seattle Longitudinal Study and Horn and Cattell's studies of fluid and crystallized intelligence.

THE SEATTLE LONGITUDINAL STUDY

In many respects middle-age people are in their cognitive prime. The Seattle Longitudinal Study of Adult Intelligence (Schaie, 1990, 1994, 1996a, 1996b, 2005; Willis & Schaie, 1999, 2006; Schaie & Willis, 2010) demonstrates this fact.

The study began in 1956 with 500 randomly chosen men and women across a variety of different age brackets ranging from 22 to 67 years of age and involved multiple waves of data collection over 5 decades. The participants were followed longitudinally and assessed every 7 years on timed tests of six primary mental abilities (Table 15.2).

Most participants showed no significant reductions in most abilities until after age 60, and then not in most areas. Virtually no one declined on all fronts, and most people improved in some areas. However, there were wide individual differences.

Additionally, there were few uniform patterns of age-related change across cognitive abilities. For example, several abilities peaked during middle age, and verbal meaning even showed improvements into old age. However, about 13 to 17 percent of adults declined in number, memory recall, or verbal fluency between ages 39 and 53. By the age of 74, there were declines in the average scores for all abilities (Schaie, 1994, 2005; Willis & Schaie, 2006; Schaie & Willis, 2010).

TABLE 15.2 Tests of Primary Mental Abilities Given in Seattle Longitudinal Study of Adult Intelligence

Test	Ability Measured	Task	Type of Intelligence*
Verbal meaning	Recognition and understanding of words	Find synonym by matching stimulus word with another word from a list	Crystallized
Word fluency	Retrieving words from long-term memory	Think of as many words as possible beginning with a given letter	Part crystallized, part fluid
Number	Performing computations	Do simple addition problems	Crystallized
Spatial orientation	Manipulating objects mentally in two-dimensional space	Select rotated examples of figure to match stimulus figure	Fluid
Inductive reasoning	Identifying patterns and inferring rules for solving logical problems	Complete a letter series	Fluid
Perceptual speed	Making quick, accurate discriminations between visual stimuli	Identify matching and nonmatching images flashed on a computer screen	Fluid

*Fluid and crystallized intelligence are defined in the next section.

Sources: Schaie, K. W. (1989). The hazards of cognitive aging. *The Gerontologist, 29*(4), 484-493; Willis, S. L., & Schaie, K. W. (1999). Intellectual functioning in midlife. In S. L. Willis & J. D. Reid (Eds.), *Life in the middle: Psychological and social development in middle age* (pp. 233–247). San Diego, CA: Academic Press.

Schaie and his colleagues also found that successive cohorts scored progressively higher at the same ages on most abilities, possibly because of improvements in education, healthy lifestyles, and other positive environmental influences (Willis & Schaie, 2006; Figure 15.1). However, once declines began, these later cohorts also showed a more rapid mortality-related decline. In other words, later cohorts performed at a higher level for longer, and the amount of time they spent at a lower level of cognitive functioning was compressed at the end of their lives (Gerstorf et al., 2011).

Individuals who scored highest tended to be free of cardiovascular and other chronic diseases, physically active, to be from a higher socioeconomic class, have high educational levels and flexible personalities at midlife, to be in an intact family, to pursue cognitively complex occupations and other activities, to be married to someone more cognitively advanced, to be satisfied with their accomplishments, and to be high in the personality dimension of openness to experience (Schaie, 2005; Willis & Schaie, 2006; Sharp et al., 2010; Schaie & Willis, 2010; Lindwall et al., 2012). Given the strong cognitive performance of most in middle age, evidence of substantial cognitive decline in persons younger than 60 may indicate a neurological problem (Schaie, 2005). In particular, midlife decline in memory recall and verbal fluency (Willis & Schaie, 2006) and perceptual processing speed (Schaie & Willis, 2010) predict cognitive impairment in old age.

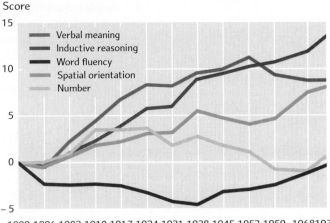

FIGURE 15.1

Cohort Differences in Scores on Tests of Primary Mental Abilities

More recent cohorts scored higher on inductive reasoning, word fluency, and spatial orientation.

Source: Schaie, K. W. (2005). *Developmental influences on adult intelligence: The Seattle Longitudinal Study.* New York, NY: Oxford University Press (Fig. 6.1, p. 137).

FLUID AND CRYSTALLIZED INTELLIGENCE

Consider a glass of water. If you tilt it, the water sloshes around in random swirls and waves. By contrast, a block of ice has a rigid crystalline structure, with every molecule in its place. This is the metaphor used by another set of cognitive researchers (Cattell, 1943; Horn & Cattell, 1967) to describe the different types of intelligence. **Fluid intelligence** is the ability to solve novel problems on the fly. Such problems require little or no previous knowledge, such as realizing that a hanger can be used to fix a leaky toilet, or discovering the pattern in a sequence of figures. It involves perceiving relations, forming concepts, and drawing inferences. **Crystallized intelligence,** by contrast, is the ability to remember and use information acquired over a lifetime, such as finding a synonym for a word or solving a math problem. Crystallized intelligence is measured by tests of vocabulary, general information, and responses to social situations and dilemmas—abilities that depend largely on education and cultural experience.

Typically, fluid intelligence peaks in young adulthood. From the age of 20 to 60 years, the average person will have lost more than one standard deviation in fluid intelligence (Salthouse, 2010). Working memory capacity also declines with age. However, many older adults perform in the real world at high levels despite the declines in fluid intelligence (Salthouse, 2012). How do we make sense of this discrepancy?

One explanation is offered by improvements in crystallized intelligence, which increase through middle age and often until near the end of life (Horn & Cattell, 1967; Cattell, 1963). Older adults can use their accumulated lifetime of knowledge to compensate for tasks in which decision making can benefit from prior experiences (Li et al., 2013). Thus you might expect that older adults would do as well, or better, on tasks such as filling out a tax return, where crystallized intelligence would be helpful, but not on tasks such as learning how to use a new smartphone, where fluid intelligence would be more important (Zaval et al., 2015).

fluid intelligence
Type of intelligence, proposed by Horn and Cattell, that is applied to novel problems and is relatively independent of educational and cultural influences.

crystallized intelligence
Type of intelligence, proposed by Horn and Cattell, involving the ability to remember and use learned information; it is largely dependent on education and culture.

People's cognitive performance offers insight into their overall health. Although crystallized intelligence is not associated with mortality risk once sociodemographic factors are considered, fluid intelligence is strongly predictive of mortality risk (Batterham et al., 2009; Aichele et al., 2015). Additionally, a large discrepancy between fluid and crystallized intelligence, particularly for highly educated people, may be an indicator of cognitive decline (O'Shea et al., 2018).

Adult Cognition

Instead of measuring the same cognitive abilities at different ages, some developmental scientists look for distinctive qualities in the thinking of mature adults.

EXPERTISE

Why do mature adults show increasing competence in solving problems in their chosen fields? One answer seems to lie in *specialized knowledge,* or *expertise*—a form of crystallized intelligence.

Because formal education is age-graded, most children learn similar things—such as how to read or complete math problems—at roughly the same time. In adulthood, however, paths of learning diverge, and adults become more or less learned in whatever domain of knowledge they pursue. These advances in expertise continue at least through middle adulthood and, for the most part, are not related to general intelligence. Moreover, they usually do not depend on the brain's information-processing machinery because some adults' fluid intelligence is characterized by **encapsulation**— that is, it becomes dedicated to handling specific kinds of knowledge. This process of encapsulation makes that knowledge easier to access, add to, and use. It may take middle-age people longer than younger people to process *new* information. But when it comes to solving problems *within* their field of expertise, their vast base of knowledge compensates for processing declines and allows them to rapidly and effectively solve a problem (Hoyer & Rybash, 1994).

Experts assimilate and interpret new knowledge more efficiently by referring to a rich, highly organized storehouse of mental representations of what they already know. For example, imaging studies show that when completing a task within their domain of expertise, adults show brain activation in areas associated with long-term memory. This allows them to integrate information in long-term memory with working memory in "chunks," and thus perform the task at a higher level than novices (Guida et al., 2012).

encapsulation
The process that allows expertise to compensate for declines in information-processing ability by bundling relevant knowledge together.

Studies of people in such diverse occupations as chess players, street vendors, abacus counters, physics experts, hospitality workers, airline counter workers, and airplane pilots illustrate how specific knowledge contributes to superior performance in a particular domain (Billet, 2001) and can help buffer age-related declines in cognitive resources when solving problems in that domain (Morrow et al., 2001).

Expert thinking often seems automatic and intuitive. Experts generally are not fully aware of the thought processes that lie behind their decisions (Charness & Schultetus, 1999; Salas et al., 2010). Such intuitive, experience-based thinking is also characteristic of what has been called postformal thought.

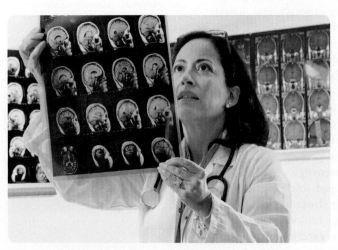

Expertise in interpreting X-rays depends on specialized knowledge. Experts often appear to be guided by intuition and cannot explain how they arrive at conclusions. Ron Levine/ Photographer's Choice RF/Getty Images

INTEGRATIVE THOUGHT

Although not limited to any particular period of adulthood, postformal thought seems well suited to the complex tasks, multiple roles, and perplexing choices and challenges of midlife, such as the need to synthesize and balance work and family demands (Sinnott, 2003). An important feature of postformal thought is its *integrative* nature (Kallio, 2011). Mature adults integrate what they read, see, or hear in terms of its meaning for them. Instead of accepting something at face value, they filter it through their life experience and previous learning.

In one study (Adams, 1991), early and late adolescents and middle-age and older adults were asked to summarize a Sufi teaching tale. Adolescents recalled more details of the story than adults did, but their summaries were largely limited to repeating the story line. Adults, especially women, gave summaries that were rich in interpretation, integrating what was in the text with its psychological and metaphorical meaning for them.

Society benefits from this integrative feature of adult thought. Generally, it is mature adults who translate their knowledge about the human condition into inspirational stories to which younger generations can turn for guidance.

CREATIVITY

Intelligence and creativity are not the same thing. Although a certain baseline general intelligence, or IQ, is needed (Guilford, 1956), creative performance is not strongly related to general intelligence once that threshold is reached (Simonton, 2000). This is true even though the baseline IQ needed for creative performance does rise for more complex creative achievements (Jauk et al., 2013).

Intelligence shows high heritability and its heritability rises with age as individuals get older and seek out more experiences in line with their proclivities (Plomin & Deary, 2015). A similar process may be operating in creativity. Earlier studies suggested many differences in creative performance were driven by environment, and that genetic contributions were weak (Runco et al., 2011; Reuter et al., 2006). More recent studies suggest that genetic influences are stronger than initially believed, and that, as with intelligence, their importance may rise with age (Vinkhuyzen et al., 2009; Piffer & Hur, 2014; Hur et al., 2014).

Highly creative people tend to be independent, nonconformist, unconventional, high in emotional intelligence, high in positive affect, and they are open to new ideas and experiences. Their thinking processes are often unconscious, leading to sudden moments of illumination (Simonton, 2000; Da Costa et al., 2015). They look at problems more deeply and come up with solutions that do not occur to others (Sternberg & Horvath, 1998). They think in flexible ways and explore many possible solutions to problems (Baas et al., 2015).

However, this is not enough. Extraordinary creative achievement requires deep, highly organized knowledge of a subject and a strong emotional attachment to the work, which spurs the creator to persevere in the face of obstacles. A person must first be thoroughly grounded in a field before she or he can see its limitations, envision radical departures, and develop a new and unique point of view (Keegan, 1996: Baer, 2015).

Not surprisingly, researchers have looked for creative problem-solving correlates in the brain. This research is challenging—creative ideas, by their very nature, are divergent and wide-ranging. One meta-analysis including 34 imaging studies showed that when people were engaged in creative tasks, they showed more activation in the prefrontal cortex regardless of what type of creative task they were performing. However, different areas became more active depending on task demands. For example, tasks that required inhibitory processes, fluency, and control were likely to generate activity in the lateral prefrontal cortex; whereas tasks that required the activation of semantic (meaning-based) associations tended to elicit more activity in the superior and inferior central gyri (Gonen-Yaacovi et al., 2013).

Creativity and Age Is there a relationship between creative performance and age? On psychometric tests of divergent thinking, age differences consistently appear. Whether data are cross-sectional or longitudinal, scores peak, on average, around the late thirties (Simonton, 1990). After this, they remain relatively flat for some time, and then decline in the seventies (Massimiliano, 2015). A similar age curve emerges when creativity is measured by variations in output (number of publications, paintings, or compositions). A person in the last decade of a creative career typically produces only about half as much as during the late thirties or early forties, though somewhat more than in the twenties (Simonton, 1990).

Middle age does not necessarily imply declines. Jennifer Lopez, 50-year-old dancer, singer, actor, fashion designer and producer, shocked and amazed audiences with her athletic performance at the 2020 Super Bowl halftime show. Focus On Sport/Getty Images

The age curve varies depending on the field. Poets, mathematicians, and theoretical physicists tend to be most prolific in their late twenties or early thirties. Research psychologists reach a peak around age 40, followed by a moderate decline. Novelists, historians, and philosophers become increasingly productive through their late forties or fifties and then level off (Dixon & Hultsch, 1999; Simonton, 1990).

However, there are some indications these data, or the interpretations, may be flawed. For instance, it is not clear that productivity should be the metric by which creativity is measured, especially as some research suggests that older adults' work remains innovative over time. For example, meta-analyses of age and creativity at work suggest there is no direct relationship between the two and that much depends on how creativity is defined (Rietzschel et al., 2016; Ng & Feldman, 2013). Additionally, patterns of creative output may have changed for more recent cohorts. For example, although previous research seemed to suggest researchers' productivity peaked in the forties, more recent data suggest that those researchers who are productive when young continue to publish scholarly articles at high rates until retirement (Stroebe, 2015).

Work and Education

In all cultures, adults need to work to support themselves and their families. In developing countries, adults often take on the same roles as their parents, and there is less occupational choice. In industrialized societies, there are a multitude of life paths, and the work people do reflects this. Moreover, retirement is more likely to be an option.

WORK VERSUS EARLY RETIREMENT

Before 1985, the average age of retirement moved steadily downward. Since then, the trend has reversed. Before bringing their working lives to a complete stop, people may reduce work hours or days, gradually moving into retirement over a number of years. This practice is called *phased retirement.* Or they may switch to another company or a new line of work, a practice called *bridge employment* (Czaja, 2006). A majority of older Americans now remain active in the labor force after retirement from their career job (Cahill et al., 2013), although the opportunities for such employment have become limited due to the high unemployment and job losses resulting from the COVID-19 pandemic (Bureau of Labor Statistics, 2020).

Many older adults may continue working to maintain their physical and emotional health and their personal and social roles, or simply because they enjoy the stimulation of work (Czaja, 2006; Sterns & Huyck, 2001). Often, people work primarily for financial reasons. For example, data show that the implementation of the Affordable Care Act (ACA) in 2010, which increased the affordability of comprehensive health care for many, led to increased early retirement and increases in part-time work (which does not generally include health benefits) in women and low-income men (Heim & Lim, 2017).

The rise in the Social Security retirement age to 67 for full benefits offers an inducement to keep working. The Age Discrimination in Employment Act, which eliminated mandatory retirement ages for most occupations, and the Americans with Disabilities Act, which requires employers to make reasonable accommodations for workers with disabilities, have helped mature workers to keep their jobs.

WORK AND COGNITIVE DEVELOPMENT

Cognitive skills, like muscles, must be used to remain healthy. Occupational choice can affect this process in adults in an interactive fashion. For example, people with high cognitive ability tend to seek out, obtain, and be good at substantively complex work—work that requires thought and independent judgment. In turn, complex work is associated with the retention of cognitive abilities. Those cognitive abilities then allow older adults to keep working as effectively as a younger person, even in the face of general age-related declines in cognitive processes (Fisher et al., 2017). Work need not necessarily be construed in the traditional way, and the same is true of men and women engaged in complex household work, such as planning a budget or making complicated repairs like putting in new plumbing (Caplan & Schooler, 2006). Regardless of the specifics, people who are deeply engaged in complex work or cognitively stimulating lifestyles tend to show stronger cognitive performance and fewer declines than their peers as they age, even if they retire (La Rue, 2010; Fisher et al., 2017).

This suggests that if work, both on the job and at home, could be made meaningful and challenging, more adults might retain or improve their cognitive abilities. This seems to be happening to some extent. The gains in cognitive abilities seen in older cohorts may reflect workplace changes that put a premium on adaptability, initiative, and decentralized decision making.

THE MATURE LEARNER

Expanding technology and shifting job markets often entail a need for more training or education. In 2016, 23.6 percent of U.S adults 45 to 54 years of age and 20.2 percent of adults 55 to 65 years of age completed a work experience or credential program (National Center for Education Statistics, 2018).

Adult Education and Work Skills Technological skills are increasingly necessary for success in the modern world and are a major component of work-related adult education. With experience, middle-age people can perform computer-based tasks as well as young adults (Czaja, 2006).

Employers see benefits of workplace education in improved morale, increased quality of work, better teamwork and problem solving, and greater ability to cope with new technology and other changes in the workplace. Moreover, in addition to the employee benefits, employers increasingly report benefits for the company as a whole, including higher economic returns and improved employee skills (Conference Board, 2000).

Literacy Training **Literacy** is a fundamental requisite for participation not only in the workplace but in all facets of a modern, information-driven society. At the start of the twentieth century, a person with a fourth-grade education was considered literate; today, a high school diploma is barely adequate.

Globally, 507 million adults age 25 to 64—about 14 percent of adults in that age range—are illiterate, mostly in sub-Saharan Africa and East and South Asia. Women make up 63 percent of illiterate adults worldwide. Illiteracy is especially common among women in developing nations, where education typically is considered unimportant for them. The United Nations Educational, Scientific, and Cultural Organization (UNESCO) is currently involved in Capacity Development for Education (CapED), providing targeted evidence-based assistance with educational reform to vulnerable countries (UNESCO, 2017).

In 2014, 17 percent of U.S. adults could not locate clearly identifiable information in brief English prose, 27 percent could not perform simple numerical operations such as addition, and 23 percent could not use simple technological tools such as e-mail or the Internet. Middle-age and older adults tend to have lower literacy levels than young adults, but the average literacy level of adults ages 50 to 59 has increased since 1992. Adults below basic literacy are less likely to be employed than adults at higher literacy levels. In the United States, the National Literacy Act requires the states to establish literacy training centers with federal funding assistance. Compared to other countries, the United States ranks about average on literacy tests. However, U.S. adults are clustered at both the high and low ends of the scale (Rampey et al., 2016).

literacy
In an adult, ability to use printed and written information to function in society, achieve goals, and develop knowledge and potential.

summary and key terms

Middle Age: A Social Construct

- The concept of middle age is a social construct. It came into use in industrial societies as an increasing life span led to new roles at midlife.
- The span of middle adulthood is often subjective.
- Most middle-age people are in good physical, cognitive, and emotional condition.

Physical Changes

- Although some physiological changes result from aging and genetic makeup, behavior and lifestyle can affect their timing and extent.
- Most middle-age adults compensate well for gradual, minor declines in sensory and psychomotor abilities. Losses in bone density and vital capacity are common.
- Symptoms of menopause and attitudes toward it may depend on cultural factors and natural changes of aging.
- Although men can continue to father children until late in life, many middle-age men experience a decline in fertility and in frequency of orgasm.
- A large proportion of middle-age men experience erectile dysfunction.
- Sexual activity generally diminishes gradually in middle age.

  presbyopia, myopia, presbycusis, basal metabolism, vital capacity, menopause, perimenopause, erectile dysfunction

Physical and Mental Health

- Most middle-age people are healthy; however, baby boomers may be less healthy than previous generations at middle age.
- Hypertension is a major health problem beginning in midlife. Cancer has passed heart disease as the number one cause of death in midlife. The prevalence of diabetes has doubled.
- The presence of chronic health conditions worsens the prognosis for those infected with COVID-19.
- Diet, exercise, alcohol use, and smoking affect present and future health.
- Low income is associated with poorer health.
- Racial and ethnic disparities in health and health care have decreased but still persist.
- Postmenopausal women become more susceptible to heart disease as well as to bone loss leading to osteoporosis. Chances of developing breast cancer also increase with age.
- While hormone therapy appears to be the most effective treatment for menopausal symptoms, the associated risks warrant caution in its use.

Design Credit: (globe) janrysavy/Getty Images

- Stress occurs when the body's ability to cope is not equal to the demands on it. Stress is often greatest in middle age. Severe stress can affect immune functioning.
- Role and career changes and other experiences typical of middle age can be stressful, but resilience is common.
- Psychological distress becomes more prevalent in middle age.
- Personality and negative emotionality can affect health. Positive emotions tend to be associated with good health.

  hypertension, diabetes, osteoporosis, mammography, hormone therapy (HT), stress, stressors

Cognitive Performance

- The Seattle Longitudinal Study found that several of the primary mental abilities remain strong during middle age, but there is great individual variability.
- Fluid intelligence declines earlier than crystallized intelligence.

  fluid intelligence, crystallized intelligence

Adult Cognition

- Some theorists propose that cognition takes distinctive forms at midlife.
- Expertise allows older adults to perform at high levels in areas they are familiar with despite the processing declines typical of age. This is because encapsulation allows them to use information more effectively.
- Postformal thought seems especially useful in situations calling for integrative thinking.
- Creative performance depends on personal attributes and environmental forces.
- Creativity is not strongly related to intelligence.
- An age-related decline appears in psychometric tests of divergent thinking and creative output, but peak ages for output vary by occupation. How creativity is defined also affects findings.

  encapsulation

Work and Education

- A shift away from early retirement and toward more flexible options is occurring.
- Complex work may improve cognitive flexibility.
- Many adults participate in educational activities, often to improve work-related skills and knowledge.
- Literacy training is an urgent need in the United States and globally.

  literacy

Psychosocial Development in Middle Adulthood

chapter 16

BrankoPhoto/iStock/Getty Images

learning objectives

Discuss stability and change in development in middle adulthood.

Summarize personality development and psychological adjustment in middle age.

Identify some important aspects of close relationships in middle adulthood.

In this chapter we look at theoretical perspectives and research on psychosocial issues and themes at midlife. We then focus on intimate relationships: marriage, cohabitation, and divorce; gay and lesbian relationships; friendships; and relationships with maturing children, aging parents, siblings, and grandchildren. All these may be woven into the rich texture of the middle years.

Change at Midlife

In psychosocial terms, middle adulthood once was considered a relatively stable period of development, where little change occurred. In part because of these assumptions, middle-age adults were rarely the object of direct study.

However, there is a renewed interest in midlife research. The changing demographics of countries such as the United States, where large proportions of middle-age adults are moving into late adulthood, has made studying the dynamics of this age more vital. In the following section, we first focus on the most influential model in this area and then issues related to personality, identity, and well-being.

Psychosocial Theory and Midlife

Erik Erikson, the most influential of what are known as normative-stage theorists, provided a frame of reference for much developmental theory and research on middle adulthood.

GENERATIVITY VERSUS STAGNATION

Erikson believed that the years around age 40 were a time when people entered their seventh psychosocial stage: **generativity versus stagnation. Generativity,** as Erikson defined it, involved finding meaning through contributing to society and leaving a legacy for future generations. The virtue of this period is *care:* "a widening commitment to *take care* of the persons, the products, and the ideas one has learned *to care for*" (Erikson, 1985, p. 67). People who do not find an outlet for generativity run the risk of becoming self-absorbed, self-indulgent, and stagnant. Adults who slide into stagnation may find themselves disconnected from their communities because of their failure to find a way to contribute.

Erikson believed that generativity was especially salient during midlife because of the demands placed on adults through work and family. Research supports that middle-age people do score higher on generativity than younger and older ones. The age at which individuals achieve generativity varies, as does its strength at any particular time, and some people are more generative than others (McAdams, 2006; Stewart & Vandewater, 1998).

Typically, generativity is expressed by being a parent or grandparent, although this is not the only path. Generativity can derive from involvement in multiple roles (McAdams, 2013; Chen et al., 2019). For instance, it can be expressed through teaching or mentorship, productivity or creativity, and self-generation or self-development or as Erikson called it, "maintenance of the world." Regardless of its form, generativity tends to be associated with prosocial behavior (McAdams, 2006). So, for example, volunteering for community service or for a political cause is an expression of generativity (Hart et al., 2003; Matsuba et al., 2012).

High levels of generativity are linked to positive outcomes. For example, highly generative people tend to report greater well-being and satisfaction in midlife (McAdams, 2001) and in later adulthood (Sheldon & Kasser, 2001), perhaps through the sense of having contributed meaningfully to society. Moreover, the positive effects are also physical in nature; generativity is also associated with good health, and a decreased risk of disability or mortality (Gruenewald et al., 2012). Highly generative people stay continually engaged in life, and this builds competencies, strengthens social bonds, improves self-image, and provides meaning (Kruse & Schmitt, 2012).

Cultural Influences on Generativity Although Erikson himself stressed the role of culture, relatively little research has focused on generativity across different cultural settings. However, because individualism is more likely to involve a concern with the self, and collectivism is more likely to involve concern for others, cultural differences would be predicted to play a role.

For instance, research conducted in Cameroon, Costa Rica, and Germany showed that a generativity model could be successfully applied to all cultures. However, the variables of import differed across cultures. Cameroonian participants scored higher on generativity and generative concern, a finding in line with the collectivistic values of their culture. Germans, whose culture is more individualistic than the other groups, scored lowest on their motivation to volunteer in the community (Hofer et al., 2008). Culture can also affect the consequences of generativity. A comparison of the Czech Republic, Germany, and Hong Kong showed differences in the link between generative concern and positive emotions. Although in all cultures this link was mediated by individual achievement goals, only in the more collectivistic Hong Kong did altruism also serve as a mediator (Au et al., 2019). Generativity may also not be age graded to the same degree in other cultures. In Argentina, for example, young, middle-age, and older adults engage in similar levels of generative activity (de Espanes et al., 2015).

Within a large country such as the United States, there are multitudes of different ethnic and cultural groups, and cultural differences in generativity also exist across different groups. For example, as a whole, religious and spiritual adults tend to be more generative than are those who are less religious (Emmons & Paloutzian, 2003; Dillon et al., 2003). This process interacts with race and ethnicity. In one study, generativity was associated with church attendance and involvement in church activities, but African Americans scored higher on generativity and religious variables than did white participants (Hart et al., 2001). Political ideology matters as well, although its effects may be nuanced. For example, because issues like climate change and pollution may affect later generations, generativity and environmentalism would be predicted to be positively correlated. People who are politically conservative are generally more generative, but less supportive of environmentalism. However, highly generative conservatives are more pro-environment (Barnett et al., 2019).

The research conducted in this area suggests that although generativity in midlife is common across cultures, the form it takes, the consequences it has, and the prevalence of it across different age groups may differ. However, generativity leads to positive outcomes and behaviors regardless of where the individual is from.

Religious and spiritual adults tend to be more generative than those who are less religious. digitalskillet/iStock/Getty Images

Issues and Themes

Whether we look at middle-age people objectively, in terms of their outward behavior, or subjectively, in terms of how they describe themselves, certain issues and themes emerge.

THE SOCIAL CLOCK

Every culture has a social clock describing the ages at which people are expected to reach certain milestones. Timing of events models suggests that, rather than being based on years lived, development is more affected by *when* events occur in a person's life. In other words, what matters is not that a person turns 67 but that the person retires.

Because there are culturally proscribed beliefs about the appropriate timing of events, Erikson (1950) believed that some adults could get "off time." In previous generations, the timing of major events in the social clock was fairly predictable. When occupational patterns were more stable and retirement at age 65 was almost universal, the meaning of work was more similar for all adults nearing retirement age. Similarly, when most women's lives revolved around bearing and rearing children, the end of the reproductive years meant something different. Today middle-age people may be raising children, being parents to adolescents and young adults, or serving as caregivers to aging parents. Because the pathways people take are more varied, so are the boundaries of middle age.

Research suggests that adults who get "off track" may have more difficulties than those who follow the expected trajectory for individuals in their culture. For example, one study of almost 700 Turkish adults found that those who perceived themselves as married "on time" showed higher levels of well-being, autonomy, competence, and relatedness than those who perceived themselves as early or late (Pekel-Uludağlı & Akbaş, 2019). Similarly, longitudinal research with 405 Canadian adults found on time or late marriage, but not early marriage, was associated with a lower risk of depression in middle age. Additionally, high self-esteem was associated with marrying on time (Johnson et al., 2017).

There are many norms regarding the "correct" timing for life events, and one particularly strong influence, especially for women, involves norms surrounding parenting. Early parenting, for instance, has been associated with declines in well-being and an increased

research in action

MIDLIFE CAREER CHANGE

As originally described by Erik Erikson, midlife is characterized as including a period of "life review" that involves evaluating past and present priorities, shifting responsibilities, and seeking out rewarding activities. One area in which people may experience life review relates to their career.

In prior generations, people often stayed employed with the same company from young adulthood to old age. However, there are now a diverse array of paths often resulting in midlife career change. Corporate restructuring, organizational downsizing, layoffs, and rapid technological change may eliminate certain classes of jobs (Myers & Harper, 2014). For some middle-age adults, appraisal of career satisfaction prompts change and leads them to voluntarily seek new careers as well-seasoned professionals in midlife.

Motivations for voluntary midlife career change include personal fulfillment, career satisfaction, contributing to greater societal good, increased prestige, or intentionally pursuing career paths put on hold during early adulthood (Etaugh, 2013). Phanse and Kaur (2015) conducted interviews with managers near the peak of their careers who opted for career change. Multiple reasons were cited, but the majority centered around themes of "self-renewal" and desire to perform new, more creative work. Other common reasons include lack of challenge, stress and anxiety due to job insecurity, workplace bullying, and conflicts with management (Barclay et al., 2011).

Many describe midlife career change as "soul searching" and "stressful," but it can also be rewarding. Self-efficacy and confidence work as catalysts for successful midlife career change (Etaugh, 2013). "Survival needs," or being able to financially provide for family, are linked to psychological well-being and are a chief area of consideration in midlife career change (Kim et al., 2018).

what's your view What would you recommend to those seeking a midlife career transition? What approaches could workplaces take in better supporting needs of middle-age professionals?

---

risk of depression when compared to on-time parenting (Koropeckyj-Cox et al., 2007; Pekel-Uludağlı & Akbaş, 2019). Late parenting also violates social norms. In survey data collected from 25 European countries involving more than 43,000 people, 57.2 percent of respondents said that women over the age of 40 were generally too old to consider having a child (Billari et al., 2010) despite estimates that only about 17 percent of 40-year-old women are definitely infertile (Leridon, 2008). Still, because of the intense time-graded social norms regarding motherhood, women are likely to feel increasing pressure to have children with age, and this affects adjustment to midlife. Whereas women who have children report declines in reproductive anxiety over time, women who do not have children are more likely to express anxiety about reproductive aging (Barrett & Toothman, 2017). This process can interact with culture. For instance, research in 12 European countries found that those women who had children more than 2 years later than their country's average age for their cohort were, in old age, lonelier than those who had children "on time." Moreover, this effect was stronger in more traditionalist countries (Zoutewelle-Terovan & Liefbroer, 2018).

THE MIDLIFE CRISIS

The middle-age man who impulsively buys an expensive sports car or the woman who abruptly leaves her job and home to travel to find herself are familiar stereotypes. Often, changes in personality and lifestyle such as these during the early to middle forties are attributed to what has been called a **midlife crisis.** At about this age, many people realize they will not be able to fulfill the dreams of their youth or fulfillment of their dreams has not brought the satisfaction they expected, and they become more aware of their own mortality. The midlife crisis is a supposedly stressful period triggered by this review and reevaluation of one's life (see Research in Action).

midlife crisis
In some normative-crisis models, stressful life period precipitated by the review and reevaluation of one's past, typically occurring in the early to middle forties.

There is both longitudinal and cross-sectional evidence from multiple countries that, on average, both men's and women's well-being gradually drops until they reach midlife. At that point, it gradually and smoothly increases until at least the age of 70, although this shift occurs sooner for those people who are temperamentally higher in well-being or who come from countries with higher levels of well-being as a whole (Cheng et al., 2017; Graham & Pozuelo, 2017).

Despite the midlife dip in well-being, the term *midlife crisis* is now considered an inaccurate representation of what most people experience in midlife (Wethington, 2000). Crises are not experienced only during midlife, although they are somewhat more common during that time, and not all people experience them. For example, from their twenties to their forties, 39 to 46 percent of men and 49 to 59 percent of women report a crisis (Robinson & Wright, 2013). People who do have crises at midlife generally also have crises at other times in their lives as well, so a midlife crisis may be a manifestation of a neurotic personality rather than a developmental phase (Lachman et al., 2015).

Crises are sometimes triggered by events or circumstances. So, for example, in one study, older Korean adults with higher education and economic status were less likely to experience a midlife crisis, whereas poor health, low social support, and high stress were associated with a greater likelihood of experiencing a midlife crisis (Chang, 2018). Men and women also differ with respect to the types of issues that precipitate a crisis. Men report more crises centered upon work, and women report more concerns regarding relationships and family issues (Robinson & Wright, 2013).

It may be best to consider midlife to be one of life's **turning points**—psychological transitions that involve significant change or transformation in the perceived meaning, purpose, or direction of a person's life. Turning points may be triggered by major life events, normative changes, or a new understanding of past experience, either positive or negative, and they may be stressful. However, turning points can sometimes also lead to positive growth from successful resolution of stressful situations (Wethington et al., 2004; Figure 16.1).

Turning points often involve an introspective review and reappraisal of values and priorities (Bauer & McAdams, 2004). The **midlife review** involves recognizing the finiteness of life and can be a time of taking stock, discovering new insights about the self, and spurring midcourse corrections in the design and trajectory of one's life. However, it can also involve regret over failure to achieve a dream or a keener awareness of *developmental deadlines*—time constraints on, say, the ability to have a child or to make up with an estranged friend or family member (Heckhausen et al., 2001).

Whether a turning point becomes a crisis may depend less on age than on individual circumstances and personal resources. People with **ego resiliency**—the ability to adapt flexibly and resourcefully to potential sources of stress—and those who have a sense of mastery and control are more likely to navigate the midlife crossing successfully (Heckhausen, 2001; Lachman, 2004; Kremen et al., 2012). They recover from stress more rapidly (Tugade et al., 2004), are less likely to become depressed

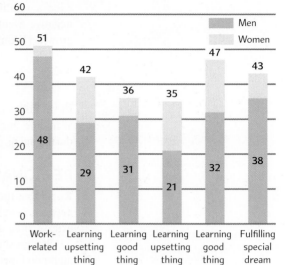

Percentage reporting

A midlife review might inspire a woman who senses her biological clock ticking to move forward on her wish to have a child. thechatat/Shutterstock

FIGURE 16.1

Turning Points Reported by 25- to 74-Year-Olds as Having Occurred in the Past 5 Years

Source: Wethington, E., Kessler, R. C., & Pixley, J. E. (2004). Turning points in adulthood. In O. G. Brim, C. D. Ryff, & R. C. Kessler (Eds.), *How healthy are we? A national study of well-being at midlife* (Figure 3, p. 600), Chicago, IL: University of Chicago Press.

turning points
Psychological transitions that involve significant change or transformation in the perceived meaning, purpose, or direction of a person's life.

midlife review
Introspective examination that often occurs in middle age, leading to reappraisal and revision of values and priorities.

ego resiliency
The ability to adapt flexibly and resourcefully to potential sources of stress.

after experiencing a trauma (Frederickson, et al., 2003), and are less likely to experience a midlife crisis (Chang, 2018). For people with resilient personalities, even negative events, such as an unwanted divorce, can become springboards for positive growth (Klohnen, 1996; Moen & Wethington, 1999).

Change and Stability in Midlife

In the following section, we focus on the processes involved with change and stability at midlife, and on the maintenance of psychological well-being and positive mental health during aging.

PERSONALITY

Recall that the best known trait model of personality described the individual differences between people as consisting of five factors: openness to experience, conscientiousness, extraversion, agreeableness, and neuroticism (Costa & McCrae, 1980).

Studies show there are normative developmental trends in personality. Specifically, in adulthood, people generally show increases in agreeableness, conscientiousness, and emotional stability and decreases in extraversion, neuroticism, and openness to experience (Roberts et al., 2006; Milojev & Sibley, 2017). This is important because subjective well-being (how happy a person feels) is related to personality traits, especially neuroticism. People who are high in neuroticism are more likely to experience a low sense of subjective well-being. High extraversion and conscientiousness, by contrast, are associated with high subjective well-being (Weiss et al., 2008; Anglim & Grant, 2016; Grant et al., 2009).

People also show individual change in response to unique life trajectories. For example, compared to people who continue to work, retirees tend to increase in agreeableness—being straightforward, altruistic, and modest—and decrease in activity (Lockenhoff et al., 2009). However, those who, against their will, become unemployed show decreases in agreeableness and conscientiousness. This relationship is stronger, especially in men, the longer the unemployment persists (Boyce et al., 2015). Social relationships matter too. Middle-age men who remarry tend to become less neurotic (Roberts & Mroczek, 2008). Men who divorce decrease in extraversion, and increases in extraversion and agreeableness, along with decreases in neuroticism, are associated with high perceived social support (Allemand et al., 2015).

Culture and Personality Are the Big Five a human universal? It does appear that, at least in literate, urban adults across a large number of cultures, the Big Five traits are a good representation of personality (McCrae & Costa, 1997; McCrae & Terracciano, 2005). However, either the traits themselves or the processes that underlie them are likely not universal. For example, in one study, researchers found the same traits represented in Japanese and American samples over a 9-year period; however, there were much greater fluctuations in trait levels in the Japanese than in the American sample (Chopik & Kitayama, 2018). This process interacts with gender. Research across 55 nations has shown that gender differences in personality traits are larger in more prosperous nations where women have more equality. In such nations, women tend to report higher levels of neuroticism, extraversion, agreeableness, and conscientiousness than men (Schmitt et al., 2008).

Moreover, the same five factors may not exist in all cultures. A study involving individuals of the Tsimané, a preliterate, hunter-gatherer indigenous society, did not find the same five-factor personality structure. The structure that emerged from their data could more accurately be characterized as two primary factors organized around "prosociality" and "industriousness," perhaps more important in a society dependent on subsistence labor to survive (Gurven et al., 2013). Thus culture may affect which features of the personality emerge as important, or the processes that involve personality change over time.

EMOTIONAL DEVELOPMENT

Studies show a gradual decline in negative emotions and an increase in positive emotions through early adulthood to old age (Carstensen et al., 2011; Diehl et al., 2011). According to research, women report slightly more negative emotionality (such as anger, fear, and anxiety) at all ages than men. Positive emotionality (such as cheerfulness) increases, on average, among men but falls among women in middle age and then rises sharply for both sexes, but especially men, in late adulthood (Mroczek, 2004). Generally, increasing age is associated with more effective emotional regulation, greater emotional well-being, and more co-occurrence of positive and negative emotions (Carstensen et al., 2011).

Relationships can also affect emotional experiences and hence stress. Married people at midlife tended to report more positive emotions and fewer negative emotions than unmarried people (Mroczek, 2004), but the quality of the relationship affects this process. Continuously married people, and especially those who reported an increase in marital satisfaction over time, showed markers associated with good cardiovascular health when compared to remarried adults. This suggests that the marital discord and strain experienced by the remarried adults had lasting effects on their health (Donoho et al., 2015).

IDENTITY DEVELOPMENT

In the following section, we discuss identity processes through three perspectives. First, we discuss the narrative approach to identity development. Then, we discuss cognitive aspects of shifting identity in midlife as informed by Piaget's work. Last, through the lens of Erikson's work, we discuss the particular issues women face in this area.

Narrative Psychology We all carry with us the story of who we are: how we came to be the person we are today, what shaped us over time and how, and who we wish to be in the future. The field of *narrative psychology* views the development of the self as a continuous process of constructing one's life story—a dramatic narrative, or personal myth, to help make sense of one's life and connect the past and present with the future (McAdams, 2006). This evolving story provides a person with a "narrative identity" (Singer, 2004). Indeed, some narrative psychologists view identity itself as this internalized *script* or story. People follow the script they have created as they act out their identity (McAdams et al., 1997). Midlife often is a time for revision of the life story (McAdams, 1993; Rosenberg et al., 1999).

Studies in narrative psychology are based on a standardized 2-hour life-story interview. Research using this technique has found that people's life stories tend to reflect their personalities (McAdams, 2006). Highly generative adults tend to construct *generativity scripts.* These scripts often feature a theme of *redemption,* or deliverance from suffering, and are associated with psychological well-being (McAdams et al., 2001; Bauer et al., 2008). In one such story, a nurse devotes herself to the care of a good friend during a fatal illness. Although devastated by her friend's death, she comes out of the experience with a renewed sense of confidence and determination to help others (McAdams, 2006). The tendency to develop narratives in which events are generally interpreted as being positive and negative events are closely examined and processed for their meaning is associated with well-being and adjustment (Lilgendahl & McAdams, 2011; Weststrate & Gluck, 2017).

Identity Process Theory According to the **identity process theory** (IPT) (Whitbourne, 1996), physical characteristics, cognitive abilities, and personality traits are incorporated into **identity schemas**. These self-perceptions are continually confirmed or revised in response to incoming information.

Piaget described two processes that have been applied toward understanding identity development. Assimilation is the interpretation of new information via existing cognitive structures. Accommodation involves changing cognitive

identity process theory (IPT)
Whitbourne's theory of identity development based on processes of assimilation and accommodation.

identity schemas
Accumulated perceptions of the self shaped by incoming information from intimate relationships, work-related situations, and community and other experiences.

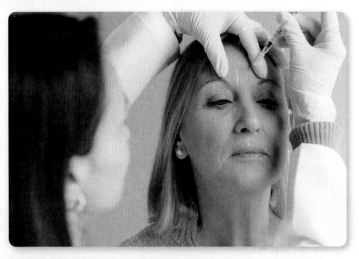

Overuse of identity assimilation may result in attempts to hold on to a consistent sense of self by trying to minimize signs of aging, as with the use of Botox to hide wrinkles. Rick Gomez/ The Image Bank/Getty Images

structures to more closely align with what is encountered. **Identity assimilation** involves holding onto a consistent sense of self in the face of new experiences that do not fit the current understanding of the self. Contradictory or confusing information is absorbed without changing one's identity schema. However, if discrepant events or experiences happen too frequently, eventually, the view of the self must change. For example, if an older adult repeatedly is unable to finish running a trail she had previously been able to complete, eventually she must reframe her understanding of what her body can do. **Identity accommodation** involves adjusting the identity schema to fit these new experiences.

Overuse of either assimilation or accommodation is unhealthy. People who constantly assimilate may seek to maintain a youthful self-image and ignore what is going on in their body. This process of denial may make it harder for them to confront the reality of aging. By contrast, people who constantly accommodate are weak and highly vulnerable to criticism. They may overreact to early signs of aging, such as the first gray hair and their pessimism may hasten physical and cognitive declines. Ideally, people are able to achieve **identity balance** and maintain a stable sense of self while adjusting their self-schemas to incorporate new information. People who achieve identity balance recognize changes and respond flexibly; they seek to control what can be controlled and accept what cannot.

Overall, both identity assimilation (to a point) and identity balance are associated with positive effects on health, well-being, and perceptions of aging (Sneed & Whitbourne, 2005), and identity accommodation is associated with declines in self-esteem (Skultety & Whitbourne, 2004). However, culture can affect this process. For example, American, German, and Norwegian adults all rate themselves as feeling younger than their chronological age, presumably as a means by which to maintain self-esteem. However, this effect is larger in Americans than in Germans and Norwegians. Moreover, whereas in Germans and Americans, feeling younger than actual age is associated with increases in life satisfaction and positive affect, only in Americans does it also influence negative affect. Last, Americans are more likely to use assimilative identity processes than Norwegians, suggesting they are more reluctant to incorporate beliefs about aging into their self-concept. These results are all consistent with American culture's greater emphasis on health and youth (Westerhof et al., 2003; Westerhof & Barrett, 2005).

Generativity and Identity Processes in Women A particularly fruitful place to examine the intersection of generativity and identity is in women. Working outside the home often requires balancing the demands of home and family, something that is generally more difficult for women than for men (Allen & Finkelstein, 2014). The process of fulfilling multiple roles is also likely to affect identity processes. Moreover, work and children are areas in which people often seek generative action. Thus most work in this area has focused on women.

Research has found that for women, inhabiting multiple roles early in life—whether or not they were married, had children, or worked outside the home—impacted identity development. Those women who filled more social roles were more likely to develop a firm sense of identity, and, once developed, their identity balance was associated with generativity and consequently well-being, psychological health, and successful resolution of work-family conflict (Vandewater et al., 1997; DeHaan & MacDermid, 1994; Peterson & Stewart, 1996).

Once established, generativity paves the way for positive life outcomes. For example, generativity has been associated with positive feelings about marriage, motherhood, and the care of aging parents, and an increased certainty about identity and sense of confidence late in life (Peterson & Duncan, 2007; Peterson, 2002; Zucker et al., 2002). Generative behaviors can have long-term health consequences. In one study, highly generative people from the ages of 60 to 75 years were found to have more frequent social contact with and provide more support to others, volunteer more, have lower levels of negative affect, be more likely to be married, have higher levels of education, and be less likely to smoke, all variables that affect health. Over the course of 10 years, they were also found to have a lower risk of impairment in activities of daily living or mortality (Gruenewald et al., 2012).

Positive Mental Health at Midlife

Positive mental health involves life satisfaction and a sense of psychological well-being, which go hand in hand with a healthy sense of self (Keyes & Shapiro, 2004).

Life Satisfaction Although many international surveys originally reported that most adults of all ages, both sexes, and all races report being satisfied with their lives (Myers, 2000; Walker et al., 2003), more recent data suggest that when very poor or troubled nations are included in analyses, we cannot characterize all people as being satisfied with their lives. However, it is still the case that the majority of societies meet enough basic human needs so that happiness is the default condition for people in many cultures (Diener et al., 2018). One reason for this general finding of life satisfaction under many circumstances is that the positive emotions associated with pleasant memories tend to persist, whereas the negative feelings associated with unpleasant memories fade. Most people also have good coping skills (Walker et al., 2003).

Social support—friends and spouses—and religiosity are important contributors to life satisfaction (Diener, 2000; Myers, 2000). So are certain personality dimensions—extraversion, emotional stability, and conscientiousness (Duckworth et al., 2012)—and the quality of work and leisure. Moreover, the relationship between work and life satisfaction is interactive—being happy at work is associated with higher life satisfaction, which then predicts work productivity and occupational commitment (Erdogan et al., 2012). Not surprisingly, income affects life satisfaction as well. Adults who make more money report higher life satisfaction, and this relationship is strongest in middle adulthood (Cheung & Lucas, 2015) and in poorer countries (Oishi et al., 2009). People in wealthier nations report greater subjective well-being than those in poorer nations (Ng & Diener, 2018). However, purchasing material goods does not increase life satisfaction, although spending money for experiences does. This may be because experiences enhance social relations more than material goods and are more likely to be incorporated into the self-image (Gilovich et al., 2015). Exercise is also associated with life satisfaction (Maher et al., 2015) although this association may be driven by overall physical health, as healthier people are more likely to engage in physical activity.

Although a majority of older adults report rising levels of life satisfaction as they age, this is certainly not the case for every adult. Adults who report poor social relationships and a lack of a sense of control tend to report declines in life satisfaction (Rocke & Lachman, 2008). There are also developmental changes that can best be described as fitting a U-shaped curve. Generally, life satisfaction is lower in early adulthood, rises in mid-adulthood, and then declines again in late adulthood (Maher et al., 2015; Mroczek & Spiro, 2005; Helson & Wink, 1992).

Well-Being Within the discipline of psychology, a subjective sense of happiness is characterized as well-being. Although people generally have an overall sense of how happy they are, happiness is multidimensional, and people can be more or less pleased with various aspects of their life. Carol Ryff and colleagues developed a model that includes six dimensions of well-being referred to as the Ryff Well-Being Inventory (Ryff, 1989; Ryff & Keyes, 1995; Ryff & Singer, 1998; Ryff, 2014). The six dimensions of the model are self-acceptance, positive relations with others, autonomy, environmental mastery, purpose in life, and personal growth.

Studies using Ryff's scale have shown midlife to be a period of generally positive mental health. In cross-sectional research, middle-age people were more autonomous than younger adults but less purposeful and focused on personal growth. Environmental mastery, on the other hand, increased for all groups over time. Self-acceptance was relatively stable for all age groups. Overall, men's and women's well-being were quite similar, but women had more positive social relationships (Ryff & Singer, 1998; Ryff, 2014; Springer et al., 2011).

Exercise has been consistently associated with life satisfaction. Yoshiyoshi Hirokawa/DigitalVision/Getty Images

When Ryff's scale was used to measure the psychological well-being of minority group members, the collective portrait replicated these age-related patterns. However, Black and Hispanic women scored lower than Black and Hispanic men in several areas. Yet when employment and marital status were controlled, minority status predicted positive well-being in several areas. It may be that such factors as self-regard, mastery, and personal growth are strengthened by meeting the challenges of minority life (Ryff et al., 2004).

Research suggests that more recent immigrants to the United States may be more physically and mentally healthy than those who have been here for two or more generations. Resistance to assimilation may promote well-being in these immigrants. Researchers have proposed the term *ethnic conservatism* for this tendency to resist assimilation and cling to familiar values and practices that give meaning to life. Ethnic conservatism is less effective in promoting well-being among the second generation, who may find it harder to resist the pull of assimilation (Horton & Schweder, 2004). By contrast, bicultural identity—being able to identify with both minority and majority cultures—is associated with well-being for them (Yamaguchi et al., 2016; Ferrari et al., 2015).

Generally, religion has a positive influence on well-being (Green & Elliot, 2010). However, contextual variables affect these processes. When religion is widely and freely practiced by a population, or when religion is highly regulated by the government but normative in the population, then religion is positively associated with health and happiness. However, when religion is rare in a population, *and* when the government restricts religious practices, it is then associated with negative effects on well-being (Hayward & Elliot, 2014). There is a caveat. A study conducted with immigrant populations across the United States, Australia, and Western Europe found positive effects for the relationship between religion and well-being for all religious immigrant groups in all countries (Connor, 2012). It may be that acculturation involves unique stressors—including discrimination, financial strain, acculturation, disruptions in relationships and uncertainty about status—for which religion offers succor.

In much of Europe and the United States, the proportion of people who do not identify with any religion has been rising, especially in younger cohorts (Lipka & McClendon, 2017). Most studies show the religiously unaffiliated with lower levels of well-being, some studies show no differences, and others show a benefit to being unaffiliated (Zuckerman, 2009; Weber et al., 2012). Some of the discrepancy may be driven by *which* atheists and agnostics are assessed. Research on atheists and agnostics found a curvilinear relationship between religious belief and atheism. People who strongly and confidently believed in religion were more likely to be high in well-being, but so were those who strongly and confidently believed in their atheism. Those people who were unsure showed lower levels of well-being (Galen & Kloet, 2011).

Previous research has suggested that the positive effects of religion may be mediated by transcendent emotions. In other words, religion leads to emotions such as awe, love, peace, and gratitude, which then exert a positive influence on well-being (Van Cappellan et al., 2016). However atheists, too, experience these emotions. For example, one study examining atheists, Buddhists, and Christians found similar levels of well-being in all groups. But, rather than citing spiritual or magical beliefs as the cause, atheists reported finding meaning and purpose in life through logic and rationality. They also reported feeling awe, wonder, and joy, not through participation in religious activities, but through nature, art, science, music, and the appreciation of humanity (Caldwell-Harris et al., 2011).

Relationships at Midlife

It is hard to generalize about the meaning of relationships in middle age today. Not only does that period cover a quarter century of development; it also embraces a greater multiplicity of life paths than ever before.

THEORIES OF SOCIAL CONTACT

According to **social convoy theory,** people move through life surrounded by *social convoys:* circles of close friends and family members of varying degrees of closeness, on whom

social convoy theory
Theory, proposed by Kahn and Antonucci, that people move through life surrounded by concentric circles of intimate relationships on which they rely for assistance, well-being, and social support.

they can rely for assistance, well-being, and social support, and to whom they in turn also offer care, concern, and support. Characteristics of the person (gender, race, religion, age, education, and marital status) together with characteristics of that person's situation (role expectations, life events, financial stress, daily hassles, demands, and resources) influence the size and composition of the convoy, the amount and kinds of social support a person receives, and the satisfaction derived from this support (Antonucci et al., 2009).

Overall, the size of the global social network peaks in young adulthood and declines thereafter. The declines in size of the social network in adulthood are primarily seen in friendship networks; the size of the family network remains relatively stable over time. Researchers have variously described this decline in friendship networks as due to changing circumstances (e.g., the increase in time demands of work and family life) or motivational goals (e.g., staying most close to people who help us regulate emotions). The size of the friendship network is also affected by culture. People from individualistic cultures have larger friendship networks. Because individualism places less emphasis on the in-group, adults from individualistic countries place more value on relationships outside the family, and sometimes use friends to fulfill relationship needs rather than family. Other relationships, such as those with coworkers or neighbors, tend to be important during particular times. For example, when changing jobs or moving, people in the social network may drop out, or new people may be included (Wrzus et al., 2013).

Socioemotional selectivity theory (Carstensen, 1991; Carstensen et al., 1999) offers a life-span perspective on how people choose with whom to spend their time. According to this approach, social interaction has three main goals: (1) it is a source of information; (2) it helps people develop and maintain a sense of self; and (3) it is a source of pleasure, comfort, and emotional well-being. In infancy, the third goal, the need for emotional support, is paramount. From childhood through young adulthood, information-seeking comes to the fore. By middle age, although information-seeking remains important, the original, emotion-regulating function of social contacts begins to reassert itself (Fung et al., 2001). To put it simply, middle-age people increasingly seek out others who help them feel good (Figure 16.2). In support of this, although their social networks were smaller than those of younger adults, older adults described their social network members more positively and less negatively. In other words, older adults chose to limit their interactions to those people whom they found to be emotionally fulfilling and supportive of them (English & Carstensen, 2014; Carmichael et al., 2015).

socioemotional selectivity theory Theory, proposed by Carstensen, that people select social contacts on the basis of the changing relative importance of social interaction as a source of information, as an aid in developing and maintaining a self-concept, and as a source of emotional well-being.

RELATIONSHIPS AND WELL-BEING

For most middle-age adults, relationships are key to well-being (Thomas et al., 2017). For example, social support from spouses, and to a lesser extent from children and friends, is related to well-being in older adults (Chen & Feeley, 2014; Lee & Szinovacz, 2016), and social support is related to life satisfaction at all ages (Siedlecki et al., 2014).

However, relationships, or the lack of them, can also present stressful demands. Being single, divorced, or widowed is associated with depression, loneliness, and decreases in happiness (Koropeckyj-Cox et al., 2007). Having a tense relationship with a spouse, mother, or sibling, in other research, was also associated with a risk of depression, especially for women (Gilligan et al., 2017). This may be because women tend to feel a greater sense of responsibility and concern for others. This may impair a woman's well-being when problems or misfortunes beset others; men are less likely to be affected in this way. This greater concern for the welfare of others may also help explain why across a variety of cultures, middle-age women tend to be unhappier with their marriages than are men (Heiman et al, 2011).

Importance of motives for social contact

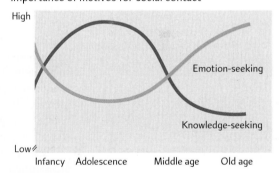

FIGURE 16.2

How Motives for Social Contact Change across the Life Span

According to socioemotional selectivity theory, infants seek social contact primarily for emotional comfort. In adolescence and young adulthood, people tend to be most interested in seeking information from others. From middle age on, emotional needs increasingly predominate.

Source: Carstensen, L. L., Gross, J. J., & Fung, H. H. (1998). The social context of emotional experience. In K. Warner Schaie and M. Powell Lawton (Eds.), *Annual review of gerontology and geriatrics* (Vol. 17, p. 331, Figure 12.2). New York, NY: Springer.

In the remaining sections of this chapter, we examine how intimate relationships develop during the middle years. We look first at relationships with spouses, cohabiting partners, homosexual partners, and friends; next at bonds with maturing children; and then at ties with aging parents, siblings, and grandchildren.

Consensual Relationships

Marriages, cohabitations, homosexual unions, and friendships typically involve two people of the same generation who mutually choose each other. How do these relationships fare in middle age?

MARRIAGE

Midlife marriage is very different from what it used to be. When life expectancies were shorter, couples who remained together for 25, 30, or 40 years were rare. The most common pattern was for marriages to be broken by death and for survivors to remarry. Additionally, people had many children and expected them to live at home until they married. It was unusual for a middle-age husband and wife to be alone together. Today, more marriages end in divorce, but couples who stay together can often look forward to 20 or more years of married life after the last child leaves home.

Researchers used to believe that marriages followed a U-shaped curve, where marriages were marked by declining levels of satisfaction until roughly 2 decades in, upon which time marriages would begin to once again turn more positive. By the third and fourth decade, it was believed, marital satisfaction was as high as in the first few years of marriage (Rollins & Feldman, 1970; Orbuch et al., 1996). However, it now appears this was incorrect. Marriages generally follow a developmental sequence, with initial sharp declines in marriage satisfaction followed by a plateau, then further, slower declines over the longer term. Not surprisingly, people who divorce report even lower marital satisfaction (Bradbury et al., 2000; Kurdek, 1999).

Why do we see these changes in marital satisfaction? One factor that has been consistently found to negatively impact marital satisfaction is the birth of a child (Twenge et al., 2003). Both mothers and fathers report a decline in satisfaction following this event, although many couples rebound as children get older, somewhat more self-sufficient, and particularly when they enter primary school (Keizer & Schenk, 2012). Marital satisfaction can also suffer in middle age when many couples have teenage children and are heavily involved in careers (Orbuch et al., 1996). Despite the stereotypes surrounding the empty nest, on average, the departure of children from the family home is usually met with an average rise in marital satisfaction for parents, although it also increases the risk of marital dissolution slightly (Bouchard, 2014). Satisfaction usually reaches a height when children are grown, many people are retired or entering retirement, and a lifetime accumulation of assets helps ease financial worries (Orbuch et al., 1996).

Sexual satisfaction also affects marital satisfaction and stability. Those couples who are satisfied with their sex lives tend to be satisfied with their marriages (Fallis et al., 2016), and better marital quality leads to longer marriages for both men and women (Yeh et al., 2006). Similar results have been found in Brazil, Germany, Japan, Spain, and the United States (Heiman et al., 2011).

In countries such as the United States, marriages are generally based on love. However, in many countries arranged marriages are the norm. Arranged marriages are partnerships formed between families where parents of the husband and wife-to-be negotiate the marriage, basing the union on pragmatic concerns including socioeconomic status, religion, family values, and physical appearance. Arranged marriages are more common in collectivistic cultures, where family bonds are viewed as more important than individual desires.

Although arranged marriages are declining in some countries (Rubio, 2013), they remain common in many parts of the world. However, in the modern era the husband and wife-to-be are more often given veto power over potential marriage partners and are more active participants in the marriage decision process (Allendorf & Pandian, 2016). Although data are scarce, the available research indicates that adults in arranged marriages show similar levels of marital satisfaction as do those in love marriages. For example, studies on love-based and arranged marriages in Indian couples living either in the United States or in India show no differences in their levels of marital satisfaction (Regan et al., 2012; Myers et al., 2005). However, parents' opinions still seem to matter. A study of different types of marriages in Pakistan showed that adults in love and arranged marriages were equally satisfied as long as their parents approved of the decision. However, those adults in love marriages where parents did not approve of the match had lower marital satisfaction (Arif & Fatima, 2015).

Marriage and Health Across a large number of studies, married people at midlife appear to be healthier, both physically and mentally, and they tend to live longer than single, separated, or divorced people. Although these results are more modest than initially thought, they nonetheless exist across a large number of countries and cultures, in both cross-sectional and prospective studies (Tantagelo et al., 2017; Umberson et al., 2013; Kaplan & Kronick, 2006). Overall, married people, and especially men, enjoy better health, lower mortality, better cardiovascular health, and a lower risk of stroke and cancer than their single counterparts (Robles et al., 2014; Wang et al., 2020).

But why would marriage (a social relationship) affect health (a biological state)? Two classes of theories have been advanced to explain these findings. The first posits that marriage is associated with the encouragement of health-promoting behaviors. So, for example, a husband might persuade or encourage his wife to stop smoking. Although there is some support for this idea, the story is more nuanced. Marriage seems to decrease the levels of hedonic risks such as going out to bars, drinking heavily, smoking, or dangerous driving. However, marriage *increases* homebody risks such as a sedentary lifestyle, a high fat diet, and being overweight (Ross et al., 2016).

The second theory focuses on the stress response system. In this view, the social support provided by marriage buffers individuals against life stressors. As chronic stress negatively affects health, married people are thus protected against some of its effects (Robles et al., 2014). Some of this may be mediated by immune function. Long-term stress depresses immune system functioning (Dhabhar, 2014). Being in a good marriage, with its protective social support, can thus bolster the immune system (Graham et al., 2006). In one study, adults in high-quality marriages had lower blood pressure, lower stress, less depression, and higher life satisfaction than single adults (Holt-Lunstad et al., 2008).

Marital quality is key. Whereas a good marital relationship can buffer people against life stressors, a poor marital relationship can make people more vulnerable to them. For example, marital strains increased both men's and women's aging-related declines in health, and this effect was stronger the older a couple was (Umberson et al., 2006). In addition, women who are in unsatisfying married or cohabiting relationships are at higher risk for cardiovascular disease and other health problems, especially if marital conflict is involved (Gallo et al., 2003; Kiecolt-Glaser & Newton, 2001).

COHABITATION

Rates of cohabitation have increased globally in recent decades. Across 36 countries in the Americas, Asia, and Europe, the average cohabitation rate is approximately 10 percent (Organisation for Economic Co-operation and Development, 2016). The rate of cohabitation in African countries varies widely. For example, in countries such as the Central African Republic (80 percent), Mozambique (74 percent), and Gabon (61 percent) rates are high, but in Muslim countries such as Niger (0.1 percent) and Senegal (0.3 percent) it is almost nonexistent (Odimegwu et al., 2018). Nonmarital relationships, or *zina*, are forbidden in Islamic law (Pereira, 2005); therefore, cohabitation is rare in such countries.

Cohabitation has increased greatly in the United States and is now more common than marriage. In 2016 there were approximately 18 million cohabiting opposite-sex adults, an increase of almost a third since 2007. About 8 percent of adults age 35 to 49 and 4 percent of adults 50 and older were cohabiting in 2016 (Stepler, 2017), and 71 percent of adults age 31 to 44 years have cohabitated at some point in their life (Horowitz et al., 2019). Baby boomers have shown the largest percent increase in cohabitation rates of any age group (Manning, 2013). When older adults do cohabitate, their relationships are generally more stable than those of younger cohabiting adults, and cohabitation is more often viewed as an alternative to marriage rather than a prelude to it (Brown et al., 2012).

What explains the rise in cohabitation for older adults? One reason is a desire for an intimate companion without the commitment of formal marriage—a commitment that, in middle age, may come to mean the possibility of having to care for an infirm partner. Whereas the majority of younger cohabitants have not been previously married, the majority of older cohabitants have (Stepler, 2017). Moreover, cohabiting adults with disabled or ill partners, as a whole, provide less care than do married partners in the same situation (Noel-Miller, 2011). This process appears to be most relevant for widowed women (Davidson, 2001). Aging men, alternatively, may be motivated to cohabitate because they anticipate needing the kind of care that wives traditionally provide and may worry about not getting it otherwise (Brown et al., 2005).

On average, cohabiting couples report worse mental health than do married couples. The disparity between married and cohabiting couples is affected by context, with the largest disparities found in religious, collectivistic countries in which cohabitation is rare and there are traditional gender roles (Amato, 2014). However, the outcomes of cohabitation differ by country. For example, though cohabitation does not provide the same level of health benefits as marriage in the United States, Britain, and Australia, cohabiting adults and married adults are equally healthy in Norway and Germany. In Australia, cohabiting women, but not men, are as healthy as married people (Perelli-Harris et al., 2017).

DIVORCE

One of the major societal shifts of the twentieth century was the global increase in the divorce rate. Much of this increase can be attributed to economic development and industrialization, and especially to increases in women's educational and occupational status. Religion is also important, and both Catholicism and Islam are negatively associated with divorce. Last, cultural values such as freedom, consent, and gender equality are associated with divorce (Wang & Schofer, 2018).

Divorce rates vary widely across countries. Russia (4.8 divorces per 1,000 people) and Belarus (4.1 divorces per 1,000) top the list. Sri Lanka (0.15 divorces per 1,000) and Vietnam (0.4 divorces per 1,000) lie at the bottom (World Population Review, 2020). In the United States, the divorce rate is 2.9 divorces per 1,000 people (Centers for Disease Control and Prevention, 2018).

Divorce rates for middle-age adults are rising. From 1990 to 2015, the divorce rate for adults age 40 to 49 years rose by 14 percent, and the divorce rate for adults older than 50 years rose by a stunning 109 percent (Stepler, 2017). The number one reason Americans cite for divorce is partner abuse—verbal, physical, or emotional. Other frequent reasons are differing values or lifestyles, infidelity, alcohol or drug abuse, relationship problems, and simply falling out of love (Marks & Lambert, 1998; Cohen & Finzi-Dottan, 2012).

Although divorce in midlife is more common than in the past, the breakup can still be traumatic. In a survey of adults who had been divorced at least once in their forties, fifties, or sixties, most respondents described the experience as more emotionally devastating than losing a job and about as devastating as a major illness, though less devastating than a spouse's death. Midlife divorce seems especially hard for women, who are more negatively affected psychologically by divorce at any age than men are (Marks & Lambert, 1998; Montenegro, 2004).

With respect to physical health, marital dissolution is associated with contradictory health outcomes (Sbarra et al., 2015). First, divorce is associated with an elevated chance of chronic health conditions and mortality in both sexes, but especially in men

(Sbarra & Coan, 2017; Hughes & Waite, 2009; Amato, 2010). Second, most people adjust well to divorce and ultimately do well (Amato, 2010; Mancini et al., 2011; Luhmann et al., 2012). How do we explain these diverse threads of research?

It may be that individual differences in the response to divorce explain the discrepancy in findings. For instance, a relatively small proportion of adults may show an extreme response to divorce and exhibit health-related consequences such as blood pressure increases or cardiovascular disease. Other adults may be more resilient and adjust well, explaining other findings. Thus, to understand the effects of divorce, we must examine individual risk and resilience factors (Sbarra et al., 2015).

Long-standing marriages may be less likely to break up than more recent ones. One possible explanation for this lies with the concept of **marital capital.** The longer a couple is married, the more likely they are to have built up joint financial assets, to share the same friends, to go through important experiences together, and to get used to the emotional benefits that marriage can provide. This accumulated "capital" can be difficult to give up (Becker, 1991; Jones et al., 1995).

marital capital
Financial and emotional benefits built up during a long-standing marriage, which tend to hold a couple together.

Another important factor that keeps many couples from divorcing is finances. Higher socioeconomic status is associated with lower risk of divorce in the United States, Israel, and Finland (Kaplan & Herbst, 2015; Jalovaara, 2003, 2001). Additionally, research has shown that marriage stability and consumer debt are associated, and stable marriages are also more likely to have low debt and be high in financial satisfaction (Dew, 2011; Archuleta et al., 2011). Financial disagreements also predict divorce (Dew et al., 2012). One interpretation of these findings is that healthy marriages are more likely to have healthy finances and thus presumably more to lose on both fronts in the event of divorce. However, gender interacts with income. When women outearn their husbands, the risk of divorce increases (Kaplan & Herbst, 2015; Jalovaara, 2003, 2001). Most of the time, however, when marriages end, middle-age divorcees, especially women who do not remarry, tend to be less financially secure than those who remain married (Wilmoth & Koso, 2002; Lin et al., 2017).

Even in long marriages, the increasing number of years that people can expect to live in good health after child rearing ends may make the dissolution of a marginal marriage an attractive option and, at least for women, growing economic independence makes it more practical to consider as well. Moreover, although it may be stressful, divorce can also lead to personal growth (Aldwin & Levenson, 2001; Luhmann et al., 2012). Older adults' better emotional regulatory strategies and greater life knowledge may make them better able to weather the storms of marriage dissolution.

Divorce is not just a feature of the modern world. It is also common in hunter-gatherer cultures (Bird-David, 1987). For example, among the Chabu of Ethiopia, almost half of adults have been divorced, and 22 percent have divorced more than once (Dira & Hewlett, 2018). In the nomadic Hadza of Tanzania, approximately 80 percent of marriages end, and divorce is common (Marlowe, 2004). Common reasons given for divorce in hunter-gatherer cultures include infertility, infidelity, and laziness (Marlowe, 2004; Dira & Hewlett, 2018). The availability of other fertile women in the group is also predictive of marriage instability (Jones et al., 2017).

GAY AND LESBIAN RELATIONSHIPS

The cohort of gays and lesbians now in middle age grew up at a time when homosexuality was not as accepted as it is now. At that time, homosexuals tended to be isolated not only from the larger community but also from each other. It was not until the 1990s that acceptance of homosexual relationships began to increase sharply, and the general public's negative perception of gays and lesbians became more positive (Keleher & Smith, 2012; Hicks & Lee, 2006).

One factor that seems to affect relationship quality in gays and lesbians is whether or not they have internalized society's negative views on homosexuality. Overall, homosexual people who have internalized a negative view of their sexuality report higher levels of depression and lower relationship quality (Cao et al., 2017; Frost & Meyer, 2009).

Research conducted after the passage of marriage equality in the United States indicates gay and lesbian couples show marriage benefits similar to those experienced by heterosexual couples.
Lars A. Niki

This may be because when faced with an episode of discrimination—which is common for sexual minorities—gays and lesbians who have internalized negative beliefs about themselves are more likely to respond with anxiety or depression than those who have not internalized those beliefs (Feinstein et al., 2012).

Although times have changed and society is more accepting of homosexual relationships, many older gays and lesbians are still reluctant to fully come out of the closet. For example, one recent study showed that about a third of older adults still feared being completely open about their sexuality (Gardner et al., 2014).

On June 26, 2015, same-sex marriage became the law of the land in the United States. Given the already established findings on the benefit of marriage for heterosexual couples, did the same dynamics exist in gay and lesbian couples?

Although more work needs to be done, initial data on marriage equality show that, as in heterosexual couples, gay and lesbian couples also benefit from marriage. In one study of 1,166 adults, married gay, lesbian, and bisexual couples reported less distress than their single counterparts, as did married heterosexuals when compared to single adults (Wight et al., 2013). As with heterosexual couples, marriage seems to have a greater effect on well-being than cohabitation (Chen & van Ours, 2018).

The availability of health insurance matters as well. Prior to marriage equality laws, same-sex couples were often excluded from their partners' health insurance coverage, even in relatively accommodating states specifying guidelines for civil unions (Ponce et al., 2010). Once marriage was possible, many more people became eligible for health insurance through their same-sex spouses. Thus, following the passage of marriage equality laws, gay and lesbian couples showed increases in health insurance coverage rates and access to health care, and research showed evidence for greater utilization of preventive health care outcomes for men (Carpenter et al., 2018; Downing & Cha, 2020).

Earlier research suggested gay and lesbian couples were more likely to break up than heterosexual couples, but as marriage was unavailable to many, data were scarce and studies had methodological problems. More recent nationally representative U.S. data suggest that both heterosexual and homosexual couples have similar rates of relationship duration and stability (Rosenfeld, 2014).

FRIENDSHIPS

Social relationships are vitally important; both their quantity and quality are predictive of mental health, physical health, and mortality (Holt-Lunstad et al., 2010). As socioemotional selectivity theory predicts, social networks tend to become smaller and more intimate at midlife. Still, friendships persist and are a strong source of emotional support and well-being, especially for women (Carmichael et al., 2015; Antonucci et al., 2001). However, their importance varies with cultural context. In individualistic cultures, not having friends or a lack of interaction with friends is associated with loneliness. In collectivistic cultures, it is not, as family members are more likely to fill relationship needs (Lykes & Kemmelmeier, 2014).

Especially during a crisis, such as a divorce or a problem with an aging parent, adults turn to friends for emotional support, practical guidance, comfort, companionship, and talk (Antonucci & Akiyama, 1997; Hartup & Stevens, 1999). The quality of such friendships can affect health, as can lack of friendships. Loneliness, for example, is predictive of increases in blood pressure, even when such variables as age, gender, race, and cardiovascular risk factors are taken into account (Hawkley et al., 2010).

Although in early adulthood, loneliness, depression, well-being, and social integration are affected by the number of friends a person has, in late adulthood, the quality of friends is what matters. More older adults lack a confidant and often feel lonely as a result, but when they do have good friends, they report more satisfaction as a result of contact with their friends than do younger adults (Nicolaisen & Thorsen, 2017). Those older adults with higher-quality friendships have better psychosocial well-being (Carmichael et al., 2015). This is especially true in times of crisis: Depressed adults with high-quality friendships have a lower suicide risk than those who do not have good friends (Marver et al., 2017).

Relationships with Maturing Children

With contemporary trends toward delayed marriage and parenthood, some middle-age people face such issues as finding a good day care or helping their grade-school child with homework. However, most parents in middle age must cope with a different set of issues that arise from living with children who will soon be leaving home. Moreover, middle-age parents increasingly have to deal with an adult child continuing to live in the family home or leaving it only to return.

ADOLESCENT CHILDREN

Ironically, the people at the two times of life popularly linked with emotional crises—adolescence and midlife—often live in the same household. Despite dealing with their own special concerns, parents have to cope daily with young people who are undergoing great physical, emotional, and social changes.

Generally, most parents at midlife are happy with their parenting role and derive satisfaction from it. For example, mutual warmth and acceptance has been associated with parenting satisfaction in both Chinese and European American middle-age mothers (Chang & Greenberger, 2012). Moreover, being involved with and committed to the parenting relationship, feeling confident in parenting abilities, and successfully managing parenting role conflict is positively related to well-being in Israeli parents (Cohen & Bocos, 2016) and associated with positive family adjustment and solidarity in Italian parents (Delvecchio et al., 2016). However, contextual and relational variables affect happiness. For example, parents are more likely to report happiness when they are financially secure, healthy, close to their child, retired, or younger parents (Mitchell, 2010). Parenting satisfaction is also positively related to parental education level and marital status, and negatively related to conflict between the parents (Downing-Matibag, 2009).

Negative emotions are also possible. Parental satisfaction declines when parents perceive their adolescent children as being involved in negative behaviors or failing to meet the challenges of life (Downing-Matibag, 2009). And, when parents do not approve of their child's choices, they are more likely to perceive their child's striving for autonomy as hostile or immature (Kloep & Hendry, 2010). However, a healthy attachment between parent and teen can, somewhat paradoxically, make the separation process of adolescence and early adulthood proceed more smoothly (Ponappa et al., 2014; Inguglia et al., 2015).

Some parents, known as *helicopter parents*, have more difficulty granting autonomy. These parents are over-involved in their child's lives, especially with respect to schooling issues, and intrusively interfere with the development of their child's autonomy. This well-intentioned but misguided parenting is associated with low autonomy granting, school disengagement, depression, anxiety, low life satisfaction, low self-efficacy, and poor adjustment to college (Padilla-Walker et al., 2012; Schiffrin et al., 2014; Darlow et al., 2017).

THE EMPTY NEST

Research is challenging popular ideas about the **empty nest** transition that occurs when the youngest child leaves home. Generally, parents whose children have left the nest report higher levels of well-being, at least when their children stay in frequent contact with them (Bouchard, 2014; Gorchoff et al., 2008). They are particularly likely to adjust well when their children leave "on time," when they are perceived to be successful, moral people, and when they have good family bonds (Mitchell, 2010). Whether or not families are blended also matters. Stepmothers and fathers whose children with previous partners move out report greater increases in life satisfaction at the launching of children from the family home than other groups (Ivanova, 2019).

When children are not accomplished, however, this process may be more difficult. Typically, when adult children have greater needs, parents provide more material and financial support to them (Fingerman et al., 2009), a process that can provide parents some relief from negative moods (Huo et al., 2019). Given this tendency, it is not

empty nest
Transitional phase of parenting following the last child's leaving the parents' home.

surprising to also find that such parents are likely to feel torn between wanting their adult children to assert their independence and a desire to step in and help. Men, in particular, seem to be more affected by their children's successes and failures (Birditt et al., 2010). If children return home, parents tend to show a temporary increase in depression and stress hormone levels (Tosi, 2020; Birditt et al., 2017).

The departure of children from the family home generally increases marital satisfaction, perhaps because of the additional time partners now have to spend with each other (Bouchard, 2014; Gorchoff et al., 2008). The empty nest may be harder on couples whose identity is dependent on the parental role, or who now must face marital problems they had previously pushed aside under the press of parental responsibilities (Antonucci et al., 2001).

Race, ethnicity, and cultural context can affect the dynamics of leaving the nest. For example, white parents generally provide more financial support to their adult children than do African American parents. Part of this is driven by available resources as white parents are more likely to be of higher socioeconomic status. However, child status (specifically, being a student) and cultural beliefs about helping are also an influence (Fingerman et al., 2011).

In much of the world, including many parts of Europe, Asia, and Latin America, the normative expectation regarding the living status of adult children is that they will remain in their parents' home until marriage (Buhl & Lance, 2007; Rosenberger, 2007; Fierro & Moreno, 2007). Because of the different expectations for adult children, the responses to their exit also vary. For example, multiple studies with Chinese samples have demonstrated Chinese parents whose adult children move out are more likely to show declines in well-being and increases in loneliness and depression than are those whose children remain in the family home (Bouchard, 2014). Within cultures such as these, leaving the family home before marriage can be perceived not as a healthy step towards adult independence, but as a sign of the breakdown in family bonds (Goldscheider & Goldscheider, 1999).

ADULT CHILDREN

Middle-age parents generally give their children more help and support than they get from them as the young adults establish careers and families (Antonucci et al., 2001). This assistance improves their chances of attending college, establishing careers, or buying homes (Johnson & Benson, 2012). Approximately 60 percent of parents with children give financial assistance to their 18- to 29-year-old children at least once a year (Barroso et al., 2019). Parents give the most help to children who need it most, typically those who are single or are single parents, or who are criminal offenders (Blieszner & Roberto, 2006; Siennick, 2011).

A grown child's delayed departure from the nest or return to it may produce family stress (Antonucci et al., 2001; Aquilino, 1996). From the adult child's point of view, the provision of financial support from a parent can threaten self-efficacy (Mortimer et al., 2016), and although living with parents can provide much needed financial and emotional support, it can also threaten a sense of independence (Burn & Szoeke, 2016). Moreover, the provision of financial assistance may be perceived by both parents and children as lending some legitimacy to parental efforts to control children (Padilla-Walker et al., 2014), undermining child autonomy.

The nonnormative experience of parent-child coresidence is becoming less. For example, in 2008, American researchers found the presence of adult children living at home was associated with a decline in marital quality. However, from 2008 to 2012, the percentage of U.S. adult children who returned to live at home as a result of the great recession rose to 36 percent. When the researchers again collected data in 2013, the presence of adult children in the home was no longer associated with low marital quality unless the child also had problems. The researchers argued that child coresidence was damaging to marital quality only when it was nonnormative. When the economy made coresidence increasingly common, this altered the interpretation and consequences of coresidence (Davis et al., 2016).

Since the 1980s, in most Western nations, more and more adult children have delayed leaving home until the late twenties or beyond (Mouw, 2005). Furthermore, the **revolving door syndrome**, sometimes called the boomerang phenomenon, has become more common. Increasing numbers of young adults, especially men, return to their parents' home, sometimes more than once, and sometimes with their own families (Blieszner & Roberto, 2006; Putney & Bengtson, 2001). Often a return to the family home is precipitated by emotional or financial concerns, or alcohol problems (Sandberg-Thoma et al., 2015; Smits et al., 2010). Sometimes adult children move back home to care for ailing parents (South & Lei, 2015).

Prolonged parenting may lead to intergenerational tension when it contradicts parents' normative expectations. As children move from adolescence to young adulthood, parents typically expect them to become independent, and children expect to do so.

revolving door syndrome
Tendency for young adults who have left home to return to their parents' household in times of financial, marital, or other trouble.

VOLUNTARY CHILDLESSNESS

The number of women without children has been rising sharply in recent decades (Frejka, 2017). Almost 27 percent of women age 30 to 39 and slightly over 15 percent of women age 40 to 50 have never given birth to a child (U.S. Census Bureau, 2019). Similar trends have been found in other countries as well, including Austria, Germany, the Netherlands, Switzerland, and the United Kingdom, and to a lesser extent Central and Eastern Europe (Kreyenfeld & Konietzka, 2017).

Although involuntary childlessness—or infertility—has a negative effect on well-being (Luk & Loke, 2015), voluntary childlessness does not. Generally, people who are childless by choice have higher well-being and better psychological health than parents, especially those who had children when young, and empty nesters (Koropeckyj-Cox et al., 2007; Hansen, 2012; Umberson et al., 2010; Bures et al., 2009). This same pattern is found across a number of countries, although it is less pronounced in countries that have stronger norms regarding parenthood (Huijt et al., 2012).

In later adulthood, research has shown that childless women tend to fare well, but childless men are more vulnerable. For example, in one study, never-married, divorced, or widowed men were at higher risk for depression than their female counterparts (Zhang & Hayward, 2001). Similarly, research conducted in Austria, Finland, and the Netherlands showed that divorced childless men were at risk for poor health, whereas divorced childless women were not (Kendig et al., 2007). One possible explanation focuses on social connections. Childless older women tend to be very active socially and have particularly robust social networks and community connections. Married childless men often depend on their wives to link them to this support network. Thus, when both unmarried and childless, these men are more prone to difficulties (Wenger et al., 2007).

Other Kinship Ties

At midlife, responsibility for care and support of aging parents may begin to shift to their middle-age children. In addition, a new relationship often begins at this time of life: grandparenthood.

RELATIONSHIPS WITH AGING PARENTS

Even when they do not live close to each other, most middle-age adults and their parents have warm, affectionate relationships based on frequent contact, mutual help, feelings of attachment, and shared values. Positive relationships with parents contribute to a strong sense of self and to emotional well-being at midlife (Blieszner & Roberto, 2006).

Most commonly, help and assistance continues to flow from adults to their own children rather than to their parents. However, with the changing demographics of the United States, particularly the lengthening of the life span, many middle-age adults gradually take on more responsibilities for their parents. For example, a son might realize that his mother is no longer able to drive and might decide to stop by the grocery store

window

on the world

THE GLOBAL SANDWICH GENERATION

In recent years researchers have called those in their forties and fifties who are squeezed between caring for both their own children and their aging parents the sandwich generation. According to the Pew Research Center, 47 percent of middle-age adults are part of the sandwich generation in the United States. About 15 percent of U.S. middle-age adults are providing financial support in some way to both a parent and a child. In addition, 61 percent of these adults are also providing emotional support and day-to-day assistance to both their aging parents and their own children (Parker & Patten, 2013). About 29 percent of adult children up to age 30 still live with their parents or have returned home after college, being at least partially supported by their parents (Parker, 2012).

Similar trends have been found in other parts of the world as well. It is estimated that by 2050, worldwide there will be three times more people in the sandwich generation caring for approximately 2 billion aging parents (United Nations, 2007). In Australia, 2.6 million people are considered "sandwich carers"; in the United Kingdom an additional 2.4 million fall into this group (Carers UK, 2012; Carers Australia, 2012).

In many parts of the world, particularly in developing countries, it is common for multiple generations of families to live together. For example, in Japan, nearly 50 percent of elders live with their children (National Institutes of Health, 2007), and in China 35 to 45 percent of the elderly live with their children (Ren & Treiman, 2014). Even if elders do not live with their children, family support is very important in Japan and China, and adult children are often available for daily care and assistance.

Caring for aging parents can be a daunting, stressful, and sometimes overwhelming task. In one study, 40 percent of 35- to 55-year-olds who were caregivers for both parents and children reported extreme levels of stress, stating that family was the top source of their stress. This stress takes a toll on family relationships and the well-being of the caretakers themselves (American Psychological Association, 2007). It is important for caretakers to recharge and take care of themselves physically and mentally. Though it may feel like a challenge at times, those being cared for are usually the people who are most important to the caretakers, and their care is an act of dedicated love for their family members.

what's your view How would you handle the responsibilities of caring for aging parents? What can you do to support a loved one who finds himself or herself in this situation?

---

filial crisis
In Marcoen's terminology, normative development of middle age, in which adults learn to balance love and duty to their parents with autonomy within a two-way relationship.

sandwich generation
Middle-age adults squeezed by competing needs to raise or launch children and to care for elderly parents.

once a week for her. This normative development is seen as the healthy outcome of a **filial crisis**, in which adults learn to balance love and duty to their parents with autonomy in a two-way relationship.

The majority of help consists of assistance with everyday needs and, less commonly, emergencies and crises. This pattern is true of most families; however, the dynamics change in situations in which parents are disabled or experience some sort of crisis themselves. Not surprisingly, in these cases, adult children often provide resources to their middle-age parents (Fingerman et al., 2010).

Members of this generation, sometimes called the **sandwich generation,** may be caught in a squeeze between the competing needs of their children and the emerging needs of their parents (see Window on the World).

Caregiving is typically a female function (Kinsella & Velkoff, 2001). When an ailing mother is widowed or a divorced woman can no longer manage alone, it is most likely that a daughter will take on the caregiving role (Pinquart & Sörensen, 2006; Schulz & Martire, 2004). Daughters and older mothers tend to be especially close (Fingerman & Dolbin-MacNab, 2006). Sons do contribute to caregiving, but they are less likely to provide primary, personal care (Blieszner & Roberto, 2006; Marks, 1996). The proportion of sons and daughters in a family affect this process. If a woman has brothers, she tends to provide more care. If a man has sisters, he tends to provide less care (Grigoryeva, 2017).

Ethnic and Cultural Differences in Caregiving Expectations and beliefs about care provided to parents differ by race and ethnicity. For example, African American and Hispanic adults are more likely than white adults to provide assistance to aging parents (Cohen et al., 2019; Ellison & Xu, 2016). Similarly, Asian, Hispanic, and foreign-born Americans are more likely to live in multigenerational households, which can include aging parents, than are white Americans (Cohn & Passel, 2018). These findings may result, in part, because of socioeconomic differences between people of different ethnicities. In particular, African American and Hispanic adults are more likely to have limited resources and so less frequently use formal caregiving services for their parents (Dilworth-Anderson et al., 2002).

Most middle-age adults and their aging parents have warm, affectionate relationships. bo1982/iStock/ Getty Images

Religion also affects the tendency to offer help. Protestants, Mormons, and Catholics, particularly those who are more conservative, are more likely to endorse having aging parents live with them than are Jewish, mainline Protestants, or religiously unaffiliated adults (Ellison & Xu, 2016). These religions share a concern for conventional family values and respect for elders.

Family caregiving beliefs also vary across cultures. As with many cultural differences, the collectivism/individualism dimension is important. Adults from collectivistic cultures that stress interconnections and the greater social good, not surprisingly, tend to be more supportive of parental caregiving. Adults from individualistic cultures, with their emphasis on autonomy, are more likely to view caring for their parents as a barrier to their personal goals (Mitchell, 2014).

Familism is another important cultural variable. Familism places family well-being over individual concerns, and people from cultures high in familism are more likely to care for aging parents themselves rather than using a formal system. Filial responsibility is related to this and involves feeling duty-bound to support aging parents. Not fulfilling filial obligations can often be seen as shameful. Hispanic families and many Asian cultures share a strong sense of these obligations. For example, one study found more caregiving of aging parents was provided by Asian and Hispanic adults, and less by non-Hispanic white adults (Miyawaki, 2016).

Strains of Caregiving The generations typically get along best while parents are healthy and vigorous. When older people become infirm, the burden of caring for them may strain the relationship (Antonucci et al., 2001; Marcoen, 1995). Given the high cost of nursing homes and most older people's reluctance to stay in them, many dependent elders receive long-term care in their own home or that of a caregiver.

Caregiving can be stressful. Many caregivers find the task a physical, emotional, and financial burden, especially if they work full-time, have limited financial resources, or lack support and assistance (Lund, 1993; Schulz & Martire, 2004). It is hard for women who work outside the home to assume an added caregiving role, and reducing work hours or quitting a job to meet caregiving obligations can increase financial stress.

Emotional strain may come not only from caregiving itself but also from the need to balance it with the many other responsibilities of midlife (Antonucci et al., 2001; Climo & Stewart, 2003). Elderly parents may become dependent at a time when middle-age adults need to launch their children or, if parenthood was delayed, to raise them. Caregiving can also lead to marriage problems. Adult caregivers report less marital happiness, great marital inequality, more hostility, and, for women, a greater degree of depressive symptomatology and depression over time (Bookwala, 2009). Some research has shown that caregiving is associated with a greater risk of relationship dissolution for women in cohabiting relationships, but not necessarily for men or for married women (Penning & Wu, 2019). Moreover, a middle-age child, who may be preparing to retire, can ill afford the additional costs of caring for a frail older person or may have health problems of his or her own (Kinsella & Velkoff, 2001).

Estimates are that approximately 59 percent of family caregivers are caring for a parent with physical impairments. It can be even more difficult to care for someone with dementia, a situation faced by 26 percent of caregivers. Moreover, 37 percent of care recipients have more than one condition or illness (National Alliance for Caregiving, 2015).

Dementia and related conditions are among the hardest to cope with. In addition to being unable to carry on basic functions of daily living, people with dementia may be incontinent, suspicious, agitated or depressed, subject to hallucinations, likely to wander about at night, dangerous to self and others, and in need of constant supervision (Schulz & Martire, 2004). Sometimes the caregiver becomes physically or mentally ill under the strain (Richardson et al., 2013). Because women are more likely than men to give personal care, their mental health and well-being may be more likely to suffer (Friedemann & Buckwalter, 2014; van der Lee et al., 2014; Caceres et al., 2016). Sometimes the stress created by the incessant, heavy demands of caregiving is so great as to lead to abuse, neglect, or even abandonment of the dependent elderly person.

caregiver burnout
Condition of physical, mental, and emotional exhaustion affecting adults who provide continuous care for sick or aged persons.

A result of these and other strains may be **caregiver burnout,** physical, mental, and emotional exhaustion that can affect adults who care for aged relatives (Hategan et al., 2018). Even the most patient, loving caregiver may become frustrated, anxious, or resentful under the constant strain of meeting an older person's seemingly endless needs. Often families and friends fail to recognize that caregivers have a right to feel discouraged, frustrated, and put upon. Caregivers need a life of their own, beyond the loved one's disability or disease. Sometimes other arrangements, such as institutionalization, assisted living, or a division of responsibilities among siblings, must be made (Shuey & Hardy, 2003).

Community support programs can reduce the strains and burdens of caregiving. Support services may include meals and housekeeping; transportation and escort services; and adult day care centers, which provide supervised activities and care while caregivers work or attend to personal needs. *Respite care* (substitute supervised care by visiting nurses or home health aides) gives regular caregivers some time off. Through counseling, support, and self-help groups, caregivers can share problems, gain information about community resources, and improve skills.

Some family caregivers, looking back, regard the experience as uniquely rewarding. Caregiving can be an opportunity for personal growth in competence, compassion, self-knowledge, and self-transcendence. Moreover, family caregivers report a sense of spiritual and religious growth and fulfilling a sense of duty (Lloyd et al., 2016; Bengtson, 2001; Climo & Stewart, 2003; Lund, 1993). When family caregivers can identify and articulate the positive aspects of caring for a person with dementia, they are less likely to experience depression and more likely to report higher well-being, life satisfaction, and self-efficacy (Quinn & Toms, 2018).

RELATIONSHIPS WITH SIBLINGS

Sibling ties are the longest-lasting relationships in most people's lives. In some cross-sectional research, sibling relationships over the life span look like an hourglass, with the most contact at the two ends—childhood and middle to late adulthood—and the least contact during the child-raising years. After establishing careers and families, siblings may renew their ties (White, 2001; Putney & Bengtson, 2001; Conger & Little, 2010). Other studies indicate a decline in contact throughout adulthood. Sibling conflict tends to diminish with age—perhaps because siblings who do not get along see each other less (Putney & Bengtson, 2001).

Relationships with siblings who remain in contact can be central to psychological well-being in midlife (Thomas, 2010; Spitze & Trent, 2006). As in young adulthood, sisters tend to be closer than brothers (Blieszner & Roberto, 2006; Spitze & Trent, 2006). Sibling relationships may be particularly beneficial for those adults who did not have children. For instance, siblings sometimes serve as caregivers for each other, and when they do, they are less negatively affected by doing so than are caregivers for parents or spouses (Namkung, et al., 2016).

Dealing with the care of aging parents can bring siblings closer together but also can cause resentment and conflict. Disagreements may arise over the division of care or over an inheritance, especially if the sibling relationship has not been good (Ngan-gana et al., 2016; Blieszner & Roberto, 2006). Problems may also emerge if there are perceptions of favoritism, either as perceived currently or as remembered from child-hood, particularly for the maternal relationship (Peng et al., 2018; Suitor et al., 2017).

GRANDPARENTHOOD

Adults in the United States become grandparents, on average, around age 45 (Blieszner & Roberto, 2006). In 2014, the United States had a population of 69.5 million grandparents (Monte, 2017). Fifty-one percent of people age 50 to 64 years have grandchildren, and about a third of them list grandparenting as the most valued aspect of getting older (Livingston & Parker, 2010).

Grandparenthood today is different in other ways from grandparenthood in the past. Most U.S. grandparents have fewer grandchildren than their parents or grandparents did (Blieszner & Roberto, 2006). With the rising incidence of midlife divorce, many grandparents are divorced, widowed, or separated (Davies & Williams, 2002), and many are step-grandparents. Middle-age grandparents tend to be married, active in their communities, and employed and thus less available to help out with their grandchildren. They also are more likely to be raising one or more children of their own (Blieszner & Roberto, 2006).

In general, grandmothers have closer, warmer, more affectionate relationships with their grandchildren (especially granddaughters) than grandfathers do and see them more (Putney & Bengtson, 2001). Grandparents who have frequent contact with their grand-children, feel good about grandparenthood, attribute importance to the role, and have high self-esteem tend to be more satisfied with being grandparents (Reitzes & Mutran, 2004). Grandparents sometimes have difficulty balancing their connection with their grandchildren and allowing their children to parent their family in accordance with their own beliefs and values (Breheny et al., 2013).

Cultural Differences in Grandparenting In many developing societies, such as those in Latin America and Asia, extended-family households predominate, and grandparents play an integral role in child raising and family decisions. In Asian countries such as Thailand and Taiwan, about 40 percent of the 50 and older population lives in the same household with a minor grandchild, and half of those with grandchildren age 10 or younger—usually grandmothers—provide care for the child (Kinsella & Velkoff, 2001). In China and Romania, mothers' migration in search of work resulted in large numbers of young children being "left behind" with family members, usually grandmothers (Ban et al., 2017; Piperno, 2012). In some countries in sub-Saharan Africa, high mortality rates in young adults as a consequence of AIDS make grandparents a critical resource for the children left orphaned by disease (Uhlenberg & Cheuk, 2010). Grandparent care is common in Europe, with slightly over 40 percent of grandparents providing regular or occasional care for their grandchildren. The provision of regular day care is somewhat more common in Southern than Northern Europe (Glaser et al., 2013; Iacovou & Skew, 2011). In short, grandparents—globally—are an important part of their grandchildren's lives.

In the United States, the extended family household is common in some minority communities, but the dominant house-hold pattern is the nuclear family. In 2014, estimates are that approximately 4 percent of U.S. grandparents lived in house-holds with their grandchildren (Glaser et al., 2018). Although 68 percent of the grandparents in an AARP survey see at least one grandchild every 1 or 2 weeks, 45 percent live too far away to see their grandchildren regularly (Davies & Williams, 2002). However, distance does not necessarily affect the quality of rela-tionships with grandchildren (Kivett, 1996).

Across many cultures, grandparents play an integral role in raising their grandchildren. Don Hammond/Design Pics

About 22 percent of U.S. grandparents provide child care for working parents (Krogstad, 2015). Indeed, grandparents are almost as likely to be child care providers as organized child care centers or preschools; 23.7 percent of children under age 5 and 31.7 percent of children overall with employed mothers are under a grandparent's care while the mothers are at work (Laughlin, 2013). In countries where the government spends more funds on child care assistance, grandparent care is less common. For example, in Denmark and Sweden, approximately 2 percent of families use grandparent care, contrasted with 15 percent in Germany and around 30 percent in Italy and Spain (Del Boca, 2015). Geographical proximity of grandparents who are willing to assist with child care, including both regular care and unanticipated "emergency" care, has a positive effect on the probability of women working outside the home (Compton & Pollak, 2014).

Raising Grandchildren Many grandparents are their grandchildren's sole or primary caregivers. One reason, in developing countries, is the migration of rural parents to urban areas to find work. These *skip-generation* families exist in all regions of the world, particularly in Afro-Caribbean countries. In sub-Saharan Africa, the AIDS epidemic has left many orphans whose grandparents step into the parents' place (Kinsella & Velkoff, 2001).

In the United States, about 1 in 10 grandparents is raising a grandchild, and this number is rising (U.S. Census Bureau, 2014). Many are serving as *parents by default* for children whose parents are unable to care for them—often as a result of teenage pregnancy, substance abuse, illness, divorce, or death. Increasingly, the opioid epidemic is taking a toll as well, and increasing numbers of children are entering the foster care system or being cared for by grandparents as a result of parental death, incarceration, or addiction (United, 2018).

Surrogate parenting by grandparents is a well-established pattern in African American and Latino families. It is more common in grandmothers, especially those living in poverty. They are also likely to be younger and have lower educational levels (Blieszner & Roberto, 2006; Dolbin-McNab & Hayslip, 2014; Dunifon et al., 2014).

Unexpected surrogate parenthood can be a physical, emotional, and financial drain on middle-age or older adults (Blieszner & Roberto, 2006). They may have to quit their jobs, shelve their retirement plans, drastically reduce their leisure pursuits and social life, and endanger their health.

Most grandparents who take on the responsibility to raise their grandchildren do it because they do not want their grandchildren placed in a stranger's foster home. Grandparents often have to deal with a sense of guilt because the adult children they raised have failed their own children and also with the rancor they may feel toward these adult children. For some caregiver couples, the strains produce tension in their relationship. If one or both parents resume their normal roles, it may be emotionally wrenching to return the child (Crowley, 1993).

Taking over the full care of grandchildren can be psychologically and physically taxing (Hadfield, 2014). With respect to physical health, studies have indicated custodial grandparents are at higher risk of poor physical health (Neely-Barnes et al., 2010; Musil et al., 2010). Custodial grandparents also report higher levels of anxiety, stress, and particularly depression, and those who are caring for children with social, behavioral, or emotional problems are particularly at risk (Doley et al., 2015; Minkler & Fuller-Thomson, 2001; Neely-Barnes et al., 2010). High levels of social support can help grandparents deal with the difficulties of parenting their grandchildren and are associated with better psychological health (Hayslip et al., 2014).

Grandparents providing **kinship care** who do not become foster parents or gain custody have no legal status and few rights. They may face many practical problems, from enrolling the child in school and gaining access to academic records to obtaining medical insurance for the child. Grandchildren are usually not eligible for coverage under employer-provided health insurance even if the grandparent has custody. Moreover, kinship families are not legally entitled to as many benefits as foster families (Lin, 2014), despite research showing that kinship care allows children to remain connected to their family networks and cultural traditions (Kiraly & Humphreys, 2013). Like working

kinship care
Care of children living without parents in the home of grandparents or other relatives, with or without a change of legal custody.

parents, working grandparents need good, affordable child care and family-friendly work-place policies, such as time off to care for a sick child. The federal Family and Medical Leave Act of 1993 does cover grandparents who are raising grandchildren, but many do not realize it.

Grandparents can be sources of guidance, companions in play, links to the past, and symbols of family continuity. They express generativity, a longing to transcend mortality by investing themselves in the lives of future generations. Men and women who do not become grandparents may fulfill generative needs by becoming foster grandparents or volunteering in schools or hospitals. By finding ways to develop what Erikson called the virtue of *care*, adults prepare themselves to enter the culminating period of adult development.

summary and key terms

Change at Midlife

- Developmental scientists previously believed little change occurred in midlife; however, there is growing consensus that midlife development shows change as well as stability.

Psychosocial Theory and Midlife

- Erikson's seventh psychosocial stage is generativity versus stagnation. Generativity is most commonly expressed through parenting, but can be expressed in other ways. The virtue of this period is *care*.
- Although generativity concerns in midlife are common across many cultures, the form generativity takes and its consequences vary. In particular, adults from collectivistic cultures and religious or spiritual adults show more concern with social goals.

    generativity versus stagnation, generativity

Issues and Themes

- The greater fluidity of the life cycle today has partly undermined the assumption of a "social clock," although people who are "on time" generally report higher well-being.
- Research does not support a normative midlife crisis. It is more accurate to refer to a transition that may be a psychological turning point.

    midlife crisis, turning points, midlife review, ego resiliency, identity process theory (IPT), identity schemas, identity assimilation, identity accommodation, identity balance

Change and Stability in Midlife

- There are normative developmental changes in personality traits with age; however, individual experiences can also result in unique changes in personality.

- Generally, there is a shift toward experiencing more positive emotions and fewer negative emotions in midlife. Emotional regulation capabilities and relationships may influence emotional experience.
- Narrative psychology describes identity development as a continuous process of constructing a life story. Highly generative people tend to focus on a theme of redemption.
- According to identity process theory, people continually confirm or revise their perceptions about themselves on the basis of experience and feedback from others. Some of these processes differ across cultures.
- Women have a more difficult time than men managing work-family conflict. However, successful management leads to generativity, which is then associated with positive outcomes.

Positive Mental Health at Midlife

- Research based on Ryff's six-dimensional scale has found that midlife is generally a period of positive mental health and well-being, though wealth, both individually and countrywide, is an issue.

Relationships at Midlife

- Two theories of the changing importance of relationships are Kahn and Antonucci's social convoy theory and Carstensen's socioemotional selectivity theory.
- Relationships at midlife are important to physical and mental health but also can present stressful demands.

    social convoy theory, socioemotional selectivity theory

Consensual Relationships

- Research on the quality of marriage suggests a dip in marital satisfaction during the years of child rearing, followed by an improved relationship after the children leave home.

- Globally, cohabitation has become more common. The influence of cohabitation on outcomes varies with cultural context.
- Divorce at midlife can be stressful and life changing. Marital capital tends to dissuade midlife divorce.
- Divorce today may be less threatening to well-being in middle age than in young adulthood.
- Married people tend to be happier at middle age than people with any other marital status.
- Gay and lesbian adults who have internalized negative views of homosexuality have more difficulty in their relationships. The passage of marriage equality in the United States showed homosexual couples benefit from marriage similarly to heterosexual couples.
- Middle-age people tend to invest less time in friendships than younger adults do but depend on friends for emotional support.

marital capital

Relationships with Maturing Children

- Parents of adolescents have to come to terms with a loss of control over their children's lives.
- The emptying of the nest is liberating for many women but may be stressful for couples whose identity is dependent on the parental role or those who now must face previously submerged marital problems.
- Middle-age parents tend to remain involved with their adult children. Conflict may arise over grown children's need to be treated as adults and parents' continuing concern about them.

- Today, more young adults are delaying departure from their childhood home or are returning to it. Adjustment tends to be smoother if the parents see the adult child as moving toward autonomy.
- Increasing numbers of adults are choosing not to have children. Generally, childlessness is associated with high well-being.

empty nest, revolving door syndrome

Other Kinship Ties

- Relationships between middle-age adults and their parents are usually characterized by a strong bond of affection.
- As life lengthens, more aging parents become dependent for care on their middle-age children. Acceptance of these dependency needs is the mark of filial maturity.
- The chances of becoming a caregiver to an aging parent increase in middle age, especially for women.
- Caregiving can be a source of considerable stress but also of satisfaction. Community support programs can help prevent caregiver burnout.
- Although siblings tend to have less contact at midlife than before and after, most middle-age siblings remain in touch, and their relationships are important to well-being.
- Most U.S. adults become grandparents in middle age and have fewer grandchildren than in previous generations.
- Divorce and remarriage of an adult child can affect grandparent-grandchild relationships.
- A growing number of grandparents are raising grandchildren whose parents are unable to care for them. Raising grandchildren can create physical, emotional, and financial strains.

filial crisis, sandwich generation, caregiver burnout, kinship care

Physical and Cognitive Development in Late Adulthood

Tim Pannell/Fuse/Getty Images

learning objectives

Discuss the causes and impact of the aging population.

Characterize longevity and discuss biological theories of aging.

Describe physical changes in late adulthood.

Identify factors that influence health and well-being in late adulthood.

Describe the cognitive functioning of older adults.

In this chapter, we begin by sketching demographic trends among today's older population. We look at the increasing length and quality of life in late adulthood and at causes of biological aging. We examine physical changes and health. We then turn to cognitive development: changes in intelligence and memory, the emergence of wisdom, and the influence of continuing education in late life.

Old Age Today

In Japan, old age is a status symbol; travelers checking into hotels there are often asked their age to ensure that they will receive proper deference. In the United States, by contrast, aging is generally seen as undesirable. In research, the most consistent stereotypes that have emerged regarding the elderly are that although older people are generally seen as warm and loving, they are incompetent and of low status (Cuddy et al., 2005; Cary & Chasteen, 2015). These stereotypes about aging may unconsciously affect older people's expectations about themselves and act as self-fulfilling prophecies (Levy, 2003).

ageism
Prejudice or discrimination against a person (most commonly an older person) based on age.

Today, efforts to combat **ageism**—prejudice or discrimination based on age—are making headway. Reports about aging achievers appear more frequently in the media. In entertainment media, older people are less often portrayed as dotards and more often as level-headed, respected, and wise, a shift that may be important in the reduction of negative stereotypes about the elderly (Bodner, 2009).

We need to look beyond distorted images of age to its true, multifaceted reality. What does today's older population look like?

THE GRAYING OF THE POPULATION

In 2018, the world reached a milestone: For the first time, people 65 years and older outnumbered children. In 2019, 1 in 11 people worldwide were age 65 or older, and projections are that by 2050, 1 in 6 people will be over 65 years old (United Nations, 2019).

The most rapid increases will be in developing countries, where the number of older people is projected to increase more than 250 percent by 2050 (National Institute on Aging, 2011; Figure 17.1). Aging populations result from declines in fertility accompanied by economic growth, better nutrition, healthier lifestyles, improved control of infectious disease, safer water and sanitation facilities, and advances in science, technology, and medicine (He et al., 2016; Dobriansky et al., 2007).

Active, healthy older adults such as actress Diana Rigg are changing the perception of old age. At age 75, she played the brilliant, sharp-tongued Lady Olenna Tyrell in Game of Thrones. She continued to work until her death in 2020 at age 82.
HBO/Kobal/Shutterstock

In many parts of the world, the fastest-growing age group consists of people in their eighties and older (Window on the World). The population of people 80 and older is projected to almost triple between 2019 and 2050, from 143 million to 426 million (United Nations, 2019). By contrast, the percentage rate increase predicted for adults aged 65 and older is about 1.5 times the current numbers, and there is an almost flat percentage change predicted in people under the age of 20 (He et al., 2016).

In the United States, the graying of the population is due to high birthrates and high immigration rates during the early to mid-twentieth century and a current trend toward smaller families, which has reduced the relative size of younger age groups. It is also due to aging of baby boomers—the surge of people born following World War II. Since 1900, the proportion of Americans age 65 and up has more than tripled, from 4.1 to 16 percent in 2019. The first of the baby boomers turned 65 in 2011, and by 2060 population projections suggest there will be almost 95 million adults age 65 and over in the United States. The 85 and older population is also expected to increase to approximately 14.4 million people in 2040—an increase of 123 percent over 2018 (Administration for Community Living, 2020).

Although racial and ethnic minority populations in the United States are, as a whole, younger than the white population, ethnic diversity among older adults is nonetheless increasing. In 2019, 23 percent of Americans age 65 and older were members of minority groups; by 2040, 34 percent will be. The largest group is African American (9 percent) followed by Asian or Pacific Islander (5 percent), Native American or Alaska native (0.5 percent), Native Hawaiian/Pacific Islander (0.1 percent), and multiracial adults (0.8 percent). Hispanics, who can be any race, are approximately 8 percent of the population (Administration for Community Living, 2020).

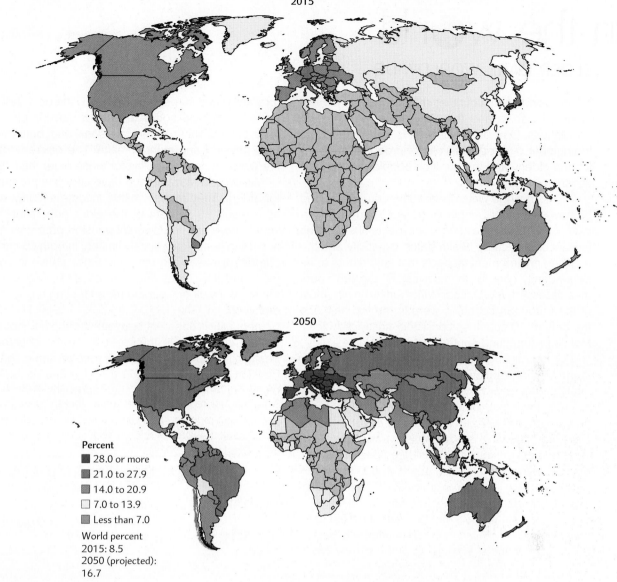

2050

Percent
- ■ 28.0 or more
- ■ 21.0 to 27.9
- ■ 14.0 to 20.9
- □ 7.0 to 13.9
- ■ Less than 7.0

World percent
2015: 8.5
2050 (projected):
16.7

FIGURE 17.1

Percentage of Population Age 65 and Older: 2015 and 2050

The growth of the population age 65 and up is projected to increase rapidly in coming decades. Growth will be greatest in much of the developing world.

Source: He, W., Goodkind, D., & Kowal, P. (2016). *U.S. Census Bureau, International Population Reports, P95/16-1, An Aging World: 2015.* Washington, DC: U.S. Government Publishing Office.

CONCEPTUALIZATIONS OF AGING

The economic impact of a graying population depends on the proportion of the population that is healthy and able-bodied. In this regard, the trend is encouraging. Many problems that we used to think were the result of age have been determined to be due to lifestyle factors or disease.

Primary aging is a gradual, inevitable process of bodily deterioration that begins early in life and continues through the years irrespective of what people do to stave it off. In this view, aging is an unavoidable consequence of getting older. **Secondary aging** results from disease, abuse, and disuse—factors that are often within a person's control (Horn & Meer, 1987). These two philosophies of aging can be likened to the familiar

primary aging
Gradual, inevitable process of bodily deterioration throughout the life span.

secondary aging
Aging processes that result from disease and bodily abuse and disuse and are often preventable.

window on the world

ELDER CARE WORLDWIDE

As the world ages, countries must adjust to their demographic shifts and the changing needs of their populations. One pressing need is elder care. Both the number of people eligible for programs supporting the elderly and the duration people require their assistance is growing.

The Global Age Watch Index ranks countries based on how well older people are doing (HelpAge International, 2015). It measures four aspects of elder welfare: income security, health status, capability, and the enabling environment (aspects that help elders to independently care for themselves). Of the 195 countries assessed, the United States ranked ninth. Most of the European countries were in the top half, and the bottom 20 countries consisted mostly of African, Middle Eastern, and Southeast Asian countries.

The top ranking went to Switzerland—where one-fourth of the population is over 60—because of its many programs promoting health, capability, and activity for the aging population, as well as universal health care and pension plans for all citizens. Nearly one-third of Japan's population is over 60, yet at the number eight ranking, it is considered one of the oldest and healthiest countries in the world. Japan has comprehensive policies in place for the elderly, including universal health care and pension plans.

Both India (ranked 71) and China (ranked 52) have many elderly adults and major disparities in quality of health care. In India, 80 percent of the elderly live in rural areas and 40 percent live below the poverty line; there is no official social security or pension plan for the elderly. Chinese elders fare somewhat better with both physical and mental health. The discrepancies are worse in both countries for those older than 75.

Malawi and Mozambique have very few programs for elders. They rank lowest in income security, and as a result 95 percent of the elder population still work. There are no universal pension programs and access to health care is very limited. In both countries chronic diseases are rampant. Elder abuse is common, and it includes financial, physical, and sexual abuse. Many elderly people report feeling unsafe and devalued.

Inequality is apparent between the top and bottom ranked countries. In the highest-income countries, nearly all people older than 65 receive some sort of pension and health care. In the low- and middle-income countries, about 25 percent receive a pension or quality health care. Much still needs to be done to equalize elder care worldwide.

what's your view In countries with limited budgets, what priority should the elderly hold when considering funding for social services? Are they equally, more, or less important than other age groups? Why?

---

nature-nurture debate. Primary aging is a nature process governed by biology. Secondary aging is the result of nurture, the environmental insults that accrue over the course of a lifetime. As always, the truth lies somewhere in between and both factors matter.

Today, social scientists who specialize in the study of aging refer to three groups of older adults: the "young old," "old old," and "oldest old." These terms represent social constructions similar to the concept of adolescence. Chronologically, *young old* generally refers to people ages 65 to 74, who are usually active, vital, and vigorous. The *old old,* ages 75 to 84, and the *oldest old,* age 85 and above, are more likely to be frail and infirm and to have difficulty managing **activities of daily living (ADL).** As a result, the oldest old consume a disproportionate number of resources such as pensions or health care costs given their population size (Kinsella & He, 2009).

A more meaningful classification is **functional age:** how well a person functions in a physical and social environment in comparison with others of the same chronological age. For example, a person of 90 who is still in good health and can live independently may be functionally younger than a 75-year-old suffering the effects of dementia.

The use of these terms and age distinctions has arisen out of research and service needs. **Gerontology** is the study of the aged and aging processes. Gerontologists are interested in differences between elderly people because these differences can influence

activities of daily living (ADL)
Essential activities that support survival, such as eating, dressing, bathing, and getting around the house.

functional age
Measure of a person's ability to function effectively in his or her physical and social environment in comparison with others of the same chronological age.

gerontology
Study of the aged and the process of aging.

outcomes. Likewise, researchers and service providers in **geriatrics,** the branch of medicine concerned with aging, are concerned with differences among the elderly. Understanding differences among the elderly is vital for the provision of support services for different age groups.

Physical Aging and Longevity

Life expectancy is the age to which a person born at a certain time and place is statistically likely to live, given his or her current age and health status. Life expectancy is based on the average **longevity,** or actual length of life, of members of a population. Gains in life expectancy reflect declines in *mortality rates,* or death rates (the proportions of a total population or of certain age groups who die in a given year). The human **life span** is the longest period that members of our species can live. The longest documented life span thus far is that of Jeanne Calment, a French woman who died at 122 years of age.

CORRELATES OF LIFE EXPECTANCY

A baby born in the United States in 2017 can expect to live to 78.6 years, more than 30 years longer than a baby born in 1900 and more than 4 times longer than a baby born at the dawn of human history (National Center for Health Statistics, 2019; Wilmoth, 2000; Figure 17.2). Much of this increase can be attributed to the influence of antibiotics, vaccination programs, and improved sanitary practices. Life expectancy rates then began to be affected more by deaths from chronic diseases. Most recently, life expectancy in the United States has shown a slight decline, in part because of unintentional drug overdoses (National Center for Health Statistics, 2019). Globally, life expectancy is projected to continue to rise in industrialized countries (Kontis et al., 2017).

Gender Differences Nearly all over the world, women live longer and have lower mortality rates at all ages than men. By the age of 65, there are approximately 80.3 men for every 100 women, by age 85 there are only 50 men for every 100 women, and by age 100 women outnumber men by 4 to 1 (He et al., 2016). The gender gap is widest in high-income industrialized nations, where female mortality dropped sharply with improvements in prenatal and obstetric care. Women's longer lives also have been attributed to their greater tendency to take care of themselves and to seek medical care, the higher level of social support they enjoy, improvements in child mortality for girls, and the rise in women's socioeconomic status in recent decades. Further, men are more likely to smoke, drink, and be exposed to dangerous toxins (Kinsella & He, 2009; Ortiz-Ospina & Beltekian, 2018).

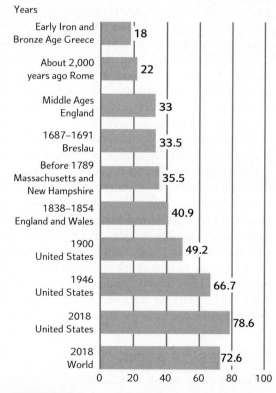

Years

Early Iron and Bronze Age Greece	18
About 2,000 years ago Rome	22
Middle Ages England	33
1687–1691 Breslau	33.5
Before 1789 Massachusetts and New Hampshire	35.5
1838–1854 England and Wales	40.9
1900 United States	49.2
1946 United States	66.7
2018 United States	78.6
2018 World	72.6

0   20   40   60   80   100

FIGURE 17.2

Changes in Life Expectancy from Ancient to Modern Times

Source: Adapted from Katchadourian, H. A. (1987). *Fifty: Midlife in perspective.* New York, NY: W. H. Freeman; World Bank. (2019). Life expectancy at birth, total (years) [Interactive graph]. Retrieved from https://data.worldbank.org/indicator/SP.DYN.LE00.IN

TABLE 17.1 U.S. Life Expectancy in Years	
	At Birth
Hispanic men	79.1
Hispanic women	84.3
White men	76.1
White women	81.0
African American men	71.5
African American women	78.1

Source: National Center for Health Statistics. (2018). *Health, United States, 2018*. Hyattsville, MD: U.S. Department of Health and Human Services.

Jeanne Calment was a French woman with the longest confirmed human life span. She lived a total of 122 years and 164 days. Pascal Parrot/Sygma/Getty Images

senescence
Period of the life span marked by declines in physical functioning usually associated with aging; begins at different ages for different people.

genetic-programming theories
Theories that explain biological aging as resulting from a genetically determined developmental timeline.

In the United States, women's life expectancy in 1900 was only 2 years longer than men's. The gender gap widened to 7.8 years in the late 1970s, mainly because more men were dying from smoking-related illnesses (heart disease and lung cancer) and fewer women were dying in childbirth. Since then the gap has narrowed to just under 5 years (National Center for Health Statistics, 2019). The gender disparity in the United States mirrors the global rates. At the age of 65, there are approximately 100 men for every 120 women. This disparity increases with advancing age; by the age of 85, there are 100 men for every 184 women (Federal Interagency Forum on Aging-Related Statistics, 2016).

Regional and Racial/Ethnic Differences In the pre-modern world, life expectancy was probably about 30 years (Ortiz-Ospina & Beltekian, 2018). In 2018, the global life expectancy rate was 72.6 years (World Bank, 2020). However, the gap in life expectancies between developed and developing countries is vast. In the Central African Republic, a person born in 2019 could expect to live 53 years, as compared to 83 years for a person born in Japan (Roser et al., 2019). The most dramatic improvements in life expectancy between 2000 and 2015 occurred in Africa, where improvements in child survival and the treatment of malaria and HIV increased life expectancy by 9.4 years (World Health Organization, 2016).

Wide racial/ethnic, socioeconomic, and geographic disparities in life expectancy exist in the United States. On average, white Americans live 3.6 years longer (78.5 years) than African Americans (74.9 years). African Americans, especially men, are more vulnerable than white Americans to illness and death from infancy through middle adulthood. Somewhat surprisingly, Hispanic Americans have the highest life expectancy (81.8 years) (National Center for Health Statistics, 2018; Table 17.1). The reasons for this are somewhat unclear but may include cultural lifestyle issues or migration effects (e.g., those who migrate to the United States tend to be healthier) (Arias, 2010).

A new way to look at life expectancy is in terms of the number of years a person can expect to live in good health, free of disabilities. Globally, healthy life expectancy (HLE) is 62 years for men and 64.8 years for women. In the United States, HLE is currently estimated to be 68.5 years of age (World Health Organization, 2018).

THEORIES OF AGING

As we get older, we may feel the effects of various chronic conditions or diseases. This process is known as **senescence,** the decline in body functioning associated with aging. Why does senescence occur? Most theories about biological aging fall into one of two categories: *genetic-programming theories* and *variable-rate theories*.

Genetic-Programming Theories Is aging an inevitable biological process? **Genetic-programming theories** propose that people's bodies age according to instructions built into the genes, and that aging is a normal part of development.

Twin studies have shown that genetic differences account for about one-fourth of the variance in the adult human life span. The genetic influences on aging appear to become stronger over time, especially after age 60 (Willcox et al., 2008; Finkel et al., 2014). With the exception of some rare genetic disorders, there is not "a" gene for aging. Rather, aging in typical people involves many gene variants, each with small effects.

Aging also may be influenced by specific genes "switching off," after which age-related losses (such as declines in vision, hearing, and motor control) occur. This process, broadly described as *epigenesis*, involves genes being turned on and off by molecular "tags," or instructions. Epigenetic changes do not involve changes in the underlying genetic code; rather, they involve changes in how genes are expressed. The accumulation of epigenetic changes is partly responsible for aging (Kim et al., 2018; D'Aquila et al., 2013: Sierra et al., 2015). Because epigenetic changes are dynamic and modifiable by environmental influences, positive interventions may be able to combat the effects of aging (Kim et al., 2018; Gravina & Vijg, 2010). For example, diet and lifestyle changes can affect our epigenetic expression and slow the rate of decline (Pal & Tyler, 2016).

Another cellular process involves *telomeres,* the repetitive fragments of DNA on the tips of chromosomes. Every time a cell divides, replicating its genetic code, the telomeres become shorter. Some theorists argue that cells can only divide a fixed number of times—eventually they run out of telomeres. Leonard Hayflick (1974) found that human cells will divide in the laboratory no more than 50 times. This is called the **Hayflick limit,** and it has been shown to be genetically controlled. Hayflick (1981) argued cells go through the same process in the body as in a laboratory culture. Once cells can no longer replicate, the body loses its ability to repair damaged tissue, and thus begins to age.

In support of this theory, research shows that telomeres shorten with age, and that the rate of telomere shortening is related to the rate of aging (Shammas, 2011). Shorter telomeres result in accelerated aging and risk of early death, and they are associated with increased risk of cancer, stroke, diabetes, dementia, chronic obstructive pulmonary disease, and skin disorders (Chilton et al., 2017). The rate of telomere change interacts with environmental influences in a complex fashion over the course of the life span (Honig et al., 2015; Dugdale & Richardson, 2018). Environmental factors known to be associated with disease and mortality, such as stress, smoking, alcohol use, and physical inactivity, can all affect the rate of telomere shortening (Puterman et al., 2015; Shalev et al., 2013; Latifovic et al., 2016; Astuti et al., 2017; Li et al., 2018; Arsenis et al., 2017). Additionally, people who have genetic disorders in which they age prematurely also have shorter telomere length (Burtner & Kennedy, 2010; Decker et al., 2009).

According to *endocrine theory,* the biological clock acts through genes that control hormonal changes. Loss of muscle strength, accumulation of fat, and atrophy of organs may be related to declines in hormonal activity (Lamberts et al., 1997). For example, mutations in the genes that code for hormones involved in the regulation of blood sugar have been linked in various other species to either increased or decreased life span, and it is likely they function similarly in humans (Van Heemst, 2010). *Immunological theory* proposes a similar process; that certain genes may cause problems in the immune system (Holliday, 2004; Kiecolt-Glaser & Glaser, 2001) that then leads to an increased susceptibility to diseases, infections, and cancer (Fulop et al., 2014).

According to the *evolutionary theory of aging,* reproductive fitness is the primary aim of natural selection. Therefore, natural selection acts most strongly on the young, who have many years of potential reproduction ahead of them. If a trait favoring reproductive output in the young is present, it will be spread throughout the population, even if the effects are damaging to the individual later in life (Hamilton, 1966; Baltes, 1997). Moreover, natural selection results in energy resources being allocated to protect and maintain the body until reproduction, but not necessarily after. After reproduction has ceased, the molecular integrity of the body cells and systems eventually deteriorate beyond the body's ability to repair them (Hayflick, 2004). This deterioration occurs because there is no selective pressure to prevent it once genes have been passed on to the next generation.

Hayflick limit
Genetically controlled limit, proposed by Hayflick, on the number of times cells can divide in members of a species.

Variable-Rate Theories Why might one older adult suffer from arthritis, poor health, and declining perceptual abilities and another remain active and engaged? According to **variable-rate theories,** aging is the result of random processes that vary from person to person. They are also called *error theories* because these processes often involve damage due to chance errors in, or environmental assaults on, biological systems.

One such theory, *wear-and-tear theory,* holds that the body ages as a result of accumulated damage to the system at the molecular level. Like an old car, the parts of the body eventually wear out (Jin, 2010). Some theorists have argued that although this sounds commonsensical, there is no fundamental reason bodies could not be made to continually regenerate, as they do in youth (Mitteldorf, 2010).

Another theory of aging, known as the *free-radical theory,* proposes that aging results from the formation of **free radicals,** a by-product of metabolic processes (Harman, 1956). Free radicals are molecules with unpaired electrons. This makes them very reactive because they seek to pair their electrons and will "steal" electrons from neighboring atoms. According to the theory, this process can ultimately damage cell membranes, structures and proteins, fats, carbohydrates, and even DNA. Moreover, free-radical damage accumulates with age and has been associated with cardiovascular disease, cancer, inflammatory diseases such as arthritis, heart disease, neurological disorders such as Parkinson's disease and Alzheimer's disease, gastric ulcers, and many others (Lobo et al., 2010).

This theory was expanded to the *mitochondrial theory of aging.* Mitochondria—tiny organisms that generate chemical energy for cells and tissues—play an important role in helping cells survive under stress and powering the body. However, when mitochondria generate energy, they also create free radicals as by-products of that process. These free radicals can negatively affect surrounding tissues, including their own mitochondrial DNA. This leads to even more free radical release, more damage, and the aging process (Harman, 2006; Ziegler et al., 2015). In this view, the action of free radicals affects the rate of aging, but it does so via damage to mitochondrial genes. Free radicals, although potentially damaging, may also have a signaling role to play by helping regulate genes necessary for cell growth and differentiation (Wojcik et al., 2010; Schieber & Chandel, 2014).

The *rate-of-living theory* postulates that there is a balance between metabolism, or energy use, and life span. The faster a body's metabolism, the shorter its life span, and vice versa (Pearl, 1928). So, for example, a hummingbird would be predicted to have a far shorter life than a sloth. This theory is useful in describing some phenomena, for example, when broadly comparing small and large animals to each other, but it does not explain many aspects of aging. For example, exercise, which increases metabolic activity, would be predicted to shorten life span. In reality, it has the opposite effect (Hulbert et al., 2007).

Genetic-programming and variable-rate theories have practical implications. If human beings are programmed to age at a certain rate, they can do little to retard the process. If, on the other hand, aging is variable, then lifestyle practices may influence it.

Some researchers have suggested that rather than focusing on how to extend the human life span, it makes more sense to consider how we can improve human health *while* aging (Partridge, 2010). Still, interest in increasing the life span remains. Controllable environmental and lifestyle factors may interact with genetic factors to determine how long a person lives and in what condition.

EXTENDING THE LIFE SPAN

Most people understand that more people survive to the age of 40 than to 60, and that more people survive to the age of 60 than to 80. When translated into statistical terms, this concept is known as a **survival curve.** A survival curve represents the percentage of people or animals alive at various ages. Survival curves support the idea of a biological limit to the life span because more members of a species die as they approach the upper limit. With respect to humans, the curve currently ends around age 100, meaning few people survive past this age.

This Japanese woman's active lifestyle has contributed to her long healthy life. GCShutter/E+/Getty Images

variable-rate theories
Theories that explain biological aging as a result of processes that involve damage to biological systems and that vary from person to person.

free radicals
Unstable, highly reactive atoms or molecules, formed during metabolism, that can cause internal bodily damage.

survival curve
A curve on a graph showing the percentage of people or animals alive at various ages.

THE OLDEST OLD

Some people will far outlive the average life expectancy of 78.6 years for Americans (National Center for Health Statistics, 2019). Research has increasingly been able to pinpoint factors that keep the "oldest-old" alive, often decades longer, than their peers.

Nearly no one reaches advanced age without health issues, but a characteristic shared by the oldest-old is resilience against disease. Their bodies are subject to extended aging processes, much greater risk for disease than younger people, and they are more likely to be frail or dependent (Sole-Auro & Crimmins, 2013). However, they are still around.

Genetics appears to be important and can explain about 25 percent of the variation in human longevity (Passarino et al., 2016). Centenarians appear to possess longevity-assuring genes. These genes seem to counteract age-related molecular damage, loss in function, and cognitive decline (Arai et al., 2014, Arai, 2017). Although discovering the genetic variants that lead to longevity might provide us with clues to help us, the research is challenging to conduct. Sample sizes are only as large as the minority of individuals who reach exceptionally old age (Santos-Lozano et al., 2016).

Lifestyle factors are also key influencers of longevity and successful aging. Health status in old age represents a lifetime accumulation of behaviors. Avoidance of obesity and smoking and engaging in regular exercise are critical lifestyle factors for healthy aging (Ferdows et al., 2017). The most important of these factors may be exercise. Exercise is clearly beneficial from a physical point of view by, for example,

reducing the risk of obesity and cardiovascular disease. However, it is perhaps even more important with respect to the maintenance of cognitive abilities. Meta-analysis examining the longitudinal impact of physical activity on cognitive decline has found physical activity is associated with a long-term 18 percent reduction in risk of dementia. Exercise is linked to increased oxygen consumption and cerebral brain flow, which may explain why it helps preserve brain health and cognitive performance (Blondell et al., 2014).

Successful aging also has much to do with psychosocial factors. For instance, social interactions are strongly associated and interact with positive affect. Although all people benefit from social interaction, those who have the greatest levels of education and better cognitive functioning are able to engage in more frequent and intense social interactions, which, in turn, contribute to higher levels of positive affect (Cho et al., 2015). Similarly, family contact, specifically when such interaction is positive, may help stave off depressive symptoms and promote well-being (Fuller-Iglesias et al., 2015).

what's your view

Have you ever known someone who lived past 100 years old? To what did that person attribute his or her longevity?

Because genetics plays at least a partial role in human longevity (Coles, 2004), some believe the idea of an exponential increase in the human life span is unrealistic. It has been assumed that gains in life expectancy have come from reductions in age-related diseases, such as heart disease, cancer, and stroke. Thus further gains should be far more difficult to achieve unless scientists find ways to modify the basic processes of aging (Hayflick, 2004; Holliday, 2004).

However, this assumption is now being questioned (Vaupel, 2010). Scientists have extended the healthy life spans of worms, fruit flies, and mice through slight genetic mutations (Ishii et al., 1998; Kolata, 1999; Lin et al., 1998; Parkes et al., 1998; Pennisi, 1998). In human beings, of course, genetic control of a biological process may be far more complex. Moreover, because no single gene or process seems responsible for senescence and the end of life, we are less likely to find genetic quick fixes for human aging (Holliday, 2004). Last, techniques that show promise in shorter-lived species may not apply to humans.

Optimists, however, point to data showing continued increase in longevity. In the United States, the number of centenarians increased from roughly 50,000 people in 2000 to 82,248 in 2017 (Administration for Community Living, 2019; Research in Action).

Data show that although different dynamics are playing out in different countries, the increase in longevity is not uncommon (World Health Organization, 2016). In the countries with the highest life expectancy, longevity has increased by 2.5 years every decade (Oeppen & Vaupel, 2002). Interestingly, death rates actually *decrease* after 100 (Coles, 2004). People at 110 are no more likely to die in a given year than people in their 80s (Vaupel et al., 1998). In other words, people hardy enough to reach a certain age are likely to go on living a while longer.

When people who live to be very old are examined, it appears that morbidity—or being in a state of disease—is being compressed. In other words, these people are reaching old age in relatively good health. However, once they begin to deteriorate, they do so very quickly. So although the overall rate of aging is unchanged, the process of aging itself seems to have been postponed, presumably because of good health (Andersen et al., 2012). Given this finding, the question then becomes: Can we postpone aging even more, delay aging until even later, and thus increase the life span? This has been termed the *longevity riddle* (Vaupel, 2010).

The answer to this question remains to be seen; however, it raises important issues. It suggests that increasing the healthy life span—a goal worthy in itself—may itself increase life expectancy. It also suggests the most fruitful area for longevity interventions should be focused on risk reduction and living a healthy lifestyle (Fries et al., 2011). There are possible economic benefits to this approach. Morbidity compression could lead to people living longer lives, while simultaneously decreasing medical costs because of the compression of poor health at the tail end of the life span (Cutler et al., 2013).

One line of research—inspired by rate-of-living theories that view energy use as the crucial determinant of aging—is on dietary restriction. Drastic caloric reduction has been found to greatly extend life in worms, fish, and monkeys—in fact, in nearly all animal species on which it has been tried (Colman et al., 2014; Heilbronn & Ravussin, 2003). A review of 15 years of research suggests that calorie restriction can have beneficial effects on human aging and life expectancy (Fontana & Klein, 2007). Calorie-restricted monkeys also show less of the brain atrophy that sometimes accompanies aging (Colman et al., 2009), a promising finding that may have implications for brain health. There are multiple studies in both humans and other primates demonstrating that calorie restriction, as long as nutrients such as vitamins and minerals are consumed in adequate amounts, is associated with positive changes in markers related to disease risk and aging. For instance, in humans, calorie restriction is associated with a reduced incidence of heart disease, cancer, and diabetes, as well as reduced damage or loss of neurons, fewer age-related declines in muscle tissue and less hearing loss (Most et al., 2017).

Given a very-low-calorie diet takes great discipline to maintain, there is increasing interest in developing drugs that mimic the effects of caloric restriction (Fontana et al., 2010). Additionally, intermittent fasting, where food is eaten only during some hours of the day, holds some promise as well. Research suggests it may exert a similar effect on metabolic processes as calorie restriction (Martin et al., 2006) while being easier to maintain on a long-term basis. Last, a more general and holistic approach to aging, with medications used *before* the advent of aging-related disease, might show more promise for extending life in humans (Partridge, 2010).

Physical Changes

With age, skin tends to become paler and less elastic, and, as fat and muscle shrink, the skin may wrinkle. Varicose veins may appear on the legs. The hair on the head thins and turns gray and then white, and body hair becomes sparser. Older adults become shorter as the disks between their spinal vertebrae atrophy. In addition, the chemical composition of the bones changes, creating a greater risk of fractures. Less visible but equally important changes affect internal organs and body systems; the brain; and sensory, motor, and sexual functioning.

ORGANIC AND SYSTEMIC CHANGES

Changes in organic and systemic functioning are highly variable. Some body systems decline rapidly, and others hardly at all (Figure 17.3). There are, however, typical age-related declines in most people. The lungs, for example, become less effective because of reductions in lung volume, atrophy in the muscles involved with breathing, and reductions in the ability of cilia (hairlike structures that clear mucus and dirt out of the lungs) to function effectively (Lowery et al., 2013). Although there are normative age-related declines in immune system functioning, stress can exacerbate this process, making older people more susceptible to developing disease or worsening preexisting conditions (Morey et al., 2015). Heart health suffers as well. Elderly adults are more likely to suffer from arrhythmia (irregular heartbeat), the muscle walls of the heart may thicken, and the valves that control the flow of blood in and out of the heart may no longer open completely. These heart changes result in impaired capacity for pumping blood, and thus decreases in cardiovascular fitness (Lee et al., 2011). Chronic stress in older adults is also related to chronic low-grade inflammation, putting older adults at risk for cognitive declines and disease (Jurgens & Johnson, 2012; Wirtz & von Kanel, 2017; Heffner, 2011). Problems with swallowing food, gastric reflux, indigestion, irritable bowel syndrome, constipation, and reduced absorption of nutrients become more common with age (Grassi et al., 2011). This puts elderly people at higher risk of malnutrition (Harris et al., 2008), especially if they have chronic diseases or are dependent on others for assistance in daily activities (Ulger et al., 2010; Saka et al., 2010).

Reserve capacity is the backup capacity that helps body systems function to their utmost limits in times of stress. With age, reserve levels tend to drop, and many older people cannot respond to extra physical demands as they once did. For example, a person who used to be able to shovel snow from the entire driveway easily may become exhausted from shoveling just the front entry.

THE AGING BRAIN

As people become older, there are declines in the brain's ability to process information rapidly, in executive functioning, and in episodic memory (Hughes et al., 2018; Fjell & Walhovd, 2010). However, in normal, healthy people, changes in the aging brain are generally subtle and make little difference in functioning. This is because the brain retains a significant degree of plasticity and can compensate for the challenges of aging by reorganizing neural circuitry and working around the problem (Cabeza et al., 2018; Park & Gutchess, 2006). Thus the declines seen in the aging brain are not as severe. For example, there are age-related changes in functional connectivity, the ways in which different areas of the brain coordinate with each other during a task. In general, imaging studies have found reduced functional connectivity during tasks. However, there is more diffuse activation (more brain areas are used for completing tasks) to compensate. This is particularly true when tasks are challenging (Sala-Llonch et al., 2015; Geerligs et al., 2014).

Some areas of the brain may even become more active with age. For example, there are increases in prefrontal activity (associated with effortful, controlled tasks) with age (Eyler et al., 2011; Park & Reuter-Lorenz, 2009). This results in a shift toward "semanticized cognition" in older adults. In other words, older adults utilize their vast store of knowledge to strategically bolster their diminishing processing capacities, allowing them to compensate with slower, although often better, decision making (Spreng & Turner, 2019).

In late adulthood, the brain gradually diminishes in volume and weight, particularly in the frontal and temporal regions (Fjell & Walhovd, 2010; Lockhart & DeCarli, 2014). The hippocampus—the seat of memory—also shrinks (Raz et al., 2010). There is also a reduction in cortical thickness (Lemaitre et al., 2012). This gradual shrinkage was formerly

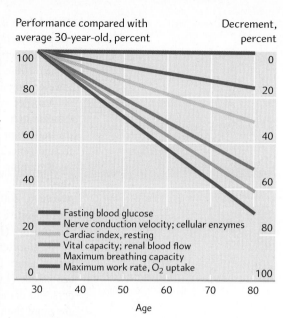

FIGURE 17.3

Declines in Organ Functioning

Differences in functional efficiency of various internal body systems are typically slight in young adulthood but widen by old age.

Source: Katchadourian, H. (1987). *Fifty: Midlife in perspective.* New York, NY: W. H. Freeman.

reserve capacity
The backup capacity that helps body systems function to their utmost limits in times of stress.

attributed to a loss of neurons (nerve cells). However, most researchers now agree that—except in certain specific brain areas, such as the cerebellum, which coordinates sensory and motor activity—neuronal loss is not substantial and does not affect cognition (Burke & Barnes, 2006; Finch & Zelinski, 2005). When the pace of these brain changes increases, however, cognitive declines are increasingly likely (Carlson et al., 2008).

Another typical change is a decrease in the number, or density, of dopamine neurotransmitters due to losses of synapses (neuronal connections). Dopamine receptors are important as they help in regulating attention (Park & Reuter-Lorenz, 2009). This decline generally results in slowed response time.

Beginning in the midfifties, the myelin sheathing that enables neuronal impulses to travel rapidly between brain regions begins to thin (Natrajan et al., 2015; Hinman & Abraham, 2007). This deterioration of the brain's myelin, or white matter, is associated with cognitive and motor declines (Liu et al., 2017), although physical exercise can slow this process (Fleischman et al., 2015).

Postmortem examinations of brain tissue have found significant DNA damage in certain genes that affect learning and memory in most very old people and some middle-age people (Lu et al., 2004). Such changes are associated with neurodegenerative disorders and dementia (Madabhushi et al., 2014). Although adults over the age of 90 years are more than 25 times more likely to develop dementia than those age 65 to 69 years (Brayne, 2007), such deterioration is not inevitable.

Not all changes in the brain are destructive. Researchers have discovered that older brains can grow new nerve cells from stem cells—something once thought impossible. Evidence of cell division has been found in the hippocampus, a portion of the brain involved in learning and memory (Seib & Martin-Villalba, 2015; Chaker et al., 2016). It appears likely that in humans, physical activity paired with cognitive challenges may be most effective in promoting the growth of new cells in the hippocampus (Kempermann, 2015; Di Bennedetto et al., 2017). Moreover, those older adults who maintain a sense of purpose later in life retain a larger volume of gray matter in their insular cortex when compared to adults without this orientation (Ryff et al., 2016). Findings such as these highlight the plasticity and possibility for positive change in the aging brain even late in life.

SENSORY AND PSYCHOMOTOR FUNCTIONING

Individual differences in sensory and motor functioning increase with age. Some older people experience sharp declines; others find their abilities virtually unchanged. Visual and hearing problems may deprive them of social relationships and independence, and motor impairments may limit everyday activities.

Vision and Hearing Older eyes need more light to see, are more sensitive to glare, and may have trouble locating and reading signs. Thus driving may become hazardous, especially at night. Older adults may have difficulty with depth or color perception or with such daily activities as reading, sewing, shopping, and cooking (Desai et al., 2001). Losses in visual contrast sensitivity can cause difficulty reading very small or very light print (Owsley, 2011). Vision problems can also cause accidents and falls (Lord et al., 2010). Many community-dwelling older adults report difficulty with bathing, dressing, and walking around the house, in part because they are visually impaired (Desai et al., 2001; Kempen et al., 2012).

People with moderate visual losses often can be helped by corrective lenses or changes in the environment. Although only 2.3 percent of U.S adults from 40 to 49 years of age have a visual impairment, by 80 years old, 50 percent of adults—currently about 1.61 million people—need glasses to see well (Varma et al., 2016). Women are more likely to have a visual impairment or be blind than men are (Bourne et al., 2017). Globally, estimates are that 2.2 billion people have some form of visual impairment (World Health Organization, 2020).

Cataracts, cloudy or opaque areas in the lens of the eye, are common in older adults and eventually cause blurred vision. Approximately 26 million Americans are currently affected by cataracts (Wittenborn & Rein, 2014), which are more common

cataracts
Cloudy or opaque areas in the lens of the eye, which cause blurred vision.

in white than African American and Hispanic populations (National Eye Institute, 2019). Worldwide, 94 million people are visually impaired and 20 million are blind because of cataracts (Lee & Afshari, 2017; Pascolini & Mariotti, 2012). Surgery to remove cataracts is one of the most frequent operations among older Americans and is generally quite successful. Cataract surgery is associated with a reduction in mortality risk of up to 60 percent (Tseng et al., 2017; Tseng et al., 2016). Presumably the reduction in mortality risk results from a number of factors tied to vision, such as greater ease and accuracy in taking medications, greater likelihood of staying physically active, and lower accident risk.

The leading cause of visual impairment in older adults is **age-related macular degeneration.** The macula is a small spot in the center of the retina that helps us keep objects directly in our line of sight in sharp focus. In the most common form of macular degeneration, the retinal cells in this area degenerate over time, and the center of the retina gradually loses the ability to sharply distinguish fine details. Activities such as reading and driving become extremely problematic, as the exact area in which a person focuses becomes blurry. In some cases, treatments using antioxidant and zinc supplements and drugs that block the growth of abnormal blood vessels under the retina can prevent further vision loss, but cannot reverse loss that has already occurred (Foundation Fighting Blindness, 2017).

Glaucoma is irreversible damage to the optic nerve caused by increased pressure in the eye. Glaucoma can be treated with eye drops, pills, or surgery. Early treatment can lower elevated pressure in the eye and delay the onset of the condition. However, even with treatment, 10 percent of people who get glaucoma will eventually go blind. In the United States, approximately 120,000 people are blind from glaucoma (Glaucoma Research Foundation, 2017). Worldwide, glaucoma is the second leading cause of blindness (World Health Organization, 2020), and in 2013 approximately 64.3 million people were affected by glaucoma (Tham et al. 2014).

Globally, about 432 million adults have disabling hearing loss—a permanent hearing loss in the better ear of more than 40 decibels (World Health Organization, 2020). In the United States, approximately 42 million adults have some form of hearing loss (National Health Interview Survey, 2018; U.S. Census Bureau, 2020).

Hearing impairments increase with age. About 17.8 percent of adults aged 45 to 64 have difficulty hearing. By 65 to 74 years, the proportion of affected adults rises to 31.6 percent, and then 47.2 percent for people 75 and older. Men are approximately 1½ times as likely to experience a hearing impairment, and American Indians, Alaska natives, and white people are more likely to be affected than those of other ethnicities (National Health Interview Survey, 2018). Hearing loss tends to have a negative impact

age-related macular degeneration Condition in which the center of the retina gradually loses its ability to discern fine details; leading cause of irreversible visual impairment in older adults.

glaucoma Irreversible damage to the optic nerve caused by increased pressure in the eye.

In age-related macular degeneration the center of the retina gradually loses visual acuity. In these photos, the left is an image as seen by a person with normal vision and the right is the same image as seen by a person with macular degeneration. National Eye Institute, National Institutes of Health

on the well-being of the impaired person and is associated with loneliness, isolation, disrupted social and family relationships, and decline in social activities (Ciorba et al., 2012). Hearing aids can help but are expensive and may magnify background noises as well as the sounds a person wants to hear. Only 1 in 3 adults aged 70 or older who would benefit from the use of hearing aids uses them (National Institute on Deafness and Other Communication Disorders, 2016).

Changes in environmental design, such as brighter reading lights, a closed captioning option on television sets, and built-in telephone amplifiers can help many older adults with sensory limitations.

Physical Changes with Aging Generally, aging results in a variety of changes related to physical abilities, including increases in body fat and declines in muscle strength, aerobic capacity, flexibility, and agility. Generally, the loss of strength is greater for lower than for upper limbs. The average loss in strength for older adults is approximately 1 to 2 percent annually, a rate that likely increases after age 75 in the absence of physical activity. Flexibility also declines, although less so for women than for men. The declines are related to aging as well as to decreases in physical activity (Milanovic et al., 2013).

These physical changes contribute to falls (Trombetti et al., 2016). Falls, the most common cause of fractures, become increasingly common with age (National Center for Injury Prevention and Control, 2016). At age 65 to 74, the rate of fractures is approximately 9 per 1,000 adults. By 85 years of age and older, the rate of fractures reaches 51 per 1,000 adults (Levant et al., 2015). Many falls are preventable by eliminating hazards commonly found in the home. Additionally, some physical changes of age contributing to falls can be reversed or slowed. A recent review showed that exercise interventions using multiple-component exercises, resistance training, balance training, and endurance training reduced the risk of falls and improved balance, endurance, and elderly people's ease of walking (Cadore et al., 2013).

functional fitness
Exercises or activities that improve daily activity.

Functional fitness refers to exercises or activities that improve daily activity. It has implications for all ages, but it is perhaps most relevant to elderly adults, who may have increasing difficulty in performing the activities of daily living necessary for independence. Levels of functional fitness decline with age in concert with physical activity in a bidirectional fashion (Milanovic et al., 2013). In other words, becoming less physically active over time results in declines in functional fitness. Those functional fitness declines then lead to less physical activity as movements become harder to execute.

Although intervention programs using resistance training in the elderly have shown that it is possible to increase muscle strength, there is limited data on how simple increases in strength transfer to everyday movements. Research does show that strength training interventions can help active older adults improve balance and mobility (Copeland et al., 2019). However, functional fitness interventions that specifically mimic desired actions show more practical success. For example, rather than using a seated leg press, an elderly person might be coached by being asked to sit down and rise from a chair while wearing a weighted vest. A meta-analysis of 13 studies on functional fitness intervention programs showed that such programs were effective in increasing performance in everyday life, and that they were more effective than merely focusing on muscle strength (Liu et al., 2014).

Part of the reason for these gains is that the primary factor in older adults is likely to be a training-induced adaptation in the brain's ability to coordinate motor and brain activity (Voss et al., 2010; Barry & Carson, 2004). For example, vacuuming requires muscle strength in the arms and legs, dynamic balance, control of range of motion, gross and fine motor movements, and the coordination of all movements together (Liu et al., 2014). Thus functional fitness is as much cognitive as it is physical.

Currently, a large literature exists documenting the positive effects of exercise on cognition. Exercise improves cognitive health in chronically ill adults, helps prevent cognitive declines in healthy adults, and appears to do so regardless of when started and what particular type of exercise is done (Northey et al., 2018; Cai et al., 2017; Gomes-Osman et al., 2018; Bherer et al., 2013).

SLEEP

Older people tend to sleep and dream less than before. Their hours of deep sleep are more restricted, and they may awaken more easily and earlier in the morning (Pace-Schott & Spencer, 2014). To some extent, this is driven by normative changes in circadian (daily) rhythms. However, the assumption that sleep problems are normal in old age can be dangerous (Mattis & Sehgal, 2016). Poor sleep quality or chronic insomnia can contribute to depression, neurodegenerative disorders such as dementia, and cognitive declines (Baglioni et al., 2011; Lee et al., 2013; Miyata et al., 2013). Either too much sleep or too little sleep is associated with an increased risk of mortality (Gangwisch et al., 2008; Chen et al., 2013).

The American College of Physicians (ACP) recommends that the first line of defense against insomnia and sleep disorders is the use of cognitive-behavioral therapy (Qaseem et al., 2016). Such therapy may include instructions on, for example, staying in bed only when asleep, getting up at the same time each morning, and learning about false beliefs pertaining to sleep needs. This type of therapy has produced improvements, with or without drug treatment (Lovato et al., 2014; Reynolds et al., 1999). However, if it is not effective, the ACP recommends short-term use medications be considered. The most commonly prescribed drugs include benzodiazepines (e.g., Halcion, Ativan), non-benzodiazepine hypnotics (e.g., Ambien), and suvorexant (e.g., Belsomra), a drug that works via altering the signaling of neurotransmitters that regulate sleep.

SEXUAL FUNCTIONING

Contrary to stereotypes, a sizable number of adults remain sexually active late into adulthood. In a national survey, 38.9 percent of U.S. men age 75 to 85 and 16.8 percent of women reported being sexually active (Lindau & Gavrilova, 2010). Men retain more sexual desire; however, both men and women report a decline in sexual desire with age (Aggarwal, 2013) and women report a greater decline in sexual activity (Lee et al., 2016). Ageism and stereotypes about the elderly may negatively influence sexual desire in older adults (Heywood et al., 2017), although more recent cohorts report a more positive attitude about sexuality in old age, higher satisfaction in their sex lives, less sexual dysfunction, and higher rates of sexual activity than previous cohorts (DeLamater, 2012).

Sex is different in late adulthood from what it was earlier. Men typically take longer to develop an erection and to ejaculate, may need more manual stimulation, may experience longer intervals between erections, or may have difficult achieving an erection. Women report more difficulties with becoming aroused and experiencing orgasm, breast engorgement and other signs of sexual arousal are less intense than before, and they may experience issues with lubrication (Lee et al., 2016; Lindau et al., 2007). Health problems are more likely to affect the sex life of women than men, but poor mental health and relationship dissatisfaction are associated with sexual dysfunction in both men and women (Laumann et al., 2008).

Sexual activity in older people is normal and healthy. Housing arrangements and care providers should consider the sexual needs of elderly people. Satisfaction with life, cognitive functioning, and psychological well-being are all strongly related to interest in and having sex (Syme, 2014; Trudel et al., 2008). However, the most consistent predictors are health status and the presence of a relationship partner (Schick et al., 2010; DeLamater, 2012). Physicians should avoid prescribing drugs that interfere with sexual functioning if alternatives are available and, when such a drug must be taken, should alert the patient to its effects.

Physical and Mental Health

Increasing life expectancy is raising pressing questions about the relationship between longevity and health, both physical and mental. How healthy are older adults today, and how can they stave off declines in health?

HEALTH STATUS

Poor health is not an inevitable consequence of aging. About 78 percent of U.S. adults age 65 and older consider themselves in good to excellent health (Federal Interagency Forum on Aging-Related Statistics, 2016). As earlier in life, poverty is strongly related to poor health and to limited access to, and use of, health care (National Center for Health Statistics, 2018). For instance, poverty is related to a higher incidence of arthritis, diabetes, high blood pressure, heart disease, depression, and stroke in the elderly (Menec et al., 2010).

COVID-19 Risk and Age As the COVID-19 pandemic progressed, it became increasingly clear older people were at higher risk of serious complications, hospitalizations, and death than younger people (World Health Organization, 2020), with the greatest risk occurring for those adults over 85 years of age (CDC COVID-19 Response Team 2020). The presence of comorbid chronic health conditions, most commonly high blood pressure, obesity, and diabetes, significantly elevated risk as well (Richardson et al., 2020). As of August 2020, deaths from COVID-19 were on track to becoming the third leading cause of death in the United States (Kochanek et al., 2019), and the pandemic was expected to continue to exert effects in the coming year.

There has been controversy about how best to count the death toll in the wake of the pandemic. When people become ill and die from COVID-19 infection, their deaths may be either the direct result of the virus or due to complications associated with preexisting chronic diseases. Additionally, any people who died from COVID-19 but were not tested for its presence might not have been included in the official count. Last, because of infection concerns, many people were not visiting doctors or hospitals when they previously would have. Thus the effects of avoiding preventative health care are also an indirect influence on overall death rates, even though they are not directly tied to COVID-19 infections.

In late August 2020, estimates of American deaths resulting directly from COVID-19 infection surpassed 187,000 (Worldometer, 2020). However, the true cost is much higher. Another way to estimate the death toll is to compare expected deaths to actual deaths regardless of the cause of death. In other words, by comparing how many people have *usually* died at a particular time of year to how many people *actually* died, we can get a more accurate representation of how COVID-19 has affected mortality. When viewed in this way, it is clear that COVID-19 is resulting in much higher death tolls in places in which the virus has spread (Centers for Disease Control and Prevention, 2020). The full extent of the virus' impact is yet to be seen; however, all indications are it will exert a brutally high cost on human lives across the globe.

CHRONIC CONDITIONS AND DISABILITIES

More than 2 out of 3 Americans have multiple chronic conditions. People with chronic health conditions are likely to have a lower quality of life and are at risk of disability and death (Gill & Moore, 2013).

Common Chronic Conditions In 2016, the six top leading causes of death in the United States—heart disease, cancer, chronic lower respiratory disease, stroke, Alzheimer's disease, and diabetes—were chronic conditions (Federal Interagency Forum on Aging-Related Statistics, 2016). More than two-thirds of health care costs involve the management of chronic disease (Gill & Moore, 2013). Worldwide, the leading causes of death at age 50 to 69 and older are heart disease, cancers, respiratory disease, and digestive disease. By 70 years and older, dementia becomes the fourth leading cause of death (Ritchie & Roser, 2019).

Many of these deaths could be prevented through healthier lifestyles. If Americans were to quit smoking, eat a healthier diet, and engage in higher levels of physical activity, estimates are that approximately 35 percent of deaths could be prevented in the elderly (Centers for Disease Control & Merck Company Foundation, 2007). The overall need for health care services for this population is expected to increase markedly over the next two decades (Centers for Disease Control and Prevention, 2013).

Rates of death as a result of diabetes declined recently, although it is still the sixth leading cause of death. Approximately 23 percent of men and 19 percent of women report being diagnosed with diabetes in the United States. Hypertension has increased in prevalence, affecting about 55 percent of men and 58 percent of women (Federal Interagency Forum on Aging-Related Statistics, 2016). Hypertension, which can affect blood flow to the brain, is related to declines in attention, learning, memory, executive functions, psychomotor abilities, and visual, perceptual, and spatial skills and is a risk factor for stroke. Aside from hypertension and diabetes, the most common chronic conditions are arthritis (43 percent of men and 54 percent of women), heart disease (35 percent of men and 25 percent of women), and cancer (26 percent of men and 21 percent of women) (Federal Interagency Forum on Aging-Related Statistics, 2016).

Chronic conditions vary by race/ethnicity. For example, in 2013–2014, 71 percent of older Blacks had hypertension, compared with 54 percent of older whites and Hispanics. Older Blacks and Hispanics were significantly more likely than older whites to have diabetes—both 32 percent, as compared with 18 percent for older whites (Federal Interagency Forum on Aging-Related Statistics, 2016).

Disabilities and Activity Limitations The proportion of older adults in the United States with chronic physical disabilities or activity limitations has declined since the late 1990s (Federal Interagency Forum on Aging-Related Statistics, 2016), perhaps due in part to the increasing number of older people who are educated and knowledgeable about preventive measures. However, the proportion of people who have difficulty with functional activities rises sharply with age (National Center for Health Statistics, 2010). Approximately 34 percent of people age 65 to 74 have functional impairments, compared with 48 percent of those 75 to 84 and 74 percent of those 85 and above (Federal Interagency Forum on Aging-Related Statistics, 2016).

In the presence of chronic conditions and loss of reserve capacity, even a minor illness or injury can have serious repercussions. In one study looking at older adults hospitalized after a fall, those adults were more likely to die or be placed in a nursing home than adults admitted to the hospital for reasons unrelated to a fall (Aitken et al., 2010).

LIFESTYLE INFLUENCES ON HEALTH AND LONGEVITY

The chances of remaining healthy and fit in late life often depend on lifestyle choices, especially related to smoking, heavy drinking, and exercise (Vu et al., 2009).

Physical Activity A lifelong program of exercise may prevent many physical changes once associated with normal aging. Regular exercise can strengthen the heart and lungs and decrease stress. It can protect against hypertension, hardening of the arteries, heart disease, osteoporosis, and diabetes. It helps maintain speed, stamina, strength, and endurance, and such basic functions as circulation and breathing. It reduces the chance of injuries by making joints and muscles stronger and more flexible, and it helps prevent or relieve lower-back pain and symptoms of arthritis. It can enable people with such conditions as lung disease and arthritis to remain independent and can help prevent the development of limitations on mobility. In addition, it may improve mental alertness and cognitive performance, help relieve anxiety and mild depression, and enhance feelings of mastery and well-being (Bauman et al., 2016; Wilson et al., 2016; Stubbs et al., 2017; Colberg et al., 2016; Cartee et al., 2016).

*In*activity contributes to heart disease, diabetes, colon cancer, and high blood pressure. It may lead to obesity, which affects the circulatory system, the kidneys, and sugar metabolism; contributes to degenerative disorders; and tends to

Exercise helps these men live longer, healthier lives, and the social aspect of their shared activities keeps them mentally healthy. Uwe Krejci/Stone/Getty Images

shorten life. Unfortunately, many older adults do not do enough. Current recommendations call for a minimum of 150 minutes of moderate aerobic activity over the course of a week, or slightly more than 20 minutes a day. Additional exercise is ideal, but anything is better than nothing (Centers for Disease Control and Prevention, 2018). Almost 28 percent of adults 50 years and older without a chronic disease are physically inactive. Moreover, adults who have at least one chronic disease are 40 percent less likely to be physically active (Watson et al., 2016).

Nutrition Almost 80 percent of Americans age 71 and older fail to meet the criteria for a healthy diet, most notably by eating too many empty calories (Krebs-Smith et al., 2010). Generally, older women (when compared to older men) (Ervin, 2008) and people of higher economic status (Wang et al., 2014) consume a healthier diet.

Nutrition plays a large part in susceptibility to such chronic illnesses as atherosclerosis, heart disease, and diabetes as well as functional and activity limitations. Excessive body fat, particularly from a diet heavy in red and processed meats and alcohol, has been linked to several types of cancer (World Cancer Research Fund, 2007). Although weight gain is not healthy for older adults, neither is excessive weight loss. Excessive weight loss can lead to muscle weakness and general frailty, and it can be as debilitating to older adults as weight gain (Schlenker, 2010).

A healthy diet can reduce risks of obesity as well as of high blood pressure and cholesterol (Federal Interagency Forum on Aging-Related Statistics, 2016). A diet high in olive oil, whole grains, vegetables, and nuts has been found to reduce cardiovascular risk (Esposito et al., 2004) and—in combination with physical activity, moderate alcohol use, and refraining from smoking—cut 10-year mortality from all causes in healthy 70- to 90-year-old Europeans by nearly two-thirds (Rosamond et al., 2008). Eating fruits and vegetables—especially those rich in vitamin C, citrus fruits and juices, green leafy vegetables, broccoli, cabbage, cauliflower, and Brussels sprouts—lowers the risk of cancer and heart disease (Takachi et al., 2007). Overall, a healthy diet is associated with a higher quality of life in older adults (Govindaraju et al., 2018).

Periodontal disease is a chronic inflammation of the gums caused by the bacteria in plaque. It can result in tender or bleeding gums and eventual tooth loss. Although more aging Americans are keeping their natural teeth than ever before, 16 percent of adults age 65 to 74 and 31 percent of those 75 and older have no teeth (Federal Interagency Forum on Aging-Related Statistics, 2016). Those older adults with fewer than 20 teeth may suffer from malnutrition (Hassan et al., 2017) as a result of the increased difficulty in adequately chewing food. Periodontal disease has also been related to cognitive declines (Kaye et al., 2010) and cardiovascular disease (Blaizot et al., 2009). Some suggest it may impair the regulation of blood sugar as well (Zadik et al., 2010).

MENTAL AND BEHAVIORAL PROBLEMS

Only 6.3 percent of Americans 75 years and older report frequent mental distress (Centers for Disease Control and Prevention, 2013). However, mental and behavioral disturbances that do occur can result in functional impairment in major life activities as well as cognitive decline (van Hooren et al., 2005).

Depression Across the world, approximately 264 million people are affected by depression. Although depression can be treated with therapy and drugs, between 76 and 85 percent of people in low- to middle-income families are not able to access treatment. Reasons for the lack of access include a lack of medical and health care resources, poverty, incorrect diagnosis, and social stigma associated with mental disorders (World Health Organization, 2020).

In the United States, rates of reported depressive symptomatology stayed relatively stable since the late 1990s. In 2016, 11 percent of older men and 16 percent of older women in the United States reported symptoms of clinical depression (Federal Interagency Forum on Aging-Related Statistics, 2016). The COVID-19 pandemic resulted in somewhat higher rates of depression in the elderly, but less so than in other age groups (Centers for Disease Control and Prevention, 2020).

Heredity has been estimated to account for 37 percent of the risk for major depression; however, genetic influences may be more important in women than in men (Mullins & Lewis, 2017; Petkus et al., 2017). Genes for depression do not work on their own—they interact with environmental risk factors to raise vulnerability. Special risk factors in late adulthood include chronic illness or disability, cognitive decline, and divorce, separation, or widowhood (Harvard Medical School, 2003; Mueller et al., 2004). In men, low social support, most commonly the result of living alone and having a small social circle, is strongly related to depression risk (Sonnenberg et al., 2013). Depression plays a more pervasive role in mental functional status, disability, and quality of life than do physical ailments such as diabetes or arthritis (Noël et al., 2004).

Depression can be treated by antidepressant drugs, psychotherapy, or both, and antidepressant drugs appear to work equally as well as they do at younger ages (Blazer, 2009). Regular exercise can reduce symptoms of mild to moderate depression (Stanton & Reaburn, 2014; Dunn et al., 2005), although this may not be true for very frail older adults (Underwood et al., 2013).

Dementia Sixty-nine-year-old Rose has become increasingly forgetful. Although her memory for long ago events is sharp, she often repeats herself or finds herself standing in her kitchen, unsure of why she walked in. She has multiple unpaid bills and got lost driving home from the store in the past week. Rose may be experiencing dementia.

Dementia is the general term for physiologically caused cognitive and behavioral decline sufficient to interfere with daily activities. Cognitive decline becomes increasingly common with advanced age, affecting 11 percent of men and 13 percent of women age 75 to 84, and 24 percent of men and 30 percent of women 85 and over (Federal Interagency Forum on Aging-Related Statistics, 2016). Worldwide, there are approximately 50 million people with dementia, 60 percent of whom live in low- and middle-income countries. Approximately 10 million new cases develop every year, and estimates are that by 2030, there will be 82 million adults worldwide suffering from dementia (World Health Organization, 2020). Although there are about 50 causes of dementia of known origin, the vast majority of cases (about two-thirds) are caused by **Alzheimer's disease,** a progressive, degenerative brain disorder (Hamza et al., 2011).

Parkinson's disease, the second most common disorder involving progressive neurological degeneration, is characterized by tremor, stiffness, slowed movement, and unstable posture. Although estimates vary widely, at 60 years of age, slightly less than half of 1 percent of people are affected with Parkinson's disease. By 80, the proportion of affected people rises to slightly under 2 percent, with the proportion of affected men rising with increasing age (Pringsheim et al., 2014).

Another condition leading to cognitive difficulties is *multi-infarct dementia* (MD). MD is the result of a series of small strokes resulting in lesions in both white and gray matter in the brain. MD often leads to difficulties with attention, memory, abnormalities in emotional expression, and difficulty walking (McKay & Counts, 2017). MD likely coexists with Alzheimer's disease in many older adults; 25 to 80 percent of adults diagnosed with Alzheimer's disease also show evidence of lesions (Jellinger, 2013).

Alzheimer's Disease Alzheimer's disease (AD) is one of the most common and most feared terminal illnesses among aging persons. It gradually robs patients of intelligence, awareness, and even the ability to control their bodily functions—and finally kills them. The disease affected more than 50 million people in 2018 and is expected to more than triple to 152 million by 2050 (Patterson, 2018).

Alzheimer's disease is the sixth leading cause of the death in the United States, and the fifth leading cause for those 65 years and older. Approximately 5.8 million Americans are living with AD, 80 percent of whom are over 75 years of age. Almost two-thirds of affected individuals are women. Older African Americans have about double the risk and Hispanics have about 1½ times the risk for AD or other cognitive impairments as

dementia
Deterioration in cognitive and behavioral functioning due to physiological causes.

Alzheimer's disease
Progressive, irreversible, degenerative brain disorder characterized by cognitive deterioration and loss of control of bodily functions, leading to death.

Parkinson's disease
Progressive, irreversible degenerative neurological disorder, characterized by tremor, stiffness, slowed movement, and unstable posture.

do non-Hispanic white adults, likely due to variations in medical conditions, health-related behaviors, and poverty (Alzheimer's Association, 2020).

Symptoms The classic symptoms of Alzheimer's disease are memory impairment, deterioration of language, and deficits in visual and spatial processing. The most prominent early symptom is inability to recall recent events or take in new information. A person may repeat questions that were just answered or leave an everyday task unfinished. These early signs may be overlooked because they look like ordinary forgetfulness or may be interpreted as signs of normal aging.

Personality changes—for instance, rigidity, apathy, egocentricity, and impaired emotional control—tend to occur early in the disease's development (Balsis et al., 2005). There are indications that these personality changes may be useful in predicting which healthy adults might be at risk of developing dementia (Duchek et al., 2007). More symptoms follow: irritability, anxiety, depression, and, later, delusions, delirium, and wandering. Long-term memory, judgment, concentration, orientation, and speech all become impaired, and patients have trouble handling basic activities of daily life. By the end, the patient cannot understand or use language, does not recognize family members, cannot eat without help, cannot control the bowels and bladder, and loses the ability to walk, sit up, and swallow solid food (Alzheimer's Association, 2020).

Causes and Risk Factors Accumulation of an abnormal protein called *beta amyloid peptide* appears to be the main culprit contributing to the development of Alzheimer's disease (Sadigh-Eteghad et al., 2015; Selkoe & Hardy, 2016). The brain of a person with AD contains excessive amounts of **neurofibrillary tangles** (twisted masses of dead neurons) and large waxy clumps of **amyloid plaque** (nonfunctioning tissue formed by beta amyloid in the spaces between neurons). Because these plaques are insoluble, the brain cannot clear them away. They may become dense, spread, and destroy surrounding neurons.

There is growing evidence that one of the primary mechanisms driving the progression of neurodegenerative disease is the breakdown of myelin, the fatty substance that coats axons and allows neural impulses to travel more rapidly. Myelin affords our brains some of their great complexity, but it also makes us vulnerable to neurodegenerative disease in old age, particularly in late developing areas of the brain (Bartzokis et al., 2007;

neurofibrillary tangles
Twisted masses of protein fibers found in brains of persons with Alzheimer's disease.

amyloid plaque
Waxy chunks of insoluble tissue found in brains of persons with Alzheimer's disease.

Esther Lipman Rosenthal's battle with Alzheimer's disease is evident in her artwork. She created the picture on the top, showing her husband golfing, at age 55, and the picture on the bottom, showing him on cross-country skis, at age 75, during the early and middle stages of her disease. Photos courtesy of Linda Goldman. Artwork by Esther Lipman Rosenthal. Photos ©Linda Lee Goldman

Wang et al., 2018). In this theory, neurodegenerative disease is a consequence of the brain's efforts to repair broken-down myelin, which result in the release of neurofibrillary tangles and amyloid plaques. These substances can damage neurons directly, but the brain is also affected by the compromised myelin (Papuc & Rejdak, 2017; Amlien & Fjell, 2014). When attempts to restore myelin are successful, disease progression is slow. However, when this process fails, neurodegenerative disease progresses (Bartzokis, 2011).

Alzheimer's disease is influenced by genetics. Some rare variants caused by dominant mutations and occurring less than 1 percent of the time are associated with early onset dementia (Hsu et al., 2018). However, the majority of dementia cases involve multifactorial effects, where any one of a number of genetic variants may put people at elevated risk. The more variants a person has and the more environmental risk factors they accumulate over the course of a lifetime, the higher the chance of developing AD. Epigenetic modifications that determine whether a particular gene is turned on are important (Lord & Cruchaga, 2014).

For example, a variant of the APOE gene has been found to contribute to susceptibility to both early- and late-onset AD (Van Cauwenberghe et al., 2016). Sex modifies this association; the gene puts women at greater risk than men (Altmann et al., 2014). A variant of another gene called SORL1 has been found to stimulate the formation of amyloid plaques (Reitz et al., 2011). Another gene variant involved in the manufacture of amyloid precursors, Cathepsin D, moderately increases the risk as well (Schuur et al., 2011). A recent meta-analysis of over 450,000 people identified 29 new risk genetic loci that were more common in people with AD (Jansen et al., 2019), and new genes are continually being identified (Lambert et al., 2013). Epigenetic modifications that determine whether a particular gene is activated may also play a part (Lord & Cruchaga, 2014). However, identified genes are thought to explain no more than half of all AD cases.

Although a NIH Consensus Development statement (Daviglus et al., 2010) stated that no firm conclusions could be drawn about lifestyle modifications that might decrease risk for AD, a recent report by the Alzheimer's Association (Baumgart et al., 2015) argued there is enough evidence to provide general guidelines. Regular physical activity and the management of cardiovascular risk factors (diabetes, obesity, hypertension, and smoking), a healthy diet, and remaining cognitively active throughout the life span all offer a protective advantage.

Foods rich in vitamin E, vitamin B-12, omega-3 fatty acids, and unhydrogenated unsaturated fats—such as nuts, seeds, fish, and eggs—may be protective against AD, whereas foods high in saturated and transunsaturated fats, such as red meats, butter, and ice cream, may be harmful. Low levels of vitamin D are also associated with dementia (Barnard et al., 2014; Morris, 2004; Cao et al., 2016). A lack of regular physical activity also puts people at risk for later dementia (Baumgart et al., 2015), and instituting an exercise program even late in life may help reverse some of the early signs of cognitive impairment in otherwise healthy adults (Lautenschlager et al., 2008).

Smokers have increased risk of AD (Saito et al., 2017; Durazzo et al., 2014). The consumption of aluminum has also been associated with dementia (Cao et al., 2016). Nonsteroidal anti-inflammatory drugs such as aspirin and ibuprofen were originally thought to cut the risk of AD (Vlad et al., 2008); however, randomized controlled studies have not found an association (Wang et al., 2015).

Cognitive impairment is more likely in people with poor health, especially those who experience strokes or diabetes (Tilvis et al., 2004). Additionally, depression, high blood pressure, obesity, and physical inactivity increase risk (Deckers et al., 2015; Bellou et al., 2017). Because dementia is associated with overall physical health, many of the risk factors for dementia are modifiable. Estimates are that 35 percent of dementia cases could be prevented by modifying a series of risk factors including education, hearing loss, obesity and hypertension, depression, smoking, physical inactivity, diabetes, and social isolation (Yaffe, 2018).

Education and cognitively stimulating activities have been associated with reduced risk of the disorder (Sattler et al., 2012; Xu et al., 2016; Sharp & Gatz, 2011), as has a challenging job (Smart et al., 2014; Seidler et al., 2004), and bilingualism, even in those who are illiterate (Bialystok et al., 2007; Alladi et al., 2013). Essentially, an active mind stays healthy longer. The protective effect may be due not to the particulars of a situation, but rather to the fact that some people tend to be more cognitively active (Wilson & Bennett, 2003). Cognitive activity may build **cognitive reserve** and thus delay the onset of dementia (Stern, 2012). Cognitive reserve, like organ reserve, may enable a deteriorating brain to continue to function under stress, up to a point, without showing signs of impairment.

Certain personality traits seem to confer protection. In particular, high conscientiousness and low neuroticism offer advantages (Low et al., 2013; McCann, 2019). Staying engaged with others may be also be beneficial, but results are unclear. Some studies, particularly those that look at adults of different ages, show reductions in dementia risk with social interaction and engagement. Other studies, particularly longitudinal work, show little effect of social networks on dementia (Baumgart et al., 2015; Marioni et al., 2015).

Diagnosis AD is generally diagnosed via medical assessment. A medical history of the patient is taken, including mental status, mood testing, a physical and neurological exam, and blood and imaging tests in order to rule out alternative explanations (Alzheimer's Association, 2020).

Neuroimaging is becoming an increasingly useful tool and shows great promise for future diagnostic purposes. The identification of AD prior to symptom onset has a variety of important applications, from assessing those individuals at risk of developing dementia, to monitoring interventions and drug treatments, and to allowing people time to plan for their future. A number of organizations, including the U.S. Preventive Services Task Force Recommendation Services, The Society of Nuclear Medicine and Molecular Imaging, the Alzheimer's Association Imaging Taskforce, and the European Federation of the Neurological Societies, have published guidelines about the use of and applications for imaging techniques in diagnosis and study. All agree that currently, brain imaging is not sufficient for diagnosis, but it holds great promise (Moyer, 2014; Johnson et al., 2013; Filippi et al., 2012). A particularly promising avenue involves the use of machine learning methods. Currently, computer-assisted algorithms have become proficient at distinguishing healthy brains from those suffering the effects of dementia but are not yet able to differentiate between different types of dementia (Ahmed et al., 2019; Pellegrini et al., 2018).

Another diagnostic approach has focused on finding biomarkers—a measurable indicator of a biological process—to diagnose early manifestations of the disease. Currently, three biomarkers have been strongly associated with dementia risk: tau proteins, amyloid plaques, and neurofilament light chains (NFLs). Tau proteins help deliver materials to neurons; however, in AD they become twisted into neurofibrillary tangles. Amyloid is a protein found throughout the body that in AD results in plaques of sticky buildup. NFL is a protein released when myelin is tangled. Researchers have used technology to detect all three substances in the cerebral and spinal fluid of people with AD (Olsson et al., 2016; Georganopoulou et al., 2005). Importantly, biomarker tests also show promise for ruling out AD in people showing impairment (Molinuevo et al., 2014).

Despite the identification of several genes associated with AD (Kim et al., 2014), genetic testing so far has a limited role in prediction and diagnosis. Still, it may be useful in combination with cognitive tests, brain scans, clinical evidence of symptoms, and predictive AI technology (Graham et al., 2020). There is evidence that people alter their health behaviors if told they have genes making them vulnerable to dementia (Chao et al., 2008), so such information may someday become part of the way in which the medical profession addresses risk in individuals. Genetic profiles may also offer a means by which to predict which drugs might be most effective in different individuals (Roses et al., 2014).

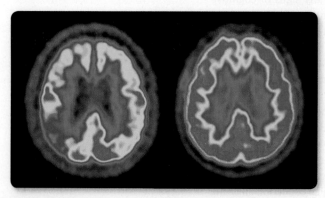

These PET (positron emission tomography) scans show a significant decrease of glucose cerebral metabolism and reduced activity (left) in a patient with Alzheimer's disease, compared to the greater activity levels seen in an unaffected brain (right). DIOMEDIA /ISM /Centre Jean PERRIN

cognitive reserve
Hypothesized fund of energy that may enable a deteriorating brain to continue to function normally.

Whatever the technique used, the identification of AD prior to symptom onset has a variety of important applications, from assessing those individuals at risk of developing dementia to monitoring interventions and drug treatments of affected people, to allowing people time to plan for their future.

Treatment Although no cure has yet been found, early diagnosis and treatment of Alzheimer's disease can improve quality of life. Currently, none of the five drugs approved by the U.S. Food and Drug Administration slows or stops the progression of Alzheimer's disease. However, four have a beneficial effect on cognitive processes by temporarily increasing the levels of available neurotransmitters in the brain. Memantine (commercially known as Namenda) works by blocking the excess stimulation of receptors, thereby limiting damage to nerve cells (Alzheimer's Association, 2020).

Another experimental approach involved immunotherapy (Solomon & Frenkel, 2010). In this approach, a "vaccine" was developed that trained the immune system to attack amyloid plaques. Although there was some success in early trials, they were halted because some patients developed meningoencephalitis, or swelling of their brain tissue, and others showed little change (Panza et al., 2014).

In the absence of a cure, management of the disease is critical. In the early stages, cognitive training interventions demonstrated gains in both cognitive and behavioral areas (Sitzer et al., 2006). More current research suggests the gains may be more modest. Recent meta-analyses have shown that although cognitive interventions do sometimes result in small cognitive gains, the benefits are not usually clinically significant and there are few improvements in everyday functioning (Kallio et al., 2017; Huntley et al., 2015). Moreover, whereas cognitive training improves performance in healthy older adults, there is little evidence that it delays cognitive declines or dementia (Butler et al., 2018).

However, behavioral symptoms can be managed. Behavioral therapies can slow deterioration, improve communication, and reduce disruptive behavior. Drugs can relieve agitation, lighten depression, and help patients sleep. Proper nourishment and fluid intake together with exercise, physical therapy, and control of other medical conditions are important, and cooperation between the physician and the caregiver is essential (Alzheimer's Association, 2020).

Cognitive Changes

Let's look first at intelligence and general processing abilities, then at memory, and then at wisdom, which is popularly associated with the later years.

INTELLIGENCE AND PROCESSING ABILITIES

Does intelligence diminish in late adulthood? The answer depends on what abilities are being measured and how. Some abilities, such as speed of mental processes and abstract reasoning, may decline in later years, but other abilities tend to improve throughout most of adult life.

The Wechsler Adult Intelligence Scale To measure the intelligence of older adults, researchers often use the **Wechsler Adult Intelligence Scale (WAIS)**. The WAIS is a standardized measure that allows assessment of a person's intellectual functioning at different ages. Scores on the WAIS subtests yield a verbal IQ, a performance IQ, and a total IQ. Older adults tend not to perform as well as younger adults on the WAIS, but the difference is primarily in processing speed and nonverbal performance. On the five subtests in the performance scale (such as identifying the missing part of a picture or mastering a maze), scores drop with age, but on the six tests making up the verbal scale—particularly tests of vocabulary, information, and comprehension—scores fall only slightly (Figure 17.4). This is called the *classic aging pattern* (Botwinick, 1984). This age disparity in performance, particularly for processing speed, is smaller in more recent cohorts (Miller et al., 2009)

Wechsler Adult Intelligence Scale (WAIS)
Intelligence test for adults that yields verbal and performance scores as well as a combined score.

WAIS-R, scaled scores

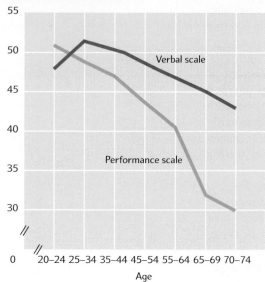

FIGURE 17.4

Classic Aging Pattern on the Revised Version of the Wechsler Adult Intelligence Scale (WAIS-R)

Scores on the performance subtests decline far more rapidly with age than scores on the verbal subtests.

Source: Botwinick, J. (1984). *Aging and behavior* (3rd ed.). New York, NY: Springer.

and does not appear to differ between men and women (Saggino et al., 2014). Variability in scores—meaning that some people score higher than others—increases with age, and particularly in those areas in which average declines are more apparent (Wisdom et al., 2012).

This pattern is likely a consequence of muscular and neurological slowing. For tasks that do not require speed, declines are less likely. For example, verbal items that hold up with age are based on knowledge and do not require the test-taker to figure out or do anything new. The performance tasks involve the processing of new information and require perceptual speed and motor skills.

The Seattle Longitudinal Study In some ways, the mind can be thought of as a muscle. It too responds to use, and it too declines if not engaged in the world around us. This "use it or lose it" dynamic is illustrated with research from the Seattle Longitudinal Study of Adult Intelligence. Researchers measured six primary mental abilities: verbal meaning, word fluency, number (computational ability), spatial orientation, inductive reasoning, and perceptual speed. Consistent with other studies, perceptual speed tends to decline earliest and most rapidly. Cognitive decline in other respects is slower and more variable. Very few people weaken in all abilities, and many improve in some areas. Most fairly healthy older adults show only small losses until the late sixties or seventies. Not until the eighties do they consistently fall below the average performance of younger adults, and even then, only in about half of people, and less so in verbal abilities and reasoning (Schaie & Willis, 2010; Schaie, 2005).

The most striking feature of the Seattle findings is the tremendous variation among individuals. Some participants show declines during their forties, but a few maintain full functioning very late in life. Those most likely to show declines are men who have low educational levels, are dissatisfied with their success in life, and exhibit a significant decrease in flexibility of personality. Some health-related variables are also important, most notably, hypertension and diabetes. Participants who engaged in cognitively complex work, who were in good health, and who exercised tended to retain their abilities longer. Engaging in activities that challenge cognitive skills promotes the retention or growth of those skills and, as mentioned earlier, may protect against dementia (Schaie & Willis, 2010; Willis & Schaie, 2005; Lindwall et al., 2012).

Cognitive deterioration, then, often may be related to disuse. Much as many aging athletes can call on physical reserves, older people who get training, practice, and social support seem to be able to draw on mental reserves.

Changes in Processing Abilities In many older adults, a general slowdown in central nervous system functioning is a major contributor to losses of efficiency of information processing and changes in cognitive abilities. Speed of processing, one of the first abilities to decline, is related to health status, balance, and gait and to performance of activities of daily living, such as looking up phone numbers and counting out change (Ball et al., 2007; Bezdicek et al., 2016).

One ability that tends to slow with age is ease in switching attention from one task to another (Bucur & Madden, 2010). This finding may help explain why many older adults have difficulty driving, which requires rapid attentional shifts (Duley & Adams, 2013; Bialystok et al., 2004). Training can improve older adults' performance. Participation in such programs has been shown to extend the period of time before older adults are forced to stop driving, to allow them to more effectively and independently complete activities of daily living to a later age, and to reduce symptoms of depression (Edwards et al., 2009; Wolinsky et al., 2015).

Although age-related declines in processing abilities occur, it is not inevitable in daily life. Older adults use their vast reservoirs of knowledge to work around problems and compensate for declines that do occur (Peters et al., 2007). Generally, older adults tend to do better on tasks that depend on ingrained habits and knowledge (Bialystok et al., 2004). It is likely that older adults are using alternative, although complementary, neural circuits for more difficult tasks. In support of this, imaging research shows differences in how older adults process information relative to younger adults. In particular, decreases in processing speed are associated with decreased specialization in areas of the brain—a process known as *dedifferentiation* (Park & McDonough, 2013). It may be that cognitive interventions are exerting their influence by restructuring the pathways used to complete difficult tasks (Park & Reuter-Lorenz, 2009).

Everyday Problem Solving The purpose of intelligence, of course, is not to take tests or process information as quickly as possible but to deal with the challenges of daily life. In many studies, the quality of practical decisions (such as what car to buy or how to compare insurance policies) bore only a modest relationship, if any, to performance on tasks like those on intelligence tests (Blanchard-Fields, 2007; Meyer et al., 1995). Similarly, much research on everyday problem solving (such as what to do about a flooded basement) has not found as early a decline as is often seen in measures of fluid intelligence, and some research has found marked improvement (Blanchard-Fields et al., 2004; Mienaltwoski, 2011), particularly when the contexts being assessed are those that older people are familiar with (Artistico et al., 2010).

Age differences are reduced in studies that focus on *interpersonal* problems—such as how to deal with a new mother who insists on showing her older mother-in-law how to hold the baby—rather than on *instrumental* problems—such as how to return defective merchandise (Thornton & Dumke, 2005). Older adults have more extensive repertoires of strategies to apply to interpersonal situations than younger adults do, they tend to minimize tension and disagreement and emphasize positive emotions, they are more likely to chose a highly effective strategy than are younger adults, and they are more likely to use their past successes or failures when asked to make a choice about something (Blanchard-Fields et al., 2007; Fingerman & Charles, 2010; Worthy & Maddox, 2012).

Cognitive Functioning and Mortality Risk Psychometric intelligence may be a predictor of how long and in what condition adults will live. In one longitudinal study, people who scored high in intelligence as children were less likely to suffer from poor health or have chronic health conditions at age 50 (Wraw et al., 2015). Other longitudinal work showed high intelligence in childhood was associated with a lower risk of mortality at age 79 (Cukic et al., 2017). Cognitive performance is also linked to physical health in adulthood as well. For example, physically frail older adults are at higher risk for cognitive impairment (Robertson et al., 2013), and people who have been critically ill often show cognitive impairments for up to a year after they recover (Pandharipande et al., 2013). Moreover, the inability to complete activities of daily living is associated with more rapid cognitive declines (Gerstorf et al., 2013).

Some researchers argue the link between intelligence and mortality is an artifact of methodological confounds in research. For example, studies that include childhood adversity within the models are less likely to find a link between intelligence and mortality (Kilgour et al., 2010). Socioeconomic status (SES) may also matter. Some studies have found that childhood SES does not seem to attenuate the link between intelligence and health (Der et al., 2009). However, when adult SES is included in models, the strength of the relationship between health and intelligence is lessened (Calvin et al., 2010). Yet another interpretation is that, as many diseases such as diabetes and hypertension may lead *both* to cognitive declines earlier in life *and* an earlier death, data showing a link between the two may reflect the action of the disease instead of an association between IQ and mortality (Batty et al., 2007).

MEMORY

Failing memory is often considered a sign of aging. Thirty-five percent of older Americans report their top concern about aging is loss of memory (National Council on Aging, 2015).

Moreover, 53 percent of adults without dementia age 40 to 79 years report experiencing memory concerns (Luck et al., 2018) and slightly under 19 percent of adults age 65 and older have cognitive impairment without dementia (Langa et al., 2017).

Short-Term Memory Researchers assess short-term memory by asking a person to repeat a sequence of numbers, either in the order in which they were presented (*digit span forward*) or in reverse order (*digit span backward*). Digit span forward ability holds up well with advancing age (Craik & Jennings, 1992; Wingfield & Stine, 1989) but digit span backward performance does not (Craik & Jennings, 1992; Lovelace, 1990). Why? One reason may involve the differentiation of sensory and working memory. **Sensory memory** involves the brief storage of sensory information. For example, when you see the trail left behind by a Fourth of July sparkler, you are seeing the trace left by your sensory memory. **Working memory** involves the short-term storage of information being actively processed, such as when you calculate the tip for a restaurant bill in your head. Some theorists argue that forward repetition requires only sensory memory, which retains efficiency throughout life. Therefore, declines in this area are more rare. However, backward repetition requires the manipulation of information in working memory, which gradually shrinks in capacity with age (Hale et al., 2011).

A key factor in memory performance is the complexity of the task (Park & Reuter-Lorenz, 2009). Tasks that require only *rehearsal,* or repetition, show very little decline. Tasks that require *reorganization* or *elaboration* show greater falloff (Emery et al., 2008). If you are asked to verbally rearrange a series of items (such as "Band-Aid, elephant, newspaper") in order of increasing size ("Band-Aid, newspaper, elephant"), you must call to mind your previous knowledge of Band-Aids, newspapers, and elephants (Cherry & Park, 1993). More mental effort is needed to keep this additional information in mind, using more of the limited capacity of working memory.

Long-Term Memory Information-processing researchers divide long-term memory into three major systems: *episodic memory, semantic memory,* and *procedural memory.*

Do you remember what you had for breakfast this morning? Such information is stored in **episodic memory,** the long-term memory system most likely to deteriorate with age (Park & Gutchess, 2005; Tromp et al., 2015). Episodic memory is linked to specific events; you retrieve an item by reconstructing the original experience in your mind. Older adults are less able than younger people to do so, perhaps because they focus less on context (where something happened, who was there), and rely more on gist than details (Dodson & Schacter, 2002). Because of this, they have fewer connections to jog their memory (Lovelace, 1990). Also, older people have had many similar experiences that tend to run together. When older people perceive an event as distinctive, they can remember it nearly as well as younger people (Geraci et al., 2009). Declines in episodic memory can be predicted on the basis of declines in working memory, perhaps because it becomes more difficult for older adults to integrate new information with existing memory structures (Memel et al., 2019).

Some types of long-term memories remain vigorous as people age. **Semantic memory** consists of meanings, facts, and concepts accumulated over a lifetime of learning. Semantic memory shows little decline with age, although infrequently used or highly specific information may sometimes be difficult to retrieve (Luo & Craik, 2008). Indeed, some aspects of semantic memory, such as vocabulary and knowledge of rules of language, may even increase with age (Camp, 1989).

Another long-term memory system that remains relatively unaffected is procedural memory. **Procedural memory** includes motor skills (like riding a bike) and habits (like taking a particular street home) that, once learned, take little conscious effort. It is relatively unaffected by age (Fleischman et al., 2004; Lezak et al., 2012). Moreover, new procedural memories that are formed in old age may be retained for at least 2 years (Smith et al., 2005) even though they may take a bit more time to learn initially (Iaria et al., 2009).

sensory memory
Initial, brief, temporary storage of sensory information.

working memory
Short-term storage of information being actively processed.

episodic memory
Long-term memory of specific experiences or events, linked to time and place.

semantic memory
Long-term memory of general factual knowledge, social customs, and language.

procedural memory
Long-term memory of motor skills, habits, and ways of doing things, which can be recalled without conscious effort; sometimes called *implicit memory.*

Riding a bicycle requires procedural memory. Once learned, procedural skills can be activated without conscious effort, even after a long period of disuse.
shapecharge/E+/Getty Images

Aging Effects on Speech and Memory As people become older, they often begin to have minor difficulties with language. However, these experiences are not generally due to issues related to language per se but rather are the result of problems accessing and retrieving information from memory. The core language processes remain relatively unchanged across age (Shafto & Tyler, 2014). Thus issues are considered memory problems rather than language problems.

For example, have you ever been unable to come up with a word that you knew perfectly well? This is known as the tip-of-the-tongue (TOT) phenomenon; it occurs in people of all ages but becomes more common in late adulthood (Abrams & Davis, 2016). Presumably, the TOT phenomenon results from a failure in working memory (Schwartz, 2008) and is not a consequence of older adults having a larger vocabulary, and thus more interference when searching for words (Shafto et al., 2017). Other problems in verbal retrieval include errors in naming pictures of objects aloud, more ambiguous references and slips of the tongue in everyday speech, more use of nonfluencies (such as "um" and "er") in speech, and a tendency to misspell words (such as *indict*) that are spelled differently than they sound (Burke & Shafto, 2004).

Correlates of Memory System Declines What explains older adults' memory losses? Investigators have offered several hypotheses. One approach focuses on biological structures and the other on the processing of information.

Neurological Change Theory suggests that declines in cognitive performance should be associated with structural changes in the brain, which research has generally confirmed. For example, myelin in the brain allows for faster conduction of nerve impulses, which should theoretically affect processing speed. Research has shown that processing speed and myelin integrity follow a similar trajectory: a U-shaped curve peaking at midlife (Bartzokis et al., 2010). As another example, working memory declines are associated in healthy older adults with decreased cortical surface area in the right frontal regions of the brain (Nissim et al., 2017).

Different memory systems depend on different brain structures. Thus a disorder that damages a particular brain structure may impair the type of memory associated with it. For example, Alzheimer's disease disrupts working memory (located in the prefrontal cortex at the front of the frontal lobes) as well as semantic and episodic memory (located in the frontal and temporal lobes); Parkinson's disease affects procedural memory, located in the cerebellum, basal ganglia, and other areas (Budson & Price, 2005).

The main structures involved in normal memory processing and storage include the *frontal lobes* and the *hippocampus.* The *frontal lobes* are active in both encoding and retrieval of episodic memories. Dysfunction of the frontal lobes may cause false memories—"remembering" events that never occurred. Specifically, changes in the prefrontal cortex and medial temporal lobes seem to be most responsible (Devitt & Schacter, 2016).

The *hippocampus,* a small, centrally located structure deep in the temporal lobe, seems critical to the ability to store new information in episodic memory and is broadly important for memory processes. Research with adults in their seventies and older has shown that better memory is associated with larger hippocampal volume. In one study, adults who were 75 years of age and older who performed well on memory tests had larger hippocampal volume (Dekhtyar et al., 2017; O'Shea et al., 2016).

The brain often compensates for age-related declines in specialized regions by tapping other regions to help. Younger adults are more likely to use localized areas of the brain during challenging tasks, whereas older adults are more likely to use more diffuse activation and utilize more or different brain areas as compensatory mechanisms for declines (Sala-Llonch et al., 2015). The brain's ability to shift functions may help explain why symptoms of Alzheimer's disease often do not appear until the disease is well advanced and previously unaffected regions of the brain, which have taken over for impaired regions, lose their own working capacity. By the time signs of damage show, the disease has likely existed for decades.

Problems in Encoding, Storage, and Retrieval Episodic memory is particularly vulnerable to the effects of aging, an effect that is aggravated as memory tasks become more complex or demanding (Cansino, 2009). Older adults seem to have more difficulty *encoding* new episodic memories, presumably because of difficulties in forming and later recalling a coherent and cohesive episode. Because of more limited processing resources, they tend to be less efficient and precise than younger adults in the use of strategies to make it easier to remember—for example, by arranging material alphabetically or creating mental associations (Craik et al., 2012). Most studies have found that older and younger adults are about equally knowledgeable as to effective encoding strategies but that older adults tend to use them less frequently (Salthouse, 1991). Some research has found that training older adults in memory strategies results in fewer age-related declines and that the larger the number of strategies taught, the larger the effect on memory (Gross et al., 2012; Naveh-Benjamin et al., 2007). However, other researchers have argued that the memory gains are limited, do not generalize to tasks other than those participants are trained in, and do not result in improvements in general memory performance (Bellander et al., 2017).

Another hypothesis is that material in *storage* may deteriorate to the point where retrieval becomes difficult or impossible. Some research suggests that a small increase in "storage failure" may occur with age (Lustig & Flegal, 2008). However, traces of decayed memories are likely to remain, and it may be possible to reconstruct them, or at least to relearn the material speedily (Camp & McKitrick, 1989; Chafetz, 1992). In particular, it appears as if memories that contain an emotional component are more resistant to the effects of decay (Kensinger, 2009). For example, studies have found that older adults are motivated to preserve memories that have positive emotional meaning to them (Reed et al., 2014; Carstensen & Mikels, 2005). Thus emotional factors need to be considered in studying memory changes in old age.

We should keep in mind that most of the research on encoding, storage, and retrieval has been done in the laboratory and that results may not transfer to the real world (Kempe et al., 2015). For example, in daily diary studies, older adults were more likely to report memory failures on days when they experienced stress, suggesting stress is relevant (Neupert et al., 2006). As another example, memory failures of older adults in daily life often include prospective memory failures. Prospective memory involves remembering to do something in the future, such as remembering to call a friend later. Prospective memory declines with age and is a significant issue for many older adults. However, the research in this area is incomplete and does not illuminate the central processes that govern failure (Kliegel et al., 2016).

WISDOM

Wisdom has been defined as "exceptional breadth and depth of knowledge about the conditions of life and human affairs and reflective judgment about the application of this knowledge. It may involve insight and awareness of the uncertain, paradoxical nature of reality and may lead to *transcendence,* detachment from preoccupation with the self" (Kramer, 2003, p. 132). Quite simply, wisdom is the ability to navigate the messiness of life. It involves understanding how people work and how to accomplish goals. People who are wise, according to psychologists, are also comfortable with uncertainty and understand that different people have different viewpoints and that sometimes there is no one right answer.

The most extensive research on wisdom as a cognitive ability has been done by the late Paul Baltes and his colleagues. In a series of studies, they asked adults of various ages and occupations to think aloud about hypothetical dilemmas. Responses were rated according to whether they showed rich factual and procedural knowledge about the human condition and about dealing with life's problems. Other criteria were awareness that contextual circumstances can influence problems, that problems tend to lend themselves to multiple interpretations and solutions, and that choices of solutions depend on individual values, goals, and priorities (Baltes & Staudinger, 2000; Pasupathi et al., 2001).

In general, people who are older are better at negotiating social problems than those who are younger (Grossman et al., 2010). Wisdom is not just a property of old age—or of any age. Instead, it appears to be a rather rare and complex phenomenon that shows relative stability or slight growth in certain individuals (Staudinger & Baltes, 1996; Staudinger et al., 1992). A variety of factors, including personality, life experiences, and self-reflective tendencies (Weststrate & Gluck, 2017; Wink & Staudinger, 2016; Shedlock & Cornelius, 2003), affect the propensity to be wise. Culture is also an influence. For example, whereas age and wisdom are associated in American samples, in Japanese samples, younger- and middle-age adults reason as wisely as older adults (Grossman et al., 2012).

Research on physical functioning, cognition, and aging is more encouraging than some might expect. Older adults tend to make the most of their abilities, often exploiting gains in one area to offset declines in another. Wisdom, for example, is associated with well-being, particularly for nursing home residents and hospice patients as compared to healthy older adults (Ardelt & Edwards, 2016). Research highlights the widely varying paths of physical and cognitive development among individuals.

summary and key terms

Old Age Today

- Efforts to combat ageism are making headway.
- The proportion of older people in the United States and world populations is greater than ever before and is expected to continue to grow. People over 80 are the fastest-growing age group.
- Although effects of primary aging may be beyond people's control, they often can avoid effects of secondary aging.
- Specialists in the study of aging sometimes refer to people between age 65 and 74 as the *young old*, those over 75 as the *old old*, and those over 85 as the *oldest old*. However, these terms may be more useful when used to refer to functional age.

ageism, primary aging, secondary aging, activities of daily living (ADL), functional age, gerontology, geriatrics

Physical Aging and Longevity

- Life expectancy has increased dramatically.
- In general, life expectancy is greater in developed countries than in developing countries, among Hispanics and white Americans than among African Americans, and among women as compared to men.
- Recent gains in life expectancy come largely from progress toward reducing death rates from diseases affecting older people.
- Many older people are staying healthier longer, but then decline rapidly once their health starts to fail. This is known as morbidity compression and may offer clues to increasing life expectancy.
- Theories of biological aging fall into two categories: genetic-programming theories and variable-rate, or error, theories.
- Research on extension of the life span through genetic manipulation or caloric restriction has challenged the idea of a biological limit to the life span.

life expectancy, longevity, life span, senescence, genetic-programming theories, Hayflick limit, variable-rate theories, free radicals, survival curve

Physical Changes

- Changes in body systems and organs are highly variable. Reserve capacity declines.
- Although the brain changes with age, the changes are usually modest. They include loss of volume and weight and a slowing of responses. However, the brain can compensate for some problems by changing how it processes information.
- Vision and hearing problems may interfere with daily life but often can be corrected. Irreversible damage may result from age-related macular degeneration or glaucoma. Losses in taste and smell may lead to poor nutrition.
- Functional fitness interventions show promise. Training can improve muscular strength, balance, and reaction time. Older adults tend to be susceptible to accidents and falls.
- Older people tend to sleep less and dream less than before. Chronic insomnia or poor sleep can contribute to health problems.
- Many older adults remain sexually active.

reserve capacity, cataracts, age-related macular degeneration, glaucoma, functional fitness

Physical and Mental Health

- Most older people are reasonably healthy. Many have chronic conditions, but these usually do not greatly limit activities or interfere with daily life. Chronic conditions are less likely with a healthy lifestyle.
- Older people are more likely than younger people to suffer from complications or death from COVID-19. Their risk is especially high if they also have chronic conditions.

- Exercise and diet are important influences on health. Loss of teeth can seriously affect nutrition.
- Most older people are in good mental health. Depression, alcoholism, and many other conditions can be reversed with treatment; a few, such as Alzheimer's disease, are irreversible.
- Alzheimer's disease becomes more prevalent with age. It is highly heritable, but diet, exercise, and other lifestyle factors may play a part. Cognitive activity may be protective by building up a cognitive reserve that enables the brain to function under stress. Behavioral and drug therapies can slow deterioration. Researchers are developing tools for early diagnosis.

  dementia, Alzheimer's disease, Parkinson's disease, neurofibrillary tangles, amyloid plaque, cognitive reserve

Aspects of Cognitive Development

- Older adults do better on the verbal portion of the Wechsler Adult Intelligence Scale than on the performance portion.
- The Seattle Longitudinal Study found that cognitive functioning in late adulthood is highly variable. Few people decline in all or most areas, and many people improve in some.

- Older adults are more effective in solving practical problems.
- A general slowdown in central nervous system functioning may affect the speed of information processing.
- Intelligence may be a predictor of longevity.
- Sensory memory, semantic memory, and procedural memory appear nearly as efficient in older adults as in younger adults. The capacity of working memory and episodic memory are often less efficient.
- Older adults have more problems with oral word retrieval and spelling than younger adults. Grammatical complexity and content of speech decline.
- Neurological changes and problems in encoding, storage, and retrieval may account for much of the decline in memory functioning in older adults. However, the brain can compensate for some age-related declines.
- Older people show considerable plasticity in cognitive performance and can benefit from training.
- According to Baltes's studies, wisdom is not age-related, but people of all ages give wiser responses to problems affecting their own age group.

  Wechsler Adult Intelligence Scale (WAIS), sensory memory, working memory, episodic memory, semantic memory, procedural memory

Design Credit: (globe) janrysavy/Getty Images

Psychosocial Development in Late Adulthood

chapter 18

Visoot Uthairam/EyeEm/Getty Images

learning objectives

Discuss theories and research on personality changes in late adulthood.

Identify strategies and resources that contribute to older adults' well-being and mental health.

Discuss aging and adaptation to work and retirement.

Characterize the social relationships of aging adults.

In this chapter, we look at theory and research on psychosocial development in late adulthood and discuss such late-life options as work, retirement, and living arrangements and their impact on society's ability to support and care for an aging population. Finally, we look at relationships with families and friends, which greatly affect the quality of these last years.

Dr. Anthony Fauci, one of the world's leading experts on infectious diseases, served as an advisor to every president since Ronald Reagan and became a leading member of the White House Coronavirus Task Force in 2020 at age 79. dpa picture alliance/Alamy Stock Photo

ego integrity versus despair
According to Erikson, the eighth and final stage of psychosocial development, in which people in late adulthood either achieve a sense of integrity of the self by accepting the lives they have lived, and thus accept death, or yield to despair that their lives cannot be relived.

Personality Development in Late Adulthood

Most theorists view late adulthood as a developmental stage with its own special issues and tasks. It is a time when people can reexamine their lives, complete unfinished business, and decide how best to channel their energies and spend their remaining days, months, or years.

EGO INTEGRITY VERSUS DESPAIR

For Erikson, the crowning achievement of late adulthood is a sense of *ego integrity,* or integrity of the self. In the eighth and final stage of the life span, **ego integrity versus despair,** older adults need to evaluate and accept their lives so as to accept death. Building on the outcomes of the seven previous stages, they struggle to achieve a sense of coherence and wholeness, rather than give way to despair over their inability to relive the past differently (Erikson et al., 1986). People who succeed in this final, integrative task gain a sense of the meaning of their lives within the larger social order. The virtue that may develop during this stage is *wisdom,* an "informed and detached concern with life itself in the face of death itself" (Erikson, 1985, p. 61). Wisdom, said Erikson, means accepting the life one has lived, without major regrets: without dwelling on "might-have-beens." It means accepting imperfection in the self, in parents, in children, and in life.

Although integrity must outweigh despair if this stage is to be resolved successfully, Erikson maintained that some despair is inevitable. People need to mourn—not only for their own misfortunes and lost chances but also for the vulnerability and transience of the human condition.

PERSONALITY TRAITS IN OLD AGE

Does personality change in late life? What is the average pattern of personality change across the life course?

Personality Stability and Change in Late Adulthood Questions about the stability of personality have been an enduring debate. Generally, personality stability follows an inverted U-shaped curve. It is lowest in adolescence, peaks in mid-adulthood, and then declines slightly in late adulthood (Specht et al., 2011; Terracciano et al., 2010). Most of the personality changes seen in late adulthood are in the direction of increased stability, adaptability, and adjustment (Soto et al., 2011; Hopwood et al., 2011).

Although Costa and McCrae reported long-term stability in their data, the stability was in terms of *average levels* of various traits within a population, and people generally maintained their rank order. In other words, particularly outgoing people were likely to remain more outgoing than their peers, even if everyone became slightly more so over time.

Longitudinal and cross-sectional studies using a modified version of their original model have found continued change in late adulthood. Research has shown increases in agreeableness, self-confidence, warmth, emotional stability, and conscientiousness and declines in neuroticism, social vitality (gregariousness), and openness to experience (Soto et al., 2011; Roberts & Mroczek, 2008; Leszko et al., 2016). Contrary to stereotypes of the elderly as rigid and set in their ways, there appear to be no age-related trends in inflexibility (Window on the World reports on stereotypes of older people worldwide). In fact, more recent cohorts, as a whole, seem to be more flexible (that is, less rigid) than previous cohorts (Schaie, 2005).

According to Erikson, ego integrity in late adulthood requires continuing stimulation and challenge, which may come from creative work. Andrea Pistolesi/Stone/Getty Images

on the world

AGING STEREOTYPES AND AGEISM

In America, Australia, the United Kingdom, and many other countries around the world, youth and beauty are idealized, and the elderly are often seen as frail, useless, childlike, and a burden to society. In the media, elders are often portrayed as sick, lonely, and mentally incompetent. Late adulthood is thought of as a time of decline, worry, fear, and loss (Quine et al., 2007).

These negative age stereotypes endorse segregation and discrimination in society, especially in the workplace and health care facilities. Ageism directly undermines political support for programs benefitting older people, including access to health care and medical treatments (Cheng & Heller, 2009). Ageism can directly affect the elderly as they often internalize societal views, hastening physical and mental decline. It has been found that adopting these negative stereotypes can decrease life span up to 7.5 years (Scheve & Venzon, 2017).

The way we view the aging process influences how we age. In cultures in which aging is viewed differently, it is experienced differently as well. For example, in the Tarahumara society in Mexico the belief is that people get stronger as they age. Many elders run great distances and lead healthy active lives

(Scheve & Venzon, 2017). Another example is 106-year-old Fauja Singh from India. He ran his first marathon in his late eighties. His advice: "Exercise daily, eat less, and resist meaningless temptations; with time my vision and hearing have deteriorated, but I'm very fit for my age" (Singh, 2017). Research has shown that elders with positive attitudes about aging show lower rates of mental illness, quicker recovery times from illness and stress, and less cognitive decline, and they live longer (McGuire, 2017).

Social policies are being created focused on increasing education, developing positive images of the elderly, and supporting the continuation of independence and resources for elders. The goals are to increase hope for the future and reduce fears among the elderly and include assisting with financial and health struggles (Quine et al., 2007).

what's your view

What do you think we can do to combat negative stereotypes about the elderly? How can you challenge your own beliefs about the elderly?

Why do people show normative changes in personality characteristics? Some researchers argue that these processes are driven primarily by intrinsic genetic differences between people that unfold over time (Costa & McCrae, 2013). Other researchers argue that life experiences—getting married, joining the workforce, and so on—are the primary drivers of personality change (Roberts et al., 2005). Still others argue explicitly for a consideration both of genetic and environmental influences (Hopwood et al., 2011).

Newer, finer grained analysis suggests that personality change consists of both stability and change and different patterns of change in different individuals, perhaps helping explain the diversity of findings in the literature (Leszko et al., 2016). For instance, there are individual differences in personality stability, peaking at midlife (Schwaba & Bleidorn, 2018). Although personality is a largely stable trait across the life span, there is also partial support for a U-shaped trend in stability with increasing instability later in life. Moreover, some traits, such as extraversion, are relatively stable. Others, such as agreeableness, are more likely to change in response to temporary events (Wagner et al., 2019).

The Influence of Personality on Health and Well-Being Personality is a strong predictor of emotionality and subjective well-being—stronger in most respects than social relationships and health (Isaacowitz & Smith, 2003). A recent meta-synthesis (a secondary meta-analysis of 36 meta-analyses) of more than 500,000 participants examined the influence of the Big Five traits on mental health, physical health, and health-related behaviors. As a whole, there was a strong link between personality and mental health, a moderate link between personality and health-related behaviors, and a weak link between personality and physical health. Moreover, when the personality traits were examined independently, agreeableness, conscientiousness, and neuroticism were stronger predictors than were extraversion and openness to experience (Strickhouser et al., 2017).

Personality can affect mental health through a variety of mechanisms. For instance, low extraversion, high neuroticism, and low conscientiousness predict depression. One possible explanation for this association is that both a particular personality profile and depression might stem from a common cause. Another model posits that personality is a risk factor that might contribute to depression. Yet another model states that although personality does not cause depression, once depression sets in, personality can influence the severity or course depression might take (Hakulinen et al., 2015). Other aspects of mental health might work in a similar fashion.

Why does personality affect physical health? Personality traits influence behavior, and behavior influences health. Highly neurotic people have lower survival rates, possibly because they are likely to smoke or use alcohol or drugs to help calm their negative emotions and because they are ineffective in managing stress (Mroczek & Spiro, 2007). By contrast, conscientiousness might predict health and mortality because conscientious people tend to avoid risky behaviors and to engage in activities that promote their health, such as regular visits to the doctor or the gym (Friedman & Kern, 2014). The riskiest combination appears to be when individuals are both high in neuroticism and low in conscientiousness, as both these patterns are associated with a higher risk of inflammatory responses in the body (Sutin et al., 2010).

Neuroticism appears to be a particularly important trait. People with neurotic personalities (moody, touchy, anxious, and restless) tend to report negative and not positive emotions, and they tend to become even less positive as they age (Charles et al., 2001; Isaacowitz & Smith, 2003). Neuroticism is a far more powerful predictor of moods and mood disorders than variables such as age, health status, education, or gender (Siedlecki et al., 2008; Magee et al., 2013). Neuroticism is in many respects a characteristically negative way of viewing the world. Therefore, it is not surprising that personality variables might be related to general well-being and satisfaction with life (Lucas & Diener, 2009).

The realization that personality *change* can also be predictive moved research away from a primary focus on the static examination of personality to the exploration of how dynamic changes might impact health indices (Leszko et al., 2016). For example, people who remain stable on openness to experience and neuroticism enjoy better reasoning abilities and faster reaction time than those individuals whose levels change (Graham & Lachman, 2012). Additionally, instability in these areas, specifically when neuroticism increases and openness to experience declines, is associated with deterioration in cognitive processing and greater difficulty with activities of daily living (Pocnet et al., 2013).

Some changes are beneficial. For instance, increases in agreeableness, conscientiousness, and extraversion are associated with improved physical and mental health (Magee et al., 2013; Turiano et al., 2011) and social well-being (Hill et al., 2012). Moreover, effects appear to be interactive. For example, in one 4-year longitudinal study of over 16,000 Australian adults, agreeableness, conscientiousness, and extraversion predicted well-being. Those adults who were high in well-being then became even more agreeable, conscientious, and extraverted over time. Thus both personality and well-being exerted reciprocal influences on each other (Soto, 2015).

Well-Being in Late Adulthood

In general, older adults have fewer mental disorders and are happier than younger adults (Mroczek & Kolarz, 1998; Yang, 2008). In fact, a recent study of 340,000 adults showed that happiness is high at approximately 18 years of age, declines until people reach 50 years of age, and then tends to rise again until 85 years of age—at that point reaching levels even higher than in the teenage years (Stone et al., 2010). Once people reach older adulthood, the prevalence of psychiatric disorders tends to decrease through the later decades of life, and gender differences tend to even out (Reynolds et al., 2015).

The rise in happiness seen in American adults later in life may reflect the selective survival of happier people, especially after the age of 70 (Segerstrom et al., 2016). Still, some cohort variations and social disparities exist. For example, baby boomers report lower levels of happiness than do earlier and later cohorts, perhaps due to the immense size of their generation and the resulting competitive strains for schooling, jobs, and economic security, as well as the turbulent societal events of their formative years (Yang, 2008).

Older adults are also better at regulating their emotions, thus they tend to be happier and more cheerful than younger adults and to experience negative emotions less often and more fleetingly (Urry & Gross, 2010; Jacques et al., 2009). Older adults also show a bias in their information processing known as the positivity effect. They are more likely to pay attention to, and then later remember, positive events than negative events (Reed et al., 2014). However, the reciprocal effect between personality and aspects of mental health and well-being exists in both a positive and negative direction—a similar dynamic has been found with personality change and depressive symptoms (Hakulinen et al., 2015).

In some adults there is a sharp and rapid decline in well-being and life satisfaction approximately 3 to 5 years before death known as a "terminal drop." Events more common in the last years of life—the loss of a spouse, increasing mobility limitations, deteriorating health, or the knowledge that the end of life is drawing near—may lead to the declines (Gerstorf et al., 2010; St. John et al., 2015). Researchers have also pointed out that satisfaction with various parts of life need to be examined separately. For example, satisfaction with health, housing, and recreation has not been found to be associated with mortality risk, whereas low satisfaction with religion, self-esteem, and finances has (St. John et al., 2015).

WELL-BEING IN SEXUAL MINORITIES

Those adults who are members of any marginalized group are subject to increased stressors that exert a negative effect on health and well-being. Thus it is not surprising to find that this is true of lesbian, gay, bisexual, and transgender (LGBT) adults. Moreover, for aging gays and lesbians who recognized their homosexuality before the rise of the gay liberation movement, their self-concept tended to be shaped by the then-prevailing stigma and bigotry leveled against sexual minorities. Many older LGBT adults must deal not only with the stigma of being a sexual minority member, but also with stigma leveled against the elderly (Van Wagenen et al., 2013).

LGBT adults report higher rates of depression and are more likely to smoke and drink excessively than heterosexual adults. Moreover, a full 82 percent of LGBT adults report being victimized at least once because of their sexual orientation or gender identity, and 64 percent report being victimized 3 or more times. Approximately 9 percent are HIV positive, and more than half of Americans now living with HIV disease are 50 years or older (Fredericksen-Goldsen et al., 2011). Moreover, few services exist targeting LGBT seniors, often leaving them without an adequate safety net (Abatiell & Adams, 2011). Many have been denied appropriate health care, and more than 20 percent do not disclose their sexual orientation to their health care providers (Fredericksen-Goldsen et al., 2011). Although all LGBT adults are at higher risk than the general population, transgender adults appear to be at even higher risk. When compared to gay, lesbian, and bisexual adults, transgender adults are more likely to suffer from poor physical health, depression, and high stress. They are also likely to report fear of accessing health care services, internalized stigma, and a lack of social support (Frederiksen-Goldsen et al., 2014).

However, not all the news is bad. Most LGBT adults are able to show resilience, and only a minority report failing to cope in a meaningful way (Van Wagenen et al., 2013). Ninety-one percent participate in wellness activities and 82 percent exercise. Moreover, approximately 90 percent report belonging to and feeling good about their community and report adequate social support. As discussed in the following section, religion can also provide protection against life's stressors, and 38 percent of LGBT adults report participating in religious or spiritual activities (Fredericksen-Goldsen et al., 2011).

THE EFFECT OF RELIGION AND ETHNICITY ON WELL-BEING

As a whole, older adults today are more religious than younger adults. In a survey of 106 countries worldwide, younger adults were less likely to say that religion was very important to them in 46 of the countries. In only 2 of the 106 countries were older adults less religious than younger adults (Pew Research Center, 2018). In the United States, 38 percent of younger millennials (born between 1990 and 1996) say religion is very important in their lives. However, 59 percent of baby boomers (born from 1946 to 1964) say the same, and for those over the age of 72, the number rises to 67 percent (Pew Research Center, 2015).

Religion seems to play a supportive role for many older people and can be part of their coping strategy (Melendez et al., 2012). For instance, adults who have been diagnosed with Alzheimer's disease show diminished use of problem-focused coping strategies and increasing use of religion, presumably as a way of managing their declines in functioning (Melendez et al., 2018). Religion may benefit older people by providing social support, encouraging a healthy lifestyle, giving the perception of control over life through prayer, fostering positive emotional states, reducing stress, and using faith in God as a way of interpreting misfortunes (Seybold & Hill, 2001). But does religion actually improve health and well-being?

Many studies suggest a positive link between religion or spirituality and health (Lawler-Row & Elliott, 2009; Powell et al., 2003). Overall, those people who identify with a religion and who attend services at least once a month are more likely to describe themselves as "very happy" than those people who are not actively religious (Marshall, 2019). Other research has found positive associations between religiosity or spirituality and measures of health, well-being, marital satisfaction, and psychological functioning, and negative associations with depression, suicide, delinquency, criminality, and drug and alcohol use (Koenig, 2012; Seybold & Hill, 2001; Bjorklof et al., 2013; Green & Elliott, 2010).

Relatively little of the research on religion and spirituality has been done with racial/ethnic minorities, although many of the patterns that have been found across groups are similar. For example, older Mexican Americans who attend church once a week have a 32 percent lower mortality risk than those who never attend (Hill et al., 2005). Similar results were found in China, with a 21 percent reduction in mortality risk for elderly adults who participated in religious activities on a regular basis as compared to those who did not (Zeng et al., 2011).

An important factor may be the social support provided by church membership and the religious community (Taylor et al., 2017). It appears this support is related to a reduced risk of depression (Chatters et al., 2015). In one national study of over 2,000 Asian Americans, church attendance was associated with a decreased risk of depression. However, this relationship was mediated by social support. In other words, the social support provided by attending church, rather than church attendance per se, was the crucial factor in risk reduction (Ai et al., 2013).

For racial and ethnic minorities, who must deal with the continuing influence of racism and discrimination, religion may play a more important role in their efforts to cope than it does for white Americans (Tabak & Mickelson, 2009). For example, religion is closely related to life satisfaction and well-being in elderly Black people (Park et al., 2018; Krause, 2004). One factor is the belief held by many Black people that the church helps sustain them in confronting racial injustice (Ellison et al., 2017; Ellison et al., 2008).

Another reason for the positive links between health and spirituality is that people who belong to a church are more likely to engage in healthy behaviors (Lawler-Row & Elliott, 2009). Research has shown that this is true with Black adults, and that religious beliefs are associated with greater fruit and vegetable consumption, reductions in alcohol consumption, and

Religious activity seems to help many people cope with stress and loss in later life, and it is associated with health and well-being. ESB Professional/Shutterstock

increases in physical activity (Holt et al., 2014; Debnan et al., 2012). This is true not just within churchgoers in the United States, but globally as well. For example, in one international study, actively religious people were less likely to smoke in 17 of 19 countries surveyed, and in 11 of the 19 countries they were less likely to drink several times a week (Marshall, 2019).

COPING AND MENTAL HEALTH

Coping is adaptive thinking or behavior aimed at reducing or relieving stress that arises from harmful, threatening, or challenging conditions. In the next section, we examine some models of coping.

Cognitive-Appraisal Model In the **cognitive-appraisal model** (Lazarus & Folkman, 1984), people respond to stressful or challenging situations on the basis of two types of analyses. In *primary appraisal,* people analyze a situation and decide, at some level, whether or not the situation is a threat to their well-being. In *secondary appraisal,* people evaluate what can be done to prevent harm and choose a coping strategy to handle the situation. Coping includes anything an individual thinks or does in trying to adapt to stress, regardless of how well it works. Choosing the most appropriate strategy and adapting to the various stressors of life requires a continuous reappraisal of the relationship between person and environment.

Problem-Focused versus Emotion-Focused Coping strategies may be either problem-focused or emotion-focused. **Problem-focused coping** involves the use of *instrumental,* or action-oriented, strategies to eliminate, manage, or improve a stressful condition. For example, some students may feel they are capable of learning the relevant material and can do well on an upcoming exam if they try hard enough. To achieve this, they may use such problem-focused coping strategies as going to the professor for extra help or spending more time studying. By addressing the source of stress, people using problem-focused coping seek to lessen any harm to the self.

Emotion-focused coping, by contrast, involves attempting to manage the emotional response to a stressful situation to relieve its physical or psychological impact. People are more likely to use this coping strategy when they conclude that little or nothing can be done about the situation itself. Thus they direct their energy toward "feeling better" rather than toward any actions meant to change the situation. For example, when faced with a difficult test, some students may select coping strategies that focus on emotions rather than actions. They might ignore the upcoming test and go out with friends instead of studying or become angry with the professor for being unfair. There are two types of emotion-focused coping: *proactive* (confronting or expressing one's emotions or seeking social support) and *passive* (avoidance, denial, suppression of emotions, or acceptance of the situation as it is).

Age Differences in Coping Styles Older adults tend to do more emotion-focused coping than younger people (Trouillet et al., 2011; Melendez et al., 2012); this is particularly true when looking at the oldest old (Martin et al., 2008). Moreover, adults with cognitive impairments and Alzheimer's disease are less likely to use problem-focused coping strategies, in all likelihood because their impairments reduce their capacity for doing so (Meléndez et al., 2018).

Generally, emotion-focused coping is less adaptive than problem-focused coping, but this is only true when something can realistically be done about the problem. When a solution is not available, it may be more adaptive to control negative or unpleasant emotions. Ideally both emotion- and problem-focused coping are available for use, thus allowing a more flexible range of responses to stressful events.

Coping styles are related to physical well-being. In one study of more than 500 older adults, those adults who used problem-focused coping strategies and sought social support in the face of stressful events showed lower levels of cortisol, a stress hormone, over the

coping
Adaptive thinking or behavior aimed at reducing or relieving stress that arises from harmful, threatening, or challenging conditions.

cognitive-appraisal model
Model of coping, proposed by Lazarus and Folkman, that holds that, on the basis of continuous appraisal of their relationship with the environment, people choose appropriate coping strategies to deal with situations that tax their normal resources.

problem-focused coping
In the cognitive-appraisal model, coping strategy directed toward eliminating, managing, or improving a stressful situation.

emotion-focused coping
In the cognitive-appraisal model, coping strategy directed toward managing the emotional response to a stressful situation so as to lessen its physical or psychological impact.

course of the day (O'Donnell et al., 2008). Coping need not be problem-focused for elderly adults to be effective, however. For example, in another study, when older adults had chronic age-related and largely uncontrollable stressors, shifting the emotion state with self-compassion (kindness and concern, rather than pity or self-criticism) was associated with lower cortisol levels (Herriot et al., 2018). The management of stress hormone levels is important because higher cortisol can lead to declines in health over time. For instance, in another study, older adults who did not use adaptive coping strategies and who had high cortisol showed more functional disabilities (i.e., more problems with activities of daily life) over time. Neither those adults who had high cortisol and coped effectively nor those adults who had low cortisol showed similar declines (Wrosch et al., 2009).

MODELS OF SUCCESSFUL AGING

With a growing number of active, healthy older adults, the concept of aging has shifted. *Successful,* or *optimal, aging* has largely replaced the idea that aging results from inevitable, intrinsic processes of loss and decline

A considerable body of work has identified three main components of successful aging: (1) avoidance of disease or disease-related disability, (2) maintenance of high physical and cognitive functioning, and (3) sustained, active engagement in social and productive activities (activities, paid or unpaid, that create social value). Successful agers tend to have social support, both emotional and material, that aids mental health, and they tend to stay active and productive and to perceive low levels of stress in their lives (Rowe & Kahn, 1997; Moore et al., 2015). Another approach emphasizes subjective well-being and satisfaction with life (Jopp & Smith, 2006; Cho et al., 2014). A meta-analysis of studies that included quantitative data as well as a definition of "successful aging" found that approximately one-third of adults over the age of 60 engage in successful aging (Depp & Jeste, 2009).

Many people argue that the definitions of *successful,* or *optimal, aging* are value-laden. These terms may put pressure on elderly people to meet standards they cannot or do not wish to meet. Moreover, the concept of successful aging is culturally bound. Western ideals such as independence, autonomy, control, and continued productivity are presented as the ideal. However, different cultures may not view these traits in the same way (Lamb, 2014).

Keeping these concerns in mind, let's look at some classic and current theories and research about aging well.

disengagement theory
Theory of aging that holds that successful aging is characterized by mutual withdrawal of the older person and society.

activity theory
Theory of aging that holds that to age successfully a person must remain as active as possible.

Disengagement Theory versus Activity Theory Who is making a healthier adjustment to old age: a person who peacefully watches the world go by from a rocking chair or one who keeps busy from morning till night? According to **disengagement theory,** a normal part of aging involves a gradual reduction in social involvement and greater preoccupation with the self. According to **activity theory,** the more active older people remain, the better they age.

Disengagement theory was one of the first theories in gerontology. Its proponents (Cumming & Henry, 1961) regarded disengagement as a normative, or typical, part of aging. They argued that awareness of the approach of death and declines in physical functioning resulted in a gradual, inevitable withdrawal from social roles. Moreover, because society stops providing useful roles for the older adult, the disengagement is mutual—others do not try to stop it.

For a time this approach was influential, but more than five decades of research has provided little support for disengagement theory, and its influence has largely waned (Achenbaum & Bengtson, 1994). This approach may have reflected beliefs about aging at the time it was developed (Moody, 2009) rather than describing a normative and healthy developmental process.

The second approach, *activity theory,* takes the opposing viewpoint. In this theory, we are what we do (Moody, 2009). Rather than retreating from life, adults who age successfully tend to remain engaged with social roles and connections. The more active they remain in those roles, the more satisfied with life they are likely to be. When they lose a role, such as when they retire, they find a substitute role, such as volunteering (Lemon et al., 1972; Neugarten et al., 1968). Research generally supports this approach, showing that people who retain their major role identities tend to report greater well-being and better mental health (Greenfield & Marks, 2004). For example, retired adults who continued or began to volunteer during the course of one longitudinal study were less likely to show the declines in well-being that other adults did (Wahrendorf & Siegrist, 2010).

As originally framed, activity theory is now regarded as overly simplistic (Bengtson & DeLiema, 2016). For example, although early research did suggest that activity was associated with life satisfaction (Neugarten et al., 1968), the interpretation of this finding may have been flawed. Rather than activity driving satisfaction, it may have been relationships that were responsible for the effect. People who remain active are more likely to maintain high-quality social relationships, and the presence of these relationships is likely to positively affect life satisfaction (Litwin & Shiovitz-Ezra, 2006). In addition, a good proportion of disengaged people are nonetheless happy with their lives, and recent research suggests that disengagement and activity theory may both speak to successful aging. Specifically, adults who believed themselves to be aging successfully struck a balance between self-acceptance and being happy with themselves as they were and remaining simultaneously engaged and involved with life (Reichstadt et al., 2010). Findings such as these suggest that activity may work best for most people but disengagement may be appropriate for others, and that it may be unwise to make generalizations about a particular pattern of successful aging (Moen et al., 1992; Musick et al., 1999).

Continuity Theory Are you happiest being out and about and staying busy? Or do you prefer a quiet night at home? What you prefer prior to the later stages of life may influence what you prefer when you reach them. In other words, if you are happy being active now, you are likely to be happy being active later. However, if you are happy being less active now, you may prefer a quieter lifestyle later in life too (Pushkar et al., 2009). This is the primary premise of **continuity theory** (Atchley, 1989). In this approach, people's need to maintain a connection between past and present is emphasized, and activity is viewed as important, not for its own sake but because it represents continuation of a previous lifestyle. Many retired people are happiest pursuing work or leisure activities similar to those they enjoyed in the past (Pushkar et al., 2010). For example, many professors, when given the choice, will opt not to retire (Dorfman, 2009). Moreover, even after they retire, the majority remain involved in professional activities similar to those they participated in when working (Dorfman & Kolarik, 2005). People who, in middle age, enjoyed leisure activities such as reading books, pursuing a hobby, or gardening tended to engage in these activities in old age as well (Agahi et al., 2006).

Continuity in activities is not always possible because some older adults must cut back on participation in favorite events due to visual, motor, or cognitive impairments. Older adults are likely to be happier, however, if they can maintain their favorite activities to some extent. So, for instance, if adults who are forced to retire are able to find bridge employment (a job following retirement), they tend to show fewer declines in health and well-being, and fewer functional limitations (Dingemans & Henkens, 2015; Zhan et al., 2009).

The Role of Productivity Some researchers focus on productive activity, any action that provides a contribution to society, as a key to aging well. Productive activity, whether paid or unpaid, has been found to have positive effects on older adults. For example, a recent meta-analysis found that across 73 studies, volunteering was associated with a host of positive outcomes, including reduced depression, better health and functional ability, and lower mortality risk. The authors suggest that participating in volunteering keeps older adults physically, cognitively, and socially active, and this increased engagement then positively affects health indices (Anderson et al., 2014). Generally, the more activities adults are involved in and the more time spent on them, the greater the positive effects (Vozikaki et al., 2017; Baker et al., 2005). Similar effects have been found for working, but not for caregiving activities (Choi et al., 2013; Stav et al., 2012; Pinquart & Sorenson, 2003).

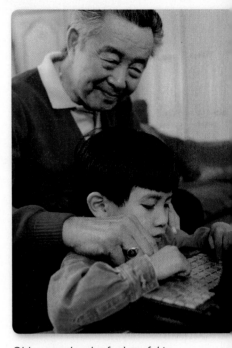

Older people who feel useful to others, as this grandparent does to his grandson, are more likely to age successfully. Steve Mason/Photodisc/Getty Images

continuity theory
Theory of aging, described by Atchley, that holds that in order to age successfully people must maintain a balance of continuity and change in both the internal and external structures of their lives.

Some research suggests that frequent participation in leisure activities can be as beneficial to health and well-being as participation in productive activities, although this effect may be stronger for women (Agahi & Parker, 2008). Social relationships appear to be important here (Stav et al., 2012). Those adults who perceive their social relationships as positive are more likely to engage in leisure activities, and leisure activities are then associated with better health outcomes (Chang et al., 2014). However, this does not mean leisure activities that are more solitary in nature do not have any benefits. For example, meditation, gardening, reading, and listening to the radio have been associated with well-being and quality of life (Geiger et al., 2016; Wang & MacMillan, 2013; Menec, 2003; Machón et al., 2017).

Selective Optimization with Compensation According to Paul Baltes and his colleagues (Baltes, 1997), successful aging involves strategies that enable people to adapt to the changing balance of growth and decline throughout life. Older adults allocate these resources via a process called **selective optimization with compensation (SOC).** SOC involves developing abilities that allow for maximum gain, as well as developing abilities that compensate for decline and could lead to loss. According to SOC, older adults conserve their resources by:

- *Selecting* fewer and more meaningful activities or goals.
- *Optimizing,* or making the most of, the resources they have to achieve their goals.
- *Compensating* for losses by using resources in alternative ways to achieve their goals.

For example, the celebrated concert pianist Arthur Rubenstein gave his farewell concert at age 89. He was able to compensate for his age-related memory loss by selecting a smaller repertoire of material to play and by practicing longer each day to optimize his performance. He also compensated for declines in motor abilities by slowing down his playing immediately before fast movements, thus heightening the contrast and making the music sound faster (Baltes & Baltes, 1990).

Research has found that use of SOC is associated with positive developmental outcomes, including greater well-being and increased happiness, and fewer sick days, falls, and less use of pain medications (Baltes & Smith, 2004; Teshale & Lachman, 2016; Zhang & Radhakrishnan, 2018). Eventually, though, older people may reach the limit of their available resources, and compensatory efforts may no longer seem to work. Adjusting one's personal standards to changes in what is possible to achieve may be essential to maintaining a positive outlook on life.

Practical and Social Issues Related to Aging

Whether and when to retire are among the most crucial lifestyle decisions people make as they approach late adulthood, affecting their financial situation, emotional state, the ways they spend their waking hours, and how they relate to family and friends. The need to provide financial support and appropriate living arrangements and care for large numbers of retired older people also has serious implications for society.

WORK AND RETIREMENT

Retirement took hold in many industrialized countries during the late nineteenth and early twentieth centuries as life expectancy increased. In the United States, the creation of the Social Security system in the 1930s, together with company-sponsored pension plans negotiated by labor unions, made it possible for many older workers to retire with financial security.

Today in the United States there are no longer strong norms concerning the timing of retirement. Often, a desire to pursue activities other than work or to spend time with family are the impetus for retirement. However, with increasing age, many adults retire

selective optimization with compensation (SOC)
Enhancing overall cognitive functioning by using stronger abilities to compensate for those that have weakened.

because of health reasons (Larrimore et al., 2018). There are multiple interrelated issues that determine retirement age, including marital status, current assets and liabilities, the status of dependents, the nature of the work and whether or not age will make that challenging, and the current state of the job market (Gibaldi, 2013).

Trends in Late-Life Work and Retirement Internationally, the average age of retirement across OECD countries is 64.2 years for men and 63.5 for women (Organisation for Economic Co-operation and Development, 2019). However, retirement ages vary across the world, as do resources available for aging adults. For example, 68 percent of people worldwide receive some form of retirement benefits. In North America (almost 100 percent) and Europe (95 percent), most adults receive some form of pension. In Central and Southern Asia (26 percent) and sub-Saharan Africa (23 percent), funding for retirement is more limited (United Nations, 2017). Cultures with high levels of poverty or with harsh living conditions provide less care for the elderly. The treatment of elders depends much on their usefulness and contributions they can provide to others (McGuire, 2017). Without an income source, these older adults may be forced to continue working late into life even if health problems emerge.

In the United States, most adults who *can* retire *do* retire, and, with increasing longevity, they spend more time in retirement than in the past (Dobriansky et al., 2007). In 2016, the average age of retirement for men was 65 years and for women 63 years (Center for Retirement Research, 2018).

However, the proportion of workers older than 65 years has increased sharply. Many older Americans continue to work because they are forced by their financial situation and escalating medical costs (Sterns, 2010). Only 40 percent of those older adults who stop working in their fifties and sixties stop for good; the remainder go back to work either part- or full-time before permanently exiting the workforce (Maestas, 2010). A 2019 survey showed 29 percent of Americans age 65 to 72 years were either working or looking for work (Fry, 2019).

Prior to the COVID-19 pandemic, this graying of the working population was expected to continue to increase through 2024 and was the fastest-growing labor participation group (U.S. Bureau of Labor Statistics, 2019). However, the economic declines that are occurring as a result of the pandemic are expected to have a devastating effect on employment opportunities available to older workers. The highest job losses in April 2020 were experienced by adults age 55 years and older. Although older adults were less likely to work in the hardest-hit areas—hospitality and leisure industries—they were more likely to work as part-time employees and less likely to be able to work remotely. Moreover, those older adults able to retain their jobs face an increased risk of infection or the loss of their health care while being the group most vulnerable to complications from COVID-19 infection (Morrisey, 2020; Bureau of Labor Statistics, 2020, 2020).

Aging and Job Performance Contrary to ageist stereotypes, older workers can be as productive as younger workers. Although they may work more slowly than younger people, they are more accurate and perform equally well on most jobs (Czaja & Sharit, 1998; Salthouse & Maurer, 1996; McDaniel et al., 2012). Moreover, older employees are often better workers, showing less absenteeism, higher commitment, more knowledge, more professionalism, and loyalty to their companies (Roscigno et al., 2007; Rozman et al., 2016). The greatest declines in productivity for older workers are seen when problem solving, learning, or speed are important. When experience or verbal abilities matter more, productivity of older workers matches or even exceeds that of younger workers (McDaniel et al., 2012; Skirbekk, 2008).

In the United States, the Age Discrimination in Employment Act (ADEA), which applies to firms with 20 or more employees, protects workers ages 40 and older from being denied a job, fired, paid less, or forced to retire because of age. Still, many employers exert subtle pressures on older employees (Landy, 1994), and age discrimination is still a factor in employment for older adults (Neumark, 2008). More than 80 percent of older workers experience at least one instance of age discrimination a year (Chou & Choi, 2011).

During the early months of the COVID-19 pandemic, masks were in short supply. Volunteering—in this case, by sewing cotton masks—is positively associated with well-being. Milan Markovic/E+/Getty Images

Life after Retirement Retirement is not a single event but a dynamic adjustment process that is best conceptualized as a form of decision making. There are five broad categories of resources that help determine how well a person adjusts to retirement: (1) individual attributes such as health and financial status; (2) preretirement job-related variables such as job stress; (3) family-related variables such as marriage quality and dependents; (4) retirement transition-related variables such as retirement planning; and (5) post-retirement activities such as bridge employment and volunteer work (Wang et al., 2011).

The research on adjustment to retirement has supported this model. For example, both physical health and financial situation predict retirement adjustment (Barbosa et al., 2016; Earl et al., 2015). Additionally, people who retire from jobs they find unpleasant or stressful show increases in well-being upon retirement (Wang, 2007). In further support of the model, retirees in happy marriages with fewer dependents show higher levels of well-being than other groups (Wang & Shi, 2014; Pinquart & Schindler, 2007). When a spouse dies, this negatively affects retirement adjustment (van Solinge & Henkens, 2008).

Whether, how well, and if people are able to plan for retirement also impacts adjustment. Those people who retire earlier than planned or against their will show declines in well-being (Barbosa et al., 2016; Wang & Shi, 2014), whereas the opportunity to plan retirement is associated with well-being and life satisfaction (Wang, 2007). Bridge employment also appears to be beneficial, and in recent research across 16 European countries it was found to be particularly important for older adults of lower socioeconomic status living without a partner (Dingemans & Henkens, 2019).

People transitioning from working to retirement are particularly likely to volunteer (Tang, 2016), and those who do volunteer are more likely to experience high levels of well-being during retirement (Hao, 2008). Volunteering during retirement has been positively associated with good health and negatively associated with depression, functional limitations, and mortality (Wahrendorf et al., 2016). Volunteering also predicts positive emotionality and protects against declines in well-being associated with major role-identity losses and declines in mental health (Greenfield & Marks, 2004; Hao, 2008). Although older adults who volunteer are more likely to be higher in resources than those who do not (Li & Ferraro, 2005), it nonetheless does appear that volunteering has a positive effect on older adults.

AGING AND FINANCIAL CONCERNS

Since the 1960s, Social Security has provided the largest share of older Americans' income—33 percent in 2019 (Social Security Administration, 2019). Eighty-six percent of people aged 65 and older receive Social Security. Other sources of income include income from assets (67 percent of people), private pensions or annuities (41 percent), and earnings (40 percent). Dependence on Social Security and asset income rises dramatically with age and decreases with income level (Federal Interagency Forum on Aging-Related Statistics, 2016).

Social Security and other government programs, such as Medicare, which covers basic health insurance for U.S. residents who are 65 or older or are disabled, have enabled today's older Americans, as a group, to live fairly comfortably. In 2017, 86 percent of retirees used Medicare (Larrimore et al., 2018). The proportion of older adults living in poverty has fallen from 35 percent in 1959, to 29 percent in 1966, and then to 10 percent in 2014 (Administration on Aging, 2016; Federal Interagency Forum on Aging-Related Statistics, 2016). The poverty rate for older adults, although still lower than that of the total population, was the only demographic group to show an increase in 2016 (Semega et al., 2017). As the U.S. population grays, and as proportionately fewer workers contribute to the Social Security system, it seems likely that benefits will decline (Sawicki, 2005).

Women—especially if they are single, widowed, separated, or divorced or if they were previously poor or worked only part-time in middle age—are more likely (10.5 percent) than men (7.5 percent) to live in poverty in old age. There are also ethnic differences. Older African Americans and Hispanic Americans, at rates of 19.3 and 17 percent, respectively, are more likely to live in poverty than older white Americans at 7.8 percent. The overall poverty rate for adults over the age of 65 is 9.2 percent. The highest poverty rates are among older Hispanic (36.8 percent), Asian (30 percent), and African American women (30 percent) who live alone (U.S. Department of Health and Human Services, 2019).

LIVING ARRANGEMENTS

In developing countries, older adults typically live with adult children and grandchildren in multigenerational households, though this custom is declining. In developed countries, most older people live alone or with a partner or spouse (Kinsella & Phillips, 2005).

In the United States, in 2014, about 7 percent of adults age 65 and older lived in senior housing of various types. Because of women's greater life expectancy, about 70 percent of noninstitutionalized men but only about 45 percent of noninstitutionalized women lived with a spouse. Twenty percent of the men and 36 percent of the women lived alone, although the proportion living alone increases with advancing age. Approximately 10 percent of the men and 19 percent of the women lived with other relatives or nonrelatives, including partners and children (Figure 18.1). Minority elders, especially Asian and Hispanic Americans, in keeping with cultural traditions, were more likely to live in extended family households (Federal Interagency Forum on Aging-Related Statistics, 2016).

Aging in Place Most older adults in industrialized countries prefer, if possible, to stay in their own homes and communities (Aurand et al., 2014). This option, called **aging in place,** makes sense for those who can manage on their own or with minimal help. Most informal caregivers, such as family, who provide aging in place care do so willingly, but it can be a significant source of stress and worry for them (Sanders et al., 2010).

aging in place
Remaining in one's own home, with or without assistance, in later life.

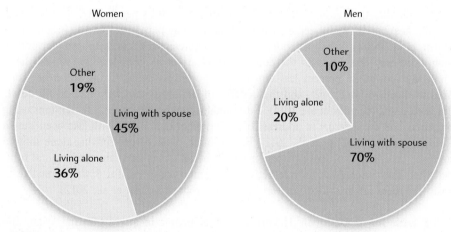

FIGURE 18.1
Living Arrangements of Noninstitutionalized Men and Women Age 65 and Over, United States, 2015

Women are more likely to live alone (especially as they get older), whereas men are more likely to live with a spouse. The "Other" category includes those living with adult children, other relatives, or nonrelatives.

Source: Federal Interagency Forum on Aging-Related Statistics. (2016). *Older Americans update 2016: Key indicators of well-being.* Washington, DC: U.S. Government Printing Office.

Not surprisingly, available resources affect the ability to age in place. For example, in the United States, older adult caretaker households are more likely to rent their homes and have a lower income (Johnson & Appold, 2017). This process intersects with culture. In collectivistic countries such as China, coresidence with grown children or grandchildren is more normative than in individualistic countries such as the United States. However, resources still affect preferences. Elderly adults who have more family resources and higher socioeconomic status prefer to live independently, whereas ethnic minority and older Chinese adults preferred to live with their children (Sereny, 2011).

For older people with impairments that make it hard to get along entirely on their own, minor support—such as meals, transportation, and home health aides—often can help them stay put. So can ramps, grab bars, and other relatively low-cost home modifications (Newman, 2003). Most older people do not need much help, and those who do can often remain in the community if they have at least one person to depend on. In fact, the single most important factor keeping people out of institutions is being married (Nihtilä & Martikainen, 2008). Increasingly, technological aids such as activity monitoring, wandering detection, and e-health applications are being used to help keep older adults physically safe and connected to others (Peek et al., 2014). With such help, aging in place can help older adults delay entry into nursing homes (Young et al., 2015).

Living Alone The growth of elderly single-person households has been spurred by greater longevity, increased benefits and pensions, increased home ownership, more elder-friendly housing, more availability of community support, and reduced public assistance with nursing home costs. Because women live longer than men and are more likely to be widowed, older women in the most developed countries are more likely than older men to live alone (Kinsella & Phillips, 2005). In the United States, about 28 percent of all noninstitutionalized older adults live alone, a greater proportion of which are women. Forty-four percent of women age 75 and over live alone (Administration on Aging, 2018). Older people living alone are more likely than older people with spouses to be poor (Administration on Aging, 2016) and to end up in institutions (Kasper et al., 2010).

Older people who live alone, particularly the oldest old, are more lonely than those who live with others. This is particularly true for women of low socioeconomic level with low education, and for those in poor health. Structural factors, such as unsafe neighborhoods, inaccessible housing, or inadequate opportunity for socialization matter too (Cohen-Mansfield et al., 2016). However, such factors as personality, cognitive abilities, physical health, and a depleted social network may play a greater role in loneliness (Martin et al., 2007). Social activities, such as volunteer work, can help an older person living alone stay connected to the community (Carr et al., 2017). Pets, too, can help. One study showed 36 percent less loneliness reported by adults living with a pet compared to those without a pet, and the benefits of pet ownership were highest for adults who lived alone (Stanley et al., 2014). Additionally, technology-based interventions using computers and the Internet to address social and emotional needs have also been shown to reduce loneliness (Choi et al., 2012). For example, elderly women living alone showed decreases in salivary cortisol (a stress marker), better sleep, and improved mental function when they were given an interactive communication robot for 8 weeks relative to those who were not provided with an interactive robot (Tanaka et al., 2012).

Living with Adult Children Historically, older people in many African, Asian, and Latin American societies could expect to live and be cared for in their children's or grandchildren's homes, but this pattern is changing. Although in recent decades there are generally a greater number of surviving generations in a family, they are also less likely to live in the same household (World Health Organization, 2019). This varies by country. Coresidence with adult children is most common in Asia and least common in Africa (Bongaarts & Zimmer, 2002) and is more common in Southern Europe than in Northern European countries (Hank, 2007).

Most older people in developed countries, even when in difficult circumstances, prefer not to live with their children (Kinsella & Phillips, 2005). They are reluctant to burden their families and to give up their freedom. The parent may feel useless, bored, and isolated from friends. If the adult child is married and the spouse and parent do not get along well, or caregiving duties become too burdensome, the marriage may be threatened (Shapiro & Cooney, 2007). Often, moving in with adult children is a consequence of economic pressures; parents move in not because they want to, but because they have little choice (Isengard & Szydlik, 2012). Adults, especially women, who move in with relatives are at higher risk of loneliness than those that are able to continue to live with a spouse or partner (Henning-Smith, 2016; Greenfield & Russell, 2011).

Whether or not living with adult children will be successful depends largely on the quality of the relationship that existed in the past and on the ability of both generations to communicate fully and frankly. Often, friction increases as adult children and their aging parents navigate the shifting power dynamics of the relationship. Actions seen by adult children as serving to keep parents safe, such as driving parents to the store rather than allowing them to drive themselves, may be seen by parents as an infringement upon their autonomy and be met with resistance and rejection (Heid et al., 2015). How this conflict is managed has repercussions for both parties. For instance, when adult children give in to conflict repeatedly, they are more likely to become depressed over time and relationship quality declines. However, when adult children attempt to reason with their aging parents rather than giving in, this is associated with more positive relationship quality. Being directly confrontational and arguing with parents is associated with negative relationship quality; however, it is also associated with greater provision of support (Heid et al., 2017). Importantly, the provision of support and benefits is a two-way street. Aging parents also provide benefits to their adult children, including emotional support, advice, and practical support (Huo et al., 2018). Indeed, although most informal caregivers do report time constraints and difficulty handing all aspects of caregiving, they also report positive aspects of caregiving (Federal Interagency Forum on Aging-Related Statistics, 2016).

Living in Institutions Many older adults opt to age in place if they expect their health to be good but prefer to live with relatives if they anticipate ill health or frailty (Fernández-Carro, 2016). Although aging in place is still preferred by most older adults, assisted living or retirement communities are frequently cited as preferred living situations as well, particularly by those who are already living in them (Kasper et al., 2019). However, many see institutionalization as a last resort and view the transition to a nursing home with trepidation, and fewer than half report a good quality of life once there (Toot et al., 2017). Although many would prefer not to live in nursing homes, many residents are left little choice by dementia, increasing frailty, caregiver illness, or their behavioral issues (Prince et al., 2015; Afram et al., 2014).

The use of nonfamily institutions for care of the frail elderly varies greatly around the world. Institutionalization has been rare in developing regions but is becoming more common even in countries such as Japan with traditions of elder care and filial piety. Moreover, declines in fertility have resulted in a rapidly aging population and a shortage of family caregivers (World Health Organization, 2019). Comprehensive geriatric home visitation programs in some countries, such as the United Kingdom, Denmark, and Australia, have been effective in holding down nursing home admissions (Stuck et al., 2002).

In all countries, the likelihood of living in a nursing home increases with age—in the United States, from about 1 percent at ages 65 to 74 to 9 percent at age 85 and over (Administration on Aging, 2016). Most older nursing home residents worldwide and almost 3 out of 4 in the United States are women (Federal Interagency Forum on Aging-Related Statistics, 2004; Kinsella & Velkoff, 2001). In addition to gender, being poor and living alone significantly increase the risk of entering long-term care (Martikainen et al., 2009).

In 2014, there were approximately 1.2 million adults over the age of 65 living in institutional settings (Administration on Aging, 2018). Such care is expensive: The median cost in 2019 for a private room in a nursing home in the United States was $8,517 per month (Genworth, 2020). High costs, among other factors, have spurred a

research in action

ELDER ABUSE

Elder abuse is a global issue. A recent review involving over 52 studies across 28 low-, middle-, and high-income countries estimated 15.7 percent of adults age 60 and older are abused. Prevalence rates vary, with Asia at 20.2 percent, Europe at 15.4 percent, and the Americas at 11.7 percent (Yon et al., 2017). In the United States, the estimated prevalence rate is 10 percent (Pillemer et al., 2015), and for every reported case, an estimated 23 cases remain undetected (Centers for Disease Control and Prevention, 2017).

Elder abuse can take various forms, including physical abuse, sexual abuse, emotional or psychological abuse, and neglect. Elder abuse can also include financial abuse or exploitation, which involves the use of an older person's resources, such as savings accounts or Social Security payments, for personal gain (Centers for Disease Control and Prevention, 2020). In India and some countries in Africa, childless widows may be forced to marry their late husband's brother, or they may be expelled from their homes. In sub-Saharan Africa, accusations of witchcraft are sometimes leveled against childless widows and used as justification for seizing their land or inheritance, and even for murder (Krug et al., 2002).

A number of factors increase the risk of elder abuse, including being female, having difficulty with activities of daily living, poor health, poverty, and having previously been victimized. Dementia and cognitive impairment are also strong predictors of the likelihood of abuse (Burnes et al., 2015; Friedman et al., 2015; Acierno et al., 2010). Perpetrators of abuse are most likely to be family members; to be male; to have a history of mental or physical illness, substance abuse, physical abuse, or violence; and to be unemployed or suffering from economic strain (Lachs & Pillemer, 2015).

Abuse can also occur within the context of nursing homes or residential care communities. Low pay, long hours, physical demands, and minimal education and training contribute to job burnout, demoralization, and high stress levels among staff members. Residents may also have problem behaviors and inflict violence on staff members, which increase odds of neglect or retaliation. Residents also harm one another. Although verbal mistreatment is most common, physical altercations can occur as well. Sexual abuse occurs too, with common perpetrators as staff or other residents (Castle et al., 2015; Lachs & Pillemer, 2015; Lachs et al., 2016).

In most states in the United States, physicians are obligated to screen for elder abuse (Hoover & Polson, 2014). Unfortunately, evidence has not shown that such screenings have an effect on the incidence of elder abuse (Moyer, 2013). Thus intervention services may have more utility. Although some studies have shown mixed results (Ploeg et al., 2009), others have shown success. For example, one community-based intervention program utilizing law enforcement, supportive social services, and coaching of at-risk older adults showed promise in reducing risk factors for abuse over the course of the study (Mariam et al., 2015).

what's your view How would you balance the need to keep elderly adults safe against their need for autonomy and independence? What actions or measures do you support to prevent or reduce elder mistreatment?

shift from institutionalization to less expensive alternative living options (discussed in the next section) and home health care. Nonetheless, as the baby boom generation ages and if current nursing home usage rates continue, the number of residents is projected to rise sharply (Seblega et al., 2010). Such growth would greatly burden Medicaid, the national health insurance program for low-income persons and the major source of payments for nursing home usage (Ness & Aronow, 2004).

Federal law sets strict requirements for nursing homes and gives residents the right to choose their own doctors, to be fully informed about their care and treatment, and to be free from physical or mental abuse, corporal punishment, involuntary seclusion, and physical or chemical restraints (see Research in Action for more information on elder abuse). Some states train volunteer ombudsmen to act as advocates for nursing home residents, to explain their rights, and to resolve their complaints about such matters as privacy, treatment, food, and financial issues.

Alternative Housing Options Many older adults are utilizing a relatively new but growing segment of the housing market known as age-qualified active adult communities. In these communities, limited to people age 55 and older, residents can walk out their front door and find a variety of leisure opportunities, such as fitness centers, tennis courts, and golf courses, close by. For those who cannot or prefer not to live completely independently, a wide array of group housing options have emerged. Some of these newer arrangements enable older people with health problems or disabilities to receive needed services or care without sacrificing autonomy, privacy, and dignity.

One popular option is *assisted living,* housing specifically for older adults. Assisted-living facilities enable tenants to live in their own home-like space while giving them easy 24-hour access to needed personal and health care services. In most of these facilities a person can move, when and if necessary, from relative independence (with housekeeping and meals provided) to help with bathing, dressing, managing medications, and using a wheelchair to get around. Assisted-living facilities vary widely in accommodations, operation, philosophy, and rates, and those offering adequate privacy and services are generally not affordable for moderate- and low-income persons (Hawes et al., 2003). Indeed, facilities are disproportionately found in areas with more educated residents and higher incomes (Stevenson & Grabowski, 2010).

Older adults in a retirement village with supportive living facilities can benefit by keeping their bodies and minds active. Squaredpixels/iStock/Getty Images

Personal Relationships in Late Life

Our stereotypes often lead us to believe that old age is a time of loneliness and isolation. Although it is true that older adults have far fewer people in their social networks than younger adults do (English & Carstenson, 2014), with men's social networks even smaller than those of women (McLaughlin et al., 2010), this does not mean older adults are necessarily isolated and lonely. For instance, meta-analyses including people from a variety of countries indicate that loneliness remains essentially unchanged from adolescence to old age (Mund et al., 2019), although there are some indications that it may increase in the very oldest old (Luhmann & Hawkley, 2016).

THEORIES OF SOCIAL CONTACT AND SOCIAL SUPPORT

According to *social convoy theory,* aging adults maintain their level of social support by identifying members of their social network who can best help them and avoiding those who are not supportive. As former coworkers and casual friends drop away, most older adults retain a stable inner circle of social convoys: close friends and family members on whom they can rely and who strongly affect their well-being (Antonucci & Akiyama, 1995).

A somewhat different explanation of changes in social contact comes from *socioemotional selectivity theory* (Carstensen, 1991, 1995, 1996). As remaining time becomes short, older adults choose to spend time with people and in activities that meet immediate emotional needs and provide them with emotional gratification. For example, an older adult may be less willing to spend precious time with a friend who gets on her nerves. Older adults tend to become more selective about social contacts, keeping up with friends and relatives who can best meet their current needs for emotional satisfaction. In this way, even though older adults may have fewer friends, the friends that they do have are closer and provide more rewarding social contact (English & Carstensen, 2014).

Thus, even though older adults may have smaller social networks than younger adults do, they tend to have as many very close relationships (Cornwell et al., 2008) and tend to be quite satisfied with those they have (Fiori et al., 2007). Their positive feelings toward old friends are as strong as those of young adults, and their positive feelings toward family members are stronger (Charles & Piazza, 2007). Although older adults tend to see friends less often, they see family about as frequently as before (Shaw et al., 2007).

The relationships older adults do maintain are more important to their well-being than ever (Charles & Carstensen, 2007) and help keep their minds and memories sharp (Kuiper et al., 2016).

RELATIONSHIPS AND HEALTH

Most of us want and need the support and love of others around us, and we are happier when part of a social community. Even if the size of that community might shrink with age, we need interaction. Because of this need, social isolation—or loneliness—is an important outcome variable that affects both psychological and physical health. Indeed, strong social relationships are as important for health and mortality as smoking, being obese, and abusing alcohol (Holt-Lunstad et al., 2010).

People who are socially isolated tend to show more rapid physical and cognitive declines than those who are not isolated, even very late in life (Cherry et al., 2013; Shankar et al., 2013; Luo et al., 2012). Moreover, the feeling of being useless to others is a strong factor for disabilities and mortality (Tilvis et al., 2012; Gu et al., 2017). Conversely, a recent meta-analysis including 10 studies and more than 136,000 respondents indicated having a purpose in life was associated with decreased risk of heart attack and death (Cohen et al., 2016).

Strong, positive social ties can literally be a lifesaver. One longitudinal study showed that socially isolated men were 53 percent more likely than the most socially connected men to die of cardiovascular disease and more than twice as likely to die from accidents or suicide (Eng et al., 2002). Similar data with women showed that older women who received the most social support were 2 times less likely to die during a 10-year period than those who received the least such support (Lyyra & Heikkinen, 2006). To be beneficial, however, relationships must be of good quality. If they are marked by criticism, rejection, neglect, control, or undermining behaviors, they can serve as chronic stressors (Rook, 2015).

THE MULTIGENERATIONAL FAMILY AND CULTURAL DIFFERENCES

Historically, families rarely spanned more than three generations. Today, many families in developed countries can include four or more generations, making it possible for a person to be both a grandparent and a grandchild at the same time (Costanzo & Hoy, 2007). This has led to the rise of multigenerational families, where grandparents, their adult children, and grandchildren live under the same roof.

The presence of so many family members can be enriching (McIlvane et al., 2007; Dunifon et al., 2014) but also can create special pressures. Although there is great variability, older adults are as a group more likely to suffer from debilitating disease or infirmity, and this care can be physically and emotionally draining (Gonyea, 2013). Given the rapid growth in the population of adults 85 and older (Ortman et al., 2014), many people in their late sixties or beyond, whose own health and energy may be faltering, may find themselves serving as caregivers. Generally, the burden of this intergenerational care falls to women (Gonyea, 2013; Cook & Cohen, 2018) due in part to gender role norms of women as caregivers.

The ways families deal with these issues often have cultural roots. People from cultures that strongly focus on familial bonds are, not surprisingly, more receptive to the needs of their aging parents and more likely to offer support than are people from more individualistic cultures (Kalmijn & Saraceno, 2008; Tomassini et al., 2007). For example, the nuclear family and the desire of older adults to live apart from their children reflect dominant U.S. values of individualism, autonomy, and self-reliance, whereas Hispanic and Asian American cultures traditionally emphasize *lineal,* or intergenerational, obligations (Johnson, 1995).

Most older people in Africa, Asia, the Caribbean, and Latin America live with their adult children. In Spain, Italy, and Greece, about 20 percent of older adults live with at least one child. And in Afghanistan and Pakistan, more than 90 percent of older adults lived with their children or extended family members (United Nations, 2019). These findings are broadly in line with the expected patterns given the collectivism/individualism scale. There are suggestions that the accelerating pace of globalization will result in a movement away from the more traditionally oriented family bonds found in many countries and toward the individualistic style characteristic of more economically stable nations (Costanzo & Hoy, 2007).

In 2016 in the United States, 20 percent of the population lived in multigenerational families, a number that has increased since the low of 12 percent in 1980. Not surprisingly, Asian American, Hispanic, Black, and immigrant families in the United States are more likely to live in multigenerational homes, although the increase recently seen is shared across all ethnic groups (Cohn & Passel, 2018; Dunifon et al., 2014)

Marital Relationships

Unlike other family relationships, marriage—at least in contemporary Western cultures— is generally formed by mutual consent. What happens to marital quality in late life?

LONG-TERM MARRIAGE

Because women usually marry older men and outlive them and because men are more likely to remarry after divorce or widowhood, a higher proportion of men than women throughout the world are married in late life (Roberts et al., 2018, Figure 18.2).

Married couples who are still together in late adulthood are more likely than middle-age couples to report higher satisfaction and fewer adjustment problems in their marriages (Orathinkal & Vansteenwegen, 2007). This may be because spouses who remain together are likely to have worked out their differences. Marriage satisfaction is important because it has been related not just to psychological well-being (Carr et al., 2014), but also to multiple positive health indices (Robles et al., 2014).

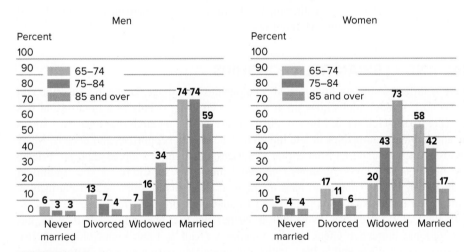

FIGURE 18.2
Marital Status of the U.S. Population Age 65 and Over by Age Group and Sex, 2016

Because of women's greater longevity, they are more likely than men to be widowed in late life, whereas men are more likely to be married or remarried in late life.

Note: Married includes married, spouse present; married, spouse absent; and separated. These data refer to the civilian noninstitutionalized population.

Source: Roberts, A. W., Ogunwole, S. U., Blakeslee, L., & Rabe, M. A. (2018). *The population 65 years and older in the United States: 2016.* Washington, DC: US Department of Commerce, Economics and Statistics Administration, US Census Bureau.

Many couples who are still together late in life say they are happier in marriage than they were in their younger years. Important benefits of marriage include intimacy, sharing, and a sense of belonging to one another.
Stockbyte/Getty Images

The way couples resolve conflicts is key to marital satisfaction throughout adulthood. Married people with more discord in their marriages tend to be anxious and depressed, whereas those with less discordant marriages tend to have higher self-esteem and report higher levels of marital satisfaction (Whisman et al., 2018; Schmitt et al., 2007). Patterns of conflict resolution tend to remain fairly constant throughout a marriage, and those couples who believe strongly in marriage, share responsibility for decision making, and share household chores are more likely to report low levels of conflict and high levels of happiness in their marriage (Kamp & Taylor, 2012). The way emotions are handled matters as well. Marriage partners, especially wives, who are able to successfully regulate negative emotions and communicate effectively are more likely to report high marriage satisfaction (Bloch et al., 2014; Tavakol et al., 2017).

A close marital relationship can moderate the negative psychological effects of functional disabilities by reducing psychological distress, anxiety and depression, and increasing self-esteem (Jean, 2017; Mancini & Bonanno, 2006). However, spouses who care for disabled partners may feel isolated, angry, and frustrated, especially if they are in poor health themselves. Such couples may be caught in a vicious cycle: The illness puts strains on the marriage, and these strains may then aggravate the illness (Karney & Bradbury, 1995), putting the caregiver's health and well-being at risk (Graham et al., 2006). For example, when one spouse is hospitalized, the other's risk of death increases (Christakis & Allison, 2006). This iterative process is exacerbated by age (Umberson et al., 2006).

Spousal caregiving late in life often ends with the institutionalization or death of one partner. A longitudinal study of over 2,000 older couples captured the fragile nature of spousal caregiving in late life. At the beginning of the study, all couples were living independently in the community. Eight years later, 20.7 percent of the husbands and 18.1 percent of the wives had been institutionalized. Moreover, 17.1 percent of husbands and 33.1 percent of wives became widowed over the course of the study (Noel-Miller, 2010).

GAY AND LESBIAN RELATIONSHIPS

There is little research on homosexual relationships in old age, largely because the current cohort of older adults grew up at a time when living openly as a homosexual was rare (Fredriksen-Goldsen & Muraco, 2010). However, the research that does exist shows gay and lesbian relationships in late life tend to be strong, supportive, and diverse. Many homosexuals have children from earlier marriages; others have adopted children. Friendship networks or support groups—a chosen family—may substitute for the traditional family (Reid, 1995). Those who have maintained close relationships and strong involvement in the homosexual community tend to adapt to aging with relative ease (Friend, 1991; Reid, 1995). However, living with a partner, whether married or cohabitating, has an additional protective effect against loneliness (Kim & Fredriksen-Goldsen, 2016). Moreover, married gay and lesbian adults and unmarried partners report better physical health than do single gay and lesbian adults (Goldsen et al., 2017).

Intimacy is important to older gay men, as it is to older heterosexual adults. Contrary to stereotype, homosexual relationships in late life are strong and supportive.
Thinkstock/Stockbyte/Getty Images

The main problems of many older gays and lesbians grow out of societal attitudes. Often there are strained relationships within the family of origin. A common issue is discrimination in nursing homes and social service agencies and discriminatory policies against same-sex living arrangements. Although marriage equality laws have reduced the extent of discrimination, unmarried individuals may face significant barriers in the event a partner falls ill or dies. They may have difficulty dealing with health care providers, managing bereavement and inheritance issues, and lack access to a partner's Social Security benefits (Orel, 2004; Kim & Fredriksen-Goldsen, 2016; Knochel et al., 2011; Rawlings, 2012; Addis et al., 2009).

WIDOWHOOD

With increasing age, death of a spouse becomes more common, and more so in women than in men. Women tend to outlive their husbands and are less likely than men to marry again. As Figure 18.2 shows, U.S. women age 65 and over are far more likely than men of the same age to be widowed (Federal Interagency Forum on Aging-Related Statistics, 2016). In most countries, more than half of older women are widows (Kinsella & Velkoff, 2001).

Widowhood has been repeatedly associated with increased mortality, with the sharpest declines seen in the first 6 months following the death of a spouse (Shor et al., 2012; Moon et al., 2011) and for unexpected deaths (Sullivan & Fenelon, 2014). Although becoming widowed is a risk for both men and women, men appear to be affected more strongly by the loss of a spouse. For example, older widowed men are far more likely to be institutionalized than older widowed women following the death of a spouse (Nihtila & Martikainen, 2008). Additionally, whereas women's mortality risk following the death of a spouse is 15 percent, men's increased risk is 27 percent (Shor et al., 2012).

DIVORCE AND REMARRIAGE

Divorce in middle-age and older adults, although still relatively rare, has risen. The divorce rate has approximately doubled since the 1990s in adults age 50 and older, and it has nearly tripled in those 65 years of age and older (Stepler, 2017). This rise can be attributed to a variety of factors. First, longer life expectancy increases the risk of divorce as people may be unwilling to spend long periods of time with a spouse they find unsuitable. As a correlate to this, remarriages, which become also more common with increasing age, are more likely to result in divorce than first marriages. Also, as divorce becomes more common, it also becomes more acceptable. Last, women's participation in the workforce has given them more economic security and hence lessened the financial burden of divorce for many women (Brown & Lin, 2012).

In 2013, 67 percent of adults age 55 to 64 years, and 50 percent of those 65 and above remarried, an increase from previous years. Men are somewhat more likely to remarry, a difference that emerges sometime in middle age. This gender gap has decreased since the 1960s and most strikingly for younger cohorts. In 1960, the gender gap was +29 for adults 55 to 64 years of age, and +28 for adults over 65. These numbers are now, respectively, +8 and +26 (Livingston, 2014). Remarriage in late life may have a special character. People in late-life remarriages seemed more trusting and accepting and less in need of deep sharing of personal feelings than in earlier marriages. Men, but not women, tend to be more satisfied in late-life remarriages than in midlife remarriages (Bograd & Spilka, 1996).

Nonmarital Lifestyles and Relationships

SINGLE LIFE

In the United States, the number of single older adults has risen in the past few decades. These demographic changes reflect a number of influences, including a decision to delay or forgo marriage, liberalization of divorce, cohabitation, widowhood, and unmarried parenthood. In the United States, approximately 37 percent of baby boomers, who began to turn 65 in 2011, are unmarried (Brown & Wright, 2017).

In most countries, 5 percent or less of older men and 10 percent or less of older women have never married. In Europe, this gender difference may reflect the toll on marriageable men taken by World War II, when today's older cohort were of marrying age. In some Latin American and Caribbean countries, proportions of never-marrieds are higher, probably due to the prevalence of consensual unions (Kinsella & Phillips, 2005). In the United States, approximately 5 percent of American men and 6 percent of American women 65 years or older have never been married (Federal Interagency Forum on Aging-Related Statistics, 2016).

When compared to divorced or widowed people, older never-married adults in the United States are more likely to prefer single life and less likely to be lonely (Dykstra, 1995), even though they are most likely to live alone and receive the least social support. They are less likely to experience "single strain"—chronic practical and emotional stressors attributed to the lack of an intimate partner (Pudrovska et al., 2006).

However, when compared to married adults, never-married people, especially men, are disadvantaged (Lin & Brown, 2012). They do not benefit from the protective effects of marriage on morbidity and mortality discussed earlier, and they are as likely to have poor health (Tamborini, 2007) and be at higher risk of death as divorced or widowed adults (Rendall et al., 2011). Moreover, they are more likely to live in poverty than married couples, as well as divorced and widowed older adults (Tamborini, 2007).

Approximately 14 percent of single adults age 57 to 85 years are in a dating relationship (Brown & Shinohara, 2013). Previously married older men are more likely to date than previously married older women, probably because of the greater availability of women in this age group. Men prefer to date women who are younger than they are, whereas women show a preference for older men until age 75, after which they prefer younger men as well (Alterovitz & Mendelsohn, 2009). Many elderly daters are sexually active but do not expect to marry. Among both whites and Blacks, men are more interested in romantic involvement than women, who may fear getting locked into traditional gender roles (Bulcroft & Bulcroft, 1991; Tucker et al., 1993).

Women gain a protective psychological benefit from dating and show similar levels of stress, depression, and loneliness whether or not they are dating, cohabiting, or married when compared to single women. However, men do not show the same benefit. Men who are dating report similar or higher levels of loneliness to single men when compared to cohabiting and married men (Wright & Brown, 2017).

Some adults classified as "single" in traditional studies are nonetheless in committed relationships. In recent decades, there has been an increase in "living apart together" (LAT) relationships in both Europe and the United States (Liefbroer et al., 2015; Strohm et al., 2009). LAT unions are monogamous intimate relationships between unmarried people who live in different households. Although reasons vary, older adults are more likely to enter into a LAT relationship rather than marriage in order to maintain their autonomy, retain control of their finances, and, particularly for women, avoid being placed in the role of caregiver (Upton-Davis, 2012). Generally, both men and women report high levels of happiness and support and low levels of strain within their LAT relationships (Lewin, 2017), perhaps because those individuals who are unhappy find it relatively easy to leave the relationship. Research suggests that although those people in LAT unions are highly attached to their partners, they do not necessarily expect the relationship to be long-lasting and show ambivalence with respect to the possibility of providing assistance in the event the relationship partner becomes ill (van der Wiel et al., 2018; Gierveld, 2015).

COHABITATION

In 2007, approximately 2.3 million adults 50 years and older were cohabiting. By 2016, this number had risen to 4 million, a 75 percent increase (Stepler, 2017). Although younger adults sometimes view cohabitation as a prelude to marriage, older adults are more likely to view it as an alternative to marriage (Brown, et al., 2012). Approximately 74 percent of cohabiting adults over the age of 50 were previously married, whereas younger cohabitants have most commonly never been married (Stepler, 2017).

Generally cohabiting relationship tend to be quite stable in older adults, a finding that is especially true for women 65 years and older (Brown et al., 2012; Vespa, 2012). Research has shown that cohabitators report equal levels of emotional satisfaction, pleasure, openness, time spent together, criticism, and demands (Brown & Kawamura, 2010). The benefits of cohabitation are most true for men. Although women derive equal benefits from merely dating, for men, living in the same home is key (Wright & Brown, 2017).

In younger adults, cohabitation is often the result of economic concerns. However, this does not seem to be the case in older adults. Factors such as wealth (Vespa, 2012), owning a home, receiving Social Security payments or a pension, or having private health insurance do not seem to affect the likelihood that a couple will choose to cohabitate (Brown, et al., 2012). Perhaps older adults, particularly women, are hesitant to marry and prefer to cohabitate because of the possibility of having to provide care to a disabled or sick partner later in life (Noel-Miller, 2011). In support of this interpretation, cohabitating women are least likely to eventually marry if they are in good health and are financially well-off (Vespa, 2013).

FRIENDSHIPS

Maintaining friendships is important for well-being. Most older people have close friends, and, as in early and middle adulthood, those with an active circle of friends tend to be healthier and happier (Golden et al., 2009; Huxhold et al., 2013). Emotional closeness seems to be a key factor. When emotional closeness is lacking, more frequent contact with friends does not impact feelings of loneliness (Drageset et al., 2011). However, regardless of closeness, those people who are not getting as much contact as they desire are more likely to feel lonely (Nicolaisen & Thorsen, 2017). People who can confide their feelings and thoughts and can talk about their worries and pain with friends tend to deal better with the changes and crises of aging (Genevay, 1986) and to live longer (Steinbach, 1992).

The element of choice in friendship may be especially important to older people (Golden et al., 2009), who may feel control over their lives slipping away (Adams, 1986). Friendship may also help older adults deal with some of the role losses of late life; those with friends tend to be happier (Adams & Taylor, 2015).

Some research has shown that many older people enjoy spending time with their friends more than time spent with their families. As earlier in life, friendships tend to revolve around pleasure and leisure, whereas family relationships tend to involve everyday needs and tasks (Antonucci & Akiyama, 1995). People usually rely on relatives for long-term commitments, such as caregiving, but friends may, on occasion, fulfill this function.

Although friends cannot replace a spouse or partner, they can help compensate for the lack of one (Hartup & Stevens, 1999) by playing the role of fictive kin, a psychological family. When family relationships are poor, older adults tend to have closer relationships with friends, and this in turn is associated with well-being (Wrzus et al., 2012). For example, never married, divorced, and widowed older adults who receive high levels of emotional and practical support from friends are less likely to be lonely (Dykstra, 1995). Similarly, social network size and social support are key protective factors against poor health, disability and depression for lesbian, gay, and bixsexual older adults (Fredriksen-Golden et al., 2013).

In line with social convoy and socioemotional selectivity theories, longtime friendships often persist into very old age (Antonucci et al., 2013). However, losing friends, because of either conflict, death, or relocation, is a relatively common experience, especially for individuals in lower socioeconomic strata (Rook & Charles, 2017; Cornwell, 2014). This is a particularly pressing issue for women, who are more likely to survive their husbands (d'Epinay et al., 2010). Although many older people do make new friends, even after age 85 (Johnson & Troll, 1994), older adults are more likely than younger adults to attribute the benefits of friendship (such as affection and loyalty) to specific individuals who cannot be replaced (de Vries, 1996) and older adults tend to have stronger positive feelings about old friends than about new friends (Charles & Piazza, 2007).

Nonmarital Kinship Ties

Some of the most lasting and important relationships in late life come not from mutual choice but from kinship bonds. Let's look at these.

RELATIONSHIPS WITH ADULT CHILDREN

Most older people have living children, but, because of global trends toward smaller families, have fewer of them than in previous generations (Dobriansky et al., 2007;

Kinsella & Phillips, 2005). In European countries, almost half of adults in their sixties live within 15 miles of their adult children, and about one-third live with an adult child (Hank, 2007). Coresidence commonly results from economic pressures (Isengard & Szydlik, 2012) and is less common in countries with strong welfare services. It is most common in the more traditional Mediterranean countries (Greece, Italy, and Spain) and least common in the Scandinavian countries (Denmark and Sweden). About half of older parents below age 80 report contact with a child, most often a daughter, at least once a week (Hank, 2007). The mother-daughter relationship tends to be especially close (Lefkowitz & Fingerman, 2003).

In the United States, about 57.1 percent of people have their nearest adult child living within a close distance to them, and 19.1 percent have an adult child living with them (Choi et al., 2018). Immigrants who arrived to the United States as older adults are most likely to live with and be dependent on adult children (Glick & Van Hook, 2002). The trend toward smaller families means fewer potential family caregivers for ailing, aging parents (Kinsella & Phillips, 2005), increasing the strains on those who do serve as caregivers—strains that may lead to mistreatment of a "difficult" frail patient.

The balance of mutual aid between parents and their adult children shifts as parents age, with children providing a greater share of support (Bengtson et al., 1990, 1996). Older adults who receive more help from their children than they give them, over time, are more likely to show increases in psychological distress (Reczek & Zhang, 2016). Although the provision of support to aging parents can result in declines in well-being for both parents and adult children, a close, high-quality relationship can buffer against this (Merz & Consedine, 2009; Merz et al., 2009).

Older parents who can do so often continue to provide financial support to children. In less-developed countries, older parents contribute through housekeeping, child care, and socialization of grandchildren (Kinsella & Phillips, 2005). Adults with children doing less well than they would like often have conflicted feelings—they are concerned and want to help, but at the same time may feel a desire to be free of responsibility toward adult children or want to encourage independence and autonomy (Birditt et al., 2010; Smith, 2012). They tend to be distressed if their children have serious problems and may consider such problems a sign of their failure as parents (Lee et al., 1995; Pillemer & Suitor, 1991; Suitor et al., 1995; Troll & Fingerman, 1996). Many older people whose adult children are mentally ill, retarded, physically disabled, or stricken with serious illnesses serve as primary caregivers for as long as both parent and child live (Greenberg & Becker, 1988; Ryff & Seltzer, 1995). The strain of this caregiving adds up over time. In middle age, parents of children with intellectual or developmental disabilities have a similar profile to parents of neurotypical children. However, as they enter old age, parents of disabled children have worse physical and mental health (Seltzer et al., 2011). Additionally, the generally unexpected loss of an adult child can result in deep psychological distress and unresolved grief (Van Humbeeck et al., 2013).

What about the increasing number of older adults without living children? Slightly over 8 percent of U.S. adults age 55 years and older do not have any children (Margolis & Verdery, 2017). Variations in kinlessness across different countries are vast. In Europe, approximately 10 percent of adults age 50 and over are childless, ranging from 6 percent in the Czech Republic to 15 percent in Switzerland (Deindl & Brandt, 2017). In China and Korea, by contrast, only about 2 percent of older adults do not have children (Verdery et al., 2019). A survey of research conducted across 66 countries found that having children is not associated with greater well-being, and in fact, it is most commonly associated with decreased well-being. However, context matters. For the oldest age groups and for widowers, the relationship reverses (Stanca, 2016).

Macrosystem variables also affect the outcomes of childlessness. In wealthier countries parents are more likely to report lower well-being, and in countries where parenting and childbearing are highly valued, childless adults are more likely to report lower life satisfaction and happiness (Stanca, 2016; Tanaka & Johnson, 2014). Thus parenthood does not guarantee well-being in old age, nor does childlessness necessarily harm it.

RELATIONSHIPS WITH SIBLINGS

Brother and sisters play an important role in older people's support networks. Relationships with siblings tend to be among the longest lasting of all relationships; 75 percent of adults 70 years of age and older have a living sibling (Cicirelli, 2013; Settersten, 2007). Siblings, more than other family members and friends, tend to provide companionship and emotional support as older adults (Bedford, 1995).

Sibling commitment, meaning the degree to which siblings keep in contact with and help each other, is relatively stable across the life span (Rittenour et al., 2007). Most older siblings say they stand ready to provide tangible help and would turn to a sibling for such help as needed, although relatively few actually do so unless facing an emergency (Cicirelli, 1995). For those that do, however, both giving support (Gierveld & Dykstra, 2008) and receiving support (Thomas, 2010) are associated with positive outcomes such as reductions in loneliness. Moreover, although caregivers are still worse off than non-caregivers, data from 19 countries show caring for a sibling is associated with less stress and greater well-being than caring for an ill spouse, child, or parent (Viana et al. 2013)

The nearer older people live to their siblings and the more siblings they have, the more they are likely to confide in them (Connidis & Davies, 1992). Reminiscing about shared early experiences becomes more frequent in old age and may help in reviewing a life and putting the significance of family relationships into perspective (Cicirelli, 1995; Eaves et al., 2005). Sisters are especially vital in maintaining family relationships and well-being, perhaps because of women's emotional expressiveness and traditional role as nurturers (Bedford, 1995; Cicirelli, 1995). Older people who are close to their sisters feel better about life and worry less about aging than those without sisters or without close ties to them (Cicirelli, 1989).

Although the death of a sibling in old age may be understood as normative and becomes increasingly common with advanced age (d'Epinay et al., 2010), survivors may grieve intensely and become lonely or depressed (Cicirelli, 2009). The loss of a sibling represents not only a loss of someone to lean on and a shift in the family constellation, but perhaps even a partial loss of identity. To mourn for a sibling is to mourn for the lost completeness of the original family within which one came to know oneself and can bring home one's own nearness to death (Cicirelli, 2013).

Bessie and Sadie Delany were best friends all their lives. Elderly siblings are an important part of each other's support network, and sisters are especially vital in maintaining family relationships. Hans L Bonnevier, Johner/Getty Images

summary ₐₙᵈ key terms

Personality Development in Late Adulthood

- Erik Erikson's final stage, ego integrity versus despair, culminates in the virtue of *wisdom*.
- Personality traits show complex patterns of stability and continued change in adulthood.
- Emotionality tends to become more positive and less negative in old age, which has implications for health.

ego integrity versus despair

Well-Being in Late Adulthood

- In general, older adults have higher well-being than younger adults.

- Sexual minority older adults are at higher risk for poor physical and mental health outcomes; however, they show resilience and strength as well.
- Religion is an important source of emotion-focused coping for many older adults. Links have been found between religion or spirituality and health, longevity, and well-being. This may be particularly true for ethnic minority adults.
- In research based on the cognitive-appraisal model, adults of all ages generally prefer problem-focused coping, but older adults use more emotional-focused coping than younger adults.
- The concept of successful aging reflects the growing number of healthy, vital older adults, but there is dispute over how to define the concept.

- Two contrasting early models of *successful, or optimal,* aging are disengagement theory and activity theory. Disengagement theory has little support, and findings on activity theory are mixed. Newer refinements of activity theory include continuity theory and an emphasis on productive activity.
- Baltes and his colleagues suggest that successful aging, in the psychosocial as well as the cognitive realm, may depend on selective optimization with compensation.

coping, cognitive-appraisal model, problem-focused coping, emotion-focused coping, disengagement theory, activity theory, continuity theory, selective optimization with compensation (SOC)

Practical and Social Issues Related to Aging

- Some older adults continue to work for pay, but most are retired. However, many retired people start new careers or do part-time paid or volunteer work. COVID-19 has been particularly damaging for the employment of older adults. Often retirement is a phased process.
- Age has both positive and negative effects on job performance, and individual differences are more significant than age differences.
- Retirement is an ongoing process. Personal, economic, and social resources may affect morale.
- The financial situation of older Americans has improved, and fewer live in poverty. Women, Hispanic Americans, and African Americans are most likely to be poor in old age.
- In developing countries, the elderly often live with children or grandchildren. In developed countries, most older people live with a spouse or live alone. Minority elders are more likely than white elders to live with extended family members.
- Most older adults in industrialized nations prefer to age in place. Most can remain in the community if they can depend on a spouse or someone else for help.
- Older women are more likely than older men to live alone.
- Older adults in developed countries typically do not expect to live with adult children and do not wish to do so.
- Institutionalization is rare in developing countries. Its extent varies in developed countries.
- Fast-growing alternatives to institutionalization include assisted-living facilities and other types of group housing.
- Elder abuse is a significant problem. Women and adults with physical limitations or health problems, living in poverty, or who were previous victims of abuse are at increased risk. Dementia is a particularly strong risk factor as well. Intervention programs may help.

aging in place

Personal Relationships in Late Life

- Relationships are important to older people, even though frequency of social contact declines in old age.

Design Credit: (globe) janrysavy/Getty Images

- According to social convoy theory, reductions or changes in social contact in late life do not impair well-being because a stable inner circle of social support is maintained. According to socioemotional selectivity theory, older people choose to spend time with people who enhance their emotional well-being.
- Social interaction is associated with good health and life satisfaction, and isolation is a risk factor for mortality.
- The way multigenerational late-life families function often has cultural roots.

Marital Relationships

- As life expectancy increases, so does the potential longevity of marriage. More men than women are married in late life. Marriages that last into late adulthood tend to be relatively satisfying.
- Although a growing proportion of men are widowed, women tend to outlive their husbands and are less likely to marry again.
- Although there is less research on sexual minority married partners, their relationships appear to be equally strong and protective against risk. Much of the risk that does occur is the result of societal stigma.
- Divorce is uncommon among older people, and most older adults who have been divorced are remarried. Remarriages may be more relaxed in late life.

Nonmarital Lifestyles and Relationships

- A small but increasing percentage of adults reach old age without marrying. Never-married adults are less likely to be lonely than divorced or widowed ones.
- Older adults are more likely to cohabit after a prior marriage than before marriage, and these unions are generally quite stable. Rates of cohabitation in older adults have risen sharply.
- Most older adults have close friends, and those who do are healthier and happier.
- Older people enjoy time spent with friends more than with family, but the family is the main source of emotional and practical support.

Nonmarital Kinship Ties

- Older parents and their adult children frequently see or contact each other, are concerned about each other, and offer each other assistance. Many older parents are caregivers for adult children, grandchildren, or great-grandchildren.
- Often siblings offer each other emotional support and sometimes more tangible support as well. Sisters, in particular, maintain sibling ties.

Dealing with Death and Bereavement

WHL/Tetra images/Getty Images

learning objectives

Describe the cultural and historical contexts of death and dying.

Discuss death and bereavement as well as attitudes about death and dying across the life span.

Identify the challenges of coping with the death of another person.

Evaluate issues involved in decisions about death.

In this chapter we discuss how people of different cultures and ages think and feel about death and dying. We examine patterns of grief and how people cope with significant loss. We look at questions raised about life support and examine whether people have the right to die. Finally, we consider how confronting death can give life greater purpose.

The Meaning of Death and Dying

Death is a biological fact, but it also has social, cultural, historical, religious, legal, psychological, developmental, medical, and ethical aspects, and often these are closely intertwined.

Let's look more closely at death and mourning in their cultural and historical context.

THE CULTURAL CONTEXT

Customs concerning disposal and remembrance of the dead, transfer of possessions, and even expression of grief vary greatly from culture to culture and often are governed by religious or legal prescriptions that reflect a society's view of what death is and what happens afterward (see Window on the World). Cultural aspects of death include care of and behavior toward the dying and the dead, the setting where death usually takes place, and mourning customs and rituals—from the all-night Irish wake, at which friends and family toast the memory of the dead person, to the weeklong Jewish *shiva*, during which family members gather at home and receive visitors. Some cultural conventions, such as flying a flag at half-mast after the death of a public figure, are codified in law.

Although there are wide variations in customs surrounding death, there are nonetheless some commonalities in the experience across cultures. Expressions of grief, anger, and fear are common across different cultures, and most cultures have a socially sanctioned way of expressing these emotions within the context of mourning or funeral practices (Parkes et al., 2015). Beliefs about the dead also show some commonalities. In most countries, although religious behavior has declined over time, most people nonetheless believe in the afterlife. Across several studies, participants from Europe, Central America, Asia, the Caribbean, and South America all shared beliefs that the "soul" of the dead person would pass on to some sort of afterlife, and they had rituals or ceremonies intended to facilitate this transition (Bechert & Quandt, 2013; Lobar et al., 2006).

THE MORTALITY REVOLUTION

Until the twentieth century, in all societies throughout history, death was a frequent, expected event, sometimes welcomed as a peaceful end to suffering. Caring for a dying loved one at home was a common experience, as it still is in some rural communities.

Great historical changes regarding death and dying have taken place since the late nineteenth century. Advances in medicine and sanitation, new treatments for many once-fatal illnesses, and a better-educated, more health-conscious population have brought about a *mortality revolution.* Women today are less likely to die in childbirth, infants are more likely to survive their first year, children are more likely to grow to adulthood, young adults are more likely to reach old age, and older people often can overcome illnesses they grew up regarding as fatal. The top causes of death in the United States in the 1900s were diseases that most often affected children and young people: pneumonia and influenza, tuberculosis, diarrhea, and enteritis. Today, despite recent increases in drug-related deaths of people in their twenties and in early middle age as well as a spike in midlife suicide, nearly three-quarters of deaths in the United States still occur among people age 65 and over, primarily from diseases such as heart disease and cancer, the top two causes of death (Kochanek, 2019). Most recently, projections for deaths resulting from COVID-19 place the virus as the third leading cause of death in 2020, although final data will not be available until 2021 (Centers for Disease Control and Prevention, 2020).

Amid all this progress in improving health and lengthening life, something important may have been lost. Looking death in the eye, bit by bit, day by day, people growing up in traditional societies absorbed an important truth: dying is part of living. As death increasingly became a phenomenon of late adulthood, it became "invisible and abstract" (Fulton & Owen, 1987–1988, p. 380). Care of the dying and the dead became largely

on the world

CULTURAL VARIATIONS IN FUNERAL CUSTOMS

Funerals in America or Europe are generally held at a church or funeral home. People dress in black, a service is held, and the deceased is either buried or cremated. There is often a visitation before the service and a gathering held at the home or church of the family. Though this is the common tradition in much of the Westernized world, it is not the only tradition.

In traditional Islamic burials, the deceased must be buried as soon as possible after death, usually within 24 hours, to free the soul from the body. The body is washed and a burial shroud is placed over it. The deceased is laid on the right side facing Mecca, without a casket, if allowed. Burial sites are marked by a simple flat marker or not marked at all. The mourning period is 3 days where the family says daily prayers for the loved one (Rahman, 2011).

For the Toraja in Indonesia, the funeral is a celebration of life. Funerals are elaborate and expensive and the whole community takes part. There is a series of ceremonies that must take place, and while this happens the deceased is embalmed and stays with the family. The person is symbolically fed and cared for, remaining part of the family until the final burial takes place on the 11th day of the ceremonies. Each year during a ritual called Ma' Nene, the bodies are exhumed, cleaned, and dressed in new clothes and walked around the village (Holloway, 2014).

In Tibet, burial rituals are based on the Buddhist belief that the spirit leaves the body the moment a person dies. The body should be returned to the earth and recycled. The sky burial is the preferred ritual. In the sky burial the body is dissected and placed on a high cliff, it is offered up to hungry vultures, a final act of kindness to other creatures, contributing to the life cycle (Kerala, 2005).

In ancient Greece, bodies of heroes were publicly burned as a sign of honor. Cremation is still widely practiced by Hindus in India and Nepal. Cremation has also become more common in South Korea due to lack of space to bury the dead. Rather than storing ashes, many people are choosing to turn their loved ones' remains into beads. The beads are colorful and are stored in glass containers to keep their loved ones close (The Week, 2012).

In Mexico and Latin America, a traditional ceremony is given at a church or the family home with a final ceremony at the burial site. Each family member, including children, throws a handful of dirt on the coffin before the grave is filled. They light a candle at church for 9 days following the death. Every year on November 2, the Day of the Dead, families gather to remember and honor those who have passed. It is often celebrated with festivals; families eat, sing, and tell stories about deceased loved ones. Families may visit the gravesite or create an altar for the family member, decorating it with candles, flowers, and the favorite foods of the deceased (Benedetti, 2017).

These varied customs and practices help people deal with death and bereavement through well-understood cultural meanings that provide a stable anchor amid the turbulence of loss.

what's your view

What are the traditions in your culture for honoring or mourning the dead? What do you think this says about your cultural values?

---

a task for professionals. Such social conventions as placing the dying person in a hospital or nursing home and refusing to openly discuss his or her condition reflected and perpetuated attitudes of avoidance and denial of death. Death—even of the very old—came to be regarded as a failure of medical treatment rather than as a natural end to life (McCue, 1995; Waldrop, 2011).

Today, this picture again is changing. **Thanatology,** the study of death and dying, is arousing interest, and educational programs have been established to help people deal with death. Because of the prohibitive cost of extended hospital care that cannot save the terminally ill as well as a movement toward a more humane end to the life span, many more deaths are now occurring at home, as they once did the world over.

thanatology
Study of death and dying.

RESPONSES TO DEATH ACROSS THE LIFE SPAN

There is no single way of viewing death at any age. As the timing-of-events model suggests, death probably does not mean the same thing to an 85-year-old man with excruciatingly painful arthritis, a 56-year-old woman at the height of a brilliant legal career who discovers she has breast cancer, and a 15-year-old who dies of an overdose of drugs.

Infancy and Childhood With respect to bereavement, if children are old enough to love, they are old enough to grieve. However, they may have difficulty expressing or understanding their grief. Like their understanding of death, this depends on cognitive and emotional development. Infants and very young children may respond to the death of a parent initially with crying, despair, and, eventually, pathological detachment. They do not understand death, but they understand loss. They may show feeding or sleeping difficulties, constipation, and previously toilet-trained toddlers may wet the bed. Depression may manifest as irritation or somatic complaints such as stomachaches (Black, 1998).

Generally, although many feel uncomfortable doing so, most parents begin to talk about death with their children at around the age of 3 years (Nguyen & Rosengren, 2004; Renaud et al., 2015). Learning about death involves understanding it is irreversible, universal (happens to everyone), nonfunctional (involves the cessation of all life function), and inevitable (Speece & Brent, 1984).

By the age of 4, children build a partial understanding of the biological nature of death. For example, 3- to 5-year-old German and Shuar children from a rural Amazon region of Ecuador were told a story and then asked questions about either a human or an animal character that either got tired and went to sleep or was killed. The 3-year-olds rarely answered correctly when asked if the character in the story who was killed could move or be afraid, whereas children at the age of 4 had little problem doing so (Barrett & Behne, 2005). However, this understanding is incomplete. In another study, preschoolers and kindergarteners expressed knowledge that a dead mouse would never be alive again or grow up to be an old mouse, but 54 percent said the mouse might still need to eat. By age 7, 91 percent of the children were consistent in their knowledge that such biological processes as eating and drinking cease at death. Generally, children have mastered the biological understanding of death by about 10 years of age (Kenyon, 2001).

Death is challenging to understand, even for adults, and can be difficult to talk about. However, 1 in 7 children will be affected by the death of a family member by the age of 10 years (Torbic, 2011). In American samples, approximately 5 to 8 percent of children experience the death of a sibling (Fletcher et al., 2013). Children can better understand death if they are introduced to the concept at an early age and are encouraged to talk about it. For example, the death of a pet or knowing another child who dies may provide an opportunity. Children's books (Malcom, 2011) and movies (Cox et al., 2005) can scaffold conversations about death, although movies, especially older ones, do not always adequately address emotional responses (Graham et al., 2018). Not surprisingly, children who have had experience with the death of a loved one have a more realistic view of death than children who have not experienced such an event (Bonoti et al., 2013; Hunter & Smith, 2008).

Although much of the research on children's understanding of death has focused on their understanding of the cessation of biological processes, it is also the case that many adults believe in the afterlife and often explicitly teach their children about it within the context of religious instruction. Within the context of these beliefs, psychological processes are presumed to carry on after death. Thus affirmative answers to questions about the persistence of thoughts, feelings, and desires after death are not necessarily reflective of immaturity (Harris, 2011). For instance, 5-year-old Vezo children from Madagascar often answered that a dead bird or man could continue to do things like sit upright or see. By the age of 7, most children responded that a dead entity could perform none of these actions. But as they grew older, children and adolescents, like adults, were increasingly likely to respond that mental processes continued after death even though biological processes ceased (Astuti & Harris, 2008). Similar findings have emerged in Spanish and British schoolchildren (Giménez & Harris, 2005; Hopkins, 2014).

Children sometimes express grief through anger, acting out, or refusing to acknowledge a death, as if the pretense a person is still alive will make it so. They may be confused by adults' euphemisms: that someone "passed on" or that the family "lost" someone or that someone is "asleep" and will never awaken. Adjusting to loss is more difficult if a child had a troubled relationship with the person who died; if a surviving parent depends too much on the child; if the death was unexpected, especially if it was a murder or suicide; if the child has had previous behavioral or emotional problems; or if family and community support are lacking (Schonfeld et al., 2016).

Parents and other adult caregivers can help children deal with bereavement by explaining that death is final and inevitable and that they did not cause the death by their misbehavior or thoughts. Children may show their grief in short spurts and then return to their daily activities, but this does not mean they are recovered. Children need reassurance that they will continue to receive care from loving adults. It is usually advisable to make as few changes as possible in a child's environment, relationships, and daily activities; to answer questions simply and honestly; and to encourage the child to talk about his or her feelings and about the person who died (Schonfeld et al., 2016; Slaven, 2017).

Adolescence For adolescents, although they are capable of a mature understanding of death, it is not something they normally think much about unless they are directly faced with it. Most teens are at the beginning of their lives, and generally their contact with death involves the death of a loved one rather than their own mortality.

In the event of a close death, teens benefit from talking about it, although support and assistance for them is not always present (Schonfeld et al., 2016). Often teens may turn to peers for such support (Dopp & Cain, 2012). At the same time teens must process their own grief they are often also asked to take on more adult responsibilities, such as helping take care of younger siblings or providing emotional support to a surviving parent (Schonfeld et al., 2016). The bereavement process can lead to academic problems, especially for juniors and seniors in high school (Schonfeld & Quackenbush, 2010), and mental health issues, particularly depression, conduct disorder, and increased likelihood of substance abuse (Brent et al., 2009; Kaplow et al., 2010).

Fortunately, much of the grief response in both children and adolescents declines over time. However, a subset of young people experience persistent or even increasing grief over time (Melhem et al., 2011). A recent meta-analysis showed that although the effect size was small to moderate, therapeutic interventions could have positive effects on the bereavement process that persisted over time. The most promising treatment approaches were musical therapy and brief psychotherapy (Rosner et al., 2010).

Adulthood Young adults are generally eager to live the lives they have been preparing for. If they are suddenly struck by a potentially fatal illness or injury, they are likely to be frustrated and angry. People who develop terminal illnesses in their twenties or thirties must face issues of death and dying at an age when they normally would be dealing with such issues of young adulthood as establishing an intimate relationship. Rather than having a long lifetime of losses as gradual preparation for the final loss of life, they find their entire world collapsing at once.

In middle age, most adults' bodies send them signals that they are not as young, agile, and hearty as they once were. More and more they think about how many years they may have left and how to make the most of those years (Neugarten, 1967). Often—especially after the death of both parents—there is a new awareness of being the older generation or the next in line to die (Scharlach & Fredriksen, 1993). Middle-age and older adults may prepare for death emotionally as well as in practical ways by making a will, planning their funerals, and discussing their wishes with family and friends.

Older adults may have mixed feelings about the prospect of dying. Physical losses and other problems may diminish their pleasure in living and their will to live (McCue, 1995). Some older adults give up on achieving unfulfilled goals. Others push harder to do what they can with life in the time they have left. Many try to extend their remaining time by adopting healthier lifestyles or struggle to live even when they are profoundly ill (Cicirelli, 2002), sometimes using religion to allay anxiety (Krause et al., 2016).

When they think or talk of their impending death, some older adults express fear or anxiety and worry about the effect their death will have on their loved ones (Missler et al., 2012). Generally, distress is greater when the discrepancy between how long they want to live and how long they think they have left is large (Cicirelli, 2006).

Facing Death and Loss

Death is an important chapter in human development. What changes do people undergo shortly before death? How do they come to terms with its imminence? How do people handle grief? How do attitudes toward death change across the life span?

FACTORS PRECEDING DEATH

Care of the Dying Along with a growing tendency to face death more honestly, movements have arisen to make dying more humane. Primary among these movements is the establishment of **hospice care** for dying persons. Hospice care is personal, patient- and family-centered, compassionate care for the terminally ill. Hospice facilities generally provide **palliative care,** which includes relief of pain and suffering, control of symptoms, alleviation of stress, and attempts to maintain a satisfactory quality of life. However, palliative care is not intended to cure or reverse the course of disease.

Hospice facilities offer a specialized type of palliative care for people whose life expectancy is 6 months or less. The goal is to allow the person to die in peace and dignity while minimizing any pain and suffering, and it often includes self-help support groups for both dying people and their families.

Hospice care may take place at home, but such care can also be given in a hospital or another institution, at a hospice center, or through a combination of home and institutional care. The provision of hospice and palliative care is associated with better outcomes. For instance, patients enrolled in hospice report greater satisfaction and pain control; they are less likely to report difficulty breathing; they spend less time in the hospital; and they are less likely to be admitted to the intensive care unit and less likely to die in the hospital. Their families are more likely to report greater satisfaction with care, higher-quality end-of-life care, and compliance with requests about end-of-life preferences (Kleinpell et al., 2019; Wright et al., 2016; Kumar et al., 2017). Death is inevitable. A bad death is not.

Hospice care is likely to have its greatest effects if it is provided early enough to improve quality of life (Gaertner et al., 2017), especially for those individuals who are unlikely to benefit from medical intervention. For example, in one study tracking newly diagnosed advanced metastatic lung cancer patients, those that began to receive palliative care immediately at the time of diagnosis had a higher quality of life, better emotional state, and even longer median survival time than patients who received standard oncological care only (Temel et al., 2010).

The Terminal Drop Even without any identifiable illness, people around the age of 100 tend to experience functional declines, lose interest in eating and drinking, and die a natural death (Johansson et al., 2004; Small et al., 2003). There also appear to be changes in life satisfaction that precede death (Windsor et al., 2015; Gerstorf et al., 2010). Such changes also have been noted in younger people whose death is near. In a 22-year longitudinal study of 1,927 men, life satisfaction showed steep declines within 1 year before death, regardless of self-rated health (Mroczek & Spiro, 2005).

Terminal drop, or *terminal decline,* refers specifically to a widely observed decline in cognitive abilities shortly before death, even when factors such as demographics and health are controlled for (Gerstorf & Ram, 2013). This effect has been found in longitudinal studies in various countries—not only of the very old, but also of adults of a wide range of ages with no signs of dementia (Johansson et al., 2004; Singer et al., 2003; Rabbitt et al., 2002; Small et al., 2003). Losses of perceptual speed have been found to predict death nearly 15 years later (Thorvaldsson et al., 2008), although most declines start at about 7.7 years before death occurs (Muniz-Terrera et al., 2013). Although more highly

hospice care
Personal, patient- and family-centered care for a person with a terminal illness.

palliative care
Care aimed at relieving pain and suffering and allowing the terminally ill to die in peace, comfort, and dignity.

Hospice care seeks to ease patients' pain and treat their symptoms to keep them as comfortable and alert as possible. It also helps families deal with illness and death. KatarzynaBialasiewicz/iStock/Getty Images

terminal drop
A frequently observed decline in cognitive abilities near the end of life. Also called *terminal decline.*

educated people generally perform better on cognitive tests, they show similar rates of decline as do less educated people. Dementia, however, accelerates the rate of decline in all people (Bendayan et al., 2017). Areas of decline include memory capacity, perceptual speed, visuospatial abilities, and everyday cognition (Gerstorf & Ram, 2013; Thorvaldsson et al., 2008).

Near-Death Experiences Some people who have come close to dying report *near-death experiences (NDE),* often involving a sense of being out of the body or sucked into a tunnel and visions of bright lights or mystical encounters. These types of experiences have been reported in many different cultures, both in modern times and in written and oral histories of nonindustrialized cultures (Tassell-Matamua, 2013). Skeptics generally interpret these reports as resulting from physiological changes that accompany the process of dying. Some researchers argue that near-death experiences reflect the common bodily structures affected by the process of dying (Mobbs & Watt, 2011), in particular, the oxygen deprivation that occurs in 9 out of 10 dying persons (Woerlee, 2005). Research in rats shows that a cardiac arrest, which brings about oxygen deprivation, also results in brain waves indicating an aroused, highly functioning brain shortly before death. This suggests humans might experience a similar type of conscious information processing during clinical death (Borjigin et al., 2013). However, not everyone who experiences oxygen deprivation experiences a NDE. In one study of cardiac patients who were "brought back" after clinical death, only about 21 percent reported a NDE (Klemenc-Ketis et al., 2010). Therefore, anoxia cannot be the sole cause of NDEs.

When a brain is deprived of oxygen, certain images arise due to alterations in the visual cortex and can result in the perception of a tunnel, like the images reported by people who have had near-death experiences. mark gibbons/Alamy Stock Photo

A variety of data from humans, including reports of NDEs in cardiac arrest survivors and individuals undergoing anesthesia; reports of NDE-like experiences in people under the influence of various drugs such as ketamine, LSD, and cannabinoids or under the influence of epilepsy or deliberately induced electrical cortical stimulation; and experiments using mild oxygen deprivation or artificially lowered blood pressure to induce NDE-like sensations, suggest that NDE phenomena are linked to stimulation or damage of various brain areas, most notably in bilateral frontal and occipital areas. The commonly reported altered sense of time, flying sensations, and light reported by some people are theorized to originate in the right hemispheric temporoparietal junction (TPJ). By contrast, the spiritual dimensions often reported, along with the sounds, music, and voices, are believed to result from the left hemispherical TPJ. Emotions and life review, another commonly experienced aspect of NDEs, are thought to originate from the hippocampus and amygdala (Blanke et al., 2016).

Regardless of their origin, NDEs are generally experienced as positive, an effect that has been proposed to occur as a result of the release of endorphins that are released during stressful experiences (Agrillo, 2011). Some people who experience NDEs report spiritual growth as one consequence, and the degree of spiritual transformation is related to the depth of the NDE (Greyson & Khanna, 2014). NDEs are predicted to occur more frequently in the coming years as survival rates continue to improve with modern resuscitation techniques (Agrillo, 2011; van Lommel, 2011).

CONFRONTING DEATH

Terror Management Theory Regardless of age, the awareness of death is distressing and has the potential to result in declines in well-being and increases in anxiety (Juhl & Routledge, 2016). One approach—terror management theory (TMT)—proposes that humans' unique understanding of death, in concert with self-preservation needs and capacity for fear, results in common emotional and psychological responses when mortality, or thoughts of death, are made salient.

One common response to thoughts of death is to become more committed to a cultural worldview (Burke et al., 2010). For example, when death is made salient, people

When death is made salient, stronger adherence to a religious ideology can provide psychological comfort. Pra Chid/ Shutterstock

are more likely to endorse their religious beliefs and they believe more strongly in the afterlife (Vail et al., 2010; Lehto & Stein, 2009). This stronger adherence to a religious ideology provides psychological comfort.

Another implication of TMT is that high self-esteem should buffer people against anxiety and fear over death. Feeling significant and valuable to others can help people believe they are more than their physical body. Generally, research has supported a link between high self-esteem and less anxiety regarding death (Burke et al., 2010).

Last, mortality salience has been associated with attachment processes. Seeking comfort from loved ones is a common response in humans undergoing threat and is a regulatory strategy to reduce anxiety. Therefore, those people who have more secure attachment relationships would be predicted to show less anxiety in the face of death, a finding that has been verified in research (Mikulincer & Florian, 2000). Moreover, when death is made salient, people are more likely to engage in behaviors to increase attachment, such as enhanced commitment, attraction, forgiveness, and intimacy (Plusnin et al., 2018).

The Five Stages of Grief The psychiatrist Elisabeth Kübler-Ross, in her pioneering work with dying people, found that most of them welcomed an opportunity to speak openly about their condition and were aware of being close to death, even when they had not been told. After speaking with some 500 terminally ill patients, Kübler-Ross (1969, 1970) outlined five stages in coming to terms with death: (1) *denial* ("This can't be happening to me!"); (2) *anger* ("Why me?"); (3) *bargaining for extra time* ("If I can only live to see my daughter married, I won't ask for anything more"); (4) *depression;* and ultimately (5) *acceptance.* She also proposed a similar progression in the feelings of people facing imminent bereavement (Kübler-Ross, 1975).

Kübler-Ross's model has been criticized and modified by other professionals who work with dying patients. Although the emotions she described are common, not everyone goes through all five stages and not necessarily in the same sequence. A person may go back and forth between anger and depression, for example, or may feel both at once.

Dying, like living, is an individual experience. For some people, denial or anger may be a healthier way to face death than calm acceptance. Kübler-Ross's findings, valuable as they are in helping us understand the feelings of those who are facing the end of life, should not be considered the sole model or criterion for a "good death."

PATTERNS OF GRIEVING

grief
Emotional response experienced in the early phases of bereavement.

bereavement
Loss, due to death, of someone to whom one feels close and the process of adjustment to the loss.

The death of a loved one is a difficult thing. First, there is **grief,** the emotional response that generally follows closely on the heels of death. This is followed by **bereavement.** Bereavement is a response to the loss of someone to whom a person feels close. But bereavement is not just an event, and it is not just grief—it is also a process of adjustment.

Bereavement often brings about a change in role or status. For example, a person may have to adjust to becoming a widow after previously being a wife, or as an orphan after previously being a son or daughter. There may be social or economic consequences as well—a loss of friends and sometimes of income. In short, bereavement can affect practically all aspects of a person's life.

grief work
Working out of psychological issues connected with grief.

The Classic Grief Work Model How do people grieve? A classic pattern of grief is three stages in which the bereaved person accepts the painful reality of the loss, gradually lets go of the bond with the dead person, and readjusts to life by developing new interests and relationships. This process of **grief work,** often takes the following path—though, as with Kübler-Ross's stages, it may vary (Brown & Stoudemire, 1983; Schulz, 1978).

1. *Shock and disbelief.* Immediately following a death, survivors often feel lost and confused. As awareness of the loss sinks in, the initial numbness gives way to overwhelming feelings of sadness and frequent crying. This first stage may last several weeks, especially after a sudden or unexpected death.

2. *Preoccupation with the memory of the dead person.* In the second stage, which may last 6 months to 2 years or so, the survivor tries to come to terms with the death but cannot yet accept it. These experiences diminish with time, though they may recur—perhaps for years—on such occasions as the anniversary of the marriage or of the death.

3. *Resolution.* The final stage has arrived when the bereaved person renews interest in everyday activities. Memories of the dead person bring fond feelings mingled with sadness rather than sharp pain and longing.

Some people recover quickly from the loss of a loved one; others never do. zakir hossain chowdhury zakir/Alamy Stock Photo

Variations in Grieving Although the pattern of grief work just described is common, grieving does not necessarily follow a straight line from shock to resolution. In the *commonly expected* pattern, the mourner goes from high to low distress. In the *absent grief* pattern, the mourner does not experience intense distress, either immediately or later. In the *chronic grief* pattern, the mourner remains distressed for a long time. Chronic grief may be especially painful and acceptance most difficult when a loss is *ambiguous,* as when a loved one is missing and presumed dead. In the final pattern, known as *resilience*, the mourner shows a low and gradually diminishing level of grief in response to the death of a loved one (Bonanno et al., 2011).

Previously, the assumption was sometimes made that something had to be wrong if a bereaved person showed only mild distress and moved on quickly from the death of a loved one. However, research suggests that over half of people can be classified as resilient (Mancini et al., 2011; Spahni et al., 2015). Moreover, resilience has been associated with positive outcomes, including reduced depression and loneliness and improved life satisfaction (Spahni et al., 2016). People who are resilient are generally low in neuroticism and high in extraversion (Mancini et al., 2015; Mancini et al., 2011). Secure attachment and an internal locus of control have also been associated with resilience (Laird et al., 2019). Older adults who are resilient also tend to have had prior experience with adversity (Seery, 2011). In other words, having had bad things happen to you and having overcome them successfully teaches you how to handle life's inevitable challenges more effectively.

The knowledge that grief takes varied forms and patterns has important implications for helping people deal with loss (Boerner et al., 2004, 2005; Bonanno et al., 2002). Table 19.1 lists suggestions for helping those who have lost a loved one. It may be unnecessary and even harmful to urge or lead mourners to work through a loss or to expect them to follow a set pattern of emotional reactions. Although bereavement therapy may help some people, the evidence suggests that many people will recover on their own if given time (Neimeyer & Currier, 2009).

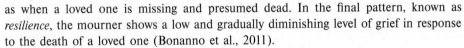

TABLE 19.1 Helping Someone Who Has Lost a Loved One
Share the sorrow. Allow—or encourage—the bereaved person to talk about feelings of loss and share memories of the deceased person.
Don't offer false comfort. Saying such things as "It's all for the best" or "You'll get over it in time" is not helpful. Instead, simply express sorrow and take time to listen.
Offer practical help. Babysitting, cooking, and running errands are ways to help someone who is grieving.
Be patient. It can take a long time to recover from a significant loss. Be available to talk and listen.
Suggest professional help when necessary. Don't hesitate to recommend professional help when it appears that someone is experiencing too much pain to cope alone.

Source: National Mental Health Association. (n.d.). *Coping with loss—bereavement and grief* [Fact sheet]. Alexandria, VA: author.

Significant Losses

Especially difficult losses that may occur during adulthood are the deaths of a spouse, a parent, or a child. The loss of a pregnancy through miscarriage or stillbirth also can be painful but usually draws less social support.

SURVIVING A SPOUSE

Because women tend to live longer than men and to be younger than their husbands, they are more likely to be widowed. They also tend to be widowed at an earlier age. Some 34 percent of U.S. women, but only 11.9 percent of U.S. men lose their spouse by age 65 (Federal Interagency Forum on Aging-Related Statistics, 2016).

The stress of widowhood often affects physical and mental health. Bereavement can lead to headaches, memory problems, difficulty with concentration, dizziness, indigestion, loss of appetite, or chest pain. It also entails higher risks of disability, drug use, anxiety, depression, insomnia, hospitalization, and even death. These reactions may range from fairly short and mild to extreme and long lasting, sometimes even for years (Stroebe et al., 2007).

A meta-analysis of mortality risk including data from over 500 million people showed that becoming a widowed person is associated with a 22 percent increase in risk of death when compared to married people, and that this risk is higher for men (27 percent) than for women (15 percent) (Moon et al., 2011). The risk of either natural death or suicide is greatest in the early months after a loss and is higher for younger adults. Indeed, the disparity in the mortality risk for men versus women as a result of becoming widowed declines with age (Shor et al., 2012).

The quality of the marital relationship that has been lost may affect the degree to which widowhood affects mental health. Higher relationship quality during the marriage has been associated with greater anger, more anxiety and depression, and feelings of yearning 6 months after the loss of the spouse (Carr & Boerner, 2009; Schaan, 2013). However, those people who are able to maintain healthy, secure attachments to other people in their lives and use them for social support are likely to show more resilience after the death of a spouse (Mancini et al., 2015).

The loss of companionship may help explain why a widowed person, especially a widower, may soon follow the spouse to the grave (Ray, 2004). However, a more practical explanation also may apply; after the death of a spouse, there may be no one to remind an older widow to take her pills or to make sure a widowed man adheres to a special diet. Those who receive such reminders (say, from children or health workers) tend to improve in health habits and reported health (Williams, 2004).

Widowhood can create practical problems too. For women, the main consequences of widowhood are more likely to be economic strain, whereas for men the chief consequences are more likely to be social isolation and loss of emotional intimacy (Pudrovska et al., 2006). Women whose husbands were the chief breadwinners may experience economic hardship or fall into poverty (Hungerford, 2001). Widowed men are more likely to become socially isolated after the death of a spouse than are widows (Isherwood et al., 2017), whereas older widows are more likely than older widowers to stay in touch with friends from whom they receive social support (Kinsella & Velkoff, 2001).

Ultimately, the distress of loss can be a catalyst for introspection and growth (Lieberman, 1996). In one study, widows continued to talk and think about their deceased husbands decades after the loss, but these thoughts rarely upset them. Instead, these women said they had become stronger and more self-confident as a result of their loss (Carnelley et al., 2006). Older widows are likely to have larger and more supportive social networks than

Older widows are more likely than older widowers to stay in touch with friends and benefit from the support of a social network.
belushi/Shutterstock

their married counterparts (Kang & Ahn, 2014), a response to spousal death likely contributing to resilience.

LOSING A PARENT IN ADULTHOOD

The loss of a parent at any time is difficult, even in adulthood (Nickerson et al., 2013). The majority of bereaved adult children still experience emotional distress—ranging from sadness and crying to depression and thoughts of suicide—after 1 to 5 years, especially following loss of a mother and most strongly in daughters (Scharlach & Fredriksen, 1993; Leopold & Lechner, 2015). However, the death of a parent can be a maturing experience. It can push adults into resolving important developmental issues: achieving a stronger sense of self and a more pressing, realistic awareness of their own mortality, along with a greater sense of purpose, responsibility, commitment, and interconnectedness to others (Pope, 2005; Moss & Moss, 1989; Scharlach & Fredriksen, 1993).

Still, the road may not be easy. Families with a history of conflict are more likely to engage in conflict when a parent is approaching death and important decisions must be made; however, when adult parents leave instructions for the type of medical treatment they desire at the end of life, this generally results in less stressful decision making for their children (Tilden et al., 2001; Kramer & Boelk, 2015). Nevertheless, regardless of the wishes of the dying parent, if siblings disagree on the treatment provided, this can damage their relationship (Su et al., 2014). Siblings are less likely to engage in conflict over end-of-life care when parents designate someone outside of the family as the person who will make decisions about such care (Khodyakov & Carr, 2009; Kramer et al., 2006)

The impact of a parent's death on siblings is equivocal. Some research suggests that following the death of a parent, siblings tend to grow less close. This may be because the link that bound them together in their adult life—a parent—is gone (Walker et al., 2005), or it may be because of conflict following parental death about such aspects as funeral arrangements or distribution of assets (Umberson, 2003). Other research suggests that parental death may lead to more close relationships. A bereaved adult child may assume more responsibility for the surviving parent and for keeping the family together (Aldwin & Levenson, 2001). Additionally, the intense emotions of bereavement may draw siblings closer, and their parent's death may eliminate previous sources of dissent and disagreement over care and medical decisions (Umberson, 2003). A longitudinal approach may help explain these disparate findings. Research shows that sibling contact intensifies after a parent dies and then declines over time. Moreover, if the second parent dies, the effect is intensified once support is no longer needed for a surviving parent (Kalmijn & Leopold, 2019)

LOSING A CHILD

A parent is rarely prepared emotionally for the death of a child. Such a death, no matter at what age, comes as a cruel, unnatural shock, an untimely event that, in the normal course of things, should never happen. The parents may feel they have failed, no matter how much they loved and cared for the child, and they may find it hard to let go.

Parents who have lost a child are at heightened risk of being depressed or hospitalized for mental illness and show poorer health-related quality of life (Rogers et al., 2008; Li et al., 2005; Song et al., 2010). The stress of a child's loss may even hasten a parent's death, most frequently via heart disease (Song et al., 2019; Rostila et al., 2012).

If a marriage is strong, the couple may draw closer together, supporting each other in their shared loss. In other cases, the loss weakens and eventually destroys the marriage (Albuquerque et al., 2016; Lyngstad, 2013). One important factor appears to be whether or not parents grieve a similar amount. Parents who perceive that their spouse is grieving more or less than they are report less satisfaction in the relationship than those who perceive greater similarity in their pain (Buyukcan-Tetik et al., 2017).

The impact of parental bereavement may vary depending on a variety of factors. Grief rises with the age of a child (up to 17) and the age of a parent (up to 40) (Wijngaards-deMeij et al., 2005; Moor & de Graaf, 2016). Parents whose child dies a traumatic death generally grieve more than those whose child dies of an illness or disorder or those who experience a stillbirth or neonatal death, and mothers tend to grieve more than fathers (Wijngaards-deMeij et al., 2005; Meert et al., 2010). Those parents who are able to make some sense of the loss generally show less intense grief (Keesee et al., 2008). Additionally, a sense of purpose in life and high levels of agreeableness are also protective (Floyd et al., 2013). As time goes by, grief tends to diminish, especially among couples who became pregnant again (Wijngaards-deMeij et al., 2005). However, even decades later, most parents express lasting grief (Rogers et al., 2008).

Many parents hesitate to discuss a terminally ill child's impending death with the child, but those who do so tend to achieve a sense of closure that helps them cope after the loss. In one study, approximately one-third of the parents said they had talked with their children about their impending death, and none of these parents regretted having done so. When asked about what they did regret following their child's death, parents regretted not bringing the subject of death up, not spending time with their child, and agreeing to surgery and additional treatment for their child (Kreicbergs et al., 2004; Brooten et al., 2019).

When asked what most helped them cope with the end of their child's life, 73 percent of parents whose children died in intensive-care units gave religious or spiritual responses. They mentioned prayer, faith, discussions with clergy, or a belief that the parent-child relationship endures beyond death. Parents also said they were guided by insight and wisdom, inner values, and spiritual virtues such as hope, trust, and love (Robinson et al., 2006). Parents who used spiritual beliefs to help them cope with their child's death showed less grief, depression, and, for mothers, less post traumatic stress and greater personal growth (Hawthorne et al., 2016). The comfort derived from religious beliefs appears to be more common in Black and Hispanic parents than in white parents (Brooten et al., 2015).

MOURNING A MISCARRIAGE

Estimates are that somewhere around one in three pregnancies end in miscarriage (Smith et al., 2003). Families, friends, and health professionals tend to avoid talking about such losses, which often are considered insignificant compared with the loss of a living child (Van, 2001). Moreover, many couples do not tell others about their pregnancy until after the first trimester, during which miscarriage is most common. So, in many cases, friends and family members may not even realize support is needed (Brier, 2008). Grief can be more wrenching without social support.

How do prospective parents cope with the loss of a child they never knew? Common responses, which are generally reported with greater intensity in women, include grief, depression, guilt, isolation, and sadness (Huffman et al., 2015; Volgsten et al., 2018). Roughly a third meet the criteria for post traumatic stress disorder (Farren et al., 2016). Generally, negative outcomes are even stronger when pregnancy losses are recurrent (Kolte et al., 2015). Often, parents who have lost a child to miscarriage or stillbirth become pregnant again, frequently within 2 to 3 months after their loss (Plana-Ripoll et al., 2018).

Whether married or living together, couples who experience a miscarriage prior to 20 weeks of gestation are 22 percent more likely to break up than couples who have a successful pregnancy. When the miscarriage occurs after 20 weeks, that risk is elevated by as much as 40 percent (Gold et al., 2010).

Medical, Legal, and Ethical Issues

Do people have a right to die? Should a terminally ill person who wants to commit suicide be allowed or helped to do so? Who decides that a life is not worth prolonging?

SUICIDE

Although suicide is no longer a crime in modern societies, there is still a stigma against it, based in part on religious prohibitions and in part on society's interest in preserving life. A person who expresses suicidal thoughts may be mentally ill, and the desire to die may be temporary and disappear when mental illness abates or circumstances change. On the other hand, a growing number of people consider a mature adult's deliberate choice of a time to end his or her life a rational decision and a right to be defended.

Suicide is a global issue. The global suicide rate was approximately 10.5 per 100,000 people in 2016, representing almost 800,000 people on a yearly basis. Although suicide can occur in people of almost any age, rates are highest in the elderly in almost all areas of the world. Men also commit suicide at higher rates than do women. Low- and middle-income countries bear the brunt of the suicide burden, accounting for 79 percent of suicides. They also tend to have higher suicide rates in young adults and older women, whereas higher-income countries have higher suicide rates in middle-age men. The most common methods used to commit suicide are self-poisoning with pesticides, hanging, and firearms (World Health Organization, 2018, 2019).

Suicide rates in the United States peaked in 1977 at 13.7 deaths per 100,000 people then slowly declined to a low of 10.4 in 2000. Since that time, however, the rate has begun to increase again, and as of 2017 was 13.0 deaths per 100,000 people, or over 47,000 people (Kochanek et al., 2019; Curtin et al., 2016). Still, this rate is lower than that in many other industrialized countries (Kinsella & Velkoff, 2001).

Statistics probably understate the number of suicides; many go unreported and some (such as traffic "accidents" and "accidental" medicinal overdoses) are not recognized as such. Also, the figures on suicides often do not include suicide *attempts*; an estimated 20 to 60 percent of people in the United States who commit suicide have tried before, and about 10 percent of people who attempt suicide will kill themselves within 10 years (Harvard Medical School, 2003; Figure 19.1).

In most nations, suicide rates rise with age (Table 19.3), and are higher among men than among women (Curtin et al., 2016; Kinsella & Velkoff, 2001; Nock et al., 2008), though more women consider or attempt suicide. Young, unmarried women with little education and those who are unusually impulsive, anxious, or depressed are most at risk for suicidal thoughts and behavior (Nock et al., 2008). Historically males were far more likely to succeed in taking their own life, but this gap has greatly diminished in recent years. Men's suicide rates are higher mainly because they are far more likely to use reliable methods, such as firearms, whereas women are more likely to choose other means, such as poisoning or hanging. Almost half of completed suicides are by gunshot, and gun deaths via suicide far outnumber those by homicide (Kochanek et al., 2019). The rates of suicide using firearms are much higher in the United States than in other similar industrialized nations (Richardson & Hemenway, 2011), presumably because of easy accessibility to firearms (Anglemyer et al., 2014). Suicide by suffocation has increased recently; approximately 1 in 4 suicides in 2014 were the result of suffocation (Curtin et al., 2016).

Suicide rates vary along ethnic and racial lines. Native American and Alaskan Natives have the highest rates, at 22.1 per 100,000 people. They are followed by whites (18.1), Asian/Pacific Islanders (7.0), African Americans (6.9), and Hispanics (6.7) (Kochanek et al., 2019). Although some people intent on suicide carefully conceal their plans, most give warning signs (Table 19.2).

Due to a jump in midlife suicide (Table 19.3), U.S. suicide rates now reach a high for adults in their forties and early fifties and then subside and rise again after age 75 (Xu et al., 2010; Kochanek et al., 2019).

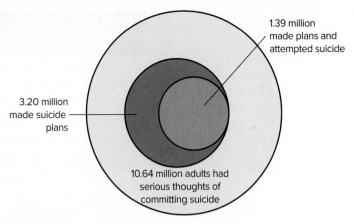

FIGURE 19.1
Suicide in the United States, 2017
About 1.39 million people attempted suicide in 2017.

Source: Substance Abuse and Mental Health Services Administration. (2018). Results from the 2017 National survey on Drug Use and Health [Data tables]. Retrieved from www. samhsa.gov/data/sites/default/files/cbhsq-reports/NSDUHDetailedTabs2017/ NSDUHDetailedTabs2017.pdf

The highest rate of suicide is among white men age 75 and over; the risk rises among men 85 and older. Older people are more likely than younger people to be depressed and socially isolated.
Anna Lurye/Shutterstock

TABLE 19.2 Preventing Suicide

WARNING SIGNS OF SUICIDE:

- Feeling depressed, down, or excessively sad.
- Feelings of hopelessness, worthlessness, or having no purpose in life, along with a loss of interest or pleasure in doing things.
- Preoccupation with death, dying, or violence, or talking about wanting to die.
- Seeking access to medications, weapons, or other means of committing suicide.
- Wide mood swings—feeling extremely up one day and terribly down the next.
- Feelings of great agitation, rage, or uncontrolled anger, or wanting to get revenge.
- Changes in eating and sleeping habits, appearance, behavior, or personality.
- Risky or self-destructive behavior, such as driving recklessly or taking illegal drugs.
- Sudden calmness (a sign that a person has made the decision to attempt suicide).
- Life crises, trauma, or setbacks, including school, work, or relationship problems, job loss, divorce, death of a loved one, financial difficulties, diagnosis of a terminal illness.
- Putting one's affairs in order, including giving away belongings, visiting family members and friends, drawing up a will, or writing a suicide note.

IF SOMEONE THREATENS SUICIDE:

- Stay calm.
- Take the threat seriously.
- Don't leave the person alone. Prevent access to firearms, knives, medications, or any other item the person may use to commit suicide.
- Don't try to handle the situation alone. Call 911 or the local emergency response number. Phone the person's doctor, the police, a local crisis intervention team, or others who are trained to help.
- While waiting for help, listen closely to the person. Let the person know you're listening by maintaining eye contact, moving closer, or holding his or her hand, if appropriate.
- Ask questions to determine what method of suicide the person is considering and whether he or she has an organized plan.
- Remind the person that help is available.
- If the person does attempt suicide, immediately call for emergency medical assistance and administer first aid, if necessary.

Source: American College of Emergency Physicians. (2008, March 10). *Know suicide's warning sign.* Irving, TX: author.

TABLE 19.3 Changes in Suicide Rates by Age, United States, 2000–2017

SUICIDE RATE, PER 100,000 PEOPLE		
Age Group	Rate in 2000	Rate in 2017
15 to 24	10.2	14.5
25 to 34	12.0	17.5
35 to 44	14.5	17.9
45 to 54	14.4	20.2
55 to 64	12.1	19.0
65 to 74	12.5	15.6
75 to 84	17.6	18.0
85 and over	19.6	20.1

Source: Kochanek, K. D., Murphy, S. L., Xu, J., & Aria, E. (2019). Deaths: Final data for 2017. *National Vital Statistics Report, 68* (9). Hyattsville, MD: National Center for Health Statistics

Although the death of a loved one is always difficult, survivors of people who take their own lives often walk an even more difficult road. Many blame themselves for failing to recognize the signs, and they suffer from feelings of guilt, shame, rejection, and isolation (Hanschmidt et al., 2016). Because of the stigma attached to suicide, these survivors often struggle with their emotions alone rather than share them with others who might understand (Schomerus et al., 2015).

HASTENING DEATH

Medical technology has outpaced our legal system and ethics. Until recent decades, the idea of helping a suffering loved one hasten death was virtually unheard of. Changing attitudes toward hastening death can be attributed largely to revulsion against technologies that keep patients alive against their will despite intense suffering, and sometimes even after the brain has stopped functioning.

Euthanasia *Euthanasia* means "good death" and is intended to end suffering or to allow a terminally ill person to die with dignity. People differ in their beliefs about this process, and some draw distinctions between the types of euthanasia used. **Passive euthanasia** involves withholding or discontinuing treatment that might extend the life of a terminally ill patient, such as medication, life support systems, or feeding tubes. Many people would characterize turning off the life support systems as passive euthanasia. Passive euthanasia is generally legal. **Active euthanasia** (sometimes called *mercy killing*) involves action taken directly or deliberately to shorten a life, and it is generally illegal. An important question regarding either form of euthanasia is whether it is done at the direct request, or to carry out the express wishes, of the person whose death results.

passive euthanasia
Withholding or discontinuation of life-prolonging treatment of a terminally ill person in order to end suffering or allow death with dignity.

active euthanasia
Deliberate action taken to shorten the life of a terminally ill person in order to end suffering or to allow death with dignity; also called *mercy killing*.

Advance Directives Some of the issues surrounding how much medical technology should be used to keep a person alive near the end of life can be addressed if people's wishes are made clear before they are incapacitated. The U.S. Supreme Court held that a person whose wishes are clearly known has a constitutional right to refuse or discontinue life-sustaining treatment (*Cruzan v. Director, Missouri Department of Health,* 1990). A mentally competent person's wishes can be spelled out in advance in a document called an **advance directive (living will),** which contains instructions for when and how to discontinue futile medical care. All 50 states have since legalized some form of advance directive or adopted other provisions governing the making of end-of-life decisions. However, only about 37 percent of people report having written down their wishes for end-of-life care and a review of past literature suggests this number has not changed significantly in the past 6 years (Yadav et al., 2017).

advance directive (living will)
Document specifying the type of care wanted by the maker in the event of an incapacitating or terminal illness.

An advance directive may take the form of a *living will* or a more formal legal document called a durable power of attorney. A living will may contain specific provisions with regard to circumstances in which treatment should be discontinued, what extraordinary measures—if any—should be taken to prolong life, and what kind of pain management is desired. A person also may specify, through a donor card or a signature on the back of his or her driver's license, that his or her organs be donated to someone in need of an organ transplant.

Some living will legislation applies only to terminally ill patients, not to those who are incapacitated by illness or injury but may live many years in severe pain. Thus advance directives may not help them. Similarly, advance directives may not help patients in comas or in persistent vegetative states. Such situations can be covered by a **durable power of attorney,** which appoints another person to make decisions if the maker of the document becomes incompetent to do so. A number of states have adopted a simple form known as a *medical durable power of attorney* expressly for decisions about health care.

durable power of attorney
Legal instrument that appoints an individual to make decisions in the event of another person's incapacitation.

Advance care planning is beneficial not just to the dying person, but also to the family. Having a plan of action when death is imminent leads to improved end-of-life care and results in higher levels of family satisfaction, and reductions in stress, anxiety, and depression in family members of the terminally ill patient (Detering et al., 2010).

research in action

PHYSICIAN-ASSISTED SUICIDE

Brittany Maynard sparked national debate on physician-assisted suicide after a diagnosis of stage 4 malignant brain cancer. At 29 years old, she was given 6 months to live. Rather than waiting for cancer to slowly overtake her brain, Brittany moved from California to Oregon, where physician-assisted suicide was legal through Oregon's Death with Dignity law. She launched an online campaign in support of expansion of legalized physician-assisted suicide for the terminally ill; her video describing her situation and decision process received over 12 million views (www.youtube.com/watch?annotation_id=annotation_1855568639&feature=iv&src_vid=1lHXH0Zb2QI&v=yPfe3rCcUeQ). She died as she wished: peacefully, at home, with her husband and family (Bever, 2014).

Physician-assisted suicide (PAS) involves a formal patient request for prescription of a lethal dosage of medication with the intent of ending life (Sulmasy et al., 2017). The patient is the one who administers the fatal dose. Over the years, public attitudes toward PAS have shifted dramatically, and many more Americans now support permitting patients a means of ending one's life in the event of terminal illness (Emanuel et al., 2016).

The American Medical Association views PAS in opposition to aims of health restoration for the sick (Yang et al., 2016). Physicians are bound by social justice principles, protecting human rights of society's most vulnerable members: the sick, disabled, poor, and minorities. Questions are raised whether these groups may be disproportionately affected by legalized PAS (Sulmasy et al., 2017).

Physicians endorse current standards of care, including patient right to refusal of treatment and further expansion of hospice and palliative care services. Palliative services deliver holistic care to patients, caregivers, and relatives with the goal of easing pain and suffering, increasing psychological and spiritual well-being, family adjustment, and a dignified transition to death (De Lima et al., 2017). Kelley and Morrison (2015) report that more than 90 percent of American adults are unaware of the existence of palliative care services, but when educated, many desire these services for end of life.

Awareness of advanced planning options and compassionate physician care are deemed essential in supporting terminally ill patients. Physicians unfortunately experience challenges in providing intensive end-of-life care in time-pressured health care environments (Sulmasy et al., 2017). Many argue for universal accessibility to palliative care services, addressing physical, emotional, and psychological needs of dying patients and their families. Medical technology is essential to prolong life, but preservation of quality at the end of life is equally important to patients.

what's your view

Do you support expansion of Death with Dignity laws to legalize physician-assisted suicide? What kinds of safeguards can be put into place to further protect patients?

They are also associated with decreased hospitalization rates, an increase in the use of preferred medical treatments, and a decrease in medical costs (Martin et al., 2016). Unfortunately, even with advance planning, directives are not always followed. Often they are unavailable during a crisis, or the wishes of the ill or dying adult are overruled in the moment (Perkins, 2007). Plans for end-of-life care are more likely to be followed if the decisions are made within the context of coordinated interventions where medical personnel, family members, and trained facilitators work together to determine a course of action (Brinkman-Stoppelenburg et al., 2014).

assisted suicide
Suicide in which a physician or someone else helps a person take his or her own life.

Assisted Suicide Assisted suicide—in which a physician or someone else helps a person bring about a self-inflicted death by, for example, prescribing or obtaining drugs or enabling a patient to inhale a deadly gas—commonly refers to situations in which people with incurable, terminal illnesses request help in ending their lives (see Research in Action). Assisted suicide is still illegal in most places but in recent years has come to the forefront of public debate. It may be similar in principle to voluntary active euthanasia, in which, for example, a patient asks for, and receives, a lethal injection, but in assisted suicide the person who wants to die performs the actual deed.

Since 1997, when a unanimous U.S. Supreme Court left regulation of physician aid-in-dying up to the states, measures to legalize assisted suicide for the terminally ill have been introduced in several states. Oregon was the first state to pass such a law, the Death with Dignity Act (DWDA). In 1994, Oregonians voted to let mentally competent patients, who have been told by two doctors that they have less than 6 months to live, request a lethal prescription with strong safeguards to make sure the request is serious and voluntary and that all other alternatives have been considered.

What has been the experience under the Oregon law? The legalization of assisted suicide has resulted in improvements of palliative care and an increased number of deaths occurring at home (88.6 percent) rather than in the hospital. In the years 1998 to 2019, 1,657 terminally ill patients took their lives, 188 of them in 2019. The concerns most frequently mentioned by patients who requested and used lethal prescriptions were decreasing ability to participate in activities that made life enjoyable (90.4 percent), loss of autonomy (86.7 percent), and loss of dignity (72.3 percent). The median age at death was 74 years, and most who chose to end their lives were white, well-educated, dying of cancer, on hospice, and had some form of health insurance (Oregon Health Authority, 2020).

As of September 2020, assisted suicide is legal in ten states (California, Colorado, Hawaii, Maine, New Jersey, Oregon, Vermont, and Washington) and Washington, D.C. (Death with Dignity, 2020). The American College of Physicians (Sulmasy & Mueller, 2017) and the American Medical Association (American Medical Association, 2018) oppose physician aid in dying as contrary to a practitioner's oath to "do no harm." The American Psychological Association takes no position, neither endorsing nor opposing assisted suicide (American Psychological Association, 2017). The American public is split with respect to the issue; 47 percent are in favor of laws to legalize assisted suicide, 49 percent are opposed (Duggan, 2014). Physician-assisted suicide opponents reject deliberate termination of life, often on moral grounds. Proponents argue for patients' autonomy, self-determination, and a compassionate end to human suffering (Levy et al., 2013; Pormeister et al., 2017).

Active euthanasia remains illegal in the United States but not in the Netherlands, where in 2002 a law permitting voluntary euthanasia for patients in a state of continuous, unbearable, and incurable suffering went into effect. In such cases, doctors can now inject a lethal dose of medication. Estimates are that somewhere around 1.8 to 2.9 percent of deaths in the Netherlands result from euthanasia or assisted suicide (Steck et al., 2013).

International Variations in End-of-Life Decisions In addition to the Netherlands, euthanasia or physician-assisted suicide (PAS) is also legal in Belgium, Canada, Colombia, and Luxembourg, with public support growing in Western Europe but declining in Central and Eastern Europe. There are suggestions that these changes are related to simultaneous changes in religiosity, particularly in post-communist Eastern Europe. The majority of PAS cases involve patients with cancer, typically older and well-educated. Although euthanasia and PAS have become increasingly legalized, fears of a "slippery slope" appear to be unfounded. In no areas, including the United States, do data indicate that vulnerable patients such as the disabled have been receiving physician-assisted suicide or euthanasia at higher rates than the general population (Radbruch et al., 2016; Emanuel et al., 2016).

The first representative study of end-of-life decisions in six European countries (Belgium, Denmark, Italy, the Netherlands, Sweden, and Switzerland) found important cultural differences. In all six countries, physicians reported withholding or withdrawing life-prolonging treatment—most typically medication, followed by hydration or nutrition—but the frequency varied greatly, from 41 percent of deaths in Switzerland to 6 percent in Italy (Bosshard et al., 2005). Active forms of physician-assisted death were most prevalent in the Netherlands and Belgium (van der Heide et al., 2003). In a later survey of physicians in the same six countries, direct physician-assisted deaths were rare, but in one-quarter to one-half of all deaths (23 percent in Italy, 51 percent in Switzerland), physicians made death-hastening decisions, such as deep sedation, sometimes accompanied by withdrawal of artificial nutrition and hydration (Bilsen et al., 2007).

In the United States support for physician-assisted suicide (PAS) varies widely, ranging from 47 to 69 percent, and it has remained essentially unchanged since the 1990s.

Fewer than 20 percent of U.S. physicians report receiving requests for PAS, and fewer than 5 percent have complied. Even in states such as Oregon and Washington, where such requests are legal, fewer than 1 percent of doctors write such prescriptions on a yearly basis (Emanuel et al., 2016).

One beneficial result of the aid-in-dying controversy has been to call attention to the need for better palliative care and closer attention to patients' motivation and state of mind. When doctors talk openly with patients about their physical and mental symptoms, their expectations, their fears and goals, their options for end-of-life care, their family concerns, and their need for meaning and quality of life, ways may be found to diminish these concerns without the taking of life (Bascom & Tolle, 2002).

End-of-Life Options and Diversity Concerns In the United States, with its ethnically diverse population, issues of social and cultural diversity need to be addressed in end-of-life decision making. Beliefs about the morality of assisted suicide vary with respect to a number of demographic variables. Race and ethnicity matter; whites are more likely (65 percent) to support the morality of assisted suicide than Hispanics (58 percent) and African Americans (52 percent). Religion also plays a major role. Only 43 percent of white Evangelicals and Black Protestants agree on the morality of suicide in the event of intractable pain. By contrast, white mainline Protestants (71 percent), Catholics (63 percent), and religiously unaffiliated adults (85 percent) believe it is a moral right. Most Americans—roughly 62 percent—support a terminally ill person's right to end their own life, and approximately 66 percent agree that there are some circumstances in which a person should be allowed to die. Only 31 percent of Americans believe everything possible should always be done to save the life of a patient (Pew Research Center, 2013).

There are also differences in how willing people are to discuss end-of-life care. Planning for death is inconsistent with traditional Navaho values, which avoid negative thinking and talk. Chinese families may seek to protect a dying person from unfavorable information, including knowledge of his or her impending death. Recent Mexican or Korean immigrants may believe less in individual autonomy than is customary in the dominant U.S. culture. Among some ethnic minorities, the value of longevity may take priority over health. Both African Americans and Hispanics, for example, are more likely than European Americans to prefer life-sustaining treatment regardless of the state of the disease and of their educational level (Pew Research Center, 2013; APA Working Group on Assisted Suicide, 2005).

Issues of hastening death will become more pressing as the population ages. In years to come, both the courts and the public will be forced to come to terms with these issues as increasing numbers of people claim a right to die with dignity and with help.

Finding Meaning and Purpose in Life and Death

The struggle to find meaning in life and in death—often dramatized in books and movies—has been borne out by research. Studies examining religion and death have found that such beliefs are generally beneficial for the dying (Edmondson et al., 2008). According to Kübler-Ross (1975), facing the reality of death is a key to living a meaningful life:

> It is the denial of death that is partially responsible for [people] living empty, purposeless lives; for when you live as if you'll live forever, it becomes too easy to postpone the things you know that you must do. In contrast, when you fully understand that each day you awaken could be the last you have, you take the time that day to grow, to become more of who you really are, to reach out to other human beings. (p. 164)

LIFE REVIEW

life review
Reminiscence about one's life in order to see its significance.

Life review is a process of reminiscence that enables a person to see the significance of his or her life. Life review can, of course, occur at any time. However, it may have special meaning in old age, when it can foster ego integrity—according to Erikson, the final critical task of the life span. As the end of their journey approaches, people may look back over their accomplishments and failures and ask themselves what their lives have meant. Awareness of mortality may be an impetus for reexamining values and seeing one's experiences and actions in a new light. Some people find the will to complete unfinished tasks, such as reconciling with estranged family members or friends, and thus to achieve a satisfying sense of closure.

Life review therapy and reminiscence interventions can help focus the natural process of life review and make it more conscious, purposeful, and efficient (Westerhof & Bohlmeijer, 2014; Lewis & Butler, 1974). Such interventions have been shown to reduce symptoms of depression and result in greater ego integrity (Pinquart & Forstmeier, 2012). Methods often used for uncovering memories in life review therapy include recording an autobiography; constructing a family tree; spending time with scrapbooks, photo albums, old letters, and other memorabilia; making a trip back to scenes of childhood and young adulthood; reuniting with former classmates or colleagues or distant family members; describing ethnic traditions; and summing up one's life's work.

Sharing memories evoked by a photo album is one way to review a life. Life review can help people recall important events and can motivate them to rebuild damaged relationships or complete unfinished tasks. REB Images/ Brand X Pictures/Getty Images

DEVELOPMENT: A LIFELONG PROCESS

On April 17, 1955, the brilliant scientist Albert Einstein experienced a painful sensation in his midsection. Grabbing the draft of a speech he was working on—which he would never complete—he was taken to a local hospital and diagnosed with a painful abdominal aortic aneurysm. Einstein refused surgery, saying, "I want to go when I want. It is tasteless to prolong life artificially. I have done my share; it is time to go. I will do it elegantly." He died a day later (Calaprice et al., 2015).

While we may vary in our ability to accept death, Einstein's view of life is worthy of admiration. In his words, "The ideals which have always shone before me and filled me with the joy of living are goodness, beauty, and truth" (Calaprice et al., 2015).

Time is relative. When we are young, the wide swath of the future stretches ahead. Near death, the end contracts and narrows. Within a limited life span, no person can realize all capabilities, gratify all desires, explore all interests, or experience all the richness that life has to offer. The tension between possibilities for growth and a finite time in which to do the growing defines human life. By choosing which possibilities to pursue and by continuing to follow them as far as possible, each person contributes to the unfinished story of human development.

summary and key terms

The Meaning of Death and Dying

- Death has biological, social, cultural, historical, religious, legal, psychological, developmental, medical, and ethical aspects.
- Customs surrounding death and mourning vary greatly from one culture to another. However, cultures share an understanding that death can bring grief, anger, and fear; provide a means by which to mourn; and have a concept of an afterlife.

- Death rates dropped drastically during the twentieth century, especially in developed countries.
- Nearly three-quarters of deaths in the United States occur among the elderly, and the top causes of death are diseases that primarily affect older adults.
- As death became primarily a phenomenon of late adulthood, it became largely "invisible," and care of the dying took place in isolation, by professionals.

- Children's understanding of death develops gradually. Young children can better understand death if it is part of their own experience.
- Adolescents generally do not think much about death, but benefit from talking to others, especially peers, in the event of the death of a loved one.
- Realization and acceptance of the inevitability of death increases throughout adulthood.

thanatology

Facing Death and Loss

- There is now an upsurge of interest in understanding and dealing realistically and compassionately with death. Examples of this tendency are a growing interest in hospice care and palliative, or comfort, care.
- People often undergo cognitive and functional declines shortly before death.
- Some people who come close to dying have "near-death" experiences that may result from physiological changes in the brain.
- Terror management theory states that mortality salience is a consequence of our ability to understand death and our self-preservation instincts. Research suggests that people may be buffered against the resulting anxiety by strong cultural beliefs, high self-esteem, or secure attachment.
- Elisabeth Kübler-Ross proposed five stages in coming to terms with dying: denial, anger, bargaining, depression, and acceptance. These stages, and their sequence, are not universal.
- There is no universal pattern of grief. The most widely studied pattern moves from shock and disbelief to preoccupation with the memory of the dead person and finally to resolution. However, research has found wide variations and resilience.

hospice care, palliative care, terminal drop, grief, bereavement, grief work

Significant Losses

- Women are more likely to be widowed, and widowed younger, than men, and they may experience widowhood somewhat differently. Physical and mental health tend to decline after widowhood, but for some people widowhood can ultimately become a positive developmental experience.
- Death of a parent can precipitate changes in the self and in relationships with others.

- The loss of a child can be especially difficult because it is not typical for most families.
- Because miscarriage and stillbirth are not generally considered significant losses in U.S. society, those who experience such losses are often left to deal with them with little social support.

Medical, Legal, and Ethical Issues

- Although suicide is no longer illegal in many modern societies, there is still a stigma attached to it. Some people maintain a "right to die," especially for people with long-term degenerative illness or pain.
- The number of suicides is probably underestimated. It is often related to depression, isolation, family conflict, financial troubles, debilitating ailments, and age. There are many more suicide attempts than actual deaths.
- Euthanasia and assisted suicide involve controversial ethical, medical, and legal issues.
- To avoid unnecessary suffering through artificial prolongation of life, passive euthanasia is generally permitted with the patient's consent or with advance directives. However, such directives are not consistently followed.
- Active euthanasia and assisted suicide are generally illegal, but public support for physician aid-in-dying has increased. Eight states and the District of Columbia have laws permitting physician-assisted suicide for the terminally ill. European countries vary with respect to the beliefs about and legality of euthanasia and assisted suicide.
- The assisted suicide controversy has focused more attention on the need for better palliative care and understanding of patients' state of mind. Issues of social and cultural diversity need to be considered.

passive euthanasia, active euthanasia, advance directive (living will), durable power of attorney, assisted suicide

Finding Meaning and Purpose in Life and Death

- The more meaning and purpose people find in their lives, the less they tend to fear death.
- Life review can help people prepare for death and give them a last chance to complete unfinished tasks.
- Even dying can be a developmental experience.

life review

Design Credit: (globe) janrysavy/Getty Images

glossary

acceleration programs Programs for educating the gifted that move them through the curriculum at an unusually rapid pace.

accommodation Piaget's term for changes in a cognitive structure to include new information.

acquired immune deficiency syndrome (AIDS) Viral disease that undermines effective functioning of the immune system.

active euthanasia Deliberate action taken to shorten the life of a terminally ill person in order to end suffering or to allow death with dignity; also called *mercy killing*.

activities of daily living (ADL) Essential activities that support survival, such as eating, dressing, bathing, and getting around the house.

activity theory Theory of aging that holds that to age successfully a person must remain as active as possible.

acute medical conditions Illnesses that last a short time.

adaptation Piaget's term for adjustment to new information about the environment, achieved through processes of assimilation and accommodation.

adolescence Developmental transition between childhood and adulthood entailing major physical, cognitive, and psychosocial changes.

adolescent growth spurt Sharp increase in height and weight that precedes sexual maturity.

adolescent rebellion Pattern of emotional turmoil, characteristic of a minority of adolescents, that may involve conflict with family, alienation from adult society, reckless behavior, and rejection of adult values.

advance directive (living will) Document specifying the type of care wanted by the maker in the event of an incapacitating or terminal illness.

age-related macular degeneration Condition in which the center of the retina gradually loses its ability to discern fine details; leading cause of irreversible visual impairment in older adults.

ageism Prejudice or discrimination against a person (most commonly an older person) based on age.

aging in place Remaining in one's own home, with or without assistance, in later life.

alcoholism Chronic disease involving dependence on use of alcohol, causing interference with normal functioning and fulfillment of obligations.

alleles Two or more alternative forms of a gene that occupy the same position on paired chromosomes and affect the same trait.

altruism Behavior intended to help others out of inner concern and without expectation of external reward; may involve self-denial or self-sacrifice.

altruistic behavior Activity intended to help another person with no expectation of reward.

Alzheimer's disease Progressive, irreversible, degenerative brain disorder characterized by cognitive deterioration and loss of control of bodily functions, leading to death.

ambivalent (resistant) attachment Pattern in which an infant becomes anxious before the primary caregiver leaves, is extremely upset during his or her absence, and both seeks and resists contact on his or her return.

amyloid plaque Waxy chunks of insoluble tissue found in brains of persons with Alzheimer's disease.

anorexia nervosa Eating disorder characterized by self-starvation.

anoxia Lack of oxygen, which may cause brain damage.

anticipatory smiling Infant smiles at an object and then gazes at an adult while still smiling.

Apgar scale Standard measurement of a newborn's condition; it assesses appearance, pulse, grimace, activity, and respiration.

art therapy Therapeutic approach that allows a person to express troubled feelings without words, using a variety of art materials and media.

assimilation Piaget's term for incorporation of new information into an existing cognitive structure.

assisted suicide Suicide in which a physician or someone else helps a person take his or her own life.

asthma A chronic respiratory disease characterized by sudden attacks of coughing, wheezing, and difficulty in breathing.

attachment Reciprocal, enduring tie between two people—especially between infant and caregiver—each of whom contributes to the quality of the relationship.

attention-deficit/hyperactivity disorder (ADHD) Syndrome characterized by persistent inattention and distractibility, impulsivity, low tolerance for frustration, and inappropriate overactivity.

authoritarian parenting In Baumrind's terminology, parenting style emphasizing control and obedience.

authoritative parenting In Baumrind's terminology, parenting style blending respect for a child's individuality with an effort to instill social values.

autonomy versus shame and doubt Erikson's second stage in psychosocial development, in which children achieve a balance between self-determination and control by others.

autosomes In humans, the 22 pairs of chromosomes not related to sexual expression.

avoidant attachment Pattern in which an infant rarely cries when separated from the primary caregiver and avoids contact on his or her return.

basal metabolism Use of energy to maintain vital functions.

basic sense of trust versus mistrust Erikson's first stage in psychosocial development, in which infants develop a sense of the reliability of people and objects.

Bayley Scales of Infant and Toddler Development Standardized test of infants' and toddlers' mental and motor development.

behavior therapy Therapeutic approach using principles of learning theory to encourage desired behaviors or eliminate undesired ones; also called *behavior modification*.

behavioral genetics Quantitative study of relative hereditary and environmental influences on behavior.

behaviorism Learning theory that emphasizes the predictable role of environment in causing observable behavior.

behaviorist approach Approach to the study of cognitive development that is concerned with basic mechanics of learning.

bereavement Loss, due to death, of someone to whom one feels close and the process of adjustment to the loss.

bilingual Fluent in two languages.

bilingual education System of teaching non-English-speaking children in their native language while they learn English, and later switching to all-English instruction.

binge drinking Consuming five or more drinks on one occasion.

binge eating disorder Eating disorder in which a person loses control over eating and binges huge quantities of food.

bioecological theory Bronfenbrenner's approach to understanding processes and contexts of human development that identifies five levels of environmental influence.

body image Descriptive and evaluative beliefs about one's appearance.

bulimia nervosa Eating disorder in which a person regularly eats huge quantities of food and then purges the body by laxatives, induced vomiting, fasting, or excessive exercise.

bullying Aggression deliberately and persistently directed against a particular target, or victim, typically one who is weak, vulnerable, and defenseless.

canalization Limitation on variance of expression of certain inherited characteristics.

caregiver burnout Condition of physical, mental, and emotional exhaustion affecting adults who provide continuous care for sick or aged persons.

case study Study of a single subject, such as an individual or a family.

cataracts Cloudy or opaque areas in the lens of the eye, which cause blurred vision.

cell death In brain development, normal elimination of excess brain cells to achieve more efficient functioning.

central nervous system Brain and spinal cord.

cephalocaudal principle Principle that development proceeds in a head-to-tail direction, that is, that upper parts of the body develop before lower parts of the trunk.

cephalocaudal principle Development proceeds "head to tail"; the upper parts of the body develop before the lower parts.

cesarean delivery Delivery of a baby by surgical removal from the uterus.

child-directed speech (CDS) Form of speech often used in talking to babies or toddlers; includes slow, simplified speech, a high-pitched tone, exaggerated vowel sounds, short words and sentences, and much repetition; also called *parentese* or *motherese*.

childhood depression Mood disorder characterized by such symptoms as a prolonged sense of friendlessness, inability to have fun or concentrate, fatigue, extreme activity or apathy, feelings of worthlessness, weight change, physical complaints, and thoughts of death or suicide.

chromosomes Coils of DNA that consist of genes.

chronic medical conditions Illnesses or impairments that persist for at least 3 months.

circular reactions Piaget's term for processes by which an infant learns to reproduce desired occurrences originally discovered by chance.

class inclusion Understanding of the relationship between a whole and its parts.

classical conditioning Learning based on associating a stimulus that does not ordinarily elicit a response with another stimulus that does elicit the response.

code mixing Use of elements of two languages, sometimes in the same utterance, by young children in households where both languages are spoken.

code switching Changing one's speech to match the situation, as in people who are bilingual.

cognitive neuroscience Study of links between neural processes and cognitive abilities.

cognitive neuroscience approach Approach to the study of cognitive development that links brain processes with cognitive ones.

cognitive perspective View that thought processes are central to development.

cognitive reserve Hypothesized fund of energy that may enable a deteriorating brain to continue to function normally.

cognitive-appraisal model Model of coping, proposed by Lazarus and Folkman, that holds that, on the basis of continuous appraisal of their relationship with the environment, people choose appropriate coping strategies to deal with situations that tax their normal resources.

cognitive-stage theory Piaget's theory that children's cognitive development advances in a series of four stages involving qualitatively distinct types of mental operations.

commitment Marcia's term for personal investment in an occupation or system of beliefs.

committed compliance Kochanska's term for wholehearted obedience of a parent's orders without reminders or lapses.

componential element Sternberg's term for the analytic aspect of intelligence.

concordant Term describing tendency of twins to share the same trait or disorder.

concrete operations Third stage of Piagetian cognitive development (approximately ages 7 to 12), during which children develop logical but not abstract thinking.

conduct disorder (CD) Repetitive, persistent pattern of aggressive, antisocial behavior violating societal norms or the rights of others.

conscience Internal standards of behavior, which usually control one's conduct and produce emotional discomfort when violated.

constructive play Play involving use of objects or materials to make something.

contextual element Sternberg's term for the practical aspect of intelligence.

contextual perspective View of human development that sees the individual as inseparable from the social context.

continuity theory Theory of aging, described by Atchley, that holds that in order to age successfully people must maintain a balance of continuity and change in both the internal and external structures of their lives.

control group In an experiment, a group of people, similar to those in the experimental group, who do not receive the treatment under study.

conventional morality (or morality of conventional role conformity) Second level in Kohlberg's theory of moral reasoning in which standards of authority figures are internalized.

convergent thinking Thinking aimed at finding the one right answer to a problem.

coping Adaptive thinking or behavior aimed at reducing or relieving stress that arises from harmful, threatening, or challenging conditions.

coregulation Transitional stage in the control of behavior in which parents exercise general supervision and children exercise moment-to-moment self-regulation.

coronavirus A large family of respiratory viruses, including those that cause the common cold, severe acute respiratory syndrome (SARS), Middle East respiratory syndrome (MERS), and COVID-19.

corporal punishment Use of physical force with the intention of causing pain but not injury so as to correct or control behavior.

correlational study Research design intended to discover whether a statistical relationship between variables exists.

COVID-19 A novel coronavirus disease causing fatigue, loss of sense of smell, cough, fever, and respiratory distress; the source of the 2019 pandemic.

creativity Ability to see situations in a new way, to produce innovations, or to discern previously unidentified problems and find novel solutions.

crisis Marcia's term for period of conscious decision making related to identity formation.

cross-modal transfer Ability to use information gained by one sense to guide another.

cross-sectional study Study designed to assess age-related differences, in which people of different ages are assessed on one occasion.

crystallized intelligence Type of intelligence, proposed by Horn and Cattell, involving the ability to remember and use learned information; it is largely dependent on education and culture.

cultural socialization Parental practices that teach children about their racial/ethnic heritage and promote cultural practices and cultural pride.

culture-fair tests Intelligence tests that deal with experiences common to various cultures, in an attempt to avoid cultural bias.

culture-free tests Intelligence tests that, if they were possible to design, would have no culturally linked content.

decoding Process of phonetic analysis by which a printed word is converted to spoken form before retrieval from long-term memory.

deductive reasoning Type of logical reasoning that moves from a general premise about a class to a conclusion about a particular member or members of the class.

deferred imitation Piaget's term for reproduction of an observed behavior after the passage of time by calling up a stored symbol of it.

dementia Deterioration in cognitive and behavioral functioning due to physiological causes.

Denver Developmental Screening Test Screening test given to children 1 month to 6 years old to determine whether they are developing normally.

deoxyribonucleic acid (DNA) Chemical that carries inherited instructions for the development of all cellular forms of life.

dependent variable In an experiment, the condition that may or may not change as a result of changes in the independent variable.

depth perception Ability to perceive objects and surfaces three-dimensionally.

diabetes (1) One of the most common diseases of childhood. It is characterized by high levels of glucose in the blood as a result of defective insulin production, ineffective insulin action, or both. (2) Disease in which the body does not produce or properly use *insulin,* a hormone that converts sugar, starches, and other foods into energy needed for daily life.

differentiation Process by which cells acquire specialized structures and functions.

discipline Methods of molding children's character and of teaching them to exercise self-control and engage in acceptable behavior.

disengagement theory Theory of aging that holds that successful aging is characterized by mutual withdrawal of the older person and society.

dishabituation Increase in responsiveness after presentation of a new stimulus.

disorganized-disoriented attachment Pattern in which an infant, after separation from the primary caregiver, shows contradictory, repetitious, or misdirected behaviors on his or her return.

divergent thinking Thinking that produces a variety of fresh, diverse possibilities.

dizygotic twins Twins conceived by the union of two different ova with two different sperm cells; also called *fraternal twins;* they are no more alike genetically than any other siblings.

dominant inheritance Pattern of inheritance in which, when a child receives different alleles, only the dominant one is expressed.

doula An experienced mentor who furnishes emotional support and information for a woman during labor.

Down syndrome Chromosomal disorder characterized by moderate-to-severe mental retardation and by such physical signs as a downward-sloping skin fold at the inner corners of the eyes. Also called *trisomy-21.*

dramatic play Play involving imaginary people or situations; also called *pretend play, fantasy play, or imaginative play.*

drug therapy Administration of drugs to treat emotional disorders.

dual representation hypothesis Proposal that children under age 3 have difficulty grasping spatial relationships because of the need to keep more than one mental representation in mind at the same time.

durable power of attorney Legal instrument that appoints an individual to make decisions in the event of another person's incapacitation.

dynamic systems theory (DST) Esther Thelen's theory, which holds that motor development is a dynamic process of active coordination of multiple systems within the infant in relation to the environment.

dynamic tests Tests based on Vygotsky's theory that emphasize potential rather than past learning.

dyslexia Developmental disorder in which reading achievement is substantially lower than predicted by IQ or age.

early intervention Systematic process of providing services to help families meet young children's developmental needs.

ecological theory of perception Theory developed by Eleanor and James Gibson, which describes developing motor and perceptual abilities as interdependent parts of a functional system that guides behavior in varying contexts.

ego control Self-control and the self-regulation of impulses.

ego integrity versus despair According to Erikson, the eighth and final stage of psychosocial development, in which people in late adulthood either achieve a sense of integrity of the self by accepting the lives they have lived, and thus accept death, or yield to despair that their lives cannot be relived.

ego resiliency (1) Dynamic capacity to modify one's level of ego control in response to environmental and contextual influences. (2) The ability to adapt flexibly and resourcefully to potential sources of stress.

elaboration Mnemonic strategy of making mental associations involving items to be remembered.

electronic fetal monitoring Mechanical monitoring of fetal heartbeat during labor and delivery.

embryonic stage Second stage of gestation (2 to 8 weeks), characterized by rapid growth and development of major body systems and organs.

emerging adulthood Proposed transitional period between adolescence and adulthood commonly found in industrialized countries.

emotion-focused coping In the cognitive-appraisal model, coping strategy directed toward managing the emotional response to a stressful situation so as to lessen its physical or psychological impact.

emotional intelligence (EI) Salovey and Mayer's term for the ability to understand and regulate emotions; an important component of effective, intelligent behavior.

emotional maltreatment Rejection, terrorization, isolation, exploitation, degradation, ridicule, or failure to provide emotional support, love, and affection; or other action or inaction that may cause behavioral, cognitive, emotional, or mental disorders.

emotions Subjective reactions to experience that are associated with physiological and behavioral changes.

empathy Ability to put oneself in another person's place and feel what the other person feels.

empty nest Transitional phase of parenting following the last child's leaving the parents' home.

encapsulation The process that allows expertise to compensate for declines in information-processing ability by bundling relevant knowledge together.

English-immersion approach Approach to teaching English as a second language in which instruction is presented only in English.

enrichment programs Programs for educating the gifted that broaden and deepen knowledge and skills through extra activities, projects, field trips, or mentoring.

epigenesis Mechanism that turns genes on or off and determines functions of body cells.

episodic memory Long-term memory of specific experiences or events, linked to time and place.

equilibration Piaget's term for the tendency to seek a stable balance among cognitive elements; achieved through a balance between assimilation and accommodation.

erectile dysfunction Inability of a man to achieve or maintain an erect penis sufficient for satisfactory sexual performance.

ethnographic study In-depth study of a culture, which uses a combination of methods including participant observation.

ethology Study of distinctive adaptive behaviors of species of animals that have evolved to increase survival of the species.

evolutionary psychology Application of Darwinian principles of natural selection and survival of the fittest to individual behavior.

evolutionary/sociobiological perspective View of human development that focuses on evolutionary and biological bases of behavior.

executive function Conscious control of thoughts, emotions, and actions to accomplish goals or solve problems.

experiential element Sternberg's term for the insightful or creative aspect of intelligence.

experiment Rigorously controlled, replicable procedure in which the researcher manipulates variables to assess the effect of one on the other.

experimental group In an experiment, the group receiving the treatment under study.

explicit memory Intentional and conscious memory, generally of facts, names, and events.

external memory aids Mnemonic strategies using something outside the person.

externalizing behaviors Behaviors by which a child acts out emotional difficulties; for example, aggression or hostility.

family therapy Psychological treatment in which a therapist sees the whole family together to analyze patterns of family functioning.

fertilization Union of sperm and ovum to produce a zygote; also called *conception*.

fetal alcohol syndrome (FAS) Combination of mental, motor, and developmental abnormalities affecting the offspring of some women who drink heavily during pregnancy.

fetal stage Final stage of gestation (from 8 weeks to birth), characterized by increased differentiation of body parts and greatly enlarged body size.

fictive kin Friends who are considered and behave like family members.

fidelity Sustained loyalty, faith, or sense of belonging that results from the successful resolution of Erikson's *identity versus identity confusion* psychosocial stage of development.

filial crisis In Marcoen's terminology, normative development of middle age, in which adults learn to balance love and duty to their parents with autonomy within a two-way relationship.

fine motor skills Physical skills that involve the small muscles and eye-hand coordination.

five-factor model Theoretical model of personality, developed and tested by Costa and McCrae, based on the "Big Five" factors underlying clusters of related personality traits: neuroticism, extraversion, openness to experience, conscientiousness, and agreeableness.

fluid intelligence Type of intelligence, proposed by Horn and Cattell, that is applied to novel problems and is relatively independent of educational and cultural influences.

foreclosure Identity status, described by Marcia, in which a person who has not spent time considering alternatives (that is, has not been in crisis) is committed to other people's plans for his or her life.

formal games with rules Organized games with known procedures and penalties.

formal operations Piaget's final stage of cognitive development, characterized by the ability to think abstractly.

free radicals Unstable, highly reactive atoms or molecules, formed during metabolism, that can cause internal bodily damage.

functional age Measure of a person's ability to function effectively in his or her physical and social environment in comparison with others of the same chronological age.

functional fitness Exercises or activities that improve daily activity.

functional play Play involving repetitive large muscular movements.

gender Significance of being male or female.

gender constancy Awareness that one will always be male or female.

gender identity Awareness, developed in early childhood, that one is male or female.

gender roles Behaviors, interests, attitudes, skills, and traits that a culture considers appropriate for each sex; differ for males and females.

gender segregation Tendency to select playmates of one's own gender.

gender stereotypes Preconceived generalizations about male or female role behavior.

gender-schema theory Theory, proposed by Bem, that children socialize themselves in their gender roles by developing a mentally organized network of information about what it means to be male or female in a particular culture.

gender-typing Socialization process by which children, at an early age, learn appropriate gender roles.

generalized anxiety disorder Anxiety not focused on any single target.

generativity Erikson's term for concern of mature adults for finding meaning through contributing to society and leaving a legacy for future generations.

generativity versus stagnation Erikson's seventh stage of psychosocial development, in which the middle-age adult develops a concern with establishing, guiding, and influencing the next generation or else experiences stagnation (a sense of inactivity or lifelessness).

genes Small segments of DNA located in definite positions on particular chromosomes; functional units of heredity.

genetic code Sequence of bases within the DNA molecule; governs the formation of proteins that determine the structure and functions of living cells.

genetic counseling Clinical service that advises prospective parents of their probable risk of having children with hereditary defects.

genetic-programming theories Theories that explain biological aging as resulting from a genetically determined developmental timeline.

genotype Genetic makeup of a person, containing both expressed and unexpressed characteristics.

genotype-environment correlation Tendency of certain genetic and environmental influences to reinforce each other; may be passive, reactive (evocative), or active. Also called *genotype-environment covariance*.

genotype-environment interaction The portion of phenotypic variation that results from the reactions of genetically different individuals to similar environmental conditions.

geriatrics Branch of medicine concerned with processes of aging and medical conditions associated with old age.

germinal stage First 2 weeks of prenatal development, characterized by rapid cell division, blastocyst formation, and implantation in the wall of the uterus.

gerontology Study of the aged and the process of aging.

gestation Period of development between conception and birth.

gestational age Age of an unborn baby, usually dated from the first day of an expectant mother's last menstrual cycle.

glaucoma Irreversible damage to the optic nerve caused by increased pressure in the eye.

goodness of fit Appropriateness of environmental demands and constraints to a child's temperament.

grief Emotional response experienced in the early phases of bereavement.

grief work Working out of psychological issues connected with grief.

gross motor skills Physical skills that involve the large muscles.

guided participation Adult's participation in a child's activity that helps to structure it and bring the child's understanding of it closer to the adult's.

habituation Type of learning in which familiarity with a stimulus reduces, slows, or stops a response.

haptic perception Ability to acquire information about properties of objects, such as size, weight, and texture, by handling them.

Hayflick limit Genetically controlled limit, proposed by Hayflick, on the number of times cells can divide in members of a species.

heritability Statistical estimate of contribution of heredity to individual differences in a specific trait within a given population.

heterozygous Possessing differing alleles for a trait.

holophrase Single word that conveys a complete thought.

Home Observation for Measurement of the Environment (HOME) Instrument to measure the influence of the home environment on children's cognitive growth.

homozygous Possessing two identical alleles for a trait.

hormone therapy (HT) Treatment with artificial estrogen, sometimes in combination with the hormone progesterone, to relieve or prevent symptoms caused by decline in estrogen levels after menopause.

hospice care Personal, patient- and family-centered care for a person with a terminal illness.

hostile attribution bias Tendency to perceive others as trying to hurt one and to strike out in retaliation or self-defense.

human genome Complete sequence of genes in the human body.

hypertension Chronically high blood pressure.

hypotheses Possible explanations for phenomena, used to predict the outcome of research.

ideal self The self one would like to be.

identification In Freudian theory, the process by which a young child adopts characteristics, beliefs, attitudes, values, and behaviors of the parent of the same sex.

identity According to Erikson, a coherent conception of the self, made up of goals, values, and beliefs to which a person is solidly committed.

identity accommodation Whitbourne's term for adjusting the self-concept to fit new experience.

identity achievement Identity status, described by Marcia, that is characterized by commitment to choices made following a crisis, a period spent in exploring alternatives.

identity assimilation Whitbourne's term for effort to fit new experience into an existing self-concept.

identity balance Whitbourne's term for a tendency to balance assimilation and accommodation.

identity diffusion Identity status, described by Marcia, that is characterized by absence of commitment and lack of serious consideration of alternatives.

identity process theory (IPT) Whitbourne's theory of identity development based on processes of assimilation and accommodation.

identity schemas Accumulated perceptions of the self shaped by incoming information from intimate relationships, work-related situations, and community and other experiences.

identity status Marcia's term for states of identity development that depend on the presence or absence of crisis and commitment.

identity versus identity confusion Erikson's fifth stage of psychosocial development, in which an adolescent seeks to develop a coherent sense of self, including the role she or he is to play in society. Also called *identity versus role confusion*.

implantation The attachment of the blastocyst to the uterine wall, occurring at about day 6.

implicit memory Unconscious recall, generally of habits and skills; sometimes called *procedural memory*.

incomplete dominance Pattern of inheritance in which a child receives two different alleles, resulting in partial expression of a trait.

independent variable In an experiment, the condition over which the experimenter has direct control.

individual psychotherapy Psychological treatment in which a therapist sees a troubled person one-on-one.

individuation (1) Adolescents' struggle for autonomy and personal identity. (2) Jung's term for emergence of the true self through balancing or integration of conflicting parts of the personality.

inductive reasoning Type of logical reasoning that moves from particular observations about members of a class to a general conclusion about that class.

inductive techniques Disciplinary techniques designed to induce desirable behavior by appealing to a child's sense of reason and fairness.

industry versus inferiority Erikson's fourth stage of psychosocial development, in which children must learn the productive skills their culture requires or else face feelings of inferiority.

infant mortality rate Proportion of babies born alive who die within the 1st year.

infertility Inability to conceive a child after 12 months of sexual intercourse without the use of birth control.

information-processing approach Approach to the study of cognitive development that analyzes processes involved in perceiving and handling information.

initiative versus guilt Erikson's third stage in psychosocial development, in which children balance the urge to pursue goals with reservations about doing so.

instrumental aggression Aggressive behavior used as a means of achieving a goal.

integration Process by which neurons coordinate the activities of muscle groups.

intellectual disability Significantly subnormal cognitive functioning. Also referred to as cognitive disability or mental retardation.

intelligent behavior Behavior that is goal oriented and adaptive to circumstances and conditions of life.

interactional synchrony The synchronized coordination of behavior and affect between a caregiver and infant.

internalization During socialization, process by which children accept societal standards of conduct as their own.

internalizing behaviors Behaviors by which emotional problems are turned inward; for example, anxiety or depression.

internet addiction A compulsive need to engage in nonwork online activities, to the point where such activities are interfering with family, social life, or work.

intimacy versus isolation Erikson's sixth stage of psychosocial development, in which young adults either form strong, long-lasting bonds with friends and romantic partners or face a possible sense of isolation and self-absorption.

invisible imitation Imitation with parts of one's body that one cannot see.

IQ (intelligence quotient) tests Psychometric tests that seek to measure intelligence by comparing a test-taker's performance with standardized norms.

kangaroo care Method of skin-to-skin contact in which a newborn is laid face down between the mother's breasts for an hour or so at a time after birth.

Kaufman Assessment Battery for Children (K-ABC-II) Nontraditional individual intelligence test designed to provide fair assessments of minority children and children with disabilities.

kinship care Care of children living without parents in the home of grandparents or other relatives, with or without a change of legal custody.

laboratory observation Research method in which all participants are observed under the same controlled conditions.

language Communication system based on words and grammar.

language acquisition device (LAD) In Chomsky's terminology, an inborn mechanism that enables children to infer linguistic rules from the language they hear.

lateralization Tendency of each of the brain's hemispheres to have specialized functions.

learning disabilities (LDs) Disorders that interfere with specific aspects of learning and school achievement.

learning perspective View of human development that holds that changes in behavior result from experience or from adaptation to the environment.

life expectancy Age to which a person in a particular cohort is statistically likely to live (given his or her current age and health status), on the basis of average longevity of a population.

life review Reminiscence about one's life in order to see its significance.

life span The longest period that members of a species can live.

linguistic speech Verbal expression designed to convey meaning.

literacy (1) Ability to read and write. (2) In an adult, ability to use printed and written information to function in society, achieve goals, and develop knowledge and potential.

longevity Length of an individual's life.

longitudinal study Study designed to assess age changes in a sample over time.

low-birth-weight babies Weight of less than 5½ pounds (2,500 grams) at birth because of prematurity or being small for date.

mammography Diagnostic X-ray examination of the breasts.

marital capital Financial and emotional benefits built up during a long-standing marriage, which tend to hold a couple together.

mechanistic model Model that views human development as a series of predictable responses to stimuli.

menarche Girl's first menstruation.

menopause Cessation of menstruation and of ability to bear children.

metacognition Thinking about thinking, or awareness of one's own mental processes.

metamemory Understanding of processes of memory.

midlife crisis In some normative-crisis models, stressful life period precipitated by the review and reevaluation of one's past, typically occurring in the early to middle forties.

midlife review Introspective examination that often occurs in middle age, leading to reappraisal and revision of values and priorities.

mirror neurons Neurons that fire when a person does something or observes someone else doing the same thing.

mnemonic device Strategy to aid memory.

monozygotic twins Twins resulting from the division of a single zygote after fertilization; also called *identical twins;* they are genetically similar.

moratorium Identity status, described by Marcia, in which a person is currently considering alternatives (in crisis) and seems headed for commitment.

multifactorial transmission Combination of genetic and environmental factors to produce certain complex traits.

mutation Permanent alteration in genes or chromosomes that may produce harmful characteristics.

mutual regulation Process by which infant and caregiver communicate emotional states to each other and respond appropriately.

myelination Process of coating neural pathways with a fatty substance called myelin, which enables faster communication between cells.

myopia Nearsightedness.

nativism Theory that human beings have an inborn capacity for language acquisition.

natural childbirth Method of childbirth that seeks to prevent pain by eliminating the mother's fear through education about the physiology of reproduction and training in breathing and relaxation during delivery.

naturalistic observation Research method in which behavior is studied in natural settings without intervention or manipulation.

neglect Failure to meet a dependent's basic needs.

neonatal jaundice Condition, in many newborn babies, caused by immaturity of liver and evidenced by yellowish appearance; can cause brain damage if not treated promptly.

neonatal period First 4 weeks of life, a time of transition from intrauterine dependency to independent existence.

neonate Newborn baby, up to 4 weeks old.

neurofibrillary tangles Twisted masses of protein fibers found in brains of persons with Alzheimer's disease.

neurons Nerve cells.

niche-picking Tendency of a person, especially after early childhood, to seek out environments compatible with his or her genotype.

nonorganic failure to thrive Slowed or arrested physical growth with no known medical cause, accompanied by poor developmental and emotional functioning.

nonshared environmental effects The unique environment in which each child grows up, consisting of distinctive influences or influences that affect one child differently than another.

normative life events In the timing-of-events model, commonly expected life experiences that occur at customary times.

normative-stage models Theoretical models that describe psychosocial development in terms of a definite sequence of age-related changes.

object permanence Piaget's term for the understanding that a person or object still exists when out of sight.

observational learning Learning through watching the behavior of others.

obsessive-compulsive disorder (OCD) Anxiety aroused by repetitive, intrusive thoughts, images, or impulses, often leading to compulsive ritual behaviors.

operant conditioning (1) Learning based on association of behavior with its consequences. (2) Learning based on reinforcement or punishment.

operational definition Definition stated solely in terms of the operations or procedures used to produce or measure a phenomenon.

oppositional defiant disorder (ODD) Pattern of behavior, persisting into middle childhood, marked by negativity, hostility, and defiance.

organismic model Model that views human development as internally initiated by an active organism and as occurring in a sequence of qualitatively different stages.

organization (1) Piaget's term for the creation of categories or systems of knowledge. (2) Mnemonic strategy of categorizing material to be remembered.

osteoporosis Condition in which the bones become thin and brittle as a result of rapid calcium depletion.

Otis-Lennon School Ability Test (OLSAT 8) Group intelligence test for kindergarten through 12th grade.

overt (direct) aggression Aggression that is openly directed at its target.

palliative care Care aimed at relieving pain and suffering and allowing the terminally ill to die in peace, comfort, and dignity.

pandemic An epidemic or disease spread across multiple countries or continents.

Parkinson's disease Progressive, irreversible degenerative neurological disorder, characterized by tremor, stiffness, slowed movement, and unstable posture.

participant observation Research method in which the observer lives with the people or participates in the activity being observed.

parturition The act or process of giving birth.

passive euthanasia Withholding or discontinuation of life-prolonging treatment of a terminally ill person in order to end suffering or allow death with dignity.

perimenopause Period of several years during which a woman experiences physiological changes of menopause; includes first year after end of menstruation; also called *climacteric*.

permissive parenting In Baumrind's terminology, parenting style emphasizing self-expression and self-regulation.

personality The relatively consistent blend of emotions, temperament, thought, and behavior that makes a person unique.

phenotype Observable characteristics of a person.

phonetic (code-emphasis) approach Approach to teaching reading that emphasizes decoding of unfamiliar words.

physical abuse Action taken deliberately to endanger another person, involving potential bodily injury.

Piagetian approach Approach to the study of cognitive development that describes qualitative stages in cognitive functioning.

plasticity (1) Range of modifiability of performance. (2) Modifiability, or "molding," of the brain through experience.

play therapy Therapeutic approach that uses play to help a child cope with emotional distress.

polygenic inheritance Pattern of inheritance in which multiple genes at different sites on chromosomes affect a complex trait.

postconventional morality (or morality of autonomous moral principles) Third level of Kohlberg's theory of moral reasoning, in which people follow internally held moral principles and can decide among conflicting moral standards.

postformal thought Mature type of thinking that relies on subjective experience and intuition as well as logic and allows room for ambiguity, uncertainty, inconsistency, contradiction, imperfection, and compromise.

postmature A fetus not yet born as of 2 weeks after the due date or 42 weeks after the mother's last menstrual period.

power assertion Disciplinary strategy designed to discourage undesirable behavior through physical or verbal enforcement of parental control.

pragmatics (1) The practical knowledge needed to use language for communicative purposes. (2) The social context of language.

preconventional morality First level of Kohlberg's theory of moral reasoning in which control is external and rules are obeyed in order to gain rewards or avoid punishment or out of self-interest.

prejudice Unfavorable attitude toward members of certain groups outside one's own, especially racial or ethnic groups.

prelinguistic speech Forerunner of linguistic speech; utterance of sounds that are not words. Includes crying, cooing, babbling, and accidental and deliberate imitation of sounds without understanding their meaning.

premenstrual syndrome (PMS) Disorder producing symptoms of physical discomfort and emotional tension for up to 2 weeks before a menstrual period.

prepared childbirth Method of childbirth that uses instruction, breathing exercises, and social support to induce controlled physical responses to uterine contractions and reduce fear and pain.

presbycusis Age-related, gradual loss of hearing, which accelerates after age 55, especially with regard to sounds at higher frequencies.

presbyopia Age-related, progressive loss of the eyes' ability to focus on nearby objects due to loss of elasticity in the lens.

preterm (premature) infants Infants born before completing the 37th week of gestation.

primary aging Gradual, inevitable process of bodily deterioration throughout the life span.

primary sex characteristics Organs directly related to reproduction, which enlarge and mature during adolescence.

problem-focused coping In the cognitive-appraisal model, coping strategy directed toward eliminating, managing, or improving a stressful situation.

procedural memory Long-term memory of motor skills, habits, and ways of doing things, which can be recalled without conscious effort; sometimes called *implicit memory*.

prosocial behavior Any voluntary behavior intended to help others.

protective factors (1) Influences that reduce the impact of potentially negative influences and tend to predict positive outcomes. (2) Influences that reduce the impact of early stress and tend to predict positive outcomes.

proximodistal principle Principle that development proceeds from within to without, that is, that parts of the body near the center develop before the extremities.

proximodistal principle The parts of the body near the center develop before the extremities.

psychoanalytic perspective View of human development as shaped by unconscious forces that motivate human behavior.

psychometric approach Approach to the study of cognitive development that seeks to measure intelligence quantitatively.

psychosexual development In Freudian theory, an unvarying sequence of stages of childhood personality development in which gratification shifts from the mouth to the anus and then to the genitals.

psychosocial development (1) Pattern of change in emotions, personality, and social relationships. (2) In Erikson's eight-stage theory, the socially and culturally influenced process of development of the ego, or self.

puberty Process by which a person attains sexual maturity and the ability to reproduce.

punishment The process by which a behavior is weakened, decreasing the likelihood of repetition.

qualitative change Discontinuous changes in kind, structure, or organization.

qualitative research Research that focuses on nonnumerical data, such as subjective experiences, feelings, or beliefs.

quantitative change Changes in the number or amount, such as in height, weight, size of vocabulary, or frequency of communication.

quantitative research Research that deals with objectively measurable data.

random assignment Assignment of participants in an experiment to groups in such a way that each person has an equal chance of being placed in any group.

random selection Selection of a sample in such a way that each person in a population has an equal and independent chance of being chosen.

reaction range Potential variability, depending on environmental conditions, in the expression of a hereditary trait.

real self The self one actually is.

receptive cooperation Kochanska's term for eager willingness to cooperate harmoniously with a parent in daily interactions, including routines, chores, hygiene, and play.

recessive inheritance Pattern of inheritance in which a child receives identical recessive alleles, resulting in expression of a nondominant trait.

reciprocal determinism Bandura's term for bidirectional forces that affect development.

reflective thinking Type of logical thinking that becomes more prominent in adulthood, involving continuous, active evaluation of information and beliefs in the light of evidence and implications.

reflex behaviors Automatic, involuntary, innate responses to stimulation.

rehearsal Mnemonic strategy to keep an item in working memory through conscious repetition.

reinforcement The process by which a behavior is strengthened, increasing the likelihood that the behavior will be repeated.

relational (social or indirect) aggression Aggression aimed at damaging or interfering with another person's relationships, reputation, or psychological well-being.

representational ability Piaget's term for capacity to store mental images or symbols of objects and events.

representational systems In neo-Piagetian terminology, the third stage in development of self-definition, characterized by breadth, balance, and the integration and assessment of various aspects of the self.

reserve capacity The backup capacity that helps body systems function to their utmost limits in times of stress.

resilient children Children who weather adverse circumstances, function well despite challenges or threats, or bounce back from traumatic events.

revolving door syndrome Tendency for young adults who have left home to return to their parents' household in times of financial, marital, or other trouble.

risky drinking Consuming more than 14 drinks a week or 4 drinks on any single day for men, and more than 7 drinks a week or 3 drinks on any single day for women.

rough-and-tumble play Vigorous play involving wrestling, hitting, and chasing, often accompanied by laughing and screaming.

sample Group of participants chosen to represent the entire population under study.

sandwich generation Middle-age adults squeezed by competing needs to raise or launch children and to care for elderly parents.

scaffolding Temporary support to help a child master a task.

schemes Piaget's term for organized patterns of thought and behavior used in particular situations.

school phobia Unrealistic fear of going to school; may be a form *of separation anxiety disorder* or *social phobia.*

scientific method System of established principles and processes of scientific inquiry, which includes identifying a problem to be studied, formulating a hypothesis to be tested by research, collecting data, analyzing the data, forming tentative conclusions, and disseminating findings.

secondary aging Aging processes that result from disease and bodily abuse and disuse and are often preventable.

secondary sex characteristics Physiological signs of sexual maturation (such as breast development and growth of body hair) that do not involve the sex organs.

secular trend Trend that can be seen only by observing several generations, such as the trend toward earlier attainment of adult height and sexual maturity, which began a century ago in some countries.

secure attachment Pattern in which an infant cries or protests when the primary caregiver leaves and actively seeks out the caregiver on his or her return.

selective optimization with compensation (SOC) Enhancing overall cognitive functioning by using stronger abilities to compensate for those that have weakened.

self-awareness Realization that one's existence and functioning are separate from those of other people and things.

self-concept Sense of self; descriptive and evaluative mental picture of one's abilities and traits.

self-conscious emotions Emotions, such as embarrassment, empathy, and envy, that depend on self-awareness.

self-definition Cluster of characteristics used to describe oneself.

self-efficacy Sense of one's capability to master challenges and achieve goals.

self-esteem The judgment a person makes about his or her self-worth.

self-evaluative emotions Emotions, such as pride, shame, and guilt, that depend on both self-awareness and knowledge of socially accepted standards of behavior.

self-regulation A child's independent control of behavior to conform to understood social expectations.

semantic memory Long-term memory of general factual knowledge, social customs, and language.

senescence Period of the life span marked by declines in physical functioning usually associated with aging; begins at different ages for different people.

sensorimotor stage Piaget's first stage in cognitive development, in which infants learn through senses and motor activity.

sensory memory Initial, brief, temporary storage of sensory information.

separation anxiety Distress shown by someone, typically an infant, when a familiar caregiver leaves.

separation anxiety disorder Condition involving excessive, prolonged anxiety concerning separation from home or from people to whom a person is attached.

sequential study Study design that combines cross-sectional and longitudinal techniques.

seriation Ability to order items along a dimension.

sex chromosomes Pair of chromosomes that determines sex: XX in the normal human female, XY in the normal human male.

sex-linked inheritance Pattern of inheritance in which certain characteristics carried on the X chromosome inherited from the mother are transmitted differently to her male and female offspring.

sexting The sharing or sending of sexually explicit or suggestive photos or videos to others.

sexual abuse Physically or psychologically harmful sexual activity or any sexual activity involving a child and an older person.

sexual orientation Focus of consistent sexual, romantic, and affectionate interest, either heterosexual, homosexual, or bisexual.

sexually transmitted infections (STIs) Infections and diseases spread by sexual contact.

shaken baby syndrome Form of maltreatment in which shaking an infant or toddler can cause brain damage, paralysis, or death.

situational compliance Kochanska's term for obedience of a parent's orders only in the presence of signs of ongoing parental control.

small-for-date (small-for-gestational-age) infants Infants whose birth weight is less than that of 90 percent of babies of the same gestational age, as a result of slow fetal growth.

social clock Set of cultural norms or expectations for the times of life when certain important events, such as marriage, parenthood, entry into work, and retirement, should occur.

social cognitive theory Albert Bandura's expansion of social learning theory; holds that children learn gender roles through socialization.

social convoy theory Theory, proposed by Kahn and Antonucci, that people move through life surrounded by concentric circles of intimate relationships on which they rely for assistance, well-being, and social support.

social learning theory Theory that behaviors are learned by observing and imitating models. Also called *social cognitive theory*.

social phobia Extreme fear and/or avoidance of social situations.

social referencing Understanding an ambiguous situation by seeking another person's perception of it.

social smiling Beginning in the 2nd month, newborn infants gaze at their parents and smile at them, signaling positive participation in the relationship.

social-contextual approach Approach to the study of cognitive development that focuses on environmental influences, particularly parents and other caregivers.

socialization Development of habits, skills, values, and motives shared by responsible, productive members of a society.

sociocultural theory Vygotsky's theory of how contextual factors affect children's development.

socioemotional selectivity theory Theory, proposed by Carstensen, that people select social contacts on the basis of the changing relative importance of social interaction as a source of information, as an aid in developing and maintaining a self-concept, and as a source of emotional well-being.

spermarche Boy's first ejaculation.

spillover hypothesis Hypothesis that there is a carryover of cognitive gains from work to leisure that explains the positive relationship between activities in the quality of intellectual functioning.

spontaneous abortion Natural expulsion from the uterus of an embryo that cannot survive outside the womb; also called *miscarriage*.

state of arousal An infant's physiological and behavioral status at a given moment in the periodic daily cycle of wakefulness, sleep, and activity.

stillbirth Death of a fetus at or after the 20th week of gestation.

Strange Situation Laboratory technique used to study infant attachment.

stranger anxiety Wariness of strange people and places, shown by some infants during the second half of the 1st year.

stress Physical or psychological demands on a person or organism.

stressors Perceived environmental demands that may produce stress.

substance abuse Repeated, harmful use of a substance, usually alcohol or other drugs.

substance dependence Addiction (physical or psychological or both) to a harmful substance.

substantive complexity Degree to which a person's work requires thought and independent judgment.

sudden infant death syndrome (SIDS) Sudden and unexplained death of an apparently healthy infant.

survival curve A curve on a graph showing the percentage of people or animals alive at various ages.

syntax Rules for forming sentences in a particular language.

systems of action Increasingly complex combinations of motor skills, which permit a wider or more precise range of movement and more control of the environment.

tacit knowledge Sternberg's term for information that is not formally taught but is necessary to get ahead.

telegraphic speech Early form of sentence use consisting of only a few essential words.

temperament Characteristic disposition, or style of approaching and reacting to situations.

teratogen Environmental agent, such as a virus, a drug, or radiation, that can interfere with normal prenatal development and cause developmental abnormalities.

terminal drop A frequently observed decline in cognitive abilities near the end of life. Also called *terminal decline*.

thanatology Study of death and dying.

theory Coherent set of logically related concepts that seeks to organize, explain, and predict data.

theory of multiple intelligences Gardner's theory that each person has several distinct forms of intelligence.

theory of sexual selection Darwin's theory that gender roles developed in response to men's and women's differing reproductive needs.

timing-of-events model Theoretical model of personality development that describes adult psychosocial development as a response to the expected or unexpected occurrence and timing of important life events.

trait models Theoretical models of personality development that focus on mental, emotional, temperamental, and behavioral traits, or attributes.

transgender Referring to individuals whose biological sex at birth and gender identity differ.

transitive inference Understanding the relationship between two objects by knowing the relationship of each to a third object.

triangular theory of love Sternberg's theory that patterns of love hinge on the balance among three elements: intimacy, passion, and commitment.

triarchic theory of intelligence Sternberg's theory describing three elements of intelligence: componential, experiential, and contextual.

turning points Psychological transitions that involve significant change or transformation in the perceived meaning, purpose, or direction of a person's life.

typological approach Theoretical approach that identifies broad personality types, or styles.

ultrasound Prenatal medical procedure using high-frequency sound waves to detect the outline of a fetus and its movements, so as to determine whether a pregnancy is progressing normally.

variable-rate theories Theories that explain biological aging as a result of processes that involve damage to biological systems and that vary from person to person.

violation of expectations Research method in which dishabituation to a stimulus that conflicts with experience is taken as evidence that an infant recognizes the new stimulus as surprising.

visible imitation Imitation with parts of one's body that one can see.

visual cliff Apparatus designed to give an illusion of depth and used to assess depth perception in infants.

visual guidance Use of the eyes to guide movements of the hands or other parts of the body.

visual preference Tendency of infants to spend more time looking at one sight than another.

visual recognition memory Ability to distinguish a familiar visual stimulus from an unfamiliar one when shown both at the same time.

visually based retrieval Process of retrieving the sound of a printed word when seeing the word as a whole.

vital capacity Amount of air that can be drawn in with a deep breath and expelled.

Wechsler Adult Intelligence Scale (WAIS) Intelligence test for adults that yields verbal and performance scores as well as a combined score.

Wechsler Intelligence Scale for Children (WISC-IV) Individual intelligence test for school-age children, which yields verbal and performance scores as well as a combined score.

whole-language approach Approach to teaching reading that emphasizes visual retrieval and use of contextual clues.

withdrawal of love Disciplinary strategy that involves ignoring, isolating, or showing dislike for a child.

working memory Short-term storage of information being actively processed.

zone of proximal development (ZPD) Vygotsky's term for the difference between what a child can do alone and what the child can do with help.

zygote One-celled organism resulting from fertilization.

"difficult" children Children with irritable temperament, irregular biological rhythms, and intense emotional responses.

"easy" children Children with a generally happy temperament, regular biological rhythms, and a readiness to accept new experiences.

"slow-to-warm-up" children Children whose temperament is generally mild but who are hesitant about accepting new experiences.

Aarts, A. A., Anderson, J. E., Anderson, C. J., Attridge, P. R., Attwood, A., Axt, J., . . . Bartmess, E. (2015). Estimating the reproducibility of psychological science. *Science, 349*(6251), 253-267.

Aassve, A., Cottini, E., & Vitali, A. (2013). Youth prospects in a time of economic recession. *Demographic Research, 29*, 949-962.

Abar, B., LaGasse, L. L., Derauf, C., Newman, E., Shah, R., Smith, L. M., . . . & Neal, C. (2013). Examining the relationships between prenatal methamphetamine exposure, early adversity, and child neurobehavioral disinhibition. *Psychology of Addictive Behaviors, 27*(3), 662.

Abatiell, P., & Adams, M. (2011). LGBT aging: a question of identity. *The Gerontologist, 51*, 880-884.

Abma, J. C., & Martinez, G. M. (2017). Sexual activity and contraceptive use among teenagers in the United States, 2011-2015. *National Health Statistics Reports*, (104), 1-23.

Abma, J. C., Martinez, G. M., & Copen, C. E. (2010). Teenagers in the United States: Sexual activity, contraceptive use, and childbearing, National Survey of Family Growth 2006-2008. *Vital Health Statistics, 23*(30). Washington, DC: National Center for Health Statistics.

Abramovitch, R., Corter, C., Pepler, D. J., & Stanhope, L. (1986). Sibling and peer interaction: A final follow-up and a comparison. *Child Development*, 217-229.

Abrams, L., & Davis, D. (2016). The tip-of-the-tongue phenomenon. In H. Wright (Ed.), *Cognition, language and aging* (pp. 13-54). Amsterdam, the Netherlands: John Benjamins.

Abubakar, I. I., Tillmann, T., & Banerjee, A. (2015). Global, regional, and national age-sex specific all-cause and cause-specific mortality for 240 causes of death, 1990-2013: A systematic analysis for the Global Burden of Disease Study 2013. *Lancet, 385*(9963), 117-171.

Achenbaum, W. A., & Bengtson, V. L. (1994). Re-engaging the disengagement theory of aging: On the history and assessment of theory development in gerontology. *Gerontologist, 34*, 756-763.

Achter, J. A., & Lubinski, D. (2003). Fostering exceptional development in intellectually talented populations. In W. B. Walsh (Ed.), *Counseling psychology and optimal human functioning* (pp. 279-296). Mahwah, NJ: Erlbaum.

Acierno, R., Hernandez, M. A., Amstadter, A. B., Resnick, H. S., Steve, K., Muzzy, W., & Kilpatrick, D. G. (2010). Prevalence and correlates of emotional, physical, sexual, and financial abuse and potential neglect in the United States: The National Elder Mistreatment Study. *American Journal of Public Health, 100*(2), 292-297.

Ackerman, B. P., Kogos, J., Youngstrom, E., Schoff, K., & Izard, C. (1999). Family instability and the problem behaviors of children from economically disadvantaged families. *Developmental Psychology, 35*(1), 258-268.

Ackerman, J. P., Riggins, T., & Black, M. M. (2010). A review of the effects of prenatal cocaine exposure among school-aged children. *Pediatrics, 125*(3), 554-565.

Adam, E. K., Gunnar, M. R., & Tanaka, A. (2004). Adult attachment, parent emotion, and observed parenting behavior: Mediator and moderator models. *Child Development, 75*, 110-122.

Adams, C. (1991). Qualitative age differences in memory for text: A life-span developmental perspective. *Psychology and Aging, 6*, 323-336.

Adams, R. G. (1986). Friendship and aging. *Generations, 10*(4), 40-43.

Adams, R. G., & Taylor, E. M. (2015). Friendship and happiness in the third age. In *Friendship and happiness* (pp. 155-169). Amsterdam, the Netherlands: Springer.

Adams, R., & Laursen, B. (2001). The organization and dynamics of adolescent conflict with parents and friends. *Journal of Marriage and the Family, 63*, 97-110.

Adamsons, K., & Johnson, S. K. (2013). An updated and expanded meta-analysis of nonresident fathering and child well-being. *Journal of Family Psychology, 27*(4), 589.

Addis, M. E., & Mahalik, J. R. (2003). Men, masculinity, and the contexts of help seeking. *American Psychologist, 58*, 5-14.

Addis, S., Davies, M., Greene, G., MacBride-Stewart, S., & Shepherd, M. (2009). The health, social care and housing needs of lesbian, gay, bisexual and transgender older people: A review of the literature. *Health & Social Care in the Community, 17*(6), 647-658.

Adey, P., Csapó, B., Demetriou, A., Hautamäki, J., & Shayer, M. (2007). Can we be intelligent about intelligence? Why education needs the concept of plastic general ability. *Educational Research Review, 2*(2), 75-97.

Administration for Children and Families. (2019). *Head Start program facts: Fiscal year 2019* [Report]. Retrieved from https://eclkc.ohs.acf.hhs.gov/about-us/article/head-start-program-facts-fiscal-year-2018

Administration for Community Living. (2019). *2018 profile of older Americans* [U.S. Department of Health and Human Services, Administration on Aging report]. Retrieved from https://acl.gov/sites/default/files/Aging%20and%20Disability%20in%20America/2018OlderAmericansProfile.pdf

Administration on Aging. (2016). *A profile of older Americans: 2016*. Retrieved from www.acl.gov/sites/default/files/Aging%20and%20Disability%20in%20America/2016-Profile.pdf

Administration on Aging. (2018). *2018 profile of aging Americans*. Retrieved from https://acl.gov/sites/default/files/Aging%20and%20Disability%20in%20America/2018OlderAmericansProfile.pdf

Administration for Community Living. (2020). *2019 profile of older Americans* [U.S. Department of Health and Human Services, Administration on Aging report]. Retrieved from https://acl.gov/sites/default/files/Aging%20and%20Disability%20in%20America/2019ProfileOlderAmericans508.pdf

Adolescent Sleep Working Group. (2014). School start times for adolescents. *Pediatrics, 134*(3), 642-649.

Adolph, K. E. (2008). Learning to move. *Current Directions in Psychological Science, 17*(3), 213-218.

Adolph, K. E., & Eppler, M. A. (2002). Flexibility and specificity in infant motor skill acquisition. In J. Fagen & H. Hayne (Eds.), *Progress in infancy research* (Vol. 2, pp. 121-167). Mahwah, NJ: Erlbaum.

Adolph, K. E., Vereijken, B., & Shrout, P. E. (2003). What changes in infant walking and why. *Child Development, 74*, 475-497.

Advocates for Youth. (2010). *Adolescents and sexually transmitted infections: A costly and dangerous global phenomenon* [Report]. Retrieved from www.advocatesforyouth.org/storage/advfy/documents/thefacts_adolescents_sti.pdf

Afram, B., Stephan, A., Verbeek, H., Bleijlevens, M. H., Suhonen, R., Sutcliffe, C., . . . Meyer, G. (2014). Reasons for institutionalization of people with dementia: Informal caregiver reports from 8 European countries. *Journal of the American Medical Directors Association, 15*(2), 108-116.

African Wedding Traditions. (2013). *Jumping the broom ceremony & African wedding traditions*. Retrieved from http://africanweddingtraditions.com/jumping-the-broom-ceremony.html

Afshin, A., Sur, P. J., Fay, K. A., Cornaby, L., Ferrara, G., Salama, J. S., . . . Afarideh, M. (2019). Health effects of dietary risks in 195 countries, 1990-2017: A systematic analysis for the Global Burden of Disease Study 2017. *The Lancet, 393*(10184), 1958-1972.

Agahi, N., & Parker, M. G. (2008). Leisure activities and mortality: Does gender matter? *Journal of Aging and Health, 20*(7), 855-871.

Agahi, N., Ahacic, K., & Parker, M. G. (2006). Continuity of leisure participation from middle age to old age. *Journal of Gerontology: Social Sciences, 61B*, S340-S346.

Aggarwal, K. K. (2013). Sexual desire and sexual activity of men and women across their lifespan. *Indian Journal of Clinical Practice, 24*(3).

Agrillo, C. (2011). Near-death experience: Out-of-body and out-of-brain? *Review of General Psychology, 15*(1), 1.

Aguilera, M., Arias, B., Wichers, M., Barrantes-Vidal, N., Moya, J., Villa, H., . . . Fañanás, L. (2009). Early adversity and 5-HTT/BDNF genes: New evidence of gene-environment interactions on depressive symptoms in a general population. *Psychological Medicine, 39*(9), 1425-1432.

Ahmed, M. R., Zhang, Y., Feng, Z., Lo, B., Inan, O. T., & Liao, H. (2019). Neuroimaging and machine learning for dementia diagnosis: Recent advancements and future prospects. *IEEE Reviews in Biomedical Engineering, 12*, 19-33.

Ahmetoglu, G., Swami, V., & Chamorro-Premuzic, T. (2010). The relationship between dimensions of love, personality, and relationship length. *Archives of Sexual Behavior, 39*(5), 1181-1190.

Ahn, D., & Shin, D. H. (2013). Is the social use of media for seeking connectedness or for avoiding social isolation? Mechanisms underlying media use and subjective well-being. *Computers in Human Behavior, 29*(6), 2453-2462.

Ahnert, L., & Lamb, M. E. (2003). Shared care: Establishing a balance between home and child care settings. *Child Development, 74*, 1044-1049.

Ahnert, L., Gunnar, M. R., Lamb, M. E., & Barthel, M. (2004). Transition to child care: Associations with infant-mother attachment, infant negative emotion and corticol elevation. *Child Development, 75*, 639-650.

Ahrons, C. R., & Tanner, J. L. (2003). Adult children and their fathers: Relationship changes 20 years after parental divorce. *Family Relations, 52*, 340-351.

Ai, A. L., Huang, B., Bjorck, J., & Appel, H. B. (2013). Religious attendance and major depression among Asian Americans from a national database: The mediation of social support. *Psychology of Religion and Spirituality, 5*(2), 78.

Aichele, S., Rabbitt, P., & Ghisletta, P. (2015). Life span decrements in fluid intelligence and processing speed predict mortality risk. *Psychology and Aging, 30*(3), 598.

Aina, T. A., Agiobu-Kemmer, I., Etta, E. F., Zeitlin, M. F., & Setiloane, K. (1993). *Early child care and nutrition in Lagos State, Nigeria.* Medford, MA: Tufts University School of Nutrition & Policy for UNICEF.

Ainsworth, M. D. S., Blehar, M. C., Waters, E., & Wall, S. (1978). *Patterns of attachment: A psychological study of the strange situation.* Hillsdale, NJ: Erlbaum.

Ainsworth, M. D. S., Blehar, M. C., Waters, E., & Wall, S. N. (2015). *Patterns of attachment: A psychological study of the strange situation.* New York, NY: Psychology Press.

Aitken, L., Burmeister, E., Lang, J., Chaboyer, W., & Richmond, T. S. (2010). Characteristics and outcomes of injured older adults after hospitalization. *Journal of the American Geriatrics Society, 58*(3), 442-449.

Ajmani, G. S., Suh, H. H., Wroblewski, K. E., & Pinto, J. M. (2017). Smoking and olfactory dysfunction: A systematic literature review and meta-analysis. *The Laryngoscope, 127*(8), 1753-1761.

Akin, A. (2012). The relationships between Internet addiction, subjective vitality, and subjective happiness. *CyberPsychology, Behavior, and Social Networking, 15*, 404-410. doi:10.1089/cyber.2011.0609.

Akinbami, L. (2006). The state of childhood asthma, United States, 1980-2005. *Advance Data from Vital and Health Statistics, 381.* Hyattsville, MD: National Center for Health Statistics.

Akinbami, L. J., Kit, B. K., Carroll, M. D., Fakhouri, T. H., & Ogden, C. L. (2017). Trends in anthropometric measures among US children 6 to 23 months, 1976-2014. *Pediatrics, 139*(3), e20163374.

Akinbami, O. J., Moorman, J. E., Bailey, C., Zahran, H. S., King, M., Johnson, C. A., & Liu, X. (2012). Trends in asthma prevalence, health care use, and mortality in the United States, 2001-2010. *NCHS Data Brief, 94.*

Aknin, L. B., Barrington-Leigh, C. P., Dunn, E. W., Helliwell, J. F., Burns, J., Biswas-Diener, R., . . . Norton, M. I. (2013). Prosocial spending and well-being: Cross-cultural evidence for a psychological universal. *Journal of Personality and Social Psychology, 104*(4), 635.

Akune, T., Muraki, S., Oka, H., Tanaka, S., Kawaguchi, H., Nakamura, K., & Yoshimura, N. (2014). Exercise habits during middle age are associated with lower prevalence of sarcopenia: The ROAD study. *Osteoporosis International, 25*(3), 1081-1088.

Al-Dhamit, Y., & Kreishan, L. (2016). Gifted students' intrinsic and extrinsic motivations and parental influence on their motivation: from the self-determination theory perspective. *Journal of Research in Special Educational Needs, 16*(1), 13-23.

Al-Namlah, A. S., Meins, E., & Fernyhough, C. (2012). Self-regulatory private speech relates to children's recall and organization of autobiographical memories. *Early Childhood Research Quarterly, 27*(3), 441-446.

Al-Naquib, N., Frankerburg, W. K., Mirza, H., Yazdi, A. W., & AlNoori, S. (1999). The standardization of the Denver developmental screening test on Arab children from the Middle East and North Africa. *Le Journal of Medical Libanais, 47,* 95-106

Alba, R. (2018). What majority-minority society? A critical analysis of the Census Bureau's projections of America's demographic future. *Socius,* 4.doi: 2378023118796932.

Albert, D., Chein, J., & Steinberg, L. (2013). The teenage brain: Peer influences on adolescent decision making. *Current Directions in Psychological Science, 22*(2), 114-120.

Albuquerque, D., Stice, E., Rodríguez-López, R., Manco, L., & Nóbrega, C. (2015). Current review of genetics of human obesity: From molecular mechanisms to an evolutionary perspective. *Molecular Genetics and Genomics, 290*(4), 1191-1221.

Albuquerque, S., Pereira, M., & Narciso, I. (2016). Couple's relationship after the death of a child: A systematic review. *Journal of Child and Family Studies, 25*(1), 30-53.

Alcohol.org. (2019). *Serving alcohol to pregnant women.* Retrieved from www.alcohol.org/laws/serving-alcohol-to-pregnant-women/

Aldwin, C. M., & Levenson, M. R. (2001). Stress, coping, and health at midlife: A developmental perspective. In M. E. Lachman (Ed.), *Handbook of midlife development* (pp. 188-214). New York, NY: Wiley.

Alexander, G. M., & Wilcox, T. (2012). Sex differences in early infancy. *Child Development Perspectives, 6*(4), 400-406.

Alexander, G. M., Wilcox, T., & Woods, R. (2009). Sex differences in infants' visual interest in toys. *Archives of Sexual Behavior, 38*(3), 427-433.

Alexander, K. L., Entwisle, D. R., & Olson, L. S. (2007). Lasting consequences of the summer learning gap. *American Sociological Review, 72,* 167-180.

Algren, M. H., Ekholm, O., Nielsen, L., Ersbøll, A. K., Bak, C. K., & Andersen, P. T. (2018). Associations between perceived stress, socioeconomic status, and health-risk behaviour in deprived neighbourhoods in Denmark: A cross-sectional study. *BMC Public Health, 18*(1), 250.

Ali, M. M., & Dwyer, D. S. (2011). Estimating peer effects in sexual behavior among adolescents. *Journal of Adolescence, 34*(1), 183-190.

Ali, M. M., Amialchuk, A., & Dwyer, D. S. (2011). Social network effects in contraceptive behavior among adolescents. *Journal of Developmental & Behavioral Pediatrics, 32*(8), 563-571.

Alibeik, H., & Angaji, S. A. (2010). Developmental aspects of left handedness. *Australian Journal of Basic and Applied Sciences, 4*(5), 881-977.

Alker, J., & Roygardner, L. (2019). *The number of uninsured children is on the rise.* Washington, DC: Georgetown University Center for Children and Families.

Alladi, S., Bak, T. H., Duggirala, V., Surampudi, B., Shailaja, M., Shukla, A. K., . . . & Kaul, S. (2013). Bilingualism delays age at onset of dementia, independent of education and immigration status. *Neurology, 81*(22), 1938-1944.

Allemand, M., Schaffhuser, K., & Martin, M. (2015). Long-term correlated change between personality traits and perceived social support in middle adulthood. *Personality and Social Psychology Bulletin, 41*(3), 420-432.

Allen, E. S., & Atkins, D. C. (2012). The association of divorce and extramarital sex in a representative US sample. *Journal of Family Issues, 33*(11), 1477-1493.

Allen, T. D., & Finkelstein, L. M. (2014). Work-family conflict among members of full-time dual-earner couples: An examination of family life stage, gender, and age. *Journal of Occupational Health Psychology, 19*(3), 376.

Allendorf, K., & Pandian, R. K. (2016). The decline of arranged marriage? Marital change and continuity in India. *Population and Development Review, 42*(3), 435.

Alloway, T. P. (2006). How does working memory work in the classroom? *Education Research and Reviews, 1,* 134-139.

Alloway, T. P., & Alloway, R. G. (2010). Investigating the predictive roles of working memory and IQ in academic attainment. *Journal of Experimental Child Psychology, 106*(1), 20-29.

Alloway, T. P., Gathercole, S. E., Kirkwood, H., & Elliot, J. (2009). The cognitive and behavioral characteristics of children with low working memory. *Child Development, 80*(2), 606-621.

Almas, A. N., Grusec, J. E., & Tackett, J. L. (2011). Children's disclosure and secrecy: Links to maternal parenting characteristics and children's coping skills. *Social Development, 20*(3), 624–643.

Almeida, S., Rato, L., Sousa, M., Alves, M. G., & Oliveira, P. F. (2017). Fertility and sperm quality in the aging male. *Current Pharmaceutical Design, 23*(30), 4429–4437.

Alterovitz, S. S. R., & Mendelsohn, G. A. (2009). Partner preferences across the life span: Online dating by older adults. *Psychology and Aging, 24*(2), 513.

Altmann, A., Tian, L., Henderson, V. W., Greicius, M. D., & Alzheimer's Disease Neuroimaging Initiative Investigators. (2014). Sex modifies the APOE-related risk of developing Alzheimer disease. *Annals of Neurology, 75*(4), 563–573.

Alzheimer's Association. (2020). *2020 Alzheimer's disease facts and figures* [Report]. Retrieved from www.alz.org/media/Documents/alzheimers-facts-and-figures.pdf

Al-Dhamit, Y., & Kreishan, L. (2016). Gifted students' intrinsic and extrinsic motivations and parental influence on their motivation: From the self-determination theory perspective. *Journal of Research in Special Educational Needs, 16*(1), 13–23.

Amato, P. R. (2000). The consequences of divorce for adults and children. *Journal of Marriage and Family, 62*, 1269–1287.

Amato, P. R. (2003). Reconciling divergent perspectives: Judith Wallerstein, quantitative family research, and children of divorce. *Family Relations, 52*, 332–339.

Amato, P. R. (2005). The impact of family formation change on the cognitive, social, and emotional well-being of the next generation. *Future of Children, 15*, 75–96.

Amato, P. R. (2010). Research on divorce: Continuing trends and new developments. *Journal of Marriage and Family, 72*(3), 650–666.

Amato, P. R. (2014). Marriage, cohabitation and mental health. *Family Matters*, (96), 5.

Amato, P. R. (2014). The consequences of divorce for adults and children: An update. *Društvena Istraživanja: Časopis za Opća Društvena Pitanja, 23*(1), 5–24.

Amato, P. R., & Anthony, C. J. (2014). Estimating the effects of parental divorce and death with fixed effects models. *Journal of Marriage and Family, 76*(2), 370–386.

Amato, P. R., Johnson, D. R., Booth, A., & Rogers, S. J. (2003). Continuity and change in marital quality between 1980 and 2000. *Journal of Marriage and Family, 65*(1), 1–22.

Amato, P. R., Kane, J. B., & James, S. (2011). Reconsidering the "good divorce." *Family Relations, 60*(5), 511–524.

American Academy of Child and Adolescent Psychiatry. (2017). *Terrorism and war: How to talk to your children*. Retrieved from www.aacap.org/AACAP/Families_and_Youth/Facts_for_Families/FFF-Guide/Talking-To-Children-About-Terrorism-And-War-087.aspx

American Academy of Pediatrics. (2019). *Benefits of breastfeeding* [Information sheet]. Retrieved from https://www.aap.org/en-us/advocacy-and-policy/aap-health-initiatives/Breastfeeding/Pages/Benefits-of-Breastfeeding.aspx

American Academy of Pediatrics. (2019). *Infant food and feeding* [Information sheet]. Retrieved from www.aap.org/en-us/advocacy-and-policy/aap-health-initiatives/HALF-Implementation-Guide/Age-Specific-Content/Pages/Infant-Food-and-Feeding.aspx

American Academy of Pediatrics Committee on Environmental Health. (2005). Lead exposure in children: Prevention, detection, and management. *Pediatrics, 116*, 1036–1046.

American Academy of Pediatrics Committee on Injury and Poison Prevention. (2000). Firearm-related injuries affecting the pediatric population. *Pediatrics, 105*(4), 888–895.

American Academy of Pediatrics Committee on Psychosocial Aspects of Child and Family Health. (1998). Guidance for effective discipline. *Pediatrics, 101*, 723–728.

American Academy of Pediatrics Committee on Public Education. (2009). Media violence-council on communications and media. *Pediatrics, 124*(5), 1495–1503.

American Academy of Pediatrics Council on Injury and Poison Prevention. (2001). Bicycle helmets. *Pediatrics, 108*(4), 1030–1032.

American Academy of Pediatrics Council on Sports Medicine and Fitness. (2001). Risk of injury from baseball and softball in children. *Pediatrics, 107*(4), 782–784.

American Academy of Pediatrics. (2004, September 30). American Academy of Pediatrics (AAP) supports Institute of Medicine's (IOM) childhood obesity recommendation [Press release].

American Academy of Pediatrics. (2006). Council on Sports Medicine and Fitness and Council on School Health. Active healthy living: Prevention of childhood obesity through increased physical activity. *Pediatrics, 117*(5), 1834–1842.

American Academy of Pediatrics. (2011). Media use by children under age 2. *Pediatrics, 128*, 1040–1045.

American Academy of Pediatrics. (2013). Children, adolescents, and the media. *Pediatrics, 132*, 958–961.

American Academy of Pediatrics. (2016). *American Academy of Pediatrics announces new guidelines for children's media use*. Retrieved from www.aap.org/en-us/about-the-aap/aap-press-room/pages/american-academy-of-pediatrics-announces-new-recommendations-for-childrens-media-use.aspx.

American Academy of Pediatrics. (2016). Media and young minds: Council on communications and media. *Pediatrics, 138*(5), 1–6.

American Cancer Society. (2011). *Guide to quitting smoking*. Retrieved from www.cancer.org/docroot/PED/content/PED_10_13X_Guide_for_Quitting_Smoking.asp?from5fast

American Cancer Society. (2017). *Breast cancer risk and prevention* [Information sheet]. Retrieved from www.cancer.org/content/dam/CRC/PDF/Public/8578.00.pdf.

American Cancer Society. (2017). *How common is breast cancer?* [Information sheet]. Retrieved from www.cancer.org/cancer/breast-cancer/about/how-common-is-breast-cancer.html

American College of Nurse-Midwives. (2016). *Position statement: Planned home births*. Silver Spring, MD: Author.

American College of Obstetricians and Gynecologists. (2013). Weight gain during pregnancy. Committee Opinion No. 548. *Obstet Gynecol, 121*, 210–212.

American College of Obstetricians and Gynecologists. (2014). Management of late-term and postterm pregnancies. Practice Bulletin No. 146. *Obstetrics and Gynecology, 124*(2, Pt. 1), 390.

American College of Obstetricians and Gynecologists. (2017). Vaginal birth after cesarean delivery. ACOG Practice Bulletin No. 184. *Obstetrics and Gynecology, 130*(5), e217–e233.

American College of Obstetricians and Gynecologists. (2018). *ACOG interim update: ACOG statement on home births*. Retrieved from www.acog.org/Clinical-Guidance-and-Publications/Committee-Opinions/Committee-on-Obstetric-Practice/Planned-Home-Birth?IsMobileSet=false

American College of Obstetricians and Gynecologists. (2019). *Exercise during pregnancy*. Retrieved from www.acog.org/Patients/FAQs/Exercise-During-Pregnancy?

American College of Obstetricians and Gynecologists. (2020). *Premenstrual syndrome* [Information sheet]. Retrieved from www.acog.org/patient-resources/faqs/gynecologic-problems/premenstrual-syndrome

American College of Obstetricians and Gynecologists. (2020). *Novel coronavirus 2019 (Covid-19)* [Practice advisory]. Retrieved from www.acog.org/clinical/clinical-guidance/practice-advisory/articles/2020/03/novel-coronavirus-2019

American Diabetes Association. (1992). *Diabetes facts*. Alexandria, VA: author.

American Diabetes Association. (2018). 13. Management of diabetes in pregnancy: Standards of Medical Care in Diabetes–2018. *Diabetes Care, 41*(Suppl. 1), S137–S143.

American Diabetes Association. (2020). *Diabetes risk: What causes diabetes? Find out and take control* [Information sheets]. Retrieved from www.diabetes.org/diabetes-risk

American Medical Association House of Delegates. (2008, June). *Resolution 205: Home deliveries*. Proceedings of the American Medical Association House of Delegates, Fifteenth Annual Meeting, Chicago, IL. Retrieved from www.ama-assn.org/ama1/pub/upload/mm/471/205.doc

American Medical Association. (2018). *Physician assisted suicide: Permitting physicians to engage in assisted suicide would ultimately cause more harm than good* [position statement]. Retrieved from www.ama-assn.org/delivering-care/physician-assisted-suicide

American Optometric Association. (2019). *Recommended eye examination frequency for pediatric patients and adults*. Retrieved from www.aoa.org/patients-and-public/caring-for-your-vision/comprehensive-eye-and-vision-examination/recommended-examination-frequency-for-pediatric-patients-and-adults

American Psychiatric Association. (2000). *Diagnostic and statistical manual of mental disorders* (4th ed., Text Revision). Washington, DC: Author.

American Psychiatric Association. (2013). *Diagnostic and statistical manual of mental disorders: DSM-5.* Washington, DC: Author.

American Psychological Association (2007). *Sandwich generation moms feeling the squeeze.* Retrieved from www.apa.org/helpcenter/sandwich-generation.aspx

American Psychological Association (APA) Working Group on Assisted Suicide and End-of-Life Decisions. (2005). *Orientation to end-of-life decision-making.* Retrieved from www.apa.org/pi/aseol/section1.html

American Psychological Association (APA). (2002). Ethical principles of psychologists and code of conduct. *American Psychologist, 57,* 1060-1073.

American Psychological Association. (2004, July). *Resolution on sexual orientation, parents, and children.* Retrieved from www.apa.org/pi/lgbc/policy/parents.html

American Psychological Association. (2016). *Stress in America: Impact of discrimination.* Retrieved from www.apa.org/news/press/releases/stress/2015/impact-of-discrimination.pdf

American Psychological Association. (2017). *Resolution on assisted dying.* Retrieved from www.apa.org/about/policy/assisted-dying-resolution.aspx

American Psychological Association. (2020). *Stress in America, 2019.* Retrieved from www.apa.org/images/stress-america-2019_tcm7-264533.pdf

American Psychological Association. (2020). *Stress in the time of COVID-19* [Report]. Retrieved from www.apa.org/news/press/releases/stress/2020/stress-in-america-covid.pdf

Amlien, I. K., & Fjell, A. M. (2014). Diffusion tensor imaging of white matter degeneration in Alzheimer's disease and mild cognitive impairment. *Neuroscience, 276,* 206-215.

Amsel, E., Goodman, G., Savoie, D., & Clark, M. (1996). The development of reasoning about causal and noncausal influences on levers. *Child Development, 67,* 1624-1646.

Amso, D., & Casey, B. J. (2006). Beyond what develops when: Neuroimaging may inform how cognition changes with development. *Current Directions in Psychological Science, 15,* 24-29.

Amso, D., & Scerif, G. (2015). The attentive brain: insights from developmental cognitive neuroscience. *Nature Reviews Neuroscience, 16*(10), 606-619.

Anastasi, A. (1988). *Psychological testing* (6th ed.). New York, NY: Macmillan.

Anastasi, A., & Schaefer, C. E. (1971). Note on concepts of creativity and intelligence. *Journal of Creative Behavior, 3,* 113-116.

Anastasiou, A., Karras, S. N., Bais, A., Grant, W. B., Kotsa, K., & Goulis, D. G. (2017). Ultraviolet radiation and effects on humans: The paradigm of maternal vitamin D production during pregnancy. *European Journal of Clinical Nutrition, 71*(11), 1268.

Andersen, A. M. N., & Urhoj, S. K. (2017). Is advanced paternal age a health risk for the offspring? *Fertility and Sterility, 107*(2), 312-318.

Andersen, S. L., Sebastiani, P., Dworkis, D. A., Feldman, L., & Perls, T. T. (2012). Health span approximates life span among many supercentenarians: Compression of morbidity at the approximate limit of life span. *Journals of Gerontology Series A: Biomedical Sciences and Medical Sciences, 67*(4), 395-405.

Anderson, A. H., Clark, A., & Mullin, J. (1994). Interactive communication between children: Learning how to make language work in dialog. *Journal of Child Language, 21,* 439-463.

Anderson, C. A., Berkowitz, L., Donnerstein, E., Huesmann, L. R., Johnson, J. D., Linz, D., Malamuth, N. M., & Wartella, E. (2003). The influence of media violence on youth. *Psychological Science in the Public Interest, 4,* 81-110.

Anderson, C. A., Bushman, B. J., Bartholow, B. D., Cantor, J., Christakis, D., Coyne, S. M., . . . Huesmann, R. (2017). Screen violence and youth behavior. *Pediatrics, 140*(Suppl. 2), S142-S147.

Anderson, C. A., Bushman, B. J., Donnerstein, E., Hummer, T. A., & Warburton, W. (2015). SPSSI research summary on media violence. *Analyses of Social Issues and Public Policy, 15*(1), 4-19.

Anderson, C. A., Suzuki, K., Swing, E. L., Groves, C. L., Gentile, D. A., Prot, S., . . . Jelic, M. (2017). Media violence and other aggression risk factors in seven nations. *Personality and Social Psychology Bulletin, 43*(7), 986-998.

Anderson, C., & Platten, C. R. (2011). Sleep deprivation lowers inhibition and enhances impulsivity to negative stimuli. *Behavioural Brain Research, 217*(2), 463-466.

Anderson, D. A., & Hamilton, M. (2005). Gender role stereotyping of parents in children's picture books: The invisible father. *Sex Roles, 52,* 145-151.

Anderson, E. L., Steen, E., & Stavropoulos, V. (2017). Internet use and Problematic Internet Use: A systematic review of longitudinal research trends in adolescence and emergent adulthood. *International Journal of Adolescence and Youth, 22*(4), 430-454.

Anderson, J. L., May, H. T., Lappe, D. L., Bair, T., Le, V., Carlquist, J. F., & Muhlestein, J. B. (2015). Impact of testosterone replacement on myocardial infarction, stroke, and death in men with low testosterone concentrations in an integrated health care system. *American Journal of Cardiology,* 117, 794-799.

Anderson, M., & Jiang, J. (2018). *Teens, social media and technology, 2018* [Pew Research Center report]. Retrieved from www.pewresearch.org/internet/2018/05/31/teens-social-media-technology-2018/

Anderson, N. D., Damianakis, T., Kröger, E., Wagner, L. M., Dawson, D. R., Binns, M. A., . . . Cook, S. L. (2014). The benefits associated with volunteering among seniors: A critical review and recommendations for future research. *Psychological Bulletin, 140*(6), 1505.

Anderson, S. (2011). *Immigrant founders and key personnel in America's 50 top venture-funded companies.* NFAP Policy Brief. Available at SSRN 2472052.

Anderson, S. E., & Whitaker, R. C. (2010). Household routines and obesity in US preschool-aged children. *Pediatrics, 125*(3), 420-428. doi: 10.1542/peds.2009-0417

Anderson, S. E., Dallal, G. E., & Must, A. (2003). Relative weight and race influence average age at menarche: Results from two nationally representative surveys of U.S. girls studied 25 years apart. *Pediatrics, 111,* 844-850.

Andreyeva, T., Kelly, I. R., & Harris, J. L. (2011). Exposure to food advertising on television: Associations with children's fast food and soft drink consumption and obesity. *Economics & Human Biology, 9*(3), 221-233.

Ang, R. P. (2015). Adolescent cyberbullying: A review of characteristics, prevention and intervention strategies. *Aggression and Violent Behavior, 25,* 35-42.

Ang, S., Rodgers, J. L., & Wanstrom, L. (2010). The Flynn Effect within subgroups in the U.S.: Gender, race, income, education, and urbanization differences in the NLSY-Children data. *Intelligence, 38*(4), 367-384.

Anglemyer, A., Horvath, T., & Rutherford, G. (2014). The accessibility of firearms and risk for suicide and homicide victimization among household members: A systematic review and meta-analysis. *Annals of Internal Medicine, 160*(2), 101-110.

Anglim, J., & Grant, S. (2016). Predicting psychological and subjective well-being from personality: Incremental prediction from 30 facets over the Big 5. *Journal of Happiness Studies, 17*(1), 59-80.

Antonarakis, S. E., & Cooper, D. N. (2019). Human Genomic Variants and Inherited Disease: Molecular Mechanisms and Clinical Consequences. In R. E. Pyeritz, B. R. Korf & W. W. Grody (Eds.), *Emery and Rimoin's Principles and Practice of Medical Genetics and Genomics* (pp. 125-200). Cambridge, MA: Academic Press.

Antonio, A. L., Chang, M. J., Hakuta, K., Kenny, D. A., Levin, S., & Milem, J. F. (2004). Effects of racial diversity on complex thinking in college students. *Psychological Science, 15,* 507-510.

Antonucci, T. C., & Akiyama, H. (1995). Convoys of social relations: Family and friendships within a life-span context. In R. Blieszner & V. Hilkevitch (Eds.), *Handbook of aging and the family* (pp. 355-371). Westport, CT: Greenwood Press.

Antonucci, T. C., Ajrouch, K. J., & Birditt, K. S. (2014). The convoy model: Explaining social relations from a multidisciplinary perspective. *The Gerontologist, 54*(1), 82-92.

Antonucci, T. C., Akiyama, H. & Merline, A. (2001). Dynamics of social relationships in midlife. In M. E. Lachman (Ed.) *Handbook of midlife development* (pp. 571-598). New York, NY: Wiley.

Antonucci, T., & Akiyama, H. (1997). Concern with others at midlife: Care, comfort, or compromise? In M. E. Lachman & J. B. James (Eds.), *Multiple paths of midlife development* (pp. 145-169). Chicago, IL: University of Chicago Press.

Aparicio-Martínez, P., Ruiz-Rubio, M., Perea-Moreno, A. J., Martínez-Jiménez, M. P., Pagliari, C., Redel-Macías, M. D., & Vaquero-Abellán, M. (2020). Gender differences in the addiction to social networks in the Southern Spanish university students. *Telematics and Informatics, 46,* 101304.

Apgar, V. (1952). A proposal for a new method of evaluation of the newborn. *Classic Papers in Critical Care, 32*(449), 97.

Aquilino, W. S. (1996). The returning adult child and parental experience at midlife. In C. Ryff & M. M. Seltzer (Eds.), *The parental experience in midlife* (pp. 423–458). Chicago, IL: University of Chicago Press.

Aquilino, W. S. (2006). Family relationships and support systems in emerging adulthood. In J. J. Arnett & J. L. Tanner (Eds.), *Emerging adults in America: Coming of age in the 21st century* (pp. 193–217). Washington, DC: American Psychological Association.

Arai, Y. (2017). The prevalence and risk factors of dementia in centenarians. *Brain Nerve, 69,* 771–780.

Arai, Y., Inagaki, H., Takayama, M., Abe, Y., Saito, Y., Takebayashi, T., Gondo, Y., & Hirose, N. (2014). Physical independence and mortality at the extreme limit of life span: Supercentenarians study in Japan. *Journals of Gerontology, 69,* 486–494.

Aram, D., Abiri, S., & Elad, L. (2014). Predicting early spelling: The contribution of children's early literacy, private speech during spelling, behavioral regulation, and parental spelling support. *Reading and Writing, 27*(4), 685–707.

Aram, D., Elad-Orbach, L., & Abiri, S. (2017). Predicting early writing: The role of parental writing mediation and children's private talk during writing. In C. McLachlan & A. Arrow (Eds.), *Literacy in the Early Years* (pp. 79–92). Singapore: Springer.

Archer, J. (2004). Sex differences in aggression in real-world settings: A meta-analytic review. *Review of General Psychology, 8,* 291–322.

Archuleta, K. L., Britt, S. L., Tonn, T. J., & Grable, J. E. (2011). Financial satisfaction and financial stressors in marital satisfaction. *Psychological Reports, 108*(2), 563–576.

Ardelt, M., & Edwards, C. A. (2016). Wisdom at the end of life: An analysis of mediating and moderating relations between wisdom and subjective well-being. *Journals of Gerontology Series B: Psychological Sciences and Social Sciences, 71*(3), 502–513.

Ardila, A., Rosselli, M., Matute, E., & Inozemtseva, O. (2011). Gender differences in cognitive development. *Developmental Psychology, 47*(4), 984.

Arias, E. (2010). United States life tables by Hispanic origin. *Vital Health Statistics, 2*(152), 1–33. Hyattsville, MD: National Center for Health Statistics.

Arias, E., MacDorman, M. F., Strobino, D. M., & Guyer, B. (2003). Annual summary of vital statistics—2002. *Pediatrics, 112,* 1215–1230.

Arif, N., & Fatima, I. (2015). Marital satisfaction in different types of marriage. *Pakistan Journal of Social and Clinical Psychology, 13*(1), 36.

Armenta, C. N., Fritz, M. M., & Lyubomirsky, S. (2016). Functions of positive emotions: Gratitude as a motivator of self-improvement and positive change. *Emotion Review.* doi: 10.1177/1754073916669596

Armour, J. A., Davison, A., & McManus, I. C. (2014). Genome-wide association study of handedness excludes simple genetic models. *Heredity, 112*(3), 221.

Arnett, J. J. (2004). *Emerging adulthood.* New York, NY: Oxford University Press.

Arnett, J. J. (2010). Oh, grow up! Generational grumbling and the new life stage of emerging adulthood. *Perspectives on Psychological Science, 5,* 89–92.

Arnett, J. J. (2014). Presidential address: The emergence of emerging adulthood: A personal history. *Emerging Adulthood, 2*(3), 155–162.

Arnett, J. J. (2015). Socialization in emerging adulthood. From the family to the wider world, from socialization to self-socialization. In J. E. Grusec & P. D. Hastings (Eds.), *Handbook of socialization: Theory and research* (pp. 85–108). New York, NY: Guilford Press.

Arnett, J. J. (2016). Does emerging adulthood theory apply across social classes? National data on a persistent question. *Emerging Adulthood, 4*(4), 227–235.

Arnold, A. P. (2017). A general theory of sexual differentiation. *Journal of Neuroscience Research, 95*(1-2), 291–300.

Arsenis, N. C., You, T., Ogawa, E. F., Tinsley, G. M., & Zuo, L. (2017). Physical activity and telomere length: Impact of aging and potential mechanisms of action. *Oncotarget, 8*(27), 45008.

Artis, J. E. (2007). Maternal cohabitation and child well-being among kindergarten children. *Journal of Marriage and Family, 69*(1), 222–236.

Artistico, D., Orom, H., Cervone, D., Krauss, S., & Houston, E. (2010). Everyday challenges in context: The influence of contextual factors on everyday problem solving among young, middle-aged and older adults. *Experimental Aging Research, 36*(2), 230–247.

Asato, M. R., Terwilliger, R., Woo, J., & Luna, B. S. (2010). White matter development in adolescence: A DTI study. *Cerebral Cortex, 20*(9), 2122–2131.

Aschersleben, G., Hofer, T., & Jovanovic, B. (2008). The link between infant attention to goal-directed action and later theory of mind abilities. *Developmental Science, 11*(6), 862–868.

Asher, M. I. (2010). Recent perspectives on global epidemiology of asthma in childhood. *Allergologia et Immunopathologia, 38*(2), 83–87.

Assari, S. (2017). Hostility, anger, and cardiovascular mortality among Blacks and whites. *Research in Cardiovascular Medicine, 6,* e34029. doi: 10.5812/cardiovascmed.34029.

Assini-Meytin, L. C., & Green, K. M. (2015). Long-term consequences of adolescent parenthood among African-American urban youth: A propensity score matching approach. *Journal of Adolescent Health, 56*(5), 529–535.

Asthana, S., Bhasin, S., Butler, R. N., Fillit, H., Finkelstein, J., Harman, S. M., . . . Urban, R. (2004). Masculine vitality: Pros and cons of testosterone in treating the andropause. *Journal of Gerontology: Medical Sciences, 59A,* 461–466.

Astuti, R., & Harris, P. L. (2008). Understanding mortality and the life of the ancestors in rural Madagascar. *Cognitive Science, 32*(4), 713–740.

Astuti, Y., Wardhana, A., Watkins, J., & Wulaningsih, W. (2017). Cigarette smoking and telomere length: A systematic review of 84 studies and meta-analysis. *Environmental Research, 158,* 480–489.

Atchley, R. C. (1989). A continuity theory of normal aging. *Gerontologist, 29,* 183–190.

Atherton, O. E., Robins, R. W., Rentfrow, P. J., & Lamb, M. E. (2014). Personality correlates of risky health outcomes: Findings from a large Internet study. *Journal of Research in Personality, 50,* 56–60.

Au, A., Lai, S., Wu, W., Hofer, J., Busch, H., Šolcová, I. P., . . . Cheng, S. T. (2019). Generativity and positive emotion in older adults: Mediation of achievement and altruism goal attainment across three cultures. *Journal of Happiness Studies,* 1–16.

Aughinbaugh, A., Robles, O., & Sun, H. (2013). Marriage and divorce: patterns by gender, race, and educational attainment. *Monthly Labor Review, 136,* 1.

Aunio, P., & Niemivirta, M. (2010). Predicting children's mathematical performance in grade one by early numeracy. *Learning and Individual Differences, 20*(5), 427–435.

Aurand, A., Miles, R., & Usher, K. (2014). Local environment of neighborhood Naturally Occurring Retirement Communities (NORCs) in a mid-sized US city. *Journal of Housing for the Elderly, 28*(2), 133–164.

Austin, E. W., Pinkleton, B. E., & Fujioka, Y. (2000). The role of interpretation processes and parental discussion in the media's effects on adolescents' use of alcohol. *Pediatrics, 105*(2), 343–349.

Auyeung, B., Baron-Cohen, S., Ashwin, E., Kinckmeyer, R., Taylor, K., Hackett, G., & Hines, M. (2009). Fetal testosterone predicts sexually differentiated childhood behavior in girls and in boys. *Psychological Science, 20,* 144–148.

Avis, J., & Harris, P. L. (1991). Belief-desire reasoning among Baka children: Evidence for a universal conception of mind. *Child Development, 62*(3), 460–467.

Avis, N. E., & Crawford, S. (2006). Menopause: Recent research findings. In S. K. Whitbourne & S. L. Willis (Eds.), *The baby boomers grow up: Contemporary perspectives on midlife* (pp. 75–109). Mahwah, NJ: Erlbaum.

Avis, N. E., Crawford, S. L., Greendale, G., Bromberger, J. T., Everson-Rose, S. A., Gold, E. B., . . . Thurston, R. C. (2015). Duration of menopausal vasomotor symptoms over the menopause transition. *JAMA Internal Medicine, 175*(4), 531–539.

Baas, M., Nijstad, B. A., & De Dreu, C. K. (2015). The cognitive, emotional and neural correlates of creativity. *Frontiers in Human Neuroscience, 9.*

Babb, S. (2017). Quitting smoking among adults—United States, 2000–2015. *Morbidity and Mortality Weekly Report, 65.*

Baber, R. J., Panay, N., & Fenton, A. (2016). 2016 IMS Recommendations on women's midlife health and menopause hormone therapy. *Climacteric, 19*(2), 109–150.

Baddeley, A. (1998). Recent developments in working memory. *Current Opinion in Neurobiology, 8,* 234–238.

Baddeley, A. D. (2001). Is working memory still working? *American Psychologist, 56,* 851–864.

Baer, J. (2015). The importance of domain-specific expertise in creativity. *Roeper Review, 37*(3), 165-178.

Baglioni, C., Battagliese, G., Feige, B., Spiegelhalder, K., Nissen, C., Voderholzer, U., . . . Riemann, D. (2011). Insomnia as a predictor of depression: A meta-analytic evaluation of longitudinal epidemiological studies. *Journal of Affective Disorders, 135*(1), 10-19.

Bahn, G. H. (2020). Coronavirus Disease 2019, School Closures, and Children's Mental Health. *Journal of the Korean Academy of Child and Adolescent Psychiatry, 31*(2), 74-79.

Baidal, J. A. W., Locks, L. M., Cheng, E. R., Blake-Lamb, T. L., Perkins, M. E., & Taveras, E. M. (2016). Risk factors for childhood obesity in the first 1,000 days: A systematic review. *American Journal of Preventive Medicine, 50*(6), 761-779.

Baillargeon, J., Urban, R.J., Ottenbacher, K.J., Pierson, K.S. & Goodwin, J.S. (2013). Trends in androgen prescribing in the United States, 2001 to 2011. *JAMA Internal Medicine*, 173, 1465-1466.

Baillargeon, R. H., Zoccolillo, M., Keenan, K., Côté, S., Pérusse, D., Wu, H.-X., . . . Tremblay, R. E. (2007). Gender differences in physical aggression: A prospective population-based survey of children before and after 2 years of age. *Developmental Psychology, 43*, 13-26.

Baillargeon, R., & Carey, S. (2012). Core cognition and beyond: The acquisition of physical and numerical knowledge. *Early Childhood Development and Later Outcome*, 33-65.

Baillargeon, R., Li, J., Gertner, Y., & Wu, D. (2011). How do infants reason about physical events. *The Wiley-Blackwell Handbook of Childhood Cognitive Development* (2nd ed., pp. 11-48). Hoboken, NJ: Wiley.

Baillargeon, R., Scott, R. M., & He, Z. (2010). False-belief understanding in infants. *Trends in Cognitive Sciences, 14*(3), 110-118.

Baio, J., Wiggins, L., Christensen, D. L., Maenner, M. J., Daniels, J., Warren, Z., . . . Durkin, M. S. (2018). Prevalence of autism spectrum disorder among children aged 8 years—autism and developmental disabilities monitoring network, 11 sites, United States, 2014. *MMWR Surveillance Summaries, 67*(6), 1.

Baiocco, R., Fontanesi, L., Santamaria, F., Ioverno, S., Baumgartner, E., & Laghi, F. (2016). Coming out during adolescence: Perceived parents' reactions and internalized sexual stigma. *Journal of Health Psychology, 21*(8), 1809-1813.

Baker, C. E. (2013). Fathers' and mothers' home literacy involvement and children's cognitive and social emotional development: Implications for family literacy programs. *Applied Developmental Science, 17*(4), 184-197.

Baker, J. L., Olsen, L. W., & Sørensen, T. I. A. (2007). Childhood body-mass index and the risk of coronary heart disease in adulthood. *New England Journal of Medicine, 357*, 2329-2336.

Baker, L. A., Cahalin, L. P., Gerst, K., & Burr, J. A. (2005). Productive activities and subjective well-being among older adults: The influence of number of activities and time commitment. *Social Indicators Research, 73*(3), 431-458.

Baker, S. (2018). The effects of parenting on emotion and self-regulation. In M. R. Sanders & A. Morawska (Eds.), *Handbook of parenting and child development across the lifespan* (pp. 217-240). Basel, Switzerland: Springer.

Balantekin, K. N., Birch, L. L., & Savage, J. S. (2018). Family, friend, and media factors are associated with patterns of weight-control behavior among adolescent girls. *Eating and Weight Disorders-Studies on Anorexia, Bulimia and Obesity, 23*(2), 215-223.

Bale, T. L., & Epperson, C. N. (2015). Sex differences and stress across the lifespan. *Nature Neuroscience, 18*(10), 1413.

Balgiu, B. A. (2017). Self-esteem, personality and resilience. Study of a students emerging adults group. *Journal of Educational Sciences and Psychology, 7*(1).

Ball, H. L. (2006). Night-time infant care: Cultural practice, evolution, and infant development. In *Childrearing and infant care issues: A cross-cultural perspective* (pp. 47-61). Melbourne, Australia: Nova Science.

Ball, K., Edwards, J. D., & Ross, L. A. (2007). The impact of speed of processing training on cognitive and everyday functions [Special issue I]. *Journal of Gerontology: Psychological Sciences, 62B*, 19-31.

Balluz, L. S., Okoro, C. A., & Strine, T. W. (2004). Access to health-care preventive services among Hispanics and non-Hispanics—United States, 2001-2002. *Morbidity and Mortality Weekly Report, 53*, 937-941.

Balsam, K. F., Rothblum, E. D., & Wickham, R. E. (2017). Longitudinal predictors of relationship dissolution among same-sex and heterosexual couples. *Couple and Family Psychology: Research and Practice, 6*(4), 247.

Balsis, S., Carpenter, B. D., & Storandt, M. (2005). Personality change precedes clinical diagnosis of dementia of the Alzheimer type. *Journal of Gerontology: Psychological Sciences, 60B*, P98-P101.

Baltes, P. B. (1987). Theoretical propositions of life-span development psychology: On the dynamics between growth and decline. *Developmental Psychology 23*(5), 611-626.

Baltes, P. B. (1997). On the incomplete architecture of human ontogeny: Selection, optimization, and compensation as foundation of developmental theory. *American Psychologist, 52*, 366-380.

Baltes, P. B., & Baltes, M. M. (1990). Psychological perspectives on successful aging: The model of selective optimization with compensation. In P. B. Baltes & M. M. Baltes (Eds.), *Successful aging: Perspectives from the behavioral sciences* (pp. 1-34). New York, NY: Cambridge University Press.

Baltes, P. B., & Smith, J. (2004). Lifespan psychology: From developmental contextualism to developmental biocultural co-constructivism. *Research in Human Development, 1*, 123-144.

Baltes, P. B., & Staudinger, U. M. (2000). Wisdom: A metaheuristic (pragmatic) to orchestrate mind and virtue toward excellence. *American Psychologist, 55*, 122-136.

Ban, L., Guo, S., Scherpbier, R. W., Wang, X., Zhou, H., & Tata, L. J. (2017). Child feeding and stunting prevalence in left-behind children: A descriptive analysis of data from a central and western Chinese population. *International Journal of Public Health, 62*(1), 143-151.

Banderali, G., Martelli, A., Landi, M., Moretti, F., Betti, F., Radaelli, G., . . . & Verduci, E. (2015). Short and long term health effects of parental tobacco smoking during pregnancy and lactation: A descriptive review. *Journal of Translational Medicine, 13*(1), 327.

Bandura, A. (1977). *Social learning theory.* Englewood Cliffs, NJ: Prentice Hall.

Bandura, A. (1986). *Social foundations of thought and action: A social cognitive theory.* Englewood Cliffs, NJ: Prentice Hall.

Bandura, A. (1989). Social cognitive theory. In R. Vasta (Ed.), *Annals of child development* (Vol. 6, pp. 1-60). Greenwich, CT: JAI.

Bandura, A., & Bussey, K. (2004). On broadening the cognitive, motivational, and sociostructural scope of theorizing about gender development and functioning: Comment on Martin, Ruble, and Szkrybalo (2002). *Psychological Bulletin, 130*(5), 691-701.

Banse, R., Gawronski, B., Rebetez, C., Gutt, H., & Bruce Morton, J. (2010). The development of spontaneous gender stereotyping in childhood: Relations to stereotype knowledge and stereotype flexibility. *Developmental Science, 13*(2), 298-306.

Banz, B. C., Fell, J. C., & Vaca, F. E. (2019). Focus: Death: Complexities of young driver injury and fatal motor vehicle crashes. *The Yale Journal of Biology and Medicine, 92*(4), 725.

Bao, A. M., & Swaab, D. F. (2010). Sex differences in the brain, behavior, and neuropsychiatric disorders. *The Neuroscientist, 16*(5), 550-565.

Barac, R., Bialystok, E., Castro, D. C., & Sanchez, M. (2014). The cognitive development of young dual language learners: A critical review. *Early Childhood Research Quarterly, 29*(4), 699-714.

Barbaresco, S., Courtemanche, C. J., & Qi, Y. (2015). Impacts of the Affordable Care Act dependent coverage provision on health-related outcomes of young adults. *Journal of Health Economics, 40*, 54-68.

Barber, J. S., Yarger, J. E., & Gatny, H. H. (2015). Black-white differences in attitudes related to pregnancy among young women. *Demography, 52*(3), 751-786.

Barbosa, L. M., Monteiro, B., & Murta, S. G. (2016). Retirement adjustment predictors—A systematic review. *Work, Aging and Retirement, 2*(2), 262-280.

Barclay, S.R., Stoltz, K.B., & Chung, Y.B. (2011). Voluntary midlife career change: Integrating the transtheoretical model and the life-span, life-space approach. *The Career Development Quarterly, 59*, 386-399.

Bariola, E., Lyons, A., Leonard, W., Pitts, M., Badcock, P., & Couch, M. (2015). Demographic and psychosocial factors associated with psychological distress and resilience among transgender individuals. *American Journal of Public Health, 105*(10), 2108-2116.

Barker, E. D., Oliver, B. R., & Maughan, B. (2010). Co-occurring problems of early onset persistent, childhood limited, and adolescent onset conduct problem youth. *Journal of Child Psychology and Psychiatry, 51*(11), 1217-1226.

Barkl, S., Porter, A., & Ginns, P. (2012). Cognitive training for children: Effects on inductive reasoning, deductive reasoning, and mathematics achievement in an Australian school setting. *Psychology in the Schools, 49*(9), 828-842.

Barkley, R. A. (1998, September). Attention-deficit hyperactivity disorder. *Scientific American,* 66-71.

Barlett, C., & Coyne, S. M. (2014). A meta-analysis of sex differences in cyber-bullying behavior: The moderating role of age. *Aggressive Behavior, 40*(5), 474-488.

Barnard, N. D., Bush, A. I., Ceccarelli, A., Cooper, J., de Jager, C. A., Erickson, K. I., . . . Morris, M. C. (2014). Dietary and lifestyle guidelines for the prevention of Alzheimer's disease. *Neurobiology of Aging, 35,* S74-S78.

Barnes, G. M., Hoffman, J. H., & Welte, J. W. (2006). Effects of parental monitoring and peer deviance in substance abuse and delinquency. *Journal of Marriage and Family, 68,* 1084-1104.

Barnes, H. F. (1949). The birth of a Ngoni child. *Man, 49,* 87-89.

Barnett, M. D., Archuleta, W. P., & Cantu, C. (2019). Politics, concern for future generations, and the environment: Generativity mediates political conservatism and environmental attitudes. *Journal of Applied Social Psychology, 49*(10), 647-654.

Barnett, R. C., & Hyde, J. S. (2001). Women, men, work, and family. *American Psychologist, 56,* 781-796.

Barnett, W. S., Jung, K., Yarosc, D. J., Thomas, J., Hornbeck, A., Stechuk, R. A., & Burns, M. S. (2008). Educational effects of the tools of the mind curriculum: A randomized trial. *Early Childhood Research Quarterly, 23*(3), 299-313.

Baron-Cohen, S. (2000). Theory of mind and autism: A review. In L. Glidden (Ed.), *International review of research in mental retardation* (Vol. 23, pp. 169-184). Cambridge, MA: Academic Press.

Barr, R. G., Konner, M., Bakeman, R., & Adamson, L. (1991). Crying in !Kung San infants: A test of the cultural specificity hypothesis. *Developmental Medicine & Child Neurology, 33*(7), 601-610.

Barr, R., Danziger, C., Hilliard, M., Andolina, C., & Ruskis, J. (2010). Amount, content and context of infant media exposure: A parental questionnaire and diary analysis. *International Journal of Early Years Education, 18,* 107-122.

Barr, R., Lauricella, A., Zack, E., & Calvert, S. L. (2010). Infant and early childhood exposure to adult-directed and child-directed television programming: Relations with cognitive skills at age four. *Merrill-Palmer Quarterly, 56*(1), 21-48.

Barr, R., Muentener, P., & Garcia, A. (2007). Age-related changes in deferred imitation from television by 6-to 18-month-olds. *Developmental Science, 10*(6), 910-921.

Barrett, A. E., & Toothman, E. L. (2017). "Explaining age differences in women's emotional well-being: The role of subjective experiences of aging": Corrigendum. *Journal of Women & Aging, 29*(1), 98-99.

Barrett, H. C., & Behne, T. (2005). Children's understanding of death as the cessation of agency: A test using sleep versus death. *Cognition, 96*(2), 93-108.

Barrett-Connor, E., Hendrix, S., Ettinger, B., Wenger, N. K., Paoletti, R., Lenfant, C. J. M., & Pinn, V. W. (2002). *Best clinical practices: Chapter 13. International position paper on women's health and menopause: A comprehensive approach.* Washington, DC: National Heart, Lung, and Blood Institute.

Barroso, A. (2020). *More than half of Americans say marriage is important but not essential for living a fulfilling life* [Pew Research Center news report]. Retrieved from www.pewresearch.org/fact-tank/2020/02/14/more-than-half-of-americans-say-marriage-is-important-but-not-essential-to-leading-a-fulfilling-life/

Barroso, A., Parker, K. & Fry, R. (2019). *Majority of Americans say parents are going too much for their adult children* [Pew Research Center report]. Retrieved from www.pewsocialtrends.org/2019/10/23/majority-of-americans-say-parents-are-doing-too-much-for-their-young-adult-children/

Barry, B. K., & Carson, R. G. (2004). The consequences of resistance training for movement control in older adults. *Journal of Gerontology: Medical Sciences, 59A,* 730-754.

Bartel, K. A., Gradisar, M., & Williamson, P. (2015). Protective and risk factors for adolescent sleep: A meta-analytic review. *Sleep Medicine Reviews, 21,* 72-85.

Bartick, M., & Reinhold, A. (2010). The burden of suboptimal breastfeeding in the United States: A pediatric cost analysis. *Pediatrics, 125,* e1048-e1056.

Barton, A. W., Yu, T., Brody, G. H., & Ehrlich, K. B. (2018). Childhood poverty, catecholamines, and substance use among African American young adults: The protective effect of supportive parenting. *Preventive Medicine, 112,* 1-5.

Bartzokis, G. (2011). Alzheimer's disease as homeostatic responses to age-related myelin breakdown. *Neurobiology of Aging, 32*(8), 1341-1371.

Bartzokis, G., Lu, P. H., & Mintz, J. (2007). Human brain myelination and amyloid beta deposition in Alzheimer's disease. *Alzheimer's & Dementia, 3*(2), 122-125.

Bartzokis, G., Lu, P. H., Tingus, K., Mendez, M. F., Richard, A., Peters, D. G., . . . Thompson, P. M. (2010). Lifespan trajectory of myelin integrity and maximum motor speed. *Neurobiology of Aging, 31*(9), 1554-1562.

Baruteau, A. E., Tester, D. J., Kapplinger, J. D., Ackerman, M. J., & Behr, E. R. (2017). Sudden infant death syndrome and inherited cardiac conditions. *Nature Reviews Cardiology, 14*(12), 715.

Basch, C. E. (2011). Teen pregnancy and the achievement gap among urban minority youth. *Journal of School Health, 81*(10), 614-618.

Basch, C. H., Zybert, P., Reeves, R., & Basch, C. E. (2017). What do popular YouTube videos say about vaccines? *Child: Care, Health and Development, 43*(4), 499-503.

Bascom, P. B., & Tolle, S. W. (2002). Responding to requests for physician-assisted suicide: "These are uncharted waters for both of us . . . ." *Journal of the American Medical Association, 288,* 91-98.

Bassuk, E. L., DeCandia, C. J, Beach, C. A. & Berman, F. (2014). *America's youngest outcasts: A report on child homelessness.* Needham, MA: National Center on Family Homelessness. Retrieved from www. HomelessChildrenAmerica.org

Baste, V., Moen, B. E., Oftedal, G., Strand, L. Å., Bjørge, L., & Mild, K. H. (2012). Pregnancy outcomes after paternal radiofrequency field exposure aboard fast patrol boats. *Journal of Occupational and Environmental Medicine, 54*(4), 431-438.

Basterfield, L., Adamson, A. J., Frary, J. K., Parkinson, K. N., Pearce, M. S., Reilly, J. J., & Gateshead Millennium Study Core Team. (2011). Longitudinal study of physical activity and sedentary behavior in children. *Pediatrics, 127*(1), e24-e30.

Batterham, P. J., Christensen, H., & Mackinnon, A. J. (2009). Fluid intelligence is independently associated with all-cause mortality over 17 years in an elderly community sample: An investigation of potential mechanisms. *Intelligence, 37*(6), 551-560.

Batty, G. D., Deary, I. J., & Gottfredson, L. S. (2007). Premorbid (early life) IQ and later mortality risk: Systematic review. *Annals of Epidemiology, 17*(4), 278-288.

Baude, A., Pearson, J., & Drapeau, S. (2016). Child adjustment in joint physical custody versus sole custody: A meta-analytic review. *Journal of Divorce & Remarriage, 57*(5), 338-360.

Bauer, J. J., & McAdams, D. P. (2004). Personal growth in adults' stories of life transitions. *Journal of Personality, 72*(3), 573-602.

Bauer, J. J., McAdams, D. P., & Pals, J. L. (2008). Narrative identity and eudaimonic well-being. *Journal of Happiness Studies, 9*(1), 81-104.

Bauer, K. W., Hearst, M. O., Escoto, K., Berge, J. M., & Neumark-Sztainer, D. (2012). Parental employment and work-family stress: Associations with family food environments. *Social Science & Medicine, 75*(3), 496-504.

Bauer, L., & Schanzenbach, D. W. (2016). The long-term impact of the Head Start program. *The Hamilton Project* [Report]. Retrieved from https://pdfs.semanticscholar.org/89fe/d0ffa9b17eab87cd45acba8720a7ebc16a18.pdf

Bauer, P. J. (2002). Long-term recall memory: Behavioral and neurodevelopmental changes in the first 2 years of life. *Current Directions in Psychological Science, 11,* 137-141.

Bauer, P. J., DeBoer, T., & Lukowski, A. F. (2007). In the language of multiple memory systems, defining and describing developments in long-term explicit memory. In L. M. Oakes & P. J. Bauer (Eds.). *Short- and long-term memory in infancy and early childhood* (pp. 240-270). New York, NY: Oxford University Press.

Bauer, P. J., Wiebe, S. A., Carver, L. J., Waters, J. M., & Nelson, C. A. (2003). Developments in long-term explicit memory late in the first year of life: Behavioral and electrophysiological indices. *Psychological Science, 14*(6), 629-635.

Bauman, A., Merom, D., Bull, F. C., Buchner, D. M., & Fiatarone Singh, M. A. (2016). Updating the evidence for physical activity: Summative reviews of the epidemiological evidence, prevalence, and interventions to promote "Active Aging." *The Gerontologist, 56*(Suppl._2), S268-S280.

Baumer, E. P., & South, S. J. (2001). Community effects on youth sexual activity. *Journal of Marriage and Family, 63*, 540-554.

Baumgart, M., Snyder, H. M., Carrillo, M. C., Fazio, S., Kim, H., & Johns, H. (2015). Summary of the evidence on modifiable risk factors for cognitive decline and dementia: A population-based perspective. *Alzheimer's & Dementia, 11*(6), 718-726.

Baumgartner, S. E., Weeda, W. D., van der Heijden, L. L., & Huizinga, M. (2014). The relationship between media multitasking and executive function in early adolescents. *Journal of Early Adolescence, 34*, 1120-1144.

Baumrind, D. (1971). Harmonious parents and their preschool children. *Developmental Psychology, 41*, 92-102.

Baumrind, D. (1972). An exploratory study of socialization effects on black children: Some black-white comparisons. *Child Development*, 261-267.

Baumrind, D. (1989). Rearing competent children. In W. Damon (Ed.), *Child development today and tomorrow* (pp. 349-378). San Francisco, CA: Jossey-Bass.

Baumrind, D. (1996). A blanket injunction against disciplinary use of spanking is not warranted by the data. *Pediatrics, 88*, 828-831.

Baumrind, D. (1996). The discipline controversy revisited. *Family Relations, 45*, 405-414.

Baumrind, D. (2005). Patterns of parental authority and adolescent autonomy. In J. Smetana (Ed.), *Changing boundaries of parental authority during adolescence* (New Directions for Child and Adolescent Development, No. 108, pp. 61-70). San Francisco, CA: Jossey-Bass.

Baumrind, D., & Black, A. E. (1967). Socialization practices associated with dimensions of competence in preschool boys and girls. *Child Development, 38*, 291-327.

Baumrind, D., Larzelere, R. E., & Owens, E. B. (2010). Effects of preschool parents' power assertive patterns and practices on adolescent development. *Parenting: Science and Practice, 10*(3), 157-201.

Bava, S., Thayer, R., Jacobus, J., Ward, M., Jernigan, T. L., & Tapert, S. F. (2010). Longitudinal characterization of white matter maturation during adolescence. *Brain Research, 1327*, 38-46.

Bayley, N. (2005). *Bayley scales of infant development*. San Antonio, TX: PsychCorp.

Bayliss, D. M., Jarrold, C., Baddeley, A. D., Gunn, D. M., & Leigh, E. (2005). Mapping the developmental constraints on working memory span performance. *Developmental Psychology, 41*(4), 579-597.

Beal, M. A., Yauk, C. L., & Marchetti, F. (2017). From sperm to offspring: Assessing the heritable genetic consequences of paternal smoking and potential public health impacts. *Mutation Research/Reviews in Mutation Research, 773*, 26-50.

Beauchamp, G. K., & Mennella, J. A. (2011). Flavor perception in human infants: Development and functional significance. *Digestion, 83*(Suppl. 1), 1-6.

Bechert, I., & Quandt, M. (Eds.). (2013). *ISSP Data Report: Religious Attitudes and Religious Change* (Vol. 13, p. 142). Cologne, Germany: GESIS.

Becker, G. S. (1991). *A treatise on the family* (Enlarged ed.). Cambridge, MA: Harvard University Press.

Becker, K. A. (2003). History of the Stanford-Binet intelligence scales: Content and psychometrics. *Stanford-Binet Intelligence Scales, Fifth Edition Assessment Service Bulletin, 1*.

Becker, M., Lüdtke, O., Trautwein, U., Köller, O., & Baumert, J. (2012). The differential effects of school tracking on psychometric intelligence: Do academic-track schools make students smarter? *Journal of Educational Psychology, 104*(3), 682.

Beckett, C., Maughan, B., Rutter, M., Castle, J., Colvert, E., Groothues, C., . . . Sonuga-Barke, E. J. S. (2006). Do the effects of severe early deprivation on cognition persist into early adolescence? Findings from the English and Romanian adoptees study. *Child Development, 77*, 696-711.

Bedford, V. H. (1995). Sibling relationships in middle and old age. In R. Blieszner & V. Hilkevitch (Eds.), *Handbook of aging and the family* (pp. 201-222). Westport, CT: Greenwood Press.

Beelmann, A., & Heinemann, K. S. (2014). Preventing prejudice and improving intergroup attitudes: A meta-analysis of child and adolescent training programs. *Journal of Applied Developmental Psychology, 35*(1), 10-24.

Behne, T., Liszkowski, U., Carpenter, M., & Tomasello, M. (2012). Twelve-month-olds' comprehension and production of pointing. *British Journal of Developmental Psychology, 30*(3), 359-375.

Behnke, M., Smith, V. C., & Committee on Substance Abuse. (2013). Prenatal substance abuse: Short and long-term effects on the exposed fetus. *Pediatrics, 131*(3), e1009-e1024.

Behrman, R. E. (1992). *Nelson textbook of pediatrics* (13th ed.). Philadelphia, PA: Saunders.

Behruzi, R., Hatem, M., Goulet, L., Fraser, W., & Misago, C. (2013). Understanding childbirth practices as an organizational cultural phenomenon: A conceptual framework. *BMC Pregnancy and Childbirth, 13*(1), 205.

Beidel, D. C., & Turner, S. M. (1998). *Shy children, phobic adults: Nature and treatment of social phobia*. Washington, DC: American Psychological Association.

Bejanyan, K., Marshall, T. C., & Ferenczi, N. (2015). Associations of collectivism with relationship commitment, passion, and mate preferences: Opposing roles of parental influence and family allocentrism. *PloS One, 10*(2).

Bell, J. F., Zimmerman, F. J., & Diehr, P. K. (2008). Maternal work and birth outcome disparities. *Maternal & Child Health Journal, 12*, 415-426.

Bell, J. T. & Spector, T. D. (2011). A twin approach to unraveling epigenetics. *Trends in Genetics, 27*, 116-125.

Bell, J. T., & Saffery, R. (2012). The value of twins in epigenetic epidemiology. *International Journal of Epidemiology, 41*(1), 140-150.

Bell, M. A. (2012). A psychobiological perspective on working memory performance at 8 months of age. *Child Development, 83*(1), 251-265.

Bell, M. A., & Fox, N. A. (1992). The relations between frontal brain electrical activity and cognitive development during infancy. *Child Development, 63,* **1142**-1163.

Bellander, M., Eschen, A., Lövdén, M., Martin, M., Bäckman, L., & Brehmer, Y. (2017). No evidence for improved associative memory performance following process-based associative memory training in older adults. *Frontiers in Aging Neuroscience, 8*, 326.

Bellieni, C. V., & Buonocore, G. (2012). Is fetal pain a real evidence? *The Journal of Maternal-Fetal & Neonatal Medicine, 25*(8), 1203-1208.

Bellinger, D. C. (2008). Lead neurotoxicity and socioeconomic status: Conceptual and analytic issues. *NeuroToxicology, 29*(5), 828-832.

Bellou, V., Belbasis, L., Tzoulaki, I., Middleton, L. T., Ioannidis, J. P., & Evangelou, E. (2017). Systematic evaluation of the associations between environmental risk factors and dementia: An umbrella review of systematic reviews and meta-analyses. *Alzheimer's & Dementia, 13*(4), 406-418.

Belsky, J., & Pluess, M. (2009). Beyond diathesis stress: Differential susceptibility to environmental influences. *Psychological Bulletin, 135*(6), 885-908. doi: 10.1037/a0017376

Belsky, J., Fish, M., & Isabella, R. (1991). Continuity and discontinuity in infant negative and positive emotionality: Family antecedents and attachment consequences. *Developmental Psychology, 27*, 421-431.

Belsky, J., Jaffee, S. R., Caspi, A., Moffitt, T., & Silva, P. A. (2003). Intergenerational relationships in young adulthood and their life course, mental health, and personality correlates. *Journal of Family Psychology, 17*, 460-471.

Belsky, J., Ruttle, P. L., Boyce, W. T., Armstrong, J. M., & Essex, M. J. (2015). Early adversity, elevated stress physiology, accelerated sexual maturation, and poor health in females. *Developmental Psychology, 51*(6), 816.

Belsky, J., Steinberg, L. D., Houts, R. M., Friedman, S. L., DeHart, G., Cauffman, E., . . . NICHD Early Child Care Research Network. (2007). Family rearing antecedents of pubertal timing. *Child Development, 78*(4), 1302-1321.

Belsky, J., Steinberg, L., Houts, R. M., & Halpern-Felsher, B. L. (2010). The development of reproductive strategy in females: Early maternal harshness—earlier menarch— increased sexual risk taking. *Developmental Psychology, 46*(1), 120-128.

Bem, S. L. (1993). *The lenses of gender: Transforming the debate on sexual inequality*. New Haven, CT: Yale University Press.

Ben-Zur, H. (2012). Loneliness, optimism, and well-being among married, divorced, and widowed individuals. *The Journal of Psychology, 146*(1-2), 23-36.

Benavides-Varela, S., Gómez, D. M., Macagno, F., Bion, R. A., Peretz, I., & Mehler, J. (2011).

Memory in the neonate brain. *PLoS One, 6*(11), e27497.

Benavides-Varela, S., Hochmann, J. R., Macagno, F., Nespor, M., & Mehler, J. (2012). Newborn's brain activity signals the origin of word memories. *Proceedings of the National Academy of Sciences, 109*(44), 17908–17913.

Bendayan, R., Piccinin, A. M., Hofer, S. M., Cadar, D., Johansson, B., & Muniz-Terrera, G. (2017). Decline in memory, visuospatial ability, and crystalized cognitive abilities in older adults: Normative aging or terminal decline? *Journal of Aging Research.*

Benedetti, A. M. (2017, December 6). *5 Dia De Los Muertos questions you were too afraid to ask.* Retrieved from www.huffingtonpost.com/2013/11/01/dia-de-los-muertos_n_4184636.html

Benenson, J. F., Philippoussis, M., & Leeb, R. (1999). Sex differences in neonates' cuddliness. *The Journal of Genetic Psychology, 160*(3), 332–342.

Bener, A., Ehlayel, M. S., Bener, H. Z., & Hamid, Q. (2014). The impact of vitamin D deficiency on asthma, allergic rhinitis and wheezing in children: An emerging public health problem. *Journal of Family & Community Medicine, 21*(3), 154.

Bengtson, V. L. (2001). Beyond the nuclear family: The increasing importance of multigenerational bonds. *Journal of Marriage and Family, 63,* 1–16.

Bengtson, V. L., & DeLiema, M. (2016). Theories of aging and social gerontology: Explaining how social factors influence well-being in later life. In M. Harrington Meyer & E. Daniele (Eds.), *Gerontology: Changes, Challenges, and Solutions.* Santa Barbara, CA: Praeger.

Bengtson, V. L., Rosenthal, C. J., & Burton, L. M. (1990). Families and aging: Diversity and heterogeneity. In R. Binstock & L. George (Eds.), *Handbook of aging and the social sciences* (3rd ed., pp. 263–287). San Diego, CA: Academic Press.

Bengtson, V. L., Rosenthal, C., & Burton, L. (1996). Paradoxes of families and aging. In R. H. Binstock & L. K. George (Eds.), *Handbook of aging and the social sciences* (4th ed., pp. 253–282). San Diego, CA: Academic Press.

Benkhadra, K., Mohammed, K., Al Nofal, A., Carranza Leon, B. G., Alahdab, F., Faubion, S., . . . Murad, M. H. (2015). Menopausal hormone therapy and mortality: A systematic review and meta-analysis. *The Journal of Clinical Endocrinology & Metabolism, 100*(11), 4021–4028.

Benner, A. D., & Graham, S. (2009). The transition to high schools as a developmental process among multiethnic urban youth. *Child Development, 80*(2), 356–376.

Benner, A. D., & Kim, S. Y. (2009). Experiences of discrimination among Chinese American adolescents and the consequences for socioemotional and academic development. *Developmental Psychology, 45*(6), 1682–1694.

Benner, A. D., Boyle, A. E., & Sadler, S. (2016). Parental involvement and adolescents' educational success: The roles of prior achievement and socioeconomic status. *Journal of Youth and Adolescence, 45*(6), 1053–1064.

Benson, E. (2003). Intelligent intelligence testing. *Monitor on Psychology, 43*(2), 48–51.

Benson, P. L., Scales, P. C., Syvertsen, A. K., & Roehlkepartain, E. C. (2012). Is youth spiritual development a universal developmental process? An international exploration. *The Journal of Positive Psychology, 7*(6), 453–470.

Bentley, M. E., Dee, D. L., & Jensen, J. L. (2003). Breastfeeding among low income, African-American women: Power, beliefs and decision making. *The Journal of Nutrition, 133*(1), 305S–309S.

Berchick, E. R., Barnett, J. C. & Upton, R. D. (2019). Health insurance coverage in the United States: 2018. *Current Population Reports, 60–267.* Washington, DC: US Government Printing Office.

Berenbaum, S. A., Bryk, K. L. K., & Beltz, A. M. (2012). Early androgen effects on spatial and mechanical abilities: Evidence from congenital adrenal hyperplasia. *Behavioral Neuroscience, 126*(1), 86.

Berends, M. (2015). Sociology and school choice: What we know after two decades of charter schools. *Annual Review of Sociology, 41,* 159–180.

Berg, C. A., & Klaczynski, P. A. (1996). Practical intelligence and problem solving: Search for perspectives. In F. Blanchard-Fields & T. M. Hess (Eds.), *Perspectives on cognitive change in adulthood and aging* (pp. 323–357). New York, NY: McGraw-Hill.

Berg, C. J., Callaghan, W. M., Syverson, C., & Henderson, Z. (2010). Pregnancy-related mortality in the United States, 1998 to 2005. *Obstetrics & Gynecology, 116*(6), 1302–1309.

Bergelson, E., & Swingley, D. (2012). At 6–9 months, human infants know the meanings of many common nouns. *Proceedings of the National Academy of Sciences, 109*(9), 3253–3258.

Bergelson, E., & Swingley, D. (2015). Early word comprehension in infants: Replication and extension. *Language Learning and Development, 11*(4), 369–380.

Bergeman, C. S., & Plomin, R. (1989). Genotype-environment interaction. In M. Bornstein & J. Bruner (Eds.), *Interaction in human development* (pp. 157–171). Hillsdale, NJ: Erlbaum.

Bergen, D. (2002). The role of pretend play in children's cognitive development. *Early Childhood Research & Practice, 4*(1). Retrieved from http://ecrp.uiuc.edu/v4n1/bergen.html

Berger, K. S. (2007). Update on bullying at school: Science forgotten? *Developmental Review, 27,* 91–92.

Berk, L. E. (1992). Children's private speech: An overview of theory and the status of research. In R. M. Diaz & L. E. Berk (Eds.), *Private speech: From social interaction to self-regulation* (pp. 17–53). Hillsdale, NJ: Erlbaum.

Berletch, J. B., Yang, F., Xu, J., Carrel, L., & Disteche, C. M. (2011). Genes that escape from X inactivation. *Human Genetics, 130*(2), 237–245.

Berlin, L. J., Ispa, J. M., Fine, M. A., Malone, P. S., Brooks-Gunn, J., Brady-Smith, C., . . . Bai, Y. (2009). Correlates and consequences of spanking and verbal punishment for low-income white, African American, and Mexican American toddlers. *Child Development, 80*(5), 1403–1420.

Berman, S. L., You, Y. F., Schwartz, S., Teo, G., & Mochizuki, K. (2011, February). Identity exploration, commitment, and distress: A cross national investigation in China, Taiwan, Japan, and the United States. *Child & Youth Care Forum, 40*(1), 65–75.

Bernardi, F., & Martínez-Pastor, J. I. (2011). Divorce risk factors and their variation over time in Spain. *Demographic Research, 24,* 771–800.

Berndt, T. J., & Perry, T. B. (1990). Distinctive features and effects of early adolescent friendships. In R. Montemayor, G. R. Adams, & T. P. Gullotta (Eds.), *From childhood to adolescence: A transitional period?* (Vol. 2, pp. 269–287). Newbury Park, CA: Sage.

Bernier, A., Carlson, S. M., & Whipple, N. (2010). From external regulation to self-regulation: Early parenting precursors of young children's executive functioning. *Child Development, 81,* 326–339. doi: 10.1111/j.1467-8624.2009.01397.x

Bernier, A., Carlson, S. M., Deschênes, M., & Matte-Gagné, C. (2012). Social factors in the development of early executive functioning: A closer look at the caregiving environment. *Developmental Science, 15*(1), 12–24.

Berrick, J. D. (1998). When children cannot remain home: Foster family care and kinship care. *Future of Children, 8,* 72–87.

Berteletti, I., Lucangeli, D., Piazza, M., Dehaene, S., & Zorzi, M. (2010). Numerical estimation in preschoolers. *Developmental Psychology, 46*(2), 545.

Bertenthal, B. I., Campos, J. J., & Kermoian, R. (1994). An epigenetic perspective on the development of self-produced locomotion and its consequences. *Current Directions in Psychological Science, 3*(5), 140–145.

Berthiaume, V. G., Shultz, T. R., & Onishi, K. H. (2013). A constructivist connectionist model of transitions on false-belief tasks. *Cognition, 126*(3), 441–458.

Berthier, N. E., & Carrico, R. L. (2010). Visual information and object size in infant reaching. *Infant Behavior and Development, 33*(4), 555–566.

Bertone-Johnson, E. R., Hankinson, S. E., Johnson, S. R., & Manson, J. E. (2008). Cigarette smoking and the development of premenstrual syndrome. *American Journal of Epidemiology, 168*(8), 938–945.

Betancourt, J. R., Green, A. R., Carrillo, J. E., & Owusu Ananeh-Firempong, I. I. (2016). Defining cultural competence: A practical framework for addressing racial/ethnic disparities in health and health care. *Public Health Reports.*

Betrán, A. P., Temmerman, M., Kingdon, C., Mohiddin, A., Opiyo, N., Torloni, M. R., . . . Downe, S. (2018). Interventions to reduce unnecessary caesarean sections in healthy women and babies. *The Lancet, 392*(10155), 1358–1368.

Betts, J. R., & Tang, Y. E. (2019). The effect of charter schools on student achievement. In M. Berends, R. J. Waddington, & J. Schoenig (Eds.), *School choice at the crossroads: Research perspectives* (pp. 67-89). New York, NY: Routledge.

Bever, L. (2014, November 2). Brittany Maynard, as promised, ends her life at 29. *The Washington Post*. Retrieved from www.washingtonpost.com/

Beyene, Y., & Martin, M. C. (2001). Menopausal experiences and bone density of Mayan women in Yucatan, Mexico. *American Journal of Human Biology, 13*(4), 505-511.

Bezdicek, O., Stepankova, H., Novakova, L. M., & Kopecek, M. (2016). Toward the processing speed theory of activities of daily living in healthy aging: Normative data of the Functional Activities Questionnaire. *Aging Clinical and Experimental Research, 28*(2), 239-247.

Bhaskaran, K., Hamouda, O., Sannesa, M., Boufassa, F., Johnson, A. M., Lambert, P. C., & Porter, K., for the CASCADE Collaboration. (2008). Changes in the risk of death after HIV seroconversion compared with mortality in the general population. *Journal of the American Medical Association, 300*, 51-59.

Bherer, L., Erickson, K. I., & Liu-Ambrose, T. (2013). A review of the effects of physical activity and exercise on cognitive and brain functions in older adults. *Journal of Aging Research*.

Bialystok, E., & Codd, J. (2000). Representing quantity beyond whole numbers: Some, none, and part. *Canadian Journal of Experimental Psychology/Revue canadienne de psychologie expérimentale, 54*(2), 117.

Bialystok, E., & Senman, L. (2004). Executive processes in appearance-reality tasks: The role of inhibition of attention and symbolic representation. *Child Development, 75*, 562-579.

Bialystok, E., Craik, F. I. M., & Freeman, M. (2007). Bilingualism as a protection against the onset of symptoms of dementia. *Neuropsychologia, 45*(2), 459-464.

Bialystok, E., Craik, F. I. M., Klein, R., & Viswanathan, M. (2004). Bilingualism, aging, and cognitive control: Evidence from the Simon task. *Psychology and Aging, 19*, 290-303.

Bianchi, S., Robinson, J., & Milkie, M. (2006). *The changing rhythms of American family life*. New York, NY: Russell Sage Foundation.

Biblarz, T. J., & Stacey, J. (2010). How does the gender of parents matter? *Journal of Marriage and Family, 72*(1), 3-22.

Biener, A., Cawley, J., & Meyerhoefer, C. (2017). The high and rising costs of obesity to the US health care system. *Journal of General Internal Medicine, 32*(1), 6-8.

Bienvenu, O. J., Nestadt, G., Samuels, J. F., Costa, P. T., Howard, W. T., & Eaton, W. W. (2001). Phobic, panic, and major depressive disorders and the five-factor model of personality. *Journal of Mental Diseases, 189*, 154-161.

Bierman, K. L. (2004). *Peer rejection: Developmental processes and intervention strategies*. New York, NY: Guilford

Bierman, K. L., Smoot, D. L., & Aumiller, K. (1993). Characteristics of aggressive rejected, aggressive (nonrejected), and rejected (non-aggressive) boys. *Child Development, 64*, 139-151.

Bigelow, A. E., & Dugas, K. (2009). Relations among preschool children's understanding of

visual perspective taking, false belief, and lying. *Journal of Cognition and Development, 9*(4), 411-433.

Biggs, W. S., & Demuth, R. H. (2011). Premenstrual syndrome and premenstrual dysphoric disorder. *American Family Physician, 84*(8).

Billari, F. C., Goisis, A., Liefbroer, A. C., Settersten, R. A., Aassve, A., Hagestad, G., & Spéder, Z. (2010). Social age deadlines for the childbearing of women and men. *Human Reproduction, 26*(3), 616-622.

Billet, S. (2001). Knowing in practice: Reconceptualising vocational expertise. *Learning and Instruction, 11*, 431-452.

Bilsen, J., Cohen, J., & Deliens, L. (2007). End of life in Europe: An overview of medical practices. *Populations and Societies* (No. 430). Paris: INED.

Bindman, S. W., Hindman, A. H., Bowles, R. P., & Morrison, F. J. (2013). The contributions of parental management language to executive function in preschool children. *Early Childhood Research Quarterly, 28*(3), 529-539.

Bird-David, N. (1987). Single persons and social cohesion in a hunter-gatherer society. In P. Hockings (Ed.), *Dimensions of social life: Essays in honor of David G. Mandelbaum* (pp. 151-165). Berlin, Germany: Mouton.

Birditt, K. S., Fingerman, K. L., & Zarit, S. H. (2010). Adult children's problems and successes: Implications for intergenerational ambivalence. *Journals of Gerontology Series B: Psychological Sciences and Social Sciences, 65*(2), 145-153.

Birditt, K. S., Manalel, J. A., Kim, K., Zarit, S. H., & Fingerman, K. L. (2017). Daily interactions with aging parents and adult children: Associations with negative affect and diurnal cortisol. *Journal of Family Psychology, 31*(6), 699.

Birmaher, B., Ryan, N. D., Williamson, D. E., Brent, D. A., Kaufman, J., Dahl, R. E., Perel, J., & Nelson, B. (1996). Childhood and adolescent depression: A review of the past 10 years. *Journal of the American Academy of Child and Adolescent Psychiatry, 35*, 1427-1440.

Biro, F. M., & Wien, M. (2010). Childhood obesity and adult morbidities. *The American Journal of Clinical Nutrition, 91*(5), 1499S-1505S.

Biro, F. M., Greenspan, L. C., Galvez, M. P., Pinney, S. M., Teitelbaum, S., Windham, G. C., . . . Kushi, L. H. (2013). Onset of breast development in a longitudinal cohort. *Pediatrics, 132*(6), 1019-1027.

Biswas, S., & Rao, C. M. (2017). Epigenetics in cancer: Fundamentals and beyond. *Pharmacology & Therapeutics, 173*, 118-134.

Bitler, M. P., Hoynes, H. W., & Domina, T. (2014). *Experimental evidence on distributional effects of Head Start* (No. w20434). Cambridge, MA: National Bureau of Economic Research.

Bixler, E. O., Vgontzas, A. N., Lin, H. M., Liao, D., Calhoun, S., Vela-Bueno, A., . . . Graff, G. (2009). Sleep disordered breathing in children in a general population sample: Prevalence and risk factors. *Sleep, 32*(6), 731-736.

Bjarnason, T., Bendtsen, P., Arnarsson, A. M., Borup, I., Iannotti, R. J., Löfstedt, P., . . . Niclasen, B. (2012). Life satisfaction among

children in different family structures: A comparative study of 36 western societies. *Children & Society, 26*(1), 51-62.

Bjorklund, D. F., & Causey, K. B. (2017). *Children's thinking: Cognitive development and individual differences* (p. 572). Thousand Oaks, CA: Sage.

Bjorklund, D. F., & Pellegrini, A. D. (2000). Child development and evolutionary psychology. *Child Development, 71*, 1687-1708.

Bjorklund, D. F., & Pellegrini, A. D. (2002). *The origins of human nature: Evolutionary developmental psychology*. Washington, DC: American Psychological Association.

Bjorklund, D. F., Miller, P. H., Coyle, T. R., & Slawinski, J. L. (1997). Instructing children to use memory strategies: Evidence of utilization deficiencies in memory training studies. *Developmental Review, 17*(4), 411-441.

Bjørkløf, G. H., Engedal, K., Selbæk, G., Kouwenhoven, S. E., & Helvik, A. S. (2013). Coping and depression in old age: a literature review. *Dementia and Geriatric Cognitive Disorders, 35*(3-4), 121-154.

Black, D. (1998). Coping with loss: Bereavement in childhood. *BMJ, 316*(7135), 931-933.

Black, L. I., Vahratian, A., & Hoffman, H. J. (2015). Communication disorders and use of intervention services among children aged 3-17 years: United States, 2012. *NCHS Data Brief, 205*.

Black, M.C., Basile, K.C., Breiding, M.J., Smith, S.G., Walters, M.L., Merrick, M.T., Chen, J., & Stevens, M.R. (2011). *The National Intimate Partner and Sexual Violence Survey (NISVS): 2010 Summary Report*. National Center for Injury Prevention and Control, Centers for Disease Control and Prevention. Retrieved from www.cdc.gov/violenceprevention/pdf/nisvs_report2010-a.pdf

Black, R. E., Allen, L. H., Bhutta, Z. A., Caulfield, L. E., De Onis, M., Ezzati, M., . . . & Maternal and Child Undernutrition Study Group. (2008). Maternal and child undernutrition: Global and regional exposures and health consequences. *The Lancet, 371*(9608), 243-260.

Black, R. E., Victora, C. G., Walker, S. P., Bhutta, Z. A., Christian, P., De Onis, M., . . . & Uauy, R. (2013). Maternal and child undernutrition and overweight in low-income and middle-income countries. *The Lancet, 382*(9890), 427-451.

Blackford, J. U., Avery, S. N., Cowan, R. L., Shelton, R. C., & Zald, D. H. (2010). Sustained amygdala response to both novel and newly familiar faces characterizes inhibited temperament. *Social Cognitive and Affective Neuroscience, 6*(5), 621-629.

Blackwell, D. L., & Clarke, T. C. (2018). State variation in meeting the 2008 federal guidelines for both aerobic and muscle-strengthening activities through leisure-time physical activity among adults aged 18-64: United States, 2010-2015. *National Health Statistics Reports, 112*, 1-22. Hyattsville, MD: National Center for Health Statistics.

Blair, C., & Raver, C. C. (2016). Poverty, stress, and brain development: New directions for prevention and intervention. *Academic Pediatrics, 16*(3), S30-S36.

Blaizot, A., Vergnes, J. N., Nuwwareh, S., Amar, J., & Sixou, M. (2009). Periodontal diseases and cardiovascular events: Meta-analysis of observational studies. *International Dental Journal, 59*(4), 197–209.

Blakemore, S. J. (2012). Development of the social brain in adolescence. *Journal of the Royal Society of Medicine, 105*(3), 111–116.

Blakemore, S., & Choudhury, S. (2006). Development of the adolescent brain: Implications for executive function and social cognition. *Journal of Child Psychology and Psychiatry, 47*(3), 296–312.

Blanchard, R. (2017). Fraternal birth order, family size, and male homosexuality: Meta-analysis of studies spanning 25 years. *Archives of Sexual Behavior*, 1–15.

Blanchard-Fields, F. (2007). Everyday problem solving and emotion: An adult developmental perspective. *Current Directions in Psychological Science, 16*(1), 26–31.

Blanchard-Fields, F., & Norris, L. (1994). Causal attributions from adolescence through adulthood: Age differences, ego level, and generalized response style. *Aging and Cognition, 1*, 67–86.

Blanchard-Fields, F., Mienaltowski, A., & Seay, R. B. (2007). Age differences in everyday problem-solving effectiveness: Older adults select more effective strategies for interpersonal problems. *Journal of Gerontology: Psychological Sciences, 62B*, P61–P64.

Blanchard-Fields, F., Stein, R., & Watson, T. L. (2004). Age differences in emotion-regulation strategies in handling everyday problems. *Journal of Gerontology: Psychological Sciences, 59B*, P261–P269.

Blanke, O., Faivre, N., & Dieguez, S. (2016). Leaving body and life behind: Out-of-body and near-death experience. In S. Laureys, O. Gosseries & G. Tononi (Eds.), *The neurology of conciousness* (pp. 323–347). Cambridge, MA: Academic Press.

Blatchford, P., Bassett, P., & Brown, P. (2011). Examining the effect of class size on classroom engagement and teacher–pupil interaction: Differences in relation to pupil prior attainment and primary vs. secondary schools. *Learning and Instruction, 21*(6), 715–730.

Blatteis, C. M. (2012). Age-dependent changes in temperature regulation-a mini review. *Gerontology, 58*(4), 289–295.

Blazer, D. G. (2009). Depression in late life: Review and commentary. *Focus, 7*(1), 118–136.

Bleicher, I., Vitner, D., Iofe, A., Sagi, S., Bader, D., & Gonen, R. (2017). When should pregnancies that extended beyond term be induced? *The Journal of Maternal-Fetal & Neonatal Medicine, 30*(2), 219–223.

Bleil, M. E., Adler, N. E., Appelhans, B. M., Gregorich, S. E., Sternfeld, B., & Cedars, M. I. (2013). Childhood adversity and pubertal timing: Understanding the origins of adulthood cardiovascular risk. *Biological Psychology, 93*(1), 213–219.

Blencowe, H., Krasevec, J., de Onis, M., Black, R. E., An, X., Stevens, G. A., . . . Shiekh, S. (2019). National, regional, and worldwide estimates of low birthweight in 2015, with trends from 2000: A systematic analysis. *The Lancet Global Health, 7*(7), e849–e860.

Blieszner, R., & Roberto, K. (2006). Perspectives on close relationships among the baby boomers. In S. K. Whitbourne & S. L. Willis (Eds.), *The baby boomers grow up: Contemporary perspectives on midlife* (pp. 261–279). Mahwah, NJ: Erlbaum.

Bloch, L., Haase, C. M., & Levenson, R. W. (2014). Emotion regulation predicts marital satisfaction: More than a wives' tale. *Emotion, 14*(1), 130.

Block, J. (1971). *Lives through time.* Berkeley, CA: Bancroft.

Block, J., & Block, J. H. (2006). Venturing a 30-year longitudinal study. *American Psychologist, 61*, 315–327.

Block, R. W., Krebs, N. F., Committee on Child Abuse and Neglect, & Committee on Nutrition. (2005). Failure to thrive as a manifestation of child neglect. *Pediatrics, 116*(5), 1234–1237.

Blondell, S. J., Hammersley-Mather, R., & Veerman, J. L. (2014). Does physical activity prevent cognitive decline and dementia?: A systematic review and meta-analysis of longitudinal studies. *BMC Public Health, 14*(1), 510.

Blum, R., & Reinhart, P. (2000). *Reducing the risk: Connections that make a difference in the lives of youth.* Minneapolis, MN: University of Minnesota, Division of General Pediatrics and Adolescent Health.

Blumenthal, H., Leen-Feldner, E. W., Babson, K. A., Gahr, J. L., Trainor, C. D., & Frala, J. L. (2011). Elevated social anxiety among early maturing girls. *Developmental Psychology, 47*(4), 1133.

Bockting, W. (2014). The impact of stigma on transgender identity development and mental health. In B. P. C. Kreukels, T. D. Steensma, & A. L. C. de Vries (Eds.), *Gender dysphoria and disorders of sex development* (pp. 319–330). Boston, MA: Springer.

Bocskay, K. A., Tang, D., Orjuela, M. A., Liu, X., Warburton, D. P., & Perera, F. P. (2005). Chromosomal aberrations in cord blood are associated with prenatal exposure to carcinogenic polycyclic aromatic hydrocarbons. *Cancer Epidemiology Biomarkers and Prevention, 14*, 506–511.

Boden, J. M., Fergusson, D. M., & John Horwood, L. (2008). Early motherhood and subsequent life outcomes. *Journal of Child Psychology and Psychiatry, 49*(2), 151–160.

Boden, J. S., Fischer, J. L., & Niehuis, S. (2010). Predicting marital adjustment from young adults' initial levels and changes in emotional intimacy over time: A 25-year longitudinal study. *Journal of Adult Development, 17*(3), 121–134.

Bodner, E. (2009). On the origins of ageism in older and younger workers. *International Psychogeriatrics, 21*, 1003–1014.

Bodrova, E. (2008). Make-believe play versus academic skills: A Vygotskian approach to today's dilemma of early childhood education. *European Early Childhood Education Research Journal, 16*(3), 357–369.

Bodrova, E., & Leong, D. J. (2005). High quality preschool programs: What would Vygotsky say? *Early Education & Development, 16*(4), 437–446.

Boerma, T., Ronsmans, C., Melesse, D. Y., Barros, A. J., Barros, F. C., Juan, L., . . . Neto, D. D. L. R. (2018). Global epidemiology of use of and disparities in caesarean sections. *The Lancet, 392*(10155), 1341–1348.

Boerner, K., Schulz, R., & Horowitz, A. (2004). Positive aspects of caregiving and adaptation to bereavement. *Psychology and Aging, 19*, 668–675.

Boerner, K., Wortman, C. B., & Bonanno, G. A. (2005). Resilient or at risk? A 4-year study of older adults who initially showed high or low distress following conjugal loss. *Journal of Gerontology: Psychological Sciences, 60B*, P67–P73.

Bogaert, A. F. (2006). Biological versus nonbiological older brothers and men's sexual orientation. *Proceedings of the National Academy of Sciences, 103*, 10771–10774.

Bogg, T., & Roberts, B. W. (2013). The case for conscientiousness: Evidence and implications for a personality trait marker of health and longevity. *Annals of Behavioral Medicine, 45*(3), 278–288.

Boggess, A., Faber, S., Kern, J., Kingston, H.M.S. (2016). Mean serum-level of common organic pollutants is predictive of behavioral severity in children with autism spectrum disorders. *Scientific Reports, 6*, 26185. http://doi.org/10.1038/srep26185

Bograd, R., & Spilka, B. (1996). Self-disclosure and marital satisfaction in mid-life and late-life remarriages. *International Journal of Aging and Human Development, 42*(3), 161–172.

Bonanno, G. A., Westphal, M., & Mancini, A. D. (2011). Resilience to loss and potential trauma. *Annual Review of Clinical Psychology, 7*, 511–535.

Bonanno, G. A., Wortman, C. B., Lehman, D. R., Tweed, R. G., Haring, M., Sonnega, J., . . . Nesse, R. M. (2002). Resilience to loss and chronic grief: A prospective study from preloss to 18-month postloss. *Journal of Personality and Social Psychology*, 1150–1164.

Bongaarts, J., & Zimmer, Z. (2002). Living arrangements of older adults in the developing world: an analysis of demographic and health survey household surveys. *The Journals of Gerontology Series B: Psychological Sciences and Social Sciences, 57*(3), S145–S157.

Bonham, V. L., Warshauer-Baker, E., & Collins, F. S. (2005). Race and ethnicity in the genome era: The complexity of the constructs. *American Psychologist, 60*(1), 9.

Bonny, J. W., & Lourenco, S. F. (2013). The approximate number system and its relation to early math achievement: Evidence from the preschool years. *Journal of Experimental Child Psychology, 114*(3), 375–388.

Bonoti, F., Leondari, A., & Mastora, A. (2013). Exploring children's understanding of death: Through drawings and the death concept questionnaire. *Death Studies, 37*(1), 47–60.

Bookwala, J. (2009). The impact of adult care on marital quality and well-being in adult daughters and sons. *Journal of Gerontology, 64B*(3), 339–347.

Boonk, L., Gijselaers, H. J., Ritzen, H., & Brand-Gruwel, S. (2018). A review of the relationship between parental involvement indicators and academic achievement. *Educational Research Review, 24*, 10–30.

Boonstra, H. D. (2010). Winning campaign: California's concerted effort to reduce its teen pregnancy rate. *Gottmacher Policy Review, 13*(2), 18-24.

Booth, J. L., & Siegler, R. S. (2006). Developmental and individual differences in pure numerical estimation. *Developmental Psychology, 42*(1), 189.

Booth-LaForce, C., & Roisman, G. I. (2014). The Adult Attachment Interview: Psychometrics, stability and change from infancy, and developmental origins: I. Introduction. *Monographs of the Society for Research in Child Development.*

Borelli, J. L., Nelson, S. K., River, L. M., Birken, S. A., & Moss-Racusin, C. (2017). Gender differences in work-family guilt in parents of young children. *Sex Roles, 76*(5-6), 356-368.

Borghuis, J., Denissen, J. J., Oberski, D., Sijtsma, K., Meeus, W. H., Branje, S., . . . Bleidorn, W. (2017). Big Five personality stability, change, and codevelopment across adolescence and early adulthood. *Journal of Personality and Social Psychology, 113*(4), 641.

Borgogna, N. C., McDermott, R. C., Aita, S. L., & Kridel, M. M. (2019). Anxiety and depression across gender and sexual minorities: Implications for transgender, gender nonconforming, pansexual, demisexual, asexual, queer, and questioning individuals. *Psychology of Sexual Orientation and Gender Diversity, 6*(1), 54.

Borjigin, J., Lee, U., Liu, T., Pal, D., Huff, S., Klarr, D., . . . Mashour, G. A. (2013). Surge of neurophysiological coherence and connectivity in the dying brain. *Proceedings of the National Academy of Sciences, 110*(35), 14432-14437.

Bornstein, M. H., & Colombo, J. (2012). Infant cognitive functioning and mental development. In S. M. Pauen (Ed.), *The Jacobs Foundation series on adolescence. Early childhood development and later outcome* (pp. 118-147). Cambridge, England: Cambridge University Press.

Bornstein, M. H., & Cote, L. R., with Maital, S., Painter, K., Park, S. Y., Pascual, L., . . . Vyt, A. (2004). Cross-linguistic analysis of vocabulary in young children: Spanish, Dutch, French, Hebrew, Italian, Korean, and American English. *Child Development, 75*, 1115-1139.

Bornstein, M. H., Haynes, O. M., O'Reilly, A. W., & Painter, K. (1996). Solitary and collaborative pretense play in early childhood: Sources of individual variation in the development of representational competence. *Child Development, 67*, 2910-2929.

Bornstein, M. H., Putnick, D. L., Cote, L. R., Haynes, O. M., & Suwalsky, J. T. D. (2015). Mother-infant contingent vocalization in eleven countries. *Psychological Science, 26*, 1272-1284.

Bornstein, M. H., Putnick, D. L., Gartstein, M. A., Hahn, C. S., Auestad, N., & O'Connor, D. L. (2015). Infant temperament: stability by age, gender, birth order, term status, and socioeconomic status. *Child Development, 86*(3), 844-863.

Borowsky, A., Shinar, D., & Oron-Gilad, T. (2010). Age, skill, and hazard perception in driving. *Accident Analysis & Prevention, 42*(4), 1240-1249.

Borowsky, I. A., Ireland, M., & Resnick, M. D. (2001). Adolescent suicide attempts: Risks and protectors. *Pediatrics, 107*(3), 485-493.

Borse, N. N., Gilchrist, J., Dellinger, A. M., Rudd, R. A., Ballesteros, M. F., & Sleet, D. A. (2008). *CDC childhood injury reports: Patterns of unintentional injuries among 0-19 year olds in the United States, 2000-2006.* Atlanta, GA: Centers for Disease Control and Prevention, National Center for Injury Prevention and Control.

Borst, G., Poirel, N., Pineau, A., Cassotti, M., & Houdé, O. (2013). Inhibitory control efficiency in a Piaget-like class-inclusion task in school-age children and adults: A developmental negative priming study. *Developmental Psychology, 49*(7), 1366.

Bosch, J., Sullivan, S., Van Dyke, D. C., Su, H., Klockau, L., Nissen, K., . . . Eberly, S. S. (2003). Promoting a healthy tomorrow here for children adopted from abroad. *Contemporary Pediatrics, 20*(2), 69-86.

Boskey, E. R. (2014). Understanding transgender identity development in childhood and adolescence. *American Journal of Sexuality Education, 9*(4), 445-463.

Bosshard, G., Nilstun, T., Bilsen, J., Norup, M., Miccinesi, G., vanDelden, J. J. M., . . . van der Heide, A., for the European End-of-Life (EURELD) Consortium. (2005). Forgoing treatment at the end of life in 6 European countries. *Archives of Internal Medicine, 165*, 401-407.

Botwinick, J. (1984). *Aging and behavior* (3rd ed.). New York, NY: Springer.

Bouchard, G. (2014). How do parents react when their children leave home? An integrative review. *Journal of Adult Development, 21*(2), 69-79.

Bouchard, T. J., & McGue, M. (2003). Genetic and environmental influences on human psychological differences. *Developmental Neurobiology, 54*(1), 4-45.

Bouchey, H. A., & Furman, W. (2003). Dating and romantic experiences in adolescence. In G. R. Adams & M. D. Berzonsky (Eds.), *Blackwell handbook of adolescence* (pp. 313-329). Oxford, England: Blackwell.

Boulianne, S. (2015). Social media use and participation: A meta-analysis of current research. *Information, Communication & Society, 18*(5), 524-538.

Boundy, E. O., Dastjerdi, R., Spiegelman, D., Fawzi, W. W., Missmer, S. A., Lieberman, E., . . . Chan, G. J. (2016). Kangaroo mother care and neonatal outcomes: A meta-analysis. *Pediatrics, 137*(1), e20152238.

Bourne, R. R., Flaxman, S. R., Braithwaite, T., Cicinelli, M. V., Das, A., Jonas, J. B., . . . Naidoo, K. (2017). Magnitude, temporal trends, and projections of the global prevalence of blindness and distance and near vision impairment: A systematic review and meta-analysis. *The Lancet Global Health, 5*(9), e888-e897.

Bowlby, J. (1951). Maternal care and mental health. *Bulletin of the World Health Organization, 3*, 355-534.

Bowlby, J. (1969). *Attachment and loss: Vol. I. Attachment.* London: Hogarth Press & the Institute of Psychoanalysis.

Bowman, J. M. (2009). Gender role orientation and relational closeness: Self-disclosive behavior in same-sex male friendships. *The Journal of Men's Studies, 16*(3), 316-330.

Bowman, N. (2013). College diversity experiences and cognitive development: A meta-analysis. *Educational Studies, (2)*, 88-132.

Bowman, N. A. (2010). College diversity experiences and cognitive development: A meta-analysis. *Review of Educational Research, 80*(1), 4-33.

Boyce, C. J., Wood, A. M., Daly, M., & Sedikides, C. (2015). Personality change following unemployment. *Journal of Applied Psychology, 100*(4), 991.

Boyce, J. A., Assa'ad, A., Burks, A. W., Jones, S. M., Sampson, H. A., Wood, R. A. . . . Schwaninger, J. M. (2010). Guidelines for the diagnosis and management of food allergy in the United States: Report of the NIAID-sponsored expert panel. *Journal of Allergy and Clinical Immunology, 126* (Suppl. 6), S1-S58.

Boyd, H., & Murnen, S. K. (2017). Thin and sexy vs muscular and dominant: Prevalence of gendered body ideals in popular dolls and action figures. *Body Image, 21*, 90-96.

Boyette, A. H. (2010). Middle childhood among Aka forest foragers of the Central African Republic: a comparative perspective. *Anthropology WSU Vancouver Education*, 1-32.

Boyle, C. (2017). "What is the impact of birth family contact on children in adoption and long-term foster care?" A systematic review. *Child & Family Social Work, 22*, 22-33.

Boyles, S. (2002, January 27). Toxic landfills may boost birth defects. *WebMD Medical News.* Retrieved from www.webmd.com/content/article/25/3606_1181.htm

Bozick, R., & DeLuca, S. (2011). Not making the transition to college: School, work, and opportunities in the lives of American youth. *Social Science Research, 40*(4), 1249-1262.

Bozoglan, B., Demirer, V., & Sahin, I. (2013). Loneliness, self-esteem, and life satisfaction as predictors of Internet addiction: A cross-sectional study among Turkish university students. *Scandinavian Journal of Psychology, 54*(4), 313-319.

Brabeck, M. M., & Shore, E. L. (2003). Gender differences in intellectual and moral development? The evidence refutes the claims. In J. Demick & C. Andreoletti (Eds.), *Handbook of adult development* (pp. 351-368). New York, NY: Plenum Press.

Bracher, G., & Santow, M. (1999). Explaining trends in teenage childbearing in Sweden. *Studies in Family Planning, 30*, 169-182.

Brackett, M. A., Cox, A., Gaines, S. O., & Salovey, P. (2005). *Emotional intelligence and relationship quality among heterosexual couples.* Unpublished data. New Haven, CT: Yale University.

Bradbery, D. (2012). *Using children's literature to build concepts of teaching about global citizenship.* Retrieved from eric.ed.gov: http://files.eric.ed.gov/fulltext/ED544512.pdf

Bradbury, M., Peterson, M. N., & Liu, J. (2014). Long-term dynamics of household size and their environmental implications. *Population and Environment, 36*(1), 73-84.

Bradbury, T. N., Fincham, F. D., & Beach, S. R. (2000). Research on the nature and determinants of marital satisfaction: A decade in review. *Journal of Marriage and Family, 62*(4), 964-980.

Braddick, O., & Atkinson, J. (2011). Development of human visual function. *Vision Research, 51*(13), 1588-1609.

Bradlee, M. L., Mustafa, J., Singer, M. R., & Moore, L. L. (2018). High-protein foods and physical activity protect against age-related muscle loss and functional decline. *The Journals of Gerontology: Series A, 73*(1), 88–94.

Bradley R. H. (2009). The home environment. In M. H. Bornstein (Ed.). *Handbook of cultural developmental science* (pp. 505–530). New York, NY: Psychology Press.

Bradley, H., Markowitz, L. E., Gibson, T., & McQuillan, G. M. (2014). Seroprevalence of herpes simplex virus types 1 and 2–United States, 1999–2010. *The Journal of Infectious Diseases, 209*(3), 325–333.

Bradley, R. H. (1989). Home measurement of maternal responsiveness. In M. H. Bornstein (Ed.), *Maternal responsiveness: Characteristics and consequences* (New Directions for Child Development, No. 43). San Francisco, CA: Jossey-Bass.

Bradley, R. H., Corwyn, R. F., Burchinal, M., McAdoo, H. P., & Coll, C. G. (2001). The home environment of children in the United States: Part II: Relations with behavioral development through age thirteen. *Child Development, 72*(6), 1868–1886.

Bradley, R. H., McRitchie, S., Houts, R. M., Nader, P., & O'Brien, M. (2011). Parenting and the decline of physical activity from age 9 to 15. *International Journal of Behavioral Nutrition and Physical Activity, 8*(1), 33.

Brady, S. A. (2011). Efficacy of phonics teaching for reading outcomes. Indications from post-NRP research. In S. A. Brady, D. Braze, & C. A. Fowler (Eds.), *New directions in communication disorders research. Explaining individual differences in reading: Theory and evidence* (pp. 69–96). London, England: Psychology Press.

Braithwaite, I., Stewart, A. W., Hancox, R. J., Beasley, R., Murphy, R., Mitchell, E. A., & ISAAC Phase Three Study Group. (2014). Fast-food consumption and body mass index in children and adolescents: an international cross-sectional study. *BMJ Open, 4*(12), e005813.

Bramham, K., Parnell, B., Nelson-Piercy, C., Seed, P. T., Poston, L., & Chappell, L. C. (2014). Chronic hypertension and pregnancy outcomes: Systematic review and meta-analysis. *BMJ, 348*, g2301.

Bramlett, M. D., & Mosher, W. D. (2002). Cohabitation, marriage, divorce, and remarriage in the United States. *Vital Health Statistics, 23*(22). Hyattsville, MD: National Center for Health Statistics.

Branche, C., Ozanne-Smith, J., Oyebite, K., & Hyder, A. A. (2008). *World report on child injury prevention.* Geneva, Switzerland: World Health Organization.

Brand, J. E., & Simon Thomas, J. (2014). Job displacement among single mothers: Effects on children's outcomes in young adulthood. *American Journal of Sociology, 119*(4), 955–1001.

Brandone, A. C. (2015). Infants' social and motor experience and the emerging understanding of intentional actions. *Developmental Psychology, 51*(4), 512.

Branum, A., & Lukacs, S. L. (2008). Food allergy among U.S. children: Trends in prevalence and hospitalizations. *NCHS Data Brief, 10*, 1–8. Hyattsville, MD: National Center for Health Statistics.

Branum, A., Sharma, A.J. & Deputy, N. (2016). QuickStats: Gestational weight gain among women with full-term, singleton births, compared with recommendations –48 states and the District of Columbia. *Morbidity and Mortality Weekly Report, 65,* **1121.** http://dx.doi.org/10.15585/mmwr.mm6540a10

Brassai, L., Piko, B. F., & Steger, M. F. (2011). Meaning in life: Is it a protective factor for adolescents' psychological health? *International Journal of Behavioral μedicine, 18*(1), 44–51.

Bratter, J. L., & King, R. B. (2008). "But will it last?": Marital instability among interracial and same-race couples. *Family Relations, 57*(2), 160–171.

Braveman, P. A., Cubbin, C., Egerter, S., Williams, D. R., & Pamuk, E. (2010). Socioeconomic disparities in health in the United States: What the patterns tell us. *American Journal of Public Health, 100*(S1), S186–S196.

Brayne, C. (2007). The elephant in the room—Healthy brains in later life, epidemiology and public health. *Neuroscience, 8*(3), 233–239.

Brecklin, L. R., & Ullman, S. E. (2010). The roles of victim and offender substance use in sexual assault outcomes. *Journal of Interpersonal Violence, 25*(8), 1503–1522. doi: 0886260509354584

Bregman, H. R., Malik, N. M., Page, M. J., Makynen, E., & Lindahl, K. M. (2013). Identity profiles in lesbian, gay, and bisexual youth: The role of family influences. *Journal of Youth and Adolescence, 42*(3), 417–430.

Breheny, M., Stephens, C., & Spilsbury, L. (2013). Involvement without interference: How grandparents negotiate intergenerational expectations in relationships with grandchildren. *Journal of Family Studies, 19*(2), 174–184.

Brendgen, M., Dionne, G., Girard, A., Boivin, M., Vitaro, F., & Perusse, D. (2005). Examining genetic and environmental effects on social aggression: A study of 6-year-old twins. *Child Development, 76*, 930–946.

Brendgen, M., Girard, A., Vitaro, F., Dionne, G., & Boivin, M. (2015). Gene-environment correlation linking aggression and peer victimization: Do classroom behavioral norms matter? *Journal of Abnormal Child Psychology, 43*(1), 19–31.

Brener, N. D., Demissie, Z., McManus, T., Shanklin, S. L., Queen, B., & Kann, L. (2017). *School health profiles 2016: Characteristics of health programs among secondary schools* [Report]. Retrieved from www.cdc.gov/healthyyouth/data/profiles/pdf/2016/2016_Profiles_Report.pdf

Brent, D. A., & Birmaher, B. (2002). Adolescent depression. *New England Journal of Medicine, 347*, 667–671.

Brent, D. A., & Mann, J. J. (2006). Familial pathways to suicidal behavior—Understanding and preventing suicide among adolescents. *New England Journal of Medicine, 355*, 2719–2721.

Brent, D., Melhem, N., Donohoe, M. B., & Walker, M. (2009). The incidence and course of depression in bereaved youth 21 months after the loss of a parent to suicide, accident, or sudden natural death. *American Journal of Psychiatry, 166*(7), 786–794.

Brent, M. R., & Siskind, J. M. (2001). The role of exposure to isolated words in early vocabulary development. *Cognition, 81,* 33–34.

Bretherton, I. (1990). Communication patterns, internal working models, and the intergenerational transmission of attachment relationships. *Infant Mental Health Journal, 11*(3), 237–252.

Brezina, P.R. & Zhao, Y. (2012). The ethical, legal, and social issues impacted by modern assisted reproductive technologies. *Obstetrics and Gynecology International.* doi:10.1155/2012/686253

Brier, N. (2008). Grief following miscarriage: A comprehensive review of the literature. *Journal of Women's Health, 17*(3), 451–464.

Briggs, G. G., Freeman, R. K., & Yaffe, S. J. (2012). *Drugs in pregnancy and lactation: A reference guide to fetal and neonatal risk.* Baltimore, MD: Lippincott Williams & Wilkins.

Briggs, J. L. (1970). *Never in anger.* Cambridge, MA: Harvard University Press.

Briggs, J. L. (1970). *Never in anger: Portrait of an Eskimo family* (Vol 12). Harvard University Press.

Briggs, S., Cantrell, E. & Karberg, E. (2019). Family instability and children's social development [Data brief]. Retrieved from www.childtrends.org/wp-content/uploads/2019/08/r03brief_ChildTrends_Aug2019.pdf

Brillo, E., Tosto, V., Ceccagnoli, A., Nikolova, N., Pinzaglia, V., Bordoni, F., . . . & Renzo, G. C. D. (2019). The effect of prenatal exposure to music on fetal movements and fetal heart rate: A pilot study. *The Journal of Maternal-Fetal & Neonatal Medicine*, 1–9.

Brinkman-Stoppelenburg, A., Rietjens, J. A., & van der Heide, A. (2014). The effects of advance care planning on end-of-life care: A systematic review. *Palliative Medicine, 28*(8), 1000–1025.

Briskin, S., LaBotz, M., Brenner, J. S., Benjamin, H. J., Cappetta, C. T., Demorest, R. A., . . . Martin, S. S. (2012). Trampoline safety in childhood and adolescence. *Pediatrics, 130*(4), 774–779.

Brito, N. H., Fifer, W. P., Myers, M. M., Elliott, A. J., & Noble, K. G. (2016). Associations among family socioeconomic status, EEG power at birth, and cognitive skills during infancy. *Developmental Cognitive Neuroscience, 19*, 144–151.

Brocca, L., McPhee, J. S., Longa, E., Canepari, M., Seynnes, O., De Vito, G., . . . Bottinelli, R. (2017). Structure and function of human muscle fibres and muscle proteome in physically active older men. *The Journal of Physiology, 595*(14), 4823–4844.

Brochado, S., Soares, S., & Fraga, S. (2017). A scoping review on studies of cyberbullying prevalence among adolescents. *Trauma, Violence, & Abuse, 18*(5), 523–531.

Brody, G. H. (1998). Sibling relationship quality: Its causes and consequences. *Annual Review of Psychology, 49*, 1–24.

Brody, G. H. (2004). Siblings' direct and indirect contributions to child development. *Current directions in psychological science, 13*(3), 124-126.

Brody, G. H., Chen, Y.-F., Murry, V. M., Ge, X., Simons, R. L., Gibbons, F. X., . . . Cutrona, C. E. (2006). Perceived discrimination and the adjustment of African American youths: A five-year longitudinal analysis with contextual moderation effects. *Child Development, 77*(5), 1170–1189.

Brody, G. H., Kim, S., Murry, V. M., & Brown, A. C. (2004). Protective longitudinal paths linking child competence to behavioral problems among African American siblings. *Child Development, 75*, 455–467.

Brodzinsky, D. M., & Pinderhughes, E. (2002). Parenting and child development in adoptive families. In M. H. Bornstein (Ed.), *Handbook of parenting* (vol. 1, pp. 279–311). Mahwah, NJ: Lawrence Erlbaum.

Broekhuizen, M. L., Van Aken, M. A., Dubas, J. S., Mulder, H., & Leseman, P. P. (2015). Individual differences in effects of child care quality: The role of child affective self-regulation and gender. *Infant Behavior and development, 40*, 216–230.

Broesch, T., & Bryant, G. A. (2018). Fathers' infant-directed speech in a small-scale society. *Child Development, 89*(2), e29–e41.

Broesch, T., Callaghan, T., Henrich, J., Murphy, C., & Rochat, P. (2011). Cultural variations in children's mirror self-recognition. *Journal of Cross-Cultural Psychology, 42*(6), 1018–1029.

Broesch, T. L., & Bryant, G. A. (2015). Prosody in infant-directed speech is similar across western and traditional cultures. *Journal of Cognition and Development, 16*, 31–43.

Bronfenbrenner, U. (1979). *The ecology of human development*. Cambridge, MA: Harvard University Press.

Bronfenbrenner, U. (1986). Ecology of the family as a context for human development: Research perspectives. *Developmental Psychology, 22*, 723–742.

Bronfenbrenner, U. (1994). Ecological models of human development. In T. Husen & T. N. Postlethwaite (Eds.), *International encyclopedia of education* (Vol. 3, 2nd ed., pp. 1643–1647). Oxford, England: Pergamon Press/Elsevier Science.

Brooks, R., & Meltzoff, A. N. (2005). The development of gaze following and its relation to language. *Developmental Science, 8*, 535–543.

Brooks, R., & Meltzoff, A. N. (2008). Infant gaze following and pointing predict accelerated vocabulary growth through two years of age: A longitudinal, growth curve modeling study. *Journal of Child Language, 35*(1), 207–220.

Brooks, R., & Meltzoff, A. N. (2015). Connecting the dots from infancy to childhood: A longitudinal study connecting gaze following, language, and explicit theory of mind. *Journal of Experimental Child Psychology, 130*, 67–78.

Brooks, S. K., Webster, R. K., Smith, L. E., Woodland, L., Wessely, S., Greenberg, N., & Rubin, G. J. (2020). The psychological impact of quarantine and how to reduce it: rapid review of the evidence. *The Lancet*.

Brooks-Gunn, J. (2003). Do you believe in magic? What can we expect from early childhood intervention programs? *SRCD Social Policy Report, 17*(1).

Brooks-Gunn, J., Han, W. J., & Waldfogel, J. (2002). Maternal employment and child cognitive outcomes in the first three years of life: The NICHD study of early child care. *Child Development, 73*(4), 1052–1072.

Brooten, D., Youngblut, J. M., Caicedo, C., & Dankanich, J. (2019). Parents: Wish I had done, wish I had not done, and coping after child NICU/PICU death. *Journal of the American Association of Nurse Practitioners, 31*(3), 175–183.

Brooten, D., Youngblut, J. M., Hannan, J., Caicedo, C., Roche, R., & Malkawi, F. (2015). Infant and child deaths: Parent concerns about subsequent pregnancies. *Journal of the American Association of Nurse Practitioners, 27*(12), 690–697.

Broude, G. J. (1995). *Growing up: A crosscultural encyclopedia*. Santa Barbara, CA: ABC-CLIO.

Brougham, R. R., Zail, C. M., Mendoza, C. M., & Miller, J. R. (2009). Stress, sex differences, and coping strategies among college students. *Current Psychology, 28*(2), 85–97.

Brown, A. (2017). 5 key findings about LGBT Americans [Pew Research Center news release]. Retrieved from www.pewresearch.org/fact-tank/2017/06/13/5-key-findings-about-lgbt-americans/

Brown, B. B., & Klute, C. (2003). Friendships, cliques, and crowds. In G. R. Adams & M. D. Berzonsky (Eds.), *Blackwell handbook of adolescence* (pp. 330–348). Malden, MA: Blackwell.

Brown, E. C., Low, S., Smith, B. H., & Haggerty, K. P. (2011). Outcomes from a school-randomized controlled trial of steps to respect: A bullying prevention program. *School Psychology Review, 40*(3).

Brown, S. L., Manning, W. D., & Stykes, J. B. (2015). Family structure and child well-being: Integrating family complexity. *Journal of Marriage and Family, 77*(1), 177–190.

Brown, J. D., & L'Engle, K. L. (2009). X-rated: Sexual attitudes and behaviors associated with US early adolescents' exposure to sexually explicit media. *Communication Research, 36*(1), 129–151.

Brown, J. T., & Stoudemire, A. (1983). Normal and pathological grief. *Journal of the American Medical Association, 250*, 378–382.

Brown, S. L. (2004). Family structure and child well-being: The significance of parental cohabitation. *Journal of Marriage and Family, 66*, 351–367.

Brown, S. L. (2010). Marriage and child well-being: Research and policy perspectives. *Journal of Marriage and Family, 72*(5), 1059–1077.

Brown, S. L., & Kawamura, S. (2010). Relationship quality among cohabitors and marrieds in older adulthood. *Social Science Research, 39*(5), 777–786.

Brown, S. L., & Lin, I. F. (2012). The gray divorce revolution: Rising divorce among middle-aged and older adults, 1990–2010. *The Journals of Gerontology: Series B, 67*(6), 731–741.

Brown, S. L., & Shinohara, S. K. (2013). Dating relationships in older adulthood: A national portrait. *Journal of Marriage and Family, 75*(5), 1194–1202.

Brown, S. L., & Wright, M. R. (2017). Marriage, cohabitation, and divorce in later life. *Innovation in Aging, 1*(2), igx015.

Brown, S. L., Bulanda, J. R., & Lee, G. R. (2005). The significance of nonmarital cohabitation: Marital status and mental health benefits among middle-aged and older adults. *Journal of Gerontology: Social Sciences, 60B*, S21–S29.

Brown, S. L., Bulanda, J. R., & Lee, G. R. (2012). Transitions into and out of cohabitation in later life. *Journal of Marriage and Family, 74*(4), 774–793.

Brown, S. L., Manning, W. D., & Payne, K. K. (2017). Relationship quality among cohabiting versus married couples. *Journal of Family Issues, 38*(12), 1730–1753.

Brownell, C. A., Ramani, G. B., & Zerwas, S. (2006). Becoming a social partner with peers: Cooperation and social understanding in one- and two-year-olds. *Child Development, 77*, 803–821.

Brownell, C. A., Svetlova, M., Anderson, R., Nichols, S. R., & Drummond, J. (2013). Socialization of early prosocial behavior: Parents' talk about emotions is associated with sharing and helping in toddlers. *Infancy, 18*(1), 91–119.

Brubacher, S. P., Glisic, U., Roberts, K. P., & Powell, M. (2011). Children's ability to recall unique aspects of one occurrence of a repeated event. *Applied Cognitive Psychology, 25*(3), 351–358.

Bruer, J. T. (2001). A critical and sensitive period primer. In D. B. Bailey, J. T. Bruer, F. J. Symons, & J. W. Lichtman (Eds.), *Critical thinking about critical periods: A series from the National Center for Early Development and Learning* (pp. 289–292). Baltimore, MD: Paul Brooks Publishing.

Bruner, J. S. (1974). From communication to language—A psychological perspective. *Cognition, 3*(3), 255–287.

Bryant, B. K. (1987). Mental health, temperament, family, and friends: Perspectives on children's empathy and social perspective taking. In N. Eisenberg & J. Strayer (Eds.), *Empathy and its development of competence in adolescence* (pp. 245–270). Cambridge, England: Cambridge University Press.

Bryden, M. P., Ardila, A., & Ardila, O. (1993). Handedness in native Amazonians. *Neuropsychologia, 31*(3), 301–308.

Bucchianeri, M. M., Fernandes, N., Loth, K., Hannan, P. J., Eisenberg, M. E., & Neumark-Sztainer, D. (2016). Body dissatisfaction: Do associations with disordered eating and psychological well-being differ across race/ethnicity in adolescent girls and boys? *Cultural Diversity and Ethnic Minority Psychology, 22*(1), 137.

Buchanan, D. W., & Sobel, D. M. (2011). Mechanism-based causal reasoning in young children. *Child Development, 82*(6), 2053–2066.

Buchanan, T. W. (2007). Retrieval of emotional memories. *Psychological Bulletin, 133*(5), 761.

Buchmann, C., & DiPrete, T. A. (2006). The growing female advantage in college completion: The role of family background and academic achievement. *American Sociological Review, 71*, 515–541.

Buchmueller, T., & Carpenter, C. (2010). Disparities in health insurance coverage, access and outcomes for individuals in same-sex versus different-sex relationships, 2000–2007. *American Journal of Public Health, 100*(3), 489–495.

Buck Louis, G., Gray, L., Marcus, M., Ojeda, S., Pescovitz, O., Witchel, S., . . . Euling, S. Y. (2008). Environmental factors and puberty timing: Expert panel research needs. *Pediatrics, 121*, S192–S207.

Buck-Morss, S. (1975). Social-economic bias in Piaget's theories and its implication for cross-cultural study. *Human Development, 18*(1-2), 35-49.

Buckingham-Howes, S., Berger, S. S., Scaletti, L. A., & Black, M. M. (2013). Systematic review of prenatal cocaine exposure and adolescent development. *Pediatrics, 131*(6), e1917-e1936.

Bucur, B., & Madden, D. J. (2010). Effects of adult age and blood pressure on executive function and speech of processing. *Experimental Aging Research, 36*(2), 153-168.

Budiman, A. & Lopez, M. H. (2017). Amid decline in international adoptions to U.S., boys outnumber girls for the first time [News report]. Retrieved from https://www.pewresearch.org/fact-tank/2017/10/17/amid-decline-in-international-adoptions-to-u-s-boys-outnumber-girls-for-the-first-time/

Budson, A. E., & Price, B. H. (2005). Memory dysfunction. *New England Journal of Medicine, 352,* 692-699.

Buehler, C. (2006). Parents and peers in relation to early adolescent problem behavior. *Journal of Marriage and Family, 68,* 109-124.

Bufferd, S. J., Dougherty, L. R., Olino, T. M., Dyson, M. W., Laptook, R. S., Carlson, G. A., & Klein, D. N. (2014). Predictors of the onset of depression in young children: a multi-method, multi-informant longitudinal study from ages 3 to 6. *Journal of Child Psychology and Psychiatry, 55*(11), 1279-1287.

Buhl, H. M., & Lanz, M. (2007). Emerging adulthood in Europe: Common traits and variability across five European countries. *Journal of Adolescent Research, 22*(5), 439-443

Buhrmester, D. (1990). Intimacy of friendship, interpersonal competence, and adjustment during preadolescence and adolescence. *Child Development, 61,* 1101-1111.

Bui, M., Benyamin, B., Shah, S., Henders, A. K., Martin, N. G., Montgomery, G. W., & McRae, A. F. (2015). Sharing a placenta is associated with a greater similarity in DNA methylation in monochorionic versus dichorionic twin pars in blood at age 14. *Twin Research and Human Genetics, 18*(6), 680-685.

Buist, K. L., Deković, M., & Prinzie, P. (2013). Sibling relationship quality and psychopathology of children and adolescents: A meta-analysis. *Clinical Psychology Review, 33*(1), 97-106.

Bulanda, J. R., & Brown, S. L. (2007). Race-ethnic differences in marital quality and divorce. *Social Science Research, 36*(3), 945-967.

Bulcroft, R. A., & Bulcroft, K. A. (1991). The nature and function of dating in later life. *Research on Aging, 13,* 244-260.

Burchinal, M. R., Roberts, J. E., Nabors, L. A., & Bryant, D. M. (1996). Quality of center child care and infant cognitive and language development. *Child Development, 67,* 606-620.

Burdelski, M. (2011). Language Socialization and Politeness Routines. In A. Durani, E. Ochs, & B. Schieffellin (Eds.), *The handbook of language socialization* (pp. 275-295). Hoboken, NJ: Blackwell Publishing.

Burdette, H. L., & Whitaker, R. C. (2005). Resurrecting free play in young children. *Archives of Pediatrics and Adolescent Medicine, 159,* 46-50.

Bureau of Labor Statistics. (2017). *Women in the labor force: A databook* [U.S. Department of Labor report]. Retrieved from www.bls.gov/opub/reports/womens-databook/2017/home.htm

Bureau of Labor Statistics. (2020). The employment situation – April 2020 [News release]. U.S. Department of Labor. Retrieved from www.bls.gov/news.release/pdf/empsit.pdf

Bureau of Labor Statistics. (2020). *The employment situation: April 2020* [Report]. Retrieved from www.bls.gov/news.release/flex2.t01.htm

Bures, R. M., Koropeckyj-Cox, T., & Loree, M. (2009). Childlessness, parenthood, and depressive symptoms among middle-aged and older adults. *Journal of Family Issues, 30*(5), 670-687.

Burgaleta, M., Johnson, W., Waber, D. P., Colom, R., & Karama, S. (2014). Cognitive ability changes and dynamics of cortical thickness development in healthy children and adolescents. *Neuroimage, 84,* 810-819.

Burke, B. L., Martens, A., & Faucher, E. H. (2010). Two decades of terror management theory: A meta-analysis of mortality salience research. *Personality and Social Psychology Review, 14*(2), 155-195.

Burke, D. M., & Shafto, M. A. (2004). Aging and language production. *Current Directions in Psychological Science, 13,* 81-84.

Burke, H., Leonardi-Bee, J., Hashim, A., Pine-Abata, H., Chen, Y., Cook, D. G., . . . McKeever, T. M. (2012). Prenatal and passive smoke exposure and incidence of asthma and wheeze: Systematic review and meta-analysis. *Pediatrics, 129*(4), 735-744.

Burke, S. N., & Barnes, C. A. (2006). Neural plasticity in the ageing brain. *Nature Review Neuroscience, 7,* 30-40.

Burn, K., & Szoeke, C. (2016). Boomerang families and failure-to-launch: Commentary on adult children living at home. *Maturitas, 83,* 9-12.

Burnes, D., Pillemer, K., Caccamise, P. L., Mason, A., Henderson, C. R., Berman, J., . . . Salamone, A. (2015). Prevalence of and risk factors for elder abuse and neglect in the community: A population-based study. *Journal of the American Geriatrics Society, 63*(9), 1906-1912.

Burnett, A. L., Nehra, A., Breau, R. H., Culkin, D. J., Faraday, M. M., Hakim, L. S., . . . Nelson, C. J. (2018). Erectile dysfunction: AUA guideline. *The Journal of Urology, 200*(3), 633-641.

Burns, B. J., Phillips, S. D., Wagner, H. R., Barth, R. P., Kolko, D. J., Campbell, Y., & Landsverk, J. (2004). Mental health need and access to mental health services by youths involved with child welfare: A national survey. *Journal of the American Academy of Child & Adolescent Psychiatry, 43,* 960-970.

Burns, K. H., Casey, P. H., Lyle, R. E., Mac Bird, T., Fussell, J. J., & Robbins, J. M. (2010). Increasing prevalence of medically complex children in US hospitals. *Pediatrics, 126*(4), 638-646.

Burrus, B. B. (2018). Decline in adolescent pregnancy in the United States: A success not shared by all. *American Journal of Public Health, 108*(Suppl. 1): S5-S6.

Burtner, C. R., & Kennedy, B. K. (2010). Progeria syndromes and ageing: What is the connection? *Nature Reviews Molecular Cell Biology, 11*(8), 567-578.

Bushman, B. J., Gollwitzer, M., & Cruz, C. (2015). There is broad consensus: Media researchers agree that violent media increase aggression in children, and pediatricians and parents concur. *Psychology of Popular Media Culture, 4*(3), 200.

Bussey, K., & Bandura, A. (1992). Self-regulatory mechanisms governing gender development. *Child Development, 63,* 1236-1250.

Bussey, K., & Bandura, A. (1999). Social cognitive theory of gender development and differentiation. *Psychological Review, 106,* 676-713.

Butler, M., McCreedy, E., Nelson, V. A., Desai, P., Ratner, E., Fink, H. A., . . . Davila, H. (2018). Does cognitive training prevent cognitive decline? A systematic review. *Annals of Internal Medicine, 168*(1), 63-68.

Buttelmann, D., Zmyj, N., Daum, M., & Carpenter, M. (2013). Selective imitation of in-group over out-group members in 14-month-old infants. *Child Development, 84*(2), 422-428.

Buttelmann, F., & Karbach, J. (2017). Development and plasticity of cognitive flexibility in early and middle childhood. *Frontiers in Psychology, 8,* 1040.

Button, K. S., Ioannidis, J. P., Mokrysz, C., Nosek, B. A., Flint, J., Robinson, E. S., & Munafò, M. R. (2013). Power failure: Why small sample size undermines the reliability of neuroscience. *Nature Reviews Neuroscience, 14*(5), 365.

Buunk, A. P., Park, J. H., & Duncan, L. A. (2010). Cultural variation in parental influence on mate choice. *Cross-Cultural Research, 44*(1), 23-40.

Buyukcan-Tetik, A., Finkenauer, C., Schut, H., Stroebe, M., & Stroebe, W. (2017). The impact of bereaved parents' perceived grief similarity on relationship satisfaction. *Journal of Family Psychology, 31*(4), 409.

Byers-Heinlein, K., Burns, T. C., & Werker, J. F. (2010). The roots of bilingualism in newborns. *Psychological Science, 21*(3), 343-348. doi:10.1177/0956797609360758

Byrnes, J. P., & Fox, N. A. (1998). The educational relevance of research in cognitive neuroscience. *Educational Psychology Review, 10,* 297-342.

Bystron, I., Rakic, P., Molnar, Z., & Blakemore, C. (2006). The first neurons of the human cerebral cortex. *Nature Neuroscience, 9*(7), 880-886.

Błachnio, A., Przepiorka, A., Benvenuti, M., Mazzoni, E., & Seidman, G. (2019). Relations between facebook intrusion, Internet addiction, life satisfaction, and self-esteem: A study in Italy and the USA. *International Journal of Mental Health and Addiction, 17*(4), 793-805.

Cabeza, R., Albert, M., Belleville, S., Craik, F. I., Duarte, A., Grady, C. L., . . . Rugg, M. D. (2018). Maintenance, reserve and compensation: The cognitive neuroscience of healthy ageing. *Nature Reviews Neuroscience, 1.*

Cabrera, N. J., Tamis-LeMonda, C. S., Bradley, R. H., Hofferth, S., & Lamb, M. E. (2000).

Fatherhood in the twenty-first century. *Child Development, 71*, 127–136.

Cabrera, S. M., Bright, G. M., Frane, J. W., Blethen, S. L., & Lee, P. A. (2014). Age of thelarche and menarche in contemporary US females: A cross-sectional analysis. *Journal of Pediatric Endocrinology and Metabolism, 27*(1–2), 47–51.

Caceres, B. A., Frank, M. O., Jun, J., Martelly, M. T., Sadarangani, T., & De Sales, P. C. (2016). Family caregivers of patients with frontotemporal dementia: An integrative review. *International Journal of Nursing Studies, 55*, 71–84.

Cacioppo, J. T., & Cacioppo, S. (2014). Social relationships and health: The toxic effects of perceived social isolation. *Social and Personality Psychology Compass, 8*(2), 58–72.

Cadore, E. L., Rodríguez-Mañas, L., Sinclair, A., & Izquierdo, M. (2013). Effects of different exercise interventions on risk of falls, gait ability, and balance in physically frail older adults: A systematic review. *Rejuvenation Research, 16*(2), 105–114.

Caetano, R., Schafer, J., & Cunradi, C.B. (2001). *Alcohol-related intimate partner violence among white, Black, and Hispanic couples in the United States.* Retrieved from https://pubs.niaaa.nih.gov/publications/arh25-1/58-65.htm

Cahill, K. E., Giandrea, M. D., & Quinn, J. F. (2013). *Bridge employment.* In M. Wang (Ed.), *The Oxford handbook of retirement* (pp. 293–310). New York, NY: Oxford University Press.

Cahn, Z., & Siegel, M. (2011). Electronic cigarettes as a harm reduction strategy for tobacco control: A step forward or a repeat of past mistakes? *Journal of Public Health Policy, 32*, 16–31. doi: 10.1057/jphp2010.41

Cai, H., Li, G., Hua, S., Liu, Y., & Chen, L. (2017). Effect of exercise on cognitive function in chronic disease patients: A meta-analysis and systematic review of randomized controlled trials. *Clinical Interventions in Aging, 12,* 773.

Cain, M. S., Leonard, J. A., Gabrieli, J. D. E., & Finn, A. S. (2016). Media multitasking in adolescence. *Psychonomic Bulletin & Review*, 23, 1932–1941.

Cairns, G., Angus, K., Hastings, G., & Caraher, M. (2013). Systematic reviews of the evidence on the nature, extent and effects of food marketing to children. A retrospective summary. *Appetite, 62*, 209–215.

Cairns, K. E., Yap, M. B. H., Pilkington, P. D., & Jorm, A. F. (2014). Risk and protective factors for depression that adolescents can modify: A systematic review and meta-analysis of longitudinal studies. *Journal of Affective Disorders, 169*, 61–75.

Calafat, A., García, F., Juan, M., Becoña, E., & Fernández-Hermida, J. R. (2014). Which parenting style is more protective against adolescent substance use? Evidence within the European context. *Drug and Alcohol Dependence, 138*, 185–192.

Calaprice, A., Kennefick, D., & Schulmann, R. (2015). *An Einstein Encyclopedia.* Princeton University Press.

Caldwell, B. M., & Bradley, R. H. (1984). *Home Observation for Measurement of the Environment.* Unpublished manuscript, University of Arkansas at Little Rock.

Caldwell, J. T., Ford, C. L., Wallace, S. P., Wang, M. C., & Takahashi, L. M. (2016). Intersection of living in a rural versus urban area and race/ethnicity in explaining access to health care in the United States. *American Journal of Public Health, 106*(8), 1463–1469.

Caldwell-Harris, C. L., Wilson, A. L., LoTempio, E., & Beit-Hallahmi, B. (2011). Exploring the atheist personality: Well-being, awe, and magical thinking in atheists, Buddhists, and Christians. *Mental Health, Religion & Culture, 14*(7), 659–672.

Çalışkan, M., Bochkov, Y. A., Kreiner-Møller, E., Bønnelykke, K., Stein, M. M., Du, G., . . . Nicolae, D. L. (2013). Rhinovirus wheezing illness and genetic risk of childhood-onset asthma. *New England Journal of Medicine, 368*(15), 1398–1407.

Calkins, S. D., & Fox, N. A. (1992). The relations among infant temperament, security of attachment, and behavioral inhibition at twenty-four months. *Child Development, 63*, 1456–1472.

Callaghan, T., Rochat, P., Lillard, A., Claux, M. L., Odden, H., Itakura, S., . . . Singh, S. (2005). Synchrony in the onset of mental-state reasoning: Evidence from five cultures. *Psychological Science, 16*(5), 378–384.

Callahan, S. T., & Cooper, W. O. (2005). Uninsurance and health care access among young adults in the United States. *Pediatrics, 116*, 88–95.

Calvin, C. M., Deary, I. J., Fenton, C., Roberts, B. A., Der, G., Leckenby, N., & Batty, G. D. (2010). Intelligence in youth and all-cause-mortality: Systematic review with meta-analysis. *International Journal of Epidemiology, 40*(3), 626–644.

Calzo, J. P., Masyn, K. E., Austin, S. B., Jun, H. J., & Corliss, H. L. (2017). Developmental latent patterns of identification as mostly heterosexual versus lesbian, gay, or bisexual. *Journal of Research on Adolescence, 27*(1), 246–253.

Camarata, S., & Woodcock, R. (2006). Sex differences in processing speed: Developmental effects in males and females. *Intelligence, 34*(3), 231–252.

Camarota, S. A., & Zeigler, K. (2016, October). Immigrants in the United States: A profile of the foreign-born using 2014 and 2015 Census Bureau data. *Center for Immigration Studies.* Retrieved from http://cis.org/sites/cis.org/files/immigrant-profile_0.pdf

Camilli, G., Vargas, S., Ryan, S., & Barnett, W. S. (2010). Meta-analysis of the effects of early education interventions on cognitive and social development. *Teachers College Record, 112*(3), 579–620.

Camp, C. J. (1989). World-knowledge systems. In L. W. Poon, D. C. Rubin, & B. A. Wilson (Eds.), *Everyday cognition in adulthood and late life.* Cambridge, England: Cambridge University Press.

Camp, C. J., & McKitrick, L. A. (1989). The dialectics of remembering and forgetting across the adult lifespan. In D. Kramer & M. Bopp (Eds.), *Dialectics and contextualism in clinical and developmental psychology: Change, transformation, and the social context* (pp. 169–187). New York, NY: Springer.

Campbell, A., Shirley, L., & Candy, J. (2004). A longitudinal study of gender-related cognition and behaviour. *Developmental Science, 7*, 1–9.

Campbell, A., Shirley, L., Heywood, C., & Crook, C. (2000). Infants' visual preference for sex-congruent babies, children, toys and activities: A longitudinal study. *British Journal of Developmental Psychology, 18*(4), 479–498.

Campbell, J. M., Lane, M., Owens, J. A., & Bakos, H. W. (2015). Paternal obesity negatively affects male fertility and assisted reproduction outcomes: A systematic review and meta-analysis. *Reproductive Biomedicine Online, 31*(5), 593–604.

Campbell-Yeo, M., Fernandes, A., & Johnston, C. (2011). Procedural pain management for neonates using nonpharmacological strategies: Part 2 mother-driven interventions. *Advances in Neonatal Care, 11*(5), 312–318.

Campione-Barr, N. (2017). The changing nature of power, control, and influence in sibling relationships. *New Directions for Child and Adolescent Development, 2017*(156), 7–14.

Campos, J. J., Sorce, J. F., Emde, R. N., & Svejda, M. (2013). Emotions as behavior regulators: Social referencing in infancy. *Emotions in Early Development, 57.*

Camras, L. A., Bakeman, R., Chen, Y., Norris, K., & Cain, T. R. (2006). Culture, ethnicity, and children's facial expressions: A study of European American, mainland Chinese, Chinese American, and adopted Chinese girls. *Emotion, 6*(1), 103.

Cansino, S. (2009). Episodic memory decay along the adult lifespan: A review of behavioral and neurophysiological evidence. *International Journal of Psychophysiology, 71*(1), 64–69.

Cantor, J. (1994). Confronting children's fright responses to mass media. In D. Zillman, J. Bryant, & A. C. Huston (Eds.), *Media, children, and the family: Social scientific, psychoanalytic, and clinical perspectives* (pp. 139–150). Hillsdale, NJ: Erlbaum.

Cao, A., & Kan, Y. W. (2013). The prevention of thalassemia. *Cold Spring Harbor Perspectives in Medicine, 3*(2), a011775.

Cao, A., Rosatelli, M. C., Monni, G., & Galanello, R. (2002). Screening for thalassemia. *Obstetrics and Gynecology Clinics, 29*(2), 305–328.

Cao, H., Zhou, N., Fine, M., Liang, Y., Li, J., & Mills-Koonce, W. R. (2017). Sexual minority stress and same-sex relationship well-being: A meta-analysis of research prior to the US Nationwide legalization of same-sex marriage. *Journal of Marriage and Family, 79*(5), 1258–1277.

Cao, L., Tan, L., Wang, H. F., Jiang, T., Zhu, X. C., Lu, H., . . . Yu, J. T. (2016). Dietary patterns and risk of dementia: A systematic review and meta-analysis of cohort studies. *Molecular Neurobiology, 53*(9), 6144–6154.

Caplan, L. J., & Schooler, C. (2006). Household work complexity, intellectual functioning, and self-esteem in men and women. *Journal of Marriage and Family, 68*, 883–900.

Caprara, G. V., Fida, R., Vecchione, M., Del Bove, G., Vecchio, G. M., Barbaranelli, C., & Bandura, A. (2008). Longitudinal analysis of the role of perceived self-efficacy for self-regulated learning in academic continuance and achievement. *Journal of Educational Psychology, 100*(3), 525–534.

Caputi, T. L., Smith, D., & Ayers, J. W. (2017). Suicide risk behaviors among sexual minority adolescents in the United States, 2015. *JAMA, 318*(23), 2349–2351.

Caraballo, R. S., Giovino, G. A., Pechacek, T. F., Mowery, P. D., Richter, P. A., Strauss, W. J., . . . Maurer, K. R. (1998). Racial and ethnic differences in serum cotinine levels of cigarette smokers. *Journal of the American Medical Association, 280*, 135-139.

Card, N., Stucky, B., Sawalani, G., & Little, T. (2008). Direct and indirect aggression during childhood and adolescence: A meta-analytic review of gender differences, intercorrelations, and relations to maladjustment. *Child Development, 79*(5), 1185-1229.

Carers Australia. (2012, September 28). *Carers caught in the 'sandwich generation'.* Retrieved from www.carersaustralia.com.au/media-centre/article/?id=carers-caught-in-the-sandwich-generation

Carers UK. (2012, November 29). *Sandwich caring.* Retrieved from www.carersuk.org/for-professionals/policy/policy-library/sandwich-caring

Carlo, G., Mestre, M. V., Samper, P., Tur, A., & Armenta, B. E. (2011). The longitudinal relations among dimensions of parenting styles, sympathy, prosocial moral reasoning, and prosocial behaviors. *International Journal of Behavioral Development, 35*(2), 116-124.

Carlson, E. A. (1998). A prospective longitudinal study of attachment disorganization/disorientation. *Child Development, 69*(4), 1107-1128.

Carlson, N. E., Moore, M. M., Dame, A., Howieson, D., Silbert, L. C., Quinn, J. F., & Kaye, J. A. (2008). Trajectories of brain loss in aging and the development of cognitive impairment. *Neurology, 79*(11), 828-833.

Carmichael, C. L., Reis, H. T., & Duberstein, P. R. (2015). In your 20s it's quantity, in your 30s it's quality: The prognostic value of social activity across 30 years of adulthood. *Psychology and Aging, 30*(1), 95.

Carnelley, K. B., Wortman, C. B., Bolger, N., & Burke, C. T. (2006). The time course of grief reactions to spousal loss: Evidence from a national probability sample. *Journal of Personality and Social Psychology, 91*, 476-492.

Carothers, S. S., Borkowski, J. G., Lefever, J. B., & Whitman, T. L. (2005). Religiosity and the socioemotional adjustment of adolescent mothers and their children. *Journal of Family Psychology, 19*, 263-275.

Carpenter, C., Eppink, S. T., Gonzales Jr, G., & McKay, T. (2018). Effects of access to legal same-sex marriage on marriage and health: Evidence from BRFSS. National Bureau of Economic Research Working Paper No. 24651.

Carr, D. C., Kail, B. L., Matz-Costa, C., & Shavit, Y. Z. (2017). Does becoming a volunteer attenuate loneliness among recently widowed older adults? *The Journals of Gerontology: Series B.*

Carr, D., & Boerner, K. (2009). Do spousal discrepancies in marital quality assessments affect psychological adjustment to widowhood? *Journal of Marriage and Family, 71*(3), 495-509.

Carr, D., Freedman, V. A., Cornman, J. C., & Schwarz, N. (2014). Happy marriage, happy life? Marital quality and subjective well-being in later life. *Journal of Marriage and Family, 76*(5), 930-948.

Carraher, T. N., Schliemann, A. D., & Carraher, D. W. (1988). Mathematical concepts in everyday life. In G. B. Saxe & M. Gearhart (Eds.), *Children's mathematics* (New Directions in Child Development, No. 41, pp. 71-87). San Francisco, CA: Jossey-Bass.

Carrion-Castillo, A., Franke, B., & Fisher, S. E. (2013). Molecular genetics of dyslexia: An overview. *Dyslexia, 19*(4), 214-240.

Carskadon, M. A. (2011). Sleep in adolescents: The perfect storm. *Pediatric Clinics, 58*(3), 637-647.

Carstensen, L. L. (1991). Selectivity theory: Social activity in life-span context. In *Annual review of gerontology and geriatrics* (Vol. 11, pp. 195-217). New York, NY: Springer.

Carstensen, L. L. (1995). Evidence for a life-span theory of socioemotional selectivity. *Current Directions in Psychological Science, 4*, 150-156.

Carstensen, L. L. (1996). Socioemotional selectivity: A life-span developmental account of social behavior. In M. R. Merrens & G. G. Brannigan (Eds.), *The developmental psychologists: Research adventures across the life span* (pp. 251-272). New York, NY: McGraw-Hill.

Carstensen, L. L., & Mikels, J. A. (2005). At the intersection of emotion and cognition: Aging and the positivity effect. *Current Directions in Psychological Science, 14*, 117-122.

Carstensen, L. L., Isaacowitz, D. M., & Charles, S. T. (1999). Taking time seriously: A theory of socioemotional selectivity. *American Psychologist, 54*, 165-181.

Carstensen, L. L., Turan, B., Scheibe, S., Ram, N., Ersner-Hershfield, H., Samanez-Larkin, G. R., . . . Nesselroade, J. R. (2011). Emotional experience improves with age: Evidence based on over 10 years of experience sampling. *Psychology and Aging, 26*(1), 21.

Cartee, G. D., Hepple, R. T., Bamman, M. M., & Zierath, J. R. (2016). Exercise promotes healthy aging of skeletal muscle. *Cell Metabolism, 23*(6), 1034-1047.

Carter, P. M., Bingham, C. R., Zakrajsek, J. S., Shope, J. T., & Sayer, T. B. (2014). Social norms and risk perception: Predictors of distracted driving behavior among novice adolescent drivers. *Journal of Adolescent Health*, 54, S32-S41.

Cary, L. A., & Chasteen, A. L. (2015). Age stereotypes and age stigma: Connections to research on subjective aging. *Annual review of gerontology and Geriatrics, 35*(1), 99-119.

Case, L. K., Brang, D., Landazuri, R., Viswanathan, P., & Ramachandran, V. S. (2017). Altered white matter and sensory response to bodily sensation in female-to-male transgender individuals. *Archives of Sexual Behavior, 46*(5), 1223-1237.

Casey, B. J., Jones, R. M., & Somerville, L. H. (2011). Braking and accelerating of the adolescent brain. *Journal of Research on Adolescence, 21*(1), 21-33.

Cash, H., Rae, C., Steel, A., & Winkler, A. (2012). Internet addiction: A brief summary of research and practice. *Current Psychiatry Reviews, 8*(4), 292-298.

Casper, W. J., Marquardt, D. J., Roberto, K. J., & Buss, C. (2016). The hidden family lives of single adults without dependent children. In T. D.

Allen & L. T. Eby (Eds.), *The Oxford handbook of work and family* (pp. 182-195). New York, NY: Oxford University Press.

Caspi, A. (1998). Personality development across the life course. In W. Damon (Series Ed.) & N. Eisenberg (Vol. Ed.), *Handbook of child psychology: Vol. 3. Social, emotional, and personality development* (5th ed., pp. 311-388). New York, NY: Wiley.

Caspi, A., Lynam, D., Moffitt, T. E., & Silva, P. A. (1993). Unraveling girls' delinquency: Biological, dispositional, and contextual contributions to adolescent misbehavior. *Developmental Psychology, 29*(1), 19-30.

Caspi, A., McClay, J., Moffitt, T. E., Mill, J., Martin, J., Craig, I. W., . . . Poulton, R. (2002). Role of genotype in the cycle of violence in maltreated children. *Science, 297*, 851-854.

Cassibba, R., Castoro, G., Costantino, E., Sette, G., & Van IJzendoorn, M. H. (2015). Enhancing maternal sensitivity and infant attachment security with video feedback: An exploratory study in Italy. *Infant Mental Health Journal, 36*(1), 53-61.

Cassidy, K. W., Werner, R. S., Rourke, M., Zubernis, L. S., & Balaraman, G. (2003). The relationship between psychological understanding and positive social behaviors. *Social Development, 12*, 198-221.

Castle, N., Ferguson-Rome, J. C., & Teresi, J. A. (2015). Elder abuse in residential long-term care: An update to the 2003 National Research Council report. *Journal of Applied Gerontology, 34*(4), 407-443.

Castro, M., Expósito-Casas, E., López-Martín, E., Lizasoain, L., Navarro-Asencio, E., & Gaviria, J. L. (2015). Parental involvement on student academic achievement: A meta-analysis. *Educational Research Review, 14*, 33-46.

Castro, V. L., Halberstadt, A. G., Lozada, F. T., & Craig, A. B. (2015). Parents' emotion-related beliefs, behaviours, and skills predict children's recognition of emotion. *Infant and Child Development, 24*(1), 1-22.

Catalano, P. M., & Shankar, K. (2017). Obesity and pregnancy: Mechanisms of short term and long term adverse consequences for mother and child. *BMJ, 356*, j1.

Cattell, R. B. (1943). The measurement of adult intelligence. *Psychological Bulletin, 40*(3), 153.

Cattell, R. B. (1963). Theory of fluid and crystallized intelligence: A critical experiment. *Journal of Educational Psychology, 54*(1), 1.

Cattuzzo, M. T., dos Santos Henrique, R., Ré, A. H. N., de Oliveira, I. S., Melo, B. M., de Sousa Moura, M., . . . Stodden, D. (2016). Motor competence and health related physical fitness in youth: A systematic review. *Journal of Science and Medicine in Sport, 19*(2), 123-129.

Caughey, A. B., Hopkins, L. M., & Norton, M. E. (2006). Chorionic villus sampling compared with amniocentesis and the difference in the rate of pregnancy loss. *Obstetrics and Gynecology, 108*, 612-616.

Cavanagh, S. E., & Huston, A. C. (2008). The timing of family instability and children's social development. *Journal of Marriage and Family, 70*(5), 1258-1270.

CDC COVID-19 Response Team. (2020). Severe outcomes among patients with coronavirus disease 2019 (COVID-19)–United States, February 12–March 16, 2020. *Morbidity and Mortality Weekly Reports, 69*(12), 343–346.

Ceci, S. J., & Williams, W. M. (1997). Schooling, intelligence, and income. *American Psychologist, 52*(10), 1051–1058.

Celis, W. (1990, August 16). More states are laying school paddle to rest. *The New York Times,* pp. A1, B12.

Center for Retirement Research. (2018). *Average retirement age for men and women* [Data table]. Retrieved from http://crr.bc.edu/wp-content/uploads/2015/10/Avg_ret_age_men.pdf

Centers for Disease Control and Prevention. (2018). *Breastfeeding* [Fact sheet]. Retrieved from www.cdc.gov/breastfeeding/breastfeeding-special-circumstances/contraindications-to-breastfeeding.html

Centers for Disease Control and Prevention. (2018). *Human immunodeficiency virus (HIV)* [Information sheet]. Retrieved from www.cdc.gov/breastfeeding/breastfeeding-special-circumstances/maternal-or-infant-illnesses/hiv.html

Centers for Disease Control and Prevention. (2019). *Data and statistics about ADHD* [Fact sheet]. Retrieved from www.cdc.gov/ncbddd/adhd/data.html

Centers for Disease Control and Prevention. (2019). *Physical activity: Why it matters.* [Fact sheet]. Retrieved from https://www.cdc.gov/physicalactivity/about-physical-activity/why-it-matters.html

Centers for Disease Control and Prevention. (2019). *Preventing bullying.* [Fact sheet]. Retrieved from https://www.cdc.gov/violenceprevention/pdf/yv/bullying-factsheet508.pdf

Centers for Disease Control and Prevention. (2020). *Mental health: Household pulse survey.* [Data report]. Retrieved from https://www.cdc.gov/nchs/covid19/pulse/mental-health.htm

Centers for Disease Control and Prevention and The Merck Company Foundation. (2007). *The state of aging and health care in America.* Whitehouse Station, NJ: The Merck Company Foundation. Retrieved from www.cdc.gov/Aging/pdf/saha_2007.pdf

Centers for Disease Control and Prevention. (2008). *Surveillance summaries.* Atlanta, GA: Author.

Centers for Disease Control and Prevention. (2010). *How tobacco smoke causes disease: The biology and behavioral basis for smoking-attributable disease: A report of the surgeon general.* Atlanta, GA: U.S. Department of Health and Human Service, National Center for Chronic Disease Prevention and Health Promotion, Office on Smoking and Health.

Centers for Disease Control and Prevention. (2010). Mortality among teenagers aged 12–19 years: United States, 1999–2006. *NCHS Data Brief.* Retrieved from www.cdc.gov/nchs/data/databriefs/db37.htm

Centers for Disease Control and Prevention. (2013). *The state of aging and health in America 2013.* Atlanta, GA: Centers for Disease Control

and Prevention, U.S. Department of Health and Human Services.

Centers for Disease Control and Prevention. (2014). *State indicator report on physical activity, 2014.* Atlanta, GA: U.S. Department of Health and Human Services. Retrieved from www.cdc.gov/physicalactivity/downloads/pa_state_indicator_report_2014.pdf

Centers for Disease Control and Prevention. (2016). *Reproductive and birth outcomes* [Information sheet]. Retrieved from https://ephtracking.cdc.gov/showRbLBWGrowthRetardationEnv.action

Centers for Disease Control and Prevention. (2016). *Reproductive and health outcomes* [Fact sheet]. Retrieved from https://ephtracking.cdc.gov/showRbLBWGrowthRetardationEnv.action

Centers for Disease Control and Prevention. (2017). *2015 Assisted Reproductive Technology National Summary Report.* Retrieved from www.cdc.gov/art/pdf/2015-report/ART-2015-National-Summary-Report.pdf

Centers for Disease Control and Prevention. (2017). *Elder abuse: Consequences.* Retrieved from www.cdc.gov/violenceprevention/elderabuse/consequences.html

Centers for Disease Control and Prevention. (2017). *Intimate partner violence.* Retrieved from www.cdc.gov/violenceprevention/intimatepartnerviolence/index.html

Centers for Disease Control and Prevention. (2017). *Marriage and divorce* [Data sheet]. Retrieved from www.cdc.gov/nchs/fastats/marriage-divorce.htm

Centers for Disease Control and Prevention. (2017). *National diabetes statistics report: Estimates of diabetes and its burden in the United States, 2017.* Atlanta, GA: US Department of Health and Human Services.

Centers for Disease Control and Prevention. (2017). *Physical activity facts.* Retrieved from www.cdc.gov/healthyschools/physicalactivity/facts.htm

Centers for Disease Control and Prevention. (2017). *Preconception health and health care.* Retrieved from www.cdc.gov/preconception/index.html

Centers for Disease Control and Prevention. (2017). *Social determinants and eliminating disparities in teen pregnancy.* Retrieved from www.cdc.gov/teenpregnancy/about/social-determinants-disparities-teen-pregnancy.htm

Centers for Disease Control and Prevention. (2017). *10 leading causes of death by age group, United States-2015* [data graphic]. Retrieved from www.cdc.gov/injury/images/lc-charts/leading_causes_of_death_age_group_2015_1050w740h.gif

Centers for Disease Control and Prevention. (2018). *Data and statistics on birth defects* [Fact sheet]. Retrieved from www.cdc.gov/ncbddd/birthdefects/data.html

Centers for Disease Control and Prevention. (2018). *Data on selected pregnancy complications in the United States* [Fact sheet]. Retrieved from www.cdc.gov/reproductivehealth/maternalinfanthealth/pregnancy-complications-data.html

Centers for Disease Control and Prevention. (2018). *Facts about Down syndrome* [Fact sheet]. Retrieved from www.cdc.gov/ncbddd/birthdefects/downsyndrome.html

Centers for Disease Control and Prevention. (2018). *Health effects: Smoking and tobacco use* [Information sheets]. Retrieved from www.cdc.gov/tobacco/basic_information/health_effects/index.htm

Centers for Disease Control and Prevention. (2018). *Immunization* [Data tables]. Retrieved from www.cdc.gov/nchs/data/hus/2017/066.pdf.

Centers for Disease Control and Prevention. (2018). *National marriage and divorce rate trends for 2000–2018* [Data tables]. Retrieved from www.cdc.gov/nchs/data/dvs/national-marriage-divorce-rates-00-18.pdf

Centers for Disease Control and Prevention. (2018). Marriage and divorce [Data sheet]. Retrieved from https://www.cdc.gov/nchs/data/dvs/national-marriage-divorce-rates-00-18.pdf

Centers for Disease Control and Prevention. (2018). *Number of infant deaths, percentage of total infant deaths, and infant mortality rate for the 10 leading causes of death in 2017, United States, 2016 and 2017* [Data table]. Retrieved from www.cdc.gov/nchs/data/databriefs/db328_tables-508.pdf#5

Centers for Disease Control and Prevention. (2018). *Physical activity guidelines for Americans, 2nd edition* [Report]. Retrieved from https://health.gov/sites/default/files/2019-09/Physical_Activity_Guidelines_2nd_edition.pdf

Centers for Disease Control and Prevention. (2018). Table C-5a. Age-adjusted percent distributions (with standard errors) of respondent-assessed health status for children under age 18 years by selected characteristics: United States, 2018 [Data table]. *Summary Health Statistics, National Health Interview Survey.* Retrieved from https://ftp.cdc.gov/pub/Health_Statistics/NCHS/NHIS/SHS/2018_SHS_Table_C-5.pdf

Centers for Disease Control and Prevention. (2018). *Youth Risk Behavior Surveillance – United States, 2017* [Data tables]. Retrieved from www.cdc.gov/healthyyouth/data/yrbs/pdf/2017/ss6708.pdf

Centers for Disease Control and Prevention. (2018). *Youth risk behavior surveillance–United States, 2017, Supplementary Tables 222-229: Obesity, overweight, and weight control* [Data tables]. Retrieved from www.cdc.gov/healthyyouth/data/yrbs/2017_tables/obesity_overweight_weight_control.htm#t222_down

Centers for Disease Control and Prevention. (2018). *Youth Risk Behavior Survey–Data Summary & Trends Report: 2007-2017* [Report]. Retrieved from www.cdc.gov/healthyyouth/data/yrbs/pdf/trendsreport.pdf

Centers for Disease Control and Prevention. (2019). *About teen pregnancy* [Fact sheet]. Retrieved from www.cdc.gov/teenpregnancy/about/index.htm

Centers for Disease Control and Prevention. (2019). *Alcohol use and your health* [Fact sheet]. Retrieved from www.cdc.gov/alcohol/fact-sheets/alcohol-use.htm

Centers for Disease Control and Prevention. (2019). *Current cigarette smoking among adults in the United States* [Fact sheet]. Retrieved from www.cdc.gov/tobacco/data_statistics/fact_sheets/adult_data/cig_smoking/index.htm

Centers for Disease Control and Prevention. (2019). *Does osteoporosis run in your family?* [Information sheet]. Retrieved from www.cdc.gov/genomics/disease/osteoporosis.htm?CDC_AA_refVal=https%3A%2F%2Fwww.cdc.gov%2Ffeatures%2Fosteoporosis%2Findex.html

Centers for Disease Control and Prevention. (2019). *Gonorrhea: Antibiotic resistance* [Report]. Retrieved from www.cdc.gov/std/gonorrhea/arg/default.htm

Centers for Disease Control and Prevention. (2019). *HIV and pregnant women, infants, and children* [Fact sheet]. Retrieved from www.cdc.gov/hiv/group/gender/pregnantwomen/index.html

Centers for Disease Control and Prevention. (2019). *HPV vaccination schedule and dosing* [Information sheet]. Retrieved from www.cdc.gov/hpv/hcp/schedules-recommendations.html

Centers for Disease Control and Prevention. (2019). *Human papilloma virus (HPV)* [Report]. Retrieved from www.cdc.gov/std/hpv/stdfact-hpv.htm

Centers for Disease Control and Prevention. (2019). *Infertility FAQs* [Fact sheet]. Retrieved from www.cdc.gov/reproductivehealth/infertility/index.htm

Centers for Disease Control and Prevention. (2019). Leading causes of death: Females, United States [Data tables]. Retrieved from www.cdc.gov/women/lcod/index.htm

Centers for Disease Control and Prevention. (2019). *Leading causes of death: Males, United States* [Data tables]. Retrieved from www.cdc.gov/healthequity/lcod/index.htm

Centers for Disease Control and Prevention. (2019). *Physical activity: Why it matters* [Fact sheet]. Retrieved from www.cdc.gov/physicalactivity/about-physical-activity/why-it-matters.html

Centers for Disease Control and Prevention. (2019). *Pregnancy and toxoplasmosis FAQs* [Information sheet]. Retrieved from www.cdc.gov/parasites/toxoplasmosis/gen_info/pregnant.html

Centers for Disease Control and Prevention. (2019). *Pregnancy mortality surveillance system* [Fact sheet]. Retrieved from www.cdc.gov/reproductivehealth/maternal-mortality/pregnancy-mortality-surveillance-system.htm

Centers for Disease Control and Prevention. (2019). *Provisional number of divorces and annulments and rate: United States, 2000–2018* [Data file]. Retrieved from www.cdc.gov/nchs/data/dvs/national-marriage-divorce-rates-00-18.pdf

Centers for Disease Control and Prevention. (2019). *Quitting smoking* [Fact sheet]. Retrieved from www.cdc.gov/tobacco/data_statistics/fact_sheets/cessation/quitting/index.htm

Centers for Disease Control and Prevention. (2019). *Sexually transmitted disease surveillance 2018* [Report]. Retrieved from www.cdc.gov/std/stats18/adolescents.htm

Centers for Disease Control and Prevention. (2019). *STDs in adolescents and young adults.* [Fact sheet]. Retrieved from www.cdc.gov/std/stats18/adolescents.htm

Centers for Disease Control and Prevention. (2019). *Weight gain during pregnancy* [Fact sheet]. Retrieved from www.cdc.gov/reproductivehealth/maternalinfanthealth/pregnancy-weight-gain.htm

Centers for Disease Control and Prevention. (2019). *STDs in adolescents and young adults* [Report]. Retrieved from www.cdc.gov/std/stats18/adolescents.htm

Centers for Disease Control and Prevention. (2020). *About electronic cigarettes (E-cigarettes)* [Fact sheet]. Retrieved from www.cdc.gov/tobacco/basic_information/e-cigarettes/about-e-cigarettes.html

Centers for Disease Control and Prevention. (2020). *Adult obesity causes and consequences* [Fact sheet]. Retrieved from www.cdc.gov/obesity/adult/causes.html.

Centers for Disease Control and Prevention. (2020). Coronavirus disease 2019 in children: United States, February 12-April 2, 2020. *Morbidity and Mortality Weekly Report.* Retrieved from http://dx.doi.org/10.15585/mmwr.mm6914e

Centers for Disease Control and Prevention. (2020). *Coronavirus disease (COVID-19) and breastfeeding* [Information sheet]. Retrieved from www.cdc.gov/breastfeeding/breastfeeding-special-circumstances/maternal-or-infant-illnesses/covid-19-and-breastfeeding.html

Centers for Disease Control and Prevention (2020). Daily updates of totals by week and state: Provisional death counts for coronavirus 2019 (COVID-19). [Data report]. Retrieved from https://www.cdc.gov/nchs/nvss/vsrr/covid19/

Centers for Disease Control and Prevention. (2020). Elder abuse [Fact sheet]. Retrieved from www.cdc.gov/violenceprevention/elderabuse/index.html

Centers for Disease Control and Prevention. (2020). Estimates of diabetes and its burden in the United States. *National Diabetes Statistics Report.* Atlanta, GA: US Department of Health and Human Services.

Centers for Disease Control and Prevention. (2020). *Excess deaths associated with COVID-19* [Report]. Retrieved from www.cdc.gov/nchs/nvss/vsrr/covid19/excess_deaths.htm

Centers for Disease Control and Prevention. (2020). Measles cases and outbreaks [Data page]. Retrieved from www.cdc.gov/measles/cases-outbreaks.html

Centers for Disease Control and Prevention. (2020). *Physical activity basics* [Fact sheet]. Retrieved from www.cdc.gov/physicalactivity/basics/index.htm

Centers for Disease Control and Prevention. (2020). *Preventing teen dating violence* [Fact sheet]. Retrieved from www.cdc.gov/violenceprevention/intimatepartnerviolence/teendatingviolence/fastfact.html

Centers for Disease Control and Prevention. (2019). *Summary health statistics tables for U.S. children: National Health Interview Survey, 2018, Table C-2a* [Data table]. Retrieved from https://ftp.cdc.gov/pub/Health_Statistics/NCHS/NHIS/SHS/2018_SHS_Table_C-2.pdf

Ceppi, G., & Zini, M. (1998). *Children, spaces, relations: Metaproject for an environment for young children.* Eggio Emilia, Italy: Municipality of Reggio Emilia Inanzia ricerca.

Cerasoli, C. P., Nicklin, J. M., & Ford, M. T. (2014). Intrinsic motivation and extrinsic incentives jointly predict performance: A 40-year meta-analysis. *Psychological Bulletin, 140*(4), 980.

Chafetz, M. D. (1992). *Smart for life.* New York, NY: Penguin Books.

Chaker, Z., George, C., Petrovska, M., Caron, J. B., Lacube, P., Caillé, I., & Holzenberger, M. (2016). Hypothalamic neurogenesis persists in the aging brain and is controlled by energy-sensing IGF-I pathway. *Neurobiology of Aging, 41,* 64–72.

Chamie, J. (2018). *Premarital sex: Increasing worldwide* [Inter Press Service News Agency report]. Retrieved from www.ipsnews.net/2018/04/premarital-sex-increasing-worldwide/

Champagne, F. A., & Mashoodh, R. (2009). Genes in context: Gene-environment interactions and the origins of individual differences in behavior. *Current Directions in Psychological Science, 18*(3), 127–131.

Chan, W. Y., Ou, S. R., & Reynolds, A. J. (2014). Adolescent civic engagement and adult outcomes: An examination among urban racial minorities. *Journal of Youth and Adolescence, 43*(11), 1829–1843.

Chandra, A., Martin, S., Collins, R., Elliott, M., Berry, S., Kanouse, D., & Miu, A. (2008). Does watching sex on television predict teen pregnancy? Findings from a National Longitudinal Survey of Youth. *Pediatrics, 122*(5), 1047–1054.

Chang, E. S., & Greenberger, E. (2012). Parenting satisfaction at midlife among European-and Chinese-American mothers with a college-enrolled child. *Asian American Journal of Psychology, 3*(4), 263.

Chang, H. K. (2018). Influencing factors on mid-life crisis. *Korean Journal of Adult Nursing, 30*(1), 98–105.

Chang, P. J., Wray, L., & Lin, Y. (2014). Social relationships, leisure activity, and health in older adults. *Health Psychology, 33*(6), 516.

Chang, S. H., Stoll, C. R., Song, J., Varela, J. E., Eagon, C. J., & Colditz, G. A. (2014). The effectiveness and risks of bariatric surgery: An updated systematic review and meta-analysis, 2003-2012. *JAMA Surgery, 149*(3), 275–287.

Chang, Y. K., Pan, C. Y., Chen, F. T., Tsai, C. L., & Huang, C. C. (2012). Effect of resistance-exercise training on cognitive function in healthy older adults: A review. *Journal of Aging and Physical Activity, 20*(4), 497–517.

Chao, R. K. (1994). Beyond parental control and authoritarian parenting style: Understanding Chinese parenting through the cultural notion of training. *Child Development, 65,* 1111–1119.

Chao, R. K. (2001). Extending research on the consequences of parenting style for Chinese Americans and European Americans. *Child Development, 72,* 1832–1843.

Chao, S., Roberts, J. S., Marteau, T. M., Silliman, R., Cupples, L. A., & Green, R. C. (2008). Health behavior changes after genetic risk assessment for Alzheimer disease: The REVEAL study. *Alzheimer Disease Association, 22*(1), 94–97.

Chaplin, T. M., & Aldao, A. (2013). Gender differences in emotion expression in children: A meta-analytic review. *Psychological Bulletin, 139*(4), 735.

Chaplin, T. M., Cole, P. M., & Zahn-Waxler, C. (2005). Parental socialization of emotion expression: gender differences and relations to child adjustment. *Emotion, 5*(1), 80.

Charles, S. T., & Carstensen, L. L. (2007). Emotion regulation and aging. In J. J. Gross (Ed.), *Handbook of emotion regulation* (pp. 307–330). New York, NY: Guilford Press.

Charles, S. T., & Piazza, J. R. (2007). Memories of social interactions: Age differences in emotional intensity. *Psychology and Aging, 22*, 300–309.

Charles, S. T., Reynolds, C. A., & Gatz, M. (2001). Age-related differences and change in positive and negative affect over 23 years. *Journal of Personality and Social Psychology, 80*, 136–151.

Charness, M. E., Riley, E. P., & Sowell, E. R. (2016). Drinking during pregnancy and the developing brain: Is any amount safe? *Trends in Cognitive Sciences, 20*(2), 80–82.

Charness, N., & Schultetus, R. S. (1999). Knowledge and expertise. In F. T. Durso (Ed.), *Handbook of applied cognition* (pp. 57–81). Chichester, England: Wiley.

Chartier, M. J., Walker, J. R., & Naimark, B. (2010). Separate and cumulative effects of adverse childhood experiences in predicting adult health and health care utilization. *Child Abuse & Neglect, 34*(6), 454–464.

Chassiakos, Y. L. R., Radesky, J., Christakis, D., Moreno, M. A., & Cross, C. (2016). Children and adolescents and digital media. *Pediatrics, 138*(5), e20162593.

Chatters, L. M., Taylor, R. J., Woodward, A. T., & Nicklett, E. J. (2015). Social support from church and family members and depressive symptoms among older African Americans. *The American Journal of Geriatric Psychiatry, 23*(6), 559–567.

Chaudry, A., & Wimer, C. (2016). Poverty is not just an indicator: The relationship between income, poverty, and child well-being. *Academic Pediatrics, 16*(3), S23–S29.

Chen, B., & Marcus, J. (2012). Students' self-presentation on Facebook: An examination of personality and self-construal factors. *Computers in Human Behavior, 28*(6), 2091–2099.

Chen, C. L., Weiss, N. S., Newcomb, P., Barlow, W., & White, E. (2002). Hormone replacement therapy in relation to breast cancer. *Journal of the American Medical Association, 287*, 734–741.

Chen, H. C., Su, T. P., & Chou, P. (2013). A nine-year follow-up study of sleep patterns and mortality in community-dwelling older adults in Taiwan. *Sleep, 36*(8), 1187–1198.

Chen, H., Chauhan, S. P., Ananth, C. V., Vintzileos, A. M., & Abuhamad, A. Z. (2013). Electronic fetal heart rate monitoring and its relationship to neonatal and infant mortality in the United States. *American Journal of Obstetrics and Gynecology, 204*(6), 491–501.

Chen, J., Krahn, H. J., Galambos, N. L., & Johnson, M. D. (2019). Wanting to be remembered: Intrinsically rewarding work and generativity in early midlife. *Canadian Review of Sociology/Revue canadienne de sociologie, 56*(1), 30–48.

Chen, L. W., Wu, Y., Neelakantan, N., Chong, M. F. F., Pan, A., & van Dam, R. M. (2016). Maternal caffeine intake during pregnancy and risk of pregnancy loss: A categorical and dose–response meta-analysis of prospective studies. *Public Health Nutrition, 19*(7), 1233–1244.

Chen, P. C., & Wang, J. D. (2006). Parental exposure to lead and small for gestational age births. *American Journal of Industrial Medicine, 49*(6), 417–422.

Chen, S., & van Ours, J. C. (2018). Subjective well-being and partnership dynamics: Are same-sex relationships different? *Demography, 55*(6), 2299–2320.

Chen, S., Yang, Y., Yimin, Q. V., Zou, Y., Huijuan, Z. H. U., Gong, F., . . . & Liu, C. (2018). Paternal exposure to medical-related radiation associated with low birthweight infants: A large population-based, retrospective cohort study in rural China. *Medicine, 97*(2).

Chen, X. (2010). Socioemotional development in Chinese children. In M. H. Bond (Ed.), *Handbook of Chinese psychology* (pp. 37–52). Oxford, England: Oxford University Press.

Chen, X. (2012). Culture, peer interaction, and socioemotional development. *Child Development Perspectives, 6*(1), 27–34.

Chen, X., Fu, R., & Zhao, S. (2014). *Culture and socialization*. In J. E. Grusec & P. D. Hastings (Eds.), *Handbook of socialization* (pp. 451–472). New York, NY: Guilford Press.

Chen, Y., & Feeley, T. H. (2014). Social support, social strain, loneliness, and well-being among older adults: An analysis of the Health and Retirement Study. *Journal of Social and Personal Relationships, 31*(2), 141–161.

Cheng, C., & Li, A. Y. L. (2014). Internet addiction prevalence and quality of (real) life: A meta-analysis of 31 nations across seven world regions. *Cyberpsychology, Behavior, and Social Networking, 17*(12), 755–760.

Cheng, M., & Berman, S. L. (2012). Globalization and identity development: A Chinese perspective. *New Directions for Child and Adolescent Development, 2012*(138), 103–121.

Cheng, S., & Heller, K. (2009). *Global aging: Challenges for community psychology*. Retrieved from dx.doi.org: doi:http://dx.doi.org/10.1007/s10464-009-9244-x

Cheng, T. C., Powdthavee, N., & Oswald, A. J. (2017). Longitudinal evidence for a midlife nadir in human well-being: Results from four data sets. *The Economic Journal, 127*(599), 126–142.

Cheng, T. L., & Goodman, E. (2015). Race, ethnicity, and socioeconomic status in research on child health. *Pediatrics, 135*(1), e225–e237.

Cheng, Y. W., Shaffer, B. L., Nicholson, J. M., & Caughey, A. B. (2014). Second stage of labor and epidural use: A larger effect than previously suggested. *Obstetrics & Gynecology, 123*(3), 527–535.

Cherlin, A. J. (2010). Demographic trends in the United States: A review of research in the 2000s. *Journal of Marriage and Family, 72*(3), 403–419.

Cherry, K. E., & Park, D. C. (1993). Individual differences and contextual variables influence spatial memory in younger and older adults. *Psychology and Aging, 8*, 517–526.

Cherry, K. E., Walker, E. J., Brown, J. S., Volaufova, J., LaMotte, L. R., Welsh, D. A., . . . Frisard, M. I. (2013). Social engagement and health in younger, older, and oldest-old adults in the Louisiana healthy aging study. *Journal of Applied Gerontology, 32*(1), 51–75.

Cheryan, S., Ziegler, S. A., Montoya, A. K., & Jiang, L. (2017). Why are some STEM fields more gender balanced than others? *Psychological Bulletin, 143*(1), 1.

Chesney, E., Goodwin, G. M., & Fazel, S. (2014). Risks of all-cause and suicide mortality in mental disorders: A meta-review. *World Psychiatry, 13*(2), 153–160.

Cheung, F., & Lucas, R. E. (2015). When does money matter most? Examining the association between income and life satisfaction over the life course. *Psychology and Aging, 30*(1), 120.

Chibwesha, C. J., & Stringer, J. S. (2019). Cervical cancer as a global concern: Contributions of the dual epidemics of HPV and HIV. *JAMA, 322*(16), 1558–1560.

Chida, Y., & Steptoe, A. (2008). Positive psychological well-being and mortality: A quantitative review of prospective observational studies. *Psychosomatic Medicine, 70*(7), 741–756.

Child Trends Databank. (2019). *Late or no prenatal care* [Fact sheet]. Retrieved from www.childtrends.org/indicators/late-or-no-prenatal-care

Child Trends DataBank. (2010). *Children in poverty*. Retrieved from www.childtrendsdatabank.org/?q=node/221

Child Trends DataBank. (2010). *Physical fighting by youth*. Retrieved from www.childtrendsdatabank.org/?q=node/136

Child Trends DataBank. (2012). *Number and percentage distribution of all children and adopted children, ages 0-17, by selected characteristics, United States, 2007* [Data file]. Retrieved from www.childtrends.org/wp-content/uploads/2012/08/113_appendix1.pdf

Child Trends DataBank. (2015). *Teen homicide, suicide and firearm deaths*. Retrieved from www.childtrends.org/wp-content/uploads/2015/12/70_Homicide_Suicide_Firearms.pdf

Child Trends DataBank. (2019). *Youth employment*. Retrieved from www.childtrends.org/indicators/youth-employment

Child Welfare Information Gateway. (2013). *Long-term consequences of child abuse and neglect*. Washington, DC: U.S. Department of Health and Human Services, Children's Bureau.

Child Welfare Information Gateway. (2016). *Trends in U.S. adoptions: 2008-2012* [Report]. Retrieved from www.childwelfare.gov/pubPDFs/adopted0812.pdf#page=1&view=Highlights

Child Welfare Information Gateway. (2019). *Child abuse and neglect fatalities 2017: Statistics and interventions*. Washington, DC: U.S. Department of Health and Human Services, Children's Bureau.

Child Welfare Information Gateway. (2019). *Long-term consequences of child abuse and neglect*. Washington, DC: U.S. Department of Health and Human Services, Administration for Children and Families, Children's Bureau

Children's Bureau. (2018). *Adoption data 2014* [Data tables]. U.S. Department of Health and Human Services. Retrieved from https://www.acf.hhs.gov/cb/resource/adoption-data-2014

Children's Defense Fund. (2019). *Child poverty.* Retrieved from www.childrensdefense.org/policy/policy-priorities/child-poverty/

Chilton, W., O'Brien, B., & Charchar, F. (2017). Telomeres, aging and exercise: Guilty by association? *International Journal of Molecular Sciences, 18*(12), 2573.

Chin, H. B., Sipe, T. A., Elder, R., Mercer, S. L., Chattopadhyay, S. K., Jacob, V., . . . & Chuke, S. O. (2012). The effectiveness of group-based comprehensive risk-reduction and abstinence education interventions to prevent or reduce the risk of adolescent pregnancy, human immunodeficiency virus, and sexually transmitted infections: Two systematic reviews for the Guide to Community Preventive Services. *American Journal of Preventive Medicine, 42*(3), 272–294.

Chingos, M. M. (2012). The impact of a universal class- size reduction policy: Evidence from Florida's statewide mandate. *Economics of Education Review, 31*(5), 543–562.

Chiriboga, C. A., Brust, J. C. M., Bateman, D., & Hauser, W. A. (1999). Dose-response effect of fetal cocaine exposure on newborn neurologic function. *Pediatrics, 103,* 79–85.

Chisholm, J. S. (2017). *Navajo infancy: An ethological study of child development.* Abingdon, England: Routledge.

Chitayat, D., Matsui, D., Amitai, Y., Kennedy, D., Vohra, S., Rieder, M., & Koren, G. (2016). Folic acid supplementation for pregnant women and those planning pregnancy: 2015 update. *The Journal of Clinical Pharmacology, 56*(2), 170–175.

Cho, H., Glewwe, P., & Whitler, M. (2012). Do reductions in class size raise students' test scores? Evidence from population variation in Minnesota's elementary schools. *Economics of Education Review, 31*(3), 77–95.

Cho, J., Martin, P., & Poon, L.W. (2015). Successful aging and subjective well-being among oldest-old adults. *The Gerontologist, 55,* 132–143.

Cho, J., Martin, P., Poon, L. W., & Georgia Centenarian Study. (2014). Successful aging and subjective well-being among oldest-old adults. *The Gerontologist, 55*(1), 132–143.

Choi, H., Schoeni, R. F., Wiemers, E. E., Hotz, V. J., & Seltzer, J. A. (2020). Spatial distance between parents and adult children in the United States. *Journal of Marriage and Family, 82*(2), 822–840.

Choi, K. S., Stewart, R., & Dewey, M. (2013). Participation in productive activities and depression among older Europeans: Survey of Health, Ageing and Retirement in Europe (SHARE). *International Journal of Geriatric Psychiatry, 28*(11), 1157–1165.

Choi, M., Kong, S., & Jung, D. (2012). Computer and internet interventions for loneliness and depression in older adults: A meta-analysis. *Healthcare Informatics Research, 18*(3), 191–198.

Chomsky, C. S. (1969). *The acquisition of syntax in children from five to ten.* Cambridge, MA: MIT Press.

Chomsky, N. (1957). *Syntactic structures.* The Hague, Netherlands: Mouton.

Chomsky, N. (1972). *Language and mind* (2nd ed.). New York, NY: Harcourt Brace Jovanovich.

Chomsky, N. (1995). *The minimalist program.* Cambridge, MA: MIT Press.

Chonchaiya, W., Tardif, T., Mai, X., Xu, L., Li, M., Kaciroti, N., . . . Lozoff, B. (2013). Developmental trends in auditory processing can provide early predictions of language acquisition in young infants. *Developmental Science, 16*(2), 159–172.

Chopik, W. J. (2017). Associations among relational values, support, health, and well-being across the adult lifespan. *Personal Relationships, 24*(2), 408–422.

Chopik, W. J., & Kitayama, S. (2018). Personality change across the life span: Insights from a cross-cultural, longitudinal study. *Journal of Personality, 86*(3), 508–521.

Chopik, W. J., O'Brien, E., & Konrath, S. H. (2017). Differences in empathic concern and perspective taking across 63 countries. *Journal of Cross-Cultural Psychology, 48*(1), 23–38.

Chopra, S., Shaw, M., Shaw, T., Sachdev, P. S., Anstey, K. J., & Cherbuin, N. (2018). More highly myelinated white matter tracts are associated with faster processing speed in healthy adults. Neuroimage, 171, 332–340.

Choquet, H., & Meyre, D. (2011). Genetics of obesity: What have we learned? *Current Genomics, 12*(3), 169–179.

Chou, R. J. A., & Choi, N. G. (2011). Prevalence and correlates of perceived workplace discrimination among older workers in the United States of America. *Ageing & Society, 31*(6), 1051–1070.

Chow, C. M., Ruhl, H., & Buhrmester, D. (2013). The mediating role of interpersonal competence between adolescents' empathy and friendship quality: A dyadic approach. *Journal of Adolescence, 36*(1), 191–200.

Chow, S. M., Henderson, S. E., & Barnett, A. L. (2001). The Movement Assessment Battery for Children: A comparison of 4-year-old to 6-year-old children from Hong Kong and the United States. *American Journal of Occupational Therapy, 55*(1), 55–61.

Christakis, N. A., & Allison, P. D. (2006). Mortality after the hospitalization of a spouse. *New England Journal of Medicine, 354,* 719–730.

Christian Home Educators Association of California. (2013). *Considering homeschooling?* Norwalk, CA: Christian Home Educators Association of California. Retrieved from www.cheaofca.org/index.cfm?fuseaction=Page.viewPage&pageId=1033

Christie, J. F. (1998). Play as a medium for literacy development. In D. P. Fromberg & D. Bergen (Eds.), *Play from birth to 12 and beyond: Contexts, perspectives, and meanings* (pp. 50–55). New York, NY: Garland.

Chryssochoou, X., & Lyons, E. (2011). Perceptions of (in) compatibility between identities and participation in the national polity of people belonging to ethnic minorities. *Identity and Participation in Culturally Diverse Societies,* 69–88.

Chung, A., Backholer, K., Wong, E., Palermo, C., Keating, C., & Peeters, A. (2016). Trends in child and adolescent obesity prevalence in economically advanced countries according to socioeconomic position: A systematic review. *Obesity Reviews, 17*(3), 276–295.

Chung, H. L., & Steinberg, L. (2006). Relations between neighborhood factors, parenting behaviors, peer deviance, and delinquency among serious juvenile offenders. *Developmental Psychology, 42,* 319–331.

Chung, T. W., Sum, S. M., & Chan, M. W. (2019). Adolescent internet addiction in Hong Kong: prevalence, psychosocial correlates, and prevention. *Journal of Adolescent Health, 64*(6), S34–S43.

Cicchetti, D., & Toth, S. L. (1998). The development of depression in children and adolescents. *American Psychologist, 53,* 221–241.

Cicchino, J. B., & Rakison, D. H. (2008). Producing and processing self-propelled motion in infancy. *Developmental Psychology, 44,* 1232–1241.

Cicchino, J. B., Aslin, R. N., & Rakison, D. H. (2011). Correspondences between what infants see and know about causal and self-propelled motion. *Cognition, 118*(2), 171–192.

Cicirelli, V. (2013). *Sibling relationships across the life span.* New York, NY: Springer Science & Business Media.

Cicirelli, V. G. (1989). Feelings of attachment to siblings and well-being in later life. *Psychology and Aging, 4*(2), 211–216.

Cicirelli, V. G. (1994). Sibling relationships in cross-cultural perspective. *Journal of Marriage and Family, 56,* 7–20.

Cicirelli, V. G. (1995). *Sibling relationships across the life span.* New York, NY: Plenum Press.

Cicirelli, V. G. (2006). Fear of death in mid-old age. *The Journals of Gerontology Series B: Psychological Sciences and Social Sciences, 61*(2), P75–P81.

Cicirelli, V. G. (2009). Sibling death and death fear in relation to depressive symptomatology in older adults. *Journals of Gerontology Series B: Psychological Sciences and Social Sciences, 64*(1), 24–32.

Cicirelli, V. G. (Ed.). (2002). *Older adults' views on death.* New York, NY: Springer.

Cillessen, A. H. N., & Mayeux, L. (2004). From censure to reinforcement: Developmental changes in the association between aggression and social status. *Child Development, 75,* 147–163.

Cillessen, A. H., & Rose, A. J. (2005). Understanding popularity in the peer system. *Current Directions in Psychological Science, 14*(2), 102–105.

Ciorba, A., Bianchini, C., Pelucchi, S., & Pastore, A. (2012). The impact of hearing loss on the quality of life of elderly adults. *Clinical Interventions in Aging, 7,* 159.

Civis Analytics. (2020). *COVID-19 impact research* [Report]. Retrieved from www.civisanalytics.com/blog/covid-19-impact-on-the-american-population/

Clark, M. A., Gleason, P. M., Tuttle, C. C., & Silverberg, M. K. (2015). Do charter schools improve student achievement? *Educational Evaluation and Policy Analysis, 37*(4), 419–436.

Clark, S., & Brauner-Otto, S. (2015). Divorce in sub-Saharan Africa: Are unions becoming less stable? *Population and Development Review, 41*(4), 583–605.

Clauss, J. A., & Blackford, J. U. (2012). Behavioral inhibition and risk for developing social anxiety disorder: A meta-analytic study. *Journal of the American Academy of Child & Adolescent Psychiatry, 51*(10), 1066–1075.

Clauss, J. A., Avery, S. N., & Blackford, J. U. (2015). The nature of individual differences in inhibited temperament and risk for psychiatric disease: A review and meta-analysis. *Progress in Neurobiology, 127*, 23–45.

Cleary, P. D., Zaborski, L. B., & Ayanian, J. Z. (2004). Sex differences in health over the course of midlife. In O. G. Brim, C. E. Ryff, & R. C. Kessler (Eds.), *How healthy are we? A national study of well-being at midlife.* Chicago, IL: University of Chicago Press.

Cleveland, H. H., & Wiebe, R. P. (2003). The moderation of adolescent-to-peer similarity in tobacco and alcohol use by school level of substance use. *Child Development, 74*, 279–291.

Cleverley, K., Szatmari, P., Vaillancourt, T., Boyle, M., & Lipman, E. (2012). Developmental trajectories of physical and indirect aggression from late childhood to adolescence: Sex differences and outcomes in emerging adulthood. *Journal of the American Academy of Child & Adolescent Psychiatry, 51*(10), 1037–1051.

Climo, A. H., & Stewart, A. J. (2003). Eldercare and personality development in middle age. In J. Demick & C. Andreoletti (Eds.), *Handbook of adult development.* New York, NY: Plenum Press.

Clinkenbeard, P. R. (2012). Motivation and gifted students: Implications of theory and research. *Psychology in the Schools, 49*(7), 622–630.

Closa-Monasterolo, R., Gispert-Llaurado, M., Canals, J., Luque, V., Zaragoza-Jordana, M., Koletzko, B., Grote, V., Weber, M., Gruszfeld, D., Scott, K., Verduci, E., ReDionigi, A., Hoyos, J., Brasselle, G., & Escribano Subias, J. (2017). The effect of postpartum depression and current mental health problems of the mother on child behavior at eight years. *Maternal and Child Health Journal, 21*, 1563–1572.

Coan, J. A., & Allen, J. J. B. (2004). The state and trait of frontal EEG activation asymmetries over the frontal cortex. In R. J. Davidson & K. Hugdahl (Eds.), *The asymmetrical brain* (pp. 565–616). Cambridge, MA: The MIT Press.

Cobb-Clark, D. A., & Schurer, S. (2012). The stability of big-five personality traits. *Economics Letters, 115*(1), 11–15.

Coelho, L., Torres, N., Fernandes, C., & Santos, A. J. (2017). Quality of play, social acceptance and reciprocal friendship in preschool children. *European Early Childhood Education Research Journal, 25*(6), 812–823.

Cohen, L. B., & Amsel, L. B. (1998). Precursors to infants' perception of the causality of a simple event. *Infant Behavior and Development, 21*, 713–732.

Cohen, L. B., & Marks, K. S. (2002). How infants process addition and subtraction events. *Developmental Science, 5*, 186–201.

Cohen, L. B., Chaput, H. H., & Cashon, C. H. (2002). A constructivist model of infant cognition. *Cognitive Development, 17*, 1323–1343.

Cohen, O., & Finzi-Dottan, R. (2012). Reasons for divorce and mental health following the

breakup. *Journal of Divorce & Remarriage, 53*(8), 581–601.

Cohen, P. (2012). *In our prime: The invention of middle age.* New York, NY: Simon and Schuster.

Cohen, R., Bavishi, C., & Rozanski, A. (2016). Purpose in life and its relationship to all-cause mortality and cardiovascular events: A meta-analysis. *Psychosomatic Medicine, 78*(2), 122–133.

Cohen, S. (2004). Social relationships and health. *American Psychologist, 59*, 676–684.

Cohen, S. A., Sabik, N. J., Cook, S. K., Azzoli, A. B., & Mendez-Luck, C. A. (2019). Differences within differences: Gender inequalities in caregiving intensity vary by race and ethnicity in informal caregivers. *Journal of Cross-Cultural Gerontology, 34*(3), 245–263.

Cohen, S. T., & Bocos, M. (2016). Relationships between perceived adult parental role, intergenerational ambivalence, and personal well-being among midlife parents. *European Proceedings of Social and Behavioral Sciences*, 601–606.

Cohen, S., & Pressman, S. D. (2006). Positive affect and health. *Current Directions in Psychological Science, 15*(3), 122–125.

Cohen, S., Doyle, W. J., Turner, R. B., Alper, C. M., & Skoner, D. P. (2003). Emotional style and susceptibility to the common cold. *Psychosomatic Medicine, 65*, 652–657.

Cohen, S., Janicki-Deverts, D., Doyle, W. J., Miller, G. E., Frank, E., Rabin, B. S., & Turner, R. B. (2012). Chronic stress, glucocorticoid receptor resistance, inflammation, and disease risk. *Proceedings of the National Academy of Sciences, 109*(16), 5995–5999.

Cohen, S., Janicki-Deverts, D., Turner, R. B., & Doyle, W. J. (2015). Does hugging provide stress-buffering social support? A study of susceptibility to upper respiratory infection and illness. *Psychological Science, 26*(2), 135–147.

Cohen-Mansfield, J., Hazan, H., Lerman, Y., & Shalom, V. (2016). Correlates and predictors of loneliness in older-adults: A review of quantitative results informed by qualitative insights. *International Psychogeriatrics, 28*(4), 557–576.

Cohn, D. (2018). *Research from 2018 demographers' conference: Migration, self-identity, marriage, and other key findings* [Pew Research Center press release]. Retrieved from www.pewresearch.org/fact-tank/2018/05/24/research-from-2018-demographers-conference-migration-self-identity-marriage-and-other-key-findings/.

Cohn, D., & Fry, R. (2010). *Women, men and the new economics of marriage.* Retrieved from http://pewsocialtrends.org/2010/01/19/women-men-and-the-new-economics-of-marriage/

Cohn, D., & Passel, J. S. (2018). *A record 64 million Americans live in multigenerational households* [Pew Research Center report]. Retrieved from www.pewresearch.org/fact-tank/2018/04/05/a-record-64-million-americans-live-in-multigenerational-households/

Cohn, D., Passel, J. S., Wang, W., & Livingston, G. (2011). *Barely half of U.S adults are married— a record low.* Retrieved from www.pewsocialtrends.org/2011/12/14/barely-half-of-u-s-adults-are-married-a-record-low/

Coie, J. D., & Dodge, K. A. (1998). Aggression and antisocial behavior. In W. Damon (Series Ed.) & N. Eisenberg (Vol. Ed.), *Handbook of child psychology: Vol. 3. Social, emotional, and personality development* (5th ed., pp. 780–862). New York, NY: Wiley.

Coifman, K. G., Flynn, J. J., & Pinto, L. A. (2016). When context matters: Negative emotions predict psychological health and adjustment. *Motivation and Emotion, 40*(4), 602–624.

Col, N. F., Guthrie, J. R., Politi, M., & Dennerstein, L. (2009). Duration of vasomotor symptoms in middle-aged women: A longitudinal study. *Menopause, 16*(3), 453–457.

Colberg, S. R., Sigal, R. J., Yardley, J. E., Riddell, M. C., Dunstan, D. W., Dempsey, P. C., . . . Tate, D. F. (2016). Physical activity/exercise and diabetes: A position statement of the American Diabetes Association. *Diabetes Care, 39*(11), 2065–2079.

Colby, A., Kohlberg, L., Gibbs, J., & Lieberman, M. (1983). A longitudinal study of moral development. *Monographs of the Society for Research in Child Development, 48*(1–2, Serial No. 200).

Colby, S. L., & Ortman, J. M. (2015). Projections of the size and composition of the US population: 2014 to 2060. Population Estimates and Projections. *Current Population Reports. P25-1143.* Washington, DC: U.S. Census Bureau.

Cole, M. (1998). *Cultural psychology: A once and future discipline.* Cambridge, MA: Belknap.

Cole, P. M., Barrett, K. C., & Zahn-Waxler, C. (1992). Emotion displays in two-year-olds during mishaps. *Child Development, 63*, 314–324.

Cole, P. M., Bruschi, C. J., & Tamang, B. L. (2002). Cultural differences in children's emotional reactions to difficult situations. *Child Development, 73*(3), 983–996.

Cole, P. M., Tamang, B. L., & Shrestha, S. (2006). Cultural variations in the socialization of young children's anger and shame. *Child Development, 77*(5), 1237–1251.

Cole, W. G., Lingeman, J. M., & Adolph, K. E. (2012). Go naked: Diapers affect infant walking. *Developmental Science, 15*(6), 783–790.

Coles, L. S. (2004). Demography of human supercentenarians. *Journal of Gerontology: Biological Sciences, 59A*, 579–586.

Coley, R. L., Morris, J. E., & Hernandez, D. (2004). Out-of-school care and problem behavior trajectories among low-income adolescents: Individual, family, and neighborhood characteristics as added risks. *Child Development, 75*, 948–965.

Coley, R. L., Votruba-Drzal, E., & Schindler, H. S. (2009). Fathers' and mothers' parenting predicting and responding to adolescent sexual risk behaviors. *Child Development, 80*(3), 808–827.

Colle, L., & Del Giudice, M. (2011). Patterns of attachment and emotional competence in middle childhood. *Social Development, 20*(1), 51–72.

Collins, R. L. (2011). Content analysis of gender roles in media: Where are we now and where should we go? *Sex Roles, 64*(3–4), 290–298.

Collins, W. A., & van Dulmen, M. (2006). Friendships and romance in emerging adulthood: Assessing the distinctiveness in close relationships. In J. J. Arnett & J. L. Tanner (Eds.), *Emerging adults in America: Coming of age in the*

21st century (pp. 219–234). Washington DC: American Psychological Association.

Colman, A. M. (2016). Race differences in IQ: Hans Eysenck's contribution to the debate in the light of subsequent research. *Personality and Individual Differences, 103*, 182–189.

Colman, R. J., Anderson, R. M., Johnson, S. C., Kastman, E. K., Kosmatka, K. J., Beasley, T. M., . . . Weindruch, R. (2009). Caloric restriction delays disease onset and mortality in rhesus monkeys. *Science, 325*(5937), 201–204.

Colman, R. J., Beasley, T. M., Kemnitz, J. W., Johnson, S. C., Weindruch, R., & Anderson, R. M. (2014). Caloric restriction reduces age-related and all-cause mortality in rhesus monkeys. *Nature Communications, 5*, 3557.

Colombo, J. (2002). Infant attention grows up: The emergence of a developmental cognitive neuroscience perspective. *Current Directions in Psychological Science, 11*, 196–200.

Colombo, J., Kannass, K. N., Shaddy, J., Kundurthi, S., Maikranz, J. M., Anderson, C. J., . . . Carlson, S. E. (2004). Maternal DHA and the development of attention in infancy and toddlerhood. *Child Development, 75*, 1254–1267.

Colombo, J., Shaddy, D. J., Anderson, C. J., Gibson, L. J., Blaga, O. M., & Kannass, K. N. (2010). What habituates in infant visual habituation? A psychophysiological analysis. *Infancy, 15*(2), 107–124.

Colonnesi, C., Stams, G. J. J., Koster, I., & Noom, M. J. (2010). The relation between pointing and language development: A meta-analysis. *Developmental Review, 30*(4), 352–366.

Comer, J.S., Bry, L.J., Poznanski, B., & Golik, A.M. (2016). Children's mental health in the context of terrorist attacks, ongoing threats, and possibilities of future terrorism. *Current Psychiatry Reports*, 18. https://doi.org/10.1007/s11920-016-0722-1

Committee on Obstetric Practice. (2002). ACOG committee opinion: Exercise during pregnancy and the postpartum period. *International Journal of Gynecology & Obstetrics, 77*(1), 79–81.

Common Sense Media. (2013). *Zero to eight: Children's media use in America* 2013. [Report]. Retrieved from www.commonsensemedia.org/research/zero-to-eight-childrens-media-use-in-america-2013

Community Paediatrics Committee, Canadian Paediatrics Society. (2005). Management of primary nocturnal enuresis. *Paediatrics and Child Health, 10*, 611–614.

Compton, J., & Pollak, R. A. (2014). Family proximity, childcare, and women's labor force attachment. *Journal of Urban Economics, 79*, 72–90.

Conference Board. (1999, June 25). *Workplace education programs are benefiting U.S. corporations and workers* [Press release]. Retrieved from www.newswise.com/articles/1999/6/WEP.TCB.html

Conger, K. J., & Little, W. M. (2010). Sibling relationships during the transition to adulthood. *Child Development Perspectives, 4*(2), 87–94.

Connellan, J., Baron-Cohen, S., Wheelwright, S., Batki, A., & Ahluwalia, J. (2000). Sex differences in human neonatal social perception. *Infant Behavior and Development, 23*(1), 113–118.

Connidis, I. A., & Davies, L. (1992). Confidants and companions: Choices in later life. *Journal of Gerontology: Social Sciences, 47*(30), S115–S122.

Connolly, M. D., Zervos, M. J., Barone II, C. J., Johnson, C. C., & Joseph, C. L. (2016). The mental health of transgender youth: Advances in understanding. *Journal of Adolescent Health, 59*(5), 489–495.

Connor, P. (2012). Balm for the soul: Immigrant religion and emotional well-being. *International Migration, 50*(2), 130–157.

Conradt, E., & Ablow, J. (2010). Infant physiological response to the still-face paradigm: Contributions of maternal sensitivity and infants' early regulatory behavior. *Infant Behavior and Development, 33*(3), 251–265.

Constant, C., Sampaio, I., Negreiro, F., Aguiar, P., Silva, A. M., Salgueiro, M., & Bandeira, T. (2011). Environmental tobacco smoke (ETS) exposure and respiratory morbidity in school age children. *Revista Portuguesa de Pneumologia (English Edition), 17*(1), 20–26.

Conteh, J. A. (2016). Dowry and bride-price. In N. Naples, R. C. Hoogland, M. Wickramasinghe & W. C. A. Wong (Eds.), *The Wiley Blackwell encyclopedia of gender and sexuality studies.* New York, NY: Wiley.

Conway, J. K. (1974). Perspectives on the history of women's education in the United States. *History of Education Quarterly, 14*(1), 1–12.

Cook, C. R., Williams, K. R., Guerra, N. G., Kim, T. E., & Sadek, S. (2010). Predictors of bullying and victimization in childhood and adolescence: A meta-analytic investigation. *School Psychology Quarterly, 25*(2), 65.

Cook, J. A., & Rabon, J. S. (2018). Maternal investments and child cognitive achievement. *Economics Bulletin, 38*(3), 1632–1654.

Cook, S. K., & Cohen, S. A. (2018). Sociodemographic disparities in adult child informal caregiving intensity in the United States: Results from the new National Study of caregiving. *Journal of gerontological Nursing, 44*(9), 15–20.

Cook-Gumperz, J., & Szymanski, M. (2001). Classroom "families": Cooperating or competing-Girls' and boys' interactional styles in a bilingual classroom. *Research on Language and Social Interaction, 34*(1), 107–130.

Cooksey-Stowers, K., Schwartz, M., & Brownell, K. (2017). Food swamps predict obesity rates better than food deserts in the United States. *International Journal of Environmental Research and Public Health, 14*(11), 1366.

Cooper, R. P., & Aslin, R. N. (1990). Preference for infant-directed speech in the first month after birth. *Child Development, 61*, 1584–1595.

Cooper, W. O., Hernandez-Diaz, S., Arbogast, P. G., Dudley, J. A., Dyer, S., Gideon, P. S., Hall, K., & Ray, W. A. (2006). Major congenital formations after first-trimester exposure to ACE inhibitors. *New England Journal of Medicine, 354*, 2443–2451.

Copeland, J. L., Good, J., & Dogra, S. (2019). Strength training is associated with better functional fitness and perceived healthy aging among physically active older adults: a cross-sectional analysis of the Canadian Longitudinal Study on Aging. *Aging Clinical and Experimental Research, 31*(9), 1257–1263.

Copeland, W., Shanahan, L., Miller, S., Costello, E. J., Angold, A., & Maughan, B. (2010). Outcomes of early pubertal timing in young women: A prospective population-based study. *American Journal of Psychiatry, 167*(10), 1218–1225.

Copen, C. E., Chandra, A., & Febo-Vazquez, I. (2016). Sexual behavior, sexual attraction, and sexual orientation among adults aged 18–44 in the United States: Data from the 2011–2013 National Survey of Family Growth. *National Health Statistics Reports*, 88, 1–14.

Copen, C. E., Chandra, A., & Martinez, G. (2012). *Prevalence and timing of oral sex with opposite-sex partners among females and males aged 15–24 years: United States, 2007–2010.* Washington, DC: U.S. Department of Health and Human Services, Centers for Disease Control and Prevention, National Center for Health Statistics.

Coplan, R. J., Ooi, L. L., & Nocita, G. (2015). When one is company and two is a crowd: Why some children prefer solitude. *Child Development Perspectives, 9*(3), 133–137.

Coplan, R. J., Ooi, L. L., Rose-Krasnor, L., & Nocita, G. (2014). 'I want to play alone': Assessment and correlates of self-reported preference for solitary play in young children. *Infant and Child Development, 23*(3), 229–238.

Coplan, R. J., Prakash, K., O'Neil, K., & Armer, M. (2004). Do you "want" to play? Distinguishing between conflicted-shyness and social disinterest in early childhood. *Developmental Psychology, 40*, 244–258.

Corbelli, J., Borrero, S., Bonnema, R., McNamara, M., Kraemer, K., Rubio, D., . . . McNeil, M. (2014). Physician adherence to U.S. Preventive Services Task Force mammography guidelines. *Women's Health Issues, 24*(3), e313–e319.

Corbetta, D., Thurman, S. L., Wiener, R. F., Guan, Y., & Williams, J. L. (2014). Mapping the feel of the arm with the sight of the object: On the embodied origins of infant reaching. *Frontiers in Psychology, 5*, 576.

Coren, S. (2012). *The left-hander syndrome: The causes and consequences of left-handedness.* New York, NY: Simon and Schuster.

Corno, L., & Voena, A. (2016). *Selling daughters: Age of marriage, income shocks and the bride price tradition* (No. W16/08). IFS Working Papers.

Cornwell, B. (2014). Social disadvantage and network turnover. *Journals of Gerontology Series B: Psychological Sciences and Social Sciences, 70*(1), 132–142.

Cornwell, B., Laumann, E. O., & Schumm, L. P. (2008). The social connectedness of older adults: A national profile. *American Sociological Review, 73*, 185–203.

Corona, G., Isidori, A. M., Buvat, J., Aversa, A., Rastrelli, G., Hackett, G., . . . Maggi, M. (2014). Testosterone supplementation and sexual function: A meta-analysis study. *The Journal of Sexual Medicine, 11*(6), 1577–1592.

Corona, G., Rastrelli, G., Morgentaler, A., Sforza, A., Mannucci, E., & Maggi, M. (2017). Meta-analysis of results of testosterone therapy on sexual function based on international index of erectile function scores. *European Urology.* http://dx.doi.org/10.1016/j.eururo.2017.03.032

Corriveau, K. H., Chen, E. E., & Harris, P. L. (2015). Judgments about fact and fiction by children from religious and nonreligious backgrounds. *Cognitive Science, 39*(2), 353–382.

Cortese, S., Kelly, C., Chabernaud, C., Proal, E., Di Martino, A., Milham, M. P., & Castellanos, F. X. (2012). Toward systems neuroscience of ADHD: A meta-analysis of 55 fMRI studies. *American Journal of Psychiatry, 169*(10), 1038–1055.

Cosgrove, K. P., Mazure, C. M., & Staley, J. K. (2007). Evolving knowledge of sex differences in brain structure, function, and chemistry. *Biological Psychiatry, 62*(8), 847–855.

Cosman, F., De Beur, S. J., LeBoff, M. S., Lewiecki, E. M., Tanner, B., Randall, S., & Lindsay, R. (2014). Clinician's guide to prevention and treatment of osteoporosis. *Osteoporosis International, 25*(10), 2359–2381.

Costa, P. T., Jr., & McCrae, R. R. (1980). Still stable after all these years: Personality as a key to some issues in adulthood and old age. In P. B. Baltes Jr. & O. G. Brim (Eds.), *Lifespan development and behavior* (Vol. 3, pp. 65–102). New York, NY: Academic Press.

Costa, P. T., Jr., & McCrae, R. R. (2006). Age changes in personality and their origins: Comments on Roberts, Walton, and Viechtbauer (2006). *Psychological Bulletin, 1,* 26–28.

Costa, P. T., Jr., & McCrae, R. R. (2013). *Personality in adulthood: A five-factor theory perspective.* Abingdon-on-Thames, England: Routledge.

Costanzo, P. R., & Hoy, M. B. (2007). Intergenerational relations: Themes, prospects, and possibilities. *Journal of Social Issues, 63*(4), 885–902.

Costello, E. J., Compton, S. N., Keeler, G., & Angold, A. (2003). Relationship between poverty and psychopathology: A natural experiment. *Journal of the American Medical Association, 290,* 2023–2029.

Cote, L. R., & Bornstein, M. H. (2009). Child and mother play in three U.S. cultural groups: Comparisons and associations. *Journal of Family Psychology, 23*(3), 355–363.

Cotrena, C., Branco, L. D., Cardoso, C. O., Wong, C. E. I., & Fonseca, R. P. (2016). The predictive impact of biological and sociocultural factors on executive processing: The role of age, education, and frequency of reading and writing habits. *Applied Neuropsychology: Adult, 23*(2), 75–84

Council on Foreign Relations. (2019). *Same-sex marriage: Global comparison* [News brief]. Retrieved from www.cfr.org/backgrounder/ same-sex-marriage-global-comparisons

Country Financial Security Index. (2018). *Survey: Americans still rely on parents to help with mobile phones, groceries and health insurance* [Report]. Retrieved from www.countryfinancial.com/en/ about-us/newsroom/year2018/Failure-to-Launch-Americans-Still-Rely-on-Parents-to-Help-with-Mobile-Phones-Gas-Groceries-and-Health-Insurance.html

Courage, M. L., & Howe, M. L. (2002). From infant to child: The dynamics of cognitive change in the second year of life. *Psychological Bulletin, 128,* 250–277.

Courtenay, W. (2011). *Dying to be men: Psychosocial, environmental, and biobehavioral directions in promoting the health of men and boys.* Abingdon-on-Thames, England: Routledge.

Couturier, J., Kimber, M., & Szatmari, P. (2013). Efficacy of family-based treatment for adolescents with eating disorders: A systematic review and meta-analysis. *International Journal of Eating Disorders, 46*(1), 3–11.

Cox, E. P., O'Dwyer, N., Cook, R., Vetter, M., Cheng, H. L., Rooney, K., & O'Connor, H. (2016). Relationship between physical activity and cognitive function in apparently healthy young to middle-aged adults: A systematic review. *Journal of Science and Medicine in Sport, 19*(8), 616–628.

Cox, M. J., & Paley, B. (2003). Understanding families as systems. *Current Directions in Psychological Science, 12*(5), 193–196.

Cox, M., Garrett, E., & Graham, J. A. (2005). Death in Disney films: Implications for children's understanding of death. *Omega-Journal of Death and Dying, 50*(4), 267–280.

Coyne, S. M., Linder, J. R., Rasmussen, E. E., Nelson, D. A., & Birkbeck, V. (2016). Pretty as a princess: Longitudinal effects of engagement with Disney princesses on gender stereotypes, body esteem, and prosocial behavior in children. *Child Development, 87*(6), 1909–1925.

Cozzi, P., Putnam, S. P., Menesini, E., Gartstein, M. A., Aureli, T., Calussi, P., & Montirosso, R. (2013). Studying cross-cultural differences in temperament in toddlerhood: United States of America (US) and Italy. *Infant Behavior and Development, 36*(3), 480–483.

Craig, L., & Mullan, K. (2011). How mothers and fathers share childcare: A cross-national time-use comparison. *American Sociological Review, 76*(6), 834–861.

Craik, F. I. M., & Jennings, J. M. (1992). Human memory. In F. I. M. Craik & T. A. Salthouse (Eds.), *Handbook of aging and cognition* (pp. 51–110). Hillsdale, NJ: Erlbaum.

Craik, F. I., & Rose, N. S. (2012). Memory encoding and aging: A neurocognitive perspective. *Neuroscience & Biobehavioral Reviews, 36*(7), 1729–1739.

Crandall, C. J., Merkin, S. S., Seeman, T. E., Greendale, G. A., Binkley, N., & Karlamangla, A. S. (2012). Socioeconomic status over the life-course and adult bone mineral density: The Midlife in the US Study. *Bone, 51*(1), 107–113.

Crawford, J. (2007). The decline of bilingual education: How to reverse a troubling trend? *International Multilingual Research Journal, 1*(1), 33–38.

Crăciun, B. (2013). Coping strategies, self-criticism and gender factor in relation to quality of life. *Procedia-Social and Behavioral Sciences, 78,* 466–470.

Creamer, M. R., Wang, T. W., Babb, S., Cullen, K. A., Day, H., Willis, G., . . . Neff, L. (2019). Tobacco product use and cessation indicators among adults—United States, 2018. *Morbidity and Mortality Weekly Report, 68*(45), 1013.

Creanga, A. A., Syverson, C., Seed, K., & Callaghan, W. M. (2017). Pregnancy-related mortality in the United States, 2011–2013. *Obstetrics and Gynecology, 130*(2), 366.

Crick, N. R., & Dodge, K. A. (1996). Social information-processing mechanisms in reactive and proactive aggression. *Child Development, 67,* 993–1002.

Crino, M., Sacks, G., Vandevijvere, S., Swinburn, B., & Neal, B. (2015). The influence on population weight gain and obesity of the macronutrient composition and energy density of the food supply. *Current Obesity Reports, 4*(1), 1–10.

Crippen, M. (2017). *The value of children's literature.* Retrieved from www. luther.edu/oneota-reading-journal/archive/2012/the-value-of-childrens-literature

Criss, M. M., Smith, A. M., Morris, A. S., Liu, C., & Hubbard, R. L. (2017). Parents and peers as protective factors among adolescents exposed to neighborhood risk. *Journal of Applied Developmental Psychology, 53,* 127–138.

Cristia, A., & Seidl, A. (2015). Parental reports on touch screen use in early childhood. *PLoS One, 10*(6), e0128338.

Cristia, A., Dupoux, E., Gurven, M., & Stieglitz, J. (2019). Child-directed speech is infrequent in a forager-farmer population: A time allocation study. *Child Development, 90*(3), 759–773.

Crocetti, E., Tagliabue, S., Sugimura, K., Nelson, L. J., Takahashi, A., Niwa, T., . . . Jinno, M. (2015). Perceptions of emerging adulthood: A study with Italian and Japanese university students and young workers. *Emerging Adulthood, 3*(4), 229–243.

Crockenberg, S. C. (2003). Rescuing the baby from the bathwater: How gender and temperament influence how child care affects child development. *Child Development, 74,* 1034–1038.

Croker, S., & Buchanan, H. (2011). Scientific reasoning in a real-world context: The effect of prior belief and outcome on children's hypothesis-testing strategies. *British Journal of Developmental Psychology, 29*(3), 409–424.

Crosnoe, R., Cavanagh, S., & Elder Jr, G. H. (2003). Adolescent friendships as academic resources: The intersection of friendship, race, and school disadvantage. *Sociological Perspectives, 46*(3), 331–352.

Crowley, S. L. (1993, October). Grandparents to the rescue. *AARP Bulletin, 1,* 16–17.

Crump, C., Sundquist, J., Winkleby, M. A., & Sundquist, K. (2019). Gestational age at birth and mortality from infancy into mid-adulthood: A national cohort study. *The Lancet Child & Adolescent Health, 3*(6), 408–417.

Cruzan v. Director, Missouri Department of Health, 110 S. Ct. 2841 (1990).

Cuddy, A. J. C., Norton, M. I., & Fiske, S. T. (2005). This old stereotype: The pervasiveness and persistence of the elderly stereotype. *Journal of Social Issues, 61*(2), 267–285.

Cuevas, K., & Bell, M. A. (2010). Developmental progression of looking and reaching performance on the A-not-B task. *Developmental Psychology, 46*(5), 1363.

Cuffee, Y., Ogedegbe, C., Williams, N. J., Ogedegbe, G., & Schoenthaler, A. (2014). Psychosocial risk factors for hypertension: An update of the literature. *Current Hypertension Reports, 16*(10), 483.

Cui, M., & Fincham, F. D. (2010). The differential effects of parental divorce and marital conflict on young adult romantic relationships. *Personal Relationships, 17*(3), 331-343.

Cui, M., Fincham, F. D., & Durtschi, J. A. (2011). The effect of parental divorce on young adults' romantic relationship dissolution: What makes a difference? *Personal Relationships, 18*(3), 410-426.

Čukić, I., Brett, C. E., Calvin, C. M., Batty, G. D., & Deary, I. J. (2017). Childhood IQ and survival to 79: Follow-up of 94% of the Scottish Mental Survey 1947. *Intelligence, 63*, 45-50.

Cumming, E., & Henry, W. (1961). *Growing old.* New York, NY: Basic Books.

Curtin, S. C., Heron, M., Minino, A. M. & Warnter, M. (2018). Recent increases in injury mortality among children and adolescents aged 10-19 years in the United States: 1999-2016. *National Vital Statistics Reports, 67*(4), 1-16. Hyattsville, MD: National Center for Health Statistics.

Curtin, S. C., Warner, M., & Hedegaard, H. (2016). *Increase in suicide in the United States, 1999-2014.* Washington, DC: U.S. Department of Health and Human Services, Centers for Disease Control and Prevention, National Center for Health Statistics.

Cutler, D. M., Ghosh, K., & Landrum, M. B. (2013). *Evidence for significant compression of morbidity in the elderly US population* (No. w19268). Cambridge, MA: National Bureau of Economic Research.

Curtis, A. C. (2015). Defining adolescence. *Journal of Adolescent and Family Health, 7*(2), 2.

Cychosz, M., Cristia, A., Bergelson, E., Casillas, M., Baudet, G., Warlaumont, A. S., . . . Seidl, A. (2019). *Canonical babble development in a large-scale crosslinguistic corpus.* Retrieved from https://doi.org/10.31234/osf.io/9vzs5

Czaja, A. J., & Sharit, J. (1998). Ability-performance relationships as a function of age and task experience for a data entry task. *Journal of Experimental Psychology–Applied, 4*, 332-351.

Czaja, S. J. (2006). Employment and the baby boomers: What can we expect in the future? In S. K. Whitbourne & S. L. Willis (Eds.), *The baby boomers grow up: Contemporary perspectives on midlife* (pp. 283-298). Mahwah, NJ: Erlbaum.

Côté, J. E. (2006). Emerging adulthood as an institutionalized moratorium: Risks and benefits to identity formation. In J. J. Arnett & J. L. Tanner (Eds.), *Emerging adults in America: Coming of age in the 21st century* (pp. 85-116). Washington, DC: American Psychological Association.

Da Costa, S., Páez, D., Sánchez, F., Garaigordobil, M., & Gondim, S. (2015). Personal factors of creativity: A second order meta-analysis. *Revista de Psicología del Trabajo y de las Organizaciones, 31*(3), 165-173.

Dabelea, D., Mayer-Davis, E. J., Saydah, S., Imperatore, G., Linder, B., Divers, J., . . . Liese, A. D. (2014). Prevalence of type 1 and type 2 diabetes among children and adolescents from 2001 to 2009. *JAMA, 311*(17), 1778-1786.

Dabul, A. J., Bernal, M. E., & Knight, G. P. (1995). Allocentric and idiocentric self-description and academic achievement among Mexican American and Anglo American adolescents. *The Journal of Social Psychology, 135*(5), 621-630.

Dagher, R. K., McGovern, P. M., Schold, J. D., & Randall, X. J. (2016). Determinants of breastfeeding initiation and cessation among employed mothers: A prospective cohort study. *BMC Pregnancy and Childbirth, 16*(1), 19

Dale, P. S., Simonoff, E., Bishop, D. V. M., Eley, T. C., Oliver, B., Price, T. S., . . . Plomin, R. (1998). Genetic influence on language delay in two-year-old children. *Nature Neuroscience, 1*, 324-328.

Danaei, G., Rimm, E. B., Oza, S., Kulkarni, S. C., Murray, C. J. L., & Ezzati, M. (2010). The promise of prevention: The effects of four preventable risk factors on national life expectancy and life expectancy disparities by race and county in the United States. *PLoS Medicine, 7*(3), e1000248. doi:10.1371/journal.pmed.1000248

Daniel, J. (2012). Making sense of MOOCs: Musing in a maze of myth, paradox and possibility. *Journal of Interactive Media in Education, 18*(3), 1-20.

Danielson, M. L., Bitsko, R. H., Ghandour, R. M., Holbrook, J. R., Kogan, M. D., & Blumberg, S. J. (2018). Prevalence of parent-reported ADHD diagnosis and associated treatment among US children and adolescents, 2016. *Journal of Clinical Child & Adolescent Psychology, 47*(2), 199-212.

Dariotis, J. K., Pleck, J. H., Astone, N. M., & Sonenstein, F. L. (2011). Pathways of early fatherhood, marriage, and employment: A latent class growth analysis. *Demography, 48*(2), 593.

Darlow, V., Norvilitis, J. M., & Schuetze, P. (2017). The relationship between helicopter parenting and adjustment to college. *Journal of Child and Family Studies, 26*(8), 2291-2298.

Dart, R. C., Surratt, H. L., Cicero, T. J., Parrino, M. W., Severtson, S. G., Bucher-Bartelson, B., & Green, J. L. (2015). Trends in opioid analgesic abuse and mortality in the United States. *New England Journal of Medicine, 372*(3), 241-248.

Dasen, P. R. (1972). Cross-cultural Piagetian research: A summary. *Journal of Cross-cultural Psychology, 3*(1), 23-40.

Dasen, P. R. (1984). The cross-cultural study of intelligence: Piaget and the Baoule. *International Journal of Psychology, 19*(1-4), 407-434.

Dasen, P. R. (1994). Culture and cognitive development from a Piagetian perspective. *Psychology and Culture,* 145-149.

Daugherty, J., & Copen, C. (2016). Trends in attitudes about marriage, childbearing, and sexual behavior: United States, 2002, 2006-2010, and 2011-2013. *National Health Statistics Reports, 92*, 1-10.

Daugherty, M., & White, C. S. (2008). Relationships among private speech and creativity in Head Start and low-socioeconomic status preschool children. *Gifted Child Quarterly, 52*(1), 30-39.

David and Lucile Packard Foundation. (2004). Children, families, and foster care: Executive summary. *Future of Children, 14*(1). Retrieved from www.futureofchildren.org

Davidson, K. (2001). Late life widowhood, selfishness and new partnership choices: A gendered perspective. *Ageing & Society, 21*(3), 297-317.

Davies, C., & Williams, D. (2002). *The grandparent study 2002 report.* Washington, DC: American Association of Retired Persons.

Daviglus, M. L., Bell, C. C., Berrettini, W., Bowen, P. E., Connolly, E. S., Cox, N. J., . . . Trevisan, M. (2010). Preventing Alzheimer's disease and cognitive decline. *NIH Consensus State-of-the-Science Statements, 27*(4), 1-30.

Davis, A. S. (2008). Children with Down syndrome: Implications for assessment and intervention in the school. *School Psychology Quarterly, 23*, 271-281.

Davis, B. E., Moon, R. Y., Sachs, H. C., & Ottolini, M. C. (1998). Effects of sleep position on infant motor development. *Pediatrics, 102*(5), 1135-1140.

Davis, E. L., Levine, L. J., Lench, H. C., & Quas, J. A. (2010). Metacognitive emotion regulation: Children's awareness that changing thoughts and goals can alleviate negative emotions. *Emotion, 10*(4), 498.

Davis, E. M., Kim, K., & Fingerman, K. L. (2018). Is an empty nest best?: Coresidence with adult children and parental marital quality before and after the great recession. *The Journals of Gerontology: Series B, 73*(3), 372-381.

Davis, E., Eivers, A., & Thorpe, K. (2012). Is quality more important if you're quirky? A review of the literature on differential susceptibility to childcare environments. *Australasian Journal of Early Childhood, 37*(4), 99-106.

Davis, O. S. P., Haworth, C. M. A., & Plomin, R. (2009). Dramatic increases in heritability of cognitive development from early to middle childhood: An 8-year longitudinal study of 8,700 pairs of twins. *Psychological Science, 20*(10), 1301-1308.

Davis, S. W., Kragel, J. E., Madden, D. J., & Cabeza, R. (2011). The architecture of cross-hemispheric communication in the aging brain: linking behavior to functional and structural connectivity. *Cerebral Cortex, 22*(1), 232-242.

Davis-Kean, P. E. (2005). The influence of parent education and family income on child achievement: The indirect role of parental expectation and the home environment. *Journal of Family Psychology, 19*(2), 294-304.

Day, J. C., Janus, A., & Davis, J. (2005). Computer and Internet use in the United States: 2003. *Current Population Reports,* P23-208. Washington, DC: U.S. Census Bureau.

Day, K. L., & Smith, C. L. (2013). Understanding the role of private speech in children's emotion regulation. *Early Childhood Research Quarterly, 28*(2), 405-414.

De Bourdeaudhuij, I., Van Cauwenberghe, E., Spittaels, H., Oppert, J. M., Rostami, C., Brug, J., . . . Maes, L. (2011). School-based interventions promoting both physical activity and healthy eating in Europe: A systematic review within the HOPE project. *Obesity Reviews, 12*(3), 205-216.

de Castro, B. O., Veerman, J. W., Koops, W., Bosch, J. D., & Monshouwer, H. J. (2002). Hostile attribution of intent and aggressive behavior: A meta-analysis. *Child Development, 73*, 916-934.

De Cosmi, V., Scaglioni, S., & Agostoni, C. (2017). Early taste experiences and later food choices. *Nutrients, 9*(2), 107.

de Espanés, G. M., Villar, F., Urrutia, A., & Serrat, R. (2015). Motivation and commitment to volunteering in a sample of Argentinian adults: What is the role of generativity? *Educational Gerontology, 41*(2), 149-161.

de Graaf, G., Buckley, F., & Skotko, B. G. (2015). Estimates of the live births, natural losses, and elective terminations with Down syndrome in the United States. *American Journal of Medical Genetics Part A, 167*(4), 756-767.

De Kovel, C. G., Carrion-Castillo, A., & Francks, C. (2019). A large-scale population study of early life factors influencing left-handedness. *Scientific Reports, 9*(1), 584.

De Lima, L., Woodruff, R., Pettus, K., Downing, J., Buitrago, R., Munyoro, E., Venkateswaran, C., Bhatnagar, S., & Radbruch, L. (2017). International Association for Hospice and Palliative Care position statement: Euthanasia and physician-assisted suicide. *Journal of Palliative Medicine, 20*, 8-14.

De Onis, M., Blössner, M., & Borghi, E. (2010). Global prevalence and trends of overweight and obesity among preschool children. *The American Journal of Clinical Nutrition, 92*(5), 1257-1264.

De Vaus, D., Gray, M., Qu, L., & Stanton, D. (2017). The economic consequences of divorce in six OECD countries. *Australian Journal of Social Issues, 52*(2), 180-199.

De Villiers, T. J., Gass, M. L. S., Haines, C. J., Hall, J. E., Lobo, R. A., Pierroz, D. D., & Rees, M. (2013). Global consensus statement on menopausal hormone therapy. *Climacteric, 16*(2), 203-204.

de Vries, B. (1996). The understanding of friendship: An adult life course perspective. In C. Magai & S. H. McFadden (Eds.), *Handbook of emotion, adult development, and aging* (pp. 249-269). San Diego, CA: Academic Press.

Dean, B. (2018). Bride service. In H. Callan (Ed.), *The international encyclopedia of anthropology.* New York, NY: Wiley.

Deary, I. J., Penke, L., & Johnson, W. (2010). The neuroscience of human intelligence differences. *Nature Reviews. Neuroscience, 11*(3), 201.

Deary, I. J., Weiss, A., & Batty, G. D. (2010). Intelligence and personality as predictors of illness and death: How researchers in differential psychology and chronic disease epidemiology are collaborating to understand and address health inequalities. *Psychological Science in the Public Interest, 11*(2), 53-79.

Death with Dignity. (2020). *Take action: Death with dignity around the U.S.* [Map]. Retrieved from www.deathwithdignity.org/take-action/

Deave, T., Heron, J., Evans, J., & Emond, A. (2008). The impact of maternal depression in pregnancy on early child development. *BJOG: An International Journal of Obstetrics & Gynaecology, 115*(8), 1043-1051.

DeBell, M., & Chapman, C. (2006). *Computer and Internet use by students in 2003: Statistical analysis report* (NCES 2006-065). Washington, DC: National Center for Education Statistics.

Debnam, K., Holt, C. L., Clark, E. M., Roth, D. L., & Southward, P. (2012). Relationship between religious social support and general social support with health behaviors in a national sample of African Americans. *Journal of Behavioral Medicine, 35*(2), 179-189.

Decety, J., Michalska, K. J., Akitsuki, Y., & Lahey, B. B. (2009). Atypical empathic responses in adolescents with aggressive conduct disorder: A functional MRI investigation. *Biological Psychology, 80*(2), 203-211.

Decker, M. L., Chavez, E., Vulto, I., & Lansdorp, P. M. (2009). Telomere length in Hutchinson-Gilford progeria syndrome. *Mechanisms of Ageing and Development, 130*(6), 377-383.

Deckers, K., van Boxtel, M. P., Schiepers, O. J., de Vugt, M., Munoz Sanchez, J. L., Anstey, K. J., . . . Ritchie, K. (2015). Target risk factors for dementia prevention: A systematic review and Delphi consensus study on the evidence from observational studies. *International Journal of Geriatric Psychiatry, 30*(3), 234-246.

Deding, U., Ejlskov, L., Grabas, M. P. K., Nielsen, B. J., Torp-Pedersen, C., & Bøggild, H. (2016). Perceived stress as a risk factor for peptic ulcers: A register-based cohort study. *BMC Gastroenterology, 16*(1), 140.

Dee, T. S., & Jacob, B. (2011). The impact of No Child Left Behind on student achievement. *Journal of Policy Analysis and Management, 30*(3), 418-446.

Degnan, K. A., Almas, A. N., Henderson, H. A., Hane, A. A., Walker, O. L., & Fox, N. A. (2014). Longitudinal trajectories of social reticence with unfamiliar peers across early childhood. *Developmental Psychology, 50*(10), 2311.

DeHaan, L. G., & MacDermid, S. M. (1994). Is women's identity achievement associated with the expression of generativity? Examining identity and generativity in multiple roles. *Journal of Adult Development, 1*, 235-247.

Dehaene-Lambertz, G. (2017). The human infant brain: A neural architecture able to learn language. *Psychonomic Bulletin & Review, 24*(1), 48-55.

Dehaene-Lambertz, G., & Spelke, E. S. (2015). The infancy of the human brain. *Neuron, 88*(1), 93-109.

Deindl, C., & Brandt, M. (2017). Support networks of childless older people: Informal and formal support in Europe. *Ageing & Society, 37*(8), 1543-1567.

Dekhtyar, M., Papp, K. V., Buckley, R., Jacobs, H. I., Schultz, A. P., Johnson, K. A., . . . Rentz, D. M. (2017). Neuroimaging markers associated with maintenance of optimal memory performance in late-life. *Neuropsychologia, 100*, 164-170.

Del Boca, D. (2015). *Child care arrangements and labor supply* (No. IDB-WP-569). IDB Working Paper Series.

del Mar Fernández, M., Saulyte, J., Inskip, H. M., & Takkouche, B. (2018). Premenstrual syndrome and alcohol consumption: A systematic review and meta-analysis. *BMJ Open, 8*(3), e019490.

Delamater, A. M., Pulgaron, E. R., & Daigre, A. (2013). Obesity in adolescence. In W. O'Donohue, L. Benuto, & L. Woodward Tolle (Eds.), *Handbook of adolescent health psychology* (pp. 597-618). New York, NY: Springer.

DeLamater, J. (2012). Sexual expression in later life: A review and synthesis. *Journal of Sex Research, 49*(2-3), 125-141.

Deli, E., Bakle, I., & Zachopoulou, E. (2006). Implementing intervention movement programs for kindergarten children. *Journal of Early Childhood Research, 4*(1), 5-18.

DeLoache, J. S. (2011). Early development of the understanding and use of symbolic artifacts. *The Wiley-Blackwell Handbook of Childhood Cognitive Development* (pp. 312-336). Hoboken, NJ: Wiley.

DeLoache, J. S., Chiong, C., Sherman, K., Islam, N., Vanderborght, M., Troseth, G. L., . . . O'Doherty, K. (2010). Do babies learn from baby media? *Psychological Science, 21*(11), 1570-1574.

DeLoache, J. S., LoBue, V., Vanderborght, M., & Chiong, C. (2013). On the validity and robustness of the scale error phenomenon in early childhood. *Infant Behavior and Development, 36*(1), 63-70.

DeLoache, J. S., Pierroutsakos, S. L., & Uttal, D. H. (2003). The origins of pictorial competence. *Current Directions in Psychological Science, 12*, 114-118.

DeLoache, J. S., Uttal, D. H., & Rosengren, K. S. (2004). Scale errors offer evidence for a perception-action dissociation early in life. *Science, 304*, 1027-1029.

DeLoache, J., & Gottlieb, A. (2000). If Dr. Spock were born in Bali: Raising a world of babies. In J. DeLoache & A. Gottlieb (Eds.), *A world of babies: Imagined childcare guides for seven societies* (pp. 1-27). New York, NY: Cambridge University Press.

Delvecchio, E., Di Riso, D., & Salcuni, S. (2016). Self-perception of parental role, family functioning, and familistic beliefs in Italian parents: Early evidence. *Frontiers in Psychology, 6*, 1983.

DeMaris, A. (2009). Distal and proximal influences on the risk of extramarital sex: A prospective study of longer duration marriages. *Journal of Sex Research, 46*(6), 597-607.

Demir, A. B., & Demir, N. (2018). Epigenetic basis of twin discordance in diseases: future benefits. *Gynecology Obstetrics & Reproductive Medicine, 24*(2), 108-118.

Denford, S., Abraham, C., Campbell, R., & Busse, H. (2017). A comprehensive review of reviews of school-based interventions to improve sexual-health. *Health Psychology Review, 11*(1), 33-52.

Deng, K., Liu, Z., Lin, Y., Mu, D., Chen, X., Li, J., . . . & Li, S. (2013). Periconceptional paternal smoking and the risk of congenital heart defects: A case-control study. *Birth Defects Research Part A: Clinical and Molecular Teratology, 97*(4), 210-216.

Deng, W., Aimone, J. B., & Gage, F. H. (2010). New neurons and new memories: How does adult hippocampal neurogenesis affect learning and memory? *Nature Reviews. Neuroscience, 11*(5), 339.

Denham, S. A., Bassett, H. H., Brown, C., Way, E., & Steed, J. (2015). "I know how you feel": Preschoolers' emotion knowledge contributes to early school success. *Journal of Early Childhood Research, 13*(3), 252-262.

Denham, S. A., Blair, K. A., DeMulder, E., Levitas, J., Sawyer, K., Auerbach-Major, S., & Queenan, P. (2003). Preschool emotional competence: Pathway to social competence? *Child Development, 74*, 238-256.

Dennis, T. (2006). Emotional self-regulation in preschoolers: The interplay of child approach reactivity, parenting, and control capacities. *Developmental Psychology, 42*, 84-97.

Denny, D. (2013). *Current concepts in transgender identity.* Abingdon, England: Routledge.

Deoni, S. C., Dean III, D. C., O'muircheartaigh, J., Dirks, H., & Jerskey, B. A. (2012). Investigating white matter development in infancy and early childhood using myelin water faction and relaxation time mapping. *Neuroimage, 63*(3), 1038-1053.

Deoni, S. C., Mercure, E., Blasi, A., Gasston, D., Thomson, A., Johnson, M., . . . Murphy, D. G. (2011). Mapping infant brain myelination with magnetic resonance imaging. *Journal of Neuroscience, 31*(2), 784-791.

Depp, C. A., & Jeste, D. V. (2009). Definitions and predictors of successful aging: A comprehensive review of larger quantitative studies. *Focus, 7,* 137-150.

Deptula, D. P., Henry, D. B., & Schoeny, M. E. (2010). How can parents make a difference? Longitudinal associations with adolescent sexual behavior. *Journal of Family Psychology, 24*(6), 731.

Deputy, N. P., Sharma, A. J., Kim, S. Y., & Hinkle, S. N. (2015). Prevalence and characteristics associated with gestational weight gain adequacy. *Obstetrics and Gynecology, 125*(4), 773.

Der, G., Batty, G. D., & Deary, I. J. (2009). The association between IQ in adolescence and a range of health outcomes at 40 in the 1979 US National Longitudinal Study of Youth. *Intelligence, 37*(6), 573-580.

Desai, M., Pratt, L. A., Lentzner, H., & Robinson, K. N. (2001). Trends in vision and hearing among older Americans. *Aging Trends,* No. 2. Hyattsville, MD: National Center for Health Statistics.

DeSalvo, K. B., Olson, R., & Casavale, K. O. (2016). Dietary guidelines for Americans. *JAMA, 315*(5), 457-458.

Deshmukh-Taskar, P. R., Nicklas, T. A., O'Neil, C. E., Keast, D. R., Radcliffe, J. D., & Cho, S. (2010). The relationship of breakfast skipping and type of breakfast consumption with nutrient intake and weight status in children and adolescents: The National Health and Nutrition Examination Survey 1999-2006. *Journal of the American Dietetic Association, 110*(6), 869-878.

Desoete, A. (2015). Predictive indicators for mathematical learning disabilities/dyscalculia in kindergarten children. In S. Chinn (Ed.), *The Routledge international handbook of dyscalculia and mathematical learning difficulties* (pp. 90-100). New York, NY: Routledge.

DeSteno, D., Gross, J. J., & Kubzansky, L. (2013). Affective science and health: The importance of emotion and emotion regulation. *Health Psychology, 32*(5), 474.

Detering, K. M., Hancock, A. D., Reade, M. C., & Silvester, W. (2010). The impact of advance care planning on end of life care in elderly patients: Randomised controlled trial. *British Medical Journal, 340,* 1345. doi:10.1136/bmj.c1345

Deters, F. G., & Mehl, M. R. (2013). Does posting Facebook status updates increase or decrease loneliness? An online social networking experiment. *Social Psychological and Personality Science, 4*(5), 579-586.

Deutsch, F. M., Servis, L. J., & Payne, J. D. (2001). Paternal participation in child care and its effects on children's self-esteem and attitudes toward gender roles. *Journal of Family Issues, 22*(8), 1000-1024.

Devereux, G. (1988). Institutionalized homosexuality of the Mohave Indians. In W. Roscoe (Ed.), *Living the spirit: A gay American Indian anthology.* New York, NY: St. Martin's Press. (Originally published 1937 in Human Biology, 9, 498-527)

Devine, R. T., & Hughes, C. (2014). Relations between false belief understanding and executive function in early childhood: A meta-analysis. *Child Development, 85*(5), 1777-1794.

Devitt, A. L., & Schacter, D. L. (2016). False memories with age: Neural and cognitive underpinnings. *Neuropsychologia, 91*, 346-359.

deVries, M. W. (1994). Kids in context: Temperament in crosscultural perspective. *Prevention and Early Intervention*, 126-139.

Dew, J. (2011). The association between consumer debt and the likelihood of divorce. *Journal of Family and Economic Issues, 32*(4), 554-565.

Dew, J., & Wilcox, W. B. (2011). If Momma ain't happy: Explaining declines in marital satisfaction among new mothers. *Journal of Marriage and Family, 73*(1), 1-12.

Dew, J., Britt, S., & Huston, S. (2012). Examining the relationship between financial issues and divorce. *Family Relations, 61*(4), 615-628.

Dewey, J. (1933). *How we think* (Rev. ed.) Boston, MA: DC Heath.

Dey, E. L., & Hurtado, S. (1999). Students, colleges and society: Considering the interconnections. In P. G. Altbach, R. O. Berndahl, & P. J. Gumport (Eds.), *American higher education in the twenty-first century: Social, political and economic challenges* (pp. 298-322). Baltimore, MD: The Johns Hopkins University Press.

DeYoung, C. G., Quilty, L. C., Peterson, J. B., & Gray, J. R. (2014). Openness to experience, intellect, and cognitive ability. *Journal of Personality Assessment, 96*(1), 46-52.

Dhabhar, F. S. (2014). Effects of stress on immune function: the good, the bad, and the beautiful. *Immunologic Research, 58*(2-3), 193-210.

Dhawan, N., Roseman, I. J., Naidu, R. K., Thapa, K., & Rettek, S. I. (1995). Self-concepts across two cultures: India and the United States. *Journal of Cross-Cultural Psychology, 26*(6), 606-621.

Di Benedetto, S., Müller, L., Wenger, E., Düzel, S., & Pawelec, G. (2017). Contribution of neuroinflammation and immunity to brain aging and the mitigating effects of physical and cognitive interventions. *Neuroscience & Biobehavioral Reviews, 75*, 114-128.

Di Mascio, D., Khalil, A., Saccone, G., Rizzo, G., Buca, D., Liberati, M., . . . D'Antonio, F. (2020). Outcome of coronavirus spectrum infections (SARS, MERS, COVID 1-19) during pregnancy: A systematic review and meta-analysis. *American Journal of Obstetrics & Gynecology MFM*, 100107.

Diamond, A. (1991). Neuropsychological insights into the meaning of object concept development. In S. Carey & R. Gelman (Eds.), *Epigensis of mind* (pp. 67-110). Hillsdale, NJ: Erlbaum.

Diamond, A. (2002). Normal development of prefrontal cortex from birth to young adulthood: Cognitive functions, anatomy, and biochemistry. In D. T. Strauss & R. T. Knight (Eds.), *Principles of frontal lobe function* (pp. 466-503). New York. NY: Oxford University Press.

Diamond, A., & Lee, K. (2011). Interventions shown to aid executive function development in children 4 to 12 years old. *Science, 333*(6045), 959-964.

Diamond, L. M., & Savin-Williams, R. C. (2003). The intimate relationships of sexual-minority youths. In G. R. Adams & M. D. Berzonsky (Eds.), *Blackwell handbook of adolescence* (pp. 393-412). Malden, MA: Blackwell.

Diamond, L. M., Pardo, S. T., & Butterworth, M. R. (2011). Transgender experience and identity. In S. J. Schwartz, K. Luyckx & V. L. Vignoles (Eds.), *Handbook of identity theory and research* (pp. 629-647). New York, NY: Springer.

Diamond, M. (2013). Transsexuality among twins: Identity concordance, transition, rearing, and orientation. *International Journal of Transgenderism, 14*(1), 24-38.

Diamond-Smith, N., Luke, N., & McGarvey, S. (2008). 'Too many girls, too much dowry': Son preference and daughter aversion in rural Tamil Nadu, India. *Culture, Health & Sexuality, 10*(7), 697-708.

Diaz, C. J., & Fiel, J. E. (2016). The effect(s) of teen pregnancy: Reconciling theory, methods, and findings. *Demography, 53*(1), 85-116.

Dick, D. M., Rose, R. J., Kaprio, J., & Viken, R. (2000). Pubertal timing and substance use: Associations between and within families across late adolescence. *Developmental Psychology, 36*, 180-189.

Dickens, W. T., & Flynn, J. R. (2006). Black Americans reduce the racial IQ gap: Evidence from standardization samples. *Psychological Science, 17*(10), 913-920.

Diehl, M., Hay, E. L., & Berg, K. M. (2011). The ratio between positive and negative affect and flourishing mental health across adulthood. *Aging & Mental Health, 15*(7), 882-893.

Diener, E. (2000). Subjective well-being: The science of happiness and a proposal for a national index. *American Psychologist, 55*, 34-43.

Diener, E., & Chan, M. Y. (2011). Happy people live longer: Subjective well-being contributes to health and longevity. *Applied Psychology: Health and Well-Being, 3*(1), 1-43.

Diener, E., Diener, C., Choi, H., & Oishi, S. (2018). Revisiting "Most People Are Happy"—and discovering when they are not. *Perspectives on Psychological Science, 13*(2), 166-170.

DiFranza, J. R., Aligne, C. A., & Weitzman, M. (2004). Prenatal and postnatal environmental tobacco smoke exposure and children's health. *Pediatrics, 113*, 1007-1015.

Dijk, D. J., Groeger, J. A., Stanley, N., & Deacon, S. (2010). Age-related reduction in daytime sleep propensity and nocturnal slow wave sleep. *Sleep, 33*(2), 211-223.

Dillon, M., Wink, P., & Fay, K. (2003). Is spirituality detrimental to generativity? *Journal for the Scientific Study of Religion, 42*(3), 427-442.

Dilworth-Anderson, P., Williams, I. C., & Gibson, B. E. (2002). Issues of race, ethnicity, and culture in caregiving research: A 20-year review (1980-2000). *The Gerontologist, 42*(2), 237-272.

Dilworth-Bart, J. E., & Moore, C. F. (2006). Mercy mercy me: Social injustice and the prevention of environmental pollutant exposures among ethnic minority and poor children. *Child Development, 77*(2), 247-265.

Dingemans, E., & Henkens, K. (2015). How do retirement dynamics influence mental well-being in later life? A 10-year panel study. *Scandinavian Journal of Work, Environment & Health, 41*(1), 16-23.

Dingemans, E., & Henkens, K. (2019). Working after retirement and life satisfaction: Cross-national comparative research in Europe. *Research on Aging, 41*(7), 648-669.

Dinsa, G. D., Goryakin, Y., Fumagalli, E., & Suhrcke, M. (2012). Obesity and socioeconomic status in developing countries: A systematic review. *Obesity Reviews, 13*(11), 1067-1079.

DiPietro, J. A., Costigan, K. A., & Voegtline, K. M. (2015). Studies in fetal behavior: Revisited, renewed, and reimagined. *Monographs of the Society for Research in Child Development, 80*(3), vii.

DiPietro, J. A., Kivlighan, K. T., Costigan, K. A., Rubin, S. E., Shiffler, D. E., Henderson, J. L., & Pillion, J. P. (2010). Prenatal antecedents of newborn neurological maturation. *Child Development, 81*(1), 115-130. doi: 10.1111/j.1467-8624.2009.01384.x

Dira, S. J., & Hewlett, B. S. (2018). The Chabu hunter-gatherers of the highland forests of Southwestern Ethiopia. *Hunter Gatherer Research, 3*(2), 323-352.

Direkvand-Moghadam, A., Sayehmiri, K., Delpisheh, A., & Kaikhavandi, S. (2014). Epidemiology of Premenstrual Syndrome (PMS): A systematic review and meta-analysis study. *Journal of Clinical and Diagnostic Research: JCDR, 8*(2), 106.

Dirix, C. E. H., Nijhuis, J. G., Jongsma, H. W., & Hornstra, G. (2009). Aspects of fetal learning and memory. *Child Development, 80*(4), 1251-1258.

Dirks, M. A., Persram, R., Recchia, H. E., & Howe, N. (2015). Sibling relationships as sources of risk and resilience in the development and maintenance of internalizing and externalizing problems during childhood and adolescence. *Clinical Psychology Review, 42*, 145-155.

Dishion, T. J., & Tipsord, J. M. (2011). Peer contagion in child and adolescent social and emotional development. *Annual Review of Psychology, 62*, 189-214.

Dittmar, H., Halliwell, E., & Ive, S. (2006). Does Barbie make girls want to be thin? The effect of experimental exposure to images of dolls on the body image of 5- to 8-year-old girls. *Developmental Psychology, 42*, 283-292.

Dixon, R. A., & Hultsch, D. F. (1999). Intelligence and cognitive potential in late life. In J. C. Cavanaugh & S. K. Whitbourne (Eds.), *Gerontology: An interdisciplinary perspective.* New York, NY: Oxford University Press.

Doak, C. M., Visscher, T. L. S., Renders, C. M., & Seidell, J. C. (2006). The prevention of overweight and obesity in children and adolescents: a review of interventions and programmes. *Obesity Reviews, 7*(1), 111-136.

Dobriansky, P. J., Suzman, R. M., & Hodes, R. J. (2007). *Why population aging matters: A global perspective.* Washington, DC: U.S. Department of State and Department of Health and Human Services, National Institute on Aging, & National Institutes of Health.

Dobson, K. G., Chow, C. H., Morrison, K. M., & Van Lieshout, R. J. (2017). Associations between childhood cognition and cardiovascular events in adulthood: A systematic review and meta-analysis. *Canadian Journal of Cardiology, 33*(2), 232-242.

Dodge, K. A., Coie, J. D., & Lynam, D. (2006). Aggression and antisocial behavior in youth. In N. Eisenberg, W. Damon, & R. Lerner (Eds.), *Handbook of child psychology: Vol. 3, Social, emotional and personality development* (6th ed., pp. 719-788). Hoboken, NJ: Wiley.

Dodge, K. A., Coie, J. D., Pettit, G. S., & Price, J. M. (1990). Peer status and aggression in boys' groups: Developmental and contextual analysis. *Child Development, 61*, 1289-1309.

Dodge, K. A., Dishion, T. J., & Lansford, J. E. (2006). Deviant peer influences in intervention and public policy for youth. *Social Policy Report, 20*(1), 1-20.

Dodge, K. A., Pettit, G. S., & Bates, J. E. (1994). Socialization mediators of the relation between socioeconomic status and child conduct problems. *Child Development, 65*, 649-665.

Dodson, C. S., & Schacter, D. L. (2002). Aging and strategic retrieval processes: Reducing false memories with a distinctiveness heuristic. *Psychology and Aging, 17*(3), 405-415.

Doherty, W. J., Kouneski, E. F., & Erickson, M. F. (1998). Responsible fathering: An overview and conceptual framework. *Journal of Marriage and Family, 60*, 277-292.

Dolan, M. A., & Hoffman, C. D. (1998). Determinants of divorce among women: A reexamination of critical influences. *Journal of Divorce and Remarriage, 28*, 97-106.

Dolbin-MacNab, M. L., & Hayslip Jr, B. (2014). Grandparents raising grandchildren. *Family Problems: Stress, Risk, and Resilience*, 133-149.

Doley, R., Bell, R., Watt, B., & Simpson, H. (2015). Grandparents raising grandchildren: investigating factors associated with distress among custodial grandparent. *Journal of Family Studies, 21*(2), 101-119.

Dombrowski, S. U., Knittle, K., Avenell, A., Araujo-Soares, V., & Sniehotta, F. F. (2014). Long term maintenance of weight loss with non-surgical interventions in obese adults: Systematic review and meta-analyses of randomised controlled trials. *BMJ, 348*, g2646.

Dominguez-Folgueras, M., & Castro-Martin, T. (2013). Cohabitation in Spain: No longer a marginal path to family formation. *Journal of Marriage and Family, 75*(2), 422-437.

Domènech Rodriguez, M. M., Donovick, M. R., & Crowley, S. L. (2009). Parenting styles in a cultural context: Observations of "protective parenting" in first-generation Latinos. *Family Process, 48*(2), 195-210.

Dong, J. Y., Zhang, Y. H., Tong, J., & Qin, L. Q. (2012). Depression and risk of stroke: A meta-analysis of prospective studies. *Stroke, 43*(1), 32-37.

Donoho, C. J., Seeman, T. E., Sloan, R. P., & Crimmins, E. M. (2015). Marital status, marital quality, and heart rate variability in the MIDUS cohort. *Journal of Family Psychology, 29*(2), 290.

Dopp, A. R., & Cain, A. C. (2012). The role of peer relationships in parental bereavement during childhood and adolescence. *Death Studies, 36*(1), 41-60.

Dorfman, L. T. (2009). Ten years later: A follow-up study of professors still working after age 70. *Educational Gerontology, 35*(11), 1032-1045.

Dorfman, L. T., & Kolarik, D. C. (2005). Leisure and the retired professor: Occupation matters. *Educational Gerontology, 31*(5), 343-361.

Dornbusch, S. M., Ritter, P. L., Leiderman, P. H., Roberts, D. F., & Fraleigh, M. J. (1987). The relation of parenting style to adolescent school performance. *Child Development, 58*(5), 1244-1257.

Doss, B. D., Rhoades, G. K., Stanley, S. M., & Markman, H. J. (2009). The effect of the transition to parenthood on relationship quality: An 8-year prospective study. *Journal of Personality and Social Psychology, 96*(3), 601-619. https://doi.org/10.1037/a0013969

Doty, R. L. (2018). Age-related deficits in taste and smell. *Otolaryngologic Clinics of North America, 51*(4), 815-825.

Doughty, S. E., Lam, C. B., Stanik, C. E., & McHale, S. M. (2015). Links between sibling experiences and romantic competence from adolescence through young adulthood. *Journal of Youth and Adolescence, 44*(11), 2054-2066.

Dow-Edwards, D., MacMaster, F. P., Peterson, B. S., Niesink, R., Andersen, S., & Braams, B. R. (2019). Experience during adolescence shapes brain development: From synapses and networks to normal and pathological behavior. *Neurotoxicology and Teratology, 76*, 106834.

Downey, D. B., Condron, D. J., & Yucel, D. (2015). Number of siblings and social skills revisited among American fifth graders. *Journal of Family Issues, 36*(2), 273-296.

Downing, J., & Cha, P. (2020). Same-sex marriage and gains in employer-sponsored insurance for US adults, 2008-2017. *American Journal of Public Health, (0)*, e1-e3.

Downing-Matibag, T. (2009). Parents' perceptions of their adolescent children, parental resources, and parents' satisfaction with the parent-child relationship. *Sociological Spectrum, 29*(4), 467-488.

Dowshen, S., Crowley, J., & Palusci, V. J. (2004). *Shaken baby/shaken impact syndrome.* Retrieved from www.kidshealth.org/parent/medical/brain/shaken.html

Drabick, D. A., Gadow, K. D., & Sprafkin, J. (2006). Co-occurrence of conduct disorder and depression in a clinic-based sample of boys with ADHD. *Journal of Child Psychology and Psychiatry, 47*(8), 766-774.

Dragan, W. Ł., Kmita, G., & Fronczyk, K. (2011). Psychometric properties of the Polish adaptation of the Infant Behavior Questionnaire–Revised (IBQ-R). *International Journal of Behavioral Development, 35*(6), 542-549.

Drageset, J., Kirkevold, M., & Espehaug, B. (2011). Loneliness and social support among nursing home residents without cognitive impairment: A questionnaire survey. *International Journal of Nursing Studies, 48*(5), 611-619.

Drake, B. (2013). *As more Americans have contacts with gays and lesbians, social acceptance rises.* Washington, DC: Pew Research Center.

Drewnowski, A. (2009). Obesity, diets, and social inequalities. *Nutrition Reviews, 67,* S36-S39.

Dreyer, B., Chung, P. J., Szilagyi, P., & Wong, S. (2016). Child poverty in the United States today: introduction and executive summary. *Academic Pediatrics, 16*(3), S1-S5.

Drijber, B. C., Reijnders, U. J. L., & Ceelen, M. (2013). Male victims of domestic violence. *Journal of Family Violence, 28,* 173-178.

Driscoll, A. K. (2014). Adult outcomes of teen mothers across birth cohorts. *Demographic Research, 30*(44), 1277.

Drolet, M., Benard, E., Perez, N., Brisson, M., & HPV Vaccination Impact Study Group. (2019). Population-level impact and herd effects following the introduction of human papillomavirus vaccination programmes: Updated systematic review and meta-analysis. *The Lancet, 394*(10197), 497-509.

Drotar, D., Olness, K., Wiznitzer, M., Schatschneider, C., Marum, L., Guay, L., . . . Mayengo, R. K. (1999). Neurodevelopmental outcomes of Ugandan infants with HIV infection: An application of growth curve analysis. *Health Psychology, 18*(2), 114.

Drukker, L., Haklai, Z., Schlesinger, M. B. Y., Bas-Lando, M., Gordon, E. S., Samueloff, A., . . . Grisaru-Granovsky, S. (2018). The next-generation: Long-term reproductive outcome of adults born at a very low birth weight. *Early Human Development, 116,* 76-80.

Drury, J., & Williams, R. (2012). Children and young people who are refugees, internally displaced persons or survivors or perpetrators of war, mass violence and terrorism. *Current Opinion in Psychiatry, 25,* 277-284.

Du, H., & Taylor, H. S. (2016). The role of HOX genes in female reproductive tract development, adult function, and fertility. *Cold Spring Harbor Perspectives in Medicine, 6*(1), a023002.

Dubicka, B., Elvins, R., Roberts, C., Chick, G., Wilkinson, P., & Goodyer, I. M. (2010). Combined treatment with cognitive-behavioural therapy in adolescent depression: Meta-analysis. *The British Journal of Psychiatry, 197*(6), 433-440.

Dubois, J., Dehaene-Lambertz, G., Kulikova, S., Poupon, C., Hüppi, P. S., & Hertz-Pannier, L. (2014). The early development of brain white matter: A review of imaging studies in fetuses, newborns and infants. *Neuroscience, 276,* 48-71.

Dubowitz, H. (1999). The families of neglected children. In M. E. Lamb (Ed.), *Parenting and child development in "nontraditional" families* (pp. 327-345). Mahwah, NJ: Erlbaum.

Dubowitz, H., Kim, J., Black, M. M., Weisbart, C., Semiatin, J., & Magder, L. S. (2011). Identifying children at high risk for a child maltreatment report. *Child Abuse & Neglect, 35*(2), 96-104.

Duchek, J. M., Balota, D. A., Storandt, M., & Larsen, R. (2007). The power of personality in discriminating between healthy aging and early-stage Alzheimer's disease. *Journals of Gerontology, 62*(6, Series A), 353-361.

Duckworth, A. L., Gendler, T. S., & Gross, J. J. (2014). Self-control in school-age children. *Educational Psychologist, 49*(3), 199-217.

Duckworth, A. L., Quinn, P. D., & Tsukayama, E. (2012). What No Child Left Behind leaves behind: The roles of IQ and self-control in predicting standardized achievement test scores and report card grades. *Journal of Educational Psychology, 104*(2), 439.

Duckworth, A. L., Weir, D. R., Tsukayama, E., & Kwok, D. (2012). Who does well in life? Conscientious adults excel in both objective and subjective success. *Frontiers in Psychology, 3,* 356.

Duckworth, A., & Seligman, M. E. P. (2005). Self-discipline outdoes IQ in predicting academic performance of adolescents. *Psychological Science, 26,* 939-944.

Duell, N., Steinberg, L., Icenogle, G., Chein, J., Chaudhary, N., Di Giunta, L., . . . Pastorelli, C. (2018). Age patterns in risk taking across the world. *Journal of Youth and Adolescence, 47*(5), 1052-1072.

Dugdale, H. L., & Richardson, D. S. (2018). Heritability of telomere variation: it is all about the environment!. *Philosophical Transactions of the Royal Society B: Biological Sciences, 373*(1741), 20160450.

Duggan, M. (2014). 5 facts about Americans' views on life-and-death issues. *Pew Research Center.* Retrieved from www.pewresearch.org/fact-tank/2014/01/5-facts-about-americans-views-on-life-and-death-issues/

Duley, J., & Adams, R. (2013). Aging and driving II: Implications of cognitive changes. *Human Performance, Situation Awareness, and Automation: Current Research and Trends HPSAA II.*

Duncan, J. R., Paterson, D. S., Hoffman, J. M., Mokler, D. J., Borenstein, N. S., Belliveau, R. A., . . . Kinney, H. C. (2010). Brainstem serotonergic deficiency in sudden infant death syndrome. *Journal of the American Medical Association, 303*(5), 430-437. doi: 10.1001/jama.2010.45

Dunfield, K., Kuhlmeier, V. A., O'Connell, L., & Kelley, E. (2011). Examining the diversity of prosocial behavior: Helping, sharing, and comforting in infancy. *Infancy, 16*(3), 227-247.

Dunham, P., Dunham, F., & O'Keefe, C. (2000). Two-year-olds' sensitivity to a parent's knowledge state: Mind reading or contextual cues? *British Journal of Developmental Psychology, 18*(4), 519-532.

Dunifon, R. E., Ziol-Guest, K. M., & Kopko, K. (2014). Grandparent coresidence and family well-being: Implications for research and policy. *The Annals of the American Academy of Political and Social Science, 654*(1), 110-126.

Dunn, A. L., Trivedi, M. H., Kampert, J. B., Clark, C. G., & Chambliss, H. O. (2005). Exercise treatment for depression: Efficacy and dose response. *American Journal of Preventive Medicine, 28,* 1-8.

Dunn, J. (1991). Young children's understanding of other people: Evidence from observations within the family. In D. Frye & C. Moore (Eds.), *Children's theories of mind: Mental states and social understanding.* Hillsdale, NJ: Erlbaum.

Dunn, J. (2006). Moral development in early childhood and social interaction in the family. In M. Killen & J. Smetana (Eds.), *Handbook of moral development* (pp. 331-350). Mahwah, NJ: Earlbaum.

Dunn, J., & Hughes, C. (2001). "I got some swords and you're dead!": Violent fantasy, antisocial behavior, friendship, and moral sensibility in young children. *Child Development, 72,* 491-505.

Dunn, J., & Munn, P. (1985). Becoming a family member: Family conflict and the development of social understanding in the second year. *Child Development, 56,* 480-492.

Dunn, R. L., & Lessen, R. (2017). The influence of human milk on flavor and food preferences. *Current Nutrition Reports, 6*(2), 134-140.

Dunson, D. B., Colombo, B., & Baird, D. D. (2002). Changes with age in the level and duration of fertility in the menstrual cycle. *Human Reproduction, 17,* 1399-1403.

Dunst, C., Gorman, E., & Hamby, D. (2012). Preference for infant-directed speech in preverbal young children. *Center for Early Literacy Learning, 5*(1), 1-13.

DuPaul, G. J., & Stoner, G. (2014). *ADHD in the schools: Assessment and intervention strategies.* New York, NY: Guilford Publications.

Dupierrix, E., de Boisferon, A. H., Méary, D., Lee, K., Quinn, P. C., Di Giorgio, E., . . . Pascalis, O. (2014). Preference for human eyes in human infants. *Journal of Experimental Child Psychology, 123,* 138-146.

DuPont, R. L. (1983). Phobias in children. *Journal of Pediatrics, 102,* 999-1002.

Durazzo, T. C., Mattsson, N., Weiner, M. W., & Alzheimer's Disease Neuroimaging Initiative. (2014). Smoking and increased Alzheimer's disease risk: a review of potential mechanisms. *Alzheimer's & Dementia, 10*(3), S122-S145.

Duriancik, D. M., & Goff, C. R. (2019). Children of single-parent households are at a higher risk of obesity: A systematic review. *Journal of Child Health Care,* 1367493519852463.

Durlak, J. A., Mahoney, J. L., Bohnert, A. M., & Parente, M. E. (2010). Developing and improving after-school programs to enhance youth's personal growth and adjustment: A special issue of AJCP. *American Journal of Community Psychology, 45*(3-4), 285-293.

Durlak, J. A., Weissberg, R. P., Dymnicki, A. B., Taylor, R. D., & Schellinger, K. B. (2011). The impact of enhancing students' social and emotional learning: A meta-analysis of school-based universal interventions. *Child Development, 82*(1), 405-432.

Dwairy, M., & Achoui, M. (2010). Adolescents-family connectedness: A first cross-cultural research on parenting and psychological adjustment of children. *Journal of Child and Family Studies, 19*(1), 8-15.

Dweck, C. S. (2008). Mindsets: How praise is harming youth and what can be done about it. *School Library Media Activities Monthly, 24*(5), 55.

Dwomoh, I., & Dinolfo, E. A. (2018). Effects of homelessness on children. *Pediatrics in Review, 39*(10), 530.

Dye, B. A., Li, X., & Beltrán-Aguilar, E. D. (2012, May). Selected oral health indicators in the United States, 2005-2008. *NCHS Data Brief,* 1-8.

Dye, J. L. (2010). *Fertility of American women: 2008.* Retrieved from www.census.gov/prod/2010pubs/p20-563.pdf

Dykas, M. J., & Cassidy, J. (2011). Attachment and the processing of social information across the life span: theory and evidence. *Psychological Bulletin, 137*(1), 19.

Dykstra, P. A. (1995). Loneliness among the never and formerly married: The importance of supportive friendships and a desire for independence. *Journal of Gerontology: Social Sciences, 50B,* S321-S329.

D'Aquila, P., Rose, G., Bellizzi, D., & Passarino, G. (2013). Epigenetics and aging. *Maturitas, 74*(2), 130-136.

D'Epinay, C. J. L., Cavalli, S., & Guillet, L. A. (2010). Bereavement in very old age: impact on health and relationships of the loss of a spouse, a child, a sibling, or a close friend. *OMEGA-Journal of Death and Dying, 60*(4), 301-325.

Earl, J. K., Gerrans, P., & Halim, V. A. (2015). Active and adjusted: Investigating the contribution of leisure, health and psychosocial factors to retirement adjustment. *Leisure Sciences, 37*(4), 354-372.

Earls, M. (2010). Incorporating recognition and management of perinatal and postpartum depression into pediatric practice. *Pediatrics, 126,* 1032-1039.

Eaves, Y. D., McQuiston, C., & Miles, M. S. (2005). Coming to terms with adult sibling grief: When a brother dies from AIDS. *Journal of Hospice & Palliative Nursing, 7*(3), 139-149.

Eccles, J. S. (2004). Schools, academic motivation, and stage-environment fit. In R. M. Lerner & L. Steinberg (Eds.), *Handbook of adolescent development* (2nd ed., pp. 125-153). Hoboken, NJ: Wiley.

Eccles, J. S., Wigfield, A., & Byrnes, J. (2003). Cognitive development in adolescence. In I. B. Weiner (Series Ed.), R. M. Lerner, M. A. Easterbrooks, & J. Mistry (Vol. Eds.), *Handbook of psychology: Vol. 6. Developmental psychology.* New York, NY: Wiley.

Eckenrode, J., Smith, E. G., McCarthy, M. E., & Dineen, M. (2014). Income inequality and child maltreatment in the United States. *Pediatrics, 133*(3), 454-461.

Eckerman, C. O., & Didow, S. M. (1996). Nonverbal imitation and toddlers' mastery of verbal means of achieving coordinated action. *Developmental Psychology, 32,* 141-152.

Eckerman, C. O., Davis, C. C., & Didow, S. M. (1989). Toddlers' emerging ways of achieving social coordination with a peer. *Child Development, 60,* 440-453.

Eckert, M. A. (2011). Slowing down: Age-related neurobiological predictors of processing speed. *Frontiers in Neuroscience, 5,* 25.

Eckert, P. (2003). Language and adolescent peer groups. *Journal of Language and Social Psychology, 22*(1), 112-118.

Eddleman, K. A., Malone, F. D., Sullivan, L., Dukes, K., Berkowitz, R. L., Kharbutli, Y., . . . D'Alton, M. E. (2006). Pregnancy loss rates after midtrimester amniocentesis. *Obstetrics and Gynecology, 108*(5), 1067-1072.

Eden, G. F., Jones, K. M., Cappell, K., Gareau, L., Wood, F. B., Zeffiro, T. A., . . . Flowers, D. L. (2004). Neural changes following remediation in adult developmental dyslexia. *Neuron, 44,* 411-422.

Edmondson, D., Park, C. L., Chaudoir, S. R., & Wortman, J. H. (2008). Death without God: Religious struggle, death concerns, and depression in the terminally ill. *Psychological Science, 19*(8), 754-758.

Edwards, C. P. (2002). Three approaches from Europe: Waldorf, Montessori, and Reggio Emilia. *Early Childhood Research and Practice, 4*(1), 14-38.

Edwards, C. P. (2003). "Fine designs" from Italy: Montessori education and the Reggio Emilia approach. *Montessori life: Journal of the American Montessori Society, 15*(1), 33-38.

Edwards, D., & Panay, N. (2016). Treating vulvovaginal atrophy/genitourinary syndrome of menopause: How important is vaginal lubricant and moisturizer composition? *Climacteric, 19*(2), 151-161.

Edwards, J. D., Delahunt, P. B., & Mahncke, H. W. (2009). Cognitive speed of processing training delays driving cessation. *Journals of Gerontology Series A: Biomedical Sciences and Medical Sciences, 64*(12), 1262-1267.

Edwards, K. J., Hershberger, P. J., Russell, R. K., & Markert, R. J. (2001). Stress, negative social exchange, and health symptoms in university students. *Journal of American College Health, 50*(2), 75-79.

Edwards, K.M., Sylaska, K.M., & Neal, A.M. (2015). Intimate partner violence among sexual minority populations: A critical review of the literature and agenda for future research. *Psychology of Violence, 5,* 112-121.

Ehrenreich, B., & English, D. (2005). *For her own good: Two centuries of the experts' advice to women.* 2nd ed. New York: Anchor Books.

Ehrenreich, B., & English, D. (2005). *For her own good: Two centuries of the experts' advice to women.* New York: Anchor.

Ehrenreich, S. E., Beron, K. J., & Underwood, M. K. (2016). Social and physical aggression trajectories from childhood through late adolescence: Predictors of psychosocial maladjustment at age 18. *Developmental Psychology, 52*(3), 457.

Eicher, J. D., & Gruen, J. R. (2013). Imaging-genetics in dyslexia: Connecting risk genetic variants to brain neuroimaging and ultimately to reading impairments. *Molecular Genetics and Metabolism, 110*(3), 201-212.

Eidelman, A. I., Schanler, R. J., Johnston, M., Landers, S., Noble, L., Szucs, K., & Viehmann, L. (2012). Breastfeeding and the use of human milk. *Pediatrics, 129*(3), e827-e841.

Eimas, P., Siqueland, E., Jusczyk, P., & Vigorito, J. (1971). Speech perception in infants. *Science, 171,* 303-306.

Einarson, A., & Boskovic, R. (2009). Use and safety of antipsychotic drugs during pregnancy. *Journal of Psychiatric Practice, 15*(3), 183-192.

Eisenberg, A. R. (1996). The conflict talk of mothers and children: Patterns related to culture, SES, and gender of child. *Merrill-Palmer Quarterly, 42,* 438-452.

Eisenberg, M. E., & Neumark-Sztainer, D. (2010). Friends' dieting and disordered eating behaviors among adolescents five years later: Findings from Project EAT. *Journal of Adolescent Health, 47*(1), 67-73.

Eisenberg, M. E., Ackard, D. M., Resnick, M. D., & Neumark-Sztainer, D. (2009). Casual sex and psychological health among young adults: Is having "friends with benefits" emotionally damaging? *Perspectives on Sexual and Reproductive Health, 41*(4), 231-237.

Eisenberg, N. (1992). *The caring child.* Cambridge, MA: Harvard University Press.

Eisenberg, N. (2000). Emotion, regulation, and moral development. *Annual Review of Psychology, 51,* 665-697.

Eisenberg, N., & Morris, A. D. (2004). Moral cognitions and prosocial responding in adolescence. In R. M. Lerner & L. Steinberg (Eds.), *Handbook of adolescent psychology* (2nd ed., pp. 155-188). Hoboken, NJ: Wiley.

Eisenberg, N., & Morris, A. S. (2004). Moral cognitions and prosocial responding in adolescence. In R. M. Lerner & L. Steinberg (Eds.), *Handbook of adolescent psychology* (pp. 155-188). New York, NY: Wiley.

Eisenberg, N., Eggum, N. D., & Di Giunta, L. (2010). Empathy-related responding: Associations with prosocial behavior, aggression, and intergroup relations. *Social Issues and Policy Review, 4*(1), 143-180.

Eisenberg, N., Eggum-Wilkens, N. D., & Spinrad, T. L. (2015). The development of prosocial behavior. In D. A. Schroeder & W. G. Graziano (Eds.), *The Oxford handbook of prosocial behavior* (pp. 114-136). Oxford, England: Oxford University Press.

Eisenberg, N., Fabes, R. A., & Murphy, B. C. (1996). Parents' reactions to children's negative emotions: Relations to children's social competence and comforting behavior. *Child Development, 67,* 2227-2247.

Eisenberg, N., Fabes, R. A., & Spinrad, T. L. (2006). Prosocial development. In W. Damon & R. M. Lerner (Series Eds.) & N. Eisenberg (Vol. Ed.), *Handbook of child psychology: Vol 3. Social, emotional and personality development* (6th ed., pp. 646-718). Hoboken: NJ: Wiley.

Eisenberg, N., Fabes, R. A., Nyman, M., Bernzweig, J., & Pinuelas, A. (1994). The relations of emotionality and regulation to children's anger-related reactions. *Child Development, 65*, 109-128.

Eisenberg, N., Spinrad, T. L., & Valiente, C. (2016). Emotion-related self-regulation, and children's social, psychological, and academic functioning. In *Child Psychology: A Handbook of Contemporary Issues* (3rd ed., pp. 219-244). Abingdon, England: Taylor and Francis.

Eisenberg, N., Spinrad, T. L., Fabes, R. A., Reiser, M., Cumberland, A., Shepard, S. A., . . . Thompson, M. (2004). The relations of effortful control and impulsivity to children's resiliency and adjustment. *Child Development, 75*, 25-46.

Eisend, M. (2010). A meta-analysis of gender roles in advertising. *Journal of the Academy of Marketing Science, 38*(4), 418-440.

Eisenegger, C., Haushofer, J., & Fehr, E. (2011). The role of testosterone in social interaction. *Trends in Cognitive Sciences, 15*(6), 263-271.

Eivers, A. R., Brendgen, M., Vitaro, F., & Borge, A. I. (2012). Concurrent and longitudinal links between children's and their friends' antisocial and prosocial behavior in preschool. *Early Childhood Research Quarterly, 27*(1), 137-146.

Ekamper, P., van Poppel, F., Stein, A. D., Bijwaard, G. E., & Lumey, L. H. (2015). Prenatal famine exposure and adult mortality from cancer, cardiovascular disease, and other causes through age 63 years. *American Journal of Epidemiology, 181*(4), 271-279.

Ekinci, B. (2014). The relationships among Sternberg's Triarchic Abilities, Gardner's multiple intelligences, and academic achievement. *Social Behavior and Personality: An International Journal, 42*(4), 625-633.

Elgamri, A. I., Ahmed, A. T., Haj-Siddig, O. E., & Chin, J. R. (2018). Infant oral mutilation (IOM) related to traditional practices among inner city pre-school children in Sudan. *African Health Sciences, 18*(2), 359-368.

Elgar, F. J., Pförtner, T. K., Moor, I., De Clercq, B., Stevens, G. W., & Currie, C. (2015). Socioeconomic inequalities in adolescent health 2002-2010: A time-series analysis of 34 countries participating in the Health Behaviour in School-aged Children study. *The Lancet, 385*(9982), 2088-2095.

Eliason, M. J. (1995). Accounts of sexual identity formation in heterosexual students. *Sex Roles, 32*, 821-834.

Eliason, S. R., Mortimer, J. T., & Vuolo, M. (2015). The transition to adulthood: Life course structures and subjective perceptions. *Social Psychology Quarterly, 78*(3), 205-227.

Eliassen, H., Colditz, G. A., Rosner, B., Willett, W. C., & Hankinson, S. E. (2006). Adult weight change and risk of postmenopausal breast cancer. *Journal of the American Medical Association, 296*, 193-201.

Elicker, J., Englund, M., & Sroufe, L. A. (1992). Predicting peer competence and peer relationships in childhood from early parent-child relationships. In R. Parke & G. Ladd (Eds.), *Family peer relationships: Modes of linkage* (pp. 77-106). Hillsdale, NJ: Erlbaum.

Elkind, D. (1967). Egocentrism in adolescence. *Child Development*, 1025-1034.

Elledge, L. C., Elledge, A. R., Newgent, R. A., & Cavell, T. A. (2016). Social risk and peer victimization in elementary school children: The protective role of teacher-student relationships. *Journal of abnormal Child Psychology, 44*(4), 691-703.

Ellis, A., & Oakes, L. M. (2006). Infants flexibly use different dimensions to categorize objects. *Developmental Psychology, 42*, 1000-1011.

Ellis, B. J., & Del Giudice, M. (2014). Beyond allostatic load: Rethinking the role of stress in regulating human development. *Development and Psychopathology, 26*(1), 1-20.

Ellis, B. J., Bates, J. E., Dodge, K. A., Fergusson, D. M., Horwood, L. J., Pettit, G. S., & Woodward, L. (2003). Does father-absence place daughters at special risk for early sexual activity and teenage pregnancy? *Child Development, 74*, 801-821.

Ellis, B. J., McFadyen-Ketchum, S., Dodge, K. A., Pettit, G. S., & Bates, J. E. (1999). Quality of early family relationships and individual differences in the timing of pubertal maturation in girls: A longitudinal test of an evolutionary model. *Journal of Personality and Social Psychology, 77*, 387-401.

Ellis, W. R., & Dietz, W. H. (2017). A new framework for addressing adverse childhood and community experiences: The building community resilience model. *Academic Pediatrics, 17*(7), S86-S93.

Ellison, C. G., & Xu, X. (2016). Religion, race/ethnicity, and norms of intergenerational assistance among older adults. *Religions, 7*(1), 5.

Ellison, C. G., DeAngelis, R. T., & Güven, M. (2017). Does religious involvement mitigate the effects of major discrimination on the mental health of African Americans? Findings from the Nashville Stress and Health Study. *Religions, 8*(9), 195.

Ellison, C. G., Musick, M. A., & Henderson, A. K. (2008). Balm in Gilead: Racism, religious involvement, and psychological distress among African-American adults. *Journal for the Scientific Study of Religion, 47*(2), 291-309.

Ellison, N. B., Steinfield, C., & Lampe, C. (2007). The benefits of Facebook "friends": Social capital and college students' use of online social network sites. *Journal of Computer-Mediated Communication, 12*(4), 1143-1168.

Else-Quest, N. M., Hyde, J. S., & Linn, M. C. (2010). Cross-national patterns of gender differences in mathematics: a meta-analysis. *Psychological Bulletin, 136*(1), 103.

ElSohly, M. A., Mehmedic, Z., Foster, S., Gon, C., Chandra, S., & Church, J. C. (2016). Changes in cannabis potency over the last 2 decades (1995-2014): Analysis of current data in the United States. *Biological Psychiatry, 79*(7), 613-619.

Ely, D. M., & Driscoll, A. K. (2019). Infant mortality in the United States, 2017: Data from the period linked birth/infant death file. *National Vital Statistics Reports, 68*(10), 1-20. Hyattsville, MD: National Center for Health Statistics.

Emanuel, E. J., Onwuteaka-Philipsen, B. D., Urwin, J. W., & Cohen, J. (2016). Attitudes and practices of euthanasia and physician-assisted suicide in the United States, Canada, and Europe. *Journal of the American Medical Association, 316*, 79-90.

Emerson, R. W., & Cantlon, J. F. (2015). Continuity and change in children's longitudinal neural responses to numbers. *Developmental Science, 18*(2), 314-326.

Emery, L., Heaven, T. J., Paxton, J. L., & Braver, T. S. (2008). Age-related changes in neural activity during performance matched working memory manipulation. *NeuroImage, 42*(4), 1577-1586.

Emmons, R. A., & Paloutzian, R. F. (2003). The psychology of religion. *Annual Review of Psychology, 54*(1), 377-402.

Endendijk, J. J., Groeneveld, M., Bakermans-Kranenburg, M. J., & Mesman, J. (2016). Gender-differentiated parenting revisited: Meta-analysis reveals very few differences in parental control of boys and girls. PLoS One, 11, 0159193. doi: 10.1371/journal. pone.0159193.

Eng, P. M., Rimm, E. B., Fitzmaurice, G., & Kawachi, I. (2002). Social ties and change in social ties in relation to subsequent total and cause-specific mortality and coronary heart disease incidence in men. *American Journal of Epidemiology, 155*, 700-709.

England, D. E., Descartes, L., & Collier-Meek, M. A. (2011). Gender role portrayal and the Disney princesses. *Sex Roles, 64*(7-8), 555-567.

Engle, P. L., & Breaux, C. (1998). Fathers' involvement with children: Perspectives from developing countries. *Social Policy Report, 12*(1), 1-21.

English, T., & Carstensen, L. L. (2014). Selective narrowing of social networks across adulthood is associated with improved emotional experience in daily life. *International Journal of Behavioral Development, 38*(2), 195-202.

Ensor, R., Spencer, D., & Hughes, C. (2011). "You feel sad?" emotion understanding mediates effects of verbal ability and mother–child mutuality on prosocial behaviors: Findings from 2 years to 4 years. *Social Development, 20*(1), 93-110.

Enwereji, E. E. (2008). Indigenous marriage institutions and divorce in Nigeria: The case of Abia state of Nigeria. *European Journal of General Medicine, 5*(3), 165-169.

Erath, S. A., El-Sheikh, M., & Cummings, E. M. (2009). Harsh parenting and child externalizing behavior: Skin conductance level reactivity as a moderator. *Child Development, 80*(2), 578-592.

Erdogan, B., Bauer, T. N., Truxillo, D. M., & Mansfield, L. R. (2012). Whistle while you work: A review of the life satisfaction literature. *Journal of Management, 38*(4), 1038-1083.

Erickson, K. I., Leckie, R. L., & Weinstein, A. M. (2014). Physical activity, fitness, and gray matter volume. *Neurobiology of Aging, 35,* S20-S28.

Erickson, L. C., & Thiessen, E. D. (2015). Statistical learning of language: Theory, validity, and predictions of a statistical learning account of language acquisition. *Developmental Review, 37,* 66-108.

Eriksen, M., Mackay, J., & Ross, H. (2013). *The tobacco atlas* (No. Ed. 4). Atlanta, GA: American Cancer Society.

Erikson broadened the concept of "crisis" and later referred instead to conflicting or competing tendencies.

Erikson, E. H. (1950). *The life cycle completed.* New York, NY: Norton.

Erikson, E. H. (1968). *Identity: Youth and crisis.* New York, NY: Norton.

Erikson, E. H. (1982). *The life cycle completed.* New York, NY: Norton.

Erikson, E. H. (1985). *The life cycle completed* (Paperback reprint ed.). New York, NY: Norton.

Erikson, E. H. Growth and crises of the healthy personality. In M. J. E. Senn (Ed.), *Symposium on the healthy personality. Suppl. 2. Transactions of the fourth conference on problems of infancy and childhood* (pp. 91-146). New York, NY: Josiah Macy Jr. Foundation.

Erikson, E. H., & Erikson, J. M. (1998). *The life cycle completed (extended version).* New York, NY: Norton.

Erikson, E. H., Erikson, J. M., & Kivnick, H. Q. (1986). *Vital involvement in old age: The experience of old age in our time.* New York, NY: Norton.

Eriksson, M., Marschik, P. B., Tulviste, T., Almgren, M., Pérez Pereira, M., Wehberg, S., . . . Gallego, C. (2012). Differences between girls and boys in emerging language skills: Evidence from 10 language communities. *British Journal of Developmental Psychology, 30*(2), 326-343.

Ertem, I. O., Krishnamurthy, V., Mulaudzi, M. C., Sguassero, Y., Balta, H., Gulumser, O., . . . Calvocoressi, L. (2018). Similarities and differences in child development from birth to age 3 years by sex and across four countries: A cross-sectional, observational study. *The Lancet Global Health, 6*(3), e279-e291.

Ervin, R. B. (2008). Healthy Index Eating scores among adults, 60 years of age and over, by sociodemographic and health characteristics: United States, 1999-2002. *Advance Data from Vital and Health Statistics,* No. 395. Hyattsville, MD: National Center for Health Statistics.

Espeland, M. A., Rapp, S. R., Shumaker, S. A., Brunner, R., Manson, J. E., Sherwin, B. B., . . . Hays, J., for the Women's Health Initiative Memory Study Investigators. (2004). Conjugated equine estrogens and global cognitive function in postmenopausal women: Women's Health Initiative Memory Study. *Journal of the American Medical Association, 21,* 2959-2968.

Esposito, K., Marfella, R., Ciotola, M., DiPalo, C., Giugliano, F., Giugliano, G., . . . Giugliano, D. (2004). Effects of a Mediterranean-style diet on endothelial dysfunction and markers of vascular inflammation in the metabolic syndrome: A randomized trial. *Journal of the American Medical Association, 292,* 1440-1446.

Estes, K. G., & Hurley, K. (2013). Infant-directed prosody helps infants map sounds to meanings. *Infancy, 18,* 797-824.

Etaugh, C.A. (2013). Midlife career transitions for women. In W. Patton (Ed.), *Conceptualising women's working lives: Moving the boundaries of discourse* (pp. 105-118). Rotterdam, the Netherlands: Sense Publishers.

Euling, S. Y., Selevan, S. G., Pescovitz, O. H., & Skakkebaek, N. E. (2008). Role of environmental factors in the timing of puberty. *Pediatrics, 121*(Suppl. 3), S167-S171.

Evans, A. D., & Lee, K. (2013). Emergence of lying in very young children. *Developmental Psychology, 49*(10), 1958.

Evans, C. E., Christian, M. S., Cleghorn, C. L., Greenwood, D. C., & Cade, J. E. (2012). Systematic review and meta-analysis of school-based interventions to improve daily fruit and vegetable intake in children aged 5 to 12 y. *The American Journal of Clinical Nutrition, 96*(4), 889-901.

Evans, G. W. (2004). The environment of childhood poverty. *American Psychologist, 59,* 77-92.

Eveleth, P. B. (2017). Timing of menarche: Secular trend and population differences. In *School-age pregnancy and parenthood* (pp. 39-52). New York, NY: Routledge.

Ewing, S. W. F., Sakhardande, A., & Blakemore, S. J. (2014). The effect of alcohol consumption on the adolescent brain: A systematic review of MRI and fMRI studies of alcohol-using youth. *NeuroImage: Clinical, 5,* 420-437.

Exner-Cortens, D., Eckenrode, J., Bunge, J., & Rothman, E. (2017). Revictimization after adolescent dating violence in a matched, national sample of youth. *Journal of Adolescent Health, 60*(2), 176-183.

Eyler, L. T., Sherzai, A., Kaup, A. R., & Jeste, D. V. (2011). A review of functional brain imaging correlates of successful cognitive aging. *Biological Psychiatry, 70*(2), 115-122.

Eze, N., Smith, L. M., LaGasse, L. L., Derauf, C., Newman, E., Arria, A., . . . & Lester, B. M. (2016). School-aged outcomes following prenatal methamphetamine exposure: 7.5-year follow-up from the Infant Development, Environment, and Lifestyle Study. *The Journal of Pediatrics, 170,* 34-38.

Fabes, R. A., & Eisenberg, N. (1992). Young children's coping with interpersonal anger. *Child Development, 63,* 116-128.

Fabes, R. A., Leonard, S. A., Kupanoff, K., & Martin, C. L. (2001). Parental coping with children's negative emotions: Relations with children's emotional and social responding. *Child Development, 72,* 907-920.

Fabes, R. A., Martin, C. L., & Hanish, L. D. (2003). Young children's play qualities in same-, other-, and mixed-gender peer groups. *Child Development, 74*(3), 921-932.

Fabricius, W. V. (2003). Listening to children of divorce: New findings that diverge from Wallerstein, Lewis, and Blakeslee. *Family Relations, 52,* 385-394.

Facebook. (2011). *Statistics.* Retrieved from www.facebook.com/press/info.php?statistics

Faedda, G. L., Marangoni, C., Serra, G., Salvatore, P., Sani, G., Vázquez, G. H., . . . Koukopoulos, A. (2015). Precursors of bipolar disorders: A systematic literature review of prospective studies. *Journal of Clinical Psychiatry, 76*(5), 614-624.

Fagot, B. I. (1997). Attachment, parenting, and peer interactions of toddler children. *Developmental Psychology, 33,* 489-499.

Fagot, B. I., Rogers, C. S., & Leinbach, M. D. (2000). Theories of gender socialization. In T. Eckes & H. M. Trautner (Eds.), *The developmental social psychology of gender.* Mahwah, NJ: Earlbaum.

Falbo, T. (2006). *Your one and only: Educational psychologist dispels myths surrounding only children.* Retrieved from www.utexas.edu/features/archive/2004/single.htm

Falbo, T. (2012). Only children: An updated review. *Journal of Individual Psychology, 68*(1).

Falbo, T., & Hooper, S. Y. (2015). China's only children and psychopathology: A quantitative synthesis. *American Journal of Orthopsychiatry, 85*(3), 259.

Falkner, B. (2010). Hypertension in children and adolescents: Epidemiology and natural history. *Pediatric Nephrology, 25*(7), 1219-1224.

Fallis, E. E., Rehman, U. S., Woody, E. Z., & Purdon, C. (2016). The longitudinal association of relationship satisfaction and sexual satisfaction in long-term relationships. *Journal of Family Psychology, 30*(7), 822.

Fandakova, Y., Selmeczy, D., Leckey, S., Grimm, K. J., Wendelken, C., Bunge, S. A., & Ghetti, S. (2017). Changes in ventromedial prefrontal and insular cortex support the development of metamemory from childhood into adolescence. *Proceedings of the National Academy of Sciences, 114*(29), 7582-7587.

Fang, L., Karakiulakis, G., & Roth, M. (2020). Are patients with hypertension and diabetes mellitus at increased risk for COVID-19 infection? *The Lancet, Respiratory Medicine.*

Fanzo, J., Hawkes, C., Udomkesmalee, E., Afshin, A., Allemandi, L., Assery, O., . . . Corvalan, C. (2018). *Global nutrition report: Shining a light to spur action on malnutrition* [Report]. Retrieved from https://globalnutritionreport.org/reports/global-nutrition-report-2018/

Fardouly, J., & Vartanian, L. R. (2016). Social media and body image concerns: Current research and future directions. *Current Opinion in Psychology, 9,* 1-5.

Farr, R. H., Forssell, S. L., & Patterson, C. J. (2010). Gay, lesbian, and heterosexual adoptive parents: Couple and relationship issues. *Journal of GLBT Family Studies, 6*(2), 199-213.

Farren, J., Jalmbrant, M., Ameye, L., Joash, K., Mitchell-Jones, N., Tapp, S., . . . Bourne, T. (2016). Post-traumatic stress, anxiety and depression following miscarriage or ectopic pregnancy: A prospective cohort study. *BMJ Open, 6*(11), e011864.

Farsani, S. F., Van Der Aa, M. P., Van Der Vorst, M. M. J., Knibbe, C. A. J., & De Boer, A. (2013). Global trends in the incidence and prevalence of type 2 diabetes in children and adolescents: A systematic review and evaluation of methodological approaches. *Diabetologia, 56*(7), 1471–1488.

Farver, J. A. M., Kim, Y. K., & Lee, Y. (1995). Cultural differences in Korean and Anglo-American preschoolers' social interaction and play behavior. *Child Development, 66,* 1088–1099.

Fasig, L. (2000). Toddlers' understanding of ownership: Implications for self-concept development. *Social Development, 9,* 370–382.

Fasula, A. M., Chia, V., Murray, C. C., Brittain, A., Tevendale, H., & Koumans, E. H. (2019). Socioecological risk factors associated with teen pregnancy or birth for young men: A scoping review. *Journal of Adolescence, 74,* 130–145.

Faure, N., Habersaat, S., Harari, M. M., Müller-Nix, C., Borghini, A., Ansermet, F., . . . Urben, S. (2017). Maternal sensitivity: A resilience factor against internalizing symptoms in early adolescents born very preterm? *Journal of Abnormal Child Psychology, 45*(4), 671–680.

Fawcett, C., & Liszkowski, U. (2015). Social referencing during infancy and early childhood across cultures. In J. Wright (Ed.), *International encyclopedia of the social & behavioral sciences* (pp. 556–562). Amsterdam, the Netherlands: Elsevier.

Fay-Stammbach, T., Hawes, D. J., & Meredith, P. (2014). Parenting influences on executive function in early childhood: A review. *Child Development Perspectives, 8*(4), 258–264.

Fear, J. M., Champion, J. E., Reeslund, K. L., Forehand, R., Colletti, C., Roberts, L., & Compas, B. E. (2009). Parental depression and interparental conflict: Children and adolescents' self-blame and coping responses. *Journal of Family Psychology, 23*(5), 762–766. doi:10.1037/a0016381

Fearon, R. P., Bakermans-Kranenburg, M. J., Van IJzendoorn, M. H., Lapsley, A.-M., & Roisman, G. I. (2010). The significance of insecure attachment and disorganization in the development of children's externalizing behavior: A meta-analytic study. *Child Development, 81,* 435–456. doi: 10.1111/j.1467-8624.2009.01405.x

Federal Interagency Forum on Aging-Related Statistics. (2004). *Older Americans 2004: Key indicators of well-being.* Washington, DC: U.S. Government Printing Office.

Federal Interagency Forum on Aging-Related Statistics. (2016). *Older Americans 2016: Key indicators of well-being.* Washington, DC: U.S. Government Printing Office.

Federal Interagency Forum on Aging-Related Statistics. (2016). *Older Americans update 2016: Key indicators of well-being.* Washington, DC: U.S. Government Printing Office.

Federal Interagency Forum on Child and Family Statistics. (2019). *America's children: Key national indicators of well-being, 2017.* Retrieved from www.childstats.gov/americaschildren/family5.asp

Federal Interagency Forum on Child and Family Statistics. (2019). *America's children: Key national indicators of well-being, 2019.* Retrieved from www.childstats.gov/americaschildren/index.asp

Fedewa, A. L., Black, W. W., & Ahn, S. (2015). Children and adolescents with same-gender parents: A meta-analytic approach in assessing outcomes. *Journal of GLBT Family Studies, 11*(1), 1–34.

Feinstein, B. A., Goldfried, M. R., & Davila, J. (2012). The relationship between experiences of discrimination and mental health among lesbians and gay men: An examination of internalized homonegativity and rejection sensitivity as potential mechanisms. *Journal of Consulting and Clinical Psychology, 80*(5), 917.

Feldman, R. (2007). Parent-infant synchrony: Biological foundations and developmental outcomes. *Current Directions in Psychological Science, 16*(6), 340–345.

Feldman, R., Magori-Cohen, R., Galili, G., Singer, M., & Louzoun, Y. (2011). Mother and infant coordinate heart rhythms through episodes of interaction synchrony. *Infant Behavior and Development, 34*(4), 569–577.

Feldman, R., Masalha, S., & Alony, D. (2006). Microregulatory patterns of family interactions: Cultural pathways to toddlers' self-regulation. *Journal of Family Psychology, 20*(4), 614.

Feng, W., Gu, B., & Cai, Y. (2016). The end of China's one-child policy. *Studies in Family Planning, 47*(1), 83–86.

Ferdows, N.B., Jensen, G.A., & Tarraf, W. (2017). Healthy aging after age 65: A life-span health production function approach. *Research on Aging.* Retrieved from https://doi.org/10.1177/0164027517713312

Ferguson, C. A. (1964). Baby talk in six languages. *American Anthropologist, 66*(6_PART2), 103–114.

Ferguson, C. J. (2010). Genetic contributions to antisocial personality and behavior: A meta-analytic review from an evolutionary perspective. *The Journal of Social Psychology, 150*(2), 160–180.

Ferguson, C. J. (2013). Violent video games and the Supreme Court: Lessons for the scientific community in the wake of Brown vs. Entertainment Merchant's Association. *American Psychologist, 68*(2), 57–74.

Ferguson, C. J. (2015). Do angry birds make for angry children? A meta-analysis of video game influences on children's and adolescents' aggression, mental health, prosocial behavior, and academic performance. *Perspectives on Psychological Science, 10*(5), 646–666.

Ferguson, C. J. (2015). Does media violence predict societal violence? It depends on what you look at and when. *Journal of Communication, 65*(1).

Ferguson, C. J., & Savage, J. (2012). Have recent studies addressed methodological issues raised by five decades of televised violence research? A critical review. *Aggression and Violent Behavior, 17,* 129–139.

Fergusson, D. M., McLeod, G. F., & Horwood, L. J. (2013). Childhood sexual abuse and adult developmental outcomes: Findings from a 30-year longitudinal study in New Zealand. *Child Abuse & Neglect, 37*(9), 664–674.

Fernald, A., & Marchman, V. A. (2012). Individual differences in lexical processing at 18 months predict vocabulary growth in typically developing and late-talking toddlers. *Child Development, 83*(1), 203–222.

Fernald, A., & Morikawa, H. (1993). Common themes and cultural variations in Japanese and American mothers' speech to infants. *Child Development, 64,* 637–656.

Fernald, A., & O'Neill, D. K. (1993). Peekaboo across cultures: How mothers and infants play with voices, faces, and expectations. In K. MacDonald (Ed.), *Parent-child play: Descriptions and implications* (pp. 259–285). Albany, NY: State University of New York Press.

Fernald, A., Perfors, A., & Marchman, V. A. (2006). Picking up speed in understanding: Speech processing efficiency and vocabulary growth across the second year. *Developmental Psychology, 42,* 98–116.

Fernald, A., Swingley, D., & Pinto, J. P. (2001). When half a word is enough: Infants can recognize spoken words using partial phonetic information. *Child Development, 72,* 1003–1015.

Fernald, A., Taeschner, T., Dunn, J., Papousek, M., de Boysson-Bardies, B., & Fukui, I. (1989). A cross-language study of prosodic modifications in mothers' and fathers' speech to preverbal infants. *Journal of Child Language, 16*(3), 477–501.

Fernald, L. C., Prado, E., Kariger, P., & Raikes, A. (2017). A toolkit for measuring early childhood development in low and middle-income countries. *World Bank.* Retrieved from http://repositorio.minedu.gob.pe/bitstream/handle/MINEDU/5723/A%20Toolkit%20for%20Measuring%20Early%20Childhood%20Development%20in%20Low%20and%20Middle-Income%20Countries.pdf?sequence=1

Fernández-Carro, C. (2016). Ageing at home, co-residence or institutionalisation? Preferred care and residential arrangements of older adults in Spain. *Ageing & Society, 36*(3), 586–612.

Ferrari, L., Rosnati, R., Manzi, C., & Benet-Martínez, V. (2015). Ethnic identity, bicultural identity integration, and psychological well-being among transracial adoptees: A longitudinal study. *New Directions for Child and Adolescent Development, 2015*(150), 63–76.

Ferraro, A. J., Malespin, T., Oehme, K., Bruker, M., & Opel, A. (2016). Advancing co-parenting education: Toward a foundation for supporting positive post-divorce adjustment. *Child and Adolescent Social Work Journal, 33*(5), 407–415.

Ferrer, E., Shaywitz, B. A., Holahan, J. M., Marchione, K., & Shaywitz, S. E. (2010). Uncoupling of reading and IQ over time: Empirical evidence for a definition of dyslexia. *Psychological Science, 21*(1), 93–101.

Ferry, A. L., Hespos, S. J., & Waxman, S. R. (2010). Categorization in 3- and 4-month-old infants: An advantage of words over tones. *Child Development, 81*(2), 472–479.

Ferry, A. L., Hespos, S. J., & Waxman, S. R. (2013). Nonhuman primate vocalizations support categorization in very young human infants. *Proceedings of the National Academy of Sciences, 110*(38), 15231–15235.

Fettro, M. N., & Manning, W. D. (2018). Child well-being in same-gender-parent families: Courts, media, and social science research. In M. Y. Janning (Ed.), *Contemporary parenting and parenthood: From news headlines to new research* (p. 283). Santa Barbara, CA: Praeger.

Field, A. E., Austin, S. B., Taylor, C. B., Malspeis, S., Rosner, B., Rockett, H. R., . . . Colditz, G. A. (2003). Relation between dieting and weight change among preadolescents and adolescents. *Pediatrics, 112*(4), 900–906.

Field, T. (2010). Postpartum depression effects on early interactions, parenting, and safety practices: A review. *Infant Behavior and Development, 33,* 1–6.

Field, T. (2010). Touch for socioemotional and physical well-being: A review. *Developmental Review, 30*(4), 367–383.

Field, T. M. (1978). Interaction behaviors of primary versus secondary caretaker fathers. *Developmental Psychology, 14,* 183–184.

Fields, J. (2004). America's families and living arrangements: 2003. *Current Population Reports,* P20-553. Washington, DC: U.S. Census Bureau.

Fierro, A. D., & Moreno, H. A. (2007). Emerging adulthood in Mexican and Spanish youth: Theories and realities. *Journal of Adolescent Research, 22*(5), 476–503.

Fihrer, I., McMahon, C. A., & Taylor, A. J. (2009). The impact of postnatal and concurrent maternal depression on child behaviour during the early school years. *Journal of Affective Disorders, 119,* 116–123.

Filippi, M., Agosta, F., Barkhof, F., Dubois, B., Fox, N. C., Frisoni, G. B., . . . Scheltens, P. (2012). EFNS task force: The use of neuroimaging in the diagnosis of dementia. *European Journal of Neurology, 19*(12), 1487–1501.

Finch, C. E., & Zelinski, E. M. (2005). Normal aging of brain structure and cognition: Evolutionary perspectives. *Research in Human Development, 2,* 69–82.

Fincham, F. D., & May, R. W. (2017). Infidelity in romantic relationships. *Current Opinion in Psychology, 13,* 70–74.

Finer, L. B., & Philbin, J. M. (2014). Trends in ages at key reproductive transitions in the United States, 1951–2010. *Women's Health Issues, 24*(3), e271–e279.

Fingerman, K. L., & Charles, S. T. (2010). It takes two to tango: Why older people have the best relationships. *Current Directions in Psychological Science, 19*(3), 172–176.

Fingerman, K. L., Pitzer, L. M., Chan, W., Birditt, K., Franks, M. M., & Zarit, S. (2010). Who gets what and why? Help middle-aged adults provide to parents and grown children. *Journal of Gerontology, 10,* 1–12.

Fingerman, K. L., VanderDrift, L. E., Dotterer, A. M., Birditt, K. S., & Zarit, S. H. (2011). Support to aging parents and grown children in Black and white families. *The Gerontologist, 51*(4), 441–452.

Fingerman, K., & Dolbin-MacNab, M. (2006). The baby boomers and their parents: Cohort influences and intergenerational ties. In S. K. Whitbourne & S. L. Willis (Eds.), *The baby boomers grow up: Contemporary perspectives on midlife* (pp. 237–259). Mahwah, NJ: Erlbaum.

Fingerman, K., Miller, L., Birditt, K., & Zarit, S. (2009). Giving to the good and to the needy: Parental support of grown children. *Journal of Marriage and Family, 71,* 1220–1233.

Fink, E., Deighton, J., Humphrey, N., & Wolpert, M. (2015). Assessing the bullying and victimisation experiences of children with special educational needs in mainstream schools: Development and validation of the Bullying Behaviour and Experience Scale. *Research in Developmental Disabilities, 36,* 611–619.

Finkel, D., Gerritsen, L., Reynolds, C. A., Dahl, A. K., & Pedersen, N. L. (2014). Etiology of individual differences in human health and longevity. *Annual Review of Gerontology and Geriatrics, 34*(1), 189–227.

Finkelhor, D., Turner, H., Wormuth, B. K., Vanderminden, J., & Hamby, S. (2019). Corporal punishment: Current rates from a national survey. *Journal of Child and Family Studies,* 1–7.

Finn, J. D. (2006). *The adult lives of at-risk students: The roles of attainment and engagement in high school* (NCES 2006-328). Washington, DC: U.S. Department of Education, National Center for Education Statistics.

Fiori, K. L., Smith, J., & Antonucci, T. C. (2007). Social network types among older adults: A multidimensional approach. *Journals of Gerontology, 62*(6, Series A), 322–330.

Fischer, K. W. (2008). Dynamic cycles of cognitive and brain development: Measuring growth in mind, brain, and education. In A. M. Battro, K. W. Fischer, & P. Léna (Eds.), *The educated brain* (pp. 127–150). Cambridge, England: Cambridge University Press.

Fischer, N., Weber, B., & Riechelmann, H. (2016). Presbycusis-age related hearing loss. *Laryngo-rhino-otologie, 95*(7), 497–510.

Fisher, C., Gertner, Y., Scott, R. M., & Yuan, S. (2010). Syntactic bootstrapping. *Wiley Interdisciplinary Reviews: Cognitive Science, 1*(2), 143–149.

Fisher, G. G., Chaffee, D. S., Tetrick, L. E., Davalos, D. B., & Potter, G. G. (2017). Cognitive functioning, aging, and work: A review and recommendations for research and practice. *Journal of Occupational Health Psychology, 22*(3), 314.

Fisher, K. R., Hirsh-Pasek, K., Newcombe, N., & Golinkoff, R. M. (2013). Taking shape: Supporting preschoolers' acquisition of geometric knowledge through guided play. *Child Development, 84*(6), 1872–1878.

Fisher, W. A., Donahue, K. L., Long, J. S., Heiman, J. R., Rosen, R. C., & Sand, M. S. (2015). Individual and partner correlates of sexual satisfaction and relationship happiness in midlife couples: Dyadic analysis of the international survey of relationships. *Archives of Sexual Behavior, 44*(6), 1609–1620.

Fitzpatrick, M. J., & McPherson, B. J. (2010). Coloring within the lines: Gender stereotypes in contemporary coloring books. *Sex Roles, 62*(1–2), 127–137.

Fivush, R. (2011). The development of autobiographical memory. *Annual Review of Psychology, 62,* 559–582.

Fivush, R., & Haden, C. A. (2006). Elaborating on elaborations: Role of maternal reminiscing style in cognitive and socioemotional development. *Child Development, 77,* 1568–1588.

Fivush, R., & Nelson, K. (2004). Culture and language in the emergence of autobiographical memory. *Psychological Science, 15,* 573–577.

Fivush, R., Habermas, T., Waters, T. E., & Zaman, W. (2011). The making of autobiographical memory: Intersections of culture, narratives and identity. *International Journal of Psychology, 46*(5), 321–345.

Fjell, A. M., & Walhovd, K. B. (2010). Structural brain changes in aging: Courses, causes and cognitive consequences. *Reviews in the Neurosciences, 21*(3), 187–222.

Fjell, A. M., Grydeland, H., Krogsrud, S. K., Amlien, I., Rohani, D. A., Ferschmann, L., . . . Bjørnerud, A. (2015). Development and aging of cortical thickness correspond to genetic organization patterns. *Proceedings of the National Academy of Sciences, 112*(50), 15462–15467.

Flannagan, C. A., Bowes, J. M., Jonsson, B., Csapo, B., & Sheblanova, E. (1998). Ties that bind: Correlates of adolescents' civic commitment in seven countries. *Journal of Social Issues, 54,* 457–475.

Flavell, J. H. (2000). Development of children's knowledge about the mental world. *International Journal of Behavioral Development, 24*(1), 15–23.

Flavell, J. H. (2016). Development of children's knowledge about the mind. In R. J. Sternberg, S. T. Fiske, & D. J. Foss (Eds.), *Scientists making a difference: One hundred eminent behavioral and brain scientists talk about their most important contributions* (pp. 198–201). Cambridge, England: Cambridge University Press.

Flavell, J. H., Flavell, E. R., & Green, F. L. (1983). Development of the appearance-reality distinction. *Cognitive Psychology, 15*(1), 95–120.

Flavell, J. H., Green, F. L., & Flavell, E. R. (1986). Development of knowledge about the appearance-reality distinction. *Monographs of the Society for Research in Child Development, 51*(1, Serial No. 212).

Flavell, J. H., Miller, P. H., & Miller, S. A. (2002). *Cognitive development.* Englewood Cliffs, NJ: Prentice Hall.

Flegal, K. M., Carroll, M. D., Ogden, C. L., & Curtin, L. R. (2010). Prevalence and trends in obesity among U.S. adults, 1999–2008. *Journal of the American Medical Association, 303,* 235–241.

Flegal, K. M., Kit, B. K., Orpana, H., & Graubard, B. I. (2013). Association of all-cause mortality with overweight and obesity using standard body mass index categories: A systematic review and meta-analysis. *JAMA, 309*(1), 71–82.

Fleischman, D. A., Wilson, R. S., Gabrieli, J. D. E., Bienias, J. L., & Bennett, D. A. (2004). A longitudinal study of implicit and explicit memory in old persons. *Psychology and Aging, 19*(4), 617–625. doi: 10.1037/0882-7974. 19.4.617

Fleischman, D. A., Yang, J., Arfanakis, K., Arvanitakis, Z., Leurgans, S. E., Turner, A. D., . . . & Buchman, A. S. (2015). Physical activity, motor function, and white matter hyperintensity burden in healthy older adults. *Neurology, 84*(13), 1294–1300.

Fletcher, J., Mailick, M., Song, J., & Wolfe, B. (2013). A sibling death in the family: Common and consequential. *Demography, 50*(3), 803–826.

Flewitt, R., Messer, D., & Kucirkova, N. (2015). New directions for early literacy in a digital age: The iPad. *Journal of Early Childhood Literacy, 15*(3), 289-310.

Flook, L., Repetti, R. L., & Ullman, J. B. (2005). Classroom social experiences as predictors of academic performance. *Developmental Psychology, 41*, 319-327.

Flores, A. R., Brown, T. N., & Herman, J. (2016). *Race and ethnicity of adults who identify as transgender in the United States.* Los Angeles, CA: Williams Institute, UCLA School of Law.

Flores, A. R., Herman, J. L., Gates, G. J., & Brown, T. N. T. (2017). *How many adults identify as transgender in the United States?* Los Angeles, CA: The Williams Institute.

Floyd, F. J., & Bakeman, R. (2006). Coming-out across the life course: Implications of age and historical context. *Archives of Sexual Behavior, 35*(3), 287-296.

Floyd, F. J., Mailick Seltzer, M., Greenberg, J. S., & Song, J. (2013). Parental bereavement during mid-to-later life: Pre- to postbereavement functioning and intrapersonal resources for coping. *Psychology and Aging, 28*(2), 402.

Flynn, H. K., Felmlee, D. H., & Conger, R. D. (2017). The social context of adolescent friendships: Parents, peers, and romantic partners. *Youth & Society, 49*(5), 679-705.

Flynn, J. (2013). The changing face of pediatric hypertension in the era of the childhood obesity epidemic. *Pediatric Nephrology, 28*(7), 1059-1066.

Flynn, J. R. (1984). The mean IQ of Americans: Massive gains 1932 to 1978. *Psychological Bulletin, 95*, 29-51.

Flynn, J. R. (1987). Massive IQ gains in 14 nations: What IQ tests really measure. *Psychological Bulletin, 101*, 171-191.

Flynn, J. T., Kaelber, D. C., Baker-Smith, C. M., Blowey, D., Carroll, A. E., Daniels, S. R., . . . Gidding, S. S. (2017). Clinical practice guideline for screening and management of high blood pressure in children and adolescents. *Pediatrics,* e20171904

Folmer-Annevelink, E., Doolaard, S., Mascareño, M., & Bosker, R. J. (2010). Class size effects on the number and types of student-teacher interactions in primary classrooms. *The Journal of Classroom Interaction,* 30-38.

Foltz, J. L., Cook, S. R., Szilagyi, P. G., Auinger, P., Stewart, P. A., Bucher, S., & Baldwin, C. D. (2011). US adolescent nutrition, exercise, and screen time baseline levels prior to national recommendations. *Clinical Pediatrics, 50*(5), 424-433.

Fomby, P., & Cherlin, A. J. (2007). Family instability and child well-being. *American Sociological Review, 72*(2), 181-204.

Fong, A., King, E., Duffy, J., Wu, E., Pan, D., & Ogunyemi, D. (2016). Declining VBAC rates despite improved delivery outcomes compared to repeat cesarean delivery [20Q]. *Obstetrics & Gynecology, 127*, 144S.

Fonner, V. A., Armstrong, K. S., Kennedy, C. E., O'Reilly, K. R., & Sweat, M. D. (2014). School based sex education and HIV prevention in low-and middle-income countries: a systematic review and meta-analysis. *PloS One, 9*(3).

Fontana, L., & Klein, S. (2007). Aging, adiposity, and calorie restriction. *Journal of the American Medical Association, 297*, 986-994.

Fontana, L., Klein, S., & Holloszy, J. (2010). Effects of long-term calorie restriction and endurance exercise on glucose tolerance, insulin action, and adipokine production. *Age, 32*(1), 97-108. doi: 10.1007/s11357-009-9118-z

Fontanel, B., & d'Harcourt, C. (1997). *Babies, history, art and folklore.* New York, NY: Abrams.

Food and Agricultural Organization of the United Nations (2019). *The state of food security and nutrition in the world* [Report]. Retrieved from www.fao.org/state-of-food-security-nutrition/en/

Forhan, S. E., Gottlieb, S. L., Sternberg, M. R., Xu, F., Datta, D., Berman, S., & Markowitz, L. E. (2008, March 13). *Prevalence of sexually transmitted infections and bacterial vaginosis among female adolescents in the United States: Data from the National Health and Nutritional Examination Survey (NHANES) 2003-2004.* Oral presentation at the meeting of the 2008 National STD Prevention Conference, Chicago, IL.

Forouzanfar, M. H., Alexander, L., Anderson, H. R., Bachman, V. F., Biryukov, S., Brauer, M., . . . Delwiche, K. (2015). Global, regional, and national comparative risk assessment of 79 behavioural, environmental and occupational, and metabolic risks or clusters of risks in 188 countries, 1990-2013: A systematic analysis for the Global Burden of Disease Study 2013. *The Lancet, 386*(10010), 2287-2323.

Forray, A., & Foster, D. (2015). Substance use in the perinatal period. *Current Psychiatry Reports, 17.* doi: 10.1007/s11920-015-0626-5

Fosco, G. M., & Grych, J. H. (2010). Adolescent triangulation into parental conflicts: longitudinal implications for appraisals and adolescent-parent relations. *Journal of Marriage and Family, 72*(2), 254-266.

Fosco, G. M., Stormshak, E. A., Dishion, T. J., & Winter, C. E. (2012). Family relationships and parental monitoring during middle school as predictors of early adolescent problem behavior. *Journal of Clinical Child & Adolescent Psychology, 41*(2), 202-213.

Foundation for Child Development. (2019). *Children's experience with parental employment insecurity and income inequality.* Retrieved from www.fcd-us.org/childrens-experience-parental-employment-insecurity-family-income-inequality/

Foundation Fighting Blindness. (2017). *Macular degeneration: available treatments.* Retrieved from www.blindness.org/macular-degeneration#available-treatments

Fox, A. M., Himmelstein, G., Khalid, H., & Howell, E. A. (2019). Funding for abstinence-only education and adolescent pregnancy prevention: Does state ideology affect outcomes? *American Journal of Public Health, 109*(3), 497-504.

Fox, N. A., Henderson, H. A., Rubin, K. H., Calkins, S. D., & Schmidt, L. A. (2001). Continuity and discontinuity of behavioral inhibition and exuberance: Psychophysiological and behavioral influences across the first four years of life. *Child Development, 72*(1), 1-21.

Fraga, M. F., Ballestar, E., Paz, M. F., Ropero, S., Setien, F., Ballestar, M. L., . . . Esteller, M. (2005). Epigenetic differences arise during the lifetime of monozygotic twins. *Proceedings of the National Academy of Sciences of the United States of America, 102*, 10604-10609.

Franceschi, R., Gaudino, R., Marcolongo, A., Gallo, M. C., Rossi, L., Antoniazzi, F., & Tatò, L. (2010). Prevalence of polycystic ovary syndrome in young women who had idiopathic central precocious puberty. *Fertility and Sterility, 93*(4), 1185-1191.

Francis, P., Mc Cormack, W., Toomey, C., Norton, C., Saunders, J., Kerin, E., . . . Jakeman, P. (2017). Twelve weeks' progressive resistance training combined with protein supplementation beyond habitual intakes increases upper leg lean tissue mass, muscle strength and extended gait speed in healthy older women. *Biogerontology, 18*(6), 881-891.

Franconi, F., Brunelleschi, S., Steardo, L., & Cuomo, V. (2007). Gender differences in drug responses. *Pharmacological Research, 55*, 81-95.

Frank, M. C., Everett, D. L., Fedorenko, E., & Gibson, E. (2008). Number as a cognitive technology: Evidence from Pirahã language and cognition. *Cognition, 108*(3), 819-824.

Frankenburg, W. K., Dodds J., Archer R., Shapiro, H., & Bresnick, B. (1992). The Denver II: a major revision and restandardization of the Denver Developmental Screening Test. *Pediatrics, 89*, 91-97.

Franks, P. W., Hanson, R. L., Knowler, W. C., Sievers, M. L., Bennett, P. H., & Looker, H. C. (2010). Childhood obesity, other cardiovascular risk factors and premature death. *New England Journal of Medicine, 362*(6), 485-493.

Freak-Poli, R., Kirkman, M., Lima, G. D. C., Direk, N., Franco, O. H., & Tiemeier, H. (2017). Sexual activity and physical tenderness in older adults: Cross-sectional prevalence and associated characteristics. *The Journal of Sexual Medicine, 14*(7), 918-927.

Fredrickson, B. L., Tugade, M. M., Waugh, C. E., & Larkin, G. R. (2003). What good are positive emotions in crisis? A prospective study of resilience and emotions following the terrorist attacks on the United States on September 11th, 2001. *Journal of Personality and Social Psychology, 84*(2), 365.

Fredriksen-Goldsen, K. I., & Muraco, A. (2010). Aging and sexual orientation: A 25-year review of the literature. *Research on Aging, 32*(3), 372-413.

Fredriksen-Goldsen, K. I., Cook-Daniels, L., Kim, H. J., Erosheva, E. A., Emlet, C. A., Hoy-Ellis, C. P., . . . Muraco, A. (2014). Physical and mental health of transgender older adults: An at-risk and underserved population. *The Gerontologist, 54*(3), 488-500.

Fredriksen-Goldsen, K. I., Emlet, C. A., Kim, H. J., Muraco, A., Erosheva, E. A., Goldsen, J., & Hoy-Ellis, C. P. (2013). The physical and mental health of lesbian, gay male, and bisexual (LGB) older adults: The role of key health indicators and risk and protective factors. *The Gerontologist, 53*(4), 664-675.

Fredriksen-Goldsen, K. I., Kim, H. J., Emlet, C. A., Muraco, A., Erosheva, E. A., Hoy-Ellis, C. P., . . . Petry, H. (2011). *The aging and health report.* Seattle, WA: Institute for Multigenerational Health.

Freeark, K., Rosenberg, E. B., Bornstein, J., Jozefowicz-Simbeni, D., Linkevich, M., & Lohnes, K. (2005). Gender differences and dynamics shaping the adoption life cycle: Review of the literature and recommendations. *American Journal of Orthopsychiatry, 75*, 86–101.

Freeman, C. (2004). *Trends in educational equity of girls & women: 2004* (NCES 2005-016). Washington, DC: National Center for Education Statistics.

Frejka, T. (2017). Childlessness in the United States. In *Childlessness in Europe: contexts, causes, and consequences* (pp. 159–179). Cham, Switzerland: Springer.

Fremont, W.P. (2004). Childhood reactions to terrorism-induced trauma: A review of the past 10 years. *Journal of the American Academy of Child and Adolescent Psychiatry*, 43, 381–392

French, S. A., Story, M., & Jeffery, R. W. (2001). Environmental influences on eating and physical activity. *Annual Review of Public Health, 22*, 309–335.

Frenda, S. J., & Fenn, K. M. (2016). Sleep less, think worse: The effect of sleep deprivation on working memory. *Journal of Applied Research in Memory and Cognition, 5*(4), 463–469.

Freud, S. (1953). *A general introduction to psychoanalysis* (J. Rivilre, Trans.). New York, NY: Permabooks. (Original work published 1935)

Freud, S. (1964). New introductory lectures on psychoanalysis. In J. Strachey (Ed. & Trans.), *The standard edition of the complete psychological works of Sigmund Freud* (Vol. 22). London: Hogarth. (Original work published 1933)

Freud, S. (1964). An outline of psychoanalysis. In J. Strachey (Ed. & Trans.), *The standard edition of the complete psychological works of Sigmund Freud* (Vol. 23). London: Hogarth. (Original work published 1940)

Fricke, T. R., Tahhan, N., Resnikoff, S., Papas, E., Burnett, A., Ho, S. M., . . . Naidoo, K. S. (2018). Global prevalence of presbyopia and vision impairment from uncorrected presbyopia: Systematic review, meta-analysis, and modelling. *Ophthalmology*, 125(10), 1492–1499.

Friedemann, M. L., & Buckwalter, K. C. (2014). Family caregiver role and burden related to gender and family relationships. *Journal of Family Nursing, 20*(3), 313–336.

Friederici, A. D. (2011). The brain basis of language processing: From structure to function. *Physiological Reviews, 91*(4), 1357–1392.

Friedman, B., Santos, E. J., Liebel, D. V., Russ, A. J., & Conwell, Y. (2015). Longitudinal prevalence and correlates of elder mistreatment among older adults receiving home visiting nursing. *Journal of Elder Abuse & Neglect, 27*(1), 34–64.

Friedman, H. S., & Kern, M. L. (2014). Personality, well-being, and health. *Annual Review of Psychology, 65*.

Friend, R. A. (1991). Older lesbian and gay people: A theory of successful aging. In J. A. Lee (Ed.), *Gay midlife and maturity* (pp. 99–118). New York, NY: Haworth.

Fries, J. F., Bruce, B., & Chakravarty, E. (2011). Compression of morbidity 1980–2011: A focused review of paradigms and progress. *Journal of Aging Research, 2011*.

Friesen, M. D., Horwood, L. J., Fergusson, D. M., & Woodward, L. J. (2017). Exposure to parental separation in childhood and later parenting quality as an adult: Evidence from a 30-year longitudinal study. *Journal of Child Psychology and Psychiatry*, 58(1), 30–37.

Frisoli, T. M., Schmieder, R. E., Grodzicki, T., & Messerli, F. H. (2011). Beyond salt: Lifestyle modifications and blood pressure. *European Heart Journal, 32*(24), 3081–3087.

Froehlich, T. E., Lanphear, B. P., Auinger, P., Hornung, R., Epstein, J. N., Braun, J., & Kahn, R. S. (2009). Association of tobacco and lead exposures with attention-deficit/hyperactivity disorder. *Pediatrics, 124*(6), e1054–e1063. doi: 10.1542/peds.2009-0738

Frost, D. M., & Meyer, I. H. (2009). Internalized homophobia and relationship quality among lesbians, gay men and bisexuals. *Journal of Counseling Psychology, 56*(1), 97–109.

Fry, R. (2019). *U.S. household size is increasing for the first time in over 160 years.* Pew Research Center. Retrieved from www.pewresearch.org/fact-tank/2019/10/01/the-number-of-people-in-the-average-u-s-household-is-going-up-for-the-first-time-in-over-160-years/

Fryar, C. D., Ostchega, Y., Hales, C. M., Zhang, G., & Kruszon-Moran, D. (2017). Hypertension prevalence and control among adults: United States, 2015–2016. *NCHS Data Brief, No. 289*. Hyattsville, MD: National Center for Health Statistics.

Fryar, C. D., Carroll, M. D., & Ogden, C. (2016). Prevalence of overweight and obesity among children and adolescents aged 2–19 years: United States, 1963–1965 through 2013–2014. *Health E-Stats*. Hyattsville, MD: National Center for Health Statistics.

Fryar, C. D., Carroll, M. D., & Ogden, C. L. (2018). Prevalence of overweight, obesity, and severe obesity among adults aged 20 and over: United States, 1960–1962 through 2015–2016. *Health E-Stats*, 1–6. Hyattsville, MD: National Center for Health Statistics.

Fryar, C. D., Gu, Q., Ogden, C. L., & Flegal, K. M. (2016). Anthropometric reference data for children and adults: United States, 2011–2014. *Vital and Health Statistics, 3*(39).

Fryar, C. D., Carroll, M. D., & Ogden, C. L. (2018). Prevalence of overweight, obesity, and severe obesity among children and adolescents aged 2–19 years: United States, 1963–1965 through 2015–2016. *Health E-Stats*, 1–6. Hyattsville, MD: National Center for Health Statistics.

Frye, C., Bo, E., Calamandrei, G., Calza, L., Dessi-Fulgheri, F., Fernández, M., . . . Patisaul, H. B. (2012). Endocrine disrupters: a review of some sources, effects, and mechanisms of actions on behaviour and neuroendocrine systems. *Journal of Neuroendocrinology, 24*(1), 144–159.

Frye, D. (2014). *Children's theories of mind: Mental states and social understanding.* London, England: Psychology Press.

Fu, G., Evans, A. D., Wang, L., & Lee, K. (2008). Lying in the name of the collective good: A developmental study. *Developmental Science, 11*(4), 495–503.

Fu, P., Gibson, C. J., Mendes, W. B., Schembri, M., & Huang, A. J. (2018). Anxiety, depressive symptoms, and cardiac autonomic function in perimenopausal and postmenopausal women with hot flashes: A brief report. *Menopause, 25*(12), 1470.

Fui, M. N. T., Dupuis, P., & Grossmann, M. (2014). Lowered testosterone in male obesity: mechanisms, morbidity and management. *Asian Journal of Andrology, 16*(2), 223.

Fui, M.N.T., Prendergast, L.A., Dupuis, P., Raval, M., Strauss, B.J., Zajac, J.D., & Grossmann, M. (2016). Effects of testosterone treatment on body fat and lean mass in obese men on a hypocaloric diet: A randomized controlled trial. *BMC Medicine*, 14. https://doi.org/10.1186/s12916-016-0700-9

Fuller, J. N., Frost, A. M., & Burr, B. K. (2015). Exploring the impact of religiosity and socioeconomic factors on perceived ideal timing of marriage in young adults. *Journal of Student Research, 4*(1), 120–129.

Fuller-Iglesias, H.R., Webster, N.J., Antonucci, T.C. (2015). The complex nature of family support across the lifespan: Implications for psychological well-being. *Developmental Psychology*, 51, 277–288.

Fulop, T., Witkowski, J. M., Pawelec, G., Alan, C., & Larbi, A. (2014). On the immunological theory of aging. In L. Robert & T. Fulop (Eds.), *Aging* (Vol. 39, pp. 163–176). Basel, Switzerland: Karger.

Fulton, R., & Owen, G. (1987–1988). Death and society in twentieth-century America. *Omega: Journal of Death and Dying, 18*(4), 379–395.

Fung, H. H., Carstensen, L. L., & Lang, F. R. (2001). Age-related patterns in social networks among European-Americans and African-Americans: Implications for socioemotional selectivity across the life span. *International Journal of Aging and Human Development, 52*, 185–206.

Fung, J., Wong, M. S., & Park, H. (2018). Cultural background and religious beliefs. In In M. R. Sanders & A. Morawska (Eds.), *Handbook of parenting and child development across the lifespan* (pp. 469–493). Basel, Switzerland: Springer.

Funk, C. & Parker, H. (2018). *Women and men in STEM often at odds over workplace equity* [Report]. Retrieved from www.pewsocialtrends.org/2018/01/09/women-and-men-in-stem-often-at-odds-over-workplace-equity/

Fuqua, J. S. (2013). Treatment and outcomes of precocious puberty: An update. *The Journal of Clinical Endocrinology & Metabolism, 98*(6), 2198–2207.

Furman, W., & Bierman, K. L. (1983). Developmental changes in young children's conception of friendship. *Child Development, 54*, 549–556.

Furman, W., & Wehner, E. A. (1997). Adolescent romantic relationships: A developmental perspective. In S. Shulman & A. Collins (Eds.), *Romantic relationships in adolescence: Developmental perspectives* (New Directions for Child and Adolescent Development, No. 78, pp. 21–36). San Francisco, CA: Jossey-Bass.

Furstenberg, F. F., Jr., Rumbaut, R. G., & Settersten, R. A., Jr. (2005). On the frontier of adulthood: Emerging themes and new directions. In R. A. Settersten Jr., F. F. Furstenberg Jr., & R. G. Rumbaut (Eds.), *On the frontier of adulthood: Theory, research, and public policy* (pp. 3-25). Chicago, IL: University of Chicago Press.

Furukawa, E., Tangney, J., & Higashibara, F. (2012). Cross-cultural continuities and discontinuities in shame, guilt, and pride: A study of children residing in Japan, Korea and the USA. *Self and Identity, 11*(1), 90-113.

Gabhainn, S., & François, Y. (2000). Substance use. In C. Currie, K. Hurrelmann, W. Settertobulte, R. Smith, & J. Todd (Eds.), *Health behaviour in school-aged children: A WHO cross-national study (HBSC) international report* (pp. 97-114). *WHO Policy Series: Healthy Policy for Children and Adolescents, Series No. 1.* Copenhagen, Denmark: World Health Organization Regional Office for Europe.

Gabrielli, J., Traore, A., Stoolmiller, M., Bergamini, E., & Sargent, J. D. (2016). Industry television ratings for violence, sex, and substance use. *Pediatrics, 138*(3), e20160487.

Gaertner, J., Siemens, W., Meerpohl, J. J., Antes, G., Meffert, C., Xander, C., . . . Becker, G. (2017). Effect of specialist palliative care services on quality of life in adults with advanced incurable illness in hospital, hospice, or community settings: Systematic review and meta-analysis. *BMJ, 357,* j2925.

Gaillard, R., Steegers, E. A. P., Franco, O. H., Hofman, A., & Jaddoe, V. W. V. (2015). Maternal weight gain in different periods of pregnancy and childhood cardio-metabolic outcomes. The Generation R Study. *International Journal of Obesity, 39*(4), 677.

Galal, M., Symonds, I., Murray, H., Petraglia, F., & Smith, R. (2012). Postterm pregnancy. *Facts, Views & Vision in ObGyn, 4*(3), 175.

Galen, L. W., & Kloet, J. D. (2011). Mental well-being in the religious and the non-religious: Evidence for a curvilinear relationship. *Mental Health, Religion & Culture, 14*(7), 673-689.

Galland, B. C., Taylor, B. J., Elder, D. E., & Herbison, P. (2012). Normal sleep patterns in infants and children: A systematic review of observational studies. *Sleep Medicine Reviews, 16*(3), 213-222.

Gallo, L. C., Troxel, W. M., Matthews, K. A., & Kuller, L. H. (2003). Marital status and quality in middle-aged women: Associations with levels and trajectories of cardiovascular risk factors. *Health Psychology, 22,* 453-463.

Gallup News. (2017). *In U.S., 10.2% or LGBT adults now married to same-sex couple.* Retrieved from http://news.gallup.com/poll/212702/lgbt-adults-married-sex-spouse.aspx?utm_source=alert&utm_medium=email&utm_content=morelink&utm_campaign=syndication

Galotti, K. M., Komatsu, L. K., & Voelz, S. (1997). Children's differential performance on deductive and inductive syllogisms. *Developmental Psychology, 33,* 70-78.

Galvao, T. F., Silva, M. T., Zimmermann, I. R., Souza, K. M., Martins, S. S., & Pereira, M. G.

(2014). Pubertal timing in girls and depression: A systematic review. *Journal of Affective Disorders, 155,* 13-19.

Gameiro, S., & Finnigan, A. (2017). Long-term adjustment to unmet parenthood goals following ART: A systematic review and meta-analysis. *Human Reproduction Update, 23*(3), 322-337.

Gammon, K. (2020, April 18). Should you have a home birth because of coronavirus? *The New York Times.* www.nytimes.com/2020/03/30/parenting/home-birth-coronavirus-hospital.html

Ganek, H., Nixon, S., Smyth, R., & Eriks-Brophy, A. (2018). A cross-cultural mixed methods investigation of language socialization practices. *The Journal of Deaf Studies and Deaf Education, 24*(2), 128-141.

Ganger, J., & Brent, M. R. (2004). Reexamining the vocabulary spurt. *Developmental Psychology, 40,* 621-632.

Gangwisch, J. E., Heymsfield, S. B., Boden-Albala, B., Buijs, R. M., Kreier, F., Opler, M. G., . . . Pickering, T. G. (2008). Sleep duration associated with mortality in elderly, but not middle-aged, adults in a large U.S. sample. *Sleep, 31*(8), 1087-1096.

Gans, J. E. (1990). *America's adolescents: How healthy are they?* Chicago, IL: American Medical Association.

Gao, G. (2015). *Americans' ideal family size is smaller than it used to be* [News brief]. Retrieved from www.pewresearch.org/fact-tank/2015/05/08/ideal-size-of-the-american-family/

Gao, W., Alcauter, S., Smith, J. K., Gilmore, J. H., & Lin, W. (2015). Development of human brain cortical network architecture during infancy. *Brain Structure and Function, 220*(2), 1173-1186.

Garandeau, C. F., Ahn, H. J., & Rodkin, P. C. (2011). The social status of aggressive students across contexts: the role of classroom status hierarchy, academic achievement, and grade. *Developmental Psychology, 47*(6), 1699.

Garbarino, J., Governale, A., Henry, P., & Nesi, D. (2015). Children and terrorism. *Social Policy Report, 29*(2).

Garcia, F., & Gracia, E. (2009). Is always authoritative the optimum parenting style? Evidence from Spanish families. *Adolescence, 44*(173), 101.

García-Mainar, I., Molina, J.A., & Montuenga, V.M. (2011). Gender differences in childcare: time allocation in five European countries. *Feminist Economics, 17*(1), 119-150.

Gard, T., Hölzel, B. K., & Lazar, S. W. (2014). The potential effects of meditation on age-related cognitive decline: A systematic review. *Annals of the New York Academy of Sciences, 1307,* 89.

Gardiner, H. W., & Kosmitzki, C. (2005). *Lives across cultures: Cross-cultural human development.* Boston, MA: Allyn & Bacon.

Gardner, A. T., de Vries, B., & Mockus, D. S. (2014). Aging out in the desert: Disclosure, acceptance, and service use among midlife and older lesbians and gay men. *Journal of Homosexuality, 61*(1), 129-144.

Gardner, H. (1993). *Frames of mind: The theory of multiple intelligences.* New York, NY: Basic Books. (Original work published 1983)

Gardner, H. (1998). Are there additional intelligences? In J. Kane (Ed.), *Education, information, and transformation: Essays on learning and thinking.* Englewood Cliffs, NJ: Prentice Hall.

Gardner, M., & Steinberg, L. (2005). Peer influence on risk taking, risk preference, and risky decision making in adolescence and adulthood: An experimental study. *Developmental Psychology, 41,* 625-635.

Garfield, R., Claxton, G., Damico, A. & Levitt, L. (2020). *Eligibility for ACA health coverage following job loss* [Kaiser Family Foundation report]. Retrieved from www.kff.org/coronavirus-covid-19/issue-brief/eligibility-for-aca-health-coverage-following-job-loss/

Garlick, D. (2003). Integrating brain science research with intelligence research. *Current Directions in Psychological Science, 12,* 185-192.

Garn, A. C., Matthews, M. S., & Jolly, J. L. (2010). Parental influences on the academic motivation of gifted students: A self-determination theory perspective. *Gifted Child Quarterly, 54*(4), 263-272.

Garner, A.A., Fine, P.R., Franklin, C.A., Sattin, R.W., & Stavrinos, D. (2011). Distracted driving among adolescents: Challenges and opportunities. *Injury Prevention,* 17, 285.

Garner, P. W., & Estep, K. M. (2001). Emotional competence, emotional socialization, and young children's peer-related social competence. *Early Education & Development, 12*(1), 29-48.

Garnick, M.B. (2015). Testosterone replacement therapy faces FDA scrutiny. *JAMA,* 313, 563.

Garthe, R. C., Sullivan, T. N., & McDaniel, M. A. (2017). A meta-analytic review of peer risk factors and adolescent dating violence. *Psychology of Violence, 7*(1), 45.

Gartstein, M. A., Bogale, W., & Meehan, C. L. (2016). Adaptation of the infant behavior questionnaire-revised for use in Ethiopia: expanding cross-cultural investigation of temperament development. *Infant Behavior and Development, 45,* 51-63.

Gartstein, M. A., Slobodskaya, H. R., Olaf Zylicz, P., Gosztyla, D., & Nakagawa, A. (2010). A cross-cultural evaluation of temperament: Japan, USA, Poland and Russia. *International Journal of Psychology and Psychological Therapy, 10*(1).

Garve, R., Garve, M., Link, K., Türp, J. C., & Meyer, C. G. (2016). Infant oral mutilation in East Africa–therapeutic and ritual grounds. *Tropical Medicine & International Health, 21*(9), 1099-1105.

Garwood, S. K., Gerassi, L., Jonson-Reid, M., Plax, K., & Drake, B. (2015). More than poverty: The effect of child abuse and neglect on teen pregnancy risk. *Journal of Adolescent Health, 57*(2), 164-168.

Gasana, J., Dillikar, D., Mendy, A., Forno, E., & Vieira, E. R. (2012). Motor vehicle air pollution and asthma in children: A meta-analysis. *Environmental Research, 117,* 36-45.

Gates, G. J. (2013). *LBGT parenting in the United States.* Retrieved from http://williamsinstitute.law.ucla.edu/wp-content/uploads/LGBT-Parenting.pdf

Gates, G. J. (2015). Marriage and family: LGBT individuals and same-sex couples. *The Future of Children, 25*(2), 67-87.

Gathercole, S. E., & Alloway, T. P. (2008). *Working memory and learning: A practical guide.* Thousand Oaks, CA: Sage.

Gattis, K. S., Berns, S., Simpson, L. E., & Christensen, A. (2004). Birds of a feather or strange birds? Ties among personality dimensions, similarity, and marital quality. *Journal of Family Psychology, 18,* 564–574.

Gauthier, A. H., & Furstenberg, F. F., Jr. (2005). Historical trends in patterns of time use among young adults in developed countries. In R. A. Settersten Jr., F. F. Furstenberg Jr., & R. G. Rumbaut (Eds.), *On the frontier of adulthood: Theory, research, and public policy* (pp. 150–176). Chicago, IL: University of Chicago Press.

Gazes, R. P., Hampton, R. R., & Lourenco, S. F. (2017). Transitive inference of social dominance by human infants. *Developmental Science, 20*(2), e12367.

Gazzaley, A., & Nobre, A. C. (2012). Top-down modulation: Bridging selective attention and working memory. *Trends in Cognitive Sciences, 16*(2), 129–135.

GBD 2015 Obesity Collaborators. (2017). Health effects of overweight and obesity in 195 countries over 25 years. *New England Journal of Medicine, 377*(1), 13–27.

Ge, X., Brody, G. H., Conger, R. D., Simons, R. L., & Murry, V. (2002). Contextual amplification of pubertal transitional effect on African American children's problem behaviors. *Developmental Psychology, 38,* 42–54.

Ge, X., Conger, R. D., & Elder Jr, G. H. (2001). Pubertal transition, stressful life events, and the emergence of gender differences in adolescent depressive symptoms. *Developmental Psychology, 37*(3), 404.

Geangu, E., Benga, O., Stahl, D., & Striano, T. (2010). Contagious crying beyond the first days of life. *Infant Behavior and Development, 33*(3), 279–288.

Geangu, E., Hauf, P., Bhardwaj, R., & Bentz, W. (2011). Infant pupil diameter changes in response to others' positive and negative emotions. *PloS One, 6*(11), e27132.

Geary, D. C. (2006). Development of mathematical understanding. In W. Damon (Ed.), D. Kuhl & R. S. Siegler (Vol. Eds.), *Handbook of child psychology: Cognition, perception, and language, Vol 2.* (6th ed., pp. 777–810). Hoboken, NJ: Wiley.

Gedo, J. (2001). *The enduring scientific contributions of Sigmund Freud.* Retrieved from www.pep-web.org/document.php?id=AOP.029.0105A

Gee, J., Weinbaum, C., Sukumaran, L., & Markowitz, L. E. (2016). Quadrivalent HPV vaccine safety review and safety monitoring plans for nine-valent HPV vaccine in the United States. *Human Vaccines & Immunotherapeutics, 12*(6), 1406–1417.

Geen, R. (2004). The evolution of kinship care: Policy and practice. *Future of Children, 14*(1). (David and Lucile Packard Foundation.) Retrieved from www.futureofchildren.org

Geerligs, L., Renken, R. J., Saliasi, E., Maurits, N. M., & Lorist, M. M. (2014). A brain-wide study of age-related changes in functional connectivity. *Cerebral Cortex, 25*(7), 1987–1999.

Geiger, A. W. (2016). *Sharing chores a key to good marriage, say majority of married adults* [Pew Research Center report]. Retrieved from www.pewresearch.org/fact-tank/2016/11/30/sharing-chores-a-key-to-good-marriage-say-majority-of-married-adults/

Geiger, P. J., Boggero, I. A., Brake, C. A., Caldera, C. A., Combs, H. L., Peters, J. R., & Baer, R. A. (2016). Mindfulness-based interventions for older adults: A review of the effects on physical and emotional well-being. *Mindfulness, 7*(2), 296–307.

Geist, C. (2017). Marriage formation in context: Four decades in comparative perspective. *Social Sciences, 6*(1), 9.

Gelman, R. (2006). Young natural-number mathematicians. *Current Directions in Psychological Science, 15,* 193–197.

Gelman, R., Spelke, E. S., & Meck, E. (1983). What preschoolers know about animate and in-animate objects. In D. R. Rogers & J. S. Sloboda (Eds.), *The acquisition of symbolic skills* (pp. 297–326). New York, NY: Plenum Press.

Genesee, F., Nicoladis, E., & Paradis, J. (1995). Language differentiation in early bilingual development. *Journal of Child Language, 22*(3), 611–631.

Genevay, B. (1986). Intimacy as we age. *Generations, 10*(4), 12–15.

Gentile, D. A. (2011). The multiple dimensions of video game effects. *Child Development Perspectives, 5*(2), 75–81.

Gentile, D. A., Bender, P. K., & Anderson, C. A. (2017). Violent video game effects on salivary cortisol, arousal, and aggressive thoughts in children. *Computers in Human Behavior, 70,* 39–43.

Gentile, S. (2017). Untreated depression during pregnancy: Short-and long-term effects in offspring. A systematic review. *Neuroscience, 342,* 154–166.

Genworth. (2018). *Genworth cost of care survey: Median cost data tables.* Retrieved from https://pro.genworth.com/riiproweb/productinfo/pdf/282102.pdf

Genworth. (2020). Cost of care trends and insights. [Report]. Retrieved from https://www.genworth.com/aging-and-you/finances/cost-of-care/cost-of-care-trends-and-insights.html

Georganopoulou, D. G., Chang, L., Nam, J.-M., Thaxton, C. S., Mufson, E. J., Klein, W. L., & Mirkin, C. A. (2005). Nanoparticle-based detection in cerebral spinal fluid of a soluble pathogenic biomarker for Alzheimer's disease. *Proceedings of the National Academy of Sciences, 102,* 2273–2276.

George, C., Kaplan, N., & Main, M. (1985). *The Berkeley Adult Attachment Interview.* [Unpublished protocol]. Department of Psychology, University of California, Berkeley.

Geraci, L., McDaniel, M. A., Manzano, I., & Roediger, H. L. (2009). The influence of age on memory for distinctive events. *Memory & Cognition, 37*(2), 175–180.

Gergely, A., Faragó, T., Galambos, Á., & Topál, J. (2017). Differential effects of speech situations on mothers' and fathers' infant-directed and dog-directed speech: An acoustic analysis. *Scientific Reports, 7*(1), 13739.

Gernhardt, A., Rübeling, H., & Keller, H. (2014). Self-and family-conceptions of Turkish migrant, native German, and native Turkish children: A comparison of children's drawings. *International Journal of Intercultural Relations, 40,* 154–166.

Gershoff, E. T. (2010). More harm than good: A summary of scientific research on the intended and unintended effects of corporal punishment on children. *Law and Contemporary Problems, 73*(2), 31–56.

Gershoff, E. T. (2013). Spanking and child development: We know enough now to stop hitting our children. *Child Development Perspectives, 7*(3), 133–137.

Gershoff, E. T., Lansford, J. E., Sexton, H. R., Davis-Kean, P., & Sameroff, A. J. (2012). Longitudinal links between spanking and children's externalizing behaviors in a national sample of white, Black, Hispanic, and Asian American families. *Child Development, 83*(3), 838–843.

Gerstorf, D., Ram, N., Hoppmann, C., Willis, S. L., & Schaie, K. W. (2011). Cohort differences in cognitive aging and terminal decline in the Seattle Longitudinal Study. *Developmental Psychology, 47*(4), 1026.

Gerstorf, D., Ram, N., Lindenberger, U., & Smith, J. (2013). Age and time-to-death trajectories of change in indicators of cognitive, sensory, physical, health, social, and self-related functions. *Developmental Psychology, 49*(10), 1805.

Gerstorf, D., Ram, N., Mayraz, G., Hidajat, M., Lindenberger, U., Wagner, G. G., & Schupp, J. (2010). Late-life decline in well-being across adulthood in Germany, the United Kingdom, and the United States: Something is seriously wrong at the end of life. *Psychology and Aging, 25*(2), 477.

Gervain, J., & Mehler, J. (2010). Speech perception and language acquisition in the first year of life. *Annual Review of Psychology, 61,* 191–218.

Gest, S. D. (1997). Behavioral inhibition: Stability and associations with adaptation from childhood to early adulthood. *Journal of Personality and Social Psychology, 72*(2), 467.

Getzels, J. W., & Jackson, P. W. (1963). The highly intelligent and the highly creative adolescent: A summary of some research findings. In C. W. Taylor & F. Baron (Eds.), *Scientific creativity: Its recognition and development* (pp. 161–172). New York, NY: Wiley.

Geuze, R. H., Schaafsma, S. M., Lust, J. M., Bouma, A., Schiefenhövel, W., & Groothuis, T. G. (2012). Plasticity of lateralization: Schooling predicts hand preference but not hand skill asymmetry in a non-industrial society. *Neuropsychologia, 50*(5), 612–620.

Ghandour, R. M., Sherman, L. J., Vladutiu, C. J., Ali, M. M., Lynch, S. E., Bitsko, R. H., & Blumberg, S. J. (2019). Prevalence and Treatment of Depression, Anxiety, and Conduct Problems in US Children. *Journal of Pediatrics, 206,* 256–267.

Gibaldi, C. P. (2013). The changing trends of retirement: Baby boomers leading the charge. *Review of Business, 34*(1), 50.

Gibbs, J. C. (1991). Toward an integration of Kohlberg's and Hoffman's theories of moral development. In W. M. Kurtines & J. L. Gewirtz (Eds.), *Handbook of moral behavior* and development: Advances in theory, research, and application (Vol. 1). Hillsdale, NJ: Erlbaum.

Gibbs, J. C. (1995). The cognitive developmental perspective. In W. M. Kurtines & J. L. Gewirtz (Eds.), Moral development: An introduction. Boston, MA: Allyn & Bacon.

Gibbs, J. C., & Schnell, S. V. (1985). Moral development "versus" socialization. American Psychologist, 40(10), 1071–1080.

Gibson, E. J. (1969). Principles of perceptual learning and development. Englewood Cliffs, NJ: Prentice-Hall.

Gibson, E. J., & Pick, A. D. (2000). An ecological approach to perceptual learning and development. New York, NY: Oxford University Press.

Gibson, E. J., & Walker, A. S. (1984). Development of knowledge of visual tactual affordances of substance. Child Development, 55, 453–460.

Gibson, J. J. (1979). The ecological approach to visual perception. Boston, MA: Houghton-Mifflin.

Giedd, J. N., & Rapoport, J. L. (2010). Structural MRI of pediatric brain development: What have we learned and where are we going? Neuron, 67(5), 728–734.

Gierveld, J. D. J. (2015). Intra-couple caregiving of older adults living apart together: Commitment and independence. Canadian Journal on Aging/La Revue canadienne du vieillissement, 34(3), 356–365.

Gierveld, J. D. J., & Dykstra, P. A. (2008). Virtue is its own reward? Support-giving in the family and loneliness in middle and old age. Ageing and Society, 28(2), 271–287.

Gill, J., & Moore, M. J. (2013). Centers for Disease Control and Prevention. (2013). The state of aging and health in America 2013. Atlanta, GA: Centers for Disease Control and Prevention, US Department of Health and Human Services.

Gillen, M. M., & Lefkowitz, E. S. (2012). Gender and racial/ethnic differences in body image development among college students. Body Image, 9(1), 126–130.

Gillespie, B. J. (2017). Correlates of sex frequency and sexual satisfaction among partnered older adults. Journal of Sex & Marital Therapy, 43(5), 403–423.

Gilligan, C. (1982/1993). In a different voice: Psychological theory and women's development. Cambridge, MA: Harvard University Press.

Gilligan, M., Suitor, J., Nam, S., Routh, B., Rurka, M., & Con, G. (2017). Family networks and psychological well-being in midlife. Social Sciences, 6(3), 94.

Gilmore, D. D. (1990). Manhood in the making: Cultural concepts of masculinity. New Haven, CT: Yale University Press.

Gilmore, J., Lin, W., Prastawa, M. W., Looney, C. B., Vetsa, Y. S. K., Knickmeyer, R. C., . . . Gerig, G. (2007). Regional gray matter growth, sexual dimorphism, and cerebral asymmetry in the neonatal brain. Journal of Neuroscience, 27(6), 1255–1260.

Gilovich, T., Kumar, A., & Jampol, L. (2015). A wonderful life: Experiential consumption and the pursuit of happiness. Journal of Consumer Psychology, 25(1), 152–165.

Giménez, M., & Harris, P. (2005). Children's acceptance of conflicting testimony: The case of death. Journal of Cognition and Culture, 5(1–2), 143–164.

Ginsberg, H. P., & Opper, S. (1988). Piaget's theory of intellectual development: An introduction (3rd ed.). Englewood Cliffs, NJ: Prentice-Hall.

Giscombé, C. L., & Lobel, M. (2005). Explaining disproportionately high rates of adverse birth outcomes among African Americans: The impact of stress, racism, and related factors in pregnancy. Psychological Bulletin, 131, 662–683.

Gjersoe, N. L., Hall, E. L., & Hood, B. (2015). Children attribute mental lives to toys when they are emotionally attached to them. Cognitive Development, 34, 28–38.

Glaser, D. (2000). Child abuse and neglect and the brain: A review. Journal of Child Psychiatry, 41, 97–116.

Glaser, K., Price, D., Di Gessa, G., Ribe, E., Stuchbury, R., & Tinker, A. (2013). Grandparenting in Europe: Family policy and grandparents' role in providing childcare. London, England: Grandparents Plus.

Glaser, K., Stuchbury, R., Price, D., Di Gessa, G., Ribe, E., & Tinker, A. (2018). Trends in the prevalence of grandparents living with grandchild(ren) in selected European countries and the United States. European Journal of Ageing, 15(3), 237–250.

Glass, H. C., Costarino, A. T., Stayer, S. A., Brett, C., Cladis, F., & Davis, P. J. (2015). Outcomes for extremely premature infants. Anesthesia and Analgesia, 120(6), 1337.

Glass, J., Simon, R. W., & Andersson, M. A. (2016). Parenthood and happiness: Effects of work-family reconciliation policies in 22 OECD countries. American Journal of Sociology, 122(3), 886–929.

Glaucoma Research Foundation. (2017). Four key facts about glaucoma. Retrieved from www.glaucoma.org/glaucoma/glaucoma-facts-and-stats.php

Glick, G. C., & Rose, A. J. (2011). Prospective associations between friendship adjustment and social strategies: Friendship as a context for building social skills. Developmental Psychology, 47(4), 1117.

Glick, J. E., & Van Hook, J. (2002). Parents' coresidence with adult children: Can immigration explain racial and ethnic variation? Journal of Marriage and Family, 64, 240–253.

Glick, S. N., Cleary, S. D., & Golden, M. R. (2015). Brief report: Increasing acceptance of homosexuality in the United States across racial and ethnic subgroups. JAIDS Journal of Acquired Immune Deficiency Syndromes, 70(3), 319–322.

Global Breastfeeding Collective, UNICEF, & World Bank. (2018). Breastfeeding and HIV [Advocacy brief]. Retrieved from www.unicef.org/nutrition/files/Global_Breastfeeding_Collective_Advocacy_Brief_Breastfeeding_and_HIV.pdf

Goble, P., Martin, C. L., Hanish, L. D., & Fabes, R. A. (2012). Children's gender-typed activity choices across preschool social contexts. Sex Roles, 67(7–8), 435–451.

Goel, I. (2016). Hijra communities of Delhi. Sexualities, 19(5–6), 535–546.

Goertz, C., Lamm, B., Graf, F., Kolling, T., Knopf, M., & Keller, H. (2011). Deferred imitation in 6-month-old German and Cameroonian Nso infants. Journal of Cognitive Education and Psychology, 10(1), 44.

Goetz, P. J. (2003). The effects of bilingualism on theory of mind development. Bilingualism: Language and Cognition, 6, 1–15.

Goffin, K. C., Boldt, L. J., & Kochanska, G. (2018). A secure base from which to cooperate: Security, child and parent willing stance, and adaptive and maladaptive outcomes in two longitudinal studies. Journal of Abnormal Child Psychology, 46(5), 1061–1075.

Gogtay, N., & Thompson, P. M. (2010). Mapping gray matter development: Implications for typical development and vulnerability to psychopathology. Brain and Cognition, 72(1), 6–15.

Gold, K. J., Sen, A., & Hayward, R. A. (2010). Marriage and cohabitation outcomes after pregnancy loss. Pediatrics, 125(5), e1202–e1207.

Goldberg, W. A., Prause, J., Lucas-Thompson, R., & Himsel, A. (2008). Maternal employment and children's achievement in context: A meta-analysis of four decades of research. Psychological Bulletin, 134(1), 77.

Goldblum, P., Testa, R. J., Pflum, S., Hendricks, M. L., Bradford, J., & Bongar, B. (2012). The relationship between gender-based victimization and suicide attempts in transgender people. Professional Psychology: Research and Practice, 43(5), 468.

Golden, J., Conroy, R. M., & Lawlor, B. A. (2009). Social support network structure in older people: Underlying dimensions and association with psychological and physical health. Psychology, Health & Medicine, 14(3), 280–290.

Goldin, C., & Lleras-Muney, A. (2019). XX> XY?: The changing female advantage in life expectancy. Journal of Health Economics, 67, 102224.

Goldin-Meadow, S. (2007). Pointing sets the stage for learning language—And creating language. Child Development, 78(3), 741–745.

Goldscheider, F., & Goldscheider, C. (1999). The changing transition to adulthood: Leaving and returning home (Vol. 17). Thousand Oaks, CA: Sage Publications.

Goldscheider, F., & Sassler, S. (2006). Creating stepfamilies: Integrating children into the study of union formation. Journal of Marriage and Family, 68, 275–291.

Goldschmidt, L., Richardson, G. A., Willford, J. A., Severtson, S. G., & Day, N. L. (2012). School achievement in 14-year-old youths prenatally exposed to marijuana. Neurotoxicology and Teratology, 34(1), 161–167.

Goldsen, J., Bryan, A. E., Kim, H. J., Muraco, A., Jen, S., & Fredriksen-Goldsen, K. I. (2017). Who says I do: The changing context of marriage and health and quality of life for LGBT older adults. The Gerontologist, 57(suppl_1), S50–S62.

Goldstein, J., McCoach, D. B., & Yu, H. (2017). The predictive validity of kindergarten readiness judgments: Lessons from one state. The Journal of Educational Research, 110(1), 50–60.

Goldstein, M. H., Schwade, J. A., & Bornstein, M. H. (2009). The value of vocalizing: Five-month-old infants associate their own noncry vocalizations with responses from caregivers. *Child Development, 80*(3), 636–644.

Goldstein, M., King, A., & West, M. (2003). Social interaction shapes babbling: Testing parallels between birdsong and speech. *Proceedings of the National Academy of Sciences, USA, 100,* 8030–8035.

Goldstein, S. E., Davis-Kean, P. E., & Eccles, J. E. (2005). Parents, peers, and problem behavior: A longitudinal investigation of the impact of relationship perceptions and characteristics on the development of adolescent problem behavior. *Developmental Psychology, 2,* 401–413.

Golinkoff, R. M., & Hirsh-Pasek, K. (2006). Baby wordsmith. *Current Directions in Psychological Science, 15,* 30–33.

Golinkoff, R. M., Can, D. D., Soderstrom, M., & Hirsh-Pasek, K. (2015). (Baby) talk to me: The social context of infant-directed speech and its effects on early language acquisition. *Current Directions in Psychological Science, 24*(5), 339–344.

Golmaryami, F. N., Frick, P. J., Hemphill, S. A., Kahn, R. E., Crapanzano, A. M., & Terranova, A. M. (2016). The social, behavioral, and emotional correlates of bullying and victimization in a school-based sample. *Journal of Abnormal Child Psychology, 44*(2), 381–391.

Golombok, S., Mellish, L., Jennings, S., Casey, P., Tasker, F., & Lamb, M. E. (2013). Adoptive gay father families: Parent–child relationships and children's psychological adjustment. *Child Development.* doi: 10.1111/cdev.12155

Golombok, S., Rust, J., Zervoulis, K., Croudace, T., Golding, J., & Hines, M. (2008). Developmental trajectories of sex-typed behaviors in boys and girls: A longitudinal general population study of children aged 2.5–8 years. *Child Development, 79,* 1583–1593.

Golub, M. S., Collman, G. W., Foster, P. M., Kimmel, C. A., Rajpert-De Meyts, E., Reiter, E. O., . . . Toppari, J. (2008). Public health implications of altered puberty timing. *Pediatrics, 121*(Suppl. 3), S218–S230.

Goman, A. M., & Lin, F. R. (2016). Prevalence of hearing loss by severity in the United States. *American Journal of Public Health, 106*(10), 1820–1822.

Gomes-Osman, J., Cabral, D. F., Morris, T. P., McInerney, K., Cahalin, L. P., Rundek, T., . . . Pascual-Leone, A. (2018). Exercise for cognitive brain health in aging: A systematic review for an evaluation of dose. *Neurology: Clinical Practice, 8*(3), 257–265.

Gomez, S. H., Tse, J., Wang, Y., Turner, B., Millner, A. J., Nock, M. K., & Dunn, E. C. (2017). Are there sensitive periods when child maltreatment substantially elevates suicide risk? Results from a nationally representative sample of adolescents. *Depression and Anxiety, 34*(8), 734–741.

Gómez-Robles, A., Hopkins, W. D., & Sherwood, C. C. (2013, June). Increased morphological asymmetry, evolvability and plasticity in human brain evolution. *Proceedings of the Royal Society B, 280*(1761), 20130575.

Gomez-Scott, J., & Cooney, T. M. (2014). Young women's education and behavioural risk trajectories: Clarifying their association with unintended-pregnancy resolution. *Culture, Health & Sexuality, 16*(6), 648–665.

Göncü, A., Mistry, J., & Mosier, C. (2000). Cultural variations in the play of toddlers. *International Journal of Behavioral Development, 24*(3), 321–329.

Gonen-Yaacovi, G., de Souza, L. C., Levy, R., Urbanski, M., Josse, G., & Volle, E. (2013). Rostral and caudal prefrontal contribution to creativity: A meta-analysis of functional imaging data. *Frontiers in Human Neuroscience, 7.*

Gonyea, J. G. (2013). Changing family demographics, multigenerational bonds, and care for the oldest old. *Public Policy and Aging Report, 23*(2), 11–15.

Gooch, D., Thompson, P., Nash, H. M., Snowling, M. J., & Hulme, C. (2016). The development of executive function and language skills in the early school years. *Journal of Child Psychology and Psychiatry, 57*(2), 180–187.

Goodchild, M., Nargis, N., & d'Espaignet, E. T. (2018). Global economic cost of smoking-attributable diseases. *Tobacco Control, 27*(1), 58–64.

Goodman, G. S., Emery, R. E., & Haugaard, J. J. (1998). Developmental psychology and law: Divorce, child maltreatment, foster care, and adoption. In W. Damon (Series Ed.), I. E. Sigel & K. A. Renninger (Vol. Eds.), *Handbook of Child Psychology* (Vol. 4, pp. 775–874). New York, NY: Wiley.

Goossens, G., Kadji, C., & Delvenne, V. (2015). Teenage pregnancy: A psychopathological risk for mothers and babies. *Psychiatria Danubina, 27*(1), 499–503.

Gorchoff, S. M., John, O. P., & Helson, R. (2008). Contextualizing change in marital satisfaction during middle age. *Psychological Science, 19*(11), 1194–1200.

Gordon, I., Zagoory-Sharon, O., Leckman, J. F., & Feldman, R. (2010). Oxytocin, cortisol, and triadic family interactions. *Physiology & Behavior, 101*(5), 679–684.

Gordon, L., Joo, J. E., Andronikos, R., Ollikainen, M., Wallace, E. M., Umstad, M. P., . . . Craig, J. M. (2011). Expression discordance of monozygotic twins at birth: Effect of intrauterine environment and a possible mechanism for fetal programming. *Epigenetics, 6,* 579–592.

Gorman, J. (2006). Gender differences in depression and response to psychotropic medication. *Gender Medicine, 3*(2), 93–109.

Gottfried, A. E., & Gottfried, A. W. (Eds.). (2013). *Maternal employment and children's development: Longitudinal research.* Berlin, Germany: Springer Science & Business Media.

Gottlieb, G. (1991). Experiential canalization of behavioral development theory. *Developmental Psychology, 27*(1), 4–13.

Gottlieb, G. (1997). *Synthesizing nature-nurture: Prenatal roots of instinctive behavior.* Mahwah, NJ: Erlbaum.

Goubet, N., & Clifton, R. K. (1998). Object and event representation in 6½-month-old infants. *Developmental Psychology, 34,* 63–76.

Gould, E., Reeves, A. J., Graziano, M. S. A., & Gross, C. G. (1999). Neurogenesis in the neocortex of adult primates. *Science, 286,* 548–552.

Govindaraju, T., Sahle, B. W., McCaffrey, T. A., McNeil, J. J., & Owen, A. J. (2018). Dietary patterns and quality of life in older adults: A systematic review. *Nutrients, 10*(8), 971.

Grabe, S., Ward, L. M., & Hyde, J. S. (2008). The role of the media in body image concerns among women: A meta-analysis of experimental and correlational studies. *Psychological Bulletin, 134*(3), 460.

Graber, J. A., Lewinsohn, P. M., Seeley, J. R., & Brooks-Gunn, J. (1997). Is psychopathology associated with the timing of pubertal development? *Journal of the American Academy of Child & Adolescent Psychiatry, 36*(12), 1768–1776.

Grace, D. M., David, B. J., & Ryan, M. K. (2008). Investigating preschoolers' categorical thinking about gender through imitation, attention, and the use of self-categories. *Child Development, 79*(6), 1928–1941.

Gracia, C. R., & Freeman, E. W. (2018). Onset of the menopause transition: The earliest signs and symptoms. *Obstetrics and Gynecology Clinics, 45*(4), 585–597.

Grady, J. S. (2018). Parents' reactions to toddlers' emotions: Relations with toddler shyness and gender. *Early Child Development and Care, 1–8.*

Graf, F., Borchert, S., Lamm, B., Goertz, C., Kolling, T., Fassbender, I., . . . Keller, H. (2014). Imitative learning of Nso and German infants at 6 and 9 months of age: Evidence for a cross-cultural learning tool. *Journal of Cross-Cultural Psychology, 45*(1), 47–61.

Graf, F., Lamm, B., Goertz, C., Kolling, T., Freitag, C., Spangler, S., . . . Lohaus, A. (2012). Infant contingency learning in different cultural contexts. *Infant and Child Development, 21*(5), 458–473.

Graf, S. (2019). *Key findings on marriage and cohabitation in the U.S.* [Pew Research Center report]. Retrieved from www.pewresearch.org/fact-tank/2019/11/06/key-findings-on-marriage-and-cohabitation-in-the-u-s/

Graham, C., & Pozuelo, J. R. (2017). Happiness, stress, and age: How the U curve varies across people and places. *Journal of Population Economics, 30*(1), 225–264.

Graham, E. K., & Lachman, M. E. (2012). Personality stability is associated with better cognitive performance in adulthood: Are the stable more able? *Journals of Gerontology Series B: Psychological Sciences and Social Sciences, 67*(5), 545–554.

Graham, J. A., Yuhas, H., & Roman, J. L. (2018). Death and coping mechanisms in animated Disney movies: A content analysis of Disney films (1937–2003) and Disney/Pixar films (2003–2016). *Social Sciences, 7*(10), 199.

Graham, J. E., Christian, L. M., & Kiecolt-Glaser, J. K. (2006). Marriage, health and immune function: A review of key findings and the role of depression. In S. Beach & M. Wimboldt (Eds.), *Relational processes in mental health*

(Vol. 11, pp. 61–76). Arlington, VA: American Psychiatric Publishing.

Graham, K. L., & Burghardt, G. M. (2010). Current perspectives on the biological study of play: Signs of progress. *The Quarterly Review of Biology, 85,* 393–418.

Graham, S. A., Lee, E. E., Jeste, D. V., Van Patten, R., Twamley, E. W., Nebeker, C., . . . Depp, C. A. (2020). Artificial intelligence approaches to predicting and detecting cognitive decline in older adults: A conceptual review. *Psychiatry Research, 284,* 112732.

Grandner, M. A., Williams, N. J., Knutson, K. L., Roberts, D., & Jean-Louis, G. (2016). Sleep disparity, race/ethnicity, and socioeconomic position. *Sleep Medicine, 18,* 7–18.

Grant, S., Langan-Fox, J., & Anglim, J. (2009). The Big Five traits as predictors of subjective and psychological well-being. *Psychological Reports, 105*(1), 205–231.

Grassi, M., Petraccia, L., Mennuni, G., Fontana, M., Scarno, A., Sabetta, S., & Fraioli, A. (2011). Changes, functional disorders, and diseases in the gastrointestinal tract of elderly. *Nutricion Hospitalaria, 26*(4).

Gravina, S., & Vijg, J. (2010). Epigenetic factors in aging and longevity. *Pflugers Archives, European Journal of Physiology, 459*(2), 241–258. doi: 10.1007/s00424-009-0730-7 Ch. 17

Gray, J. R., & Thompson, P. M. (2004). Neurobiology of intelligence: Science and ethics. *Neuroscience, 5,* 471–492.

Gray, P. (2011). The special value of children's age-mixed play. *American Journal of Play, 3*(4), 500–522.

Grayer, A. (2020, July). Several big U.S. school districts are extending remote classes into the fall. *CNN.* Retrieved from https://www.cnn.com/2020/07/13/us/school-reopening-plans-major-cities/index.html

Grazzani, I., Ornaghi, V., Conte, E., Pepe, A., & Caprin, C. (2018). The relation between emotion understanding and theory of mind in children aged 3 to 8: The key role of language. *Frontiers in Psychology, 9.*

Green, M., & Elliott, M. (2010). Religion, health, and psychological well-being. *Journal of Religion and Health, 49*(2), 149–163.

Greenberg, J., & Becker, M. (1988). Aging parents as family resources. *Gerontologist, 28*(6), 786–790.

Greene, K. M., & Maggs, J. L. (2015). Revisiting the time trade-off hypothesis: Work, organized activities, and academics during college. *Journal of Youth and Adolescence, 44*(8), 1623–1637.

Greene, M. L., Way, N., & Pahl, K. (2006). Trajectories of perceived adult and peer discrimination among Black, Latino, and Asian American adolescents: patterns and psychological correlates. *Developmental Psychology, 42*(2), 218.

Greenfield, E. A., & Marks, N. F. (2004). Formal volunteering as a protective factor for older adults' psychological well-being. *Journal of Gerontology: Social Sciences, 59B,* S258–S264.

Greenfield, E. A., & Russell, D. (2011). Identifying living arrangements that heighten risk for loneliness in later life: Evidence from the US National Social Life, Health, and Aging Project. *Journal of Applied Gerontology, 30*(4), 524–534.

Greenfield, P. M. (2009). Technology and informal education: What is taught, what is learned. *Science, 323*(5910), 69–71. doi: 10.1126/science.1167190

Greenwood, D. C., Thatcher, N. J., Ye, J., Garrard, L., Keogh, G., King, L. G., & Cade, J. E. (2014). Caffeine intake during pregnancy and adverse birth outcomes: A systematic review and dose-response meta-analysis. *European Journal of Epidemiology, 29*(10), 725.

Gregory, S., Simmons, A., Kumari, V., Howard, M., Hodgins, S., & Blackwood, N. (2012). The antisocial brain: Psychopathy matters: A structural MRI investigation of antisocial male violent offenders. *Archives of General Psychiatry, 69*(9), 962–972

Grenier, A. (2014, April 11). Majority of U.S. patents granted to foreign individuals. American *Immigration Council Immigration Impact.* Retrieved from http://immigrationimpact.com/2014/04/11/majority-of-u-s-patents-granted-to-foreign-individuals/

Gress-Smith, J. L., Roubinov, D. S., Andreotti, C., Compas, B. E., & Luecken, L. J. (2015). Prevalence, severity and risk factors for depressive symptoms and insomnia in college undergraduates. *Stress and Health, 31*(1), 63–70.

Greyson, B., & Khanna, S. (2014). Spiritual transformation after near-death experiences. *Spirituality in Clinical Practice, 1*(1), 43.

Griffin, K. W., Botvin, G. J., Scheier, L. M., Diaz, T., & Miller, N. L. (2000). Parenting practices as predictors of substance use, delinquency, and aggression among urban minority youth: Moderating effects of family structure and gender. *Psychology of Addictive Behaviors: Journal of the Society of Psychologists in Addictive Behaviors, 14*(2), 174.

Griffith, K. N. (2020). Changes in insurance coverage and access to care for young adults in 2017. *Journal of Adolescent Health, 66*(1), 86–91.

Grigorenko, E. L., Meier, E., Lipka, J., Mohatt, G., Yanez, E., & Sternberg, R. J. (2004). Academic and practical intelligence: A case study of the Yup'ik in Alaska. *Learning and Individual Differences, 14*(4), 183–207.

Grigoryeva, A. (2017). Own gender, sibling's gender, parent's gender: The division of elderly parent care among adult children. *American Sociological Review, 82*(1), 116–146.

Grimbos, T., Dawood, K., Burriss, R. P., Zucker, K. J., & Puts, D. A. (2010). Sexual orientation and the second to fourth finger length ratio: A meta-analysis in men and women. *Behavioral Neuroscience, 124*(2), 278–287.

Grinshteyn, E., & Hemenway, D. (2016). Violent death rates: I US compared with other high-income OECD countries, 2010. *The American Journal of Medicine, 129*(3), 266–273.

Groen, R. S., Bae, J. Y., & Lim, K. J. (2012). Fear of the unknown: ionizing radiation exposure during pregnancy. *American Journal of Obstetrics and Gynecology, 206*(6), 456–462.

Groenen, A. A., Kruijsen, A. J., Mulvey, G. M., & Ulrich, B. D. (2010). Constraints on early movement: Tykes, togs, and technology. *Infant Behavior and Development, 33*(1), 16–22.

Groh, A. M., Fearon, R. P., Bakermans-Kranenburg, M. J., Van IJzendoorn, M. H., Steele, R. D., &

Roisman, G. I. (2014). The significance of attachment security for children's social competence with peers: A meta-analytic study. *Attachment & Human Development, 16*(2), 103–136.

Gross, A. L., Parisi, J. M., Spira, A. P., Kueider, A. M., Ko, J. Y., Saczynski, J. S., . . . Rebok, G. W. (2012). Memory training interventions for older adults: A meta-analysis. *Aging & Mental Health, 16*(6), 722–734.

Grossman, A. H., & D'Augelli, A. R. (2007). Transgender youth and life-threatening behaviors. *Suicide and Life-Threatening Behavior, 37*(5), 527–537.

Grossman, A. H., D'augelli, A. R., & Frank, J. A. (2011). Aspects of psychological resilience among transgender youth. *Journal of LGBT Youth, 8*(2), 103–115.

Grossman, A. H., D'Augelli, A. R., Howell, T. J., & Hubbard, S. (2005). Parent reactions to transgender youth, gender nonconforming expression and identity. *Journal of Gay & Lesbian Social Services, 18*(1), 3–16.

Grossmann, I., Karasawa, M., Izumi, S., Na, J., Varnum, M. E., Kitayama, S., & Nisbett, R. E. (2012). Aging and wisdom: Culture matters. *Psychological Science, 23*(10), 1059–1066.

Grossmann, I., Na, J., Varnum, M. E., Park, D. C., Kitayama, S., & Nisbett, R. E. (2010). Reasoning about social conflicts improves into old age. *Proceedings of the National Academy of Sciences, 107*(16), 7246–7250.

Grotevant, H. D., McRoy, R. G., Wrobel, G. M., & Ayers-Lopez, S. (2013). Contact between adoptive and birth families: Perspectives from the Minnesota/Texas Adoption Research Project. *Child Development Perspectives, 7*(3), 193–198.

Grotevant, H.D. (2012). What works in open adoption. In P. A. Curtis & G. Alexander (Eds). *What works in child welfare.* Washington, DC: Child Welfare League of America.

Grov, C., Bimbi, D. S., Nanin, J. E., & Parsons, J. T. (2006). Race, ethnicity, gender and generational factors associated with the coming-out process among gay, lesbian and bisexual individuals. *Journal of Sex Research, 43*(2), 115–121.

Gruber, K. J., Cupito, S. H., & Dobson, C. F. (2013). Impact of doulas on healthy birth outcomes. *The Journal of Perinatal Education, 22*(1), 49.

Gruenewald, T. L., Liao, D. H., & Seeman, T. E. (2012). Contributing to others, contributing to oneself: Perceptions of generativity and health in later life. *Journals of Gerontology Series B: Psychological Sciences and Social Sciences, 67*(6), 660–665.

Grundgeiger, T., Bayen, U. J., & Horn, S. S. (2014). Effects of sleep deprivation on prospective memory. *Memory, 22*(6), 679–686.

Grusec, J. E. (2006). The development of moral behavior and conscience from a socialization perspective. In M. Killen & J. G. Smetana (Eds.), *Handbook of Moral Development* (pp. 243–265). Mahwah, NJ: Lawrence Erlbaum.

Grusec, J. E., & Goodnow, J. J. (1994). Impact of parental discipline methods on the child's internalization of values: A reconceptualization of current points of view. *Developmental Psychology, 30,* 4–19.

Gu, D., Dupre, M. E., & Qiu, L. (2017). Self-perception of uselessness and mortality among older adults in China. *Archives of Gerontology and Geriatrics, 68,* 186–194.

Guallar, E., & Laine, C. (2014). Controversy over clinical guidelines: listen to the evidence, not the noise. *Annals of Internal Medicine, 160*(5), 361–362.

Guberman, S. R. (1996). The development of everyday mathematics in Brazilian children with limited formal education. *Child Development, 67,* 1609–1623.

Guendelman, S., Kosa, J. L., Pearl, M., Graham, S., Goodman, J., & Kharrazi, M. (2009). Juggling work and breastfeeding: Effects of maternity leave and occupational characteristics. *Pediatrics, 123,* e38–e46.

Guerra, V. M., & Giner-Sorolla, R. S. (2015). Investigating the three ethics in emerging adulthood: A study in five countries. In L. A. Jensen (Ed.), *Moral development in a global world: Research from a cultural-developmental perspective* (pp. 117–140). Cambridge, England: Cambridge University Press.

Guglielmo, D., Gazmararian, J. A., Chung, J., Rogers, A. E., & Hale, L. (2018). Racial/ethnic sleep disparities in US school-aged children and adolescents: A review of the literature. *Sleep Health, 4*(1), 68–80.

Guida, A., Gobet, F., Tardieu, H., & Nicolas, S. (2012). How chunks, long-term working memory and templates offer a cognitive explanation for neuroimaging data on expertise acquisition: A two-stage framework. *Brain and Cognition, 79*(3), 221–244.

Guilamo-Ramos, V., Lee, J. J., Kantor, L. M., Levine, D. S., Baum, S., & Johnsen, J. (2015). Potential for using online and mobile education with parents and adolescents to impact sexual and reproductive health. *Prevention Science, 16*(1), 53–60.

Guilford, J. P. (1956). Structure of intellect. *Psychological Bulletin, 53,* 267–293.

Guilford, J. P. (1986). *Creative talents: Their nature, uses and development.* Buffalo, NY: Bearly.

Guilleminault, C., Palombini, L., Pelayo, R., & Chervin, R. D. (2003). Sleeping and sleep terrors in prepubertal children: What triggers them? *Pediatrics, 111,* e17–e25.

Guillery, R. W. (2005). Is postnatal neocortical maturation hierarchical? *Trends in Neurosciences, 28*(10), 512–517.

Guiney, H., Lucas, S. J., Cotter, J. D., & Machado, L. (2015). Evidence cerebral blood-flow regulation mediates exercise–cognition links in healthy young adults. *Neuropsychology, 29*(1), 1.

Gunderson, E. A., Gripshover, S. J., Romero, C., Dweck, C. S., Goldin-Meadow, S., & Levine, S. C. (2013). Parent praise to 1- to 3-year-olds predicts children's motivational frameworks 5 years later. *Child Development, 84*(5), 1526–1541.

Gunn, J. K. L., Rosales, C. B., Center, K. E., Nuñez, A., Gibson, S. J., Christ, C., & Ehiri, J. E. (2016). Prenatal exposure to cannabis and maternal and child health outcomes: a systematic review and meta-analysis. *BMJ Open, 6*(4), e009986.

Gunnar, M. R., Kryzer, E., Van Ryzin, M. J., & Phillips, D. A. (2010). The rise in cortisol in family day care: Associations with aspects of care quality, child behavior, and child sex. *Child Development, 81,* 851–869. doi: 10.1111/j.1467-8624.2010.01438.x

Guo, G., Roettger, M., & Cai, T. (2008). The integration of genetic propensities into social-control models of delinquency and violence among male youths. *American Sociological Review, 73,* 543–568.

Gupta, B. P., Murad, M. H., Clifton, M. M., Prokop, L., Nehra, A., & Kopecky, S. L. (2011). The effect of lifestyle modification and cardiovascular risk factor reduction on erectile dysfunction: A systematic review and meta-analysis. *Archives of Internal Medicine, 171*(20), 1797–1803.

Gupta, K. K., Gupta, V. K., & Shirasaka, T. (2016). An update on fetal alcohol syndrome—pathogenesis, risks, and treatment. *Alcoholism: Clinical and Experimental Research, 40*(8), 1594–1602.

Guralnik, J. M., Butterworth, S., Wadsworth, M. E. J., & Kuh, D. (2006). Childhood socioeconomic status predicts physical functioning a half century later. *Journal of Gerontology: Medical Sciences, 61A,* 694–701.

Gurin, P. Y., Dey, E. L., Gurin, G., & Hurtado, S. (2003). How does racial/ethnic diversity promote education? *Western Journal of Black Studies, 27*(1), 20.

Gurrentz, B. (2018). *Living with an unmarried partner now more common for young adults* [U.S. Census Bureau news report]. Retrieved from www.census.gov/library/stories/2018/11/cohabitaiton-is-up-marriage-is-down-for-young-adults.html

Gurrentz, B. (2019). *Cohabitating partners older, more racially diverse, more educated, higher earners* [U.S. Census Bureau news report]. Retrieved from www.census.gov/library/stories/2019/09/unmarried-partners-more-diverse-than-20-years-ago.html

Gurteen, P. M., Horne, P. J., & Erjavec, M. (2011). Rapid word learning in 13- and 17-month-olds in a naturalistic two-word procedure: Looking versus reaching measures. *Journal of Experimental Child Psychology, 109*(2), 201–217.

Gurven, M., Von Rueden, C., Massenkoff, M., Kaplan, H., & Lero Vie, M. (2013). How universal is the Big Five? Testing the five-factor model of personality variation among forager–farmers in the Bolivian Amazon. *Journal of Personality and Social Psychology, 104*(2), 354.

Gusarova, I., Fraser, V., & Alderson, K. G. (2012). A quantitative study of "friends with benefits" relationships. *The Canadian Journal of Human Sexuality, 21*(1), 41.

Guthold, R., Stevens, G. A., Riley, L. M., & Bull, F. C. (2020). Global trends in insufficient physical activity among adolescents: A pooled analysis of 298 population-based surveys with 1.6 million participants. *The Lancet Child & Adolescent Health, 4*(1), 23–35.

Guttmacher Institute. (2013). *Facts on American teens' sexual and reproductive health.* Retrieved from www.guttmacher.org/pubs/FB-ATSRH.html#6

Guttmacher Institute. (2016). *American teens' sexual and reproductive health* [Fact sheet]. Retrieved from www.guttmacher.org/fact-sheet/american-teens-sexual-and-reproductive-health-old

Guttmacher Institute. (2017). *The looming threat to sex education: A resurgence of federal funding for abstinence-on programs?* [News release]. Retrieved from www.guttmacher.org/gpr/2017/03/looming-threat-sex-education-resurgence-federal-funding-abstinence-only-programs.

Guttmacher Institute. (2018). *The teen pregnancy prevention program was on the right track and now it's being dismantled* [Blog post]. Retrieved from www.guttmacher.org/article/2018/05/teen-pregnancy-prevention-program-was-right-track-now-its-being-dismantled.

Gwynn, J. D., Hardy, L. L., Wiggers, J. H., Smith, W. T., D'Este, C. A., Turner, N., . . . Attia, J. R. (2010). The validation of a self-report measure and physical activity of Australian Aboriginal and Torres Strait Islander and non-indigenous rural children. *Australian and New Zealand Journal of Public Health, 34,* S57–S65.

Haar, J. M., Russo, M., Suñe, A., & Ollier-Malaterre, A. (2014). Outcomes of work–life balance on job satisfaction, life satisfaction and mental health: A study across seven cultures. *Journal of Vocational Behavior, 85*(3), 361–373.

Haas, C., Takayoshi, P., Carr, B., Hudson, K., & Pollock, R. (2011). Young people's everyday literacies: The language features of instant messaging. *Research in the Teaching of English,* 378–404.

Habak, P. J., & Kole, M. (2018). Pregnancy, vaginal birth after cesarean delivery (VBAC). In *StatPearls* [Internet]. Treasure Island, FL: StatPearls Publishing.

Hackman, D. A., Farah, M. J., & Meaney, M. J. (2010). Socioeconomic status and the brain: mechanistic insights from human and animal research. *Nature Reviews Neuroscience, 11*(9), 651.

Hadfield, J. C. (2014). The health of grandparents raising grandchildren: A literature review. *Journal of Gerontological Nursing, 40*(4), 32–42.

Hafford, C. (2010). Sibling caretaking in immigrant families: Understanding cultural practices to inform child welfare practice and evaluation. *Evaluation and Program Planning, 33*(3), 294–302.

Hagan, Jr., J.F., Committee of Psychosocial Aspects of Child and Family Health, & Task Force on Terrorism (2005). Psychosocial implications of disaster or terrorism on children: A guide for the pediatrician. *Pediatrics, 116,* 787–795.

Haglund, K. A., & Fehring, R. J. (2010). The association of religiosity, sexual education, and parental factors with risky sexual behaviors among adolescents and young adults. *Journal of Religion and Health, 49*(4), 460–472.

Haider, B. A., & Bhutta, Z. A. (2017). Multiple-micronutrient supplementation for women during pregnancy. *Cochrane Database of Systematic Reviews,* 4.

Haidt, J., Koller, S. H., & Dias, M. G. (1993). Affect, culture, and morality, or is it wrong to eat your dog? *Journal of Personality and Social Psychology, 65*(4), 613.

Haight, S. C., Ko, J. Y., Tong, V. T., Bohm, M. K., & Callaghan, W. M. (2018). Opioid use disorder documented at delivery hospitalization—United

States, 1999–2014. *Morbidity and Mortality Weekly Report, 67*(31), 845.

Hair, N. L., Hanson, J. L., Wolfe, B. L., & Pollak, S. D. (2015). Association of child poverty, brain development, and academic achievement. *JAMA Pediatrics, 169*(9), 822–829.

Haith, M. M. (1986). Sensory and perceptual processes in early infancy. *Journal of Pediatrics, 109*(1), 158–171.

Haith, M. M. (1998). Who put the cog in infant cognition? Is rich interpretation too costly? *Infant Behavior and Development, 21*(2), 167–179.

Hakeem, G. F., Oddy, L., Holcroft, C. A., & Abenhaim, H. A. (2015). Incidence and determinants of sudden infant death syndrome: A population-based study on 37 million births. *World Journal of Pediatrics, 11*(1), 41–47.

Hakulinen, C., Elovainio, M., Pulkki-Råback, L., Virtanen, M., Kivimäki, M., & Jokela, M. (2015). Personality and depressive symptoms: Individual participant meta-analysis of 10 cohort studies. *Depression and Anxiety, 32*(7), 461–470.

Hale, S., Rose, N. S., Myerson, J., Strube, M. J., Sommers, M., Tye-Murray, N., & Spehar, B. (2011). The structure of working memory abilities across the adult life span. *Psychology and Aging, 26*(1), 92.

Hales, C. M., Carroll, M. D., Fryar, C. D., & Ogden, C. L. (2017). *Prevalence of obesity among adults and youth: United States, 2015–2016.* Atlanta, GA: U.S. Department of Health and Human Services, Centers for Disease Control and Prevention, National Center for Health Statistics.

Hales, C., Carroll, M. D., Fryar, C. D. & Ogden, C. L. (2020). Prevalence of obesity and severe obesity among adults: United States, 2017–2018. *NCHS Data Brief, No. 360.* Hyattsville, MD: National Center for Health Statistics.

Halgunseth, L. C., Ispa, J. M., & Rudy, D. (2006). Parental control in Latino families: An integrated review of the literature. *Child Development, 77*, 1282–1297.

Halim, M. L., Ruble, D. N., Tamis-LeMonda, C. S., Zosuls, K. M., Lurye, L. E., & Greulich, F. K. (2014). Pink frilly dresses and the avoidance of all things "girly": Children's appearance rigidity and cognitive theories of gender development. *Developmental Psychology, 50*(4), 1091.

Hall, J. A. (2011). Sex differences in friendship expectations: A meta-analysis. *Journal of Social and Personal Relationships, 28*(6), 723–747.

Hall, J. H., & Fincham, F. D. (2006). Relationship dissolution after infidelity. In M. Fine & J. Harvey (Eds.), *Handbook of divorce and relationship dissolution* (pp. 153–168). Hillsdale, NJ: Erlbaum.

Hallers-Haalboom, E. T., Mesman, J., Groeneveld, M. G., Endendijk, J. J., Van Berkel, S. R., Van der Pol, L. D., & Bakermans-Kranenburg, M. J. (2014). Mothers, fathers, sons, and daughters: Parental sensitivity in families with two children. *Journal of Family Psychology, 28,* 138–147. doi: 10.1037/a0036004

Halpern, C. T., & Kaestle, C. E. (2014). Sexuality in emerging adulthood. In D. L. Tolman, L. M. Diamond, J. A. Bauermeister, W. H. George, J. G. Pfaus, & L. M. Ward (Eds.), *APA handbook of sexuality and psychology, Vol. 1: Person-based approaches.* (pp. 487–522). Washington, DC: American Psychological Association.

Halpern, C., Young, M., Waller, M., Martin, S., & Kupper, L. (2003). Prevalence of partner violence in same-sex romantic and sexual relationships in a national sample of adolescents. *Journal of Adolescent Health, 35*(2), 124–131.

Halpern, D. F., Benbow, C. P., Geary, D. C., Gur, R. C., Hyde, J. S., & Gernsbacher, M. A. (2007). The science of sex differences in science and mathematics. *Psychological Science in the Public Interest, 8*, 1–51.

Halpern, H. P., & Perry-Jenkins, M. (2016). Parents' gender ideology and gendered behavior as predictors of children's gender-role attitudes: A longitudinal exploration. *Sex Roles, 74*(11–12), 527–542.

Halpern, S. C., Schuch, F. B., Scherer, J. N., Sordi, A. O., Pachado, M., Dalbosco, C., . . . Von Diemen, L. (2018). Child maltreatment and illicit substance abuse: A systematic review and meta-analysis of longitudinal studies. *Child Abuse Review, 27*(5), 344–360.

Hamilton, B. E., & Ventura, S. J. (2012). *Birth rates for US teenagers reach historic lows for all age and ethnic groups* (Vol. 89). Hyattsville, MD: US Department of Health and Human Services, Centers for Disease Control and Prevention, National Center for Health Statistics.

Hamilton, J. L., Nesi, J., & Choukas-Bradley, S. (2020). *Teens and social media during the COVID-19 pandemic: Staying socially connected while physically distant.*

Hamilton, M. C., Anderson, D., Broaddus, M., & Young, K. (2006). Gender stereotyping and under-representation of female characters in 200 popular children's picture books: A twenty-first century update. *Sex Roles, 55*(11–12), 757–765.

Hamilton, S. F., & Hamilton, M. A. (2006). School, work, and emerging adulthood. In J. J. Arnett & J. L. Tanner (Eds.), *Emerging adults in America: Coming of age in the 21st century* (pp. 257–277). Washington, DC: American Psychological Association.

Hamilton, W. D. (1966). The moulding of senescence by natural selection. *Journal of Theoretical Biology, 12*(1), 12–45.

Hamlin, J. K., & Wynn, K. (2011). Young infants prefer prosocial to antisocial others. *Cognitive Development, 26*(1), 30–39.

Hammerton, G., Heron, J., Mahedy, L., Maughan, B., Hickman, M., & Murray, J. (2018). Low resting heart rate, sensation seeking and the course of antisocial behaviour across adolescence and young adulthood. *Psychological Medicine, 48*(13), 2194–2201.

Hammond, S. I., Müller, U., Carpendale, J. I., Bibok, M. B., & Liebermann-Finestone, D. P. (2012). The effects of parental scaffolding on preschoolers' executive function. *Developmental Psychology, 48*(1), 271.

Hampton, K. N., Goulet, L. S., Rainie, L., & Purcell, K. (2011). *Social networking sites and our lives.* Pew Research Center's Internet and American Life Project. Retrieved from www.namingandtreating.com/wp-content/uploads/2011/07/PIP-Social-networking-sites-and-our-lives.pdf

Hamza, T. H., Chen, H., Hill-Burns, E. M., Rhodes, S. L., Montimurro, J., Kay, D. M., . . . Yearout, D. (2011). Genome-wide gene-environment study identifies glutamate receptor gene GRIN2A as a Parkinson's disease modifier gene via interaction with coffee. *PLoS Genetics, 7*(8), e1002237

Han, J. A., Cho, Y., & Kim, J. (2014). Effects of preschool children's gender, temperament, emotional regulation and maternal parenting stress on children's overt aggression and relational aggression. *Korean Journal of Human Ecology, 23*(4), 599–611.

Han, W. J., Miller, D. P., & Waldfogel, J. (2010). Parental work schedules and adolescent risky behaviors. *Developmental Psychology, 46*(5), 1245.

Han, Z., Lutsiv, O., Mulla, S., McDonald, S. D., & Group, K. S. (2012). Maternal height and the risk of preterm birth and low birth weight: A systematic review and meta-analyses. *Journal of Obstetrics and Gynaecology Canada, 34*(8), 721–746.

Handmaker, N. S., Rayburn, W. F., Meng, C., Bell, J. B., Rayburn, B. B., & Rappaport, V. J. (2006). Impact of alcohol exposure after pregnancy recognition on ultrasonographic fetal growth measures. *Alcoholism: Clinical and Experimental Research, 30*, 892–898.

Hank, K. (2007). Proximity and contacts between older parents and their children: A European comparison. *Journal of Marriage and Family, 69*(1), 157–173.

Hankin, B. L., Mermelstein, R., & Roesch, L. (2007). Sex differences in adolescent depression: Exposure and reactivity models. *Child Development, 78*, 279–295.

Hannigan, J. H., & Armant, D. R. (2000). Alcohol in pregnancy and neonatal outcome. *Seminars in Neonatology, 5,* 243–254.

Hanschmidt, F., Lehnig, F., Riedel-Heller, S. G., & Kersting, A. (2016). The stigma of suicide survivorship and related consequences—a systematic review. *PLoS One, 11*(9).

Hanscombe, K. B., Trzaskowski, M., Haworth, C. M., Davis, O. S., Dale, P. S., & Plomin, R. (2012). Socioeconomic status (SES) and children's intelligence (IQ): In a UK-representative sample SES moderates the environmental, not genetic, effect on IQ. *PLoS One, 7*(2), e30320.

Hansen, S. N., Schendel, D. E., & Parner, E. T. (2015). Explaining the increase in the prevalence of autism spectrum disorders: The proportion attributable to changes in reporting practices. *JAMA Pediatrics, 169*(1), 56–62.

Hansen, T. (2012). Parenthood and happiness: A review of folk theories versus empirical evidence. *Social Indicators Research, 108*(1), 29–64.

Hanson, L. (1968). *Renoir: The man, the painter, and his world.* New York, NY: Dodd, Mead.

Hao, Y. (2008). Productive activities and psychological well-being among older adults. *Journals of Gerontology, 63*(2, Series A), S64–S72.

Hara, Y., Waters, E. M., McEwen, B. S., & Morrison, J. H. (2015). Estrogen effects on cognitive and synaptic health over the lifecourse. *Physiological Reviews, 95*(3), 785–807.

Hardy, S. A., Pratt, M. W., Pancer, S. M., Olsen, J. A., & Lawford, H. L. (2011). Community and religious involvement as contexts of identity change across late adolescence and emerging adulthood. *International Journal of Behavioral Development, 35*(2), 125–135.

Hare, D. L., Toukhsati, S. R., Johansson, P., & Jaarsma, T. (2014). Depression and cardiovascular disease: A clinical review. *European Heart Journal, 35*(21), 1365–1372.

Hareli, S., Kafetsios, K., & Hess, U. (2015). A cross-cultural study on emotion expression and the learning of social norms. *Frontiers in Psychology, 6*, 1501.

Hargreaves, A. L., Nowak, G., Frew, P., Hinman, A. R., Orenstein, W. A., Mendel, J., . . . Omer, S. B. (2020). Adherence to timely vaccinations in the United States. *Pediatrics, 145*(3).

Harlow, H. F., & Harlow, M. K. (1962). The effect of rearing conditions on behavior. *Bulletin of the Menninger Clinic, 26*, 213–224.

Harman, D. (1956). Aging: a theory based on free radical and radiation chemistry. *Journal of Gerontology, 11*(3), 298–300.

Harman, D. (2006). Free radical theory of aging: An update. *Annals of the New York Academy of Sciences, 1067*(1), 10–21.

Harold, G. T., & Sellers, R. (2018). Annual research review: Interparental conflict and youth psychopathology: An evidence review and practice focused update. *Journal of Child Psychology and Psychiatry, 59*(4), 374–402.

Harper, G. W., Serrano, P. A., Bruce, D., & Bauermeister, J. A. (2016). The Internet's multiple roles in facilitating the sexual orientation identity development of gay and bisexual male adolescents. *American Journal of Men's Health, 10*(5), 359–376.

Harper, J. M., Padilla-Walker, L. M., & Jensen, A. C. (2016). Do siblings matter independent of both parents and friends? Sympathy as a mediator between sibling relationship quality and adolescent outcomes. *Journal of Research on Adolescence, 26*(1), 101–114.

Harper, S. R., Patton, L. D., & Wooden, O. S. (2009). Access and equity for African American students in higher education: A critical race historical analysis of policy efforts. *The Journal of Higher Education, 80*(4), 389–414.

Harriger, J. A., Schaefer, L. M., Thompson, J. K., & Cao, L. (2019). You can buy a child a curvy Barbie doll, but you can't make her like it: Young girls' beliefs about Barbie dolls with diverse shapes and sizes. *Body Image, 30*, 107–113.

Harris, A. M., Iqbal, K., Schillie, S., Britton, J., Kainer, M. A., Tressler, S., & Vellozzi, C. (2016). Increases in acute hepatitis B virus infections—Kentucky, Tennessee, and West Virginia, 2006–2013. *Morbidity and Mortality Weekly Report, 65*(3), 47–50.

Harris, D. G., Davies, C., Ward, H., & Haboubi, N. Y. (2008). An observational study of screening for malnutrition in elderly people living in sheltered accommodation. *Journal of Human Nutrition and Dietetics, 21*(1), 3–9.

Harris, P. L. (2011). Conflicting thoughts about death. *Human Development, 54*(3), 160–168.

Harrist, A. W., Zain, A. F., Bates, J. E., Dodge, K. A., & Pettit, G. S. (1997). Subtypes of social withdrawal in early childhood: Sociometric status and social-cognitive differences across four years. *Child Development, 68*, 278–294.

Hart, C. H., DeWolf, M., Wozniak, P., & Burts, D. C. (1992). Maternal and paternal disciplinary styles: Relations with preschoolers' playground behavioral orientation and peer status. *Child Development, 63*, 879–892.

Hart, D., Hofmann, V., Edelstein, W., & Keller, M. (1997). The relation of childhood personality types to adolescent behavior and development: A longitudinal study of Icelandic children. *Developmental Psychology, 33*, 195–205.

Hart, D., Southerland, N., & Atkins, R. (2003). Community service and adult development. In J. Demick & C. Andreoletti (Eds.), *Handbook of adult development* (pp. 585–597). New York, NY: Plenum Press.

Hart, H. M., McAdams, D. P., Hirsch, B. J., & Bauer, J. J. (2001). Generativity and social involvement among African Americans and white adults. *Journal of Research in Personality, 35*(2), 208–230.

Harter, S. (1993). Developmental changes in self-understanding across the 5 to 7 shift. In A. Sameroff & M. Haith (Eds.), *Reason and responsibility: The passage through childhood* (pp. 207–236). Chicago, IL: University of Chicago Press.

Harter, S. (1996). Developmental changes in self-understanding across the 5 to 7 shift. In A. J. Sameroff & M. M. Haith (Eds.), *The five to seven year shift: The age of reason and responsibility* (pp. 207–235). Chicago, IL: University of Chicago Press.

Harter, S. (1998). The development of self-representations. In W. Damon (Series Ed.) & N. Eisenberg (Vol. Ed.), *Handbook of child psychology: Vol. 3. Social, emotional, and personality development* (5th ed., pp. 553–617). New York, NY: Wiley.

Harter, S. (2006). The self. In W. Damon & R. M. Lerner (Series Eds.) & N. Eisenberg (Vol. Ed.), *Handbook of child psychology: Vol 3. Social, emotional and personality development* (pp. 505–570). Hoboken, NJ: Wiley.

Hartl, A. C., Laursen, B., & Cillessen, A. H. (2015). A survival analysis of adolescent friendships: The downside of dissimilarity. *Psychological Science, 26*(8), 1304–1315.

Hartshorn, K., Rovee-Collier, C., Gerhardstein, P., Bhatt, R. S., Wondoloski, R. L., Klein, P., . . . Campos-de-Carvalho, M. (1998). The ontogeny of long-term memory over the first year-and-a-half of life. *Developmental Psychobiology, 32*, 69–89.

Hartup, W. W. (1992). Peer relations in early and middle childhood. In V. B. Van Hasselt & M. Hersen (Eds.), *Handbook of social development: A lifespan perspective* (pp. 257–281). New York, NY: Plenum Press.

Hartup, W. W., & Stevens, N. (1999). Friendships and adaptation across the life span. *Current Directions in Psychological Science, 8*, 76–79.

Harvard Medical School. (2003, May). Confronting suicide—Part I. *Harvard Mental Health Letter, 19*(11), 1–4.

Harvard Medical School. (2004, December). Children's fears and anxieties. *Harvard Mental Health Letter, 21*(6), 1–3.

Harwood, R. L., Handwerker, W. P., Schoelmerich, A., & Leyendecker, B. (2001). Ethnic category labels, parental beliefs, and the contextualized individual: An exploration of the individualism-sociocentrism debate. *Parenting: Science and Practice, 1*(3), 217–236.

Hassan, N. M. M., Akhter, R., Staudinger, L., Tarpey, N., Basha, S., Cox, S., & Kashiwazaki, H. (2017). Oral disease and malnutrition in the elderly—Impact of oral cancer. *Current Oral Health Reports, 4*(2), 64–69.

Hasstedt, K. (2018). Ensuring adolescents' ability to obtain confidential family planning services in Title X. *Guttmacher Policy Review, 21*, 48–54.

Hategan, A., Bourgeois, J. A., Cheng, T., & Young, J. (2018). Caregiver burnout. In *Geriatric psychiatry study guide* (pp. 433–442). Cham, Switzerland: Springer.

Hatzenbuehler, M. L., O'Cleirigh, C., & Bradford, J. (2012). Effect of same-sex marriage laws on health care use and expenditures on sexual minority men: A quasi-natural experiment. *American Journal of Public Health, 102*(2), 285–291.

Hauck, F. R., Tanabe, K. O., & Moon, R. Y. (2011, August). Racial and ethnic disparities in infant mortality. In *Seminars in perinatology* (Vol. 35, No. 4, pp. 209–220). Philadelphia, PA: W.B. Saunders.

Haugaard, J. J. (1998). Is adoption a risk factor for the development of adjustment problems? *Clinical Psychology Review, 18*, 47–69.

Haun, D. B., & Tomasello, M. (2011). Conformity to peer pressure in preschool children. *Child Development, 82*(6), 1759–1767.

Hawes, C., Phillips, C. D., Rose, M., Holan, S., & Sherman, M. (2003). A national survey of assisted living facilities. *Gerontologist, 43*, 875–882.

Hawkley, L. C., Thisted, R. A., Masi, C. M., & Cacioppo, J. T. (2010). Loneliness predicts increased blood pressure: 5-year cross-lagged analyses in middle-aged and older adults. *Psychology and Aging, 25*(1), 132.

Haworth, C. M., Wright, M. J., Luciano, M., Martin, N. G., De Geus, E. J. C., Van Beijsterveldt, C. E. M., . . . Kovas, Y. (2010). The heritability of general cognitive ability increases linearly from childhood to young adulthood. *Molecular Psychiatry, 15*(11), 1112.

Hawthorne, D. M., Youngblut, J. M., & Brooten, D. (2016). Parent spirituality, grief, and mental health at 1 and 3 months after their infant's/child's death in an intensive care unit. *Journal of Pediatric Nursing, 31*(1), 73–80.

Hay, C., Meldrum, R. C., Widdowson, A. O., & Piquero, A. R. (2017). Early aggression and later delinquency: Considering the redirecting role of good parenting. *Youth Violence and Juvenile Justice, 15*(4), 374–395.

Hay, D. F., Pawlby, S., Waters, C. S., Perra, O., & Sharp, D. (2010). Mothers' antenatal depression and their children's antisocial outcomes. *Child Development, 81*(1), 149–165.

Hay, D. F., Pedersen, J., & Nash, A. (1982). Dyadic interaction in the first year of life. In K.

H. Rubin & H. S. Ross (Eds.), *Peer relationships and social skills in children*. New York, NY: Springer.

Hay, D., Caplan, M., & Nash, A. (2018). The beginnings of peer relations. In K. Rubin, W. Bukowski, & B. Laursen (Eds.), *Handbook of peer interactions, relationships, and groups* (pp. 200-221). New York, NY: Guilford Press.

Hayflick, L. (1974). The strategy of senescence. *Gerontologist, 14*(1), 37-45.

Hayflick, L. (1981). Intracellular determinants of aging. *Mechanisms of Aging and Development, 28*, 177.

Hayflick, L. (2004). Aging: The reality: "Anti-aging" is an oxymoron. *The Journals of Gerontology Series A: Biological Sciences and Medical Sciences, 59*(6), B573-B578.

Hayflick, L. (2004). "Anti-aging" is an oxymoron. *Journal of Gerontology: Biological Sciences, 59A*, 573-578.

Hayne, H., Boniface, J., & Barr, R. (2000). The development of declarative memory in human infants: Age-related changes in deffered imitation. *Behavioral Neuroscience, 114*(1), 77.

Hayslip Jr., B., Blumenthal, H., & Garner, A. (2014). Social support and grandparent caregiver health: One-year longitudinal findings for grandparents raising their grandchildren. *Journals of Gerontology Series B: Psychological Sciences and Social Sciences, 70*(5), 804-812.

Hayward, R. D., & Elliott, M. (2014). Cross-national analysis of the influence of cultural norms and government restrictions on the relationship between religion and well-being. *Review of Religious Research, 56*(1), 23-43.

He, W., Goodkind, D., & Kowal, P. R. (2016). *An aging world: 2015*. Washington, DC: United States Census Bureau.

Healy, A. J., Malone, F. D., Sullivan, L. M., Porter, T. F., Luthy, D. A., Comstock, C. H., . . . D'Alton, M. E. (2006). Early access to prenatal care: Implications for racial disparity in perinatal mortality. *Obstetrics and Gynecology, 107*, 625-631.

Heath, S. B. (1989). Oral and literate tradition among Black Americans living in poverty. *American Psychologist, 44*, 367-373.

Heatherington, E. M. (2006). The influence of conflict, marital problem solving and parenting on children's adjustment in nondivorced, divorced and remarried families. In A. Clarke-Stewart & J. Dunn (Eds.), *Families count: Effects on child and adolescent development* (pp. 203-237). New York, NY: Cambridge University Press.

Heckhausen, J. (2001). Adaptation and resilience in midlife. In M. E. Lachman (Ed.), *Handbook of midlife development* (pp. 345-394). New York, NY: Wiley.

Heckhausen, J., Wrosch, C., & Fleeson, W. (2001). Developmental regulation before and after a developmental deadline: The sample case of biological clock for childbearing. *Psychology and Aging, 16*, 400-413.

Hedman, A. M., van Haren, N. E., Schnack, H. G., Kahn, R. S., & Hulshoff Pol, H. E. (2012). Human brain changes across the life span: A review of 56 longitudinal magnetic resonance imaging studies. *Human Brain Mapping, 33*(8), 1987-2002.

Heffner, K. L. (2011). Neuroendocrine effects of stress on immunity in the elderly: implications for inflammatory disease. *Immunology and Allergy Clinics of North America, 31*(1), 95-108.

Heffner, L. J. (2004). Advanced maternal age—How old is too old? *New England Journal of Medicine, 351*, 1927-1929.

Heid, A. R., Zarit, S. H., & Fingerman, K. L. (2016). "My parent is so stubborn!"— Perceptions of aging parents' persistence, insistence, and resistance. *Journals of Gerontology Series B: Psychological Sciences and Social Sciences, 71*(4), 602-612.

Heid, A. R., Zarit, S. H., & Fingerman, K. L. (2017). Adult children's responses to parent "stubbornness." *The Gerontologist, 57*(3), 429-440.

Heidenreich, A., Bellmunt, J., Bolla, M., Joniau, S., Mason, M., Matveev, V., . . . Zattoni, F. (2011). EAU guidelines on prostate cancer. Part 1: Screening, diagnosis, and treatment of clinically localised disease. *European Urology, 59*(1), 61-71.

Heikamp, T., Trommsdorff, G., & Fäsche, A. (2013). Development of self-regulation in context. In G. seebab, M. Schmitz, & P. M. Gollwitzer (Eds.), *Acting intentionally and its limits: Individuals, groups, institutions* (pp. 193-222). Boston, MA: Gruyter.

Heiland, F., & Liu, S. H. (2006). Family structure and wellbeing of out-of-wedlock children: The significance of the biological parents' relationship. *Demographic Research, 15*, 61-104.

Heilbronn, L. K., & Ravussin, E. (2003). Calorie restriction and aging: Review of the literature and implications for studies in humans. *American Journal of Clinical Nutrition, 78*, 361-369.

Heim, B. T., & Lin, L. (2017). Does health reform lead to an increase in early retirement? Evidence from Massachusetts. *ILR Review, 70*(3), 704-732.

Heim, C., & Binder, E. B. (2012). Current research trends in early life stress and depression: Review of human studies on sensitive periods, gene-environment interactions, and epigenetics. *Experimental Neurology, 233*(1), 102-111.

Heiman, J. R., Long, J. S., Smith, S. N., Fisher, W. A., Sand, M. S., & Rosen, R. C. (2011). Sexual satisfaction and relationship happiness in midlife and older couples in five countries. *Archives of Sexual Behavior, 40*(4), 741-753.

Heine, S. J., Lehman, D. R., Markus, H. R., & Kitayama, S. (1999). Is there a universal need for positive self-regard? *Psychological Review, 106*(4), 766.

Heiss, G., Wallace, R., Anderson, G. L., Aragaki, A., Beresford, S. A. A., Brzyski, R., . . . Stefanick, M. L., for the WHI Investigators. (2008). Health risks and benefits 3 years after stopping randomized treatment with estrogen and progestin. *Journal of the American Medical Association, 299*, 1036-1045.

Helms, H. M., Crouter, A. C., & McHale, S. M. (2003). Marital quality and spouses' marriage work with close friends and each other. *Journal of Marriage and Family, 65*, 963-977.

Helms, J. E. (1992). Why is there no study of cultural equivalence in standardized cognitive ability testing? *American Psychologist, 47*, 1083-1101.

HelpAge International. (2015). *Global AgeWatch Index 2015: Insight report*. Retrieved from www.ageinternational.org.uk/Documents/Global_AgeWatch_Index_2015_HelpAge.pdf

Helson, R., & Roberts, B. W. (1994). Ego development and personality change in adulthood. *Journal of Personality and Social Psychology, 66*, 911-920.

Helson, R., & Wink, P. (1992). Personality change in women from the early 40s to the early 50s. *Psychology and Aging, 7*(1), 46-55.

Helwig, C. C., & Jasiobedzka, U. (2001). The relation between law and morality: Children's reasoning about socially beneficial and unjust laws. *Child Development, 72*, 1382-1393.

Henning-Smith, C. (2016). Quality of life and psychological distress among older adults: The role of living arrangements. *Journal of Applied Gerontology, 35*(1), 39-61.

Henrique, R. S., Ré, A. H., Stodden, D. F., Fransen, J., Campos, C. M., Queiroz, D. R., & Cattuzzo, M. T. (2016). Association between sports participation, motor competence and weight status: A longitudinal study. *Journal of Science and Medicine in Sport, 19*(10), 825-829.

Henry, M., Mahathey, R. M., Robinson, A., Azim, A. & Watt, R. (2018). *The 2018 Annual Homeless Assessment Report (AHAR) to Congress*. Washington, DC: US Department of Housing and Urban Development, Office of Community Planning and Development.

Hepach, R., Vaish, A., & Tomasello, M. (2012). Young children are intrinsically motivated to see others helped. *Psychological Science, 23*(9), 967-972.

Herbig, B., Büssing, A., & Ewert, T. (2001). The role of tacit knowledge in the work context of nursing. *Journal of Advanced Nursing, 34*, 687-695.

Herek, G. M. (2006). Legal recognition of same-sex unions in the United States: A social science perspective. *American Psychologist, 61*, 607-621.

Herman-Giddens, M. E., Steffes, J., Harris, D., Slora, E., Hussey, M., Dowshen, S. A., . . . Reiter, E. O. (2012). Secondary sexual characteristics in boys: Data from the Pediatric Research in Office Settings Network. *Pediatrics, 130*(5), e1058-e1068.

Hernandez, D. J., & Macartney, S. E. (2008, January). *Racial-ethnic inequality in child well-being from 1985-2004: Gaps narrowing, but persist* (No. 9). New York, NY: Foundation for Child Development.

Hernandez, S. J. (2004, Summer). Demographic change and the life circumstances of immigrant families. *Future of Children, 14*(2).

Heron, M. (2019). Deaths: Leading causes for 2017. *National Vital Statistics Reports, 68*(6), 1-77. Hyattsville, MD: National Center for Health Statistics.

Heron, M. P., Hoyert, D. L., Murphy, S. L., Xu, J. Q., Kochanek, K. D., & Tejada-Vera, B. (2009). Deaths: Final data for 2006. *National Vital Statistics Reports, 57*(14). Hyattsville, MD: National Center for Health Statistics.

Heron, M.P. (2018). Deaths: Final data for 2016. *National Vital Statistics Reports, 67*(6), 1-77. Hyattsville, MD: National Center for Health Statistics.

Herriot, H., Wrosch, C., & Gouin, J. P. (2018). Self-compassion, chronic age-related stressors, and diurnal cortisol secretion in older adulthood. *Journal of Behavioral Medicine, 41*(6), 850–862.

Herrnstein, R. J., & Murray, C. (1994). *The bell curve: Intelligence and class structure in American life.* New York, NY: Free Press.

Hertenstein, M. J., & Campos, J. J. (2004). The retention effects of an adult's emotional displays on infant behavior. *Child Development, 75*, 595–613.

Hertlein, K. M., & Piercy, F. P. (2006). Internet infidelity: A critical review of the literature. *The Family Journal, 14*(4), 366–371.

Hespos, S. J., & Baillargeon, R. (2008). Young infants' actions reveal their developing knowledge of support variables: Converging evidence for violation-of-expectation findings. *Cognition, 107*(1), 304–316.

Hess, R. D., & Azuma, H. (1991). Cultural support for schooling: Contrasts between Japan and the United States. *Educational Researcher, 20*(9), 2–9.

Hesso, N. A., & Fuentes, E. (2005). Ethnic differences in neonatal and postneonatal mortality. *Pediatrics, 115,* e44–e51.

Hetherington, E. M., Reiss, D., & Plomin, R. (2013). *Separate social worlds of siblings: The impact of nonshared environment on development.* Milton Park, Abingdon, England: Routledge.

Hewes, J. (2014). Seeking balance in motion: The role of spontaneous free play in promoting social and emotional health in early childhood care and education. *Children, 1,* 280–301.

Hewlett, B. S. (1987). Intimate fathers: Patterns of paternal holding among Aka pygmies. In M. E. Lamb (Ed.), *The father's role: Cross-cultural perspectives* (pp. 295–330). Hillsdale, NJ: Erlbaum.

Hewlett, B. S. (1992). Husband-wife reciprocity and the father-infant relationship among Aka pygmies. In B. S. Hewlett (Ed.), *Father-child relations: Cultural and biosocial contexts* (pp. 153–176). New York, NY: de Gruyter.

Hewlett, B. S., Lamb, M. E., Shannon, D., Leyendecker, B., & Schölmerich, A. (1998). Culture and early infancy among central African foragers and farmers. *Developmental Psychology, 34*(4), 653–661.

Heylens, G., De Cuypere, G., Zucker, K. J., Schelfaut, C., Elaut, E., Bossche, H. V., . . . T'Sjoen, G. (2012). Gender identity disorder in twins: A review of the case report literature. *The Journal of Sexual Medicine, 9*(3), 751–757.

Heymann, J., Siebert, W. S., & Wei, X. (2007). The implicit wage costs of family friendly work practices. *Oxford Economic Papers, 59*(2), 275–300.

Heywood, W., Minichiello, V., Lyons, A., Fileborn, B., Hussain, R., Hinchliff, S., . . . Dow, B. (2017). The impact of experiences of ageism on sexual activity and interest in later life. *Ageing & Society.*

Hiatt, C., Laursen, B., Mooney, K. S., & Rubin, K. H. (2015). Forms of friendship: A person-centered assessment of the quality, stability, and outcomes of different types of adolescent friends. *Personality and Individual Differences, 77,* 149–155.

Hicks, G. R., & Lee, T. T. (2006). Public attitudes toward gays and lesbians: Trends and predictors. *Journal of Homosexuality, 51*(2), 57–77.

Hilgard, J., Engelhardt, C. R., Rouder, J. N., Segert, I. L., & Bartholow, B. D. (2019). Null effects of game violence, game difficulty, and 2D: 4D digit ratio on aggressive behavior. *Psychological Science, 30*(4), 606–616.

Hill, C., & Holzer, H. (2007). Labor market experiences and the transition to adulthood. In S. Danziger & C. Rouse (Eds.), *The price of independence: The economics of early adulthood* (pp. 141–169). New York, NY: Russell Sage Foundation.

Hill, N. E., & Taylor, L. C. (2004). Parental school involvement and children's academic achievement: Pragmatics and issues. *Current Directions in Psychological Science, 13,* 161–168.

Hill, N., & Tyson, D. (2009). Parental involvement in middle school: A meta-analytical assessment of the strategies that promote achievement. *Developmental Psychology, 45*(3), 740–763.

Hill, P. L., Turiano, N. A., Mroczek, D. K., & Roberts, B. W. (2012). Examining concurrent and longitudinal relations between personality traits and social well-being in adulthood. *Social Psychological and Personality Science, 3*(6), 698–705.

Hill, T. D., Angel, J. L., Ellison, C. G., & Angel, R. J. (2005). Religious attendance and mortality: An 8-year follow-up of older Mexican Americans. *Journal of Gerontology: Social Sciences, 60B,* S102–S109.

Hilliard, L. J., & Liben, L. S. (2010). Differing levels of gender salience in preschool classrooms: Effects on children's gender attitudes and intergroup bias. *Child Development, 81*(6), 1787–1798.

Hillier, L. (2002). "It's a catch-22": Same-sex-attracted young people on coming out to parents. In S. S. Feldman & D. A. Rosenthal (Eds.), *Talking sexuality* (New Directions for Child and Adolescent Development, No. 97, pp. 75–91). San Francisco, CA: Jossey-Bass.

Hinds, D. A., Stuve, L. L., Nilsen, G. B., Halperin, E., Eskin, E., Ballinger, D. G., . . . Cox, D. R. (2005). Whole-genome patterns of common DNA variation in three human populations. *Science, 307,* 1072–1079.

Hingson, R. W., Heeren, T., & Winter, M. R. (2006). Age at drinking onset and alcohol dependence: Age at onset, duration, and severity. *Archivers of Pediatrics & Adolescent Medicine, 160,* 739–746.

Hinman, J. D., & Abraham, C. R. (2007). What's behind the decline? The role of white matter in brain aging. *Neurochemical Research, 32*(12), 2023–2031.

Hirschl, T. A., Altobelli, J., & Rank, M. R. (2003). Does marriage increase the odds of affluence? Exploring the life course probabilities. *Journal of Marriage and Family, 65*(4), 927–938.

Hirsh-Pasek, K. (1991). Pressure or challenge in preschool: How academic environments affect children. In L. Rescorla, M. Hyson, K. Hirsh-Pasek (Eds.), *Academic instruction in early childhood: Challenge or pressure?* (pp. 39–45). San Francisco, CA: Jossey-Bass.

Hirsh-Pasek, K., Adamson, L. B., Bakeman, R., Owen, M. T., Golinkoff, R. M., Pace, A., . . .

Suma, K. (2015). The contribution of early communication quality to low-income children's language success. *Psychological Science, 26*(7), 1071–1083.

Hitzert, M. M., Van Braeckel, K. N., Bos, A. F., Hunnius, S., & Geuze, R. H. (2014). Early visual attention in preterm and fullterm infants in relation to cognitive and motor outcomes at school age: An exploratory study. *Frontiers in Pediatrics, 2.*

HIV.gov. (2020). *U.S. statistics: Fast facts* [Data sheet]. Retrieved from www.hiv.gov/hiv-basics/overview/data-and-trends/statistics

Ho, R. C. M., Neo, L. F., Chua, A. N. C., Cheak, A. A. C., & Mak, A. (2010). Research on psychoneuroimmunology: Does stress influence immunity and coronary artery disease? *Annals Academy of Medicine Singapore, 39,* 191–196.

Hoang, T. D., Reis, J., Zhu, N., Jacobs, D. R., Launer, L. J., Whitmer, R. A., . . . Yaffe, K. (2016). Effect of early adult patterns of physical activity and television viewing on midlife cognitive function. *JAMA Psychiatry, 73*(1), 73–79.

Hoban, T. F. (2004). Sleep and its disorders in children. *Seminars in Neurology, 24,* 327–340.

Hobbs, W. R., Burke, M., Christakis, N. A., & Fowler, J. H. (2016). Online social integration is associated with reduced mortality risk. *Proceedings of the National Academy of Sciences, 113*(46), 12980–12984.

Hodges, E. V. E., Boivin, M., Vitaro, F., & Bukowski, W. M. (1999). The power of friendship: Protection against an escalating cycle of peer victimization. *Developmental Psychology, 35,* 94–101.

Hofer, J., Busch, H., Chasiotis, A., Kärtner, J., & Campos, D. (2008). Concern for generativity and its relation to implicit pro-social power motivation, generative goals, and satisfaction with life: A cross-cultural investigation. *Journal of Personality, 76*(1), 1–30.

Hoff, E. (2003). The specificity of environmental influence: Socioeconomic status affects early vocabulary development via maternal speech. Child Development, 74, 1368–1378.

Hoff, E. (2006). How social contexts support and shape language development. *Developmental Review, 26,* 55–88.

Hofferth, S. L. (2006). Residential father family type and child well-being: Investment versus selection. *Demography, 43*(1), 53–77.

Hoffman, G. F., Davies, M., & Norman, R. (2007). The impact of lifestyle factors on reproductive perfomance in the general population and those undergoing infertility treatment: A review. *Human Reproduction Update, 13*(3), 209–223.

Hoffman, J. (2020, April 23). Vaccine rates drop dangerously as parents avoid doctor's visits. *The New York Times.* www.nytimes.com/2020/04/23/health/coronavirus-measles-vaccines.html

Hoffman, M. C., Mazzoni, S. E., Wagner, B. D., & Laudenslager, M. L. (2016). Measures of maternal stress and mood in relation to preterm birth. *Obstetrics and Gynecology, 127*(3), 545.

Hoffman, M. L. (1970). Conscience, personality, and socialization techniques. *Human Development, 13,* 90–126.

Hofmann, S. G., Asnaani, A., Vonk, I. J., Sawyer, A. T., & Fang, A. (2012). The efficacy of cognitive behavioral therapy: A review of meta-analyses. *Cognitive Therapy and Research, 36*(5), 427–440.

Hogge, W. A. (2003). The clinical use of karyotyping spontaneous abortions. *American Journal of Obstetrics and Gynecology, 189,* 397–402.

Holfelder, B., & Schott, N. (2014). Relationship of fundamental movement skills and physical activity in children and adolescents: A systematic review. *Psychology of Sport and Exercise, 15*(4), 382–391.

Holland, G., & Tiggemann, M. (2016). A systematic review of the impact of the use of social networking sites on body image and disordered eating outcomes. *Body Image, 17,* 100–110.

Holliday, R. (2004). The multiple and irreversible causes of aging. *Journal of Gerontology: Biological Sciences, 59A,* 568–572.

Holloway, A. (2014, January 24). *The Toraja people and the most complex funeral rituals in the world.* Retrieved from www.ancient-origins.net/ancient-places-asia/toraja-people-and-most-complex-funeral-rituals-world-001268

Holmbeck, G. N. (2018). A model of family relational transformations during the transition to adolescence: Parent–adolescent conflict and adaptation. In J. A. Graber, J. Brooks-Gunn, A. C. Petersen (Eds.), *Transitions through adolescence* (pp. 167–199). London, England: Psychology Press.

Holmes, R. M. (2012). The outdoor recess activities of children at an urban school: Longitudinal and intraperiod patterns. *American Journal of Play, 4*(3), 327.

Holt, C. L., Clark, E. M., Debnam, K. J., & Roth, D. L. (2014). Religion and health in African Americans: The role of religious coping. *American Journal of Health Behavior, 38*(2), 190–199.

Holt-Lunstad, J., Birmingham, W., & Jones, B. Q. (2008). Is there something unique about marriage? The relative impact of marital status, relationship quality, and network social support on ambulatory blood pressure and mental health. *Annals of Behavioral Medicine, 35*(2), 239–244.

Holt-Lunstad, J., Smith, T. B., & Layton, J. B. (2010). Social relationships and mortality risk: A meta-analytic review. *PLoS Medicine, 7*(7), e1000316. doi:10.1371/journal.pmed.1000316

Holt-Lunstad, J., Smith, T. B., Baker, M., Harris, T., & Stephenson, D. (2015). Loneliness and social isolation as risk factors for mortality: A meta-analytic review. *Perspectives on Psychological Science, 10*(2), 227–237.

Hong, J. S., & Espelage, D. L. (2012). A review of research on bullying and peer victimization in school: An ecological system analysis. *Aggression and Violent Behavior, 17*(4), 311–322.

Hong, Z., Ng, K. K., Sim, S. K., Ngeow, M. Y., Zheng, H., Lo, J. C., . . . Zhou, J. (2015). Differential age- dependent associations of gray matter volume and white matter integrity with processing speed in healthy older adults. *Neuroimage, 123,* 42–50.

Honig, L. S., Kang, M. S., Cheng, R., Eckfeldt, J. H., Thyagarajan, B., Leiendecker-Foster, C., . . . Lee, J. H. (2015). Heritability of telomere length in a study of long-lived families. *Neurobiology of Aging, 36*(10), 2785–2790

Hoorn, J., Dijk, E., Meuwese, R., Rieffe, C., & Crone, E. A. (2016). Peer influence on prosocial behavior in adolescence. *Journal of Research on Adolescence, 26*(1), 90–100.

Hoover, R. M., & Polson, M. (2014). Detecting elder abuse and neglect: Assessment and intervention. *American Family Physician, 89*(6).

Hopkins, B., & Westra, T. (1988). Maternal handling and motor development: An intracultural study. *Genetic, Social and General Psychology Monographs, 14,* 377–420.

Hopkins, B., & Westra, T. (1990). Motor development, maternal expectations and the role of handling. *Infant Behavior and Development, 13,* 117–122.

Hopkins, M. (2014). *The development of children's understanding of death.* Doctoral dissertation, University of East Anglia.

Hopwood, C. J., Donnellan, M. B., Blonigen, D. M., Krueger, R. F., McGue, M., Iacono, W. G., & Burt, S. A. (2011). Genetic and environmental influences on personality trait stability and growth during the transition to adulthood: A three-wave longitudinal study. *Journal of Personality and Social Psychology, 100*(3), 545.

Horn, J. C., & Meer, J. (1987, May). The vintage years. *Psychology Today,* 76–90.

Horn, J. L., & Cattell, R. B. (1967). Age differences in fluid and crystallized intelligence. *Acta Psychologica, 26,* 107–129.

Hornung, O., & Heim, C. (2014). Gene-environment interactions and intermediate phenotypes: Early trauma and depression. *Frontiers in Endocrinology, 5,* 14.

Horowitz, B. N., Neiderhiser, J. M., Ganiban, J. M., Spotts, E. L., Lichtenstein, P., & Reiss, D. (2010). Genetic and environmental influences on global family conflict. *Journal of Family Psychology, 24*(2), 217–220.

Horowitz, J. M., Graf, N. & Livingston, G. (2019). *Marriage and cohabitation in the U.S.* [Pew Research Center report]. Retrieved from www.pewsocialtrends.org/2019/11/06/marriage-and-cohabitation-in-the-u-s/

Horton, R., & Shweder, R. A. (2004). Ethnic conservatism, psychological well-being, and the downside of mainstreaming: Generational differences. In O. G. Brim, C. D. Ryff, & R. C. Kessler (Eds.), *How healthy are we? A national study of well-being at midlife* (pp. 373–397). Chicago, IL: University of Chicago Press.

Hoskins, D. H. (2014). Consequences of parenting on adolescent outcomes. *Societies, 4*(3), 506–531.

Hostinar, C. E., & Miller, G. E. (2019). Protective factors for youth confronting economic hardship: Current challenges and future avenues in resilience research. *American Psychologist, 74*(6), 641.

Houltberg, B. J., Henry, C. S., & Morris, A. S. (2012). Family interactions, exposure to violence, and emotion regulation: Perceptions of children and early adolescents at risk. *Family Relations, 61,* 283–296. doi: 10.1111/j.1741-3729.2011.00699.x

Howard, K. S., Lefever, J. B., Borkowski, J. G., & Whitman, T. L. (2006). Fathers' influence in the lives of children with adolescent mothers. *Journal of Family Psychology, 20,* 468–476.

Howe, N., Rinaldi, C. M., Jennings, M., & Petrakos, H. (2002). "No! The lambs can stay out because they got cozies": Constructive and destructive sibling conflict, pretend play, and social understanding. *Child Development, 73*(5), 1460–1473.

Howell, R. T., Kern, M. L., & Lyubomirsky, S. (2007). Health benefits: Meta-analytically determining the impact of well-being on objective health outcomes. *Health Psychology Review, 1*(1), 83–136.

Howlader N., Noone A.M., Krapcho M., Miller, D., Brest A., . . . Cronin, K.A. (2019). *SEER Cancer Statistics Review, 1975–2016.* Bethesda, MD: National Cancer Institute. Retrieved from https://seer.cancer.gov/csr/1975_2016/

Howland, M., Armeli, S., Feinn, R., & Tennen, H. (2017). Daily emotional stress reactivity in emerging adulthood: Temporal stability and its predictors. *Anxiety, Stress, & Coping, 30*(2), 121–132.

Hoxby, C. M. (2000). The effects of class size on student achievement: New evidence from population variation. *The Quarterly Journal of Economics, 115*(4), 1239–1285.

Hoyer, W. J., & Rybash, J. M. (1994). Characterizing adult cognitive development. *Journal of Adult Development, 1*(1), 7–12.

Hsu, S., Gordon, B. A., Hornbeck, R., Norton, J. B., Levitch, D., Louden, A., . . . McDade, E. (2018). Discovery and validation of autosomal dominant Alzheimer's disease mutations. *Alzheimer's Research & Therapy, 10*(1), 67.

Huang, G. C., Unger, J. B., Soto, D., Fujimoto, K., Pentz, M. A., Jordan-Marsh, M., & Valente, T. W. (2014). Peer influences: The impact of online and offline friendship networks on adolescent smoking and alcohol use. *Journal of Adolescent Health, 54*(5), 508–514.

Hudak, M. L., & Tan, R. C. (2012). Neonatal drug withdrawal. *Pediatrics, 129*(2), e540–e560.

Hudd, S., Dumlao, J., Erdmann-Sager, D., Murray, D., Phan, E., & Soukas, N. (2000). Stress at college: Effects on health habits, health status and self-esteem. *College Students Journal, 34*(2), 217–227.

Hudley, A. H. C., & Mallinson, C. (2015). *Understanding English language variation in US schools.* New York, NY: Teachers College Press.

Huesmann, L. R. (2007). The impact of electronic media violence: Scientific theory and research. *Journal of Adolescent health, 41*(6), S6–S13.

Huffman, C. S., Schwartz, T. A., & Swanson, K. M. (2015). Couples and miscarriage: The influence of gender and reproductive factors on the impact of miscarriage. *Women's Health Issues, 25*(5), 570–578.

Hug, L., Sharrow, D., Zhong, K., & You, D., (2018). *Levels & Trends in Child Mortality: Report 2018.* Estimates developed by the United Nations Inter-agency Group for Child Mortality Estimation. New York, NY: United Nations Children's Fund.

Hughes, C. (2011). Changes and challenges in 20 years of research into the development of executive functions. *Infant and Child Development, 20*(3), 251–271.

Hughes, C., Devine, R. T., Ensor, R., Koyasu, M., Mizokawa, A., & Lecce, S. (2014). Lost in translation? Comparing British, Japanese, and Italian children's theory-of-mind performance. *Child Development Research*.

Hughes, D., Rodriguez, J., Smith, E. P., Johnson, D. J., Stevenson, H. C., & Spicer, P. (2006). Parents' ethnic-racial socialization practices: A review of research and directions for future study. *Developmental Psychology, 42*(5), 747.

Hughes, M. E., & Waite, L. J. (2009). Marital biography and health at mid-life. *Journal of Health and Social Behavior, 50*(3), 344–358.

Hughes, M. L., Agrigoroaei, S., Jeon, M., Bruzzese, M., & Lachman, M. E. (2018). Change in cognitive performance from midlife into old age: Findings from the Midlife in the United States (MIDUS) study. *Journal of the International Neuropsychological Society, 24*(8), 805–820.

Huijts, T., Kraaykamp, G., & Subramanian, S. V. (2013). Childlessness and psychological well-being in context: A multilevel study on 24 European countries. *European Sociological Review, 29*(1), 32–47.

Hujoel, P. P., Bollen, A. M., Noonan, C. J., & del Aguila, M. A. (2004). Antepartum dental radiography and infant low birth weight. *Journal of the American Medical Association, 291*, 1987–1993.

Hulbert, A. J., Pamplona, R., Buffenstein, R., & Buttemer, W. A. (2007). Life and death: metabolic rate, membrane composition, and life span of animals. *Physiological Reviews, 87*(4), 1175–1213.

Hummel, A., Shelton, K. H., Heron, J., Moore, L., & van den Bree, M. B. (2013). A systematic review of the relationships between family functioning, pubertal timing and adolescent substance use. *Addiction, 108*(3), 487–496.

Hunger Notes. (2016). *2016 World Hunger and Poverty Facts and Statistics*. Retrieved from www.worldhunger.org/2015-world-hunger-and-poverty-facts-and-statistics/#progress

Hungerford, T. L. (2001). The economic consequences of widowhood on elderly women in the United States and Germany. *Gerontologist, 41*, 103–110.

Hunt, G. E., Malhi, G. S., Cleary, M., Lai, H. M. X., & Sitharthan, T. (2016). Comorbidity of bipolar and substance use disorders in national surveys of general populations, 1990–2015: Systematic review and meta-analysis. *Journal of Affective Disorders, 206*, 321–330.

Hunt, G. E., Malhi, G. S., Lai, H. M. X., & Cleary, M. (2020). Prevalence of comorbid substance use in major depressive disorder in community and clinical settings, 1990–2019: Systematic review and meta-analysis. *Journal of Affective Disorders*.

Hunter, S. B., & Smith, D. E. (2008). Predictors of children's understandings of death: Age, cognitive ability, death experience and maternal communicative competence. *OMEGA-Journal of Death and Dying, 57*(2), 143–162.

Huntley, J. D., Gould, R. L., Liu, K., Smith, M., & Howard, R. J. (2015). Do cognitive interventions improve general cognition in dementia? A meta-analysis and meta-regression. *BMJ Open, 5*(4), e005247.

Huo, M., Graham, J. L., Kim, K., Birditt, K. S., & Fingerman, K. L. (2019). Aging parents' daily support exchanges with adult children suffering problems. *The Journals of Gerontology: Series B, 74*(3), 449–459.

Huo, M., Graham, J. L., Kim, K., Zarit, S. H., & Fingerman, K. L. (2018). Aging parents' disabilities and daily support exchanges with middle-aged children. *The Gerontologist, 58*(5), 872–882.

Hur, Y. M., Jeong, H. U., & Piffer, D. (2014). Shared genetic and environmental influences on self-reported creative achievement in art and science. *Personality and Individual Differences, 68*, 18–22.

Hurley, K. M., Black, M. M., Papas, M. A., & Quigg, A. M. (2008). Variation in breastfeeding behaviors, perceptions, and experiences by race/ethnicity among a low-income statewide sample of Special Supplemental Nutrition Program for Women, Infants, and Children (WIC) participants in the United States. *Maternal & Child Nutrition, 4*(2), 95–105.

Husby, I. M., Stray, K. M. T., Olsen, A., Lydersen, S., Indredavik, M. S., Brubakk, A. M., . . . Evensen, K. A. I. (2016). Long-term follow-up of mental health, health-related quality of life and associations with motor skills in young adults born preterm with very low birth weight. *Health and Quality of Life Outcomes, 14*(1), 56.

Hussein, N., Weng, S. F., Kai, J., Kleijnen, J., & Qureshi, N. (2018). Preconception risk assessment for thalassaemia, sickle cell disease, cystic fibrosis and Tay-Sachs disease. *Cochrane Database of Systematic Reviews*, (3).

Hutchinson, E. A., De Luca, C. R., Doyle, L. W., Roberts, G., Anderson, P. J., & Victorian Infant Collaborative Study Group. (2013). School-age outcomes of extremely preterm or extremely low birth weight children. *Pediatrics*, peds-2012.

Huttenlocher, J., Levine, S., & Vevea, J. (1998). Environmental input and cognitive growth: A study using time period comparisons. *Child Development, 69*, 1012–1029.

Huttenlocher, J., Vasilyeva, M., Cymerman, E., & Levine, S. (2002). Language input and child syntax. *Cognitive Psychology, 45*, 337–374.

Huxhold, O., Miche, M., & Schüz, B. (2013). Benefits of having friends in older ages: Differential effects of informal social activities on well-being in middle-aged and older adults. *Journals of Gerontology Series B: Psychological Sciences and Social Sciences, 69*(3), 366–375.

Hyde, J. S. (2005). The gender similarity hypothesis. *American Psychologist, 60*, 581–592.

Hyde, J. S. (2014). Gender similarities and differences. *Annual Review of Psychology, 65*, 373–398.

Hyde, J., Lindberg, S., Linn, M., Ellis, A., & Williams, C. (2008). Gender similarities characterize math performance. *Science, 321*, 494–495.

Iacoboni, M. (2008). *Mirroring people: The new science of how we connect with others*. New York, NY: Farrar, Straus & Giroux.

Iacoboni, M., & Mazziotta, J. C. (2007). Mirror neuron system: Basic findings and clinical applications. *Annals of Neurology, 62*, 213–218.

Iacovou, M., & Skew, A. J. (2011). Household composition across the new Europe: Where do the new member states fit in? *Demographic Research, 25*, 465–490.

Ialongo, N. S., Edelsohn, G., & Kellam, S. G. (2001). A further look at the prognostic power of young children's reports of depressed mood and feelings. *Child Development, 72*, 736–747.

Iannotti, R. J., Kogan, M. D., Janssen, I., & Boyce, W. F. (2009). Patterns of adolescent physical activity, screen-based media use, and positive and negative health indicators in the US and Canada. *Journal of Adolescent Health, 44*(5), 493–499.

Iaria, G., Palermo, L., Committeri, G., & Barton, J. J. S. (2009). Age differences in the formation and use of cognitive maps. *Behavioural Brain Research, 196*(2), 187–191.

Ida, Y., & Mandal, M. (2003). Cultural difference in side bias: Evidence from Japan and India. *Laterality: Asymmetries of Body, Brain and Cognition, 8*(2), 121–133.

Iervolino, A. C., Hines, M., Golombok, S. E., Rust, J., & Plomin, R. (2005). Genetic and environmental influences on sex-types behavior during the preschool years. *Child Development, 76*, 826–840.

Ihmeideh, F. M. (2014). The effect of electronic books on enhancing emergent literacy skills of pre-school children. *Computers & Education, 79*, 40–48.

Imada, T., Zhang, Y., Cheour, M., Taulu, S., Ahonen, A., & Kuhl, P. (2006). Infant speech perception activates Broca's area: A developmental magnetoencephalography study. *NeuroReport, 17*, 957–962.

Imai, M., Li, L., Haryu, E., Okada, H., Hirsh-Pasek, K., Golinkoff, R. M., & Shigematsu, J. (2008). Novel noun and verb learning in Chinese-, English-, and Japanese-speaking children. *Child Development, 79*(4), 979–1000.

Imdad, A., & Bhutta, Z. A. (2011). Effect of balanced protein energy supplementation during pregnancy on birth outcomes. *BMC Public Health, 11*(3), S17.

Imoscopi, A., Inelmen, E. M., Sergi, G., Miotto, F., & Manzato, E. (2012). Taste loss in the elderly: Epidemiology, causes and consequences. *Aging Clinical and Experimental Research, 24*(6), 570–579.

Imperatore, G., Boyle, J. P., Thompson, T. J., Case, D., Dabelea, D., Hamman, R. F., . . . Rodriguez, B. L. (2012). Projections of type 1 and type 2 diabetes burden in the US population aged, 20 years through 2050: Dynamic modeling of incidence, mortality, and population growth. *Diabetes Care, 35*(12), 2515–2520.

Imuta, K., Henry, J. D., Slaughter, V., Selcuk, B., & Ruffman, T. (2016). Theory of mind and prosocial behavior in childhood: A meta-analytic review. *Developmental Psychology, 52*(8), 1192.

Ingalhalikar, M., Smith, A., Parker, D., Satterthwaite, T. D., Elliott, M. A., Ruparel, K., . . . Verma, R. (2014). Sex differences in the structural connectome of the human brain. *Proceedings of the National Academy of Sciences, 111*(2), 823–828.

Inguglia, C., Ingoglia, S., Liga, F., Coco, A. L., & Cricchio, M. G. L. (2015). Autonomy and relatedness in adolescence and emerging adulthood: Relationships with parental support and psychological distress. *Journal of Adult Development, 22*(1), 1-13.

Innocenti, G. M., & Price, D. J. (2005). Exuberance in the development of cortical networks. *Nature Reviews Neuroscience, 6*(12), 955.

Isaacowitz, D. M., & Smith, J. (2003). Positive and negative affect in very old age. *Journal of Gerontology: Psychological Sciences, 58B,* P143-P152.

Isengard, B., & Szydlik, M. (2012). Living apart (or) together? Coresidence of elderly parents and their adult children in Europe. *Research on Aging, 34*(4), 449-474.

Isherwood, L. M., King, D. S., & Luszcz, M. A. (2017). Widowhood in the fourth age: Support exchange, relationships and social participation. *Ageing & Society, 37*(1), 188-212.

Ishida, M., & Moore, G. E. (2013). The role of imprinted genes in humans. *Molecular Aspects of Medicine, 34*(4), 826-840.

Ishii, N., Fujii, M., Hartman, P. S., Tsuda, M., Yasuda, K., Senoo-Matsuda, N., . . . Suzuki, K. (1998). A mutation in succinate dehydrogenase cytochrome *b* causes oxidative stress and ageing in nematodes. *Nature, 394,* 694-697.

Islam, R. M., Bell, R. J., Rizvi, F., & Davis, S. R. (2017). Vasomotor symptoms in women in Asia appear comparable with women in Western countries: A systematic review. *Menopause, 24*(11), 1313-1322.

Ivanova, K. (2019). My children, your children, our children, and my well-being: Life satisfaction of "empty nest" biological parents and stepparents. *Journal of Happiness Studies,* 1-21.

Iverson, J. M., Capirci, O., Volterra, V., & Goldin-Meadow, S. (2008). Learning to talk in a gesture-rich world: Early communication in Italian vs. American children. *First Language, 28*(2), 164-181.

Izard, V., Sann, C., Spelke, E. S., & Streri, A. (2009). Newborn infants perceive abstract numbers. *Proceedings of the National Academy of Sciences, 106*(25), 10382-10385.

Izumi-Taylor, S., Samuelsson, I. P., & Rogers, C. S. (2010). Perspectives of play in three nations: A comparative study in Japan, the United States, and Sweden. *Early Childhood Research & Practice, 12*(1), n1.

Jaccard, J., & Dittus, P. J. (2000). Adolescent perceptions of maternal approval of birth control and sexual risk behavior. *American Journal of Public Health, 90,* 1426-1430.

Jackson, J. B., Miller, R. B., Oka, M., & Henry, R. G. (2014). Gender differences in marital satisfaction: A meta-analysis. *Journal of Marriage and Family, 76*(1), 105-129.

Jackson, J. K., Weiss, M. A., Schwarzenberg, A. B. & Nelson, R. M. (2020). *Global economic effects of COVID-19* [Congressional Research Service report]. Retrieved from https://fas.org/sgp/crs/row/R46270.pdf

Jackson, K. D., Howie, L. D., & Akinbami, L. J. (2013). Trends in allergic conditions among children: United States, 1997-2011. *NCHS Data Brief, 121.* Hyattsville, MD: National Center for Health Statistics.

Jacobi, T. (2012, April 17). Without immigrant labor, the economy would crumble. *The New York Times.* Retrieved from www.nytimes.com/roomfordebate/2011/08/17/could-farms-survive-without-illegal-labor/without-immigrant-labor-the-economy-would-crumble

Jacobs, M., Zhang, G., Chen, S., Mullins, B., Bell, M., Jin, L., . . . Pereira, G. (2017). The association between ambient air pollution and selected adverse pregnancy outcomes in China: A systematic review. *Science of the Total Environment, 579,* 1179-1192.

Jacobson, J. L., & Wille, D. E. (1984). Influence of attachment and separation experience on separation distress at 18 months. *Developmental Psychology, 20*(3), 477.

Jacobson, J. L., & Wille, D. E. (1986). The influence of attachment pattern on developmental changes in peer interaction from the toddler to the preschool period. *Child Development, 57,* 338-347.

Jacques, P. L. S., Bessette-Symons, B., & Cabeza, R. (2009). Functional neuroimaging studies of aging and emotion: fronto-amygdalar differences during emotional perception and episodic memory. *Journal of the International Neuropsychological Society, 15*(6), 819-825.

Jadallah, M., Anderson, R. C., Nguyen-Jahiel, K., Miller, B. W., Kim, I. H., Kuo, L. J., . . . Wu, X. (2011). Influence of a teacher's scaffolding moves during child-led small-group discussions. *American Educational Research Journal, 48*(1), 194-230.

Jadva, V., Hines, M., & Golombok, S. (2010). Infants' preferences for toys, colors, and shapes: Sex differences and similarities. *Archives of Sexual Behavior, 39*(6), 1261-1273.

Jaffari-Bimmel, N., Juffer, F., van IJzendoorn, M. H., Bakermans-Kranenburg, M. J., & Mooijaart, A. (2006). Social development from infancy to adolescence: Longitudinal and concurrent factors in an adoption sample. *Developmental Psychology, 42,* 1143-1153.

Jaffee, S., & Hyde, J. S. (2000). Gender differences in moral orientation: A meta-analysis. *Psychological Bulletin, 126,* 703-726.

Jakicic, J. M., Powell, K. E., Campbell, W. W., Dipietro, L., Pate, R. R., Pescatello, L. S., . . . Piercy, K. L. (2019). Physical activity and the prevention of weight gain in adults: A systematic review. *Medicine & Science in Sports & Exercise, 51*(6), 1262-1269.

Jalovaara, M. (2001). Socio-economic status and divorce in first marriages in Finland 1991-93. *Population Studies, 55*(2), 119-133.

Jalovaara, M. (2003). The joint effects of marriage partners' socioeconomic positions on the risk of divorce. *Demography, 40*(1), 67-81.

James, C., Davis, K., Charmaraman, L., Konrath, S., Slovak, P., Weinstein, E., & Yarosh, L. (2017). Digital life and youth well-being, social connectedness, empathy, and narcissism. *Pediatrics, 140*(Suppl. 2), S71-S75.

Janecka, M., Mill, J., Basson, M. A., Goriely, A., Spiers, H., Reichenberg, A., . . . & Fernandes, C. (2017). Advanced paternal age effects in neurodevelopmental disorders—review of potential underlying mechanisms. *Translational Psychiatry, 7*(1), e1019.

Jankowiak, W. (1992). Father-child relations in urban China. In B. S. Hewlett (Ed.), *Father-child relations: Cultural and bi-social contexts* (pp. 345-363). New York, NY: de Gruyter.

Jankowiak, W. R., & Fischer, E. F. (1992). A cross-cultural perspective on romantic love. *Ethnology, 31*(2), 149-155.

Jankowski, J. J., Rose, S. A., & Feldman, J. F. (2001). Modifying the distribution of attention in infants. *Child Development, 72,* 339-351.

Jansen, I. E., Savage, J. E., Watanabe, K., Bryois, J., Williams, D. M., Steinberg, S., . . . Voyle, N. (2019). Genome-wide meta-analysis identifies new loci and functional pathways influencing Alzheimer's disease risk. *Nature Genetics.*

Jarman, H. (2016). Curvy Barbie: A step in the right direction, but is it far enough? *Journal of Aesthetic Nursing, 5,* 396-397.

Jarvis, P., Newman, S., & Swiniarski, L. (2014). On becoming social: The importance of collaborative free play in childhood. *International Journal of Play, 3,* 53-68.

Jauk, E., Benedek, M., Dunst, B., & Neubauer, A. C. (2013). The relationship between intelligence and creativity: New support for the threshold hypothesis by means of empirical breakpoint detection. *Intelligence, 41*(4), 212-221.

Jay, T., King, K., & Duncan, T. (2006). Memories of punishment for cursing. *Sex Roles, 55*(1-2), 123-133.

Jean, R. B. (2017). The influence of health over time on psychological distress among older couples: The moderating role of marital functioning. *Sexuality & Ageing.*

Jee, S. H., Sull, J. W., Park, J., Lee, S., Ohrr, H., Guallar, E., & Samet, J. M. (2006). Body-mass index and mortality in Korean men and women. *New England Journal of Medicine, 355,* 779-787.

Jeha, D., Usta, I., Ghulmiyyah, L., & Nassar, A. (2015). A review of the risks and consequences of adolescent pregnancy. *Journal of Neonatal-Perinatal Medicine, 8*(1), 1-8.

Jellinger, K. A. (2013). Pathology and pathogenesis of vascular cognitive impairment—a critical update. *Frontiers in Aging Neuroscience, 5,* 17.

Jenkins, J. V. M., Woolley, D. P., Hooper, S. R., & De Bellis, M. D. (2014). Direct and indirect effects of brain volume, socioeconomic status and family stress on child IQ. *Journal of Child and Adolescent Behavior, 1*(2).

Jennings, K. D., Sandberg, I., Kelley, S. A., Valdes, L., Yaggi, K., Abrew, A., & Macey-Kalcevic, M. (2008). Understanding of self and maternal warmth predict later self-regulation in toddlers. *International Journal of Behavioral Development, 32,* 108-118. doi: 10.1177/0165025407087209

Jensen, A. R. (1969). How much can we boost IQ and scholastic achievement? *Harvard Educational Review, 39,* 1-123.

Jensen, L. A. (1998). Moral divisions within countries between orthodoxy and progressivism: India and the United States. *Journal for the Scientific Study of Religion,* 90-107.

Jensen, L. A. (2011). The cultural development of three fundamental moral ethics: Autonomy, community, and divinity. *Zygon, 46*(1), 150-167.

Jenson, L. A. (1997). Different worldviews, different morals: America's culture war divide. *Human Development, 40,* 325-344.

Ji-Yeon, K., McHale, S. M., Crouter, A. C., & Osgood, D. W. (2007). Longitudinal linkages between sibling relationships and adjustment from middle childhood through adolescence. *Developmental Psychology, 43*(4), 960–973.

Jia, Y., Way, N., Ling, G., Yoshikawa, H., Chen, X., Hughes, D., . . . Lu, Z. (2009). The influence of student perceptions of school climate on socioemotional and academic adjustment: A comparison of Chinese and American adolescents. *Child Development, 80*(5), 1514–1530.

Jiao, W. Y., Wang, L. N., Liu, J., Fang, S. F., Jiao, F. Y., Pettoello-Mantovani, M., & Somekh, E. (2020). Behavioral and emotional disorders in children during the COVID-19 epidemic. *The Journal of Pediatrics*.

Jin, K. (2010). Modern biological theories of aging. *Aging and Disease, 1*(2), 72.

Jipson, J. L., & Gelman, S. A. (2007). Robots and rodents: Children's inferences about living and nonliving kinds. *Child Development, 78*(6), 1675–1688.

Johansson, B., Hofer, S. M., Allaire, J. C., Maldonado-Molina, M. M., Piccinin, A. M., Berg, S., . . . McClearn, G. E. (2004). Change in cognitive capabilities in the oldest old: The effects of proximity to death in genetically related individuals over a 6-year period. *Psychology and Aging, 19*, 145–156.

Johansson, H., Kanis, J. A., Odén, A., McCloskey, E., Chapurlat, R. D., Christiansen, C., . . . Glüer, C. C. (2014). A meta-analysis of the association of fracture risk and body mass index in women. *Journal of Bone and Mineral Research, 29*(1), 223–233.

Johnell, O., & Kanis, J. A. (2006). An estimate of the worldwide prevalence and disability associated with osteoporotic fractures. *Osteoporosis International, 17*(12), 1726–1733.

Johns, M. M., Lowry, R., Andrzejewski, J., Barrios, L. C., Demissie, Z., McManus, T., . . . & Underwood, J. M. (2019). Transgender identity and experiences of violence victimization, substance use, suicide risk, and sexual risk behaviors among high school students—19 states and large urban school districts, 2017. *Morbidity and Mortality Weekly Report, 68*(3), 67.

Johnson Jr., J. H., & Appold, S. J. (2017). *US older adults: Demographics, living arrangements, and barriers to aging in place*. White paper, Kenan Institute.

Johnson, A. J., Becker, J. A. H., Craig, E. A., Gilchrist, E. S., & Haigh, M. M. (2009). Changes in friendship commitment: Comparing geographically close and long-distance young-adult friendships. *Communication Quarterly, 57*(4), 395–415.

Johnson, C. L. (1995). Cultural diversity in the late-life family. In R. Blieszner & V. Hilkevitch (Eds.), *Handbook of aging and the family* (pp. 307–331). Westport, CT: Greenwood Press.

Johnson, C. L., & Troll, L. E. (1994). Constraints and facilitators to friendships in late late life. *Gerontologist, 34*, 79–87.

Johnson, III, J. A., & Johnson, A. M. (2015). Urban-rural differences in childhood and adolescent obesity in the United States: A systematic review and meta-analysis. *Childhood Obesity, 11*(3), 233–241.

Johnson, J. M., Nachtigall, L. B., & Stern, T. A. (2013). The effect of testosterone levels on mood in men: A review. *Psychosomatics, 54*(6), 509–514.

Johnson, K. A., Minoshima, S., Bohnen, N. I., Donohoe, K. J., Foster, N. L., Herscovitch, P., . . . Hedrick, S. (2013). Appropriate use criteria for amyloid PET: A report of the Amyloid Imaging Task Force, the Society of Nuclear Medicine and Molecular Imaging, and the Alzheimer's Association. *Journal of Nuclear Medicine, 54*(3), 476–490.

Johnson, K., Caskey, M., Rand, K., Tucker, R., & Vohr, B. (2014). Gender differences in adult-infant communication in the first months of life. *Pediatrics, 134*, 1603–1610.

Johnson, M. D., & Galambos, N. L. (2014). Paths to intimate relationship quality from parent– adolescent relations and mental health. *Journal of Marriage and Family, 76*(1), 145–160.

Johnson, M. D., Krahn, H. J., & Galambos, N. L. (2017). Better late than early: Marital timing and subjective well-being in midlife. *Journal of Family Psychology, 31*(5), 635.

Johnson, M. K., & Benson, J. (2012). The implications of family context for the transition to adulthood. In A. Booth, S. L. Brown, N. S. Landale, W. D. Manning, & S. M. McHale (Eds.), *Early adulthood in a family context* (pp. 87–103). New York, NY: Springer.

Johnson, S., & Marlow, N. (2014, April). Growing up after extremely preterm birth: Lifespan mental health outcomes. *Seminars in Fetal and Neonatal Medicine, 19*(2), 97–104.

Johnson, S., & Marlow, N. (2017). Early and long-term outcome of infants born extremely preterm. *Archives of Disease in Childhood, 102*(1), 97–102.

Johnston, J., Riley, J., Ryan, C., & Kelly-Vance, L. (2015). Evaluation of a summer reading program to reduce summer setback. *Reading & Writing Quarterly, 31*(4), 334–350.

Johnston, L. D., O'Malley, P. M., Bachman, J. G., & Schulenberg, J. E. (2013). *Monitoring the Future: National results on drug use: 2012 Overview, key findings on adolescent drug use*. Ann Arbor, MI: Institute for Social Research, The University of Michigan.

Johnston, L. D., O'Malley, P. M., Miech, R. A., Bachman, J. G., & Schulenberg, J. E. (2017). Monitoring the Future National Survey Results on Drug Use, 1975–2016: Overview, key findings on adolescent drug use. *Institute for Social Research*.

Jones, C. L., Tepperman, L., & Wilson, S. J. (1995). *The future of the family*. Englewood Cliffs, NJ: Prentice Hall.

Jones, D. E., Greenberg, M., & Crowley, M. (2015). Early social-emotional functioning and public health: The relationship between kindergarten social competence and future wellness. *Journal Information, 105*(11).

Jones, E. K., Jurgenson, J. R., Katzenellenbogen, J. M., & Thompson, S. C. (2012). Menopause and the influence of culture: another gap for indigenous Australian women? *BMC Women's Health, 12*(1), 43.

Jones, G. W. (2015). Divorce trends and patterns in Asia. In *Routledge handbook of families in Asia* (pp. 332–344). Abingdon, England: Routledge.

Jones, H., Barber, C. C., Nikora, L. W., & Middlemiss, W. (2017). Māori child rearing and infant sleep practices. *New Zealand Journal of Psychology, 46*(3), 30–37.

Jones, N. G. B., Marlowe, F. W., Hawkes, K., & O'Connell, J. F. (2017). Paternal investment and hunter-gatherer divorce rates. In L. Cronk, N. Chagnon & W. Irons (Eds.), *Adaptation and human behavior* (pp. 69–90). Abingdon, England: Routledge.

Jopp, D., & Smith, J. (2006). Resources and life management strategies as determinants of successful aging: On the protective effect of selection, optimization, and compensation. *Psychology and Aging, 21*, 253–265.

Jordan, B., & Davis-Floyd, R. (1993). *Birth in four cultures. A crosscultural investigation of childbirth in Yucatan, Holland, Sweden and the United States*. Long Grove, IL: Waveland Press.

Jordan, K. (2014). Initial trends in enrolment and completion of massive open online courses. *The International Review of Research in Open and Distributed Learning, 15*(1).

Jordan, N. C., Glutting, J., & Ramineni, C. (2010). The importance of number sense to mathematics achievement in first and third grades. *Learning and Individual Differences, 20*(2), 82–88.

Jordan, N. C., Kaplan, D., Oláh, L. N., & Locuniak, M. N. (2006). Number sense growth in kindergarten: A longitudinal investigation of children at risk for mathematics difficulties. *Child Development, 77*, 153–175.

Jordan, R. E., Adab, P., & Cheng, K.K. (2020). Covid-19: Risk factors for severe disease and death. *British Medical Journal, 368*. doi: 10.1136/bmj.m1198

Jose, A., O'Leary, K. D., & Moyer, A. (2010). Does premarital cohabitation predict subsequent marital stability and marital quality? A meta-analysis. *Journal of Marriage and Family, 72*(1), 105–116.

Joyce, A., Martin, J. A., Hamilton, B. E., Osterman, M. J. K., & Driscoll, A. K. (2019). Births: Final data for 2018. *National Vital Statistics Reports, 67*, 1–55. Hyattsville, MD: National Center for Health Statistics.

Ju, H., Jones, M., & Mishra, G. (2014). The prevalence and risk factors of dysmenorrhea. *Epidemiologic Reviews, 36*(1), 104–113.

Juffer, F., Palacios, J., Le Mare, L., Sonuga-Barke, E. J., Tieman, W., Bakermans-Kranenburg, M. J., . . . Verhulst, F. C. (2011). II. Development of adopted children with histories of early adversity. *Monographs of the Society for Research in Child Development, 76*(4), 31–61.

Juhl, J., & Routledge, C. (2016). Putting the terror in terror management theory: Evidence that the awareness of death does cause anxiety and undermine psychological well-being. *Current Directions in Psychological Science, 25*(2), 99–103.

Julian, M. M. (2013). Age at adoption from institutional care as a window into the lasting effects of early experiences. *Clinical Child and Family Psychology Review, 16*(2), 101–145.

Jurewicz, J., & Hanke, W. (2008). Prenatal and childhood exposure to pesticides and neurobehavioral development: Review of epidemiological studies. *International Journal of Occupational Medicine and Environmental Health, 21*(2), 121-132.

Jurgens, H. A., & Johnson, R. W. (2012). Dysregulated neuronal-microglial cross-talk during aging, stress and inflammation. *Experimental Neurology, 233*(1), 40-48.

Jusczyk, P. W., & Hohne, E. A. (1997). Infants' memory for spoken words. *Science, 277,* 1984-1986.

Juster, F. T., Ono, H., & Stafford, F. P. (2004). *Changing times of American youth: 1981-2003* (Child Development Supplement). Ann Arbor, MI: University of Michigan Institute for Social Research.

Kaewsarn, P., Moyle, W., & Creedy, D. (2003). Traditional postpartum practices among Thai women. *Journal of Advanced Nursing, 41*(4), 358-366.

Kagan, J. (1976). Emergent themes in human development: Some basic assumptions about the development of cognitive and affective structures and their stability from infancy to later childhood are reexamined in light of new evidence from a variety of sources. *American Scientist, 64*(2), 186-196.

Kagan, J. (1997). Temperament and the reactions to unfamiliarity. *Child Development, 68,* 139-143.

Kagan, J. (2008). In defense of qualitative changes in development. *Child Development, 79*(6), 1606-1624.

Kagan, J. (2012). The biography of behavioral inhibition. In M. Zentner & R. Shiner (Eds.), *Handbook of temperament* (pp. 69-82). New York, NY: Guilford Press.

Kagan, J., & Snidman, N. (2004). *The long shadow of temperament.* Cambridge, MA: Belknap Press.

Kagan, J., Reznick, J. S., Clarke, C., Snidman, N., & Garcia-Coll, C. (1984). Behavioral inhibition to the unfamiliar. *Child Development,* 2212-2225.

Kagan, J., Reznick, J. S., Snidman, N., Gibbons, J., & Johnson, M. O. (1988). Childhood derivatives of inhibition and lack of inhibition to the unfamiliar. *Child Development,* 1580-1589.

Kahn, M., Sheppes, G., & Sadeh, A. (2013). Sleep and emotions: Bidirectional links and underlying mechanisms. *International Journal of Psychophysiology, 89*(2), 218-228.

Kahn, S., Zimmerman, G., Csikszentmihalyi, M., & Getzels, J. W. (2014). Relations between identity in young adulthood and intimacy at midlife. In *Applications of flow in human development and education* (pp. 327-338). Amsterdam, the Netherlands: Springer.

Kaiser Family Foundation, Hoff, T., Greene, L., & Davis, J. (2003). *National survey of adolescents and young adults: Sexual health knowledge, attitudes and experiences.* Menlo Park, CA: Henry J. Kaiser Foundation.

Kaiser Family Foundation. (2017). OECD Health Data: Health status: Health status indicators. *OECD Health Statistics database.*

Kalil, A., & Ziol-Guest, K. M. (2005). Single mothers' employment dynamics and adolescent well-being. *Child Development, 76,* 196-211.

Kalkbrenner, A. E., Schmidt, R. J., & Penlesky, A. C. (2014). Environmental chemical exposures and autism spectrum disorders: A review of the epidemiological evidence. *Current Problems in Pediatric Adolescent Health Care, 44,* 277-318.

Kalkhoran, S., & Glantz, S. A. (2016). E-cigarettes and smoking cessation in real-world and clinical settings: a systematic review and meta-analysis. *The Lancet Respiratory Medicine, 4*(2), 116-128.

Kallio, E. (2011). Integrative thinking is the key: An evaluation of current research into the development of adult thinking. *Theory & Psychology, 21*(6), 785-801.

Kallio, E. L., Öhman, H., Kautiainen, H., Hietanen, M., & Pitkälä, K. (2017). Cognitive training interventions for patients with Alzheimer's disease: A systematic review. *Journal of Alzheimer's Disease, 56*(4), 1349-1372.

Kalmijn, M., & Leopold, T. (2019). Changing sibling relationships after parents' death: The role of solidarity and kinkeeping. *Journal of Marriage and Family, 81*(1), 99-114.

Kalmijn, M., & Saraceno, C. (2008). A comparative perspective on intergenerational support: Responsiveness to parental needs in individualistic and familialistic cultures. *European Societies, 10*(3), 479-508.

Kamal, R., Hudman, J., & McDermott, E. (2019). What do we know about infant mortality in the U.S. and comparable countries? [Report]. *Peterson-KFF Health System Tracker.* Retrieved from www.healthsystemtracker.org/chart-collection/infant-mortality-u-s-compare-countries/#item-start

Kamp, D. C. M., & Taylor, M. G. (2012). Trajectories of marital conflict across the life course: Predictors and interactions with marital happiness trajectories. *Journal of Family Issues, 33*(3), 341-368.

Kamp, K. A. (2001). Where have all the children gone? The archaeology of childhood. *Journal of Archaeological Method and Theory, 8,* 1-34.

Kang, H. S., & Ahn, B. (2014). Resilient widowed older adults and their family and friend relations. *International Letters of Social and Humanistic Sciences, 42,* 62-71.

Kanis, J. A. (2007). *Assessment of osteoporosis at the primary health-care level.* Sheffield, England: WHO Collaborating Centre for Metabolic Bone Diseases, University of Sheffield.

Kann, L., Kinchen, S., Shanklin, S. L., Flint, K. H., Hawkins, J., Harris, W. A., . . . Whittle, L. (2014). Youth risk behavior surveillance—United States, 2013. *MMWR. Surveillance Summaries, 63.*

Kann, L., McManus, T., Harris, W. A., Shanklin, S. L., Flint, K. H., Queen, B., . . . Lim, C. (2018). Youth risk behavior surveillance—United States, 2017. *MMWR Surveillance Summaries, 67*(8), 1.

Kann, L., McManus, T., Harris, W.A., et al., (2018). Youth risk behavior surveillance — United States, 2017. *Morbidity and Mortality Weekly Reports, 67*(SS-8), 1-114. http://dx.doi.org/10.15585/mmwr.ss6708a1

Kanugo, S. & Patel, D. R. (2016). Universal newborn hearing screening in the United States. *International Public Health Journal, 8*(4), 421.

Kaplan, A., & Herbst, A. (2015). Stratified patterns of divorce: Earnings, education, and gender. *Demographic Research, 32,* 949-982.

Kaplan, H., & Dove, H. (1987). Infant development among the Ache of East Paraguay. *Developmental Psychology, 23,* 190-198.

Kaplan, R. M., & Kronick, R. G. (2006). Marital status and longevity in the United States population. *Journal of Epidemiological Community Health, 60,* 760-765.

Kaplow, J. B., Saunders, J., Angold, A., & Costello, E. J. (2010). Psychiatric symptoms in bereaved versus nonbereaved youth and young adults: A longitudinal epidemiological study. *Journal of the American Academy of Child & Adolescent Psychiatry, 49*(11), 1145-1154.

Kaplowitz, P. B. (2010). Delayed puberty. *Pediatrics in Review, 31*(5), 189.

Karably, K., & Zabrucky, K. M. (2017). Children's metamemory: A review of the literature and implications for the classroom. *International Electronic Journal of Elementary Education, 2*(1), 32-52.

Karasik, L. B., Tamis-LeMonda, C. S., & Adolph, K. E. (2011). Transition from crawling to walking and infants' actions with objects and people. *Child Development, 82*(4), 1199-1209.

Karim, J., & Weisz, R. (2010). Cross-cultural research on the reliability and validity of the Mayer-Salovey-Caruso Emotional Intelligence Test (MSCEIT). *Cross-Cultural Research, 44*(4), 374-404.

Karimi-Zarchi, M., Neamatzadeh, H., Dastgheib, S. A., Abbasi, H., Mirjalili, S. R., Behforouz, A., . . . Bahrami, R. (2020). Vertical transmission of coronavirus disease 19 (COVID-19) from infected pregnant mothers to neonates: A review. *Fetal and Pediatric Pathology, 1-5.*

Karney, B. R., & Bradbury, T. N. (1995). The longitudinal course of marital quality and stability: A review of theory, method, and research. *Psychological Bulletin, 118,* 3-34.

Karoly, L. A. (2016). The economic returns to early childhood education. *The Future of Children, 26*(2), 37-55.

Kashimada, K., & Koopman, P. (2010). SRY: The master switch in mammalian sex determination. *Development, 137*(23), 3921-3930.

Kasper, J. D., Pezzin, L. E., & Rice, J. B. (2010). Stability and changes in living arrangements: Relationship to nursing home admission and timing of placement. *Journals of Gerontology, 65B*(Series B), 783-791.

Kasper, J. D., Wolff, J. L., & Skehan, M. (2019). Care arrangements of older adults: What they prefer, what they have, and implications for quality of life. *The Gerontologist, 59*(5), 845-855.

Katis, D., & Selimis, S. (2005, June). The development of metaphoric motion: Evidence from Greek children's narratives. In *Annual Meeting of the Berkeley Linguistics Society* (Vol. 31, No. 1, pp. 205-216).

Katz-Wise, S. L., Budge, S. L., Fugate, E., Flanagan, K., Touloumtzis, C., Rood, B., . . . Leibowitz, S. (2017). Transactional pathways of transgender identity development in transgender and gender-nonconforming youth and caregiver perspectives from the Trans Youth Family Study. *International Journal of Transgenderism, 18*(3), 243-263.

Katzman, R. (1993). Education and prevalence of Alzheimer's disease. *Neurology, 43,* 13-20.

Katzmarzyk, P. T., Barreira, T. V., Broyles, S. T., Champagne, C. M., Chaput, J. P., Fogelholm, M., . . . Lambert, E. V. (2015). Relationship between lifestyle behaviors and obesity in children ages 9-11: Results from a 12-country study. *Obesity, 23*(8), 1696-1702.

Kaufman, A. S., & Kaufman, N. L. (1983). *Kaufman Assessment Battery for Children: Administration and scoring manual.* Circle Pines, MN: American Guidance Service.

Kaufman, A. S., & Kaufman, N. L. (2003). *Kaufman Assessment Battery for Children* (2nd ed.). Circle Pines, MN: American Guidance Service.

Kaufman, S. B., Quilty, L. C., Grazioplene, R. G., Hirsh, J. B., Gray, J. R., Peterson, J. B., & DeYoung, C. G. (2016). Openness to experience and intellect differentially predict creative achievement in the arts and sciences. *Journal of Personality, 84*(2), 248-258.

Kaushik, R., Krisch, I. M., Schroeder, D. R., Flick, R., & Nemergut, M. E. (2015). Pediatric bicycle-related head injuries: A population-based study in a county without a helmet law. *Injury Epidemiology, 2*(1), 16.

Kavanaugh, M. L., & Jerman, J. (2018). Contraceptive method use in the United States: trends and characteristics between 2008, 2012 and 2014. *Contraception, 97*(1), 14-21.

Kawabata, Y., & Crick, N. (2008). The roles of cross-racial/ethnic friendships in social adjustment. *Developmental Psychology, 44*(4), 1177-1183.

Kawabata, Y., Alink, L. R., Tseng, W. L., Van Ijzendoorn, M. H., & Crick, N. R. (2011). Maternal and paternal parenting styles associated with relational aggression in children and adolescents: A conceptual analysis and meta-analytic review. *Developmental Review, 31*(4), 240-278.

Kaye, E. K., Valencia, A., Baba, N., Spiro, A., Dietrich, T., & Garcia, R. I. (2010). Tooth loss and periodontal disease predict poor cognitive function in older men. *Journal of the American Geriatrics Society, 58*(4), 713-718.

Kazdin, A. E., & Benjet, C. (2003). Spanking children: Evidence and issues. *Current Directions in Psychological Science, 12,* 99-103.

Kazemi, A., Ardabili, H. E., & Solokian, S. (2010). The association between social competence in adolescents and mothers' parenting style: A cross sectional study on Iranian girls. *Child and Adolescent Social Work Journal, 27*(6), 395-403.

Keag, O. E., Norman, J. E., & Stock, S. J. (2018). Long-term risks and benefits associated with cesarean delivery for mother, baby, and subsequent pregnancies: Systematic review and meta-analysis. *PLoS medicine, 15*(1), e1002494.

Keegan, R. T. (1996). *Creativity from childhood to adulthood: A difference of degree and not of kind* (New Directions for Child Development, No. 72, pp. 57-66). San Francisco, CA: Jossey-Bass.

Keeney, B., & Keeney, H. (2013). Reentry into First Creation: A contextual frame for the Ju/'hoan Bushman performance of puberty rites, storytelling, and healing dance. *Journal of Anthropological Research, 69*(1), 65-86.

Keesee, N. J., Currier, J. M., & Neimeyer, R. A. (2008). Predictors of grief following the death of one's child: The contribution of finding meaning. *Journal of Clinical Psychology, 64*(10), 1145-1163.

Kefalas, M., Furstenberg, F., & Napolitano, L. (2005, September). Marriage is more than being together: The meaning of marriage among young adults in the United States. Network on Transitions to Adulthood Research Working Paper.

Keijsers, L., Branje, S. J. T., Frijns, T., Finkenauer, C., & Meeus, W. (2010). Gender differences in keeping secrets from parents in adolescence. *Developmental Psychology, 46*(1), 293-298.

Keijsers, L., Branje, S. J., VanderValk, I. E., & Meeus, W. (2010). Reciprocal effects between parental solicitation, parental control, adolescent disclosure, and adolescent delinquency. *Journal of Research on Adolescence, 20*(1), 88-113.

Keizer, R., & Schenk, N. (2012). Becoming a parent and relationship satisfaction: A longitudinal dyadic perspective. *Journal of Marriage and Family, 74*(4), 759-773.

Keleher, A., & Smith, E. R. (2012). Growing support for gay and lesbian equality since 1990. *Journal of Homosexuality, 59*(9), 1307-1326.

Keller, B. (1999, February 24). *A time and place for teenagers.* Retrieved from www.edweek.org/ew/vol-18/24studen.h18

Keller, H., Kärtner, J., Borke, J., Yovsi, R., & Kleis, A. (2005). Parenting styles and the development of the categorical self: A longitudinal study on mirror self-recognition in Cameroonian Nso and German families. *International Journal of Behavioral Development, 29*(6), 496-504.

Keller, H., Yovsi, R., Borke, J., Kärtner, J., Jensen, H., & Papaligoura, Z. (2004). Developmental consequences of early parenting experiences: Self-recognition and self-regulation in three cultural communities. *Child Development, 75*(6), 1745-1760.

Kelley, A.S. & Morrison, R.S. (2015). Palliative care for the seriously ill. *New England Journal of Medicine, 373,* 747-755.

Keller, B. (1999). A time and place for teenagers. *Education Week 18* (24), 27-31, https://www.edweek.org/ew/articles/1999/02/24/24studen.h18.html.

Kelley, M. L., Smith, T. S., Green, A. P., Berndt, A. E., & Rogers, M. C. (1998). Importance of fathers' parenting to African-American toddlers' social and cognitive development. *Infant Behavior & Development, 21,* 733-744.

Kellman, P. J., & Arterberry, M. E. (1998). *The cradle of knowledge: Development of perception in infancy.* Cambridge, MA: MIT Press.

Kellogg, N., & the Committee on Child Abuse and Neglect. (2005). The evaluation of sexual abuse in children. *Pediatrics, 116*(2), 506-512.

Kelly, D. J., Liu, S., Ge, L., Quinn, P. C., Slater, A. M., Lee, K., Liu, Q., & Pascalis, O. (2007). Cross-race preferences for same-race faces extend

beyond the African versus Caucasian contrast in 3-month-old infants. *Infancy, 11,* 87-95.

Kelly, D. J., Quinn, P. C., Slater, A. M., Lee, K., Gibson, A., Smith, M., Ge, L., & Pascalis, O. (2005). Three-month-olds, but not newborns, prefer own-race faces. *Developmental Science, 8,* 31-36.

Kelly, D. M., & Jones, T. H. (2014). Testosterone and cardiovascular risk in men. *Cardiovascular Issues in Endocrinology, 43,* 1-20.

Kelly, J. B., & Emery, R. E. (2003). Children's adjustment following divorce: Risk and resiliency perspectives. *Family Relations, 52,* 352-362.

Kelly, R. R., McDonald, L. T., Jensen, N. R., Sidles, S. J., & LaRue, A. C. (2019). Impacts of psychological stress on osteoporosis: Clinical implications and treatment Interactions. *Frontiers in Psychiatry, 10,* 200.

Kelly, Y., Sacker, A., Schoon, I., & Nazroo, J. (2006). Ethnic differences in achievement of developmental milestones by 9 months of age: The Millennium Cohort Study. *Developmental Medicine and Child Neurology, 48*(10), 825-830.

Kemmler, W., Bebenek, M., Kohl, M., & von Stengel, S. (2015). Exercise and fractures in postmenopausal women. Final results of the controlled Erlangen Fitness and Osteoporosis Prevention Study (EFOPS). *Osteoporosis International, 26*(10), 2491-2499.

Kempe, M., Kalicinski, M., & Memmert, D. (2015). Naturalistic assessment of everyday memory performance among older adults. *Experimental Aging Research, 41*(4), 426-445.

Kempen, G. I., Ballemans, J., Ranchor, A. V., van Rens, G. H., & Zijlstra, G. R. (2012). The impact of low vision on activities of daily living, symptoms of depression, feelings of anxiety and social support in community-living older adults seeking vision rehabilitation services. *Quality of Life Research, 21*(8), 1405-1411.

Kempermann, G. (2015). Activity dependency and aging in the regulation of adult neurogenesis. *Cold Spring Harbor Perspectives in Biology, 7*(11), a018929.

Kena, G., Aud, S., Johnson, F., Wang, X., Zhang, J., Rathbun, A., Wilkinson-Flicker, S., & Kristapovich, P. (2014). *The condition of education 2014 (NCES 2014-083).* Washington, DC: U.S. Department of Education, National Center for Education Statistics. Retrieved from http://nces.ed.gov/pubsearch

Kendig, H., Dykstra, P. A., van Gaalen, R. I., & Melkas, T. (2007). Health of aging parents and childless individuals. *Journal of Family Issues, 28*(11), 1457-1486.

Kennedy, S., & Ruggles, S. (2013). *Breaking up is hard to count: The rise of divorce and cohabitation instability in the United States, 1980-2010.* Working Paper 2013-01. Minneapolis, MN: University of Minnesota, Minnesota Population Center.

Kennedy, S., & Ruggles, S. (2014). Breaking up is hard to count: The rise of divorce in the United States, 1980-2010. *Demography, 51*(2), 587-598.

Kenny, U., O'Malley-Keighran, M. P., Molcho, M., & Kelly, C. (2017). Peer influences on adolescent body image: Friends or foes? *Journal of Adolescent Research, 32*(6), 768-799.

Kensinger, E. A. (2009). How emotion affects older adults' memories for event details. *Memory, 17*(2), 208-219.

Kenyon, B. L. (2001). Current research in children's conceptions of death: A critical review. *OMEGA- Journal of Death and Dying, 43*(1), 63-91.

Kerala, N. (2005, September 1). *After death, Tibetans still prefer sky burial.* Retrieved from www.buddhistchannel.tv/index. php?id=1,1614,0,0,1,0#.Wjb-nN-nGCi

Kern, M. L., & Friedman, H. S. (2008). Do conscientious individuals live longer?: A quantitative review. *Health Psychology, 27*(5), 505-512.

Kerr, D. C. R., Lopez, N. L., Olson, S. L., & Sameroff, A. J. (2004). Parental discipline and externalizing behavior problems in early childhood: The roles of moral regulation and child gender. *Journal of Abnormal Child Psychology, 32*(4), 369-383.

Kerr, M., Stattin, H., & Özdemir, M. (2012). Perceived parenting style and adolescent adjustment: Revisiting directions of effects and the role of parental knowledge. *Developmental Psychology, 48*(6), 1540.

Kessler, R. C., Berglund, P. A., Chiu, W. T., Deitz, A. C., Hudson, J. I., Shahly, V., . . . Bruffaerts, R. (2013). The prevalence and correlates of binge eating disorder in the World Health Organization World Mental Health Surveys. *Biological Psychiatry, 73*(9), 904-914.

Keyes, C. L. M., & Shapiro, A. D. (2004). Social well-being in the United States: A descriptive epidemiology. In O. G. Brim, C. D. Ryff, & R. C. Kessler (Eds.), *How healthy are we? A national study of well-being at midlife* (pp. 350-372). Chicago, IL: University of Chicago Press.

Khamis, R. Y., Ammari, T., & Mikhail, G. W. (2016). Gender differences in coronary heart disease. *Heart, 102*(14), 1142-1149.

Khandwala, Y. S., Zhang, C. A., Lu, Y., & Eisenberg, M. L. (2017). The age of fathers in the USA is rising: An analysis of 168 867 480 births from 1972 to 2015. *Human Reproduction, 32*(10), 2110-2116.

Khaw, K. T., Wareham, N., Bingham, S., Welch, A., Luben, R., & Day, N. (2008). Combined impact of health behaviours and mortality in men and women: The EPIC-Norfolk Prospective Population Study. *PLoS Medicine, 5*(1), e12. doi: 10.1371/journal.pmed.0050012

Khera, R., Murad, M. H., Chandar, A. K., Dulai, P. S., Wang, Z., Prokop, L. J., . . . Singh, S. (2016). Association of pharmacological treatments for obesity with weight loss and adverse events: A systematic review and meta-analysis. *JAMA, 315*(22), 2424-2434.

Khodyakov, D., & Carr, D. (2009). The impact of late-life parental death on adult sibling relationships: Do parents' advance directives help or hurt? *Research on Aging, 31*(5), 495-519.

Kiblawi, Z. N., Smith, L. M., Diaz, S. D., LaGasse, L. L., Derauf, C., Newman, E., . . . & Strauss, A. (2014). Prenatal methamphetamine exposure and neonatal and infant neurobehavioral outcome: Results from the IDEAL study. *Substance Abuse, 35*(1), 68-73.

Kids Count Data Center. (2019). *Progress stalls on child poverty.* Retrieved from https://datacenter. kidscount.org/updates/show/253-progress-stalls-on-child-poverty

Kiecolt-Glaser, J. K., & Glaser, R. (2001). Stress and immunity: Age enhances the risks. *Current Directions in Psychological Science, 10*, 18-21.

Kiecolt-Glaser, J. K., & Newton, T. L. (2001). Marriage and health: His and hers. *Psychological Bulletin, 127*, 472-503.

Kiel, E. J., Premo, J. E., & Buss, K. A. (2016). Maternal encouragement to approach novelty: A curvilinear relation to change in anxiety for inhibited toddlers. *Journal of Abnormal Child Psychology, 44*(3), 433-444.

Kier, C., & Lewis, C. (1998). Preschool sibling interaction in separated and married families: Are same-sex pairs or older sisters more sociable? *The Journal of Child Psychology and Psychiatry and Allied Disciplines, 39*(2), 191-201.

Kilgour, A. H., Starr, J. M., & Whalley, L. J. (2010). Associations between childhood intelligence (IQ), adult morbidity and mortality. *Maturitas, 65*(2), 98-105.

Killewald, A. (2016). Money, work, and marital stability: Assessing change in the gendered determinants of divorce. *American Sociological Review, 81*(4), 696-719.

Kim, D. H., Yeo, S. H., Park, J. M., Choi, J. Y., Lee, T. H., Park, S. Y., . . . & Cha, H. J. (2014). Genetic markers for diagnosis and pathogenesis of Alzheimer's disease. *Gene, 545*(2), 185-193.

Kim, D. J., Davis, E. P., Sandman, C. A., Sporns, O., O'Donnell, B. F., Buss, C., & Hetrick, W. P. (2016). Children's intellectual ability is associated with structural network integrity. *Neuroimage, 124*, 550-556.

Kim, H. J., & Fredriksen-Goldsen, K. I. (2016). Living arrangement and loneliness among lesbian, gay, and bisexual older adults. *The Gerontologist, 56*(3), 548-558.

Kim, J., McHale, S. M., Osgood, D. W., & Crouter, A. C. (2006). Longitudinal course and family correlates of sibling relationships from childhood through adolescence. *Child Development, 77*, 1746-1761.

Kim, S. Y., Fouad, N., Maeda, H., Xie, H., & Nazan, N. (2018). Midlife work and psychological well-being: A test of the psychology of working theory. *Journal of Career Assessment, 26*(3), 413-424.

Kim, S., Nordling, J. K., Yoon, J. E., Boldt, L. J., & Kochanska, G. (2013). Effortful control in "hot" and "cool" tasks differentially predicts children's behavior problems and academic performance. *Journal of Abnormal Child Psychology, 41*(1), 43-56.

Kim, S., Wyckoff, J., Morris, A. T., Succop, A., Avery, A., Duncan, G. E., & Jazwinski, S. M. (2018). DNA methylation associated with healthy aging of elderly twins. *GeroScience, 40*(5-6), 469-484.

Kim-Cohen, J., Moffitt, T. E., Caspi, A., & Taylor, A. (2004). Genetic and environmental processes in young children's resilience and vulnerability to socioeconomic deprivation. *Child Development, 75*, 651-668.

Kimball, M. M. (1986). Television and sex-role attitudes. In T. M. Williams (Ed.), *The impact of television: A natural experiment in three communities* (pp. 265-301). Orlando, FL: Academic Press.

Kincaid, C., Jones, D. J., Sterrett, E., & McKee, L. (2012). A review of parenting and adolescent sexual behavior: The moderating role of gender. *Clinical Psychology Review, 32*(3), 177-188.

King, K. M., Meehan, B. T., Trim, R. S., & Chassin, L. (2006). Market or mediator? The effects of adolescent substance use on young adult educational attainment. *Addiction, 101*, 1730-1740.

King, M., & Bartlett, A. (2006). What same sex civil partnerships may mean for health. *Journal of Epidemiology and Community Health, 60*, 188-191.

King, P. M., & Kitchener, K. S. (2004). Reflective judgment: Theory and research on the development of epistemic assumptions through adulthood. *Educational Psychologist, 39*(1), 5-18.

King, V., Amato, P. R., & Lindstrom, R. (2015). Stepfather–adolescent relationship quality during the first year of transitioning to a stepfamily. *Journal of Marriage and Family, 77*(5), 1179-1189.

King, W. J., MacKay, M., Sirnick, A., & The Canadian Shaken Baby Study Group. (2003). Shaken baby syndrome in Canada: Clinical characteristics and outcomes of hospital cases. *Canadian Medical Association Journal, 168*, 155-159.

Kinsella, K., & He, W. (2009). *An aging world: 2008. International Population Reports* (P95/09-1). Washington, DC: U.S. Government Printing Office.

Kinsella, K., & Phillips, P. (2005, March). Global aging: The challenges of success. *Population Bulletin,* No. 1. Washington, DC: Population Reference Bureau.

Kinsella, K., & Velkoff, V. A. (2001). *An aging world: 2001* (U.S. Census Bureau, Series P95/01-1). Washington, DC: U.S. Government Printing Office.

Kiraly, M., & Humphreys, C. (2013). Family contact for children in kinship care: A literature review. *Australian Social Work, 66*(3), 358-374.

Kirby, D., & Laris, B. (2009). Effective curriculum-based sex and STD/HIV education programs for adolescents. *Child Development Perspectives, 3*, 21-29.

Kirkorian, H. L., Wartella, E. A., & Anderson, D. R. (2008). Media and young children's learning. *The Future of Children, 18*(1), 39-61.

Kisilevsky, B. S., & Hains, S. M. J. (2010). Exploring the relationship between fetal heart rate and cognition. *Infant and Child Development, 19*, 60-75.

Kisilevsky, B. S., Hains, S. M. J., Jacquet, A. Y., Granier-Deferre, C., & Lecanuet, J. P. (2004). Maturation of fetal responses to music. *Developmental Science, 7*(5), 550-559.

Kisilevsky, B. S., Hains, S. M., Brown, C. A., Lee, C. T., Cowperthwaite, B., Stutzman, S. S., . . . Ye, H. H. (2009). Fetal sensitivity to properties of maternal speech and language. *Infant Behavior and Development, 32*(1), 59-71.

Kisilevsky, B. S., Muir, D. W., & Low, J. A. (1992). Maturation of human fetal responses to vibroacoustic stimulation. *Child Development, 63,* 1497–1508.

Kitamura, C., Thanavishuth, C., Burnham, D., & Luksaneeyanawin, S. (2001). Universality and specificity in infant-directed speech: Pitch modifications as a function of infant age and sex in a tonal and non-tonal language. *Infant Behavior and Development, 24*(4), 372–392.

Kitamura, C., Winskel, H., & Padakannaya, P. (2014). Infant-directed speech: Social and linguistic pathways in tonal and non-tonal languages. *South and Southeast Asian Psycholinguistics,* 36–44.

Kitzman, K. M., Dalton, W. T., III, Stanley, C. M., Beech, B. M., Reeves, T. P., Bescemi, J., . . . Midgett, E. L. (2010). Lifestyle interventions for youth who are overweight: A meta-analytic review. *Health Psychology, 29*(1), 91–101.

Kivett, V. R. (1996). The saliency of the grandmother-granddaughter relationship: Predictors of association. *Journal of Women and Aging, 8,* 25–39.

Klahr, A. M., & Burt, S. A. (2014). Elucidating the etiology of individual differences in parenting: A meta-analysis of behavioral genetic research. *Psychological Bulletin, 140*(2), 544.

Klauer, S. G., Guo, F., Simons-Morton, B. G., Ouimet, M. C., Lee, S. E., & Dingus, T. A. (2014). Distracted driving and risk of road crashes among novice and experienced drivers. *New England Journal of Medicine, 370*(1), 54–59.

Klein, J. D. (2020). Reversing Obamacare erodes coverage for young adults. *Journal of Adolescent Health, 66*(1), 6–7.

Klein, J. D., & the American Academy of Pediatrics Committee on Adolescence. (2005). Adolescent pregnancy: Current trends and issues. *Pediatrics, 116,* 281–286.

Kleinpell, R., Vasilevskis, E. E., Fogg, L., & Ely, E. W. (2019). Exploring the association of hospice care on patient experience and outcomes of care. *BMJ Supportive & Palliative Care, 9*(1), e13.

Klemenc-Ketis, Z., Kersnik, J., & Grmec, S. (2010). The effect of carbon dioxide on near-death experiences in out-of-hospital cardiac arrest survivors: A prospective observational study. *Critical Care, 14*(2), R56.

Kletke, B., Hallford, D.J., & Mellor, D.J. (2014). Sexting prevalence and correlates: A systematic literature review. *Clinical Psychology Review, 34,* 44–53.

Klibanoff, R. S., Levine, S. C., Huttenlocher, J., Vasilyeva, M., & Hedges, L. V. (2006). Preschool children's mathematical knowledge: The effect of teacher "math talk." *Developmental Psychology, 42,* 59–69.

Kliegel, M., Ballhausen, N., Hering, A., Ihle, A., Schnitzspahn, K. M., & Zuber, S. (2016). Prospective memory in older adults: Where we are now and what is next. *Gerontology, 62*(4), 459–466.

Kline, D. W., & Scialfa, C. T. (1996). Visual and auditory aging. In J. E. Birren & K. W. Schaie (Eds.), *Handbook of the psychology of aging* (pp. 191–208). San Diego, CA: Academic Press.

Klingberg, T. (2010). Training and plasticity of working memory. *Trends in Cognitive Sciences, 14*(7), 317–324.

Kloep, M., & Hendry, L. B. (2010). Letting go or holding on? Parents' perceptions of their relationships with their children during emerging adulthood. *British Journal of Developmental Psychology, 28*(4), 817–834.

Klohnen, E. C. (1996). Conceptual analysis and measurement of the construct of ego-resiliency. *Journal of Personality and Social Psychology, 70,* 1067–1079.

Knafo, A., & Plomin, R. (2006). Parental discipline and affection and children's prosocial behavior: Genetic and environmental links. *Journal of Personality and Social Psychology, 90,* 147–164.

Knafo-Noam, A., Vertsberger, D., & Israel, S. (2018). Genetic and environmental contributions to children's prosocial behavior: Brief review and new evidence from a reanalysis of experimental twin data. *Current Opinion in Psychology, 20,* 60–65.

Knickmeyer, R. C., Gouttard, S., Kang, C., Evans, D., Wilber, K., Smith, J. K., . . . Gilmore, J. H. (2008). A structural MRI study of human brain development from birth to 2 years. *Journal of Neuroscience, 28*(47), 12176–12182.

Knobloch, S., Callison, C., Chen, L., Fritzsche, A., & Zillmann, D. (2005). Children's sex-stereotyped self-socialization through selective exposure to entertainment: Cross-cultural experiments in Germany, China, and the United States. *Journal of Communication, 55*(1), 122–138.

Knochel, K. A., Quam, J. K., & Croghan, C. F. (2011). Are old lesbian and gay people well served? Understanding the perceptions, preparation, and experiences of aging services providers. *Journal of Applied Gerontology, 30*(3), 370–389.

Ko, T. J., Tsai, L. Y., Chu, L. C., Yeh, S. J., Leung, C., Chen, C. Y., . . . Hsieh, W. S. (2014). Parental smoking during pregnancy and its association with low birth weight, small for gestational age, and preterm birth offspring: a birth cohort study. *Pediatrics & Neonatology, 55*(1), 20–27.

Kobayashi, C., Glover, G. H., & Temple, E. (2007). Cultural and linguistic effects on neural bases of 'theory of mind' in American and Japanese children. *Brain Research, 1164,* 95–107.

Kochanek, K. D., Murphy, S. L., Xu, J. & Arias, E. (2019). Deaths: Final data for 2017. *National Vital Statistics Reports, 68*(9). Hyattsville, MD: National Center for Health Statistics.

Kochanek, K. D., Murphy, S. L., Xu, J. Q. & Arias E. A. (2019). Deaths: Final data for 2014. *National Vital Statistics Reports, 68*(9), 1–77. Hyattsville, MD: National Center for Health Statistics.

Kochanek, K. D., Murphy, S. L., Xu, J. Q. & Bastian, B., Arias, E. (2019). Deaths: Final data for 2017. *National Vital Statistics Reports, 68*(9), 1–77. Hyattsville, MD: National Center for Health Statistics.

Kochanska, G. (1993). Toward a synthesis of parental socialization and child temperament in early development of conscience. *Child Development, 64*(2), 325–347.

Kochanska, G. (2001). Emotional development in children with different attachment histories: The first three years. *Child Development, 72,* 474–490.

Kochanska, G., & Aksan, N. (1995). Mother-child positive affect, the quality of child compliance to requests and prohibitions, and maternal control as correlates of early internalization. *Child Development, 66,* 236–254.

Kochanska, G., Aksan, N., & Joy, M. E. (2007). Children's fearfulness as a moderator of parenting in early socialization: Two longitudinal studies. *Developmental Psychology, 43,* 222–237.

Kochanska, G., Askan, N., Prisco, T. R., & Adams, E. E. (2008). Mother-child and father-child mutually responsive orientation in the first two years and children's outcomes at preschool age: Mechanisms of influence. *Child Development, 79,* 30–44.

Kochanska, G., Boldt, L. J., Kim, S., Yoon, J. E., & Philibert, R. A. (2015). Developmental interplay between children's biobehavioral risk and the parenting environment from toddler to early school age: Prediction of socialization outcomes in preadolescence. *Development and Psychopathology, 27*(3), 775–790.

Kochanska, G., Coy, K. C., & Murray, K. T. (2001). The development of self-regulation in the first four years of life. *Child Development, 72*(4), 1091–1111.

Kochanska, G., Friesenborg, A. E., Lange, L. A., & Martel, M. M. (2004). Parents' personality and infants' temperament as contributors to their emerging relationship. *Journal of Personality and Social Psychology, 86,* 744–759.

Kochanska, G., Gross, J. N., Lin, M. H., & Nichols, K. E. (2002). Guilt in young children: Development, determinants, and relations with a broader system of standards. *Child Development, 73*(2), 461–482.

Kochanska, G., Tjebkes, T. L., & Forman, D. R. (1998). Children's emerging regulation of conduct: Restraint, compliance, and internalization from infancy to the second year. *Child Development, 69*(5), 1378–1389.

Kochanska, G., Woodard, J., Kim, S., Koenig, J. L., Yoon, J. E., & Barry, R. A. (2010). Positive socialization mechanisms in secure and insecure parent–child dyads: Two longitudinal studies. *Journal of Child Psychology and Psychiatry, 51*(9), 998–1009.

Koechlin, E., Basso, G., Pietrini, P., Panzer, S., & Grafman, J. (1999). The role of the anterior prefrontal cortex in human cognition. *Nature, 399,* 148–151.

Koenig, H. G. (2012). Religion, spirituality, and health: The research and clinical implications. *ISRN Psychiatry, 2012.*

Koenig, L. B., McGue, M., & Iacono, W. G. (2008). Stability and change in religiousness during emerging adulthood. *Developmental Psychology, 44*(2), 532.

Koenig, H. G., King, D., & Carson, V. B. (2012). *Handbook of religion and health* (2nd ed.). New York, NY: Oxford University Press.

Kogan, M. D., Newacheck, P. W., Honberg, L., & Strickland, B. (2005). Association between underinsurance and access to care among children with special health care needs in the United States. *Pediatrics, 116,* 1162–1169.

Kohl III, H. W., & Cook, H. D. (2013). *Status and trends of physical activity behaviors and related school policies.* Washington, DC: The National Academies Press.

Kohlberg, L. (1966). A cognitive-developmental analysis of children's sex role concepts and attitudes. In E. E. Maccoby (Ed.), *The development of sex differences.* Stanford, CA: Stanford University Press.

Kohlberg, L. (1969). Stage and sequence: The cognitive-developmental approach to socialization. In D. A. Goslin (Ed.), *Handbook of socialization theory and research.* Chicago, IL: Rand McNally.

Kohlberg, L. (1973). Continuities in childhood and adult moral development revisited. In P. Baltes & K. W. Schaie (Eds.), *Life-span developmental psychology: Personality and socialization* (pp. 180–207). New York, NY: Academic Press.

Kohlberg, L. (1981). *Essays on moral development.* San Francisco, CA: Harper & Row.

Kohlberg, L., & Ryncarz, R. A. (1990). Beyond justice reasoning: Moral development and consideration of a seventh stage. In C. N. Alexander & E. J. Langer (Eds.), *Higher stages of human development* (pp. 191–207). New York, NY: Oxford University Press.

Kohn, D., & Passel, J. S. (2018). Record 64 million Americans live in multigenerational households. *Pew Research Center.* Retrieved from www.pewresearch.org/fact-tank/2018/04/05/a-record-64-million-americans-live-in-multigenerational-households/

Kohn, J. L., Rholes, S. W., Simpson, J. A., Martin III, A. M., Tran, S., & Wilson, C. L. (2012). Changes in marital satisfaction across the transition to parenthood: The role of adult attachment orientations. *Personality and Social Psychology Bulletin, 38*(11), 1506–1522.

Kohn, M. L. (1980). Job complexity and adult personality. In N. J. Smelser & E. H. Erikson (Eds.), *Themes of work and love in adulthood.* Cambridge, MA: Harvard University Press.

Kokkinaki, T. (2019). Structural variations, quantitative differences and similarities between maternal and paternal infant-directed speech. *Early Child Development and Care, 189*(12), 1925–1942.

Kolata, G. (1999, March 9). Pushing limits of the human life span. *The New York Times.* Retrieved from www.nytimes.com/library/national/science/030999sci-aging.html

Kolb, B., Harker, A., & Gibb, R. (2017). Principles of plasticity in the developing brain. *Developmental Medicine & Child Neurology, 59*(12), 1218–1223.

Kolb, B., Mychasiuk, R., Muhammad, A., Li, Y., Frost, D. O., & Gibb, R. (2012). Experience and the developing prefrontal cortex. *Proceedings of the National Academy of Sciences, 109*(Suppl. 2), 17186–17193.

Kolbert, E. (1994, January 11). Canadians curbing TV violence. *The New York Times,* pp. C15, C19.

Kolesinska, Z., Ahmed, S. F., Niedziela, M., Bryce, J., Molinska-Glura, M., Rodie, M., . . . Hiort, O. (2014). Changes over time in sex assignment for disorders of sex development. *Pediatrics, 134*(3), e710–e715.

Kolling, T., Graf, F., & Knopf, M. (2016). Cross-cultural perspectives on declarative and nondeclarative memory from infancy to early childhood. *Child Development Perspectives, 10*(1), 28–32.

Kolte, A. M., Olsen, L. R., Mikkelsen, E. M., Christiansen, O. B., & Nielsen, H. S. (2015). Depression and emotional stress is highly prevalent among women with recurrent pregnancy loss. *Human Reproduction, 30*(4), 777–782.

Komarraju, M., & Nadler, D. (2013). Self-efficacy and academic achievement: Why do implicit beliefs, goals, and effort regulation matter? *Learning and Individual Differences, 25,* 67–72.

Konijnenberg, C. (2015). Methodological issues in assessing the impact of prenatal drug exposure. *Substance abuse: Research and Treatment, 9,* SART-S23544.

Konjarski, M., Murray, G., Lee, V. V., & Jackson, M. L. (2018). Reciprocal relationships between daily sleep and mood: A systematic review of naturalistic prospective studies. *Sleep Medicine Reviews, 42,* 47–58.

Konner, M. (2017). Hunter-gatherer infancy and childhood: The !Kung and others. In B. Hewlett & M. Lamb (Eds.), *Hunter-gatherer childhoods* (pp. 19–64). Abingdon, England: Routledge.

Konner, M., & Shostak, M. (1987). Timing and management of birth among the! Kung: Biocultural interaction in reproductive adaptation. *Cultural Anthropology, 2*(1), 11–28.

Konrad, K., Firk, C., & Uhlhaas, P. J. (2013). Brain development during adolescence: Neuroscientific insights into this developmental period. *Deutsches Ärzteblatt International, 110*(25), 425.

Kontis, V., Bennett, J. E., Mathers, C. D., Li, G., Foreman, K., & Ezzati, M. (2017). Future life expectancy in 35 industrialized countries: Projections with a Bayesian model ensemble. *The Lancet, 389*(10076), 1323–1335.

Korat, O., & Or, T. (2010). How new technology influences parent–child interaction: The case of e-book reading. *First Language, 30*(2), 139–154.

Korbin, B., & Spilsbury, J. C. (1999). Cultural competence and child neglect. In H. Dubowitz (Ed.), *Neglected children: Research, practice, and policy* (p. 69). Thousand Oaks, CA: Sage Publications.

Korchmaros, J. D., Ybarra, M. L., & Mitchell, K. J. (2015). Adolescent online romantic relationship initiation: Differences by sexual and gender identification. *Journal of Adolescence, 40,* 54–64.

Korda, H., & Itani, Z. (2013). Harnessing social media for health promotion and behavior change. *Health Promotion Practice, 14*(1), 15–23.

Koren, G., Pastuszak, A., & Ito, S. (1998). Drugs in pregnancy. *New England Journal of Medicine, 338,* 1128–1137.

Koropeckyj-Cox, T., Pienta, A. M., & Brown, T. H. (2007). Women of the 1950s and the "normative" life course: The implications of childlessness, fertility timing, and marital status for psychological well-being in late midlife. *The International Journal of Aging and Human Development, 64*(4), 299–330.

Kost, K., Henshaw, S., & Carlin, L. (2013). *U.S. teenage pregnancies, births and abortions: National and state trends and trends by race and ethnicity, 2010.* Retrieved from www.guttmacher.org/pubs/USTPtrends.pdf

Kostović, I., & Judaš, M. (2010). The development of the subplate and thalamocortical connections in the human foetal brain. *Acta Paediatrica, 99*(8), 1119–1127.

Kotlęga, D., Gołąb-Janowska, M., Masztalewicz, M., Ciećwież, S., & Nowacki, P. (2016). The emotional stress and risk of ischemic stroke. *Neurologia i Neurochirurgia Polska, 50*(4), 265–270.

Kousta, E., Papathanasiou, A., & Skordis, N. (2010). Sex determination and disorders of sex development according to the revised nomenclature and classification in 46, XX individuals. *Hormones, 9*(3), 218–231.

Kovacs, M., Obrosky, S., & George, C. (2016). The course of major depressive disorder from childhood to young adulthood: Recovery and recurrence in a longitudinal observational study. *Journal of Affective Disorders, 203,* 374–381.

Kovas, Y., Hayiou-Thomas, M. E., Dale, P. S., Bishop, D. V. M., & Plomin, R. (2005). Genetic influences in different aspects of language development: The etiology of language skills in 4.5-year-old twins. *Child Development, 76,* 632–651.

Kovács, Á. M. (2012). Early bilingualism and theory of mind: Bilinguals' advantage in dealing with conflicting mental representations. *Access to Language and Cognitive Development,* 192–218.

Kowalski, R. M., Giumetti, G. W., Schroeder, A. N., & Lattanner, M. R. (2014). Bullying in the digital age: A critical review and meta-analysis of cyberbullying research among youth. *Psychological Bulletin, 140*(4), 1073–1137.

Kozhimannil, K. B., Hardeman, R. R., Alarid-Escudero, F., Vogelsang, C. A., Blauer-Peterson, C., & Howell, E. A. (2016). Modeling the cost-effectiveness of doula care associated with reductions in preterm birth and cesarean delivery. *Birth, 43*(1), 20–27.

Kozlowska, K., & Hanney, L. (1999). Family assessment and intervention using an interactive art exercise. *Australia and New Zealand Journal of Family Therapy, 20*(2), 61–69.

Kramer, B. J., & Boelk, A. Z. (2015). Correlates and predictors of conflict at the end of life among families enrolled in hospice. *Journal of Pain and Symptom Management, 50*(2), 155–162.

Kramer, B. J., Boelk, A. Z., & Auer, C. (2006). Family conflict at the end of life: Lessons learned in a model program for vulnerable older adults. *Journal of Palliative Medicine, 9*(3), 791–801.

Kramer, D. A. (2003). The ontogeny of wisdom in its variations. In J. Demick & C. Andreoletti (Eds.), *Handbook of adult development* (pp. 131–151). New York, NY: Plenum Press.

Kramer, L. (2010). The essential ingredients of successful sibling relationships: An emerging framework for advancing theory and practice. *Child Development Perspectives, 4*(2), 80–86.

Kramer, L., & Kowal, A. K. (2005). Sibling relationship quality from birth to adolescence: The enduring contributions of friends. *Journal of Family Psychology, 19*(4), 503.

Kramer, S. (2019). U.S. has world's highest rate of children living in single-parent households [Report]. *Pew Research Center.* Retrieved from www.pewresearch.org/fact-tank/2019/12/12/u-s-children-more-likely-than-children-in-other-countries-to-live-with-just-one-parent/

Kraschnewski, J. L., Boan, J., Esposito, J., Sherwood, N. E., Lehman, E. B., Kephart, D. K., & Sciamanna, C. N. (2010). Long-term weight loss maintenance in the United States. *International Journal of Obesity, 34*(11), 1644.

Krashen, S., & McField, G. (2005). What works? Reviewing the latest evidence on bilingual education. *Language Learner 1*(2), 7–10, 34.

Krause, C., Longo, D., & Shuwairi, S. (2019). Increased visual interest and affective responses to impossible figures in early infancy. *Infant Behavior and Development, 57*, 101341.

Krause, N. (2004). Common facets of religion, unique facets of religion, and life satisfaction among older African Americans. *Journal of Gerontology: Social Sciences, 59B*, S109–S117.

Krause, N., Pargament, K. I., & Ironson, G. (2018). In the shadow of death: Religious hope as a moderator of the effects of age on death anxiety. *The Journals of Gerontology: Series B, 73*(4), 696–703.

Krcmar, M. (2011). Word learning in very young children from infant-directed DVDs. *Journal of Communication, 61*(4), 780–794.

Kreager, D. A., Molloy, L. E., Moody, J., & Feinberg, M. E. (2016). Friends first? The peer network origins of adolescent dating. *Journal of Research on Adolescence, 26*(2), 257–269.

Krebs-Smith, S. M., Guenther, P. M., Subar, A. F., Kirkpatrick, S. I., & Dodd, K. W. (2010). Americans do not meet federal dietary recommendations. *The Journal of Nutrition, 140*(10), 1832–1838.

Kreicbergs, U., Valdimarsdóttir, U., Onelöv, E., Henter, J. I., & Steineck, G. (2004). Talking about death with children who have severe malignant disease. *New England Journal of Medicine, 351*(12), 1175–1186.

Kreider, R. M. (2005). Number, timing, and duration of marriages and divorces: 2001. *Household Economic Studies,* P70–97. Washington, DC: U.S. Census Bureau.

Kremen, A. M., & Block, J. (1998). The roots of ego-control in young adulthood: Links with parenting in early childhood. *Journal of Personality and Social Psychology, 75*(4), 1062–1075.

Kremen, W. S., Lachman, M. E., Pruessner, J. C., Sliwinski, M., & Wilson, R. S. (2012). Mechanisms of age-related cognitive change and targets for intervention: Social interactions and stress. *Journals of Gerontology Series A: Biomedical Sciences and Medical Sciences, 67*(7), 760–765.

Kreyenfeld, M., & Konietzka, D. (2017). Analyzing childlessness. In *Childlessness in Europe: Contexts, causes, and consequences* (pp. 3–15). New York, NY: Springer.

Krishnan, A., Gandour, J. T., & Bidelman, G. M. (2010). The effects of tone language experience on pitch processing in the brainstem. *Journal of Neurolinguistics, 23*(1), 81–95.

Kroger, J. (2003). Identity development during adolescence. In G. R. Adams & M. D. Berzonsky (Eds.), *Blackwell handbook of adolescence* (pp. 205–226). Malden, MA: Blackwell.

Kroger, J., & Haslett, S. J. (1991). A comparison of ego identity status transition pathways and change rates across five identity domains. *International Journal of Aging and Human Development, 32*, 303–330.

Kroger, J., Martinussen, M., & Marcia, J. E. (2009). Identity status change during adolescence and young adulthood: A meta-analysis. *Journal of Adolescence, 33*(5), 683–698.

Krogstad, J. (2015). Facts about American grandparents [Pew Research Center news report]. Retrieved from www.pewresearch.org/fact-tank/2015/09/13/5-facts-about-american-grandparents/

Kross, E., Verduyn, P., Demiralp, E., Park, J., Lee, D. S., Lin, N., . . . Ybarra, O. (2013). Facebook use predicts declines in subjective well-being in young adults. *PloS One, 8*(8), e69841.

Krug, E. G. (2015). *Hearing loss due to recreational exposure to loud sounds: A review.* Geneva, Switzerland: World Health Organization.

Krug, E. G., Mercy, J. A., Dahlberg, L. L., & Zwi, A. B. (2002). The world report on violence and health. *The Lancet, 360*(9339), 1083–1088.

Kruse, A., & Schmitt, E. (2012). Generativity as a route to active ageing. *Current Gerontology and Geriatrics Research, 2012.*

Kuczmarski, R. J., Ogden, C. L., Grummer-Strawn, L. M., Flegal, K. M., Guo, S. S., Wei, R., . . . Johnson, C. L. (2000). *CDC growth charts: United States* (Advance Data, No. 314). Washington, DC: Centers for Disease Control and Prevention, U.S. Department of Health and Human Services.

Kuhl, P. K. (2004). Early language acquisition: Cracking the speech code. *Nature Reviews Neuroscience, 5*, 831–843.

Kuhl, P. K. (2010). Brain mechanisms in early language acquisition. *Neuron, 67*(5), 713–727.

Kuhl, P. K. (2011). Early language learning and literacy: Neuroscience implications for education. *Mind, Brain, and Education, 5*, 128–142. doi:10.1111/j.1751-228X.2011.01121.x

Kuhl, P. K., Andruski, J. E., Chistovich, I. A., Chistovich, L. A., Kozhevnikova, E. V., Ryskina, V. L., . . . Lacerda, F. (1997). Cross-language analysis of phonetic units in language addressed to infants. *Science, 277*, 684–686.

Kuhl, P. K., Conboy, B. T., Padden, D., Nelson, T., & Pruitt, J. (2005). Early speech perception and later language development: Implications for the "critical period." *Language Learning and Development, 1*, 237–264.

Kuhl, P. K., Williams, K. A., Lacerda, F., Stevens, K. N., & Lindblom, B. (1992). Linguistic experience alters phonetic perception in infants by 6 months of age. *Science, 255*, 606–608.

Kuhl, P., & Rivera-Gaxiola, M. (2008). Neural substrates of language acquisition. *Annual Review of Neuroscience, 31*, 511–534.

Kuhn, D. (2006). Do cognitive changes accompany developments in the adolescent brain? *Perspectives on Psychological Science, 1*, 59–67.

Kuiper, J. S., Zuidersma, M., Zuidema, S. U., Burgerhof, J. G., Stolk, R. P., Oude Voshaar, R. C., & Smidt, N. (2016). Social relationships and cognitive decline: A systematic review and meta-analysis of longitudinal cohort studies. *International Journal of Epidemiology, 45*(4), 1169–1206.

Kumar, P., Wright, A. A., Hatfield, L. A., Temel, J. S., & Keating, N. L. (2017). Family perspectives on hospice care experiences of patients with cancer. *Journal of Clinical Oncology, 35*(4), 432.

Kumar, S., & Kelly, A. S. (2017, February). Review of childhood obesity: From epidemiology, etiology, and comorbidities to clinical assessment and treatment. *Mayo Clinic Proceedings, 92*(2), 251–265.

Kunzman, R., & Gaither, M. (2013). Homeschooling: A comprehensive survey of the research. *Other Education, 2*(1), 4–59.

Kuperberg, A. (2014). Age at coresidence, premarital cohabitation, and marriage dissolution: 1985–2009. *Journal of Marriage and Family, 76*(2), 352–369.

Kurdek, L. A. (1999). The nature and predictors of the trajectory of change in marital quality for husbands and wives over the first 10 years of marriage. *Developmental Psychology, 35*(5), 1283.

Kurdek, L. A. (2005). What do we know about gay and lesbian couples? *Current Directions in Psychological Science, 5*, 251–254.

Kurdek, L. A. (2006). Differences between partners from heterosexual, gay, and lesbian cohabiting couples. *Journal of Marriage and Family, 68*, 509–528.

Kurdek, L. A. (2008). A general model of relationship commitment: Evidence from same-sex partners. *Personal Relationships, 15*(3), 391–405.

Kuss, D. J., Griffiths, M.D., Karila, L., & Billieux, J. (2014). Internet addiction: A systematic review of epidemiological research for the last decade. *Current Pharmaceutical Design, 20*(25), 4026–4052.

Kusunoki, Y., & Upchurch, D. M. (2011). Contraceptive method choice among youth in the United States: The importance of relationship context. *Demography, 48*(4), 1451–1472.

Kwon, A. Y., Vallotton, C. D., Kiegelmann, M., & Wilhelm, K. H. (2018). Cultural diversification of communicative gestures through early childhood: A comparison of children in English-, German-, and Chinese-speaking families. *Infant Behavior and Development, 50*, 328–339.

Kärtner, J., Keller, H., & Yovsi, R. D. (2010). Mother–infant interaction during the first 3 months: The emergence of culture-specific contingency patterns. *Child Development, 81*(2), 540–554.

Kärtner, J., Keller, H., Chaudhary, N., & Yovsi, R. D. (2012). The development of mirror self-recognition in different sociocultural contexts. *Monographs of the Society for Research in Child Development,* i–101.

Kübler-Ross, E. (1969). *On death and dying.* New York, NY: Macmillan.

Kübler-Ross, E. (1970). *On death and dying* [Paperback]. New York, NY: Macmillan.

Kübler-Ross, E. (Ed.). (1975). *Death: The final stage of growth.* Englewood Cliffs, NJ: Prentice Hall.

Kühnel, J., Zacher, H., De Bloom, J., & Bledow, R. (2017). Take a break! Benefits of sleep and short breaks for daily work engagement. *European Journal of Work and Organizational Psychology, 26*(4), 481-491.

La Rue, A. (2010). Healthy brain aging: role of cognitive reserve, cognitive stimulation, and cognitive exercises. *Clinics in Geriatric Medicine, 26*(1), 99-111.

Labbo, L. D., & Kuhn, M. R. (2000). Weaving chains of affect and cognition: A young child's understanding of CD-ROM talking books. *Journal of Literacy Research, 32*(2), 187-210.

Laberge, L., Tremblay, R. E., Vitaro, F., & Montplaisir, J. (2000). Development of parasomnias from childhood to early adolescence. *Pediatrics, 106*(1), 67-74.

Labouvie-Vief, G. (2006). Emerging structures of adult thought. In J. J. Arnett & J. L. Tanner (Eds.), *Emerging adults in America: Coming of age in the 21st century* (pp. 59-84). Washington, DC: American Psychological Association.

Labrecque, L. T., & Whisman, M. A. (2017). Attitudes toward and prevalence of extramarital sex and descriptions of extramarital partners in the 21st century. *Journal of Family Psychology, 31*(7), 952.

Lachman, M. E. (2004). Development in midlife. *Annual Review of Psychology, 55,* 305-331.

Lachman, M. E., & Firth, K. M. P. (2004). The adaptive value of feeling in control during midlife. In O. G. Brim, C. D. Ryff, & R. C. Kessler (Eds.), *How healthy are we? A national study of well-being at midlife* (pp. 320-349). Chicago, IL: University of Chicago Press.

Lachman, M. E., Teshale, S., & Agrigoroaei, S. (2015). Midlife as a pivotal period in the life course: Balancing growth and decline at the crossroads of youth and old age. *International Journal of Behavioral Development, 39*(1), 20-31.

Lachs, M., & Pillemer, K. (2015). Elder abuse. *New England Journal of Medicine, 373,* 1947-1956. doi: 10.1056/NEJMra1404688

Lachs, M. S., Teresi, J. A., Ramirez, M., van Haitsma, K., Silver, S., Eimicke, J. P., . . . Pillemer, K. A. (2016). The prevalence of resident-to-resident elder mistreatment in nursing homes. *Annals of Internal Medicine, 165,* 229-236.

Lack, G. (2008). Epidemiologic risks for food allergy. *Journal of Allergy and Clinical Immunology, 121*(6), 1331-1336.

Lackland, D. T. (2014). Racial differences in hypertension: Implications for high blood pressure management. *The American Journal of the Medical Sciences, 348*(2), 135-138.

Laconi, S., Kaliszewska-Czeremska, K., Gnisci, A., Sergi, I., Barke, A., Jeromin, F., . . . Király, O. (2018). Cross-cultural study of Problematic Internet Use in nine European countries. *Computers in Human Behavior, 84,* 430-440.

Ladd, G. W., & Sechler, C. M. (2013). Young children's peer relations and social competence. In B. Spodek & O. Saracho (Eds.), *Handbook of research on the education of young children* (pp. 47-80). New York, NY: Routledge.

Ladd, G. W., Herald-Brown, S. L., & Reiser, M. (2008). Does chronic classroom peer rejection predict the development of children's classroom participation during the grade school years? *Child Development, 79*(4), 1001-1015.

Ladegaard, H. J. (2004). Politeness in young children's speech: Context, peer group influence and pragmatic competence. *Journal of Pragmatics, 36*(11), 2003-2022.

LaFontana, K. M., & Cillessen, A. H. N. (2002). Children's perceptions of popular and unpopular peers: A multi-method assessment. *Developmental Psychology, 38,* 635-647.

LaFreniere, P. (2011). Evolutionary functions of social play: Life histories, sex differences, and emotion regulation. *American Journal of Play, 3*(4), 464-488.

Lagattuta, K. H. (2014). Linking past, present, and future: Children's ability to connect mental states and emotions across time. *Child Development Perspectives, 8*(2), 90-95.

Lago, S., Cantarero, D., Rivera, B., Pascual, M., Blázquez-Fernández, C., Casal, B., & Reyes, F. (2018). Socioeconomic status, health inequalities and non-communicable diseases: A systematic review. *Journal of Public Health, 26*(1), 1-14.

Lahey, B. B. (2009). Public health significance of neuroticism. *American Psychologist, 64*(4), 241-256.

Lai, H. M. X., Cleary, M., Sitharthan, T., & Hunt, G. E. (2015). Prevalence of comorbid substance use, anxiety and mood disorders in epidemiological surveys, 1990-2014: A systematic review and meta-analysis. *Drug and Alcohol Dependence, 154,* 1-13.

Laible, D. J., & Thompson, R. A. (2002). Mother-child conflict in the toddler years: Lessons in emotion, morality, and relationships. *Child Development, 73*(4), 1187-1203.

Laird, J., Lew, S., DeBell, M., & Chapman, C. (2006). *Dropout rates in the United States: 2002 and 2003* (NCES 2006-062). Washington, DC: U.S. Department of Education, National Center for Education Statistics.

Laird, K. T., Krause, B., Funes, C., & Lavretsky, H. (2019). Psychobiological factors of resilience and depression in late life. *Translational Psychiatry, 9*(1), 1-18.

Lake, A. (2015, November). *For every child, a fair chance: The promise of equity.* Retrieved from www.unicef.org/publications/files/For_every_child_a_fair_chance.pdf

Lamb, M. E. (1981). The development of father-infant relationships. In M. E. Lamb (Ed.), *The role of the father in child development* (2nd ed.). New York, NY: Wiley.

Lamb, M. E., & Lewis, C. (2010). The development and significance of father-child relationships in two-parent families. *The Role of the Father in Child Development, 5,* 94-153.

Lamb, M. E., Frodi, A. M., Frodi, M., & Hwang, C. P. (1982). Characteristics of maternal and paternal behavior in traditional and non-traditional Swedish families. *International Journal of Behavior Development, 5,* 131-151.

Lamb, S. (2014). Permanent personhood or meaningful decline? Toward a critical anthropology of successful aging. *Journal of Aging Studies, 29,* 41-52.

Lambert, J. C., Ibrahim-Verbaas, C. A., Harold, D., Naj, A. C., Sims, R., Bellenguez, C., . . . Grenier-Boley, B. (2013). Meta-analysis of 74,046 individuals identifies 11 new susceptibility loci for Alzheimer's disease. *Nature Genetics, 45*(12), 1452.

Lamberts, S. W. J., van den Beld, A. W., & van der Lely, A. (1997). The endocrinology of aging. *Science, 278,* 419-424.

Lamela, D., Figueiredo, B., Bastos, A., & Feinberg, M. (2016). Typologies of post-divorce coparenting and parental well-being, parenting quality and children's psychological adjustment. *Child Psychiatry & Human Development, 47*(5), 716-728.

Lamm, C., & Majdandžić, J. (2015). The role of shared neural activations, mirror neurons, and morality in empathy-a critical comment. *Neuroscience Research, 90,* 15-24.

Lamm, C., Zelazo, P. D., & Lewis, M. D. (2006). Neural correlates of cognitive control in childhood and adolescence: Disentangling the contributions of age and executive function. *Neuropsychologia, 44,* 2139-2148.

Lampit, A., Hallock, H., & Valenzuela, M. (2014). Computerized cognitive training in cognitively healthy older adults: A systematic review and meta-analysis of effect modifiers. *PLoS Medicine, 11*(11).

Lanciano, T., & Curci, A. (2015). Does emotions communication ability affect psychological well-being? A study with the Mayer-Salovey-Caruso Emotional Intelligence Test (MSCEIT) v2. 0. *Health Communication, 30*(11), 1112-1121.

Lancy, D. F. (2016). Playing with knives: The socialization of self-initiated learners. *Child development, 87*(3), 654-665.

Landazabal, M. G. (2009). A comparative analysis of empathy in childhood and adolescence: Gender differences and associated socio-emotional variables. *International Journal of Psychology and Psychological Therapy, 9*(2), 217-235.

Lande, M. B., Batisky, D. L., Kupferman, J. C., Samuels, J., Hooper, S. R., Falkner, B., . . . Adams, H. R. (2017). Neurocognitive function in children with primary hypertension. *Journal of Pediatrics, 180,* 148-155.

Lande, M. B., Kupferman, J. C., & Adams, H. R. (2018). Cognitive and behavioral aspects of childhood hypertension. *Pediatric Hypertension,* 605-616.

Landor, A., Simons, L. G., Simons, R. L., Brody, G. H., & Gibbons, F. X. (2011). The role of religiosity in the relationship between parents, peers, and adolescent risky sexual behavior. *Journal of Youth and adolescence, 40*(3), 296-330.

Landy, F. J. (1994, July-August). Mandatory retirement age: Serving the public welfare? *Psychological Science Agenda* (Science Directorate, American Psychological Association), 10-11, 20.

Lane, J. M., Liang, J., Vlasac, I., Anderson, S. G., Bechtold, D. A., Bowden, J., . . . Loudon, A. (2017). Genome-wide association analyses of sleep disturbance traits identify new loci and highlight shared genetics with neuropsychiatric and metabolic traits. *Nature Genetics, 49*(2), 274.

Langa, K. M., Larson, E. B., Crimmins, E. M., Faul, J. D., Levine, D. A., Kabeto, M. U., & Weir, D. R. (2017). A comparison of the prevalence of dementia in the United States in 2000 and 2012. *JAMA Internal Medicine, 177*(1), 51-58.

Lange, N., Froimowitz, M. P., Bigler, E. D., Lainhart, J. E., & Brain Development Cooperative Group. (2010). Associations between IQ, total and regional brain volumes, and demography in a large normative sample of healthy children and adolescents. *Developmental Neuropsychology, 35*(3), 296-317.

Lange, S., Probst, C., Rehm, J., & Popova, S. (2018). National, regional, and global prevalence of smoking during pregnancy in the general population: A systematic review and meta-analysis. *The Lancet Global Health, 6*(7), e769-e776.

Langley, K., Heron, J., Smith, G. D., & Thapar, A. (2012). Maternal and paternal smoking during pregnancy and risk of ADHD symptoms in offspring: testing for intrauterine effects. *American Journal of Epidemiology, 176*(3), 261-268.

Lanoye, A., Brown, K. L., & LaRose, J. G. (2017). The transition into young adulthood: A critical period for weight control. *Current Diabetes Reports, 17*(11), 114.

Lansford, J. E., Ceballo, R., Abbey, A., & Stewart, A. J. (2001). Does family structure matter? A comparison of adoptive, two-parent biological, single-mother, stepfather, and stepmother households. *Journal of Marriage and family, 63*(3), 840-851.

Lansford, J. E., Criss, M. M., Dodge, K. A., Shaw, D. S., Pettit, G. S., & Bates, J. E. (2009). Trajectories of physical discipline: Early childhood antecedents and developmental outcomes. *Child Development, 80*(5), 1385-1402. doi: 10.1111/j.1467-8624.2009.01340.x

Lansford, J. E., Godwin, J., Tirado, L. M. U., Zelli, A., Al-Hassan, S. M., Bacchini, D., . . . Di Giunta, L. (2015). Individual, family, and culture level contributions to child physical abuse and neglect: A longitudinal study in nine countries. *Development and Psychopathology, 27*(4pt2), 1417-1428.

Lansford, J. E., Skinner, A. T., Sorbring, E., Giunta, L. D., Deater-Deckard, K., Dodge, K. A., . . . Uribe Tirado, L. M. (2012). Boys' and girls' relational and physical aggression in nine countries. *Aggressive Behavior, 38*(4), 298-308.

Lantagne, A., & Furman, W. (2017). Romantic relationship development: The interplay between age and relationship length. *Developmental Psychology, 53*(9), 1738.

LaRocque, M., Kleiman, I., & Darling, S. M. (2011). Parental involvement: The missing link in school achievement. *Preventing School Failure, 55*(3), 115-122.

Larrimore, J., Durante, S., Kreiss, K., Park, C., & Sahm, C. (2018). *Report on the economic well-being of U.S. households in 2017-2018.* Washington, DC: Board of Governors of the Federal Reserve System.

Larson, R., & Wilson, S. (2004). Adolescents across place and time: Globalization and the changing pathways to adulthood. In R. M. Lerner & L. Steinberg (Eds.), *Handbook of adolescent psychology* (2nd ed., pp. 299-331). Hoboken, NJ: Wiley.

Laski, E. V., & Siegler, R. S. (2014). Learning from number board games: You learn what you encode. *Developmental Psychology, 50*(3), 853.

Latifovic, L., Peacock, S. D., Massey, T. E., & King, W. D. (2016). The influence of alcohol consumption, cigarette smoking, and physical activity on leukocyte telomere length. *Cancer Epidemiology and Prevention Biomarkers, 25*(2), 374-380.

Lau, C. Q. (2012). The stability of same-sex cohabitation, different-sex cohabitation, and marriage. *Journal of Marriage and Family, 74*(5), 973-988.

Lau, C. S., Chamberlain, R. S., & Sun, S. (2017). Less invasive surfactant administration reduces the need for mechanical ventilation in preterm infants: A meta-analysis. *Global Pediatric Health, 4,* 2333794X17696683.

Laughlin, L. (2013). Who's minding the kids? Child care arrangements: Spring 2011. *Current Population Reports,* P70-135. Washington, DC: U.S. Census Bureau.

Laumann, E. O., Das, W., & Waite, L. J. (2008). Sexual dysfunction among older adults: Prevalence and risk factors from a nationally representative U.S. probability sample of men and women 57-85 years of age. *Journal of Sexual Medicine, 5*(10), 2300-2311.

Lauricella, A. R., Wartella, E., & Rideout, V. J. (2015). Young children's screen time: The complex role of parent and child factors. *Journal of Applied Developmental Psychology, 36,* 11-17.

Laurin, J. C., & Joussemet, M. (2017). Parental autonomy-supportive practices and toddlers' rule internalization: A prospective observational study. *Motivation and Emotion, 41*(5), 562-575.

Laursen, B. (1996). Closeness and conflict in adolescent peer relationships: Interdependence with friends and romantic partners. In W. M. Bukowski, A. F. Newcomb, & W. W. Hartup (Eds.), *The company they keep: Friendship in childhood and adolescence* (pp. 186-210). New York, NY: Cambridge University Press.

Lautenschlager, N. T., Cox, K. L., Flicker, L., Foster, J. K., van Bockxmeer, F. M., Xiao, J., . . . Almeida, O. P. (2008). Effects of physical activity on cognitive function in older adults at risk for Alzheimer's disease. *Journal of the American Medical Association, 300*(9), 1027-1037.

Lavee, Y., & Ben-Ari, A. (2004). Emotional expressiveness and neuroticism: Do they predict marital quality? *Journal of Marriage and Family, 18,* 620-627.

Lavenex, P., & Lavenex, P. B. (2013). Building hippocampal circuits to learn and remember: insights into the development of human memory. *Behavioural Brain Research, 254,* 8-21.

Lawler, M., & Nixon, E. (2011). Body dissatisfaction among adolescent boys and girls: The effects of body mass, peer appearance culture and internalization of appearance ideals. *Journal of Youth and Adolescence, 40*(1), 59-71.

Lawler-Row, K. A., & Elliott, J. (2009). The role of religious activity and spirituality in the health and well-being of older adults. *Journal of Health Psychology, 14*(1), 43-52.

Lawrence, E., Rothman, A. D., Cobb, R., Rothman, M. T., & Bradbury, T. (2008). Marital satisfaction across the transition to parenthood. *Journal of Family Psychology, 22*(1), 41-50.

Lazarus, R. S., & Folkman, S. (1984). *Stress, appraisal, and coping.* New York, NY: Springer.

Le Bourdais, C., & Lapierre-Adamcyk, É. (2004). Changes in conjugal life in Canada: Is cohabitation progressively replacing marriage? Journal of Marriage and Family, 66(4), 929-942.

Le, H. N. (2000). Never leave your little one alone: Raising an Ifaluk child. In J. DeLoache & A. Gottlieb (Eds.), *A world of babies: Imagined child-care guides for seven societies* (pp. 199-222). New York, NY: Cambridge University Press.

Leahy-Warren, P., McCarthy, G., & Corcoran, P. (2012). First-time mothers: Social support, maternal parental self-efficacy and postnatal depression. *Journal of Clinical Nursing, 21,* 388-397.

Lean, S. C., Derricott, H., Jones, R. L., & Heazell, A. E. (2017). Advanced maternal age and adverse pregnancy outcomes: A systematic review and meta-analysis. *PloS One, 12*(10), e0186287.

Leaper, C., & Smith, T. E. (2004). A meta-analytic review of gender variations in children's language use: Talkativeness, affiliative speech, and assertive speech. *Developmental Psychology, 40,* 993-1027.

Leaper, C., Anderson, K. J., & Sanders, P. (1998). Moderators of gender effects on parents' talk to their children: A meta-analysis. *Developmental Psychology, 34*(1), 3.

LeBlanc, E. S., Patnode, C. D., Webber, E. M., Redmond, N., Rushkin, M., & O'Connor, E. A. (2018). Behavioral and pharmacotherapy weight loss interventions to prevent obesity-related morbidity and mortality in adults: Updated evidence report and systematic review for the US Preventive Services Task Force. *JAMA, 320*(11), 1172-1191.

Lecce, S., & Hughes, C. (2010). The Italian job?: Comparing theory of mind performance in British and Italian children. *British Journal of Developmental Psychology, 28*(4), 747-766.

Leclère, C., Viaux, S., Avril, M., Achard, C., Chetouani, M., Missonier, S., & Cohen, D. (2014). Why synchrony matters during mother-child interactions: A systematic review. *PloS One, 9*(12), e113571.

LeCuyer, E. A., & Zhang, Y. (2015). An integrative review of ethnic and cultural variation in socialization and children's self-regulation. *Journal of Advanced Nursing, 71*(4), 735-750.

Lederberg, A. R., Schick, B., & Spencer, P. E. (2013). Language and literacy development of deaf and hard-of-hearing children: Successes and challenges. *Developmental Psychology, 49*(1), 15.

Leduc, K., Williams, S., Gomez-Garibello, C., & Talwar, V. (2017). The contributions of mental state understanding and executive functioning to preschool-aged children's lie-telling. *British Journal of Developmental Psychology, 35*(2), 288-302.

Lee, C. M., & Afshari, N. A. (2017). The global state of cataract blindness. *Current Opinion in Ophthalmology, 28*(1), 98-103.

Lee, C., & Orazem, P. F. (2010). High school employment, school performance, and college entry. *Economics of Education Review, 29*(1), 29-39.

Lee, D. M., Nazroo, J., O'Connor, D. B., Blake, M., & Pendleton, N. (2016). Sexual health and well-being among older men and women in England: Findings from the English Longitudinal Study of Ageing. *Archives of Sexual Behavior, 45*(1), 133-144.

Lee, E., Cho, H. J., Olmstead, R., Levin, M. J., Oxman, M. N., & Irwin, M. R. (2013). Persistent sleep disturbance: A risk factor for recurrent depression in community-dwelling older adults. *Sleep, 36*(11), 1685-1691.

Lee, G. R., Netzer, J. K., & Coward, R. T. (1995). Depression among older parents: The role of intergenerational exchange. *Journal of Marriage and Family, 57,* 823-833.

Lee, G. Y., & Kisilevsky, B. S. (2014). Fetuses respond to father's voice but prefer mother's voice after birth. *Developmental Psychobiology, 56*(1), 1-11.

Lee, H. C., Huang, K. T., & Shen, W. K. (2011). Use of antiarrhythmic drugs in elderly patients. *Journal of Geriatric Cardiology: JGC, 8*(3), 184.

Lee, H. J., & Szinovacz, M. E. (2016). Positive, negative, and ambivalent interactions with family and friends: Associations with well-being. *Journal of Marriage and Family, 78*(3), 660-679.

Lee, I., Djoussé, L., & Sesso, H. D. (2010). Physical activity and weight gain prevention. *Journal of the American Medical Association, 303*(12), 1173-1179.

Lee, J. M., Appugliese, D., Kaciroti, N., Corwyn, R. F., Bradley, R., & Lumeng, J. C. (2007). Weight status in young girls and the onset of puberty. *Pediatrics, 119,* e624-e630.

Lee, J. T., & Bartolomei, M. S. (2013). X-inactivation, imprinting, and long noncoding RNAs in health and disease. *Cell, 152*(6), 1308-1323.

Lee, J., & Reeves, T. (2012). Revisiting the impact of NCLB high-stakes school accountability, capacity, and resources: State NAEP 1990-2009 reading and math achievement gaps and trends. *Educational Evaluation and Policy Analysis, 34*(2), 209-231.

Lee, K., Olson, D. R., & Torrance, N. (1999). Chinese children's understanding of false beliefs: The role of language. *Journal of Child Language, 26*(1), 1-21.

Lee, R. M., Grotevant, H. D., Hellerstedt, W. L., Gunnar, M. R., & The Minnesota International Adoption Project Team. (2006). Cultural socialization in families with internationally adopted children. *Journal of Family Psychology, 20*(4), 571-580.

Lee, R., Zhai, F., Brooks-Gunn, J., Han, W. J., & Waldfogel, J. (2014). Head Start participation and school readiness: Evidence from the early childhood longitudinal study-birth cohort. *Developmental Psychology, 50*(1), 202.

Lee, S. J., Ralston, H. J. P., Drey, E. A., Partridge, J. C., & Rosen, M. A. (2005). Fetal pain: A sys-tematic multidisciplinary review of the evidence. *Journal of the American Medical Association, 294,* 947-954.

Lee, V. E., Brooks-Gunn, J., Schnur, E., & Liaw, F. R. (1990). Are Head Start effects sustained? A longitudinal follow-up comparison of disadvantaged children attending Head Start, no preschool, and other preschool programs. *Child Development, 61*(2), 495-507.

Lee, Y., & Styne, D. (2013). Influences on the onset and tempo of puberty in human beings and implications for adolescent psychological development. *Hormones and Behavior, 64*(2), 250-261.

Leerkes, E. M., Blankson, A. N., & O'Brien, M. (2009). Differential effects of maternal sensitivity to infant distress and nondistress on social-emotional functioning. *Child Development, 80*(3), 762-775.

Leerkes, E. M., Weaver, J. M., & O'Brien, M. (2012). Differentiating maternal sensitivity to infant distress and non-distress. *Parenting, 12*(2-3), 175-184.

Lefkowitz, E. S., & Fingerman, K. L. (2003). Positive and negative emotional feelings and behaviors in mother-daughter ties in late life. *Journal of Family Psychology, 17,* 607-617.

Lefkowitz, E. S., & Gillen, M. M. (2006). "Sex is just a normal part of life": Sexuality in emerging adulthood. In J. J. Arnett & J. L. Tanner (Eds.), *Emerging adults in America: Coming of age in the 21st century* (pp. 235-255). Washington, DC: American Psychological Association.

Leger, K. A., Charles, S. T., Turiano, N. A., & Almeida, D. M. (2016). Personality and stressor-related affect. *Journal of Personality and Social Psychology, 111*(6), 917.

Lehmiller, J. J., VanderDrift, L. E., & Kelly, J. R. (2011). Sex differences in approaching friends with benefits relationships. *Journal of Sex Research, 48*(2-3), 275-284.

Lehto, R., & Stein, K. (2009). Death anxiety: An analysis of an evolving concept. *Research and Theory for Nursing Practice: An International Journal, 23,* 23-41.

Leinung, M., & Wu, C. (2017). The biologic basis of transgender identity: 2D:4D finger length ratios implicate a role for prenatal androgen activity. *Endocrine Practice, 23*(6), 669-671.

Lemaitre, H., Goldman, A. L., Sambataro, F., Verchinski, B. A., Meyer-Lindenberg, A., Weinberger, D. R., & Mattay, V. S. (2012). Normal age-related brain morphometric changes: Nonuniformity across cortical thickness, surface area and gray matter volume? *Neurobiology of Aging, 33*(3), 617-e1.

Leman, P. J., Ahmed, S., & Ozarow, L. (2005). Gender, gender relations, and the social dynamics of children's conversations. *Developmental Psychology, 41,* 64-74.

Lemon, B. W., Bengtson, V. L., & Peterson, J. A. (1972). An exploration of the activity theory of aging: Activity types and life satisfaction among in-movers to a retirement community. *Journal of Gerontology, 27*(4), 511-523.

Lenehan, M. E., Summers, M. J., Saunders, N. L., Summers, J. J., & Vickers, J. C. (2015). Relationship between education and age-related cognitive decline: A review of recent research. *Psychogeriatrics, 15*(2), 154-162.

Lennartz, C., Arundel, R., & Ronald, R. (2016). Younger adults and homeownership in Europe through the global financial crisis. *Population, Space and Place, 22*(8), 823-835.

Lenroot, R. K., & Giedd, J. N. (2006). Brain development in children and adolescents: Insights from anatomical magnetic resonance imaging. *Neuroscience & Biobehavioral Reviews, 30*(6), 718-729.

Leonardi-Bee, J., Nderi, M., & Britton, J. (2016). Smoking in movies and smoking initiation in adolescents: Systematic review and meta-analysis. *Addiction, 111*(10), 1750-1763.

Leopold, T., & Lechner, C. M. (2015). Parents' death and adult well-being: Gender, age, and adaptation to filial bereavement. *Journal of Marriage and Family, 77*(3), 747-760.

Leppink, E. W., Odlaug, B. L., Lust, K., Christenson, G., & Grant, J. E. (2016). The young and the stressed: Stress, impulse control, and health in college students. *The Journal of Nervous and Mental Disease, 204*(12), 931-938.

Leridon, H. (2008). A new estimate of permanent sterility by age: Sterility defined as the inability to conceive. *Population Studies, 62*(1), 15-24.

Lerman, R. I., Price, J., & Wilcox, W. B. (2017). Family structure and economic success across the life course. *Marriage & Family Review, 53*(8), 744-758.

Lesaux, N. K., Crosson, A. C., Kieffer, M. J., & Pierce, M. (2010). Uneven profiles: Language minority learners' word reading, vocabulary, and reading comprehension skills. *Journal of Applied Developmental Psychology, 31*(6), 475-483.

Leslie, A. M. (1995). A theory of agency. In D. Sperber, D. Premack, & A. J. Premack (Eds.), *Causal cognition* (pp. 121-149). Oxford, England: Clarendon Press.

Leslie, A. M., Friedman, O., & German, T. P. (2004). Core mechanisms in 'theory of mind.' *Trends in Cognitive Sciences, 8*(12), 528-533.

Lester, B. M., & Boukydis, C. F. Z. (1985). *Infant crying: Theoretical and research perspectives.* New York, NY: Plenum Press.

Lester, B. M., Kotelchuch, M., Spelke, E., Sellers, M. J., & Klein, R. E. (1974). Separation protest in Guatemalan infants: Cross-cultural and cognitive findings. *Developmental Psychology, 10*(1), 79.

Leszko, M., Elleman, L. G., Bastarache, E. D., Graham, E. K., & Mroczek, D. K. (2016). Future directions in the study of personality in adulthood and older age. *Gerontology, 62*(2), 210-215.

Levant, S., Chari, K., & DeFrances, C. J. (2015). Hospitalizations for patients aged 85 and over in the United States, 2000-2010. *NCHS Data Brief,* No. 182, 1-8.

LeVay, S. (1991). A difference in hypothalamic structure between heterosexual and homosexual men. *Science, 253,* 1034-1037.

Levine, C. S.; Miller, G. E.; Lachman, M. E.; Seeman, T. E., & Chen, E. (2017). Early life adversity and adult health. In C. Ryff & R. Krueger (Eds.), *Oxford handbook of integrative health science.* Oxford, England: Oxford University Press.

Available at https://cpb-us-e1.wpmucdn.com/sites.northwestern.edu/dist/6/1408/files/2016/09/Levineetal_ELA_revised-1zyee4s.pdf

Levine, L. J., & Edelstein, R. S. (2009). Emotion and memory narrowing: A review and goal-relevance approach. *Cognition and Emotion, 23*(5), 833–875.

LeVine, R. (1994). *Child care and culture: Lessons from Africa.* Cambridge, England: Cambridge University Press.

LeVine, R. A. (1980). Adulthood among the Gusii of Kenya. In N. J. Smelser & E. Homburger Erikson (Eds.), *Themes of work and love in adulthood* (pp. 77–104). Cambridge, MA: Harvard University Press.

LeVine, R. A. (1994). *Child care and culture: Lessons from Africa.* Cambridge, England: Cambridge University Press.

LeVine, R. A., & LeVine, S. (2016). *Do parents matter?: Why Japanese babies sleep soundly, Mexican siblings don't fight, and American families should just relax.* New York, NY: PublicAffairs.

Levine, R., Sato, S., Hashimoto, T., & Verma, J. (1995). Love and marriage in eleven cultures. *Journal of Cross Cultural Psychology, 26,* 554–571.

Levitt, H. M., & Ippolito, M. R. (2014). Being transgender: Navigating minority stressors and developing authentic self-presentation. *Psychology of Women Quarterly, 38*(1), 46–64.

Levy, B. R. (2003). Mind matters: Cognitive and physical effects of aging self-stereotypes. *Journal of Gerontology: Psychological Sciences, 58B,* P203–P211.

Levy, D. P., Sheiner, E., Wainstock, T., Sergienko, R., Landau, D., & Walfisch, A. (2017). Evidence that children born at early term (37–38 6/7 weeks) are at increased risk for diabetes and obesity-related disorders. *American Journal of Obstetrics and Gynecology, 217*(5), 588-e1.

Levy, T. B., Azar, S., Huberfeld, R., Siegel, A. M., & Strous, R.D. (2013). Attitudes towards euthanasia and assisted suicide: A comparison between psychiatrists and other physicians. *Bioethics, 27,* 402–408.

Lewin, A. C. (2017). Health and relationship quality later in life: A comparison of living apart together (LAT), first marriages, remarriages, and cohabitation. *Journal of Family Issues, 38*(12), 1754–1774.

Lewis, B. H., Legato, M., & Fisch, H. (2006). Medical implications of the male biological clock. *Journal of the American Medical Association, 19,* 2369–2371.

Lewis, J. M., and Kreider, R. M. (2015). *Remarriage in the United States.* Washington, DC: U.S. Census Bureau (American Community Survey Reports ACS-30).

Lewis, M. (1995). Self-conscious emotions. *American Scientist, 83,* 68–78.

Lewis, M. (1997). The self in self-conscious emotions. In S. G. Snodgrass & R. L. Thompson (Eds.), *The self across psychology: Self-recognition, self-awareness, and the self-concept: Vol. 818.* New York, NY: New York Academy of Sciences.

Lewis, M. (1998). Emotional competence and development. In D. Pushkar, W. Bukowski, A. E. Schwartzman, D. M. Stack, & D. R. White

(Eds.), *Improving competence across the life-span* (pp. 27–36). New York, NY: Plenum Press.

Lewis, M. (2007). Early emotional development. In A. Slater & M. Lewis (Eds.), *Introduction to infant development.* Malden, MA: Blackwell.

Lewis, M. I., & Butler, R. N. (1974). Life-review therapy: Putting memories to work in individual and group psychotherapy. *Geriatrics, 29,* 165–173.

Lewis, M., & Brooks, J. (1974). Self, other, and fear: Infants' reaction to people. In H. Lewis & L. Rosenblum (Eds.), *The origins of fear: The origins of behavior* (Vol. 2). New York, NY: Wiley.

Lewis-Morrarty, E., Degnan, K. A., Chronis-Tuscano, A., Rubin, K. H., Cheah, C. S., Pine, D. S., . . . Fox, N. A. (2012). Maternal over-control moderates the association between early childhood behavioral inhibition and adolescent social anxiety symptoms. *Journal of Abnormal Child Psychology, 40*(8), 1363–1373.

Lewkowicz, D. J. (1996). Perception of auditory-visual temporal synchrony in human infants. *Journal of Experimental Psychology: Human Perception and Performance, 22*(5), 1094.

Lewkowicz, D. J., & Hansen-Tift, A. M. (2012). Infants deploy selective attention to the mouth of a talking face when learning speech. *Proceedings of the National Academy of Sciences, 109*(5), 1431–1436.

Lew-Levy, S., Boyette, A. H., Crittenden, A. N., Hewlett, B. S., & Lamb, M. E. (2019). Gender-typed and gender-segregated play among Tanzanian Hadza and Congolese Bayaka hunter-gatherer children and adolescents. *Child Development.*

Lezak, M. D., Howieson, D. B., Bigler, E. D., & Tranel, D. (2012). *Neuropsychological Assessment* (5th ed.). New York, NY: Oxford University Press.

Li, J., Guan, Y., Akhtar, F., Xu, X., Yang, J. J., Chen, S., . . . Qiu, W. (2018). The association between alcohol consumption and telomere length: A meta-analysis focusing on observational studies. *BioRxiv, 374280.*

Li, J., Laursen, T. M., Precht, D. H., Olsen, J., & Mortensen, P. B. (2005). Hospitalization for mental illness among parents after the death of a child. *New England Journal of Medicine, 352*(12), 1190–1196.

Li, J., Zhao, H., Song, J. M., Zhang, J., Tang, Y. L., & Xin, C. M. (2015). A meta-analysis of risk of pregnancy loss and caffeine and coffee consumption during pregnancy. *International Journal of Gynecology & Obstetrics, 130*(2), 116–122.

Li, R., Chase, M., Jung, S., Smith, P. J. S., & Loeken, M. R. (2005). Hypoxic stress in diabetic pregnancy contributes to impaired embryo gene expression and defective development by inducing oxidative stress. *American Journal of Physiology: Endocrinology and Metabolism, 289,* 591–599.

Li, Y., & Ferraro, K. F. (2005). Volunteering and depression in later life: Social benefit or selection processes? *Journal of Health and Social Behavior, 46*(1), 68–84.

Li, Y., Baldassi, M., Johnson, E. J., & Weber, E. U. (2013). Complementary cognitive

capabilities, economic decision making, and aging. *Psychology and Aging, 28*(3), 595.

Liamputtong, P. (2009). Yu duan practices: The significance and implications for women's health in northern Thailand. *Thailand: Economic, Political and Social Issues,* 123–137.

Liamputtong, P. (Ed.). (2007). *Reproduction, childbearing and motherhood: A cross-cultural perspective.* New York, NY: Nova Science Publications.

Libertus, M. E., & Brannon, E. M. (2010). Stable individual differences in number discrimination in infancy. *Developmental Science, 13*(6), 900–906.

Lickliter, R., & Honeycutt, H. (2003). Developmental dynamics: Toward a biologically plausible evolutionary psychology. *Psychological Bulletin, 129,* 819–835.

Lidstone, J., Meins, E., & Fernyhough, C. (2011). Individual differences in children's private speech: Consistency across tasks, timepoints, and contexts. *Cognitive Development, 26*(3), 203–213.

Lie, A., Skogstad, M., Johannessen, H. A., Tynes, T., Mehlum, I. S., Nordby, K. C., . . . Tambs, K. (2016). Occupational noise exposure and hearing: A systematic review. *International Archives of Occupational and Environmental Health, 89*(3), 351–372.

Lieberman, M. (1996). *Doors close, doors open: Widows, grieving and growing.* New York, NY: Putnam.

Liefbroer, A. C., & Dourleijn, E. (2006). Unmarried cohabitation and union stability: Testing the role of diffusion using data from 16 European countries. *Demography, 43*(2), 203–221.

Liefbroer, A. C., Poortman, A. R., & Seltzer, J. A. (2015). Why do intimate partners live apart? Evidence on LAT relationships across Europe. *Demographic Research, 32,* 251.

Lien, Y. J., Chen, W. J., Hsiao, P. C., & Tsuang, H. C. (2015). Estimation of heritability for varied indexes of handedness. *Laterality: Asymmetries of Body, Brain and Cognition, 20*(4), 469–482.

Lighter, J., Phillips, M., Hochman, S., Sterling, S., Johnson, D., Francois, F., & Stachel, A. (2020). Obesity in patients younger than 60 years is a risk factor for Covid-19 hospital admission. *Clinical Infectious Diseases, 9*(10.1093).

Lilgendahl, J. P., & McAdams, D. P. (2011). Constructing stories of self-growth: How individual differences in patterns of autobiographical reasoning relate to well-being in midlife. *Journal of Personality, 79*(2), 391–428.

Lillard, A. S., & Peterson, J. (2011). The immediate impact of different types of television on young children's executive function. *Pediatrics, 128*(4), 644–649.

Lillard, A., & Curenton, S. (1999). Do young children understand what others feel, want, and know? *Young Children, 54*(5), 52–57.

Lillard, A., & Else-Quest, N. (2006). The early years: Evaluating Montessori education. *Science, 313,* 1893–1894.

Lin, C. H. (2014). Evaluating services for kinship care families: A systematic review. *Children and Youth Services Review, 36,* 32–41.

Lin, I. F., & Brown, S. L. (2012). Unmarried boomers confront old age: A national portrait. *The Gerontologist, 52*(2), 153–165.

Lin, I. F., Brown, S. L., & Hammersmith, A. M. (2017). Marital biography, social security receipt, and poverty. *Research on Aging, 39*(1), 86–110.

Lin, S., Hwang, S. A., Marshall, E. G., & Marion, D. (1998). Does paternal occupational lead exposure increase the risks of low birth weight or prematurity? *American Journal of Epidemiology, 148,* 173–181.

Lin, Y. W., & Bratton, S. C. (2015). A meta-analytic review of child-centered play therapy approaches. *Journal of Counseling & Development, 93*(1), 45–58.

Lin, Y., Seroude, L., & Benzer, S. (1998). Extended life-span and stress resistance in the Drosophila mutant methuselah. *Science, 282,* 943–946.

Lind, A., & Brzuzy, S. (2008). *Battleground: Women, gender, and sexuality.* Westport, CT: Greenwood Publishing Group.

Lindau, S. T., & Gavrilova, N. (2010). Sex, health, and years of sexually active life gained due to good health: evidence from two US population based cross sectional surveys of ageing. *BMJ, 340,* c810.

Lindau, S. T., Schumm, P., Laumann, E. O., Levinson, W., O'Muircheartaigh, C. A., & Waite, L. J. (2007). A study of sexuality and health among older adults in the United States. *New England Journal of Medicine, 357,* 762–774.

Lindberg, L. D., Maddow-Zimet, I., & Boonstra, H. (2016). Changes in adolescents' receipt of sex education, 2006–2013. *Journal of Adolescent Health, 58*(6), 621–627.

Lindberg, S. M., Hyde, J. S., Petersen, J. L., & Linn, M. C. (2010). New trends in gender and mathematics performance: a meta-analysis. *Psychological Bulletin, 136*(6), 1123.

Lindell, A. K., & Campione-Barr, N. (2017). Continuity and change in the family system across the transition from adolescence to emerging adulthood. *Marriage & Family Review, 53*(4), 388–416.

Lindsay, D. S. (2015). Replication in psychological science. *Psychological Science, 26,* 1827–1832.

Lindsay, R., Gallagher, J. C., Kleerekoper, M., & Pickar, J. H. (2002). Effect of lower doses of conjugated equine estrogens with and without medroxyprogesterone acetate on bone in early postmenopausal women. *Journal of the American Medical Association, 287,* 2668–2676.

Lindsey, E. W., Cremeens, P. R., & Caldera, Y. M. (2010). Mother–child and father–child mutuality in two contexts: Consequences for young children's peer relationships. *Infant and Child Development: An International Journal of Research and Practice, 19*(2), 142–160.

Lindwall, M., Cimino, C. R., Gibbons, L. E., Mitchell, M. B., Benitez, A., Brown, C. L., . . . MacDonald, S. W. (2012). Dynamic associations of change in physical activity and change in cognitive function: Coordinated analyses of four longitudinal studies. *Journal of Aging Research, 2012.*

Linnet, K. M., Wisborg, K., Obel, C., Secher, N. J., Thomsen, P. H., Agerbo, E., & Henriksen, T. B. (2005). Smoking during pregnancy and the risk of hyperkinetic disorder in offspring. *Pediatrics, 116,* 462–467.

Lipari, R. N., Hughes, A., & Bose, J. (2016). Driving under the influence of alcohol and illicit drugs. In *The CBHSQ Report.* Rockville, MD: Substance Abuse and Mental Health Services Administration.

Lipka, M., & McClendon, D. (2017). *Why people with no religion are projected to decline as a share of the world's population* [Fact Tank report]. Retrieved form www.pewresearch.org/fact-tank/2017/04/07/why-people-with-no-religion-are-projected-to-decline-as-a-share-of-the-worlds-population/

Lippi, G., & Cervellin, G. (2016). The interplay between genetics, epigenetics and environment in modulating the risk of coronary heart disease. *Annals of Translational Medicine, 4*(23).

Liszkowski, U., Carpenter, M., & Tomasello, M. (2008). Twelve-month-olds communicate helpfully and appropriately for knowledgeable and ignorant partners. *Cognition, 108,* 732–739.

Litt, J. S., Gerry Taylor, H., Margevicius, S., Schluchter, M., Andreias, L., & Hack, M. (2012). Academic achievement of adolescents born with extremely low birth weight. *Acta Paediatrica, 101*(12), 1240–1245.

Little, T. D., Rodkin, P. C., & Hawley, P. H. (Eds.). (2007). *Aggression and adaptation: The bright side to bad behavior.* New York, NY: Routledge.

Littleton, H., Breitkopf, C., & Berenson, A. (2006, August 13). *Correlates of anxiety symptoms during pregnancy and association with perinatal outcomes: A meta-analysis.* Presentation at the 114th annual convention of the American Psychological Association, New Orleans, LA.

Litwin, H., & Shiovitz-Ezra, S. (2006). The association between activity and well-being in later life: What really matters? *Aging and Society, 26*(2), 225–242.

Liu, C. J., Shiroy, D. M., Jones, L. Y., & Clark, D. O. (2014). Systematic review of functional training on muscle strength, physical functioning, and activities of daily living in older adults. *European Review of Aging and Physical Activity, 11*(2), 95–106.

Liu, D., Li, L., Wu, X., Zheng, D., Wang, J., Yang, L., & Zheng, C. (2020, March 18). Pregnancy and perinatal outcomes of women with coronavirus disease (COVID-19) pneumonia: A preliminary analysis. *American Journal of Roentgenology,* 1–6.

Liu, D., Sabbagh, M. A., Gehring, W. J., & Wellman, H. M. (2009). Neural correlates of children's theory of mind development. *Child Development, 80*(2), 318–326.

Liu, D., Wellman, H. M., Tardif, T., & Sabbagh, M. A. (2008). Theory of mind development in Chinese children: A meta-analysis of false-belief understanding across cultures and languages. *Developmental Psychology, 44*(2), 523.

Liu, G., Zong, G., Doty, R. L., & Sun, Q. (2016). Prevalence and risk factors of taste and smell impairment in a nationwide representative sample of the US population: A cross-sectional study. *BMJ Open, 6*(11), e013246.

Liu, H., Yang, Y., Xia, Y., Zhu, W., Leak, R. K., Wei, Z., . . . Hu, X. (2017). Aging of cerebral white matter. *Ageing Research Reviews, 34,* 64–76.

Liu, J., Raine, A., Venables, P. H., Dalais, C., & Mednick, S. A. (2003). Malnutrition at age 3 years and lower cognitive ability at age 11 years. *Archives of Pediatric and Adolescent Medicine, 157,* 593–600.

Liu, J., Zhang, A., & Li, L. (2012). Sleep duration and overweight/obesity in children: Review and implications for pediatric nursing. *Journal for Specialists in Pediatric Nursing, 17*(3), 193–204.

Liu, K., Daviglus, M. L., Loria, C. M., Colangelo, L. A., Spring, B., Moller, A. C., & Lloyd-Jones, D. M. (2012). Healthy lifestyle through young adulthood and the presence of low cardiovascular disease risk profile in middle age. *Circulation, 125*(8), 996–1004.

Liu, L., & Kager, R. (2014). Perception of tones by infants learning a non-tone language. *Cognition, 133*(2), 385–394.

Liu, M. Y., Li, N., Li, W. A., & Khan, H. (2017). Association between psychosocial stress and hypertension: A systematic review and meta-analysis. *Neurological Research, 39*(6), 573–580.

Liu, S., Xiao, W. S., Xiao, N. G., Quinn, P. C., Zhang, Y., Chen, H., . . . Lee, K. (2015). Development of visual preference for own-versus other-race faces in infancy. *Developmental Psychology, 51*(4), 500.

Livingston, G. & Thomas, D. (2019). Why is the teen birth rate falling? *FactTank: News in the Numbers, Pew Research Center.* Retrieved from www.pewresearch.org/fact-tank/2019/08/02/why-is-the-teen-birth-rate-falling/

Livingston, G. (2014). Chapter 2: *The demographics of remarriage* [Pew Research Center report]. Retrieved from www.pewsocialtrends.org/2014/11/14/chapter-2-the-demographics-of-re-marriage/

Livingston, G. (2014). Four in ten couples are saying "I do" again: Growing number of adults have remarried [Pew Research Center report]. Retrieved from www.pewsocialtrends.org/2014/11/14/four-in-ten-couples-are-saying-i-do-again/

Livingston, G. (2018). Stay-at-home moms and dads account for about one-in-five U.S. parents [Pew Social Trends news report]. Retrieved from www.pewresearch.org/fact-tank/2018/09/24/stay-at-home-moms-and-dads-account-for-about-one-in-five-u-s-parents/

Livingston, G. (2018). *The changing profile of unmarried parents.* Retrieved from www.pewsocialtrends.org/2018/04/25/the-changing-profile-of-unmarried-parents/

Livingston, G., & Parker, K. (2010, September 9). *Since the start of the Great Recession, more children raised by grandparents.* Retrieved from http://pewsocialtrends.org/2010/09/09/since-the-start-of-the-great-recession-more-children-raised-by-grandparents/

Livingston, G., & Parker, K. (2019). *8 facts about American dads* [Pew Research Center data brief]. Retrieved from www.pewresearch.org/fact-tank/2019/06/12/fathers-day-facts/

Livingston. G. (2018). *7 facts about U.S. moms* [Pew Research Center news report]. Retrieved from www.pewresearch.org/fact-tank/2018/05/10/facts-about-u-s-mothers/.

Lloyd, J., Patterson, T., & Muers, J. (2016). The positive aspects of caregiving in dementia: A critical review of the qualitative literature. *Dementia, 15*(6), 1534-1561.

Lobar, S. L., Youngblut, J. M., & Brooten, D. (2006). Cross-cultural beliefs, ceremonies, and rituals surrounding death of a loved one. *Pediatric Nursing, 32*(1), 44.

Lobo, M. A., & Galloway, J. C. (2012). Enhanced handling and positioning in early infancy advances development throughout the first year. *Child Development, 83*(4), 1290-1302.

Lobo, V., Patil, A., Phatak, A., & Chandra, N. (2010). Free radicals, antioxidants and functional foods: Impact on human health. *Pharmacognosy Reviews, 4*(8), 118.

Lobstein, T., Jackson-Leach, R., Moodie, M. L., Hall, K. D., Gortmaker, S. L., Swinburn, B. A., James, W. P. T., Wang, Y., & McPherson, K. (2015). Child and adolescent obesity: Part of a bigger picture. *Lancet, 385,* 2510-2520.

LoBue, V., & DeLoache, J. (2011). Pretty in pink: The early development of gender-stereotyped colour preferences. *British Journal of Developmental Psychology, 29*(3), 656-667. doi: 10.1111/ j.2044-835X.2011.02027.x

LoBue, V., Rakison, D. H., & DeLoache, J. S. (2010). Threat perception across the life span: Evidence for multiple converging pathways. *Current Directions in Psychological Science, 19*(6), 375-379.

Lock, A., Young, A., Service, V., & Chandler, P. (1990). Some observations on the origin of the pointing gesture. In V. Volterra & C. J. Erting (Eds.), *From gesture to language in hearing and deaf children.* New York, NY: Springer.

Lock, M. (1993). The politics of mid-life and menopause: Ideologies for the second sex in North America and Japan. In S. Lindenbaum & M. M. Lock (Eds.), *Knowledge, Power, and Practice: The Anthropology of Medicine and Every Day Life* (pp. 330-336). Oakland, CA: University of California Press.

Lockenhoff, C. E., Terracciano, A., & Costa, P. T. (2009). Five-factor model personality traits and the retirement transition: Longitudinal and cross-sectional associations. *Psychology and Aging, 24*(3), 722-728.

Lockhart, S. N., & DeCarli, C. (2014). Structural imaging measures of brain aging. *Neuropsychology Review, 24*(3), 271-289.

Lockwood, P. L., Sebastian, C. L., McCrory, E. J., Hyde, Z. H., Gu, X., De Brito, S. A., & Viding, E. (2013). Association of callous traits with reduced neural response to others' pain in children with conduct problems. *Current Biology, 23*(10), 901-905.

Lohse, N., Hansen, A. E., Pedersen, G., Kronborg, G., Gerstoft, J., Sørensen, H. T., . . . Obel, N. (2007). Survival of persons with and without HIV infection in Denmark, 1995-2005. *Annals of Internal Medicine, 146,* 87-95.

Loo, S. Y., Chen, B. Y., Yu, O. H. Y., Azoulay, L., & Renoux, C. (2017). Testosterone replacement therapy and the risk of stroke in men: A systematic review. *Maturitas, 106,* 31-37.

Looker, A. C., Sarafrazi, N. I., Fan, B., & Shepherd, J. A. (2017). FRAX-based estimates of 10-year probability of hip and major osteoporotic fracture among adults aged 40 and over:

United States, 2013 and 2014. *National Health Statistics Reports, 103,* 1-16. Hyattsville, MD: National Center for Health Statistics.

Lopes, P. N., Brackett, M. A., Nezlek, J. B., Schütz, A., Sellin, L., & Salovey, P. (2004). Emotional intelligence and social interaction. *Personality and Social Psychology Bulletin, 30,* 1018-1034.

Lopes, P. N., Grewal, D., Kadis, J., Gall, M., & Salovey, P. (2006). Evidence that emotional intelligence is related to job performance and affect and attitudes at work. *Psicothema, 18*(Suppl. 1), 132-138.

Lopes, P. N., Salovey, P., & Straus, R. (2003). Emotional intelligence, personality, and the perceived quality of social relationships. *Personality and Individual Differences, 35,* 641-658.

Lopes, V. P., Rodrigues, L. P., Maia, J. A., & Malina, R. M. (2011). Motor coordination as predictor of physical activity in childhood. *Scandinavian Journal of Medicine & Science in Sports, 21*(5), 663-669.

Lopez-Gay, A., Esteve, A., López-Colás, J., Permanyer, I., Turu, A., Kennedy, S., . . . Lesthaeghe, R. (2014). A geography of unmarried cohabitation in the Americas. *Demographic Research, 30,* 1621.

Loprinzi, P. D., & Davis, R. E. (2016). Secular trends in parent-reported television viewing among children in the United States, 2001-2012. *Child: Care, Health and Development, 42*(2), 288-291.

Lord, J., & Cruchaga, C. (2014). The epigenetic landscape of Alzheimer's disease. *Nature Neuroscience, 17*(9), 1138-1140.

Lord, S. R., Smith, S. T., & Menant, J. C. (2010). Vision and falls in older people: risk factors and intervention strategies. *Clinics in Geriatric Medicine, 26*(4), 569-581.

Lorenz, K. (1957). Comparative study of behavior. In C. H. Schiller (Ed.), *Instinctive behavior.* New York, NY: International Universities Press.

Loth, K. A., Watts, A. W., Van Den Berg, P., & Neumark- Sztainer, D. (2015). Does body satisfaction help or harm overweight teens? A 10-year longitudinal study of the relationship between body satisfaction and body mass index. *Journal of Adolescent Health, 57*(5), 559-561.

Lovato, N., Lack, L., Wright, H., & Kennaway, D. J. (2014). Evaluation of a brief treatment program of cognitive behavior therapy for insomnia in older adults. *Sleep, 37*(1), 117-126.

Lovelace, E. A. (1990). Basic concepts in cognition and aging. In E. A. Lovelace (Ed.), *Aging and cognition: Mental processes, self-awareness, and interventions* (pp. 1-28). Amsterdam, the Netherlands: North-Holland, Elsevier.

Low, L. F., Harrison, F., & Lackersteen, S. M. (2013). Does personality affect risk for dementia? A systematic review and meta-analysis. *The American Journal of Geriatric Psychiatry, 21*(8), 713-728.

Low, S., Shortt, J. W., & Snyder, J. (2012). Sibling influences on adolescent substance use: The role of modeling, collusion, and conflict. *Development and Psychopathology, 24*(1), 287-300.

Lowe, C. J., Safati, A., & Hall, P. A. (2017). The neurocognitive consequences of sleep restriction: A meta-analytic review. *Neuroscience & Biobehavioral Reviews, 80,* 586-604.

Lowe, J. R., MacLean, P. C., Duncan, A. F., Aragón, C., Schrader, R. M., Caprihan, A., & Phillips, J. P. (2012). Association of maternal interaction with emotional regulation in 4- and 9-month infants during the Still Face Paradigm. *Infant Behavior and Development, 35*(2), 295-302.

Lowery, E. M., Brubaker, A. L., Kuhlmann, E., & Kovacs, E. J. (2013). The aging lung. *Clinical Interventions in Aging, 8,* 1489.

Lozoff, B., Jordan, B., & Malone, S. (1988). Childbirth in cross-cultural perspective. *Marriage & Family Review, 12*(3-4), 35-60.

Lu, B., Kumar, A., Castellsagué, X., & Giuliano, A. R. (2011). Efficacy and safety of prophylactic vaccines against cervical HPV infection and diseases among women: A systematic review & meta-analysis. *BMC Infectious Diseases, 11*(1), 13

Lu, M. C. (2018). Reducing maternal mortality in the United States. *JAMA, 320*(12), 1237-1238.

Lu, P. H., Lee, G. J., Tishler, T. A., Meghpara, M., Thompson, P. M., & Bartzokis, G. (2013). Myelin breakdown mediates age-related slowing in cognitive processing speed in healthy elderly men. *Brain and Cognition, 81*(1), 131-138.

Lu, T., Pan, Y., Kao, S.-Y., Li, C., Cohane, I., Chan, J., & Yankner, B. A. (2004). Gene regulation and DNA damage in the ageing human brain. *Nature, 429,* 883-891.

Lubienski, C., Puckett, T., & Brewer, T. J. (2013). Does homeschooling "work"? A critique of the empirical claims and agenda of advocacy organizations. *Peabody Journal of Education, 88*(3), 378-392.

Luby, J. L. (2015). Poverty's most insidious damage: The developing brain. *JAMA Pediatrics, 169*(9), 810-811.

Lucas, A. J., & Dyment, J. E. (2010). Where do children choose to play on the school ground? The influence of green design. *Education 3-13, 38*(2), 177-189.

Lucas, R. E., & Diener, E. (2009). Personality and subjectivity of well-being. In E. Diener (Ed.), *The science of well-being: The collected works of Ed Diener* (pp. 75-102). New York, NY: Springer.

Lucas, R. E., Clark, A. E., Georgellis, Y., & Diener, E. (2003). Reexamining adaptation and the set point model of happiness: Reactions to changes in marital status. *Journal of Personality and Social Psychology, 84,* 527-539.

Lucas-Thompson, R. G., Goldberg, W. A., & Prause, J. (2010). Maternal work early in the lives of children and its distal associations with achievement and behavior problems: A meta-analysis. *Psychological Bulletin, 136* (6), 915-942.

Luciana, M. (2010). Adolescent brain development: Introduction to the special issue. *Brain and Cognition, 72*(1), 1-5.

Lucile Packard Children's Hospital at Stanford. (2009). *Failure to thrive.* Retrieved from www.lpch.org/DiseaseHealthInfo/Health/Library/growth/thrive.html

Luck, T., Roehr, S., Rodriguez, F. S., Schroeter, M. L., Witte, A. V., Hinz, A., . . . Villringer, A. (2018). Memory-related subjective cognitive symptoms in the adult population: Prevalence and associated factors–results of the LIFE-Adult-Study. *BMC Psychology, 6*(1), 23.

Luders, E., Thompson, P. M., & Toga, A. W. (2010). The development of the corpus callosum in the healthy human brain. *Journal of Neuroscience, 30*(33), 10985–10990.

Luders, E., Toga, A. W., & Thompson, P. M. (2014). Why size matters: Differences in brain volume account for apparent sex differences in callosal anatomy: The sexual dimorphism of the corpus callosum. *Neuroimage, 84*, 820–824.

Luhmann, M., & Hawkley, L. C. (2016). Age differences in loneliness from late adolescence to oldest old age. *Developmental Psychology, 52*(6), 943.

Luhmann, M., Hofmann, W., Eid, M., & Lucas, R. E. (2012). Subjective well-being and adaptation to life events: A meta-analysis. *Journal of Personality and Social Psychology, 102*(3), 592.

Luk, B. H. K., & Loke, A. Y. (2015). The impact of infertility on the psychological well-being, marital relationships, sexual relationships, and quality of life of couples: A systematic review. *Journal of Sex & Marital Therapy, 41*(6), 610–625.

Lumey, L. H., Khalangot, M. D., & Vaiserman, A. M. (2015). Association between type 2 diabetes and prenatal exposure to the Ukraine famine of 1932-33: A retrospective cohort study. *The Lancet Diabetes & Endocrinology, 3*(10), 787–794.

Lumey, L. H., Stein, A. D., & Susser, E. (2011). Prenatal famine and adult health. *Annual Review of Public Health, 32*, 237–262.

Luna, B., Garver, K. E., Urban, T. A., Lazar, N. A., & Sweeney, J. A. (2004). Maturation of cognitive processes from late childhood to adulthood. *Child Development, 75*, 1357–1372.

Lund, D. A. (1993). Caregiving. In R. Kastenbaum (Ed.), *Encyclopedia of adult development* (pp. 57–63). Phoenix, AZ: Oryx Press.

Lund, H. D., Reider, B. D., Whiting, A. B., & Prichard, J. R. (2010). Sleep patterns and predictors of disturbed sleep in a large population of college students. *Journal of Adolescent Health, 46*(2), 125–132.

Lundberg, S., & Pollak, R. A. (2014). Cohabitation and the uneven retreat from marriage in the United States, 1950-2010. In *Human capital in history: The American record* (pp. 241–272). Chicago, IL: University of Chicago Press.

Luo, L., & Craik, F. I. M. (2008). Aging and memory: A cognitive approach. *Canadian Journal of Psychiatry, 53*(6), 346–353.

Luo, R., Tamis-LeMonda, C. S., & Song, L. (2013). Chinese parents' goals and practices in early childhood. *Early Childhood Research Quarterly, 28*(4), 843–857.

Luo, Y., Hawkley, L. C., Waite, L. J., & Cacioppo, J. T. (2012). Loneliness, health, and mortality in old age: A national longitudinal study. *Social Science & Medicine, 74*(6), 907–914.

Lustig, C., & Flegal, K. (2008). Age differences in memory: Demands on cognitive control and association processes. *Advances in Psychology, 139*, 137–149.

Luthar, S. S., & Latendresse, S. J. (2005). Children of the affluent: Challenges to well-being. *Current Directions in Psychological Science, 14*, 49–53.

Lykes, V. A., & Kemmelmeier, M. (2014). What predicts loneliness? Cultural difference between individualistic and collectivistic societies in Europe. *Journal of Cross-Cultural Psychology, 45*(3), 468–490.

Lynch, A. D., Lerner, R. M., & Leventhal, T. (2013). Adolescent academic achievement and school engagement: An examination of the role of school-wide peer culture. *Journal of Youth and Adolescence, 42*(1), 6–19.

Lyngstad, T. H. (2013). Bereavement and divorce: Does the death of a child affect parents' marital stability? *Family Science, 4*(1), 79–86.

Lynn, R., & Meisenberg, G. (2010). National IQs calculated and validated for 108 nations. *Intelligence, 38*(4), 353–360.

Lynn, R., & Vanhanen, T. (2012). National IQs: A review of their educational, cognitive, economic, political, demographic, sociological, epidemiological, geographic and climatic correlates. *Intelligence, 40*(2), 226–234.

Lynn, R., Meisenberg, G., Mikk, J., & Williams, A. (2007). National IQs predict differences in scholastic achievement in 67 countries. *Journal of Biosocial Science, 39*(6), 861–874.

Lyons-Ruth, K., Alpern, L., & Repacholi, B. (1993). Disorganized infant attachment classification and maternal psychosocial problems as predictors of hostile-aggressive behavior in the preschool classroom. *Child Development, 64*, 572–585.

Lytton, H., & Romney, D. M. (1991). Parents' differential socialization of boys and girls: A meta-analysis. *Psychological Bulletin, 109*(2), 267.

Lyyra, T., & Heikkinen, R. (2006). Perceived social support and mortality in older people. *Journal of Gerontology: Social Sciences, 61B*, S147–S152.

Ma, V., & Schoeneman, T. J. (1997). Individualism versus collectivism: A comparison of Kenyan and American self-concepts. *Basic and Applied Social Psychology, 19*(2), 261–273.

Ma, W., Golinkoff, R. M., Houston, D. M., & Hirsh-Pasek, K. (2011). Word learning in infant- and adult-directed speech. *Language Learning and Development, 7*(3), 185–201.

Maccoby, E. (2000). A developmental account. In A. Pellegrini & P. Smith (Eds.), *Psychology of Education: Major Themes* (p. 323). New York, NY: Routledge.

Maccoby, E. E. (1984). Middle childhood in the context of the family. In W. A. Collins (Ed.), *Development during middle childhood.* Washington, DC: National Academy.

Maccoby, E. E. (1990). Gender and relationships: A developmental account. *American Psychologist, 45*(4), 513.

Maccoby, E. E. (1992). The role of parents in the socialization of children: A historical overview. *Developmental Psychology, 28*(6), 1006–1017.

Maccoby, E. E. (2002). Gender and group process: A developmental perspective. *Current Directions in Psychological Science, 11*, 54–58.

Maccoby, E. E., & Jacklin, C. N. (1987). Gender segregation in childhood. *Advances in Child Development and Behavior, 20*, 239–287.

Maccoby, E. E., & Martin, J. A. (1983). Socialization in the context of the family: Parent-child interaction. In P. H. Mussen (Series Ed.) & E. M. Hetherington (Vol. Ed.), *Handbook of child psychology: Vol. 4. Socialization, personality, and social development* (pp. 1–101). New York, NY: Wiley.

MacDonald, W. L., & DeMaris, A. (1996). Parenting stepchildren and biological children. *Journal of Family Issues, 17*, 5–25.

Macdonald-Wallis, K., Jago, R., Page, A. S., Brockman, R., & Thompson, J. L. (2011). School-based friendship networks and children's physical activity: A spatial analytical approach. *Social Science & Medicine, 73*(1), 6–12.

MacDorman, M. F., & Declercq, E. (2018). The failure of United States maternal mortality reporting and its impact on women's lives. *Obstetrical & Gynecological Survey, 73*(11), 615–616.

MacDorman, M. F., & Gregory, E. C. (2015). Fetal and perinatal mortality: United States, 2013. *National Vital Statistics Reports, 64*(8), 1–24. Hyattsville, MD: National Center for Health Statistics.

MacDorman, M. F., & Mathews, T. J. (2009). Behind international rankings of infant mortality: How the United States compares with Europe. *NCHS Data Brief, 23*. Hyattsville, MD: National Center for Health Statistics.

MacDorman, M. F., Menacker, F., & Declercq, E. (2010). Trends and characteristics of home and other out-of-hospital births in the United States, 1990-2006. *National Vital Statistics Reports, 58*(11), 1–14, 16.

Machaalani, R., & Waters, K. A. (2014). Neurochemical abnormalities in the brainstem of the sudden infant death syndrome (SIDS). *Paediatric Respiratory Reviews, 15*(4), 293–300.

Machón, M., Larrañaga, I., Dorronsoro, M., Vrotsou, K., & Vergara, I. (2017). Health-related quality of life and associated factors in functionally independent older people. *BMC Geriatrics, 17*(1), 19.

MacKenzie, M. J., Nicklas, E., Waldfogel, J., & Brooks-Gunn, J. (2013). Spanking and child development across the first decade of life. *Pediatrics, 132*(5), e1118–e1125.

MacLean, P. S., Wing, R. R., Davidson, T., Epstein, L., Goodpaster, B., Hall, K. D., . . . Rothman, A. J. (2015). NIH working group report: Innovative research to improve maintenance of weight loss. *Obesity, 23*(1), 7–15.

Macmillan, R., McMorris, B. J., & Kruttschnitt, C. (2004). Linked lives: Stability and change in maternal circumstances and trajectories of antisocial behavior in children. *Child Development, 75*, 205–220.

Madabhushi, R., Pan, L., & Tsai, L. H. (2014). DNA damage and its links to neurodegeneration. *Neuron, 83*(2), 266–282.

Madden, D. J., & Langley, I. K. (2003). Age-related changes in selective attention and perceptual load during visual search. *Psychology & Aging, 18*, 54–67.

Madden, M., Lenhart, A., Duggan, M., Cortesi, S., & Gasser, U. (2013). *Teens and technology 2013* (pp. 1-19). Washington, DC: Pew Internet & American Life Project.

Madigan, S., Ly, A., Rash, C. L., Van Ouytsel, J., & Temple, J. R. (2018). Prevalence of multiple forms of sexting behavior among youth: A systematic review and meta-analysis. *JAMA Pediatrics, 172*(4), 327-335.

Madigan, S., Wade, M., Tarabulsy, G., Jenkins, J. M., & Shouldice, M. (2014). Association between abuse history and adolescent pregnancy: A meta-analysis. *Journal of Adolescent Health, 55*(2), 151-159.

Maestas, N. (2010). *Encouraging work at older ages. Testimony presented before the Senate Finance Committee on July 15, 2010 (CT-350).* Rand Corporation. Retrieved from http://finance.senate.gov/imo/media/doc/071510nmtest.pdf

Magee, C. A., Heaven, P. C., & Miller, L. M. (2013). Personality change predicts self-reported mental and physical health. *Journal of Personality, 81*(3), 324-334.

Magnuson, K., & Berger, L. M. (2009). Family structure states and transitions: Associations with children's well-being during middle childhood. *Journal of Marriage and Family, 71*(3), 575-591.

Maguire, D. J., Taylor, S., Armstrong, K., Shaffer-Hudkins, E., Germain, A. M., Brooks, S. S., . . . & Clark, L. (2016). Long-term outcomes of infants with neonatal abstinence syndrome. *Neonatal Network, 35*(5), 277-286.

Mahalik, J. R., Levine Coley, R., McPherran Lombardi, C., Doyle Lynch, A., Markowitz, A. J., & Jaffee, S. R. (2013). Changes in health risk behaviors for males and females from early adolescence through early adulthood. *Health Psychology, 32*(6), 685.

Mahatmya, D., & Lohman, B. (2011). Predictors of late adolescent delinquency: The protective role of after-school activities in low-income families. *Children and Youth Services Review, 33*(7), 1309-1317.

Maher, J. P., Pincus, A. L., Ram, N., & Conroy, D. E. (2015). Daily physical activity and life satisfaction across adulthood. *Developmental Psychology, 51*(10), 1407.

Main, M. (1995). Recent studies in attachment: Overview, with selected implications for clinical work. In S. Goldberg, R. Muir, & J. Kerr (Eds.), *Attachment theory: Social, developmental, and clinical perspectives* (pp. 407-470). Hillsdale, NJ: Analytic Press.

Main, M., & Solomon, J. (1986). Discovery of an insecure, disorganized/disoriented attachment pattern: Procedures, findings, and implications for the classification of behavior. In M. Yogman & T. B. Brazelton (Eds.), *Affective development in infancy.* Norwood, NJ: Ablex.

Main, M., Kaplan, N., & Cassidy, J. (1985). Security in infancy, childhood and adulthood: A move to the level of representation. In I. Bretherton & E. Waters (Eds.), *Growing points in attachment. Monographs of the Society for Research in Child Development, 50*(1-20), 66-104.

Maisonet, M., Christensen, K. Y., & Rubin, C., Holmes, A., Flanders, A. H., Heron, J., . . . Ong, K. K. (2010). Role of prenatal characteristics and early growth on pubertal attainment of British girls. *Pediatrics, 126*(3), 591-600.

Malabarey, O. T., Balayla, J., Klam, S. L., Shrim, A., & Abenhaim, H. A. (2012). Pregnancies in young adolescent mothers: a population-based study on 37 million births. *Journal of Pediatric and Adolescent Gynecology, 25*(2), 98-102.

Malaspina, D., Gilman, C., & Kranz, T. M. (2015). Paternal age and mental health of offspring. *Fertility and Sterility, 103*(6), 1392-1396.

Malcom, N. L. (2011). Images of heaven and the spiritual afterlife: Qualitative analysis of children's storybooks about death, dying, grief, and bereavement. *OMEGA-Journal of Death and Dying, 62*(1), 51-76.

Malik, V. S., Pan, A., Willett, W. C., & Hu, F. B. (2013). Sugar-sweetened beverages and weight gain in children and adults: A systematic review and meta-analysis. *The American Journal of Clinical Nutrition, 98*(4), 1084-1102.

Malloy, M. H. (2008). Impact of Cesarean section on neonatal mortality rates among very preterm infants in the United States, 2000-2003. *Pediatrics, 122,* 285-292.

Malmqvist, E., Liew, Z., Källén, K., Rignell-Hydbom, A., Rittner, R., Rylander, L., & Ritz, B. (2017). Fetal growth and air pollution—a study on ultrasound and birth measures. *Environmental Research, 152,* 73-80.

Mampe, B., Friederici, A. D., Christophe, A., & Wermke, K. (2009). Newborns' cry melody is shaped by their native language. *Current Biology, 19*(23), 1994-1997. doi: 10.1016/j.cub.2009.09.064

Manago, A. M., Taylor, T., & Greenfield, P. M. (2012). Me and my 400 friends: The anatomy of college students' Facebook networks, their communication patterns, and well-being. *Developmental Psychology, 48*(2), 369.

Mancillas, A. (2006). Challenging the stereotypes about only children: A review of the literature and implications for practice. *Journal of Counseling & Development, 84*(3), 268-275.

Mancini, A. D., & Bonanno, G. A. (2006). Marital closeness, functional disability, and adjustment in late life. *Psychology and Aging, 21,* 600-610.

Mancini, A. D., Bonanno, G. A., & Clark, A. E. (2011). Stepping off the hedonic treadmill: Individual differences in response to marriage, divorce, and spousal bereavement. *Journal of Individual Differences, 32*(3), 144-152.

Mancini, A. D., Sinan, B., & Bonanno, G. A. (2015). Predictors of prolonged grief, resilience, and recovery among bereaved spouses. *Journal of Clinical Psychology, 71*(12), 1245-1258.

Mandara, J., Gaylord-Harden, N. K., Richards, M. H., & Ragsdale, B. L. (2009). The effects of change in racial identity and self-esteem on changes in African American adolescents' mental health. *Child Development, 80*(6), 1660-1675.

Mandler, J. M. (1998). Representation. In D. Kuhn & R. S. Siegler (Eds.), *Handbook of child psychology: Vol. 2. Cognition, perception, and language* (5th ed., pp. 255-308). New York, NY: Wiley.

Mandler, J. M. (2007). On the origins of the conceptual system. *American Psychologist, 62,* 741-751.

Manning, W. D. (2013). Trends in cohabitation: Over twenty years of change, 1987-2010. *NCFMR Family Profiles, 54,* 29-41.

Manning, W. D. (2017). Cohabitation and child well-being. In D. Besharov (Ed.), *Family and child well-being after welfare reform* (pp. 113-128). New York, NY: Routledge.

Manning, W. D., Fettro, M. N., & Lamidi, E. (2014). Child well-being in same-sex parent families: Review of research prepared for American Sociological Association Amicus Brief. *Population Research and Policy Review, 33*(4), 485-502.

Manning, W. D., Longmore, M. A., & Giordano, P. C. (2007). The changing institution of marriage: Adolescents' expectations to cohabit and to marry. *Journal of Marriage and Family, 69*(3), 559-575.

Manning, W. D., Smock, P. J., & Fettro, M. N. (2019). Cohabitation and marital expectations among single millennials in the US. *Population Research and Policy Review, 38*(3), 327-346.

Manson, J. E., & Martin, K. A. (2001). Post-menopausal hormone-replacement therapy. *New England Journal of Medicine, 345,* 34-40.

Manson, J. E., Aragaki, A. K., Rossouw, J. E., Anderson, G. L., Prentice, R. L., LaCroix, A. Z., . . . Lewis, C. E. (2017). Menopausal hormone therapy and long-term all-cause and cause-specific mortality: The Women's Health Initiative randomized trials. *JAMA, 318*(10), 927-938.

Manson, J. E., Chlebowski, R. T., Stefanick, M. L., Aragaki, A. K., Rossouw, J. E., Prentice, R. L., . . . Wactawski-Wende, J. (2013). Menopausal hormone therapy and health outcomes during the intervention and extended poststopping phases of the Women's Health Initiative randomized trials. *JAMA, 310*(13), 1353-1368.

Mar, R. A., Tackett, J. L., & Moore, C. (2010). Exposure to media and theory-of-mind development in preschoolers. *Cognitive Development, 25*(1), 69-78.

Maranon, R., & Reckelhoff, J. F. (2013). Sex and gender differences in control of blood pressure. *Clinical Science, 125*(7), 311-318.

March of Dimes Birth Defects Foundation. (2004). *Cocaine use during pregnancy* [Fact sheet]. Retrieved from www.marchofdimes.com/professionals/681_1169.asp

March of Dimes. (2014, October). *Low birthweight.* Retrieved from www.marchofdimes.org/complications/low-birthweight.aspx

Marchant, L. F., McGrew, W. C., & Eibl-Eibesfeldt, I. (1995). Is human handedness universal? Ethological analyses from three traditional cultures. *Ethology, 101*(3), 239-258.

Marchi, J., Berg, M., Dencker, A., Olander, E. K., & Begley, C. (2015). Risks associated with obesity in pregnancy, for the mother and baby: A systematic review of reviews. *Obesity Reviews, 16*(8), 621-638.

Marchman, V. A., & Fernald, A. (2008). Speed of word recognition and vocabulary knowledge in infancy predict cognitive and language outcomes in later childhood. *Developmental Science, 11,* F9-16.

Marcia, J. E. (1966). Development and validation of ego identity status. *Journal of Personality and Social Psychology, 3*(5), 551-558.

Marcia, J. E. (1979, June). *Identity status in late adolescence: Description and some clinical implications.* Address given at symposium on identity development, Rijksuniversitat Groningen, Netherlands.

Marcia, J. E. (1993). The relational roots of identity. In J. Kroger (Ed.), *Discussions on ego identity* (pp. 101-120). Hillsdale, NJ: Erlbaum.

Marcoen, A. (1995). Filial maturity of middle-aged adult children in the context of parent care: Model and measures. *Journal of Adult Development, 2,* 125-136.

Marcon, R. A. (2002). Moving up the grades: Relationship between preschool model and later school success. *Early Childhood Research & Practice, 4*(1), n1.

Mares, M. L., & Pan, Z. (2013). Effects of Sesame Street: A meta-analysis of children's learning in 15 countries. *Journal of Applied Developmental Psychology, 34*(3), 140-151.

Margolis, A. E., Herbstman, J. B., Davis, K. S., Thomas, V. K., Tang, D., Wang, Y., . . . & Rauh, V. A. (2016). Longitudinal effects of prenatal exposure to air pollutants on self-regulatory capacities and social competence. *Journal of Child Psychology and Psychiatry, 57*(7), 851-860.

Margolis, R., & Verdery, A. M. (2017). Older adults without close kin in the United States. *The Journals of Gerontology: Series B, 72*(4), 688-693.

Mariam, L. M., McClure, R., Robinson, J. B., & Yang, J. A. (2015). Eliciting Change in At-Risk Elders (ECARE): Evaluation of an elder abuse intervention program. *Journal of Elder Abuse & Neglect, 27*(1), 19-33.

Marioni, R. E., Proust-Lima, C., Amieva, H., Brayne, C., Matthews, F. E., Dartigues, J. F., & Jacqmin-Gadda, H. (2015). Social activity, cognitive decline and dementia risk: A 20-year prospective cohort study. *BMC Public Health, 15*(1), 1089.

Markant, J., & Amso, D. (2014). Leveling the playing field: Attention mitigates the effects of intelligence on memory. *Cognition, 131*(2), 195-204.

Markopoulou, P., Papanikolaou, E., Analytis, A., Zoumakis, E., & Siahanidou, T. (2019). Preterm birth as a risk factor for metabolic syndrome and cardiovascular disease in adult life: A systematic review and meta-analysis. *The Journal of Pediatrics.*

Markowitz, L. E., Gee, J., Chesson, H., & Stokley, S. (2018). Ten years of human papillomavirus vaccination in the United States. *Academic Pediatrics, 18*(2), S3-S10.

Markowitz, L. E., Hariri, S., Lin, C., Dunne, E. F., Steinau, M., McQuillan, G., & Unger, E. R. (2013). Reduction in human papillomavirus (HPV) prevalence among young women following HPV vaccine introduction in the United States, National Health and Nutrition Examination Surveys, 2003-2010. *The Journal of Infectious Diseases, 208*(3), 385-393.

Marks, N. F. (1996). Caregiving across the life-span: National prevalence and predictors. *Family Relations, 45,* 27-36.

Marks, N. F., & Lambert, J. D. (1998). Marital status continuity and change among young and midlife adults: Longitudinal effects on psychological well-being. *Journal of Family Issues, 19*(6), 652-686.

Markus, H. R., & Kitayama, S. (1991). Culture and the self: Implications for cognition, emotion, and motivation. *Psychological Review, 98*(2), 224.

Marlowe, F. (2010). *The Hadza: Hunter-gatherers of Tanzania* (Vol. 3). Berkeley, CA: University of California Press.

Marlowe, F. W. (2004). Mate preferences among Hadza hunter-gatherers. *Human Nature, 15*(4), 365-376.

Marmot, M. G., & Fuhrer, R. (2004). Socioeconomic position and health across midlife. In O. G. Brim, C. D. Ryff, & R. C. Kessler (Eds.), *How healthy are we? A national study of well-being at midlife.* Chicago, IL: University of Chicago Press.

Marsh, A. A., Finger, E. C., Schechter, J. C., Jurkowitz, I. T., Reid, M. E., & Blair, R. J. R. (2011). Adolescents with psychopathic traits report reductions in physiological responses to fear. *Journal of Child Psychology and Psychiatry, 52*(8), 834-841.

Marshall, J. (2019). *Are religious people happier, healthier? Our new global study explores this question* [Pew Research Center news report]. Retrieved from www. pewresearch.org/fact-tank/2019/01/31/are-religious-people-happier-healthier-our-new-global-study-explores-this-question/

Martikainen, P., Moustgaard, H., Murphy, M., Einio, E. K., Koskinen, S., Martelin, T., & Noro, A. (2009). Gender, living arrangements, and social circumstances as determinants of entry into and exit from long-term institutional care at older ages: A 6-year follow-up study of older Finns. *The Gerontologist, 49*(1), 34-45.

Martin, B., Mattson, M. P., & Maudsley, S. (2006). Caloric restriction and intermittent fasting: Two potential diets for successful brain aging. *Ageing Research Reviews, 5*(3), 332-353.

Martin, C. E., Longinaker, N., Mark, K., Chisolm, M. S., & Terplan, M. (2015). Recent trends in treatment admissions for marijuana use during pregnancy. *Journal of Addiction Medicine, 9*(2), 99-104.

Martin, C. L., & Fabes, R. A. (2001). The stability and consequences of young children's same-sex peer interactions. *Developmental Psychology, 37,* 431-446.

Martin, C. L., & Ruble, D. (2004). Children's search for gender cues: Cognitive perspectives on gender development. *Current Directions in Psychological Science, 13,* 67-70.

Martin, C. L., Fabes, R. A., Hanish, L., Leonard, S., & Dinella, L. M. (2011). Experienced and expected similarity to same-gender peers: Moving toward a comprehensive model of gender segregation. *Sex Roles, 65*(5-6), 421-434.

Martin, C. L., Kornienko, O., Schaefer, D. R., Hanish, L. D., Fabes, R. A., & Goble, P. (2013). The role of sex of peers and gender-typed activities in young children's peer affiliative networks: A longitudinal analysis of selection and influence. *Child Development, 84*(3), 921-937.

Martin, C. L., Ruble, D. N., & Szkrybalo, J. (2002). Cognitive theories of early gender development. *Psychological Bulletin, 128,* 903-933.

Martin, G. N., & Clarke, R. M. (2017). Are psychology journals anti-replication? A snapshot of editorial practices. *Frontiers in Psychology, 8,* 523.

Martin, J. A., & Osterman, M. J. (2019). Is twin childbearing on the decline? Twin births in the United States, 2014-2018. *NCHS Data Brief 551.* Retrieved from www.cdc.gov/nchs/products/databriefs/db351.htm

Martin, J. A., Hamilton, B. E., Osterman, M. J. & Driscoll, A. K., & Mathews, T. J. (2019). Births: Final data for 2018. *National Vital Statistics Reports, 68*(13), 1-47. Hyattsville, MD: National Center for Health Statistics.

Martin, J. A., Hamilton, B. E., Osterman, M. J. K, Driscoll, A. K., & Drake, P. (2018). Births: Final data 2017. *National Vital Statistics Reports, 67*(8). Hyattsville, MD: National Center for Health Statistics.

Martin, J. A., Hamilton, B. E., Osterman, M. J., & Driscoll, A. K. (2019). Births: Final data for 2018. *National Vital Statistics Report, 68*(13), 1-47. Hyattsville, MD: National Center for Health Statistics.

Martin, J. A., Hamilton, B. E., Osterman, M. J., Driscoll, A. K., & Mathews, T. J. (2017). Births: Final data for 2015. *National Vital Statistics Report, 66*(1), 1. Hyattsville, MD: National Center for Health Statistics.

Martin, J. A., Hamilton, B. E., Sutton, P. D., Ventura, S. J., Mathews, T. J., & Osterman, M. J. K. (2010). Births: Final data for 2008. *National Vital Statistics Reports, 59*(1). Hyattsville, MD: National Center for Health Statistics.

Martin, J. A., Hamilton, B. E., Sutton, P. D., Ventura, S. J., Menacker, F., & Munson, M. L. (2005). Births: Final data for 2003. *National Vital Statistics Reports, 54*(2). Hyattsville, MD: National Center for Health Statistics.

Martin, J. A., Hamilton, B. E., Sutton, P. D., Ventura, S. J., Menacker, F., Kirmeyer, S., & Munson, M. (2007). Births: Final data for 2005. *National Vital Statistics Reports, 56*(6). Hyattsville, MD: National Center for Health Statistics.

Martin, J. A., Kirmeyer, S., Osterman, M., & Shepherd, R. A. (2009). Born a bit too early: Recent trends in later preterm births. *NCHS Data Brief, 24.* Hyattsville, MD: National Center for Health Statistics.

Martin, J., Hamilton, B. E., & Osterman, M. J. K. (2019). Births in the United States, 2018. *NCHS Data Brief, 346.* Hyattsville, MD: National Center for Health Statistics.

Martin, M. K., & Voorhies, B. (1975). *Female of the species.* New York, NY: Columbia University Press.

Martin, P., Kliegel, M., Rott, C., Poon, L. W., & Johnson, M. A. (2007). Personality and coping among centenarians. In L. W. Poon & T. T. Perls (Eds.), *Annual review of gerontology and geriatrics, vol. 27: Biopsychosocial approaches to longevity* (pp. 89–106). New York, NY: Springer.

Martin, P., Kliegel, M., Rott, C., Poon, L. W., & Johnson, M. A. (2008). Age differences and changes of coping behavior in three age groups: Findings from the Georgia Centenarian Study. *International Journal of Aging & Human Development, 66*(2), 97–114.

Martin, R. (2017). Gender and emotion stereotypes in children's television. *Journal of Broadcasting & Electronic Media, 61*(3), 499–517.

Martin, R. S., Hayes, B., Gregorevic, K., & Lim, W. K. (2016). The effects of advance care planning interventions on nursing home residents: A systematic review. *Journal of the American Medical Directors Association, 17*(4), 284–293.

Martin, S. P., & Parashar, S. (2006). Women's changing attitudes toward divorce, 1974–2002: Evidence for an educational crossover. *Journal of Marriage and Family, 68*, 29–40.

Martinez, G., and Abma, J. C. (2015). *Sexual activity, contraceptive use, and childbearing of teenagers aged 15–19 in the United States.* Washington, DC: National Center for Health Statistics. Retrieved from www.cdc.gov/mmwr/pdf/ss/ss6304.pdf

Martinez, G., Copen, C. E., & Abma, J. C. (2011). Teenagers in the United States: Sexual activity, contraceptive use, and childbearing, 2006–2010. National Survey of Family Growth. National Center for Health Statistics. *Vital Health Statistics, 23*(31).

Martino, D., Loke, Y. J., Gordon, L., Ollikainen, M., Cruickshank, M. N., Saffrey, R., Craig, J. M. (2013). Longitudinal, genome-scale analyses of DNA methylation in twins from birth to 18 months of age reveals rapid epigenetic change in early life and pair-specific effects of discordance. *Genome Biology, 14*, R42. http://doi.org/10.1186/gb-2013-14-5-r4

Martorell, R. (2016). Improved nutrition in the first 1000 days and adult human capital and health. *American Journal of Human Biology*, 1–12.

Martorell, R., & Zongrone, A. (2012). Intergenerational influences on child growth and undernutrition. *Paediatric and Perinatal Epidemiology, 26*, 302–314.

Martorell, R., Melgar, P., Maluccio, J. A., Stein, A. D., & Rivera, J. A. (2010). The nutrition intervention improved adult human capital and economic productivity. *The Journal of Nutrition, 140*(2), 411–414.

Martorell, S., & Martorell, G. (2006). Bridging uncharted waters: Down syndrome association of Atlanta outreach to Latino/a families. *American Journal of Community Psychology, 37*, 219–225.

Martínez-Lozano, V., Sánchez-Medina, J. A., & Goudena, P. P. (2011). A cross-cultural study of observed conflicts between young children. *Journal of Cross-Cultural Psychology, 42*(6), 895–907.

Marver, J. E., Galfalvy, H. C., Burke, A. K., Sublette, M. E., Oquendo, M. A., Mann, J. J., & Grunebaum, M. F. (2017). Friendship, depression, and suicide attempts in adults: Exploratory analysis of a longitudinal follow-up study. *Suicide and Life-Threatening Behavior.*

Marván, M. L., & Alcalá-Herrera, V. (2019). Psychosocial and cultural aspects. In J. Ussher, J. Chrisler, & J. Perz (Eds.), *Routledge international handbook of women's sexual and reproductive health* (p. 28). New York, NY: Routledge.

Mascarenhas, M. N., Flaxman, S. R., Boerma, T., Vanderpoel, S., & Stevens, G. A. (2012). National, regional, and global trends in infertility prevalence since 1990: A systematic analysis of 277 health surveys. *PLoS Medicine, 9*(12), e1001356.

Masci, D., & DeSilver, D. (2019). A global snapshot of same-sex marriage. *Pew Research Center.* Retrieved from www.pewresearch.org/fact-tank/2019/10/29/global-snapshot-same-sex-marriage/

Masci, D., Sciupac, E., & Lipka, M. (2017). *Gay marriage around the world.* Washington, DC: Pew Research Center. Retrieved from www.pewforum.org/2017/08/08/gay-marriage-around-the-world-2013/.

Mashburn, A. J., Justice, L. M., Downer, J. T., & Pianta, R. C. (2009). Peer effects on children's language achievement during prekindergarten. *Child Development, 80*(3), 686–702.

Maski, K. P., & Kothare, S. V. (2013). Sleep deprivation and neurobehavioral functioning in children. *International Journal of Psychophysiology, 89*(2), 259–264.

Mason, T. B., & Pack, A. I. (2007). Pediatric parasomnias. *Sleep, 30*(2), 141–151.

Massimiliano, P. (2015). The effects of age on divergent thinking and creative objects production: A cross-sectional study. *High Ability Studies, 26*(1), 93–104.

Masten, A. S., & Coatsworth, J. D. (1998). The development of competence in favorable and unfavorable environments: Lessons from research on successful children. *American Psychologist, 53*, 205–220.

Mastin, J. D., & Vogt, P. (2016). Infant engagement and early vocabulary development: A naturalistic observation study of Mozambican infants from 1;1 to 2;1. *Journal of Child Language, 43*, 235–264.

Matcham, F., Norton, S., Scott, D. L., Steer, S., & Hotopf, M. (2016). Symptoms of depression and anxiety predict treatment response and long-term physical health outcomes in rheumatoid arthritis: secondary analysis of a randomized controlled trial. *Rheumatology, 55*(2), 268–278.

Mather, M. (2010). *U.S. children in single-mother families.* Washington, DC: Population Reference Bureau.

Mathers, M., Canterford, L., Olds, T., Hesketh, K., Ridley, K., & Wake, M. (2009). Electronic media use and adolescent health and well-being: Cross-sectional community study. *Academic Pediatrics, 9*(5), 307–314.

Mathews, T. J., & Hamilton, B. E. (2016). Mean age of mothers is on the rise: United States, 2000–2014. *NCHS Data Brief, (232)*, 1–8.

Mathews, T. J., & MacDorman, M. F. (2008). Infant mortality statistics from the 2005 period linked birth/infant death data set. *National Vital Statistics Reports, 57*(2). Hyattsville, MD: National Center for Health Statistics.

Matson, J. L., Worley, J. A., Fodstad, J. C., Chung, K. M., Suh, D., Jhin, H. K., . . . Furniss, F. (2011). A multinational study examining the cross cultural differences in reported symptoms of autism spectrum disorders: Israel, South Korea, the United Kingdom, and the United States of America. *Research in Autism Spectrum Disorders, 5*(4), 1598–1604.

Matsuba, M. K., Pratt, M. W., Norris, J. E., Mohle, E., Alisat, S., & McAdams, D. P. (2012). Environmentalism as a context for expressing identity and generativity: Patterns among activists and uninvolved youth and midlife adults. *Journal of Personality, 80*(4), 1091–1115.

Matsumoto, D., & Juang, L. (2008). *Culture and psychology* (4th ed.). Belmont, CA: Wadsworth, Cengage Learning.

Mattei, T. A., Bond, B. J., Goulart, C. R., Sloffer, C. A., Morris, M. J., & Lin, J. J. (2012). Performance analysis of the protective effects of bicycle helmets during impact and crush tests in pediatric skull models. *Journal of Neurosurgery: Pediatrics, 10*(6), 490–497.

Matthys, W., & John, E. (2017). *Oppositional defiant disorder and conduct disorder in childhood.* Hoboken, NJ: Wiley & Sons.

Mattis, J., & Sehgal, A. (2016). Circadian rhythms, sleep, and disorders of aging. *Trends in Endocrinology & Metabolism, 27*(4), 192–203.

Mattock, K., & Burnham, D. (2006). Chinese and English infants' tone perception: Evidence for perceptual reorganization. *Infancy, 10*(3), 241–265.

Maughan, B., Collishaw, S., & Stringaris, A. (2013). Depression in childhood and adolescence. *Journal of the Canadian Academy of Child and Adolescent Psychiatry, 22*(1), 35.

Maulik, P. K., Mascarenhas, M. N., Mathers, C. D., Dua, T., & Saxena, S. (2011). Prevalence of intellectual disability: A meta-analysis of population-based studies. *Research in Developmental Disabilities, 32*(2), 419–436.

Maurer, D., & Lewis, T. L. (1979). Peripheral discrimination by three-month-old infants. *Child Development, 50*, 276–279.

Mayer, A., & Träuble, B. E. (2013). Synchrony in the onset of mental state understanding across cultures? A study among children in Samoa. *International Journal of Behavioral Development, 37*(1), 21–28.

Mayeza, E. (2017). "It's not right for boys to play with dolls": Young children constructing and policing gender during "free play" in a South African classroom. *Discourse: Studies in the Cultural Politics of Education*, 1–13.

Mayhew, A., Mullins, T. L. K., Ding, L., Rosenthal, S. L., Zimet, G. D., Morrow, C., & Kahn, J. A. (2014). Risk perceptions and subsequent sexual behaviors after HPV vaccination in adolescents. *Pediatrics*, peds-2013.

Maynard, A. E. (2004). Sibling interactions. In U. P. Gielen & J. Roopnarine (Eds.), *Advances in applied developmental psychology. Childhood and adolescence: Cross-cultural perspectives and applications* (pp. 229–252). Westport, CT: Praeger Publishers/Greenwood Publishing Group.

Maynard, S. (2010). The impact of e-books on young children's reading habits. *Publishing Research Quarterly, 26*(4), 236–248.

Mazurek, M. O., & Sohl, K. (2016). Sleep and behavioral problems in children with autism spectrum disorder. *Journal of Autism and Developmental Disorders, 46*(6), 1906–1915.

Mazzio, E. A., & Soliman, K. F. (2012). Basic concepts of epigenetics: Impact of environmental signals on gene expression. *Epigenetics, 7*(2), 119–130.

Mazzocco, M. M., Feigenson, L., & Halberda, J. (2011). Impaired acuity of the approximate number system underlies mathematical learning disability (dyscalculia). *Child Development, 82*(4), 1224–1237.

Mbarek, H., Steinberg, S., Nyholt, D. R., Gordon, S. D., Miller, M. B., McRae, A. F., . . . & Davies, G. E. (2016). Identification of common genetic variants influencing spontaneous dizygotic twinning and female fertility. *The American Journal of Human Genetics, 98*(5), 898–908.

McAdams, D. (1993). *The stories we live by.* New York, NY: Morrow.

McAdams, D. P. (2001). Generativity in mid-life. In M. E. Lachman (Ed.), *Handbook of midlife development* (pp. 395–443). New York, NY: Wiley.

McAdams, D. P. (2006). The redemptive self: Generativity and the stories Americans live by. *Research in Human Development, 3*, 81–100.

McAdams, D. P. (2013). The positive psychology of adult generativity: Caring for the next generation and constructing a redemptive life. In J. D. Sinnott (Ed.), *Positive psychology* (pp. 191–205). New York, NY: Springer.

McAdams, D. P., Diamond, A., de St. Aubin, E., & Mansfield, E. (1997). Stories of commitment: The psychosocial construction of generative lives. *Journal of Personality and Social Psychology, 72*, 678–694.

McAdams, D. P., Reynolds, J., Lewis, M., Patten, A. H., & Bowman, P. J. (2001). When bad things turn good and good things turn bad: Sequences of redemption and contamination in life narrative and their relation to psychosocial adaptation in midlife adults and in students. *Personality and Social Psychology Bulletin, 27*(4), 474–485.

McAlister, A. R., & Peterson, C. C. (2013). Siblings, theory of mind, and executive functioning in children aged 3–6 years: New longitudinal evidence. *Child Development, 84*(4), 1442–1458.

McAuley, T., & White, D. A. (2011). A latent variables examination of processing speed, response inhibition, and working memory during typical development. *Journal of Experimental Child Psychology, 108*(3), 453–468.

McCabe, D. P., Roediger III, H. L., McDaniel, M. A., Balota, D. A., & Hambrick, D. Z. (2010). The relationship between working memory capacity and executive functioning: Evidence for a common executive attention construct. *Neuropsychology, 24*(2), 222.

McCabe, J., Fairchild, E., Grauerholz, L., Pescosolido, B. A., & Tope, D. (2011). Gender in twentieth-century children's books: Patterns of disparity in titles and central characters. *Gender & Society, 25*(2), 197–226.

McCabe, M. P., Sharlip, I. D., Lewis, R., Atalla, E., Balon, R., Fisher, A. D., . . . Segraves, R. T. (2016). Incidence and prevalence of sexual dysfunction in women and men: A consensus statement from the Fourth International Consultation on Sexual Medicine.

McCallum, K. E., & Bruton, J. R. (2003). The continuum of care in the treatment of eating disorders. *Primary Psychiatry, 10*(6), 48–54.

McCann, S. J. (2019). Relation of state Alzheimer's prevalence to state resident Big Five personality in the USA. *Current Psychology*, 1–10.

McCarthy, J. (2018). *Two in three Americans support same-sex marriage* [Gallup polls news release]. Retrieved from https://news.gallup.com/poll/234866/two-three-americans-support-sex-marriage.aspx

McClain, M. C., & Pfeiffer, S. (2012). Identification of gifted students in the United States today: A look at state definitions, policies, and practices. *Journal of Applied School Psychology, 28*(1), 59–88.

McClelland, E., & McKinney, C. (2016). Disruptive behavior and parenting in emerging adulthood: Mediational effect of parental psychopathology. *Journal of Child and Family Studies, 25*(1), 212–223.

McClintock, M. K., & Herdt, G. (1996). Rethinking puberty: The development of sexual attraction. *Current Directions in Psychological Science, 5*(6), 178–183.

McClure, E. B. (2000). A meta-analytic review of sex differences in facial expression processing and their development in infants, children, and adolescents. *Psychological Bulletin, 126*(3), 424.

McCord, J. (1996). Unintended consequences of punishment. *Pediatrics, 98*(4), 832–834.

McCoy, D. C., Yoshikawa, H., Ziol-Guest, K. M., Duncan, G. J., Schindler, H. S., Magnuson, K., . . . Shonkoff, J. P. (2017). Impacts of early childhood education on medium-and long-term educational outcomes. *Educational Researcher, 46*(8), 474–487.

McCoy, K. P., George, M. R., Cummings, E. M., & Davies, P. T. (2013). Constructive and destructive marital conflict, parenting, and children's school and social adjustment. *Social Development, 22*(4), 641–662.

McCoy, K., Cummings, E. M., & Davies, P. T. (2009). Constructive and destructive marital conflict, emotional security and children's prosocial behavior. *Journal of Child Psychology and Psychiatry, 50*(3), 270–279.

McCrae, R. R. (2002). Cross-cultural research on the five-factor model of personality. In W. J. Lonner, D. L. Dinnel, S. A. Hayes, & D. N. Sattler (Eds.), *Online readings in psychology and culture* (Unit 6, Chapter 1). Bellingham, WA: Center for Cross-Cultural Research, Western Washington University.

McCrae, R. R., & Costa Jr, P. T. (1997). Personality trait structure as a human universal. *American Psychologist, 52*(5), 509.

McCrae, R. R., & Terracciano, A. (2005). Universal features of personality traits from the observer's perspective: Data from 50 cultures. *Journal of Personality and Social Psychology, 88*(3), 547.

McCrae, R. R., Costa, P. T., Jr., & Busch, C. M. (1986). Evaluating comprehensiveness in personality systems: The California Q-set and the five-factor model. *Journal of Personality, 54*, 430–446.

McCrae, R. R., Costa, P. T., Jr., Ostendorf, F., Angleitner, A., Hebríckova, M., Avia, M. D., . . . Smith, P. B. (2000). Nature over nurture: Temperament, personality, and lifespan development. *Journal of Personality and Social Psychology, 78*, 173–186.

McCrink, K., Bloom, P., & Santos, L. R. (2010). Children's and adults' judgments of equitable resource distributions. *Developmental Science, 13*(1), 37–45.

McCue, J. D. (1995). The naturalness of dying. *Journal of the American Medical Association, 273*, 1039–1043.

McDaniel, M. A., Pesta, B. J., & Banks, G. C. (2012). Job performance and the aging worker. In J. Hedge & W. Borman (Eds.), *The Oxford Handbook of Work and Aging* (pp. 280–297). Oxford, England: Oxford University Press.

McDaniel, M., Paxson, C., & Waldfogel, J. (2006). Racial disparities in childhood asthma in the United States: Evidence from the National Health Interview Survey, 1997 to 2003. *Pediatrics, 117*, 868–877.

McDermott, M., & Barik, N. (2014). Developmental antecedents of proactive and reactive rebelliousness: The role of parenting style, childhood adversity, and attachment. *Journal of Motivation, Emotion, and Personality: Reversal Theory Studies, 2*(1), 22–31.

McDonald, K. L., & Gibson, C. E. (2017). Peer rejection and disruptive behavioral disorders. In J. Lochman & W. Matthys (Eds.), *The Wiley handbook of disruptive and impulse-control disorders* (pp. 323–338). New York, NY: Wiley.

McDonald, K. L., Dashiell-Aje, E., Menzer, M. M., Rubin, K. H., Oh, W., & Bowker, J. C. (2013). Contributions of racial and sociobehavioral homophily to friendship stability and quality among same-race and cross-race friends. *Journal of Early Adolescence.* doi:10.1177/0272431612472259.

McDonough, C., Song, L., Hirsh-Pasek, K., Golinkoff, R. M., & Lannon, R. (2011). An image is worth a thousand words: Why nouns tend to dominate verbs in early word learning. *Developmental Science, 14*(2), 181–189.

McDowell, M., Fryar, C., Odgen, C., & Flegal, K. (2008). Anthropometric reference data for children and adults: United States, 2003–2006. *National Health Statistics Reports* (No. 10). Hyattsville, MD: National Center for Health Statistics.

McElwain, N. L., & Volling, B. L. (2005). Preschool children's interactions with friends and older siblings: Relationship specificity and joint contributions to problem behavior. *Journal of Family Psychology, 19*(4), 486.

McFarland, J., Cui, J., Holmes, J., & Wang, X. (2019). *Trends in high school dropout and completion rates in the United States: 2019 (NCES*

2020-117). U.S. Department of Education. Washington, DC: National Center for Education Statistics. Retrieved from https://nces.ed.gov/pubsearch

McFarland, J., Hussar, B., Zhang, J., Wang, X., Wang, K., Hein, . . . Barmer, A. (2019). *The condition of education 2019* (NCES 2019-144). U.S. Department of Education. Washington, DC: National Center for Education Statistics. Retrieved from https://nces.ed.gov/pubsearch/pubsinfo.asp?pubid=2019144.

McFarland, R. A., Tune, G. B., & Welford, A. (1964). On the driving of automobiles by older people. *Journal of Gerontology, 19,* 190-197.

McGee, R. W. (2016). *In which countries is homosexuality most (and least) acceptable? A ranking of 98 countries* [Social Science Research Network data report]. Retrieved from https://papers.ssrn.com/sol3/papers.cfm?abstract_id=2799845

McGuire, S. L. (2017, September 27). *Aging education: A worldwide imperative.* Retrieved from http://file.scirp.org/pdf/CE_2017092615440943.pdf

McHale, S. M., & Huston, T. L. (1985). The effect of the transition to parenthood on the marriage relationship. *Journal of Family Issues, 6*(4), 409-433.

McHale, S. M., Bissell, J., & Kim, J. Y. (2009). Sibling relationship, family, and genetic factors in sibling similarity in sexual risk. *Journal of Family Psychology, 23*(4), 562.

McHale, S. M., Updegraff, K. A., & Whiteman, S. D. (2012). Sibling relationships and influences in childhood and adolescence. *Journal of Marriage and Family, 74*(5), 913-930.

McIlvane, J. M., Ajrouch, K. J., & Antonucci, T. C. (2007). Generational structure and social resources and social influences on health and well-being. *Journal of Social Issues, 63,* 759-774.

McKay, E., & Counts, S. E. (2017). Multi-infarct dementia: A historical perspective. *Dementia and Geriatric Cognitive Disorders Extra, 7*(1), 160-171.

McKinney, C. O., Hahn-Holbrook, J., Chase-Lansdale, P. L., Ramey, S. L., Krohn, J., Reed-Vance, M., . . . Shalowitz, M. U. (2016). Racial and ethnic differences in breastfeeding. *Pediatrics, 138*(2), e20152388.

McLanahan, S., Tach, L., & Schneider, D. (2013). The causal effects of father absence. *Annual Review of Sociology, 39,* 399-427.

McLaughlin, D., Vagenas, D., Pachana, N. A., Begum, N., & Dobson, A. (2010). Gender differences in social network size and satisfaction in adults in their 70s. *Journal of Health Psychology, 15*(5), 671-679.

McLemore, G. L., & Richardson, K. A. (2016). Data from three prospective longitudinal human cohorts of prenatal marijuana exposure and offspring outcomes from the fetal period through young adulthood. *Data in Brief, 9,* 753.

McLeod, J. D., Kruttschnitt, C., & Dornfeld, M. (1994). Does parenting explain the effects of structural conditions on children's antisocial behavior? A comparison of Blacks and whites. *Social Forces, 73*(2), 575-604.

McLeod, R., Boyer, K., Karrison, T., Kasza, K., Swisher, C., Roizen, N., . . . Toxoplamosis Study Group. (2006). Outcome of treatment for congenital toxoplasmosis, 1981-2004: The national collaborative Chicago-based, congenital toxoplasmosis study. *Clinical Infectious Diseases: An Official Publication of the Infectious Diseases Society of America, 42*(10), 1383-1394.

McLoyd, V. C., & Smith, J. (2002). Physical discipline and behavior problems in African American, European American, and Hispanic children: Emotional support as a moderator. *Journal of Marriage and Family, 64,* 40-53.

McManus, I. C., Davison, A., & Armour, J. A. (2013). The evolution of human handedness. *Annals of the New York Academy of Sciences, 1288*(1), 48.

McNamara, T. K., Pitt-Catsouphes, M., Matz-Costa, C., Brown, M., & Valcour, M. (2013). Across the continuum of satisfaction with work-family balance: Work hours, flexibility-fit, and work-family culture. *Social Science Research, 42*(2), 283-298.

McNeal, Jr., R. B. (2012). Checking in or checking out? Investigating the parent involvement reactive hypothesis. *The Journal of Educational Research, 105*(2), 79-89.

McNulty, J. K., Wenner, C. A., & Fisher, T. D. (2016). Longitudinal associations among relationship satisfaction, sexual satisfaction, and frequency of sex in early marriage. *Archives of Sexual Behavior, 45*(1), 85-97.

McQuiggan, M., & Megra, M. (2017). *Parent and family involvement in education: Results from the National Household Education Surveys Program of 2016. First Look. NCES 2017-102* [Report]. Washington, DC: National Center for Education Statistics.

McTiernan, A., Kooperberg, C., White, E., Wilcox, S., Coates, R., Adams-Campbell, L. L., . . . Ockene, J. (2003). Recreational physical activity and the risk of breast cancer in postmenopausal women: The Women's Health Initiative Cohort Study. *Journal of the American Medical Association, 290,* 1331-1336.

Meade, C. S., & Ickovics, J. R. (2005). Systematic review of sexual risk among pregnant and mothering teens in the USA: Pregnancy as an opportunity for integrated prevention of STD and repeat pregnancy. *Social Science & Medicine, 60*(4), 661-678.

Mechcatie, E., & Rosenberg, K. (2018). HPV vaccination does not change adolescent sexual behaviors. *AJN The American Journal of Nursing, 118*(11), 56.

Medland, S. E., Duffy, D. L., Wright, M. J., Geffen, G. M., Hay, D. A., Levy, F., . . . Hewitt, A. W. (2009). Genetic influences on handedness: Data from 25,732 Australian and Dutch twin families. *Neuropsychologia, 47*(2), 330-337.

Mednick, S. C., Nakayama, K., Cantero, J. L., Atienza, M., Levin, A. A., Pathak, N., & Stickgold, R. (2002). The restorative effect of naps on perceptual deterioration. *Nature Neuroscience, 5,* 677-681.

Meeker, M. (2018). *Internet trends 2018* [Report]. Retrieved from kleinerperkins.com

Meert, K. L., Donaldson, A. E., Newth, C. J., Harrison, R., Berger, J., Zimmerman, J., . . . Nicholson, C. (2010). Complicated grief and associated risk factors among parents following a child's death in the pediatric intensive care unit. *Archives of Pediatrics & Adolescent Medicine, 164*(11), 1045-1051.

Meerwijk, E. L., & Sevelius, J. M. (2017). Transgender population size in the United States: A meta-regression of population-based probability samples. *American Journal of Public Health, 107*(2), e1-e8.

Meeus, W. (2011). The study of adolescent identity formation 2000-2010: A review of longitudinal research. *Journal of research on Adolescence, 21*(1), 75-94.

Meezan, W., & Rauch, J. (2005). Gay marriage, same-sex parenting, and America's children. *Future of Children, 15,* 97-115.

Mehta, M. A., Golembo, N. I., Nosarti, C., Colvert, E., Mota, A., Williams, S. C., . . . Sonuga-Barke, E. J. (2009). Amygdala, hippocampal and corpus callosum size following severe early institutional deprivation: The English and Romanian Adoptees study pilot. *Journal of Child Psychology and Psychiatry, 50*(8), 943-951.

Mei, J. (1994). The northern Chinese custom of rearing babies in sandbags: Implications for motor and intellectual development. *Motor development: Aspects of normal and delayed development.* Amsterdam: VU Uitgeverij.

Meier, R. (1991, January-February). Language acquisition by deaf children. *American Scientist, 79,* 60-70.

Meijer, A. M., & van den Wittenboer, G. L. H. (2007). Contributions of infants' sleep and crying to marital relationship of first-time parent couples in the 1st year after childbirth. *Journal of Family Psychology, 21,* 49-57.

Meinhardt, J., Sodian, B., Thoermer, C., Döhnel, K., & Sommer, M. (2011). True-and false-belief reasoning in children and adults: An event-related potential study of theory of mind. *Developmental Cognitive Neuroscience, 1*(1), 67-76.

Meins, E. (1998). The effects of security of attachment and maternal attribution of meaning on children's linguistic acquisitional style. *Infant Behavior and Development, 21,* 237-252.

Melby-Lervåg, M., & Hulme, C. (2013). Is working memory training effective? A meta-analytic review. *Developmental Psychology, 49*(2), 270.

Meléndez, J. C., Satorres, E., Redondo, R., Escudero, J., & Pitarque, A. (2018). Well-being, resilience, and coping: Are there differences between healthy older adults, adults with mild cognitive impairment, and adults with Alzheimer-type dementia? *Archives of Gerontology and Geriatrics, 77,* 38-43.

Melhem, N. M., Porta, G., Shamseddeen, W., Payne, M. W., & Brent, D. A. (2011). Grief in children and adolescents bereaved by sudden parental death. *Archives of General Psychiatry, 68*(9), 911-919.

Melhuish, E., Ereky-Stevens, K., Petrogiannis, K., Ariescu, A., Penderi, E., Rentzou, K., . . . Leseman, P. (2015). *A review of research on the effects of Early Childhood Education and Care (ECEC) upon child development* [Monograph]. London: Birkbeck, University of London.

Meléndez, J. C., Mayordomo, T., Sancho, P., & Tomás, J. M. (2012). Coping strategies: Gender differences and development throughout life span. *The Spanish Journal of Psychology, 15*(3), 1089-1098.

Meléndez, J. C., Satorres, E., Redondo, R., Escudero, J., & Pitarque, A. (2018). Wellbeing, resilience, and coping: Are there differences between healthy older adults, adults with mild cognitive impairment, and adults with Alzheimer-type dementia? *Archives of Gerontology and Geriatrics, 77,* 38-43.

Memel, M., Woolverton, C. B., Bourassa, K., & Glisky, E. L. (2019). Working memory predicts subsequent episodic memory decline during healthy cognitive aging: Evidence from a cross-lagged panel design. *Aging, Neuropsychology, and Cognition, 26*(5), 711-730.

Menacker, F., Martin, J. A., MacDorman, M. F., & Ventura, S. J. (2004). Births to 10-14 year-old mothers, 1990-2002: Trends and health outcomes. *National Vital Statistics Reports, 53*(7). Hyattsville, MD: National Center for Health Statistics.

Mendle, J. (2014). Beyond pubertal timing: New directions for studying individual differences in development. *Current Directions in Psychological Science, 23*(3), 215-219.

Mendle, J., & Ferrero, J. (2012). Detrimental psychological outcomes associated with pubertal timing in adolescent boys. *Developmental Review, 32*(1), 49-66.

Mendle, J., Turkheimer, E., D'Onofrio, B. M., Lynch, S. K., Emery, R. E., Slutske, W. S., & Martin, N. G. (2006). Family structure and age at menarche: A children-of-twins approach. *Developmental Psychology, 42,* 533-542.

Mendonça, B., Sargent, B., & Fetters, L. (2016). Cross-cultural validity of standardized motor development screening and assessment tools: A systematic review. *Developmental Medicine & Child Neurology, 58*(12), 1213-1222.

Menec, V. H. (2003). The relation between everyday activities and successful aging: A 6-year longitudinal study. *The Journals of Gerontology Series B: Psychological Sciences and Social Sciences, 58*(2), S74-S82.

Menec, V. H., Shooshtari, S., Nowicki, S., & Fournier, S. (2010). Does the relationship between neighborhood socioeconomic status and health outcomes persist into very old age? A population-based study. *Journal of Aging and Health, 22*(1), 27-47.

Menegaux, F., Baruchel, A., Bertrand, Y., Lescoeur, B., Leverger, G., Nelken, B., . . . Clavel, J. (2006). Household exposure to pesticides and risk of childhood acute leukaemia. *Occupational and Environmental Medicine, 63*(2), 131-134.

Mennella, J. A. (2014). Ontogeny of taste preferences: Basic biology and implications for health. *The American Journal of Clinical Nutrition, 99*(3), 704S-711S.

Mennella, J. A., & Bobowski, N. K. (2015). The sweetness and bitterness of childhood: Insights from basic research on taste preferences. *Physiology & Behavior, 152,* 502-507.

Menon, U. (2001). Middle adulthood in cultural perspective: The imagined and the experienced in three cultures. In M. E. Lachman (Ed.), *Handbook of midlife development* (pp. 40-74). New York: Wiley.

Merrell, K., Gueldner, B., Ross, S., & Isava, D. (2008). How effective are school bullying intervention programs? A meta-analysis of intervention research. *School Psychology Quarterly, 23*(1), 26-42.

Merrill, S. S., & Verbrugge, L. M. (1999). Health and disease in midlife. In S. L. Willis & J. D. Reid (Eds.), *Life in the middle: Psychological and social development in middle age* (pp. 78-103). San Diego, CA: Academic Press.

Merz, E. M., & Consedine, N. S. (2009). The association of family support and wellbeing in later life depends on adult attachment style. *Attachment & Human Development, 11*(2), 203-221.

Merz, E. M., Consedine, N. S., Schulze, H. J., & Schuengel, C. (2009). Well-being of adult children and ageing parents: Associations with intergenerational support and relationship quality. *Ageing & Society, 29*(5), 783-802.

Mesman, J., & Groeneveld, M. G. (2018). Gendered parenting in early childhood: Subtle but unmistakable if you know where to look. *Child Development Perspectives, 12*(1), 22-27.

Messinger, D. S., Bauer, C. R., Das, A., Seifer, R., Lester, B. M., Lagasse, L. L., . . . Poole, W. K. (2004). The maternal lifestyle study: Cognitive, motor, and behavioral outcomes of cocaine-exposed and opiate-exposed infants through three years of age. *Pediatrics, 113,* 1677-1685.

Metayer, C., Zhang, L., Wiemels, J. L., Bartley, K., Schiffman, J., Ma, X., . . . & Ducore, J. (2013). Tobacco smoke exposure and the risk of childhood acute lymphoblastic and myeloid leukemias by cytogenetic subtype. *Cancer Epidemiology and Prevention Biomarkers, 22*(9), 1600-1611.

Metz, T. D., & Borgelt, L. M. (2018). Marijuana use in pregnancy and while breastfeeding. *Obstetrics and Gynecology, 132*(5), 1198-1210.

Metz, T. D., & Stickrath, E. H. (2015). Marijuana use in pregnancy and lactation: a review of the evidence. *American Journal of Obstetrics and Gynecology, 213*(6), 761-778.

Meyer, B. J. F., Russo, C., & Talbot, A. (1995). Discourse comprehension and problem solving: Decisions about the treatment of breast cancer by women across the life-span. *Psychology in Aging, 10,* 84-103.

Meyer, I. H. (2003). Prejudice, social stress, and mental health in lesbian, gay, and bisexual populations: Conceptual issues and research evidence. *Psychological Bulletin, 129,* 674-697.

Meyer-Bahlburg, H. F. (2005). Gender identity outcome in female-raised 46, XY persons with penile agenesis, cloacal exstrophy of the bladder, or penile ablation. *Archives of Sexual Behavior, 34*(4), 423-438.

Miao, C., Humphrey, R. H., & Qian, S. (2017). Are the emotionally intelligent good citizens or counterproductive? A meta-analysis of emotional intelligence and its relationships with organizational citizenship behavior and counterproductive work behavior. *Personality and Individual Differences, 116,* 144-156.

Michalska, K. J., Zeffiro, T. A., & Decety, J. (2016). Brain response to viewing others being harmed in children with conduct disorder symptoms. *Journal of Child Psychology and Psychiatry, 57*(4), 510-519.

Miedzian, M. (1991). *Boys will be boys: Breaking the link between masculinity and violence.* New York, NY: Doubleday.

Mienaltowski, A. (2011). Everyday problem solving across the adult life span: Solution diversity and efficacy. *Annals of the New York Academy of Sciences, 1235*(1), 75-85.

Migeon, B. R. (2006). The role of X inactivation and cellular mosaicism in women's health and sex-specific disorders. *Journal of the American Medical Association, 295,* 1428-1433.

Migration Policy Institute (2019). *Children in U.S. immigrant families* [Data chart]. Retrieved from www.migrationpolicy.org/programs/data-hub/charts/children-immigrant-families

Mikulincer, M., & Florian, V. (2000). Exploring individual differences in reactions to mortality salience: Does attachment style regulate terror management mechanisms? *Journal of Personality and Social Psychology, 79*(2), 260.

Milanović, Z., Pantelić, S., Trajković, N., Sporiš, G., Kostić, R., & James, N. (2013). Age-related decrease in physical activity and functional fitness among elderly men and women. *Clinical Interventions in Aging, 8,* 549.

Millar, W. S. (1988). Smiling, vocal, and attentive behavior during social contingency learning in seven-and ten-month-old infants. *Merrill-Palmer Quarterly (1982),* 301-325.

Miller, B., Messias, E., Miettunen, J., Alaräisänen, A., Järvelin, M. R., Koponen, H., . . . Kirkpatrick, B. (2010). Meta-analysis of paternal age and schizophrenia risk in male versus female offspring. *Schizophrenia Bulletin, 37*(5), 1039-1047.

Miller, D. I., & Halpern, D. F. (2014). The new science of cognitive sex differences. *Trends in Cognitive Sciences, 18*(1), 37-45.

Miller, D. I., Eagly, A. H., & Linn, M. C. (2015). Women's representation in science predicts national gender-science stereotypes: Evidence from 66 nations. *Journal of Educational Psychology, 107*(3), 631.

Miller, D. P. (2011). Maternal work and child overweight and obesity: The importance of timing. *Journal of Family and Economic Issues, 32*(2), 204-218.

Miller, K. D., Siegel, R. L., Lin, C. C., Mariotto, A. B., Kramer, J. L., Rowland, J. H., . . . Jemal, A. (2016). Cancer treatment and survivorship statistics, 2016. *CA: A Cancer Journal for Clinicians, 66*(4), 271-289.

Miller, K., & Kohn, M. (1983). The reciprocal effects of job condition and the intellectuality of leisure-time activities. In M. L. Kohn & C. Schooler (Eds.), *Work and personality: An inquiry into the impact of social stratification* (pp. 217-241). Norwood, NJ: Ablex.

Miller, L. J., Myers, A., Prinzi, L., & Mittenberg, W. (2009). Changes in intellectual functioning associated with normal aging. *Archives of Clinical Neuropsychology, 24*(7), 681-688. doi: 10.1093/arclin/acp072

Miller, P. J., Wang, S. H., Sandel, T., & Cho, G. E. (2002). Self-esteem as folk theory: A comparison of European American and Taiwanese mothers' beliefs. *Parenting: Science and Practice*, 2(3), 209-239.

Miller, S. A. (2009). Children's understanding of second-order mental states. *Psychological Bulletin*, 135(5), 749.

Mills, K. L., Lalonde, F., Clasen, L. S., Giedd, J. N., & Blakemore, S. J. (2012). Developmental changes in the structure of the social brain in late childhood and adolescence. *Social Cognitive and Affective Neuroscience*, 9(1), 123-131.

Mills, K. T., Bundy, J. D., Kelly, T. N., Reed, J. E., Kearney, P. M., Reynolds, K., . . . He, J. (2016). Global disparities of hypertension prevalence and control. *Circulation*, 134(6), 441-450.

Milojev, P., & Sibley, C. G. (2017). Normative personality trait development in adulthood: A 6-year cohort-sequential growth model. *Journal of Personality and Social Psychology*, 112(3), 510.

Min, M. O., Minnes, S., Lang, A., Weishampel, P., Short, E. J., Yoon, S., & Singer, L. T. (2014). Externalizing behavior and substance use related problems at 15 years in prenatally cocaine exposed adolescents. *Journal of Adolescence* 37(3), 269-279.

Mindell, J. A., & Owens, J. A. (2015). *A clinical guide to pediatric sleep: Diagnosis and management of sleep problems*. Philadelphia, PA: Lippincott Williams & Wilkins.

Mindell, J. A., Li, A. M., Sadeh, A., Kwon, R., & Goh, D. Y. (2015). Bedtime routines for young children: A dose- dependent association with sleep outcomes. *Sleep*, 38(5), 717-722.

Mindell, J. A., Sadeh, A., Kohyama, J., & How, T. H. (2010). Parental behaviors and sleep outcomes in infants and toddlers: A cross-cultural comparison. *Sleep Medicine*, 11(4), 393-399.

Mindell, J. A., Sadeh, A., Kwon, R., & Goh, D. Y. (2013). Cross-cultural differences in the sleep of preschool children. *Sleep Medicine*, 14(12), 1283-1289.

Miner, J. L., & Clarke-Stewart, A. (2009). Trajectories of externalizing behaviors from age 2 to age 9: Relations with gender, temperament, ethnicity, parenting and rater. *Developmental Psychology*, 44(3), 771-786.

Minkin, M. J., Reiter, S., & Maamari, R. (2015). Prevalence of postmenopausal symptoms in North America and Europe. *Menopause*, 22(11), 1231-1238.

Minkler, M., & Fuller-Thomson, D. E. (2001). Physical and mental health status of American grandparents providing extensive child care to their grandchildren. *Journal of the American Medical Women's Association (1972)*, 56(4), 199-205.

Miranda, L., Dixon, V., & Reyes, C. (2015). How states handle drug use during pregnancy. *ProPublica*. https://projects.propublica.org/graphics/maternity-drug-policies-by-state

Mireault, G., Poutre, M., Sargent-Hier, M., Dias, C., Perdue, B., & Myrick, A. (2012). Humour perception and creation between parents and 3- to 6-month-old infants. *Infant and Child Development*, 21(4), 338-347.

Mischel, W. (1966). A social-learning view of sex differences in behavior. *The Development of Sex Differences*, 56, 81.

Missler, M., Stroebe, M., Geurtsen, L., Mastenbroek, M., Chmoun, S., & Van Der Houwen, K. (2012). Exploring death anxiety among elderly people: A literature review and empirical investigation. *OMEGA-Journal of Death and Dying*, 64(4), 357-379.

Mitchell, B. A. (2010). Happiness in midlife parental roles: A contextual mixed methods analysis. *Family Relations*, 59(3), 326-339.

Mitchell, B. A. (2014). Generational juggling acts in midlife families: Gendered and ethnocultural intersections. *Journal of Women & Aging*, 26(4), 332-350.

Mitchell, J. E., Roerig, J., & Steffen, K. (2013). Biological therapies for eating disorders. *International Journal of Eating Disorders*, 46(5), 470-477.

Mitchell, L. L., & Syed, M. (2015). Does college matter for emerging adulthood? Comparing developmental trajectories of educational groups. *Journal of Youth and Adolescence*, 44(11), 2012-2027.

Mitteldorf, J. (2010). Aging is not a process of wear and tear. *Rejuvenation Research*, 13(2-3), 322-326.

Mix, K. S., Huttenlocher, J., & Levine, S. C. (2002). Multiple cues for quantification in infancy: Is number one of them? *Psychological Bulletin*, 128, 278-294.

Miyata, S., Noda, A., Iwamoto, K., Kawano, N., Okuda, M., & Ozaki, N. (2013). Poor sleep quality impairs cognitive performance in older adults. *Journal of Sleep Research*, 22(5), 535-541.

Miyawaki, C. E. (2016). Caregiving practice patterns of Asian, Hispanic, and non-Hispanic white American family caregivers of older adults across generations. *Journal of Cross-Cultural Gerontology*, 31(1), 35-55.

Moaddab, A., Dildy, G. A., Brown, H. L., Bateni, Z. H., Belfort, M. A., Sangi-Haghpeykar, H., & Clark, S. L. (2016). Health care disparity and state-specific pregnancy-related mortality in the United States, 2005-2014. *Obstetrics & Gynecology*, 128(4), 869-875.

Mobbs, D., & Watt, C. (2011). There is nothing paranormal about near-death experiences: How neuroscience can explain seeing bright lights, meeting the dead, or being convinced you are one of them. *Trends in Cognitive Sciences*, 15(10), 447-449.

Mode, N. A., Evans, M. K., & Zonderman, A. B. (2016). Race, neighborhood economic status, income inequality and mortality. *PloS One*, 11(5).

Modecki, K. L., Hagan, M. J., Sandler, I., & Wolchik, S. A. (2015). Latent profiles of nonresidential father engagement six years after divorce predict long-term offspring outcomes. *Journal of Clinical Child & Adolescent Psychology*, 44(1), 123-136.

Modecki, K. L., Minchin, J., Harbaugh, A. G., Guerra, N. G., & Runions, K. C. (2014). Bullying prevalence across contexts: A meta-analysis measuring cyber and traditional

bullying. *Journal of Adolescent Health*, 55(5), 602-611.

Moein, S. T., Hashemian, S. M., Mansourafshar, B., Khorram-Tousi, A., Tabarsi, P., & Doty, R. L. (2020, April). Smell dysfunction: A biomarker for COVID-19. *International Forum of Allergy & Rhinology*.

Moen, P., & Wethington, E. (1999). Midlife development in a life course context. In S. L. Willis & J. D. Reid (Eds.), *Life in the middle: Psychological and social development in middle age* (pp. 1-23). San Diego, CA: Academic Press.

Moen, P., Dempster-McClain, D., & Williams, R. M., Jr. (1992). Successful aging: Life-course perspective on women's multiple roles and health. *American Journal of Sociology*, 97, 1612-1638.

Moffitt, T. E. (1993). Adolescence-limited and life-course-persistent antisocial behavior: a developmental taxonomy. *Psychological Review*, 100(4), 674.

Mohai, P., Lantz, P. M., Morenoff, J., House, J. S., & Mero, R. P. (2009). Racial and socioeconomic disparities in residential proximity to polluting industrial facilities: Evidence from the Americans' Changing Lives study. *American Journal of Public Health*, 99, S649-S656.

Molinuevo, J. L., Blennow, K., Dubois, B., Engelborghs, S., Lewczuk, P., Perret-Liaudet, A., . . . Parnetti, L. (2014). The clinical use of cerebrospinal fluid biomarker testing for Alzheimer's disease diagnosis: A consensus paper from the Alzheimer's Biomarkers Standardization Initiative. *Alzheimer's & Dementia*, 10(6), 808-817.

Moll, H., & Meltzoff, A. N. (2011). How does it look? Level 2 perspective-taking at 36 months of age. *Child Development*, 82(2), 661-673.

Moll, H., & Tomasello, M. (2012). Three-year-olds understand appearance and reality—just not about the same object at the same time. *Developmental Psychology*, 48(4), 1124.

Molnár, G. (2011). Playful fostering of 6- to 8-year-old students' inductive reasoning. *Thinking Skills and Creativity*, 6(2), 91-99.

Monaghan, P., & Haussmann, M. F. (2015). The positive and negative consequences of stressors during early life. *Early Human Development*, 91(11), 643-647.

Monahan, K. C., Rhew, I. C., Hawkins, J. D., & Brown, E. C. (2014). Adolescent pathways to co-occurring problem behavior: The effects of peer delinquency and peer substance use. *Journal of Research on Adolescence*, 24(4), 630-645.

Monahan, K. C., Steinberg, L., Cauffman, E., & Mulvey, E. P. (2009). Trajectories of antisocial behavior and psychosocial maturity from adolescence to young adulthood. *Developmental Psychology*, 45(6), 1654.

Mondschein, E. R., Adolph, K. E., & Tamis-LeMonda, C. S. (2000). Gender bias in mothers' expectations about infant crawling. *Journal of Experimental Child Psychology (Special Issue on Gender)*, 77, 304-316.

Money, J., Hampson, J. G., & Hampson, J. L. (1955). Hermaphroditism: Recommendations concerning assignment of sex, change of sex and psychologic management. *Bulletin of the Johns Hopkins Hospital*, 97(4), 284-300.

Monger, G. P. (2013). *Marriage customs of the world: An encyclopedia of dating customs and wedding traditions.* Santa Barbara, CA: ABC-CLIO, LLC.

Monte, L. M. (2017). Fertility research brief. *Household Economic Studies Current Population Reports P70BR-147.* Washington, DC: U.S. Census Bureau.

Montenegro, X. P. (2004). *The divorce experience: A study of divorce at midlife and beyond.* Washington, DC: American Association of Retired Persons.

Montesi, L., El Ghoch, M., Brodosi, L., Calugi, S., Marchesini, G., & Dalle Grave, R. (2016). Long-term weight loss maintenance for obesity: A multidisciplinary approach. *Diabetes, Metabolic Syndrome and Obesity: Targets and Therapy, 9,* 37.

Montgomery, M. J., & Côté, J. E. (2003). College as a transition to adulthood. In G. R. Adams & M. D. Berzonsky (Eds.), *Blackwell handbook of adolescence.* Malden, MA: Blackwell.

Montirosso, R., Cozzi, P., Putnam, S. P., Gartstein, M. A., & Borgatti, R. (2011). Studying cross-cultural differences in temperament in the first year of life: United States and Italy. *International Journal of Behavioral Development, 35*(1), 27–37.

Moody, A. K. (2010). Using electronic books in the classroom to enhance emergent literacy skills in young children. *Journal of Literacy and Technology, 11*(4), 22–52.

Moody, H. R. (2009). *Aging: Concepts and controversies.* Thousand Oaks, CA: Pine Forge/Sage.

Mook-Kanamori, D. O., Steegers, E. A., Eilers, P. H., Raat, H., Hofman, A., & Jaddoe, V. W. (2010). Risk factors and outcomes associated with first-trimester fetal growth restriction. *Journal of the American Medical Association, 303*(6), 527–534. doi: 10.1001/jama.2010.78

Moon, J. R., Kondo, N., Glymour, M. M., & Subramanian, S. V. (2011). Widowhood and mortality: A meta-analysis. *PLoS One, 6*(8), e23465.

Moon, R. Y., & Hauck, F. R. (2016). SIDS risk: It's more than just the sleep environment. *Pediatrics, 137*(1), e20153665.

Moon, R. Y., & Task Force on Sudden Infant Death Syndrome. (2016). SIDS and other sleep-related infant deaths: Evidence base for 2016 updated recommendations for a safe infant sleeping environment. *Pediatrics, 138*(5), e20162940.

Mooney, C. J., Elliot, A. J., Douthit, K. Z., Marquis, A., & Seplaki, C. L. (2016). Perceived control mediates effects of socioeconomic status and chronic stress on physical frailty: Findings from the health and retirement study. *The Journals of Gerontology: Series B, 73*(7), 1175–1184.

Moor, N., & de Graaf, P. M. (2016). Temporary and long-term consequences of bereavement on happiness. *Journal of Happiness Studies, 17*(3), 913–936.

Moore, M. (2012). Behavioral sleep problems in children and adolescents. *Journal of Clinical Psychology in Medical Settings, 19*(1), 77–83.

Moore, R. C., Eyler, L. T., Mausbach, B. T., Zlatar, Z. Z., Thompson, W. K., Peavy, G., . . .

Jeste, D. V. (2015). Complex interplay between health and successful aging: Role of perceived stress, resilience, and social support. *The American Journal of Geriatric Psychiatry, 23*(6), 622–632.

Moore, S. E., Cole, T. J., Poskitt, E. M. E., Sonko, B. J., Whitehead, R. G., McGregor, I. A., & Prentice, A. M. (1997). Season of birth predicts mortality in rural Gambia. *Nature, 388,* 434.

Moran, L., Lengua, L. J., Zalewski, M., Ruberry, E., Klein, M., Thompson, S., & Kiff, C. (2017). Variable-and person-centered approaches to examining temperament vulnerability and resilience to the effects of contextual risk. *Journal of Research in Personality, 67,* 61–74.

Mordre, M., Groholt, B., Kjelsberg, E., Sandstad, B., & Myhre, A. M. (2011). The impact of ADHD and conduct disorder in childhood on adult delinquency: A 30 years follow-up study using official crime records. *BMC Psychiatry, 11*(1), 57.

Morelli, G. A., Rogoff, B., & Angellilo, C. (2003). Cultural involvement in young children's access to work or involvement in specialized child-focused activities. *International Journal of Behavioral Development, 27,* 264–274.

Moreno-Smith, M., Lutgendorf, S. K., & Sood, A. K. (2010). Impact of stress on cancer metastasis. *Future Oncology, 6*(12), 1863–1881.

Morey, J. N., Boggero, I. A., Scott, A. B., & Segerstrom, S. C. (2015). Current directions in stress and human immune function. *Current Opinion in Psychology, 5,* 13–17.

Morgan, E. M. (2013). Contemporary issues in sexual orientation and identity development in emerging adulthood. *Emerging Adulthood, 1*(1), 52–66.

Morley, T. E., & Moran, G. (2011). The origins of cognitive vulnerability in early childhood: Mechanisms linking early attachment to later depression. *Clinical Psychology Review, 31*(7), 1071–1082.

Morris, A. S., Robinson, L. R., Hays-Grudo, J., Claussen, A. H., Hartwig, S. A., & Treat, A. E. (2017). Targeting parenting in early childhood: A public health approach to improve outcomes for children living in poverty. *Child Development, 88*(2), 388–397.

Morris, M. C. (2004). Diet and Alzheimer's disease: What the evidence shows. *Medscape General Medicine, 6,* 1–5.

Morrisey, M. (2020). *Relief efforts need to do more to protect older workers in a coronavirus economic shutdown* [Economic Policy Institute report]. Retrieved from www.epi.org/blog/relief-efforts-need-to-do-more-to-protect-older-workers-in-a-coronavirus-economic-shutdown/

Morrison, K. E., Rodgers, A. B., Morgan, C. P., & Bale, T. L. (2014). Epigenetic mechanisms in pubertal brain maturation. *Neuroscience, 264,* 17–24.

Morrissey, T. W. (2013). Trajectories of growth in body mass index across childhood: Associations with maternal and paternal employment. *Social Science & Medicine, 95,* 60–68.

Morrow, D. G., Menard, W. W. E., Stine-Morrow, E. A. L., Teller, T., & Bryant, D. (2001). The

influence of expertise and task factors on age differences in pilot communication. *Psychology and Aging, 16,* 31–46.

Mortimer, J. T., Kim, M., Staff, J., & Vuolo, M. (2016). Unemployment, parental help, and self-efficacy during the transition to adulthood. *Work and Occupations, 43*(4), 434–465

Moser, A., Zimmermann, L., Dickerson, K., Grenell, A., Barr, R., & Gerhardstein, P. (2015). They can interact, but can they learn? Toddlers' transfer learning from touchscreens and television. *Journal of Experimental Child Psychology, 137,* 137–155.

Mosier, C. E., & Rogoff, B. (2003). Privileged treatment of toddlers: Cultural aspects of individual choice and responsibility. *Developmental Psychology, 39,* 1047–1060.

Moss, M. S., & Moss, S. Z. (1989). The death of a parent. In R. A. Kalish (Ed.), *Midlife loss: Coping strategies.* Newbury Park, CA: Sage.

Most, J., Tosti, V., Redman, L. M., & Fontana, L. (2017). Calorie restriction in humans: An update. *Ageing Research Reviews, 39,* 36–45.

Motta, V., Bonzini, M., Grevendonk, L., Iodice, S., & Bollati, V. (2017). Epigenetics applied to epidemiology: Investigating environmental factors and lifestyle influence on human health. *La Medicina del lavoro, 108*(1), 10–23.

Mou, Y., Province, J. M., & Luo, Y. (2014). Can infants make transitive inferences? *Cognitive Psychology, 68,* 98–112.

Mouw, T. (2005). Sequences of early adult transitions: How variable are they, and does it matter. In R. Settersten Jr., F. Furstenberg Jr., & R. Rumbaut (Eds.), *On the frontier of adulthood: Theory, research, and public policy* (pp. 256–291). Chicago, IL: University of Chicago Press.

Moyer, V. A. (2012). Screening for prostate cancer: U.S. Preventive Services Task Force recommendation statement. *Annals of Internal Medicine, 157*(2), 120–134.

Moyer, V. A. (2013). Screening for intimate partner violence and abuse of elderly and vulnerable adults: US preventive services task force recommendation statement. *Annals of Internal Medicine, 158*(6), 478–486.

Moyer, V. A. (2014). Screening for cognitive impairment in older adults: U.S. Preventive Services Task Force recommendation statement. *Annals of Internal Medicine, 160*(11), 791–797.

Mroczek, D. K. (2004). Positive and negative affect at midlife. In O. G. Brim, C. D. Ryff, & R. C. Kessler (Eds.), *How healthy are we? A national study of well-being at midlife* (pp. 205–226). Chicago, IL: University of Chicago Press.

Mroczek, D. K., & Kolarz, C. M. (1998). The effect of age on positive and negative affect: A developmental perspective on happiness. *Journal of Personality and Social Psychology, 75*(5), 1333–1349.

Mroczek, D. K., & Spiro, A. (2005). Change in life satisfaction during adulthood: Findings from the Veterans Affairs Normative Aging Study. *Journal of Personality and Social Psychology, 88,* 189–202.

Mroczek, D. K., & Spiro, A., III. (2007). Personality change influences mortality in older men. *Psychological Science, 18*(5), 371–376.

Mrug, S., Elliott, M. N., Davies, S., Tortolero, S. R., Cuccaro, P., & Schuster, M. A. (2014). Early puberty, negative peer influence, and problem behaviors in adolescent girls. *Pediatrics, 133*(1), 7–14.

Mrug, S., Molina, B. S., Hoza, B., Gerdes, A. C., Hinshaw, S. P., Hechtman, L., & Arnold, L. E. (2012). Peer rejection and friendships in children with attention-deficit/hyperactivity disorder: Contributions to long-term outcomes. *Journal of Abnormal Child Psychology, 40*(6), 1013–1026.

Mueck, A., & Ruan, X. (2017). Menopausal symptoms–Comparing East and West. *Maturitas, 100,* 111

Mueller, T. I., Kohn, R., Leventhal, N., Leon, A. C., Solomon, D., Coryell, W., . . . Keller, M. B. (2004). The course of depression in elderly patients. *American Journal of Psychiatry, 12,* 22–29.

Muentener, P., & Carey, S. (2010). Infants' causal representations of state change events. *Cognitive Psychology, 61*(2), 63–86.

Mulford, C., & Giordano, P. (2008). Teen dating violence: A closer look at adolescent romantic relationships. *National Institute of Justice Journal, 261,* 34–41.

Mullins, N., & Lewis, C. M. (2017). Genetics of depression: Progress at last. *Current Psychiatry Reports, 19*(8), 43.

Mumbare, S. S., Maindarkar, G., Darade, R., Yenge, S., Tolani, M. K., & Patole, K. (2012). Maternal risk factors associated with term low birth weight neonates: A matched-pair case control study. *Indian Pediatrics, 49*(1), 25–28.

Mund, M., Freuding, M. M., Möbius, K., Horn, N., & Neyer, F. J. (2020). The stability and change of loneliness across the life span: A meta-analysis of longitudinal studies. *Personality and Social Psychology Review.*

Muniz-Terrera, G., van den Hout, A., Piccinin, A. M., Matthews, F. E., & Hofer, S. M. (2013). Investigating terminal decline: Results from a UK population-based study of aging. *Psychology and Aging, 28*(2), 377.

Mura Paroche, M., Caton, S. J., Vereijken, C. M., Weenen, H., & Houston-Price, C. (2017). How infants and young children learn about food: A systematic review. *Frontiers in Psychology, 8,* 1046.

Murachver, T., Pipe, M., Gordon, R., Owens, J. L., & Fivush, R. (1996). Do, show, and tell: Children's event memories acquired through direct experience, observation, and stories. *Child Development, 67,* 3029–3044.

Muraco, A. (2006). Intentional families: Fictive kin ties between cross-gender, different sexual orientation friends. *Journal of Marriage and Family, 68,* 1313–1325.

Murawski, N. J., Moore, E. M., Thomas, J. D., & Riley, E. P. (2015). Advances in diagnosis and treatment of fetal alcohol spectrum disorders: from animal models to human studies. *Alcohol Research: Current Reviews, 37*(1), 97.

Muris, P., Merckelbach, H., & Collaris, R. (1997). Common childhood fears and their origins. *Behaviour Research and Therapy, 35,* 929–937.

Murphy, M. J., & Peterson, M. J. (2015). Sleep disturbances in depression. *Sleep Medicine Clinics, 10*(1), 17–23.

Murray, C. J., Abraham, J., Ali, M. K., Alvarado, M., Atkinson, C., Baddour, L. M., . . . Bolliger, I. (2013). The state of US health, 1990–2010: Burden of diseases, injuries, and risk factors. *JAMA, 310*(6), 591–606.

Murray, J., & Farrington, D. P. (2010). Risk factors for conduct disorder and delinquency: Key findings from longitudinal studies. *The Canadian Journal of Psychiatry, 55*(10), 633–642.

Murray, R., & Ramstetter, C. (2013). The crucial role of recess in school. *Pediatrics, 131*(1), 183–188.

Murray-Close, M., & Heggeness, M. L. (2018). Manning up and womaning down: How husbands and wives report their earnings when she earns more. US Census Bureau Social, Economic, and Housing Statistics Division Working Paper (2018-20).

Murry, V. M., & Lippold, M. A. (2018). Parenting practices in diverse family structures: Examination of adolescents' development and adjustment. *Journal of Research on Adolescence, 28*(3), 650–664.

Murtagh, E., & NCD Risk Factor Collaboration. (2017). Worldwide trends in children's and adolescents' body mass index, underweight, overweight and obesity, in comparison with adults, from 1975 to 2016: A pooled analysis of 2,416 population-based measurement studies with 128.9 million participants (Pre-published version).

Musick, K., & Michelmore, K. (2015). Change in the stability of marital and cohabiting unions following the birth of a child. *Demography, 52*(5), 1463–1485.

Musick, M. A., Herzog, A. R., & House, J. S. (1999). Volunteering and mortality among older adults: Findings from a national sample. *Journal of Gerontology: Psychological Sciences, 54B,* S173–S180.

Musil, C. M., Gordon, N. L., Warner, C. B., Zauszniewski, J. A., Standing, T., & Wykle, M. (2010). Grandmothers and caregiving to grandchildren: Continuity, change, and outcomes over 24 months. *The Gerontologist, 51*(1), 86–100.

Mustanski, B. S., DuPree, M. G., Nievergelt, C. M., Bocklandt, S., Schork, N. J., & Hamer, D. H. (2005). A genomewide scan of male sexual orientation. *Human Genetics, 116,* 272–278.

Mustonen, U., Huurre, T., Kiviruusu, O., Haukkala, A., & Aro, H. (2011). Long-term impact of parental divorce on intimate relationship quality in adulthood and the mediating role of psychosocial resources. *Journal of Family Psychology, 25*(4), 615.

Myers, D. G. (2000). The funds, friends, and faith of happy people. *American Psychologist, 55,* 56–67.

Myers, J. E., & Harper, M. C. (2014). Midlife concerns and caregiving experiences: Intersecting life issues affecting mental health. In R. C. Talley, G. L. Fricchione, & B. G. Druss (Eds.), *The challenges of mental health caregiving* (pp. 123–142). New York, NY: Springer.

Myers, J. E., Madathil, J., & Tingle, L. R. (2005). Marriage satisfaction and wellness in India and the United States: A preliminary comparison of arranged marriages and marriages of choice. *Journal of Counseling and Development, 83*(2), 183–190.

Myrick, S. E., & Martorell, G. A. (2011). Sticks and stones may break my bones: Protective factors for the effects of perceived discrimination on social competence in adolescence. *Personal Relationships, 18*(3), 487–501.

Márquez, I. E., Sánchez, L. M., & Ramos-Navarro, C. (2019). Long-term outcomes of preterm infants treated with less invasive surfactant technique (LISA). *The Journal of Maternal-Fetal & Neonatal Medicine,* 1–6.

Mäkinen, M., Puukko-Viertomies, L. R., Lindberg, N., Siimes, M. A., & Aalberg, V. (2012). Body dissatisfaction and body mass in girls and boys transitioning from early to mid-adolescence: Additional role of self-esteem and eating habits. *BMC Psychiatry, 12*(1), 35.

Nabi, R. L., Prestin, A., & So, J. (2013). Facebook friends with (health) benefits? Exploring social network site use and perceptions of social support, stress, and well-being. *Cyberpsychology, Behavior, and Social Networking, 16*(10), 721–727.

Nader, P. R., Bradley, R. H., Houts, R. M., McRitchie, S. L., & O'Brien, M. (2008). Moderate-to-vigorous physical activity from ages 9 to 15 years. *Journal of the American Medical Association, 300,* 295–305.

Nagaraja, J., Menkedick, J., Phelan, K. J., Ashley, P., Zhang, X., & Lanphear, B. P. (2005). Deaths from residential injuries in US children and adolescents, 1985–1997. *Pediatrics, 116,* 454–461.

Nagata, J. M., Palar, K., Gooding, H. C., Garber, A. K., Bibbins-Domingo, K., & Weiser, S. D. (2019). Food insecurity and chronic disease in US young adults: Findings from the National Longitudinal Study of Adolescent to Adult Health. *Journal of General Internal Medicine, 34*(12), 2756–2762.

Nahar, B., Hossain, M. I., Hamadani, J. D., Ahmed, T., Grantham-McGregor, S., & Persson, L. A. (2012). Effects of psychosocial stimulation on improving home environment and child-rearing practices: Results from a community-based trial among severely malnourished children in Bangladesh. *BMC Public Health, 12*(1), 622.

Naicker, K., Galambos, N. L., Zeng, Y., Senthilselvan, A., & Colman, I. (2013). Social, demographic, and health outcomes in the 10 years following adolescent depression. *Journal of Adolescent Health, 52*(5), 533–538.

Naik, S., Kolikonda, M., Prabhu, A., & Lippmann, S. (2018). Marijuana on the brain—a concern. *Innovations in Clinical Neuroscience, 15*(1–2), 12.

Naito, M., & Miura, H. (2001). Japanese children's numerical competencies: Age and school-related influences on the development of number concepts and addition skills. *Developmental Psychology, 37,* 217–230.

Naito, T., & Geilen, U. P. (2005). The changing Japanese family: A psychological portrait. In J. L. Roopnarine & U. P. Gielen (Eds.), *Families in global perspective* (pp. 63–84). Boston, MA: Allyn & Bacon.

Nakamoto, J., & Schwartz, D. (2010). Is peer victimization associated with academic achievement? A meta-analytic review. *Social Development, 19*(2), 221–242.

Namkung, E. H., Greenberg, J. S., & Mailick, M. R. (2017). Well-being of sibling caregivers: Effects of kinship relationship and race. *The Gerontologist, 57*(4), 626–636.

Nandrup, A. B. (2016). Do class size effects differ across grades? *Education Economics, 24*(1), 83–95.

Nardone, S., & Elliott, E. (2016). The interaction between the immune system and epigenetics in the etiology of autism spectrum disorders. *Frontiers in Neuroscience, 10,* 329. http://doi.org/10.3389/fnins.2016.00329

Naseem, K. (2018). Job stress, happiness and life satisfaction: The moderating role of emotional intelligence empirical study in telecommunication sector Pakistan. *Journal of Social Sciences, 4*(1), 7–14.

Nash, E., & Dreweke, J. (2019). The US abortion rate continues to drop: Once again, state abortion restrictions are not the main driver. *Guttmacher Policy Review, 22.*

National Academies of Sciences, Engineering, and Medicine. (2019). *A roadmap to reducing child poverty.* Washington, DC: The National Academies Press. https://doi.org/10.17226/25246

National Alliance for Caregiving. (2015). *2015 report: Caregiving in the U.S.* [report]. Retrieved from www.caregiving.org/wp-content/uploads/2015/05/2015_CaregivingintheUS_Final-Report-June-4_WEB.pdf

National Alliance for Public Charter Schools, (2020). *Charter school databases: Data dashboard* [Data sheet]. Retrieved from https://data.publiccharters.org/

National Center for Chronic Disease Prevention and Health Promotion. (2019). *Oral health* [Fact sheet]. Retrieved from www.cdc.gov/chronicdisease/resources/publications/aag/oral-health.htm

National Center for Education Statistics. (2003). *The condition of education, 2003 (NCES 2003-067).* Washington, DC: Author

National Center for Education Statistics. (2007). *The nation's report card: Mathematics 2007 (NCES 2007-494).* Washington, DC: Author.

National Center for Education Statistics. (2008). *1.5 million homeschooled students in the United States in 2007 (NCES 2009-030).* Washington, DC: Author.

National Center for Education Statistics. (2016). *Number and internet access of instructional computers and rooms in public schools, by selected school characteristics: Selected years, 1995 through 2008* [Data file]. Retrieved from https://nces.ed.gov/programs/digest/d15/tables/dt15_218.10.asp?

National Center for Education Statistics. (2017). *Digest of education statistics, 2018* [Report].

Retrieved from https://nces.ed.gov/programs/digest/d18/index.asp

National Center for Education Statistics. (2017). *The condition of education 2017 (NCES 2017-144).* Washington, DC: Author.

National Center for Education Statistics. (2018). *Early childhood care arrangements: Choices and costs* [Report]. Retrieved from https://nces.ed.gov/programs/coe/indicator_tca.asp

National Center for Education Statistics. (2018). *The condition of education* [Report]. Retrieved from https://nces.ed.gov/programs/coe/indicator_sae.asp

National Center for Education Statistics. (2019). *Fast facts: High school graduation rates* [Report]. Retrieved from https://nces.ed.gov/fastfacts/display.asp?id=805

National Center for Education Statistics. (2019). *The condition of education* [Report]. Retrieved from https://nces.ed.gov/programs/coe/indicator_cgg.asp

National Center for Health Statistics. (2017). *Health, United States, 2016: With chartbook on long-term trends in health.* Hyattsville, MD: Author.

National Center for Health Statistics. (1999). *Abstract adapted from Births: Final Data for 1999 by Mid-Atlantic Parents of Multiples.* Retrieved from www.orgsites.com/va/mapom/_pgg1.php3

National Center for Health Statistics. (2004). *Health, United States, 2004 with chartbook on trends in the health of Americans* (DHHS Publication No. 2004-1232). Hyattsville, MD: Author.

National Center for Health Statistics. (2010). Table 68. Hypertension and elevated blood pressure among persons 20 years of age and over, by selected characteristics: United States, 1988–1994, 1999–2002, and 2003–2006. *Health, United States, 2009: With special feature on medical technology* (DHHS Publication No. 2010-1232). Hyattsville, MD: author. Retrieved from http://www.cdc.gov/nchs/data/hus/hus09.pdf#068

National Center for Health Statistics. (2016). *Health, United States, 2015: With special feature on racial and ethnic health disparities.* Retrieved from www.ncbi.nlm.nih.gov/pubmed/27308685

National Center for Health Statistics. (2017). *Births in the United States, 2016* [Centers for Disease Control data brief]. Retrieved from www.cdc.gov/nchs/products/databriefs/db287.htm.

National Center for Health Statistics. (2018). *Tables of summary health statistics* [Data tables]. Retrieved from www.cdc.gov/nchs/nhis/SHS/tables.htm.

National Center for Health Statistics. (2019). *Health, United States 2018* [Report]. Retrieved from www.cdc.gov/nchs/data/hus/hus18.pdf

National Center for Injury Prevention and Control. (2016). *Home and recreational safety: Hip fractures among older adults.* Retrieved from www.cdc.gov/homeandrecreationalsafety/falls/adulthipfx.html

National Center for Learning Disabilities. (2014). *The state of learning disabilities, 3rd ed., 2014* [Report]. Retrieved from www.ncld.org/wp-content/uploads/2014/11/2014-State-of-LD-FINAL-FOR-RELEASE.pdf.

National Coalition for the Homeless. (2017). *Homelessness in America.* Retrieved from http://nationalhomeless.org/about-homelessness/

National Conference of State Legislators. (2020). *Health insurance and states: An NCSL overview* [Information sheet]. Retrieved from www.ncsl.org/research/health/health-insurance-and-states-overview.aspx

National Council on Aging. (2015). *The 2015 United States of Aging survey: National findings* [Report]. Retrieved from www.ncoa.org/wp-content/uploads/USA15-National-Fact-Sheet-Final.pdf

National Eye Institute. (2019). *Cataract data and statistics* [Fact sheet]. Retrieved from www.nei.nih.gov/learn-about-eye-health/resources-for-health-educators/eye-health-data-and-statistics/cataract-data-and-statistics

National Health Interview Survey. (2018). Table A-6a. *Age-adjusted percentages (with standard errors) of hearing trouble, vision trouble, and absence of teeth among adults aged 18 and over, by selected characteristics: United States, 2018* [Data tables]. Retrieved from https://ftp.cdc.gov/pub/Health_Statistics/NCHS/NHIS/SHS/2018_SHS_Table_A-6.pdf

National Highway Traffic Safety Administration. (2017). *Teen driving.* Retrieved from www.nhtsa.gov/road-safety/teen-driving

National Institute of Child Health and Human Development. (2017). *Phenylketonuria (PKU).* Retrieved from www.nichd.nih.gov/health/topics/pku/Pages/default.aspx

National Institute of Mental Health. (2018). *Eating disorders: About more than food* [Report]. Retrieved from https://www.nimh.nih.gov/health/publications/eating-disorders/eatingdisorders_148810.pdf

National Institute of Neurological Disorders and Stroke. (2006, January 25). *NINDS shaken baby syndrome* [Information page]. Retrieved from www.ninds.nih.gov/disorders/shakenbaby/shakenbaby.htm

National Institute on Aging. (2011). *Global health and aging.* Retrieved from www.nia.nih.gov/sites/default/files/nia-who_report_booklet_oct-2011_a4__1-12-12_5.pdf

National Institute on Alcohol Abuse and Alcoholism. (1996, July). *Alcohol alert* (No. 33-1996 [PH 366]). Bethesda, MD: author.

National Institute on Alcohol Abuse and Alcoholism. (2020). *Alcohol facts and statistics.* Retrieved from www.niaaa.nih.gov/alcohol-health/overview-alcohol-consumption/alcohol-facts-and-statistics

National Institute on Deafness and Other Communication Disorders. (2016). *Quick statistics about hearing.* Retrieved from www.nidcd.nih.gov/health/statistics/quick-statistics-hearing

National Institute on Drug Abuse. (2012). *Is nicotine addictive? Research report series.* Bethesda, MD: National Institutes of Health, National Institute on Drug Abuse.

National Institutes of Health. (2007). *Why populations aging matters: A global perspective* [Report]. Retrieved from www.nia.nih.gov/sites/default/files/2017-06/WPAM.pdf

National Institutes of Health. (2010, February 4). *NIH scientists identify maternal and fetal genes that increase preterm birth risk* [Press release]. Retrieved from www.nih.gov/news/health/feb2010/nichd-04.htm

National Partnership for Women. (2018). Continuous support for women during childbirth: 2017 Cochrane Review Update Key Takeaways. *The Journal of Perinatal Education, 27*(4), 193.

National Reading Panel (2000). *Report of the National Reading Panel: Teaching children to read: An evidence-based assessment of the scientific research literature on reading and its implications for reading instruction: Reports of the subgroups.* Washington, DC: National Institute of Child Health and Human Development.

National Reading Panel. (2000). *Report of the National Reading Panel. Teaching children to read: An evidence-based assessment of the scientific research literature on reading and its implications for reading instruction: Reports of the subgroups.* Washington, DC: National Institute of Child Health and Human Development.

National Research Council. (1993). *Losing generations: Adolescents in high risk settings.* Washington, DC: National Academy Press.

National Research Council. (1993). *Understanding child abuse and neglect.* Washington, DC: National Academy Press.

National Safety Council. (2020). *Drivers are falling asleep behind the wheel* [Report]. Retrieved from www.nsc.org/road-safety/safety-topics/fatigued-driving

National Sleep Foundation. (2020). *Children and sleep* [Information sheet]. Retrieved from www.sleepfoundation.org/articles/children-and-sleep

Natrajan, M. S., de la Fuente, A. G., Crawford, A. H., Linehan, E., Nuñez, V., Johnson, K. R., . . . Franklin, R. J. (2015). Retinoid X receptor activation reverses age-related deficiencies in myelin debris phagocytosis and remyelination. *Brain, 138*(12), 3581–3597.

Navarro, J., Pulido, R., Berger, C., Arteaga, M., Osofsky, H. J., Martinez, M., . . . Hansel, T. C. (2016). Children's disaster experiences and psychological symptoms: An international comparison between the Chilean earthquake and tsunami and Hurricane Katrina. *International Social Work, 59*(4), 545–558.

Naveh-Benjamin, M., Brav, T., & Levy, O. (2007). The associative memory deficit of older adults: The role of strategy utilization. *Psychology and Aging, 22*(1), 202–208.

Neely-Barnes, S. L., Graff, J. C., & Washington, G. (2010). The health-related quality of life of custodial grandparents. *Health & Social Work, 35*(2), 87–97.

Nehring, I., Kostka, T., von Kries, R., & Rehfuess, E. A. (2015). Impacts of in utero and early infant taste experiences on later taste acceptance: a systematic review. *The Journal of Nutrition, 145*(6), 1271–1279.

Neidorf, S., & Morin, R. (2011). *Four-in-ten Americans have close friends or relatives who are gay.* Retrieved from http://pewresearch.org/pubs/485/friends-who-are-gay

Neimeyer, R. A., & Currier, J. M. (2009). Grief therapy: Evidence of efficacy and emerging directions. *Current Directions in Psychological Science, 18*(6), 352–356.

Neisser, U., Boodoo, G., Bouchard, T. J., Jr., Boykin, A. W., Brody, N., Ceci, S. J., . . . Urbina, S. (1996). Intelligence: Knowns and unknowns. *American Psychologist, 51*(2), 77–101.

Neitzel, R. L., & Fligor, B. J. (2019). Risk of noise-induced hearing loss due to recreational sound: Review and recommendations. *The Journal of the Acoustical Society of America, 146*(5), 3911–3921.

Nelson, C. A. (1995). The ontogeny of human memory: A cognitive neuroscience perspective. *Developmental Psychology, 31*, 723–738.

Nelson, C. A., Zeanah, C. H., & Fox, N. A. (2019). How early experience shapes human development: The case of psychosocial deprivation. *Neural Plasticity.*

Nelson, D. B., Moniz, M. H., & Davis, M. M. (2018). Population-level factors associated with maternal mortality in the United States, 1997–2012. *BMC Public Health, 18*(1), 1007.

Nelson, K. (1993). The psychological and social origins of autobiographical memory. *Psychological Science, 47*, 7–14.

Nelson, K. (2005). Evolution and development of human memory systems. In B. J. Ellis and D. F. Bjorklund (Eds.), *Origins of the social mind: Evolutionary psychology and child development* (pp. 354–382). New York, NY: Guilford Press.

Nelson, K. B., Sartwelle, T. P., & Rouse, D. J. (2016). Electronic fetal monitoring, cerebral palsy, and caesarean section: Assumptions versus evidence. *BMJ, 355*, i6405.

Nelson, K., & Fivush, R. (2004). The emergence of autobiographical memory: A social cultural developmental theory. *Psychological Bulletin, 111*, 486–511.

Nelson, L. J., Padilla-Walker, L. M., & Nielson, M. G. (2015). Is hovering smothering or loving? An examination of parental warmth as a moderator of relations between helicopter parenting and emerging adults' indices of adjustment. *Emerging Adulthood, 3*(4), 282–285.

Nelson, S. K., Kushlev, K., English, T., Dunn, E. W., & Lyubomirsky, S. (2013). In defense of parenthood: Children are associated with more joy than misery. *Psychological Science, 24*(1), 3–10.

Neppl, T. K., Dhalewadikar, J., & Lohman, B. J. (2016). Harsh parenting, deviant peers, adolescent risky behavior: Understanding the mediational effect of attitudes and intentions. *Journal of Research on Adolescence, 26*(3), 538–551.

Neppl, T. K., Donnellan, M. B., Scaramella, L. V., Widaman, K. F., Spilman, S. K., Ontai, L. L., & Conger, R. D. (2010). Differential stability of temperament and personality from toddlerhood to middle childhood. *Journal of Research in Personality, 44*(3), 386–396.

Nesdale, D. (2011). Social groups and children's intergroup prejudice: Just how influential are social group norms? *Anales de Psicología/Annals of Psychology, 27*(3), 600–610.

Ness, J., Ahmed, A., & Aronow, W. S. (2004). Demographics and payment characteristics of nursing home residents in the United States: A 23-year trend. *Journal of Gerontology: Medical Sciences, 59A*, 1213–1217.

Neto, F. K., Noschang, R., & Nunes, M. L. (2016). The relationship between epilepsy, sleep disorders, and attention deficit hyperactivity disorder (ADHD) in children: A review of the literature. *Sleep Science, 9*(3), 158–163.

Neuburger, S., Jansen, P., Heil, M., & Quaiser-Pohl, C. (2011). Gender differences in pre-adolescents' mental-rotation performance: Do they depend on grade and stimulus type? *Personality and Individual Differences, 50*(8), 1238–1242.

Neugarten, B. L. (1967). The awareness of middle age. In R. Owen (Ed.), *Middle age.* London, England: BBC.

Neugarten, B. L., & Neugarten, D. A. (1987, May). The changing meanings of age. *Psychology Today,* 29–33.

Neugarten, B. L., Havinghurst, R. & Tobin, S. (1968). Personality and patterns of aging. In B. Neugarten (Ed.). *Middle age and aging.* Chicago, IL: University of Chicago Press.

Neugarten, B. L., Moore, J. W., & Lowe, J. C. (1965). Age norms, age constraints, and adult socialization. *American Journal of Sociology, 70*, 710–717.

Neumann, R., Steinhäuser, N., & Roeder, U. R. (2009). How self-construal shapes emotion: Cultural differences in the feeling of pride. *Social Cognition, 27*(2), 327–337.

Neumark, D. (2008). *Reassessing the age discrimination in employment act* (Research Report No. 2008-09). Washington, DC: AARP Public Policy Institute. Retrieved from www.socsci.uci.edu/~dneumark/2008_09_adea.pdf

Neupert, S. D., Almeida, D. M., Mroczek, D. K., & Spiro, A. (2006). Daily stressors and memory failures in a naturalistic setting: Findings from the VA Normative Aging Study. *Psychology and Aging, 21*, 424–429.

Newcomb, A. F., & Bagwell, C. L. (1995). Children's friendship relations: A meta-analytic review. *Psychological Bulletin, 117*(2), 306–347.

Newman, C. L., Howlett, E., & Burton, S. (2014). Implications of fast food restaurant concentration for preschool-aged childhood obesity. *Journal of Business Research, 67*(8), 1573–1580.

Newman, R. S. (2005). The cocktail party effect in infants revisited: Listening to one's name in noise. *Developmental Psychology, 41*, 352–362.

Newman, S. (2003). The living conditions of elderly Americans. *Gerontologist, 43*, 99–109.

Neyfakh, L. (2014, August 31). What "age segregation" does to America. *Boston Globe.* Retrieved from www.bostonglobe.com/ideas/2014/08/30/what-age-segregation-does-america/o568E8xoAQ7VG6F4grjLxH/story.html

Ng, F. F. Y., Pomerantz, E. M., & Lam, S. F. (2007). European American and Chinese parents' responses to children's success and failure: Implications for children's responses. *Developmental Psychology, 43*(5), 1239.

Ng, M., De Montigny, J. G., Ofner, M., Do, M. T. (2017). Environmental factors associated with autism spectrum disorder: A scoping review for the years 2003-2013. *Health Promotion and Chronic Disease Prevention in Canada, 37,* 1-23.

Ng, M., Fleming, T., Robinson, M., Thomson, B., Graetz, N., Margono, C., . . . Abraham, J. P. (2014). Global, regional, and national prevalence of overweight and obesity in children and adults during 1980-2013: A systematic analysis for the Global Burden of Disease Study 2013. *The Lancet, 384*(9945), 766-781.

Ng, T. W., & Feldman, D. C. (2013). A meta-analysis of the relationships of age and tenure with innovation-related behaviour. *Journal of Occupational and Organizational Psychology, 86*(4), 585-616.

Ng, W., & Diener, E. (2019). Affluence and subjective well-being: Does income inequality moderate their associations? *Applied Research in Quality of Life, 14*(1), 155-170.

Ngangana, P. C., Davis, B. L., Burns, D. P., McGee, Z. T., & Montgomery, A. J. (2016). Intra-family stressors among adult siblings sharing caregiving for parents. *Journal of Advanced Nursing, 72*(12), 3169-3181.

Ngun, T. C., & Vilain, E. (2014). The biological basis of human sexual orientation: Is there a role for epigenetics. *Advances in Genetics, 86,* 167-184.

Nguyen, S., & Rosengren, K. (2004). Parental reports of children's biological knowledge and misconceptions. *International Journal of Behavioral Development, 28*(5), 411-420.

Nguyen, T. K., & Astington, J. W. (2014). Reassessing the bilingual advantage in theory of mind and its cognitive underpinnings. *Bilingualism: Language and Cognition, 17*(2), 396-409.

NICHD Early Child Care Research Network. (2005). Duration and developmental timing of poverty and children's cognitive and social development from birth through third grade. *Child Development, 76,* 795-810.

Nickerson, A., Bryant, R. A., Aderka, I. M., Hinton, D. E., & Hofmann, S. G. (2013). The impacts of parental loss and adverse parenting on mental health: Findings from the National Comorbidity Survey-Replication. *Psychological Trauma: Theory, Research, Practice, and Policy, 5*(2), 119.

Nicolaisen, M., & Thorsen, K. (2017). What are friends for? Friendships and loneliness over the lifespan—From 18 to 79 years. *The International Journal of Aging and Human Development, 84*(2), 126-158.

Nielsen, M., & Tomaselli, K. (2010). Overimitation in Kalahari Bushman children and the origins of human cultural cognition. *Psychological Science, 21*(5), 729-736.

Niemi, A. K. (2017). Review of randomized controlled trials of massage in preterm infants. *Children, 4*(4), 21

Nieuwenhuijsen, M. J., Dadvand, P., Grellier, J., Martinez, D., & Vrijheid, M. (2013). Environmental risk factors of pregnancy outcomes: a summary of recent meta-analyses of epidemiological studies. *Environmental Health, 12*(1), 6.

Nihtilä, E., & Martikainen, P. (2008). Why older people living with a spouse are less likely to be institutionalized: The role of socioeconomic factors and health characteristics. *Scandinavian Journal of Public Health, 36,* 35-43.

Nikolas, M. A., & Burt, S. A. (2010). Genetic and environmental influences on ADHD symptom dimensions of inattention and hyperactivity: a meta-analysis. *Journal of Abnormal Psychology, 119*(1), 1.

Nilsen, E. S., & Graham, S. A. (2009). The relations between children's communicative perspective-taking and executive functioning. *Cognitive Psychology, 58,* 220-249.

Nisbett, R. E., Aronson, J., Blair, C., Dickens, W., Flynn, J., Halpern, D. F., & Turkheimer, E. (2012). Group differences in IQ are best understood as environmental in origin. *American Psychologist, 67,* 503-504. doi:10.1037/a0029772

Nisbett, R. E., Aronson, J., Blair, C., Dickens, W., Flynn, J., Halpern, D. F., & Turkheimer, E. (2012). Intelligence: New findings and theoretical developments. *American Psychologist, 67*(2), 130.

Nisbett, R.E. (2003). *The geography of thought: How Asians and Westerners think differently—and why.* New York, NY: Free Press.

Nissim, N. R., O'Shea, A. M., Bryant, V., Porges, E. C., Cohen, R., & Woods, A. J. (2017). Frontal structural neural correlates of working memory performance in older adults. *Frontiers in Aging Neuroscience, 8,* 328.

Niv, S., Ashrafulla, S., Tuvblad, C., Joshi, A., Raine, A., Leahy, R., & Baker, L. A. (2015). Childhood EEG frontal alpha power as a predictor of adolescent antisocial behavior: A twin heritability study. *Biological Psychology, 105,* 72-76.

Nix, R. L., Bierman, K. L., Heinrichs, B. S., Gest, S. D., Welsh, J. A., & Domitrovich, C. E. (2016). The randomized controlled trial of Head Start REDI: Sustained effects on developmental trajectories of social-emotional functioning. *Journal of Consulting and Clinical Psychology, 84*(4), 310.

Noble, Y., & Boyd, R. (2012). Neonatal assessments for the preterm infant up to 4 months corrected age: A systematic review. *Developmental Medicine & Child Neurology, 54*(2), 129-139.

Nock, M. K., Borges, G., Bromet, E. J., Alonso, J., Angermeyer, M., Beautrais, A., . . . Williams, D. (2008). Cross-national prevalence and risk factors for suicidal ideation, plans and attempts. *British Journal of Psychiatry, 192,* 98-105.

Nock, M. K., Green, J. G., Hwang, I., McLaughlin, K. A., Sampson, N. A., Zaslavsky, A. M., & Kessler, R. C. (2013). Prevalence, correlates, and treatment of lifetime suicidal behavior among adolescents: results from the National Comorbidity Survey Replication Adolescent Supplement. *JAMA Psychiatry, 70*(3), 300-310.

Nolen-Hoeksema, S., & Aldao, A. (2011). Gender and age differences in emotion regulation strategies and their relationship to depressive symptoms. *Personality and Individual Differences, 51*(6), 704-708.

Northey, J. M., Cherbuin, N., Pumpa, K. L., Smee, D. J., & Rattray, B. (2018). Exercise interventions for cognitive function in adults older than 50: A systematic review with meta-analysis. *British Journal of Sports Medicine, 52*(3), 154-160.

Northwestern University Center on Human Development. (2014). *Revised parenting in the age of digital technology: A national survey.* Retrieved from http://cmhd.northwestern.edu/wp-content/uploads/2015/06/Parenting AgeDigitalTechnology.REVISED.FINAL_. 2014.pdf

Norton, D. E. (2010). *Through the eyes of a child: An introduction to children's literature* (8th ed.). Boston., MA: Prentice-Hall.

Notterman, D. A., & Mitchell, C. (2015). Epigenetics and understanding the impact of social determinants of health. *Pediatric Clinics, 62*(5), 1227-1240.

Noël, P. H., Williams, J. W., Unutzer, J., Worchel, J., Lee, S., Cornell, J., . . . Hunkeler, E. (2004). Depression and comorbid illness in elderly primary care patients: Impact on multiple domains of health status and well-being. *Annals of Family Medicine, 2,* 555-562.

Noël-Miller, C. (2010). Spousal loss, children, and the risk of nursing home admission. *Journals of Gerontology Series B: Psychological Sciences and Social Sciences, 65*(3), 370-380.

Noël-Miller, C. M. (2011). Partner caregiving in older cohabiting couples. *Journals of Gerontology Series B: Psychological Sciences and Social Sciences, 66*(3), 341-353.

Nucci, L., Hasebe, Y., & Lins-Dyer, M. T. (2005). Adolescent psychological well-being and parental control. In J. Smetana (Ed.), *Changing boundaries of parental authority during adolescence* (New Directions for Child and Adolescent Development, No. 108, pp. 17-30). San Francisco, CA: Jossey-Bass.

O'Leary, L., Hughes-McCormack, L., Dunn, K., & Cooper, S. A. (2018). Early death and causes of death of people with Down syndrome: A systematic review. *Journal of Applied Research in Intellectual Disabilities, 31*(5), 687-708.

Oberle, E. (2009). The development of theory of mind reasoning in Micronesian children. *Journal of Cognition and Culture, 9*(1-2), 39-56.

Oberle, E., Schonert-Reichl, K. A., & Thomson, K. C. (2010). Understanding the link between social and emotional well-being and peer relations in early adolescence: Gender-specific predictors of peer acceptance. *Journal of Youth and Adolescence, 39*(11), 1330-1342.

Oberman, L. M., & Ramachandran, V. S. (2007). The simulating social mind: The role of the mirror neuron system and simulation in the social and communicative deficits of autism spectrum disorders. *Psychological Bulletin, 133,* 310-327.

Obradovic, J., Stamperdahl, J., Bush, N. R., Adler, N. E., & Boyce, W. T. (2010). Biological sensitivity to context: The interactive effects of stress reactivity and family adversity on socioemotional behavior and school readiness. *Child Development, 81,* 270-289.

Odgers, C. L., Donley, S., Caspi, A., Bates, C. J., & Moffitt, T. E. (2015). Living alongside more affluent neighbors predicts greater involvement in antisocial behavior among low-income boys. *Journal of Child Psychology and Psychiatry, 56*(10), 1055–1064.

Odgers, C., Caspi, A., Nagin, D., Piquero, A., Slutske, W., Milne, B., . . . Moffitt, T. E. (2008). Is it important to prevent early exposure to drugs and alcohol among adolescents? *Psychological Science, 19*(10), 1037–1044.

Odimegwu, C., Ndagurwa, P., Singini, M. G., & Baruwa, O. J. (2018). Cohabitation in sub-Saharan Africa: A regional analysis. *Southern African Journal of Demography, 18*(1), 111–170.

Oeppen, J., & Vaupel, J. W. (2002). Broken limits to life expectancy. *Science, 296*(5570), 1029–1031.

Oesterle, S., Hawkins, J. D., Hill, K. G., & Bailey, J. A. (2010). Men's and women's pathways to adulthood and their adolescent precursors. *Journal of Marriage and Family, 72*(5), 1436–1453.

Oesterle, S., Hawkins, J. D., & Hill, K. G. (2011). Men's and women's pathways to adulthood and associated substance misuse. *Journal of Studies on Alcohol and Drugs, 72*(5), 763–773.

Offer, D., & Church, R. B. (1991). Generation gap. In R. M. Lerner, A. C. Petersen, & J. Brooks-Gunn (Eds.), *Encyclopedia of adolescence* (pp. 397–399). New York, NY: Garland.

Offer, D., Kaiz, M., Ostrov, E., & Albert, D. B. (2002). Continuity in family constellation. *Adolescent and Family Health, 3*, 3–8.

Office of Disease Prevention and Health Promotion. (2020). *PA-3.1 Adolescents meeting federal physical activity guidelines (percent, grades 9–12) by sex, year: 2017* [Graphs]. Retrieved from www.healthypeople.gov/2020/topics-objectives/topic/physical-activity/national-snapshot

Offit, P. A., Quarles, J., Gerber, M. A., Hackett, C. J., Marcuse, E. K., Kollman, T. R., . . . Landry, S. (2002). Addressing parents' concerns: Do multiple vaccines overwhelm or weaken the infant's immune system? *Pediatrics, 109*, 124–129.

Ofori, B., Oraichi, D., Blais, L., Rey, E., & Berard, A. (2006). Risk of congenital anomalies in pregnant users of non-steroidal anti-inflammatory drugs: A nested case-control study. *Birth Defects Research Part B: Developmental and Reproductive Toxicology, 77*(4), 268–279.

Ogawa, N., & Gudykunst, W. B. (2000). *Politeness rules in Japan and the United States* (Doctoral dissertation, in partial fulfillment for M.A. in Speech Communcation, California State University, Fullerton).

Ogden, C. L., Carroll, M. D., Fakhouri, T. H., Hales, C. M., Fryar, C. D., Li, X., & Freedman, D. S. (2018). Prevalence of obesity among youths by household income and education level of head of household—United States 2011–2014. *Morbidity and Mortality Weekly Report, 67*(6), 186.

Ogden, C. L., Carroll, M. D., Fryar, C. D., & Flegal, K. M. (2015). *Prevalence of obesity among adults and youth: United States, 2011–2014* (pp. 1–8). Washington, DC: US Department of Health and Human Services, Centers for Disease Control and Prevention, National Center for Health Statistics.

Ogden, C. L., Carroll, M. D., Kit, B. K., & Flegal, K. M. (2014). Prevalence of childhood and adult obesity in the United States, 2011–2012. *JAMA, 311*(8), 806–814.

Ogden, C. L., Fryar, C. D., Hales, C. M., Carroll, M. D., Aoki, Y., & Freedman, D. S. (2018). Differences in obesity prevalence by demographics and urbanization in US children and adolescents, 2013–2016. *JAMA, 319*(23), 2410–2418.

Ogden, C. L., Lamb, M. M., Carroll, M. D., & Flegal, K. M. (2010). Obesity and socioeconomic status in children and adolescents: United States, 2005–2008. *NCHS Data Brief, 51*. Hyattsville, MD: National Center for Health Statistics.

Oishi, S., Diener, E., Lucas, R. E., & Suh, E. M. (2009). Cross-cultural variations in predictors of life satisfaction: Perspectives from needs and values. In E. Diener (Ed.), *Culture and well-being* (pp. 109–127). Dordrecht, the Netherlands: Springer.

Olatomide, O. O., & Akomolafe, M. J. (2013). Job satisfaction and emotional intelligence as predictors of organizational commitment of secondary school teachers. *Ife PsychologIA: An International Journal, 21*(2), 65–74.

Olfson, M., Blanco, C., Wang, S., Laje, G., & Correll, C. U. (2014). National trends in the mental health care of children, adolescents, and adults by office-based physicians. *JAMA Psychiatry, 71*(1), 81–90.

Olfson, M., Crystal, S., Huang, C., & Gerhard, T. (2010). Trends in antipsychotic drug use by very young, privately insured children. *Journal of Child and Adolescent Psychiatry, 49*(1), 13–23.

Olsen, S. F., Yang, C., Hart, C. H., Robinson, C. C., Wu, P., Nelson, D. A., . . . Wo, J. (2002). Maternal psychological control and preschool children's behavioral outcomes in China, Russia, and the United States. In B. K. Barber (Ed.), *Intrusive parenting: How psychological control affects children and adolescents* (pp. 235–262). Washington, DC: American Psychological Association.

Olson, M. E., Diekema, D., Elliott, B. A., & Renier, C. M. (2010). Impact of income and income inequality on infant health outcomes in the United States. *Pediatrics, 126*(6), 1165–1173.

Olsson, B., Lautner, R., Andreasson, U., Öhrfelt, A., Portelius, E., Bjerke, M., . . . Wu, E. (2016). CSF and blood biomarkers for the diagnosis of Alzheimer's disease: a systematic review and meta-analysis. *The Lancet Neurology, 15*(7), 673–684.

Olthof, T., Schouten, A., Kuiper, H., Stegge, H., & Jennekens-Schinkel, A. (2000). Shame and guilt in children: Differential situational antecedents and experiential correlates. *British Journal of Developmental Psychology, 18*, 51–64.

Ono, M., & Harley, V. R. (2013). Disorders of sex development: New genes, new concepts. *Nature Reviews Endocrinology, 9*(2), 79–91.

Onyishi, E. I., Sorokowski, P., Sorokowska, A., & Pipitone, R. N. (2012). Children and marital satisfaction in a non-Western sample: Having more children increases marital satisfaction among the Igbo people of Nigeria. *Evolution and Human Behavior, 33*(6), 771–774.

Ooi, L. L., Baldwin, D., Coplan, R. J., & Rose-Krasnor, L. (2018). Young children's preference for solitary play: Implications for socio-emotional and school adjustment. *British Journal of Developmental Psychology, 36*(3), 501–507.

Opfer, J. E., & Gelman, S. A. (2011). Development of the animate-inanimate distinction. *The Wiley-Blackwell handbook of childhood cognitive development* (2nd ed., pp. 213–238). Hoboken, NJ: Wiley.

Orathinkal, J., & Vansteenwegen, A. (2007). Do demographics affect marital satisfaction? *Journal of Sex & Marital Therapy, 33*(1), 73–85.

Orbuch, T. L., House, J. S., Mero, R. P., & Webster, P. S. (1996). Marital quality over the life course. *Social Psychology Quarterly, 59*, 162–171.

Oregon Health Authority. (2020). *Death with dignity act: 2098 data summary* [Report]. Public Health Division, Center for Health Statistics. www.oregon.gov/oha/PH/PROVIDERPARTNERRESOURCES/EVALUATIONRESEARCH/DEATHWITHDIGNITYACT/Documents/year22.pdf

Orel, N. A. (2004). Gay, lesbian, and bisexual elders: Expressed needs and concerns across focus groups. *Journal of Gerontological Social Work, 43*(2–3), 57–77.

Organisation for Economic Co-Development and Learning (2020). Average class size [Data table]. Retrieved from https://stats.oecd.org/Index.aspx?DataSetCode=EDU_CLASS

Organisation for Economic Co-operation and Development. (2013). *PISA 2012 results: What makes schools successful? Resources, policies and practices (volume IV)*. Paris, France: Author.

Organisation for Economic Co-operation and Development. (2016). *Cohabitation rate and prevalence of other forms of partnership* [Data report]. Retrieved from www.oecd.org/els/family/SF_3-3-Cohabitation-forms-partnership.pdf

Organisation for Economic Co-operation and Development. (2019). *Ageing and employment policies: Statistics on average effective age of retirement* [Data tables]. Retrieved from www.oecd.org/els/emp/average-effective-age-of-retirement.htm

Organisation for Economic Co-operation and Development. (2019). *Marriage and divorce rates* [Data sheet]. Retrieved from www.oecd.org/social/family/SF_3_1_Marriage_and_divorce_rates.pdf

Organization for Economic Co-operation and Development. (2004). Education at a glance: OECD indicators—2004. *Education & Skills, 2004*(14), 1–456.

Organization for Economic Co-operation and Development. (2015). *The ABC of gender equity in education: Aptitude, behavior, confidence.* Retrieved from www.oecd.org/pisa/keyfindings/pisa-2012-results-gender-eng.pdf

Organization for Economic Co-operation and Development. (2016). *Country note: Key findings from the PISA 2015 from the United States.* Retrieved from www.oecd.org/pisa/PISA-2015-United-States.pdf

Organization for Economic Co-operation and Development. (2016). *PISA 2015 results in focus.* Retrieved from www.oecd.org/pisa/pisa-2015-results-in-focus.pdf

Orgilés, M., Morales, A., Delvecchio, E., Mazzeschi, C., & Espada, J. P. (2020). Immediate psychological effects of the COVID-19 quarantine in youth from Italy and Spain.

Ornoy, A., Reece, E. A., Pavlinkova, G., Kappen, C., & Miller, R. K. (2015). Effect of maternal diabetes on the embryo, fetus, and children: congenital anomalies, genetic and epigenetic changes and developmental outcomes. *Birth Defects Research Part C: Embryo Today: Reviews, 105*(1), 53-72.

Ortiz-Ospina, E., & Beltekian, D. (2018, August 14). Why do women live longer than men? [Our World in Data blog]. Retrieved from https://ourworldindata.org/why-do-women-live-longer-than-men

Ortman, J. M., Velkoff, V. A., & Hogan, H. (2014). *An aging nation: the older population in the United States,* P25-1140. Washington, DC: United States Census Bureau, Economics and Statistics Administration, U.S. Department of Commerce.

Oshio, T., Nozaki, K., & Kobayashi, M. (2013). Division of household labor and marital satisfaction in China, Japan, and Korea. *Journal of Family and Economic Issues, 34*(2), 211-223.

Ossorio, P., & Duster, T. (2005). Race and genetics: Controversies in biomedical, behavioral, and forensic sciences. *American Psychologist, 60,* 115-128.

Osterberg, E.C., Bernie, A.M., & Ramasamy, R. (2014). Risks of testosterone replacement therapy in men. *Indian Journal of Urology,* 30, 2-7.

Osterman, M. J., & Martin, J. A. (2011). Epidural and spinal anesthesia use during labor: 27-state reporting area, 2008. *National Vital Statistics Reports, 59*(5), 1-13. Hyattsville, MD: National Center for Health Statistics.

Ostfeld, B. M., Esposity, L., Perl, H., & Hegyl, T. (2010). Concurrent risks in sudden infant death syndrome. *Pediatrics, 125*(3), 447-453.

Otis, A. S. (1993). *Otis-Lennon School Ability Test: OLSAT.* New York, NY: The Psychological Corp.

Ouellette, G. P., & Sénéchal, M. (2008). A window into early literacy: Exploring the cognitive and linguistic underpinnings of invented spelling. *Scientific Studies of Reading, 12*(2), 195-219.

Ouimet, M. C., Pradhan, A. K., Brooks-Russell, A., Ehsani, J. P., Berbiche, D., & Simons-Morton, B. G. (2015). Young drivers and their passengers: A systematic review of epidemiological studies on crash risk. *Journal of Adolescent Health, 57*(1), S24-S35.

Overstreet, S., Devine, J., Bevans, K., & Efreom, Y. (2005). Predicting parental involvement in children's schooling within an economically disadvantaged African American sample. *Psychology in the Schools, 42*(1), 101-111.

Owen, J., & Fincham, F. D. (2011). Effects of gender and psychosocial factors on "friends with benefits" relationships among young adults. *Archives of Sexual Behavior, 40*(2), 311-320.

Owens, J. A., Chervin, R. D., & Hoppin, A. G. (2019). *Behavioral sleep problems in children* [Fact sheet]. Retrieved from www.uptodate.com/contents/behavioral-sleep-problems-in-children.

Owens, J., & Adolescent Sleep Working Group. (2014). Insufficient sleep in adolescents and young adults: An update on causes and consequences. *Pediatrics, 134*(3), e921-e932.

Owens, R. E. (1996). *Language development* (4th ed.). Boston, MA: Allyn & Bacon.

Owsley, C. (2011). Aging and vision. *Vision Research, 51*(13), 1610-1622.

Oxley, T. J., Mocco, J., Majidi, S., Kellner, C. P., Shoirah, H., Singh, I. P., . . . Skliut, M. (2020). Large-vessel stroke as a presenting feature of Covid-19 in the young. *New England Journal of Medicine*, e60.

Oyserman, D., Coon, H. M., & Kemmelmeier, M. (2002). Rethinking individualism and collectivism: Evaluation of theoretical assumptions and meta-analyses. *Psychological Bulletin, 128*(1), 3.

Özçalışkan, Ş., & Goldin-Meadow, S. (2010). Sex differences in language first appear in gesture. *Developmental Science, 13*(5), 752-760.

Özen, S., & Darcan, Ş. (2011). Effects of environmental endocrine disruptors on pubertal development. *Journal of Clinical Research in Pediatric Endocrinology, 3*(1), 1.

Ozmeral, E. J., Eddins, A. C., Frisina, D. R., & Eddins, D. A. (2016). Large cross-sectional study of presbycusis reveals rapid progressive decline in auditory temporal acuity. *Neurobiology of Aging, 43*, 72-78.

Ozonoff, S., Young, G.S., Carter, A., Messinger, D., Yirimiya, N., Zwaigenbaum, L., . . . Stone, W.L. (2011). Recurrence risk for autism spectrum disorders: A baby siblings research consortium study. *Pediatrics, 128.* doi: 10.1542/peds.2010-2825

O'Brien, C. M., & Jeffery, H. E. (2002). Sleep deprivation, disorganization and fragmentation during opiate withdrawal in newborns. *Pediatric Child Health, 38,* 66-71.

O'Connor, C. (2019). A guiding hand or a slap on the wrist: Can drug courts be the solution to maternal opioid use. *Journal of Criminal Law & Criminology, 109,* 103.

O'Donnell, K., Badrick, E., Kumari, M., & Steptoe, A. (2008). Psychological coping styles and cortisol over the day in healthy older adults. *Psychoneuroendocrinology, 33*(5), 601-611.

O'Flynn O'Brien, K. L., Varghese, A. C., & Agarwal, A. (2010). The genetic causes of male factor infertility: A review. *Fertility and Sterility, 93,* 1-12.

O'Hara, M. W., & McCabe, J. E. (2013). Postpartum depression: Current status and future directions. *Annual Review of Clinical Psychology, 9,* 379-407.

O'Higgins, M., Roberts, I. S., Glover, V., & Taylor, A. (2013). Mother-child bonding at 1 year: Associations with symptoms of postnatal depression and bonding in the first few weeks. *Archives of Women's Mental Health, 16,* 381-389.

O'Keefe, L. (2014, June 24). Parents who read to their children nurture more than literary skills.

AAP News. Retrieved from www.aappublications.org/content/early/2014/06/24/aapnews.20140624-2

O'Leary, K., Small, B. J., Panaite, V., Bylsma, L. M., & Rottenberg, J. (2017). Sleep quality in healthy and mood-disordered persons predicts daily life emotional reactivity. *Cognition and Emotion, 31*(3), 435-443.

O'Shea, A., Cohen, R., Porges, E. C., Nissim, N. R., & Woods, A. J. (2016). Cognitive aging and the hippocampus in older adults. *Frontiers in Aging Neuroscience, 8,* 298.

O'Shea, D. M., Fieo, R., Woods, A., Williamson, J., Porges, E., & Cohen, R. (2018). Discrepancies between crystallized and fluid ability are associated with frequency of social and physical engagement in community dwelling older adults. *Journal of Clinical and Experimental Neuropsychology, 40*(10), 963-970.

Pace, G. T., Shafer, K., Jensen, T. M., & Larson, J. H. (2015). Stepparenting issues and relationship quality: The role of clear communication. *Journal of Social Work, 15*(1), 24-44.

Pace-Schott, E. F., & Spencer, R. M. (2014). Sleep loss in older adults: Effects on waking performance and sleep-dependent memory consolidation with healthy aging and insomnia. In M. T. Bianchi (Ed.), *Sleep deprivation and disease* (pp. 185-197). New York, NY: Springer.

Padilla-Walker, L. M., Nelson, L. J., & Knapp, D. J. (2014). "Because I'm still the parent, that's why!" Parental legitimate authority during emerging adulthood. *Journal of Social and Personal Relationships, 31*(3), 293-313.

Padmanabhan, V., Cardoso, R. C., & Puttabyatappa, M. (2016). Developmental programming, a pathway to disease. *Endocrinology, 157*(4), 1328-1340.

Pagani, L. S., Fitzpatrick, C., Barnett, T. A., & Dubow, E. (2010). Prospective associations between early childhood television exposure and academic, psychosocial, and physical well-being by middle childhood. *Archives of Pediatrics & Adolescent Medicine, 164*(5), 425-431.

Painter, J. N., Willemsen, G., Nyholt, D., Hoekstra, C., Duffy, D. L., Henders, A. K., . . . & Martin, N. G. (2010). A genome wide linkage scan for dizygotic twinning in 525 families of mothers of dizygotic twins. *Human Reproduction, 25*(6), 1569-1580.

Pal, S., & Tyler, J. K. (2016). Epigenetics and aging. *Science Advances, 2*(7), e1600584.

Palacios, J., & Brodzinsky, D. (2010). Adoption research: Trends, topics, outcomes. *International Journal of Behavioral Development, 34*(3), 270-284.

Pamuk, E., Makuc, D., Heck, K., Reuben, C., & Lochner, K. (1998). Socioeconomic status and health chartbook. In *Health, United States, 1998.* Hyattsville, MD: National Center for Health Statistics.

Pan, B. A., Rowe, M. L., Singer, J. D., & Snow, C. E. (2005). Maternal correlates of growth in toddler vocabulary production in low-income families. *Child Development, 76*(4), 763-782.

Pandharipande, P. P., Girard, T. D., Jackson, J. C., Morandi, A., Thompson, J. L., Pun, B. T., . . . Moons, K. G. (2013). Long-term cognitive impairment after critical illness. *New England Journal of Medicine, 369*(14), 1306–1316.

Panigrahy, A., Filiano, J., Sleeper, L. A., Mandell, F., Valdes-Dapena, M., Krous, H. F., . . . Kinney, H. C. (2000). Decreased serotonergic receptor binding in rhombic lip-derived regions of the medulla oblongata in the sudden infant death syndrome. *Journal of Neuropathology and Experimental Neurology, 59,* 377–384.

Pantasri, T., & Norman, R. J. (2014). The effects of being overweight and obese on female reproduction: A review. *Gynecological Endocrinology, 30*(2), 90–94.

Panza, F., Logroscino, G., Imbimbo, B. P., & Solfrizzi, V. (2014). Is there still any hope for amyloid-based immunotherapy for Alzheimer's disease? *Current Opinion in Psychiatry, 27*(2), 128–137.

Papadatou-Pastou, M., Martin, M., Munafo, M., & Jones, G. (2008). Sex differences in left-handedness: A meta-analysis of 144 studies. *American Psychological Association Bulletin, 134*(5), 677–699.

Papadimitriou, A. (2016). Timing of puberty and secular trend in human maturation. In P. Kumanov & A. Agarwal (Eds.), *Puberty* (pp. 121–136). Cham, Switzerland: Springer.

Papuć, E., & Rejdak, K. (2017). Does myelin play the leading role in Alzheimer's disease pathology. *Journal of Alzheimers Disease & Parkinsonism, 7*(321).

Parish-Morris, J., Mahajan, N., Hirsh-Pasek, K., Golinkoff, R. M., & Collins, M. F. (2013). Once upon a time: Parent–child dialogue and story-book reading in the electronic era. *Mind, Brain, and Education, 7*(3), 200–211.

Park, C. L., Holt, C. L., Le, D., Christie, J., & Williams, B. R. (2018). Positive and negative religious coping styles as prospective predictors of well-being in African Americans. *Psychology of Religion and Spirituality, 10*(4), 318.

Park, D. C., & Gutchess, A. H. (2005). Long-term memory and aging: A cognitive neuroscience perspective. In R. Cabeza, L. Nyberg, & D. C. Park (Eds.), *Cognitive neuroscience of aging: Linking cognitive and cerebral aging* (pp. 218–245). New York, NY: Oxford University Press.

Park, D. C., & McDonough, I. M. (2013). The dynamic aging mind: Revelations from functional neuroimaging research. *Perspectives on Psychological Science, 8*(1), 62–67.

Park, D. C., & Reuter-Lorenz, P. (2009). The adaptive brain: Aging and neurocognitive scaffolding. *Annual Review of Psychology, 60*(1), 173–176.

Park, D., & Gutchess, A. (2006). The cognitive neuroscience of aging and culture. *Current Directions in Psychological Science, 15,* 105–108.

Park, M. J., Mulye, T. P., Adams, S. H., Brindis, C. D., & Irwin, C. E. (2006). The health status of young adults in the United States. *Journal of Adolescent Health, 39,* 305–317.

Park, S., Belsky, J., Putnam, S., & Crnic, K. (1997). Infant emotionality, parenting, and 3-year inhibition: Exploring stability and lawful discontinuity in a male sample. *Developmental Psychology, 33,* 218–227.

Parke, R. D. (2004). Development in the family. *Annual Review of Psychology, 55,* 365–399.

Parke, R. D., & Buriel, R. (1998). Socialization in the family: Ethnic and ecological perspectives. In W. Damon (Series Ed.) & N. Eisenberg (Vol. Ed.), *Handbook of child psychology: Vol. 3. Social, emotional, and personality development* (5th ed., pp. 463–552). New York, NY: Wiley.

Parker, A. E., Mathis, E. T., & Kupersmidt, J. B. (2013). How is this child feeling? Preschool-aged children's ability to recognize emotion in faces and body poses. *Early Education & Development, 24*(2), 188–211.

Parker, J. D., Woodruff, T. J., Basu, R., & Schoendorf, K. C. (2005). Air pollution and birth weight among term infants in California. *Pediatrics, 115,* 121–128.

Parker, K. (2012, March 15). *The boomerang generation: Feeling OK about living with mom and dad.* Retrieved from www.pewsocialtrends.org/2012/03/15/the-boomerang-generation/

Parker, K., & Patten, E. (2013, January 30). *The sandwich generation: Rising financial burdens for middle-aged Americans.* Retrieved from www.pewsocialtrends.org/2013/01/30/the-sandwich-generation/

Parker, K., & Stepler, R. (2017). *Americans see men as the financial providers, even as women's contributions grow* [Pew Research Center report]. Retrieved from www.pewresearch.org/fact-tank/2017/09/20/americans-see-men-as-the-financial-providers-even-as-womens-contributions-grow/

Parker, K., Horowitz, J. M., & Rohal, M. (2015). *Parenting in America: Outlook, worries, aspirations are strongly linked to financial situation.* [Pew Research Center report]. Retrieved from www.pewsocialtrends.org/2015/12/17/parenting-in-america/

Parker-Lalomio, M., McCann, K., Piorkowski, J., Freels, S., & Persky, V. W. (2018). Prenatal exposure to polychlorinated biphenyls and asthma, eczema/hay fever, and frequent ear infections. *Journal of Asthma, 55*(10), 1105–1115.

Parkes, A., Henderson, M., Wight, D., & Nixon, C. (2011). Is parenting associated with teenagers' early sexual risk-taking, autonomy and relationship with sexual partners? *Perspectives on Sexual and Reproductive Health, 43*(1), 30–40.

Parkes, C. M., Laungani, P., & Young, W. (Eds.). (2015). *Death and bereavement across cultures.* Abingdon-on-Thames, England: Routledge.

Parkes, T. L., Elia, A. J., Dickinson, D., Hilliker, A. J., Phillips, J. P., & Boulianne, G. L. (1998). Extension of Drosophila lifespan by overexpression of human SOD1 in motorneurons. *Nature Genetics, 19,* 171–174.

Parkinson, J. R., Hyde, M. J., Gale, C., Santhakumaran, S., & Modi, N. (2013). Preterm birth and the metabolic syndrome in adult life: A systematic review and meta-analysis. *Pediatrics, 131*(4), e1240–e1263.

Parks, S. E., Lambert, A. B. E., & Shapiro-Mendoza, C. K. (2017). Racial and ethnic trends in sudden unexpected infant deaths: United States, 1995–2013. *Pediatrics, 139*(6), e20163844.

Parmar, P., Harkness, S., & Super, C. M. (2004). Asian and Euro-American parents' ethnotheories of play and learning: Effects on preschool children's home routines and school behaviour. *International Journal of Behavioral Development, 28*(2), 97–104.

Parsons, C. E., Young, K. S., Rochat, T. J., Kringelbach, M. L., & Stein, A. (2012). Postnatal depression and its effects on child development: A review of evidence from low- and middle-income countries. *British Medical Bulletin, 101,* 57–79.

Partanen, E., Kujala, T., Näätänen, R., Liitola, A., Sambeth, A., & Huotilainen, M. (2013). Learning-induced neural plasticity of speech processing before birth. *Proceedings of the National Academy of Sciences, 110*(37), 15145–15150.

Parten, M. B. (1932). Social play among preschool children. *Journal of Abnormal and Social Psychology, 27,* 243–269.

Partridge, L. (2010). The new biology of ageing. *Philosophical Transactions, 365*(1537), 147–154.

Partridge, S., Balayla, J., Holcroft, C. A., & Abenhaim, H. A. (2012). Inadequate prenatal care utilization and risks of infant mortality and poor birth outcome: A retrospective analysis of 28,729,765 US deliveries over 8 years. *American Journal of Perinatology, 29*(10), 787–794.

Paruthi, S., Brooks, L. J., D'Ambrosio, C., Hall, W. A., Kotagal, S., Lloyd, R. M., . . . Rosen, C. L. (2016). Recommended amount of sleep for pediatric populations: a consensus statement of the American Academy of Sleep Medicine. *Journal of Clinical Sleep Medicine, 12*(06), 785–786.

Pascalis, O., & Kelly, D. J. (2009). The origins of face processing in humans: Phylogeny and ontogeny. *Perspectives on Psychological Science, 4*(2), 200–209.

Pascolini, D., & Mariotti, S. P. (2012). Global estimates of visual impairment: 2010. *British Journal of Ophthalmology, 96*(5), 614–618.

Passarino, G., De Rango, F., & Montesanto, A. (2016). Human longevity: Genetics or lifestyle? It takes two to tango. *Immunity and Aging, 13.* doi: 10.1186/s12979-016-0066-z

Pasterski, V., Geffner, M. E., Brain, C., Hindmarsh, P., Brook, C., & Hines, M. (2011). Prenatal hormones and childhood sex segregation: Playmate and play style preferences in girls with congenital adrenal hyperplasia. *Hormones and Behavior, 59*(4), 549–555.

Pastor, P. N., & Reuben, C. A. (2008). Diagnosed attention deficit hyperactivity disorder and learning disability, United States, 2004–2006. *Vital and Health Statistics, 10*(237). Hyattsville, MD: National Center for Health Statistics.

Pastor, P. N., Duran, C., & Reuben, C. (2015). Quickstats: Percentage of children and adolescents aged 5–17 years with diagnosed attention-deficit/hyperactivity disorder (ADHD), by race and Hispanic ethnicity—National health interview survey, United States, 1997–2014. *Morbidity and Mortality Weekly Report (MMWR), 64*(33), 925–925.

Pasupathi, M., Staudinger, U. M., & Baltes, P. B. (2001). Seeds of wisdom: Adolescents' knowledge and judgment about difficult life problems. *Developmental Psychology, 37*(3), 351–361.

Patel, H., Rosengren, A., & Ekman, I. (2004). Symptoms in acute coronary syndromes: Does sex make a difference? *American Heart Journal, 148*(1), 27–33.

Patel, K. V., Coppin, A. K., Manini, T. M., Lauretani, F., Bandinelli, S., Ferrucci, L., & Guralnik, J. M. (2006, August 10). Midlife physical activity and mobility in older age: The InCHIANTI Study. *American Journal of Preventive Medicine, 31*(3), 217–224.

Pathak, P. K., Tripathi, N., & Subramanian, S. V. (2014). Secular trends in menarcheal age in India-evidence from the Indian human development survey. *PLoS One, 9*(11), e111027.

Patrick, S. W., & Schiff, D. M. (2017). A public health response to opioid use in pregnancy. *Pediatrics*, e20164070.

Patterson, C. (2018). *World Alzheimer Report 2018: The state of the art of dementia research: New frontiers.* London, England: Alzheimer's Disease International.

Patterson, C. J. (1992). Children of lesbian and gay parents. *Child Development, 63,* 1025–1042.

Patterson, C. J. (1995). Lesbian mothers, gay fathers, and their children. In A. R. D'Augelli & C. J. Patterson (Eds.), *Lesbian, gay, and bisexual identities over the lifespan: Psychological perspectives* (pp. 293–320). New York, NY: Oxford University Press.

Patterson, C. J. (1995). Sexual orientation and human development: An overview. *Developmental Psychology, 31,* 3–11.

Patterson, C., Guariguata, L., Dahlquist, G., Soltész, G., Ogle, G., & Silink, M. (2014). Diabetes in the young-a global view and worldwide estimates of numbers of children with type 1 diabetes. *Diabetes Research and Clinical Practice, 103*(2), 161–175.

Patton, G. C., Coffey, C., Sawyer, S. M., Viner, R. M., Haller, D. M., Bose, K. (2009, September 12). Global patterns of mortality in young people: A systematic analysis of population health data. *The Lancet.* Retrieved from www.thelancet.com/journals/lancet/article/PIIS0140-6736(09)60741-8/fulltext

Paulus, M. (2017). How to Dax? Preschool children's prosocial behavior, but not their social norm enforcement relates to their peer status. *Frontiers in Psychology, 8,* 1779.

Pawelski, J. G., Perrin, E. C., Foy, J. M., Allen, C. E., Crawford, J. E., Del Monte, M., . . . Tanner, J. L. (2006). The effects of marriage, civil union, and domestic partnership laws on the health and well-being of children. *Pediatrics, 118*(1), 349–364.

Pearl, R. (1928). *The rate of living.* New York, NY: Alfred A. Knopf.

Peck, J. D., Leviton, A., & Cowan, L. D. (2010). A review of the epidemiologic evidence concerning the reproductive health effects of caffeine consumption: A 2000–2009 update. *Food and Chemical Toxicology, 48*(10), 2549–2576.

Pedersen, D. E. (2017). Which stressors increase the odds of college binge drinking? *College Student Journal, 51*(1), 129–141.

Peek, S. T., Wouters, E. J., van Hoof, J., Luijkx, K. G., Boeije, H. R., & Vrijhoef, H. J. (2014). Factors influencing acceptance of technology for aging in place: A systematic review. *International Journal of Medical Informatics, 83*(4), 235–248.

Pegg, J. E., Werker, J. F., & McLeod, P. J. (1992). Preference for infant-directed over adult-directed speech: Evidence from 7 week old infants. *Infant Behavior and Development, 15,* 325–345.

Pekel-Uludağlı, N., & Akbaş, G. (2019). Young adults' perceptions of social clock and adulthood roles in the Turkish population. *Journal of Adult Development, 26*(2), 105–115.

Pellegrini, A. D., & Archer, J. (2005). Sex differences in competitive and aggressive behavior: A view from sexual selection theory. In B. J. Ellis & D. F. Bjorklund (Eds.), *Origins of the social mind: Evolutionary psychology and child development* (pp. 219–244). New York, NY: Guilford Press.

Pellegrini, A. D., & Long, J. D. (2002). A longitudinal study of bullying, dominance, and victimization during the transition from primary school through secondary school. *British Journal of Developmental Psychology, 20,* 259–280.

Pellegrini, A. D., Dupuis, D., & Smith, P.K. (2007). Play in evolution and development. *Developmental Review, 27,* 261–276.

Pellegrini, A. D., Kato, K., Blatchford, P., & Baines, E. (2002). A short-term longitudinal study of children's playground games across the first year of school: Implications for social competence and adjustment to school. *American Educational Research Journal, 39,* 991–1015.

Pellegrini, E., Ballerini, L., Hernandez, M. D. C. V., Chappell, F. M., González-Castro, V., Anblagan, D., . . . Mair, G. (2018). Machine learning of neuroimaging for assisted diagnosis of cognitive impairment and dementia: A systematic review. *Alzheimer's & Dementia: Diagnosis, Assessment & Disease Monitoring, 10,* 519–535

Pelphrey, K. A., Reznick, J. S., Davis Goldman, B., Sasson, N., Morrow, J., Donahoe, A., & Hodgson, K. (2004). Development of visuospatial short-term memory in the second half of the 1st year. *Developmental Psychology, 40*(5), 836.

Peng, S., Suitor, J. J., & Gilligan, M. (2018). The long arm of maternal differential treatment: Effects of recalled and current favoritism on adult children's psychological well-being. *The Journals of Gerontology: Series B, 73*(6), 1123–1132.

Penning, M. J., & Wu, Z. (2016). Caregiver stress and mental health: Impact of caregiving relationship and gender. *The Gerontologist, 56*(6), 1102–1113.

Pennington, B. F., Moon, J., Edgin, J., Stedron, J., & Nadel, L. (2003). The neuropsychology of Down syndrome: Evidence for hippocampal dysfunction. *Child Development, 74,* 75–93.

Pennisi, E. (1998). Single gene controls fruit fly life-span. *Science, 282,* 856.

Pepper, S. C. (1942). *World hypotheses.* Berkeley, CA: University of California Press.

Pepper, S. C. (1961). *World hypotheses.* Berkeley, CA: University of California Press.

Pereira, C. (2005). Zina and transgressive heterosexuality in northern Nigeria. *Feminist Africa, 5,* 52–79.

Pereira, M. A., Kartashov, A. I., Ebbeling, C. B., Van Horn, L., Slattery, M. L., Jacobs, D. R., Jr., & Ludwig, D. S. (2005). Fast-food habits, weight gain, and insulin resistance (the CARDIA study): 15-year prospective analysis. *Lancet, 365,* 36–42.

Perelli-Harris, B., Styrc, M. E., Addo, F., Hoherz, S., Lappegard, T., Sassler, S., & Evans, A. (2017). Comparing the benefits of cohabitation and marriage for health in mid-life: Is the relationship similar across countries? ESRC Centre for Population Change working paper 84.

Perkins, H. S. (2007). Controlling death: The false promise of advance directives. *Annals of Internal Medicine, 147*(1), 51–57.

Perkins, M. (2016). Politeness without routines: a case study in Hobongan and implications for typology. *Lodz Papers in Pragmatics, 12*(1), 3–21.

Perou, R., Bitsko, R. H., Blumberg, S. J., Pastor, P., Ghandour, R. M., Gfroerer, J. C., . . . Parks, S. E. (2013). Mental health surveillance among children—United States, 2005–2011. *MMWR Surveillance Summaries, 62*(Suppl. 2), 1–35.

Perreira, K. M., Wassink, J., & Harris, K. M. (2019). Beyond race/ethnicity: Skin color, gender, and the health of young adults in the United States. *Population Research and Policy Review, 38*(2), 271–299.

Perrin, A. (2015). *Social media usage: 2005-2015: 65% of adults now use social networking sites—a nearly tenfold jump in the past decade* [Pew Research Trust report]. Retrieved from www.pewinternet.org/2015/10/08/2015/Social-Networking-Usage-2005-2015/

Perrin, E. C., Siegel, B. S., & Committee on Psychosocial Aspects of Child and Family Health. (2013). Promoting the well-being of children whose parents are gay or lesbian. *Pediatrics, 131*(4), e1374–e1383.

Pesando, L. M., Castro, A. F., Andriano, L., Behrman, J. A., Billari, F., Monden, C., . . . & Kohler, H. P. (2018). Global family change: Persistent diversity with development. *Population and Development Review.*

Pesonen, A. K., Räikkönen, K., Strandberg, T., Keltikangas-Järvinen, L., & Järvenpää, A. L. (2004). Insecure adult attachment style and depressive symptoms: Implications for parental perceptions of infant temperament. *Infant Mental Health Journal: Official Publication of The World Association for Infant Mental Health, 25*(2), 99–116.

Pesowski, M. L., & Friedman, O. (2015). Preschoolers and toddlers use ownership to predict basic emotions. *Emotion, 15*(1), 104.

Peters, E., Hess, T. M., Västfjäll, D., & Auman, C. (2007). Adult age differences in dual information processes: Implications for the role of affective and deliberative processes in older adults' decision making. *Perspectives on Psychological Science, 2*(1), 1–23.

Petersen, A. C. (1993). Presidential address: Creating adolescents: The role of context and process in developmental transitions. *Journal of Research on Adolescents, 3*(1), 1–18.

Peterson, B. E. (2002). Longitudinal analysis of midlife generativity, intergenerational roles, and caregiving. *Psychology and Aging, 17*, 161–168.

Peterson, B. E., & Duncan, L. E. (2007). Midlife women's generativity and authoritarianism: Marriage, motherhood and 10 years of aging. *Psychology and Aging, 22*(3), 411–419.

Peterson, B. E., & Stewart, A. J. (1996). Antecedents and contexts of generativity motivation at midlife. *Psychology and Aging, 11*(1), 21.

Peterson, C. (2011). Children's memory reports over time: Getting both better and worse. *Journal of Experimental Child Psychology, 109*(3), 275–293.

Petit, D., Pennestri, M. H., Paquet, J., Desautels, A., Zadra, A., Vitaro, F., . . . Montplaisir, J. (2015). Childhood sleepwalking and sleep terrors: A longitudinal study of prevalence and familial aggregation. *JAMA Pediatrics, 169*(7), 653–658.

Petit, D., Touchette, E., Tremblay, R. E., Boivin, M., & Montplaisir, J. (2007). Dyssomnias and parasomnias in early childhoold. *Pediatrics, 119*(5), e1016–e1025.

Petitto, L. A., & Kovelman, I. (2003). The bilingual paradox: How signing-speaking bilingual children help us to resolve it and teach us about the brain's mechanisms underlying all language acquisition. *Learning Languages, 8*, 5–18.

Petitto, L. A., & Marentette, P. F. (1991). Babbling in the manual mode: Evidence for the ontogeny of language. *Science, 251*, 1493–1495.

Petitto, L. A., Holowka, S., Sergio, L., & Ostry, D. (2001). Language rhythms in babies' hand movements. *Nature, 413*, 35–36.

Petkus, A. J., Beam, C. R., Johnson, W., Kaprio, J., Korhonen, T., McGue, M., . . . IGEMS Consortium. (2017). Gene–environment interplay in depressive symptoms: Moderation by age, sex, and physical illness. *Psychological Medicine, 47*(10), 1836–1847.

Petrenko, C. L. (2015). Positive behavioral interventions and family support for fetal alcohol spectrum disorders. *Current Developmental Disorders Reports, 2*(3), 199–209.

Petrenko, C. L., & Alto, M. E. (2017). Interventions in fetal alcohol spectrum disorders: An international perspective. *European Journal of Medical Genetics, 60*(1), 79–91.

Petrosino, A., Turpin-Petrosino, C., Hollis-Peel, M. E., & Lavenberg, J. G. (2013). 'Scared Straight' and other juvenile awareness programs for preventing juvenile delinquency. *Cochrane Database Systematic Reviews.*

Pettit, G. S., & Arsiwalla, D. D. (2008). Commentary on special section on "bidirectional parent–child relationships": The continuing evolution of dynamic, transactional models of parenting and youth behavior problems. *Journal of Abnormal Child Psychology, 36*(5), 711.

Pew Research Center. (2013). *A survey of LGBT Americans: Attitudes, experiences and values in changing times* [Report]. Retrieved from www.pewsocialtrends.org/wp-content/uploads/ sites/3/2013/06/SDT_LGBT-Americans_ 06-2013.pdf

Pew Research Center. (2013). *Views on end-of-life medical treatment* [Report]. Retrieved from www.pewforum.org/2013/11/21/views-on-end-of- life-medical-treatments/

Pew Research Center. (2014). *Global morality* [Interactive data set]. Retrieved from www. pewresearch.org/global/interactives/global- morality/

Pew Research Center. (2014). *What's morally acceptable? That depends on where in the world you live* [Report]. Retrieved from www. pewresearch.org/fact-tank/2014/04/15/whats- morally-acceptable-it-depends-on-where-in-the- world-you-live/

Pew Research Center. (2015). *U.S. public becoming less religious: Modest drop in overall rates of belief, but religiously affiliated Americans are as observant as ever* [Report]. Retrieved from www. pewforum.org/2015/11/03/u-s-public-becoming- less-religious/

Pew Research Center. (2015). *Parenting in America: Outlook, worries, aspirations are strongly linked to financial situation* [Report]. Retrieved from www.pewresearch.org/wp-content/uploads/ sites/3/2015/12/2015-12-17_parenting-in-america_ FINAL.pdf

Pew Research Center. (2018). *The age gap in religion around the world* [Report]. Retrieved from www.pewforum.org/2018/06/13/the-age-gap-in- religion-around-the-world/#same-pattern-seen- over-multiple-measures-of-religious-commitment

Pew Research Center. (2019). *Attitudes on same-sex marriage* [Fact sheet]. Retrieved from www. pewforum.org/fact-sheet/changing-attitudes-on- gay-marriage/

Pew Research Center. (2019). Gay marriage around the world [Fact sheet]. Retrieved from www.pewforum.org/fact-sheet/gay-marriage- around-the-world/

Pew Research Center. (2019). *Same-sex marriage around the world* [Fact sheet]. Retrieved from www.pewforum.org/fact-sheet/gay-marriage- around-the-world/

Pew Research Center. (2017). *Religious belief and national belonging in Central and Eastern Europe* [Report]. Retrieved from www.pewforum. org/2017/05/10/religious-belief-and-national- belonging-in-central-and-eastern-europe/

Phanse, R., & Kaur, R. (2015). An exploratory study on self-renewal in mid-life voluntary career changes for managers. *Journal of Management Research and Analysis, 2*, 204–213.

Phillips, D., Crowell, N. A., Sussman, A. L., Gunnar, M., Fox, N., Hane, A. A., & Bisgaier, J. (2012). Reactive temperament and sensitivity to context in childcare. *Social Development, 21*(3), 628–643.

Phillips, J. A., & Sweeney, M. M. (2005). Premarital cohabitation and marital disruption among white, Black, and Mexican American women. *Journal of Marriage and Family, 67*, 296–314.

Phillips, T. M. (2012). The influence of family structure vs. family climate on adolescent well-being. *Child and Adolescent Social Work Journal, 29*(2), 103–110.

Phinney, J. S. (1989). Stages of ethnic identity development in minority group of adolescents. *Journal of Early Adolescence, 9*, 34–49.

Phinney, J. S. (1998). Stages of ethnic identity development in minority group adolescents. In R. E. Muuss & H. D. Porton (Eds.), *Adolescent behavior and society: A book of readings* (pp. 271–280). New York, NY: McGraw-Hill.

Phinney, J. S. (2003). Ethnic identity and acculturation. In K. Chun, P. B. Organista, & G. Marin (Eds.), *Acculturation: Advances in theory, measurement, and applied research* (pp. 63–81). Washington, DC: American Psychological Association.

Phinney, J. S. (2006). Ethnic identity exploration in emerging adulthood. In J. J. Arnett & J. L. Tanner (Eds.), *Emerging adults in America: Coming of age in the 21st century* (pp. 117–134). Washington, DC: American Psychological Association.

Phinney, J. S., Ferguson, D. L., & Tate, J. D. (1997). Intergroup attitudes among ethnic minorities. *Child Development, 68*(3), 955–969.

Phinney, J. S., Jacoby, B., & Silva, C. (2007). Positive intergroup attitudes: The role of ethnic identity. *International Journal of Behavioral Development, 31*(5), 478–490.

Phinney, J. S., Romero, I., Nava, M., & Huang, D. (2001). The role of language, parents, and peers in ethnic identity among adolescents in immigrant families. *Journal of Youth and Adolescence, 30*(2), 135–153.

Piaget, J. (1929). *The child's conception of the world.* New York, NY: Harcourt Brace.

Piaget, J. (1952). *The origins of intelligence in children.* New York, NY: International Universities Press. (Original work published 1936)

Piaget, J. (1962). *The language and thought of the child* (M. Gabain, Trans.). Cleveland, OH: Meridian. (Original work published 1923)

Piaget, J. (1964). *Six psychological studies.* New York, NY: Vintage Books.

Piaget, J., & Inhelder, B. (1967). *The child's conception of space.* New York, NY: Norton.

Piazza, J. R., Charles, S. T., Sliwinski, M. J., Mogle, J., & Almeida, D. M. (2013). Affective reactivity to daily stressors and long-term risk of reporting a chronic physical health condition. *Annals of Behavioral Medicine, 45*(1), 110–120.

Pica, P., Lemer, C., Izard, V., & Dehaene, S. (2004). Exact and approximate arithmetic in an Amazonian indigene group. *Science, 306*(5695), 499–503.

Piffer, D., & Hur, Y. M. (2014). Heritability of creative achievement. *Creativity Research Journal, 26*(2), 151–157.

Pike, A., & Oliver, B. R. (2017). Child behavior and sibling relationship quality: A cross-lagged analysis. *Journal of Family Psychology, 31*(2), 250.

Pike, A., Coldwell, J., & Dunn, J. F. (2005). Sibling relationships in early/middle childhood: Links with individual adjustment. *Journal of Family Psychology, 19*(4), 523.

Pillemer, K., & Suitor, J. J. (1991). "Will I ever escape my child's problems?" Effects of adult children's problems on elderly parents. *Journal of Marriage and Family, 53*, 585–594.

Pillemer, K., Connolly, M. T., Breckman, R., Spreng, N., & Lachs, M. S. (2015). Elder mistreatment: Priorities for consideration by the White House Conference on Aging. *The Gerontologist, 55*(2), 320-327.

Pillow, B. H. (2002). Children's and adult's evaluation of the certainty of deductive inferences, inductive inferences and guesses. *Child Development, 73*(3), 779-792.

Pinkerton, J. A. V., Aguirre, F. S., Blake, J., Cosman, F., Hodis, H., Hoffstetter, S., . . . Marchbanks, P. (2017). The 2017 hormone therapy position statement of the North American Menopause Society. *Menopause, 24*(7), 728-753.

Pino, O. (2016). Fetal memory: The effects of prenatal auditory experience on human development. *BAOJ Med Nursing, 2,* 3.

Pinquart, M. (2016). Associations of parenting styles and dimensions with academic achievement in children and adolescents: A meta-analysis. *Educational Psychology Review, 28*(3), 475-493.

Pinquart, M. (2017). Associations of parenting dimensions and styles with externalizing problems of children and adolescents: An updated meta-analysis. *Developmental Psychology, 53*(5), 873.

Pinquart, M., & Forstmeier, S. (2012). Effects of reminiscence interventions on psychosocial outcomes: A meta-analysis. *Aging & Mental Health, 16*(5), 541-558.

Pinquart, M., & Schindler, I. (2007). Changes of life satisfaction in the transition to retirement: a latent-class approach. *Psychology and Aging, 22*(3), 442.

Pinquart, M., & Sörensen, S. (2003). Associations of stressors and uplifts of caregiving with caregiver burden and depressive mood: a meta-analysis. *The Journals of Gerontology Series B: Psychological Sciences and Social Sciences, 58*(2), P112-P128.

Pinquart, M., & Sörensen, S. (2006). Gender differences in caregiver stressors, social resources, and health: An updated meta-analysis. *Journal of Gerontology: Psychological and Social Sciences, 61B,* P33-P45.

Piperno, F. (2012). The impact of female emigration on families and the welfare state in countries of origin: The case of Romania. *International Migration, 50*(5), 189-204.

Piquero, A. R., Jennings, W. G., Diamond, B., Farrington, D. P., Tremblay, R. E., Welsh, B. C., & Gonzalez, J. M. R. (2016). A meta-analysis update on the effects of early family/parent training programs on antisocial behavior and delinquency. *Journal of Experimental Criminology, 12*(2), 229-248.

Pison, G., Monden, C., & Smits, J. (2015). Twinning rates in developed countries: Trends and explanations. *Population and Development Review, 41*(4), 629-649.

Plana-Ripoll, O., Basso, O., László, K. D., Olsen, J., Parner, E., Cnattingius, S., . . . Li, J. (2018). Reproduction after the loss of a child: A population-based matched cohort study. *Human Reproduction, 33*(8), 1557-1565.

Pleis, J. R., & Lucas, J. W. (2009). Summary health statistics for U.S. adults: National health interview survey 2007. *Vital Health Statistics, 10*(240). Hyattsville, MD: National Center for Health Statistics.

Ploeg, J., Fear, J., Hutchison, B., MacMillan, H., & Bolan, G. (2009). A systematic review of interventions for elder abuse. *Journal of Elder Abuse & Neglect, 21*(3), 187-210.

Plomin, R., & Daniels, D. (2011). Why are children in the same family so different from one another? *International Journal of Epidemiology, 40*(3), 563-582.

Plomin, R., & Deary, I. J. (2015). Genetics and intelligence differences: five special findings. *Molecular Psychiatry, 20*(1), 98-108.

Plomin, R., & Kovas, Y. (2005). Generalist genes and learning disabilities. *Psychological Bulletin, 131,* 592-617.

Plomin, R., DeFries, J. C., Knopik, V. S., & Neiderhiser, J. M. (2016). Top 10 replicated findings from behavioral genetics. *Perspectives on Psychological Science, 11*(1), 3-23.

Plusnin, N., Pepping, C. A., & Kashima, E. S. (2018). The role of close relationships in terror management: A systematic review and research agenda. *Personality and Social Psychology Review, 22*(4), 307-346.

Pocnet, C., Rossier, J., Antonietti, J. P., & von Gunten, A. (2013). Personality traits and behavioral and psychological symptoms in patients at an early stage of Alzheimer's disease. *International Journal of Geriatric Psychiatry, 28*(3), 276-283.

Poehlmann-Tynan, J., Gerstein, E. D., Burnson, C., Weymouth, L., Bolt, D. M., Maleck, S., & Schwichtenberg, A. J. (2015). Risk and resilience in preterm children at age 6. *Development and Psychopathology, 27*(3), 843-858.

Polanczyk, G. V., Salum, G. A., Sugaya, L. S., Caye, A., & Rohde, L. A. (2015). Annual Research Review: A meta-analysis of the worldwide prevalence of mental disorders in children and adolescents. *Journal of Child Psychology and Psychiatry, 56*(3), 345-365.

Polderman, T. J., Benyamin, B., De Leeuw, C. A., Sullivan, P. F., Van Bochoven, A., Visscher, P. M., & Posthuma, D. (2015). Meta-analysis of the heritability of human traits based on fifty years of twin studies. *Nature Genetics, 47*(7), 702-709.

Polhamus, B., Dalenius, K., Mackintosh, H., Smith, B., and Grummer-Strawn, L. (2011). *Pediatric nutrition surveillance 2009 report.* Atlanta, GA: Department of Health and Human Services, Centers for Disease Control and Prevention.

Pomerantz, E. M., & Saxon, J. L. (2001). Conceptions of ability as stable and self-evaluative processes: A longitudinal examination. *Child Development, 72,* 152-173.

Pomerantz, E. M., & Wang, Q. (2009). The role of parental control in children's development in Western and Asian countries. *Current Directions in Psychological Science, 18*(5), 285-289.

Pomery, E. A., Gibbons, F. X., Gerrard, M., Cleveland, M. J., Brody, G. H., & Wills, T. A. (2005). Families and risk: Prospective analyses of familial and social influences on adolescent substance use. *Journal of Family Psychology, 19,* 560-570.

Ponappa, S., Bartle-Haring, S., & Day, R. (2014). Connection to parents and healthy separation during adolescence: A longitudinal perspective. *Journal of Adolescence, 37*(5), 555-566.

Ponce, N. A., Cochran, S. D., Pizer, J. C., & Mays, V. M. (2010). The effects of unequal access to health insurance for same-sex couples in California. *Health Affairs, 29*(8), 1539-1548.

Pons, F., Harris, P. L., & de Rosnay, M. (2004). Emotion comprehension between 3 and 11 years: Developmental periods and hierarchical organization. *European Journal of Developmental Psychology, 1*(2), 127-152.

Pope, A. (2005). Personal transformation in midlife orphanhood: An empirical phenomenological study. *OMEGA-Journal of Death and Dying, 51*(2), 107-123.

Pope, A. L., Murray, C. E., & Mobley, A. K. (2010). Personal, relational, and contextual resources and relationship satisfaction in same-sex couples. *Family Journal, 18,* 163-168.

Popenoe, D., & Whitehead, B. D. (2003). *The state of our unions 2003: The social health of marriage in America.* Piscataway, NJ: National Marriage Project.

Popenoe, D., & Whitehead, B. D. (Eds.). (2004). *The state of our unions 2004: The social health of marriage in America.* Piscataway, NJ: National Marriage Project, Rutgers University.

Popoola, O., & Ayandele, O. (2019). Cohabitation: Harbinger or slayer of marriage in sub-Saharan Africa? *Gender and Behaviour, 17*(2), 13029-13039.

Popova, S., Lange, S., Probst, C., Gmel, G., & Rehm, J. (2017). Estimation of national, regional, and global prevalence of alcohol use during pregnancy and fetal alcohol syndrome: A systematic review and meta-analysis. *The Lancet Global Health, 5*(3), e290-e299.

Pormeister, K., Finley, M., & Rohack, J. J. (2017). Physician assisted suicide as a means of mercy: A comparative analysis of possible legal implications in Europe and the United States. *Virginia Journal of Social Policy and the Law, 24,* 1-24.

Porter, C., Hurren, N. M., Cotter, M. V., Bhattarai, N., Reidy, P. T., Dillon, E. L., . . . Sidossis, L. S. (2015). Mitochondrial respiratory capacity and coupling control decline with age in human skeletal muscle. *American Journal of Physiology-Heart and Circulatory Physiology.*

Porter, P. (2008). "Westernizing" women's risks? Breast cancer in lower-income countries. *New England Journal of Medicine, 358,* 213-216.

Portnoy, J., & Farrington, D. P. (2015). Resting heart rate and antisocial behavior: An updated systematic review and meta-analysis. *Aggression and Violent Behavior, 22,* 33-45.

Posada, G., Gao, Y., Wu, F., Posada, R., Tascon, M., Schoelmerich, A., . . . Synnevaag, B. (1995). The secure-base phenomenon across cultures: Children's behavior, mothers' preferences, and experts' concepts. In E. Waters, B. E. Vaughn, G. Posada, & K. Kondo-Ikemura (Eds.), *Caregiving, cultural, and cognitive perspectives on secure-base behavior and working models: New growing points of attachment theory and research* (pp. 27-48). *Monographs of the Society for*

Research in Child Development, 60(2–3, Serial No. 244).

Poushter, J. (2014). *What's morally acceptable? It depends on where you live.* [Pew Research Center news report]. Retrieved from www.pewresearch.org/fact-tank/2014/04/15/whats-morally-acceptable-it-depends-on-where-in-the-world-you-live/

Povinelli, D. J., & Giambrone, S. (2001). Reasoning about beliefs: A human specialization? *Child Development, 72*, 691–695.

Powell, L. H., Shahabi, L., & Thoresen, C. E. (2003). Religion and spirituality: Linkages to physical health. *American Psychologist, 58*, 36–52.

Pratt, L. A., Dey, A. N., & Cohen, A. J. (2007). Characteristics of adults with serious psychological distress as measured by the K6 scale, United States, 2001-04. *Advance Data, 382*, 1–18.

Preddy, T. M., & Fite, P. J. (2012). Differential associations between relational and overt aggression and children's psychosocial adjustment. *Journal of Psychopathology and Behavioral Assessment, 34*(2), 182–190.

Preissler, M., & Bloom, P. (2007). Two-year-olds appreciate the dual nature of pictures. *Psychological Science, 18*(1), 1–2.

Prentice, P., & Viner, R. M. (2013). Pubertal timing and adult obesity and cardiometabolic risk in women and men: A systematic review and meta-analysis. *International Journal of Obesity, 37*(8), 1036.

Primack, B. A., Shensa, A., Escobar-Viera, C. G., Barrett, E. L., Sidani, J. E., Colditz, J. B., & James, A. E. (2017). Use of multiple social media platforms and symptoms of depression and anxiety: A nationally representative study among US young adults. *Computers in Human Behavior, 69*, 1–9.

Prince, M., Prina, M., & Guerchet, M. (2015). *World Alzheimer Report 2013: Journey of caring-analysis of long-term care for dementia.* London, England: Alzheimer's Disease International.

Pringsheim, T., Jette, N., Frolkis, A., & Steeves, T. D. (2014). The prevalence of Parkinson's disease: A systematic review and meta-analysis. *Movement Disorders, 29*(13), 1583–1590.

Profet, M. (1992). Pregnancy sickness as adaptation: A deterrent to maternal ingestion of teratogens. In L. Cosmides, J. Tooby, & J. H. Barkov (Eds.), *The adapted mind* (pp. 327–366). New York, NY: Oxford University Press.

Pruden, S. M., Hirsch-Pasek, K., Golinkoff, R. M., & Hennon, E. A. (2006). The birth of words: Ten-month-olds learn words through perceptual salience. *Child Development, 77*, 266–280.

Psacharopoulos, G., & Patrinos, H. A. (2018). Returns to investment in education: A decennial review of the global literature. *Education Economics, 26*(5), 445–458. doi: 10.1080/09645292.2018.1484426

Pudrovska, T., Schieman, S., & Carr, D. (2006). Strains of singlehood in later life: Do race and gender matter? *Journal of Gerontology: Social Sciences, 61B*, S315–S322.

Pulgarón, E. R. (2013). Childhood obesity: A review of increased risk for physical and psychological comorbidities. *Clinical Therapeutics, 35*(1), A18–A32.

Pulkkinen, L. (1996). Female and male personality styles: A typological and developmental analysis. *Journal of Personality and Social Psychology, 70*, 1288–1306.

Puma, M., Bell, S., Cook, R., Heid, C., Broene, P., Jenkins, F., . . . Downer, J. (2012). *Third grade follow-up to the Head Start impact study: Final report.* OPRE Report 2012-45. Washington, DC: Administration for Children & Families.

Purcell, K., Heaps, A., Buchanan, J. & Fried, L. (2013). *How teachers are using technology in the classroom.* Washington, DC: Pew Internet & American Life Project.

Purdue-Smithe, A. C., Manson, J. E., Hankinson, S. E., & Bertone-Johnson, E. R. (2016). A prospective study of caffeine and coffee intake and premenstrual syndrome. *The American Journal of Clinical Nutrition, 104*(2), 499–507.

Pushkar, D., Chaikelson, J., Conway, M., Etezadi, J., Giannopoulus, C., Li, K., & Wrosch, C. (2010). Testing continuity and activity variables as predictors of positive and negative affect in retirement. *Journals of Gerontology Series B: Psychological Sciences and Social Sciences, 65*(1), 42–49.

Putallaz, M., & Bierman, K. L. (Eds.). (2004). *Aggression, antisocial behavior, and violence among girls: A developmental perspective.* New York, NY: Guilford Press.

Puterman, E., Lin, J., Krauss, J., Blackburn, E. H., & Epel, E. S. (2015). Determinants of telomere attrition over 1 year in healthy older women: Stress and health behaviors matter. *Molecular Psychiatry, 20*(4), 529–535.

Putnam, K. T., Harris, W. W., & Putnam, F. W. (2013). Synergistic childhood adversities and complex adult psychopathology. *Journal of Traumatic Stress, 26*(4), 435–442.

Putney, N. M., & Bengtson, V. L. (2001). Families, intergenerational relationships, and kin-keeping in midlife. In M. E. Lachman (Ed.), *Handbook of midlife development* (pp. 528–570). New York, NY: Wiley.

Qaseem, A., Forcia, M. A., McLean, R. M., & Denberg, T. D. (2017). Treatment of low bone density or osteoporosis to prevent fractures in men and women: A clinical practice guideline update from the American College of Physiciansment of low bone density or osteoporosis to prevent fractures in men and women. *Annals of Internal Medicine.*

Qaseem, A., Kansagara, D., Forcia, M. A., Cooke, M., & Denberg, T. D. (2016). Management of chronic insomnia disorder in adults: A clinical practice guideline from the American College of Physiciansmanagement of chronic insomnia disorder in adults. *Annals of Internal Medicine, 165*(2), 125–133.

Qiu, A., Mori, S., & Miller, M. I. (2015). Diffusion tensor imaging for understanding brain development in early life. *Annual Review of Psychology, 66*, 853–876.

Quamie, L. (2010, February 2). *Paid family leave funding included in budget.* Retrieved from www.clasp.org/issues/in_focus?type=work_life_and_job_quality&id=0009

Quattrin, T., Liu, E., Shaw, N., Shine, B., & Chiang, E. (2005). Obese children who are referred to the pediatric oncologist: Characteristics and outcome. *Pediatrics, 115*, 348–351.

Quine, S., Morrell, S., & Kendig, H. (2007). *The hopes and fears of older Australians: For self, family, and society.* Retrieved from http://nclive.org/cgi-bin/nclsm?url=http://search.proquest.com/docview/216243395?accountid=10939

Quinn, C., & Toms, G. (2019). Influence of positive aspects of dementia caregiving on caregivers' well-being: A systematic review. *The Gerontologist, 59*(5), e584–e596.

Quinn, P. C., Lee, K., Pascalis, O., Tanaka, J. W. (2016). Narrowing in categorical responding to other-race face classes by infants. *Developmental Science, 19*, 362–371

Quinn, P. C., Westerlund, A., & Nelson, C. A. (2006). Neural markers of categorization in 6-month-old infants. *Psychological Science, 17*, 59–66.

Quirk, K., Owen, J., & Fincham, F. (2014). Perceptions of partner's deception in friends with benefits relationships. *Journal of Sex & Marital Therapy, 40*(1), 43–57.

Raabe, T., & Beelmann, A. (2011). Development of ethnic, racial, and national prejudice in childhood and adolescence: A multinational meta-analysis of age differences. *Child Development, 82*(6), 1715–1737.

Rabbitt, P., Watson, P., Donlan, C., McInnes, L., Horan, M., Pendleton, N., & Clague, J. (2002). Effects of death within 11 years on cognitive performance in old age. *Psychology and Aging, 17*, 468–481.

Racz, S. J., & McMahon, R. J. (2011). The relationship between parental knowledge and monitoring and child and adolescent conduct: A 10-year update. *Clinical Child and Family Psychology Review, 14*(4), 377–398.

Radbruch, L., Leget, C., Bahr, P., Müller-Busch, C., Ellershaw, J., de Conno, F., . . . board members of the EAPC. (2016). Euthanasia and physician-assisted suicide: A white paper from the European Association for Palliative Care. *Palliative Medicine, 30*(2), 104–116.

Radford, J. (2019). Key findings about U.S. immigrants. *Pew Research Center.* Retrieved from www.pewresearch.org/fact-tank/2019/06/17/key-findings-about-u-s-immigrants/

Radford, J. & Noe-Bustamante, L. (2019). Facts on U.S. immigrants, 2017: Statistical portrait of the foreign born population in the United States. *Pew Research Center.* Retrieved from www.pewresearch.org/hispanic/2019/06/03/facts-on-u-s-immigrants-trend-data/

Rahman, R. (2011, October 25). *Who, what, why: What are the burial customs in Islam?* Retrieved from www.bbc.com/news/magazine-15444275

Raju, T. N., Buist, A. S., Blaisdell, C. J., Moxey-Mims, M., & Saigal, S. (2017). Adults born preterm: A review of general health and system-specific outcomes. *Acta Paediatrica, 106*(9), 1409–1437.

Rakison, D. H. (2005). Infant perception and cognition. In B. J. Ellis & D. F. Bjorklund (Eds.), *Origins of the social mind* (pp. 317–353). New York, NY: Guilford Press.

Rakison, D. H., & Krogh, L. (2012). Does causal action facilitate causal perception in infants younger than 6 months of age? *Developmental Science, 15*(1), 43-53.

Rakison, D. H., & Yermolayeva, Y. (2010). Infant categorization. *Wiley Interdisciplinary Reviews: Cognitive Science, 1*(6), 894-905.

Raley, S., Bianchi, S. M., & Wang, W. (2012). When do fathers care? Mothers' economic contribution and fathers' involvement in child care. *American Journal of Sociology, 117*(5), 1422-1459.

Ramey, C. T. (2018). The Abecedarian approach to social, educational, and health disparities. *Clinical Child and Family Psychology Review,* 1-18.

Ramey, C. T., & Ramey, S. L. (2003, May). Preparing America's children for success in school. Paper prepared for an invited address at the White House Early Childhood Summit on Ready to Read, Ready to Learn, Denver, CO.

Rampey, B. D., Finnegan, R., Goodman, M., Mohadjer, L., Krenzke, T., Hogan, J., & Provasnik, S. (2016). *Skills of U.S. unemployed, young, and older adults in sharper focus: Results from the Program for the International Assessment of Adult Competencies (PIAAC) 2012/2014: First Look (NCES 2016-039rev).* U.S. Department of Education. Washington, DC: National Center for Education Statistics. Retrieved from http://nces.ed.gov/pubsearch

Ramsey, P. G., & Lasquade, C. (1996). Preschool children's entry attempts. *Journal of Applied Developmental Psychology, 17,* 135-150.

Rangmar, J., Hjern, A., Vinnerljung, B., Strömland, K., Aronson, M., & Fahlke, C. (2015). Psychosocial outcomes of fetal alcohol syndrome in adulthood. *Pediatrics, 135*(1), e52-e58.

Rankin, J., Matthews, L., Cobley, S., Han, A., Sanders, R., Wiltshire, H. D., & Baker, J. S. (2016). Psychological consequences of childhood obesity: Psychiatric comorbidity and prevention. *Adolescent Health, Medicine and Therapeutics, 7,* 125.

Raposa, E. B., Laws, H. B., & Ansell, E. B. (2016). Prosocial behavior mitigates the negative effects of stress in everyday life. *Clinical Psychological Science, 4*(4), 691-698.

Rapport, M. D., Orban, S. A., Kofler, M. J., & Friedman, L. M. (2013). Do programs designed to train working memory, other executive functions, and attention benefit children with ADHD? A meta-analytic review of cognitive, academic, and behavioral outcomes. *Clinical Psychology Review, 33*(8), 1237-1252.

Rasberry, C. N., Lee, S. M., Robin, L., Laris, B. A., Russell, L. A., Coyle, K. K., & Nihiser, A. J. (2011). The association between school-based physical activity, including physical education, and academic performance: A systematic review of the literature. *Preventive Medicine, 52,* S10-S20.

Rathbun, A., West, J., & Germino-Hausken, E. (2004). *From kindergarten through third grade: Children's beginning school experiences* (NCES 2004-007). Washington, DC: National Center for Education Statistics.

Rauh, V. A., Whyatt, R. M., Garfinkel, R., Andrews, H., Hoepner, L., Reyes, A., . . . Perera, F. P. (2004). Developmental effects of exposure to environmental tobacco smoke and material hardship among inner-city children. *Neurotoxicology and Teratology, 26,* 373-385.

Raver, C. C. (2002). Emotions matter: Making the case for the role of young children's emotional development for early school readiness. *Social Policy Report, 16*(3).

Raver, C. C., Blair, C., & Willoughby, M. (2013). Poverty as a predictor of 4-year-olds' executive function: New perspectives on models of differential susceptibility. *Developmental Psychology, 49*(2), 292.

Rawlings, D. (2012). End-of-life care considerations for gay, lesbian, bisexual, and transgender individuals. *International Journal of Palliative Nursing, 18*(1), 29-34.

Ray, B. D. (2010). Academic achievement and demographic traits of homeschool students: A nationwide study. *Academic Leadership,* Winter, 8(1).

Ray, D. C., Armstrong, S. A., Balkin, R. S., & Jayne, K. M. (2015). Child-centered play therapy in the schools: Review and meta-analysis. *Psychology in the Schools, 52*(2), 107-123.

Ray, O. (2004). How the mind hurts and heals the body. *American Psychologist, 59,* 29-40.

Rayfield, S., & Plugge, E. (2017). Systematic review and meta-analysis of the association between maternal smoking in pregnancy and childhood overweight and obesity. *Journal of Epidemiology and Community Health, 71*(2), 162-173

Raymo, J. M., Iwasawa, M., & Bumpass, L. (2009). Cohabitation and family formation in Japan. *Demography, 46*(4), 785-803.

Raz, N., Ghisletta, P., Rodrigue, K. M., Kennedy, K. M., & Lindenberger, U. (2010). Trajectories of brain aging in middle-aged and older adults: Regional and individual differences. *Neuroimage, 51*(2), 501-511.

Raznahan, A., Shaw, P., Lalonde, F., Stockman, M., Wallace, G. L., Greenstein, D., . . . Giedd, J. N. (2011). How does your cortex grow? *Journal of Neuroscience, 31*(19), 7174-7177.

Reardon, S. F. (2011). The widening academic achievement gap between the rich and the poor: New evidence and possible explanations. In G. Duncan & R. Murnane (Eds.), *Whither opportunity?* (pp. 91-116). New York, NY: Russell Sage Foundation.

Reardon, S. F. (2013). The widening income achievement gap. *Educational Leadership, 70*(8), 10-16.

Reby, D., Levréro, F., Gustafsson, E., & Mathevon, N. (2016). Sex stereotypes influence adults' perception of babies' cries. *BMC Psychology, 4*(1), 19.

Recchia, H. E., & Howe, N. (2009). Associations between social understanding, sibling relationship quality, and siblings' conflict strategies and outcomes. *Child Development, 80*(5), 1564-1578.

Reczek, C., & Zhang, Z. (2016). Parent-child relationships and parent psychological distress: How do social support, strain, dissatisfaction, and equity matter? *Research on Aging, 38*(7), 742-766.

Reddy, U. M., Davis, J. M., Ren, Z., & Greene, M. F. (2017). Opioid Use in Pregnancy, Neonatal Abstinence Syndrome, and Childhood Outcomes: Executive Summary of a Joint Workshop by the Eunice Kennedy Shriver National Institute of Child Health and Human Development, American Congress of Obstetricians and Gynecologists, American Academy of Pediatrics, Society for Maternal-Fetal Medicine, Centers for Disease Control and Prevention, and the March of Dimes Foundation. *Obstetrics and Gynecology, 130*(1), 10.

Reddy, U. M., Wapner, R. J., Rebar, R. W., & Tasca, R. J. (2007). Infertility, assisted reproductive technology, and adverse pregnancy outcomes: Executive summary of a National Institute of Child Health and Human Development Workshop. *Obstetrics and Gynecology, 109,* 967-977.

Reed, A. E., Chan, L., & Mikels, J. A. (2014). Meta-analysis of the age-related positivity effect: Age differences in preferences for positive over negative information. *Psychology and Aging, 29*(1), 1-15.

Reese, D. (1998, May). *Mixed-age grouping: What does the research say, and how can parents use this information.* Retrieved from www.kidsource.com/mixed-age-grouping-what-does-research-say-and-how-can-parents-use-information#sthash.2Ywwka9z.7w0B5qlt.dpbs

Reese, E. (1995). Predicting children's literacy from mother-child conversations. *Cognitive Development, 10,* 381-405.

Reese, E., Sparks, A., & Leyva, D. (2010). A review of parent interventions for preschool children's language and emergent literacy. *Journal of Early Childhood Literacy, 10*(1), 97-117.

Reeve, S., Emsley, R., Sheaves, B., & Freeman, D. (2018). Disrupting sleep: the effects of sleep loss on psychotic experiences tested in an experimental study with mediation analysis. *Schizophrenia Bulletin, 44*(3), 662-671.

Regan, P. C., Lakhanpal, S., & Anguiano, C. (2012). Relationship outcomes in Indian-American love-based and arranged marriages. *Psychological Reports, 110*(3), 915-924.

Rehm, C. D., Peñalvo, J. L., Afshin, A., & Mozaffarian, D. (2016). Dietary intake among US adults, 1999-2012. *JAMA, 315*(23), 2542-2553.

Reichstadt, J., Sengupta, G., Depp, C. A., Palinkas, L. A., & Jeste, D. V. (2010). Older adults' perspectives on successful aging: Qualitative interviews. *American Journal of Geriatric Psychiatry, 18*(7), 567-575.

Reid, I. R. (2014). Should we prescribe calcium supplements for osteoporosis prevention? *Journal of Bone Metabolism, 21*(1), 21-28.

Reid, J. D. (1995). Development in late life: Older lesbian and gay life. In A. R. D'Augelli & C. J. Patterson (Eds.), *Lesbian, gay, and bisexual identities over the lifespan: Psychological perspectives* (pp. 215-240). New York, NY: Oxford University Press.

Reid, N., Dawe, S., Shelton, D., Harnett, P., Warner, J., Armstrong, E., . . . O'Callaghan, F. (2015). Systematic review of fetal alcohol spectrum disorder interventions across the life span. *Alcoholism: Clinical and Experimental Research, 39*(12), 2283-2295.

Reilly, D., Neumann, D. L., & Andrews, G. (2015). Sex differences in mathematics and science achievement: A meta-analysis of National Assessment of Educational Progress assessments. *Journal of Educational Psychology, 107*(3), 645.

Reilly, J. J., & Kelly, J. (2011). Long-term impact of overweight and obesity in childhood and adolescence on morbidity and premature mortality in adulthood: Systematic review. *International Journal of Obesity, 35*(7), 891.

Reinehr, T., & Roth, C. L. (2019). Is there a causal relationship between obesity and puberty? *The Lancet Child & Adolescent Health, 3*(1), 44–54.

Reiner, M., Niermann, C., Jekauc, D., & Woll, A. (2013). Long-term health benefits of physical activity–a systematic review of longitudinal studies. *BMC Public Health, 13*(1), 813.

Reiner, W. G. (2005). Gender identity and sex-of-rearing in children with disorders of sexual differentiation. *Journal of Pediatric Endocrinology and Metabolism, 18*(6), 549–554.

Reiner, W. G., & Gearhart, J. P. (2004). Discordant sexual identity in some genetic males with cloacal exstrophy assigned to female sex at birth. *New England Journal of Medicine, 350*(4), 333–341.

Reisner, S. L., Poteat, T., Keatley, J., Cabral, M., Mothopeng, T., Dunham, E., . . . Baral, S. D. (2016). Global health burden and needs of transgender populations: A review. *The Lancet, 388*(10042), 412–436.

Reiss, A. L., Abrams, M. T., Singer, H. S., Ross, J. L., & Denckla, M. B. (1996). Brain development, gender and IQ in children: A volumetric imaging study. *Brain, 119*, 1763–1774.

Reissland, N., Francis, B., & Mason, J. (2013). Can healthy fetuses show facial expressions of "pain" or "distress"? *PloS One, 8*(6), e65530.

Reitz, C., Cheng, R., Rogaeva, E., Lee, J. H., Tokuhiro, S., Zou, F., . . . Shibata, N. (2011). Meta-analysis of the association between variants in SORL1 and Alzheimer disease. *Archives of Neurology, 68*(1), 99–106.

Reitzes, D. C., & Mutran, E. J. (2004). Grandparenthood: Factors influencing frequency of grandparent-grandchildren contact and role satisfaction. *Journal of Gerontology: Social Sciences, 59*, S9–S16.

Rekker, R., Pardini, D., Keijsers, L., Branje, S., Loeber, R., & Meeus, W. (2015). Moving in and out of poverty: The within-individual association between socioeconomic status and juvenile delinquency. *PLoS One, 10*(11), e0136461.

Remez, L. (2000). Oral sex among adolescents: Is it sex or is it abstinence? *Family Planning Perspectives, 32*, 298–304.

Ren, Q., & Treiman, D. J. (2014, January). *Population Studies Center research reports.* Retrieved from https://www.psc.isr.umich.edu/pubs/pdf/rr14-814.pdf

Renaud, S. J., Engarhos, P., Schleifer, M., & Talwar, V. (2015). Children's earliest experiences with death: circumstances, conversations, explanations, and parental satisfaction. *Infant and Child Development, 24*(2), 157–174.

Rendall, M. S., Weden, M. M., Favreault, M. M., & Waldron, H. (2011). The protective effect of marriage for survival: A review and update. *Demography, 48*(2), 481.

Rende, R., Slomkowski, C., Lloyd-Richardson, E., & Niaura, R. (2005). Sibling effects on substance use in adolescence: Social contagion and genetic relatedness. *Journal of Family Psychology, 19*, 611–618.

Resing, W. C. (2013). Dynamic testing and individualized instruction: Helpful in cognitive education? *Journal of Cognitive Education and Psychology, 12*(1), 81.

Resnick, L. B. (1989). Developing mathematical knowledge. *American Psychologist, 44*, 162–169.

Reuter, M., Roth, S., Holve, K., & Hennig, J. (2006). Identification of first candidate genes for creativity: A pilot study. *Brain Research, 1069*, 190–197.

Reynolds, A. J., Temple, J. A., Ou, S. R., Arteaga, I. A., & White, B. A. (2011). School-based early childhood education and age-28 well-being: Effects by timing, dosage, and subgroups. *Science, 333*(6040), 360–364.

Reynolds, C. F., III, Buysse, D. J., & Kupfer, D. J. (1999). Treating insomnia in older adults: Taking a long-term view. *Journal of the American Medical Association, 281*, 1034–1035.

Reynolds, G. D., Guy, M. W., & Zhang, D. (2011). Neural correlates of individual differences in infant visual attention and recognition memory. *Infancy, 16*(4), 368–391.

Reynolds, K., Pietrzak, R. H., El-Gabalawy, R., Mackenzie, C. S., & Sareen, J. (2015). Prevalence of psychiatric disorders in US older adults: Findings from a nationally representative survey. *World Psychiatry, 14*(1), 74–81.

Rhee, E., Uleman, J. S., Lee, H. K., & Roman, R. J. (1995). Spontaneous self-descriptions and ethnic identities in individualistic and collectivistic cultures. *Journal of Personality and Social Psychology, 69*(1), 142.

Rhee, S. H., & Waldman, I. D. (2002). Genetic and environmental influences on antisocial behavior: A meta-analysis of twin and adoption studies. *Psychological Bulletin, 128*, 490–529.

Rhodes, R. E., Janssen, I., Bredin, S. S., Warburton, D. E., & Bauman, A. (2017). Physical activity: Health impact, prevalence, correlates and interventions. *Psychology & Health, 32*(8), 942–975.

Ricciuti, H. N. (1999). Single parenthood and school readiness in white, Black, and Hispanic 6- and 7-year-olds. *Journal of Family Psychology, 13*, 450–465.

Ricciuti, H. N. (2004). Single parenthood, achievement, and problem behavior in white, Black, and Hispanic children. *Journal of Educational Research, 97*, 196–206.

Rice, K., Prichard, I., Tiggemann, M., & Slater, A. (2016). Exposure to Barbie: Effects on thin-ideal internalization, body esteem, and body dissatisfaction among young girls. *Body Image, 19*, 142–149.

Rice, M. L. (1982). Child language: What children know and how. In T. M. Field, A. Hudson, H. C. Quay, L. Troll, & G. E. Finley (Eds.), *Review of human development research.* New York, NY: Wiley.

Rice, M. L., Smolik, F., Perpich, D., Thompson, T., Rytting, N., & Blossom, M. (2010). Mean length of utterance levels in 6-month intervals for children 3 to 9 years with and without language impairments. *Journal of Speech, Language, and Hearing Research, 53*(2), 333–349.

Rice, M. L., Taylor, C. L., & Zubrick, S. R. (2008). Language outcomes of 7-year-old children with or without a history of late language emergence at 24 months. *Journal of Speech, Language, and Hearing Research, 51*, 394–407.

Richards, J. B., Zheng, H. F., & Spector, T. D. (2012). Genetics of osteoporosis from genome-wide association studies: advances and challenges. *Nature Reviews Genetics, 13*(8), 576–588.

Richards, R., Merrill, R. M., & Baksh, L. (2011). Health behaviors and infant health outcomes in homeless pregnant women in the United States. *Pediatrics, 128*(3), 438–446.

Richardson, C. R., Kriska, A. M., Lantz, P. M., & Hayward, R. A. (2004). Physical activity and mortality across cardiovascular disease risk groups. *Medicine and Science in Sports and Exercise, 36*, 1923–1929.

Richardson, E. G., & Hemenway, D. (2011). Homicide, suicide, and unintentional firearm fatality: comparing the United States with other high-income countries, 2003. *Journal of Trauma and Acute Care Surgery, 70*(1), 238–243.

Richardson, G. A., & Day, N. L. (2018). Longitudinal studies of the effects of prenatal cocaine exposure on development and behavior. In *Handbook of Developmental Neurotoxicology* (pp. 379–388). Cambridge, MA: Academic Press.

Richardson, G. A., De Genna, N. M., Goldschmidt, L., Larkby, C., & Donovan, J. E. (2019). Prenatal cocaine exposure: Direct and indirect associations with 21-year-old offspring substance use and behavior problems. *Drug and Alcohol Dependence, 195*, 121–131.

Richardson, J. (1995). *Achieving gender equality in families: The role of males* (Innocenti Global Seminar, Summary Report). Florence, Italy: UNICEF International Child Development Centre, Spedale degli Innocenti.

Richardson, K. J., Lewis, K. H., Krishnamurthy, P. K., Kent, C., Wiltshire, A. J., & Hanlon, H. M. (2018). Food security outcomes under a changing climate: Impacts of mitigation and adaptation on vulnerability to food insecurity. *Climatic Change, 147*(1–2), 327–341.

Richardson, S., Hirsch, J. S., Narasimhan, M., Crawford, J. M., McGinn, T., Davidson, K. W., . . . Cookingham, J. (2020). Presenting characteristics, comorbidities, and outcomes among 5700 patients hospitalized with COVID-19 in the New York City area. *Journal of the American Medical Association, 323* (20), 2052–2059.

Richardson, T. J., Lee, S. J., Berg-Weger, M., & Grossberg, G. T. (2013). Caregiver health: health of caregivers of Alzheimer's and other dementia patients. *Current Psychiatry Reports, 15*(7), 367.

Richert, R. A., Robb, M. B., Fender, J. G., & Wartella, E. (2010). Word learning from baby videos. *Archives of Pediatrics & Adolescent Medicine, 164*(5), 432–437.

Richman, A. L., Miller, P. M., & LeVine, P. A. (2010). Cultural and educational variations in maternal responsiveness. In R. A. LeVine (Ed.), *Psychological anthropology: A reader on self in culture* (pp. 181–192). Malden, MA: Wiley-Blackwell.

Richman, A. L., Miller, P. M., & LeVine, R. A. (1992). Cultural and educational variations in maternal responsiveness. *Developmental Psychology, 28*(4), 614.

Richman, L. S., Kubzansky, L., Maselko, J., Kawachi, I., Choo, P., & Bauer, M. (2005). Positive emotion and health: Going beyond the negative. *Health Psychology, 24*, 422–429.

Riddell, R. R. P., Racine, N. M., Gennis, H. G., Turcotte, K., Uman, L. S., Horton, R. E., . . . Lisi, D. M. (2015). Non-pharmacological management of infant and young child procedural pain. *Cochrane Database of Systematic Reviews, 12*.

Rideout, V. J., Foehr, U. G., & Roberts, D. F. (2010). *Generation M^2: Media in the lives of 8- to 18-year-olds.* Menlo Park, CA: Henry J. Kaiser Family Foundation.

Ridgers, N. D., Fairclough, S. J., & Stratton, G. (2010). Variables associated with children's physical activity levels during recess: The A-CLASS project. *International Journal of Behavioral Nutrition and Physical Activity, 7*(1), 74.

Ridgers, N. D., Salmon, J., Parrish, A. M., Stanley, R. M., & Okely, A. D. (2012). Physical activity during school recess: A systematic review. *American Journal of Preventive Medicine, 43*(3), 320–328.

Riegle-Crumb, C., Farkas, G., & Muller, C. (2006). The role of gender and friendship in advanced course taking. *Sociology of Education, 79*(3), 206–228.

Riem, M. M., Bakermans-Kranenburg, M. J., van IJzendoorn, M. H., Out, D., & Rombouts, S. A. (2012). Attachment in the brain: Adult attachment representations predict amygdala and behavioral responses to infant crying. *Attachment & Human Development, 14*(6), 533–551.

Riemann, M. K., & Kanstrup Hansen, I. L. (2000). Effects on the fetus of exercise in pregnancy. *Scandinavian Journal of Medicine & Science in Sports, 10*(1), 12–19.

Rietzschel, E. F., Zacher, H., & Stroebe, W. (2016). A lifespan perspective on creativity and innovation at work. *Work, Aging and Retirement, 2*(2), 105–129.

Riggle, E. D. B., Rotosky, S. S., & Riggle, S. G. (2010). Psychological distress, well-being and legal recognition in same-sex couple relationships. *Journal of Family Psychology, 24*(1), 82–86.

Riggle, E. D., Rostosky, S. S., McCants, L. E., & Pascale-Hague, D. (2011). The positive aspects of a transgender self-identification. *Psychology & Sexuality, 2*(2), 147–158.

Rious, J. B., & Cunningham, M. (2018). Altruism as a buffer for antisocial behavior for African American adolescents exposed to community violence. *Journal of Community Psychology, 46*(2), 224–237.

Riphagen, S., Gomez, X., Gonzalez-Martinez, C., Wilkinson, N., & Theocharis, P. (2020). Hyperinflammatory shock in children during COVID-19 pandemic. *The Lancet.*

Ritchie, H., & Roser, M. (2019). *Causes of death* [Our World in Data fact sheet]. Retrieved from https://ourworldindata.org/causes-of-death#breakdown-of-deaths-by-age

Ritchie, S. J., Bates, T. C., & Deary, I. J. (2015). Is education associated with improvements in general cognitive ability, or in specific skills? *Developmental Psychology, 51*(5), 573.

Ritchie, S. J., Bates, T. C., Der, G., Starr, J. M., & Deary, I. J. (2013). Education is associated with higher later life IQ scores, but not with faster cognitive processing speed. *Psychology and Aging, 28*(2), 515.

Rittenour, C. E., Myers, S. A., & Brann, M. (2007). Commitment and emotional closeness in the sibling relationship. *Southern Communication Journal, 72*(2), 169–183.

Ritz, B. R., Chatterjee, N., Garcia-Closas, M., Gauderman, W. J., Pierce, B. L., Kraft, P., . . . McAllister, K. (2017). Lessons learned from past gene-environment interaction successes. *American Journal of Epidemiology, 186*(7), 778–786.

Rivas-Drake, D., Seaton, E. K., Markstrom, C., Quintana, S., Syed, M., Lee, R. M., . . . Ethnic and Racial Identity in the 21st Century Study Group. (2014). Ethnic and racial identity in adolescence: Implications for psychosocial, academic, and health outcomes. *Child Development, 85*(1), 40–57.

Rivas-Drake, D., Syed, M., Umaña-Taylor, A., Markstrom, C., French, S., Schwartz, S. J., . . . Ethnic and Racial Identity in the 21st Century Study Group. (2014). Feeling good, happy, and proud: A meta-analysis of positive ethnic–racial affect and adjustment. *Child Development, 85*(1), 77–102.

Rivers, S. E., Brackett, M. A., Omori, M., Sickler, C., Bertoli, M. C., & Salovey, P. (2013). Emotion skills as a protective factor for risky behaviors among college students. *Journal of College Student Development, 54*(2), 172–183.

Robbins, C. L., Schick, V., Reece, M., Herbenick, D., Sanders, S. A., Dodge, B., & Fortenberry, J. D. (2011). Prevalence, frequency, and associations of masturbation with partnered sexual behaviors among US adolescents. *Archives of Pediatrics & Adolescent Medicine, 165*(12), 1087–1093.

Roberts, A. W., Ogunwole, S. U., Blakeslee, L., & Rabe, M. A. (2018). *The population 65 years and older in the United States: 2016.* Washington, DC: US Department of Commerce, Economics and Statistics Administration, US Census Bureau.

Roberts, B. W., Walton, K. E., & Viechtbauer, W. (2006). Patterns of mean-level change in personality traits across the life course: A meta-analysis of longitudinal studies. *Psychological Bulletin, 132*(1), 1.

Roberts, B. W., Wood, D., & Smith, J. L. (2005). Evaluating five factor theory and social investment perspectives on personality trait development. *Journal of Research in Personality, 39*(1), 166–184.

Roberts, B., & Mroczek, D. (2008). Personality trait change in adulthood. *Current Directions in Psychological Science, 17*(1), 31–35.

Robertson, D. A., Savva, G. M., & Kenny, R. A. (2013). Frailty and cognitive impairment—a review of the evidence and causal mechanisms. *Ageing Research Reviews, 12*(4), 840–851.

Robins, R. W., John, O. P., Caspi, A., Moffitt, T. E., & Stouthamer-Loeber, M. (1996). Resilient, overcontrolled, and undercontrolled boys: Three replicable personality types. *Journal of Personality and Social Psychology, 70*, 157–171.

Robinson, M., Thiel, M. M., Backus, M. M., & Meyer, E. C. (2006). Matters of spirituality at the end of life in the pediatric intensive care unit. *Pediatrics, 118*, 719–729.

Robinson, O. C., & Wright, G. R. (2013). The prevalence, types and perceived outcomes of crisis episodes in early adulthood and midlife: A structured retrospective-autobiographical study. *International Journal of Behavioral Development, 37*(5), 407–416.

Robles, T. F., Slatcher, R. B., Trombello, J. M., & McGinn, M. M. (2014). Marital quality and health: A meta-analytic review. *Psychological Bulletin, 140*(1), 140.

Rodenhizer, K. A. E., & Edwards, K. M. (2019). The impacts of sexual media exposure on adolescent and emerging adults' dating and sexual violence attitudes and behaviors: A critical review of the literature. *Trauma, Violence, & Abuse, 20*(4), 439–452.

Rodgers, E., D'Agostino, J. V., Harmey, S. J., Kelly, R. H., & Brownfield, K. (2016). Examining the nature of scaffolding in an early literacy intervention. *Reading Research Quarterly, 51*(3), 345–360.

Rodriguez, J. M., Karlamangla, A. S., Gruenewald, T. L., Miller-Martinez, D., Merkin, S. S., & Seeman, T. E. (2019). Social stratification and allostatic load: Shapes of health differences in the MIDUS study in the United States. *Journal of Biosocial Science, 51*(5), 627–644.

Roess, A. A., Jacquier, E. F., Catellier, D. J., Carvalho, R., Lutes, A. C., Anater, A. S., & Dietz, W. H. (2018). Food consumption patterns of infants and toddlers: Findings from the Feeding Infants and Toddlers Study (FITS) 2016. *The Journal of Nutrition, 148*(9S), 1525S–1535S.

Rogers, C. H., Floyd, F. J., Seltzer, M. M., Greenberg, J., & Hong, J. (2008). Long-term effects of the death of a child on parents' adjustment in midlife. *Journal of Family Psychology, 22*(2), 203.

Rogler, L. H. (2002). Historical generations and psychology: The case of the Great Depression and World War II. *American Psychologist, 57*(12), 1013–1023.

Rogoff, B. (2003). *The cultural nature of human development.* Oxford, England: Oxford University Press.

Rogoff, B., & Morelli, G. (1989). Perspectives on children's development from cultural psychology. *American Psychologist, 44*(2), 343.

Rogoff, B., Mistry, J., Göncü, A., & Mosier, C. (1993). Guided participation in cultural activity by toddlers and caregivers. *Monographs of the Society for Research in Child Development, 58*(8, Serial No. 236).

Rogoff, B., Morelli, G. A., & Chavajay, P. (2010). Children's integration in communities and segregation from people of differing ages. *Perspectives on Psychological Science, 5*(4), 431–440.

Roisman, G. I., Clausell, E., Holland, A., Fortuna, K., & Elieff, C. (2008). Adult romantic relationships as contexts of human development: A multimethod comparison of same-sex couples with opposite-sex dating, engaged, and married dyads. *Developmental Psychology, 44,* 91–101.

Roisman, G. I., Masten, A. S., Coatsworth, J. D., & Tellegen, A. (2004). Salient and emerging developmental tasks in the transition to adulthood. *Child Development, 75,* 123–133.

Rojas-Flores, L., Clements, M. L., Hwang Koo, J., & London, J. (2017). Trauma and psychological distress in Latino citizen children following parental detention and deportation. *Psychological Trauma: Theory, Research, Practice, and Policy, 9*(3), 352.

Rollins, B. C., & Feldman, H. (1970). Marital satisfaction over the family life cycle. *Journal of Marriage and the Family,* 20–28.

Romano, E., Babchishin, L., Marquis, R., & Fréchette, S. (2015). Childhood maltreatment and educational outcomes. *Trauma, Violence, & Abuse, 16*(4), 418–437.

Romano, E., Tremblay, R. E., Boulerice, B., & Swisher, R. (2005). Multi-level correlates of childhood physical aggression and prosocial behavior. *Journal of Abnormal Child Psychology, 33*(5), 565–578.

Ronfard, S., & Corriveau, K. H. (2016). Teaching and preschoolers' ability to infer knowledge from mistakes. *Journal of Experimental Child Psychology, 150,* 87–98.

Rook, K. S. (2015). Social networks in later life: Weighing positive and negative effects on health and well-being. *Current Directions in Psychological Science, 24*(1), 45–51.

Rook, K. S., & Charles, S. T. (2017). Close social ties and health in later life: Strengths and vulnerabilities. *American Psychologist, 72*(6), 567.

Roopnarine, J. L. (2011). Cultural variations in beliefs about play, parent-child play, and children's play: Meaning for childhood development. In A. D. Pellegrini (Ed.), *Oxford library of psychology. The Oxford handbook of the development of play* (pp. 19–37). Oxford, England: Oxford University Press.

Roopnarine, J. L., & Davidson, K. L. (2015). Parent-child play across cultures: Advancing play research. *American Journal of Play, 7*(2), 228–252.

Roopnarine, J. L., & Honig, A. S. (1985). The unpopular child. *Young Children, 40*(6), 59–64.

Roopnarine, J. L., Hooper, F. H., Ahmeduzzaman, M., & Pollack, B. (1993). Gentle play partners: Mother-child and father-child play in New Delhi, India. In K. MacDonald (Ed.), *Parent-child play* (pp. 287–304). Albany, NY: State University of New York Press.

Roosa, M. W., Deng, S., Ryu, E., Burrell, G. L., Tein, J., Jones, S., Lopez, V., & Crowder, S. (2005). Family and child characteristics linking neighborhood context and child externalizing behavior. *Journal of Marriage and Family, 667,* 515–529.

Rosamond, W., Flegal, K., Furie, K., Go, A., Greenlund, K., Haase, N., . . . Hong, Y. (2008). Heart disease and stroke statistics—2008 update: A report from the American Heart Association Statistics Committee and Stroke Statistics Subcommittee. *Circulation, 117*(4), e25–e146.

Rosario, M., Schrimshaw, E. W., & Hunter, J. (2011). Different patterns of sexual identity development over time: Implications for the psychological adjustment of lesbian, gay, and bisexual youths. *Journal of Sex Research, 48*(1), 3–15.

Roscigno, V., Mong, S., Bryon, R., & Tester, G. (2007). *Age discrimination, social closure and employment.* Retrieved from http://nclive.org/cgi-bin/nclsm?url=http://search.proquest.com/docview/229891354?accountid=10939

Rose, A. J., & Smith, R. L. (2018). Gender and peer relationships. In W. M. Bukowski, B. Laursen, & K. H. Rubin (Eds.), *Handbook of peer interactions, relationships, and groups* (pp. 571–589). New York, NY: The Guilford Press.

Rose, S. A., Feldman, J. F., & Jankowski, J. J. (2002). Processing speed in the 1st year of life: A longitudinal study of preterm and full-term infants. *Developmental Psychology, 38,* 895–902.

Rose, S. A., Feldman, J. F., Jankowski, J. J., & Van Rossem, R. (2012). Information processing from infancy to 11 years: Continuities and prediction of IQ. *Intelligence, 40*(5), 445–457.

Roseberry, S., Hirsh-Pasek, K., & Golinkoff, R. M. (2014). Skype me! Socially contingent interactions help toddlers learn language. *Child Development, 85*(3), 956–970.

Rosen, E. D., Kaestner, K. H., Natarajan, R., Patti, M. E., Sallari, R., Sander, M., & Susztak, K. (2018). Epigenetics and epigenomics: Implications for diabetes and obesity. *Diabetes, 67*(10), 1923–1931.

Rosen, R. C., & Kupelian, V. (2016). Epidemiology of erectile dysfunction and key risk factors. In T. S. Köhler & K. T. McVary (Eds.), *Contemporary treatment of erectile dysfunction* (pp. 45–56). Cham, Switzerland: Humana Press.

Rosenbaum, J. E. (2009). Patient teenagers? A comparison of the sexual behavior of virginity pledgers and matched nonpledgers. *Pediatrics, 123,* e110–e120.

Rosenberg, S. D., Rosenberg, H. J., & Farrell, M. P. (1999). The midlife crisis revisited. In S. L. Willis & J. D. Reid (Eds.), *Life in the middle* (pp. 47–73). San Diego, CA: Academic Press.

Rosenberger, N. (2007). Rethinking emerging adulthood in Japan: Perspectives from long-term single women. *Child Development Perspectives, 1*(2), 92–95.

Rosenbluth, S. C., & Steil, J. M. (1995). Predictors of intimacy for women in heterosexual and homosexual couples. *Journal of Social and Personal Relationships, 12*(2), 163–175.

Rosenfeld, M. J. (2014). Couple longevity in the era of same-sex marriage in the United States. *Journal of Marriage and Family, 76*(5), 905–918.

Rosengren, A., Smyth, A., Rangarajan, S., Ramasundarahettige, C., McKee, M., Yusuf, S., & PURE study investigators. (2018). P3410 Variations in socioeconomic status and cardiovascular disease: Risk factors, incidence and case fatality. Rates and management in 20 countries. *European Heart Journal, 39*(suppl_1), ehy563-P3410.

Rosenthal, B. P., & Fischer, M. (2014). Functional vision changes in the normal and aging eye. In T. L. Kauffman, R. W. Scott, J. O. Barr, & M. L. Moran (Eds.), *Comprehensive Guide to Geriatric Rehabilitation* (p. 381). London, England: Churchill Livingstone.

Roser, M. (2017). Fertility rate. *Our World in Data* [Report]. Retrieved from https://ourworldindata.org/fertility-rate?utm_source=DI&utm_medium=referral

Roser, M. Ortiz-Ospina, E., & Beltekian, D. (2019, October). *Life expectancy* [Our World in Data report]. Retrieved from https://ourworldindata.org/life-expectancy

Roser, M., & Ortiz-Espina, E. (2018). *Literacy.* OurWorldInData.org. United Nations Educational, Scientific and Cultural Organization (UNESCO). Retrieved from https://ourworldindata.org/literacy

Roses, A. D., Saunders, A. M., Lutz, M. W., Zhang, N., Hariri, A. R., Asin, K. E., . . . Brannan, S. K. (2014). New applications of disease genetics and pharmacogenetics to drug development. *Current Opinion in Pharmacology, 14,* 81–89.

Rosner, B., Cook, N. R., Daniels, S., & Falkner, B. (2013). Childhood blood pressure trends and risk factors for high blood pressure: the NHANES experience 1988–2008. *Hypertension, 62*(2), 247–254.

Rosner, R., Kruse, J., & Hagl, M. (2010). A meta-analysis of interventions for bereaved children and adolescents. *Death Studies, 34*(2), 99–136.

Ross, C. E., Hill, T. D., & Mirowsky, J. (2016). Reconceptualizing health lifestyles: The case of marriage. *Research in the Sociology of Health Care, 34,* 243–260.

Ross, S. E., Flynn, J. I., & Pate, R. R. (2016). What is really causing the obesity epidemic? A review of reviews in children and adults. *Journal of Sports Sciences, 34*(12), 1148–1153.

Rossi, A. S. (2004). The menopausal transition and aging process. In O. G. Brim, C. D. Ryff, & R. C. Kessler (Eds.), *How healthy are we? A national study of well-being at midlife.* Chicago, IL: University of Chicago Press.

Rostila, M., Saarela, J., & Kawachi, I. (2012). Mortality in parents following the death of a child: a nationwide follow-up study from Sweden. *Journal of Epidemiology and Community Health, 66*(10), 927–933.

Rothbart, M. K., Ahadi, S. A., & Evans, D. E. (2000). Temperament and personality: Origins and outcomes. *Journal of Personality and Social Psychology, 78,* 122–135.

Rothbart, M. K., Ahadi, S. A., Hershey, K. L., & Fisher, P. (2001). Investigations of temperament at three to seven years: The Children's Behavior Questionnaire. *Child Development, 72*(5), 1394–1408.

Rothbart, M. K., Sheese, B. E., Rueda, M. R., & Posner, M. I. (2011). Developing mechanisms of self-regulation in early life. *Emotion Review, 3*(2), 207-213.

Rouse, C., Brooks-Gunn, J., & McLanahan, S. (2005). Introducing the issue. *Future of Children, 15*(1), 5-14.

Roussotte, F. F., Bramen, J. E., Nunez, C., Quandt, L. C., Smith, L., O'Connor, M. J., ... Sowell, E. R. (2011). Abnormal brain activation during working memory in children with prenatal exposure to drugs of abuse: The effects of methamphetamine, alcohol, and polydrug exposure. *NeuroImage, 54*(4), 3067-3075.

Rovee-Collier, C. (1996). Shifting the focus from what to why. *Infant Behavior and Development, 19,* 385-400.

Rovee-Collier, C. (1999). The development of infant memory. *Current Directions in Psychological Science, 8,* 80-85.

Rowe, J. W., & Kahn, R. L. (1997). Successful aging. *Gerontologist,* 37, 433-440.

Rowe, M. L. (2012). A longitudinal investigation of the role of quantity and quality of child-directed speech in vocabulary development. *Child Development, 83*(5), 1762-1774.

Roy, S., Aggarwal, A., Dhangar, G., & Aneja, A. (2016). Mercury in vaccines: A review. *Global Vaccines and Immunology, 1.* doi: 10.15761/GVI.1000119

Rozman, M., Treven, S., & Cancer, V. (2016). *Stereotypes of older employees compared to younger employees in Slovenian companies.* Retrieved from http://nclive.org/cgi-bin/nclsm?url-http://search.proquest.com/docview/1854196758?accountid=10939

Rubin, D. C., Berntsen, D., & Hutson, M. (2009). The normative and the personal life: Individual differences in life scripts and life story events among USA and Danish undergraduates. *Memory, 17*(1), 54-68.

Rubin, D. H., Krasilnikoff, P. A., Leventhal, J. M., Weile, B., & Berget, A. (1986, August 23). Effect of passive smoking on birth weight. *Lancet,* 415-417.

Rubin, K. H., Bukowski, W., & Parker, J. G. (1998). Peer interactions, relationships, and groups. In W. Damon (Series Ed.) & N. Eisenberg (Vol. Ed.), *Handbook of child psychology: Vol. 3. Social, emotional, and personality development* (5th ed., pp. 619-700). New York, NY: Wiley.

Rubin, K. H., Burgess, K. B., Dwyer, K. M., & Hastings, P. D. (2003). Predicting preschoolers' externalizing behavior from toddler temperament, conflict, and maternal negativity. *Developmental Psychology, 39*(1), 164-176.

Rubio, G. (2013). The love revolution: Decline in arranged marriages in Asia, the Middle East and Sub-Saharan Africa. Mimeo, University of California, Los Angeles.

Ruble, D. N., & Martin, C. L. (1998). Gender development. In W. Damon (Series Ed.) & N. Eisenberg (Vol. Ed.), *Handbook of child psychology: Vol. 3. Social, emotional, and personality development* (5th ed., pp. 933-1016). New York, NY: Wiley.

Ruble, D. N., Martin, C. L., & Berenbaum, S. A. (2006). Gender development. In W. Damon & R. M. Lerner (Series Eds.) & D. Kuhn & R. S. Seigler (Vol. Eds.), *Handbook of child psychology: Vol 2. Cognition, perception, and language* (pp. 858-932). Hoboken: NJ: Wiley.

Rudasill, K. M., Hawley, L. R., LoCasale-Crouch, J., & Buhs, E. S. (2017). Child temperamental regulation and classroom quality in Head Start: Considering the role of cumulative economic risk. *Journal of Educational Psychology, 109*(1), 118.

Rudolph, K. D., Lambert, S. F., Clark, A. G., & Kurlakowsky, K. D. (2001). Negotiating the transition to middle school: The role of self-regulatory processes. *Child Development, 72*(3), 929-946.

Rudy, D., & Grusec, J. E. (2006). Authoritarian parenting in individualistic and collectivistic groups: Associations with maternal emotion and cognition and children's self-esteem. *Journal of Family Psychology, 20,* 68-78.

Rueda, M. R., Posner, M. I., & Rothbart, M. K. (2005). The development of executive attention: Contributions to the emergence of self-regulation. *Developmental Neuropsychology, 28*(2), 573-594.

Ruigrok, A. N., Salimi-Khorshidi, G., Lai, M. C., Baron-Cohen, S., Lombardo, M. V., Tait, R. J., & Suckling, J. (2014). A meta-analysis of sex differences in human brain structure. *Neuroscience & Biobehavioral Reviews, 39,* 34-50.

Runco, M. A., Noble, E. P., Reiter-Palmon, R., Acar, S., Ritchie, T., & Yurkovich, J. M. (2011). The genetic basis of creativity and ideational fluency. *Creativity Research Journal, 23*(4), 376-380.

Rundle, A. G., Park, Y., Herbstman, J. B., Kinsey, E. W., & Wang, Y. C. (2020). COVID-19 related school closings and risk of weight gain among children. *Obesity.*

Runyan, D. K., Shankar, V., Hassan, F., Hunter, W. M., Jain, D., Paula, C. S., ... Bordin, I. A. (2010). International variations in harsh child discipline. *Pediatrics, 126*(3), e701-e711.

Rushton, J. P., & Ankney, C. D. (2009). Whole brain size and general mental ability: A review. *International Journal of Neuroscience, 119*(5), 692-732.

Rushton, J. P., & Jensen, A. R. (2005). Thirty years of research on race differences in cognitive ability. *Psychology, Public Policy, and Law, 11,* 235-294.

Russ, S. A., Larson, K., Franke, T. M., & Halfon, N. (2009). Associations between media use and health in US children. *Academic Pediatrics, 9*(5), 300-306.

Rutter, M. (2012). Gene-environment interdependence. *European Journal of Developmental Psychology, 9*(4), 391-412.

Rutter, M., Caspi, A., Fergusson, D., Horwood, L. J., Goodman, R., Maughan, B., ... Carroll, J. (2004b). Sex differences in developmental reading disability: New findings from 4 epidemiological studies. *JAMA, 291*(16), 2007-2012.

Rutter, M., O'Connor, T. G., & English & Romanian Adoptees (ERA) Study Team. (2004). Are there biological programming effects for psychological development? Findings from a study of Romanian adoptees. *Developmental Psychology, 40,* 81-94.

Ryan, A. S., Wenjun, Z., & Acosta, A. (2002). Breastfeeding continues to increase into the new millennium. *Pediatrics, 110,* 1103-1109.

Ryan, C., Russell, S. T., Huebner, D., Diaz, R., & Sanchez, J. (2010). Family acceptance in adolescence and the health of LGBT young adults. *Journal of Child and Adolescent Psychiatric Nursing, 23*(4), 205-213.

Rychlak, J. F. (2003). *The human image in postmodern America.* Washington, DC: American Psychological Association.

Ryff, C. D. (1989). Happiness is everything, or is it? Explorations on the meaning of psychological well-being. *Journal of Personality and Social Psychology, 57*(6), 1069.

Ryff, C. D. (2014). Psychological well-being revisited: Advances in the science and practice of eudaimonia. *Psychotherapy and Psychosomatics, 83*(1), 10-28.

Ryff, C. D., & Keyes, C. L. M. (1995). The structure of psychological well-being revisited. *Journal of Personality and Social Psychology, 69,* 719-727.

Ryff, C. D., & Seltzer, M. M. (1995). Family relations and individual development in adulthood and aging. In R. Blieszner & V. Hilkevitch (Eds.), *Handbook of aging and the family* (pp. 95-113). Westport, CT: Greenwood Press.

Ryff, C. D., & Singer, B. (1998). Middle age and well-being. In H. S. Friedman (Ed.), *Encyclopedia of mental health* (pp. 707-719). San Diego, CA: Academic Press.

Ryff, C. D., Heller, A. S., Schaefer, S. M., Van Reekum, C., & Davidson, R. J. (2016). Purposeful engagement, healthy aging, and the brain. *Current Behavioral Neuroscience Reports, 3*(4), 318-327.

Ryff, C. D., Singer, B. H., & Palmersheim, K. A. (2004). Social inequalities in health and well-being: The role of relational and religious protective factors. In O. G. Brim, C. D. Ryff, & R. C. Kessler (Eds.), *How healthy are we? A national study of well-being at midlife.* Chicago, IL: University of Chicago Press.

Röcke, C., & Lachman, M. E. (2008). Perceived trajectories of life satisfaction across past, present and future: Profiles and correlates of subjective change in young, middle-aged, and older adults. *Psychology and Aging, 23*(4), 833-847.

Rübeling, H., Keller, H., Yovsi, R. D., Lenk, M., Schwarzer, S., & Kühne, N. (2011). Children's drawings of the self as an expression of cultural conceptions of the self. *Journal of Cross-Cultural Psychology, 42*(3), 406-424.

Saarni, C., Campos, J. J., Camras, A., & Witherington, D. (2006). Emotional development: Action, communication, and understanding. In N. Eisenberg, W. Damon, & R. Lerner (Eds.), *Handbook of child psychology: Vol. 3, Social, emotional and personality development* (6th ed., pp. 226-299). Hoboken, NJ: Wiley.

Sabol, B., Denman, M. A., & Guise, J. (2015). Vaginal birth after cesarean: An effective method to reduce cesarean. *Clinical Obstetrics and Gynecology, 58*(2), 309-319.

Sacks, J. J., Gonzales, K. R., Bouchery, E. E., Tomedi, L. E., & Brewer, R. D. (2015). 2010 national and state costs of excessive alcohol consumption. *American Journal of Preventive Medicine, 49*(5), e73–e79.

Sadeh, A., Mindell, J., & Rivera, L. (2011). "My child has a sleep problem": A cross-cultural comparison of parental definitions. *Sleep Medicine, 12*(5), 478–482.

Sadigh-Eteghad, S., Sabermarouf, B., Majdi, A., Talebi, M., Farhoudi, M., & Mahmoudi, J. (2015). Amyloid- beta: A crucial factor in Alzheimer's disease. *Medical Principles and Practice, 24*(1), 1

Sadruddin, A. F., Ponguta, L. A., Zonderman, A. L., Wiley, K. S., Grimshaw, A., & Panter-Brick, C. (2019). How do grandparents influence child health and development? [A systematic review]. *Social Science & Medicine, 239,* 1–32. doi. org/10.1016/j.socscimed.2019.112476

Saez, M. (2011). Same-sex marriage, same-sex cohabitation, and same-sex families around the world: Why "same" is so different? *American University Journal of Gender, Social Policy & the Law,* 19, 1.

Saggino, A., Pezzuti, L., Tommasi, M., Cianci, L., Colom, R., & Orsini, A. (2014). Null sex differences in general intelligence among elderly. *Personality and Individual Differences, 63,* 53–57.

Sahoo, K., Sahoo, B., Choudhury, A. K., Sofi, N. Y., Kumar, R., & Bhadoria, A. S. (2015). Childhood obesity: Causes and consequences. *Journal of Family Medicine and Primary Care, 4*(2), 187.

Saigal, S., Stoskopf, B., Streiner, D., Boyle, M., Pinelli, J., Paneth, N., & Goddeeris, J. (2006). Transition of extremely low-birth-weight infants from adolescence to young adulthood: Comparison with normal birth-weight controls. *Journal of the American Medical Association, 295,* 667–675.

Saint-Georges, C., Chetouani, M., Cassel, R., Apicella, F., Mahdhaoui, A., Muratori, F., ... & Cohen, D. (2013). Motherese in interaction: At the cross-road of emotion and cognition? [A systematic review]. *PloS One, 8*(10), e78103.

Saito, E. K., Diaz, N., Chung, J., & McMurtray, A. (2017). Smoking history and Alzheimer's disease risk in a community-based clinic population. *Journal of Education and Health Promotion, 6.*

Saka, B., Kaya, O., Ozturk, G. B., Erten, N., & Karan, M. A. (2010). Malnutrition in the elderly and its relationship with other geriatric syndromes. *Clinical Nutrition, 29*(6), 745–748.

Sala-Llonch, R., Bartrés-Faz, D., & Junqué, C. (2015). Reorganization of brain networks in aging: A review of functional connectivity studies. *Frontiers in Psychology, 6.*

Salami, A., Eriksson, J., Nilsson, L. G., & Nyberg, L. (2012). Age-related white matter microstructural differences partly mediate age-related decline in processing speed but not cognition. *Biochimica et Biophysica Acta (BBA)-Molecular Basis of Disease, 1822*(3), 408–415.

Salas, E., Rosen, M. A., & DiazGranados, D. (2010). Expertise-based intuition and decision making in organizations. *Journal of Management, 36*(4), 941–973.

Saleem, S., Tikmani, S. S., McClure, E. M., Moore, J. L., Azam, S. I., Dhaded, S. M., ... Tenge, C. (2018). Trends and determinants of

stillbirth in developing countries: Results from the Global Network's Population-Based Birth Registry. *Reproductive Health, 15*(1), 100.

Salk, R. H., Hyde, J. S., & Abramson, L. Y. (2017). Gender differences in depression in representative national samples: meta-analyses of diagnoses and symptoms. *Psychological Bulletin, 143*(8), 783.

Salk, R. H., Petersen, J. L., Abramson, L. Y., & Hyde, J. S. (2016). The contemporary face of gender differences and similarities in depression throughout adolescence: Development and chronicity. *Journal of Affective Disorders, 205,* 28–35.

Salkind, N. J. (Ed.). (2005). Smiling. *The encyclopedia of human development.* Thousand Oaks, CA: Sage.

Salomo, D., & Liszkowski, U. (2013). Sociocultural settings influence the emergence of prelinguistic deictic gestures. *Child Development, 84*(4), 1296–1307.

Salovey, P., & Mayer, J. D. (1990). Emotional intelligence. *Imagination, Cognition, and Personality, 9,* 185–211.

Salovey, P., Rothman, A. J., Detweiler, J. B., & Steward, W. T. (2000). Emotional states and physical health. *American Psychologist, 55,* 110–121.

Salthouse, T. (2012). Consequences of age-related cognitive declines. *Annual Review of Psychology, 63,* 201–226.

Salthouse, T. A. (1991). *Theoretical perspectives on cognitive aging.* Hillsdale, NJ: Erlbaum.

Salthouse, T. A. (2010). *Major issues in cognitive aging.* New York, NY: Oxford University Press.

Salthouse, T. A., & Maurer, T. J. (1996). Aging, job performance, and career development. In J. E. Birren, K. W. Schaie, R. P. Abeles, M. Gatz, & T. A. Salthouse (Eds.), *Handbook of the psychology of aging* (pp. 353–364). Cambridge, MA: Academic Press.

Samdal, O., & Dür, W. (2000). The school environment and the health of adolescents. In C. Currie, K. Hurrelmann, W. Settertobulte, R. Smith, & J. Todd (Eds.), *Health and health behaviour among young people: A WHO cross-national study (HBSC) international report* (pp. 49–64). (WHO Policy Series: Health Policy for Children and Adolescents, Series No. 1.) Copenhagen, Denmark: World Health Organization Regional Office for Europe.

Samuels, H. R. (1980). The effect of an older sibling on infant locomotor exploration of a new environment. *Child Development,* 607–609.

Samuelson, L. K., & McMurray, B. (2017). What does it take to learn a word? *Wiley Interdisciplinary Reviews: Cognitive Science, 8*(1-2), e1421

Sandall, J., Tribe, R. M., Avery, L., Mola, G., Visser, G. H., Homer, C. S., ... Taylor, P. (2018). Short-term and long-term effects of caesarean section on the health of women and children. *The Lancet, 392*(10155), 1349–1357.

Sandberg-Thoma, S. E., Snyder, A. R., & Jang, B. J. (2015). Exiting and returning to the parental home for boomerang kids. *Journal of Marriage and Family, 77*(3), 806–818.

Sanders, A. R., Martin, E. R., Beecham, G. W., Guo, S., Dawood, K., Rieger, G., ... Duan, J. (2015). Genome-wide scan demonstrates

significant linkage for male sexual orientation. *Psychological Medicine, 45*(7), 1379–1388.

Sanders, A., Stone, R., Meador, R., & Parker, V. (2010). Aging in place partnerships: A training program for family caregivers of residents living in affordable senior housing. *Cityscape: A Journal of Policy Development and Research, 12*(2), 85–104.

Sanders, L. D., Stevens, C., Coch, D., & Neville, H. J. (2006). Selective auditory attention in 3-to 5-year-old children: An event-related potential study. *Neuropsychologia, 44*(11), 2126–2138.

Sandin, S., Lichtenstein, P., Kuja-Halkola, R., Larsson, H., Hultman, C.M., & Reichenberg, A. (2014). The familial risk of autism. *Journal of the American Medical Association, 311,* 1770–1777.

Sandnabba, H. K., & Ahlberg, C. (1999). Parents' attitudes and expectations about children's cross-gender behavior. *Sex Roles, 40,* 249–263.

Sann, C., & Streri, A. (2007). Perception of object shape and texture in human newborns: evidence from cross-modal transfer tasks. *Developmental Science, 10*(3), 399–410.

Santelli, J. S., Kantor, L. M., Grilo, S. A., Speizer, I. S., Lindberg, L. D., Heitel, J., ... Heck, C. J. (2017). Abstinence-only-until-marriage: An updated review of US policies and programs and their impact. *Journal of Adolescent Health, 61*(3), 273–280.

Santini, Z. I., Koyanagi, A., Tyrovolas, S., Mason, C., & Haro, J. M. (2015). The association between social relationships and depression: A systematic review. *Journal of Affective Disorders, 175,* 53–65.

Santos-Lozano, A., Santamarina, A., Pareja-Galeano, H., Sanchis-Gomar, F., Fiuza-Luces, C., Cristi-Montero, C., Bernal-Pino, A., Lucia, A., & Garatachea, N. (2016). The genetics of exceptional longevity: Insights from centenarians. *Maturitas, 90,* 49–57.

Sapolsky, R. M. (1992). Neuroendocrinology of the stress-response. *Behavioral Endocrinology,* 287–324.

Saraiya, A., Garakani, A., & Billick, S.B. (2013). Mental health approaches to child victims of acts of terrorism. *Psychiatric Quarterly, 84,* 115–124.

Sargent, J. D., & Dalton, M. (2001). Does parental disapproval of smoking prevent adolescents from becoming established smokers? *Pediatrics, 108*(6), 1256–1262.

Sarnecka, B. W., & Carey, S. (2007). How counting represents number: What children must learn and when they learn it. *Cognition, 108*(3), 662–674.

Sartorius, G., Spasevska, S., Idan, A., Turner, L., Forbes, E., Zamojska, A., ... Handelsman, D. J. (2012). Serum testosterone, dihydrotestosterone and estradiol concentrations in older men self-reporting very good health: The healthy man study. *Clinical Endocrinology, 77*(5), 755–763.

Sarvet, A. L., Wall, M. M., Fink, D. S., Greene, E., Le, A., Boustead, A. E., ... Hasin, D. S. (2018). Medical marijuana laws and adolescent marijuana use in the United States: A systematic review and meta-analysis. *Addiction, 113*(6), 1003–1016.

Sattar, N., McInnes, I. B., & McMurray, J. J. (2020). Obesity a risk factor for severe COVID-19 infection: Multiple potential mechanisms. *Circulation*.

Satterwhite, C. L., Torrone, E., Meites, E., Dunne, E. F., Mahajan, R., Ocfemia, M. C. B., . . . Weinstock, H. (2013). Sexually transmitted infections among US women and men: Prevalence and incidence estimates, 2008. *Sexually Transmitted Diseases, 40*(3), 187-193.

Sattler, C., Toro, P., Schönknecht, P., & Schröder, J. (2012). Cognitive activity, education and socioeconomic status as preventive factors for mild cognitive impairment and Alzheimer's disease. *Psychiatry Research, 196*(1), 90-95.

Sauter, D. A., Panattoni, C., & Happé, F. (2013). Children's recognition of emotions from vocal cues. *British Journal of Developmental Psychology, 31*(1), 97-113.

Savic, I., & Lindström, P. (2008). PET and MRI show differences in cerebral asymmetry and functional connectivity between homo- and heterosexual subjects. *Proceedings of the National Academy of Sciences, USA, 105,* 9403-9408. doi: 10.1073/pnas.0801566105

Savin-Williams, R. C. (2006). Who's gay? Does it matter? *Current Directions in Psychological Science, 15,* 40-44.

Savin-Williams, R. C. (2011). Identity development among sexual-minority youth. In S. J. Schwartz, K. Luyckx, & V. L. Vignoles (Eds.), *Handbook of identity theory and research* (pp. 671-689). New York, NY: Springer.

Sawicki, M. B. (2005, March 16). *Collision course: The Bush budget and Social Security* (EPI Briefing Paper No. 156). Retrieved from www.epinet.org/content.cfm/bp156

Saxe, R., Tenenbaum, J. B., & Carey, S. (2005). Secret agents: Inferences about hidden causes by 10- and 12-month old infants. *Psychological Science, 16,* 995-1001.

Sayal, K., Prasad, V., Daley, D., Ford, T., & Coghill, D. (2018). ADHD in children and young people: prevalence, care pathways, and service provision. *The Lancet Psychiatry, 5*(2), 175-186.

Sbarra, D. A. (2015). Divorce and health: Current trends and future directions. *Psychosomatic Medicine, 77*(3), 227.

Sbarra, D. A., & Coan, J. A. (2017). Divorce and health: Good data in need of better theory. *Current Opinion in Psychology, 13,* 91-95.

Sbarra, D. A., Hasselmo, K., & Bourassa, K. J. (2015). Divorce and health: Beyond individual differences. *Current Directions in Psychological Science, 24*(2), 109-113.

Scales, P. C., Benson, P. L., Oesterle, S., Hill, K. G., Hawkins, J. D., & Pashak, T. J. (2016). The dimensions of successful young adult development: A conceptual and measurement framework. *Applied Developmental Science, 20*(3), 150-174

Scarr, S. (1992). Developmental theories for the 1990s: Development and individual differences. *Child Development, 63,* 1-19.

Scarr, S., & McCartney, K. (1983). How people make their own environments: A theory of genotype-environment effects. *Child Development, 54,* 424-435.

Schaan, B. (2013). Widowhood and depression among older Europeans—The role of gender, caregiving, marital quality, and regional context. *Journals of Gerontology Series B: Psychological Sciences and Social Sciences, 68*(3), 431-442.

Schaap, L. A., Koster, A., & Visser, M. (2013). Adiposity, muscle mass, and muscle strength in relation to functional decline in older persons. *Epidemiologic Reviews, 35*(1), 51-65.

Schafft, K. A., Jensen, E. B., & Hinrichs, C. C. (2009). Food deserts and overweight school children: Evidence from Pennsylvania. *Rural Sociology, 74,* 153-177.

Schaie, K. W. (1990). Intellectual development in adulthood. In J. E. Birren & K. W. Schaie (Eds.), *Handbook of the psychology of aging* (pp. 291-309). San Diego, CA: Academic Press.

Schaie, K. W. (1994). The course of adult intellectual development. *American Psychologist, 49*(4), 304-313.

Schaie, K. W. (1996). Intellectual development in adulthood. In J. E. Birren & K. W. Schaie (Eds.), *Handbook of the psychology of aging* (4th ed., pp. 266-286). San Diego, CA: Academic Press.

Schaie, K. W. (1996). *Intellectual development in adulthood: The Seattle Longitudinal Study.* Cambridge, England: Cambridge University Press.

Schaie, K. W. (2005). *Developmental influences on adult intelligence: The Seattle longitudinal study.* New York, NY: Oxford University Press.

Schaie, K. W., & Willis, S. L. (2010). The Seattle Longitudinal Study of adult cognitive development. *ISSBD Bulletin, 57*(1), 24.

Scharf, M., & Goldner, L. (2018). "If you really love me, you will do/be. . .": Parental psychological control and its implications for children's adjustment. *Developmental Review*.

Scharf, M., Mayseless, O., & Kivenson-Baron, I. (2004). Adolescents' attachment representations and developmental tasks in emerging adulthood. *Developmental Psychology, 40,* 430-444.

Scharf, R. J., Stroustrup, A., Conaway, M. R., & DeBoer, M. D. (2016). Growth and development in children born very low birthweight. *Archives of Disease in Childhood-Fetal and Neonatal Edition, 101*(5), F433-F438.

Scharlach, A. E., & Fredriksen, K. I. (1993). Reactions to the death of a parent during midlife. *Omega, 27,* 307-319.

Scheiber, C., Reynolds, M. R., Hajovsky, D. B., & Kaufman, A. S. (2015). Gender differences in achievement in a large, nationally representative sample of children and adolescents. *Psychology in the Schools, 52*(4), 335-348.

Scheid, V. (2007, March). *Traditional Chinese medicine—What are we investigating?: The case of menopause.* Retrieved from U.S. National Library of Medicine National Institutes of Health: www.ncbi.nlm.nih.gov/pmc/articles/PMC2233879/

Scher, A., Epstein, R., & Tirosh, E. (2004). Stability and changes in sleep regulation: A longitudinal study from 3 months to 3 years. *International Journal of Behavioral Development, 28*(3), 268-274.

Schetter, C. D. (2009). Stress processes in pregnancy and preterm birth. *Current Directions in Psychological Science, 18*(4), 205-209.

Schetter, C. D., & Tanner, L. (2012). Anxiety, depression and stress in pregnancy: Implications for mothers, children, research, and practice. *Current Opinion in Psychiatry, 25*(2), 141.

Scheve, T., & Venzon, C. (2017). *10 stereotypes about aging (that just aren't true).* Retrieved from https://health.howstuffworks.com/wellness/aging/aging-process/5-stereotypes-about-aging.htm

Schick, V., Herbenick, D., Reece, M., Sanders, S. A., Dodge, B., Middlestadt, S. E., & Fortenberry, J. D. (2010). Sexual behaviors, condom use, and sexual health of Americans over 50: Implications for sexual health promotion for older adults. *The Journal of Sexual Medicine, 7,* 315-329.

Schickedanz, A., Dreyer, B. P., & Halfon, N. (2015). Childhood poverty: Understanding and preventing the adverse impacts of a most-prevalent risk to pediatric health and well-being. *Pediatric Clinics, 62*(5), 1111-1135.

Schieber, M., & Chandel, N. S. (2014). ROS function in redox signaling and oxidative stress. *Current Biology, 24*(10), R453-R462.

Schiffrin, H. H., Liss, M., Miles-McLean, H., Geary, K. A., Erchull, M. J., & Tashner, T. (2014). Helping or hovering? The effects of helicopter parenting on college students' well-being. *Journal of Child and Family Studies, 23*(3), 548-557.

Schlaerth, A., Ensari, N., & Christian, J. (2013). A meta-analytical review of the relationship between emotional intelligence and leaders' constructive conflict management. *Group Processes & Intergroup Relations, 16*(1), 126-136.

Schlegel, A., & Barry, H., III. (1991). *Adolescence: An anthropological inquiry.* New York, NY: Free Press.

Schlegel, A. (2011). Adolescent Ties to Adult Communities. *Bridging cultural and developmental approaches to psychology: New syntheses in theory, research, and policy,* 138.

Schlegel, A. (2013). A cross-cultural approach to adolescence. In D. Browning (Ed.), *Adolescent identities* (pp. 49-62). Abingdon, England: Routledge.

Schlenker, E. D. (2010). Healthy aging: Nutrition concepts for older adults. In T. Wilson, N. J. Temple, G. A. Bray, & M. B. Struble (Eds.), *Nutrition guide for physicians* (pp. 215-226). New York, NY: Humana Press.

Schmidt, J. A., Shumow, L., & Kackar, H. (2007). Adolescents' participation in service activities and its impact on academic, behavioral, and civic outcomes. *Journal of Youth and Adolescence, 36*(2), 127-140.

Schmitt, D. P., & Allik, J. (2005). Simultaneous administration of the Rosenberg Self-Esteem Scale in 53 nations: Exploring the universal and culture-specific features of global self-esteem. *Journal of Personality and social Psychology, 89*(4), 623.

Schmitt, D. P., Realo, A., Voracek, M., & Allik, J. (2008). Why can't a man be more like a woman? Sex differences in Big Five personality traits across 55 cultures. *Journal of Personality and Social Psychology, 94*(1), 168.

Schmitt, M. T., Branscombe, N. R., Postmes, T., & Garcia, A. (2014). The consequences of perceived discrimination for psychological well-being: A meta-analytic review. *Psychological Bulletin, 140*(4), 921.

Schmitt, M., Kliegel, M., & Shapiro, A. (2007). Marital interaction in middle and old age: A predictor of marital satisfaction? *International Journal of Aging & Human Development, 65*(4), 283–300.

Schmitt, S. A., Simpson, A. M., & Friend, M. (2011). A longitudinal assessment of the home literacy environment and early language. *Infant and Child Development, 20*(6), 409–431.

Schnaas, L., Rothenberg, S. J., Flores, M., Martinez, S., Hernandez, C., Osorio, E., . . . Perroni, E. (2006). Reduced intellectual development in children with prenatal lead exposure. *Environmental Health Perspectives, 114*(5), 791–797.

Schnack, H. G., Van Haren, N. E., Brouwer, R. M., Evans, A., Durston, S., Boomsma, D. I., . . . Hulshoff Pol, H. E. (2014). Changes in thickness and surface area of the human cortex and their relationship with intelligence. *Cerebral Cortex, 25*(6), 1608–1617.

Schneider, B. H., Atkinson, L., & Tardif, C. (2001). Child-parent attachment and children's peer relations: A quantitative review. *Developmental Psychology, 37*, 86–100.

Schneider, J. P., Weiss, R., & Samenow, C. (2012). Is it really cheating? Understanding the emotional reactions and clinical treatment of spouses and partners affected by cybersex infidelity. *Sexual Addiction & Compulsivity, 19*(1–2), 123–139.

Schneider, M. (2002). *Do school facilities affect academic outcomes?* Washington, DC: National Clearinghouse for Educational Facilities.

Schneider, W. (2008). The development of metacognitive knowledge in children and adolescents: Major trends and implications for education. *Mind, Brain, and Education, 2*(3), 114–121.

Schoenborn, C. A. (2004). Marital status and health: United States, 1999–2002. *Advance Data from Vital and Health Statistics, No. 351.* Hyattsville, MD: National Center for Health Statistics.

Scholten, C. M. (1985). *Childbearing in American society: 1650–1850.* New York, NY: New York University Press.

Schomerus, G., Evans-Lacko, S., Rüsch, N., Mojtabai, R., Angermeyer, M. C., & Thornicroft, G. (2015). Collective levels of stigma and national suicide rates in 25 European countries. *Epidemiology and Psychiatric Sciences, 24*(2), 166–171.

Schondelmyer, E. (2017). *Fewer married households and more living alone.* Retrieved from www.census.gov/library/stories/2017/08/more-adults-living-without-children.html

Schonfeld, D. J., & Quackenbush, M. (2010). *The grieving student: A teacher's guide.* Baltimore, MD: Paul H. Brookes Publishing Co.

Schonfeld, D. J., Demaria, T., & Committee on Psychosocial Aspects of Child and Family Health, Disaster Preparedness Advisory Council. (2016). Supporting the grieving child and family. *Pediatrics*, e20162147.

Schredl, M., Anders, A., Hellriegel, S., & Rehm, A. (2008). TV viewing, computer game playing and nightmares in school children. *Dreaming, 18*(2), 69–76. http://dx.doi.org.vwu.idm.oclc.org/10.1037/1053-0797.18.2.69

Schredl, M., Fricke-Oerkermann, L., Mitschke, A., Wiater, A., & Lehmkuhl, G. (2009). Longitudinal study of nightmares in children: Stability and effect of emotional symptoms. *Child Psychiatry and Human Development, 40*(3), 439–449.

Schulenberg, J. E., Johnston, L. D., O'Malley, P. M., Bachman, J. G., Miech, R. A. & Patrick, M. E. (2017). *Monitoring the Future national survey results on drug use, 1975–2016: Volume II, College students and adults ages 19–55.* Ann Arbor: Institute for Social Research, The University of Michigan. Available at http://monitoringthefuture.org/pubs.html#monographs

Schulenberg, J., O'Malley, P., Bachman, J., & Johnston, L. (2005). Early adult transitions and their relation to well-being and substance use. In R. A. Settersten Jr., F. F. Furstenberg Jr., & R. G. Rumbaut (Eds.), *On the frontier of adulthood: Theory, research, and public policy* (pp. 417–453). Chicago, IL: University of Chicago Press.

Schulz, M. S., Cowan, C. P., & Cowan, P. A. (2006). Promoting healthy beginnings: A randomized controlled trial of a preventive intervention to preserve marital quality during the transition to parenthood. *Journal of Consulting and Clinical Psychology, 74*, 20–31.

Schulz, R. (1978). *A psychology of death, dying, and bereavement.* Reading, MA: Addison-Wesley.

Schulz, R., & Martire, L. M. (2004). Family caregiving of persons with dementia: Prevalence, health effects, and support strategies. *American Journal of Geriatric Psychiatry, 12*, 240–249.

Schurz, M., Aichhorn, M., Martin, A., & Perner, J. (2013). Common brain areas engaged in false belief reasoning and visual perspective taking: a meta-analysis of functional brain imaging studies. *Frontiers in Human Neuroscience, 7.*

Schuur, M., Ikram, M. A., Van Swieten, J. C., Isaacs, A., Vergeer-Drop, J. M., Hofman, A., . . . Van Duijn, C. M. (2011). Cathepsin D gene and the risk of Alzheimer's disease: a population-based study and meta-analysis. *Neurobiology of Aging, 32*(9), 1607–1614.

Schwaba, T., & Bleidorn, W. (2018). Individual differences in personality change across the adult life span. *Journal of Personality, 86*(3), 450–464.

Schwartz, B. L. (2008). Working memory load differentially affects tip-of-the-tongue states and feeling-of-knowing judgments. *Memory & Cognition, 36*(1), 9–19.

Schwartz, D. A., & Graham, A. L. (2020). Potential maternal and infant outcomes from (Wuhan) coronavirus 2019-nCoV infecting pregnant women: Lessons from SARS, MERS, and other human coronavirus infections. *Viruses, 12*(2), 194.

Schwartz, D., Chang, L., & Farver, J. M. (2001). Correlates of victimization in Chinese children's peer groups. *Developmental Psychology, 37*(4), 520–532.

Schwartz, D., McFadyen-Ketchum, S. A., Dodge, K. A., Pettit, G. S., & Bates, J. E. (1998). Peer group victimization as a predictor of children's behavior problems at home and in school. *Development and Psychopathology, 10*, 87–99.

Schwartz, S. J., Zamboanga, B. L., Luyckx, K., Meca, A., & Ritchie, R. A. (2013). Identity in emerging adulthood: Reviewing the field and looking forward. *Emerging Adulthood, 1*(2), 96–113.

Schwarz, J., Axelsson, J., Gerhardsson, A., Tamm, S., Fischer, H., Kecklund, G., & Åkerstedt, T. (2019). Mood impairment is stronger in young than in older adults after sleep deprivation. *Journal of Sleep Research, 28*(4), e12801.

Schweinhart, L. J. (2007). Crime prevention by the High/Scope Perry preschool program. *Victims & Offenders, 2*(2), 141–160.

Schweinhart, L. J., Barnes, H. V., & Weikart, D. P. (1993). *Significant benefits: The High/Scope Perry Preschool Study through age 27* (Monographs of the High/Scope Educational Research Foundation No. 10). Ypsilanti, MI: High/Scope.

Schöber, C., Schütte, K., Köller, O., McElvany, N., & Gebauer, M. M. (2018). Reciprocal effects between self-efficacy and achievement in mathematics and reading. *Learning and Individual Differences, 63*, 1–11.

Scott, M. E., Booth, A., King, V., & Johnson, D. R. (2007). Postdivorce father-adolescent closeness. *Journal of Marriage and Family, 69*(5), 1194–1209.

Scott, R. M., & Baillargeon, R. (2009). Which penguin is this? Attributing false beliefs about object identity at 18 months. *Child Development, 80*(4), 1172–1196.

Scott, S., Doolan, M., Beckett, C., Harry, S., & Cartwright, S. (2012). *How is parenting style related to child antisocial behaviour? Preliminary findings from the Helping Children Achieve study* [Research report]. Retrieved from http://dera.ioe.ac.uk/13827/1/DFE-RR185a.pdf

Seabra, L., Loureiro, M., Pereira, H., Monteiro, S., Marina Afonso, R., & Esgalhado, G. (2017). Relationship between internet addiction and self-esteem: Cross-cultural study in Portugal and Brazil. *Interacting with Computers, 29*(5), 767–778.

Seaman, J. E., Allen, I. E., & Seaman, J. (2018). Grade increase: Tracking distance education in the United States. Babson Survey Research Group.

Seblega, B. K., Zhang, N. J., Unruh, L. Y., Breen, G. M., Paek, S. C., & Wan, T. T. (2010). Changes in nursing home staffing levels, 1997 to 2007. *Medical Care Research and Review, 67*(2), 232–246.

Seehagen, S., & Herbert, J. S. (2011). Infant imitation from televised peer and adult models. *Infancy, 16*(2), 113–136.

Seery, M. D. (2011). Resilience: A silver lining to experiencing adverse life events? *Current Directions in Psychological Science, 20*(6), 390-394.

Segerstrom, S. C., & Miller, G. E. (2004). Psychological stress and the human immune system: A meta-analytic study of 30 years of inquiry. *Psychological Bulletin, 130*(4), 601.

Segerstrom, S. C., Combs, H. L., Winning, A., Boehm, J. K., & Kubzansky, L. D. (2016). The happy survivor? Effects of differential mortality on life satisfaction in older age. *Psychology and Aging, 31*(4), 340.

Segrin, C., & Flora, J. (2017). Family conflict is detrimental to physical and mental health. In J. A. Samp (Ed.), *Communicating interpersonal conflict in close relationships: Contexts, challenges and opportunities,* 207-224. Abingdon, England: Routledge/Taylor & Francis Group.

Seib, D. R., & Martin-Villalba, A. (2015). Neurogenesis in the normal ageing hippocampus: A mini-review. *Gerontology, 61*(4), 327-335.

Seidler, A., Neinhaus, A., Bernhardt, T., Kauppinen, T., Elo, A. L., & Frolich, L. (2004). Psychosocial work factors and dementia. *Occupational and Environmental Medicine, 61,* 962-971.

Seiffge-Krenke, I. (2016). Leaving home: Antecedents, consequences, and cultural patterns. In J. Arnett (Ed.), *The Oxford handbook of emerging adulthood* (pp. 177-189). New York, NY: Oxford University Press.

Selkie, E. M., Fales, J. L., & Moreno, M. A. (2016). Cyberbullying prevalence among US middle and high school-aged adolescents: A systematic review and quality assessment. *Journal of Adolescent Health, 58*(2), 125-133.

Seiter, L. N., & Nelson, L. J. (2011). An examination of emerging adulthood in college students and nonstudents in India. *Journal of Adolescent Research, 26*(4), 506-536.

Selkoe, D. J., & Hardy, J. (2016). The amyloid hypothesis of Alzheimer's disease at 25 years. *EMBO Molecular Medicine, 8*(6), 595-608.

Selman, R. L. (1980). *The growth of interpersonal understanding: Developmental and clinical analyses.* New York, NY: Academic Press.

Selman, R. L., & Selman, A. P. (1979, April). Children's ideas about friendship: A new theory. *Psychology Today,* 71-80.

Seltzer, J. A. (2000). Families formed outside of marriage. *Journal of Marriage and Family, 62,* 1247-1268.

Seltzer, M. M., Floyd, F., Song, J., Greenberg, J., & Hong, J. (2011). Midlife and aging parents of adults with intellectual and developmental disabilities: impacts of lifelong parenting. *American Journal on Intellectual and Developmental Disabilities, 116*(6), 479-499.

Semega, J. L., Fontenot, K. R., and Kollar, M. A. (2017). *U.S. Census Bureau, Current Population Reports, P60-259, Income and Poverty in the United States: 2016.* Washington, DC: U.S. Government Printing Office.

Sen, A., Partelow, L., & Miller, D. C. (2005). *Comparative indicators of education in the United States and other G8 countries: 2004* (NCES 2005-021). Washington, DC: National Center for Education Statistics.

Sengoelge, M., Hasselberg, M., & Laflamme, L. (2010). Child home injury mortality in Europe: A 16-country analysis. *European Journal of Public Health, 21*(2), 166-170.

Serdiouk, M., Rodkin, P., Madill, R., Logis, H., & Gest, S. (2015). Rejection and victimization among elementary school children: The buffering role of classroom-level predictors. *Journal of Abnormal Child Psychology, 43*(1), 5-17.

Sereny, M. (2011). Living arrangements of older adults in China: The interplay among preferences, realities, and health. *Research on Aging, 33*(2), 172-204.

Sethi, A., Mischel, W., Aber, J. L., Shoda, Y., & Rodriguez, M. L. (2000). The role of strategic attention deployment in development of self-regulation: Predicting preschoolers' delay of gratification from mother-toddler interactions. *Developmental Psychology, 36,* 767-777.

Settersten Jr., R. A. (2007). Social relationships in the new demographic regime: Potentials and risks, reconsidered. *Advances in Life Course Research, 12,* 3-28.

Sexton, C. E., Betts, J. F., Demnitz, N., Dawes, H., Ebmeier, K. P., & Johansen-Berg, H. (2016). A systematic review of MRI studies examining the relationship between physical fitness and activity and the white matter of the ageing brain. *Neuroimage, 131,* 81-90.

Seybold, K. S., & Hill, P. C. (2001). The role of religion and spirituality in mental and physical health. *Current Directions in Psychological Science, 10,* 21-24.

Shafto, M. A., & Tyler, L. K. (2014). Language in the aging brain: The network dynamics of cognitive decline and preservation. *Science, 346*(6209), 583-587.

Shafto, M. A., James, L. E., Abrams, L., & Tyler, L. K. (2017). Age-related increases in verbal knowledge are not associated with word finding problems in the Cam-CAN cohort: What you know won't hurt you. *The Journals of Gerontology: Series B, 72*(1), 100-106.

Shager, H. M., Schindler, H. S., Magnuson, K. A., Duncan, G. J., Yoshikawa, H., & Hart, C. M. (2013). Can research design explain variation in Head Start research results? A meta-analysis of cognitive and achievement outcomes. *Educational Evaluation and Policy Analysis, 35*(1), 76-95.

Shah, P. S. (2010). Parity and low birth weight and preterm birth: A systematic review and meta-analyses. *Acta Obstetricia et Gynecologica Scandinavica, 89*(7), 862-875.

Shah, T., Sullivan, K., & Carter, J. (2006). Sudden infant death syndrome and reported maternal smoking during pregnancy. *American Journal of Public Health, 96*(10), 1757-1759.

Shahaeian, A., Peterson, C. C., Slaughter, V., & Wellman, H. M. (2011). Culture and the sequence of steps in theory of mind development. *Developmental Psychology, 47*(5), 1239.

Shalev, I., Entringer, S., Wadhwa, P. D., Wolkowitz, O. M., Puterman, E., Lin, J., & Epel, E. S. (2013). Stress and telomere biology: A lifespan perspective. *Psychoneuroendocrinology, 38*(9), 1835-1842.

Shamir, A., & Shlafer, I. (2011). E-books effectiveness in promoting phonological awareness and concept about print: A comparison between children at risk for learning disabilities and typically developing kindergarteners. *Computers & Education, 57*(3), 1989-1997

Shamir, A., Korat, O., & Fellah, R. (2012). Promoting vocabulary, phonological awareness and concept about print among children at risk for learning disability: Can e-books help? *Reading and Writing, 25*(1), 45-69.

Shammas, M. A. (2011). Telomeres, lifestyle, cancer, and aging. *Current Opinion in Clinical Nutrition and Metabolic Care, 14*(1), 28.

Shankar, A., Hamer, M., McMunn, A., & Steptoe, A. (2013). Social isolation and loneliness: Relationships with cognitive function during 4 years of follow-up in the English Longitudinal Study of Ageing. *Psychosomatic Medicine, 75*(2), 161-170.

Shankaran, S., Das, A., Bauer, C. R., Bada, H. S., Lester, B., Wright, L. L., & Smeriglio, V. (2004). Association between patterns of maternal substance use and infant birth weight, length, and head circumference. *Pediatrics, 114,* e226-e234.

Shannon, J. D., Tamis-LeMonda, C. S., London, K., & Cabrera, N. (2002). Beyond rough and tumble: Low income fathers' interactions and children's cognitive development at 24 months. *Parenting: Science & Practice, 2*(2), 77-104.

Shao, H., Breitner, J. C., Whitmer, R. A., Wang, J., Hayden, K., Wengreen, H., . . . Welsh-Bohmer, K. (2012). Hormone therapy and Alzheimer disease dementia New findings from the Cache County Study. *Neurology, 79*(18), 1846-1852.

Shapiro, A., & Cooney, T. M. (2007). Interpersonal relations across the life course. *Advances in Life Course Research, 12,* 191-219.

Sharapova, S. R., Phillips, E., Sirocco, K., Kaminski, J. W., Leeb, R. T., & Rolle, I. (2018). Effects of prenatal marijuana exposure on neuropsychological outcomes in children aged 1-11 years: A systematic review. *Paediatric and Perinatal Epidemiology, 32*(6), 512-532.

Sharma, A. R., McGue, M. K., & Benson, P. L. (1996). The emotional and behavioral adjustment of United States adopted adolescents, Part I: An overview. *Children and Youth Services Review, 18,* 83-100.

Sharma, R., Agarwal, A., Rohra, V. K., Assidi, M., Abu-Elmagd, M., & Turki, R. F. (2015). Effects of increased paternal age on sperm quality, reproductive outcome and associated epigenetic risks to offspring. Reproductive Biology and Endocrinology, 13(1), 35.

Sharma, V., Coleman, S., Nixon, J., Sharples, L., Hamilton-Shield, J., Rutter, H., & Bryant, M. (2019). A systematic review and meta-analysis estimating the population prevalence of comorbidities in children and adolescents aged 5 to 18 years. *Obesity Reviews, 20*(10), 1341-1349.

Sharp, E. H., Tucker, C. J., Baril, M. E., Van Gundy, K. T., & Rebellon, C. J. (2015). Breadth of participation in organized and unstructured leisure activities over time and rural adolescents' functioning. *Journal of Youth and Adolescence, 44*(1), 62-76.

Sharp, E. S., & Gatz, M. (2011). The relationship between education and dementia: An updated systematic review. *Alzheimer Disease and Associated Disorders, 25*(4), 289.

Sharp, E. S., Reynolds, C. A., Pedersen, N. L., & Gatz, M. (2010). Cognitive engagement and cognitive aging: Is openness protective? *Psychology and Aging, 25*(1), 60-73.

Shatz, M., & Gelman, R. (1973). The development of communication skills: Modifications in the speech of young children as a function of listener. *Monographs of the Society for Research in Child Development, 38*(5, Serial No. 152).

Shaw, B. A., Krause, N., Liang, J., & Bennett, J. (2007). Tracking changes in social relations throughout late life. *Journal of Gerontology: Social Sciences, 62B,*S90-S99.

Shayer, M., Ginsburg, D., & Coe, R. (2007). Thirty years on—A large anti-Flynn effect? The Piagetian Test Volume & Heaviness norms 1975-2003. *British Journal of Educational Psychology, 77*(1), 25-41.

Shaywitz, S. (2003). *Overcoming dyslexia: A new and complete science-based program for overcoming reading problems at any level.* New York: Knopf.

Shaywitz, S. E. (1998). Current concepts: Dyslexia. *New England Journal of Medicine, 338,* 307-312.

Shaywitz, S. E., Mody, M., & Shaywitz, B. A. (2006). Neural mechanisms in dyslexia. *Current Directions in Psychological Science, 15,* 278-281.

Shea, K. M., Little, R. E., & the ALSPAC Study Team. (1997). Is there an association between preconceptual paternal X-ray exposure and birth outcome? *American Journal of Epidemiology, 145,* 546-551.

Shedlock, D. J., & Cornelius, S. W. (2003). Psychological approaches to wisdom and its development. In J. Demick & C. Andreoletti (Eds.), *Handbook of adult development* (pp. 153-167). New York, NY: Plenum Press.

Shekerdemian, L. S., Mahmood, N. R., Wolfe, K. K., Riggs, B. J., Ross, C. E., McKiernan, C. A., . . . Burns, J. P. (2020). Characteristics and outcomes of children with coronavirus disease 2019 (COVID-19) infection admitted to US and Canadian pediatric intensive care units. *Journal of the American Medical Association, Pediatrics.* Published online May 11, 2020. doi:10.1001/jamapediatrics.2020.1948

Sheldon, K. M., & Kasser, T. (2001). Getting older, getting better? Personal strivings and psychological maturity across the life span. *Developmental Psychology, 37,* 491-501.

Shephard, R. J. (2007). Fitness of Canadian children: Range from traditional Inuit to sedentary city dwellers, and assessment of secular changes. *Medicine and Sport Science, 50,* 91-103.

Shepherd-Banigan, M., Basu, A., Bell, J. F., Booth-LaForce, C., & Harris, J. R. (2019). Is maternal income in childhood associated with adolescent health and behavioral outcomes? *Journal of Family Issues, 40*(7), 911-928.

Shetgiri, R., Espelage, D. L., & Carroll, L. (2015). Bullying trends, correlates, consequences, and characteristics. In *Practical strategies for clinical management of bullying* (pp. 3-11). New York, NY: Springer International Publishing.

Shigehara, K., Konaka, H., Koh, E., Izumi, K., Kitagawa, Y., & Mizokami, A. (2015). Effects of testosterone replacement therapy on nocturia and quality of life with hypogonadism: A subanalysis of a previous prospective randomized controlled study in Japan. *The Aging Male,* 18, 169-174.

Shimahara, N. K. (1986). The cultural basis of student achievement in Japan. *Comparative Education, 22*(1), 19-26.

Shin, Y., & Raudenbush, S. W. (2011). The causal effect of class size on academic achievement: Multivariate instrumental variable estimators with data missing at random. *Journal of Educational and Behavioral Statistics, 36*(2), 154-185.

Shiner, R. L., Buss, K. A., McClowry, S. G., Putnam, S. P., Saudino, K. J., & Zentner, M. (2012). What is temperament now? Assessing progress in temperament research on the twenty-fifth anniversary of Goldsmith et al. *Child Development Perspectives, 6*(4), 436-444.

Shinya, Y., Kawai, M., Niwa, F., & Myowa-Yamakoshi, M. (2016). Associations between respiratory arrhythmia and fundamental frequency of spontaneous crying in preterm and term infants at term-equivalent age. *Developmental Psychobiology, 58*(6), 724-733.

Shonkoff, J., & Phillips, D. (2000). Growing up in child care. In I. Shonkoff & D. Phillips (Eds.), *From neurons to neighborhoods* (pp. 297-327). Washington, DC: National Research Council/Institute of Medicine.

Shor, E., Roelfs, D. J., Curreli, M., Clemow, L., Burg, M. M., & Schwartz, J. E. (2012). Widowhood and mortality: A meta-analysis and meta-regression. *Demography, 49*(2), 575-606.

Short, S. E., Yang, Y. C., & Jenkins, T. M. (2013). Sex, gender, genetics, and health. *American Journal of Public Health, 103*(S1), S93-S101.

Shriver, L. H., Marriage, B. J., Bloch, T. D., Spees, C. K., Ramsay, S. A., Watowicz, R. P., & Taylor, C. A. (2018). Contribution of snacks to dietary intakes of young children in the United States. *Maternal & Child Nutrition, 14*(1).

Shuey, K., & Hardy, M. A. (2003). Assistance to aging parents and parents-in-law: Does lineage affect family allocation decisions? *Journal of Marriage and Family, 65,* 418-431.

Shulman, S., & Connolly, J. (2013). The challenge of romantic relationships in emerging adulthood: Reconceptualization of the field. *Emerging Adulthood, 1*(1), 27-39.

Shulman, S., Scharf, M., Lumer, D., & Maurer, O. (2001). Parental divorce and young adult children's romantic relationships: Resolution of the divorce experience. *American Journal of Orthopsychiatry, 71,* 473-478.

Shumaker, S. A., Legault, C., Kuller, L., Rapp, S. R., Thal, L., Lane, D. S., . . . Coker, L. H., for the Women's Health Initiative Memory Study Investigators. (2004). Conjugated equine estrogens and incidence of probable dementia and mild cognitive impairment in postmenopausal women: Women's Health Initiative Memory Study. *Journal of the American Medical Association, 291,* 2947-2958.

Shweder, R. A., Goodnow, J., Hatano, G., Levine, R. A., Markus, H., & Miller, P. (2006). The cultural psychology of development: One mind, many mentalities. In W. Damon (Ed.), *Handbook of child development* (pp. 865-937). New York, NY: Wiley.

Shweder, R. A., Much, N. C., Mahapatra, M., & Park, L. (1997). The "big three" of morality (autonomy, community, divinity) and the "big three" explanations of suffering. *Morality and Health, 119,* 119-169.

Sicherer, S. H., & Sampson, H. A. (2018). Food allergy: A review and update on epidemiology, pathogenesis, diagnosis, prevention, and management. *Journal of Allergy and Clinical Immunology, 141*(1), 41-58.

Siddeek, B., Mauduit, C., Simeoni, U., & Benahmed, M. (2018). Sperm epigenome as a marker of environmental exposure and lifestyle, at the origin of diseases inheritance. *Mutation Research/Reviews in Mutation Research, 778,* 38-44.

Sidney, S., Quesenberry, C. P., Jaffe, M. G., Sorel, M., Go, A. S., & Rana, J. S. (2017). Heterogeneity in national US mortality trends within heart disease subgroups, 2000-2015. *BMC Cardiovascular Disorders, 17*(1), 192.

Sidney, S., Quesenberry, C. P., Jaffe, M. G., Sorel, M., Nguyen-Huynh, M. N., Kushi, L. H., . . . Rana, J. S. (2016). Recent trends in cardiovascular mortality in the United States and public health goals. *JAMA Cardiology, 1*(5), 594-599.

Siedlecki, K. L., Salthouse, T. A., Oishi, S., & Jeswani, S. (2014). The relationship between social support and subjective well-being across age. *Social Indicators Research, 117*(2), 561-576.

Siedlecki, K., Tucker-Drop, E. M., Oishi, S., & Salthouse, T. A. (2008). Life satisfaction across adulthood: Different determinants at different ages? *Journal of Positive Psychology, 3*(3), 153-164.

Siegel, M. B., Tanwar, K. L., & Wood, K. S. (2011). Electronic cigarettes as a smoking-cessation tool: Results from an online survey. *American Journal of Preventive Medicine.* doi: 10.1016/j.amepre.2010.12.006

Siegel, R. L., Miller, K. D., & Jemal, A. (2015). Cancer statistics, 2015. *CA: a Cancer Journal for Clinicians, 65*(1), 5-29.

Siegler, R. S. (1998). *Children's thinking* (3rd ed.). Upper Saddle River, NJ: Prentice Hall.

Siegler, R. S. (2009). Improving the numerical understanding of children from low-income families. *Child Development Perspectives, 3*(2), 118-124.

Siegler, R. S., & Booth, J. L. (2004). Development of numerical estimation in young children. *Child Development, 75*(2), 428-444.

Siegler, R. S., & Opfer, J. E. (2003). The development of numerical estimation: Evidence for multiple representations of numerical quantity. *Psychological Science, 14*(3), 237-250.

Siennick, S. E. (2011). Tough love? Crime and parental assistance in young adulthood. *Criminology, 49*(1), 163-195.

Sierra, M., Fernández, A., & Fraga, M. (2015). Epigenetics of aging. *Current Genomics, 16*(6), 435–440.

Sieving, R. E., McNeely, C. S., & Blum, R. W. (2000). Maternal expectations, mother-child connectedness, and adolescent sexual debut. *Archives of Pediatric & Adolescent Medicine, 154*, 809–816.

Silberg, J. L., Maes, H., & Eaves, L. J. (2012). Unraveling the effect of genes and environment in the transmission of parental antisocial behavior to children's conduct disturbance, depression and hyperactivity. *Journal of Child Psychology and Psychiatry, 53*(6), 668–677.

Silventoinen, K., Rokholm, B., Kaprio, J., & Sørensen, T. I. A. (2010). The genetic and environmental influences on childhood obesity: A systematic review of twin and adoption studies. *International Journal of Obesity, 34*(1), 29.

Simmonds, M., Llewellyn, A., Owen, C. G., & Woolacott, N. (2016). Predicting adult obesity from childhood obesity: A systematic review and meta-analysis. *Obesity Reviews, 17*(2), 95–107.

Simmons, R. G., Blyth, D. A., & McKinney, K. L. (1983). The social and psychological effect of puberty on white females. In J. Brooks-Gunn & A. C. Petersen (Eds.), *Girls at puberty: Biological and psychological perspectives.* New York, NY: Plenum Press.

Simons, E., To, T., Moineddin, R., Stieb, D., & Dell, S. D. (2014). Maternal second-hand smoke exposure in pregnancy is associated with childhood asthma development. *The Journal of Allergy and Clinical Immunology: In Practice, 2*(2), 201–207.

Simonton, D. K. (1990). Creativity and wisdom in aging. In J. E. Birren & K. W. Schaie (Eds.), *Handbook of the psychology of aging* (pp. 320–329). New York, NY: Academic Press.

Simonton, D. K. (2000). Creativity: Cognitive, personal, developmental, and social aspects. *American Psychologist, 55*, 151–158.

Simpson, J. A., Collins, A., Tran, S., & Haydon, K. C. (2007). Attachment and the experience and expression of emotions in romantic relationships: A developmental perspective. *Journal of Personality and Social Psychology, 92*, 355–367.

Sin, N. L. (2016). The protective role of positive well-being in cardiovascular disease: review of current evidence, mechanisms, and clinical implications. *Current Cardiology Reports, 18*(11), 106.

Sinclair, J., & Milner, D. (2005). On being Jewish: A qualitative study of identity among British Jews in emerging adulthood. *Journal of Adolescent Research, 20*(1), 91–117.

Sines, E., Syed, U., Wall, S., & Worley, H. (2007). Postnatal care: A critical opportunity to save mothers and newborns. *Policy Perspectives on Newborn Health.* Washington, DC: Save the Children and Population Reference Bureau.

Singer, J. L. (2004). Narrative identity and meaning-making across the adult lifespan. *Journal of Personality, 72*, 437–459.

Singer, J. L., & Singer, D. G. (1998). Barney & Friends as entertainment and education: Evaluating the quality and effectiveness of a television series for preschool children. In J. K. Asamen & G. L. Berry (Eds.), *Research paradigms, television, and social behavior* (pp. 305–367). Thousand Oaks, CA: Sage.

Singer, L. T., Minnes, S., Short, E., Arendt, K., Farkas, K., Lewis, B., . . . Kirchner, H. L. (2004). Cognitive outcomes of preschool children with prenatal cocaine exposure. *Journal of the American Medical Association, 291*, 2448–2456.

Singer, T., Verhaeghen, P., Ghisletta, P., Lindenberger, U., & Baltes, P. B. (2003). The fate of cognition in very old age: Six-year longitudinal findings in the Berlin Aging Study (BASE). *Psychology and Aging, 18*, 318–331.

Singh, A. S., Mulder, C., Twisk, J. W., Van Mechelen, W., & Chinapaw, M. J. (2008). Tracking of childhood overweight into adulthood: A systematic review of the literature. *Obesity Reviews, 9*(5), 474–488.

Singh, G. K., Yu, S. M., & Kogan, M. D. (2013). Health, chronic conditions, and behavioral risk disparities among US immigrant children and adolescents. *Public Health Reports, 128*(6), 463–479.

Singh, L., & Fu, C. S. (2016). A new view of language development: The acquisition of lexical tone. *Child Development, 87*(3), 834–854.

Singh, L., Nestor, S., Parikh, C., & Yull, A. (2009). Influences of infant-directed speech on early world recognition. *Infancy, 14*, 654–666.

Singh, M. K. (2017, March 30). *At almost 106 years old Fauja Singh reveals the secret of his youthfulness.* Retrieved from http://file.scirp.org/pdf/CE_2017092615440943.pdf

Sink, A., & Mastro, D. (2017). Depictions of gender on primetime television: A quantitative content analysis. *Mass Communication and Society, 20*(1), 3–22.

Sinnott, J. D. (2003). Postformal thought and adult development. In J. Demick & C. Andreoletti (Eds.), *Handbook of adult development.* New York, NY: Plenum Press.

Sitzer, D. I., Twamley, E. W., & Jeste, D. V. (2006). Cognitive training in Alzheimer's disease: A meta-analysis of the literature. *Acta Psychiatrica Scandinavica, 114*(2), 75–90.

Skaalvik, E. M., Federici, R. A., & Klassen, R. M. (2015). Mathematics achievement and self-efficacy: Relations with motivation for mathematics. *International Journal of Educational Research, 72*, 129–136.

Skinner, A. C., Perrin, E. M., Moss, L. A., & Skelton, J. A. (2015). Cardiometabolic risks and severity of obesity in children and young adults. *New England Journal of Medicine, 373*(14), 1307–1317.

Skinner, A. C., Ravanbakht, S. N., Skelton, J. A., Perrin, E. M., & Armstrong, S. C. (2018). Prevalence of obesity and severe obesity in US children, 1999–2016. *Pediatrics, 141*(3), e20173459.

Skinner, B. F. (1957). *Verbal behavior.* New York, NY: Appleton-Century-Crofts.

Skinner, D. (1989). The socialization of gender identity: Observations from Nepal. In J. Valsiner (Ed.), *Child development in cultural context* (pp. 181–192). Toronto, Ontario, Canada: Hogrefe & Huber.

Skirbekk, V. (2008). Age and productivity capacity: Descriptions, causes and policy options. *Ageing Horizons, 8*(4), 12.

Skoric, M. M., Zhu, Q., Goh, D., & Pang, N. (2016). Social media and citizen engagement: A meta-analytic review. *New Media & Society, 18*(9), 1817–1839.

Skorska, M. N., Blanchard, R., VanderLaan, D. P., Zucker, K. J., & Bogaert, A. F. (2017). Gay male only-children: Evidence for low birth weight and high maternal miscarriage rates. *Archives of Sexual Behavior, 46*(1), 205–215.

Skultety, K. M., & Whitbourne, S. K. (2004). Gender differences in identity processes and self-esteem in middle and later adulthood. *Journal of Women & Aging, 16*(1-2), 175–188.

Slagt, M., Dubas, J. S., Deković, M., & van Aken, M. A. (2016). Differences in sensitivity to parenting depending on child temperament: A meta-analysis. *Psychological Bulletin, 142*(10), 1068.

Slattery, T. L., & Meyers, S. A. (2014). Contextual predictors of adolescent antisocial behavior: The developmental influence of family, peer, and neighborhood factors. *Child and Adolescent Social Work Journal, 31*(1), 39–59.

Slaughter, V., Imuta, K., Peterson, C. C., & Henry, J. D. (2015). Meta-analysis of theory of mind and peer popularity in the preschool and early school years. *Child Development, 86*(4), 1159–1174.

Slaven, M. (2017). Best practices in children's bereavement: A qualitative analysis of needs and services. *Journal of Pain Management, 10*(1), 119.

Slayton, S. C., D'Archer, J., & Kaplan, F. (2010). Outcome studies on the efficacy of art therapy: A review of findings. *Art Therapy, 27*(3), 108–118.

Sliwinska-Kowalska, M., & Davis, A. (2012). Noise-induced hearing loss. *Noise and Health, 14*(61), 274.

Slobin, D. (1990). The development from child speaker to native speaker. In J. W. Stigler, R. A. Schweder, & G. H. Herdt (Eds.), *Cultural psychology: Essays on comparative human development* (pp. 233–258). New York, NY: Cambridge University Press.

Slyper, A. H. (2006). The pubertal timing controversy in the USA, and a review of possible causative factors for the advance in timing of onset of puberty. *Clinical Endocrinology, 65*, 1–8.

Small, B. J., Fratiglioni, L., von Strauss, E., & Bäckman, L. (2003). Terminal decline and cognitive performance in very old age: Does cause of death matter? *Psychology and Aging, 18*, 193–202.

Smart, E. L., Gow, A. J., & Deary, I. J. (2014). Occupational complexity and lifetime cognitive abilities. *Neurology, 83*(24), 2285–2291.

Smedley, A., & Smedley, B. D. (2005). Race as biology is fiction, racism as a social problem is real: Anthropological and historical perspectives on the social construction of race. *American Psychologist, 60*, 16–26.

Smedley, B. D., Stith, A. Y., & Nelson, A. R. (Eds.). (2002). *Unequal treatment: Confronting racial and ethnic disparities in health care.* Washington, DC: National Academy Press.

Smetana, J. G., Metzger, A., Gettman, D. C., & Campione-Barr, N. (2006). Disclosure and secrecy in adolescent-parent relationships. *Child Development, 77*, 201–217.

Smetana, J., Crean, H., & Campione-Barr, N. (2005). Adolescents' and parents' changing conceptions of parental authority. In J. Smetana (Ed.), *Changing boundaries of parental authority during adolescence* (New Directions for Child and Adolescent Development, No. 108, pp. 31–46). San Francisco, CA: Jossey-Bass.

Smilansky, S. (1968). *The effects of sociodramatic play on disadvantaged preschool children.* New York, NY: Wiley.

Smischney, T. M., Roberts, M. A., Gliske, K., Borden, L. M., & Perkins, D. F. (2018). Developing youth competencies: The impact of program quality. *Journal of Youth Development, 13*(4), 29–48.

Smith, A. M., Mioduszewski, O., Hatchard, T., Byron- Alhassan, A., Fall, C., & Fried, P. A. (2016). Prenatal marijuana exposure impacts executive functioning into young adulthood: An fMRI study. *Neurotoxicology and Teratology, 58,* 53–59.

Smith, A. R., Chein, J., & Steinberg, L. (2014). Peers increase adolescent risk taking even when the probabilities of negative outcomes are known. *Developmental Psychology, 50*(5), 1564.

Smith, A., Rissel, C. E., Richters, J., Grulich, A. E., & Visser, R. O. (2003). Sex in Australia: Reproductive experiences and reproductive health among a representative sample of women. *Australian and New Zealand Journal of Public Health, 27*(2), 204–209.

Smith, C. D., Walton, A., Loveland, A. D., Umberger, G. H., Kryscio, R. J., & Gash, D. M. (2005). Memories that last in old age: Motor skill learning and memory preservation. *Neurobiology of Aging, 26*(6), 883–890.

Smith, C. L., & Bell, M. A. (2010). Stability in infant frontal asymmetry as a predictor of toddlerhood internalizing and externalizing behaviors. *Developmental Psychobiology, 52*(2), 158–167.

Smith, C., & Snell, P. (2009). *Souls in transition: The religious and spiritual lives of emerging adults.* Oxford, England: Oxford University Press.

Smith, C., Snell, P., & Longest, K. (2010). Religious trajectories from the teenage years into the emerging adult years. *Lifelong Faith Journal, 4,* 14–27.

Smith, J. R. (2012). Listening to older adult parents of adult children with mental illness. *Journal of Family Social Work, 15*(2), 126–140.

Smith, L. A., Geller, N. L., Kellams, A. L., Colson, E. R., Rybin, D. V., Heeren, T., & Corwin, M. J. (2016). Infant sleep location and breastfeeding practices in the United States, 2011–2014. *Academic Pediatrics, 16*(6), 540–549.

Smith, L. M., LaGasse, L. L., Derauf, C., Grant, P., Shah, R., Arria, A., . . . Lester, B. M. (2006). The infant development, environment, and lifestyle study: Effects of prenatal methamphetamine exposure, polydrug exposure, and poverty on intrauterine growth. *Pediatrics, 118,* 1149–1156.

Smith, P. J., Blumenthal, J. A., Hoffman, B. M., Cooper, H., Strauman, T. A., Welsh-Bohmer, K., . . . Sherwood, A. (2010). Aerobic exercise and neurocognitive performance: A meta-analytic review of randomized controlled trials. *Psychosomatic Medicine, 72*(3), 239.

Smith, P. K. (2005). Play: Types and functions in human development. In A. D. Pellegrini & P. K. Smith (Eds.), *The nature of play* (pp. 271–291). New York, NY: Guilford Press.

Smith, P. K. (2005). Social and pretend play in children. In A. D. Pellegrini & P. K. Smith (Eds.), *The nature of play* (pp. 173–209). New York, NY: Guilford Press.

Smith, P. K., & Pellegrini, A. D. (2013). Learning through play. In R. E. Tremblay, M. Boivin, & R. Peters, R. (Eds.), *Encyclopedia on early childhood development* [online]. www.child-encyclopedia. com/play/according-experts/learning-through-play

Smith, R. L., Rose, A. J., & Schwartz-Mette, R. A. (2010). Relational and overt aggression in childhood and adolescence: Clarifying mean-level gender differences and associations with peer acceptance. *Social Development, 19*(2), 243–269.

Smith, S. L., & Boyson, A. R. (2002). Violence in music videos: Examining the prevalence and context of physical aggression. *Journal of Communication, 52*(1), 61–83.

Smith, S. L., Pieper, K. M., Granados, A., & Choueiti, M. (2010). Assessing gender-related portrayals in top-grossing G-rated films. *Sex Roles, 62,* 774–786. doi: 10-1007/s11199-009-9736z

Smith, T. B., & Silva, L. (2011). Ethnic identity and personal well-being of people of color: A meta-analysis. *Journal of Counseling Psychology, 58*(1), 42.

Smith, T. W. (2003). *American sexual behavior: Trends, socio-demographic differences, and risk behavior* (GSS Topical Report No. 25). Chicago, IL: National Opinion Research Center, University of Chicago.

Smith, T. W. (2006). Personality as risk and resilience in physical health. *Current Directions in Psychological Science, 15,* 227–231.

Smithsonian. (2014, December 8). *Queen Victoria dreamed up the white wedding dress in 1840.* Retrieved from www.smithsonianmag.com/smart-news/queen-victoria-sparked-white-wedding-dress-trend-1840-180953550/

Smits, A., Van Gaalen, R. I., & Mulder, C. H. (2010). Parent-child coresidence: Who moves in with whom and for whose needs? *Journal of Marriage and Family, 72*(4), 1022–1033.

Smits, J., & Monden, C. (2011). Twinning across the developing world. *PLoS One, 6*(9), e25239.

Smock, P. J., & Schwartz, C. R. (2020). The demography of families: A review of patterns and change. *Journal of Marriage and Family, 82*(1), 9–34.

Smorti, M., & Ponti, L. (2018). How does sibling relationship affect children's prosocial behaviors and best friend relationship quality? *Journal of Family Issues, 39*(8), 2413–2436.

Sneed, J. R., & Whitbourne, S. K. (2005). Models of the aging self. *Journal of Social Issues, 61*(2), 375–388.

Snow, M. E., Jacklin, C. N., & Maccoby, E. E. (1983). Sex-of-child differences in father-child interaction at one year of age. *Child Development, 54,* 227–232.

Snyder, J., Bank, L., & Burraston, B. (2005). The consequences of antisocial behavior in older male siblings for younger brothers and sisters. *Journal of Family Psychology, 19,* 643–653.

Snyder, J., Cramer, A., Afrank, J., & Patterson, G. R. (2005). The contributions of ineffective discipline and parental hostile attributions of child misbehavior to the development of conduct problems at home and school. *Developmental Psychology, 41*(1), 30.

Snyder, T. D., de Brey, C., and Dillow, S. A. (2016). *Digest of education statistics 2015 (NCES 2016-014).* Washington, DC: National Center for Education Statistics, Institute of Education Sciences, U.S. Department of Education.

Sobolewski, J. M., & Amato, P. J. (2005). Economic hardship in the family of origin and children's psychological well-being in adulthood. *Journal of Marriage and Family, 67,* 141–156.

Social Security Administration. (2019). *Fact sheet.* Retrieved from www.ssa.gov/news/press/factsheets/basicfact-alt.pdf

Society for Neuroscience. (2008). Neural disorders: Advances and challenges. In *Brain facts: A primer on the brain and nervous system* (pp. 36–54). Washington, DC: Author.

Society for Research in Child Development (SRCD). (2007). Ethical standards for research with children. (Updated by SRCD Governing Council, March 2007.) Retrieved from www.srcd.org/ethicalstandards.html

Soderstrom, M. (2007). Beyond babytalk: Re-evaluating the nature and content of speech input to preverbal infants. *Developmental Review, 27*(4), 501–532.

Soehner, A. M., & Harvey, A. G. (2012). Prevalence and functional consequences of severe insomnia symptoms in mood and anxiety disorders: Results from a nationally representative sample. *Sleep, 35*(10), 1367–1375.

Soenens, B., Vansteenkiste, M., Luyckx, K., & Goossens, L. (2006). Parenting and adolescent problem behavior: An integrated model with adolescent self-disclosure and perceived parental knowledge as intervening variables. *Developmental Psychology, 42,* 305–318.

Sofi, F., Valecchi, D., Bacci, D., Abbate, R., Gensini, G. F., Casini, A., & Macchi, C. (2011). Physical activity and risk of cognitive decline: A meta-analysis of prospective studies. *Journal of Internal Medicine, 269*(1), 107–117.

Sokol, R. Z., Kraft, P., Fowler, I. M., Mamet, R., Kim, E., & Berhane, K. T. (2006). Exposure to environmental ozone alters semen quality. *Environmental Health Perspectives, 114*(3), 360–365.

Sole-Auro, A. & Crimmins, E.M. (2013). The oldest old: Health in Europe and the United States. In J. Robine, C. Jagger, & E.M. Crimmins (Eds)., *Annual review of gerontology and geriatrics: Health longevity, a global approach, Vol. 33* (pp. 3–34). New York, NY: Springer.

Soleimanloo, S. S., White, M. J., Garcia-Hansen, V., & Smith, S. S. (2017). The effects of sleep loss on young drivers' performance: A systematic review. *PLoS One, 12*(8).

Soley, G., & Hannon, E. E. (2010). Infants prefer the musical meter of their own culture: A cross-cultural comparison. *Developmental Psychology, 46*(1), 286.

Soliman, A., De Sanctis, V., & Elalaily, R. (2014). Nutrition and pubertal development. *Indian Journal of Endocrinology and Metabolism, 18*(Suppl. 1), S39.

Solmeyer, A. R., McHale, S. M., & Crouter, A. C. (2014). Longitudinal associations between sibling relationship qualities and risky behavior across adolescence. *Developmental Psychology, 50*(2), 600.

Solomon, B., & Frenkel, D. (2010). Immunotherapy for Alzheimer's disease. *Neuropharmacology, 59*(4-5), 303-309.

Solomon, J., & George, C. (2011). The disorganized attachment–caregiving system. *Disorganized Attachment & Caregiving*, 25-51.

Sommers, B. D., Gunja, M. Z., Finegold, K., & Musco, T. (2015). Changes in self-reported insurance coverage, access to care, and health under the Affordable Care Act. *JAMA, 314*(4), 366-374.

Sommerville, J. A., Schmidt, M. F., Yun, J. E., & Burns, M. (2013). The development of fairness expectations and prosocial behavior in the second year of life. *Infancy, 18*(1), 40-66.

Song, J., Floyd, F. J., Seltzer, M. M., Greenberg, J. S., & Hong, J. (2010). Long-term effects of child death on parents' health-related quality of life: A dyadic analysis. *Family Relations, 59*(3), 269-282.

Song, J., Mailick, M. R., Greenberg, J. S., & Floyd, F. J. (2019). Mortality in parents after the death of a child. *Social Science & Medicine, 239*, 112522.

Song, Y., Ma, J., Agardh, A., Lau, P. W., Hu, P., & Zhang, B. (2015). Secular trends in age at menarche among Chinese girls from 24 ethnic minorities, 1985 to 2010. *Global Health Action, 8*(1), 26929.

Sonnenberg, C. M., Deeg, D. J. H., Van Tilburg, T. G., Vink, D., Stek, M. L., & Beekman, A. T. F. (2013). Gender differences in the relation between depression and social support in later life. *International Psychogeriatrics, 25*(1), 61-70.

Sontag, L. M., Graber, J. A., & Clemans, K. H. (2011). The role of peer stress and pubertal timing on symptoms of psychopathology during early adolescence. *Journal of Youth and Adolescence, 40*(10), 1371-1382.

Sonuga-Barke, E. J., Kennedy, M., Kumsta, R., Knights, N., Golm, D., Rutter, M., . . . Kreppner, J. (2017). Child-to-adult neurodevelopmental and mental health trajectories after early life deprivation: The young adult follow-up of the longitudinal English and Romanian Adoptees study. *The Lancet, 389*(10078), 1539-1548.

Sophian, C., Wood, A., & Vong, K. I. (1995). Making numbers count: The early development of numerical inferences. *Developmental Psychology, 31*, 263-273.

Soto, C. J. (2015). Is happiness good for your personality? Concurrent and prospective relations of the big five with subjective well-being. *Journal of Personality, 83*(1), 45-55.

Soto, C. J., John, O. P., Gosling, S. D., & Potter, J. (2011). Age differences in personality traits from 10 to 65: Big Five domains and facets in a large cross-sectional sample. *Journal of Personality and Social Psychology, 100*(2), 330.

South, S. J., & Lei, L. (2015). Failures-to-launch and boomerang kids: Contemporary determinants of leaving and returning to the parental home. *Social Forces, 94*(2), 863-890.

Spahni, S., Bennett, K. M., & Perrig-Chiello, P. (2016). Psychological adaptation to spousal bereavement in old age: The role of trait resilience, marital history, and context of death. *Death Studies, 40*(3), 182-190.

Spahni, S., Morselli, D., Perrig-Chiello, P., & Bennett, K. M. (2015). Patterns of psychological adaptation to spousal bereavement in old age. *Gerontology, 61*(5), 456-468.

Spear, L. P. (2014). Adolescents and alcohol: Acute sensitivities, enhanced intake, and later consequences. *Neurotoxicology and Teratology, 41*, 51-59.

Spear, L. P. (2018). Effects of adolescent alcohol consumption on the brain and behaviour. *Nature Reviews Neuroscience, 19*(4), 197.

Specht, J., Egloff, B., & Schmukle, S. C. (2011). Stability and change of personality across the life course: The impact of age and major life events on mean-level and rank-order stability of the Big Five. *Journal of Personality and Social Psychology, 101*(4), 862.

Spector-Bagdady, K., De Vries, R., Harris, L. H., & Low, L. K. (2017). Stemming the standard-of-care sprawl: Clinician self-interest and the case of electronic fetal monitoring. *Hastings Center Report, 47*(6), 16-24.

Speece, M. W., & Brent, S. B. (1984). Children's understanding of death: A review of three components of a death concept. *Child Development, 55*, 1671-1686.

Spelke, E. S. (2005). Sex differences in intrinsic aptitude for mathematics and science? A critical review. *American Psychologist, 60*, 950-958.

Spelke, E. S. (2017). Core knowledge, language, and number. *Language Learning and Development, 13*(2), 147-170.

Spencer, J. P., Clearfield, M., Corbetta, D., Ulrich, B., Buchanan, P., & Schöner, G. (2006). Moving toward a grand theory of development: In memory of Esther Thelen. *Child Development, 77*, 1521-1538.

Spicer, P. (2010). Cultural influences on parenting. *Zero to Three, 30*(4), 28.

Spiegel, C., & Halberda, J. (2011). Rapid fast-mapping abilities in 2-year-olds. *Journal of Experimental Child Psychology, 109*(1), 132-140.

Spinath, F. M., Price, T. S., Dale, P. S., & Plomin, R. (2004). The genetic and environmental origins of language disability and ability. *Child Development, 75*, 445-454.

Spinrad, T. L., Eisenberg, N., Harris, E., Hanish, L., Fabes, R. A., Kupanoff, K., . . . Holmes, J. (2004). The relation of children's everyday nonsocial peer play behavior to their emotionality, regulation, and social functioning. *Developmental Psychology, 40*, 67-80.

Spirduso, W. W., & MacRae, P. G. (1990). Motor performance and aging. In J. E. Birren & K. W. Schaie (Eds.), *Psychology of aging* (3rd ed., pp. 183-200). New York, NY: Academic Press.

Spiro, A., III. (2001). Health in midlife: Toward a life-span view. In M. E. Lachman (Ed.), *Handbook of midlife development* (pp. 156-187). New York, NY: Wiley.

Spitze, G., & Trent, K. (2006). Gender differences in adult sibling relations in two-child families. *Journal of Marriage and Family, 68*, 977-992.

Spreng, R. N., & Turner, G. R. (2019). The shifting architecture of cognition and brain function in older adulthood. *Perspectives on Psychological Science, 14*(4), 523-542.

Springer, K. W., Pudrovska, T., & Hauser, R. M. (2011). Does psychological well-being change with age? Longitudinal tests of age variations and further exploration of the multidimensionality of Ryff's model of psychological well-being. *Social Science Research, 40*(1), 392-398.

Sroufe, L. A. (1997). *Emotional development.* Cambridge, England: Cambridge University Press.

Sroufe, L. A., Carlson, E., & Shulman, S. (1993). Individuals in relationships: Development from infancy through adolescence. In D. C. Funder, R. D. Parke, C. Tomlinson-Keasey, & K. Widaman (Eds.), *Studying lives through time: Personality and development* (pp. 315-342). Washington, DC: American Psychological Association.

Sroufe, L. A., Coffino, B., & Carlson, E. A. (2010). Conceptualizing the role of early experience: Lessons from the Minnesota Longitudinal Study. *Developmental Review, 30*(1), 36-51.

Sroufe, L. A., Egeland, B., Carlson, E. A., & Collins, W. A. (2005). *The development of the person: The Minnesota study of risk and adaptation from birth to adulthood.* New York, NY: Guilford Press.

St. John, P. D., Mackenzie, C., & Menec, V. (2015). Does life satisfaction predict five-year mortality in community-living older adults? *Aging & Mental Health, 19*(4), 363-370.

Staff, J., Mortimer, J. T., & Uggen, C. (2004). Work and leisure in adolescence. In R. M. Lerner & L. Steinberg (Eds.), *Handbook of adolescent development* (2nd ed., pp. 429-450). Hoboken, NJ: Wiley.

Staff, J., Schulenberg, J. E., & Bachman, J. G. (2010). Adolescent work intensity, school performance, and academic engagement. *Sociology of Education, 83*(3), 183-200.

Stallman, H. M., & Kohler, M. (2016). Prevalence of sleepwalking: A systematic review and meta-analysis. *PloS One, 11*(11), e0164769.

Stallman, H. M., & Ohan, J. L. (2016). Parenting style, parental adjustment, and co-parental conflict: Differential predictors of child psychosocial adjustment following divorce. *Behaviour Change, 33*(2), 112-126.

Stanca, L. (2016). The geography of parenthood and well-being: Do children make us happy, where and why. *World Happiness Report*, 88-102.

Staneva, A., Bogossian, F., Pritchard, M., & Wittkowski, A. (2015). The effects of maternal depression, anxiety, and perceived stress during pregnancy on preterm birth: A systematic review. *Women and Birth, 28*(3), 179-193.

Stanley, I. H., Conwell, Y., Bowen, C., & Van Orden, K. A. (2014). Pet ownership may attenuate loneliness among older adult primary care patients who live alone. *Aging & Mental Health*, *18*(3), 394–399.

Stanton, R., & Reaburn, P. (2014). Exercise and the treatment of depression: A review of the exercise program variables. *Journal of Science and Medicine in Sport*, *17*(2), 177–182.

Starr, A., Libertus, M. E., & Brannon, E. M. (2013). Number sense in infancy predicts mathematical abilities in childhood. *Proceedings of the National Academy of Sciences*, *110*(45), 18116–18120.

Staudinger, U. M., & Baltes, P. B. (1996). Interactive minds: A facilitative setting for wisdom-related performance? *Journal of Personality and Social Psychology*, *71*, 746–762.

Staudinger, U. M., Smith, J., & Baltes, P. B. (1992). Wisdom-related knowledge in a life review task: Age differences and the role of professional specialization. *Psychology and Aging*, *7*, 271–281.

Stav, W. B., Hallenen, T., Lane, J., & Arbesman, M. (2012). Systematic review of occupational engagement and health outcomes among community-dwelling older adults. *American Journal of Occupational Therapy*, *66*(3), 301–310.

Steck, N., Egger, M., Maessen, M., Reisch, T., & Zwahlen, M. (2013). Euthanasia and assisted suicide in selected European countries and US states: Systematic literature review. *Medical Care*, *51*(10), 938–944.

Steensma, T. D., McGuire, J. K., Kreukels, B. P., Beekman, A. J., & Cohen-Kettenis, P. T. (2013). Factors associated with desistence and persistence of childhood gender dysphoria: a quantitative follow-up study. *Journal of the American Academy of Child & Adolescent Psychiatry*, *52*(6), 582–590.

Steinbach, U. (1992). Social networks, institutionalization, and mortality among elderly people in the United States. *Journal of Gerontology: Social Sciences*, *47*(4), S183–S190.

Steinberg, L. (2005). Psychological control: Style or substance? In J. Smetana (Ed.), *Changing boundaries of parental authority during adolescence* (New Directions for Child and Adolescent Development, No. 108, pp. 71–78). San Francisco, CA: Jossey-Bass.

Steinberg, L., & Darling, N. (1994). The broader context of social influence in adolescence. In R. Silberstein & E. Todt (Eds.), *Adolescence in context*. New York, NY: Springer.

Steinberg, L., Eisengard, B., & Cauffman, E. (2006). Patterns of competence and adjustment among adolescents from authoritative, authoritarian, indulgent, and neglectful homes: A replication in a sample of serious juvenile offenders. *Journal of Research on Adolescence*, *16*(1), 47–58.

Steinberg, L., Lamborn, S. D., Darling, N., Mounts, N. S., & Dornbusch, S. M. (1994). Over-time changes in adjustment and competence among adolescents from authoritative, authoritarian, indulgent, and neglectful families. *Child Development*, *65*(3), 754–770.

Steinhausen, H. C. (2002). The outcome of anorexia nervosa in the 20th century. *American Journal of Psychiatry*, *159*, 1284–1293.

Stelmach, A., & Nerlich, B. (2015). Metaphors in search of a target: The curious case of epigenetics. *New Genetics and Society*, *34*(2), 196–218.

Stepanikova, I., Nie, N. H., & He, X. (2010). Time on the Internet at home, loneliness, and life satisfaction: Evidence from panel time-diary data. *Computers in Human Behavior*, *26*(3), 329–338.

Stepien-Sporek, A., & Ryznar, M. (2016). The consequences of cohabitation. *USFL Rev.*, *50*, 75.

Stepler, R. (2017). *Led by baby boomers, divorce rates climb for America's 50+ population* [Pew Research Center report]. Retrieved from www.pewresearch.org/fact-tank/2017/03/09/led-by-baby-boomers-divorce-rates-climb-for-americas-50-population/

Stepler, R. (2017). *Number of U.S. adults cohabiting with a partner continues to rise, especially among those 50 and older* [Pew Research Center news release]. Retrieved from www.pewresearch.org/fact-tank/2017/04/06/

Stern, Y. (2012). Cognitive reserve in ageing and Alzheimer's disease. *The Lancet Neurology*, *11*(11), 1006–1012.

Sternberg, R. (2020). *The real-time impact of COVID-19 on small business employees* [Report]. Retrieved from https://gusto.com/company-news/smb-employee-covid-19-impact

Sternberg, R. J. (1985). *Beyond IQ: A triarchic theory of human intelligence*. New York, NY: Cambridge University Press.

Sternberg, R. J. (1985). *Beyond IQ: A triarchic theory of human intelligence*. Cambridge, England: Cambridge University Press.

Sternberg, R. J. (1986). A triangular theory of love. *Psychological Review*, *93*(2), 119.

Sternberg, R. J. (1987, September 23). The use and misuse of intelligence testing: Misunderstanding meaning, users over-rely on scores. *Education Week*, *22*, 28.

Sternberg, R. J. (1993). *Sternberg Triarchic Abilities Test*. Unpublished manuscript.

Sternberg, R. J. (1998). *Cupid's arrow: The course of love through time*. Cambridge, England: Cambridge University Press.

Sternberg, R. J. (2004). Culture and intelligence. *American Psychologist*, *59*, 325–338.

Sternberg, R. J. (2005). There are no public policy implications: A reply to Rushton and Jensen (2005). *Psychology, Public Policy, and Law*, *11*, 295–301.

Sternberg, R. J. (2006) A duplex theory of love. In R. J. Sternberg & K. Weis (Eds.), *The new psychology of love* (pp. 184–199). New Haven, CT: Yale University Press.

Sternberg, R. J., & Horvath, J. A. (1998). Cognitive conceptions of expertise and their relations to giftedness. In R. C. Friedman & K. B. Rogers (Eds.), *Talent in context: Historical and social perspectives on giftedness* (pp. 177–191). Washington, DC: American Psychological Association.

Sternberg, R. J., Castejón, J. L., Prieto, M. D., Hautamäki, J., & Grigorenko, E. L. (2001). Confirmatory factor analysis of the Sternberg Triarchic Abilities Test in three international samples: An empirical test of the triarchic theory of intelligence. *European Journal of Psychological Assessment*, *17*(1), 1.

Sternberg, R. J., Grigorenko, E. L., & Oh, S. (2001). The development of intelligence at midlife. In M. E. Lachman (Ed.), *Handbook of midlife development* (pp. 217–247). New York, NY: Wiley.

Sternberg, R. J., Wagner, R. K., Williams, W. M., & Horvath, J. A. (1995). Testing common sense. *American Psychologist*, *50*, 912–927.

Sterns, H. L. (2010). New and old thoughts about aging and work in the present and future. *The Gerontologist*, *50*(4), 568–571.

Sterns, H. L., & Huyck, M. H. (2001). The role of work in midlife. In M. E. Lachman (Ed.), *Handbook of midlife development* (pp. 447–486). New York, NY: Wiley.

Sterry, T. W., Reiter-Purtill, J., Gartstein, M. A., Gerhardt, C. A., Vannatta, K., & Noll, R. B. (2010). Temperament and peer acceptance: The mediating role of social behavior. *Merrill-Palmer Quarterly (1982)*, 189–219.

Stevens, W. D., Hasher, L., Chiew, K. S., & Grady, C. L. (2008). A neural mechanism underlying memory failure in older adults. *Journal of Neuroscience*, *28*(48), 12820–12824.

Stevenson, D. G., & Grabowski, D. C. (2010). Sizing up the market for assisted living. *Health Affairs*, *29*(1), 35–43.

Stevenson, D. K., Verter, J., Fanaroff, A. A., Oh, W., Ehrenkranz, R. A., Shankaran, S., . . . Korones, S. B. (2000). Sex differences in outcomes of very low birthweight infants: The newborn male disadvantage. *Archives of Disease in Childhood-Fetal and Neonatal Edition*, *83*(3), F182–F185.

Stevenson, H. W., Lee, S. Y., Chen, C., Stigler, J. W., Hsu, C. C., Kitamura, S., & Hatano, G. (1990). Contexts of achievement: A study of American, Chinese, and Japanese children. *Monographs of the Society for Research in Child Development*, *55*, i–119. https://doi.org/10.2307/1166090

Stevenson-Hinde, J., & Shouldice, A. (1996). Fearfulness: Developmental consistency. In A. J. Sameroff & M. M. Haith (Eds.), *The five- to seven-year shift: The age of reason and responsibility* (pp. 237–252). Chicago, IL: University of Chicago Press.

Stewart, A. J., & Vandewater, E. A. (1998). The course of generativity. In D. P. McAdams & D. de St. Aubin (Eds.), *Generativity and adult development: How and why we care for the next generation*. Washington, DC: American Psychological Association.

Stewart, A. M., Lewis, G. F., Heilman, K. J., Davila, M. I., Coleman, D. D., Aylward, S. A., & Porges, S. W. (2013). The covariation of acoustic features of infant cries and autonomic state. *Physiology & Behavior*, *120*, 203–210.

Stewart, E. A., & Simons, R. L. (2010). Race, code of the street, and violent delinquency: A multilevel investigation of neighborhood street culture and individual norms of violence. *Criminology*, *48*(2), 569–605.

Stewart, R. B. (1983). Sibling attachment relationships: Child–infant interaction in the strange situation. *Developmental Psychology*, *19*(2), 192.

Stigler, J. W., & Stevenson, H. W. (1992). *The learning gap: Why our schools are failing and what we can learn from Japanese and Chinese education.* New York, NY: Summit Books.

Stiles, J., Brown, T. T., Haist, F., & Jernigan, T. L. (2015). Brain and cognitive development. In L. S. Liben, U. Muller, & R. M. Lerner (Eds.), *Handbook of child psychology and developmental science* (pp. 9–62). New York, NY: Wiley.

Stipek, D. J., Gralinski, H., & Kopp, C. B. (1990). Self-concept development in the toddler years. *Developmental Psychology, 26,* 972–977.

Stock, H., Devries, K., Rotstein, A., Abrahams, N., Campbell, J., Watts, C., & Moreno, C.G. (2013). The global prevalence of intimate partner homicide: A systematic review. *Lancet, 382,* 859–865.

Stone, A. A., Schwartz, J. E., Broderick, J. E., & Deaton, A. (2010). A snapshot of the age distribution of psychological well-being in the United States. *Proceedings of the National Academy of Sciences of the U.S.A., 107*(22), 9985–9990.

Storebø, O. J., & Simonsen, E. (2016). The association between ADHD and antisocial personality disorder (ASPD) a review. *Journal of Attention Disorders, 20*(10), 815–824.

Strathearn, L. (2011). Maternal neglect: oxytocin, dopamine and the neurobiology of attachment. *Journal of Neuroendocrinology, 23*(11), 1054–1065.

Strathearn, L., Fonagy, P., Amico, J., & Montague, P. R. (2009). Adult attachment predicts maternal brain and oxytocin response to infant cues. *Neuropsychopharmacology, 34*(13), 2655.

Straus, M. A. (1999). The benefits of avoiding corporal punishment: New and more definitive evidence. Submitted for publication in K. C. Blaine (Ed.), *Raising America's children.*

Strauss, N., Giessler, K., & McAllister, E. (2015). How doula care can advance the goals of the Affordable Care Act: A snapshot from New York City. *The Journal of Perinatal Education, 24*(1), 8.

Strayer, D. L., Drews, F. A., & Crouch, D. F. (2006). A comparison of the cell phone driver and the drunk driver. *Human Factors, 48,* 381–391.

Strenze, T. (2007). Intelligence and socioeconomic success: A meta-analytic review of longitudinal research. *Intelligence, 35*(5), 401–426.

Strickhouser, J. E., Zell, E., & Krizan, Z. (2017). Does personality predict health and well-being? A metasynthesis. *Health Psychology, 36*(8), 797.

Stright, A. D., Gallagher, K. C., & Kelley, K. (2008). Infant temperament moderates relations between maternal parenting in early childhood and children's adjustment in first grade. *Child Development, 79*(1), 186–200.

Stroebe, M., Schut, H., & Stroebe, W. (2007). Health outcomes of bereavement. *Lancet, 370,* 1960–1973.

Stroebe, W. (2015). Age and scientific creativity. In S. Whitbourne (Ed.), *The encyclopedia of adulthood and aging.* New York, NY: Wiley.

Strohm, C. Q., Seltzer, J. A., Cochran, S. D., & Mays, V. M. (2009). "Living apart together" relationships in the United States. *Demographic Research, 21,* 177.

Strohschein, L. (2012). Parental divorce and child mental health: Accounting for predisruption differences. *Journal of Divorce & Remarriage, 53,* 489–502. doi:10.1080/10502556.2012.682903

Strouse, G. A., & Ganea, P. A. (2017). Toddlers' word learning and transfer from electronic and print books. *Journal of Experimental Child Psychology, 156,* 129–142.

Stubbs, B., Vancampfort, D., Rosenbaum, S., Firth, J., Cosco, T., Veronese, N., . . . Schuch, F. B. (2017). An examination of the anxiolytic effects of exercise for people with anxiety and stress-related disorders: A meta-analysis. *Psychiatry Research, 249,* 102–108.

Stuck, A. E., Egger, M., Hammer, A., Minder, C. E., & Beck, J. C. (2002). Home visits to prevent nursing home admission and functional decline in elderly people: Systematic review and meta-regression analysis. *JAMA, 287*(8), 1022–1028.

Stueve, A., & O'Donnell, L. N. (2005). Early alcohol initiation and subsequent sexual and alcohol risk behaviors among urban youths. *American Journal of Public Health, 95,* 887–893.

Stutzer, A., & Frey, B. S. (2006). Does marriage make people happy, or do happy people get married?. *The Journal of Socio-Economics, 35*(2), 326–347.

Su, C. T., McMahan, R. D., Williams, B. A., Sharma, R. K., & Sudore, R. L. (2014). Family matters: Effects of birth order, culture, and family dynamics on surrogate decision-making. *Journal of the American Geriatrics Society, 62*(1), 175–182.

Su, W., Han, X., Jin, C., Yan, Y., & Potenza, M. N. (2019). Are males more likely to be addicted to the internet than females? A meta-analysis involving 34 global jurisdictions. *Computers in Human Behavior, 99,* 86–100.

Suanda, S. H., Tompson, W., & Brannon, E. M. (2008). Changes in the ability to detect ordinal numerical relationships between 9 and 11 months of age. *Infancy, 13*(4), 308–337.

Subrahmanyam, K. & Greenfield, P. (2008). Online communication and adolescent relationships. *The Future of Children* 18, 119–146.

Subrahmanyam, K., Reich, S. M., Waecheter, N., & Espinoza, G. (2008). Online and offline social networks: Use of social networking sites by emerging adults. *Journal of Applied Developmental Psychology, 29*(6), 420–433.

Substance Abuse and Mental Health Services Administration. (2013). *Results from the 2012 National Survey on Drug Use and Health: Summary of National Findings.* Rockville, MD: Substance Abuse and Mental Health Services Administration.

Substance Abuse and Mental Health Services Administration. (2018). *Key substance use and mental health indicators in the United States: Results from the 2017 National Survey on Drug Use and Health* (HHS Publication No. SMA 18-5068, NSDUH Series H-53). Rockville, MD: Center for Behavioral Health Statistics and Quality, Substance Abuse and Mental Health Services Administration. Retrieved from www.samhsa.gov/data/

Substance Abuse and Mental Health Services Administration. (2019*). Key substance use and mental health indicators in the United States: Results from the 2018 National Survey on Drug Use and Health* (HHS Publication No. PEP19-5068, NSDUH Series H-54). Rockville, MD: Center for Behavioral Health Statistics and Quality, Substance Abuse and Mental Health Services Administration. Retrieved from https://www.samhsa.gov/data/

Substance Abuse and Mental Health Services Administration. (2019). Results from the 2018 national survey on drug use and health: Detailed tables. Retrieved from www.samhsa.gov/data/report/2018-nsduh-detailed-tables

Sugden, N. A., & Marquis, A. R. (2017). Meta-analytic review of the development of face discrimination in infancy: Face race, face gender, infant age, and methodology moderate face discrimination. *Psychological Bulletin, 143*(11), 1201–1244.

Suitor, J. J., Gilligan, M., Peng, S., Jung, J. H., & Pillemer, K. (2017). Role of perceived maternal favoritism and disfavoritism in adult children's psychological well-being. *Journals of Gerontology Series B: Psychological Sciences and Social Sciences, 72*(6), 1054–1066.

Suitor, J. J., Pillemer, K., Keeton, S., & Robison, J. (1995). Aged parents and aging children: Determinants of relationship quality. In R. Blieszner & V. Hilkevitch (Eds.), *Handbook of aging and the family* (pp. 223–242). Westport, CT: Greenwood Press.

Sullivan, A. R., & Fenelon, A. (2014). Patterns of widowhood mortality. *Journals of Gerontology Series B: Psychological Sciences and Social Sciences, 69*(1), 53–62.

Sullivan, K. T., Pasch, L. A., Johnson, M. D., & Bradbury, T. N. (2010). Social support, problem solving, and the longitudinal course of newlywed marriage. *Journal of Personality and Social Psychology, 98*(4), 631–644.

Sulmasy, L.S., Mueller, P.S., Ethics, Professionalism, and Human Rights Committee of the American College of Physicians. (2017). Ethics and the legalization of physician-assisted suicide: An American College of Physicians position paper. *Annals of Internal Medicine, 167*(8), 576–578.

Sumter, S. R., Valkenburg, P. M., & Peter, J. (2013). Perceptions of love across the lifespan: Differences in passion, intimacy, and commitment. *International Journal of Behavioral Development, 37*(5), 417–427.

Sundet, J., Barlaug, D., & Torjussen, T. (2004). The end of the Flynn Effect? A study of secular trends in mean intelligence test scores of Norwegian conscripts during half a century. *Intelligence, 32,* 349–362.

Sung, J., Beijers, R., Gartstein, M. A., de Weerth, C., & Putnam, S. P. (2015). Exploring temperamental differences in infants from the USA and the Netherlands. *European Journal of Developmental Psychology, 12*(1), 15–28.

Suomi, S., & Harlow, H. (1972). Social rehabilitation of isolate-reared monkeys. *Developmental Psychology, 6,* 487–496.

Suprawati, M., Anggoro, F. K., & Bukatko, D. (2014). "I think I can": Achievement-oriented themes in storybooks from Indonesia, Japan, and the United States. *Frontiers in Psychology, 5,* 167.

Susman, E. J., & Rogol, A. (2004). Puberty and psychological development. In R. M. Lerner & L. Steinberg (Eds.), *Handbook of adolescent psychology* (2nd ed., pp. 15–44). Hoboken, NJ: Wiley.

Susperreguy, M. I., & Davis-Kean, P. E. (2016). Maternal math talk in the home and math skills in preschool children. *Early Education and Development, 27*(6), 841–857.

Sutin, A. R., Terracciano, A., Deiana, B., Naitza, S., Ferrucci, L., Uda, M., . . . Costa, P. T. (2010). High neuroticism and low conscientiousness are associated with interleukin-6. *Psychological Medicine, 40*(9), 1485–1493.

Suzuki, N., Nakanishi, K., Yoneda, M., Hirofuji, T., & Hanioka, T. (2016). Relationship between salivary stress biomarker levels and cigarette smoking in healthy young adults: An exploratory analysis. *Tobacco Induced Diseases, 14*(1), 20.

Swain, I., Zelano, P., & Clifton, R. (1993). Newborn infants' memory for speech sounds retained over 24 hours. *Developmental Psychology, 29,* 312–323.

Swallen, K. C., Reither, E. N., Haas, S. A., & Meier, A. M. (2005). Overweight, obesity, and health-related quality of life among adolescents: The National Longitudinal Study of Adolescent Health. *Pediatrics, 115,* 340–347.

Swamy, G. K., Ostbye, T., & Skjaerven, R. (2008). Association of preterm birth with long-term survival, reproduction, and next-generation preterm birth. *Journal of the American Medical Association, 299,* 1429–1436.

Swanson, S. A., Crow, S. J., Le Grange, D., Swendsen, J., & Merikangas, K. R. (2011). Prevalence and correlates of eating disorders in adolescents: Results from the national comorbidity survey replication adolescent supplement. *Archives of General Psychiatry, 68*(7), 714–723.

Sweeney, M. M. (2010). Remarriage and stepfamilies: Strategic sites for family scholarship in the 21st century. *Journal of Marriage and Family, 72*(3), 667–684.

Swift, D. L., McGee, J. E., Earnest, C. P., Carlisle, E., Nygard, M., & Johannsen, N. M. (2018). The effects of exercise and physical activity on weight loss and maintenance. *Progress in Cardiovascular Diseases, 61*(2), 206–213.

Swingley, D. (2008). The roots of the early vocabulary in infants' learning from speech. *Current Directions in Psychological Science, 17,* 308–312.

Swingley, D., & Fernald, A. (2002). Recognition of words referring to present and absent objects by 24-month-olds. *Journal of Memory and Language, 46,* 39–56.

Syed, M., & Azmitia, M. (2008). A narrative approach to ethnic identity in emerging adulthood: Bringing life to the identity status model. *Developmental Psychology, 44*(4), 1012.

Syme, M. (2014). The evolving concept of older adult sexual behavior and its benefits. *Generations, 38*(1), 35–41.

Symoens, S., Bastaits, K., Mortelmans, D., & Bracke, P. (2013). Breaking up, breaking hearts? Characteristics of the divorce process and well-being after divorce. *Journal of Divorce & Remarriage, 54*(3), 177–196.

Tabak, M. A., & Mickelson, K. D. (2009). Religious service attendance and distress: The moderating role of stressful life events and race/ethnicity. *Sociology of Religion, 70*(1), 49–64.

Tach, L., & Halpern-Meekin, S. (2009). How does premarital cohabitation affect trajectories of marital quality? *Journal of Marriage and Family, 71,* 298–317.

Tackett, J. L., Krueger, R. F., Iacono, W. G., & McGue, M. (2005). Symptom-based subfactors of DSM-defined conduct disorder: Evidence for etiologic distinctions. *Journal of Abnormal Psychology, 114,* 483–487.

Tackett, J. L., Kushner, S. C., Herzhoff, K., Smack, A. J., & Reardon, K. W. (2014). Viewing relational aggression through multiple lenses: Temperament, personality, and personality pathology. *Development and psychopathology, 26*(3), 863–877.

Tadros, M. A., Lim, R., Hughes, D. I., Brichta, A. M., & Callister, R. J. (2015). Electrical maturation of spinal neurons in the human fetus: Comparison of ventral and dorsal horn. *Journal of Neurophysiology, 114*(5), 2661–2671.

Tai, T. O., Baxter, J., & Hewitt, B. (2014). Do co-residence and intentions make a difference? Relationship satisfaction in married, cohabiting, and living apart together couples in four countries. *Demographic Research, 31,* 71–104.

Tajfel, H. (1981). *Human groups and social categories.* Cambridge, UK: Cambridge University Press.

Takachi, R., Inoue, M., Ishihara, J., Kurahashi, N., Iwasaki, M., Sasazuki, S., . . . Tsugane, S. (2007). Fruit and vegetable intake and risk of total cancer and cardiovascular disease: Japan Public Health Center-based Prospective Study. *American Journal of Epidemiology, 167*(1), 59–70.

Talens, R. P., Christensen, K., Putter, H., Willemsen, G., Christiansen, L., Kremer, D., . . . & Heijmans, B. T. (2012). Epigenetic variation during the adult lifespan: Cross-sectional and longitudinal data on monozygotic twin pairs. *Aging Cell, 11*(4), 694–703.

Taliaferro, L. A., & Muehlenkamp, J. J. (2014). Risk and protective factors that distinguish adolescents who attempt suicide from those who only consider suicide in the past year. *Suicide and Life-Threatening Behavior, 44*(1), 6–22.

Tallent-Runnels, M., Thomas, J. A., Lan, W. Y., Cooper, S., Ahern, T. C., Shaw, S. M., & Liu, X. (2006). Teaching courses online: A review of the research. *Review of Educational Research, 76*(1), 93–135.

Talwar, V., & Lee, K. (2002). Development of lying to conceal a transgression: Children's control of expressive behaviour during verbal deception. *International Journal of Behavioral Development, 26*(5), 436–444.

Tamborini, C. R. (2007). The never-married in old age: Projections and concerns for the near future. *Social Security Bulletin, 67,* 25.

Tamnes, C. K., Østby, Y., Walhovd, K. B., Westlye, L. T., Due-Tønnessen, P., & Fjell, A. M. (2010). Intellectual abilities and white matter microstructure in development: A diffusion tensor imaging study. *Human Brain Mapping, 31*(10), 1609–1625.

Tanaka, K., & Johnson, N. E. (2016). Childlessness and mental well-being in a global context. *Journal of Family Issues, 37*(8), 1027–1045.

Tanaka, M., Ishii, A., Yamano, E., Ogikubo, H., Okazaki, M., Kamimura, K., . . . Watanabe, Y. (2012). Effect of a human-type communication robot on cognitive function in elderly women living alone. *Medical Science Monitor: International Medical Journal of Experimental and Clinical Research, 18*(9), CR550.

Tang, F. (2016). Retirement patterns and their relationship to volunteering. *Nonprofit and Voluntary Sector Quarterly, 45*(5), 910–930.

Tassell-Matamua, N. (2013). Phenomenology of near-death experiences: An analysis of a Maori case study. *Journal of Near-Death Studies, 32,* 107–117.

Tatangelo, G., McCabe, M., Campbell, S., & Szoeke, C. (2017). Gender, marital status and longevity. *Maturitas, 100,* 64–69.

Tau, G. Z., & Peterson, B. S. (2010). Normal development of brain circuits. *Neuropsychopharmacology, 35*(1), 147.

Tavakol, Z., Nikbakht Nasrabadi, A., Behboodi Moghadam, Z., Salehiniya, H., & Rezaei, E. (2017). A review of the factors associated with marital satisfaction. *Galen Medical Journal, 6*(3).

Taveras, E. M., Capra, A. M., Braveman, P. A., Jensvold, N. G., Escobar, G. J., & Lieu, T. A. (2003). Clinician support and psychosocial risk factors associated with breastfeeding discontinuation. *Pediatrics, 112,* 108–115.

Taylor, L. E., Swerdfeger, A. L., & Eslick, G. D. (2014). Vaccines are not associated with autism: An evidence-based meta-analysis of case-control and cohort studies. *Vaccine, 32*(29), 3623–3629.

Taylor, R. J., Chatters, L. M., Lincoln, K. D., & Woodward, A. T. (2017). Church-based exchanges of informal social support among African Americans. *Race and Social Problems, 9*(1), 53–62.

Teasdale, T. W., & Owen, D. R. (2008). Secular declines in cognitive test scores: A reversal of the Flynn effect. *Intelligence, 36,* 121–126.

Teck, J. T. W., & McCann, M. (2018). Tracking internet interest in anabolic-androgenic steroids using Google Trends. *The International Journal on Drug Policy, 51,* 52.

Temel, J. S., Greer, J. A., Muzikanskym, A., Gallagher, E. R., Admane, S., Jackson, V. A., . . . Lynch, T. J. (2010). Early palliative care for patients with metastatic non-small-cell lung cancer. *New England Journal of Medicine, 363*(8), 733–742.

Tenenbaum, H. R., & Leaper, C. (2002). Are parents' gender schemas related to their children's gender-related cognitions? A meta-analysis. *Developmental Psychology, 38*(4), 615.

Teo, A. R., Choi, H., & Valenstein, M. (2013). Social relationships and depression: Ten-year follow-up from a nationally representative study. *PloS One, 8*(4).

Teo, A. R., Lerrigo, R., & Rogers, M. A. (2013). The role of social isolation in social anxiety disorder: A systematic review and meta-analysis. *Journal of Anxiety Disorders, 27*(4), 353–364.

Tepper, P. G., et al. (2016). *Characterizing the trajectories of vasomotor symptoms across the menopausal transition.* Retrieved from Swanstudy.org: www.swanstudy.org/wps/wp-content/uploads/2016/08/TepperVMSMenopause2016.pdf

Terracciano, A., McCrae, R. R., & Costa, P. T. (2010). Intra-individual change in personality stability and age. *Journal of Research in Personality, 44*(1), 31–37.

Terribilli, D., Schaufelberger, M. S., Duran, F. L., Zanetti, M. V., Curiati, P. K., Menezes, P. R., . . . Busatto, G. F. (2011). Age-related gray matter volume changes in the brain during non-elderly adulthood. *Neurobiology of Aging, 32*(2), 354–368.

Teshale, S. M., & Lachman, M. E. (2016). Managing daily happiness: The relationship between selection, optimization, and compensation strategies and well-being in adulthood. *Psychology and Aging, 31*(7), 687.

Testa, R. J., Jimenez, C. L., & Rankin, S. (2014). Risk and resilience during transgender identity development: The effects of awareness and engagement with other transgender people on affect. *Journal of Gay & Lesbian Mental Health, 18*(1), 31–46.

Teubert, D., & Pinquart, M. (2010). The association between coparenting and child adjustment: A meta-analysis. *Parenting: Science and Practice, 10*(4), 286–307.

Tham, Y. C., Li, X., Wong, T. Y., Quigley, H. A., Aung, T., & Cheng, C. Y. (2014). Global prevalence of glaucoma and projections of glaucoma burden through 2040: A systematic review and meta-analysis. *Ophthalmology, 121*(11), 2081–2090.

Thapar, A., Collishaw, S., Pine, D. S., & Thapar, A. K. (2012). Depression in adolescence. *The Lancet, 379*(9820), 1056–1067.

Thapar, A., Fowler, T., Rice, F., Scourfield, J., van den Bree, M., Thomas, H., Harold, G., & Hay, D. (2003). Maternal smoking during pregnancy and attention deficit hyperactivity disorder symptoms in offspring. *American Journal of Psychiatry, 160*, 1985–1989.

The Aspen Institute. (2018). Sport participation and physical activity rates [Data sheet]. Retrieved from www.aspenprojectplay.org/kids-sports-participation-rates

The Aspen Institute. (2018). *The state of play 2018: Trends and development* [Report]. Retrieved from https://assets.aspeninstitute.org/content/uploads/2018/10/StateofPlay2018_v4WEB_2-FINAL.pdf

The Conference Board, USA. (2000). *Turning skills into profit: Economic benefits of workplace education programs.* New York: Author.

The Week. (2012, January 24). *Turning the dead into beads: South Korea's "odd" new trend.* Retrieved from theweek.com/articles/478701/turning-dead-into-beads-south-koreas-odd-new-trend

The World Bank. (2020). *Food security and COVID-19* [News brief]. Retrieved from www.worldbank.org/en/topic/agriculture/brief/food-security-and-covid-19

Thelen, E., & Fisher, D. M. (1982). Newborn stepping: An explanation for a "disappearing" reflex. *Developmental Psychology, 18*, 760–775.

Thelen, E., & Fisher, D. M. (1983). The organization of spontaneous leg movements in newborn infants. *Journal of Motor Behavior, 15*, 353–377.

Thoits, P. A. (2010). Stress and health: Major findings and policy implications. *Journal of Health and Social Gehavior, 51*(1_suppl), S41–S53.

Thoits, P. A. (2011). Mechanisms linking social ties and support to physical and mental health. *Journal of Health and Social Behavior, 52*(2), 145–161.

Thomas, A. G., Dennis, A., Bandettini, P. A., & Johansen-Berg, H. (2012). The effects of aerobic activity on brain structure. *Frontiers in Psychology, 3*.

Thomas, A., & Chess, S. (1977). *Temperament and development.* New York, NY: Brunner/Mazel.

Thomas, A., & Chess, S. (1984). Genesis and evolution of behavioral disorders: From infancy to early adult life. *American Journal of Orthopsychiatry, 141*(1), 1–9.

Thomas, A., Chess, S., & Birch, H. G. (1968). *Temperament and behavior disorders in children.* New York, NY: New York University Press.

Thomas, H. N., Hamm, M., Borrero, S., Hess, R., & Thurston, R. C. (2018). Body image, attractiveness, and sexual satisfaction among midlife women: A qualitative study. *Journal of Women's Health, 28*(1), 100–106.

Thomas, H. N., Hess, R., & Thurston, R. C. (2015). Correlates of sexual activity and satisfaction in midlife and older women. *The Annals of Family Medicine, 13*(4), 336–342.

Thomas, J. G., Bond, D. S., Phelan, S., Hill, J. O., & Wing, R. R. (2014). Weight-loss maintenance for 10 years in the National Weight Control Registry. *American Journal of Preventive Medicine, 46*(1), 17–23.

Thomas, P. A. (2010). Is it better to give or to receive? Social support and the well-being of older adults. *Journals of Gerontology Series B: Psychological Sciences and Social Sciences, 65*(3), 351–357.

Thomas, P. A., Liu, H., & Umberson, D. (2017). Family relationships and well-being. *Innovation in Aging, 1*(3), igx025

Thompson, J. A., Olyaei, A., Skeith, A., & Caughey, A. B. (2019). Cesarean prevalence rates for different races by maternal characteristics [20B]. *Obstetrics & Gynecology, 133*, 25S–26S.

Thompson, P. M., Cannon, T. D., Narr, K. L., van Erp, T., Poutanen, V., Huttunen, M., . . . Toga, A. W. (2001). Genetic influences on brain structure. *Nature Neuroscience, 4*, 1253–1258.

Thompson, P. M., Giedd, J. N., Woods, R. P., MacDonald, D., Evans, A. C., & Toga, A. W. (2000). Growth patterns in the developing brain detected by using continuum mechanical tensor maps. *Nature, 404*, 190–193.

Thompson, R. A. (2011). Emotion and emotion regulation: Two sides of the developing coin. *Emotion Review, 3*(1), 53–61.

Thomsen, M. R., Nayga, Jr., R. M., Alviola, P. A., & Rouse, H. L. (2016). The effect of food deserts on the body mass index of elementary schoolchildren. *American Journal of Agricultural Economics, 98*, 1–18.

Thomson, E., & McLanahan, S. S. (2012). Reflections on "Family structure and child well-being: Economic resources vs. parental socialization." *Social Forces, 91*(1), 45–53.

Thornton, W. J. L., & Dumke, H. A. (2005). Age differences in everyday problem-solving and decision-making effectiveness: A meta-analytic review. *Psychology and Aging, 20*, 85–99.

Thorvaldsson, V., Hofer, S. M., Berg, S., Skoog, I., Sacuiu, S., & Johansson, B. (2008). Onset of terminal decline in cognitive abilities in individuals without dementia. *Neurology.* Advance online publication. doi: 10.1212/01.wnl.0000312379.02302.ba

Thurston, R. C., Johnson, B. D., Shufelt, C. L., Braunstein, G. D., Berga, S. L., Stanczyk, F. Z., . . . Kelsey, S. F. (2017). Menopausal symptoms and cardiovascular disease mortality in the Women's Ischemia Syndrome Evaluation (WISE). *Menopause, 24*(2), 126.

Tilden, V. P., Tolle, S. W., Nelson, C. A., & Fields, J. (2001). Family decision-making to withdraw life-sustaining treatments from hospitalized patients. *Nursing Research, 50*(2), 105–115.

Tilvis, R. S., Kahonen-Vare, M. H., Jolkkonen, J., Valvanne, J., Pitkala, K. H., & Stradnberg, T. E. (2004). Predictors of cognitive decline and mortality of aged people over a 10-year period. *Journal of Gerontology: Medical Sciences, 59A*, 268–274.

Tilvis, R. S., Laitala, V., Routasalo, P., Strandberg, T. E., & Pitkala, K. H. (2012). Positive life orientation predicts good survival prognosis in old age. *Archives of Gerontology and Geriatrics, 55*(1), 133–137.

Tippett, N., & Wolke, D. (2015). Aggression between siblings: Associations with the home environment and peer bullying. *Aggressive Behavior, 41*(1), 14–24.

Tither, J., & Ellis, B. (2008). Impact of fathers on daughter's age at menarche: A genetically and environmentally controlled sibling study. *Developmental Psychology, 44*(5), 1409–1420.

Tobin, J. (2005). Quality in early childhood education: An anthropologist's perspective. *Early Education and Development, 16*(4), 421–434.

Tobin, J. J., Wu, D. Y., & Davidson, D. H. (1989). *Preschool in three cultures: Japan, China, and the United States.* New Haven, CT: Yale University Press.

Toga, A. W., Thompson, P. M., & Sowell, E. R. (2006). Mapping brain maturation. *Trends in Neurosciences, 29*(3), 148–159.

Toga, A., & Thompson, P. M. (2005). Genetics of brain structure and intelligence. *Annual Review of Neurology, 28*, 1–23.

Tokariev, A., Videman, M., Palva, J. M., & Vanhatalo, S. (2016). Functional brain connectivity develops rapidly around term age and changes between vigilance states in the human newborn. *Cerebral Cortex, 26*(12), 4540–4550.

Tolan, P. H., Gorman-Smith, D., & Henry, D. B. (2003). The developmental ecology of urban males' youth violence. *Developmental Psychology, 39*, 274-291.

Tolppanen, A. M., Solomon, A., Kulmala, J., Kåreholt, I., Ngandu, T., Rusanen, M., . . . Kivipelto, M. (2015). Leisure-time physical activity from mid-to late life, body mass index, and risk of dementia. *Alzheimer's & Dementia, 11*(4), 434-443.

Tomasello, M. (2007). Cooperation and communication in the 2nd year of life. *Child Development Perspectives, 1*(1), 8-12.

Tomasello, M., & Moll, H. (2010). The gap is social: Human shared intentionality and culture. In P. M. Kappeler & J. B. Silk (Eds.), *Mind the gap* (pp. 331-349). Berlin, Germany: Springer-Verlag.

Tomassini, C., Glaser, K., & Stuchbury, R. (2007). Family disruption and support in later life: A comparative study between the United Kingdom and Italy. *Journal of Social Issues, 63*(4), 845-863.

Tomkinson, G. R., & Olds, T. S. (2007). Secular changes in pediatric aerobic fitness test performance: The global picture. In *Pediatric Fitness* (Vol. 50, pp. 46-66). Basel, Switzerland: Karger Publishers.

Toomey, R. B., Syvertsen, A. K., & Shramko, M. (2018). Transgender adolescent suicide behavior. *Pediatrics, 142*(4), e20174218.

Toot, S., Swinson, T., Devine, M., Challis, D., & Orrell, M. (2017). Causes of nursing home placement for older people with dementia: A systematic review and meta-analysis. *International Psychogeriatrics, 29*(2), 195-208.

Topor, D. R., Keane, S. P., Shelton, T. L., & Calkins, S. D. (2010). Parent involvement and student academic performance: A multiple mediational analysis. *Journal of Prevention & Intervention in the Community, 38*(3), 183-197.

Torbic, H. (2011). Children and grief: but what about the children? *Home Healthcare Now, 29*(2), 67-77.

Torrance, E. P. (1974). *The Torrance Tests of Creative Thinking: Technical norms manual.* Bensonville, IL: Scholastic Testing Service.

Torrance, E. P., & Ball, O. E. (1984). *Torrance Tests of Creative Thinking: Streamlined (revised) manual, Figural A and B.* Bensonville, IL: Scholastic Testing Service.

Tosi, M. (2020). Boomerang kids and parents' well-being: Adaptation, stressors, and social norms. *European Sociological Review.*

Totsika, V., & Sylva, K. (2004). The Home Observation for Measurement of the Environment revisited. *Child and Adolescent Mental Health, 9*, 25-35.

Towle, E. B., & Morgan, L. M. (2002). Romancing the transgender native: Rethinking the use of the "third gender" concept. *GLQ: A Journal of Lesbian and Gay Studies, 8*(4), 469-497.

Townsend, N. W. (1997). Men, migration, and households in Botswana: An exploration of connections over time and space. *Journal of Southern African Studies, 23*, 405-420.

Toy, C. C., Deitz, J., Engel, J. M., & Wendel, S. (2000). Performance of 6-month-old Asian American infants on the Movement Assessment of Infants: A descriptive study. *Physical & Occupational Therapy in Pediatrics, 19*(3-4), 5-23.

Trachtenberg, F. L., Haas, E. A., Kinney, H. C., Stanley, C., & Krous, H. F. (2012). Risk factor changes for sudden infant death syndrome after initiation of Back- to-Sleep campaign. *Pediatrics,* peds-2011.

Traditional Chinese Weddings. (2014). Retrieved from http://traditions.cultural-china.com/en/14Traditions30.html

Trafimow, D., Triandis, H. C., & Goto, S. G. (1991). Some tests of the distinction between the private self and the collective self. *Journal of Personality and Social Psychology, 60*(5), 649.

Trahan, L. H., Stuebing, K. K., Fletcher, J. M., & Hiscock, M. (2014). The Flynn effect: A meta-analysis. *Psychological Bulletin, 140*(5), 1332.

Trautner, H. M., Ruble, D. N., Cyphers, L., Kirsten, B., Behrendt, R., & Hartmann, P. (2005). Rigidity and flexibility of gender stereotypes in childhood: Developmental or differential? *Infant and Child Development, 14*(4), 365-381.

Treas, J., Lui, J., & Gubernskaya, Z. (2014). Attitudes on marriage and new relationships: Cross-national evidence on the deinstitutionalization of marriage. *Demographic Research, 30*, 1495.

Treit, S., Zhou, D., Chudley, A. E., Andrew, G., Rasmussen, C., Nikkel, S. M., . . . & Beaulieu, C. (2016). Relationships between head circumference, brain volume and cognition in children with prenatal alcohol exposure. *PLoS One, 11*(2), e0150370.

Tremblay, M. S., Barnes, J. D., González, S. A., Katzmarzyk, P. T., Onywera, V. O., Reilly, J. J., & Tomkinson, G. R. (2016). Global matrix 2.0: Report card grades on the physical activity of children and youth comparing 38 countries. *Journal of Physical Activity and Health, 13*(s2), S343-S366.

Tremblay, M. S., Gray, C. E., Akinroye, K., Harrington, D. M., Katzmarzyk, P. T., Lambert, E. V., . . . Prista, A. (2014). Physical activity of children: A global matrix of grades comparing 15 countries. *Journal of Physical Activity and Health, 11*(s1), S113-S125.

Tremblay, R. E., Nagin, D. S., Séguin, J. R., Zoccolillo, M., Zelazo, P. D., Boivin, M., . . . Japel, C. (2004). Physical aggression during early childhood: Trajectories and predictors. *Pediatrics, 114*(1), e43-e50.

Troll, L. E., & Fingerman, K. L. (1996). Connections between parents and their adult children. In C. Magai & S. H. McFadden (Eds.), *Handbook of emotion, adult development, and aging* (pp. 185-205). San Diego, CA: Academic Press.

Trombetti, A., Reid, K. F., Hars, M., Herrmann, F. R., Pasha, E., Phillips, E. M., & Fielding, R. A. (2016). Age-associated declines in muscle mass, strength, power, and physical performance: Impact on fear of falling and quality of life. *Osteoporosis International, 27*(2), 463-471.

Trommsdorff, G., & Cole, P. M. (2011). Emotion, self-regulation, and social behavior in cultural contexts. In X. Chen & K. H. Rubin (Eds.), *Socioemotional development in cultural context.* New York, NY: Guilford.

Tromp, D., Dufour, A., Lithfous, S., Pebayle, T., & Després, O. (2015). Episodic memory in normal aging and Alzheimer disease: Insights from imaging and behavioral studies. *Ageing Research Reviews, 24*, 232-262.

Tronick, E. (1972). Stimulus control and the growth of the infant's visual field. *Perception and Psychophysics, 11*, 373-375.

Tronick, E. Z. (1989). Emotions and emotional communication in infants. *American Psychologist, 44*(2), 112-119.

Tronick, E. Z., Morelli, G. A., & Ivey, P. (1992). The Efe forager infant and toddler's pattern of social relationships: Multiple and simultaneous. *Developmental Psychology, 28*(4), 568-577.

Tropp, L. R., O'Brien, T. C., & Migacheva, K. (2014). How peer norms of inclusion and exclusion predict children's interest in cross-ethnic friendships. *Journal of Social Issues, 70*(1), 151-166.

Troseth, G. L., & DeLoache, J. S. (1998). The medium can obscure the message: Young children's understanding of video. *Child Development, 69*, 950-965.

Troseth, G. L., Saylor, M. M., & Archer, A. H. (2006). Young children's use of video as a source of socially relevant information. *Child Development, 77*, 786-799.

Trouillet, R., Doan-Van-Hay, L. M., Launay, M., & Martin, S. (2011). Impact of age, and cognitive and coping resources on coping. *Canadian Journal on Aging/La Revue canadienne du vieillissement, 30*(4), 541-550.

Trudel, G., Villeneuve, V., Anderson, A., & Pilon, G. (2008). Sexual and marital aspects of old age: An update. *Sexual and Relationship Therapy, 23*(2), 161-169.

Tsai, J. L., Louie, J. Y., Chen, E. E., & Uchida, Y. (2007). Learning what feelings to desire: Socialization of ideal affect through children's storybooks. *Personality and Social Psychology Bulletin, 33*(1), 17-30.

Tsang, T. W., & Elliott, E. J. (2017). High global prevalence of alcohol use during pregnancy and fetal alcohol syndrome indicates need for urgent action. *The Lancet Global Health, 5*(3), e232-e233.

Tsao, F. M., Liu, H. M., & Kuhl, P. K. (2004). Speech perception in infancy predicts language development in the second year of life: A longitudinal study. *Child Development, 75*, 1067-1084.

Tseng, V. L., Chlebowski, R. T., Yu, F., Cauley, J. A., Li, W., Thomas, F., . . . Coleman, A. L. (2017). Association of cataract surgery with mortality in older women: Findings from the women's health initiative. *JAMA Ophthalmology.*

Tseng, V. L., Yu, F., Lum, F., & Coleman, A. L. (2016). Cataract surgery and mortality in the United States Medicare population. *Ophthalmology, 123*(5), 1019-1026.

Tucker, M. A., Morris, C. J., Morgan, A., Yang, J., Myers, S., Pierce, J. G., . . . Scheer, F. A. (2017). The relative impact of sleep and circadian drive on motor skill acquisition and memory consolidation. *Sleep, 40*(4).

Tucker, M. B., Taylor, R. J., & Mitchell-Kernan, C. (1993). Marriage and romantic involvement among aged African Americans. *Journal of Gerontology: Social Sciences, 48*, S123–S132.

Tucker-Drob, E. M., & Bates, T. C. (2016). Large cross-national differences in gene × socioeconomic status interaction in intelligence. *Psychological Science, 27*(2), 138–149.

Tugade, M. M., Fredrickson, B. L., & Feldman Barrett, L. (2004). Psychological resilience and positive emotional granularity: Examining the benefits of positive emotions on coping and health. *Journal of Personality, 72*(6), 1161–1190.

Turanovic, J. J., Pratt, T. C., & Piquero, A. R. (2017). Exposure to fetal testosterone, aggression, and violent behavior: A meta-analysis of the 2D: 4D digit ratio. *Aggression and Violent Behavior, 33*, 51–61.

Turati, C., Simion, F., Milani, I., & Umilta, C. (2002). Newborns' preference for faces: What is crucial? *Developmental Psychology, 38*, 875–882.

Turcotte Benedict, F., Vivier, P. M., & Gjelsvik, A. (2015). Mental health and bullying in the United States among children aged 6 to 17 years. *Journal of Interpersonal Violence, 30*(5), 782–795.

Turiano, N. A., Pitzer, L., Armour, C., Karlamangla, A., Ryff, C. D., & Mroczek, D. K. (2011). Personality trait level and change as predictors of health outcomes: Findings from a national study of Americans (MIDUS). *Journals of Gerontology Series B: Psychological Sciences and Social Sciences, 67*(1), 4–12.

Turner, P. J., & Gervai, J. (1995). A multi-dimensional study of gender typing in preschool children and their parents: Personality, attitudes, preferences, behavior, and cultural differences. *Developmental Psychology, 31*, 759–772.

Twenge, J. M., Campbell, W. K., & Foster, C. A. (2003). Parenthood and marital satisfaction: A meta-analytic review. *Journal of Marriage and Family, 65*(3), 574–583.

Twenge, J. M., Sherman, R. A., & Wells, B. E. (2015). Changes in American adults' sexual behavior and attitudes, 1972–2012. *Archives of Sexual Behavior, 44*(8), 2273–2285.

Uecker, J. E., & Stokes, C. E. (2008). Early marriage in the United States. *Journal of Marriage and Family, 70*(4), 835–846.

Uhlenberg, P., & Cheuk, M. (2010). The significance of grandparents to grandchildren: An international perspective. In D. Dannefer & C. Phillipson (Eds.), *The SAGE handbook of social gerontology* (pp. 447–458). Thousand Oaks, CA: Sage.

Ülger, Z., Halil, M., Kalan, I., Yavuz, B. B., Cankurtaran, M., Güngör, E., & Arıoğul, S. (2010). Comprehensive assessment of malnutrition risk and related factors in a large group of community-dwelling older adults. *Clinical Nutrition, 29*(4), 507–511.

Umberson, D. (2003). *Death of a parent.* New York, NY: Cambridge University Press.

Umberson, D., Pudrovska, T., & Reczek, C. (2010). Parenthood, childlessness, and well-being: A life course perspective. *Journal of Marriage and Family, 72*(3), 612–629.

Umberson, D., Thomeer, M. B., Kroeger, R. A., Lodge, A. C., & Xu, M. (2015). Challenges and opportunities for research on same-sex relationships. *Journal of Marriage and Family, 77*(1), 96–111.

Umberson, D., Thomeer, M. B., & Williams, K. (2013). Family status and mental health: Recent advances and future directions. In C. S. Aneshensel, J. C. Phelan, & A. Bierman (Eds.), *Handbook of the sociology of mental health* (pp. 405–431). Dordrecht, the Netherlands: Springer.

Umberson, D., Williams, K., Powers, D. A., Liu, H., & Needham, B. (2006). You make me sick: Marital quality and health over the life course. *Journal of Health and Social Behavior, 47*, 1–16.

UNAIDS. (2019). *World AIDS Day 2019* [Fact sheet]. Retrieved from www.unaids.org/sites/default/files/media_asset/UNAIDS_FactSheet_en.pdf

Underwood, M., Lamb, S. E., Eldridge, S., Sheehan, B., Slowther, A. M., Spencer, A., . . . Diaz-Ordaz, K. (2013). Exercise for depression in elderly residents of care homes: A cluster-randomised controlled trial. *The Lancet, 382*(9886), 41–49.

UNESCO Institute for Statistics. (2017). Literacy rates continue to rise from one generation to the next. *Fact Sheet No. 45 FS/2017/LIT/45.*

UNESCO. (2017). *School violence and bullying: Global status report.* Retrieved from http://unesdoc.unesco.org/images/0024/002469/246970e.pdf

UNESCO. (2019). *Behind the numbers: Ending school violence and bullying* [Report]. Retrieved from https://unesdoc.unesco.org/ark:/48223/pf0000366483

UNESCO. (2020). *COVID-19 educational disruption and response* [Information sheet]. Retrieved from https://en.unesco.org/covid19/educationresponse

UNICEF & WHO. (2019). *Low birthweight estimates: Levels and trends 2000–2015.* Geneva: World Health Organization. Licence: CC BY-NC-SA 3.0 IGO. Retrieved from www.unicef.org/media/53711/file/UNICEF-WHO%20Low%20birthweight%20estimates%202019%20.pdf

UNICEF. (2019). *Maternal and newborn health: Newborns and mothers are still dying in appalling numbers–mostly from preventable causes* [Report]. Retrieved from www.unicef.org/health/maternal-and-newborn-health

UNICEF Millennium Development Goals. (2015). *Goal: Reduce child mortality.* Retrieved from www.un.org/sustainabledevelopment

UNICEF. (2014). *A statistical snapshot of violence against adolescent girls* [Report]. Retrieved from www.unicef.org/publications/files/A_Statistical_Snapshot_of_Violence_Against_Adolescent_Girls.pdf

UNICEF. (2014, September). *Hidden in Plain Sight: A statistical analysis of violence against children.* Retrieved from www.unicef.org/publications/index_74865.html

UNICEF. (2015). *Goal: Eradicate extreme poverty and hunger.* Retrieved from www. unicef.org/mdg/poverty.html

UNICEF. (2015). *UNICEF data: Monitoring the situation for children and women: Maternal mortality.* Retrieved from https://data.unicef.org/topic/maternal-health/maternal-mortality/#

UNICEF. (2017). *UNICEF data: Monitoring the situation for children and women: Immunizations.* Retrieved from https://data.unicef.org/topic/child-health/immunization/#

UNICEF. (2019). *A world ready to learn: Prioritizing quality early childhood education* [Report]. Retrieved from https://data.unicef.org/resources/a-world-ready-to-learn-report/

UNICEF. (2019). *Immunization* [Fact sheet]. Retrieved from https://data.unicef.org/topic/child-health/immunization/

UNICEF. (2019). *Levels and trends in child mortality* [Report]. Retrieved from https://data.unicef.org/resources/levels-and-trends-in-child-mortality/

UNICEF. (2019). *Low birthweight* [Fact sheet]. Retrieved from https://data.unicef.org/topic/nutrition/low-birthweight/

UNICEF. (2019). *More women and children survive today than ever before* [Report]. Retrieved from www.unicef.org/press-releases/more-women-and-children-survive-today-ever-un-report

UNICEF. (2019). *The state of the world's children 2019: Children, food and nutrition* [Report]. Retrieved from https://data.unicef.org/resources/state-of-the-worlds-children-2019/

UNICEF. (2019). Under-five mortality [Data sheet]. Retrieved from https://data.unicef.org/topic/child-survival/under-five-mortality/

UNICEF. (2008). *State of the world's children 2009: Maternal and newborn health.* New York, NY: Author.

United Nations Educational, Scientific and Cultural Organization. (2017). Literacy rates continue to rise from one generation to the next. *Fact Sheet No. 45 FS/2017/LIT/45.*

United Nations. (2007). *World population ageing* [Report]. Retrieved from www.un.org/en/development/desa/population/publications/pdf/ageing/WorldPopulationAgeingReport2007.pdf

United Nations. (2017). *Old age: Responding to a rapidly aging population* [Article]. Retrieved from www.un.org/development/desa/dspd/wp-content/uploads/sites/22/2018/07/Chapter-IVOld-age-responding-to-a-rapidly-ageing.pdf

United Nations. (2018). *ICTs, LCDs and the SDGs: Achieving universal and affordable Internet in the least developed countries* [Report]. Retrieved from http://unohrlls.org/custom-content/uploads/2018/01/

United Nations. (2018). *United Nations demographic yearbook 2017* [Data report]. Retrieved from https://unstats.un.org/unsd/demographic-social/products/dyb/dyb_2017/

United Nations. (2019). *Ageing* [Fact sheet]. Retrieved from www.un.org/en/sections/issues-depth/ageing/

United Nations. (2019). *Living arrangements of older persons around the world* [Department of Economic and Social Affairs: Population Division report]. Retrieved from www.un.org/en/development/desa/population/publications/pdf/popfacts/PopFacts_2019-2.pdf

United, G. (2016). *Raising the children of the opioid epidemic: Solutions and support for grandfamilies* [Generations United report]. Retrieved from www.grandfamilies.org/Portals/0/2016%20State%20of%20 Grandfamilies%20Report%20FINAL.pdf

Uphoff, E., Cabieses, B., Pinart, M., Valdés, M., Antó, J. M., & Wright, J. (2015). A systematic review of socioeconomic position in relation to asthma and allergic diseases. *European Respiratory Journal, 46*(2), 364–374.

Uphold-Carrier, H., & Utz, R. (2012). Parental divorce among young and adult children: A long-term quantitative analysis of mental health and family solidarity. *Journal of Divorce & Remarriage, 53*(4), 247–266.

Upton-Davis, K. (2012). Living apart together relationships (LAT): Severing intimacy from obligation. *Gender Issues, 29*(1–4), 25–38.

Urry, H. L., & Gross, J. J. (2010). Emotion regulation in older age. *Current Directions in Psychological Science, 19*(6), 352–357.

U.S. Bureau of Labor Statistics (2019). *Employment characteristics of families summary* [News release]. Retrieved from https://www.bls.gov/news.release/famee.nr0.htm

U.S. Bureau of Labor Statistics. (2008, May 30). *Employment characteristics of families in 2007* [News release]. Washington, DC: U.S. Department of Labor.

U.S. Bureau of Labor Statistics. (2017). *Highlights of women's earnings in 2017* [Report]. Retrieved from www.bls.gov/opub/reports/womens-earnings/2017/pdf/home.pdf

U.S. Bureau of Labor Statistics. (2019). *Employment characteristics of families: 2018* [Economic news release]. Retrieved from www.bls.gov/news.release/famee.nr0.htm

U.S. Bureau of Labor Statistics. (2020). *Employment characteristics of families: 2019* [Economic news release]. Retrieved from https://www.bls.gov/news.release/pdf/famee.pdf

U.S. Census Bureau. (2019). *Historical living arrangements of children, Table CH-1. Living-arrangements of children under 18 years old: 1960 to present* [Data table]. Retrieved from www.census.gov/data/tables/time-series/demo/families/children.html

U.S. Census Bureau. (2007). *The population profile of the United States: Dynamic version.* Retrieved from www.census.gov/population/www/pop-profile/profiledynamic.html

U.S. Census Bureau. (2014). *10 percent of grandparents live with a grandchild* [News report]. Retrieved from www.census.gov/newsroom/press-releases/2014/cb14-194.html

U.S. Census Bureau. (2016). *America's families and living arrangements: 2016* [Data tables]. Retrieved from www.census.gov/data/tables/2016/demo/families/cps-2016.html

U.S. Census Bureau. (2018). *Characteristics of same-sex couple households, 2005 to present* [Data tables]. Retrieved from www.census.gov/data/tables/time-series/demo/same-sex-couples/ssc-house-characteristics.html

U.S. Census Bureau. (2018). Percent married among 18- to 34-year-olds: 1978 and 2018 [Census Library graph]. Retrieved from www.census.gov/library/visualizations/2018/comm/percent-married.html

U.S. Census Bureau. (2019). *Annual estimates of the resident population for selected age groups by sex for the United States, counties, and Puerto Rico Commonwealth and Municipios: April 1, 2010 to July 1, 2018* [Data tables]. Retrieved from https://factfinder.census.gov/faces/tableservices/jsf/pages/productview.xhtml?pid=PEP_2018_PEPAGESEX&prodType=table

U.S. Census Bureau. (2019). *Decennial Censuses, 1890 to 1940, and Current Population Survey. Annual Social and Economic Supplements, 1947 to 2019* [Graph]. Retrieved from www.census.gov/content/dam/Census/library/visualizations/time-series/demo/families-and-households/ms-2.pdf

U.S. Census Bureau. (2019). *Fertility of women in the United States: 2018* [Data tables]. Retrieved from www.census.gov/data/tables/2018/demo/fertility/women-fertility.html#par_list_58

U.S. Census Bureau. (2019). *U.S. Census Bureau releases CPS estimates of same-sex households* [Report]. Retrieved from www.census.gov/newsroom/press-releases/2019/same-sex-households.html

U.S. Census Bureau. (2020). *Historical marital status tables* [Data tables]. Retrieved from www.census.gov/data/tables/time-series/demo/families/marital.html

U.S. Census Bureau. (2020). *Quick facts, United States* [Data sheet]. Retrieved from www.census.gov/quickfacts/fact/table/US/PST045219#PST045219

U.S. Department of Agriculture. (2019). *Food security in the U.S.* [Fact sheet]. Retrieved from www.ers.usda.gov/topics/food-nutrition-assistance/food-security-in-the-us/key-statistics-graphics.aspx

U.S. Department of Education. (2017). *School discipline laws and regulation by category* [Interactive database]. Retrieved from https://safesupportivelearning.ed.gov

U.S. Department of Health & Human Services, Administration for Children and Families, Administration on Children, Youth, and Families, Children's Bureau. (2017). *Child maltreatment 2015.* Available from www.acf.hhs.gov/programs/cb/research-data-technology/statistics-research/child-maltreatment

U.S. Department of Health & Human Services, Administration on Children, Youth, and Families, Children's Bureau. (2019). *Child maltreatment 2017.* Available from www.acf.hhs.gov/sites/default/files/cb/cm2017.pdf

U.S. Department of Health and Human Services. (1999). *Mental health: A report of the surgeon general.* Rockville, MD: U.S. Department of Health and Human Services, Substance Abuse and Mental Health Services Administration, National Institutes of Health, National Institute of Mental Health.

U.S. Department of Health and Human Services. (2014). *Facts about bullying.* Retrieved from www.stopbullying.gov/media/facts/index.html

U.S. Department of Health and Human Services. (2018). *Physical activity guidelines for Americans,* 2nd ed. Washington, DC: U.S. Department of Health and Human Services.

U.S. Department of Health and Human Services. (2018). *Recommended Uniform Screening Panel.* Retrieved from www.hrsa.gov/advisory-committees/heritable-disorders/rusp/index.html

U.S. Department of Health and Human Services. (2019). *2018 profile of older Americans.* Administration for Community Living, Administration on Aging. Retrieved from https://acl.gov/sites/default/files/Aging%20and%20Disability%20in%20America/2018OlderAmericansProfile.pdf

U.S. Department of Health and Human Services. (2020). *Oral health* [Data report]. Retrieved from www.healthypeople.gov/2020/topics-objectives/topic/oral-health

U.S. Department of Health and Human Services. (2020). *Trends in teen pregnancy and childbearing* [Office of Adolescent Health report]. Retrieved from www.hhs.gov/ash/oah/adolescent-development/reproductive-health-and-teen-pregnancy/teen-pregnancy-and-childbearing/trends/index.html

U.S. Department of Justice Drug Intelligence Center. (2011). *The economic impact of illicit drug use on American society.* Retrieved from www.justice.gov/archive/ndic/pubs44/44731/44731p.pdf

U.S. Department of Labor, Bureau of Labor Statistics. (2013). Tabulations retrieved November 22, 2013, from www.bls.gov/cps/cpsaat07.htm.

U.S. Food and Drug Administration. (2016). *FDA Communication: FDA cautions about using testosterone products for low testosterone due to aging; requires labeling change to inform of possible increased risk of heart attack and stroke with use.* Retrieved from www.fda.gov/Drugs/DrugSafety/ucm436259.htm

U.S. Interagency Council on Homelessness. (2018). *Homelessness in America: Focus on families with children* [Report]. Retrieved from www.usich.gov/resources/uploads/asset_library/Homeslessness_in_America_Families_with_Children.pdf

U.S. Office of Personnel Management. (2019). *Paid parental leave for federal employees* [Memorandum]. Retrieved from www.chcoc.gov/content/paid-parental-leave-federal-employees

U.S. Preventive Services Task Force. (2006). Screening for speech and language delay in preschool children: Recommendation statement. *Pediatrics, 117,* 497–501. Uttal, D. H., Meadow, N. G., Tipton, E., Hand, L. L., Alden, A. R., Warren, C., & Newcombe, N. S. (2013). The malleability of spatial skills: A meta-analysis of training studies. *Psychological Bulletin, 139,* 352–402. doi:10.1037/a0028446

Vagi, K. J., Olsen, E. O. M., Basile, K. C., & Vivolo-Kantor, A. M. (2015). Teen dating violence (physical and sexual) among US high school students: Findings from the 2013 National Youth Risk Behavior Survey. *JAMA Pediatrics, 169*(5), 474–482.

Vagi, K. J., Rothman, E. F., Latzman, N. E., Tharp, A. T., Hall, D. M., & Breiding, M. J. (2013). Beyond correlates: A review of risk and protective factors for adolescent dating violence perpetration. *Journal of Youth and Adolescence, 42*(4), 633–649.

Vail, K. E., Rothschild, Z. K., Weise, D. R., Solomon, S., Pyszczynski, T., & Greenberg, J.

(2010). A terror management analysis of the psychological functions of religion. *Personality and Social Psychology Review, 14*(1), 84–94.

Vaillant-Molina, M., & Bahrick, L. E. (2012). The role of intersensory redundancy in the emergence of social referencing in 5½-month-old infants. *Developmental Psychology, 48*(1), 1.

Vaiserman, A. M. (2015). Epigenetic programming by early-life stress: Evidence from human populations. *Developmental Dynamics, 244*(3), 254–265.

Vaish, A., & Striano, T. (2004). Is visual reference necessary? Contributions of facial versus vocal cues in 12-month-olds' social referencing behavior. *Developmental Science, 7*(3), 261–269.

Valero, S., Daigre, C., Rodríguez-Cintas, L., Barral, C., Gomà-i-Freixanet, M., Ferrer, M., . . . Roncero, C. (2014). Neuroticism and impulsivity: their hierarchical organization in the personality characterization of drug-dependent patients from a decision tree learning perspective. *Comprehensive Psychiatry, 55*(5), 1227–1233.

Valkenburg, P. M., & Peter, J. (2008). Adolescents' identity experiments on the Internet: Consequences for social competence and self-concept unity. *Communication Research, 35*(2), 208–231.

Valkenburg, P. M., & Peter, J. (2009). Social consequences of the Internet for adolescents: A decade of research. *Current Directions in Psychological Science, 18*(1), 1–5.

Valtorta, N. K., Kanaan, M., Gilbody, S., Ronzi, S., & Hanratty, B. (2016). Loneliness and social isolation as risk factors for coronary heart disease and stroke: Systematic review and meta-analysis of longitudinal observational studies. *Heart, 102*(13), 1009–1016.

Van Cappellen, P., Toth-Gauthier, M., Saroglou, V., & Fredrickson, B. L. (2016). Religion and well-being: The mediating role of positive emotions. *Journal of Happiness Studies, 17*(2), 485–505.

Van Cauwenberghe, C., Van Broeckhoven, C., & Sleegers, K. (2016). The genetic landscape of Alzheimer disease: clinical implications and perspectives. *Genetics in Medicine, 18*(5), 421–430.

Van Cleave, J., Gortmaker, S. L., & Perrin, J. M. (2010). Dynamics of obesity and chronic health conditions among children and youth. *Journal of the American Medical Association, 303*(7), 623–630.

Van de Bongardt, D., Reitz, E., Sandfort, T., & Deković, M. (2015). A meta-analysis of the relations between three types of peer norms and adolescent sexual behavior. *Personality and Social Psychology Review, 19*(3), 203–234.

Van den Bergh, B. R., van den Heuvel, M. I., Lahti, M., Braeken, M., de Rooij, S. R., Entringer, S., . . . & Schwab, M. (2017). Prenatal developmental origins of behavior and mental health: The influence of maternal stress in pregnancy. *Neuroscience & Biobehavioral Reviews*.

Van den Eijnden, R. J., Meerkerk, G. J., Vermulst, A. A., Spijkerman, R., & Engels, R. C. (2008). Online communication, compulsive Internet use, and psychosocial well-being among adolescents: A longitudinal study. *Developmental Psychology, 44*(3), 655.

Van der Graaff, J., Branje, S., De Wied, M., Hawk, S., Van Lier, P., & Meeus, W. (2014). Perspective taking and empathic concern in adolescence: Gender differences in developmental changes. *Developmental Psychology, 50*(3), 881.

van der Heide, A., Deliens, L., Faisst, K., Nilstun, T., Norup, M., Paci, E., . . . van der Maas, P. J., on behalf of the EURELD consortium. (2003). End-of-life decision making in six European countries: Descriptive study. *Lancet, 362*, 345–350.

van der Heijden, K. B., Vermeulen, M. C., Donjacour, C. E., Gordijn, M. C., Hamburger, H. L., Meijer, A. M., . . . Weysen, T. (2018). Chronic sleep reduction is associated with academic achievement and study concentration in higher education students. *Journal of Sleep Research, 27*(2), 165–174.

van der Lee, J., Bakker, T. J., Duivenvoorden, H. J., & Dröes, R. M. (2014). Multivariate models of subjective caregiver burden in dementia: A systematic review. *Ageing Research Reviews, 15*, 76–93.

van der Stel, M., & Veenman, M. V. (2014). Metacognitive skills and intellectual ability of young adolescents: A longitudinal study from a developmental perspective. *European Journal of Psychology of Education, 29*(1), 117–137.

van der Wiel, R., Mulder, C. H., & Bailey, A. (2018). Pathways to commitment in living-apart-together relationships in the Netherlands: A study on satisfaction, alternatives, investments and social support. *Advances in Life Course Research, 36*, 13–22.

Van Geel, M., Vedder, P., & Tanilon, J. (2014). Relationship between peer victimization, cyberbullying, and suicide in children and adolescents: A meta-analysis. *JAMA Pediatrics, 168*(5), 435–442.

Van Goozen, S. H., & Fairchild, G. (2008). How can the study of biological processes help design new interventions for children with severe antisocial behavior? *Development and Psychopathology, 20*(3), 941–973.

Van Goozen, S., Fairchild, G., Snoek, H., & Harold, G. (2007). The evidence for a neurobiological model of childhood antisocial behavior. *Psychological Bulletin, 133*, 149–182.

Van Heemst, D. (2010). Insulin, IGF-1 and longevity. *Aging and Disease, 1*(2), 147.

van Hooren, S. A. H., Valentijn, S. A. M., Bosma, H., Ponds, R. W. H. M., van Boxtel, M. P. J., & Jolles, J. (2005). Relation between health status and cognitive functioning: A 6-year follow-up of the Maastricht Aging Study. *Journal of Gerontology: Psychological Sciences, 60B*, P57–P60.

Van Horn, N. L., & Street, M. (2019). *Night terrors*. Treasure Island, FL: StatPearls Publishing.

Van Humbeeck, L., Piers, R. D., Van Camp, S., Dillen, L., Verhaeghe, S. T., & Van Den Noortgate, N. J. (2013). Aged parents' experiences during a critical illness trajectory and after the death of an adult child: A review of the literature. *Palliative Medicine, 27*(7), 583–595.

Van IJzendoorn, M. H., & Kroonenberg, P. M. (1988). Cross-cultural patterns of attachment: A meta-analysis of the Strange Situation. *Child Development, 59*, 147–156.

Van IJzendoorn, M. H., & Sagi, A. (1999). Cross-cultural patterns of attachment: Universal and contextual dimensions. In J. Cassidy & P. R. Shaver (Eds.), *Handbook of attachment: Theory, research, and clinical applications* (pp. 713–734). New York, NY: Guilford Press.

Van IJzendoorn, M. H., Bakermans-Kranenburg, M. J., & Ebstein, R. P. (2011). Methylation matters in child development: Toward developmental behavioral epigenetics. *Child Development Perspectives, 5*(4), 305–310.

Van IJzendoorn, M. H., Schuengel, C., & Bakermans-Kranenburg, M. J. (1999). Disorganized attachment in early childhood: Meta-analysis of precursors, concomitants, and sequelae. *Development and Psychopathology, 11*, 225–250.

Van Lancker, W., & Parolin, Z. (2020). COVID-19, school closures, and child poverty: A social crisis in the making. *The Lancet Public Health, 5*(5), e243–e244.

Van Lier, P. A., Vitaro, F., Barker, E. D., Brendgen, M., Tremblay, R. E., & Boivin, M. (2012). Peer victimization, poor academic achievement, and the link between childhood externalizing and internalizing problems. *Child Development, 83*(5), 1775–1788.

Van Lieshout, C. F. M., Haselager, G. J. T., Riksen-Walraven, J. M., & van Aken, M. A. G. (1995, April). Personality development in middle childhood. In D. Hart (Chair), *The contribution of childhood personality to adolescent competence: Insights from longitudinal studies from three societies*. Symposium conducted at the biennial meeting of the Society for Research in Child Development, Indianapolis, IN.

Van Lommel, P. (2011). Near-death experiences: the experience of the self as real and not as an illusion. *Annals of the New York Academy of Sciences, 1234*(1), 19–28.

Van Ouytsel, J., Van Gool, E., Walrave, M., Ponnet, K., & Peeters, E. (2016). Exploring the role of social networking sites within adolescent romantic relationships and dating experiences. *Computers in Human Behavior, 55*, 76–86.

Van Ryzin, M. J., Stormshak, E. A., & Dishion, T. J. (2012). Engaging parents in the family checkup in middle school: Longitudinal effects on family conflict and problem behavior through the high school transition. *Journal of Adolescent Health, 50*(6), 627–633.

Van Solinge, H., & Henkens, K. (2008). Adjustment to and satisfaction with retirement: Two of a kind? *Psychology and Aging, 23*(2), 422.

Van Steenbergen, E. F., Kluwer, E. S., & Karney, B. R. (2011). Workload and the trajectory of marital satisfaction in newlyweds: Job satisfaction, gender, and parental status as moderators. *Journal of Family Psychology, 25*(3), 345.

Van Wagenen, A., Driskell, J., & Bradford, J. (2013). "I'm still raring to go": Successful aging among lesbian, gay, bisexual, and transgender older adults. *Journal of Aging Studies, 27*(1), 1–14.

Van Zalk, M. H. W., & Kerr, M. (2014). Developmental trajectories of prejudice and tolerance toward immigrants from early to late adolescence. *Journal of Youth and Adolescence, 43*(10), 1658-1671.

Van, P. (2001). Breaking the silence of African American women: Healing after pregnancy loss. *Health Care Women International, 22,* 229-243.

Vandell, D. L., & Bailey, M. D. (1992). Conflicts between siblings. In C. U. Shantz & W. W. Hartup (Eds.), *Conflict in child and adolescent development* (pp. 242-269). New York, NY: Cambridge University Press.

VanderLaan, D. P., Blanchard, R., Wood, H., Garzon, L. C., & Zucker, K. J. (2015). Birth weight and two possible types of maternal effects on male sexual orientation: A clinical study of children and adolescents referred to a Gender Identity Service. *Developmental Psychobiology, 57*(1), 25-34.

Vandewater, E. A., Ostrove, J. M., & Stewart, A. J. (1997). Predicting women's well-being in midlife: The importance of personality development and social role involvements. *Journal of Personality and Social Psychology, 72*(5), 1147.

Vandivere, S., Malm, K., & Radel, L. (2009). *Adoption USA: A chartbook based on the 2007 National Survey of Adoptive Parents.* Washington, DC: U.S. Department of Health and Human Services, Office of the Assistant Secretary for Planning and Evaluation.

Vandorpe, B., Vandendriessche, J., Vaeyens, R., Pion, J., Matthys, S., Lefevre, J., . . . Lenoir, M. (2012). Relationship between sports participation and the level of motor coordination in childhood: A longitudinal approach. *Journal of Science and Medicine in Sport, 15*(3), 220-225.

van't Veer, A. E., & Giner-Sorolla, R. (2016). Preregistration in social psychology—A discussion and suggested template. *Journal of Experimental Social Psychology, 67,* 2-12.

Varela, R. E., Vernberg, E. M., Sanchez-Sosa, J. J., Riveros, A., Mitchell, M., & Mashunkashey, J. (2004). Parenting style of Mexican, Mexican American, and Caucasian-non-Hispanic families: Social context and cultural influences. *Journal of Family Psychology, 18*(4), 651.

Varma, R., Vajaranant, T. S., Burkemper, B., Wu, S., Torres, M., Hsu, C., . . . McKean-Cowdin, R. (2016). Visual impairment and blindness in adults in the United States: Demographic and geographic variations from 2015 to 2050. *JAMA Ophthalmology, 134*(7), 802-809.

Vasilyeva, M., Huttenlocher, J., & Waterfall, H. (2006). Effects of language intervention on syntactic skill levels in preschoolers. *Developmental Psychology, 42,* 164-174.

Vaterlaus, J. M., Tulane, S., Porter, B. D., & Beckert, T. E. (2017). The perceived influence of media and technology on adolescent romantic relationships. *Journal of Adolescent Research.* doi: 10.1177/0743558417712611

Vaupel, J. W. (2010). Biodemography of human ageing. *Nature, 464*(7288), 536-542.

Vaupel, J. W., Carey, J. R., Christensen, K., Johnson, T. E., Yashin, A. I., Holm, N. V., . . . Curtsinger, J. W. (1998). Biodemographic trajectories of longevity. *Science, 280,* 855-860.

Veenstra, R., Lindenberg, S., Oldehinkel, A. J., De Winter, A. F., Verhulst, F. C., & Ormel, J. (2005). Bullying and victimization in elementary schools: A comparison of bullies, victims, bully/victims, and uninvolved preadolescents. *Developmental Psychology, 41,* 672-682.

Venetsanou, F., & Kambas, A. (2010). Environmental factors affecting preschoolers' motor development. *Early Childhood Education Journal, 37*(4), 319-327.

Venkatraman, A., Garg, N., & Kumar, N. (2015). Greater freedom of speech on Web 2.0 correlates with dominance of views linking vaccines to autism. *Vaccine, 33*(12), 1422-1425.

Ventola, C. L. (2016). Immunization in the United States: Recommendations, barriers, and measures to improve compliance: Part 1: Childhood vaccinations. *Pharmacy and Therapeutics, 41*(7), 426.

Ventura, A. K., & Worobey, J. (2013). Early influences on the development of food preferences. *Current Biology, 23*(9), R401-R408.

Verdery, A. M., Margolis, R., Zhou, Z., Chai, X., & Rittirong, J. (2019). Kinlessness around the world. *The Journals of Gerontology: Series B, 74*(8), 1394-1405.

Verdoni, L., Mazza, A., Gervasoni, A., Martelli, L., Ruggeri, M., Ciufredda, M., Bonanoni, E., & D'Antiga, L. (2020). An outbreak of severe Kawasaki-like disease at the Italian epicenter of the SARS-CoV-2 epidemic. *The Lancet.* https://doi.org/10.1016/S0140-6736(20)31103-X

Vereecken, C., & Maes, L. (2000). Eating habits, dental care and dieting. In C. Currie, K. Hurrelmann, W. Settertobulte, R. Smith, & J. Todd (Eds.), *Health and health behaviour among young people: A WHO cross-national study (HBSC) international report* (pp. 83-96). WHO Policy Series: Healthy Policy for Children and Adolescents, Series No. 1. Copenhagen, Denmark: World Health Organization Regional Office for Europe.

Verhulst, B., Neale, M. C., & Kendler, K. S. (2015). The heritability of alcohol use disorders: a meta-analysis of twin and adoption studies. *Psychological Medicine, 45*(5), 1061-1072.

Vernon-Feagans, L., Willoughby, M., & Garrett-Peters, P. (2016). Predictors of behavioral regulation in kindergarten: Household chaos, parenting, and early executive functions. *Developmental Psychology, 52*(3), 430.

Verschueren, K., Buyck, P., & Marcoen, A. (2001). Self-representations and socioemotional competence in young children: A 3-year longitudinal study. *Developmental Psychology, 37,* 126-134.

Verschueren, K., Marcoen, A., & Schoefs, V. (1996). The internal working model of the self, attachment, and competence in five-year-olds. *Child Development, 67,* 2493-2511.

Vespa, J. (2012). Union formation in later life: Economic determinants of cohabitation and remarriage among older adults. *Demography, 49*(3), 1103-1125.

Vespa, J. (2013). Relationship transitions among older cohabitors: The role of health, wealth, and family ties. *Journal of Marriage and Family, 75*(4), 933-949.

Viana, M. C., Gruber, M. J., Shahly, V., Alhamzawi, A., Alonso, J., Andrade, L. H., . . . Girolamo, G. D. (2013). Family burden related to mental and physical disorders in the world: Results from the WHO World Mental Health (WMH) surveys. *Revista Brasileira de Psiquiatria, 35*(2), 115-125.

Victor, J. L. (2015). Young people housing in Hong Kong: Why failure to launch? *Proceedings of the Korean Housing Association Conference,* 305-309.

Victora, C. G., Adair, L., Fall, C., Hallal, P. C., Martorell, R., Richter, L., . . . Maternal and Child Undernutrition Study Group. (2008). Maternal and child undernutrition: Consequences for adult health and human capital. *The Lancet, 371*(9609), 340-357.

Victora, M., Victora, C., & Barros, F. (1990). Cross-cultural differences in developmental rates: A comparison between British and Brazilian children. *Child: Care, Health and Development, 16,* 151-164

Vieno, A., Nation, M., Pastore, M., & Santinello, M. (2009). *Developmental Psychology, 45*(6), 1509-1519.

Vikraman, S., Fryar, C. D., & Ogden, C. L. (2015, September). Caloric intake from fast food among children and adolescents in the United States, 2011-2012. *NCHS Data Brief,* 1-8.

Vinden, P. G. (1999). Children's understanding of mind and emotion: A multi-culture study. *Cognition & Emotion, 13*(1), 19-48.

Vinkhuyzen, A. A., Van der Sluis, S., Posthuma, D., & Boomsma, D. I. (2009). The heritability of aptitude and exceptional talent across different domains in adolescents and young adults. *Behavior Genetics, 39*(4), 380-392.

Viola, T. W., Salum, G. A., Kluwe-Schiavon, B., Sanvicente-Vieira, B., Levandowski, M. L., & Grassi-Oliveira, R. (2016). The influence of geographical and economic factors in estimates of childhood abuse and neglect using the Childhood Trauma Questionnaire: A worldwide meta-regression analysis. *Child Abuse & Neglect, 51,* 1-11.

Virtala, P., Huotilainen, M., Partanen, E., Fellman, V., & Tervaniemi, M. (2013). Newborn infants' auditory system is sensitive to Western music chord categories. *Frontiers in Psychology, 4.*

Vita, A. J., Terry, R. B., Hubert, H. B., & Fries, J. F. (1998). Aging, health risk, and cumulative disability. *New England Journal of Medicine, 338,* 1035-1041.

Viteri, O. A., Soto, E. E., Bahado-Singh, R. O., Christensen, C. W., Chauhan, S. P., & Sibai, B. M. (2015). Fetal anomalies and long-term effects associated with substance abuse in pregnancy: A literature review. *American Journal of Perinatology, 32*(05), 405-416.

Vittrup, B., Snider, S., Rose, K. K., & Rippy, J. (2016). Parental perceptions of the role of media and technology in their young children's lives. *Journal of Early Childhood Research, 14,* 43-54.

Vlachou, M., Andreou, E., Botsoglou, K., & Didaskalou, E. (2011). Bully/victim problems among preschool children: A review of current research evidence. *Educational Psychology Review, 23*(3), 329.

Vlad, S. C., Miller, D. R., Kowall, N. W., & Felson, D. T. (2008). Protective effects of NSAIDs on the development of Alzheimer disease. *Neurology, 70,* 1672-1677.

Vliegen, N., Casalin, S., & Luyten, P. (2014). The course of postpartum depression: A review of longitudinal studies. *Harvard Review of Psychiatry, 22,* 1-22.

Vocks, S., Tuschen-Caffier, B., Pietrowsky, R., Rustenbach, S. J., Kersting, A., & Herpertz, S. (2010). Meta-analysis of the effectiveness of psychological and pharmacological treatments for binge eating disorder. *International Journal of Eating Disorders, 43*(3), 205-217.

Voegtline, K. M., Costigan, K. A., Pater, H. A., & DiPietro, J. A. (2013). Near-term fetal response to maternal spoken voice. *Infant Behavior and Development, 36*(4), 526-533.

Vogl, K., & Preckel, F. (2014). Full-time ability grouping of gifted students: Impacts on social self-concept and school-related attitudes. *Gifted Child Quarterly, 58*(1), 51-68.

Vohr, B. R., Wright, L. L., Poole, K., & McDonald, S. A., for the NICHD Neonatal Research Network Follow-up Study. (2005). Neurodevelopmental outcomes of extremely low birth weight infants<30 weeks' gestation between 1993 and 1998. *Pediatrics, 116,* 635-643.

Volgsten, H., Jansson, C., Svanberg, A. S., Darj, E., & Stavreus-Evers, A. (2018). Longitudinal study of emotional experiences, grief and depressive symptoms in women and men after miscarriage. *Midwifery, 64,* 23-28.

Volkow, N. D., Baler, R. D., Compton, W. M., & Weiss, S. R. (2014). Adverse health effects of marijuana use. *New England Journal of Medicine, 370*(23), 2219-2227.

Volling, B. L., Kennedy, D. E., & Jackey, L. M. (2010). The development of sibling jealousy. In S. L. Hart & M. Legerstee (Eds.), *Handbook of jealousy: Theory, research, and multidisciplinary approaches* (pp. 387-4317). Chicester, England: Blackwell Publishing.

Volling, B. L., Mahoney, A., & Rauer, A. J. (2009). Sanctification of parenting, moral socialization, and young children's conscience development. *Psychology of Religion and Spirituality, 1*(1), 53.

Von dem Knesebeck, O., Verde, P. E., & Dragano, N. (2006). Education and health in 22 European countries. *Social Science & Medicine, 63*(5), 1344-1351.

von Gontard, A., Heron, J., & Joinson, C. (2011). Family history of nocturnal enuresis and urinary incontinence: results from a large epidemiological study. *The Journal of Urology, 185*(6), 2303-2307.

von Hofsten, C. (2004). An action perspective on motor development. *Cognitive Sciences, 8*(1), 266-272.

Vondra, J. I., & Barnett, D. (1999). A typical attachment in infancy and early childhood among children at developmental risk. *Monographs of the Society for Research in Child Development, 64*(3, Serial No. 258).

Voorveld, H.A.M. & van der Goot, M. (2013). Age differences in media multitasking: A diary study. *Journal of Broadcasting & Electronic Media,* 57, 392-408.

Voss, M. W., Prakash, R. S., Erickson, K. I., Basak, C., Chaddock, L., Kim, J. S., . . . & Wójcicki, T. R. (2010). Plasticity of brain networks in a randomized intervention trial of exercise training in older adults. *Frontiers in Aging Neuroscience, 2.*

Voss, W., Jungmann, T., Wachtendorf, M., & Neubauer, A. P. (2012). Long-term cognitive outcomes of extremely low-birth-weight infants: The influence of the maternal educational background. *Acta Paediatrica, 101*(6), 569-573.

Votruba-Drzal, E., Li-Grining, C. R., & Maldonado-Carreno, C. (2008). A developmental perspective on full-versus part-day kindergarten and children's academic trajectories through fifth grade. *Child Development, 79,* 957-978.

Voydanoff, P. (2004). The effects of work demands and resources on work-to-family conflict and facilitation. *Journal of Marriage and Family, 66,* 398-412.

Voyer, D., & Voyer, S. D. (2014). Gender differences in scholastic achievement: A meta-analysis. *Psychological Bulletin, 140*(4), 1174.

Vozikaki, M., Linardakis, M., Micheli, K., & Philalithis, A. (2017). Activity participation and well-being among European adults aged 65 years and older. *Social Indicators Research, 131*(2), 769-795.

Vu, T., Liu, T., Garside, D. B., & Daviglus, M. L. (2009). Unhealthy lifestyle choices in older age and subsequent health-related quality of life: The Chicago Heart Association Detection Project. *Circulation, 120,* S482-S483.

Vygotsky, L. S. (1962). *Thought and language.* Cambridge, MA: MIT Press. (Original work published 1934)

Vygotsky, L. S. (1978). *Mind in society: The development of higher psychological processes.* Cambridge, MA: Harvard University Press.

Véronneau, M. H., & Dishion, T. J. (2011). Middle school friendships and academic achievement in early adolescence: A longitudinal analysis. *The Journal of Early Adolescence, 31*(1), 99-124.

Véronneau, M. H., Vitaro, F., Brendgen, M., Dishion, T. J., & Tremblay, R. E. (2010). Transactional analysis of the reciprocal links between peer experiences and academic achievement from middle childhood to early adolescence. *Developmental Psychology, 46*(4), 773.

Waggoner, L. W. (2015). With marriage on the decline and cohabitation on the rise, what about marital rights for unmarried partners? University of Michigan Public Law Research Paper No. 477.

Waggoner, L. W. (2016). Marriage is on the decline and cohabitation is on the rise: At what point, if ever, should unmarried partners acquire marital rights? *Family Law Quarterly, 50*(2), 215.

Wagle, K. C., Carrejo, M. H., & Tan, R. S. (2012). The implications of increasing age on erectile dysfunction. *American Journal of Men's Health, 6*(4), 273-279.

Wagner, J., Lüdtke, O., & Robitzsch, A. (2019). Does personality become more stable with age? Disentangling state and trait effects for the big five across the life span using local structural equation modeling. *Journal of Personality and Social Psychology.*

Wahrendorf, M., & Siegrist, J. (2010). Are changes in productive activities of older people associated with changes in their well-being? Results of a longitudinal European study. *European Journal of Ageing, 7*(2), 59-68.

Wahrendorf, M., Blane, D., Matthews, K., & Siegrist, J. (2016). Linking quality of work in midlife to volunteering during retirement: A European study. *Journal of Population Ageing, 9*(1-2), 113-130.

Wainright, J. L., & Patterson, C. J. (2006). Delinquency, victimization, and substance use among adolescents with female same-sex parents. *Journal of Family Psychology, 20*(3), 526.

Wainright, J. L., Russell, S. T., & Patterson, C. J. (2004). Psychosocial adjustment, school outcomes, and romantic relationships of adolescents with same-sex parents. *Child Development, 75,* 1886-1898.

Waite, L. J., Luo, Y., & Lewin, A. C. (2009). Marital happiness and marital stability: Consequences for psychological well-being. *Social Science Research, 38*(1), 201-212.

Waldfogel, J., Craigie, T. A., & Brooks-Gunn, J. (2010). Fragile families and child wellbeing. *The Future of Children/Center for the Future of Children, the David and Lucile Packard Foundation, 20*(2), 87.

Waldrop, D. P. (2011). Denying and defying death: The culture of dying in 21st century America. *The Gerontologist, 51,* 571-576.

Walen, H. R., & Lachman, M. E. (2000). Social support and strain from partner, family, and friends: Costs and benefits for men and women in adulthood. *Journal of Social and Personal Relationships, 17*(1), 5-30.

Walk, R. D., & Gibson, E. J. (1961). A comparative and analytical study of visual depth perception. *Psychology Monographs, 75*(15).

Walker, A. J., Allen, K. R., & Connidis, I. A. (2005). Theorizing and studying sibling ties in adulthood. *Sourcebook of Family Theory and Research,* 167-190.

Walker, C. M., Walker, L. B., & Ganea, P. A. (2013). The role of symbol-based experience in early learning and transfer from pictures: Evidence from Tanzania. *Developmental Psychology, 49*(7), 1315.

Walker, R. E., Keane, C. R., & Burke, J. G. (2010). Disparities and access to healthy food in the United States: A review of food deserts literature. *Health & Place, 16*(5), 876-884.

Walker, T. Y., Elam-Evans, L. D., Yankey, D., Markowitz, L. E., Williams, C. L., Fredua, B., . . . Stokley, S. (2019). National, regional, state, and selected local area vaccination coverage among adolescents aged 13-17 years—United States, 2018. *Morbidity and Mortality Weekly Report, 68*(33), 718.

Walker, W. R., Skowronski, J. J., & Thompson, C. P. (2003). Life is pleasant—And memory helps to keep it that way! *Review of General Psychology, 7,* 203-210.

Wallentin, M. (2009). Putative sex differences in verbal abilities and language cortex: A critical review. *Brain and Language, 108*(3), 175-183.

Wallis, C. (2011). Performing gender: A content analysis of gender display in music videos. *Sex Roles, 64*(3-4), 160-172.

Wallis, C. J. D., Lo, K., Lee, Y., Krakowsky, Y., Garbens, A., Satkunasivam, R., . . . Nam, R.K. (2016). Survival and cardiovascular events in men treated with testosterone replacement therapy: An intention-to-treat observational cohort study. *The Lancet Diabetes & Endocrinology*, 4, 498-506.

Walpole, M. (2003). Socioeconomic status and college: How SES affects college experiences and outcomes. *The Review of Higher Education, 27*(1), 45-73.

Wan, H. C., Downey, L. A., & Stough, C. (2014). Understanding non-work presenteeism: Relationships between emotional intelligence, boredom, procrastination and job stress. *Personality and Individual Differences, 65*, 86-90.

Wang, C. T. L., & Schofer, E. (2018). Coming out of the penumbras: World culture and cross-national variation in divorce rates. *Social Forces, 97*(2), 675-704.

Wang, D. D., Leung, C. W., Li, Y., Ding, E. L., Chiuve, S. E., Hu, F. B., & Willett, W. C. (2014). Trends in dietary quality among adults in the United States, 1999 through 2010. *JAMA Internal Medicine, 174*(10), 1587-1595.

Wang, D., & MacMillan, T. (2013). The benefits of gardening for older adults: A systematic review of the literature. *Activities, Adaptation & Aging, 37*(2), 153-181.

Wang, J., Tan, L., Wang, H. F., Tan, C. C., Meng, X. F., Wang, C., . . . Yu, J. T. (2015). Anti-inflammatory drugs and risk of Alzheimer's disease: An updated systematic review and meta-analysis. *Journal of Alzheimer's Disease, 44*(2), 385-396.

Wang, L., Wang, X., Wang, W., Chen, C., Ronnennberg, A. G., Guang, W., . . . Xu, X. (2004). Stress and dysmenorrhea: A population-based prospective study. *Occupational and Environmental Medicine, 61*, 1021-1026.

Wang, M. (2007). Profiling retirees in the retirement transition and adjustment process: Examining the longitudinal change patterns of retirees' psychological well-being. *Journal of Applied Psychology, 92*(2), 455.

Wang, M. T., & Degol, J. L. (2017). Gender gap in science, technology, engineering, and mathematics (STEM): Current knowledge, implications for practice, policy, and future directions. *Educational Psychology Review, 29*(1), 119-140.

Wang, M. T., Eccles, J. S., & Kenny, S. (2013). Not lack of ability but more choice: Individual and gender differences in choice of careers in science, technology, engineering, and mathematics. *Psychological Science, 24*(5), 770-775.

Wang, M., & Shi, J. (2014). Psychological research on retirement. *Annual Review of Psychology, 65*, 209-233.

Wang, M., Henkens, K., & van Solinge, H. (2011). Retirement adjustment: A review of theoretical and empirical advancements. *American Psychologist, 66*(3), 204.

Wang, Q. (2004). The emergence of cultural self-constructs: Autobiographical memory and self-description in European American and Chinese children. *Developmental Psychology, 40*(1), 3.

Wang, S. S., Zhang, Z., Zhu, T. B., Chu, S. F., He, W. B., & Chen, N. H. (2018). Myelin injury in the central nervous system and Alzheimer's diseases. *Brain Research Bulletin.*

Wang, W., & Parker, K. C. (2014). *Record share of Americans have never married: As values, economics and gender patterns change.* Washington, DC: Pew Research Center, Social & Demographic Trends Project.

Wang, Y. (2002). Is obesity associated with early sexual maturation? A comparison of the association in American boys versus girls. *Pediatrics, 110*(5), 903-910.

Wang, Y., & Lim, H. (2012). The global childhood obesity epidemic and the association between socio-economic status and childhood obesity. *International Review of Psychiatry, 24*(3), 176-188.

Wang, Y., Jiao, Y., Nie, J., O'Neil, A., Huang, W., Zhang, L., . . . Woodward, M. (2020). Sex differences in the association between marital status and the risk of cardiovascular, cancer, and all-cause mortality: A systematic review and meta-analysis of 7,881,040 individuals. *Global Health Research and Policy, 5*(1), 1-16.

Wardle, J., Carnell, S., Haworth, C. M., & Plomin, R. (2008). Evidence for a strong genetic influence on childhood adiposity despite the force of the obesogenic environment. *The American Journal of Clinical Nutrition, 87*(2), 398-404.

Ware, J. J., & Munafò, M. R. (2015). Genetics of smoking behaviour. In *The Neurobiology and Genetics of Nicotine and Tobacco* (pp. 19-36). New York, NY: Springer International Publishing.

Warneken, F., & Tomasello, M. (2006). Altruistic helping in human infants and young chimpanzees. *Science, 311*, 1301-1303.

Warneken, F., & Tomasello, M. (2008). Extrinsic rewards undermine altruistic tendencies in 20-month-olds. *Developmental Psychology, 44*, 1785-1788.

Warraich, H. J., & Califf, R. M. (2019). Differences in health outcomes between men and women: Biological, behavioral, and societal factors. *Clinical Chemistry, 65*(1), 19-23.

Warren, J. R., & Lee, J. C. (2003). The impact of adolescent employment on high school drop-out: Differences by individual and labor-market characteristics. *Social Science Research, 32*(1), 98-128.

Warshak, R. A. (2014). Social science and parenting plans for young children: A consensus report. *Psychology, Public Policy, and Law, 20*(1), 46.

Wasik, B. H., Ramey, C. T., Bryant, D. M., & Sparling, J. J. (1990). A longitudinal study of two early intervention strategies: Project CARE. *Child Development, 61,* 1682-1696.

Wass, S., Porayska-Pomsta, K., & Johnson, M. (2011). Training attentional control in infancy. *Current Biology.* doi:10.1016/j.cub.2011.08.00

Watamura, S. E., Donzella, B., Alwin, J., & Gunnar, M. R. (2003). Morning-to-afternoon increases in cortisol concentrations for infants and toddlers at child care: Age differences and behavioral correlates. *Child Development, 74*, 1006-1020.

Waters, E., & Deane, K. E. (1985). Defining and assessing individual differences in attachment relationships: Q-methodology and the organization of behavior in infancy and early childhood. *Monographs of the Society for Research in Child Development*, 41-65.

Watkins, D., Akande, A., Fleming, J., Ismail, M., Lefner, K., Murani, R., . . . Wondimu, H. (1998). Cultural dimensions, gender, and the nature of self-concept: A fourteen-country study. *International Journal of Psychology, 33*(1), 17-31.

Watson, A. C., Nixon, C. L., Wilson, A., & Capage, L. (1999). Social interaction skills and theory of mind in young children. *Developmental Psychology, 35*(2), 386-391.

Watson, J. B., & Rayner, R. (1920). Conditioned emotional reactions. *Journal of Experimental Psychology, 3*, 1-14.

Watson, K. B., Carlson, S. A., Gunn, J. P., Galuska, D. A., O'Connor, A., Greenlund, K. J., & Fulton, J. E. (2016). Physical inactivity among adults aged 50 years and older—United States, 2014. *Morbidity and Mortality Weekly Report, 65*(36), 954-958.

Watson, K., Handal, B., Maher, M., & McGinty, E. (2013). Globalising the class size debate: Myths and realities. *Journal of International and Comparative Education*, 72-85.

Waugh, W. E., & Brownell, C. A. (2015). Development of body-part vocabulary in toddlers in relation to self-understanding. *Early Child Development and Care, 185*(7), 1166-1179.

Waxman, S., Fu, X., Arunachalam, S., Leddon, E., Geraghty, K., & Song, H. J. (2013). Are nouns learned before verbs? Infants provide insight into a long-standing debate. *Child Development Perspectives, 7*(3), 155-159.

Wayne, J., Musisca, N., & Fleeson, W. (2004). Considering the role of personality in the work-family experience: Relationships of the big five to work–family conflict and facilitation. *Journal of Vocational Behavior, 64*(1), 108-130.

Weaver, J. M., & Schofield, T. J. (2015). Mediation and moderation of divorce effects on children's behavior problems. *Journal of Family Psychology, 29*(1), 39.

Weber, A., Fernald, A., & Diop, Y. (2017). When cultural norms discourage talking to babies: Effectiveness of a parenting program in rural Senegal. *Child Development.* doi:10.1111/cdev.12882

Weber, S., Jud, A., & Landolt, M. A. (2016). Quality of life in maltreated children and adult survivors of child maltreatment: a systematic review. *Quality of Life Research, 25*(2), 237-255.

Weber, S. R., Pargament, K. I., Kunik, M. E., Lomax, J. W., & Stanley, M. A. (2012). Psychological distress among religious nonbelievers: A systematic review. *Journal of Religion and Health, 51*(1), 72-86.

Weeden, K. A., Cha, Y., & Bucca, M. (2016). Long work hours, part-time work, and trends in the gender gap in pay, the motherhood wage penalty, and the fatherhood wage premium.

RSF: The Russell Sage Foundation Journal of the Social Sciences, 2(4), 71-102.

Wei, Y., Schatten, H., & Sun, Q. Y. (2015). Environmental epigenetic inheritance through gametes and implications for human reproduction. *Human Reproduction Update, 21*(2), 194-208.

Weinberg, M. K., Tronick, E. Z., Cohn, J. F., & Olson, K. L. (1999). Gender differences in emotional expressivity and self-regulation during early infancy. *Developmental Psychology, 35*(1), 175.

Weinmayr, G., Forastiere, F., Büchele, G., Jaensch, A., Strachan, D. P., Nagel, G., & ISAAC Phase Two Study Group. (2014). Overweight/obesity and respiratory and allergic disease in children: International study of asthma and allergies in childhood (ISAAC) phase two. *PloS One, 9*(12), e113996.

Weinstock, H., Berman, S., & Cates, W., Jr. (2004). Sexually transmitted diseases among American youth: Incidence and prevalence estimates, 2000. *Perspectives on Sexual and Reproductive Health, 36*, 6-10.

Weisberg, D. S., Hirsh-Pasek, K., Golinkoff, R. M., Kittredge, A. K., & Klahr, D. (2016). Guided play: Principles and practices. *Current Directions in Psychological Science, 25*(3), 177-182.

Weisberg, D. S., Sobel, D. M., Goodstein, J., & Bloom, P. (2013). Young children are reality-prone when thinking about stories. *Journal of Cognition and Culture, 13*(3-4), 383-407.

Weisgram, E. S., Fulcher, M., & Dinella, L. M. (2014). Pink gives girls permission: Exploring the roles of explicit gender labels and gender-typed colors on preschool children's toy preferences. *Journal of Applied Developmental Psychology, 35*(5), 401-409.

Weisleder, A., & Fernald, A. (2013). Talking to children matters: Early language experience strengthens processing and builds vocabulary. *Psychological Science, 24*(11), 2143-2152.

Weisner, T. S. (1993). Ethnographic and ecocultural perspectives on sibling relationships. In Z. Stoneman & P. W. Berman (Eds.), *The effects of mental retardation, visibility, and illness on sibling relationships* (pp. 51-83). Baltimore, MD: Brooks.

Weisner, T. S., Gallimore, R., Bacon, M. K., Barry III, H., Bell, C., Novaes, S. C., . . . Koel, A. (1977). My brother's keeper: Child and sibling caretaking [and comments and reply]. *Current Anthropology, 18*(2), 169-190.

Weiss, A., Bates, T. C., & Luciano, M. (2008). Happiness is a personal (ity) thing. The genetics of personality and well-being in a representative sample. *Psychological Science, 19*, 205-210.

Weisz, J. R., Weiss, B., Han, S. S., Granger, D. A., & Morton, T. (1995). Effects of psychotherapy with children and adolescents revisited: A meta-analysis of treatment outcome studies. *Psychological Bulletin, 117*(3), 450-468.

Weitzman, L. J., Eifler, D., Hokada, E., & Ross, C. (1972). Sex-role socialization in picture books for preschool children. *American Journal of Sociology, 77*(6), 1125-1150.

Wellman, H. M. (2014). *Making minds: How theory of mind develops.* Oxford, England: Oxford University Press.

Wellman, H. M., Fang, F., Liu, D., Zhu, L., & Liu, G. (2006). Scaling of theory-of-mind understandings in Chinese children. *Psychological Science, 17*(12), 1075-1081.

Wellman, H. M., Lopez-Duran, S., LaBounty, J., & Hamilton, B. (2008). Infant attention to intentional action predicts preschool theory of mind. *Developmental Psychology, 44,* 618-623.

Wen, X., Wen, S. W., Fleming, N., Demissie, K., Rhoads, G. G., & Walker, M. (2007). Teenage pregnancy and adverse birth outcomes: A large population based retrospective cohort study. *International Journal of Epidemiology, 36*(2), 368-373.

Wendelken, C., Baym, C. L., Gazzaley, A., & Bunge, S. A. (2011). Neural indices of improved attentional modulation over middle childhood. *Developmental Cognitive Neuroscience, 1*(2), 175-186.

Wenger, G. C., Dykstra, P. A., Melkas, T., & Knipscheer, K. C. (2007). Social embeddedness and late-life parenthood: Community activity, close ties, and support networks. *Journal of Family Issues, 28*(11), 1419-1456.

Wentworth, N., Benson, J. B., & Haith, M. M. (2000). The development of infants' reaches for stationary and moving targets. *Child Development, 71,* 576-601.

Wentzel, K. R. (2017). Peer relationships, motivation, and academic performance at school. In A. J. Elliot, C. S. Dweck, & D. S. Yeager (Eds.), *Handbook of competence and motivation: Theory and application* (pp. 586-603). New York, NY: The Guilford Press.

Wentzel, K. R., & Muenks, K. (2016). Peer influence on students' motivation, academic achievement, and social behavior. In K. R. Wentzel & G. B. Ramani (Eds.). *Handbook of social influences in school contexts: Social-emotional, motivation, and cognitive outcomes* (pp. 13-30). New York, NY: Routledge.

Werker, J. F., Yeung, H. H., & Yoshida, K. A. (2012). How do infants become experts at native-speech perception? *Current Directions in Psychological Science, 21*(4), 221-226.

Wermke, K., Teiser, J., Yovsi, E., Kohlenberg, P. J., Wermke, P., Robb, M., . . . Lamm, B. (2016). Fundamental frequency variation within neonatal crying: Does ambient language matter? *Speech, Language and Hearing, 19*(4), 211-217.

Werner, E. E. (1993). Risk and resilience in individuals with learning disabilities: Lessons learned from the Kauai longitudinal study. *Learning Disabilities Research and Practice, 8,* 28-34.

Westen, D. (1998). The scientific legacy of Sigmund Freud: Toward a psychodynamically informed psychological science. *Psychological Bulletin, 124,* 333-371.

Westerhof, G. J., & Barrett, A. E. (2005). Age identity and subjective well-being: A comparison of the United States and Germany. *The Journals of Gerontology Series B: Psychological Sciences and Social Sciences, 60*(3), S129-S136.

Westerhof, G. J., & Bohlmeijer, E. T. (2014). Celebrating fifty years of research and applications in reminiscence and life review: State of the art and new directions. *Journal of Aging Studies, 29,* 107-114.

Westerhof, G. J., Barrett, A. E., & Steverink, N. (2003). Forever young? A comparison of age identities in the United States and Germany. *Research on Aging, 25*(4), 366-383.

Westling, E., Andrews, J. A., Hampson, S. E., & Peterson, M. (2008). Pubertal timing and substance use: The effects of gender, parental monitoring and deviant peers. *Journal of Adolescent Health, 42*(6), 555-563.

Weststrate, N. M., & Glück, J. (2017). Hard-earned wisdom: Exploratory processing of difficult life experience is positively associated with wisdom. *Developmental Psychology, 53*(4), 800.

Wethington, E. (2000). Expecting stress: Americans and the "midlife crisis." *Motivation and Emotion, 24*(2), 85-103.

Wethington, E., Kessler, R. C., & Pixley, J. E. (2004). Turning points in adulthood. In O. G. Brim, C. D. Ryff & R. C. Kessler (Eds.), *How healthy are we? A national study of well-being at midlife* (pp. 586-613). Chicago, IL: University of Chicago Press.

Wexler, I. D., Branski, D., & Kerem, E. (2006). War and children. *Journal of the American Medical Association, 296,* 579-581.

Wheaton, A. G., Jones, S. E., Cooper, A. C., & Croft, J. B. (2018). Short sleep duration among middle school and high school students—United States, 2015. *Morbidity and Mortality Weekly Report, 67*(3), 85.

Whisman, M. A., Robustelli, B. L., & Labrecque, L. T. (2018). Specificity of the association between marital discord and longitudinal changes in symptoms of depression and generalized anxiety disorder in the Irish longitudinal study on ageing. *Family Process, 57*(3), 649-661.

Whitbourne, S. K. (1996). Psychosocial perspectives on emotions: The role of identity in the aging process. In C. Magai & S. H. McFadden (Eds.), *Handbook of emotion, adult development, and aging* (pp. 83-98). Cambridge, MA: Academic Press.

Whitbourne, S. K. (2001). The physical aging process in midlife: Interactions with psychological and sociocultural factors. In M. E. Lachman (Ed.), *Handbook of midlife development* (pp. 109-155). New York, NY: Wiley.

White, L. (2001). Sibling relationships over the life course: A panel analysis. *Journal of Marriage and Family, 63*(2), 555-568.

White, R. (2002). Indigenous young Australians, criminal justice and offensive language. *Journal of Youth Studies, 5*(1), 21-34.

Whitebread, D., Coltman, P., Pasternak, D. P., Sangster, C., Grau, V., Bingham, S., . . . Demetriou, D. (2009). The development of two observational tools for assessing metacognition and self-regulated learning in young children. *Metacognition and Learning, 4*(1), 63-85.

Whitehurst, G. J., & Lonigan, C. J. (1998). Child development and emergent literacy. *Child Development, 69,* 848-872.

Whitehurst, G. J., & Lonigan, C. J. (2001). Emergent literacy: Development from prereaders to readers. In S. B. Neuman & D. K. Dickinson (Eds.), *Handbook of early literacy research* (pp. 11-29). New York, NY: Guilford Press.

Whitmer, R. A., Quesenberry, C. P., Zhou, J., & Yaffe, K. (2011). Timing of hormone therapy and dementia: the critical window theory revisited. *Annals of Neurology, 69*(1), 163-169.

Whitmire, R. (2020, May). Due to COVID-19, thousands of low-income students are deferring and dropping college plans. *The Hill*. Retrieved from https://thehill.com/opinion/education/498231-due-to-covid-19-thousands-of-low-income-students-are-deferring-and-dropping

Whitney, P., Hinson, J. M., Satterfield, B. C., Grant, D. A., Honn, K. A., & Van Dongen, H. P. (2017). Sleep deprivation diminishes attentional control effectiveness and impairs flexible adaptation to changing conditions. *Scientific Reports, 7*(1), 1-9.

Whittington, J. R., Simmons, P. M., Phillips, A. M., Gammill, S. K., Cen, R., Magann, E. F., & Cardenas, V. M. (2018). The use of electronic cigarettes in pregnancy: A review of the literature. *Obstetrical & Gynecological Survey, 73*(9), 544-549.

Whitty, M. T. (2003). Pushing the wrong buttons: Men's and women's attitudes toward online and offline infidelity. *CyberPsychology & Behavior, 6*(6), 569-579.

WHO Multicentre Growth Reference Study Group & de Onis, M. (2006). Assessment of sex differences and heterogeneity in motor milestone attainment among populations in the WHO Multicentre Growth Reference Study. *Acta Paediatrica, 95*, 66-75.

Whyte, J. C., & Bull, R. (2008). Number games, magnitude representation, and basic number skills in preschoolers. *Developmental Psychology, 44*(2), 588.

Wichstrøm, L., & von Soest, T. (2016). Reciprocal relations between body satisfaction and self-esteem: A large 13-year prospective study of adolescents. *Journal of Adolescence, 47*, 16-27.

Widen, S. C., & Russell, J. A. (2008). Children acquire emotion categories gradually. *Cognitive Development, 23*(2), 291-312.

Widman, L., Choukas-Bradley, S., Helms, S. W., & Prinstein, M. J. (2016). Adolescent susceptibility to peer influence in sexual situations. *Journal of Adolescent Health, 58*(3), 323-329.

Widom, C. S. (2017). Long-term impact of childhood abuse and neglect on crime and violence. *Clinical Psychology: Science and Practice, 24*(2), 186-202.

Wiesmann, C. G., Schreiber, J., Singer, T., Steinbeis, N., & Friederici, A. D. (2017). White matter maturation is associated with the emergence of theory of mind in early childhood. *Nature Communications, 8*, 14692.

Wight, R. G., LeBlanc, A. J., & Lee Badgett, M. V. (2013). Same-sex legal marriage and psychological well-being: Findings from the California Health Interview Survey. *American Journal of Public Health, 103*(2), 339-346.

Wijngaards-de Meij, L., Stroebe, M., Schut, H., Stroebe, W., van den Bout, J., van der Heijden, P., & Dijkstra, I. (2005). Couples at risk following the death of their child: Predictors of grief versus depression. *Journal of Consulting and Clinical Psychology, 73*(4), 617.

Wikoff, D., Welsh, B. T., Henderson, R., Brorby, G. P., Britt, J., Myers, E., . . . Tenenbein, M. (2017). Systematic review of the potential adverse effects of caffeine consumption in healthy adults, pregnant women, adolescents, and children. *Food and Chemical Toxicology, 109*, 585-648.

Wilcox, B., & DeRose, L. (2017). *In Europe, cohabitation is stable, right? The Brookings Institute* [News memo]. Retrieved from www.brookings.edu/blog/social-mobility-memos/2017/03/27/in-europe-cohabitation-is-stable-right/

Wilcox, W. B., & Nock, S. L. (2006). What's love got to do with it? Equality, equity, commitment and women's marital quality. *Social Forces, 84*, 1321-1345.

Wilder, S. (2014). Effects of parental involvement on academic achievement: A meta-synthesis. *Educational Review, 66*(3), 377-397.

Wildsmith, E., Schelar, E., Peterson, K., & Manlove, J. (2010). *Sexually transmitted diseases among young adults: Prevalence, perceived risk and risk-taking behaviors* (2010-21). Retrieved from www.childtrends.org/Files/Child_Trends-2010_05_01_RB_STD.pdf

Willcox, B. J., Donlon, T. A., He, Q., Chen, R., Grove, J. S., Yano, K., . . . Curb, J. D. (2008). FOXO3A genotype is strongly associated with human longevity. *Proceedings of the National Academy of Sciences of the United States of America, 105*(37), 13987-13992.

Williams, D. R. (2012). Miles to go before we sleep: Racial inequities in health. *Journal of Health and Social Behavior, 53*(3), 279-295.

Williams, D. R., Priest, N., & Anderson, N. B. (2016). Understanding associations among race, socioeconomic status, and health: Patterns and prospects. *Health Psychology, 35*(4), 407.

Williams, E. P., Mesidor, M., Winters, K., Dubbert, P. M., & Wyatt, S. B. (2015). Overweight and obesity: Prevalence, consequences, and causes of a growing public health problem. *Current Obesity Reports, 4*(3), 363-370.

Williams, K. (2004). The transition to widowhood and the social regulation of health: Consequences for health and health risk behavior. *Journal of Gerontology: Social Sciences, 59B*, S343-S349.

Williams, K., & Dunne-Bryant, A. (2006). Divorce and adult psychological well-being: Clarifying the role of gender and child age. *Journal of Marriage and Family, 68*, 1178-1196.

Williams, L. R., & Steinberg, L. (2011). Reciprocal relations between parenting and adjustment in a sample of juvenile offenders. *Child Development, 82*(2), 633-645.

Williams, P. D., & Williams, A. R. (1987). Denver Developmental Screening Test norms: A cross-cultural comparison. *Journal of Pediatric Psychology, 12*(1), 39-59.

Williams, S. T., Ontai, L. L., & Mastergeorge, A. M. (2010). The development of peer interaction in infancy: Exploring the dyadic processes. *Social Development, 19*(2), 348-368.

Willingham, D. T. (2004). Reframing the mind. *Education Next, 4*, 19-24.

Willis, S. L., & Schaie, K. W. (1999). Intellectual functioning in midlife. In S. L. Willis & J. D.

Reid (Eds.), *Life in the middle: Psychological and social development in middle age* (pp. 233-247). San Diego, CA: Academic Press.

Willis, S. L., & Schaie, K. W. (2005). Cognitive trajectories in midlife and cognitive functioning in old age. In S. L. Willis & M. Martin (Eds.), *Middle adulthood: A lifespan perspective* (pp. 243-276). Thousand Oaks, CA: Sage.

Willis, S. L., & Schaie, K. W. (2006). Cognitive functioning in the baby boomers: Longitudinal and cohort effects. In S. K. Whitbourne & S. L. Willis (Eds.), *The baby boomers grow up: Contemporary perspectives on midlife* (pp. 205-234). Mahwah, NJ: Erlbaum.

Willis, T. A., & Gregory, A. M. (2015). Anxiety disorders and sleep in children and adolescents. *Sleep Medicine Clinics, 10*(2), 125-131.

Willoughby, B. J., & Belt, D. (2016). Marital orientation and relationship well-being among cohabiting couples. *Journal of Family Psychology, 30*(2), 181.

Willoughby, B. J., Farero, A. M., & Busby, D. M. (2014). Exploring the effects of sexual desire discrepancy among married couples. *Archives of Sexual Behavior, 43*(3), 551-562.

Willoughby, B. J., Hall, S. S., & Goff, S. (2015). Marriage matters but how much? Marital centrality among young adults. *The Journal of Psychology, 149*(8), 796-817.

Wilmoth, J. R. (2000). Demography of longevity: Past, present, and future trends. *Experimental Gerontology, 35*, 1111-1129.

Wilmoth, J., & Koso, G. (2002). Does marital history count? Marital status and wealth outcomes among preretirement adults. *Journal of Marriage and Family, 64*, 254-268.

Wilson, B. J. (2008). Media and children's aggression, fear, and altruism. *Future of Children, 18*, 87-118.

Wilson, D. R. (2010). Health consequences of childhood sexual abuse. *Perspectives in Psychiatric Care, 46*(1), 56-64.

Wilson, G. T., Grilo, C. M., & Vitousek, K. M. (2007). Psychological treatment of eating disorders. *American Psychologist, 62*, 199-216.

Wilson, M. G., Ellison, G. M., & Cable, N. T. (2016). Basic science behind the cardiovascular benefits of exercise. *British Journal of Sports Medicine, 50*(2), 93-99.

Wilson, R. S., & Bennett, D. A. (2003). Cognitive activity and risk of Alzheimer's disease. *Current Directions in Psychological Science, 12*, 87-91.

Windsor, T. D., Gerstorf, D., & Luszcz, M. A. (2015). Social resource correlates of levels and time-to-death-related changes in late-life affect. *Psychology and Aging, 30*(1), 136.

Wingfield, A., & Stine, E. A. L. (1989). Modeling memory processes: Research and theory on memory and aging. In G. C. Gilmore, P. J. Whitehouse, & M. L. Wykle (Eds.), *Memory, aging, and dementia: Theory, assessment, and treatment* (pp. 4-40). New York, NY: Springer.

Wink, P., & Staudinger, U. M. (2016). Wisdom and psychosocial functioning in later life. *Journal of Personality, 84*(3), 306-318.

Winner, E. (2000). The origins and ends of giftedness. *American Psychologist, 55*, 159-169.

Wirtz, P. H., & von Känel, R. (2017). Psychological stress, inflammation, and coronary heart disease. *Current Cardiology Reports, 19*(11), 111.

Wisdom, N. M., Mignogna, J., & Collins, R. L. (2012). Variability in Wechsler Adult Intelligence Scale-IV subtest performance across age. *Archives of Clinical Neuropsychology, 27*(4), 389–397.

Wittenborn, J., & Rein, D. (2014). The future of vision: Forecasting the prevalence and costs of vision problems. *Prevent Blindness.*

Woerlee, G. M. (2005). *Mortal minds: The biology of the near-death experience.* New York, NY: Prometheus Books.

Wohlfahrt-Veje, C., Mouritsen, A., Hagen, C. P., Tinggaard, J., Mieritz, M. G., Boas, M., ... Main, K. M. (2016). Pubertal onset in boys and girls is influenced by pubertal timing of both parents. *The Journal of Clinical Endocrinology & Metabolism, 101*(7), 2667–2674.

Wojcik, M., Burzynska-Pedziwiatr, I., & Wozniak, L. A. (2010). A review of natural and synthetic antioxidants important for health and longevity. *Current Medicinal Chemistry, 17*(28), 3262–3288.

Wolf, S., Magnuson, K. A., & Kimbro, R. T. (2017). Family poverty and neighborhood poverty: Links with children's school readiness before and after the Great Recession. *Children and Youth Services Review, 79,* 368–384.

Wolff, P. H. (1969). The natural history of crying and other vocalizations in early infancy. In B. M. Foss (Ed.), *Determinants of infant behavior* (Vol. 4). London: Methuen.

Wolinsky, F. D., Vander Weg, M. W., Howren, M. B., Jones, M. P., & Dotson, M. M. (2015). The effect of cognitive speed of processing training on the development of additional IADL difficulties and the reduction of depressive symptoms: Results from the IHAMS randomized controlled trial. *Journal of Aging and Health, 27*(2), 334–354.

Wolke, D., Bilgin, A., & Samara, M. (2017). Systematic review and meta-analysis: fussing and crying durations and prevalence of colic in infants. *The Journal of Pediatrics, 185,* 55–61.

Woltering, S., & Shi, Q. (2016). On the neuroscience of self-regulation in children with disruptive behavior problems: Implications for education. *Review of Educational Research, 86*(4), 1085–1110.

Wong, C. A., Scavone, B. M., Peaceman, A. M., McCarthy, R. J., Sullivan, J. T., Diaz, N. T., ... Grouper, S. (2005). The risk of cesarean delivery with neuraxial analgesia given early versus late in labor. *New England Journal of Medicine, 352,* 655–665.

Wong, C. C. Y., Caspi, A., Williams, B., Craig, I. W., Houts, R., & Ambler, A. (2010). A longitudinal study of epigenetic variation in twins. *Epigenetics, 5,* 516–526.

Wong, C. C. Y., Meaburn, E. L., Ronald, A., Price, T. S., Jeffries, A. R., Schalkwyk, L. C., ... Mill, J. (2014). Methylomic analysis of monozygotic twins discordant for autism spectrum disorder and related behavioural traits. *Molecular Psychiatry, 19*(4), 495–503.

Wong, C. T., Wais, J., & Crawford, D. A. (2015). Prenatal exposure to common environment factors affects brain lipids and increases risk of developing autism spectrum disorders. *European Journal of Neuroscience, 42,* 2742–2760.

Wong, H., Gottesman, I., & Petronis, A. (2005). Phenotypic differences in genetically identical organisms: The epigenetic perspective. *Human Molecular Genetics, 14* (Review Issue 1), R11–R18.

Wong, K.M., Mastenbroek, S., & Repping, S. (2014). Cryopreservation of human embryos and its contribution to in vitro success rates. *Fertility and Sterility,* 102, 19–26.

Wong, M. M., Nigg, J. T., Zucker, R. A., Puttler, L. I., Fitzgerald, H. E., Jester, J. M., ... Adams, K. (2006). Behavioral control and resiliency in the onset of alcohol and illicit drug use: A prospective study from preschool to adolescence. *Child Development, 77,* 1016–1033.

Wong, S. S., Zhou, B., Goebert, D., & Hishinuma, E. S. (2013). The risk of adolescent suicide across patterns of drug use: a nationally representative study of high school students in the United States from 1999 to 2009. *Social Psychiatry and Psychiatric Epidemiology, 48*(10), 1611–1620.

Wood, R. M., & Gustafson, G. E. (2001). Infant crying and adults' anticipated caregiving responses: Acoustic and contextual influences. *Child Development, 72,* 1287–1300.

Wood, W., & Eagly, A. (2002). A cross-cultural analysis of the behavior of women and men: Implications for the origins of sex differences. *Psychological Bulletin, 128,* 699–727.

Wood, W., & Eagly, A. H. (2012). Biosocial construction of sex differences and similarities in behavior. *Advances in Experimental Social Psychology, 46*(1), 55–123.

Woodruff, T. J., Axelrad, D. A., Kyle, A. D., Nweke, O., Miller, G. G., & Hurley, B. J. (2004). Trends in environmentally related childhood illnesses. *Pediatrics, 113,* 1133–1140.

Woodward, A. L., Markman, E. M., & Fitzsimmons, C. M. (1994). Rapid word learning in 13- and 18-month-olds. *Development Psychology, 30,* 553–566.

Woolley, J. D., & Cox, V. (2007). Development of beliefs about storybook reality. *Developmental Science, 10*(5), 681–693.

World Bank. (2018). *World Development Report 2018: Learning to Realize Education's Promise.* Washington, DC: World Bank. doi:10.1596/978-1-4648-1096-1.

World Bank. (2019). *Life expectancy at birth, total (years)* [Interactive data tables]. Retrieved from https://data.worldbank.org/indicator/sp.dyn.le00.in

World Bank. (2019). Poverty [Data sheet]. Retrieved from www.worldbank.org/en/topic/poverty/overview

World Bank. (2020). Life expectancy at birth, total (years) [Interactive data tables]. Retrieved from https://data.worldbank.org/indicator/SP.DYN.LE00.IN

World Cancer Research Fund. (2007, November). *Food, nutrition, physical activity, and the prevention of cancer: A global perspective.* London, England: author.

World Health Organization & UNICEF. (2009). *WHO child growth standards and the identification of severe acute malnutrition in infants and children: Joint statement by the World Health Organization and the United Nations Children's Fund* [Data report]. Retrieved from https://apps.who.int/iris/bitstream/handle/10665/44129/9789241598163_eng.pdf?ua=1

World Health Organization. (2016). *Child maltreatment* [Fact sheet]. Retrieved from www.who.int/news-room/fact-sheets/detail/child-maltreatment

World Health Organization. (2016). *Growing antibiotic resistance forces updates for recommended treatment for sexually transmitted infections* [News release]. Retrieved from www.who.int/news-room/detail/30-08-2016-growing-antibiotic-resistance-forces-updates-to-recommended-treatment-for-sexually-transmitted-infections

World Health Organization. (2016). *World health statistics 2016: Monitoring health for the Sustainable Development Goals.* Geneva, Switzerland: World Health Organization.

World Health Organization. (2016, November 7). *New guidelines on antenatal care for a positive pregnancy experience.* Retrieved from www.who.int/reproductivehealth/news/antenatal-care/en

World Health Organization. (2016, November). *Maternal mortality.* Retrieved from www.who.int/mediacentre/factsheets/fs348/en

World Health Organization. (2017). *Cardiovascular disease* [Fact sheet]. Retrieved from www.who.int/news-room/fact-sheets/detail/cardiovascular-diseases-(cvds)

World Health Organization. (2017). *Sugars and dental caries* [WHO technical information note]. Retrieved from https://apps.who.int/iris/bitstream/handle/10665/259413/WHO-NMH-NHD-17.12-eng.pdf?sequence=1

World Health Organization. (2017). *Growing up unequal* [HBSC 2016 study (2013/2014 survey)]. Retrieved from www.euro.who.int/en/publications/abstracts/growing-up-unequal.-hbsc-2016-study-20132014-survey

World Health Organization. (2018). *Adolescence: Health risks and solutions* [Data sheet]. Retrieved from www.who.int/en/news-room/fact-sheets/detail/adolescents-health-risks-and-solutions

World Health Organization. (2018). Alcohol [Fact sheet]. Retrieved from www.who.int/news-room/fact-sheets/detail/alcohol

World Health Organization. (2018). *Diabetes* [Fact sheet]. Retrieved from www.who.int/news-room/fact-sheets/detail/diabetes

World Health Organization. (2018). *Female genital mutilation* [Data sheet]. Retrieved from www.who.int/news-room/fact-sheets/detail/female-genital-mutilation

World Health Organization. (2018). *Global nutrition report* [Report]. Retrieved from https://globalnutritionreport.org/reports/global-nutrition-report-2018/

World Health Organization. (2018). *Harmful use of alcohol kills more than 3 million people each year, most of them men* [News release]. Retrieved from www.who.int/news-room/detail/21-09-2018-harmful-use-of-alcohol-kills-more-than-3-million-people-each-year-most-of-them-men

World Health Organization. (2018). *Healthy life expectancy (HALE) at birth* [Data table]. Retrieved from http://apps.who.int/gho/data/view.main.HALEXREGv?lang=en

World Health Organization. (2018). *National suicide prevention strategies: Progress, examples, indicators* [Report]. Geneva: World Health Organization. Licence: CC BY-NC-SA 3.0 IGO. Retrieved from https://apps.who.int/iris/bitstream/han dle/10665/279765/9789241515016-eng.pdf?ua=1

World Health Organization. (2018). *Obesity and overweight* [Fact sheet]. Retrieved from www.who.int/news-room/fact-sheets/detail/obesity-and-overweight

World Health Organization. (2018). *Obesity and overweight: Key facts* [Fact sheet]. Retrieved from www.who.int/en/news-room/fact-sheets/detail/obesity-and-overweight

World Health Organization. (2019). *Adolescents overview* [Fact sheet]. Retrieved from https://data.unicef.org/topic/adolescents/overview/

World Health Organization. (2019). *Ageing and life course* [Report]. Retrieved from www.who.int/ageing/healthy-ageing/en/

World Health Organization. (2019). *Aging and health* [Information sheet]. Retrieved from www.who.int/news-room/fact-sheets/detail/ageing-and-health

World Health Organization. (2019). *Child malnutrition* [Data sheet]. Retrieved from www.who.int/gho/child-malnutrition/en/

World Health Organization. (2019). *Child maltreatment* [Fact sheet]. Retrieved from www.who.int/news-room/fact-sheets/detail/child-maltreatment.

World Health Organization. (2019). *Children: Reducing mortality* [Fact sheet]. Retrieved from www.who.int/en/news-room/fact-sheets/detail/children-reducing-mortality

World Health Organization. (2019). *Hepatitis B* [Fact sheet]. Retrieved from www.who.int/news-room/fact-sheets/detail/hepatitis-b

World Health Organization. (2019). *HIV/AIDS* [Fact sheet]. Retrieved from www.who.int/health-topics/hiv-aids/#tab=tab_1

World Health Organization. (2019). *Hypertension* [Fact sheet]. Retrieved from www.who.int/news-room/fact-sheets/detail/hypertension

World Health Organization. (2019). *Levels and trends in child mortality* [Report]. Retrieved from www.unicef.org/media/60561/file/UN-IGME-child-mortality-report-2019.pdf

World Health Organization. (2019). *Maternal mortality* [Fact sheet]. Retrieved from www.who.int/news-room/fact-sheets/detail/maternal-mortality

World Health Organization. (2019). *Sexually transmitted infections (STIs)* [Fact sheet]. Retrieved from www.who.int/news-room/fact-sheets/detail/sexually-transmitted-infections-(stis)

World Health Organization. (2019). *Suicide* [Fact sheet]. Retrieved from www.who.int/news-room/fact-sheets/detail/suicide

World Health Organization. (2019). *Tobacco* [Fact sheet]. Retrieved from www.who.int/news-room/fact-sheets/detail/tobacco

World Health Organization. (2019). *Violence against children* [Report]. Retrieved from www.who.int/news-room/fact-sheets/detail/violence-against-children

World Health Organization. (2019). *World health statistics 2019: Monitoring health for the SDGs, sustainable development goals* [Report]. Retrieved from https://apps.who.int/iris/bitstream/handle/10665/311696/WHO-DAD-2019.1-eng.pdf

World Health Organization. (2019). *World hunger is still not going down after 3 years and obesity is still growing – UN report* [News release]. Retrieved from www.who.int/news-room/detail/15-07-2019-world-hunger-is-still-not-going-down-after-three-years-and-obesity-is-still-growing-un-report

World Health Organization. (2019). *Global status report on alcohol and health 2018*. Geneva, Switzerland: Author.

World Health Organization. (2019). *Levels and trends in child mortality* [Report]. Retrieved from www.unicef.org/media/60561/file/UN-IGME-child-mortality-report-2019.pdf

World Health Organization. (2020). *Adolescent pregnancy* [Fact sheet]. Retrieved from www.who.int/news-room/fact-sheets/detail/adolescent-pregnancy

World Health Organization. (2020). *Blindness and visual impairment* [Report]. Retrieved from www.who.int/health-topics/blindness-and-vision-loss#tab=tab_1

World Health Organization. (2020). *Breast cancer* [Information sheet]. Retrieved from www.who.int/cancer/prevention/diagnosis-screening/breast-cancer/en/

World Health Organization. (2020). *Deafness and hearing loss* [Report]. Retrieved from www.who.int/news-room/fact-sheets/detail/deafness-and-hearing-loss

World Health Organization. (2020). *Dementia* [Fact sheet]. Retrieved from www.who.int/news-room/fact-sheets/detail/dementia

World Health Organization. (2020). *Depression* [Fact sheet]. Retrieved from www.who.int/news-room/fact-sheets/detail/depression

World Health Organization. (2020). *Overweight and obesity: Key facts* [Information sheet]. Retrieved from www.who.int/en/news-room/fact-sheets/detail/obesity-and-overweight

World Health Organization. (2020). *Q & A: Older people and COVID-19* [Information sheet]. Retrieved from www.who.int/emergencies/diseases/novel-coronavirus-2019/question-and-answers-hub/q-a-detail/q-a-on-on-covid-19-for-older-people

World Health Organization. (2020). *Sexually transmitted infections* [Fact sheet]. Retrieved from www.who.int/news-room/fact-sheets/detail/sexually-transmitted-infections-(stis)

World Health Organization. (2020). *Tobacco* [Fact sheet]. Retrieved from www.who.int/news-room/fact-sheets/detail/tobacco

World Health Organization. (2020). *What are the health consequences of being overweight?* [Q & A]. Retrieved from www.who.int/news-room/q-a-detail/what-are-the-health-consequences-of-being-overweight

World Population Review. (2020). *Divorce rates by country, 2020* [Report]. Retrieved from http://worldpopulationreview.com/countries/divorce-rates-by-country/

Worldometer. (2020). *United States: Coronavirus cases* [Data portal]. Retrieved from www.worldometers.info/coronavirus/country/us/

Worobey, J. & Worobey H.S. (2014). Body-size stigmatization by preschool girls: In a doll's world, it is good to be "Barbie." *Body Image, 11,* 171–174.

Woroniecki, R. P., Kahnauth, A., Panesar, L. E., & Supe-Markovina, K. (2017). Left ventricular hypertrophy in pediatric hypertension: A mini review. *Frontiers in Pediatrics, 5,* 101.

Worthy, D. A., & Maddox, W. T. (2012). Age-based differences in strategy use in choice tasks. *Frontiers in Neuroscience, 5,* 145.

Wraw, C., Deary, I. J., Gale, C. R., & Der, G. (2015). Intelligence in youth and health at age 50. *Intelligence, 53,* 23–32.

Wright, A. A., Keating, N. L., Ayanian, J. Z., Chrischilles, E. A., Kahn, K. L., Ritchie, C. S., . . . Landrum, M. B. (2016). Family perspectives on aggressive cancer care near the end of life. *JAMA, 315*(3), 284–292.

Wright, A. J. (2016). Childhood enuresis. *Paediatrics and Child Health, 26*(8), 353–359.

Wright, J. D., Hirsch, R., & Wang, C. (2009). One-third of adults embraced most heart healthy behaviors in 1999–2002. *NCHS Data Brief, 17.* Hyattsville, MD: National Center for Health Statistics.

Wright, M. R., & Brown, S. L. (2017). Psychological well-being among older adults: The role of partnership status. *Journal of Marriage and Family, 79*(3), 833–849.

Wrosch, C., Miller, G. E., & Schulz, R. (2009). Cortisol secretion and functional disabilities in old age: importance of using adaptive control strategies. *Psychosomatic Medicine, 71*(9), 996.

Wrzus, C., Hänel, M., Wagner, J., & Neyer, F. J. (2013). Social network changes and life events across the life span: A meta-analysis. *Psychological Bulletin, 139*(1), 53.

Wrzus, C., Wagner, J., & Neyer, F. J. (2012). The interdependence of horizontal family relationships and friendships relates to higher well-being. *Personal Relationships, 19*(3), 465–482.

Wrzus, C., Zimmermann, J., Mund, M., & Neyer, F. J. (2017). Friendships in young and middle adulthood: Normative patterns and personality differences. In M. Hojjat & A. Moyer (Eds.), *The psychology of friendship* (pp. 21–38). New York, NY: Oxford University Press.

Wu, C., & Leinung, M. C. (2015). The biologic basis of transgender Identity: Finger length ratios in transgender individuals implicates a role for prenatal androgen activity. *Basic and Clinical Aspects of Sexual Development,* SAT-081.

Wu, K. G., Chang, C. Y., Yen, C. Y., & Lai, C. C. (2019). Associations between environmental heavy metal exposure and childhood asthma: A population-based study. *Journal of Microbiology, Immunology and Infection, 52*(2), 352–362.

Wu, Z., & Hart, R. (2002). The effects of marital and nonmarital union transition on health. *Journal of Marriage and Family, 64,* 420–432.

Wulczyn, F. (2004). Family reunification. In David and Lucile Packard Foundation, Children, families, and foster care. *Future of Children, 14*(1). Retrieved from www.futureofchildren.org

Wynn, K. (1990). Children's understanding of counting. *Cognition, 36,* 155–193.

Wynn, K. (1992). Addition and subtraction by human infants. *Nature, 358.*

Wörmann, V., Holodynski, M., Kärtner, J., & Keller, H. (2012). A cross-cultural comparison of the development of the social smile: A longitudinal study of maternal and infant imitation in 6-and 12-week-old infants. *Infant Behavior and Development, 35*(3), 335–347.

Xiao, N. G., Quinn, P. C., Liu, S., Ge, L., Pascalis, O., & Lee, K. (2018). Older but not younger infants associate own-race faces with happy music and other-race faces with sad music. *Developmental Science, 21*(2), e12537.

Xie, X., Ding, G., Cui, C., Chen, L., Gao, Y., Zhou, Y., . . . & Tian, Y. (2013). The effects of low-level prenatal lead exposure on birth outcomes. *Environmental Pollution, 175,* 30–34.

Xu, F., Bao, X., Fu, G., Talwar, V., & Lee, K. (2010). Lying and truth-telling in children: From concept to action. *Child Development, 81*(2), 581–596.

Xu, J. Q., Kochanek, K. D., Murphy, S. L., & Tejada-Vera, B. (2010). Deaths: Final data for 2007. *National Vital Statistics Report, 58*(19). Hyattsville, MD: National Center for Health Statistics.

Xu, J., Kochanek, K. D., Murphy, S. L., & Tejada-Vera, B. (2016). Deaths: Final data for 2014. *National Vital Statistics Report, 65*(4). Hyattsville, MD: National Center for Health Statistics.

Xu, W., Tan, L., Wang, H. F., Tan, M. S., Tan, L., Li, J. Q., . . . Yu, J. T. (2016). Education and risk of dementia: dose-response meta-analysis of prospective cohort studies. *Molecular Neurobiology, 53*(5), 3113–3123.

Yadav, K. N., Gabler, N. B., Cooney, E., Kent, S., Kim, J., Herbst, N., . . . Courtright, K. R. (2017). Approximately one in three U.S. adults completes any type of advance directive for end-of-life care. *Health Affairs, 36*(7), 1244–1251.

Yadav, R., Khanna, A., & Singh, D. (2017). Exploration of relationship between stress and spirituality characteristics of male and female engineering students: A comprehensive study. *Journal of Religion and Health, 56*(2), 388–399.

Yaffe, K. (2018). Modifiable risk factors and prevention of dementia: What is the latest evidence? *JAMA Internal Medicine, 178*(2), 281–282.

Yamaguchi, A., Kim, M. S., Oshio, A., & Akutsu, S. (2016). Relationship between bicultural identity and psychological well-being among American and Japanese older adults. *Health Psychology Open, 3*(1), 2055102916650093.

Yaman, A., Mesman, J., van IJzendoorn, M. H., & Bakermans-Kranenburg, M. J. (2010). Parenting and toddler aggression in second-generation immigrant families: The moderating role of child temperament. *Journal of Family Psychology, 24*(2), 208.

Yang, B., Ollendick, T. H., Dong, Q., Xia, Y., & Lin, L. (1995). Only children and children with siblings in the People's Republic of China: Levels of fear, anxiety, and depression. *Child Development, 66*(5), 1301–1311.

Yang, L., Neale, B. M., Liu, L., Lee, S. H., Wray, N. R., Ji, N., . . . & Faraone, S. V. (2013). Polygenic transmission and complex neuro developmental network for attention deficit hyperactivity disorder: Genome-wide association study of both common and rare variants. *American Journal of Medical Genetics Part B: Neuropsychiatric Genetics, 162*(5), 419–430.

Yang, Y. (2008). Social inequalities in happiness in the United States, 1972 to 2004: An age-period-cohort analysis. *American Sociological Review, 73,* 204–226.

Yang, Y. T., & Curlin, F. A. (2016). Why physicians should oppose assisted suicide. *Journal of the American Medical Association, 315,* 247–248.

Yap, Y., Rice-Lacy, R. C., Bei, B., & Wiley, J. F. (2018). 0178 Bidirectional relations between stress and sleep: An intensive daily study. *Sleep, 41*(suppl_1), A70–A70.

Yatsenko, A. N., & Turek, P. J. (2018). Reproductive genetics and the aging male. *Journal of Assisted Reproduction and Genetics, 35*(6), 933–941.

Yau, J. P., Tausopoulos-Chan, M., & Smetana, J. G. (2009). Disclosure to parents about everyday activities among American adolescents from Mexican, Chinese and European backgrounds. *Child Development, 80*(5), 1481–1498.

Ybarra, M. L., & Mitchell, K. J. (2014). "Sexting" and its relation to sexual activity and sexual risk behavior in a national survey of adolescents. *Journal of Adolescent Health, 55*(6), 757–764.

Ybarra, M. L., Strasburger, V. C., & Mitchell, K. J. (2014). Sexual media exposure, sexual behavior, and sexual violence victimization in adolescence. *Clinical Pediatrics, 53*(13), 1239–1247.

Yeh, H., Lorenz, F. O., Wickrama, K. A. S., Conger, R. D., & Elder, G. H. (2006). Relationships among sexual satisfaction, marital quality, and marital instability at midlife. *Journal of Family Psychology, 20,* 339–343.

Yeung, H. H., Chen, K. H., & Werker, J. F. (2013). When does native language input affect phonetic perception? The precocious case of lexical tone. *Journal of Memory and Language, 68*(2), 123–139.

Yeung, W. J., Sandberg, J. F., Davis-Kean, P. E., & Hofferth, S. L. (2001). Children's time with fathers in intact families. *Journal of Marriage and Family, 63,* 136–154.

Yip, T. (2014). Ethnic identity in everyday life: The influence of identity development status. *Child Development, 85*(1), 205–219.

Yip, T., Seaton, E. K., & Sellers, R. M. (2006). African American racial identity across the lifespan: Identity status, identity content, and depressive symptoms. *Child Development, 77,* 1504–1517.

Yon, Y., Mikton, C. R., Gassoumis, Z. D., & Wilber, K. H. (2017). Elder abuse prevalence in community settings: A systematic review and meta-analysis. *The Lancet Global Health, 5*(2), e147–e156.

Yoon, P. W., Bastian, B., Anderson, R. N., Collins, J. L., & Jaffe, H. W. (2014). Potentially preventable deaths from the five leading causes of death—United States, 2008-2010. *Morbidity and Mortality Weekly Report, 63*(17), 369.

Yoon, V., Maalouf, N. M., & Sakhaee, K. (2012). The effects of smoking on bone metabolism. *Osteoporosis International, 23*(8), 2081–2092.

Yoshikawa, H. (1994). Prevention as cumulative protection: Effects of early family support and education on chronic delinquency and its risks. *Psychological Bulletin, 115*(1), 28–54.

Yoshikawa, H., Aber, J. L., & Beardslee, W. R. (2012). The effects of poverty on the mental, emotional, and behavioral health of children and youth: Implications for prevention. *American Psychologist, 67*(4), 272.

Young, M., & Schieman, S. (2018). Scaling back and finding flexibility: Gender differences in parents' strategies to manage work–family conflict. *Journal of Marriage and Family, 80*(1), 99–118.

Young, Y., Kalamaras, J., Kelly, L., Hornick, D., & Yucel, R. (2015). Is aging in place delaying nursing home admission? *Journal of the American Medical Directors Association, 16*(10), 900-e1.

Youngblade, L. M., & Belsky, J. (1992). Parent-child antecedents of 5-year-olds' close friendships: A longitudinal analysis. *Developmental Psychology, 28,* 700–713.

Yu, J., & Xie, Y. (2015). Cohabitation in China: Trends and determinants. *Population and Development Review, 41*(4), 607–628.

Yucel, D., Bobbitt-Zeher, D., & Downey, D. B. (2018). Quality matters: Sibling relationships and friendship nominations among adolescents. *Child Indicators Research, 11*(2), 523–539.

Yudell, M., Roberts, D., DeSalle, R., & Tishkoff, S. (2016). Taking race out of human genetics. *Science, 351*(6273), 564–565.

Yunger, J. L., Carver, P. R., & Perry, D. G. (2004). Does gender identity influence children's psychological well-being? *Developmental Psychology, 40,* 572–582.

Zadik, Y., Bechor, R., Galor, S., & Levin, L. (2010). Periodontal disease might be associated even with impaired fasting glucose. *British Dental Journal, 208*(10), E20–E20.

Zahn-Waxler, C., Friedman, R. J., Cole, P. M., Mizuta, I., & Hiruma, N. (1996). Japanese and U.S. preschool children's responses to conflict and distress. *Child Development, 67,* 2462–2477.

Zahodne, L. B., Glymour, M. M., Sparks, C., Bontempo, D., Dixon, R. A., MacDonald, S. W., & Manly, J. J. (2011). Education does not slow cognitive decline with aging: 12-year evidence from the Victoria Longitudinal Study. *Journal of the International Neuropsychological Society, 17*(6), 1039–1046.

Zajdel, R. T., Bloom, J. M., Fireman, G., & Larsen, J. T. (2013). Children's understanding and experience of mixed emotions: The roles of age, gender, and empathy. *The Journal of Genetic Psychology, 174*(5), 582–603.

Zandi, P. P., Anthony, J. C., Hayden, K. M., Mehta, K., Mayer, L., & Breitner, J. C. S. (2002). Reduced incidence of AD with NSAID but no H^2 receptor antagonists. *Neurology, 59,* 880–886.

Zangl, R., & Mills, D. L. (2007). Increased brain activity to infant-directed speech in 6- and 13-month old infants. *Infancy, 11*, 31-62.

Zanto, T. P., & Gazzaley, A. (2014). Attention and ageing. In A. Nobre & S. Kastner (Eds.), *The Oxford handbook of attention* (pp. 927-971). New York, NY: Oxford University Press.

Zapolski, T. C., Clifton, R. L., Banks, D. E., Hershberger, A., & Aalsma, M. (2019). Family and peer influences on substance attitudes and use among juvenile justice-involved youth. *Journal of Child and Family Studies, 28*(2), 447-456.

Zare, B. (2011, July). Review of studies on infidelity. *3rd International Conference on Advanced Management Science IPEDR, 19*, 182-186.

Zaval, L., Li, Y., Johnson, E. J., & Weber, E. U. (2015). Complementary contributions of fluid and crystallized intelligence to decision making across the life span. In T. M. Hess, J. Strough, & C. E. Löckenhoff (Eds.), *Aging and decision making* (pp. 149-168). Cambridge, MA: Academic Press.

Zeinali, A., Sharifi, H., Enayati, M., Asgari, P., & Pasha, G. (2011). The mediational pathway among parenting styles, attachment styles and self-regulation with addiction susceptibility of adolescents. *Journal of Research in Medical Sciences: The Official Journal of Isfahan University of Medical Sciences, 16*(9), 1105.

Zeitlin, M. (2011). *New information on West African traditional education and approaches to its modernization.* Dakar, Senegal: Tostan.

Zelazo, P. D., & Carlson, S. M. (2012). Hot and cool executive function in childhood and adolescence: Development and plasticity. *Child Development Perspectives, 6*(4), 354-360.

Zelazo, P. D., Müller, U., Frye, D., & Marcovitch, S. (2003). The development of executive function in early childhood. *Monographs of the Society for Research in Child Development, 68*(3, Serial No. 274).

Zelazo, P. R., Kearsley, R. B., & Stack, D. M. (1995). Mental representations for visual sequences: Increased speed of central processing from 22 to 32 months. *Intelligence, 20*, 41-63.

Zeng, L., Xia, S., Yuan, W., Yan, K., Xiao, F., Shao, J., & Zhou, W. (2020, March 26). Neonatal early-onset infection with SARS-CoV-2 in 33 neonates born to mothers with COVID-19 in Wuhan, China. *JAMA Pediatrics.*

Zeng, Y., Gu, D., & George, L. K. (2011). Association of religious participation with mortality among Chinese old adults. *Research on Aging, 33*(1), 51-83.

Zeserson, J. M. (2001). Chi no michi as metaphor: Conversations with Japanese women about menopause. *Anthropology & Medicine, 8*(2-3), 177-199.

Zhai, F., Brooks-Gunn, J., & Waldfogel, J. (2014). Head Start's impact is contingent on alternative type of care in comparison group. *Developmental Psychology, 50*(12), 2572.

Zhan, Y., Wang, M., Liu, S., & Shultz, K. S. (2009). Bridge employment and retirees' health: A longitudinal investigation. *Journal of Occupational Health Psychology, 14*(4), 374.

Zhang, C., & Morrison, J. W. (2010). Imparting cultural values to Chinese children through literature. *International Journal of Early Childhood, 42*(1), 7-26.

Zhang, K., & Wang, X. (2013). Maternal smoking and increased risk of sudden infant death syndrome: A meta-analysis. *Legal Medicine, 15*(3), 115-121.

Zhang, L. F. (2004). The Perry scheme: Across cultures, across approaches to the study of human psychology. *Journal of Adult Development, 11*(2), 123-138.

Zhang, W., & Radhakrishnan, K. (2018). Evidence on selection, optimization, and compensation strategies to optimize aging with multiple chronic conditions: A literature review. *Geriatric Nursing, 39*(5), 534-542.

Zhang, Z., & Hayward, M. D. (2001). Childlessness and the psychological well-being of older persons. *The Journals of Gerontology Series B: Psychological Sciences and Social Sciences, 56*(5), S311-S320.

Zhao, Y. (2002, May 29). Cultural divide over parental discipline. *The New York Times.* Retrieved from www.nytimes.com/2002/05/29/nyregion/29DISC.html?ex

Zheng, Y., Manson, J. E., Yuan, C., Liang, M. H., Grodstein, F., Stampfer, M. J., . . . Hu, F. B. (2017). Associations of weight gain from early to middle adulthood with major health outcomes later in life. *JAMA, 318*(3), 255-269.

Zhong, J., & Arnett, J. J. (2014). Conceptions of adulthood among migrant women workers in China. *International Journal of Behavioral Development, 38*(3), 255-265.

Zhou, J. N., Hofman, M. A., Gooren, L. J., & Swaab, D. F. (1995). A sex difference in the human brain and its relation to transsexuality. *Nature, 378*(6552), 68.

Zhou, S., Rosenthal, D. G., Sherman, S., Zelikoff, J., Gordon, T., & Weitzman, M. (2014). Physical, behavioral, and cognitive effects of prenatal tobacco and postnatal secondhand smoke exposure. *Current Problems in Pediatric and Adolescent Health Care, 44*(8), 219-241.

Zhu, J., & Chan, Y. M. (2017). Adult consequences of self-limited delayed puberty. *Pediatrics, 139*(6), e20163177.

Ziegler, D. V., Wiley, C. D., & Velarde, M. C. (2015). Mitochondrial effectors of cellular senescence: Beyond the free radical theory of aging. *Aging Cell, 14*(1), 1-7.

Ziemer, C. J., & Snyder, M. (2016). A picture you can handle: Infants treat touch-screen images more like photographs than objects. *Frontiers in Psychology, 7*, 1253.

Zigler, E., & Styfco, S. J. (2001). Extended childhood intervention prepares children for school and beyond. *Journal of the American Medical Association, 285*, 2378-2380.

Zigler, E., Taussig, C., & Black, K. (1992). Early childhood intervention: A promising preventative for juvenile delinquency. *American Psychologist, 47*, 997-1006.

Zizza, C., Siega-Riz, A. M., & Popkin, B. M. (2001). Significant increase in young adults' snacking between 1977-1978 and 1994-1996 represents a cause for concern! *Preventive Medicine, 32*, 303-310.

Zlotnick, C., Tam, T. W., & Soman, L. A. (2012). Life course outcomes on mental and physical health: the impact of foster care on adulthood. *American Journal of Public Health, 102*(3), 534-540.

Zlotnick, C., Tam, T., & Zerger, S. (2012). Common needs but divergent interventions for US homeless and foster care children: Results from a systematic review. *Health & Social Care in the Community, 20*(5), 449-476.

Zmyj, N., & Seehagen, S. (2013). The role of a model's age for young children's imitation: A research review. *Infant and Child Development, 22*(6), 622-641.

Zolotor, A. J., Theodore, A. D., Runyan, D. K., Chang, J. J., & Laskey, A. L. (2011). Corporal punishment and physical abuse: Population-based trends for three-to-11-year-old children in the United States. *Child Abuse Review, 20*(1), 57-66.

Zosuls, K. M., Andrews, N. C., Martin, C. L., England, D. E., & Field, R. D. (2016). Developmental changes in the link between gender typicality and peer victimization and exclusion. *Sex Roles, 75*(5-6), 243-256.

Zoutewelle-Terovan, M., & Liefbroer, A. C. (2018). Swimming against the stream: Non-normative family transitions and loneliness in later life across 12 nations. *The Gerontologist, 58*(6), 1096-1108.

Zubiaurre-Elorza, L., Junque, C., Gómez-Gil, E., Segovia, S., Carrillo, B., Rametti, G., & Guillamon, A. (2012). Cortical thickness in untreated transsexuals. *Cerebral Cortex, 23*(12), 2855-2862.

Zucker, A. N., Ostrove, J. M., & Stewart, A. J. (2002). College-educated women's personality development in adulthood: Perceptions and age differences. *Psychology and Aging, 17*, 236-244.

Zucker, K. J. (2017). Epidemiology of gender dysphoria and transgender identity. *Sexual Health, 14*(5), 404-411.

Zuckerman, P. (2009). Atheism, secularity, and well-being: How the findings of social science counter negative stereotypes and assumptions. *Sociology Compass, 3*(6), 949-971.

Zufferey, S. (2016). Pragmatic acquisition. In J.-O. Östman & J. Verschueren (Eds.), *Handbook of pragmatics.* Amsterdam, the Netherlands: John Benjamins.

Zuffianò, A., Alessandri, G., Gerbino, M., Kanacri, B. P. L., Di Giunta, L., Milioni, M., & Caprara, G. V. (2013). Academic achievement: The unique contribution of self-efficacy beliefs in self-regulated learning beyond intelligence, personality traits, and self-esteem. *Learning and Individual Differences, 23*, 158-162.

Zwergel, C., & von Kaisenberg, C. S. (2019). Maternal and fetal risks in higher multiple cesarean deliveries. In *Recent Advances in Cesarean Delivery.* London: IntechOpen.

Zylstra, R.G., Prater, C.D., Walthour, A.E., & Aponte, A.F. (2014). Autism: Why the rise in rates? Our improved understanding of the disorder and increasingly sensitive diagnostic tools are playing a role—but so are some other factors. *Journal of Family Practice, 63*, 316-320.

Zyngier, D. (2014). Class size and academic results, with a focus on children from culturally, linguistically and economically disenfranchised communities. *Evidence Base, 1*(3), 1-24.

Bernal, M. E., 297
Bernal-Pino, A., 417
Bernardi, F., 358
Berndt, A. E., 138, 140
Berndt, T. J., 310
Bernhardt, T., 429
Bernie, A.M., 368
Bernier, A., 149, 228
Berns, S., 346
Berntsen, D., 345
Bernzweig, J., 211
Beron, K. J., 259
Berrettini, W., 429
Berrick, J. D., 157
Berry, S., 305
Berteletti, I., 227
Bertenthal, B. I., 98
Berthiaume, V. G., 177
Berthier, N. E., 100
Bertoli, M. C., 333
Bertone-Johnson, E. R., 330
Bertrand, Y., 66
Bescemi, J., 221
Bessette-Symons, B., 443
Betancourt, J. R., 169
Betti, F., 63
Betts, J. F., 364
Betts, J. R., 240
Bevans, K., 238
Bever, L., 480
Beyene, Y., 366
Bezdicek, O., 432
Bhadoria, A. S., 165, 220–221, 277
Bhardwaj, R., 134
Bhasin, S., 367
Bhaskaran, K., 329
Bhatnagar, S., 480
Bhatt, R. S., 106
Bhattarai, N., 363
Bherer, L., 422
Bhutta, Z. A., 60
Bialystok, E., 127, 177, 227, 430, 432, 433
Bianchi, S., 355
Bianchi, S. M., 356
Bianchini, C., 422
Bibbins-Domingo, K., 321
Biblarz, T. J., 254
Bibok, M. B., 228
Bidelman, G. M., 124
Bienias, J. L., 434
Bienvenu, O. J., 346
Bierman, K. L., 152, 187, 210, 214, 257
Bigelow, A. E., 176
Biggs, W. S., 330
Bigler, E. D., 231, 434
Bijwaard, G. E., 60
Bilgin, A., 133
Billari, F. C., 386
Billet, S., 378
Billick, S.B., 265
Billieux, J., 323
Bilsen, J., 481
Bimbi, D. S., 329
Binder, E. B., 319
Bindman, S. W., 229
Bingham, C. R., 292
Bingham, S., 180
Binkley, N., 365
Binns, M. A., 447
Bion, R. A., 114
Birch, H. G., 136
Birch, L. L., 278
Bird-David, N., 397
Birditt, K., 399, 402
Birditt, K. S., 399–400, 462
Birkbeck, V., 202
Birken, S. A., 357
Birmaher, B., 282
Birmingham, W., 326, 395
Biro, F. M., 165, 272
Biryukov, S., 369
Bisgaier, J., 153

Bishop, D. V. M., 185, 241
Bissell, J., 256
Biswas, S., 46
Biswas-Diener, R., 288
Bitler, M. P., 186
Bitsko, R. H., 242, 262–263
Bixler, E. O., 160
Bjarnason, T., 253
Bjerke, M., 430
Bjorck, J., 444
Bjørge, L., 66
Bjørkløf, G. H., 444
Bjorklund, D. F., 26, 115, 199, 202–203, 205, 220, 230
Bjørnerud, A., 231
Black, A. E., 208
Black, D., 468
Black, K., 314
Black, L. I., 185
Black, M. M., 63, 88
Black, M.C., 358
Black, R. E., 60, 80
Black, W. W., 254, 309
Blackburn, E. H., 415
Blackford, J. U., 137
Blackwell, D. L., 321, 370
Blackwood, N., 313
Blaga, O. M., 115
Blair, C., 195, 229, 232, 238
Blair, K. A., 193
Blair, R. J. R., 313
Blais, L., 61
Blaisdell, C. J., 82
Blaizot, A., 426
Blake, J., 367
Blake, M., 272, 423
Blake-Lamb, T. L., 89
Blakemore, C., 92
Blakemore, S. J., 275, 281
Blakeslee, L., 457
Blanchard, R., 300
Blanchard-Fields, F., 332, 433
Blanco, C., 264
Blane, D., 450
Blanke, O., 471
Blankson, A. N., 133
Blasi, A., 93
Blatchford, P., 220, 239
Blatteis, C. M., 365
Blauer-Peterson, C., 77
Blazer, D. G., 427
Blázquez-Fernández, C., 325
Bledow, R., 322
Blehar, M. C., 141–142
Bleicher, I., 82
Bleidorn, W., 346, 441
Bleijlevens, M. H., 453
Bleil, M. E., 272
Blencowe, H., 80
Blennow, K., 430
Blethen, S. L., 272
Blieszner, R., 400–402, 404–406
Bloch, L., 458
Bloch, T. D., 219
Block, J. H., 346
Block, R. W., 155
Blondell, S. J., 370, 417
Blonigen, D. M., 440–441
Bloom, J. M., 246
Bloom, P., 111, 176, 227
Blössner, M., 165
Blossom, M., 126
Blowey, D., 310
Blum, R. W., 301, 306
Blumberg, S. J., 242, 262–263
Blumenthal, H., 273, 406
Blumenthal, J. A., 202, 259, 364
Blyth, D. A., 273
Bo, E., 272
Boan, J., 320
Boas, M., 272
Bobbitt-Zeher, D., 310
Bobowski, N. K., 96

Bochkov, Y. A., 223
Bocklandt, S., 300
Bockting, W., 343
Bocos, M., 399
Bocskay, K. A., 65
Boda, J. M., 341
Boden, J. S., 344
Boden-Albala, B., 423
Bodner, E., 410
Bodrova, E., 120, 205
Boehm, J. K., 443
Boeije, H. R., 452
Boelk, A. Z., 321
Boerma, T., 75, 330
Boerner, K., 473–474
Bogaert, A. F., 300
Bogale, W., 137
Bogg, T., 346
Boggero, I. A., 419, 448
Boggess, A., 92
Bøggild, H., 376
Bogossian, F., 65
Bograd, R., 459
Bohlmeijer, E. T., 483
Bohm, M. K., 61
Bohnen, N. I., 251, 430
Bohnert, A. M., 249
Boivin, M., 162, 210–211, 238, 261, 314
Bolan, G., 454
Boldt, L. J., 136, 150, 194, 247
Bolger, N., 474
Bolla, M., 372
Bollati, V., 317
Bollen, A. M., 66
Bolliger, I., 169
Bolt, D. M., 82
Bonanno, G. A., 397, 458, 473–474
Bonanoni, E., 222
Bond, B. J., 224
Bond, D. S., 320
Bongaarts, J., 452
Bongar, B., 299
Boniface, J., 118
Bønnelykke, K., 223
Bonnema, R., 373
Bonny, J. W., 118
Bonoti, F., 468
Bontempo, D., 364
Bonzini, M., 317
Boodoo, G., 232
Bookwala, J., 403
Boomsma, D. I., 231, 379
Boonk, L., 291
Boonstra, H., 305
Boonstra, H. D., 304–305
Booth, A., 308, 354
Booth, J. L., 227
Booth-LaForce, C., 144, 309
Borchert, S., 119
Borden, L. M., 249
Bordin, I. A., 207
Bordoni, F., 59
Borelli, J. L., 357
Borenstein, N. S., 85
Borgatti, R., 137
Borge, A. I., 213
Borgelt, L. M., 63
Borges, G., 477
Borghi, E., 165
Borghini, A., 82
Borghuis, J., 346
Borgogna, N. C., 300
Borjigin, J., 471
Borke, J., 147
Borkowski, J. G., 305
Bornstein, J., 255
Bornstein, M. H., 13, 109, 114, 125, 133, 206
Borowsky, A., 284, 364
Borowsky, I. A., 284
Borrero, S., 367, 373
Borse, N. N., 85
Borst, G., 226

Borup, I., 253
Bos, A. F., 115
Bosch, J., 255
Bosch, J. D., 259
Bose, J., 324
Bose, K., 68
Bosker, R. J., 239
Boskey, E. R., 299
Boskovic, R., 96
Bosma, H., 426
Bossche, H. V., 198
Bosshard, G., 481
Botsoglou, K., 213
Bottinelli, R., 363
Botvin, G. J., 309
Botwinick, J., 431–432
Bouchard, G., 394, 399–400
Bouchard, T. J., Jr., 181, 232
Bouchery, E. E., 61
Bouchey, H. A., 298, 311
Boufassa, F., 329
Boukydis, C. F. Z., 121
Boulerice, B., 211
Boulianne, G. L., 417
Boulianne, S., 348
Bouma, A., 164
Boundy, E. O., 81
Bourassa, K., 434
Bourassa, K. J., 396–397
Bourgeois, J. A., 404
Bourne, R. R., 420
Bourne, T., 476
Boustead, A. E., 281
Bowden, J., 160
Bowen, C., 452
Bowen, P. E., 429
Bowker, J. C., 257
Bowles, R. P., 229
Bowman, J. M., 348
Bowman, N. A., 332
Bowman, P. J., 389
Boyce, C. J., 388
Boyce, J. A., 167
Boyce, W. F., 310
Boyce, W. T., 272
Boyd, H., 222
Boyd, R., 93
Boyer, K., 64
Boyette, A. H., 152, 212
Boykin, A. W., 232
Boyle, C., 255
Boyle, J. P., 223
Boyle, M., 82, 259
Boyles, S., 66
Boyson, A. R., 259
Bozick, R., 293
Bozoglan, B., 323
Braams, B. R., 275
Brabeck, M. M., 288, 334
Bracher, G., 306
Bracke, P., 359
Brackett, M. A., 333
Bradbury, T. N., 354, 394, 458
Braddick, O., 96
Bradford, J., 299, 326, 443
Bradlee, M. L., 363
Bradley, H., 303
Bradley, R. H., 107, 138, 219–220, 248, 272, 303
Brady, S. A., 236
Brady-Smith, C., 207
Braeken, M., 65
Brain, C., 197
Braithwaite, T., 420
Brake, C. A., 448
Bramen, J. E., 64
Bramham, K., 81
Branche, C., 224
Branco, L. D., 364
Brand, J. E., 309
Brand-Gruwel, S., 291
Brandone, A. C., 116

Brandt, M., 462
Brang, D., 198
Branje, S., 288, 314, 346
Branje, S. J. T., 308
Brann, M., 463
Brannan, S. K., 430
Brannon, E. M., 118, 173
Branscombe, N. R., 256
Branski, D., 265
Branum, A., 59, 167
Brassai, L., 301
Brasselle, G., 145
Bratter, J. L., 357
Bratton, S. C., 264
Brauer, K., 369
Braun, J., 62, 63
Brauner-Otto, S., 251
Braunstein, G. D., 365
Brav, T., 436
Braveman, P. A., 88, 169, 318
Braver, T. S., 434
Brayne, C., 420, 430
Breau, R. H., 367
Breaux, C., 138
Brecklin, L. R., 324
Breckman, R., 454
Bredin, S. S., 370
Breen, G. M., 454
Bregman, H. R., 299
Breheny, M., 405
Brehmer, Y., 436
Breiding, M. J., 312, 358
Breitkopf, C., 64
Breitner, J. C. S., 374
Brendgen, M., 210, 211, 213, 238, 291, 314
Brener, N. D., 305
Brenner, J. S., 224
Brent, D. A., 282, 284, 469
Brent, M. R., 125, 128
Brent, S. B., 468
Bresnick, B., 97
Brest A., 372
Bretherton, I., 144
Brett, C. E., 81, 433
Brewer, R. D., 61
Brewer, T. J., 240
Brezina, P.R., 331
Brichta, A. M., 59
Brier, N., 476
Briggs, G. G., 61
Briggs, S., 251
Bright, G. M., 272
Brillo, E., 59
Brindis, C. D., 318
Brinkman-Stoppelenburg, A., 480
Briskin, S., 224
Brito, N. H., 127
Britt, J., 63
Britt, S. L., 397
Brittain, A., 304
Britton, J., 282, 303
Broaddus, M., 201
Brocca, L., 363
Brochado, S., 311
Brockman, R., 257
Broderick, J. E., 442
Brodosi, L., 320
Brody, G. H., 150, 250, 256, 273, 298, 301, 310
Brody, N., 232
Brodzinsky, D., 255
Brodzinsky, D. M., 255
Broekhuizen, M. L., 153
Broene, P., 186
Broesch, T., 147
Bromberger, J. T., 366
Bromet, E. J., 477
Bronfenbrenner, U., 25
Brook, C., 197
Brooks, J., 147
Brooks, L. J., 276
Brooks, R., 115
Brooks, S. K., 240

Di Gessa, G., 405
Di Giorgio, E., 97
Di Giunta, L., 156, 247, 275
Dijk, D. J., 365
Dijk, E., 288
Dijkstra, I., 476
Dildy, G. A., 68
Dillen, L., 462
Dillikar, D., 223
Dillon, E. L., 363
Dillon, M., 385
Dillow, S. A., 336
Dilworth-Anderson, P., 403
Dilworth-Bart, J. E., 170
Di Martino, A., 242
Di Mascio, D., 77
Dinella, L. M., 139, 205
Ding, E. L., 426
Ding, G., 66
Ding, L., 303
Dingemans, E., 447, 450
Dingus, T. A., 283
Dinsa, G. D., 166
Dionne, G., 210-211, 314
DiPalo, C., 426
DiPietro, J. A., 58-59, 64-65
Dipietro, L., 370
DiPrete, T. A., 336
Dira, S. J., 397
Direk, N., 367
Direkvand-Moghadam, A., 330
Di Riso, D., 399
Dirix, C. E. H., 59
Dirks, H., 93
Dirks, M. A., 310
Dishion, T. J., 249, 256-258, 291, 307, 314
Disteche, C. M., 44
Dittmar, H., 222
Dittus, P. J., 301
Divers, J., 223
Dixon, R. A., 364, 380
Dixon, V., 38
Djoussé, L., 272
Do, M. T., 92
Doak, C. M., 278
Doan-Van-Hay, L. M., 445
Dobriansky, P. J., 410, 449
Dobson, A., 455
Dobson, C. F., 76
Dobson, K. G., 231
Dodd, K. W., 426
Dodds J., 97
Dodge, B., 300, 423
Dodge, K. A, 211
Dodge, K. A., 205, 210, 211, 248, 257-259, 261, 272, 301, 313, 314
Dodson, C. S., 434
Dogra, S., 422
Doherty, W. J., 138
Döhnel, K., 177
Dolan, M. A., 358
Dolbin-MacNab, M. L., 402, 406
Doley, R., 406
Dombrowski, S. U., 320
Domina, T., 186
Dominguez-Folgueras, M., 351
Domitrovich, C. E., 187
Donahoe, A., 119
Donahue, K. L., 367, 368
Donaldson, A. E., 476
Dong, J. Y., 374
Dong, Q., 213
Donjacour, C. E., 322
Donlan, C., 470
Donlon, T. A., 415
Donnellan, M. B., 136, 440-441
Donnerstein, E., 259, 260, 271
D'Onofrio, B. M., 272
Donoho, C. J., 389
Donohoe, K. J., 251, 430
Donohoe, M. B., 469
Donovan, J. E., 63
Donzella, B., 153
Doolaard, S., 239
Doolan, M., 207
Dopp, A. R., 469
Dorfman, L. T, 447
Dornbusch, S. M., 209
Dornfeld, M., 209
Dorronsoro, M., 448
dos Santos Henrique, R., 163
Dotson, M. M., 432
Dotterer, A. M., 400
Doty, R. L., 363
Dougherty, L. R., 263
Doughty, S. E., 310
Dourleijn, E., 253
Douthit, K. Z., 370
Dove, H., 99
Dow, B., 423
Dow-Edwards, D., 275
Downer, J., 186
Downer, J. T., 183
Downey, D. B., 151, 310
Downey, L. A., 333
Downing, J., 398, 480
Downing-Matibag, T., 399
Dowshen, S., 155
Dowshen, S. A., 272
Doyle, L. W., 82
Doyle, W. J., 325, 375
Doyle Lynch, A., 371
Drabick, D. A., 313
Dragan, W. £., 137
Dragano, N., 325
Drageset, J., 461
Drake, B., 157, 350
Drake, P., 42, 65, 67-68
Drapeau, S., 252
Dreweke, J., 304
Drews, F. A., 292
Drey, E. A., 96
Driscoll, A. K., 42, 65, 67, 68, 72, 74-75, 80-82, 84-85, 304, 345, 355
Driskell, J., 443
Dröes, R. M., 404
Du, G., 223
Dua, T., 241
Duan, J., 300
Duarte, A., 419
Dubas, J. S., 136, 153
Dubbert, P. M., 320
Duberstein, P. R., 393, 398
Dubois, B., 145, 430
Dubow, E., 178
Duckworth, A., 289
Duckworth, A. L., 149, 231, 391
Ducore, J., 66
Dudley, J. A., 61
Duelle, N., 275
Due-Tønnessen, P., 231
Duffy, D. L., 41, 164
Duffy, J., 75
Dufour, A., 434
Dugas, K., 176
Dugdale, H. L., 415
Duggan, M., 291, 481
Duggirala, V., 430
Duivenvoorden, H. J., 404
Dukes, K., 66
Duley, J., 432
Dumke, H. A., 433
Dumlao, J., 321
Duncan, A. F., 145
Duncan, G. E., 386, 415
Duncan, G. J., 187
Duncan, J. R., 85
Duncan, L. E., 390
Duncan, T., 184
Dunfield, K., 135
Dunham, E., 197
Dunham, F., 125
Dunham, P., 125
Dunifon, R. E., 406, 456-457
Dunn, A. L., 427
Dunn, E. C., 157
Dunn, E. W., 356
Dunn, J., 151, 177, 205
Dunn, J. F., 151, 213, 256
Dunn, K., 50
Dunn, R. L., 96
Dunne, E. F., 303, 329
Dunne-Bryant, A., 359
Dunson, D. B., 330
Dunst, B., 243, 379
Dunst, C., 129
Dunstan, D. W., 425
DuPaul, G. J., 242
Dupierrix, E., 97
DuPont, R. L., 211
Dupoux, E., 129
Dupre, M. E., 456
DuPree, M. G., 300
Dupuis, D., 203
Dupuis, P., 367-368
Dür, W., 291
Duran, C., 242
Duran, F. L., 364
Durante, S., 449-450
Durazzo, T. C., 429
Duriancik, D. M., 253
Durkin, M. S., 92
Durlak, J. A., 249-250
Durston, S., 231
Durtschi, J. A., 311
Düzel, S., 420
Dwairy, M., 307
Dweck, C. S., 193
Dwomoh, I., 170
Dworkis, D. A., 418
Dwyer, D. S., 301-302
Dwyer, K. M., 211
Dye, B. A., 218
Dyer, S., 61
Dykas, M. J., 144
Dykstra, P. A., 401, 460-461, 463
Dyment, J. E., 220
Dymnicki, A. B., 250
Dyson, M. W., 263

Eagly, A., 199
Eagly, A. H., 198, 336
Eagon, C. J., 320, 448
Earl, J. K., 450
Earls, M., 145
Earnest, C. P., 321
Eaton, W. W., 346
Eaves, L. J., 313
Eaves, Y. D., 463
Ebbeling, C. B., 319
Eberly, S. S., 255
Ebmeier, K. P., 364
Ebstein, R. P., 46
Eccles, J. E., 307
Eccles, J. S., 278, 285, 288, 289, 291-293, 336
Eckenrode, J., 313
Eckerman, C. O., 151-152
Eckert, M. A., 364
Eckert, P., 386
Eckfeldt, J. H., 415
Eddins, A. C., 363
Eddins, D. A., 363
Eddleman, K. A., 66
Edelsohn, G., 263
Edelstein, R. S., 180
Edelstein, W., 346
Eden, G. F., 241
Edgin, J., 50
Edmondson, D., 482
Edwards, C. A, 437
Edwards, C. P., 186
Edwards, D., 437
Edwards, J. D., 432
Edwards, K. J., 326
Edwards, K. M., 305
Edwards, K.M., 358
Efreom, Y., 238
Egeland, B., 144
Egerter, S., 169, 318
Egger, M., 453, 481
Eggum, N. D., 247
Eggum-Wilkens, N. D., 210
Egloff, B., 346, 440
Ehiri, J. E., 63
Ehlayel, M. S., 223
Ehrenkranz, R. A., 139
Ehrenreich, S. E., 259
Ehsani, J. P., 283
Eibl-Eibesfeldt, I., 164
Eicher, J. D., 241
Eid, M., 397
Eidelman, A. I., 88
Eilers, P. H., 63
Eimas, P., 96
Eimicke, J. P., 454
Einarson, A., 96
Einio, E. K., 453
Eisenberg, A. R., 246
Eisenberg, M. E., 278, 349
Eisenberg, N., 149-150, 193, 205, 210-211, 213-214, 247, 266, 278, 287-288, 358
Eisend, M., 202
Eisenegger, C., 197
Eisengard, B., 208
Eivers, A., 153
Eivers, A. R., 213
Ejlskov, L., 376
Ekamper, P., 60
Ekholm, O., 370
Ekinci, B., 234
Ekman, I., 369
Elad, L., 184
Elad-Orbach, L., 184
Elalaily, R., 271-272
Elam-Evans, L. D., 303
Elaut, E., 198
Elder, D. E., 79, 160
Elder, G. H., 394
Elder, R., 305
Elder Jr, G. H., 273, 291
Eldridge, S., 427
Eley, T. C., 185
El-Gabalawy, R., 443
Elgamri, A. I., 87
Elgar, F. J., 275
El Ghoch, M., 320
Elia, A. J., 417
Eliason, M. J., 343
Eliason, S. R., 341
Eliassen, H., 373
Elicker, J., 144
Elieff, C., 350
Elkind, D., 285
Elledge, A. R., 238
Elledge, L. C., 238
Elleman, L. G., 440-442
Ellershaw, J., 481
Elliot, A. J., 370
Elliot, J., 229
Elliott, A. J., 127
Elliott, B. A., 169
Elliott, E., 92
Elliott, E. J., 61
Elliott, M., 305, 392, 444
Elliott, M. A., 290
Elliott, M. N., 273
Ellis, A., 116, 290
Ellis, B., 272
Ellis, B. J., 272, 301
Ellis, W. R., 250
Ellison, C. G., 403, 444
Ellison, G. M., 425
Ellison, N. B., 325
Elo, A. L., 429
Elovainio, M., 442-443
Else-Quest, N., 186
Else-Quest, N. M., 237
El-Sheikh, M., 206
ElSohly, M. A., 281
Ely, D. M., 80, 84-85
Ely, E. W., 470
Emanuel, E. J., 480-482
Emde, R. N., 98
Emerson, R. W., 118
Emery, L., 434
Emery, R. E., 251, 255, 272
Emlet, C. A., 443, 461
Emmons, R. A., 385
Emond, A., 65
Emsley, R., 322
Enayati, M., 144
Endendijk, J. J., 139
Eng, P. M., 456
Engarhos, P., 468
Engedal, K., 444
Engel, J. M., 99
Engelborghs, S., 430
Engelhardt, C. R., 260
Engels, R. C., 310
England, D. E., 201-202
Engle, P. L., 138
English, T., 356, 393, 455
Englund, M., 144
Ensari, N., 333
Ensor, R., 178, 210
Entringer, S., 65, 415
Entwisle, D. R., 238
Enwereji, E. E., 251
Epel, E. S., 415
Epperson, C. N., 139
Eppink, S. T., 398
Eppler, M. A., 101
Epstein, J. N., 62-63
Epstein, L., 320
Epstein, R., 79
Erath, S. A., 206
Erchull, M. J., 399
Erdmann-Sager, D., 321
Erdogan, B., 391
Ereky-Stevens, K., 108
Erickson, K. I., 364, 422, 429
Erickson, L. C., 123
Erickson, M. F., 138
Eriksen, M., 281
Erikson, E. H., 20, 140, 147, 194, 195, 246, 285, 296, 343, 384, 440
Eriksson, J., 364
Eriksson, M., 196
Erjavec, M., 125
Erosheva, E. A., 443, 461
Ersbøll, A. K., 370
Ersner-Hershfield, H., 389
Ertem, I. O., 100
Erten, N., 419
Ervin, R. B., 426
Eschen, A., 436
Escobar, G. J., 88
Escobar-Viera, C. G., 348
Escoto, K., 309
Escribano Subias, J., 145
Escudero, J., 444
Esgalhado, G., 323
Eskin, E., 371
Eslick, G. D., 86, 92
Espada, J. P., 264
Espehaug, B., 461
Espelage, D. L., 261
Espeland, M. A., 374
Espinoza, G., 348
Esposito, J., 320
Esposito, K., 426
Esposity, L., 85
Essex, M. J., 272
Esteller, M., 46
Estep, K. M., 193
Esteve, A., 351
Etaugh, C.A., 386
Etezadi, J., 447
Etta, E. F., 107
Ettinger, B., 371, 373
Euling, S. Y, 270
Euling, S. Y., 271
Evangelou, E., 429
Evans, A., 231, 396

Graham, J. E., 395
Graham, J. L., 399, 453
Graham, K. L., 203
Graham, S. A., 88, 174, 292, 430
Gralinski, H., 147
Granados, A., 202, 259, 342, 364
Grandner, M. A., 79
Granger, D. A., 264
Granier-Deferre, C., 59
Grant, D. A., 322
Grant, J. E., 321
Grant, P., 63, 64
Grant, S., 388
Grant, W. B., 60
Grantham-McGregor, S., 107
Grassi, M., 419
Grassi-Oliveira, R., 156
Grau, V., 180
Graubard, B. I., 319, 370
Grauerholz, L., 201
Gravina, S., 415
Gray, C. E., 272
Gray, J. R., 231–232, 346
Gray, L., 270
Gray, M., 354
Gray, P., 152, 212
Graziano, M. S. A., 93
Grazioplene, R. G., 346
Grazzani, I., 177
Green, A. P., 138, 140
Green, A. R., 169
Green, F. L., 176
Green, J. G., 284
Green, J. L., 280
Green, K. M., 341
Green, M., 392, 444
Green, R. C., 430
Greenberg, J., 462, 472, 475–476
Greenberg, J. S., 404, 475, 476
Greenberg, M., 187
Greenberg, N., 240
Greenberger, E., 364
Greendale, G., 366
Greendale, G. A., 365
Greene, E., 281
Greene, G., 458
Greene, K. M., 337
Greene, M. F., 61
Greene, M. L., 298
Greenfield, E. A., 447, 450, 453
Greenfield, P., 312
Greenfield, P. M., 291, 348
Greenlund, K., 426
Greenlund, K. J., 426
Greenspan, L. C., 272
Greenstein, D., 218
Greenwood, D. C., 63, 221
Greer, J. A., 470
Gregorevic, K., 480
Gregorich, S. E., 272
Gregory, A. M., 160
Gregory, E. C., 57, 82, 83
Gregory, S., 313
Greicius, M. D., 429
Grellier, J., 66
Grenell, A., 111
Grenier-Boley, B., 429
Gress-Smith, J. L., 322
Greulich, F. K., 205
Grevendonk, L., 317
Grewal, D., 333
Greyson, B., 471
Griffin, K. W., 309
Griffith, K. N., 318
Griffiths, M.D., 323
Grigorenko, E. L., 234, 333
Grigoryeva, A., 402
Grilo, C. M., 279–280
Grilo, S. A., 306
Grimbos, T., 300
Grimm, K. J., 230
Grimshaw, A., 7
Grinshteyn, E., 283
Grmec, S., 471

Grodstein, F., 363
Grodzicki, T., 369
Groeger, J. A., 365
Groen, R. S., 66
Groenen, A. A., 99
Groeneveld, M., 139
Groeneveld, M. G., 139–140
Groh, A. M., 143
Groholt, B., 262
Groothues, C., 95
Groothuis, T. G., 164
Gross, A. L., 436
Gross, C. G., 93
Gross, J. J., 149, 375, 443
Gross, J. N., 207
Grossberg, G. T., 404
Grossman, A. H., 299–300, 436
Grossmann, I., 436–437
Grossmann, M., 367–368
Grote, V., 145
Grotevant, H. D., 254–255
Group, K. S., 81
Grouper, S., 46, 76
Grov, C., 329
Grove, J. S., 415
Groves, C. L., 260, 311
Gruber, K. J., 76
Gruber, M. J., 463
Gruen, J. R., 241
Gruenewald, T. L., 371, 384, 390
Grulich, C. A., 180
Grummer-Strawn, L., 89
Grundgeiger, T., 322
Grunebaum, M. F., 398
Grusec, J. E., 207, 211, 246, 248
Gruszfeld,D., 145
Grych, J. H., 252
Grydeland, H., 231
Gu, B., 213
Gu, D., 444, 456
Gu, Q., 160, 217
Gu, X., 262
Guallar, E., 370, 372
Guan, Y., 100, 415
Guang, W., 330
Guariguata, L., 223
Guberman, S. R., 228
Gubernskaya, Z., 351
Gudykunst, W. B., 184
Gueldner, B., 262
Guendelman, S., 88
Guenther, P. M., 426
Guerchet, M., 453
Guerra, N. G., 262
Guerra, V. M., 334
Guglielmo, D., 218
Guida, A., 378
Guilamo-Ramos, V., 305
Guilford, J. P., 243, 379
Guillamon, A., 198
Guilleminault, C., 160
Guillery, R. W., 93
Guillet, L. A., 461, 463
Guiney, H., 321
Guise, J., 75
Gulumser, O., 100
Gunderson, E. A., 193
Güngör, E., 419
Gunja, M. Z., 318
Gunn, D. M., 229
Gunn, J. K. L., 63
Gunn, J. P., 426
Gunnar, M., 153
Gunnar, M. R., 143, 153–154, 255
Guo, F., 283
Guo, G., 313
Guo, S., 300, 405
Gupta, B. P., 371
Gupta, K. K., 62
Gupta, V. K., 62
Gur, R. C., 196, 237, 238, 290, 336
Guralnik, J. M., 370
Gurin, G., 332
Gurin, P. Y., 332

Gurrentz, B., 351
Gurteen, P. M., 125
Gurven, M., 129, 388
Gusarova, I., 349
Gustafson, G. E., 132
Gustafsson, E., 139
Gutchess, A., 419
Gutchess, A. H., 419, 434
Guthold, R., 276
Guthrie, J. R., 366
Gutt, H., 200
Güven, M., 444
Guy, M. W., 115, 314
Guyer, B., 81, 84
Gwynn, J. D., 219

Haar, J. M., 357
Haas, C., 286
Haas, E. A., 85
Haas, S. A., 277
Haase, C. M., 458
Haase, N., 426
Habak, P. J., 75
Habermas, T., 180
Habersaat, S., 82
Haboubi, N. Y., 419
Hack, M., 82
Hackett, C. J., 86
Hackett, G., 197, 367
Hackman, D. A., 238
Haden, C. A., 180
Hadfield, J. C., 406
Hafford, C., 255
Hagan, Jr., J.F., 265
Hagan, M. J., 308
Hagen, C. P., 272
Hagestad, G., 386
Haggerty, K. P., 262
Hagl, M., 469
Haglund, K. A., 301
Hahn, C. S., 13, 136
Hahn-Holbrook, J., 88
Haider, B. A., 60
Haidt, J., 334
Haight, S. C., 61
Haines, C. J., 372–374
Hains, S. M. J., 59, 114
Hair, N. L., 238
Haist, F., 162, 163
Haith, M. M., 96, 100, 117, 118
Hajovsky, D. B., 237
Haj-Siddig, O. E., 87
Hakeem, G. F., 85
Hakim, L. S., 367
Hakulinen, C., 442, 443
Hakuta, K., 332
Halberda, J., 125, 173, 183
Halberstadt, A. G., 7, 140, 246, 290
Hale, L., 218
Hales, C., 370
Hales, C. M., 84, 165, 221, 278, 319, 369
Halfon, N., 310
Halgunseth, L. C., 248
Halil, M., 419
Halim, M. L., 205
Halim, V. A., 450
Hall, D. M., 312
Hall, E. L., 173
Hall, J. A., 348
Hall, J. E., 372–374
Hall, J. H., 358
Hall, K., 61
Hall, K. D., 166, 320
Hall, P. A., 322
Hall, S. S., 353
Hall, W. A., 276
Hallal, P. C., 60
Hallenen, T., 447–448
Haller, D. M., 68
Hallers-Haalboom, E. T., 139
Hallford, D.J., 312
Halliwell, E., 222
Hallock, H., 364

Halperin, E., 371
Halpern, C., 312
Halpern, C. T., 343
Halpern, D. F., 195–196, 232, 237–238, 290, 336
Halpern, H. P., 201
Halpern, S. C., 157
Halpern-Felsher, B. L., 272–273
Halpern-Meekin, S., 358
Hamadani, J. D., 107
Hambrick, D. Z., 179
Hamburger, H. L., 322
Hamby, D., 129
Hamby, S., 207
Hamer, D. H., 300
Hamer, M., 456
Hamid, Q., 223
Hamilton, B., 177
Hamilton, B. E., 42, 62, 65, 67–68, 72, 74–75, 80–82, 304, 345–355, 452
Hamilton, J. L., 311
Hamilton, M., 202
Hamilton, M. A., 336
Hamilton, M. C., 201
Hamilton, S. F., 336
Hamilton, W. D., 415
Hamilton-Shield, J., 277
Hamlin, J. K., 134
Hamm, M., 367
Hamman, R. F., 223
Hammer, A., 453
Hammersley-Mather, R., 370, 417
Hammersmith, A. M., 397
Hammerton, G., 313
Hammond, S. I., 228
Hamouda, O., 329
Hampson, J. G., 197
Hampson, J. L., 197
Hampson, S. E., 273
Hampton, K. N., 348
Hampton, R. R., 226
Hamza, T. H., 427
Han, A., 278
Han, J. A., 211
Han, S. S., 264
Han, W. J., 107, 186, 309
Han, X., 323
Han, Z., 81
Hancock, A. D., 479
Handal, B., 239
Handelsman, D. J., 367
Handmaker, N. S., 62
Handwerker, W. P., 193
Hane, A. A., 153, 204
Hänel, M., 347, 393
Hanioka, T., 321
Hanish, L., 205
Hanish, L. D., 152, 201
Hank, K., 452, 462
Hanke, W., 170
Hankin, B. L., 282
Hankinson, S. E., 330, 373
Hanlon, H. M., 320
Hannan, P. J., 278
Hanney, L., 264
Hannigan, J. H., 62
Hannon, E. E., 96
Hanratty, B., 325
Hanschmidt, F., 479
Hanscombe, K. B., 182, 232
Hansel, T. C., 265
Hansen, A. E., 329
Hansen, S. N., 92
Hansen, T., 97
Hansen-Tift, A. M., 97
Hanson, J. L., 238
Hanson, R. L., 221
Hao, Y., 450
Happé, F., 194
Hara, Y., 371
Harari, M. M., 82
Harbaugh, A. G., 262
Hardeman, R. R., 77

Hardy, J., 428
Hardy, L. L., 219
Hardy, M. A., 404
Hardy, S. A., 341
Hare, D. L., 374
Hareli, S., 132
Hargreaves, A. L., 86
Haring, M., 473
Hariri, A. R., 430
Hariri, S., 303
Harker, A., 95
Harkness, S., 205
Harley, V. R., 43
Harlow, H., 141
Harlow, H. F., 141
Harlow, M. K., 141
Harman, D., 416
Harman, S. M., 367
Harmey, S. J., 182
Harnett, P., 62
Haro, J. M., 325–326
Harold, D., 429
Harold, G., 242, 262
Harold, G. T., 248–249, 251
Harper, G. W., 298, 310, 335, 386
Harper, J. M., 298, 310, 335, 386
Harper, M. C., 386
Harper, S. R., 335
Harriger, J. A., 222
Harrington, D. M., 272
Harris, A. M., 303
Harris, D., 272
Harris, D. G., 419
Harris, E., 205
Harris, J. L., 219
Harris, J. R., 309
Harris, K. M., 318
Harris, L. H., 75
Harris, P. L., 176, 178, 194, 368, 468, 498
Harris, T., 325
Harris, W. A., 276, 301
Harris, W. W., 264
Harris, W.A., 276
Harrison, F., 430
Harrison, R., 476
Harrist, A. W., 205
Harry, S., 207
Hars, M., 422
Hart, C. H., 208, 213
Hart, D., 346, 384
Hart, H. M., 385
Hart, S., 326
Harter, S., 146, 191–193, 246
Hartl, A. C., 310
Hartman, P. S., 417
Hartmann, P., 200
Hartshorn, K., 106
Hartup, W. W., 213, 257–258, 310, 398, 461
Hartwig, S. A., 8, 250
Harvey, A. G., 322
Harwood, R. L., 193
Haryu, E., 125, 183
Hasebe, Y., 307
Haselager, G. J. T., 346
Hashemian, S. M., 363
Hasher, L., 364
Hashim, A., 223
Hashimoto, T., 353
Hasin, D. S., 281
Haslett, S. J., 297
Hassan, F., 207
Hassan, N. M. M., 426
Hasselberg, M., 167
Hasselmo, K., 396, 397
Hasstedt, M., 302
Hastings, G., 219
Hastings, P. D., 211
Hatano, G., 288, 334
Hatchard, T., 63, 119, 330
Hategan, A., 404
Hatem, M., 72
Hatfield, L. A., 470

Hulme, C., 228, 229
Hulshoff Pol, H. E., 231, 364
Hultman, C.M., 92
Hultsch, D. F., 380
Hummel, A., 273
Hummer, T. A., 259, 260
Humphrey, N., 260
Humphrey, R. H., 333
Humphreys, C., 406
Hungerford, T. L., 474
Hunkeler, E., 427
Hunnius, S., 115
Hunt, G. E., 327
Hunter, J., 298
Hunter, S. B., 468
Hunter, W. M., 207
Huntley, J. D., 431
Huo, M., 399, 453
Huotilainen, M., 96, 116
Hur, Y. M., 379
Hurley, B. J., 170, 241–242
Hurley, K. M., 88
Hurren, N. M., 363
Hurtado, S., 332–336
Husby, I. M., 82
Hussar, B., 291, 292, 335–337
Hussein, N., 51
Hussey, M., 272
Huston, A. C., 251
Huston, S., 397
Hutchinson, E. A., 82
Hutchison, B., 454
Hutson, M., 345
Huttenlocher, J., 117, 173, 183, 231
Huttunen, M., 231
Huurre, T., 252
Huxhold, O., 461
Huyck, M. H., 380
Hwang, C. P., 140
Hwang, I., 284
Hwang, S. A., 66, 417
Hwang Koo, J., 264
Hyde, J., 290
Hyde, J. S., 195, 196, 210–211, 237,
  238, 278, 288, 290, 327–328,
  336, 357
Hyde, M. J., 82
Hyde, Z. H., 262
Hyder, A. A., 224

Iacoboni, M., 135
Iacono, W. G., 313, 342, 440–441
Iacovou, M., 405
Ialongo, N. S., 263
Iannotti, R. J., 253, 310
Iaria, G., 434
Ibrahim-Verbaas, C. A., 429
Icenogle, G., 275
Ickovics, J. R., 301
Ida, Y., 164
Idan, A., 367
Iervolino, A. C., 196, 201
Ihle, A., 436
Ihmeideh, F. M., 237
Ikram, M. A., 429
Imada, T., 127
Imai, M., Li, L., 125, 183
Imbimbo, B. P., 431
Imdad, A., 60
Imoscopi, A., 363
Imperatore, G., 223
Imuta, K., 152, 175, 210, 257
Inagaki, H., 417
Inan, O. T., 430
Indredavik, M. S., 82
Inelmen, E. M., 363
Ingalhalikar, M., 290
Ingoglia, S., 399
Inguglia, C., 399
Inhelder, B., 174, 226
Innocenti, G. M., 162
Inoue, M., 426
Inozemtseva, O., 195

Inskip, H. M., 330
Ioannidis, J. P., 37, 429
Iodice, S., 317
Iofe, A., 82
Ioverno, S., 299
Ippolito, M. R., 343
Iqbal, K., 303
Ireland, M., 284
Ironson, G., 111
Irwin, C. E., 318
Irwin, M. R., 423
Isaacowitz, D. M., 393, 441–442
Isaacs, A., 429
Isabella, R., 136
Isava, D., 262
Isengard, B., 453, 462
Isherwood, L. M., 474
Ishida, M., 47
Ishihara, J., 426
Ishii, A., 452
Ishii, N., 417
Isidori, A. M., 367
Islam, N., 128
Islam, R. M., 366
Ismail, M., 297
Ispa, J. M., 207, 248
Israel, S., 210
Itakura, S., 178
Itani, Z., 348
Ito, S., 61
Ivanova, K., 399
Ive, S., 222
Iverson, J. M., 124
Ivey, P., 138, 140
Iwamoto, K., 423
Iwasaki, M., 426
Iwasawa, M., 351
Izard, C., 266
Izard, V., 118
Izquierdo, M., 422
Izumi, K., 368
Izumi, S., 437
Izumi-Taylor, S., 205

Jaarsma, T., 374
Jaccard, J., 301
Jackey, L. M., 150
Jacklin, C. N., 140, 205
Jackson, J. B., 354
Jackson, J. C., 433
Jackson, J. K., 347
Jackson, K. D., 167
Jackson, M. L., 322
Jackson, P. W., 243
Jackson, V. A., 470
Jackson-Leach, R., 166
Jacob, B., 239
Jacob, V., 305
Jacobs, D. R., 370
Jacobs, D. R., Jr., 319
Jacobs, H. I., 435
Jacobs, M., 65
Jacobson, J. L., 142, 144
Jacobus, J., 274
Jacoby, B., 342
Jacqmin-Gadda, H., 430
Jacques, P. L. S., 443
Jacquet, A. Y., 59
Jacquier, E. F., 89
Jadalla, M., 182
Jaddoe, V. W., 63
Jaddoe, V. W. V., 59
Jadva, V., 200
Jaensch, A., 223
Jaffari-Bimmel, N., 144
Jaffe, H. W., 319
Jaffe, M. G., 369
Jaffee, S., 288
Jaffee, S. R., 347, 371
Jago, R., 257
Jain, D., 207
Jakeman, P., 363
Jakicic, J. M., 370
Jalmbrant, M., 476

Jalovaara, M., 397
James, A. E., 348
James, C., 311
James, L. E., 435
James, N., 422
James, S., 252
James, W. P. T., 166
Jampol, L., 391
Janecka, M., 66
Janicki-Deverts, D., 325, 375
Jankowiak, W., 138
Jankowiak, W. R., 311, 348
Jankowski, J. J., 82, 114–115
Jansen, I. E., 429
Janssen, I., 310, 370
Jansson, C., 476
Janus, A., 239
Japel, C., 210
Jarman, H., 222
Jarrold, C., 229
Jarvelin, M. R., 66
Järvenpää, A. L., 144
Jarvis, P., 203
Jauk, E., 243, 379
Jay, T., 184
Jayne, K. M., 264
Jazwinski, S. M., 386, 415
Jean, R. B., 458
Jean-Louis, G., 79
Jee, S. H., 370
Jeffery, H. E., 63
Jeffery, R. W., 219
Jeffries, A. R., 46, 331
Jeha, D., 305
Jekauc, D., 321
Jelic, M., 260, 311
Jellinger, K. A., 427
Jemal, A., 373
Jen, S., 458
Jenkins, F., 186
Jenkins, J. M., 304
Jenkins, J. V. M., 181
Jenkins, T. M., 44
Jennekens-Schinkel, A., 247
Jennings, J. M., 434
Jennings, K. D., 139
Jennings, M., 24, 115, 146, 150, 212
Jennings, S., 254
Jennings, W. G., 314
Jensen, A. C., 298, 310, 335, 386
Jensen, A. R., 232
Jensen, E. B., 166
Jensen, G.A., 417
Jensen, H., 147
Jensen, J. L., 88, 89
Jensen, L. A., 334–335
Jensen, N. R., 376
Jensen, T. M., 359
Jenson, L. A., 334
Jensvold, N. G., 88
Jeon, M., 419
Jeong, H. U., 379
Jerman, J., 328
Jernigan, T. L., 162–163, 274
Jeromin, F., 323
Jerskey, B. A., 93
Jeste, D. V., 419, 430–431, 446–447
Jester, J. M., 282
Jeswani, S., 393
Jette, N., 427
Jhin, H. K., 92
Ji, N., 45
Jia, Y., 291
Jiang, J., 310
Jiang, L., 292
Jiang, T., 429
Jiao, F. Y., 264
Jiao, W. Y., 264
Jiao, Y., 395
Jimenez, C. L., 300
Jin, C., 323
Jin, K., 416

Jin, L., 65
Jinno, M., 317
Jipson, J. L., 173
Ji-Yeon, K., 150
Joash, K., 476
Johannessen, H. A., 363
Johannsen, N. M., 321
Johansson, B., 470–471
Johansson, H., 372
Johansson, P., 374
John, E., 262
John, O. P., 346, 399–400, 440
Johnell, O., 372
John Horwood, L., 341
Johns, H., 429, 430
Johns, M. M., 300
Johnsen, J., 305
Johnson, A. M., 221, 329
Johnson, B. D., 365
Johnson, C. A., 223
Johnson, C. C., 343
Johnson, C. L., 456, 461
Johnson, D., 318, 363
Johnson, D. J., 192, 298
Johnson, D. R., 308, 354
Johnson, E. J., 377
Johnson, F., 187
Johnson, III, J. A., 221
Johnson, J. D., 259–260, 271
Johnson, J. M., 251, 430
Johnson, K. A., 251, 430, 435
Johnson, K. R., 420
Johnson, M. A., 33, 65, 93,
  445, 452
Johnson, M. D., 311, 354,
  384–385
Johnson, M. K., 400
Johnson, M. O., 137
Johnson, N. E., 462
Johnson, R. W., 419
Johnson, S., 82
Johnson, S. C., 418
Johnson, S. K., 251
Johnson, S. R., 330
Johnson, T. E., 418
Johnson, W., 217, 231, 427
Johnson Jr., J. H., 452
Johnston, C., 96
Johnston, J., 238,
  280–282, 327
Johnston, L., 311, 341
Johnston, L. D., 280–281
Johnston, M., 88
Joinson, C., 162
Jokela, M., 442–443
Jolkkonen, J., 429
Jolles, J., 426
Jolly, J. L., 243
Jonas, J. B., 420
Jones, B. Q., 326, 395
Jones, C. L., 397
Jones, D. E., 187
Jones, D. J., 301
Jones, E. K., 366
Jones, G., 164
Jones, G. W., 251
Jones, H., 138, 397
Jones, K. M., 241
Jones, L. Y., 422
Jones, M., 330
Jones, M. P., 432
Jones, N. G. B., 138, 397
Jones, R. M., 274–275
Jones, S., 262
Jones, S. E., 276
Jones, S. M., 167
Jones, T. H., 367
Jongsma, H. W., 59
Joniau, S., 372
Jonson-Reid, M., 157
Jonsson, B., 288
Joo, J. E., 46
Jopp, D., 446

Jordan, B., 72
Jordan, K., 335
Jordan, N. C., 173
Jordan, R. E., 369
Jordan-Marsh, M., 60, 282
Jorm, A. F., 282
Jose, A., 351
Joseph, C. L., 343
Joshi, A., 313
Josse, G., 379
Jovanovic, B., 177
Joy, M. E., 150
Jozefowicz-Simbeni, D., 255
Ju, H., 330
Juan, L., 75
Juan, M., 248
Juang, L., 233
Judaš, M., 59
Juffer, F., 144, 255
Juhl, J., 471
Julian, M. M., 255
Jun, H. J., 298
Jun, J., 404
Jung, J. H., 405
Jung, K., 24
Jung, S., 64
Jungmann, T., 82
Junque, C., 198
Junqué, C., 419, 435
Jurewicz, J., 170
Jurgens, H. A., 419
Jurgenson, J. R., 366
Jurkowitz, I. T., 313
Jusczyk, P., 96
Jusczyk, P. W., 121
Juster, F. T., 219
Justice, L. M., 183

Kabeto, M. U., 434
Kaciroti, N., 127, 272
Kackar, H., 288
Kadis, J., 333
Kadji, C., 65
Kaelber, D. C., 310
Kaestle, C. E., 343
Kaestner, K. H., 46
Kaewesarn P., 72
Kafetsios, K., 132
Kagan, J., 118, 136–137, 142
Kager, R., 124
Kahn, J. A., 303
Kahn, K. L., 470
Kahn, M., 322
Kahn, R. E., 261
Kahn, R. L., 446
Kahn, R. S., 62–63, 364
Kahn, S., 344
Kahnauth, A., 223
Kahonen-Vare, M. H., 429
Kai, J., 51
Kaikhavandi, S., 330
Kail, B. L., 452
Kainer, M. A., 303
Kaiz, M., 306
Kalamaras, J., 452
Kalan, I., 419
Kalicinski, M., 436
Kalil, A., 309
Kaliszewska-Czeremska, K., 323
Kalkbrenner, A. E., 92
Kalkhoran, S., 324
Källén, K., 65
Kallio, E., 379
Kallio, E. L., 431
Kalmijn, M., 456, 475
Kamal, R., 84
Kambas, A., 99
Kamimura, K., 452
Kaminski, J. W., 63
Kamp, D. C. M., 458
Kamp, K. A., 203
Kampert, J. B., 427
Kan, Y. W., 51
Kanaan, M., 325

Murray-Close, M., 353
Murry, V., 273
Murry, V. M., 250, 298, 308
Murta, S. G., 450
Murtagh, E., 277
Musco, T., 318
Musick, K., 253
Musick, M. A., 444, 447
Musil, C. M., 406
Musisca, N., 346
Must, A, 259-260, 271-272
Mustafa, J., 363
Mustanski, B. S., 300
Mustonen, U., 252
Mutran, E. J., 405
Muzikanskym, A., 470
Muzzy, W., 454
Mychasiuk, R., 119
Myers, A., 431
Myers, D. G., 348, 354, 391
Myers, E., 63
Myers, J. E., 353, 386, 395
Myers, M. M., 127
Myers, S., 322
Myers, S. A., 463
Myhre, A. M., 262
Myowa-Yamakoshi, M., 133
Myrick, A., 133
Myrick, S. E., 298

Na, J., 436-437
Näätänen, R., 96
Nabi, R. L., 348
Nabors, L. A., 154
Nachtigall, L. B., 251, 430
Nadel, L., 50
Nader, P., 220
Nader, P. R., 219
Nadler, D., 289
Nagaraja, J., 167
Nagata, J. M., 321
Nagel, G., 223
Nagin, D., 282
Nagin, D. S., 210
Nahar, B., 107
Naicker, K., 282
Naidoo, A., 63
Naidoo, K. S., 362
Naidu, R. K., 297
Naik, S., 63
Naimark, B., 157
Naito, M., 173
Naito, T., 353
Naitza, S., 442
Naj, A. C., 429
Nakagawa, A., 137
Nakamoto, J., 238, 291
Nakamura, K., 370
Nakanishi, K., 321
Nakayama, K., 322
Nam, J.-M., 430
Nam, R.K., 368
Nam, S., 393
Namkung, E. H., 404
Nandrup, A. B., 239
Nanin, J. E., 329
Napolitano, L., 353
Narasimhan, A., 424
Narciso, I., 475
Nardone, S., 92
Nargis, N., 322
Narr, K. L., 231
Naseem, K., 333
Nash, A., 151, 152
Nash, E., 304
Nash, H. M., 228
Nassar, A., 305
Natarajan, R., 46
Nation, M., 314
Natrajan, M. S., 420
Nava, M., 298
Navarro, J., 265
Navarro-Asencio, E., 246, 290
Naveh-Benjamin, M., 436

Nayga, R. M., Jr., 166
Nazan, N, 386, 415
Nazroo, J., 99, 272, 423
Ndagurwa, P., 351, 395
Nderi, M., 282
Neal, A.M., 358
Neal, B., 165
Neal, C., 64
Neale, B. M., 45
Neale, M. C., 327
Neamatzadeh, H., 64
Nebeker, C., 430
Needham, B., 395, 458
Neely-Barnes, S. L., 406
Neff, L., 370
Negreiro, F., 170
Nehra, A., 367, 371
Nehring, I., 58
Neiderhiser, J. M., 54
Neidorf, S., 350
Neimeyer, R. A., 473, 476
Neinhaus, A., 429
Neisser, U., 232
Neitzel, R. L., 363
Nelken, B., 66
Nelson, A. R., 325
Nelson, B., 282
Nelson, C. A., 95, 110, 119, 475
Nelson, C. J., 367
Nelson, D. A., 202, 208
Nelson, D. B., 72
Nelson, K., 180
Nelson, K. B., 75, 109, 118, 180
Nelson, L. J., 317, 347, 400
Nelson, R. M., 347
Nelson, S. K., 356-357
Nelson, T., 11, 123
Nelson, V. A., 431
Nelson-Piercy, C., 81
Nemergut, M. E., 224
Neo, L. F., 321
Neppl, T. K., 136, 313
Nerlich, B., 46
Nesdale, D., 256
Nesi, D., 265
Nesi, J., 311
Nespor, M., 114
Ness, J., 454
Nesse, R. M., 473
Nesselroade, J. R., 389
Nestadt, G., 346
Neto, D. D. L. R., 75
Neto, F. K., 161
Netzer, J. K., 462
Neubauer, A. C., 243, 379
Neubauer, A. P., 82
Neugarten, B. L., 345, 447, 469
Neugarten, D. A., 345
Neumann, D. L., 237
Neumann, R., 297
Neumark, D., 449
Neumark- Sztainer, D., 278
Neumark-Sztainer, D., 278, 309, 310
Neupert, S. D., 436
Neville, H. J., 229
Newacheck, P. W., 222
Newcomb, A. F., 258
Newcomb, P., 373
Newcombe, N., 120
Newgent, R. A., 238
Newman, C. L., 166
Newman, E., 64
Newman, R. S., 124
Newman, S., 203, 452
Newth, C. J., 476
Neyer, F. J., 347, 393, 455, 461
Neyfakh, L., 212
Nezlek, J. B., 333
Ng, F. F. Y., 193
Ng, K. K., 364
Ng, M., 92, 165
Ng, T. W., 380
Ng, W., 391

Ngandu, T., 370
Ngangana, P. C., 405
Ngeow, M. Y., 364
Ngun, T. C., 300
Nguyen, S., 468
Nguyen, T. K., 177
Nguyen-Huynh, M. N., 369
Nguyen-Jahiel, K., 182
Niaura, R., 282, 310
Nichols, K. E., 207
Nicholson, C., 476
Nicholson, J. M., 76, 323
Nickerson, A., 475
Nicklas, E., 207
Nicklas, T. A., 219
Nicklett, E. J., 444
Nicklin, J. M., 289
Niclasen, B., 253
Nicoladis, E., 127
Nicolae, D. L., 223
Nicolaisen, M., 398, 461
Nicolas, S., 378
Nie, J., 395
Nie, N. H., 35
Niedziela, M., 197
Niehuis, S., 344
Nielsen, B. J., 376
Nielsen, H. S., 476
Nielsen, L., 370
Nielsen, M., 135
Nielson, M. G., 347
Niemi, A. K., 81
Niemivirta, M., 225
Niermann, C., 321
Niesink, R., 275
Nieuwenhuijsen, M. J., 66
Nievergelt, C. M., 300
Nigg, J. T., 282
Nihiser, A. J., 220
Nihtilä, E., 452
Nijhuis, J. G., 59
Nijstad, B. A., 379
Nikbakht Nasrabadi, A., 458
Nikkel, S. M., 62
Nikolas, M. A., 242
Nikolova, N., 59
Nikora, L. W., 138, 397
Nilsen, E. S., 174
Nilsen, G. B., 371
Nilsson, L. G., 364
Nilstun, T., 481
Nisbett, R. E., 195, 232, 238, 436, 437
Nisbett, R.E., 178
Nissen, C., 423
Nissen, K., 255
Nissim, N. R., 435
Niv, S., 313
Niwa, F., 133
Niwa, T., 317
Nix, R. L., 187
Nixon, C., 301
Nixon, C. L., 177
Nixon, J., 277
Noble, E. P., 379
Noble, K. G., 127
Noble, L., 88
Noble, Y., 93
Nobre, A. C., 229
Nóbrega, C., 319
Nocita, G., 204
Nock, M. K., 157, 284, 477
Nock, S. L., 354
Noda, A., 423
Noël, P. H., 427
Noël-Miller, C. M., 396, 458, 461
Nolen-Hoeksema, S., 322
Noll, R. B., 214
Noom, M. J., 124
Noonan, C. J., 66
Noone A.M., 372
Nordby, K. C., 363
Nordling, J. K., 194, 247
Norman, J. E., 75

Norman, R., 331
Norman, R. J., 331
Noro, A., 453
Norris, J. E., 384
Norris, K., 194
Norris, L., 332
Northey, J. M., 422
Norton, C., 363
Norton, J. B., 429
Norton, M. E., 66
Norton, M. I., 288, 410
Norton, S., 374
Norup, M., 481
Norvilitis, J. M., 399
Nosarti, C., 95
Noschang, R., 161
Nosek, B. A., 37
Novaes, S. C., 309
Novakova, L. M., 432
Nowacki, P., 376
Nowak, G., 86
Nowicki, S., 424
Nozaki, K., 356
Nucci, L., 307
Nunes, M. L., 161
Nuñez, A., 63
Nunez, C., 64
Nuñez, V., 420
Nuwwareh, S., 426
Nweke, O., 170, 241-242
Nyberg, L., 364
Nygard, M., 321
Nyholt, D., 41
Nyholt, D. R., 41
Nyman, M., 211

Oakes, L. M., 116
Obel, C., 63
Obel, N., 329
Oberle, E., 178, 257
Oberman, L. M., 135
Oberski, D., 346
O'Brien, B., 415
O'Brien, C. M., 63
O'Brien, E., 247, 326
O'Brien, M., 121, 133, 219, 220
O'Brien, T. C., 256
Obrosky, S., 263
O'Callaghan, F., 62
Ocfemia, M. C. B., 329
Ockene, J., 373
O'Cleirigh, C., 326
O'Connell, J. F., 138, 397
O'Connell, L., 135
O'Connor, A., 426
O'Connor, C., 61
O'Connor, D. B., 272, 423
O'Connor, D. L., 13, 136
O'Connor, E. A., 320
O'Connor, H., 364
O'Connor, M. J., 64
O'Connor, T. G, 196, 241
Odden, H., 178
Oddy, L., 85
Odén, A., 372
Odgers, C., 282
Odimegwu, C., 351, 395
Odlaug, B. L., 321
O'Doherty, K., 128
O'Donnell, B. F., 231
O'Donnell, K., 446
O'Donnell, L. N., 282
O'Dwyer, N., 364
Oehme, K., 252
Oeppen, J., 418
Oesterle, S., 341
Offer, D., 306
Offit, P. A., 86
O'Flynn O'Brien, K. L., 330
Ofner, J., 92
Ofori, B., 61
Oftedal, G., 66
Ogawa, E. F., 415

Ogawa, N., 184
Ogden, C., 217, 220, 319
Ogden, C. L., 84, 89, 139, 160, 165, 217, 219, 221, 278, 319, 370
Ogedegbe, C., 325
Ogedegbe, G., 325
Ogikubo, H., 452
Ogle, G., 223
Ogunwole, S. U., 457
Ogunyemi, D., 75
Oh, S., 234, 333
Oh, W., 139, 257
Ohan, J. L., 251-252
O'Hara, M. W., 145
O'Higgins, M., 145
Öhman, H., 431
Öhrfelt, A., 430
Ohrr, H., 370
Oimet, M. C., 283
Oishi, S., 391, 393, 442
Ojeda, S., 270
Oka, H., 370
Oka, M., 354
Okada, H., 125, 183
Okazaki, M., 452
O'Keefe, C., 125
Okely, A. D., 220
Okoro, C. A., 371
Okuda, M., 423
Olaf Zylicz, P., 137
Oláh, L. N., 173
Olander, E. K., 59
Olatomide, O. O., 333
Oldehinkel, A. J., 261
Olds, T., 310
Olds, T. S., 219
O'Leary, K., 322
O'Leary, K. D., 351
O'Leary, L., 50
Olfson, M., 264
Olino, T. M., 263
Oliveira, P. F., 367
Oliver, B., 185
Oliver, B. R., 212, 313
Ollendick, T. H., 213
Ollier-Malaterre, A., 357
Ollikainen, M., 46
Olmstead, R., 423
Olsen, A., 82
Olsen, E. O. M., 312
Olsen, J., 64, 476
Olsen, J. A., 341
Olsen, L. R., 476
Olsen, L. W., 221
Olsen, S. F., 208
Olson, D. R., 178
Olson, K. L., 139
Olson, L. S., 238
Olson, M. E., 169
Olson, R., 219
Olson, S. L., 207
Olsson, B., 430
Olthof, T., 247
Olyaei, A., 75
O'Malley, P., 317, 341
O'Malley, P. M., 280-281, 327
O'Malley-Keighran, M. P., 278
Omer, S. B., 86
Omori, M., 333
O'Muircheartaigh, C. A., 423
O'muircheartaigh, J., 93
O'Neil, A., 395
O'Neil, C. E., 219
O'Neil, K., 204, 205
O'Neill, D. K., 110-111
Onelöv, E., 476
Onishi, K. H., 177
Ono, H., 219
Ono, M., 43
Ontai, L. L., 136, 151
Onwuteaka-Philipsen, B. D., 480, 481, 482
Onyishi, E. I., 356
Onywera, V. O., 219

Reitzes, D. C., 405
Rejdak, K., 429
Rekker, R., 314
Remez, L., 301
Ren, Q., 402
Ren, Z., 61
Renaud, S. J., 468
Rendall, M. S., 460
Rende, R., 282, 310
Renders, C. M., 278
Renier, C. M., 169
Renken, R. J., 419
Renoux, C., 368
Rentfrow, P. J., 346
Rentz, D. M., 435
Rentzou, K., 108
Renzo, G. C. D., 59
Repacholi, B., 144
Repetti, R. L., 238
Repping, S., 46, 331
Resing, W. C., 234
Resnick, H. S., 454
Resnick, L. B., 227–228
Resnick, M. D., 284, 349
Resnikoff, S., 362
Rettek, S. I., 297
Reuben, C., 242, 325
Reuben, C. A., 242
Reuter, M., 379
Reuter-Lorenz, P., 419–420, 433, 434
Rey, E., 61
Reyes, A., 63
Reyes, C., 38
Reyes, F., 325
Reynolds, A. J., 115, 289, 314
Reynolds, C. A., 377, 415, 442
Reynolds, C. F., III, 423
Reynolds, G. D., 115, 314
Reynolds, J., 389
Reynolds, K., 369, 443
Reynolds, M. R., 237
Rezaei, E., 458
Reznick, J. S., 119, 136–137
Rhee, E., 297
Rhee, S. H., 313
Rhew, I. C., 282
Rhoads, G. G., 305
Rhodes, R. E., 370
Rhodes, S. L., 427
Rholes, S. W., 356
Ribe, E., 405
Ricciuti, H. N., 253, 309
Rice, F., 242
Rice, J. B., 452
Rice, K., 222
Rice, M. L., 126, 184, 185
Rice-Lacy, R. C., 322
Richard, A., 93, 435
Richards, J. B., 372
Richards, M. H., 298
Richards, R., 170
Richardson, C. R., 370
Richardson, D. S., 415
Richardson, E. G., 477
Richardson, G. A., 63
Richardson, J., 138
Richardson, K. A., 63
Richardson, K. J., 320
Richardson, S., 424
Richardson, T. J., 404
Richert, R. A., 128
Richman, L. S., 374–375
Richmond, T. S., 425
Richter, L., 60
Richter, P. A., 325
Richters, J., 476
Riddell, M. C., 425
Riddell, R. R. P., 96
Rideout, V. J., 292
Ridgers, N. D., 220
Ridley, K., 310
Riechelmann, H., 362
Riedel-Heller, S. G., 479

Rieder, M., 60
Rieffe, C., 288
Rieger, G., 300
Riegle-Crumb, C., 291
Riem, M. M., 143
Riemann, D., 423
Riemann, M. K., 60
Rietjens, J. A., 480
Rietzschel, E. F., 380
Riggins, T., 63
Riggle, E. D., 343
Riggle, E. D. B., 350
Riggle, S. G., 350
Riggs, B. J., 222
Rignell-Hydbom, A., 65
Riksen-Walraven, J. M., 346
Riley, E. P., 62
Riley, J., 238
Riley, L. M., 276
Rimm, E. B., 369, 456
Rinaldi, C. M., 24, 115, 146, 150, 212
Rious, J. B., 314
Riphagen, S., 222
Rippy, J., 112
Rissel, C. E., 476
Ritchie, C. S., 470
Ritchie, H., 424
Ritchie, K., 429
Ritchie, S. J., 232, 364
Ritchie, T., 379
Rittenour, C. E., 463
Ritter, P. L., 209
Rittirong, J., 462
Rittner, R., 65
Ritz, B., 65
Ritz, B. R., 318
Ritzen, H., 291
Rivas-Drake, D., 342
River, L. M., 357
Rivera, B., 325
Rivera, J. A., 167
Rivera-Gaxiola, M., 123, 127–128
Riveros, A., 209
Rivers, S. E., 333
Rizvi, F., 366
Rizzo, G., 77
Robb, M., 59, 121
Robb, M. B., 128
Robbins, C. L., 300
Robbins, J. M., 222
Roberto, K., 400–402, 404–406
Roberto, K. J., 348
Roberts, A. W., 457
Roberts, B., 346, 388, 440
Roberts, B. A., 433
Roberts, B. W., 346, 388, 441, 442
Roberts, D., 79
Roberts, D. F., 209, 292
Roberts, G., 82
Roberts, I. S., 145
Roberts, J. E., 154
Roberts, J. S., 430
Roberts, K. P., 180
Roberts, L., 249
Roberts, M. A., 249
Robertson, D. A., 433
Robin, L., 220
Robins, R. W., 346
Robinson, A., 169
Robinson, C. C., 208
Robinson, E. S., 37
Robinson, J., 355
Robinson, J. B., 454
Robinson, K. N., 420
Robinson, L. R., 8, 250
Robinson, M., 165, 476
Robinson, O. C., 387
Robison, J., 462
Robitzsch, A., 441
Robles, O., 357
Robles, T. F., 326, 395, 457
Robustelli, B. L., 458

Rochat, P., 147, 178
Rochat, T. J., 145
Röcke, C., 391
Rockett, H. R., 278
Rodenhizer, K. A. E., 305
Rodgers, A. B., 47
Rodgers, E., 182
Rodgers, J. L., 232
Rodie, M., 197
Rodkin, P., 238
Rodkin, P. C., 259
Rodrigue, K. M., 419
Rodrigues, L. P., 163
Rodriguez, B. L., 223
Rodriguez, F. S., 434
Rodriguez, J., 192, 298
Rodriguez, J. M., 371
Rodriguez, M. L., 149
Rodríguez-Cintas, L., 346
Rodríguez-López, R., 319
Rodríguez-Mañas, L., 422
Roeder, U. R., 297
Roediger, H. L., 434
Roediger III, H. L., 179
Roehlkepartain, E. C., 342
Roehr, S., 434
Roelfs, D. J., 459, 474
Roerig, J., 280
Roesch, L., 282
Roess, A. A., 89
Roettger, M., 313
Rogaeva, E., 429
Rogers, A. E., 218
Rogers, C. H., 475–476
Rogers, C. S., 201, 205
Rogers, M. A., 325
Rogers, M. C., 138, 140
Rogers, S. J., 354
Rogoff, B., 32, 119–120, 148, 203, 212, 285
Rogol, A., 269–271, 273, 278
Rohack, J. J., 481
Rohal, M., 207
Rohani, D. A., 231
Rohde, L. A., 263
Rohra, V. K., 66
Roisman, G. I., 143–144, 344, 350
Roizen, N., 64
Rojas-Flores, L., 264
Rokholm, B., 278
Rolle, I., 63
Rollins, B. C., 394
Roman, J. L., 468
Roman, R. J., 297
Romano, E., 157, 211
Rombouts, S. A., 143
Romero, C., 193
Romero, I., 298
Romney, D. M., 140
Ronald, A., 46, 331
Ronald, R., 347
Roncero, C., 346
Ronfard, S., 175
Ronnennberg, A. G., 330
Ronsmans, C., 75
Ronzi, S., 325
Rood, B., 343
Rook, K. S., 456, 461
Rooney, K., 364
Roopnarine, J. L., 140, 152, 186
Roosa, M. W., 262
Ropero, S., 46
Rosales, C. B., 63
Rosamond, W., 426
Rosario, M., 298
Rosatelli, M. C., 51
Roscigno, V., 449
Rose, A. J., 202, 256, 258–259, 342, 364
Rose, G., 415
Rose, K. K., 112
Rose, M., 455
Rose, N. S., 436

Rose, R. J., 273
Rose, S. A., 82, 114–115
Roseberry, S., 128
Rose-Krasnor, L., 204
Roseman, I. J., 297
Rosen, C. L., 276
Rosen, E. D., 46
Rosen, M. A., 96, 378
Rosen, R. C., 367, 368, 393–394
Rosenbaum, J. E., 305
Rosenbaum, S., 425
Rosenberg, E. B., 255
Rosenberg, H. J., 389
Rosenberg, K., 303
Rosenberg, S. D., 389
Rosenberger, N., 400
Rosenbluth, S. C., 348
Rosenfeld, M. J., 398
Rosengren, A., 325, 369
Rosengren, K., 468
Rosengren, K. S., 111
Rosenthal, B. P., 362
Rosenthal, C., 462
Rosenthal, C. J., 462
Rosenthal, D. G., 66
Rosenthal, S. L., 303
Roser, M., 236, 355, 414, 424
Rosnati, R., 392
Rosner, B., 223, 278, 373
Rosner, R., 469
Ross, C. E., 222, 278, 395
Ross, H., 281
Ross, J. L., 197
Ross, L. A., 432
Ross, S., 262
Ross, S. E., 278, 395
Rosselli, M., 195
Rossi, A. S., 368
Rossi, L., 273
Rossier, J., 442
Rossouw, J. E., 373
Rostami, C., 221
Rostila, M., 475
Roth, C. L., 272
Roth, D. L., 445
Roth, M., 318
Roth, S., 379
Rothbart, M. K., 136, 149, 194
Rothblum, E. D., 350, 358
Rothenberg, S. J., 66
Rothman, A. J., 320, 374
Rothman, E., 313
Rothman, E. F., 193
Rothschild, Z. K., 472
Rotosky, S. S., 350
Rotstein, A., 358
Rott, C., 65, 445, 452
Rottenberg, J., 322
Roubinov, D. S., 322
Rouder, J. N., 260
Rourke, M., 177
Rouse, C., 238
Rouse, D. J., 75
Rouse, H. L., 166
Roussotte, F. F., 64
Routasalo, P., 456
Routh, B., 393
Routledge, C., 471
Rovee-Collier, C., 105–106
Rowe, J. W., 446
Rowe, M. L., 129
Rowland, J. H., 373
Roy, S., 92
Roygardner, L., 169
Rozanski, A., 456
Rozman, M., 449
Ruan, X., 366
Rübeling, H., 192
Rubin, C., 272
Rubin, D. C., 345
Rubin, D. H., 66
Rubin, G. J., 240

Rubin, K. H., 137, 204–205, 211, 257, 310
Rubin, S. E., 64, 65
Rubio, D., 373
Rubio, G., 394
Ruble, D., 199–200
Ruble, D. N., 196, 199–201, 205
Rudd, R. A., 85
Rudolph, K. D., 263
Rudy, D., 248
Rueda, M. R., 149, 194
Ruffman, T., 175, 210
Rugg, M. D., 419
Ruggeri, M., 222
Ruggles, S., 357
Ruhl, H., 310
Ruigrok, A. N., 139, 197, 290
Ruiz-Rubio, M., 323
Rumbaut, R. G., 317
Runco, M. A., 379
Rundek, T., 422
Rundle, A. G., 240
Runions, K. C., 262
Runyan, D. K., 156, 207
Ruparel, K., 290
Rurka, M., 393
Rusanen, M., 370
Rüsch, N., 479
Rushkin, M., 320
Rushton, J. P., 231–232
Ruskis, J., 112, 178
Russ, A. J., 454
Russ, S. A., 310
Russell, D., 453
Russell, J. A., 194
Russell, L. A., 220
Russell, R. K., 326
Russell, S. T., 254, 299
Russo, C., 433
Russo, M., 357
Rust, J., 195, 196, 201
Rustenbach, S. J., 280
Rutherford, G., 283, 477
Rutter, H., 277
Rutter, M., 53, 95, 196, 241
Ruttle, P. L., 272
Ryan, A. S., 88
Ryan, C., 238, 299
Ryan, M. K., 110
Ryan, N. D., 282
Ryan, S., 108, 186
Rybash, J. M., 378
Rybin, D. V., 63, 119
Rychlak, J. F., 193
Ryff, C. D., 391, 392, 420, 442, 462
Rylander, L., 65
Ryncarz, R. A., 334
Ryskina, V. L., 129
Rytting, N., 126
Ryu, E., 262
Ryznar, M., 351

Saarela, J., 475
Saarni, C., 194, 246
Sabbagh, M. A., 177–178
Sabermarouf, B., 428
Sabetta, S., 419
Sabik, N. J., 403
Sabol, B., 75
Saccone, G., 77
Sachdev, P. S., 364
Sachs, H. C., 99
Sacker, A., 99
Sacks, G., 165
Sacks, J. J., 61
Sacuiu, S., 470–471
Saczynski, J. S., 436
Sadarangani, T., 404
Sadeh, A., 79, 160–161, 322
Sadigh-Eteghad, S., 428
Sadruddin, A. F., 7
Saez, M., 349
Safati, A., 322

Page numbers in **boldface** indicate key terms. Page numbers followed by *t* indicate tables; page numbers followed by *f* indicate figures.

K-ABC-II (Kaufman Assessment
    Battery for Children), **234**
kangaroo care, **81**
karyotype, 51, 51*f*
Kaufman Assessment Battery for
    Children (K-ABC-II), **234**
kindergarten, 187
kinetic cues, 100
kinship care, **406**
kinship ties, 401–407, 461–463

laboratory experiments, 34
laboratory observation, 29*t*, 30
LAD (language acquisition
    device), **121**
Lamaze method, 76
language, **120**, 125
    acquisition. *See* language
        acquisition
    development. *See* language
        development
    gender differences and, 196
language acquisition
    in adolescence, 285–286
    brain development and, 127
    caregiver influence, 121, 128
    child-directed speech, 129
    children's books and, 128
    delayed development, 185
    in early childhood, 182–185
    early development, 121–126,
        122*t*, 127–129
    early vocalization, 121
    first sentences, 125–126
    first words, 124–125
    gestures, 124
    in infancy and toddlerhood,
        120–129
    in middle childhood, 235–237
    milestones, 122*t*
    perception of sounds and
        structure, 122–123
    pragmatics, 183–184
    private speech, 184
    second-language learning,
        235–236
    social interaction and, 127–129
    social speech, 183–184
    vocabulary development,
        182–183, 235
language acquisition device
    (LAD), **121**
language development, 123–124
    variations in, 126–127
lanugo, 77
late adulthood
    ageism and, 410
    aging. *See* aging
    aging in place, 451–452
    alternative housing options, 455
    chronic conditions, 424–425
    cognitive changes, 431–437
    cohabitation, 460–461
    coping strategies, 445–446
    disabilities and activity
        limitations, 425
    elder abuse, 454
    elder care, 412
    financial concerns, 450–451
    friendships, 461
    gay and lesbian relationships, 458
    graying of population, 410, 411*f*
    health status, 424
    intelligence, 431–433
    kinship ties, 461–463
    lifestyle influences on health and
        longevity, 425–426
    living alone in, 452
    living arrangements,
        451–455, 451*f*
    living in institutions, 453–454
    living with adult children,
        452–453
    longevity and aging, 413–418

marital relationships, 457–459
    memory, 433–436
    nonmarital lifestyles and
        relationships, 459–461
    personality, 440–442
    personal relationships in,
        455–457
    physical and mental health,
        423–431
    physical changes in, 418–423
    psychosocial development,
        439–463
    relationships in, 455–457
    relationships with adult children,
        461–462
    relationships with siblings, 463
    retirement and, 448–450
    single life in, 459–460
    typical developments, 5*t*
    well-being, 442–448
    wisdom and, 436–437
    work and, 448–450
latency stage, 19, 20*t*
lateralization, **90**
Latino Americans. *See also*
        Hispanic Americans
    cesarean birth rate, 75
    early childhood health, 318
    identity formation and, 298
    living with adult children, 452
    obesity in children, 89
    perceived discrimination and, 298
    raising grandchildren, 406
    spanking among, 207
laughing, 133
LDs (learning disabilities), **241**
lead
    as environmental hazard, 66
    intellectual disability and, 241
learning disabilities (LDs), **241**
learning perspective, 18*t*, 21–22
LeBoyer method, 76
leptin, 272
lesbian, gay, bisexual,
        or transgender (LGBT)
    adults, 443
    parents, 355
LH (lutenizing hormone), 269
life expectancy, **413–414**, 413*f*
life review, **482–483**
life satisfaction, 391
life span, **413**
    extending, 416–418
    periods of, 3–5, 4*t*–5*t*
    responses to death across,
        468–470
life-span development, **2**
life-span developmental
        approach, 12
limbic system, 275
linguistic intelligence, 232, 234*t*
linguistic speech, **124**
literacy, **128**, **381**
    adult training, 381
    emergent literacy, 185
    historical and global trends
        in, 236
    middle childhood development
        and, 236–237
"living apart together" (LAT)
    relationships, 460
living arrangements in late
        adulthood, 451–455
living will, **479**
locomotion, 98–99
locomotor play, 202
logical-mathematical intelligence,
        232, 234*t*
longevity, **413–418**
    lifestyle influences, 425–426
longitudinal studies, 34–36, 35*t*
long-term marriage, 457–458
long-term memory, **179**, 434
loss, ambiguous, 473

love
    in emerging and young
        adulthood, 348
    triangular theory of, 348
    withdrawal of, 207–**208**
low-birth-weight babies, 67–68, **80**
    outcomes, 81
    risk factors, 81
    risk factors for, 81
    treatment, 81
lutenizing hormone (LH), 269

macrosystem, 25*f*, 26
macular degeneration,
        age-related, **421**
magnetic resonance imaging
        (MRI), 217
malnutrition, 60, 165–166
    infants, 89–90
    in late adulthood, 419
    stillbirth and, 82–83
maltreatment
    in infancy and toddlerhood,
        154–157
    long-term effects, 157
mammography, **373**
marijuana
    adolescence, use in, 280–281
    consumption during
        pregnancy, 63
    emerging and young adulthood,
        use in, 327
    prenatal development and, 63, 66
marital capital, **397**
marital happiness, 354
marital satisfaction, 354
    health and, 395
    in middle adulthood, 394–395
    parenthood and, 356
marriage. *See also* remarriage
    after cohabitation, 351
    arranged, 353, 394–395
    cultural and contextual influences,
        351–353
    divorce, 357–359, 459
    emerging and young adults views
        on, 352
    extramarital sexual activity,
        353–354
    first, age at, 353
    gay and lesbian, 349–350,
        397–398
    and health, 395
    influence on health, 326
    long-term, 457–458
    in middle adulthood, 394–395
    relationships in late adulthood,
        457–459
    same-sex, 328, 349–350, 397–398
    satisfaction in, 354
    "semi-arranged," 353
    traditions across cultures, 352
    wedding traditions, 352
    widowhood, 459
massive, open, online courses
        (MOOCs), 335
masturbation, 300
maternal blood tests, 67*t*
maternal mortality rates, 68, 72
maternal weight, prenatal
        development and, 59–60
mathematics
    early childhood cognitive
        development, 173
    middle childhood cognitive
        development, 227
maturation, **6**
mature-onset diabetes. *See* type 2
        diabetes
measles-mumps-rubella (MMR)
        vaccine, 86
measurement estimation, 227
mechanistic model, **16**
    quantitative change and, 17

meconium, 78
media use
    academic achievement and,
        239–240
    adolescents and, 292
    aggression and, 259–260, 260*f*
    in early childhood, 178–179
    in infancy and toddlerhood, 112
    infidelity and, 354
    research-based recommendations
        for babies and, 112
    violence and, 259–260
media violence, influence on
        aggression, 259–260
Medicaid, 450
medical durable power of
        attorney, 479
Medicare, 450
meiosis, 42
melatonin, 276
memory. *See also* working memory
    aging and, 435
    Alzheimer's disease and, 428
    autobiographical memory, 180
    basic processes and
        capacities, 179
    childhood memories, 180
    declarative memory, 118
    declining of, 435–436
    early childhood development,
        179–180
    episodic memory, 180, 434
    explicit memory, 118
    generic memory, 180
    implicit memory, 118
    infant development, 105–106
    in late adulthood, 433–436
    long-term memory, 179, 434
    metamemory, 230
    mnemonics, 229
    procedural memory, 118, 434
    recall, 179–180
    recognition, 179–180
    retention, 180
    semantic memory, 434
    sensory memory, 179, 434
    short-term memory, 434
    visual recognition memory, 114
menarche, **271**, 273–274
Mendel, Gregor, 44
menopausal transition, 365
menopause, **365**–367
    cultural differences in, 366
menopause hormone therapy
        (MHT), 366–367
menstruation, 271, 330
mental health
    in adolescence, 280–284
    anxiety disorders, 262–263
    childhood depression, 263
    children's, 240, 263–264
    common problems, 262–264
    disruptive conduct disorders, 262
    effect of COVID-19 on, 328
    emotions and, 374–375
    in emerging and young adulthood,
        326–328
    in late adulthood, 426–431
    in middle adulthood, 374–375,
        391–392
    in middle childhood, 262–266
    personality and, 442
    positive, 391–392
    resilience, 265–266
mental states, knowledge of, 175
mercury, 66, 241
mesosystem, 25*f*, 26
messenger RNA (m-RNA), 42
metacognition, **230**, 285
metamemory, **230**
metaphor, 235
methamphetamine, 64
MHT (menopause hormone
        therapy), 366–367

micronutrients, 60
microsystem, 25–26, 25*f*
middle adulthood
    aging parents, relationships with,
        401–404
    brain development, 363–364
    career change and, 386
    change and stability in, 388–390
    change at, 384
    cohabitation, 395–396
    consensual relationships in,
        394–398
    creativity in, 379–380
    divorce and, 396–397
    emotions in, 388–389
    empty nest, 399–400
    expertise and, 378
    fitness and, 363
    friendships in, 398
    gay and lesbian relationships,
        397–398
    health in, 368–376
    identity in, 226, 389–390
    integrative thought, 378–379
    kinship ties, 401–407
    marriage, 394–395
    maturing children and, 399–401
    mental abilities in, 376*t*, 377*f*
    mental health at, 374–375,
        391–392
    midlife change, 384
    personality in, 388
    physical changes in, 362–368
    psychosocial development,
        384–407
    psychosocial theory and,
        384–385
    relationships in, 392–407
    sensory changes during, 362–363
    sexual activity in, 367–368
    sexual and reproductive
        functioning, 365–368, 365*t*
    sibling relationships, 404–405
    as social construct, 362
    social contact theories,
        392–393, 393*f*
    stress at, 375–376
    structural and systemic changes,
        364–365
    voluntary childlessness, 401
middle age. *See* middle adulthood
middle childhood
    aggression and, 258–262
    anxiety disorders, 262–263
    brain development, 217–218, 218*f*
    and changes in brain's
        structure, 217
    childhood depression, 263
    cognitive development,
        224–228, 225*t*
    common emotional problems,
        262–264
    developing self, 246–247
    disruptive conduct disorders,
        262
    education and, 237–243
    emotional development, 246–247
    executive functioning, 228–229
    family influences, 247–256
    growth patterns, 217*t*
    health and safety, 218–224
    information-processing approach,
        228–230
    language and, 235–237
    language development, 122*t*
    literacy and, 235–237
    medical conditions, 222–224
    memory, 229
    mental health and, 262–266
    obesity in, 220–221
    peer influences, 256–262
    physical development, 217–218
    Piagetian approach, 224–228
    prosocial behavior, 247

psychometric approach, 230–234
psychosocial development, 245–266
selective attention, 229
midlife. *See* middle adulthood
midlife crisis, **385**–388
midlife review, **387**
mindset, self-esteem and, 192–193
mirror neurons, **135**
mirror self-recognition, 147
miscarriage. *See* spontaneous abortion
mitochondrial theory of aging, 416
mitosis, 42–43, 57
MMR vaccine, 86
mnemonic device, **229**
mnemonic strategies, metamemory and, 229–230
modeling, 22
modesty, 193
monkeys, and attachment, 141
monozygotic twins, **41**–42
Montessori method, 186
MOOCs (massive, open, online courses), 335
moral development
    in adolescence, 286–288
moral reasoning
    culture and, 334–335
    levels and stages of, 286
    prosocial, 288–289
moratorium status, 341
Moro reflex, 94*t*
mortality rates
    adolescence, 283, 283*f*
    under age 5, 83, 83*f*, 167, 168, 168*f*
    anorexia nervosa, 280
    infants. *See* infant mortality rates
    life expectancy and, 413
    life span and, 416
mortality revolution, 466–467
motherese, 129
mothers
    age at first birth, 355*f*
    bedtime, 79
    effects of employment, 152–153, 249, 309
    relationships with adult children, 462
    role in caregiving, 138
    teenagers, 304–305
    timing of puberty and, 272
motor coordination, 163
motor cortex, 127
motor development
    dynamic systems theory, 101
    in early childhood, 163–164
    ecological theory of perception, 100–101
    ethnic and cultural influences, 99–100
    infants, 97–101, 98*t*
    milestones for infants, 97, 98*t*
    perception and, 100
MRI (magnetic resonance imaging), 217
multifactorial transmission, **45**
multigenerational households. *See* extended family
multilingual households, 126–127
multiple births, 41–42, 68
    IVF and, 331
multiplicity, 332
musical intelligence, 232–233, 234*t*
mutation, **43**
mutual help, 401
mutual regulation, **144**
myelin. *See* white matter
myelination, **93**
myopia, **362**

naproxen, 61
narrative psychology, 389

National Assessment of Educational Progress (NAEP), 239
National Institute of Child Health and Human Development (NICHD), 79
Native Americans
    academic achievement and, 289–290
    age at first birth, 355
    alcohol use among, 324
    diabetes and, 223
    health status in emerging and young adulthood, 318
    infant mortality among, 84, 84*f*
    media use and, 239
    miscarriages among, 57
    populations, 410
    SIDS and, 85
    suicide and, 283, 477
    teenage pregnancy and, 304
nativism, **121**
natural childbirth, **75**
natural experiments, 34
naturalistic observation, 29*t*, 30
naturalist intelligence, 232–233, 234*t*
natural selection, 26
nature *versus* nurture debate
    canalization, 53
    genotype-environment correlation, 53–54
    genotype-environment interaction, 53
    heredity and environment, 51–54
    language acquisition, 120–121
    nonshared environmental effects, 54
    reaction range, 52–53
near-death experiences (NDEs), 471
negative emotions, 374
negative interactions, 326
negative nomination, 257
negative peer influence, 256
negativism, 148
neglect
    cultural influences, 156
    in infancy and toddlerhood, **154**–157
    long-term effects, 157
neglectful parenting, 208
neonatal jaundice, **78**
neonatal period, **77**–79
neonate, **77**
neurobehavioral abnormalities, methamphetamine and, 64
neurobiological deficits, 313
neurodevelopmental disorders
See also autism spectrum disorders (ASD)
    vaccines and, 86
neurofibrillary tangles, **428**
neurons, **91**–93
neuroticism
    in emerging and young adulthood, 345*f*, 346
    in late adulthood, 442
    in middle adulthood, 388
neurotransmitters, 93
newborn babies, 59
    behavioral assessment, 78–79
    body systems, 78
    low birth weight, 80–82
    medical assessment, 78–79
    perception of sounds and structure, 122
    postmaturity and, 82
    sensory capacities, 95–97
    size and appearance, 77
    sleep patterns, 79
    states of arousal, 79
    stillborns, 82–83
NICHD (National Institute of Child Health and Human Development), 79

niche-picking, **54**
nicotine, 62, 66, 323–324
nightmares, 162
night terrors, 162
noble savage theory of development, 16
No Child Left Behind (NCLB) Act of 2001, 239
nocturnal emission, 271
non-college-bound students, 293
noninvasive screening tests, 50
nonnormative influences, **11**
nonorganic failure to thrive, **155**
nonshared environmental effects, **54**
nonsiblings, toddler contact with, 151–152
nonsocial play, 204*t*
nonsteroidal anti-inflammatory drugs (NSAIDs), 61
normative age-graded events, 11, 345
normative history-graded events, 11
normative influences, **11**
normative life events, **345**
normative-stage models
    in emerging and young adulthood, 343–344, 344*t*
nouns, 125
novelty preference, 114
nuclear family, **6**–7
number line estimation, 227
number patterns, 173
numbers
    early childhood understanding of, 173
    middle childhood understanding of, 227
    toddler understanding of, 117–118
number sense, 173
number transformations, 173
numerosity estimation, 227
nursing homes, 453–454
nutrition, 219
    in adolescence, 276–280
    breast *versus* bottle, 88–89
    caloric reduction and longevity, 418
    in infancy, 88–89
    influence on health, 319
    in late adulthood, 426
    in middle childhood, 219
nutritional supplements, infants and toddlers, 90

obesity. *See also* overweight
    in adolescence, 277–278
    causes, 220–221
    epidemic, 319–320, 320*f*
    in infants, 89
    in middle childhood, 220–221
    outcomes, 221
    prenatal development and, 60
    prevention in middle childhood, 221
    rates, 221
    treatment, 221
object concept, 110–111
object permanence, **110**–111, 116–117, 117*f*
objects in space, understanding of, 172, 225
observational learning, **22**
obsessive-compulsive disorder (OCD), **263**
occipital lobe, 91, 91*f*
OCD (obsessive-compulsive disorder), **263**
ODD (oppositional defiant disorder), **262**
Oedipus complex, 19
oldest old, 412, 417

old old, 412
OLSAT8 (Otis-Lennon School Ability Test), **231**
one-parent families, 252–253. *See also* single-mother families
only child, 213
open adoption, 254
open-ended interviews, 29
open science movement, 36–37
operant conditioning, 21–**22**, **105**
operational definition, **30**
opiates, 61
opioid abuse, 280
oppositional defiant disorder (ODD), **262**
oral stage, 19, 20*t*
ordinality, 173
organismic model, **16**–17
organization, **23**, **230**
organogenesis, 57
osteoporosis, **372**
Otis-Lennon School Ability Test (OLSAT8), **231**
overextended word meanings, 126
overt aggression, **210**, 259
overweight, 165, 220, 319–320, 320*f*. *See also* obesity
    in adolescence, 277–278
    outcomes, 221
ovulation, 41

pain, 96
pain cry, 132
palliative care, **470**
pandemic, **64**. *See also* COVID-19
parental monitoring and self-disclosure, 307–308
parental self-reports, 29
parental *versus* adolescent authority, 308*t*
parentese, 129
parents/parenting, 82
    abusive and neglectful, 155–156
    academic achievement and, 238, 290–291
    adolescents, relationships with, 306–309
    adult children and, 400–401
    aggression and, 211
    antisocial behavior and, 313–314
    Baumrind's model of parenting styles, 208–209, 208*t*
    and child vaccination, 86
    control strategies, coregulation and, 248
    cultural and contextual influences, 355
    cultural differences in parenting styles, 209
    by default, 406
    discipline and, 206–208
    early childhood and, 206–211
    early media use and, 112
    early social experiences and, 138
    emerging adults, relationships with, 346–348
    emerging and young adults as, 355–357
    fearfulness in early childhood, 211
    helicopter, 399
    and inductive techniques, 207
    influence on gender differences, 139–140
    lesbian, gay, bisexual, or transgender (LGBT), 355
    marital satisfaction and, 356
    in middle childhood, 248
    neglectful parenting, 208
    permissive parenting, 208
    poverty and, 249–250
    and recognition of emotions, 246
    sandwich generation and, 402
    social interaction model and, 180
    stepparenthood, 359

styles of, 208–209, 208*t*, 307
    substance use in adolescence, 282
    terrible twos and, 148
    uninvolved parenting, 208
parietal lobe, 91, 91*f*, 127
Parkinson's disease, **427**
participant observation, **31**
parturition, **73**
passion, 348
passive correlations, 53
passive euthanasia, **479**
peekaboo games, 110–111
peers
    academic achievement and, 238, 290–291
    aggression, 258–262
    friendship, 257–258, 258*t*
    gender-typing and, 201
    influence, 256–262
    influences, 150–152
    influences in adolescence, 310–313
    middle childhood and, 256–262
    popularity, 257
    and positive/negative pressure, 201
    substance use in adolescence and, 282
pelvic inflammatory disease (PID), 303
perception
    depth perception, 100
    of discrimination, 298
    ecological theory of, 100–101
    haptic perception, 100
    motor development and, 100
perceptual awareness, 118
perceptual development, cultural differences in, 123–124
perceptual processes, 114–115
performance measures, 29*t*, 30
perimenopause, **365**
periodontal disease, 426
permissive parenting, **208**
personal agency, 146
personal fable, 285
personality, **132**. *See also* normative-stage models
    Alzheimer's disease and, 428
    culture and, 388
    ego-resilient, 346
    influence on health and well-being, 441–442
    in late adulthood, 440–442
    in middle adulthood, 388
    models of development, 343–346, 344*t*
    overcontrolled, 346
    resilience and, 266
    stability and change in late adulthood, 440–441
    timing-of-events models, 344*t*, 345
    trait models, 344*t*, 345–346
    traits in old age, 440–442
    typological models, 344*t*, 346
    undercontrolled, 346
pesticide exposure, 170
PET (positron emission tomography), 30, 415
p-hacking, 37
phallic stage, 19, 20*t*
phased retirement, 380
phenotype, **44**–45
phenylketonuria (PKU), 48*t*, 79
phonemes, 122–123
phonetic approach, **236**
physical abuse, **154**, 454
physical activity
    in adolescence, 275–276
    adult lifestyle habits, 425–426
    benefits of, 275
    and body weight, 321
    and fitness, 219–220
    in late adulthood, 422, 425–426
    in middle childhood, 221
    during pregnancy, 60–61

physical development, **3**
adolescence, 269–274
early childhood, 160–170
infants, 86–97
in middle adulthood, 362–376
middle childhood, 217–218
physical fitness
behavioral influences on,
319–324, 369–370
in emerging and young
adulthood, 317–328
in middle adulthood, 363
in middle childhood, 218–224
physical punishment, 107, 207
African Americans and, 209
physician-assisted suicide (PAS),
480–482
Piagetian approach, 20*t*,
22–24, **105**
cultural influences on, 227–228
early childhood development
and, 170–179
evaluation of theory, 285
formal operations, 284–285
imitation, 109–110
infant and toddler development
and, 108–113, 109*t*
information processing and,
115–118
middle childhood development
and, 224–228
object concept, 110–113
preoperational stage, 170–175
research evaluation, 113–114
sensorimotor stage substages,
108–109, 109*t*
symbolic development, 111–113
theory of mind, 175–178
pictorial competence, 111
PID (pelvic inflammatory
disease), 303
pincer grasp, 97, 98
PKU. See phenylketonuria (PKU)
placebo, 33
placenta, 57
plasticity, **12**, 14, **95**
play
adaptive value of, 203
cognitive levels of, 202–203
constructive play, 203
cultural influences on, 205–206
dramatic play, 203, 205
in early childhood, 202–206
fantasy play, 172
formal games with rules, 203
functional play, 202
gender differences in, 205
imaginative play, 203
locomotor play, 202
pretend play, 203
reticent play, 205
rough-and-tumble play, 220
social dimension of,
204–205, 204*t*
social play, 204–205, 204*t*
playmates in early childhood,
213–214
play style
culture and, 140
gender differences and, 139
play therapy, **264**
pleasure principle, 19
PMS (premenstrual syndrome),
329–330
politeness, 184
polycystic kidney disease, 48*t*
polygenic inheritance, **44**
pons, 127
popularity, 257
positive emotions, 374–375
positive mental health, in middle
adulthood, 391–392
positive nomination, 257
positive peer influence, 256

positron emission tomography
(PET), 30, 415
postformal thought, 331–**332**
postmature, **82**
postpartum depression (PPD), 145
poverty
abuse and neglect and, 155
academic achievement and, 289
aggressiveness and, 211
antisocial behavior and, 314
dropping out of high school and,
291–292
early childhood health and, 169
in emerging and young
adulthood, 319
failure to thrive and, 155
food insecurity and, 321
health in middle age and, 370
immigrant families and, 10
IQ and, 182
in late adulthood, 451
low-birth-weight babies and, 81
media use and, 239
parenting and, 249–250
prenatal care and, 68
statistics, 8
power assertion, **208**
PPD (postpartum depression), 145
Prader-Willi syndrome, 47
pragmatics, **183**–184, **235**
preconception care, 69
prediction of development, 2
prefrontal cortex, 119, 275
pregnancy. See also childbirth;
prenatal development
during adolescence,
304–305, 304*f*
and alcohol, 38, 62
impact of pandemic on, 64
marijuana consumption
during, 63
postpartum depression, 145
prevention programs, 304
smoking and, 62–63
weight gain during, 59–60
preimplantation genetic
diagnosis, 67*t*
prejudice, **256**
prelinguistic speech, **121**
premarital sex, 328
premature babies. See preterm
babies
premenstrual syndrome (PMS),
329–330
prenatal care, 69
disparities, 67–69
globally, 68
low birth weight, risk factors
for, 81
prenatal development, 4*t*
alcohol taken during, 61–62
assessment techniques, 67*t*
brain development during,
89–91, 91*f*
caffeine and, 63
cocaine and, 63
diabetes and, 64, 65
embryonic stage, 57
fetal stage, 58–59
genetic and chromosomal
abnormalities, 47–50, 48*t*
germinal stage, 57
marijuana and, 63
material drug intake, 61–64
material illness and, 64
maternal age and, 65
maternal influences, 59–66
maternal malnutrition, 60
maternal physical activity and
strenuous work, 60–61
maternal stress and depression,
64–65
maternal weight, 59–60
medical drugs taken during, 61

methamphetamine and, 64
monitoring, 66–69
nicotine and, 62–63
opioids taken during, 61
outside environmental hazards,
65–66
paternal influences, 66
sensory capacities, 95–97
stages, 54–59
time line, 55*t*–56*t*
prenatal screening, 66–69, 67*t*
preoperational stage, 20*t*, **170**
preoperational thought
advances of, 170–173, 171*t*
immature aspects of, 171*t*,
173–175
prepared childbirth, **75**
presbycusis, 362
presbyopia, 362
preschool education, 185
advancement in math and, 173
compensatory programs,
186–187
cultural variations in, 185–186
types of, 186
preschoolers. See early childhood
pretend play, 172, 203
preterm babies, 67–68, **80**, 83
primary aging, **411**–412
primary appraisal, 445
primary reflexes, 93
primary sex characteristics, **269**
primitive reflexes, 93
privacy, 37
private speech, **184**
proactive aggression, 258
problem-focused coping, 322, **445**
problem solving
creativity and, 379
development in middle
childhood, 231
expertise, 378
hypothetical-deductive reasoning
and, 284–285
late adult cognition and, 433
play and, 205
procedural memory, 118, **434**
progesterone, 373
Project CARE, 107
Project Head Start, 186–187, 187*f*
prosocial behavior, **210**
in adolescence, 288
in early childhood, 210
in middle childhood, 247
prosocial moral reasoning,
288–289
protective factors, **265**
protective headgear, usage of, 224
proximity-seeking, 26
proximodistal principle, **56**, **86**
psychoanalytic perspective,
17–21, 18*t*
gender and, 199
psychological control, 307
psychological well-being.
See well-being
psychometric approach, **105**,
106–108
development testing, 106
early home environment
assessment, 107
early intervention, 107–108
intelligence testing, 106, 181–182
in late adulthood, 433
middle childhood development
and, 230–234
testing infants and toddlers, 106
psychosexual development,
18–**19**, 20*t*
psychosocial development, **3**,
19–21, **20**, 20*t*
in adolescence, 295–314
altruistic helping, 134–135
attachments and, 140–144
autonomy, 147–148

conscience, 149–150
contact with other children,
211–214
crying, 132–133
developing self, 191–195,
246–247
in early childhood, 190–214
in emerging and young
adulthood, 340–359
emotions, 132–135
empathy, 134–135
family interactions and, 138
foundations of, 132–140
gender differences, 139–140
in infancy and toddlerhood,
131–157, 132*t*
in late adulthood, 439–463
laughing, 133
maltreatment and, 154–157
in middle adulthood, 383–407
in middle childhood, 245–266
mutual regulation, 144
postpartum depression in
mother, 145
self-regulation, 149
sense of self, 146–147
smiling, 133
socialization processes, 148–150
social referencing, 146
temperament, 135–138
trust and, 140
psychosocial moratorium, 296
psychosocial theory, 296
and middle adulthood, 384–385
puberty, **269**
adolescent growth spurt, 271
cultural context of, 273–274
hormonal changes in, 269, 270*f*
menstruation, 271
primary sex characteristics,
269–270
secondary sex characteristics,
269–270
sexual maturity, 271
signs of, 270–271
timing, consequences of,
272–273
timing, influences on, 271–272
pudendal block, 76
punishment, **22**, 107, 207

qualitative change, **17**
qualitative research, 27–**28**
quantitative research *vs.*, 28
quality of child care, 153–154, 154*t*
quantitative change, **17**
quantitative research, 27–**28**
qualitative research *vs.*, 28
quarantine, COVID-19 and, 240
quasi-experiments, 34
questionnaires, 29, 29*t*

race, 10
and access to health
insurance, 169
adolescent mortality and, 283
chronic conditions in late
adulthood and, 425
college enrollment and, 335–336
health in middle age, 370–371
influence on health, 325
influences on pubertal timing, 272
life expectancy and, 414
and mortality ratio, 72
puberty and, 272
and self-definition, 191–192
tooth decay and dental care, 218
racial identity formation, 298
random assignment, 33–34
random selection, 28
rapid eye movement (REM)
sleep, 79
rate-of-living theory, 416
reaction range, **52**–53

reactive aggression, 258–259
reactive correlations, 54
reading. See also literacy
middle childhood and, 236–237
reality, fantasy *vs.*, 176
reality principle, 19
real self, **191**
rebellion, adolescent, **306**
recall, 179–180
receptive cooperation, **150**
receptive vocabulary, 125
recess, 219–220
recessive inheritance, **44**, 45*f*
reciprocal determinism, **22**
recognition, 179–180
redemption, 389
reflective thinking, **332**
reflex behavior, **93**, 94*t*
reflexes, 93–95, 108
Reggio Emilia approach, 186
Reggio Emilia model, 186
regional anesthesia, 76
rehearsal, **230**, 434
reinforcement, **22**, 206
relational aggression, **210**, 258
relationships. See also friendship;
gay relationships; marriage
in adolescence, 306–309
with aging parents, 401–404
consensual, 394–398
dynamics, 355–356
in emerging adults, 346–348
in emerging and young
adulthood, 346–348
and health, 456
in late adulthood, 455–463
"living apart together" (LAT), 460
with maturing children, 399–401
in middle adulthood, 392–407
with other children, 211–214
stress, 326
and well-being, 393–394
relativistic thinking, 332
religion, 334–335, 350, 392, 396,
444–445, 482
religious identity formation,
342–343
remarriage
in late adulthood, 459
post-divorce, 359
REM sleep, 79
reorganization, 434
representational ability, **109**
representational systems, **246**
reproducibility crisis, 36
reproductive health. See also
sexually transmitted
infections (STIs)
in emerging and young
adulthood, 328–331
in late adulthood, 423
male sexual functioning, 367
menopause, 365–367
in middle adulthood,
365–368, 365*t*
research
with human participants, 37
process, theories of human
development and, 27
research designs
attachment, study of, 143
basic, 31–34, 31*t*
case studies, **31**, 31*t*
correlational studies, 31, 31*t*
cross-sectional studies, 34–36, 35*t*
developmental, 34–36, 35*f*
ethnographic studies, 31, 31*t*
experiments, 31*t*, 33–34
longitudinal studies, 34–36, 35*t*
sequential studies, 34–36, 35*t*, 36*f*
research ethics, 36–37
research methods
data collection, 29–30
groups and variables, 33

theory, **16**
theory of mind, **175**
 brain development and, 177
 cultural influences on, 177–178
 early childhood and, 175–178
 fantasy *vs.* reality, 176
 individual differences in
   development of, 177
theory of multiple intelligences,
   232–233, 234*t*
theory of sexual selection, **198**
thimerosal, 92
thinking
 convergent thinking, **243**
 divergent thinking, **243**
 interactive, 379
 knowledge of, 175
 postformal thought, 331–332
 reflective thinking, 332
 relativistic thinking, 332
three-mountain task, 174, 174*f*
timing-of-event models, 344*t*, **345**
tip-of-the-tongue phenomenon
   (TOT), **435**
tobacco. *See* smoking
toddlerhood. *See* infancy and
   toddlerhood
tonic neck reflex, 94*t*
tooth decay, 218
Torrance Tests of Creative Thinking
   (TTCT), 243
TOT (tip-of-the-tongue
   phenomenon), 435
touch, 96
toxoplasmosis, 64
trait models, 344*t*, 345–346
transcendence, 436
transduction, **172**
transgender, 197–198, **298**–299
 identity development, 343
 youth, 299–300
transitive inferences, **225**, 225*t*
transracial adoption, 255
trauma
 children's responses to, 265
 stress and, 375
treatment groups, 33

triangular theory of love, **348**
triarchic theory of intelligence,
   233, 333
trimesters, 57
trust, development of, 140
TTCT (Torrance Tests of Creative
   Thinking), 243
turning points, **387**, 387*f*
type 2 diabetes, 223, 369
typological approach, 344*t*, **346**

ultrasound, **58**, 67*t*
umbilical cord sampling, 67*t*
underextended word meanings, 126
undernutrition, 165–167.
   See also malnutrition
uninvolved parenting, 208
United Nations Convention on the
   Rights of Children, 207

vaccinations
 autism spectrum disorder, 92
 childhood disease prevention, 86
 exemptions for religious/
   philosophical reasons, 86
 HPV, 302–303
vaginal birth after cesarean
   (VBAC), 75
vaginal delivery, 75
variable-rate theories, **416**
variables, 33
vehicle accidents, adolescent
   mortality, 283
vernix caseosa, 77
victims
 bullying and, 260–262
 intimate partner violence, 358
video games, violent, 259–260
violation of expectations, **117**
violence
 intimate partner, 358
 media, influence on aggression,
   259–260
 in teen dating, 311–313
virtue, 20
visible imitation, **109**
vision. *See* sight

visual cliff, **100**
visual fixation, infants, 97
visual guidance, **100**
visually based retrieval, **236**
visual preference, **114**, 147
visual recognition memory, 114
visual reports, 29, 29*t*
vital capacity, **365**
vitamin supplements
 infants and toddlers, 90
vocabulary development
 in adolescence, 286
 in early childhood, 182–183
 in middle childhood, 235
vocational issues, 292–293
voluntary childlessness, 401
volunteering
 in late adulthood, 447, 450

WAIS-R (Wechsler Adult
   Intelligence Scale),
   431–432, 432*f*
walking, 99
walking reflex, 94*t*, 101
wear-and-tear theory, 416
Wechsler Adult Intelligence Scale
   (WAIS-R), **431**–432, 432*f*
Wechsler Intelligence Scale for
   Children (WISC-IV), **230**
Wechsler Preschool and Primary
   Scale of Intelligence, Revised
   (WPPSI-IV), **181**
wedding traditions, 352
wedding veil, 352
weight. *See also* obesity
 in adolescence, 276–280
 in early childhood, 160, 160*t*
 low-birth-weight babies, 80–82
 in middle adulthood, 370
 in middle childhood, 217, 217*t*
 puberty and, 272, 273
well-being
 effect of religion and ethnicity
   on, 444–445
 influence of personality on,
   441–442
 in late adulthood, 442–448

in middle adulthood, 391–392
 relationships and, 393–394
 in sexual minorities, 443
 voluntary childlessness and, 401
wet dream, 271
white Americans
 academic achievement and, 289
 adolescent mortality and, 283
 alcohol use among, 325
 body image and, 278
 chronic conditions and, 425
 cohabitation attitudes of, 351
 dropping out of high school, 291
 health status in emerging and
   young adulthood, 318
 infant mortality among, 84, 84*f*
 life expectancy and, 414, 414*t*
 media use and, 239
 obesity and, 319
 osteoporosis in, 372
 puberty in, 272
 sexual behavior in
   adolescence, 300
 smoking among, 323
 spanking among, 207
 suicide and, 477
 teen dating violence and, 312
white matter
 in adolescence, 274, 274*f*
 binge drinking and, 281
 brain development and, 217
 gender development and, 197
whole-language approach, **236**
widowhood, 459, 474
WISC-IV (Wechsler Intelligence
   Scale for Children), **230**
wisdom, 436–437, 440
witch's milk, 77
withdrawal of love, 207–**208**
women. *See also* single-mother
   families
 generativity and, 390
 health in middle age, 371–374
 identity development in middle
   adulthood, 390
 life expectancy, 413–414
 osteoporosis in, 371

pay gap, 337
poverty in late adulthood, 451
 without children, 401
word meanings, 126
work
 in adolescence, 293
 adult education and, 381
 cognitive growth during, 338,
   380–381
 college attendance and,
   337–338
 dual-income families and,
   356–357
 early retirement *versus*, 380
 in emerging and young
   adulthood, 337–338
 in late adulthood, 448–450
 in middle age, 380–381
 midlife career change, 386
 mothers working, 249, 309
 parents impacted by, 249
work-family balance, 356–357
working memory
 in early childhood, 179
 in infancy and toddlerhood, 119
 in late adulthood, 434
 in middle childhood, 229
working parents, children of, 249
World Health Organization, 68
WPPSI-IV (Wechsler Preschool
   and Primary Scale of
   Intelligence, Revised), **181**
writing in middle childhood,
   236–237

X chromosomes, 43–44

Y chromosomes, 43
young adulthood. *See* emerging and
   young adulthood
young old, 412

zone of proximal development
   (ZPD), **24**, **182**
 intelligence tests and, 234
zygote, **41**, 42–43, 43*f*